JANUARY 1977 – VOLUME 6, NUMBER 1

ONTEMPORARY SOCIOLOGY

A JOURNAL OF REVIEWS

IN THIS ISSUE

For Marx or for Sociology: recent books on Marxism and Sociology by Michael Burawoy.

Edward Tiryakian on important new Durkheim editions in French.

Reviews of nine recent books in the Sociology of Education.

"'Inevitability' means never having to say you're sorry." Rayna Rapp Reiter on Patriarchy.

Bruce Hackett reviews *The Reality of Ethnomethodology.*

Benton Johnson on Robert Bellah's *The Broken Covenant.*

Jane Prather reviews *The Sociology of Housework.*

Mike Miller on *Three Centuries of Social Mobility in America.*

Gregory Stone on the Sociology of Sport.

Taking Chances: Ruth Dixon reviews Kristin Lukër's work on abortion and the decision not to contracept.

Letters from three editors of Sociology journals.

Theda Skocpol on Urban Networks.

UBLICATION OF THE AMERICAN SOCIOLOGICAL ASSOCIATION

contemporary sociology

a journal of reviews

January 1977 • Volume 6, Number 1

Concerning advertising, change of address and subscriptions, address: Executive Office, American Sociological Association, 1722 N Street, N.W., Washington, D.C. 20036.

Concerning manuscripts and book reviews, address: Editor, *Contemporary Sociology: A Journal of Reviews,* C-002, University of California, San Diego, La Jolla, California, 92093.

Contemporary Sociology: A Journal of Reviews is published at 49 Sheridan Avenue, Albany, N.Y. 12210, bi-monthly in January, March, May, July, September, and November.

Annual membership dues in the American Sociological Association, $30.00–$50.00. Student Member, $15; Associate, $20; International Associate, $12; Student Associate, $10.

Subscription rate for members, $10; non-members, $15; institutions and libraries, $20; non-member students, $10. Single issues $4.

New subscriptions and renewals will be entered on a calendar year basis only.

Change of address: Six weeks advance notice to the Executive Office, and old address as well as new, are necessary for change of subscriber's address.

Claims for undelivered copies must be made within the month following the regular month of publication. The publishers will supply missing copies when losses have been sustained in transit and when the reserve stock will permit.

Second class postage paid at Washington, D.C. and at additional mailing offices.

Book reviews from *CS* are indexed in *Book Review Index,* published by Gale Research Company.

ASA Multiple Submission Policy: Submission of a manuscript to a professional journal clearly implies commitment to publish in that journal. The competition for journal space requires a great deal of time and effort on the part of editorial readers whose main compensation for this service is the opportunity to read papers prior to publication and the gratification associated with discharge of professional obligation. For these reasons, *the American Sociological Association regards submission of a manuscript to a professional journal while that paper is under review by another journal as unacceptable.*

Cover designed by Kenneth E. Anderson, A.I.A.

TABLE OF CONTENTS

LETTERS 5

FEATURE ESSAYS

Marxism and Sociology .... Michael Burawoy 9
On Discovering Durkheim .... Edward A. Tiryakian 17

RECENT WORK IN EDUCATION

Bowles and Gintis: *Schooling in Capitalist America: Educational Reform and the Contradictions of Economic Life* .... Michael Useem 19
Denton: *Existentialism and Phenomenology in Education: Collected Essays* .... John M. Johnson 22
Feinberg and Rosemont: *Work, Technology, and Education: Dissenting Essays in the Intellectual Foundations of American Education* .... Zelda F. Gamson 23
Gras: *Sociologie de l'education: Textes fondamentaux* .... Remi Clignet 24
Gurin and Epps: *Black Consciousness, Identity, and Achievement: A Study of Students in Historically Black Colleges* .... A. E. Paris 25
Neave: *How They Fared: The Impact of the Comprehensive School upon the University* .... John C. Weidman 26
Sharp and Green: *Education and Social Control: A Study in Progressive Primary Education* .... Rosalie Cohen 27
Stebbins: *Teachers and Meaning: Definitions of Classroom Situations*.... Thomas J. Cottle 28
Wolters: *The New Negro on Campus: Black College Rebellions of the 1920's* .... Ronald W. Saufley 29

BOOK REVIEWS

CRIME, LAW, AND DEVIANCE

Ahlström-Laakso: *Drinking Habits among Alcoholics* .... Odis E. Bigus 30
Edwards and Wilson: *Social Deviance in Australia* .... Frances H. Lovejoy 30
Brodsky: *The Female Offender* .... Harriet Engel Gross 31
Hunt and Chambers: *The Heroin Epidemics: A Study of Heroin Use in the United States, 1965–75* .... Paul Attewell 31
McConville: *The Use of Imprisonment: Essays in the Changing State of English Penal Policy;*
Stratton: *Who Guards the Guards?;* and
Williams: *Changing Prisons* .... Robert Sommer 32
Monkkonen: *The Dangerous Class: Crime and Poverty in Columbus, Ohio, 1860–1885* .... David Lewis Smith 33
Murton: *The Dilemma of Prison Reform;*
Orland: *Prisons: Houses of Darkness;* and
Rudoff: *Work Furlough and the County Jail* .... W. David Watts 34
Roebuck and Frese: *The Rendezvous: A Case Study of an After-Hours Club* .... Edward F. Vacha 35

DEMOGRAPHY, POPULATION, AND MIGRATION

Berelson: *The Great Debate on Population Policy: An Instructive Entertainment* .... Nancy E. Williamson 35
Jones: *Population Growth and Educational Planning in Developing Nations* .... Pranab Chatterjee 36
Karp and Kelly: *Toward an Ecological Analysis of Intermetropolitan Migration* .... Gregory Williams 37
Mesarovic and Pestel: *Mankind at the Turning Point: The Second Report to the Club of Rome;* and
Olson and Landsberg: *The No-Growth Society* .... J. Allen Whitt 38
Pessen: *Three Centuries of Social Mobility in America* .... S. M. Miller 40
Pullum: *Measuring Occupational Inheritance* .... Paul H. Tress 41
Spengler: *Population and America's Future* .... Paul R. Williams 43

FAMILY AND INTIMATE LIFESTYLES

Askham: *Fertility and Deprivation: A Study of Differential Fertility amongst Working-Class Families in Aberdeen* .... Hyman Rodman 44
Constantine and Constantine: *Group Marriage: A Study of Contemporary Multilateral Marriage* .... Stephen K. Sanderson 44

Greenblat, Stein, and Washburne: *The Marriage Game: Understanding Marital Decision Making* .... Charles T. Hill 45
Chekki: *Modernization and Kin Network* .... A. A. Khatri 46
Michel: *Sociologie de la famille et du mariage* .... Saskia Sassen-Koob 47
Oppong: *Marriage among a Matrilineal Elite: A Family Study of Ghanaian Senior Civil Servants* .... John Mogey 47
Spillane and Ryser: *Male Fertility Survey: Fertility Knowledge, Attitudes, and Practices of Married Men* .... Teresa D. Marciano 48

MEDICAL
Camp: *Magic, Myth and Medicine* .... Miriam Sonn 49
Ford: *The Physician's Assistant: A National and Local Analysis* .... Michael Yedidia 49
Kane: *The Challenges of Community Medicine* and
Salber: *Caring and Curing: Community Participation in Health Services* .... Laurie Engelberg 50
Luker: *Taking Chances: Abortion and the Decision Not to Contracept* .... Ruth B. Dixon 51
Rushing: *Community, Physicians, and Inequality: Sociological Study of the Maldistribution of Physicians* .... Victor W. Marshall 52

OCCUPATIONS AND WORK
Blackburn: *Perceptions of Work: Variations within a Factory* and
Mann: *Workers on the Move: The Sociology of Relocation* .... James W. Rinehart 53
Brugger: *Democracy and Organisation in Chinese Industrial Enterprise, 1948–1953* .... Gary G. Hamilton 53
Bulmer: *Working-Class Images of Society* .... Patricia Voydanoff 54
Davis and Cherns: *The Quality of Working Life. Volume 2: Cases and Commentary;*
Fairfield: *Humanizing the Workplace;*
Katzell and Yankelovich: *Work, Productivity, and Job Satisfaction: An Evaluation of Policy-Related Research;*
O'Toole: *Work and the Quality of Life: Resource Papers for "Work in America";*
Rosow: *The Worker and the Job: Coping with Change;* and
Stewart and Cantor: *Varieties of Work Experience: The Social Control of Occupational Groups and Roles* .... Craig C. Lundberg 55
Geer: *Learning to Work* and
Ornstein: *Entry into the American Labor Force* .... Jeylan T. Mortimer 57
Horn: *The Rise and Fall of the Victorian Servant* and
Oakley: *The Sociology of Housework* .... Jane E. Prather 58
Rueschemeyer: *Lawyers and Their Society: A Comparative Study of the Legal Profession in Germany and in the United States* .... Albert J. Bergesen 59

ORGANIZATIONS
Becker and Neuhauser: *The Efficient Organization* .... Gerald R. Salancik 59
Edelstein and Warner: *Comparative Union Democracy: Organisation and Opposition in British and American Unions* .... Edna E. Raphael 60
Lorsch and Morse: *Organizations and Their Members: A Contingency Approach* .... Johannes M. Pennings 61
Wexley and Yukl: *Organizational Behavior and Industrial Psychology: Readings with Commentary* .... Bert R. Brown 62

POLITICAL
Beres and Targ: *Planning Alternative World Futures: Values, Methods, and Models* .... Elise Boulding 62
Blume: *Toward a Political Sociology of Science* .... Lowell L. Hargens 64
Katz et al.: *Bureaucratic Encounters: A Pilot Study in the Evaluation of Government Services* .... Theodore L. Reed 64
Mantell: *True Amerianism: Green Berets and War Resisters* .... Charles P. Flynn 65
Oxaal, Barnett, and Booth: *Beyond the Sociology of Development: Economy and Society in Latin America and Africa* .... Patricia Madoo Lengermann 65
Somerville: *The Peace Revolution: Ethos and Social Process* .... Duane K. Friesen 66
Wilson: *Immigrants and Politics* .... Mark Tannenbaum 67
Wolfe: *The Seamy Side of Democracy: Repression in America* .... Albert Szymanski 68

RACE AND ETHNIC
Adams: *Prison of Grass: Canada from the Native Point of View;*
Guillemin: *Urban Renegades: The Cultural Strategy of American Indians;* and
Wax and Buchanan: *Solving "The Indian Problem": The White Man's Burdensome Business* .... Joe T. Darden 69

Althauser and Spivak: *The Unequal Elites* .... Ray C. Rist 69
Bianco: *The Two Rosetos* .... Paul J. Campisi 70
Blackwell and Janowitz: *Black Sociologists: Historical and Contemporary Perspectives* .... Albert J. McQueen 71
Chatterjee: *Local Leadership in Black Communities: Organizational and Electoral Developments in Cleveland in the Nineteen Sixties* and
Cole: *Blacks in Power: A Comparative Study of Black and White Elected Officials* .... Leslie G. Carr 73
Cordasco: *Studies in Italian American Social History;*
Kayal and Kayal: *The Syrian-Lebanese in America: A Study in Religion and Assimilation;* and
Rogers: *Americans of Portuguese Descent: A Lesson in Differentiation* .... William P. Nye 74
Despres: *Ethnicity and Resource Competition in Plural Societies* .... Aubrey W. Bonnett 75
Feldstein and Costello: *The Ordeal of Assimilation: A Documentary History of the White Working Class* .... Harry Cohen 76
Henriques: *Children of Conflict: A Study of Interracial Sex and Marriage* .... Robert Staples 76
Krickus: *Pursuing the American Dream: White Ethnics and the New Populism* .... Paul D. Starr 77
Kuper: *Race, Science and Society* .... Hugh H. Smythe 77
Loehlin, Lindzey, and Spuhler: *Race Differences in Intelligence* .... Edward E. Harris 78
McCagg: *Jewish Nobles and Geniuses in Modern Hungary* .... Robert Blumstock 78
Rose, Rothman, and Wilson: *Through Different Eyes: Black and White Perspectives on American Race Relations* .... John W. Martin 79
Stoddard: *Mexican Americans* .... Jaime Sena-Rivera 80
Wintersmith: *Police and the Black Community* .... Gwynne Peirson 80

RELIGION
Beckford: *Religious Organization: A Trend Report and Bibliography* .. Wade F. Hook 81
Bellah: *The Broken Covenant: American Civil Religion in Time of Trial* .... Benton Johnson 82
Campbell: *Toward a Sociology of Irreligion* .... Rolfe Schulze 84
Frazier and Lincoln: *The Negro Church in America* and *The Black Church Since Frazier* .... Russell R. Dynes 84
Hostetler: *Hutterite Society* .... Allan W. Eister 85
Lewy: *Religion and Revolution* .... Roger O'Toole 86
Tomasi: *Piety and Power: The Role of the Italian Parishes in the New York Metropolitan Area, 1880–1930* .... Oscar Handlin 88

SEX ROLES AND SEXUALITY
Arafat and Yorburg: *The New Women: Attitudes, Behavior, and Self-Image* .... Nona Glazer 89
Barker-Benfield: *The Horrors of the Half-Known Life: Male Attitudes toward Women and Sexuality in Nineteenth-Century America* .... Michael Gordon 89
Bogdan: *Being Different: The Autobiography of Jane Fry* .... Imogene L. Simmons 90
Goldberg: *The Inevitability of Patriarchy* .... Rayna Rapp Reiter 91
Kessler: *Women: An Anthropological View* and
Rohrlich-Leavitt: *Women Cross-Culturally: Change and Challenge* ...... Judith Caditz 92
Mednick, Tangri, and Hoffman: *Women and Achievement: Social and Motivational Analyses* .... Sandra Harley Carey 93

SOCIAL PSYCHOLOGY
Bartos: *Process and Outcome of Negotiations* .... Bernard P. Cohen 94
Lyman and Scott: *The Drama of Social Reality* .... James M. Henslin 95
Smith: *Flags through the Ages and across the World* .... Sasha R. Weitman 96

THEORY
Bershady: *Ideology and Social Knowledge* .... Barclay D. Johnson 97
Birnbaum and Chazel: *Théorie Sociologique* .... Phillip Bosserman 99
Droz and Rahmy: *Understanding Piaget* and
Piaget and Inhelder: *The Origin of the Idea of Chance in Children* . Kathryn P. Meadow 100
Marcus: *Engels, Manchester, and the Working Class* .... Evan Stark 100
Mehan and Wood: *The Reality of Ethnomethodology* .... Bruce M. Hackett 101
Skidmore: *Theoretical Thinking in Sociology* and
Skidmore: *Sociology's Models of Man: The Relationships of Models of Man to Sociological Explanation in Three Sociological Theories* .... Deena Weinstein 103

Thoresen: *Toward a Science of Man: Essays in the History of Anthropology* .... Lola Romanucci-Ross 103

URBAN

Fainstein and Fainstein: *Urban Political Movements: The Search for Power by Minority Groups in American Cities;*
Lamb: *Political Power in Poor Neighborhoods;* and
O'Brien: *Neighborhood Organization and Interest-Group Processes* .. George W. Dowdall 104

Hardoy: *Urbanization in Latin America: Approaches and Issues* and
Wilsher and Righter: *The Exploding Cities* .... J. John Palen 105

Liu: *Quality of Life Indicators in U.S. Metropolitan Areas: A Statistical Analysis* .... Kirsten A. Grønbjerg 107

Rossi, Berk, and Eidson: *The Roots of Urban Discontent: Public Policy, Municipal Institutions, and the Ghetto* .... Albert J. Reiss, Jr. 108

Whyte: *Organizing for Agricultural Development: Human Aspects in the Utilization of Science and Technology* .... E. A. Wilkening 109

ADDITIONAL REVIEWS

Atchley: *The Sociology of Retirement* .... Sarah Matthews 109

Ball and Loy: *Sport and Social Order: Contributions to the Sociology of Sport* .... Gregory P. Stone 110

Anderson and Carter: *Human Behavior in the Social Environment: A Social Systems Approach* .... Gregory Williams 112

Bunce: *Television in the Corporate Interest;*
Groombridge: *Television and the People: A Programme for Democratic Participation;* and
Williams: *Television: Technology and Cultural Form* .... Robert G. Dunn 113

Bogdan and Taylor: *Introduction to Qualitative Research Methods: A Phenomenological Approach to the Social Sciences;* and
Fletcher: *Beneath the Surface: An Account of Three Styles of Sociological Research* .... Kathy Calkins Charmaz 114

Caplovitz: *Consumers in Trouble: A Study of Debtors in Default* .... Julius A. Roth 115

Daniels: *Living in Fear: A History of Horror in the Mass Media* and
Howitt and Cumberbatch: *Mass Media, Violence and Society* .... Nathan Weinberg 116

Friedmann: *Youth and Society* and
Havighurst and Dreyer: *Youth: The Seventy-fourth Yearbook of the National Society for the Study of Education, Part I* .... Judith D. Handel 116

Goldhamer: *The Soviet Soldier: Soviet Military Management at the Troop Level* .... David R. Segal 117

Lazarsfeld and Reitz: *An Introduction to Applied Sociology* .... Michael Hennessy 118

Levitan and Johnston: *The Job Corps: A Social Experiment that Works* .... William S. Bennett 119

Mileti, Drabek, and Haas: *Human Systems in Extreme Environments: A Sociological Perspective* .... Verta A. Taylor 119

Rogers: *Children and Language: Readings in Early Language and Socialization* .... Robert Williams 120

Rozman: *Urban Networks in Ch'ing China and Tokugawa Japan* and
Rozman: *Urban Networks in Russia, 1750–1800, and Premodern Periodization* .... Theda Skocpol 120

Struening and Guttentag: *Handbook of Evaluation Research, vols. 1 & 2* .... Howard E. Freeman 122

Scott: *Aggression* and
Selg: *The Making of Human Aggression: A Psychological Approach* .. Karl Schonborn 123

Weber: *Socioeconomic Methods in Educational Analysis* .... David E. Drew 124

Weil and Hartley: *The Sociology of the Arts* .... Richard W. Christopherson 125

Weizenbaum: *Computer Power and Human Reason: From Judgement to Calculation* .... John F. Crowther 125

PUBLICATIONS RECEIVED 126

LETTERS

(Letters which comment on particular reviews are routinely sent to reviewers for a reply. Where no reply by reviewers appears in these columns, it is usually because they chose not to reply.)

Editor's Note:

The following three letters, from editors of sociology journals, were written in response to the letter from Norbert Wiley in *CS*' issue of November, 1976.

BENNETT M. BERGER

To the Editor:

No scientist would decry the use of ideas, even creative fancy in the process of inquiry. No one censures Goffman for lack of path analysis. One might suppose that, in Professor Pangloss's world, one would find both big ideas and their testing in any serious search for reliable knowledge. This would include discussions in review journals where one should not be surprised to find a degree of intellectual excitement. (I don't minimize the artistry and professional competence of our colleagues, Wrong and Berger. I express my surprise that one should be surprised at the use of book reviews to generate intriguing debate and insight, a notion which antedates 1966.)

I wish I could follow the pattern that seems sometimes to characterize sociologists' interchange, elevating one's own stature by cutting the other guy off at the knees. What a pleasure it would be for *Social Forces* to become a third major journal, cracking into the circle of the big two, unwholesomely bloated with power. (Sotto voce, we *are* the third major journal. And we delight in a catholic range of content and methods investing reports of empirical research set against a backdrop of pertinent theory.) But in truth, I'm not sure why they shouldn't be the big two. *AJS* set up shop in 1895, one year before Durkheim's *Année sociologique* commenced publication. It has a great tradition and enormous accumulated experience. Until *SF* began publication in 1922 it was *the* means of professional exchange among sociologists. Nor is it clear why a professional association should not have a medium, independent of any university or particular subfield, one not "bloated with power" but preeminent in representing the field and conveying the prestige of the profession.

Obviously it's imperative that with such power these journals be responsibly edited. This means (and I could not agree more with Professor Wiley) that the principal media available for sociologists' publications should be hospitable to a wide range of methods and orientations and, certainly, should be indifferent to imputed ideology and miscellaneous ascriptive traits.

So far so good. But pieties don't produce MSS., much less good ones. Longing for virtue in others won't actualize the splendid journal. I remember Karl Schuessler, one of *ASR*'s very good editors, lamenting the dearth of stimulating papers in theory among MSS. submitted. But I fear Professor Wiley's strictures underplay such realities. He seems to lean toward a-sociological, great-man/devil explanations of editorial policies. (How else interpret such phrases as the "aura the two top editors give their journals," or the "editorial procedures they adopt and how they apply them"?) Is Buzz Zelditch unaffected by the ASA's Publication Committee? by the ASA Council? by his own identity as a sociologist? by his editorial associates? This is not to say that editors, succeeding one another through short terms, have no impact on the journal's routines. But certainly the influence on policy is modest. And sometimes the idiosyncratic impact is not registered in much beyond a new logo. My review of more than 2,000 MSS. over the few years I've edited *SF* suggests that we might entertain some other explanations of our present publication pattern.

For example: the range of MSS. published accurately reflects the actual distribution of current sociological research—in method, content and theory. Corollary: the incidence of k'vetching is inversely related to the production of research in sociology.

Or: There is a positive relationship between the quality of a MS. and the probability of publication. Corollary: Rejected MSS. are generally poorer than those published—poorer both in the logic of inquiry and in the collection and manipulation of data; poorer as communications to colleagues, revelling in polysyllabic smokescreens and substituting esoteric signs such as MCA for ideas; poorer in theory, the justification of the hypotheses being tested. (Dustbowl empiricism still trivializes some of our research.)

Or: There is an inverse relationship between rejection of a MS. and the likelihood that its findings can be generalized to any known population. (Alas, those 30 Ss drawn from an introductory sociology class seem to reappear regularly in the daily flow of MSS. This might be acceptable were they redeemed by stunning ideas: we should tolerate poor samples, or nonsamples when they are so recognized and when they effectively challenge Accepted Truth. We want above all to discover the exception that proves—meaning tests—the rule.)

Or: the larger the N (pages) the greater the possible range of MSS. (in content, method and theoretical orientation). We have waited too long to increase the number of pages in *CS* and to give *ASR*'s editor an additional 90 pages for a bit of intellectual leeway. (We would have done better to buy more pages with the money used to junkett staff people for ASA's minority programs when phone and stamps would have done as well.) A paucity of pages limits range. The very *CS* policy that Professor Wiley applauds is one that contributes to an end he must deplore: it preempts pages some of which might otherwise go to reducing the appalling number of books that must now go unreviewed.

These words, too, whittle away at available space. So I must quit without raising questions about a number of statements: the contention that sociological research usually treats "social problems defined by government," the implied antithesis between ideas and method, the notion that some sort of method is mandatory, the incompatibility of formal rationality and the nature of a "living society" . . . I conclude by assuring Professor Wiley that, if editorial performance/ ain't in accordance/with what he and I might prefer, it's less likely owing to intellectual bigotry than to the current state of the field, reflected in our colleagues' work; together with an indigence (and an allocation of funds?) unbecoming a professional society.

EVERETT K. WILSON
Social Forces

To the Editor:

Some of what *Contemporary Sociology* (*CS*) is doing would be superfluous if the other American Sociological Association (ASA) journals were doing their job. This seems to be Norbert Wiley's main point. My own view, contrary to his, is that the other journals are doing their job and none of what *CS* is doing is potentially superfluous.

At the moment, *CS* is living up to the terms of its prospectus. The committee report (*The American Sociologist,* Vol. 5, pp. 405–406) which led to its establishment envisaged "review essays and symposia, composite reviews covering a number of similar books . . . and articles reviewing recent sociological literature. . ." It went on to suggest that commentary from readers concerning previously published reviews might become a regular feature of the new journal. This policy, it was argued, "would encourage more responsibile reviewing, and would permit scholarly debate over the merits of controversial books." The report generally called for a flexible editorial policy.

An implication is that the editor of *CS* is more or less obliged to find new ways of packaging ideas about new books. This is not to detract from the accomplishments of Editor Berger and his predecessor Dennis Wrong, but simply to note that better designs for the critical evaluation of books were contemplated from the start. The editors of the other journals probably enjoy less freedom to act ad libitum.

As with *CS,* the other ASA journals are doing what their founders had in mind. *The American Sociological Review* (*ASR*) was created in the mid-1930s to get away from armchair sociology and to foster empirical investigations; *Sociological Methodology* (*SM*) was created in the late 1960s to give sociologists more ready access to promising methods for doing social research. Neither were set up as a forum for the exchange of opinions, although such exchanges are not barred from their pages. Nevertheless, they are primarily a means for disseminating significant studies.

But one might argue that what is significant in sociology is debatable; that what has significance for one circle of sociologists may have none for another; and that a significant line of investigation may be excluded from the journals because its representatives hold no editorships. Although such uneven representation may occur, the chances are against the exclusion of truly significant works for the following reasons.

(1) ASA editors are searched and screened. Tolerance and impartiality are given due weight in selecting editors.

(2) Since ASA editors are appointed for short terms, none of them singly can do much damage before his/her term has expired. A partisan editor has little time in which to push his/her favorite brand of sociology at the expense of others.

(3) Editors have practically nothing to do with the subjects on which sociologists spend their time; hence, they have little to do with the content of what is published. If most studies for the time being are on the subject of occupational mobility, most published papers for a time will be on that subject. The editor must either publish what sociologists are doing or nothing at all.

(4) Nor are editors free of the influence of long term trends in sociology. Not too long ago I did an analysis of ASR for the first 30 years. Among other things, I discovered that the trend in statistical papers was steadily upward during that period. In the late 1930s, approximately one third of the papers were statistical; in the early 1960s, around two thirds were of that character. During this period, none of the editors featured a statistical background and most had the reputation of being eclectics in theory and method. The steady increase in the number of statistical articles reflected not the bias of individual editors, but rather the greater use of the statistical method in sociology.

(5) Nor does an editor have much to do with what is submitted for review. In the case of *SM,* the editors have gone to some pains to publicize their interest in methods for doing field research. But few papers of this nature have been forthcoming. Editors can only publish what they have an opportunity to publish.

(6) Editors do not make decisions, they announce them. Since editors are 99 percent dependent on their reviewers, it is essential that their reviewers be dependable. Dependable and

knowledgeable reviewers lessen the risk of publishing bad papers. Of course, a scoundrel may favor his/her friends by getting "reviews" from friendly "reviewers." Conscientious editors collectively are the best safeguard against that danger.

My conclusion is that the shortcomings of published sociology reflect not the bias of editors but rather the poverty of sociology. What exists only in the imagination cannot be submitted for publication; what remains unsubmitted cannot be judged; and what is judged to add little or nothing to knowledge cannot be published. Brilliant essays are especially liable to these hazards. Many never get written; many never get submitted; and many are judged to add nothing to sociology, whatever their literary value. Turning this around, ASA editors publish what is accepted; reviewers judge what is submitted; and authors submit what they have done. ASA editors are not political commissars; they do not set goals and priorities. Their main goal is to get into print what is considered to be worthwhile, and to keep out of print what is considered to be worthless.

KARL SCHUESSLER
Sociological Methodology

To the Editor:

The editors of the *American Journal of Sociology* for some time have been thinking hard about certain of the important questions raised by Norbert Wiley. As a result, we have published in recent issues of the journal a statement of editorial policy that we take seriously and that we hope our colleagues will take seriously too.

Our statements reads as follows:

The editors of the *American Journal of Sociology* are actively seeking articles that make major contributions to theory building and research in sociology or set important new agendas for the discipline. The overwhelming proportion of papers that we now receive report research. We will always be eager to publish research papers if they are truly first-rate. But there are other kinds of papers, equally important, that we see all too seldom. If we are currently receiving our share of these papers, then we would like to have more than our share.

We are looking especially for presentations of original theoretical arguments, descriptions and illustrations of important new methods, and critical syntheses and evaluations of the state of knowledge or method in major areas of the discipline. We also would like to publish papers that point up important connections between theory and method in sociology and other disciplines.

We will do our best to insure that these papers receive prompt, trenchant, and appropriate reviews.

CHARLES E. BIDWELL
American Journal of Sociology

To the Editor:

While normally we would not concern ourselves with replying to reviews such as Margaret Sery Young's, simply because of its relatively unsophisticated content, this particular review raises an important matter of principle to which attention should be called.

The review of our *The Imperial Animal* (May, 1976) appeared five years after the publication of the book in question and since a book like this is a year in press this is effectively six years after the authors finished work on it. The reviewer chooses to criticize certain aspects of the data and argument on the basis of subsequent work by other authors, largely primatologists. As she rightly claims, hindsight is a great help in these matters and indeed, had we had all this material available in 1969 and 1970 when we were writting the manuscript, it would no doubt have been different. What is remarkable, however, is that the reviewer treats our work as though it ended in 1970 and makes absolutely no reference to the considerable body of material we have since produced which has taken care of many of the objections, expanded the argument in other directions, and moved towards a position more consistent with the new information. This we understand to be the normal course of scientific activity and unless the reviewer assumes that we've been on permanent vacation since the book was published, why does she not give us credit for in fact participating in this normal course of events? None of this work has appeared in particularly obscure places and is certainly well known to our well-informed contemporaries. Neither reviewers nor editors should be allowed to have a monopoly on hindsight when reviewing books half a decade after the event.

While we appreciate the extensive amount of time which must have been devoted to the preparation of this review, it has not prevented an error on detail in the publication description. The paperback edition did not appear in 1971 and was not published by the hardback publisher, Holt, Rhinehart and Winston. It appeared in 1972 and was published by Delta Books.

ROBIN FOX
LIONEL TIGER
Rutgers University

To the Editor:

I understand the dismay of Professors Tiger and Fox at the four-year delay in the appearance of my review of *The Imperial Animal*. Part of the delay was my fault and I apologize for it. However, the wide circulation of the book among social scientists seemed to require that it be reviewed, however belatedly.

As I stated in the review, the book's inadequacies were apparent at the time of publication. As a matter of principle, in an effort to be fair and not to take advantage of hindsight, I used only findings that were available prior to 1971.

I used the dates in the bibliography and notes in *The Imperial Animal* as guides to what I could consider available to the authors at the time of writing. When I used sources other than those referenced by Tiger and Fox, I limited myself to pre-1971 sources. Most of what I used was available five years before *The Imperial Animal* was written. Perhaps I should have made that point more forcefully in the review.

Also, perhaps that is a reason for the "relatively unsophisticated content" of the review. Most of the early ethological studies, including those in primatology relevant to the concern of Tiger and Fox, were relatively unsophisticated in technique, involving careful description rather than analysis. They were, however, appropriate to the stage of development of the discipline. It is from this descriptive research, and the more analytic research deriving from it, that the more recent and more sophisticated techniques and theoretical statements are developing.

I do not believe that in drawing mainly from primatological sources I was being unfair. The authors purported their work to be ethological and to examine man as a primate. It is not unreasonable, therefore, to expect them to have expertise in primatology. Where I used examples from primatology, it was to show that there is evidence to lead one to question the generalizability of some of the examples from primatology which Tiger and Fox themselves used.

I made no assumption in the review that the authors were no longer pursuing scientific research in the area of human ethology. In fact, I expressed my confidence, as well as my hope, that future professional discourse would further illuminate the subject of their work. If I implied that they would be barred from participating in that discourse, the implication was unintentional, and I apologize for it. I still believe, regretfully, that subsequent contributions are unlikely to have the broad circulation and appeal of *The Imperial Animal*.

I was invited to review the hardcover edition published in 1971. The copy of the review which I submitted did not mention any other edition. I addressed my review to the 1971 edition on the basis of information available when it was written. The review was not intended as a survey review or a review essay. Other readers and reviewers will be able to evaluate the contribution of subsequent works.

MARGARET SERY YOUNG
Guilford College

FEATURE ESSAYS

Marxism and Sociology

Marxist Sociology, by TOM BOTTOMORE. New York: Holmes & Meier Publishers, 1975. 78 pp. $7.00 cloth $3.00 paper.

Karl Marx: Economy, Class and Social Revolution, edited by Z. A. JORDAN. New York: Charles Scribner's Sons, 1975. 332 pp. $10.00 cloth.

Karl Marx on Society and Social Change, edited by NEIL J. SMELSER. Chicago: University of Chicago Press, 1973. 206 pp. $12.50 cloth. $3.25 paper.

Marx and Modern Social Theory, by ALAN SWINGEWOOD. New York: Halsted Press, 1975. 248 pp. $17.95 cloth.

MICHAEL BURAWOY
University of California, Berkeley

If we believe, for whatever reasons, that the revolution is imminent, then the immediate issues for Marxists are ones of strategy and organization. In such historical circumstances practice and theory directly affect and inform one another. Just as the organization of class struggle responds to the theory of revolution, so the theory of revolution moves with the class struggle through which it is carried out. Voluntarism and determinism are joined.

Few Marxists regarded the third quarter of the twentieth century as the historical location for such a revolutionary conjuncture, except perhaps in the underdeveloped world. Indeed, as capitalism has expanded it has displayed an astonishing capacity to overcome the crises it generates, to absorb or repel alternatives, and to incorporate change and criticism. Such non-revolutionary conditions have increased the distinctions between the polarities; people "make their own history . . . but under circumstances directly found . . ." (*The Eighteenth Brumaire*)—between voluntarism and determinism; revolution and science; freedom and necessity. For Marx the two perspectives stood opposed; during unpropitious times they develop independent traditions. On the one hand, we look for an explanation for the "appearance" of durability—that what exists is natural and inevitable. In other words, we attempt to construct a theory of ideology. In this view we also look for patterns of determination which illuminate the trajectories of capitalism, the displacement and condensation of primary contradictions, and the emergence of new classes and with them new contradictions. In short, we search for a Marxist science which will transform the appearances of everyday life into a knowledge of underlying patterns of development and change. On the other hand, we abandon the consolations and discomforts of determinism and "sociological fatalism" and proclaim that the conditions for revolution are indeed ripe. What little attempt is made to explain, call it theory if you must, is justified and validated not by its plausibility but by its purpose. Here we find "messianic utopianism"—Lukács's judgment of his own early work.

Therefore, the first theme I wish to explore in this essay concerns the divergence, within Marxism and in interpretations of Marx, of voluntarism and determinism, particularly as it occurs in periods defined as non-revolutionary. I propose to use the four assigned books to illustrate this thesis and to show how attempts to bridge the gulf lead into a political and intellectual abyss or into discourse outside the Marxist tradition.

The second theme of my discussion concerns the current relevance of Marx's work. Is Marx to be regarded as a grandmaster who shaped the development of sociology but whose thought has been assimilated into the main body of social theory? If so, has he been superseded and are his most trenchant insights limited to the particular era in which he lived? Can sociology continue to benefit from his work in the analysis of advanced capitalism? Or, alternatively, is Marx the founder of an independent tradition which cannot be absorbed into the main body of social theory along with Durkheim and Weber without distortion? Are his theoretical structures incompatible with those of modern social theory? Must Marxism be seen in terms of its own distinctive premises? In other words, in referring to or using Marx's work, are we "for sociology" or "for Marx"? Although none of the four books under review is concerned with recent developments in Marxism, it will nevertheless be necessary to invoke such work in order to arrive at tentative conclusions about the viability of an autonomous Marxist tradition.

Empiricism

Introducing his book devoted to Marxist sociology, Bottomore writes: "the working out of these two themes—science and revolution—constitutes the history of Marxist thought during the past century" (p. 13). Bottomore claims that Marxist positivism has been most significantly advanced in the little translated works of the Austrian school.[1] However, he also stresses the opposition to this positivist tradition from both Marxists and non-Marxists, from the Hegelian tradition with its explicit refutation of positivism, from the dogmatism always haunting Marxism (which has secured a stranglehold over its development in most socialist countries), and from the dominant cultural and educational institutions of capitalism which have always shunned Marxist thought.

What, then, is left of Marxist sociology? Not much, claims Bottomore, dismayed by its failure to fulfill its promise. Influenced by an empiricist tradition, Bottomore is skeptical of determinate or global "laws." He prefers "significant correlations" and "causal explanations" and the final comment of the book is, "the idea of the inevitability of socialism has tended to impoverish and deform Marxist thought" (p. 75). By the same token Bottomore embraces "free conscious activity" which may change those "correlations" and "explanations." Between theory and practice there must be continual interaction, but Bottomore gives us little indication of where and how to begin.

In defining the elements of a Marxist sociology, Bottomore draws upon the later work of Korsch—not long before the latter abandoned Marxism altogether. They are: (1) the primacy of the economic structure (a position which Bottomore seems to reject as being unrealistic, though without any serious consideration of what "primacy" might mean); (2) the historical specificity of all social phenomena; (3) the setting of empirical studies within an historical context; (4) the recognition of revolutionary as well as of evolutionary change (though again Bottomore has some misgivings). Needless to say Weber's or even Durkheim's work could be easily absorbed into this notion of sociology; not much, that is, is left of Marxism. In trying to weave the two Marxist traditions together, Bottomore loses sight of all that is distinctively Marxist. He poses the problem but his empiricist epistemological commitment to inductive "correlations" rather than deductive "laws" leads into a cul-de-sac.

Curiously, Bottomore notes early in his book that Marx himself was never able to fuse the positivist and Hegelian elements into a superior synthesis. This does not daunt Bottomore in his own attempts at reconciliation. But it should come as no surprise that he finds himself outside the realm of Marxist discourse. As I suggested earlier, a return to Marx involves a choice rather than a reconciliation; a choice between the primacy of "voluntarism" as in Swingewood's treatment or of "determinism" as in the treatments of Smelser and Jordan.

Voluntarism

In a text touching on a vast range of theoretical issues, Swingewood defines his position unequivocally: "Thus there is a clear link between the development of modern social theory and the works of Marx, between the 'degeneration' of Marxism at the end of the nineteenth century and the revitalisation of sociology in the work of Weber, Simmel and Schutz; and between 'voluntaristic' Marxism and 'voluntaristic' sociology. This book is an attempt to explore this relationship" (p. 9). In Marx's writings, Swingewood claims, lies buried a voluntarism containing many of the insights of the masters of sociology. His arguments in behalf of this claim are not convincing—relying more on dogmatic and cursory illumination than a sustained analysis of either Marx or modern social theory.

Swingewood takes voluntarism to its logical conclusion. Like Bottomore, he will have no part of any determinism, whether Hegelian evanescence or the inevitable crash of capitalism. Where Bottomore lampoons Marcuse for his "stubborn commitment to a subjective, arbitrary interpretation of history which is no longer connected either with a social movement or with a publicly accessible body of knowledge and criteria of validity by which

[1] By positivism Bottomore understands, "an approach to the social sciences which regards them as being essentially the same as natural sciences, aiming at the formulation of general causal laws, resting their claims to valid knowledge upon the analysis of some empirical reality, not upon philosophical intuition, and thus asserting the unity of scientific method; and which makes a sharp distinction between scientific statements and value judgements" (p. 9). Therefore, Bottomore does not make the distinction within positivism between laws derived deductively (Marxist positivism) and laws derived inductively (empiricist positivism). His conclusion that Marxist sociology is underdeveloped is partly a consequence of defining sociology, and in particular Marxist sociology, as an empiricist positivism.

its assertions might be judged" (p. 46), Swingewood lambasts both Marcuse and Parsons for their different species of sociological fatalism. What is missing from their mechanical analyses, argues Swingewood, is the "dialectic" in which a contradictory movement *always* asserts itself. But, in rejecting one determinism, he immediately falls prey to another.

The dialectical movement, according to Swingewood, is as inevitable as it is ubiquitous. But what precisely is it? It is a method to penetrate "beneath the surface of particular phenomena and disclose its [sic] contradictory movement and structure" (p. 136), "a social analysis consisting of a constant shuttling between the parts and the whole, not simply in one direction but in both" (p. 44). Were Swingewood to develop such notions as "structure," "contradictory movement," "totality," or restrict himself to consistent usage, his analysis would make more progress. In practice, he calls upon the dialectic when confronting any significant antinomy, any apparent paradox. Whenever an important distinction is required, he smudges, blurrs, and eliminates it by verbal fiat—introducing dialectics to foreclose prematurely any further discussion.

My objection is not to the use of the dialectic per se, but Swingewood's failure to specify its meaning. However, Swingewood is not alone in making up his mind prematurely about the dialectic. Thus, it is slightly surprising to read Smelser's comment, "He [Marx] aggressively embraced the Hegelian principle of dialectic" (p. xii), as if in serene oblivion of the decades of debate within the Marxist tradition on the specificity of the materialist dialectic. Confusion is only compounded when Jordan, in his introduction, writes: "Marx was a naturalist philosopher . . . and not a materialist. Still less was he a dialectical materialist" (p. 10)! Bottomore, who picks his words and concepts carefully, only refers to the dialectic once, when criticizing Gramsci for not specifying its meaning.

But Swingewood is not content to rely on just a spiritual contraceptive. As a final precaution against intellectual germination, Swingewood invokes the more concrete idea of class struggle. Laws of capitalism (what they are is left to the imagination) constitute the objective conditions for change, the potential of which is only realized in class struggle. But what is this? Struggles between classes or struggles which produce classes? What are classes? Are struggles reflected in conflict between different modes of production or within a single mode of production? What is struggle about, that is, what is the object of struggle? Is it the same for political, economic, and ideological class struggles? Are these different types of struggles or aspects of the same struggles? Are we to conceive of classes as carrying their own distinctive ideologies (in Poulantzas's graphic terms, as football players carry number plates on their backs), the "class-in-itself-class-for-itself" problematique of *Poverty of Philosophy?* If so, class struggles are struggles *between* different ideologies. *Or* are we to assert, with Gramsci, that classes are inserted into a dominant (hegemonic) ideology, the problematique of *The German Ideology* (the ruling ideas are the ideas of the ruling class)? If so, then class struggles take place within the context defined by the hegemonic ideology. Above all, what determines class struggles—the form they take, the level of struggle and their development? Or are they spontaneous eruptions as unpredictable as earthquakes? Ever since Marx put pen to paper (and indeed before), these issues have been the subject of furious debate, but one wouldn't know it from Swingewood's treatment.

In his introduction to a selection of works by Marx, Jordan displays more sensitivity to these issues. He distinguishes between classes defined sociologically (as sets of places determined by relations to the means of production) and classes defined historically (as social and political forces—agents of change). Like Bottomore, but now in a specific context, Jordan doubts whether Marx ever reconciled these two notions. A Marxist theory of class must confront the problem and not indulge in Swingewood's obfuscation: "Class involved both the subjective factor of consciousness and the objective element of organization, bound together by the relationship to the means of production" (p. 139). Swingewood uncritically adopts the scheme of "class-in-itself-class-for-itself" with the merger conditional on political and ideological factors. He says, for example, "Class consciousness is compounded from the most diverse contradictions embracing the fetishism of commodities, nationalist sentiments, political reformism *and* class identification" (p. 133). However, outside the teleology of Lukács, which Swingewood emphatically rejects, the in-itself-for-itself problematique loses all meaning. By what criterion can we assert an a priori "class-in-itself"? Once we have left Lukács behind, the appearance of a class as a force is not a primordial given, but a consequence, a combined effect of a set of objective structures (political, ideological, and economic) related to one another in ways that have to be explored.

Again, let me stress, I am not saying that class struggles are unimportant; on the contrary they are central to *any* Marxist theory. But classes and struggles do not appear by immaculate conception, either at random or from teleology; like everything else they have to be produced; they are organized and they affect conditions just as they are in turn affected by conditions—all of which require careful study.

Determinism

Marx had not one but two motors of history. In the *Communist Manifesto,* for example, Marx and Engels refer to history as the history of class struggles, while in *Capital* considerable weight is given to competition as a propellant of capitalist development. However, rather than posing the problem of the *relationship* between struggle, which governs relations *between* classes, and competition, which governs relations *within* classes, the authors tend to emphasize one or the other. As we have seen, Swingewood focuses on class struggle as the agent of revolutionary transformation and virtually ignores competition. By contrast Smelser emphasizes competition as the engine of capitalism. In his perspective, classes appear more as carriers of contradictions or laws; their emergence and struggle is conditioned by the development of capitalism. With some qualifications Jordan adopts a similar view: "According to this new conception, society is brought about by natural causes which originate with men but are subject to laws in the same sense as are other phenomena of nature, that is, regardless of what men intend or fail to do" (p. 12).

But what are these contradictions and laws? Where are they to be found? Which structures do they implicate? How do we know they exist? What meaning shall we attach to the concepts in the first place? The four writers take different if not always clearly defined positions. Drawing on an Hegelian idiom, Swingewood employs contradiction, negative and dialectic, in bewildering succession, while Jordan and Bottomore studiously avoid such concepts. Smelser confesses that he finds the dialectic confusing, though he is less perturbed by the concept of contradiction: "Marx's concept of contradiction rests on a certain *relationship* between the mode of production and relations of production" (p. xvi). Swingewood and Jordan *also* regard this as a central contradiction or conflict examined by Marx. But what precisely is the contradiction between the forces of production and the relations of production? Since capitalist relations of production are based on *private* ownership, while the development of the forces of production involves their *socialization* (the rise of the collective worker and the interdependence of productive activities), "contradiction" is conventionally assumed. But why?

At this point it becomes clear that failure to consider developments in Marxism renders obsolete parts of the analyses of Jordan, Smelser, and Swingewood. Whether we have read his works or not, we all have our own Marx—worker and capitalist, student and teacher, journalist and politician. Moreover, we frequently cling to our stereotype so tenaciously that we ignore or peremptorily dismiss the on-going, thriving tradition of Marxist science and scholarship. So, for example, few serious Marxists continue to regard the relationship between the forces of production and relations of production as a fundamental contradiction within capitalism. First, socialization of the ownership of the means of production has not brought changes anticipated by the elimination of a "fundamental" contradiction within capitalism. Nationalization of industry has been incorporated within capitalist relations of production. Despite the prominence given to planning and collective ownership, Bettleheim and Marglin have argued that the driving mechanisms within the political economy of the Soviet Union are similar to those found under advanced capitalism. Second, Braverman, Gorz, Marglin, and others have argued that the forces of production, far from being the dominant element of the principal contradiction, are themselves at least in part subordinated to the relations of production. More specifically, the instruments of production (such as the assembly line) and the division of labor (fractionalization, hierarchy, and so forth) constitute a means of reproducing and obscuring rather than undermining relations of ownership and exploitation. Their thesis dovetails with the views of Marcuse and Habermas that "technology" and "rationality" have been turned into a means of ideological domination within the framework of capitalist relations of production. In other words, the liberating potential embodied in the development of the forces of production is never realized. Far from being "contradictory" the forces of production and the relations of production constitute a mutually reinforcing pair.

So what are the primary contradictions of capitalism? There are, of course, various post-Marx answers, from the realization crises of Luxemburg to the fiscal crisis of O'Connor. But restricting oneself to Marx's own writings, one can note the resurgence of interest in the "law of the falling rate of profit." Indeed, Smelser himself appears to find the *form* of the dynamics associated with this law as one of the more sociologically attractive parts of Marx's work. Bottomore, Jordan, and Swingewood pay little attention to the falling rate of profit. They refer to it only to reject it as empirically invalid or grounded on false assumptions. We shall return to issues of validity later; for the moment I am concerned with its theoretical significance.

As a result of competition and in order to survive, capitalists are compelled to accumulate profit. In so doing each capitalist also irrevocably contributes to a diminishing overall rate of profit. In other words capitalists are involved in a gigantic Prisoner's Dilemma Game where the interests of the *individual capitalist in his or her own survival* are bound into an inescapable conflict with the common interests of the entire bourgeoisie, that is, with the interests of the *capitalist class in the survival of capitalism.* Here, at last, we have a relatively clear notion of contradiction as a process which irreversably undermines the requirements of its own reproduction and sows the seeds of its own destruction.

Structuralist Modification of Determinism

The structure of the economy continually propels capitalists into undermining the system as a whole and thereby defines, theoretically, a set of counter-tendencies inscribed in other structures (which we will call the state). The state must absorb the disruptive consequences if the system as a whole is to survive. The manner in which men and women must transform nature in order to live —the mode of production—implies a set of conditions which must exist if production is to continue to be organized in the same way. The structure of economic practices implies (1) a corresponding set of reproduction requirements performed (or not performed) by (a) a structure of political practices which reproduces (or transforms) social relations and (b) a structure of ideological practices which reproduces (or transforms a specific type of consciousness, *and* (2) a set of relations among these three structures. Under the feudal mode of production, the political is *dominant,* whereas under the capitalist mode of production the economic is *dominant.* In both cases the economic is *determinant,* its primacy residing in the fact that it *determines the relations among structures;* it establishes a totality of "structures in dominance," as Althusser says, based on the reproduction requirements of the particular mode of production.

We must take the argument one step further before returning to Smelser et al. Under what conditions will these dominant structures *actually* reproduce the characteristic relations of production? Under what conditions will the system break down? To answer this question, we must return to the conceptual level of class struggles but go beyond Swingewood's spontaneity and Smelser's reductionism. The *capacity* of the state (the political and ideological structures) to preserve the cohesion of the entire system or social formation depends on the level or intensity of economic class struggles. As Glynn and Sutcliffe, Gough, and others have suggested, the level and indeed the success of economic class struggles in Britain are making it increasingly difficult for the state to reproduce capitalist relations of production. Apart from the question of capacity there is the question of *orientation*—will the state even "attempt" to reproduce capitalist relations of production? This is contingent on the level of *political* class struggles, that is, struggles which have as their object the control of the state. In a situation of political class balance the state may move to undermine the dominant mode of production. The study of class struggle permits us to understand the actual *operation* of reproductive mechanisms.

However, these class struggles are themselves structured and organized. In any given conjuncture, economic class struggles are determined *within limits* by the form of economic relations; but these limits may themselves be modified as class struggle in turn affects (again within limits) the form of economic relations. A similar double limiting process takes place between political class struggles and the organization of the state. Then, there is also the problem of conceptualizing the relationship between political and economic class struggles themselves—a subject which excited a great deal of attention in the Marxist literature of the Second International. In summary, the mode of determination of class struggles operates on the basis of structurally defined limits which themselves may be shifted by the level of class struggle, and conceivably bring the system to the point of collapse. The development of capitalism, that is, the outcome of competition and struggle, is therefore *indeterminate but not arbitrary*. (Przeworski has recently proposed a theory of the relationship between crises, political competition, and economic class struggles.)

The State

Seeds of the above formulation can be found in Smelser's discussion of the state's capacity to "soften the contradictions" (p. xviii), that is, to preserve the system as a whole. Unfortunately he does not relate this to his interpretation of economic primacy or to the intervention of class struggles. But even such a rudimentary characterization of the functions of the state is more sophisticated than Jordan's conventional understanding (misunderstanding?) based on a quote (misquote?) from the *Communist Manifesto*. "The executive of the modern State is but a committee for managing the common affairs of the whole bourgeoisie" is frequently rendered "the state is the executive committee of the bourgeoisie." (Jordan, p. 56, does not make the exact citation, but he certainly adopts and therefore dismisses the instrumentalist view of the state based on his reading of the *Communist Manifesto*.) Moreover, the omission does make a difference.

First, if the state is to protect the *common* interests of the *entire* bourgeoisie, then clearly it cannot side with any one capitalist or group of capitalists in the competition among capitalists or groups of capitalists. That is, the state must be to some degree autonomous from all capitalists. A relative autonomy is inscribed in the very definition of its function. Second, what are the common interests of the entire bourgeoisie, if capitalists are always competing with one another? They can only be the preservation of the capitalist system, i.e., capitalist relations of production. These interests are immediately threatened when the state assumes an "absolute" autonomy, as in circumstances of class balance (*The 18th Brumaire*), or when the state becomes the instrument of a particular "power bloc" within the capitalist class (Watergate?). Far from being an instrument of an economically dominant class for the pursuit of narrow economic interests and the oppression of subordinate classes, the state as Poulantzas has pointed out, is organized to present the interests of the capitalist class as the interests of all and to insert *all* agents of production (irrespective of their relationship to the means of production) into political and ideological activities as free and equal citizens. In so doing, the state necessarily grants concessions to the subordinate classes but such concessions, as Gramsci says, "cannot touch the essential." This perspective has, of course, been the subject of considerable debate, kindled by the work of Miliband and Poulantzas and elaborated by others such as O'Connor, Offe, and Mandel. Marxist theory of the state is now an arena of thriving discourse.

The Labor Theory of Value and Marxian Dynamics

A major problem with all these characterizations of the capitalist state is that they rest on an unstated (and unknown?) theory of the dynamics of the economy. I propose, therefore, to return briefly to the question of dynamics and in particular the validity of the falling rate of profit. For Jordan the issue is simple: "Since the consequences deriving from the theory of surplus value are disconfirmed by historical developments, the validity of the theory is doubtful and a radical modification or abandonment of it is imperative. . . . The fate of the theory of surplus value does not affect Marx's contribution to the sociology of capitalism" (p. 46). Smelser says much the same, "Many parts of Marx's synthesis—most notably the theory of value—have been discredited and are no longer taken seriously by committed Marxists" (p. xii).[2] Who, pray, are these "committed Marxists" who can so casually sweep away the foundation of the entire Marxian edifice? They are certainly not the contributors to *New Left Review, Monthly Review, Economy and Society*, or *Les Temps Modernes!* If Samuelson has to reconsider his position and devote serious attention to the labor theory of value (in connection with the recent "capital controversy" between Cambridge, England and Cambridge, United States), then perhaps the time has come for sociologists to acquaint

[2] Moreover, the authors do not specify what they understand to be the labor theory of value. Is it a theory of exploitation? A theory of the economy? A particular way of stating that the relations of production determine relations of exchange and distribution? For me it is the postulate that the socially necessary labor time embodied in a commodity bears a definite but complex relation to its price.

themselves with the real issues rather than offer outdated epitaphs. Following Sraffa's path-breaking rehabilitation of Ricardian economics and critique of marginalist economics, other British economists such as Dobb, Meek, and Morishima have injected new life into the labor theory of value. Furthermore, it is increasingly apparent that no other theory of value can account for the distribution of wealth under capitalism. To be sure, the labor theory of value has its problems, the most intransigent being the relationship of price and value—the so-called transformation problem. But even this is solvable in principle.

So what can we say about the falling rate of profit? First, the original formulae were presented in terms of value, whereas subsequent empirical invalidations have been in terms of price. Second, even if Marx's forecasts were wrong, it could be that his inferences were false rather than the assumptions embodied in the labor theory of value. The derivation of dynamics through the three volumes of *Capital* is based on primitive mathematics, using ceteris paribus arguments. A rewriting of *Capital,* with more sophisticated mathematics, is now required in order to discover which of Marx's inferences were logically sound and the additional ad hoc assumptions he was forced to make to come to his conclusions. Third, there are a wide range of countertendencies, such as reducing the cost of reproducing labor power, which off-set the falling rate of profit. In addition, competition, like struggle, is only determined within limits. It may be mitigated by the formation of coalitions, as in any Prisoner's Dilemma Game, that is through monopolies, but this by no means eliminates competition.

The destiny of the labor theory of value is not only crucial to the dynamics of capitalism and therefore to a theory of the state, but also to the Marxian notion of class. Debates are raging as to what constitutes productive labor; which workers produce surplus value (for example, Gough, Poulantzas, and O'Connor). If certain workers such as police do not produce surplus value can they still be exploited? Are janitors in government offices, schools, and factories members of the same class? Or does this depend on the conjuncture? These theoretical issues have been thrown into prominence by the feminist movement. Is housework productive labor (indirectly productive?)? Are housewives exploited or merely oppressed? These are difficult problems and cannot be treated apart from the ideological struggles that contribute to their solution.

Marxism and Functionalism

So far, we have brought together a Marxian dynamics based on competition, Smelser's stabilizing institutions, and Swingewood's class struggles. We are now in a position to consider the relationship between Marxism and structural functionalism. Swingewood's criticisms of Parsons are important but predictable; "The voluntaristic social theory which Parsons announced in *The Structure of Social Action* turns out to be no more than cultural and psychological determinism" (p. 207). In coming to this conclusion Swingewood collapses three very different theoretical structures, developed at different stages in Parsons's career, into a single framework, as if Parsons never changed his mind. (Swingewood does much the same for Marx.) It is true that in the "mature" Parsons, there is little recognition of class struggle and consciousness, and the framework is above all ahistorical. But there are reasons for this. Whereas Marx *both* develops a set of abstract concepts (as in the preface and introduction to *A Contribution to the Critique of Political Economy*—mode of production, forces of production, relations of production) *and* examines these concepts in their concrete historical form (*capitalist* mode of production), Parsons confines himself to the development of abstract or general concepts. Parsons has no criterion for periodizing history and never systematically develops a theory involving the concrete application of his abstract concepts, in the sense that Marx had a theory of capitalism. In this regard Smelser's own efforts to specify Parsons's concepts can be seen as retracing the steps of Lenin, Trotsky, Luxemburg, Lukács, Hilferding, Gramsci, Thompson, etc.

In his treatment of Marxism and functionalism, Smelser appears as a paragon of circumspection not only against the sniping of Swingewood but also against Parsons's recent dismissal of Marx as an ideologue and apostle of class struggle. (Parsons's Marx is a close kin of Swingewood's Marx.) Thus, Smelser invites Marx into the League of Functionalists. But he makes two provisos, first: "Marxism opting for the primacy of economic relations, functionalism opting for a principle of mutual interdependence of structures"; second: "Marxism giving more emphasis to the destructive impact of a single kind of contradiction, and functionalism, while acknowledging dysfunctions, tending to give more emphasis to the adjustive or reconstitutive processes" (p. xxi). Regarding the first qualification, there is obvious confusion. In writing of primacy, Smelser fails to distinguish between "determination" and "dominance" (see previous discussion) and therefore never arrives at the mutual interdependence of structures which lies at the core of the Marxian social structure. A more interesting focus would have been to compare the *form* of interdependence inscribed in Balibar's "determination in the last instance" on the one hand and in Parsons's hierarchies of control and conditioning on the other.

Implicit in the second qualification is the view that Marx had a theory of social change, the absence of which makes structural functionalism atheoretical. For Parsons has no dynamics; he has no *theory* of social change. In *The Social System* he offers a global array of possible strains that appear in ad hoc, unpredictable, and largely unstructured ways. The social structure is conceived of as a medley of jostling forces in which only chaos can be discerned, but held together by the cement of value consensus. By contrast, Marx's entire theoretical effort is to search for an underlying dynamic which will explain the apparent anarchy. In Parsons's and Smelser's *Economy and Society* (chapter 5) both the source and the consequences of "strain" are not just indeterminate but also arbitrary. In his recent work, Parsons has at best emerged with a set of concepts (differentiation, value generalization, adaptive upgrading, and inclusion) which may be used to empirically describe social change. Why change takes place at all and why it assumes any particular form is not clear.

On one issue both Swingewood and Smelser agree; that neither Marxism nor functionalism can be reduced to simple "conflict" or "consensus" models of society. Yet in pointing to the commonality of the theoretical systems they obscure a fundamental difference, namely the nature of consensus. For Parsons, value consensus is somehow given and primordial, whereas for Marx, it is organized—a consequence rather than a prior condition. For Parsons the "non-contractual elements of contract" are given prior to exchange relations, whereas for Marx consent is a *result* of exchange. The elaboration of this Marxist perspective has been the great contribution of Gramsci—a point Bottomore overlooks in his hasty dismissal of Gramsci (p. 37).

A Marxist reconstruction of Parsons would introduce a structure of the cultural system involving some notion of dynamics, periodization, and possibly contradiction, as well as a totality of structures governed by the conditions for reproducing a specific "cultural system." Habermas's combination of productive activities based on instrumental rationality and communicative interaction based on consensual norms moves some distance toward such a formulation. But, as Bottomore comments, Habermas, as a member of "the last generation of the Frankfurt School before its virtual dissolution at the end of the 1960s," has "lost any distinctive relation to Marxist theory" (p. 45). Again, our first hypothesis is upheld, namely a synthesis of "objective" and "subjective" components is impossible within the Marxist tradition.

For Marx or For Sociology?

In concluding, I wish to draw together my various references to the rapidly expanding Marxist literature, as it bears upon the viability of an autonomous Marxist tradition distinct from modern social theory. Whereas I have had space to consider only a fraction of current Marxist work in Europe and the United States, Jordan and Smelser have chosen to ignore all such contributions. In their view the major insights of Marx have already been incorporated into the body of sociology. For Jordan, Marx's analysis of the division of labor is one of his most distinctive contributions. For Smelser, what is sociologically valuable is to be found in Marx's "more concrete discussions of the composition, structure, and functioning of societies; and in his empirically informed—'middle range' if you will—analyses of the processes and mechanisms of change" (p. xxxvii). As pointed out earlier, Bottomore's outline of a "Marxist sociology" loses any distinctive relation to Marxist theory. In the light of Bottomore's immense contributions in bringing Marx and Marxism to sociology, it is strange to find him adopting such a negative view. All three are "for sociology."

Only Swingewood is "for Marx": "The task of Marxist social theory is to assimilate the strong side of non-Marxist thought and yet remain Marxist" (p. 227). As a final sentence, it may portend a future work, but in the present volume Swingewood consistently dissociates Marx from Weber, Durkheim, Schutz, and others. If indeed it is the voluntaristic components of sociology from which Swingewood is hoping to borrow, then he may well heed Bottomore's warning that in the merging of Marxist and non-Marxist "subjectivism," such as in phenomenology, "something distinctive has been lost" (p. 48). Where Swingewood sees the potential resurrection of Marxism, Bottomore sees its potential abdication.

One condition for the assimilation of non-Marxist thought, while remaining Marxist, is the definition of what is specific to Marxism, to its method, its theory, and its philosophy. Swingewood makes an attempt in his exposition of the dialectic and totality, but the result is confusing and unconvincing. While both Jordan and Smelser examine Marx the scientist, they are not interested in the distinctiveness of Marxian science in relation to other sciences or even other social sciences. Bottomore is more interested in this question. However, after inveighing against the dangers of dogmatism, he cavalierly dismisses as "an obscure body of thought" (p. 72) the school of French structuralists associated with Althusser, Balibar, Godelier, Poulantzas, and Therborn, and ignores such Italians as Della Volpe and his student Colletti. All these students of Marx are vigorously trying to establish the basis of a Marxist science—a true *Marxist* sociology.

With a secure epistemological and theoretical foundation, it will no longer be important (if it ever was) to rescue or defend Marx against his detractors—to claim, for example, on the basis of isolated citations from *Theories of Surplus Value* that Marx did indeed have a theory of the destruction and creation of places in the capitalist social structure (Swingewood, pp. 116–117). The analysis of the transformation of the occupational structure under capitalism is long overdue—but can not be done by saying that Marx knew about it all along. The man was human. He is now dead. He doesn't have to be saved. So long as we are true to a Marxist problematique, we can be more humble and less defensive about his achievements.

On Discovering Durkheim

Textes, by Emile Durkheim. *Volume 1: Eléments d'une Théorie Sociale. Volume 2: Religion, Morale, Anomie. Volume 3: Fonctions Sociales et Institutions.* Presentation by Victor Karady. Paris: Editions de Minuit, 1975. 512, 512, and 568 pp. No price listed.

Edward A. Tiryakian
Duke University

Durkheim buffs the world over—and they seem to be a growing legion—will rejoice at the publication of this three-volume set; this is undoubtedly one of the most important publication events of the decade for sociologists having more than a passing interest in the figure who, after all, secured the foundations of modern sociology. Durkheim's fame, renown, even notoriety, essentially rest upon four major books, easily available in translation (*The Division of Labor, Suicide, The Rules,* and *The Elementary Forms*); several courses that he gave have posthumously been published as books, and for the most part are readily accessible also. But there is a much larger output of his writings, which while assuredly of lesser importance than the "big four" sociological symphonies he composed are nevertheless significant in a number of ways: as early drafts or sketches for the later, more polished, mature works; as preliminary and necessary scaffolding for Durkheim's sociological enterprise; as loci of debates he was engaging in with both academic and extra-academic audiences; and lastly, as personal documents which reveal something of the "inner man," whose outer self so totally identified with sociology that Durkheim the total man has yet to be discovered. Victor Karady, research associate of the French Centre National de la Recherche Scientifique, has combed high and low to put together in these volumes writings of Durkheim which are not available in book form; left out are Durkheim's essays and extended book reviews which he published in *l'Année Sociologique,* because these have been available in a single volume, *Journal Sociologique,* by Jean Davignaud. The result is an outstanding labor of love and a real service to the profession, since it places at our disposal writings published in journals and annuals which at best only a handful of libraries and collections in the United States have; moreover, there are also unpublished items—such as letters—that have previously not appeared in print.

In *Volume 1* (which Karady has designated by the thematic title of *Elements of a Social Theory*), most of the writings deal with Durkheim's delineations of sociology as a discipline. These include the analytical differentiation of sociology from other social sciences, the relation of sociology to still other disciplines such as philosophy and history, and the state of sociology in France. An important section of this volume, chapter 3, is devoted to writings of Durkheim, done in his early formative period, which pertain to social science studies in Germany. Of particular interest are the two major articles that Durkheim published in *La Revue philosophique* in the 1880s following his study tour in Germany; one can see from these and other items the important stimulus of Wilhelm Wundt and Albert Schaeffle, in particular, on the young but already intellectually mature Durkheim. Wundt's laboratory and comparative studies of folkways and mores may well have served Durkheim later as the inspiration for the *Année Sociologique.* Also in this section are to be found his comments on Toennies's *Gemeinschaft und Gesellschaft,* which Durkheim reviewed in 1889; the review (p. 390) hints at the need for a book which would provide a thorough critique of Toennies's thesis concerning the evolutionary aspects of modern society, from organic to mechanical solidarity. That critique, of course, became Durkheim's doctoral dissertation four years later, and in *Volume 2,* Karady has appropriately included the extensive portion of the introduction to the first edition (which is the appendix to the Simpson translation of *The Division of Labor*). However fruitful Durkheim's early contacts with German social thought were, they also made Durkheim suspect in some conservative circles as being unduly under German influence; his letters on the subject (pp. 400–407), indicate how rankled he was at the unfairness of the accusations. The volume's concluding section or "annex" has various materials, which, though not sociological, present us with a spectrum of his concerns. They range from his first writing (1883), an address to the graduating class at the Lycée de Sens (which this reviewer had the pleasure of discovering in the archives of Durkheim's hometown of Epinal and which is now available in English in Robert N. Bellah, ed., *Emile Durkheim on Morality and Society*), to one of his last written items: a description of the history and structure of life at the University of Paris. The latter is part of a collective work that was designed during the war to make the United States have greater familiarity, understanding, and sympathy for France; Durkheim's piece is not only highly informative but also is part of his "war effort" for France, alongside his more partisan tracts written to persuade international public opinion of the rightfulness of the French cause against Germany (his two major pamphlets, written in 1915, are not reprinted in the present set). Also included in this section are writings which take us deeply into the "inner man," namely four necrological notices Durkheim wrote about persons very close to him: his dearest friend at the Ecole Normale, Victor Hommay; Octave Hamelin, a philosopher of great promise and one of Durkheim's closest colleagues at Bordeaux; Robert Hertz, one of the greatest of the great team Durkheim had organized in pre-war France; and André Durkheim, his only son, killed, like Hertz, during World War I. The notices that Durkheim wrote are not maudlin; they tell us about the essence of each unfortunate victim, but they also indicate that Durkheim was as full of deep feelings as he was of profound thoughts.

Volume 2: Religion, Morale, Anomie takes us to what we may regard as the core contributions of Durkheim to sociology, namely the elucidation and conceptualization of the moral dimensions of the social order (including its threatened dissolution or destruction in the phenomena of anomie). Well in advance of the 1912 publication of *The Elementary Forms,* Durkheim gave repeated attention to the relation of religion to society. The volume opens with a letter written in 1889 in which Durkheim suggests that while religiosity is very diffuse and complex, it is not an individual creation; he also states that myths and rituals are interrelated components of any religion. Reports by observers of Durkheim's conferences and lectures on religion are also made available in this volume; this includes a very extensive summary (pp. 65–122) of a course Durkheim taught in 1906–07 on the origins of religion, wherein he developed the structures for his later crowning achievement, *The Elementary Forms of the Religious Life.* But in addition to the scholarly writings on the structure and origin of religious life, there are also materials Durkheim wrote or presented in public debates on the future of religion in modern society, on the separation of church and state, and other related topics. Other writings of Durkheim to be found in this volume pertain to various aspects of "anomie and social health," including pieces on divorce, illegitimacy, and sexual education; yet another major section presents various of Durkheim's approaches to morality, which of course he wished to develop into an objective, scientific field of investigation inasmuch as Durkheim approached it as a social phenomenon.

The "annex" of this volume, like the preceding one, is extremely rewarding in uncovering dimensions of Durkheim the person. Victor Karady has managed to gather nearly one hundred pages of letters Durkheim wrote. The largest set (pp. 389–439) was made available to the editor by the daughter of Celestin Bouglé, one of the initial collaborators of the *Année Sociologique* who eventually became Director of the Ecole Normale. The entire correspondence was written while Durkheim was at Bordeaux, during the years

1896–1902, and certainly informs us of the toils involved in the early years of the *Année Sociologique.* Other letters in this section are to François Simiand, Octave Hamelin, Louis Havet, and Xavier Léon, the latter being the enterprising young publisher of *La Revue de Métaphysique et de Morale* and founder of the French Society of Philosophy. A close friendship developed between the two, which one can follow through the letters.

The third volume (*Social Functions and Institutions*) presents us with Durkheim's writings on a variety of institutional structures and practices, notably marriage and kinship (this includes his inaugural lecture of the course on the family he taught in his second year at Bordeaux, pp. 9–34), the polity, law, and jurisprudence. The closing section presents diverse materials on pedagogy and the university teaching of philosophy in France and Germany. In lieu of an "annex," Karady has provided us with a fifty-page bibliography of primary sources thoughtfully categorized and arranged by year of publication. I should add at this point that, unlike too many French scholarly publications, Karady fortunately provides in this and in each of the other two volumes a useful summary, as well as a name and a subject index.

I trust that from what I have said, readers of this review will feel prompted to have their libraries acquire this major collection of Durkheim materials. Perhaps some altruistic soul will feel the call to translate these volumes so as to broaden further the American readership. Durkheim's *Textes* make for amply rewarding reading by filling in some of the lacunae of the man and his works; they will remain required readings for some time to come.

RECENT WORK IN EDUCATION

Schooling in Capitalist America: Educational Reform and the Contradictions of Economic Life, by SAMUEL BOWLES and HERBERT GINTIS. New York: Basic Books, 1976. 340 pp. $13.95 cloth.

MICHAEL USEEM
Boston University

Traditional paradigms are undermined when seemingly anomalous "facts" accumulate and demand radically new ways of viewing the world. For at least a decade now, such problems threatened the classical liberal vision of the American system as an instrument for equalizing opportunity and creating a more harmonious social order. Indeed, problems with the liberal paradigm materialized as soon as its empirical wing initiated assessments of the impact of schooling in America. But James Coleman's *Equality of Educational Opportunity,* Christopher Jencks's *Inequality,* and related studies offered no new frameworks to explain the failure of schools to achieve liberal goals, leaving those troubled by their findings little option but to cling to tradition. Unlike its predecessors, however, *Schooling in Capitalist America* provides an innovative context for understanding education. Carefully selecting from the empirical materials left by those who have shown that education is not the great equalizer, Samuel Bowles and Herbert Gintis establish a persuasive new paradigm. Thus, failure of schools to achieve cognitive equality and reduce social inequality are not viewed as aberrations, but rather as the predictable consequences of schooling in a capitalist society. The authors bring order to an array of formerly inexplicable facts, making it likely that this seminal work will structure debate and research on American education for at least a decade.

The new paradigm for understanding schooling is self-consciously neo-Marxist. The economy is seen as the dominant institution in American society, and education is consigned to a largely subordinate status, taking its shape from capitalist demands, and, at times, popular counter-demands. Other familiar Marxist tenets are present as well—including the assertion that an institution can only be analyzed within a broad theory of the social order. Consistent with strands of contemporary Marxist thought in the US, Bowles and Gintis place particular stress on the alienation induced by hierarchic organization and the emergence of new "human needs" that can only be satisfied through wholesale reorganization of American society.

Three other aspects of Bowles and Gintis's approach require mention. First, the authors insist on verification, in contrast to the convention in some Marxist circles where points are made by quoting sacred texts or relying on purely theoretical discourse. *Schooling in Capitalist America* is representative of the empirically oriented, Marxist analysis now ascendent in American social science, an analysis that effectively overcomes the anti-theoretical bias of US inquiry and the anti-positivist bent of European Marxism. Second, important components of the Bowles-Gintis explanations have been shaped by the political and intellectual movement—the Union of Radical Political Economists (URPE)—that the authors played a key role in mobilizing. Breaking with the neo-classical and Keynesian orthodoxies of American economics, this movement has brought fresh, provocative interpretations to topics ranging from imperialism to urban squalor and the fiscal crisis of the public sector. URPE's influence here can be seen in the book's stress on the latent control value of the division of labor and in the authors' hidden dialogue with the human capital school in economics.

Finally, Bowles and Gintis make effective use of a common tool of sociological analysis—functionalism. Their analysis focuses on education's twin functions of meeting the demands of both capital accumulation and class reproduction. Yet, rather than leading to lifeless abstraction, functionalist analysis in the authors' hands becomes a creative instrument for studying relations between two nominally distinct institutions, the economy and education. By positing that education helps maintain conditions necessary for capitalist activity, testable hypotheses that are not otherwise deducible can be formulated. For example, since women are channeled into dead-end jobs in the economy or kept out of the labor market altogether, one can expect a comparable channeling of women in education. And, as it turns out, not only are these hypotheses generally confirmed, but they also prove to be more credible explanations for the present structure of education than the common presumption that education is an autonomous system largely subject to its own special laws.

Working within this framework, Bowles and Gintis offer a meticulous analysis of the central features of American education. They start with the premise that any "explanation must begin with the fact that schools produce workers" (p. 10). The type of workers depends, of course, on the kinds of jobs available. Accordingly, Bowles and Gintis present a highly condensed description of the American economy. In their view, business firms are founded around the imperatives of profit and domination. These imperatives result in continuous management efforts to press labor to work as hard as possible for the least remuneration, often in degrading conditions and always within an autocratic decision-making hierarchy. This manager-worker conflict tends to intensify over time, since, say the authors, capitalists share with bicycle riders the problem that stability is contingent on forward motion. The results include sharp disparities in income, widespread worker alienation, and unequal schooling. Up to this point the book does not purport to break new ground.

Education's subordinate role in serving the capitalist economy—the book's predominant premise—is demonstrated with the concept known as the "correspondence principle." This principle states that school structure closely parallels job structure in a number of respects. First, not only does school curriculum mirror the range of special skills required by employers, but the authoritarian structure of the school is a reproduction of the bureaucratic hierarchy of the work place. Thus, neither students nor workers are allowed to exercise any significant influence over the purpose and organization of their activity. At the same time, the fragmentation of work tasks is reflected in curricular specialization. Further, sex, race, and class discrimination in hiring, wages, and promotion are mirrored in the distribution of educational resources. Regardless of any special capacities for academic achievement, white, upper-class men are provided the best educational opportunities. Meanwhile, attempts to legitimate the hierarchic and exploitative division of labor in America also have their parallels in education. The use of IQ testing and the ideology of "meritocracy," for instance, are familiar devices for masking the perpetuation of class privilege in both sectors. Finally, the wage is the standard device for motivating laborers to undertake alienating work; and, in like fashion, the school grade is nearly universally employed to ensure student submission to an intrinsically unrewarding experience.

Two examples illustrate how the authors make their case. If the correspondence principle is accurate, personality traits rewarded in schools should parallel those emphasized in the work place. Bowles and Gintis note a striking consistency between the results of a study of the personality correlates of students with high grade-point averages and the findings of a separate examination of the character correlates of high supervisor rating of workers in several bureaucracies. Compliance with authority, dependability, and internalization of behavioral norms all enable one to predict which workers and students will be rewarded in both settings. Applying this model further, it is also anticipated that the personality traits emphasized in school will vary with the probable occupational destination of the student. A vertical differentiation is likely, with students destined for managerial positions being encouraged to develop leadership and decision-making skills, while students channeled to subordinate positions are socialized to comply with authority. Such a pattern is found in a comparative study of colleges whose student bodies vary sharply in their likely adult occupations.

Schooling, then appears to reproduce the future work conditions of students as a form of anticipatory socialization. The political process by which schools adopt policies corresponding to those of business organization is, of course, critically important. Unless political influences can be identified, correspondence may be no more than temporal coincidence and economic change will not result in altered educational programs. Unfortunately, political connections receive only the scantest attention in *Schooling in Capitalist America.* Since this is probably the least researched issue in American education, Bowles and Gintis had virtually no material on which to construct a case. They do, however, suggest two mechanisms by which the concerns of business are transmitted into educational programs. One consists of the unplanned response of individual students, teachers, parents, and school administrators to "economic reality." Parents, for instance, pressure schools to offer programs that will make their children employable and the result is the establishment of very vocationally-oriented programs that business people themselves would urge on the system. The second mechanism is significant only in time of crisis. When major education principles are at stake, social classes become self-interested actors. The capitalist class, by virtue of its strategic position on governing boards and its control over financial resources, consciously intervenes to ensure that the emergent policies conform to changing economic demands.

Yet other classes have not passively accepted the capitalist-determined educational policies. According to Bowles and Gintis, contradictions of the broader society also find their correspondence in the social system. Just as labor has collectively resisted exploitative and alienating management policies, students often have banded together to challenge similar policies imposed by school administrators. The college rebellions of the late 1960s, for example, can be seen, in part, as a student response to the bureaucratization of the campus induced by the expansion and degradation of white collar work in the US. These political struggles emanating from educational contradictions, themselves rooted in economic contradictions, are a central dynamic behind educational change. To illuminate this general concept, Bowles and Gintis extensively survey three critical junctures in the history of American education: the emergence of the public school system in the mid-nineteenth century, the educational reforms of the Progressive Era, and the massive expansion and transformation of higher education since World War II.

Ultimately, Bowles and Gintis present a compelling case, but it is an unproven one. Even readers with relaxed standards of empirical verification will recognize that the correspondence principle is in a tentative stage of formulation. Similarly, though the authors seem to be on firm footing when they argue that the primary purpose of schooling is not the inculcation of cognitive skills, more research is needed before it can be concluded safely that the character development is the more significant feature of education's role in reproducing the class structure. The book contains a plausible but not fully documented analysis and it offers an implicit research agenda for sociologists and economists for years to come.

Conceptual problems weaken certain arguments of the book. The translation of economic interests into educational policies, for instance, is held to be mediated by the capitalist class during periods of overt conflict. Yet this would seem to be predicated on the collective consciousness, cohesion, and unity of action in the capitalist class that is rarely, if ever, seen in the US. More generally, the book's political sociology is underdeveloped; and lacking an adequate theory of the state and political process, the book tends to fall back on ad hoc explanations for linkages between the economy and education. The absence of adequate theoretical anchoring is also apparent in the concept of alienation, which at times is without social organizational roots, and therefore, significant political potential. Another weakness is that only marginal connections are apparent between the strategies for educational change occupying the book's closing pages and the previously developed analytic scheme. Finally, a book purporting to offer an encompassing analysis of education is bound to leave most readers a bit disappointed that their favorite topics are treated inadequately. For instance, readers primarily interested in the role of teachers or the place of academic research will find little analysis here.

Nonetheless, *Schooling in Capitalist America* is a work of exemplary scholarship. It is a graphic demonstration of the effectiveness of neo-Marxist analysis in arranging an array of evidence into an appealing framework for the interpretation of a major American institution. The authors lean heavily on research conducted not only by economists and sociologists, but also by historians, psychologists, and political scientists, making the work a model of inter-disciplinary analysis. In line with contemporary concerns, Bowles and Gintis are explicitly policy oriented, though not toward educational administrators. Rather, numerous policy proposals are offered to students, teachers, activists, and others who would democratize education, reorient it to serve working class and minority interests better, and otherwise radically alter the organization of education. In the meantime, the book provides a realistic and comprehensive, albeit tentative, explanation for the structure and purpose of schooling in America that has never before been available.

Existentialism and Phenomenology in Education: Collected Essays, edited by DAVID E. DENTON. New York: Teachers College Press, 1974. 220 pp. $9.95 cloth.

JOHN M. JOHNSON
Arizona State University

The essays in this volume are intended to present a comprehensive view of the leading edge of existential and phenomenological thought regarding educational philosophy, theory, and practice. They originated from the 1971 meetings of the Philosophy of Education Society, and seek to update and redefine the relevance of existential-phenomenological thinking for education since the publication of the only major works in this area, George Kneller's 1958 *Existentialism and Education* and Van Cleve Morris's 1966 *Existentialism in Education*. The volume includes ten essays, eight of which are published here for the first time, and these are presented in four untitled sections, an appropriate format for their thematic diversity.

The volume's lengthiest essay is Leroy Troutner's comprehensive overview of the similarities and differences between the educational thought of John Dewey and that of the leading existentialist and phenomenological thinkers, especially Husserl, Heidegger, Kierkegaard, Schiller, and Tillich. There can be little doubt that John Dewey's educational thought has been, and still is, the bedrock of liberal educational theory in the US, and an extensive discussion of him is appropriate and just. Troutner challenges the contemporary relevance of the taken-for-granted ideas of educational liberalism, and charges that Dewey's pragmatism and experimentalism insufficiently appreciate the relative independence of individuals from their immediate environments, the reflexive nature of the self, and the processes of an individual's becoming. These are some of the key ideas to be found in the writings of some of the important existential thinkers. The objective of Troutner's discussion is to propose a philosophical anthropology of education which adequately appreciates the respective educational contributions of Dewey and Heidegger, one which hopefully eliminates their respective problems and weaknesses as well.

The four essays of part II explore issues related to the promotion and practice of aesthetic education. Taken together, they criticize the rationalism, materialism, scientism, and abstract wordsmithing extant in our pedagogical institutions (or tell why earlier existentialists were so critical of these), and they call for (abstractly) a new awareness of existential possibilities, of caring, of radical individual freedom, of reflexivity, of commitment, of becoming. Eugene Kaelin tries to set forth the existential grounds for aesthetic education in his chapter by that title, and Maxine Greene and Philip Phenix examine the relevance of many of the literary contributions of the early and contemporary existentialists in their respective chapters. David Denton's "That Mode of Being Called Teaching" presents a hypothetical dialogue which intends a reflexive understanding of teaching as a distinctive and irreducible way of being. Each of these chapters presupposes the reader's familiarity with past and present scholarship and literature, as do some of the others as well, and they are ill-suited for those who are seeking an "introduction" to existential or phenomenological thought.

Part III includes Gordon Chamberlin's "Phenomenological Methodology and Understanding Education," an exceptionally well done exposition of the relevence of Edmund Husserl's difficult thought for educational theory and practice. Also, Clinton Collins's "The Multiple Realities of Schooling" is a fine analysis of Alfred Schutz's writings and their relevance for understanding the different levels of meaning which inhere in the educational process. The final part of the volume includes Troutner's phenomenological analysis of time, a favorite topic for phenomenologists, and the practical (and policy) relevancies of such an analysis. The concluding essay is Donald Vandenberg's excellent discussion of the prevailing assumptions of educational theory and research, and includes some innovative suggestions for advancing toward a more meaningful educational theory and understanding.

Existentialism and Phenomenology in Education is a mixed bag of essays, covering diverse topics with varied intelligibility and quality. Those unschooled in the existential-phenomenological style-of-hyphenated-exposition and concepts-which-insist-on-processual-and-relational-primacy will likely conclude that much old wine is being poured into some new bottles here. But the essays do reveal the potential creativity and insight of phenomenological analyses, and they are likely to make for an especially meaningful contribution for those who grasped their essential truth before reading them.

Work, Technology, and Education: Dissenting Essays in the Intellectual Foundations of American Education, edited by WALTER FEINBERG and HENRY ROSEMONT, JR. Urbana: University of Illinois Press, 1975. 220 pp. $10.00 cloth.

ZELDA F. GAMSON
University of Michigan, Ann Arbor

A paradox: This book could not have been written if its argument applied to its authors. By now, the radical critique of American education should be familiar to the readers of *Contemporary Sociology*. Best spelled out in the introductory essay by Feinberg and Rosemont and in the chapter by Herbert Gintis and Samuel Bowles, it goes like this: The schools have always been intimately related to the surrounding society. A correct understanding of this relationship should pay particular attention to the requisites and social relations in the workplace. As the social relations of production have changed (or not changed), so have the schools. Industrial capitalism needs a work force which can perform in a differentiated, hierarchically organized occupational structure. The generation, stabilization, and selection of cognitive and psychomotor skills, personality traits, and self-presentational styles for later performance of work roles fall to the family and the schools. The family and the schools work together to reinforce class-based characteristics which determines access to and participation in different levels of the organization of production.

A correspondence principle holds, such that the form and content of social relations in family life, education, and production show great similarity. Parents whose jobs require the observance of rules and punctuality will tend to rear their children according to these requisites, will send their children to schools which are organized to "reproduce" these traits in youngsters, who in turn will enter jobs requiring them, and so on. At the other end, parents whose jobs require internalized standards and independence will value these characteristics in their children and in their children's schools. The end result is that the system of education, through its production of a well-tuned labor force, neither promotes individual self-development nor equality of opportunity: "Under corporate capitalism, the correspondence between the social relation of production and the social relation of reproduction . . . precludes egalitarian humane education . . ." (p. 120).

This analysis of the functions of education builds on, and contributes to, the burgeoning revisionist literature on the history of American education, particularly of reform movements. The use of public education as a way of controlling and socializing immigrants and lower class youth to the needs of an increasingly industrialized and technological economic order is the theme of works published elsewhere by Michael Katz. In this volume, Joel Spring examines the development of the modern high school and James Anderson reinterprets the educational reform movement for blacks in the South at the turn of the century. Feinberg and Rosemont, in "Training for the Welfare State: The Progressive Education Movement" and Gintis and Bowles, in "The Contradictions of Liberal Educational Reform" argue that the progressives of yesterday and today have failed to change education in any serious way because they either did not recognize the dependency of schooling on social and economic forces or accepted that dependency and worked to make it more effective.

The radical critique is now a well-developed framework for interpreting the relations between schooling and society. Here and elsewhere, the economists Bowles and Gintis have drawn in a sophisticated way from the work on educational and class stratification, on childrearing values and techniques, and on industrial psychology. One can argue with their interpretation of the sociological and social psychological research, but the more important point lies in the "correspondence principle" itself. Under their Marxist approach lurks a rather simple-minded functionalism which sees things fitting together all too neatly. The educational system has not been *that* successful, nor has industrial capitalism. Non-capitalist industrial societies seem to fit the argument just as well, if not better. Individuals and groups have broken out of the cycle. Contradictions are engendered by the very nature of education, whereby the system the authors describe can be criticized and attacked, resisted and undermined. The authors themselves are examples, as are rebels and reformers of recent years who are products of the educational system which was to "reproduce" them.

It is important to pay attention to these exceptions; they sharpen the focus considerably. Furthermore, for both theory and practice, the radicals must begin to conduct systematic research at a macro-level on the effects of technology on the educational process (the essays by Kenneth Benne, Max Wartofsky, Don Ihde and Noam Chomsky in this volume begin such an analysis but do not draw on empirical work), and on the *mechanisms* by which society has its effects on schools. Who have been the policy-makers for educational institutions at various levels? How has policy been made and implemented? What have been the relationships between industrial elites and educational elites? How have resources been distributed through the educational system? Exactly how has the school curriculum, hidden and otherwise, been shaped by the occupational and economic structure? Anderson's historical essay on black education is exemplary in tracing the answers to some of these questions. We need more evidence from other time and other places.

Sociologie de l'education: Textes fondamentaux, by Alain Gras. Paris: Larousse Libraire, 1974. 382 pp. No price listed, paper.

Remi Clignet
Northwestern University

As the author notes, sociological studies of education have increased, as a response to the anxieties and concerns that the multifaceted educational crises of the last decade have generated among various segments of the population.

This book, an edited collection of articles, is unusual in French publishing, which, up to now, has rarely issued anthologies in the field of social sciences. Such books raise three kinds of questions for a reviewer. Is the technique appropriate to the needs of the market? Are the articles chosen representative of the most significant theories and methodologies in the field? Last, does the editing per se make sense and what does the entire volume tell us about the discipline?

To deal with the first question first, I respectfully submit that I do not think that a collection of articles written by different authors is necessarily an appropriate tool for stimulating educational communications between teachers and students. Often enough, disparities in the vocabulary or strategies used by various authors for idiosyncratic reasons lower the general level of understanding. At the same time, it is certainly essential to be exposed to such disparities in order to achieve a better appreciation of the tension between essence and existence. But who is going to profit most from this kind of experience? The problem is worth researching.

As is always the case, the selection of articles will make some readers happy and will leave some others dissatisfied. Happy, because some of the works presented are original, and it is not often that one can read about Swedish educational policies or about Chinese controversies and polemics on the functions of education. Further, the editor stresses the significance of the variations taken by educational phenomena in distinctive historical and cultural contexts and this is very important in view of his orientations. In this regard, it is always refreshing to read an author such as Isambert Jamati who is not getting the fame she deserves (another topic of research). But some readers will be unhappy because the editor relies too often upon reviews of original texts or researches rather than upon such texts themselves. For example, the reader learns about the views of

Basil Bernstein through the reviews of Denis Lawson whose glasses are not always rosy as far as Bernstein is concerned. In addition, some of the selections appear to have been chosen because they were fashionable. Durkheim and Illich, Parsons and McLuhan are very strange bedfellows, and their proximity is more esthetic than scientific.

Last, the organization of the themes makes sense. The editor begins with a macro sociological view of the functions served by formal schooling. After reviewing the profile of the major actors present in the educational scene and their roles, he returns to a macro sociological level to examine the screening and weeding out functions that schools perform. At the same time, however, the editor falls in one of the major traps of the current sociological profession; it is highly fashionable to stress the fact that schools and educational roles replicate more significant social arrangements, and that educational institutions tend for that reason to be the dependents of industries or commercial organizations. So far so good. But to the extent that economists and sociologists have established that there is not one but several labor markets characterized by differing organizational and behavioral patterns, one would expect the same hypothesis of differentiation to be applied to the educational context. Yet, the author prefers to remain at an ideological level and to acclaim the contributors who treat knowledge as an undifferentiated whole, or to claim it himself. But if the industrial world influences the educational universe, there is no reason to assume that there is *not* a segmentation of the forms of knowledge and hence of the forms of educational communication analogous to that operating in the labor market. I have said "*no* reason to assume that there is *not*": sociology does not only include the presentation of ideological themes but it also requires the testing of hypotheses, toward which a researcher may have a varying amount of sympathy, but feels obliged, all the same, to evaluate.

Black Consciousness, Identity, and Achievement: A Study of Students in Historically Black Colleges, by PATRICIA GURIN and EDGAR EPPS. New York: John Wiley & Sons, 1975. 545 pp. $13.95 cloth.

A. E. PARIS
Cornell University

In focusing upon Black students from predominantly Black colleges, Gurin and Epps have seized upon a population and a series of issues of real importance. The findings and results of research in this area affect not only national educational policy, but, if embodied in policy guidelines and legislation, will have direct impact on the structure of opportunities for large numbers of Black young people about to enter or already within the nation's higher education facilities. Further, the population with which they deal has heretofore not received a great deal of systematic attention. A project such as this one which collected both longitudinal (1964–70) and cross-sectional (eight schools, enrolling some 18,000 students) data constitutes a valuable base for understanding the characteristics of an often ignored population. This research therefore offers an addition and a needed corrective to previous interpretations built upon scanty data and faulty assumptions.

The authors make it clear that these students do not suffer from the "burden of Black Higher Miseducation." In fact, in their diversity, motivation, achievement, etc., they look much like their peers in other groups and in other schools. There are differences to be sure (e.g., more than 35% of the entering Black students at these schools have family incomes under $4,000 a year) but such differences have not amounted to fatal defects. Along the way, several items in the conventional wisdom regarding (Black) college populations are effectively challenged. The data demonstrate an equality of motivation and performance between Black lower and upper income students; the insignificance of family background on student performance; the absolute irrelevance of paternal presence or absence on individual achievement; Black female dominance was likewise shown up as mythic. Black college-educated women were found to be less ambitious than men, their goals reflected lower educational and occupational aspirations, and they suffered the effects of race and sex-discrimination in their work lives as well. Black activism (within the parameters of social psychological discussion) was redefined more adequately as an expression of ideology and sophisticated political understanding rather than as alienation and powerlessness, as in previous research.

Of crucial importance at this political moment was the data-backed demonstration of equality of motivation and performance among the lower and upper income Black students. Minority students have become increasingly restive over the last few years over policies designed to limit, if not actively discourage, the admission of lower income students to higher education. Students have charged that administrators are acting under the presumption that lower income students are more politicized—hence activist—than more affluent students, and these policies are therefore designed to preserve stability. Administrators, insofar as they have responded, have claimed that lower income students are less competent and therefore less worthy of admission than the more affluent. Such findings of equality of motivation and performance undercut these administrative rationales and pull the covers from often overtly political educational policy.

There is, however, a key objection to be leveled at the work. It may well be that the overall form in which the research results are cast constitutes a strait-jacket on innovative and critical thinking. In choosing to focus on the achievement of Black students, the authors locate their effort within a well-established social-psychological discussion, but one whose relevance and utility is currently being questioned. The authors themselves note (chapter 15) that achievement is tied to a complex of ideas rooted in individualism: an individualism tied to a specific American Liberalism, antithetical to collective commitments and family loyalties, valuing competition rather than cooperation, etc. This sociopolitical paradigm is, in turn, linked to the ideological hegemony of the American middle classes. As the intellectual grip of these strata has weakened, the political and ideological roots of academic discussions centering on achievement, etc., have become increasingly clear.

By constraining themselves within the bounds of the conventional social-psychological discussion, the authors are locked into a political stance vis-á-vis that discussion. This gives their work a flavor of defensive apologia and detracts from its potential originality. The question is not whether Black students are as achievement oriented as Whites but rather what original or different perspectives and conceptions can be brought to bear to illuminate the experience encapsulated within this data set. This larger and more critical task is not addressed by the authors and consequently their book suffers.

In calling the larger paradigm into question, one must remain sensitive to the situation of non-White social scientists. They must often do battle against implicit or overtly biased theories and formulations. In this instance, the discussions regarding the ideological bias of the Internal-External Scale, and the data-backed challenge to formulations over-emphasizing Black psychopathology are valuable counters to current discussion. It is not that these are useless efforts but that they are the small details of a larger edifice. It is the whole edifice that is in need of substantial renovation. It is to be hoped that this work is but a prolegomenon to that larger project.

How They Fared: The Impact of the Comprehensive School upon the University, by GUY R. NEAVE. Boston: Routledge & Kegan Paul, 1975. 249 pp. No price listed, cloth.

JOHN C. WEIDMAN
University of Minnesota, Minneapolis

This volume addresses an important concern of national educational policy around the world, namely, what is the relationship between the organizational structure of secondary education, especially its differentiation of students by ability, and the social class distribution of entrants to higher education?

Neave has surveyed almost a thousand graduates of state-supported "comprehensive" schools (primary aim: "to provide secondary education for all children in a given neighborhood") who were enrolled in universities. Graduates enrolled in post-secondary institutions for engineering or teacher education are excluded. The comprehensive school, a relatively recent arrival on the British scene, is portrayed as an increasingly popular alternative to the traditional state-supported grammar school, where admission is based on selection at the age of eleven (using scores on the standardized, Eleven Plus exam), and the curriculum is oriented solely toward preparation for university attendance. The general findings are that comprehensive schools have improved access by social class to all universities (with the notable exception of the elite Oxbridge), both by postponing selection until much later in secondary school, and by providing more open access for students to college-preparatory curricula. While the tables included in the book do not always support the conclusions drawn from them. Neave's treatment of the rich data is reasonably good.

One paradox does appear, to the eyes of this reviewer from the other side of the Atlantic, in Neave's concluding suggestion that the British higher education system would be wise to follow the model of the standardized test used widely for college admission in the United States, the SAT exam. Neave is willing to settle for reducing one type of social class bias by postponing selection until graduation from secondary school, while retaining a corresponding social class bias introduced by the use of SAT and kindred exams that has, in fact, led to reduced emphasis on such exams for college admissions in the United States.

On the whole, this is a very informative volume. While dealing with the British educational system, the findings have significant implications for other national systems where students are differentiated by ability and selected for college-preparatory study relatively early in their school years.

Education and Social Control: A Study in Progressive Primary Education, by RACHEL SHARP and ANTHONY GREEN. Boston: Routledge & Kegan Paul, 1975. 256 pp. $21.75 cloth. $12.00 paper.

ROSALIE COHEN
Temple University

The title of this book may be somewhat misleading, suggesting a macro-sociological analysis of a school system. It is, instead, a micro-analysis of the teacher's role, in interaction with pupils; it uses a phenomenological approach and ideal-type case analysis to illustrate how teachers create and manage academic stratification in the classroom, and thus determine the life chances of their pupils. During the initial phases of the study, a shift had been made from a symbolic interactionist approach to the phenomenological which, resulted in a long (and unnecessary) justification for this change in the early chapters. And, although the original study design called for two schools for comparison and contrast, apparent difficulties in establishing rapport for the study in the second school resulted in discarding it as a study arena, weakening the outcomes of the research considerably. Comparison and contrast of ideal-type reaction characteristics of teachers and pupils in the remaining school, however, and the conclusions drawn from them, were sufficiently interesting to warrant further study.

The research done here by the authors bears upon major educational change themes in modern countries. It illuminates methods to achieve equalization of educational opportunity goals in England, as a country influenced by the American school and its contemporary crises. The arena for the study was Mapledene Lane School in a housing development (estate) for low income families in an English urban industrial community. A child-centered curriculum had been selected as especially appropriate for these children, and, in this new school, it had been established as the prevailing ethos. The authors illustrate how, despite the requirements to meet pupil "needs, interests and readiness levels," and despite describable variations among teachers in how they viewed the pupils and the teaching-learning process, literacy and numeracy were still the expected outcomes of the educational enterprise; little effort had been made to establish additional criteria for educational accountability appropriate to the new methods, and "busyness" had become the established norm for purposes of classroom management. Because no new educational theories had been put forth to undergird the child-centered classroom, teachers had strengthened genetic explanations and adopted psychiatric ones for good or poor performance; and major changes in teacher education for teaching in such schools had been modified to include sub-specialties in these areas. The authors comment, "the frequently found relationship between child-centered approaches to pedagogy and a social pathology approach to certain categories of pupils would be interpreted not merely as some accidental or contingent association, but logically related to certain types of structural conditions . . ." apparent in the classroom. The effect of these new approaches (if these results can be generalized) has been, thus, to reduce the extant number of alternative explanations of deviance to a single, "fuzzy" explanation—an observation which has been made in other countries, including the US, by other researchers.

One chapter of special interest to sophisticated readers comments on the absence of a language to describe non-traditional expectations of the child-centered approach. To fall back on the available language of psychiatry without due consideration and acceptance of one or another of their clearly definable theories of mental development is viewed, thus, as a lack of responsibility on the parts of education-centered researchers and professionals.

In general, the phenomenological approach used by the authors was a productive one, drawing out, with considerable sensitivity, the motivations behind ideal-typical modes of response to classroom expectations. Despite the exploratory character of this study and the limits of the study design, this study provides some provocative insights into the directions of contemporary educational change.

Teachers and Meaning: Definitions of Classroom Situations, by ROBERT A. STEBBINS. Leiden: E. J. Brill, 1975. 140 pp. No price listed, cloth.

THOMAS J. COTTLE
The Children's Defense Fund of the Washington Research Project

Of the many sociological traditions of inquiry, that involved with defining the situation is one of the richest. Its intellectual predispositions in symbolic interactionism, Weber's concept of Verstehen, the social phenomenological work of Schutz, and general social perception are strong and viable. Contemporary research in ethnomethodology, participant observation, and ecological psychology reveal that the tradition remains ripe and promising. In one respect, it is not uncommon for those working in this fascinating field to write a complex prose, almost as if their new work in the structure and nature of social action demanded that they create new linguistic forms and neologisms to convey their findings and the newness of the territory they have claimed. But this last phrase should be amended. For the new territory is in fact old but unstudied territory for the rest of us, in the sense that it is everyday, familiar, even routine behavior that these scientists are studying.

With *Teachers and Meaning,* Robert A. Stebbins has made still another valuable contribution to the tradition of defining the situation. More specifically, he has attempted to create a series of hypotheses that help us to understand the meaning of certain classroom actions and activities to teachers. Focusing on the manner in which teachers in two schools, one in Jamaica the other in Newfoundland, deal with the *meaning* of disorderly behavior, academic performance, and tardiness, surely a less studied variable, he leads us through most interesting and soundly written discussions of the definition of the situation. Acknowledging his own intellectual progenitors, Dewey, Thomas, Znaniecki, Goffman, and the writings of Willard Waller, Professor Stebbins lays out three modes of situational definitions: cultural, habitual personal, and unique personal. He then presents a series of thirteen operational statements which have guided his classroom observations and interviews with teachers. In a sense, these statements reflect the phases of actors as they define situations. In perceiving others, looking at ourselves in the situation and reacting to ourselves and others during and after the completion of a particular action, as for example, chastising a student for being tardy, we begin to see the phase development of situational definitions. In simplest terms, we make a teaching plan, enact it or change it, all of which requires leisurely or spontaneous reflection. Then we react to the enactment of the plan.

From the outset, Professor Stebbins's purpose is clear and forthright. He wishes to produce "general statements about *classes* of definitions used by identifiable groups . . . in particular but recurrent situations." His research problems involve systematically examining first, the cultural or habitual definitions available to people in a given situation, and second, the common predispositions activated by a situation and ultimately influencing the definition of that situation.

With this in mind, Stebbins's observations and recordings of classroom behavior (teacher behavior really) find a useful if not wholly ingenious context. His observations are hardly new, nor do the people he is studying come alive, which is not necessarily a worthwhile criterion of successful research. As he rightly claims, his theories and methods may help teachers define their situations, although I question his assertion that teachers, like other professionals, are unable to provide descriptions and organizations of their work routines. Too often we forget that some of the limitations of human behavior we claim to observe are the results of our inquiries, *our* conceptions, and preconceptions.

Clearly, there is value in studies of this sort, but the exact value is, well, yet to be defined. For in this type of work we not only inquire into the meanings people proffer about their situations, but we teach them how to think about their situations. Thus, the very same tensions inherent in the teacher-student relationship emerge in the teacher-researcher relationship. All of us in this business have our special fields of information to impart, a need for social order, and highly mannered and ritualistic forms of social observation, self perception, and assessment of performance which may or may not enlighten those we teach. Hopefully, *Teachers and Meaning* is a step toward this enlightenment.

The New Negro on Campus: Black College Rebellions of the 1920's, by RAYMOND WOLTERS. Princeton, N.J.: Princeton University Press, 1975. 348 pp. $15.00 cloth.

RONALD W. SAUFLEY
University of California, Santa Cruz

By 1920, many of the nation's black colleges were in extremely precarious positions. They generally existed in hostile environments and were primarily led by men, mostly white, who felt it imperative to placate either the white South or the Northern philanthropists who, to insure economic expansion, had acceded to the South's view on Negro education. This view emphasized that "higher education" for blacks should primarily consist of vocational training designed to assure docile black graduates taking subordinate positions in a white dominated society.

As a result of the Hampton and Tuskegee models stressing job training and moral piety and the enormous influence of Booker T. Washington who was convinced that manual skills and property were prerequisite for white acceptance of blacks, many of the black colleges over the previous twenty-five years had moved away from "Classical" education to primarily vocational programs. This played directly into white hands. Any moves toward restrengthening the liberal arts were met with hostility and were regarded as dangerous because already decreasing philanthropic support might be cut-off.

At the same time, while white colleges had greatly loosened student controls, most black colleges still retained rigid tutelary discipline to reassure Southern whites that Negroes would always know their place. The implications were not lost on black students.

By 1920, however, the New Negro movement was gaining speed. Racial pride and the egalitarianism of DuBois were taking hold. The rising tide of black "consciousness" would ultimately demand that blacks take greater control of their own institutions.

In *The New Negro on Campus,* Raymond Wolters skillfully examines the clash between conservative forces still trying to mold black colleges to their own philosophy in the 1920s, and the New Negro who demanded far greater control over institutions that shaped black lives. The majority of the book is comprised of case studies of differing rebellions at a variety of black campuses which led to the resignations of several college presidents and aroused the anger of black alumni. Included are studies of Fisk, the leading liberal arts college; Hampton and Tuskegee, the vocational powers; Howard, the only black multiversity; two state-supported land grant colleges; and white and black church-controlled institutions. The case studies are supplemented by two detailed chapters which put the 1920s rebellions within the context of black college history.

While black control is the underlying issue, there are several other themes which permeate the book. Always there is the looming figure of DuBois battling against the Booker Washington/Tuskegee legacy which often led vocationally oriented blacks to cooperate with the white power structure. Academic politics are stressed; but political machinations often rose far above the academic level. R. R. Moton's fight for black control of Tuskegee Veterans' Hospital continually involved the President of the United States. Nathan Young's fight to make Lincoln (Missouri) a real university involved three governors and an incredible story of corrupt state-wide politics, graft, and battles for control of university patronage. Another continuing theme, often prevalent today, concerns the extent to which a black college can allow itself to be co-opted in order to secure necessary resources.

Wolters's book is a well-researched historical exposition remarkably devoid of jargon. It is also eminently readable. In the preface the author notes that above all he was "trying to tell an interesting story." He has!

BOOK REVIEWS

Crime, Law, and Deviance

Drinking Habits among Alcoholics, by SALME AHLSTRÖM-LAAKSO. Helsinki: The Finnish Foundation for Alcohol Studies. Distributed by Rutgers Center of Alcohol Studies, New Brunswick, N.J., 1975. 215 pp. $8.00 cloth.

ODIS E. BIGUS
University of Tulsa

This book presents findings from a two stage panel survey, conducted during 1968 and 1969 in three Finnish locations (Helsinki and two rural communities). The surveys were conducted under the auspices of the Finnish Foundation for Alcohol Studies and the Social Research Institute of Alcohol Studies, to ascertain the effects on the drinking behavior of alcoholics of a new Finnish Alcohol Act, which in several ways extended the availability of alcoholic beverages.

The general design, sampling, and measurement techniques are replete with problems (probably the most serious of which involve sampling and the reliability of alcoholic self-reports on surveys), as are probably all attempts to survey largely non-institutionalized alcoholic populations. The author clearly recognizes and discusses most of these problems, but as he himself acknowledges, recognition and discussion will not make them disappear. He reasonably (although somewhat more optimistically than this reviewer would) represents the validity of his findings by stating, "It was a foregone conclusion that the results would be rough approximations." Because space restrictions prohibits an adequate airing here, the question as to whether or not these problems, added together, are severe enough to undermine the usefulness of the findings must be left up to the individual who chooses to read the book.

However, several specific findings are so strong as to erase any doubt that they were produced primarily by the changes in the Alcohol Act. Notably, the increase in overall consumption, as reported by the respondents (who were 849 in number and all men between the ages of 21 and 59 years) was 46%. Also, the increase in consumption of medium strength beer, which was made more available by the act, was four times in Helsinki, 12 times in one rural community, and 28 times in the other rural community. Many of the other findings inspire less confidence because of their failure to indicate strong patterns across the three subsamples, and the fact that they could rather easily have been produced by sampling and measurement problems or variables not attended to in the study. They are, however, as valid as could be expected with the difficulties inherent in surveying alcoholic populations.

The book, which was originally written in Finnish, is well written and well translated (although it suffers from an overabundance of typographical errors).

This book might be of interest to persons who are intent on keeping abreast of the most recent "findings" in the area of alcohol abuse, and possibly those interested in the effects of official control policies on behavior. It is void of conceptualization and theory, and thus has few if any implications beyond these areas.

Social Deviance in Australia, edited by ANNE R. EDWARDS and PAUL R. WILSON. Melbourne, Australia: Cheshire, 1975. 294 pp. $6.95 paper.

FRANCES H. LOVEJOY
University of New South Wales

Two sections of this book are outstanding. Part one competently reviews the symbolic interactionist perspective of the sociology of deviance. Part five, "Whither Deviance?," contains a brilliant critique of symbolic interactionism by Dennis Altman (who is both a social scientist and—as the author of *Homosexual Oppression and Liberation*—one of Australia's most articulate deviants). Altman attacks the "tolerant" stance of the interactionist which "acts so as to diminish the potential of deviance in bringing about political change, and in effect trivializes those who are stigmatized." He also documents ways in which the political dimension is ignored in such deviance studies.

Parts two, three, and four contain articles set in Australia on the labeling process, lawbreaking deviants, and other rule-breakers respectively. Unfortunately their substantive content is insufficient for them to remedy adequately the lack of an anthology of field studies for Australian deviance courses. Each section is preceded by an overview which links it to the central theoretical concerns of part one.

Its extensive bibliographies, careful linking of fieldwork to theory, and quota of specific studies make it a useful text. It also deserves to be read by researchers and militant deviants for its theoretical analyses.

The Female Offender, edited by ANNETTE M. BRODSKY. Beverly Hills, Calif.: Sage Publications, 1975. 108 pp. $3.95 paper.

HARRIET ENGEL GROSS
Governors State University

Slim volume, "slim pickins," at least for the academic sociologist. The articles were originally gathered for a special journal edition, but unlike the best of such editions, the collection is a thinly threaded mélange. One gets the distinct impression that the conference at which some of the papers were delivered took all comers, as did the editor of this volume. This may have been supportable when the book was put together, but such works as Rita Simon's *Women and Crime* and Freda Adler's *Sisters in Crime*, published in the same year, speak to the previous neglect of the subject much more substantively. With the exception of the first article which gives a presentable, if less than exhaustive, review of the literature, and the last article (editor's contribution) which offers reasonable suggestions for future planning (e.g., include in plans for women the fact that their ties with family members are important to their well-being), the gist of the remaining articles can be summarized quickly. We "learn" such less than astonishing facts that attractive female offenders get a better deal than unattractive female offenders, and that the personality profiles of men and women inmates differ with women showing such traits as greater "sensitivity of feeling" (p. 44). There's a feminist activitist's discussion of the women's movement's relation to the topic with the revealingly astructural assertion "that one of the most important things feminists can do with women in jail and in the criminal justice system is to teach more assertive behavior" (p. 8). A director of a prison then notes that the status of women offenders differs from that of men in lower recidivism rates, smaller facilities, and relatively more personal relations with institutional personnel. An ex-offender reaffirms the dire need for vocational training that inculcates marketable skills. More imaginatively, she calls for efforts to educate the public about ex-offenders as an antidote to the nearly exclusive rehabilitative concern with changing the offender herself. In sum, the collection lacks theoretical sophistication but may provide practioners with some useful directives.

The Heroin Epidemics: A Study of Heroin Use in the United States, 1965–75, by LEON GIBSON HUNT and CARL D. CHAMBERS. New York: Spectrum Publications, 1976. 145 pp. No price listed, cloth.

PAUL ATTEWELL
University of California, San Diego

The demographic or epidemiological examination of deviant behavior is an extraordinarily difficult undertaking. The deviants themselves spend much of their time trying to avoid appearing in the statistics (i.e., arrest records, entries to treatment, etc.), and the interpretation of available data is both complex and error-prone.

In recent years, a good deal of work has been done on the demographic/epidemiological characterization of heroin abuse, and Hunt and Chambers's book is the first comprehensive exposition of the methods and findings of this approach. There will probably be considerable debate over some of the methods and interpretations: however, this is clearly destined to be the definitive analysis of the micro-transmission of heroin use from individual to individual, and the macro-diffusion of use across the US.

The book is also an extremely lucid and interesting account of heroin phenomena, and is written such that even non-mathematical readers will learn much about heroin, despite the proliferation of statistical models, simulations, and formulae.

Its basic findings fly in the face of much popular mythology concerning heroin addiction. At the micro level, heroin typically spreads by peer contact among youths age 15 to 21. Once a person has been addicted for any length of time his/her peer group has probably also turned to heroin, and the addict is enclosed within a small social network of fellow users. What this means is that long-time addicts are highly unlikely to have anything to do with "straights"—they are not the ones who turn new kids into users. On the contrary the avant garde of heroin addiction are young users who have not themselves been into heroin very long, and who are busily turning all their friends on. This is a classic youth culture phenomenon.

The geographical incidence of heroin epidemics is also interesting. Starting in big cities on the East and West coasts, epidemics have successively appeared in the seventies in smaller and smaller cities and in less and less densely populated areas, while incidence of new use in the big cities has peaked and even declined. The authors specifically point out the similiarities between this process and the spread of other cultural innovations. The spread of heroin epidemics from big to small population centers closely paralleled that of television in the 40s and 50s and the transmission of various more recent cultural fads and fashions. Unfortunately, as the authors point out, the Federal Government has consistently been a few years behind the epidemic front, with unfortunate consequences for intervention and treatment.

There is much else in this book for anyone interested in issues of heroin addiction and treatment. It is highly recommended.

The Use of Imprisonment: Essays in the Changing State of English Penal Policy, edited by SEAN MCCONVILLE. Boston: Routledge & Kegan Paul, 1976. 128 pp. $8.25 paper.

Who Guards the Guards?, 2nd ed., by BRIAN STRATTON. London: PROP, 1973. 143 pp. No price listed, paper.

Changing Prisons, by J. E. HALL WILLIAMS. Toronto: Macmillan of Canada, 1975. 210 pp. $14.50 cloth.

ROBERT SOMMER
University of California, Davis

The British penal system faces most of the same problems that confront the American penal system and is meeting them in much the same way. This is the conclusion I would draw from these three books. The first is a textbook of British penal practice, the second, a diatribe by an embittered ex-convict, and the third, a detached overview of the system. One can readily find counterparts to each of these books in American penal literature. If one central theme is to be discerned in all three volumes, it is that treatment/therapy/training doesn't work in a prison environment.

The Use of Imprisonment is a collection of essays on prison issues intended for use as a text by students in social science, law, social work, and corrections. The individual essays are well-written and current. That they deal entirely with the British penal system diminishes their usefulness for American undergraduates or professional students, but the book remains an exceedingly good reference work. Graham Zellick provides a history of prisoners' rights in Great Britain. Until recently the situation was much the same as it was in the United States, where the rule of law stopped at the prison gates, but things are changing. Norman Jepson discusses staff training and recruitment and the problems created by the expansion of the British prison system over the last twenty-five years as it tripled in almost all aspects —in number of inmates, staff, and in number of institutions. Mark Williams rejects "humane containment" as necessarily defeatist which is the goal of prison psychologists. Unfortunately the evidence he provides on the ability of psychologists (or anyone else) to accomplish more than this is discouraging. Frances Heidensohn argues for treating women offenders differently than men since women present less of a danger to society. Her expressed hope is that non-institutional alternatives will replace prison for all but a few high security risk women offenders. Hugh Klare and Keith Hawkins provide a comprehensive but not terribly rosy picture of alternatives to imprisonment. Martin Wright documents 200 years of penal reform, from Sheriff John Howard in the Eighteenth century to the prisoners' rights organizations of today. McConville closes the book with a rejection of the treatment model of imprisonment and leaves humane containment as virtually its sole objective.

Brian Stratton's *Who Guards the Guards?* provides an insider's view of several British prisons. Comparing Stratton's account to autobiographies of American inmates, we find that although there does not seem to be the terrible racial animosity in British prisons that exists here, nor as much gang violence, nor hard drug use, in general, a British lag would feel at home in the cell of an American con, and vice versa.

The book is a litany of charges about poor food, poor medical treatment, poor living conditions, and rampant brutality toward inmates on the part of guards. Stratton not only had difficulty in the maximum security institution at Parkhurst, but also was unable to adapt himself to the more benign regime of the model prison at Blundeston. His attitude that "a screw is still a screw" continually got him into trouble.

Sadly, this is not a very good book. It was rejected by most of the major publishers and finally published by PROP, the militant prisoners' organization. The problem with the book is that Stratton is too involved in his own case to make generalizations or sound recommendations. Perhaps the book was written too soon after the author's release. Had he waited a year or two, or revised the book in a few years' time, it might have been much improved. An important feature of life in a total institution, is that small details of routine and privilege become exceedingly important. This does not necessarily make them interesting to the reader. The book is more an extended list of personal grievances than an exposé of the British prison system.

The avowed goal of J. E. Hall Williams's *Changing Prisons* is to hold a mirror up to the British penal system. This metaphor is both apt and curious. The mirror Williams holds reflects the image of the prison system as seen by others. There is a noticeable absence of original research and fact-finding by Williams and of first-person statements from prison officials and inmates.

In general, the author sees no reason to be ashamed of the English prison system. He attempts to counteract the "penological pessimism" engendered by the end of a treatment era. He is decidedly hostile to the prison rights movement as represented by the English PROP, the Norwegian KROM, or the Prisoners' Union in the United States. He accepts the view that prison will always be necessary for some offenders, but does not directly concern himself with the large number of people in custody who, he admits, do not need to be there. The implications of discharging the unnecessarily confined prisoners for the subsequent handling of the remaining 15–25% are not discussed.

The book presents no radical solutions or reform proposals—this was not the author's intention. However, it is a well-balanced and thoughtful analysis of current trends and views.

The Dangerous Class: Crime and Poverty in Columbus, Ohio, 1860–1885, by Eric H. Monkkonen. Cambridge, Mass.: Harvard University Press, 1975. 186 pp. $13.50 cloth.

David Lewis Smith
Emory University

Criminologists and sociologists, move over; here come the historians! This short monograph, a revised dissertation by a historian, has the explicit goal of providing a causal analysis of crime and poverty. Historians have long been accused of ignoring the "common person" aspect of history; however, Monkkonen's history from the "bottom up" is refreshing as well as instructive. The author and reviewer caution the reader not to expect a traditional presentation, as the "dangerous class" apparently left no diaries, letters, or other accounts from which to construct generalizations about daily activity. Instead, the "modern" analytic tools of factor analysis and correlation-regression, buttressed by a deluge of tables (far too many in the opinion of the reviewer), are utilized. While there are both theoretical and methodological flaws, students of criminology, poverty, and urbanization will find this work worthy of perusal.

The existence of a dangerous class overarching both the disreputable poor and the criminal, long a concern of sociologists, has been directly linked with the twin processes of urbanization and industrialization. In questioning this traditional wisdom, Monkkonen joins the burgeoning ranks of sociological investigators who, equipped with contemporary survey findings, have disconfirmed the equation of urbanization/industrialization with pathology.

Monkkonen's work would have proven more useful to sociologists and historians alike had it examined historical evidence from 1860 to the present. A longer time span and the concurrent increases in urbanization might document important impacts on crime and poverty, i.e., war, economic depression, and rapid increases in prosperity.

The minor nuisances of occasional questionable assumptions and conclusions will not be detailed here; instead, a sample of interesting conclusions are:

Criminals more frequently became paupers than paupers criminals.

Criminals were economically and occupationally "better off" than paupers.

Urbanization was not associated with crime or poverty in any simple fashion.
Thefts by trick and deception were distinct urban crimes and increased urbanization.
The poor house had an unexpected youthful population.
There was some evidence of a "dangerous class."

The question of urban influence is not so much rejected as modified, and the complexity of the relationship is demonstrated if not unraveled. Hopefully, additional case studies similar to this will further understanding of this complex and crucial question as researchers make greater utilization of historical materials.

The Dilemma of Prison Reform, by THOMAS O. MURTON. New York: Holt, Rinehart and Winston, 1976. 285 pp. No price listed, paper.

Prisons: Houses of Darkness, by LEONARD ORLAND. New York: Free Press, 1975. 224 pp. $10.00 cloth.

Work Furlough and the County Jail, by ALVIN RUDOFF. Springfield, Ill.: Charles C Thomas, 1975. 198 pp. $12.50 cloth.

W. DAVID WATTS
Ohio University, Athens

Prison is a difficult institution. A product of good intentions and reform, it produces degredation, humiliation, and little rehabilitation. The key resocialization agency of our "criminal justice system," prisons are centers of resistance and rebellion. These three books suggest more reforms for prison.

Thomas Murton is an experienced prison administrator and reformer. In 1968, he directed the uncovering of three inmate bodies allegedly killed by officials and inmate guards at Arkansas's Cummins Prison Farm. A month later, he was fired. In *The Dilemma of Prison Reform*, he explores the "cyclical nature of prison reform." He summarizes the history of the prison, including material on self government. Murton believes prison reform fails because of an inadequate power base for change and the culpability of prison administrators. He types reformer roles and reform efforts putting them together into a "theory of reform." He applies his theory to two cases he was involved with—in Alaska and Arkansas. Administrators mask atrocities in their institutions and block efforts at "real reform" in order to retain their positions and authority. Murton describes medical, psychiatric, and work rehabilitation programs in prison as farcical. He recommends the establishment of participatory management, where prisoners, staff, and administrators govern their institution together. The alternative to real reform, Murton believes, is revolt. The tone of *The Dilemma of Prison Reform* is bitter and angry. Murton is convinced that the only way to reform is to do what he did: never compromise, never yield. The outcome is a dilemma: reformers who never compromise get fired; and compromisers, at least in Murton's eyes, never accomplish anything.

Prisons: Houses of Darkness, is a reasoned, well-written description and critique of American prisons. Orland, a lawyer and ex-parole board member, believes that law is coming to the prison. Recent Supreme Court decisions have affected freedom of religion in prisons, jailhouse lawyers, parole and probation revocation hearings, and prisoners' mail. Many of these reforms have been accomplished by prisoners themselves acting through the courts. Orland believes that more court action will extend the rule of law to prison. He urges action by legislatures to create codes of conduct in prison and to establish Ombudsman programs.

Orland also criticizes the processes that send persons to prison and control their release. Sentences in the United States are the "highest in the Western world." We punish harshly and offer little lenience. Orland believes the indeterminate sentence, the ideal of prison reformers for decades, is counterproductive. The arbitrary power of judges, parole boards, and sentencing boards should be curtailed. He proposes "radical" and "reformist" models for change. A sober, rational approach to prison reform, *Prisons: Houses of Darkness*, assumes that courts and legislatures will respond to prisoners. That remains to be seen.

The third book is an empirical study of a traditional alternative to incarceration. Work release or work furlough was designed to stop criminals from lying idle at taxpayers' expense, while honest citizens had to work for a living. Work furlough defrayed the costs of incarceration and lowered welfare payments to prisoners' families. A nice by-product might be rehabilitation. Rudoff studied California's Santa Clara County, where about one-third of the male inmates participated in work furlough. Work furlough is associated with a *deterioration* in law abiding attitudes. Work furlough tends to be more available for Mexican-Americans because of their experience in agricultural labor. Work furlough participants, while committing crimes after sentence completion, tend to wait longer and commit less serious crimes. Work furlough, in summary, reduces costs associated with prison, provides an assured employment reserve and seems to be associated with only minimal changes in prisoner attitudes and behavior. Still, work furlough was preferred by most inmates. While essentially non-rehabilitative and perhaps exploitive, it seems to be a more attractive way to "do time."

These three books propose seemingly futile reforms. Inmate self government is not a widely adopted procedure. Radical reformers, like Murton, have very limited opportunities to effect change. Work furlough, while better than sitting in a cell, is not clearly successful. Legal reforms have occurred and may continue. Yet, the recent Supreme Court decision upholding the death penalty and limiting federal jurisdiction over the exclusionary rule suggests that law may not penetrate the prison. Even if all three reforms were adopted, the prison would remain.

The Rendezvous: A Case Study of an After-Hours Club, by JULIAN B. ROEBUCK and WOLFGANG FRESE. New York: Free Press, 1976. 278 pp. $10.95 cloth.

EDWARD F. VACHA
Project SELF
Santa Maria, California

What distinguishes this book from most participant observation studies of public places is the authors' attempt to supplement observations with lengthy interviews of forty patrons and employees and the use of several informants (patrons, employees, and the owner) to provide data not easily obtained through participant observation alone. The result is that the authors have been able to develop a typology of patrons and employees, and, more importantly, they have sketched the organized perspectives and situational identities adopted by the various kinds of patrons (including "squares," call girls, party girls, thieves, and other deviant and marginally deviant types). It is this specification of the actors organized perspectives toward the setting, each other, and (in very brief sketches) the "straight" world that is the major contribution of this book.

In addition, the authors have provided a better picture of the role of employees in creating and sustaining the kind of behavior characteristic of the setting than most investigations of public places. In this respect, the authors' discussions of the employees' use of "front" or presentation of self, their control of the kinds of patrons admitted, and their protection of the setting and their patrons from police harassment are particularly interesting.

In short, the contributions of this book are primarily descriptive. The authors have combined two previously developed conceptual frameworks, the "behavior setting" approach used by Sherri Cavan in her study of bars (*Liquor License*) and a symbolic interactionist framework (largely based on McCall and Simmons's formulations) to describe the patrons' and employees' behavior and perspectives. In fact, except for the discussions of backstage behavior and the actors' perspectives, the findings of this book confirm Cavan's findings.

In addition to those interested in drinking behavior and behavior in public places, this book may be useful as a supplementary text to those teaching introductory sociology and deviance courses. The descriptions of the perspectives and identities of the various deviant types who frequent the club are lively and entertaining and may stimulate students to read more detailed accounts and analyses of deviant behavior. The book also provides a very good summary of the literature on bars and bar behavior, and a summary discussion of the literature on sociability (including Simmel's work) and play.

Demography, Population, and Migration

The Great Debate on Population Policy: An Instructive Entertainment, by BERNARD BERELSON. New York: The Population Council, 1975. 40 pp. $2.00 paper.

NANCY E. WILLIAMSON
Maternal and Child Health/Family Planning Project
Tagbilaran City, Bohol, Philippines

Soon after he resigned as President of The Population Council, Bernard Berelson wrote a brief one-act play on population policy. The three characters are: FamPlan, who advocates increased efforts to bring family planning to couples around the world;

DevDev, who asserts that poverty is the main problem, not population growth, and that our efforts should concentrate on increased production and redistribution of wealth; and AcCrit, the academic critic, who warns about the seriousness of the population problem, the extent of our ignorance about demographic phenomena, the basic pro-natalism of most societies, and the need for more research.

These three characters explore the nature of the population problem, the range of solutions, the role of family planning programs, and whether they have been successful and by what criteria. The purpose of this exercise is to push the debate beyond the negativism of the last decade. The actors speak, for the most part, using actual words from the population literature which the author carefully documents.

Although Berelson attempts to make the positions confront each other directly, this is difficult since people holding these views emphasize different problems and solutions and are bored with the subject matter of others. DevDev, for example, has no real objection to family planning programs. It is just that they do not excite him.

In the play, each of the three characters is referred to as "he." This suggests the debate is among men. It sounds a bit like a variation on the controversy begun by Freud. ("What do women want? Large families or small families? What should we give them? Family planning or sewing machines?")

In my view, the position of AcCrit does not hang together as well as the other two. It is a pastiche of Kingsley Davis, Paul Ehrlich, Anne Ehrlich, Garret Hardin, and Ansley Coale, among others. However, since I am closer to this position than the other two, I may see greater diversity. It must be a sociological axiom that one can see finer distinctions within a group one is familiar with than an outsider could, or would want to, make.

Finally, all three characters ignore one importantly reality. Because of enormous worldwide expenditures on the military, the resources available for both development and population control are much less than they could be. Perhaps it would be healthier if this level of military spending were not just taken as given.

Regardless of these or other limitations, this play is a most pleasant and "instructive entertainment" on the current population policy controversy and a good way to get into the literature.

Population Growth and Educational Planning in Developing Nations, by GAVIN JONES. New York: Irvington Publishers, 1975. Distributed by Halsted Press. 238 pp. $14.95 cloth.

PRANAB CHATTERJEE
Case Western Reserve University

The purpose of this work is to explore how population growth affects educational progress in developing countries and, in turn, how educational progress affects population growth. Toward that end, the author reviews population trends and the educational patterns in the developing countries with per capita GNP below $700, analyzes the specific cases of Thailand, Sri Lanka, and Singapore, and upon drawing his conclusions, proceeds to draw several policy implications.

The reciprocal relationship between population growth and educational progress has been of interest to demographers, educators, and planners for a considerable period of time. This book reviews the problems of understanding such a relationship very well: the role(s) of educational policy and educational expenditures; the need for an increasing share of GNP for education in most cases; the effect of migration to the cities in the developing countries, calling for vastly differing levels of school enrollment in the urban areas than in the rural areas; the shortage of teachers; the teacher/student ratio and teacher requirements; etc. Before embarking on the case studies of the three nations, this work also points out several important issues in isolating the demographic factor from others in the process of educational progress. Then, as the author reviews the three cases, he illustrates how increased fertility has retarded educational progress in Thailand, how the "timing of fertility decline" may affect the same in Sri Lanka, and how Singapore is "reaizing the benefits of declining fertility." Upon presenting these cases, the author then examines the role(s) of the said reciprocal relationship on economic development and labor force trends.

For the most part, this work really examines a one-way relationship of the effect of fertility on educational progress. The author himself acknowledges this at the beginning of chapter 10 (the first of the three concluding chapters), and attempts a flow diagram to return to his concern about the mutually reinforcing properties of the two variables. And, it is in this attempt that the author's attempts are in no way as detailed or well-developed as they are in his examination of the impact of fertility on educational progress.

The flow diagram in chapter 10 proposes many other variables (norms about family size, delayed age at marriage, etc., etc.) which may show how educational progress develops and that in turn, leads to fertility decline. It is in this effort that the author's efforts are noteworthy, but somewhat limited.

For one, to examine the complex relationship between the two variables the author chooses three Asian countries of rather small size. It is the size of some these countries which, during their historical development in the immediate and extended past, led to different levels of urbanization and political socialization of the masses.

For two, the political boundaries of nation-states are not always a good unit of analysis for understanding the complex reciprocal relationship which is being examined here, because (and especially in large countries) in some cases the within-nation variations are possibly as wide as between-nation variations.

For three, the author has approached a macro sociological problem, but proposes mostly micro sociological variables when he begins to examine the actual reciprocal part of the relationship.

In summary, the work is a scholarly effort in the understanding of the impact of fertility in the developing nations, and contributes in this field precisely because it helps raise several theoretical (in the choice of the variables) and the methodological (in the choice of alternative units of analysis) questions of extreme importance.

Toward an Ecological Analysis of Intermetropolitan Migration, by HERBERT H. KARP and K. DENNIS KELLY. Chicago: Markham Publishing Company, 1974 (originally published in 1971). 132 pp. No price listed, cloth.

GREGORY WILLIAMS
The University of Akron

Substantially, this monograph will not have wide appeal. If however, one's special interest centers on the research and theory relating to the ecological approach to migration, the book should be considered.

This slender volume presents two empirical studies. Part I, "Migration Models of Stouffer and Zipf: A Critique," is perhaps mistitled. True, the authors criticize past studies based on the work of Stouffer and Zipf for not having adequate definitions and concepts and for not using measures of migration independent of their independent variables; nevertheless, the main body of this section is devoted to the authors' own work. Following the earlier work of Anderson, Bogue, Watson, and Zipf the authors employ regression analysis to test a series of hypotheses suggesting an association between migration rate and such variables as: city population size, distance, percent unemployed, percent engaged in manufacture, percent of families with incomes under $3,000, and Index of Climate. They contend that not only will these variables explain much of the variance in migration rates but that the characteristics for the city of destination will be more important in explaining the variance than will the characteristics of the city of origin. The data used are migration rates and a measure of each of the independent variables listed above for two-way migration streams between New York, Los Angeles, Chicago, and Denver SMAs and two-way migration streams between these four areas and thirteen other large SMAs for the period 1955–1960. While this sample is the same as that used earlier by Galle and Taeuber, it does seem a rather limited one and, by the authors' own admission, all but one of the cities are among the older and larger SMAs in the nation. Stepwise regression reveals that five variables account for 71% of the variance (Index of Climate of destination, 32%; population of destination, 19%; distance, 8%; percent of families with incomes under $3,000, 7%; Index of Climate of origin, 6%). Unlike the results of previous studies, climate appears to be much more significant than any of the economic factors, the latter accounting for little of the variance. The authors briefly provide a number of possible explanations for these results: climate was not included in previous studies, their measure of migration was theoretically and operationally independent of their other variables, and social and economic factors might account for the remaining unexplained variance. Since this finding is contradictory to their own expectations and to previous findings, it seems that a more substantial attempt at explaining their results might have been in order.

Part II of this study presents an analysis of migration and economic base. The authors are proponents of the "export base theory of economic growth." Utilizing a great many quotes, they devote the first chapter of this section to presenting this theory and responding to its critics. In the remaining pages, they attempt to test the following hypotheses: (1) net population growth attributable to migration will vary in correspondence with the extent of the community's export base, (2) net migration will vary inversely with population size, (3) net migration will vary directly with the community's involvement in service or tertiary industry, and (4) net migration for a particular community will vary inversely with accessibility of that community to other communities. The data used are for a sample of 89 SMSAs with populations of 250,000 or more in 1960. Migration is measured for the period 1955–60 by frequency of net migration for each SMSA, frequency of net population change attributable to migration, and the frequency of migration along each of the 7,832 separate migration streams. Independent variables are: size; distance of each SMSA to the nearest larger SMSA; percent of each SMSA's employed labor force in service activity, 1950; a basic-nonbasic (Bn) activity ratio for each SMSA, 1950 (taken from the regression equations generated by Ullman and Dacey); distance in miles to the nearest neighboring SMSA; and total population potential, 1950.

After interpreting a series of complex regression equations, the authors discovered that the relationships between growth due to intermetropolitan migration and export base and between net migration and export base are essentially the same. That is, size of community and basic-nonbasic activity factors constitute a single factor in explaining a significant proportion of variation in net intermetropolitan migration and net migration from all sources. Further, the overall relationship between the Bn-size factor and net migration is accounted for by such a relationship among the largest SMSAs (400,000+) in their sample. The third hypothesis concerning the relationship between net migration and a community's involvement in service activity was not substantiated. As for the fourth hypothesis, the authors found that there is a direct relationship between population growth attributable to net migration for an SMSA and distance to the nearest larger SMSA, the larger SMSAs (400,000+) again accounting for the association. For the smallest SMSAs, generalized accessibility to other SMSAs rather than distance is significant in explaining net migration. Finally, a very brief discussion of the relationship between the 7,832 migration streams and the potential for functional expansion provides little of value, the findings being negative. The authors, however, do infer that functional expansion, while it does not affect in-migration, may discourage out-migration.

In general, I would prefer to be sympathetic to empirical work of the sort presented here. In this case, I find it difficult. For all the effort which must have gone into this work, one is left with the wish that there had been something more substantial and valuable in the way of findings. And from a stylistic point of view, the writing, while intended to be technical, is often too much so, making the study rather uninteresting to read and, in spots, difficult to follow without very careful reading.

Mankind at the Turning Point: The Second Report to the Club of Rome, by MIHAJLO MESAROVIC and EDUARD PESTEL. New York: New American Library, 1976. 210 pp. $1.95 paper.

The No-Growth Society, edited by MANCUR OLSON and HANS H. LANDSBERG. New York: W. W. Norton & Company, 1974. 259 pp. $10.00 cloth. $2.95 paper.

J. ALLEN WHITT
Brown University

Are we on the brink of wrenching global crises that will result in profound changes in the quality of our lives, the shape of contemporary and future societies, and the nature of the relations among the nations and people of the world? These books address this central question: both are concerned with the consequences of population and economic growth on our finite planet.

Of the two works, the Olson and Landsberg collection, a reprint of the Fall 1973 issue of *Daedalus*, is generally less urgent in tone, the essential message being that it probably makes more sense to "reform" growth rather than stop it entirely. The editors, both economists, conclude that the composition of economic output could be made more socially and environmentally benign by means of "effluent fees, environmental regulations, public expenditures, institutional modifications, and behavioral changes." The fourteen articles included in the volume provide a more well-developed discussion of economic implications and remedies (such as the price mechanism and effluent fees) than of "institutional modifications and behavioral changes," yet it is precisely these latter issues that will most engage the interests and expertise of sociologists. This selection of articles probably reflects fairly accurately the state of knowledge in the area at the time (1973), for the crucial sociological questions surrounding the growth/no-growth issue are the more complex and difficult ones.

Despite the somewhat uneven quality of the articles (as is usually true in edited works), and a style that is often dry, the book does contain several useful and stimulating pieces. For example, Kingsley Davis provides a good explanation and defense of the ZPG (Zero Population Growth) position. E. J. Mishan and Kenneth Boulding have literate statements detailing the need to reduce or eliminate economic growth, with Mishan taking the firmer position for no-growth and Boulding giving a sober assessment of the difficult social adjustments that curtailed growth will necessitate. An important article by Lester Brown argues that the increasing interdependency of rich and poor countries in our finite world means that we are compelled "to address the issue of social justice on a world wide scale and in a new context." The issue of social justice is also taken up by Willard R. Johnson in a cogent and well-written article entitled "Should the Poor Buy No Growth?" His novel conclusion is that the issue of growth versus no-growth is largely irrelevant to the needs of the poor. What is needed, he argues, is redistribution of income. William Alonso gives us a forceful critique of the efforts by local urban areas to limit population, arguing that such policies are likely to be ineffective (because of larger demographic factors) or regressive in that they may amount to methods for keeping the poor and other outsiders from living in desirable locations. However, more recent work (e.g., Harvey Molotch, "The City as a Growth Machine," *AJS*, September, 1976) suggests that the validity of some of Alonso's conclusions is open to question.

In short, the Olson and Landsberg book does a competent job of bringing together the basic arguments for and against no-growth policies. It also indirectly demonstrates the need for additional sociological (and other) analyses of the political, cultural, and social implications of reduced economic and population growth.

A greater sense of mission and urgency is conveyed by the Mesarovic and Pestel book, the successor to the original 1972 Club of Rome report, *The Limits to Growth.* The general thrust of the book is much the same as the earlier work: unless the rapid expansion of global population, energy and resource use, and pollution is brought under control, catastrophe of enormous proportions will befall human civilization in a few decades at most. Mass starvation, to-the-death conflicts over increasingly scarce resources, economic collapse, widening gaps between rich and poor, increasing deaths due to pollution, and destruction of the natural environment will come about unless concerted and effective action is soon taken by the nations of the world to develop technological, social, and political means to regulate growth.

The real news concerning the Mesarovic and Pestel work is that it contains three significant modifications of the original *Limits to Growth* model and approach. These represent responses to the considerable criticism of the earlier work (e.g., *Models of Doom,* edited by H. S. D. Cole et al.). First, instead of conceiving of the world as a homogeneous unit, the globe is subdivided into ten regions made up of roughly similar countries (e.g., Western Europe, Latin America, "Centrally Planned Asia"). This is intended to reflect the fact that different regions face different problems, and that their responses to regional crisis may vary considerably.

Second, Mesarovic and Pestel do not condemn growth per se, but only the kind they label "undifferentiated." Such growth involves simple replication of existing forms, as in cell division, and is "unbalanced" and "cancerous." Much current world population and economic growth is of this dangerous form. What is needed, the authors assert, in a word well-known to sociologists, is a turn toward differentiated or "organic" growth. Harmonious, organic growth patterns, according to a "master plan" or "blueprint," will have to be cooperatively and systematically created by the increasingly interdependent nations. This represents a considerable softening of the no-growth line set forth in *Limits to Growth.* It is now argued that while certain kinds of growth may have to be reduced or eliminated in certain areas (e.g., population growth in Southeast Asia), it is desirable to permit other kinds of growth in other areas (e.g., food production for the underfed countries).

Third, there has also been a modification in the computer simulation procedure used to predict the consequences of global growth.

Critics had charged that the *Limits to Growth* model had been too much based on physical and mechanistic constraints on growth and did not sufficiently take into account the adaptative capabilities of social institutions and human action. This new model now uses "conversational analysis": as the program is running, the operator or "decision analyst" can observe the effects of incremental inputs and can choose, within specified constraints, the priorities to be emphasized, cost to be incurred, and risks to be taken. The authors state that they have thus "programmed on the computer some of the decision-processes which constitute the purposive system and the norms which govern the decision, or selection, processes." At this point, the ears of the sociologist prick up. Unfortunately, due to obscurities in the text, and to technical "Briefs" that are sometimes too brief, it is unclear just what these decision-processes and norms may be.

Mankind at the Turning Point is a more sophisticated presentation than was *Limits to Growth*. However, one may still wonder if "disaggregation" of data has yet been carried far enough. Perhaps what is needed is data by nations, or even by subdivisions of nations, such as by ethnic groups or social classes, in order to adequately assess the causes and consequences of growth. Also, there are those who will feel that computer models dealing with such macroanalysis in the face of exceedingly complex relationships and incomplete data exemplify premature quantification and may be worthless or, worse, seriously misleading. Finally, even though certain sociological factors have presumably been included in the model along with the complex array of important physical and economic variables, it appears that much has been left out in terms of the role of human perception, social interaction, culture, politics, the impact of social institutions and organizations, and the possibilities for social change. Sociologists will have much to add in these areas.

Three Centuries of Social Mobility in America, edited by EDWARD PESSEN. Lexington, Mass.: D. C. Heath & Company, 1974. 313 pp. No price listed, paper.

S. M. MILLER
Boston University

The field of history is today the most interesting and innovating of the social sciences. I am not thinking primarily of the application of high-powered techniques, like econometrics, to historical material. More impressive is the basic, slogging work of scrutinizing archives to find out, for example, who was imprisoned in the counter-revolution in the Vendee. The analysis of detailed census records may mean that we know more about the residents of a block in Philadelphia in 1870 than we know about its residents today. Feminist historians are revealing an occupational life and pattern of social networks in nineteenth century America which sharply modify our understanding of daily life. The recent profound and detailed analyses of slavery relate ideology and interest, the process by which ideological hegemony develops. Radical reinterpretations of the Progressive Movement and the difficulties of immigrants in schools have reinvigorated US history and made it compelling and basic to sociological theorizing.

As a schoolboy, I thought that American history was dull compared to European. It was taught as homogenized, uncontroversial, idealized, or whitewashed official history, a US version of what the British call "the Whig interpretation of history." It is different today. We are now getting a history from below and a history based on specific and widely-ranging data. Old complacencies are breaking up. While the historians of Europe engage in prodigious feats of uncovering the past, American historians are at least as industrious, willing to learn new techniques, and discard old ideas, though they are perhaps less willing to speculate and theorize. Still, controversy abounds; official history is floundering.

Sociologists will be forced to abandon or drastically modify the basic assumptions about historical developments which underlay much of sociological theorizing. Our concepts of and beliefs about industrialization, modernization, the nuclear family, Gemeinschaft-Gesellschaft, and the like are not sustainable. Historical fact is undermining sociological theory.

In their studies of social mobility, American historians are making a specific major contribution to sociology. They are sophisticated about sociological approaches and are uncovering through archival sources the social origins and career histories of people of past areas.

The work of Stephen Thernstrom on Newburyport and Boston in the late nineteenth century is, of course, well known to sociologists. But other historians, many influenced directly or indirectly by his work, have also been digging. Edward Pessen has brought together many of these studies in an unusually interesting portrayal of intra- and inter-generational social mobility. In a few years another volume will be necessary as the analysis of hard-won data becomes available in the studies supported by the National Science Foundation and the Center for Metropolitan Problems of the National Institute of Mental Health.

The Pessen book, which contains only reprinted articles and selections from books, is divided into four sections. Section I, "The Mixed Pattern of the Colonial and Revolutionary Periods," deals mainly with agricultural classes and, to a lesser extent, merchants. It contains Jackson Turner Main's work on social mobility in revolutionary American. Section II, "The Surprising Immobility of the 'Era of the Common Man,' 1820–1850," includes Pessen's important article on antebellum social mobility but not his work on wealth. Section III, "The Complex Mobility Patterns of the Early Industrial Era, 1860–1900," reprints Thernstrom on Newburyport, Herbert Gutman on Paterson entrepreneurs, and the work on the industrial elite of the 1870s and 1900 by Frances Gregory, Irene Neu, and William Miller. Section IV, "The Twentieth Century: New Dimensions, New Approaches, Inconclusive Mobility Patterns," is a grabbag of sociological articles, displaying excerpts from Lipset and Bendix, Blau and Duncan, Glen Elder, Gordon Lewis, and Bradley Schiller's interesting article on the opportunities of welfare children. The introduction and concluding bibliographic essay are competent and instructive for neophytes; the brief section and head notes are very useful and should have been expanded.

What the anthology lacks is a summary or interpretation of the studies which range from Reavis's study of the gentry in mid-seventeenth century Maryland to Blau and Duncan's survey of US males in 1962. But it does introduce us to a wide range of historical materials. Historians have progressed from studies of business elites in the post-Civil War period to earlier and much broader studies of elites and have added non-elite groups as well. Soon, for some cities, we will learn what happened to all or most of the residents of neighborhoods so that we will have a detailed reckoning of past eras.

The main issue of the book is whether or not mobility rates have declined in the United States. Pessen's anthology makes clear that the question in that simple form cannot be answered. One has to specify time and place, what specific groups of people, what kind of mobility. What was true in seventeenth century Maryland with its open land was not true in Dedham, Massachusetts. Or, the high percentage of post-1860 Paterson manufacturers who had artisan working-class origins contrasted with the small percentage of heads of large corporations who had similar origins.

The findings which most interest me are: (1) "perhaps the clearest as well as the most significant finding of the historical studies is that vertical mobility before the twentieth century was not nearly so pervasive as sociologists and general readers thought it was" (p. XXII); (2) in some areas in Maryland, in the seventeenth century, very high rates of mobility prevailed, while in others mobility rates were much lower; (3) patterns and rates changed over time; even within the seventeenth century mobility declined, especially for indentured servants in Maryland; (4) the eighteenth century appears to have had more upward mobility than the nineteenth; (5) while many rich Americans were self-made, most of the rich in the prebellum period came from well-to-do families and were able to turn their headstarts into enormous gains (Pessen, p. 114); (6) post-Civil War business leaders predominantly came from well-to-do families; the issue of rags-to-riches is a question of increase or decrease in the proportion from poor families, never a predominance of them; and (7) upward mobility among working-class males in the third quarter of the nineteenth century was usually not spectacular.

Unfortunately, many historians are not very good at or are reluctant to explain why things happened as they did. That is where historically sensitive sociologists can perform important roles. Historians are certainly doing their share. What is lacking today are explanations and hypotheses about the connections between changing industrial and occupational formations and mobility. Some writers on mobility seem to believe that occupational classifications are technologically given and fixed and that individuals are then appropriately sorted into these boxes. Such mechanistic approaches are misleading (see Katherine Stone, "Origins of Job Structures in the Steel Industry," *Review of Radical Political Economics,* Vol. 6, #2, pp. 113–173), and we should be analyzing how labor force distributions come to be what they are and how individuals move through jobs.

The improved techniques and understanding of social mobility studies have shunted sociologists away from historical perspectives. Perhaps the lively new interest among sociologists in historical development may intensify the fusion of technique with historical sensitivity and knowledge.

Measuring Occupational Inheritance, by THOMAS W. PULLUM. New York: Elsevier Scientific Publishing Company, 1975. 184 pp. $12.75 cloth.

PAUL H. TRESS
Purdue University, Calumet

Models of social mobility are usually one of two types. The first type represents mobility as the end result of regression procedures, e.g., the work of Blau and Duncan, while the second type represents mobility as movement among a set of cells in a cross-classification table, e.g., stochastic models. Pullum's monograph is a major contribution toward the realization and resolution of methodological problems in the more general cross-classification approach. The cross-classification approach does not assume parametric data like the regression approach. The classifications are usually mutually exclusive and exhaustive at two different time points.

Pullum's main thesis is that mobility represented by the cross-classification approach is a function of two types of mobility: forced mobility representing substantive social structural factors, antecedent to mobility, that affect mobility (e.g., differential fertility and changes of the age-sex composition of the occupational structure), and implied or stable mobility representing residual, random, and unidentified circulatory factors. Hence, Pullum feels the analysis of social mobility must measure the relative effects of both types of mobility on the mobility process.

Pullum initially analyzes forced mobility by elaborating on current models that incorporate the effects of differential age-specific fertility rates on the number of individuals in a given occupational state. By adding information on whether or not the individual has ever been a member of the labor force, Pullum advances the explanatory power of these models. This is a needed type of analysis given the age and sex composition of a population on the labor market in societies undergoing rapid economic changes. However, Pullum feels there are limits to the analysis of forced mobility since introduction of the age of the individual results in great problems in modeling the joint distribution of age and occupation, resulting in the need to make substantively unsupported assumptions on the nature of the constraints on the distribution. Pullum concludes that the analysis of "forced" mobility is a deadend and consequently begins to examine the other component of mobility, implied or stable mobility. The reasons for the deadend nature of the forced approach are not well articulated. This is a major fault of the monograph since many social processes may be viewed as forced by substantive factors.

The stable mobility is analyzed in terms of the degree to which the observed patterns of moves depart from a baseline model of independence, where the cells of the cross-classification are a simple multiplicative function of the appropriate cell row and cell column which reflect the origin and destination of the move. Pullum develops three alternatives to the independence model. The first, quasi-independence, blocks movement along the diagonals, covering individuals with a tendency to stay in an occupation, with the added restriction that only moves in the upward or downward direction are permitted for only one state. The second and third alternatives to the independence model block movement among the lower and upper triangles of the cross-classification tables respectively, with the added restriction that no state has only one blocked cell. The independence and alternative models are then applied to sets of cross-national data and compared by measures developed by Pullum that attempt to see the degree to which the models correctly predict observed patterns of mobility. Pullum finds the alternative models are better predictors of mobility than the independence model, with the quasi-independence model more powerful than the upward or downward model. Pullum concluded that mobility is better explained by exchanges between two sets of occupational states than among a set of occupational states.

The methodological and substantive contributions of Pullum's work are obscured his turgid writing style, despite the fact that the more difficult formal material is in a set of appendices. Pullum is very modest in writing on the implications of his separation of social mobility, into two types of processes, one due to substantive and one due to random factors. Many social processes in different substantive areas are represented by cross-classification tables and could be analyzed by Pullum's techniques. For example, the use of blocked cells in the alternatives to the independence models provides a different technique from the use of absorbing states in a simple Markov Chain, yielding a more substantive, appealing approach. Due to the implications of his approach, Pullum's monograph is as significant a contribution to the analysis of cross-classifications as Goodman's statistical developments or Coleman's models of response uncertainty. However, the technical level of Pullum's monograph presumes a level of mathematical statistics well beyond that of the majority of sociologists. I only hope another author translates the implications of Pullum's argument for the mass audience of sociologists who do not have this training.

Population and America's Future, by JOSEPH J. SPENGLER. San Francisco: W. H. Freeman & Company, 1975. 260 pp. $9.00 cloth. $3.95 paper.

PAUL R. WILLIAMS
University of Rochester

Joseph Spengler is a highly respected authority on the interrelations between population size and factors relating to growth and economic development. Much of his previous work has focused on these interrelations as they have operated historically in what are now referred to as economically developed countries and in some instances, in less developed societies. Although some attention is given to historical developments in both population and economy in the United States, as the title suggests, the emphasis of this work is on the current situation in the United States and future prospects. As indicated in his introduction, the book can be conveniently divided into three parts. The first part deals with the proximate determinants of population growth, i.e., death rates, birth rates, and immigration, their past and prospective trends and the natural environment in which population growth has occurred. Attention is also given in this part to how changes in population size and composition have been related to economic growth.

The second section of the book deals with the "effects" of population change. Considered here are such things as Age Composition, Population Concentration and Megalopolitanization, Numbers: Costs and Benefits, and Numbers, Interest, Policy. An attempt is made to analyze subjective costs and benefits of reproductive behavior and population growth, i.e., those that exist in the "mind of the decision maker," and objective costs and benefits that accrue to individuals, families and economies, as well as to deal with such topics as population optima, optimal distribution, population quality, and the impact of population growth on international relations and public policy.

In the third and final section of the book the author discusses in detail the implications of prospective population growth (or non-growth as is assumed eventually) including again such things as age structure, population quality, the physical environment, the economy, socioeconomic pressure, the distribution of income and consumption, and international pressures.

What is good about this book? The author alerts us to many of the costs and dangers of continued population growth. This is not especially exciting since it has been done by so many so frequently. His exposition on the aging of the population and the potential for intergenerational conflict under conditions of non-growth is well developed and interesting. He wisely disarms critics of non-growth who might use this as a basis for their arguments by indicating how such conflicts can be averted. I am more concerned about the things that are not done well, especially since they are the work of such a highly respected author who commands attention. First, there is perhaps the trivial. Spengler uses demographic terms which might be unfamiliar to non-demographers without providing adequate, accurate, and appropriately placed definitions (examples, the crude birth rate is defined as the "births per 1000 female inhabitants per year" and the concept "stationary population" is used throughout the work but is not defined until page 153 and then very loosely). In a similar vein, the discussion of tables frequently refers to data not included in them. Finally, as indicated by the outline of the contents, there is a considerable tendency toward redundancy.

More important than the flaws mentioned above however is the author's tendency to adhere strictly to economic interpretations of reproduction without acknowledgment that such interpretations have been subjected to serious criticism and debate. Similarly, the benefits of population growth are discussed in a cursory manner on two thirds of a page. Certainly more can be said, if for no other reason than to counter those who argue strenuously that the benefits are great.

Finally, in discussing the matter of reducing fertility and fertility differentials, Spengler stresses the notion that the "external" costs of excessive fertility must be "internalized," i.e., those who have too many children must pay for their own excesses. How? And with what moral and ethical implications? He answers neither. Nor does he seem to be aware of the considerable reductions in differential fertility that have already occurred as a result of enlightened government policies regarding the provision of contraceptive services and abortions. There are many other points that could be made. This book should be read, but cautiously.

Family and Intimate Lifestyles

Fertility and Deprivation: A Study of Differential Fertility amongst Working-Class Families in Aberdeen, by JANET ASKHAM. New York: Cambridge University Press, 1975. 188 pp. $14.50 cloth.

HYMAN RODMAN
University of North Carolina, Greensboro

The book's basic question, as familiar as Rainwater, is why the poor have more children. Askham personally interviewed ninety wives in Aberdeen, Scotland, selected from the unskilled and skilled working classes. Within each class, a group with two children, and another group with four or more children, were interviewed in 1970. It is a retrospective study of intact families carried out ten years after marriage.

A series of variables are separately explored in relation to achieved family size and to social class. Askham reports few differences among the four groups on several cultural variables. But there are differences by family size on such variables as family-size preferences and contraceptive behavior. Moreover, on many variables—e.g., deprivation, time between meeting and marriage, birth control KAP measures—the contrast is sharpest between the skilled-2 child and the unskilled-4 child groups, with the other two groups in an intermediate position.

Askham concludes that greater deprivation leads to lower-working-class orientations which involve less planning for the future. Hence, more children. Here, the study stumbles over a key problem—orientations are inferred from fertility and other behavior and are then used to explain fertility behavior.

The book anticipates Norman B. Ryder's call for more focused studies, and it illuminates the question of cultural versus situational explanations of fertility.

Group Marriage: A Study of Contemporary Multilateral Marriage, by LARRY L. CONSTANTINE and JOAN M. CONSTANTINE. New York: Collier Books, 1973. 299 pp. $2.95 paper.

STEPHEN K. SANDERSON
Indiana University of Pennsylvania

This book represents an attempt to explore the recently emerging phenomenon that the authors refer to as "multilateral marriage," i.e., "marriages" of three or more people. More specifically, the authors examine a variety of sociological and psychological issues related to multilateral marriage such as: who participates and why, the origins and dissolution of multilateral marriages, social network and role structure, patterns of leadership and control, economic arrangements, sexual interaction, child-rearing, the contribution of multilateral marriage to psycho-social growth and personal gratification, patterns of conflict and accommodation among members, special difficulties of multilateral marriages, and how such expanded families accommodate themselves to the larger society.

Unfortunately, the authors leave us with an unsettling mixture of fact and value. They alternate between presenting empirical data on the nature of multilateral marriage and proselytizing for the wondrous benefits to be gained from this emerging phenomenon (though, to the authors' credit, they make no pretense of falsely disguising their values through a facade of supposed objectivity). This leaves the authors with an uncertain audience (as they themselves clearly realize). Thus, social scientists may be put off by the loose, almost novelistic, value-oriented style, and the general reader may be baffled by the statistical analyses of data.

This double-edged nature of the book presents more serious problems, however. From a social-scientific point of view, the most serious shortcoming appears to involve the choice of respondents. It is never clear just who or how many are being studied or how they were selected in the first place. Furthermore, the presentation of data is generally incomplete, often confusing, and almost invariably mixed with digressions into the authors' value preferences. In this latter regard, it is particularly distressing to note the way in which the authors quickly gloss over or ignore the many difficulties presented by these expanded marriages. For example, the authors' own data show that the dissolution rate of multilateral marriages approaches 100%, but they quickly and naively dismiss this piece of data by simply commenting that conventional marriages in our own society also have a high rate of dissolution. While the explaining away of unsettling findings is not uncommon in the social sciences, in this case it stretches one's imagination a bit too far. The authors are clearly aware that multilateral marriage is not all a bed of roses, but their heavily biased attitude in favor of it nevertheless prevents the kind of balanced assessment that seems to be needed here.

Despite these shortcomings, the Constantines present some potentially valuable data and raise a variety of important and interesting questions concerning a poorly understood phenomenon. The book should be of benefit to social scientists who are concerned about such new horizons in marital and family relationships.

The Marriage Game: Understanding Marital Decision Making, by CATHY S. GREENBLAT, PETER J. STEIN, and NORMAN F. WASHBURNE. New York: Random House, 1974. 135 pp. $4.95 paper.

CHARLES T. HILL
University of Washington

As the subtitle implies, *The Marriage Game* is intended to facilitate learning major elements of the marriage system and their interconnections by having students make decisions and experience the consequence of those decisions without suffering the costs of real-life mistakes. It is primarily intended for use as a supplement for courses on marriage and the family (although it is also recommended for use in premarital and marital counseling). Students play the game in a series of seven to ten (or more) rounds, each of which (except the first) takes a fifty minute class period. In each round there are six steps as follows: stating your value preferences on seven values (e.g., security, freedom), calculating your resources (e.g., choosing to work full or part time or not at all and noting the consequences for income, leisure time, etc.), making basic budget decisions (e.g., how much to pay for rent, food), interacting with others (allocating free time to particular activities, finding a partner, exchanging sex gratification cards), reacting to your partner (e.g., giving and receiving ego support points, deciding on your marital status for the next round), and calculating your final score for the round (calculating your marital happiness based on your value weightings and obtained points). Each of the decisions made in a round has implications for points on the following value dimensions: security, esteem, freedom, enjoyment, sex gratification, marital and parental status, and ego support. In addition, each decision has implications for other decisions to be made in the same and subsequent rounds (e.g., children acquired in one round require income and freedom resources in subsequent rounds). The game attempts to incorporate the major decisions that are made in relation to marriage, and illustrate some of the important implications that those decisions might have.

The description of the game is delightful to read—in discovering what things are included and how they are operationalized. For example, if one chooses to exchange sex gratification cards with a partner and has chosen not to spend money for contraception, one draws chance cards to determine whether or not pregnancy occurs taking into account the number of sex gratification cards exchanged. The book includes not only a description of the game and a useful summary of the rules for each step, it also includes all game materials, suggestions for altering the game (e.g., to reflect social class differences or equality of the sexes), a set of readings, questions for discussion, and advice for the instructor on running the game. In short, the authors have attempted to provide all of the materials necessary for the successful use of the game. (Each participant needs a copy of the book.)

But how adequate is the model employed in the game? In constructing the game the authors have tried to base decision consequences on research findings as much as possible (e.g., probabilities of illness or pregnancy, average income levels for each sex). When necessary, however, they have relied on intuition and their collective best guess. For the purposes intended by the authors, the model appears to be fairly adequate. The whole thrust of the presentation of the game in the book is to raise issues concerning the "facts" reflected in the game. The description of the game spells out ways in which the game is like and unlike real life, and the study questions constantly ask the student to identify factors not included in the game. The game would be especially useful in raising issues concerning the differential impact of marriage on men and women—since it incorporates sex differences in income, esteem, freedom when there are children, etc. But while the game and book would be successful in raising questions, they may be less successful in answering them. The readings included in the book are generally good and also relevant, but they are brief and by themselves insufficient. As the authors recommend, the book and game should be used as a supplement (e.g., in discussion sessions); the game can stimulate interest in but not substitute for other course materials. In addition, the book lacks specific references for the research findings incorporated in the game. A version of the game description which identifies best guesses and sources of existing data ought to be part of the game documentation and should have been available at least to the instructor (e.g., in an appendix).

But while the model used in the game appears adequate for raising certain issues concerning marital decision making, it probably would be less adequate for certain other purposes. In particular it may be less adequate for teaching decision strategies and giving people training experience in the making of marital decisions. Omissions in the game which are useful in generating discussion may be misleading in the development of decision strategies. The latter use of course was not intended by the authors of this game, but is one way in which "decision games" are often used (e.g., in "operations research" in business and military applications). A game adequate for one purpose may be inadequate for another purpose, and to some extent different criteria may be appropriate for evaluating games for different applications.

In sum, *The Marriage Game* could be useful for raising issues and stimulating discussion, but for classroom use it needs to be accompanied by other materials providing both greater depth and greater breadth.

Modernization and Kin Network, by DANESH A. CHEKKI. Leiden, The Netherlands: E. J. Brill, 1974. 184 pp. No price listed, cloth.

A. A. KHATRI
University of Alabama, Birmingham

Chekki's book reports his 1962–63 empirical study of modernization and kin network of agriculturist Lingayats and white collar Brahmans in Dharwar, India. The author conducted extensive interviews with 115 respondents from each caste, collected their detailed genealogies, supplemented the data with observation, home visits, and interviews with other resource persons.

This comparative study explores kin universe of the two castes and focuses on their social interaction, mate selection, matrimonial bonds (in the contexts of sub-caste endogamy, socio-economic status, preference for uncle-niece and bilateral cross-cousin marriages), intra-familial roles, and relationships among the extended kin. The author examines the impact of legislation, welfare programs, and other modernizing forces and summarizes his findings concerning change and continuity in "order to provide a model of urban kin network in a modernizing society" (p. 18).

The findings refute Goode's hypothesis of the Indian family moving toward the Western nuclear family model. The study "suggests that despite modernization and some changes in urban family and kinship, the nuclear family, far from being isolated, and atomized, appears to be organically fused with the extended kin network" (p. 155). This modified extended family "is adapting itself to suit modern environmental needs and pressures" (p. 157). Modernization in India has not followed Western lines and "depends upon and frequently finds structural support from tradition" (p. 160).

Brahmans are reported to be modernizing at a faster rate than the Lingayats due to their higher levels of education, social mobility, and other influences. However, this reviewer's examination of the reported data concerning *the behavior* of Brahmans does not reveal a significant impact of modernization in familial and kinship areas. Marriages continue to be arranged by the family and kin with traditional considerations of sub-caste endogamy, hypergamy, and exchange of dowry (insisted upon by educated Brahman youth). Not a single case of widow re-marriage was evident over the last century among these "modernized" Brahmans nor was any case of divorce. The author has reported wide spread prevalence of child marriages and other traditional family-relevant *behavior* among the predominantly agriculturist Lingayats.

The author has not presented the criteria of selection of specific groups of 115 interviewees from each caste. He would have enhanced the scientific value of the study by reporting on the reliability of investigative methods used, e.g., the extent of congruence of data obtained separately from husband and wife in the same household. The documentation of changes with statistical support from the author's data concerning modernization would have been more convincing than loose generalizations "seen mainly through the eyes of the aged informants" (p. 153) whose number is not specified. The book would have benefited from additional juxtaposition of findings concerning the two castes in tabular form, more sophisticated statistical presentation, and addition of an interview guide.

Despite these and other limitations, the author deserves high praise for his lucid style of presentation, for his systematic organization, and for his excellent contribution to our understanding of modernization and kin network among the Lingayats and Brahmans in Southwestern India. The book is a must for students interested in continuity and change in contemporary Indian society—specifically family and kinship.

Sociologie de la famille et du mariage, by ANDREE MICHEL. Paris: Presses Universitaries de France, 1972. 200 pp. No price listed, paper.

SASKIA SASSEN-KOOB
Queens College/CUNY

Michel's concise study of the discipline is part of the basic P.U.F. series in sociology which includes works such as Lefebvre's *Sociology of Marx,* Aron's *Contemporary German Sociology* and Boudon's *Mathematics in Sociology*. Not surprisingly then, this is a serious little book with considerable analytical power and an intelligent use of existing data on the family. Since it is mostly a study of the functions, structure, and internal interaction of urban families in industrialized societies and most empirical work in this area has been done in the US, the analysis is largely US based and oriented—ongoing comparisons with findings for Europe, both Western and Eastern, and Japan, fail to mitigate this preponderance. The inclusion of opinions and findings of family experts like Kharchev from the Soviet Union, and the thoughts of Gramsci, an author not usually quoted in family text-books, is stimulating.

Michel's analysis of the subject is good. The author breaks down conceptual schemas, most importantly Parsons's, into their components and confronts these with the facts. This confrontation is generally dynamic in that it does not sacrifice complexity for the sake of elegance. And it is dotted with ingenious insights and theses. Although the author places herself within the situational approach to the study of the family, I did not find that this limited or enhanced her analysis. All in all, this study is but a modest addition to sociology of the family as we know it in the US due to the bias in the data base.

More novel and interesting for US sociologists are the approximately sixty pages analyzing the work on the family by Engels, Mauss, Lévi-Strauss, and G. Tillion. To my delight, these authors reappear frequently in the overall study and indeed appear to influence Michel's analysis more so than her own situational approach. Since Tillion is the least known to US sociologists, here follow a few remarks on her work. Tillion seeks to explain social change in family structures and to understand the historical and pre-historical origins of the deep-seated resistance in contemporary industrialized societies to such matters as equality for women, birth-control, and abortion. Her analysis is in terms of total social phenomena. Thereby she avoids the pitfall of structuralism which leaves out demographic, economic, and cultural factors and that of an evolutionism which imputes determining causality to one factor (density for Durkheim, technology for Morgan and Gordon Childe). Further, Tillion locates our civilization and our ideas about the family and natality simultaneously in a synchronic and diachronic historical context, therewith avoiding unilinear evolutionism in her explanations. History is used as a lively source for understanding certain tensions and incongruencies in contemporary industrial societies.

Marriage among a Matrilineal Elite: A Family Study of Ghanaian Senior Civil Servants, by CHRISTINE OPPONG. New York: Cambridge University Press, 1974. 187 pp. $13.95 cloth.

JOHN MOGEY
Boston University

Matrilineal societies are fragile things; the society of the Akan peoples of Ghana, West Africa was cracked, but not broken, by the combined impact of missionaries and money a little over a generation ago. Jack Caldwell showed in some detail how Christian schools and cash from cocoa farming had affected fertility aspirations and desires: this is part of his *Population and Family Changes in Africa* (Australian National University Press, 1968). He showed how the concepts of demography and survey analysis could be used in Africa. Christine Oppong, though trained as a social anthropologist, shows that the concepts of sociology as developed mainly in the USA can be applied to the study of an African people and that they work beautifully. Here, data acquired by questionnaire and by patient participation in household events, are used to analyze the dynamics of domestic life among the top layer of decision makers in an important new nation state.

The Akan decision makers who now run the government bureaus in Ghana and their Akan wives come from a matrilineal background. Since they move around for periods of a year or two to regional centers, and since their wives are educated and want to work, their households usually have some kinfolk helping with cooking and childcare. While they strive to conform to an ideal of a Christian conjugal stable marriage, they need help on many occasions from their close relatives. These helpers may be equally intelligent but through social accidents are illiterate and polygamous and work as cocoa-farmers, or roadside traders. In a vivid set of chapters, covering allocation of resources, decision making, and change, the tensions inherent in these domestic groups are explored.

The principal locus of tensions is not the enormous differences in wealth, in financial security, or in style of life, but the tensions inherent in the conjugal pair within a matrilineal society. The loyalty felt by a husband to his sons and his desire to provide for their education and advancement comes into conflict with his traditional duty to devote his resources to his sister's sons and daughters. In matrilineal societies sets of siblings control the resources of a lineage; wives and husbands often do not live in the same households. So, wives see their husbands spending savings and time on the affairs of their maternal relatives. In Africa, parenthood is usually more important than marriage, marriage is a graduated set of ceremonies, and in matrilineal societies, since the children take their mother's name and inherit from her relatives, it is not important that the children be stable. The changes in Ghana involve the ideals of loyalty between husband and wife, monogamy, the nuclear family as a residential group, and taking pride and responsibility for the children of that union. Most of these civil servants began their married life with a traditional ceremony and followed this months or years later by official registration; this registration makes divorce more difficult. In only about a quarter of the whole group of eighty-five had both parents and present generation bothered to register their marriages.

To explore marital behavior, Oppong uses the results of a questionnaire to supplement her case study material. The central concept is openness or segregation of marital roles. Acceptance of an open marital relation, which involves mutual self revelation and equality in decision making, is mainly the result of education, particularly from having educated parents or grandparents. Most marriages are now monogamous, but extra-marital wives and their children, legitimated by customary law in the villages, are often tolerated. African women expect to work to support their own children and to contribute to the groceries. These educated working wives find the major source of tension in the demands of their husband's brothers and sisters that he support their children at the expense of his own.

This elegant and clearly presented study deserves to be read by all sociologists interested in discovering what massive social change does to the ruling elite of the society. Although the strains and tensions originate from changes in family role expectations, they bear directly on our understanding as sociologists of what happens when new norms are successfully introduced into a social system. The strains and tensions of this elite should have parallels in the communist elites who run the ten socialist states of Europe. This book can be recommended for classes in family sociology or in social change.

Male Fertility Survey: Fertility Knowledge, Attitudes, and Practices of Married Men, by WILLIAM H. SPILLANE and PAUL E. RYSER. Cambridge, Mass.: Ballinger Publishing Company, 1975. 191 pp. No price listed, cloth.

TERESA D. MARCIANO
Fairleigh Dickinson University

Male attitudes and practices, considered important influences on fertility in the Third World, deserve more attention in developed countries. This book provides a good amount of such descriptive material within a modest geographical and substantive scope, while the questions it raises and implies indicate needed further research.

A generally positive orientation to family planning was found in a random sample of married men in the city of Pittsburgh. Given this, its finding of the influence of peer group on contraceptive method suggests tests of group-based contraceptive programs for men. Also, an impression the authors report is a distinction between male and female fertility attitudes, linked for females more immediately to pregnancy and for males to the sexual encounter. One would wish for more research here, given the concerns of women over family formation and career, and in light of the study finding that slightly higher numbers of children are desired by husbands, compared to wives' perceived desires.

This book is a useful resource, as it includes a description of necessary adaptations for all-male samples (e.g., entree and question phrasing), as well as the conditions of random sample attrition, and the difficulty of contacting low-income men.

Medical

Magic, Myth and Medicine, by JOHN CAMP. New York: Taplinger Publishing Company, 1974. 192 pp. $8.50 cloth.

MIRIAM SONN
Massachusetts General Hospital, Boston

This volume describes a wide assortment of beliefs and practices concerning health and illness. The scope of the material is very broad, extending temporally from the ancient Egyptians and Greeks to modern times, spatially across continents, and thematically through fertility, birth and death, contraception and abortion, self-medication, herbal remedies, quacks, faith and healing, osteopathy, and acupuncture.

The author seems to maintain an uneasy attitude toward these beliefs and practices. He vacillates between amazement at people's beliefs in the efficacy of various herbal remedies to a view of those remedies as nuggets of value in the world of healing. He praises the blending of modern medicine and ancient remedies in India, China, and Japan and lambasts Western herbalists for not being more precise and scientific, but does not find fault with modern medical researchers and practitioners for ignoring much of the empirical, if unscientific, wisdom of those herbalists.

Camp writes in a pleasing and entertaining style and offers a catalogue of exotic anecdotes to titillate and nourish the imagination of the reader. Efforts at organizing and analyzing the material, however, are paper-thin or absent. Several chapter headings hint at some underlying conception of the material, but no conceptual framework ever follows. A few lines outline patterns of causative factors as viewed by some tribal peoples. Before that surface is scratched, however, the reader is buried in anecdotes from which there is virtually no let-up throughout the book. In the chapter on household cures and self-medication, several enticing words appear about the role of the dispensing chemist as an alternative to visiting the doctor and about some of the tensions between pharmacists and physicians. Again, the direction is maneuvered back to the descriptive level where it remains. Thus, the presentation never rises above the level of tales of folklore and assorted superstitions.

The Physician's Assistant: A National and Local Analysis, by ANN SUTER FORD. New York: Praeger Publishers, 1975. 245 pp. $17.50 cloth.

MICHAEL YEDIDIA
Brandeis University

In her book, Ann Ford aims to enrich our understanding of the dynamics of achieving innovation in the health care delivery system. The intent is to integrate social theory and empirical findings in an analysis of the problems and prospects facing the physician's assistant. In addition to its substantive contribution to the health personnel field, this approach promises a sociological yield as well. One expects that the outcome will offer valuable insight into the relevance of sociological inquiry to planned social change.

The author has selected an appropriate and timely focus for this effort. Large-scale introduction of physician's assistants is increasingly viewed as a viable mechanism for augmenting the availability of services, elevating the quality of care, and curbing costs. As such, it is regarded by many as the panacea for our health care crisis.

Ford lays the groundwork for her analysis by cataloguing existing literature on diffusion of innovation, organizational conflict, and health personnel development. This section is informative and suggests avenues for research. Unfortunately, however, the author does not undertake a synthesis nor critique of these materials and, consequently, does not emerge with an adequate conceptual framework for maximizing the analytic yield from the empirical chapters which follow.

The strength of the book lies in the presentation of the data from the three surveys conducted by the author—two national questionnaires concerning physician's assistant and nurse practitioner programs and one case study of the attitudes of physicians, nurses, and patients toward a program for obstetrical physician's assistants. In reporting the results, physician's assistant and nurse practitioner programs are compared, and changes over time are emphasized. Ford is very thorough in selecting parameters for data collection, focusing on issues of role delineation, professional identity, level of autonomy, source of recruitment, acceptance by consumers and health professionals, legal concerns, and costs. In each of these areas, she draws upon earlier studies for complementary data and insights. The end product is a useful compilation of information for those who have an interest in this substantive field.

The major shortcoming of the book is its failure to fulfill its potential to make a significant sociological contribution. The author juxtaposes relevant theory with empirical findings without crystallizing those issues which emerge from the intersection of the two. Unaddressed, for example, is the dilemma concerning the extent to which the innovative possibilities accompanying planned social change can be conserved while satisfying the requirements of acceptance. Posed in substantive terms, will the physician's assistant inevitably take on the very attributes which, when displayed by other health practitioners, have contributed to a mode of care which is prohibitively expensive, depersonalized and fragmented, and of insufficient supply to serve the needs of the population? While readers may draw upon Ford's data to make their own suppositions, it is disconcerting that the author does not take the initiative in this sphere. She has forfeited an opportunity to contribute evidence for an affirmative response to the persistent query: What does sociological theory have to offer those attempting to instigate systematic changes in our social structure?

The Challenges of Community Medicine, edited by ROBERT L. KANE. New York: Springer Publishing Company, 1974. 369 pp. No price listed, cloth.

Caring and Curing: Community Participation in Health Services, by EVA J. SALBER. New York: Prodist, 1975. 166 pp. $3.95 paper.

LAURIE ENGELBERG
University of California, Los Angeles

Community medicine is in the process of emerging as an important medical specialty, albeit, primarily academic. It is more concerned than other medical specialties with identifying and examining the social factors which ultimately affect individual health. While both books under review fall under the rubric "Community Medicine," they are quite different in focus and intent.

The Salber book is a series of excerpts from unstructured interviews with community residents associated with Bracken Field Health Center. Salber, an M.D., was the original director of the health center—a center located in a low-income housing project. Unfortunately, Salber never makes explicit the intended functions of this particular health project. Salber was well acquainted with the people she interviewed and thus there is no attempt at unbiased sampling. Her book, does, however, offer a view of community health care almost entirely from a consumer's viewpoint.

Salber set out to demonstrate: that consumer input serves to improve the quality of health care services; that community involvement is personally (i.e., psychosocially) valuable to participants; and that an understanding of human needs is necessary for providing good medical care. While an argument is made for consumer participation in health care and health planning, Salber not only fails to demonstrate that such participation actually improves health services, she also never indicates *how* such improvement could occur. Rather, the bulk of the book is an account of how involvement in the health center favorably altered participants' lives.

Salber's humanistic approach to health care results in enthusiastic support of community projects without locating them in a concrete political, social, and economic context. With only minimal attention to the politics, profits, and ripoffs which often accompany community health projects, Salber's book encourages complacency rather than critical examination.

The Kane book is a more rigorous and less intimate view of community medicine and consequently is likely to be of greater interest to sociologists. Each of the fifteen articles included in this anthology is intended to acquaint the reader with factors affecting the health of a community. All except two of the articles were prepared especially for this volume.

A primary theme of this anthology is the multidisciplinary nature of community medicine. Several disciplines have unique and important contributions to make and a number of the articles include arguments for the inclusions of specific fields in the study of community medicine. These arguments are sometimes slightly overstated and tend to obscure more important concerns such as the specific goals of community medicine.

Other foci of the papers include: (1) the methods utilized in community medicine: community diagnosis, health services research, and epidemiology; (2) the relationship between medical care systems and the health of a community, including issues such as preventive medicine, consumer demands/participation, and the limitations of contemporary medicine; (3) the role of evaluation in community health care and health care programs; and (4) social and environmental influences on health: personal stress, pollution, occupationally related exposure to toxins, and the consequences of overpopulation. The articles are primarily discussions, but draw from original research for elaboration. Throughout, there is an attempt to show that medical care is not always synonymous with health.

Like a number of anthologies, Kane's book suffers from unevenness in tone and style. The volume's integration is, however, greatly improved by Kane's contribution. Not only are his section introductions helpful in orienting the reader toward particular areas of interest, but his articles in the collection offer a great deal of additional insight.

What the Salber book carries to extremes, the Kane book lacks: a connection between community medicine and people's lives. While the book fails to live up to its title in demonstrating the *challenges* of community medicine, as an introductory text it is a success. It provides a nice overall orientation for students of community medicine.

Taking Chances: Abortion and the Decision Not to Contracept, by KRISTEN LUKER. Berkeley: University of California Press, 1975. 219 pp. $10.95 cloth.

RUTH B. DIXON
University of California, Davis

California women in 1971–72 had almost three hundred abortions for every thousand live births. Unlike Latin America or Eastern European countries in which women turn to abortion (legal or illegal) because contraceptives are scarce, in California contraceptives are easy to get. The central question that Luker addresses is "Why women who have easily available, inexpensive, efficient, and presumably convenient contraceptives within their reach should turn to an expensive, at times humiliating, and often traumatic procedure to end a pregnancy, especially in a social context which severely disapproves of discretionary abortions . . ." (pp. 10–11).

Taking Chances is an intelligent, beautifully argued reconstruction of a process of contraceptive risk taking that typifies a group of women seeking abortion in a Northern California clinic. Although 73% of the first 500 clients had used effective methods of contraception in the past (pill, diaphragm, IUD, condom, foam) only 6% had done so since their last menstrual period, even though their presence at the abortion clinic suggests that they wished to avoid pregnancy. Such risk taking, usually labeled by social scientists and helping agencies alike as irrational, neurotic, or self-destructive, is reinterpreted in the light of the women's own definitions of their situations. The perceived social, physical, and economic costs of initiating and maintaining contraception are weighed against the perceived benefits of pregnancy (testing the partner's commitment, testing fertility) and against the subjective probability of pregnancy which, for most clients, is surprisingly low (two-thirds had been told by a doctor that they would experience difficulty conceiving). Given this (usually implicit) cost-benefit calculation and the availability of legal therapeutic abortion to correct a faulty decision, the women's behavior in avoiding the high costs of contraception in view of the perceived low probability and low cost of pregnancy becomes reasonable and logical. In arriving at this conclusion, Luker adds to a growing body of literature on fertility decision making that challenges the concepts of ignorance or irrationality as explanations of reproductive behavior bewildering to "outsiders." Mahmood Mamdani's analysis, in *The Myth of Population Control,* of why Indian villagers in the Punjab did not adopt contraception in spite of the pressure of population on the land is another example: the villagers themselves viewed the economic and social advantages of many children, especially sons, as far outweighing their costs and were able to present convincing (though untested by Mamdani) arguments in support of this assertion.

Luker develops her theory of contraceptive risk-taking from in-depth interviews with a sample of fifty women seeking abortions, almost all of whom had practiced effective contraception in the past but who took risks before this pregnancy, that is, could not blame the pregnancy on contraceptive failure. Most were young, single, and white. The key to understanding their contraceptive risk taking is that "In making decisions about contraception they try to attain many goals, *only one of which is not getting pregnant*" (p. 16, emphasis added). Luker's contribution as a sociologist is to place these other goals firmly in a social structural context rather than looking to personality traits for explanations of such "deviant" behavior.

The process of decision making is artfully reconstructed through grounded theory developed from interviews so that the underlying logic of risk-taking becomes clear. My one hesitation with the approach is that virtually all behavior becomes rational almost by definition: if a person acted this way, then she had a logical reason for doing so. Is there any way of proving this assumption wrong? Did any of the fifty interviewed clients act irrationally in taking contraceptive risks (or in terminating the pregnancy) *given their own perceptions* of the weighting of costs and benefits? Luker's challenging model is a major substantive contribution and a welcome stimulant to further theorizing in the complex field of reproductive decision making.

Community, Physicians, and Inequality: Sociological Study of the Maldistribution of Physicians, by WILLIAM A. RUSHING. Lexington, Mass.: Lexington Books, 1975. 255 pp. $15.00 cloth.

VICTOR W. MARSHALL
McMaster University

The causes of the geographical maldistribution of US physicians, Rushing argues, lie not with any characteristics of individual practitioners or the organization of medicine, but with "the structure of *society* and of *general* social and economic differences between *communities*." This argument is made by analyzing the following, theoretically-selected variables: community wealth (operationalized as median family income), urbanization (percent of residents living in urban areas), community population size, community hospital facilities, community background of physicians, and physician specialty. The unit of analysis is the county, with all 2,971 counties from 47 states included.

Along with confirmation of many commonsensical ideas, we find refreshing insights. The distribution of physicians conforms to the general pattern of the distribution of professionals. This is not surprising, but is seldom recognized. A flight, especially of non-specialists, to the suburbs is described. Moreover, community size and urbanization interact, such that in highly urban counties doctors are attracted to the suburbs, whereas in rural areas they are attracted to larger cities. Thus, neither population size nor extent of urbanization can be considered uniform in their effects on physician distribution. Likewise, hospital facilities are more powerful in attracting physicians in affluent, urbanized communities with highly skilled occupational-service sectors than in less affluent, less urbanized communities with low skilled occupational-service sectors. Findings such as these (and there are many similar findings) serve to support Rushing's argument that community characteristics, and not the pecuniary motivations of practioners, or the organization factors of health care, are of central importance in explaining physician distribution.

At first blush this book might appear to contain all one ever wanted to know about the causes of the unequal geographical distribution of physicians. However, those not enthusiastic about secondary analysis of demographic data will find themselves begging for one, just one, real live doctor to leap from the pages to tell his or her story. Use of grouped data both necessitates strong assumptions in statistical interpretation (noted but made by Rushing) and leads to a sense of distance from the situation being described. Rushing's theory of community differences *causing* geographical differences in physician distribution employs a reified notion of causality which heightens this sense of distance, as does his indexing of community differences (his major explanatory factor) by only two variables (median family income and percent urban).

Despite these weaknesses, which will not in any case seriously disturb most "number-crunchers," a major strength of the book is Rushing's painstaking attention to the details of, and the restrictions in using, this methodological approach. The book can be read as a refresher course (it is too difficult for a first course) in the statistical analysis of large data sets. Text, footnotes, and two appendices seem to consider every possible limitation of the data or the statistical techniques (largely correlation and regression analyses), making the book a model of careful scholarship within this genre of sociology. This does not, however make for ease or joy of reading.

The major weakness of this book is its failure to escape the narrow confines of American health policy in considering possible solutions to the physician distribution problem. Health care innovations of other countries are not considered, and Rushing's own policy recommendation, to form "inter-community medical networks" linking advantaged and disadvantaged communities, seems rather melioristic and unimaginative. Indeed, as he admits (p. 219), "All that may be new [in his plan] is the rationalization and systematization of a process that already exists to some extent."

It will nevertheless be unfortunate if policy-makers in the health care field do not read this book, for the concluding four chapters systematically analyze various "solutions" to the unequal distribution problem, employing the data and analyses of the earlier chapters in the book. The evaluation of policy in the light of data is rare and should be welcomed.

Occupations and Work

Perceptions of Work: Variations within a Factory, by H. Beynon and R. M. Blackburn. New York: Cambridge University Press, 1972. 179 pp. $6.95 paper.

Workers on the Move: The Sociology of Relocation, by Michael Mann. New York: Cambridge University Press, 1973. 265 pp. $4.95 paper. $15.00 cloth.

James W. Rinehart
University of Western Ontario

Beynon and Blackburn examine work attitudes in an English factory dominated by mass production technology. Responses to fixed-alternative questions showed (not surprisingly) that attitudes are a function of objective employment factors and orientations to work which are woven from life experiences.

Women who work part-time in the factory, performing repetitive tasks, expressed general satisfaction with their employment because they expected little else from work than wages to supplement family income. Men who worked on the night-shift (mainly assemblers) were also satisfied. This attitude reflected family responsibilities, resultant instrumental orientations to work, and the belief that all jobs that pay decent wages are stultifying. The greatest discontent was expressed by day-shift males, whose jobs were objectively the most desirable. Their youth and lack of family obligations led to a relative disinterest in wage levels and to (unfulfilled) expectations for gratifying jobs.

This descriptive account of job attitudes is not nearly as informative as Beynon's *Working for Ford.* Based on depth-interviews with workers, the latter study reveals complexities and conflicts of work life which elude survey research.

The second book is an excellent case study of a successful factory relocation. Mann develops and tests a theory of differential propensities to relocate. Non-work considerations (particularly British council houses) affected relocation decisions. But decisions to move were explained largely by "employment dependence," based on wages, fringe benefits, and security. It also entailed a reliance on the firm's internal labor market for the maintenance of job status. For example, part of the workforce was engaged in continuous process work in which job ratings and earnings were inflated by management's need for reliable workers. Process workers had been recruited from a pool of the low-skilled. Had they stayed behind, they would have had little chance of finding comparable employment.

The book is sprinkled with interesting results. Manual workers were no more attached to neighbors and kin than salaried personnel. No support was found for Blauner's sanguine analysis of automation. This plant was dirty; the workforce showed few signs of "integration"; and the much-vaunted responsibility of process operatives was dismissed by a worker, who said: "The thing about these jobs is the responsibility. That means you musn't fall asleep."

Democracy and Organisation in Chinese Industrial Enterprise, 1948–1953, by William Brugger. New York: Cambridge University Press, 1975. 374 pp. $27.50 cloth.

Gary G. Hamilton
University of California, Davis

Western observers in the late nineteenth century wrote a great deal about the democratic aspects of everyday life in China. Their concern was not with formal political democracy, but rather with the apparent paucity of stable hierarchical authority relations in Chinese organizational life. With the collapse of Imperial China, this theme lost favor among twentieth century China scholars until very recently. Now, with the People's Republic as the subject for academic scrutiny, interest has again turned toward the analysis of democracy in China. This book is one of the better examples of this genre in recent China scholarship.

The primary focus of the book is the analysis of how the new regime established its control over, and instituted patterns of, worker participation within China's industrial factories. This topic is superficially bracketed by nods in the direction of organizational theory and cross-cultural comparisons. For theory, Brugger contrasts the often critiqued "logic of industrialism" developed by Clark Kerr and associates with a theory derived from the Chinese experience. The contrast is not particularly incisive or theoretically revealing. Besides this contrast, which is interspersed throughout the book at appropriate points, the author devotes his first chapter to comparing China's nineteenth and early twentieth century industrial beginnings with those of Russia and Japan. Though interesting, the comparisons are not well developed, are not integrated into the remainder of the book, and provide little thematic forecast of what is to follow. The chapter, as Brugger implicitly acknowledges, seems to have been written as an afterthought, an ex post facto attempt to gain macro-sociological relevance for a micro-sociological analysis.

Fortunately, the merits of this book lie in the strength of the author's micro-sociological analysis. Here one sees the real theme that integrates the study. In the years immediately following the Communist takeover, China's political leaders tried, in various ways, to implement what they perceived was the Soviet organizational model of industrialization, a system of "one-person management." This model emphasizes the establishment of rigid vertical relationships between staff and line workers, a formal bureaucratization of both staff positions and worker participation within the enterprise, and subservience to centralized authority. The core of this book insightfully analyzes why this model was not successfully implemented in the Chinese context. In so doing, Brugger shows the origins of a distinctly Chinese model of industrialization, one which, according to Brugger, developed as adaptation of the origanizational ideology used by the Chinese Communists in the 1930s and 1940s. As opposed to the Soviet model, the Chinese model stresses individual participation and loyalty within small groups, the establishment and politicization of horizontal lines of integration, and the imposition of political control without using a middle management. The importance of this book comes from the detailed treatment with which Brugger describes the often simultaneous implementation of these two contradictory models in such areas as labor agreements, fiscal control, incentive programs, party organization, and command structures. The study presents a convincing portrait of the tentative, sometimes conflictive but never easy, formation of a decentralized approach (i.e., democracy) to industrialization in China that arose out of the failure to implement the Soviet model. As such, this book should be of interest to comparativists analyzing comparable phenomena in other societies and to students of China examining the institutional origins of contemporary society.

Working-Class Images of Society, edited by MARTIN BULMER. Boston: Routledge & Kegan Paul, 1975. 278 pp. $13.75 paper.

PATRICIA VOYDANOFF
Merrill-Palmer Institute

In 1966 David Lockwood published a paper, "Sources of Variation in Working-Class Images of Society," in which he outlined two types of traditional workers and the work and community factors associated with each type. The proletarian traditional worker is characterized by a two-class power model of society and is found in isolated occupations having occupational communities. The deferential traditional worker holds a hierarchical prestige model of society and is found in occupations with much interaction between employer and employee, in small firms, and in small towns with interactional status systems. These traditional workers are contrasted with the privatized workers analyzed in the reports of the Affluent Worker Project. This paper served as the springboard for a conference held in 1972 in which recent British research and theory on working-class social imagery was presented. This book includes Lockwood's article, two integrating articles by the editor, and conference papers presented by D. H. Allcorn, E. Batstone, C. Bell, R. M. Blackburn, R. Brown, J. Cousins, R. L. Davis, R. H. Fryer, D. Lockwood, M. Mann, C. M. Marsh, R. Martin, R. S. Moore, H. Newby, G. Salaman, J. H. Westergaard, and A. Willener.

The studies include samples of workers who were expected to be either proletarian (miners and shipbuilders) or deferential (agricultural workers and employees of small firms) according to Lockwood's conceptualization. As might be expected the results do not fit Lockwood's neat ideal types. The context in which the results are presented is somewhat disturbing since the researchers seem to use Lockwood's ideal types more as formal hypotheses to be tested than as an initial formulation to be explored and built upon. In spite of this emphasis, some empirical and conceptual development is accomplished in the course of the papers. The variety of images of the stratification system and the extent of ambivalence are greater than expected on the basis of Lockwood's types. In addition, several factors relevant to the relationship between work and community structure and images are located, e.g., the role of religion and other ideas, the extent of bureaucratization, and the influence of skill differences in the formation of occupational communities. The two papers analyzing the concept of occupational community are among the most interesting in the volume.

The research focuses on results from surveys using standardized interview items to measure class images. Since the study of class images is not developed enough conceptually to allow the formulation of valid survey items, informal interviewing or other qualitative methods should result in a better understanding of the domain to be included in future measures. The editor discusses this and other theoretical and methodological issues in his two excellent introductory papers.

In general this book is more valuable from the perspective of the theoretical and methodological issues covered in the analysis of working-class images of society than for the substantive results presented in the research papers. It could serve as a useful case study of the relationship between theory and research within a social action frame of reference.

The Quality of Working Life. Volume 2: Cases and Commentary, edited by LOUIS E. DAVIS and ALBERT B. CHERNS. New York: Free Press, 1975. 387 pp. $12.95 cloth. $4.95 paper.

Humanizing the Workplace, edited by ROY P. FAIRFIELD. Buffalo: Prometheus Books, 1974. 264 pp. $11.95 cloth.

Work, Productivity, and Job Satisfaction: An Evaluation of Policy-Related Research, by RAYMOND A. KATZELL and DANIEL YANKELOVICH. New York: The Psychological Corporation, 1975. 432 pp. $5.95 paper.

Work and the Quality of Life: Resource Papers for "Work in America," by JAMES O'TOOLE. Cambridge, Mass.: MIT Press, 1974. 414 pp. $15.00 cloth. $5.95 paper.

The Worker and the Job: Coping with Change, by JEROME M. ROSOW. Englewood Cliffs, N.J.: Prentice-Hall, 1974. 208 pp. $6.95 cloth. $2.45 paper.

Varieties of Work Experience: The Social Control of Occupational Groups and Roles, edited by PHYLLIS STEWART and MURIEL CANTOR. New York: John Wiley & Sons, 1974. 407 pp. $12.50 cloth. $5.95 paper.

CRAIG C. LUNDBERG
Oregon State University

In 1973, a special task force reporting to the then Secretary of Health, Education and Welfare, Elliot Richardson, published the controversial *Work in America.* The quality of life for Americans was the theme and how critically important work is was the focus. The often negative effects of the organization of and for work, on productivity, physical and mental health, family stability, and even political behavior were the findings. That volume symbolized a turning point in what may turn out to be a social movement of more major significance than women's liberation or the Black movement. Prior to *Work in America,* conditions of work had been experimented with in piecemeal ways and had been improving. Popular books such as Studs Terkel's *Working* have helped to bring widespread attention to the problem. The energy crises, foreign competition, and environmental concerns have no doubt raised our collective awareness to quality-of-life matters. The H.E.W. report, however, symbolized a major turning point. It crystallized many of the issues and prompted much more concerted inquiries and thinking into the experience and consequences of work in America. In the last few years there has been an ever increasing record of these inquiries, among which are the books under review here.

Work and the Quality of Life is a selected set of papers commissioned for the *Work in America* report. It includes sections paralleling its parent volume, asking who is dissatisfied, what are the problems of American workers, how does work affect health, how might jobs be redesigned, what are the present and needed opportunities for organizational/vocational education, and what changes in national employment and welfare policy are required? The theme is the concern for changing the institution of work so as to improve the quality of life. Striking to this reviewer is the myth-busting quality of the papers. It seems inevitable that the perspective gained by reviewing and evaluating many, many studies and practices leads to departures from conventional analysis. The holistic and humanistic orientation that pervades this book is a refreshing alternative to the prevailing mode of public policy thinking that has been dominated by economists and administrators.

In many ways the Rosow edited book, *The Worker and the Job,* parallels the above volume. The seven authors and the editor—all participants in a 1973 Arden House conference—debate the pros and cons of whether, and how much, improving work-life can contribute to the general quality of life. Changing success definitions, a spreading psychology of entitlement, disillusionment with the cult of efficiency, less economic insecurity, changing characteristics of the labor force, and similar basic disruptive changes are discussed against findings about worker satisfaction and adjustment, evolving labor relations institutions and practices, and national productivity. The book concludes with a discussion of future concerns with job design, organizational experiments, and policy issues. The chapters are all careful, not always consistent, and, from the perspective of three additional years, not all that bold. This reviewer, however, found it more provocative in total than *Work and the Quality of Life,* even though three of the contributors are common to both books.

Worker satisfaction and alienation are topics running through all of the books under review. *Humanizing the Workplace* and *Work, Productivity and Job Satisfaction* deal with these topics most directly. The former volume once again is a collection of twenty-one essays with editorial bridges which look at the variety of analyses of the problem as well as the variety of organizational, definitional, and motivational applications of ideas about humanizing work. As can be expected, there is much controversy, yet the recommendations seem short on social vision. The solutions offered are familiar ones: job enrichment, job enlargement, and participatory management. Basically, however, this is a volume of hope, although the hope stems as much from perceived opportunities as current realities. The humanizing theme and careful editing make it a readable book and an excellent primer on the issues and contemporary innovations regarding the place of work in life and vice-versa. The Katzell, Yankelovich volume on the other hand is a book of hope based on research. Job satisfaction and productivity are the topics; labor and management leaders and empirical research are the sources; the findings contain realistic and useful information for future policies. The main findings are summarized quickly: piecemeal efforts are limited in effect compared to larger socio-technical systems efforts that attend to interweaving appropriate compensation, job-person fit, contribution opportunities, support resources and hygiene factors. In addition, it was found that both labor and management share goals for improvement and, with more knowledge and political sensitivity, probably can bring about improvements, especially with a coordinated drive by multiple societal agencies and components. Clearly a message of hope. As a research report, however, this book will appeal mostly to professionals and may not have the wider impact it deserves.

Sociologists will probably be more interested in the final two books under review. The Davis and Cherns book, vol. 2 of *The Quality of Working Life* has three salient parts. The first examines the status of cases in science and the uses and abuses of action research. The older research strategy implied is a lot less in vogue these days but the editors provide both a cogent defense of cases as a unit of analysis and one of the better summaries of the pros and cons of comparable case usage. Part two offers fifteen cases about industrial participation, system design and redesign, and job design. These are detailed in their description and insightful in their commentary. They provide the most comprehensive set of case materials related to innovation focused on improving the quality of work-life presently available. Part three of the book offers abstracts of other case studies and the reports of five task groups who used the cases to examine such topics as diffusion, intervention strategy, and institution building. This is a rich volume for student and professional alike.

Varieties of Work Experience is the book of the current set which is not directly concerned with the quality-of-work-life theme. Ostensibly it is a "reader" on occupational autonomy and the sources of control that regulate autonomy. Social structure's impact on occupational norms and relationships is what is unique. The twenty-one contributions report on diverse occupations—from cab driving to CPAs, from ballet to housewifery—sometimes descriptively sometimes theoretically. The editors provide excellent conceptual summaries too on cultural, organizational, occupational, and client control. The volume is dedicated to Melvin Dalton and many of his associates and students are contributors, thus the systematic comparative cases is the genre. The separate chapters are in fact fairly uneven, but usefully studded with insight and questions. As a text this book should have limited appeal except for very specialized courses; however, as a reference work for serious investigators it offers a wealth of leads. Occupational autonomy clearly is a theoretical point of leverage overlooked in other work on the quality of work-life. One wonders if a more discrete conceptual focus such as is represented in this volume is what is really needed now that the "concern generator" books previously noted exist.

Clearly the quality of work-life is a vital area for research and scholarship. Speculation and secondary analysis are having their day. Many research issues have as yet to be dealt with, for example, comparative micro studies versus more pointed surveys. Definitionally, the area needs a lot of effort. The books reviewed here do admirably call our attention to the area; however, only the last two discussed offer very much in the way of suggestions for going forward.

Learning to Work, edited by BLANCHE GEER. Beverly Hills, Calif.: Sage Publications, 1972. 109 pp. $3.95 paper.

Entry into the American Labor Force, by MICHAEL D. ORNSTEIN. New York: Academic Press, 1976. 220 pp. $12.50 cloth.

JEYLAN T. MORTIMER
University of Minnesota, Minneapolis

These books, both broadly concerned with entering the work force, exemplify the diversity in our field. *Learning to Work* derives from an exploratory study of vocational education directed by Blanche Geer and Howard Becker. The accounts of the fieldwork are tied loosely together by their common symbolic interactionist perspective. While some practices, such as "binging" or "running the iron" might seem strange, most of the problems observed in the diverse educational contexts (a skid row barber college, ironworking site, butcher shop, beauty school, door-to-door sales course, electronics factory, and county jail school) will be familiar. But in spite of frequently outmoded programs, poor fit between what was taught and what was needed to be learned, education by peers, and anxious disenchanted students, trainees' abilities and work orientations seemed to be influenced. When training was on the job, practitioners were often too busy to teach, and too eager to assign the novice the least skilled tasks (e.g., wrapping instead of cutting meat) which would not detract from other organizational objectives (selling meat, servicing clients, or constructing buildings). Trainees thus learned only part of the "bundle of tasks" of future occupational roles—those that were lucky enough to observe or were assertive enough to persuade others to teach them. Still, Becker emphasizes that the apprentice will not be distracted by "making the grade," learning irrelevancies which often are the basis of student evaluation.

This book would be a stimulating supplement for courses in occupational sociology, sociology of education, or a unit on socialization.

Ornstein's work, a product of the Social Accounts Project at Johns Hopkins, conceptualizes labor force entry *as a process* and presents important findings regarding its implications for mobility. Arguing that previous "static" definitions of entry limit the explained variance in later attainments, Ornstein studied experiences during the first two years after "a firm commitment to the labor force is made." He utilized interview data, providing a wealth of retrospective work information, obtained by NORC from 1,588 American men, aged 30–39 in 1968 (with an oversampling of Blacks to 46% of the total). Among the variables studied are family background, education, pre-entry jobs, job finding techniques, first job duration, prestige and wages of early jobs, number of job changes, industries, unemployment, marital status, and geographic mobility. Racial variations in pre-entry work experience, in the determinants of early job quality and changes, and in the consequences of background and entry experiences for mobility during the following eight years are examined using regression and path techniques. Of particular interest are the different structures of wage and prestige attainment, the implications of military service, and the increasing relative disadvantage of Blacks resulting from their initial characteristics and, to a lesser extent, from the structure of their attainment process.

Unfortunately, little discussion, explanation, or theoretical linkage accompanies the findings. For example, since direct application was found to lead to better jobs than did informal methods, reasons for the discrepancy with Granovetter's *Getting a Job* should have been considered. In one section, he departs from conventional variable ordering in regression, finds that the number of job changes *over one and two year periods* have negative effects, with education controlled, on *first* job prestige (the dependent variable, though temporally prior to job changes), and concludes that "the prestige score of the first job, rather than its wages, appears to provide the motivation . . . to change jobs" (p. 113). Later, after showing that increases in wage rates explain over 40% of the variance in the first job's duration, he changes his position: "the predominant factor in determining first job duration is the amount of wage increase in the job" (p. 124). But because wage increases are often tied to seniority, the causal ordering of the variables is problematic. In sum, this is a book for those whose interest in the process of status attainment provides the motivation to glean through and interpret the many findings, discount occasional leaps from findings to conclusions, and correct the typos in moving from text to table.

The Rise and Fall of the Victorian Servant, by PAMELA HORN. New York: St. Martin's Press, 1975. 185 pp. $10. 95 cloth.

The Sociology of Housework, by ANN OAKLEY. New York: Pantheon Paperbacks, 1974. 242 pp. $3.95 paper.

JANE E. PRATHER
California State University, Northridge

Sociologists have long neglected any study of the houseworker—the dominant occupation pursued by a majority of the population. As sociological awareness of sexism increases, interest arises for an analysis of the occupation of houseworker utilizing a Sociology of Work perspective. These two books attempt to fill this void. Though both writers and their subjects are British, the findings and analyses are highly relevant to American society.

Horn, an historian, draws upon literary as well as historical accounts written by servants and their masters to describe in a rich and convincing manner the lives of British domestic servants in the Victorian era. The book contains outstanding photographs of their assorted uniforms, and indicates the servants' appropriate demeanor.

Oakley's book, derived from her dissertation, consists of data obtained from indepth interviews with forty housewives in Britain. The reader may experience the actual data analysis (chapters 4–9) as proceeding in a detailed but snail-like pace. Reading only the succinct summaries will provide the essential review of each chapter. Of special interest for sociologists are the brief and fascinating accounts of the perspectives of five founding fathers (Marx, Weber, Comte, Spencer, and Durkheim) on women's roles and rights.

Despite the basic difference of whether they receive direct monetary compensation for their work, the domestic servant and the houseworker (as Oakley calls the housewife) experience three important similarities in their work setting. (1) In both occupations, beliefs prevail that women are inherently better suited for performing domestic work than are men. Although male servants in Britain received higher wages than female servants, the British government imposed a heavier tax on male than female servants to discourage employers from hiring men whose labor was sought in other occupations. (2) Both the housekeeper and the domestic servant voice similar complaints about their work—long hours, fragmented work schedule, monotony, routine, low prestige, and lack of control over the work flow. (3) Neither the domestic servant nor the houseworker receive high wages. Presumably their alleged fringe benefits such as security, protection, room and board, compensate for the lack of high wages.

A striking difference between the domestic worker and the houseworker is their perception of power. Oakley discovers the houseworker feels she has autonomy in her work because she is her own boss; yet she experiences little power in her marital relationship. Thus, she has power as a worker in her home but not as a wife. The domestic servant as portrayed by Horn did not possess power and her work was carefully and thoroughly monitored by higher ranking servants as well as the master and mistress of the household.

In summation, these volumes provide a fascinating look for sociologists into the world of housework and in turn the role of houseworker. Oakley painstakingly differentiates between the role of houseworker and the feelings the women experience about performing housework. While most of Oakley's houseworkers express satisfaction with their roles as houseworkers, only a few report positive feelings about doing housework. From a social movement perspective, both books contain interesting accounts of the effect of labor saving devices upon housework from both the houseworker's and the servant's perspectives. An analysis of the domestic servant provides insights for the future of the contemporary houseworker. Just as Horn identifies the decline of the domestic servant as being related to the availability of employment opportunities for women following World War I, today's sociologist can predict that as more women enter the labor force, the number of full-time, life-long houseworkers will decrease. In the words of a former Victorian servant, "Only since the first war did things change. The wealthy then realized we were worth more than they paid us." It will be interesting to see if in the future the houseworker—whether a woman or a man—will finally be recognized as worthy of monetary compensation!

Lawyers and Their Society: A Comparative Study of the Legal Profession in Germany and in the United States, by DIETRICH RUESCHEMEYER. Cambridge, Mass.: Harvard University Press, 1973. 254 pp. $13.00 cloth.

ALBERT J. BERGESEN
University of Arizona

Imagine trying to list all the differences you could think of between the organization and practice of law in Germany and the United States in one breath. That is the experience of this book. Obvious differences are glossed over at such a rapid rate that there is no time for elaboration or any decent explanation. The book is a rambling account of somewhat commonplace observations on similarities and differences between these two legal systems: "Germany has four times as many professionally trained judges as the United States" (p. 34), "Procedure is generally more flexible and nontechnical than in American courts" (p. 44), or "Initial contacts and connections are probably more important in the American than in the German bar" (p. 44). No conceptual framework is offered in which to interpret these differences. Nor is the book an in-depth study of any particular facet of law, or an historical study of the evolution of law in both countries. The data are secondary, being findings reported from other studies. What explanation there is, is composed of a breezy sociology of statements like, "Any group that is fairly differentiated tends to show some forms of stratification . . ." (p. 48), and casual references to the presence and absence of a feudal tradition in Germany and the United States and an everyday approach to cause and effect—"A field may be for one or another reason unattractive to many lawyers, and this may constitute the basis of specialization for a minority, often reached by default" (p. 46).

The problem with this book is simple. It is neither a conceptual nor a theoretical piece nor is it a good job of researching differences between the two systems. The comparisons that are made are, as mentioned before, largely commonplace and hence not of great interest in and of themselves. And since they are not used to make some larger point they are really of very little value. The book seems more like a literature review of some possible topics of comparative research that might be worth investigation, with the book comparing German and American legal systems still to be written.

Organizations

The Efficient Organization, by SELWYN W. BECKER and DUNCAN NEUHAUSER. New York: Elsevier Scientific Publishing Company, 1975. 237 pp. $12.50 cloth.

GERALD R. SALANCIK
University of Illinois, Urbana

One must always pause to admire writers who can encapsulate the complexity of their thought with the adjectival brevity of "the efficient organization." The title is the best part of the book, though its tease turns to torment when one does not find a single declarative that says, "The efficient organization is. . . ." Instead of answers to aid disorganized administrators one is faced with an overwhelming, confusing, and complicated discussion of Becker's (and Gerald Gordon's) Entrepreneurial Theory of Formal Organizations, parts I and II. The book's thesis is simple enough: Owners who know what they are doing, know what they want and know how to get it, will have more efficient organizations if they specify procedures to those they hire to work for them. If they do not know what they are doing, they should leave it up to someone else to decide, called a professional. And if they are smart, the owners will keep track of what they are getting from those whom they hire. It escapes me why it takes ninety-five pages to state this in burdensome phrases like the "complete, truncated and enucleated bureaucracies." I suspect it has something to do with the efficient language of scholars. In some ten pages, for instance, one learns that success is the attainment of a goal, and goal attainment in turn is the discounted present value of the ratio of benefits to costs (in comparison to other alternatives) which in turn is output divided by input, but that all of this cannot be measured because we cannot locate the owners and they may not know what their goals are, so instead we compare organizations which seem to have similar goals (but in fact may not) and see which are getting theirs for less.

The authors examine their thesis in light of information on twenty-seven Chicago hospitals; the presentation, though excessive (fifty pages), is uninformative and inaccurate. One cannot determine how measures were made, and the appendix which claims to reproduce the "measuring instruments" does not. Some of the same data is presented twice in separate chapters with remarkable effect; the ostensibly same correlations increase in magnitude (one from .50 to .738), which can only be attributed to the progress of science. The authors construct a sentence that should make even an unschooled student blanch, "We claim support for the hypothesis despite the number of 'nonsignificant' correlations." The measures of efficiency do not relate to the authors' own conception of the term.

Yet, these minor points aside, the major finding is that the cost of a day of patient care (diet, cleaning, lab services) is less in hospitals which write job descriptions for employees servicing the care, and this is particularly true in hospitals that offer fewer technical services. Unfortunately, this has nothing to do with efficiency, since the cost index is a product of the cost per unit of care multiplied by the number of units administered. According to this index, a hospital that changes your bed once in two days and charges $3.00 is more efficient than one which changes it once a day for $1.00. In contrast to the authors, I would consider the latter not only more efficient but a bit more decent to boot. The authors also examine "quality of care," which for unknowable reasons they call a measure of efficiency. The findings: hospitals with physicians who have influence (over what is unspecified) have lower death rates, as do hospitals which do more autopsies. Unfortunately, the authors do not combine their analysis of costs with their analysis of quality care and thus never test whether the output (quality care) is due to the use of more input (cost of care) or more efficient use of input (specification of job procedures and watchdogging of employees). The authors also do not publish the most useful information they do have: the names of the hospitals and their death rates. This is more a personal than a professional criticism, as my father lives in Chicago and is getting on in years.

In short, the book offers a simple thesis made complicated by unreadable language and presents, with great labor and questionable analyses, a study which does not test the thesis. With a purchase order and $12.50, one can become the efficient spendthrift.

Comparative Union Democracy: Organisation and Opposition in British and American Unions, by J. David Edelstein and Malcolm Warner. New York: Halsted Press, 1976. 378 pp. $19.95 cloth.

Edna E. Raphael
Pennsylvania State University
University Park

This is the concluding report of a relatively long-term study of formal organizational features and political outcomes among the national level labor union organizations of England and the United States. It is comparative also in the fact that a sample of these organizations is considered within each country. Variables are included which represent predetermined operations of a theoretical model of influences on democratic outcomes in labor union organizations. When compared with other models in sociology which similarly are not mathematical, the authors suggest that theirs is a "multiple-characteristic" model. They also recognize that the model preferably might be termed a typology, since full delineation of relationships among the parts of the system is not achieved.

Central to the study is the measure of democratic political organization, which is termed the "effectiveness of opposition" to incumbent elected officials at the top of the national level of these organizations. In England these officials often are elected for life, or age of compulsory retirement. In the US elections for officials at equivalent organizational levels are periodic. This democracy is operationalized through measures of "closeness of votes or frequency of defeat" of incumbents instead of the presence of organized political opposition. However, a detailed reading of the materials presented reveals that what is being measured within the British trade unions is in fact organized political opposition within the British Labour Party, a condition which does not exist in the United States.

Numerous predictor variables are correlated with the outcome, "closeness of elections," and factor analyses among these correlations also are pursued. These statistics are considered and presented separately for national level elections in fifty-one labor union organizations in the United States, and for sixteen wherein officials are elected periodically and fifteen where they are elected permanently in England. Detailed case study materials of one of each of these two types of British unions, the Amalgamated Engineering and Foundry Workers Union (AEF) where elections are periodic and the National Union of Mineworkers (NUM) where elected officials hold office permanently, are presented in separate lengthy chapters. Other formal structural features in the two organizations for the most part are identical in these two cases where "closeness of elections" have been a characteristic outcome over a relatively extended period of time. But it is another commonality there, and one which is not introduced as a feature of the authors' theoretical model (in fact it is not even mentioned) which is the most important of all. British labor union organizations essentially constitute the British Labour Party, which has governed the country intermittenly since World War II. Ideological organized left-right political struggles within the Labour Party anteceded the more recent election victories, and remain common within the Party and its Trade Union Congress. The chapters which detail the NUM and AEF make this abundantly clear. Particularly since the deliberate removal of left-wing forces in the late 1940s, political ideologies have not been a source of electoral opposition in American labor union organizations. Neglect of consideration of the demonstrable relationships between political social organization in labor unions and the societies in which they are imbedded is the book's most serious deficiency. Implicit here also is a criticism of neglect of consideration of the future of democratic trade-unionism as an outcome of the politics of their respective societies. Electoral opposition can, in fact, be staged if it is not a politically organized opposition. There is at least one case at hand of proceedings brought by an individual member, under provisions of the Landrum-Griffith Act, in a US federal court against incumbent officials who were prosecuted for such actions. Finally, to write about labor union organizations as monolithic formal structures is to miss the point that, at least in the US, it is the informal as well as formal structure at the local union level of organization which is at the heart of the matter, together with the structures of the industry and the community with which the membership contends. Nevertheless, this is an important book and I found the opening discussion chapter especially stimulating and illuminating.

Organizations and Their Members: A Contingency Approach, by JAY W. LORSCH and JOHN J. MORSE. New York: Harper & Row Publishers, 1974. 177 pp. $12.95 cloth.

JOHANNES M. PENNINGS
Carnegie-Mellon University

This book is an extension of previous research by Jay W. Lorsch and Paul Lawrence on the so-called structural contingency theory. This "theory" holds that organizations have to show a congruence between environmental and structural variables to ensure optimum performance. This line of thinking is expanded here by incorporating the notion of congruence between environmental and structural variables on the one hand and personality characteristics of the members on the other hand.

A comparison of four manufacturing plants and six research and development laboratories seems to corraborate the notion of fit or congruence. The implication of such findings from the point of view of the practioner (for whom the book is intended) is that there is no single best way for designing or managing an organization; nor should an organization select personnel according to some universal standards since different people may differentially fit different types of organizations and hence differentially contribute to their performance.

The book is well written and does not require prior knowledge of the literature. Like earlier publications from this "school," the methodological rigor is absent and integration with the sociological literature is rather limited. The results do not always seem to warrant the sweeping conclusions. Some results seem to be consistent with alternative, but more specific, interpretations. For example, the differences in effectiveness among the research and development laboratories (as indicated by the judgment of a manager) may be more a function of the bureaucratic-professional role conflict and may be better explained by such a middle-range theory. The conceptual formulations of the study are somewhat eclectic and do not become integrated through some notion of congruence or fit or through some other line of thinking.

However, for a practitioner who is searching for intuitive or phenomonological insight, such flaws are probably insignificant.

Organizational Behavior and Industrial Psychology: Readings with Commentary, edited by KENNETH N. WEXLEY and GARY A. YUKL. New York: Oxford University Press, 1975. 641 pp. $8.95 paper.

BERT R. BROWN
Rutgers University

This collection of fifty-two recent articles is grouped into eight sections: Job Satisfaction, Leadership, Organization Structure, Organizational Development and Conflict Management, Performance Appraisal, Personnel Selection, Training, and Human Factors. There is an effort by the editors to achieve a balance between integrative reviews and conceptual and empirical papers in each of the areas covered. The sections on job Satisfaction and Organizational Development include outstanding papers by Paul Goodman and Abraham Friedman on Adams's Theory of Inequity and by Wendell French and Cecil Bell, Jr. on Organizational Development interventions. The least well developed area is that of Organizational Conflict, consisting of only one (nonetheless excellent) paper by Richard Walton and John Dutton, which presents a model on the management of interdepartmental conflict. The interstitial sections prepared by the editors are very brief and represent only a limited attempt to integrate the material presented in each section. This book would be useful as an ancillary resource in conjunction with more comprehensive texts in organizational psychology or sociology courses.

Political

Planning Alternative World Futures: Values, Methods, and Models, edited by LOUIS RENÉ BERES and HARRY R. TARG. New York: Praeger Publishers, 1975. 312 pp. $20.00 cloth. $6.95 paper.

ELISE BOULDING
University of Colorado, Boulder

This book is described in a foreword by Chadwick Alger as a "jailbreak" by US international relations scholars too long constrained by certain definitions of appropriate data and relevant actors in world affairs. While on the whole it is a very modest jailbreak, more from a maximum security prison to a minimum security prison than into "freedom," it is nevertheless a significant and honest presentation of the state of the field of world order studies from the political science perspective. The substantial overlap between chapters (reading the book is a bit like flying around the world and finding that all airports look alike) is inevitable given that the fourteen contributing scholars are still in the process of "inventing the field" and all feel an overriding need to state a persuasive rationale for a global frame of reference and an orientation toward futures creation. As in any new field, there is both wide divergence in sources used, and a noticeable convergence in ways of thinking. Of the 370 or so scholars whose work is referenced (I am indebted to William Boulding for this analysis of the references) in the fourteen chapters, only one Norwegian sociologist Johan Galtung, is mentioned by as many as half of the authors. Three scholars were cited by six different authors (Falk, Targ and Wager) and two were cited by five different authors (Haas and Meadows). On the other hand, concepts developed in the Institute of World Order's World Order Models Project, directed by Saul Mendlowitz (one of the contributing authors) and concepts developed in the Club of Rome studies, are freely used by all the authors whether referenced or not.

The chief defect of the book is the defect of the field of world order studies: that conceptualizations at the global level are of such a high order of abstraction that it is hard to avoid purely verbal manipulations that trap the mind and let reality escape. My own prescription for avoiding excessive scholarly abstraction is to establish a sequence of apprenticeships for all would-be-world order scholars in a couple of transnational nongovernmental associations, on a UN agency committee or two, on the staff of an intergovernmental development body, and finally in the statistics division of the UN itself. Yes Virginia, there *is* a real world order It is just possible that there might have been more grounding in the social reality if some of the twenty-two women scholars referenced in the book (many of them more data-oriented than the all-male roster of authors) had been included as contributing authors.

The book is in part a "how-to-do-it" on global modeling of alternative futures, and Kent, Beres, Washburn, and Bobrow are the most successful in teaching modeling as process. Targ's treatment of this is also interesting, especially his discussion of the superiority of misery-avoidance over enjoyment as a modeling dynamic. All the authors are careful to distinguish between forecasting and design, and are careful to critique underlying assumptions about human behavior and the social order that shape the modeling effort (Soroos and Washburn are especially good on this). Most of them also call for visioning and the use of the intuitive faculties in futures creation. Unsurprisingly, there is a gap between the designing they do and the visioning they call for. Stohl's chapter on images helps somewhat to close the gap. Had he used some of the new case studies of twentieth century anarchism instead of classical theoretical formulations in his discussion of anarchism, more insight on the relationship between vision and design might have emerged.

All the authors are normatively oriented and wish to be policy relevant, but the breakthrough on identification of world order values made by the world order models team (described in the Mendlowitz and Weiss chapter and referred to frequently by other authors) has yet to be followed by a breakthrough in understanding about valuing as process. Constructing and choosing desired futures is a social learning process, and there must be a continuous feedback between the social environment and the conceptualizer for that learning to take place. Beres's treatment of social learning, in both of the chapters authored by him, is a strong presentation of this problem. Beres also deals with this, and his otherwise excellent overview would have been stronger if he had included some mention of relevant sociological and social-psychological research. Wager, the only historian among the authors, also contributes substantially to our understanding of social learning with an eloquent statement of the role of humanistic and historical studies in developing the human capacity for visualizing futures. The general bias against treatment of social learning inheres in the proposition accepted by most world order modelers that systemic change takes priority over behavior change, which thus becomes a secondary phenomenon.

The dichotomy is a false one, since neither system change nor social learning can take place except through extensive operationalization of concepts and subsequent mapping of data in reference to the real world. While most of the authors in this book talk about operationalization, very few of them to do it. The failure to operationalize becomes particularly glaring in discussions of transition models and theories of social change. There is a tendency to list concepts and potential variables without specification of empirical referents or the relationship between variables. Falk's transition model, while filled with interesting concepts, falls into this trap. While he specifies sequences, he doesn't indicate relationship or process.

Bobrow and Doran "save" the book by dealing in depth with problems of operationalization. Bobrow's chapter is brilliant and should be read by all students of modeling. His spelling out of modeling in terms of performance goals, operational requirements and action instruction statements brings the process down to the level of testable social reality. His insistence on attention to indicators that can help us monitor processes, on getting feedback on model performance and on continuous evaluation of that feedback, is a needed corrective to excessive abstraction. His specific advice to world order modelers on transition strategies will I hope be taken seriously by all practitioners in the field.

Doran's excellent chapter on alternative "growth" models is somewhat marred by a failure to provide diagrams for the models he discusses in the text, and a failure to present the data on which the analysis is based in a form understandable directly in the context of the chapter. Only readers already familiar with the Forrester-Meadows work will be able to interpret the data he belatedly offers in his appendix.

Beres and Targ are to be congratulated for having brought together this collection of papers on the state of the world order futures field, because in thus signalling both the weaknesses and strengths of the new discipline they are providing the conditions for further growth. One important aspect of that growth, I believe, will be for the political scientists now liberated from an unhappy marriage with the old international relations data to begin to prepare for a cautious courtship with socio-economic data of various kinds, including indicator data and historical data, on a variety of global actors and entities—transnational, regional, cultural, as well as international and national. Such a step will make new social maps of the past, present, and future possible, and will make the world order field more useful to policy makers, activists, students, and teachers—as well as to themselves in their own futures construction.

Toward a Political Sociology of Science, by STUART S. BLUME. New York: Free Press, 1974. 288 pp. $9.95 cloth.

LOWELL L. HARGENS
Indiana University, Bloomington

Although billed on its dust cover as "a radical departure from standard sociological studies of science," this book is actually a straightforward extension of past work on the relations of science and scientists to contemporary political structures, with emphasis on the US and Great Britain. In some respects, the book updates Bernard Barber's *Science and the Social Order,* a classic treatment published a quarter of a century ago. Thus, readers who are seeking either a discussion of contemporary science from a radical political perspective, or a new theoretical framework for analyzing the relations between science and the political order are likely to be disappointed by Blume's book. On the other hand, those who are looking for a systematic discussion of relations between science and politics from a comparative and historical perspective will find much of value in the book.

Blume argues that science is increasingly dependent on the political and economic structures of society for support. As a result, scientists are becoming increasingly aware of their obligations to society as a whole and suspicious of the alleged value neutrality of science and the motives of its chief supporters. Blume claims that these trends are reflected in a new "professionalism" among scientists which stresses their obligations to provide the public with information about possible uses and misuses of scientific knowledge and with accurate information about the effects of the products and policies of their supporters (especially business and government). He traces the impact of this new professionalism on traditional scientific associations, on the development of labor unions and political interest groups among scientists, and on relations between scientific and political elites. Blume is clearly enthusiastic about the emergence of the new professionalism, but he is also sensitive to the possibilities it opens up for public conflict among scientists and the consequent loss of public respect for the scientific enterprise. Although he treats the emergence of the new professionalism in the US and Great Britain in some detail, little consideration is given to possible mechanisms by which it may become institutionalized. Indeed, toward the end of his analysis Blume admits that the developments he analyzes may disappear in the future. Blume does not attempt to show relations between these developments and patterns of cognitive change in science; his analysis is primarily a study of the political behavior of scientists rather than a sociology of their intellectual products.

Blume presents several excellent case studies of historical trends in scientists' organizational activities, and these are the highpoints of the book. His analysis of the histories of the American Chemical Society, the Chemical Society in Britain, and the British and American Associations for the Advancement of Science are provocative and should be of interest to sociologists concerned with the political consequences of the organizational structures of scientific associations. Blume's comparative analysis of the unionization movements among British and American scientists, and the triadic relations between political elites, scientific elites, and scientific "masses" are also valuable.

Blume is less successful in his attempts to provide a theoretical framework for his discussions. It is sometimes difficult to follow the thread of his arguments in chapters explicitly devoted to theoretical explication. While a variety of conceptual schemes are introduced in the book, they remain largely undeveloped and do not provide theoretical coherence. Furthermore, Blume devotes a major effort to a quixotic attack on the position that science can best be studied as an autonomous subsystem of society. Unnamed "Mertonians" are alleged to be the perpetrators of this position (although a minimal familiarity with the work of Merton himself will force one to conclude that Merton is not one of Blume's Mertonians), but the extent of allegiance to such a silly view is considerably overestimated by Blume. As a result, at points this valuable addition to the literature on the political behavior of modern scientists appears to be a misguided polemic.

Bureaucratic Encounters: A Pilot Study in the Evaluation of Government Services, by DANIEL KATZ, BARBARA A. GUTEK, ROBERT L. KAHN, and EUGENIA BARTON. Ann Arbor: Institute for Social Research/ University of Michigan, 1975. 264 pp. No price listed, paper.

THEODORE L. REED
Temple University

Bureaucratic Encounters is about citizen utilization and evaluation of governmental bureaucracy and the relationship of these bureaucratic encounters to various measures of generalized support of the political system. The findings are based on questions from an ISR national omnibus survey (spring 1973) in which fewer than 60% of the respondents reported any contact with governmental bureaucracies. The results are reported in about 140 tables (mostly bivariate frequency) with associated interpretation. There is no integrative theoretical framework. An opening chapter reviews marginally relevant evaluation studies. A conclusion summarizes the findings and sketches a program of further research. The monograph does not meet the high standards associated with the past work of the authors.

A digest of the findings—and non-findings—includes: (1) governmental services are under utilized by 1/3 of the sample; (2) only 15% of the sample report problems (not encounters) with constraint agencies; (3) there are substantial differences in the evaluation of service agencies; Social Security is most positively evaluated (86% satisfied), hospital/medical services (57% satisfied), and welfare (61% satisfied) are least positively evaluated; (4) governmental services have no overall redistributive effect; services tend to serve different segments of the population; (5) nine demographic factors explain about 21% of the variance in utilization of service agencies and only about 12% of the variance in problems with control agencies; (6) seven demographic factors and agency characteristics explained only 14% of the variance in satisfaction with service agency encounters; (7) attitudes derived from people's specific experiences with government bureaucracies (pragmatic support) are more positive than their general attitudes (ideological support); and (8) the young express less positive evaluations of bureaucratic encounters and slightly less system support than their elders.

True Americanism: Green Berets and War Resisters, by DAVID MARK MANTELL. New York: Teachers College Press/Columbia University, 1974. 285 pp. $5.95 paper. $10.00 cloth.

CHARLES P. FLYNN
Miami University, Oxford, Ohio

Despite the central significance of war as a social phenomenon, there is a dearth of sociological theory and research dealing with such important topics as social background and attitudinal factors as related to favorability toward participation in war, as well as willingness to become part of the military. Mantell's study helps remedy this lack. Employing a judgment sample of twenty-five Special Forces "Green Beret" troops and twenty-five war resisters, Mantell comparatively analyzes, using primarily depth interviews, the socialization experiences, intrafamilial relationships, and war-related attitudes of the two groups. Among his more salient findings: the Green Berets tended to have experienced a lack of positive affective relationships with parents; had participated in hunting much more than the war-resisters; had witnessed violent incidents, such as accidents, when children or adolescents; and tended to have an instrumental, amoral attitude toward the brutal aspects of their military functioning, regarding themselves as highly skilled technicians. Most surprising, to Mantell, was the Green Berets' lack of patriotic, or indeed any sort of ideological motivation. Rather, they saw themselves as professionals who would be willing to hire themselves out to the highest bidder regardless of the cause for which they might be asked to fight. It is this instrumental, technicist attitude that allows the Green Berets to feel little or no distress or qualms at committing various kinds of brutalities and even atrocities, many times against innocent Vietnamese, that are described in detail in the anecdotal material Mantell interweaves in his analysis.

This book is excellent in all respects. It is very systematic in its methodology, sensitive to the moral issues and dilemmas associated with differential degrees of willingness to participate in war, and contributive of important insights into the nature of soldierly motivations as well as the empathy failure that has come to characterize modern, technologically-oriented warfare. Mantell has provided a valuable contribution to the sparse sociological literature dealing with the humanistic aspects of war.

Beyond the Sociology of Development: Economy and Society in Latin America and Africa, edited by IVAR OXAAL, TONY BARNETT, and DAVID BOOTH. Boston: Routledge & Kegan Paul, 1975. 295 pp. $21.75 cloth. $12.25 paper.

PATRICIA MADOO LENGERMANN
George Washington University

This collection of papers by British-based social scientists explores conceptually and emprically the "dependency" approach to Third World social change, an approach which most American sociologists have been introduced to through the writings of Andre Gunnar Frank. Derived from Marxism, dependency theory holds that there has been a long historical relationship between Third World and the North Atlantic societies, a relationship which persists today; that this has been and is an exploitative relationship in which the latter nations have used Third World economies in the interests of their own capitalist expansion; and that this relationship, together with resulting social structures internal to Third World societies, explains the continuing underdevelopment of the Third World. As Americans move away from their own "developmentalist" perspective on Third World issues, and begin to explore dependency theory, they will find this a useful and persuasive book, for it weds that style of judicious scholarship typical of British work to an orientation which many have dismissed, for all its attractiveness, as primarily ideological.

Despite their obvious debt to Frank, these writers seek to expand and strengthen his thesis in three ways. First they critically scrutinize his writings. Weaknesses that they point to include his focus on relationships of exchange rather than on relationships of production, and the mechanical, overgeneral nature of his metropolis/satellite model. Second they demonstrate, through careful review articles, the complementarity between Frank's general thesis and a much broader literature which includes the writings of Latin American social scientists, the Caribbean New World group, French economic anthropologists, and the theories of a plural society and of internal colonialism. This effort enhances the stature of dependency theory, adding new dimensions to it, and shows it to be the culmination of multiple trends in the international social science community's approach to the Third World. Third, a series of rigorously empirical case studies (of Kenya, Tanzania, the Sudan, Guyana, and Peru) reveal the methodological implications of this orientation. We learn that one must analyze concrete instances of dependency in historical and contemporary detail, focusing on the economic institution and particularly on the details of incorporation into world capitalism; and that one must trace this process from local through national and international systems, scrutinizing the mechanisms of transition between levels and the processes by which these dynamics influence social class and other socio-cultural features of the dependent society.

One weakness of the book is that empirically it focuses on the microdynamics of peasant economies, with much scanter attention to national systems and only the most impressionistic approach to the relationship between nations, yet theoretically this last relationship is the ultimate cause of local exploitation and underdevelopment. The other striking weakness of the book is its failure to grapple conceptually or empirically with the phenomenon of "nonprogressive" attitudes within Third World societies. Indeed, in touching on the phenomenon of racial prejudice in South Africa, Guyana, and Peru the authors tend to imply naively that these attitudes are merely epiphenomal to the economic situation. That "factors of consciousness" can be given a more sophisticated role in Marxist-derived theory has been demonstrated by the Critical Frankfurt School, another block of literature which, ideally, the editors might have linked to dependency theory in a review paper. All in all, though, this is a valuable book which adds importantly to our understanding of the details of dependency theory.

The Peace Revolution: Ethos and Social Process, by JOHN SOMERVILLE. Westport, Conn.: Greenwood Press, 1975. 236 pp. $12.95 cloth.

DUANE K. FRIESEN
Bethel College, North Newton, Kansas

The purpose of this book is to describe the revolution that is necessary in our habits of thinking and acting in order to prevent a nuclear war. Somerville is a nuclear pacifist. He argues that the present policy of governments of nuclear deterrence based upon threat is both dangerous and absurd.

At several points Somerville refers to the Cuban missile crisis as an example of the bankruptcy of nuclear policy. Kennedy told the Soviets that they must remove their missiles from Cuba without any conditions, even though according to Robert Kennedy's memoirs, Kennedy recognized it was reasonable for the Soviets to demand that the US remove its bases from Turkey. Kennedy in fact did not expect the Soviets to meet his demands and expected furthermore to have to bomb the bases in Cuba which would wipe out everyone. Somerville's position is that one should never commit oneself to a course of action that would involve the use of nuclear weapons for any reason whatsoever, not to "save face" and not even to retaliate if one has been attacked with nuclear weapons. Any position which would destroy everything including oneself is both absurd and morally wrong.

Arguing from the above premises, Somerville outlines in the bulk of the book the conditions and processes which are necessary to eliminate the nuclear threat. A peace revolution demands new politics, new education, new semantics, new morality, a new human individual, and a new science of peace. Though Somerville presses for a new kind of economics which leads to the social ownership of the means of production for the sake of the general welfare rather than a capitalist system involving competition for private profit, he recognizes that these fundamental economic changes are not likely for a long time. In the competitive economic framework, however, capitalist and socialist nations must both recognize that nothing would be gained by nuclear war.

The book is based upon sound scholarship, though Somerville fails to make use of and make the reader aware of the large amount of peace research literature that is available today to those interested in the prevention of war. The political dimensions of the problem of preventing nuclear war are also not sufficiently emphasized and analyzed. Overall, however, the book's strength derives from the multifaceted way in which the problem of preventing nuclear war is viewed.

Immigrants and Politics, by PAUL R. WILSON. Canberra: Australian National University Press, 1973. 175 pp. $10.50 cloth.

MARK TANNENBAUM
Harvard Law School and *University of Michigan, Ann Arbor*

The open chapter of *Immigrants and Politics* claims the following objectives: to achieve a clear understanding of the manner in which people participate in the political process; to ascertain the relationship between migrant assimilation and political participation; to determine the impact of immigration on the political system itself; and to explain differences in political behavior between major Australian immigrant groups and between immigrants and native born Australians. The agenda is long and the book is short. I would have been more satisfied had the agenda been shorter and the analysis of each issue more focused and thorough.

The book reports the results of a political attitudes and behavior survey conducted among British and Italian post-war immigrants to Brisbane to discover why Italian Australians confess to abysmally low levels of political activity. Two measures of political "behavior" are constructed: interest in politics ("Do you talk about politics with . . .?") and self reported political activism ("Have you ever sent a letter to . . .?"). Arguably, these indexes tap some dimension of political interest and/or participation. After showing that these measures of participation are indeed related, the search commences for variables to explain British-Italian differences; namely, past political involvement in the migrant's native land, length of residence in Australia, occupational status (whose relation is reported but never demonstrated), and the cultural assimilation variables which occupy the major thrust of the theoretical exposition. Finally, we are treated to a model of political participation which includes and orders the variables irrespective of any demonstrated statistical justification. Somehow, everything —the weak, the strong, and the non-existent —gets thrown in.

It is all rather exasperating. A word of advice to prospective readers: equip yourself with a sharp pencil and a calculator, for if you bother to reanalyze the data, as I did, you will find they bear little relation to the theoretical exposition. Immigrants' length of residence in Australia, to be sure, is related to interest in politics; but the assimilation variables add little, if anything, beyond its contribution. By failing to pull his tables apart, the author fails to see this; consequently, the theoretical discussion is hopelessly detached from the data analysis. Some gratuitous explanations for the relationship between residence and political interest are offered (SES, leisure time availability), and plausible though they may be, the data presented offer no support. Some variables that do seem to make a difference may be confounded with the dependent variables (e.g., group membership).

Perhaps most frustrating is Wilson's failure to pursue his questions beyond the most cursory level of inquiry. The data are not analyzed really: they are culled for bits and pieces of prima facie relationships which lend deceptive support to the assimilationist theory the book touts. Counter evidence, when recognized explicity, is promptly forgotten. All too often the author leaves the foray midway through, and charges on to other battles, other tables. But neither the tables, nor the reader is won over.

The Seamy Side of Democracy: Repression in America, by ALAN WOLFE. New York: David McKay, 1973. 306 pp. $7.95 cloth.

ALBERT SZYMANSKI
University of Oregon

Alan Wolfe's thesis is that political repression is an integral and normal part of the American system. Repression is seen as "a process by which those in power keep themselves in power by consciously attempting to destroy and render harmless organizations and ideologies that threaten those in power." The author thus makes the vitally important observation that political repression consists of far more than the jailing and physical harassment of those who oppose the capitalist system. Repression is seen as a mechanism which ensures that existing power relationships will be reproduced from generation to generation.

Wolfe reviews the history of the use of the police, national guard, FBI, HUAC, industrial spies, conspiracy trials, the Smith Act, etc., throughout the 20th Century. He cites the 471 uses of the National Guard against strikes, students, and national minorities from 1919 to 1969, the systematic harassment and virtual destruction of the Black Panthers and the wiping out of the IWW during and immediately after World War I as case studies in what happens to those that oppose the American way of life.

Wolfe emphasizes the class nature of the state and the asymmetrical way it deals with different classes of the population. The state, he convincingly argues, typically supports the privileged in struggles among the classes. In support of his argument he reminds us of the differential treatment of upper and lower class lawbreakers by the courts, e.g., corporate violators of the anti-trust laws typically receive slaps on the wrist, although their actions defraud the public of many millions of dollars, while leaders of the IWW, the Socialist and Communist Parties, have received harsh prison sentences for merely verbally expressing their convictions.

Perhaps the major contribution of the book is its treatment of the manipulation of the political ideas held by the masses as a major form of political repression. Wolfe points out that if the government can convince the overwhelming majority of people that left-wing ideologies are evil, then dissenting groups will gain few adherents. Indeed he goes on to argue that the most repressive system possible would not be fascism, but a society in which, because of the efficiency of ideological manipulation, there was nothing to police. Wolfe briefly analyzes the role of education and the mass media as well as the use of public relations techniques as mechanisms of ideological repression. On the one hand the omnipresent hawking of the basic values of liberal society: individualism, competition, fatalism, distrust, parochialism, respect for authority, etc., serves as a prophylactic against socialist/communist ideas and makes the individual relatively content with capitalism. On the other hand the overt multifacited propaganda against socialism and communism serves to discredit these alternative ways of life in the eyes of the masses of American people so that they will not turn to social movements which threaten the power and privilege of the US ruling class.

Wolfe points out that historically it has been liberal Democrats more than conservative Republicans who have been responsible for the use of violent repression against the Left in the US, e.g., the repression of the IWW, the jailing of Eugene Debs, the harassment of the Socialist Party and the Palmer raids all occurred during Woodrow Wilson's administration, and the jailing of the C. P. leadership occurred during Harry Truman's.

In general *The Seamy Side of Democracy* is a very useful and most timely book. The revelations of the last two years about the various disruptive efforts of the US intelligence agencies, the most infamous of which are the FBI's Cointelpro program aimed at sowing divisiveness and demoralization among Black, Old Left, and New Left groups, and the CIA's overseas "destabilization" campaigns underscore Wolfe's points about repression.

The book would be stronger had the author researched a little more thoroughly the various instances of repression against the Left, e.g., the repression of the Communist Party in the late 1940s and 1950s, rather than relying so heavily on the examples of the IWW and Black Panthers. The book also suffers from a lack of attention to the defenses which the lower classes and oppositional movements have against the two forms of repression. A brief discussion of how the Communist movements in China and Indochina and the left working class movements in Europe have been able to survive, and in many cases make revolution, in the face of repression far more brutal than that used by the US ruling class, would have been most instructive. The concluding chapter also suffers from the naive and moralistic argument that "to build a non-repressive society it is necessary to have a non-repressive movement." Wolfe's position leaves him to a rejection of Leninism and a flirtation with anarchism. If the history of modern liberation movements, as well as the examples Wolfe provides, tell us anything, it is that the ruling class will leave no stone unturned to preserve its privileges and, in the last analysis, understands nothing but superior force.

Race and Ethnic

Prison of Grass: Canada from the Native Point of View, by HOWARD ADAMS. Toronto: New Press, 1975. 238 pp. $12.95 cloth.

Urban Renegades: The Cultural Strategy of American Indians, by JEANNE GUILLEMIN. New York: Columbia University Press, 1975. 336 pp. $10.95 cloth.

Solving "The Indian Problem": The White Man's Burdensome Business, edited by MURRAY L. WAX and ROBERT W. BUCHANAN. New York: New Viewpoints, 1975. 237 pp. $12.50 cloth. $4.95 paper.

JOE T. DARDEN
Michigan State University

Prison of Grass is an unusual book. It deals primarily with the Indians and Metis (mixed blood, i.e., part Indian and part white) of the western plains of Canada. The author, who is a Metis, has presented an historical account of the effects of 300 years of white supremacy, imperialism, colonization, and capitalism on the native people and their nation and he has done it from the perspective of the native.

It is indeed refreshing to review a book about the history of a colonized and exploited people which has been written by a member of the exploited group. Such books, especially about Native Americans are so rare. Not only is this book rare because it is written by a member of the colonized, but it is also rare because it is well written, well researched, scholarly, and very interesting. It is far superior to the other two books listed above and should rank at the top of the list among any recent books dealing with Native Americans.

Adams used both primary and secondary sources and relied heavily on *L'Histoire de la Nation Metisse dans l'Ouest Canadien,* by A. H. de Tremaudan.

Only a Metis or an Indian could have written this book. Because to have written it, one must have experienced it. For a revealing and interesting account of Indian-white relations in Canada, I highly recommend *Prison of Grass.*

Urban Renegades is not a book about "Urban Indians." Instead it is a book about a single tribe, the Micmac, a tribe of 10,000 members that compose about ninety percent of the Indians in Boston. The Micmac's social organization is the basic focus of the book.

The author based the work primarily on urban ethnographic fieldwork conducted from 1969 to 1971. The book is primarily descriptive with very little analysis and not a work that I would recommend for a course on Urban Indians.

Solving "The Indian Problem": The White Man's Burdensome Business, is a book of essays and *New York Times* news stories which focuses on the ways that whites have interpreted their relationships to the various Indian tribes and how whites have attempted to solve the "Indian problem." The editors argue that the "Indian problem" is linked to the ideological and political problem of the United States, i.e., the problem of determining whether the United States is, or should be a "melting pot," an amalgamation of ethnicities or a pluralistic society where ethnic and racial groups can remain socially and culturally distinctive. The conflict between these two ideologies and its impact on Indian policy is the major focus of this book.

There is little that one learns about how to "solve the Indian problem" after reading this journalistic compilation of newspaper articles. The book does, however, put the dilemma of the "Indian problem" into a philosophical perspective which can be understood by the laity. To that end, it serves a useful purpose.

The Unequal Elites, by ROBERT P. ALTHAUSER and SYDNEY S. SPIVAK. New York: John Wiley & Sons, 1975. 204 pp. $12.50 cloth.

RAY C. RIST
National Institute of Education/HEW

Since the period of Reconstruction, it has been a widely held belief that providing education for Black Americans would be the surest and most effective way of eventually attaining parity with white Americans, be it economic, political, or occupational. Such a view has been so pervasive as to transcend racial, ideological, and social class lines. The redemption of a legacy of racism, discrimination, and segregation has been sought in the American creed of education.

The outcomes, however, have not met the expectations. This present study by Althauser and Spivak provides yet further evidence that equal educational attainment in and of itself has not brought equality in other areas. Rather, what one finds is that the inequalities evident elsewhere in the society manifest themselves as well in the "output" function of education. Thus the sobering conclusion of the authors that at the time of this study (1967), comparable higher educational attainments between blacks and whites did not result in comparable rewards and benefits.

On the first page of their study, the authors pose this question, "Do black and white men find that their resources, when equal, produce rewards of equal value in the marketplace of human competition?" Adopting a quasi-experimental design in an effort to control for other variables confounding the assessment of education on occupational achievement and income, the authors selected a sample of approximately 800 white and black college graduates whose academic achievement and social class were held constant. Focusing on graduates from three universities (two predominantly white and one predominantly black), they compared small closely matched samples of white and black graduates from between 1932 and 1964. It quickly becomes apparent that scope was sacrificed for specificity. Both the limited population and particular time frame (prior to the rapid increase of black students in higher education and the civil rights movement in general) were recognized by the authors. Thus they wisely made no claims or sought grand extrapolations to other populations or periods.

Throughout this study, there is evidence of the gradual shift occurring in studies of education and stratification away from a focus on "inputs" and towards the study of variations in outcomes. In the present instance, it is the impact of educational attainment upon career rewards. The findings are mixed. Perhaps the most general conclusion to come from the study is the following:

> Thus, in our moderately controlled comparison, an equal starting point was converted into one form of equal results–equal average job status. However, these equalities did not produce equal income, either median or average. The median income differences of roughly $500 favoring whites and, to a lesser extent, the $1,500 difference (favoring whites) between white and Frazier [predominantly black university] black graduates are smaller than from previous (though not exactly comparable) analysis using 1960 census data (pp. 120–21).

Though these findings are modified based on regional variations, differences in salaries between the public and private sectors, and additional educational experience, the fact remains—equal educational attainment does not translate into equal control over economic resources. For the latter to be accomplished, blacks must compensate for the realities of discrimination by having to obtain more education in order to achieve parity of economic resources with whites who have less education.

The Two Rosetos, by CARLA BIANCO. Bloomington: Indiana University Press, 1974. 234 pp. $10.00 cloth.

PAUL J. CAMPISI
Southern Illinois University, Edwardsville

The Two Rosetos is a participant observer study of the folkways of two related communities, one in Italy and the other in the United States. Using folklore as the basis of her evaluation of the acculturation process, the author attempts to examine the relationship between old world traits and the content and structure of the Italian American experience. It is the first important comparative folklore study since the publication in 1939 of Phyllis Williams', *Southern Italian Folkways in Europe and America.*

The old world community of Roseto Valfortore, Foggia, Italy is located in that highly neglected area south of Naples which has traditionally experienced such oppressive social and economic hardships that the only rational alternative for millions of its peasant inhabitants has been to emigrate regardless of their close attachment to home and country.

In 1882 eleven immigrants from Roseto Valfortore arrived in New York. They came as farmers but found work in the slate quarries near Bangor, Pennsylvania. There they settled in a "Little Italy" adjacent to East Bangor and founded the town of Roseto, Pennsylvania, the focal point of this research report. For the next 90 years these people and those who followed were to develop a way of life reminiscent of the one they had known in Roseto Valfortore but transformed and shaped to meet the new definitions, meanings, and cultural expectations of the new American world. Today, Roseto, Pennsylvania's population of about 2,000 persons is still completely Italian. Ninety-five percent of its residents are descended from the namesake town of Roseto Valfortore, and it is probably one of the most homogeneous ethnic enclaves in America. Although Rosetans continue to work in the slate quarries and related industries, many have prospered and are the owners of small businesses, modest garment factories, and are even directors or owners of two slate quarries, the very kind in which their early forebears had worked for as little as 40 cents a day.

In 1963 Roseto achieved national attention from a widely published medical study which indicated an unusually low incidence of death from heart disease. This was an astounding finding in view of the heavy Italian diet which Rosetans continued to use. Although the author does not comment on the ethnic implications of the medical survey, some students of ethnicity would not hesitate to hypothesize that acceptance of one's ethnic self correlates positively with lack of stress, feelings of well being, and personal good health.

The second part of this report contains the verbatim transcripts of the taped interviews conducted in English and Italian. In this section which is packed with tales of bandits, witches, heroes, migration woes, and magical cures, the author has caught the peasant's marvelous sensitivity to the comical as well as the tragic.

Carla Bianco concludes that both the structure and social processes of Rosetan culture have been altered by deep changes in both communities. Though the future of Roseto seems in doubt, particularly because of the inclination of the third generation Italian-Americans to move increasingly within the core American culture, there is no question but that the transition from the old world to the new was made much easier by the presence of old world Rosetan folkways. In many ways this study supports the hypothesis that cultural pluralism in America is a very real and positive force for both the individual and the nation.

Black Sociologists: Historical and Contemporary Perspectives, edited by JAMES E. BLACKWELL and MORRIS JANOWITZ. Chicago: University of Chicago Press, 1974. 415 pp. $16.00 cloth. $4.95 paper.

ALBERT J. MCQUEEN
Oberlin College

Historically the sociological profession, while proclaiming liberal values, has displayed little vigor in examining its own practices or in initiating institutional changes to foster optimal professional development and participation of minority sociologists. Only with the advent of pressures from black sociologists in the late 1960s were there significant movements in this direction. Before then it was convenient to avoid the conflicts that fundamental changes would have generated by taking note of the progressive liberalism permeating the profession in race relations, and in the fact that the American Sociological Association had, in 1948, honored a black sociologist, E. Franklin Frazier, with its presidency.

This book, the first in-depth study of black sociologists, is the product of difficult, sometimes excruciating processes of reorientation and change that have gripped the profession in recent years. It is appropriate that this volume should be the outgrowth of a conference initiated by committees of the Caucus of Black Sociologists (CBS) and ASA, and sponsored and supported by the University of Chicago. This institution should be acclaimed for its towering influence in the race relations field and for being in the forefront of all universities in producing black Ph.D.s in sociology and encouraging their scholarship. I think it would have been *more* appropriate, however, had this endeavor been jointly sponsored with one or more black universities, such as Fisk, Atlanta, Tuskegee, or Howard. These institutions were home bases where black sociologists, from the earliest beginnings of sociology in this country and usually against great odds, built traditions of teaching, research, and scholarship that paralleled but seldom intersected with mainstream activities in the field. In any case, the book succeeds handsomely and makes important contributions by revealing the main features of that history, as well as the dilemmas and constraints that shaped the adaptations of black sociologists.

One of the limitations of a pioneering study of such broad scope is that a single conference is not (in the nature of conferences) the best vehicle for shaping a balanced and penetrating set of investigations of the many facets of the subject. This can be seen in the heavy emphasis placed on the careers of those three acknowledged giants among sociologists, black or white: DuBois, Johnson, and Frazier. By contrast, the circumstances and contributions of many other important figures are only touched on lightly or mentioned in passing. Despite their stature and the pervasiveness of their influence as scholars and activists, the question should remain open whether it is proper to designate this trio exclusively as the "founding figures" in the professional realm of black sociologists. For example, it is doubtful whether the scope and influence of DuBois, *as a sociologist and in the context of the times,* was greater than that of George E. Haynes, who in 1910, shortly after co-founding the organization that became the National Urban League, established the Social Science Department at Fisk University and headed it with scholarly and administrative distinction until 1921. The point is not to quibble over who was "first" or "most important"; it is simply to recognize that the book contains interpretations that are likely to be controversial, has gaps in its coverage, and is considerably uneven.

The book is organized around careers of particular sociologists and their institutional and professional adaptations in a segregated society; it has contemporary data on black sociologists, an excursus into certain theoretical and ideological questions, and points out some institutional consequences of a number of recent changes.

The descriptions and analyses of careers and historical developments take up more than half of the book and supply the most interesting and insightful materials. The two closely related themes dominating these discussions are today compelling factors in the professional lives of black sociologists, just as they were four or five decades ago. The first theme is the integration or balance between the role of black sociologists as advocates of black rights and development, and their role, as sociologists, to adhere to professional standards and expectations extant in the social sciences at a given time. The second theme deals with problems of constructing relatively satisfactory professional relationships across largely separate but interrelated institutional spheres. The obvious backdrop to these two sets of problems is the structuring and control of critical resources, standards, and opportunities by white persons whose orientations and interests have usually run counter to those of black sociologists, whether as citizens or as professionals. Each of the fourteen articles (sixteen authors: eleven blacks, five whites) explores certain topics that bear upon these core themes.

Sociologists of African descent, for reasons made clear in this book, have tended to be self-consciously *black* in professional orientation. Most have specialized in race relations or some area of black life. They also have shown strong commitment to and widespread participation in militant civil rights activities. Charles U. Smith and Lewis Killian, despite having to work with a small sample, demonstrate this nicely in their article on social protest. At the same time, faith in the efficacy of social scientific research for improving the conditions of black existence, forcefully projected by W. E. B. DuBois as early as 1895, has been a prominent feature of the professional heritage of black sociologists. As social scientists, they pursued dual aims: to develop the black community internally and to influence external centers of power and decision-making. Reconciling the roles of advocate and scientist has been heavily dependent on external circumstances that structure available options. The essential fact here, until recent times, is that the main outlet for black sociologists has been to teach in black institutions where resources were woefully scarce and conditions tended not to be conducive to research and scholarship. Butler Jones describes, at times with sardonic realism, how in that world buttressed by broader professional mores most black sociologists were professionally invisible and only a few managed to gain professional prominence. In this book the lesser known ones—and some who are more meritorious—remain largely invisible, and the image of black sociologists is projected by the reputations and accomplishments of the famous few.

Just as the academic base of black sociologists was separated from the mainstream, so their participation in the affairs of ASA was sparse and marginal. Small numbers was undoubtedly one of the inhibiting factors. At the time their article was written (1972), James Conyers and Edgar Epps were able to identify only 160 black sociologists with Ph.D.s. Black females are even more seriously underrepresented. Jacquelyn Jackson reports that women constituted only 15% of blacks receiving doctorates between 1945 and 1972. Despite disadvantages of size, CBS was founded in 1968 as an interest group exercising leverage to bring about major changes within ASA and to influence other organizational spheres bearing upon black interests. James Blackwell, a key figure in its birth and one who did much of the organizational work vital to its early successes, has carefully chronicled CBS's history and achievements in his article.

The presence of CBS and the emergence of radical black ideologies are factors associated in the minds of many persons with a sense of black-white polarization in the profession. A crucial question in this regard is whether the mobilization of black sociologists is merely an organizational weapon to insure full incorporation into the profession or a more substantive and theoretical movement toward an autonomous intellectual position and a competing association. There are black sociologists who support both positions. Perhaps the line between them is most sharply drawn around the possibility and desirability of attempting to formulate what has become known as "black sociology." In this volume, William Wilson takes on the task of identifying and critically appraising certain tenets of black sociology. Taking Merton's criticisms of the black "insider doctrine" as his point of departure, Wilson convincingly argues that there is no support in the logic of scientific inquiry for the notion that black social scientists somehow have exclusive access to "true" knowledge about black people not available to white social scientists or, indeed, to those of whatever background. Furthermore, in examining certain writings of black sociologists on the black family, a topic of intense interest, he pretty much demolishes the idea that a unique, coherent black perspective has emerged in this area. At the same time, Wilson's seemingly uncritical acceptance of Merton's lengthy, harshly polemical arguments probably causes him to dismiss the very idea of black perspectives as invalid and not to consider the possibility that insider perspectives may, under some circumstances, have important, indeed, crucial scientific value. Also I think it is a mistake to overlook the fact that research and scholarship are carried on in sociopolitical contexts where realistic conflicts often stem from divergences of interests. Wilson understandably recoils from the risk that research and teaching in the race relations field may be undermined, perhaps irreparably, by the aggressive actions of some proponents of black studies and black sociology. These feelings are reinforced by the hard data Wilson Record presents in his article reporting research on responses of a national sample of sociologists to black studies. Yet the possibility should not be ignored that the dialectics of conflict precipitated by black developments in substantive areas may well yield valuable creative consequences for both theory and research.

The other two articles dealing with black perspectives in substantive terms do not go far in elucidating contentious issues. Nathan Hare's brief paper, long on generalizations and short on analysis, is essentially a defense of black studies and its legitimacy in the eyes of the "new breed" of young black sociologists. Walter Wallace makes a case for utilizing sound, general sociological theory in research and analysis of black culture and social organization at all levels, from the interpersonal to the intersocietal. His "interpretative framework" is designed for systematic, critical analyses of ideas and hypotheses about black life and for formulating "new theoretical propositions" for research on blacks. Because Wallace's discussion in this paper is general and somewhat disjointed, judgments about the analytical power and promise of his ideas will have to await further applications.

Black sociologists, not being homogeneous in either ideological or specialty terms, can be expected to develop along several paths as their ranks are infused with fresh perspectives and energies from increasing numbers of young Ph.D.s and as they are influenced by developments in the profession and society at large. At a time when the profession seems to have embarked upon a continuous process of self-evaluation and innovation, special efforts should be made to deepen understanding of the professional situations and prospects of black sociologists. The time is long overdue for vague impressions, misinformation, and plain ignorance to be replaced by facts and well-considered interpretations. As a basic source book, this volume marks a strong, praiseworthy beginning in this neglected area. While it may have particular interest for specialists in race relations, black studies, and minority affairs generally, I heartily recommend it to all sociologists. The paperback edition should find wide use as a source of selected readings in both upper level undergraduate and graduate courses.

Local Leadership in Black Communities: Organizational and Electoral Developments in Cleveland, in the Nineteen Sixties, by PRANAB CHATTERJEE. Cleveland: Case Western Reserve University, School of Applied Sciences, 1975. 238 pp. No price listed, paper.

Blacks in Power: A Comparative Study of Black and White Elected Officials, by LEONARD A. COLE, Princeton, N.J.: Princeton University Press, 1976. 234 pp. $13.50 cloth.

LESLIE G. CARR
The University of Akron

Chatterjee's monograph is concerned with the changes in black political leadership and organization which occurred in Cleveland in the decade of the 1960s. It was there in 1967 that Carl Stokes became the first black mayor of a major American city.

The election of Stokes is attributed to the "commodity" riots in the Hough area in 1966, the charisma of Stokes, the general decay of the city, and the ineptitude of the previous administration. Stokes was able to put together a diffuse coalition which crossed class and race boundaries. Stokes appealed to the "representation" goals of the middle-class black as well as to the "personification" or identity goals of the underclass black. Many white voters apparently believed that a black mayor could prevent further rioting. Stokes had the backing of the leaders of many major corporations as well as that of small business and the white liberal community.

Stokes was re-elected in 1969 but he declined to run for a third term in 1971. In his second term Stokes had difficulty with the police force, scandals, a proposed tax plan, the city council, and the Democratic party. With the original coalition unraveling, Stokes indicated a desire to move into national politics but he was unable to find a way to do this. He took a job with a New York TV station. He was unable to pick his successor and a white mayor was elected in 1971. Critics suggest that Stokes did not represent the interests of the underclass and that he was an opportunist.

Unfortunately, the major part of Chatterjee's monograph is devoted to an exercise in social science which could not succeed. It attempts to create typologies of organizations and leadership, to derive propositions from these typologies, and to test them. There is no attempt to relate these propositions to any existing theoretical framework. The data consist of newspaper accounts, personal papers, and interviews. As the author acknowledges at the beginning of chapters five and nine and in appendix I, such data cannot be used to empirically test propositions. Nevertheless, the author's observations and insights into the processes leading to the election of Stokes are intrinsically interesting and the typologies and propositions may be of value in future research.

This is one of the few accounts available of the Stokes election. It may be of value to persons interested in community power studies, political sociology, and race relations.

While Chatterjee's monograph conveys a tone of skepticism about the real accomplishments of black politicians, Cole sees the process of black entry into politics as a triumph for American pluralism. The process is seen as a refutation of the ideas of black separatism identified with black radicals such as Seale, Baraka, Newton, and Carmichael. The process has occurred because of the newfound identify of black people and the fact that whites now see blacks "almost the same way as other ethnic or religious groups."

Cole conducted taped and questionnaire interviews with black and white elected officials in sixteen New Jersey cities. He interviewed a sample of citizens in those cities by telephone and he analyzed the voting in the city councils. He found that black officials are different from white officials in that white officials are better educated, have better occupations, and had spent less time in party politics. Like their white counterparts, black officials had few clear objectives or platforms of specific programs. White support was necessary for election of black officials and the lower the annual income of city residents the less likely the city's blacks were proportionately represented. Votes in city councils were unanimous around 90% of the time. There was little bloc voting by race, but black interests were represented and often supported by white officials. Unlike Chatterjee, Cole does not feel that the blacks who have gained office are generally middle class persons representing middle class interests which detracts significantly from this victory for American pluralism.

Studies in Italian American Social History, edited by FRANCESCO CORDASCO. Totowa, N. J.: Roman & Littlefield, 1975. 264 pp. $25.00 cloth.

The Syrian-Lebanese in America: A Study in Religion and Assimiliation, by PHILIP M. KAYAL, and JOSEPH M. KAYAL, Boston: Twayne Publishers, 1975. 260 pp. $12.50 cloth.

Americans of Portuguese Descent: A Lesson in Differentiation, by FRANCIS M. ROGERS. Beverly Hills, Calif.: Sage Publications, 1974. $3.00 paper.

WILLIAM P. NYE
Hollins College

The three books under review have the common feature of being written by persons with the "appropriate" ethnic affiliation. All three also put in a strong plug for the misunderstood virtues of the particular American minority under investigation and all take the now familiar swipe at assimilationist ideology in favor of cultural pluralism.

The volume edited by Cordasco is a *festschrift* to Leonard Covello and suffers from a general unevenness and lack of originality. The contributors are mostly historians and the topics tend toward either the anecdotal or the obscure. For example, Michael Parenti reminisces on his father's troubles as a small businessman in the bread baking industry and Jean Anne Scarpaci gives an account of Italians in Louisiana's sugar parishes. The level of scholarship varies with the particular author but the book should hold some interest for the specialist in Italian studies.

The work on Portuguese Americans is more of a paper than a book. The author is a Professor of Romance Languages and Literature, though the seventy-page essay is cast as a Sage Research Paper in the Social Sciences. Rogers writes well and passionately on his chosen topic and presents an interesting, sociohistorical abstract of a major work in progress.

The Kayals' book is the most consistently sociological of the three and the Syrian-Lebanese-Americans are indeed an interesting and widely misunderstood group. The general lack of knowledge concerning who they are, how they conceive of themselves as well as how many there are serves to highlight the problems of many of the "lesser" minorities in American society. Unfortunately, the Kayals' thorough presentation verges on redundancy and this takes away from the inherent interest of their topic. They also manage to insert a goodly amount of political rhetoric with regard to the Middle East situation, but this proves only mildly distracting.

I suppose that all three books belong in any "respectable" library collection on ethnic studies. Each makes at least some substantive contribution to our factual knowledge of American ethnic relations. None, however, makes any noteworthy contribution to our general understanding of intergroup relations on a theoretical level.

Ethnicity and Resource Competition in Plural Societies, edited by LEO A. DESPRES. The Hague: Mouton Publishers, 1975 (distributed by Aldine Publishing Company). 221 pp. $12.50 cloth.

AUBREY W. BONNETT
Hunter College/CUNY

With this collection of eight previously published papers, Leo Despres hopes to stimulate interest in a comparative theory of ethnic phenomena. These first rate papers, initially written for the IXth International Congress of Anthropological and Ethnological Sciences, attempt to apply revitalized anthropological conceptual approaches to understanding the structure of "Plural Societies." But the book goes further. This is not a book about anthropology per se, but rather impinges on the area of the other social sciences, especially sociology. Sociologists who have broad theoretical interests will find it interesting and relatively readable.

The first five papers are drawn primarily from studies of New World populations in Guyana, Ecuador, Peru, and Panama. The remaining essays deal with populations in Africa and South India. They all, to some extent, attempt to deal with what one of the essayists, Skinner, describes as "the ethnic group competition for the strategic resources of their respective societies." The best papers in my opinion were written by Despres, not only because he tries in the final essay to refine a conceptual framework, but also because of his superb analysis of Guyana, the plural society par excellence. Some of my criticisms are therefore directed toward the Despres analysis.

The plural society theory stresses unequal power relationships and the super-imposition of cleavages. When this framework is used to study race or ethnicity, class, and competition for scarce resources one has to take into account the role of ethnic leaders in the interethnic bargaining process. Often these leaders can utilize their charisma to gain favorable access to scarce resources for their respective constituents. The flexibility of these leaders, their ability to use their charisma to initiate or impede social change are all factors that must be clearly seen as independent variables in the competition for scarce resources.

Greater attention must also be paid to the role of extrinsic factors, namely, the ability of the former colonial power to maintain control of the internal and external economies in these plural societies. In this regard it is interesting to see how the spread of cooperativism in Guyana will mollify the formerly intense overt conflict.

For Sociologists this book can adequately supplement another similar effort by N. Glazer and D. Moynihan in their *Ethnicity: Theory and Experience.* It is a must in courses in Race Relations, Sociology of Development, Comparative Sociology, and Political Sociology.

I highly recommend this book not only for the academician, but for the scholar/statesperson and consciousness raised American students who wish to escape the usual ethnocentric research of American scholars.

The Ordeal of Assimilation: A Documentary History of the White Working Class, edited by STANLEY FELDSTEIN and LAWRENCE COSTELLO. Garden City, N.Y. Anchor Books, 1974. 500 pp. $4.95 paper.

HARRY COHEN
Iowa State University

In recent years we have been witness to a new cycle in the fad of social concern for the downtrodden working and lower disenfranchised classes: Blacks, Chicanos, American Indians, and women. Sociologists, government, universities, and students rush on to compensate by rediscovering the plight of these poor folk. Studies, courses, grants show that the social heart can also bleed for the masses. Unnoticed is the condition of other suffering people whose day for concern has passed or which has not yet come. This book attempts to remedy the imbalance by focusing attention on the white ethnic working classes. That the study of and care for these ethnics may yet become a fad too, displacing the other worthies, detracts little from the social value of this book of readings, so written that in the flowing transition one fortunately forgets that these are readings and not one text.

This book is mainly an historical account drawn from many sources and documents, tracing the documentary history of the white working class, 1830s–1970s. Sociologists will find good background material for their own work, even an occasional sociological type study (one done in 1870) but will have to search elsewhere for the kind of theory, generalization, and sociologese preferred in the sociological discipline.

Children of Conflict: A Study of Interracial Sex and Marriage, by FERNANDO HENRIQUES. New York: E. P. Dutton, 1975. 196 pp. $8.95 cloth. $3.95 paper.

ROBERT STAPLES
University of California, San Francisco

The title of this book is somewhat misleading. It has little to do with children nor is it in an empirical study of interracial sex and marriage. Most of the book is devoted to the history of miscegnation in the United States, West Indies, Africa, and Europe. Henriques covers quite well the racial attitudes and social mores which shaped the anti-miscegnation laws and practices in those societies. Beside the excellent historical and cross-cultural analysis, the author is to be commended for including the cross-fertilization that took place within the non-white community as well as between whites and non-whites.

Starting with race attitudes and relations in ancient Greece and Egypt, where there was racial awareness but not prejudice, Henriques takes us to the bastion of racial purity —the United States. Four of his ten chapters are devoted to miscegnation in this country, but they are mainly a compilation of legal statutes and opinions proscribing racial mixture. His other sources are documents and narratives of white participants in, and observers of, interracial sex in the last three centuries. We get little of Black attitudes toward race mixing in these chapters. The chapter on Black and White sexuality in contemporary America is the most disappointing of all. Many of the references cited are dated and others are of dubious validity. Taken together they represent the personal opinions of about ten men. None of the various research studies on interracial dating and marriage are cited. What we get, instead, are the insights of Eldridge Cleaver, pop sociologist Calvin Hernton, psychiatrists, and the like. Moreover, there is no acknowledgement of the changes that have occurred in Black/White mating in the last ten years.

When discussing interracial unions in Europe, Africa, and the West Indies, Henriques is on surer ground. Being of African, Indian, and European ancestry, he brings to his analysis an experiental insight which is sorely lacking in the discussion on American miscegenation. He captures the subtle nuances and variations in attitudes toward miscegenation by noting the class and racial differences in Britain, skin-color ranking in the West Indies, and the relationships between the various ethnic groups which inhabit that area.

In the beginning of the book, Henriques makes clear his subjective view of the interracial unions. (His parents were of mixed background and he is married to an English woman.) While this is refreshing, the end result in this book is a vigorous, often harsh, denunciation of all views opposing interracial marriage. Henriques makes the rather naive statement that "if the world is to solve the problem of interracial conflict the only sure foundation is interracial marriage." Such a position ignores the political and economic conditions associated with interracial conflict. And, one might ask the question: To whose benefit has racial amalgamation worked in the past?

I regret the lack of of a final chapter which would have tied some loose ends together or at least have expanded upon his thesis that interracial marriage would solve the race problem. Overall, Henriques's book is a real contribution to the literature on this subject. The aforementioned limitations make it something less than a definitive work.

Pursuing the American Dream: White Ethnics and the New Populism, by RICHARD KRICKUS. Garden City, N.Y.: Anchor Books, 1976. 424 pp. $3.95 paper.

PAUL D. STARR
Auburn University

"Why is it that college professors and journalists who write sympathetically about the frustrations and rage which produces a Rap Brown fail to realize that they also produce a Tony Imperiale?" This question, put to Krickus by an activist from Newark's white working class, reflects a major concern of this book—the "New Ethnicity," a heightened political consciousness and militancy among non-wasp whites in America, primarily those of Italian, Irish, and Slavic descent from the industrial mid-west to points north and east. Selectively drawing upon historical and sociological sources, Krickus, argues against the stereotypes of white ethnics as reactionary bigots, successfully articulates many of their problems, and proposes a political strategy by which they could achieve, in cooperation with other groups, greater social justice. Most of the problems of the white ethnics center around a sense of relative deprivation and those political and economic institutions, both public and private, that shape their lives but over which they have little or no influence.

Contrary to the author's argument, however, there is evidence that ethnocentrism on the part of some members of ethnic groups (Black militants for example) combined with government attempts to selectively redress inequalities tends to bring about neo-conservative responses by other ethnic groups. This state of affairs is one of the important barriers to achieving the "New Populism" the author proposes.

Although the book focuses on a significant trend in American society, discusses many of the issues involved and proposes a direction for their solution, it will be of limited use to most sociologists. The book's emphasis on interpreting current political trends and strategies includes questions which have been answered by recent elections. Some of the issues raised have been discussed in greater depth by Greeley and Novak, and there has been no effort to deal with theoretical aspects of ethnicity. The topic is, nevertheless, a very important one which requires our attention.

Race, Science and Society, edited by LEO KUPER. New York: Columbia University Press, 1975. 370 pp. $12.00 cloth. $4.95 paper.

HUGH H. SMYTHE
Brooklyn College and the Graduate School/ CUNY

Two decades ago, in 1956, UNESCO published the results of a series of conferences it had held on *The Race Question in Modern Science.* The volume under review is a revised, easy to read, updated version of that earlier work and comes at a most opportune time. Divided into three major parts, the first, "Defense Against Racism," sets forth the position of late internationally-known geneticist, L. C. Dunn, whose 1958 work on *Heredity and Evolution in Human Populations* is still looked upon as an indispensable source of scientific data on race. He opined "Genetics is more than the study of heredity," exposed the fallacy of the old "blood theory" notion of parental blending, undercut former views of fixed and absolute biological differences among races, and showed that subgrouping does not imply a basic difference of race. Additional well written chapters deal with race as it relates to contemporary genetics, history, culture, and psychology.

Part two, concerned with social structure and racism, analyzes race, caste, ethnicity, tribalism, and has a useful and perceptive unit on the position of the Chinese minority in Southeast Asia arising from their role in the economy of regional nations. The third section reviews changing perspectives as related to scientific theories about the nature of people and their societies, social conflict, modern technology, the impact of politics, and alternative lines of development on the thesis of race and racism, with the volume closing with an appendix of four major official statements on the race question, and an index.

This is an especially timely publication. The race question is now receiving more attention worldwide than ever before. The American Association for the Advancement of Science, in its annual meeting in February, 1976, debated the matter with the proceedings reflecting a real change—no participants argued that nonwhites, on the average, are lower in intelligence than whites. In 1973, the United Nations proclaimed a decade for action to combat racism. Third World nations, practically all nonwhite, have become increasingly vociferous in the U.N. and elsewhere—challenging the superiority and power of a largely white Western world, and revealing the unscientific shallowness of much of the racial thinking of past generations.

Almost every major question related to race and racism and the role science has played and continues to play is focused upon here. While important for its authority, amplification, and coverage, the collection is outstandingly valuable for showing that scientific objectivity is a chimera; that pretending we can operate in a vacuum when functioning in our role of scientist is a naive delusion which may lead us to hide our biases but not eliminate their effect upon our thinking.

Race Differences in Intelligence, by JOHN C. LOEHLIN, GARDNER LINDZEY, and J. W. SPUHLER. San Francisco: W. H. Freeman, 1975. 380 pp. $12.00 cloth. $5.95 paper.

EDWARD E. HARRIS
Indiana University—Purdue University

The book provides a scholarly examination of the relative importance of biological and environmental factors as determinants of behavior.

Considerable attention is given to defining the meaning of race, intelligence, and intelligence tests. The concept of race is discussed in terms of what it meant to different writers during different times. The discussion on intelligence focuses on the nature of intelligence, how it is measured, the innate versus learned controversy, its evolution, its relation to culture, its world distributions, and what the testing instruments predict in view of these and other questions. Other preliminary discussion deals with questions on the extent to which intelligence is inheritable by using various heritability coefficients. The authors acknowledge that environment has a covariance and interaction impact on heritability estimates.

Part two of the book examines a variety of studies. Data are presented from the perspectives of genetic designs (using several types of independent variables, e.g., measures of IQ, and in some instances social class as an intervening and/or control variable). Some studies employ a temporal model whereby IQ change is studied over time with regard to race or race and sex within the intergeneration or intrageneration perspective. Diverse measures of IQ are employed. Other studies include considerations of regional differences in IQ in the United States. Another model involves combinations of race, ethnicity, and social status. A final group of studies includes the relevance of nutritional factors.

In this discussion of the relative importance of biological and environmental factors, the present reviewer believes that sociologists would conclude that the authors are hampered by their inability to illustrate the time order or other ways in which various variables may be interrelated. The demonstration of this type of systematic interrelationship is not possible from the review of the various studies described. In some instances, the sociological implication has to be assumed or inferred. In others, one finds it difficult to assume what causal mechanisms may be at work. The summary statements provide the foundation for systematic theory building on the assumption that data are acquired to test hypotheses and their interrelationships. Policy implications are also discussed. This book is recommended for all sociologists.

Jewish Nobles and Geniuses in Modern Hungary, by WILLIAM O. MCCAGG, JR., New York: East European Monographs. Distributed by Columbia University Press, 1972. 245 pp. $12.50 cloth.

ROBERT BLUMSTOCK
McMaster University

The arresting title of this book results from two anomalous aspects of Hungarian Jewish life which developed during the period 1848–1918. On the one hand, there is the relatively welcome reception of Jews in Hungary and their consequent success in central areas of the developing economy. On the other hand, a goodly number of this Jewish haute bourgoisie achieved considerable eminence in international scientific and intellectual circles.

In McCagg's attempt to make sense of this relationship he deftly wanders through the maze of political intrigues, economic adventures, social skirmishes, and cultural gaucheries which were generated as a result of Jewish emancipation and Hungarian economic development within the political morass of the Austrian Empire. The book produced is a remarkable achievement in its thorough review of archival material, documents, and literature not normally available to Western social scientists.

The major strength of the book lies in its uncovering of Jewish family histories, the areas in which entrepreneurial success obtained, and the patterns involved in the ennoblement process. The thrust of the argument is that the nascent Jewish bourgoisie, cum nobility, linked its future to a moribund feudal aristocracy in order to continue to amass wealth, while at the same time attempting to firm up its niche in an otherwise friendless political environment. As the Empire creaked to its final senescence, the pattern of ennoblement took on greater importance. For those Jews fortunate enough to achieve this recognition, the conferring of nobility presented both legitimacy and the possibility of sharing political power. For the aristocracy, it was a means to consolidate and strengthen Magyar dominance in a multi-national state. The choices for both sides were limited and the exchange of services one-sided. This became evident when the Jews were no longer useful as buffers against the encroachments of various nationalities in 1920, after the short lived Councils Republic. At this point Jews were "exposed" as an alien element in the country and legislated restrictions, which predate the infamous Nuremberg Laws by more than a decade, were placed on their participation in the institutional structure of the country.

At this point the established noble-Jewish generation continued to maintain its influence for a considerable period, by adjusting, negotiating, and compromising. At the same time, however, the next generation saw the bleakness of its future in Hungary and began its migration to the West. This step was taken, not because of a feeling of immediate threat, but simply because Hungary was for this generation an obvious scientific and intellectual dead-end. The relative stability of the early years of the inter-war period allowed gifted individuals to continue, with limited disruption to their careers, an active and creative life outside the confines of a truncated country with a reactionary regime.

While the main argument is well presented, there are two minor blemishes which mar an otherwise excellent book. One is that the central argument tends to give a singular emphasis to achievement in science while ignoring the host of Jewish poets, writers, playwrights, journalists, and artists who chose to remain in Hungary. This cultural and artistic cohort was neither as prescient nor as mobile as those who had the skills and talents which were in high demand in the West. By choosing careers which tied them linguistically to Hungary, these individuals made an error which cost many of them their lives as well as their careers. Their names are not as well known as those central to this study, yet many continued to work in an environment which has only posthumously granted them recognition.

In addition, there are many families, whose history and accomplishments are traced in considerable detail, who produced no heirs who achieved singular eminence, while the family ties of those more central to the study such as Teller, Szilard, and Von Neumann are only sketchily outlined.

These minor cautions, however, do not alter the impact of the book, which presents a lively review of events in an area at once peripheral, yet very much a part of the West. The problems of modernization, the marginal situation of the Jews in central Europe, the sources of Fascism, contrast with the uniqueness of political democracy and are well highlighted in this useful and interesting work.

Through Different Eyes: Black and White Perspectives on American Race Relations, edited by PETER I. ROSE, STANLEY ROTHMAN, and WILLIAM J. WILSON. New York: Oxford University Press, 1973. 453 pp. $12.50 cloth. $3.95 paper.

JOHN W. MARTIN
University of Illinois, Chicago Circle

The turbulence of the 1960s both reflected and exacerbated the historic polarization of the races in America. This period was characterized, among other things, by the intensification of ethnocentrism, the re-emergence of cultural nationalism, the push for programs of Black Studies staffed exclusively by black professors, and, in some instances, the re-evaluation and even rejection of White Sociology. Merton has labeled the increasing claims to group-based truths Insider and Outsider doctrines. The emergence of these doctrines, due in part to limitations in the development of race relations theory, would appear to necessitate a revitalization of explorations in the sociology of knowledge.

Edited by three social scientists—all of whom share a number of common characteristics, but who differ racially and in other aspects of their background—*Through Different Eyes* represents a limited, but important, inquiry into the sociology of knowledge. It is a project which, in the editors' words, "is a result of our own differences *and* mutual concerns."

The primary objective of this collection of essays is to present a variety of black and white perspectives on race and ethnic relations. To this end, a number of black and white scholars of diverse cultural and social backgrounds were asked to prepare essays on race relations as seen through the eyes of specified segments of the two racial communities.

Among the twenty contributors, many of them experts on their assigned subjects, are Joyce Ladner, R. S. Bryce-Laporte, Edgar Epps, J. Herman Blake, Sethard Fisher, Chuck Stone, Lewis Killian, Andrew Greeley, Murray Friedman, Robert Blauner, Norbert Wiley, and Jan Dizard. Their essays are on black adolescent females, black immigrants, integrationists, black nationalists, black politicians, black professors, white Southerners, the Irish, the Jews, white professors, the silent majority, and radical students, respectively.

Although some readers may disagree with the interpretations set forth in certain of these essays, they should find it difficult to disagree with at least two general conclusions that emerge: (1) there is neither a black nor white perspective on race relations, although the views of the former appear to be significantly less diverse than those of the latter; and (2) there is no consensus to be found within identifiable segments of either community, for example, the black middle class or white professors.

In the epilogue, William Wilson correctly argues, in a brief analysis of the essays, that perceptions of race relations are in some degree determined by "race" but also by socioeconomic position and the frequently attendant feelings of security or insecurity in the struggle over scarce resources.

In an equally illuminating essay, Stanley Rothman develops an eight-category typology of black and white perceptions of racial and ethnic conflict ranging from conservative through liberal-integrationist to radical and including the cross-cutting category "black nationalist."

The essays, as variable in style and tone as Peter Rose forewarns, are nevertheless welcome contributions to the literature. Bryce-Laporte's essay on black immigrants from places such as Jamaica, Trinidad, Haiti, and Panama fills a conspicuous gap in an area in which only a paucity of systematic knowledge currently exists.

Through Different Eyes recommends itself as an excellent supplement to the materials currently used in the introductory race relations course.

Mexican Americans, by ELLWYN R. STODDARD. New York: Random House, 1973. 269 pp. $3.95 paper.

JAIME SENA-RIVERA
University of Notre Dame

The author's expressed intent, as "an external observer who is not Mexican American by birth," is to give the most accurate picture possible of the heterogeneity of the Mexican American social structure. One is unsure of his definition of "social structure," but let me say, adopting Stoddard's tone, as an internal observer who is a Chicano by birth, that this is one of the better short accounts by a gringo of Mexican American history, social-psychological identity definitions, institutional (church and family), review, cultural attributes and the problems connected to them (including within dominant culture educational institutions, and attendant to socioeconomic class and status), and political and other organizational development. It is perhaps in this last effort that Stoddard excels. For as an external observer (one sees him here and there in the Southwest at Chicano events, discrete, observant, probing), Stoddard has very capably outlined the range of ideologies and quality of political and organizational development of Mexican Americans up to about 1971. More recent important events and developments have yet to be comprehensively reported. Stoddard's work is still useful, especially to the serious student just beginning to study the subject of Mexican Americans.

Police and the Black Community, by ROBERT F. WINTERSMITH. Lexington, Mass.: Lexington Books, 1974. 149 pp. $12.50 cloth.

GWYNNE PEIRSON
Howard University

The author's thesis is that police attitudes toward, and treatment of, Black Americans are based on this country's history of slavery. Wintersmith argues that a full understanding of our past history in this area is therefore a necessary ingredient for a "correct and comprehensive" grasp of the present day police-Black relationships.

In an attempt to validate his hypothesis, the author devotes four chapters to the history of slavery and the political and social psychology of the South, both before and after the Civil War. Based on this background, he concludes that the defeat of the South in the Civil War divested the Southern ruling class of its power base. Allegedly, this "exiled Southern ruling class" again gained control twenty-two years after that war's end. Joined by the "ruling class" from the North, they began to construct a new order from which Blacks were excluded.

In following up this hypothesis, Wintersmith determines that the second-class citizenship accorded Blacks was codified so that violence, intimidation, and even murder became the tools by which the police have maintained Southern ideology and custom. To a very large extent, Wintersmith uses this theme to attribute the overall existence of present day police brutality toward Blacks to Southern and Northern "ruling class" whites. The degree of the author's commitment to this very questionable thesis is indicated in chapter 5, where he states, "The foregoing chapters have attempted to consider chronologically the political, economic, and social-psychological factors that have contributed historically to police-Black-community relations." In part, the weakness in Wintersmith's research is that his focus is too narrow. He accepts Levy's findings (Burton Levy, "The Police and the Negro: Myth and Reality.") that the police recruit "a significant number of bigots," (p. 55) and Rubin's (Jesse Rubin, "Police Identity and the Police Role") position that "problems" between the police and the Black community can be attributed to police role conflicts.

The weakness in this position, as with the findings of several other researchers who have published their analysis and explanation of the "problem," e.g., Skolnick, James Q. Wilson, Westley, Reiss, Neiderhoffer, Bordua, etc., is the willingness to minimize or ignore the extent of institutionalized racism throughout white society, and failure to recognize that the police merely reflect and act out the racism existant throughout that society. The author even refers to the attitude of white supremacy and Black inferiority in the past tense, infering that these conditions only existed "during this nation's early history" (p. 107).

Wintersmith's scholarship compares favorably to the more widely recognized writings in this field. While being more insightful in some areas, his conclusions tend to be a "rubber stamp" of the Skolnick-Wilson-Westley-Bordua findings. It is obvious that the book is not directed toward the class of Americans who have been the victims of police practices and attitudes. In all probability it will be accepted favorably by academically oriented analysts of our criminal justice system, and by police administrators. When the author overlooked the findings of knowledgeable Blacks, e.g., Haywood Burns, Lewis Killian, Charles Grigg, Joyce Ladner, etc., he was able to effectively ignore not only the findings of the Kerner Commission that America is a racist society, but that the problem of racism is not limited to the police. Rather, it is a condition that exists throughout white dominated institutions. A more important finding which eluded Wintersmith was that police racism cannot be eliminated by restructuring or changing the police role. Racism will only cease to exist when its institutionalized system of rewards and punishments is eliminated throughout white society.

Religion

Religious Organization: A Trend Report and Bibliography, by James A. Beckford. The Hague: Mouton, 1973. 170 pp. No price listed, paper.

Wade F. Hook
Gettysburg College

The objective of this report, which is to summarize the major findings on the sociology of religious organization from 1960–74, has been successfully achieved. This high-quality research presents a well-organized argument supporting the importance of the study of religious organization and claiming diversion from attention to religious structures by sociologists in the past.

There is a candid explanation for the under-development of sociological interest in the study of Western religious groups: generalized resistance to the scientific study of religion; priority given to the inner life and to "spirit" in religious forms and activities; anxieties about the survival of the groups under study; limited resources and cooperation except when research is sponsored and designed by the groups themselves, etc.

Appropriate references are made to the pioneering efforts of Max Weber and Ernst Troeltsch in the delineation of religious groups for special study. Acquaintance with the works of such men as H. Richard Niebuhr, Bryan Wilson, J. Milton Yinger, Gibson Winter, T. F. O'Dea is a requirement for maximum comprehension. The references in rapid sequence to so many authors and their findings would leave one, who is without a fair orientation to the literature in the sociology of religion, breathless from a strenuous exercise in name calling and encyclopedic exposure to the major findings of the respective researchers. Few names and titles are missing from the extensive bibliography. Perhaps the most noticeable omission is Robert Bellah, whose work could have been mentioned when references or illustrations were drawn from Far Eastern religions.

Sociologists of religion will find the book to be of immense value. It is a challenge to researchers and specialists to substitute theoretical relevance for inconsonant ideas and facts and to be more cautious in their use of time-worn typologies (church and sect). More use of the theory of formal organizations, the "open-systems" perspective in studying religious groups, focus upon internal dynamics of religious organizations, the use of conceptual guidelines, and the construction of new typologies with organizational and ideological dimensions are sound suggestions for more effective and intensive research into religious organization.

Theologians and church historians interested in sociological approaches to religion will also find this volume highly useful. Likewise, administrators and policy-makers of national religious bodies in the US (Protestant, Catholic, and Jewish) could benefit from analysis of extracted findings: ignorance on the part of laity of the basic tenets of their professed faiths; devaluation of the teaching function of ministers, priests, and rabbis; high numbers of denominational switches to conservative groups; low priorities given to member-recruitment in mainstream Protestant churches; most autocratic leadership in groups with the least formal organization; the seminary curriculum debate of scholarly versus practical subjects; and the implications of the fact that in religious groups the highly committed do not exceed 10% of the total membership.

The superiority claimed for the study of religious organization does not eliminate the assertion that modes of religious consciousness and behavior are not totally dependent upon social structures, nor the likelihood that a certain abstractness about religious groups will continue to defy researchers.

The Broken Covenant: American Civil Religion in Time of Trial, by ROBERT N. BELLAH. New York: Seabury Press, 1975. 172 pp. $7.95 cloth.

BENTON JOHNSON
University of Oregon

Robert Bellah's *Broken Covenant* is a sequel to his celebrated and controversial essay on American civil religion that appeared in 1967. In that essay he advanced the thesis that throughout American history the nation has been informed by a religiously inspired vision that has given meaning and purpose to both public and private undertakings. Although this guiding vision is largely Christian, in fact Puritan, in origin, it has been the exclusive property of no single denomination. Its prophets, among whom Abraham Lincoln is perhaps the greatest, have included government leaders and intellectuals. It has provided a heroic and lofty national charter to which even Jews and Catholics have given ready assent. The American civil religion is not a mere inventory of what the various religions of the nation can agree upon, for it is a coherent religious tradition in its own right. Nor does it simply lend legitimacy to the institutional status quo, for its transcendental precepts provide a lever for pronouncing judgment on national sins. The civil religion has been forged and transformed in two great times of national trial: the period of the foundation of the Republic and the period of the Civil War. Now, according to Bellah, the nation faces a third time of trial.

In the current book Bellah develops these and related points in greater depth and detail than he did in his original essay. He devotes a great deal of attention to the Puritan foundations of the civil religion, to its periodic perversion as a cover for racism and imperialism, to its antipathy to utilitarianism and its various heirs, to the American aversion to socialism, and to the current time of national trial. One of Bellah's major arguments is that the Puritan notion of the covenant involved both an outer and an inner reference. The outward covenant was a framework of communal purposes and obligations, a framework later embodied in the Constitution and its various amendments and official interpretations. The inward covenant was the free and voluntary commitment of the individual to the duties set forth in the outward covenant. This commitment was liberating in the sense that it promised freedom from torment and oppression, but a condition of this freedom was a life of discipline and virtue. Among the Puritans, as Bellah puts it, "individualism only made sense within the collective context."

Now although this dual notion of the covenant has influenced the American conception of the relation between the citizen and the structures of public authority, it has been undermined since the eighteenth century by utilitarian thought, with its legitimation of the pursuit of individual and group interest apart from "any encompassing context of loyalties and obligations." Neither the ideology of laissez-faire capitalism nor the currrent ideology of liberal technocracy is grounded in a society-wide consensus concerning what larger ends are collectively worth pursuing. But there is another and more intriguing reason for Bellah's critique of utilitarianism. Together with capitalism and modern science, utilitarianism has fostered what William Blake called "single vision," namely a view of the world that relies solely on reason and discards "the imaginative vision long nurtured in the religious and poetic traditions of the West." Twofold vision, on the other hand, enables one to perceive and symbolize the many shades of meaning obscured by the surface appearance of things. Twofold vision is essential in the creation of myths, which endow history and human activity with drama and purpose. Myths, and the symbols embedded in them, mobilize private energies for public purposes by interpreting aspects of common experience in terms of the deepest human fears and hopes. Myth is an indispensable component of any civil religion. But the current cult of single vision has almost banished myth from the realm of public discourse; it survives only in the shadows, in poetry and in unconscious fantasy, where it often operates in "dark and devious ways." As a result, America's "precious cup" of collective meaning is nearly empty. The nation cannot solve its collective problems until the cup of myth runneth over once again.

Bellah was a student of Talcott Parsons and his theoretical perspective embodies many Parsonian motifs. He assumes that social coherence is impossible without a shared body of values and norms, he assigns culture an active role in shaping social structure and personality, and he believes that "religion is the key to culture." There is no hint in *The Broken Covenant* that class influences may have shaped the content of the civil religion. Like Parsons, Bellah places classical Marxism outside the realm of plausible sociology (at one point he quips that Marx should have read less Ricardo and more Blake!). But his treatment of the current American situation is drastically different from anything Parsons could have written. By and large, Parsons's analyses of American life have been implicitly optimistic, even pollyannish, in temper. Bellah, on the other hand, has joined the ranks of those who believe the country is in grave danger. "The main drift," he writes, "is to the edge of the abyss." He sees growing cynicism, a distrust of public institutions, a preoccupation with personal gratification, and a general disinclination to take obligations seriously. The most striking of his departures from the Parsonian posture, however, is his advocacy of socialism. For him, the "most decisive" aspects of America's third time of trial is capitalism with its "tyranny of profits," its destructive addiction to growth, and its cult of consumption. Capitalism itself is legitimated by philosophies alien to the spirit of the civil religion and has constantly undermined that spirit. Capitalism can only be overthrown by a national movement that is moral and religious in character, a movement analogous to the Great Awakenings of the eighteenth and nineteenth centuries. A new version of the civil religion must be forged by an imaginative synthesis of old myths and transcendent, or ecstatic, reason.

Robert Bellah is one of a very small number of contemporary pioneers in the sociology of religion. Like many original thinkers, however, his insights sometimes run ahead of his ability to make them clear and plausible to the critical reader. His magnificent phrasing occasionally obscures a sketchiness of argument and evidence. The notion of myth, for example, is central to his treatment of the civil religion. Myth, he says, is not a description of reality but rather a way of transfiguring it. A myth can be true or false, but the test of its truth is not scientific in nature. What, then, is the test of its truth? He does not say. The question is not trivial. It is relevant to the critical problem of what the intellectual foundations of a new civil religion might be. He says next to nothing about how old myth and ecstatic reason might be combined so as to enlist the commitment of enough people to mount a national movement for socialism that has some prospect of success. In short, there is a great deal that is missing from this book. But Bellah is in his prime and we can expect to hear more from him soon.

Toward a Sociology of Irreligion, by COLIN CAMPBELL. London: The Macmillan Press, 1971. 171 pp. No price listed, cloth.

ROLF SCHULZE
San Diego State University

This slim volume may have broken the apparent taboo preventing "the serious study of the social phenomenon of the rejection of religion." In the process of outlining the relationship of religion and irreligion, Campbell provides us with a long overdue critique of the functionalist position in the sociology of religion. It is Campbell's examination of irreligion which reveals major flaws in the functionalist conception of religion as the major integrative institution and as the provider of solutions to the "ultimate problems" of human existence. Campbell argues that the functionalist view of religion owes more to theology than sociology. He demonstrates that the kinds of definitions used by functionalists such as Parsons, Bellah, Lenski, and Yinger permit any belief system (including irreligion) to perform the vital functions of social integration and provide "ultimate" solutions to our most fundamental questions. He clarifies why sociologists of religion have either neglected irreligion altogether or have treated it as a residual category. Some, Lenski in particular, have simply included any and all belief systems (including explicitly anti- and unreligious ideologies such as communism) in their definition. They have therefore been able to refrain from almost all discussion of the sociologically important category of irreligion. By so doing they have avoided raising and answering some of the disturbing questions posed by Campbell and others interested in the phenomenon of modern and contemporary irreligion.

The publication of Campbell's book is both an indication of change in the sociology of religion, as well as an indictment of the discipline for having taken so long to address the problems raised by the author of the study under review.

Society and sociology have both undergone significant and related changes in the preceding two hundred years. While various interrelated scientific, technological, economic, political, and cultural revolutions profoundly changed society and contributed to the ongoing trend of secularization, sociology has traversed from Comte's early efforts to develop a Religion of Humanity (including an elaborate ritual) to the contemporary materialism of neo-Marxists and other insurgent sociologists. It is quite possible that the steady expansion of secularization in the West has brought about conditions which permit the simultaneous existence of intensely religious revival movements as well as large masses of people (perhaps the majority) which one could only classify as functionally irreligious, despite their nominally religious status. It is under these conditions that one finds both sufficient adherents for various sectarian revivals (Billy Graham, the Reverend Moon, the Hare Krishna societies, and other Far Eastern Gurus) as well as renewed attention to irreligion in its various forms. It is to Campbell's credit that he has alerted us to these phenomena and their meaning for the sociology of religion notwithstanding the orthodox bias of the more eminent students in the field.

Despite the relative brevity of Campbell's monograph, he presents a number of important issues in the emerging sociological study of irreligion. Among them he discusses the role of irreligious movements, individuals, and organizations in the secularization of modern society. This is another subject largely overlooked by students of social movements. He also manages to shed new light on the definition of religion—a task made necessary by the effort to define irreligion—and finally, he provides some important conceptional tools for the further study of irreligion.

Despite a number of typographical errors, some of which are capable of altering the meaning of the relevant passage, Campbell's pioneering study will surely set the tone for much subsequent work. His monograph is mandatory reading for all who wish to be fully informed in the sociology of religion. It is the first book which provides a much needed balance to the sociology of religion. Campbell's work also makes it possible to study irreligion in its own right, and to treat religion as a residual.

The Negro Church in America and *The Black Church since Frazier*, by E. FRANKLIN FRAZIER and C. ERIC LINCOLN. New York: Schocken Books, 1974. 216 pp. $10.00 cloth. $2.95 paper.

RUSSELL R. DYNES
Ohio State University, Columbus

Modern packagers, including book publishers, often present the old with minor alterations and add the new to create novelty. This book packages two long essays together.

Both the essays have been previously published and both are important in their own right; the packaging implies continuity yet demands comparison.

Frazier's essay, first prepared as the Frazier Lecture at the University of Liverpool in 1953, was first published in the US in 1964, two years after his death. The essay states the now familiar theme that the conditions of slavery destroyed the remnants of social cohesion among American Negroes. In their subsequent social isolation, the Christian religion provided a new basis for social cohesion. Frazier traces the institutionalization process through American history from the "invisible" institution during slavery to the emergence of the institutionalized church. He then follows the consequences of urban migration for their differentiation among the religious consciousness of Negroes—pointing out the tendancies of withdrawal of the Negro middle class, the indications of rejection of old forms by other segments, and the positive affirmation of "new" religions. With such a broad sweep of sources and scope, it is not surprising that Frazier's interpretation has attracted revisionists, most of them sectarian in contrast to Frazier's catholicism.

If Frazier's view was retrospective and panoramic, Lincoln's view is contemporary and focused. In his essay, he does not wish to quibble with Frazier but to extend his work. He too picks up the theme that religion is a reflection of group consciousness. He contends that Frazier's "Negro Church" died in the turmoil of the sixties, and that out of the ashes of that decade emerged a bold, self confident phoenix, the contemporary Black Church. He goes on to discuss this emergence from Martin Luther King to the Black Manifesto. He discusses the New Black Theology, its meaning and its relevance to the Black community. He concludes with a final chapter on the Nation of Islam, based on his excellent and well known book. He also includes a number of appendices with illustrative documents of that period.

In reading the two essays, one comes to the conclusion that the old (Frazier) is still new but the new (Lincoln) is already old. The sixties, however exciting and productive, are gone and now we can gain some perspective. Not everything was burned. There are still other birds around beside the phoenix and even the phoenix has aged and lost some of its wingspread. Lincoln, as the logical successor to Frazier in understanding the Black Church, needs to go back and sift through the ashes again to see what he finds now. He had a narrower frame to examine than did Frazier and it is a frame that keeps changing. No one will be able to focus the contemporary issues until they are no longer contemporary. I hope that Lincoln will continue to go back and examine the Black Church.

The package is still valuable. It is perhaps the best single source of both the old and the new of the Negro-Black Church. Much of its worth is Frazier's essay. Lincoln's phoenix is an appropriate image for some of the changes of the sixties but it does not exhaust either the immediate past, the present, nor the future.

Hutterite Society, by JOHN A. HOSTETLER. Baltimore, Md.: Johns Hopkins University Press, 1974. 403 pp. $14.00 cloth.

ALLAN W. EISTER
Wellesley College

Generally speaking, communally organized groups, religiously or otherwise inspired, have not been thought of as long-lasting enterprises. The Hutterian Brethren, however, of whom there are presently over 20,000, living in some 229 colonies in the United States and Canada alone, can trace a history spanning four centuries, and they give every evidence, according to data presented in this monographic account, of continuing strongly into a fifth.

Specifically sociological questions have guided Hostetler's inquiry: the relationship of internal problems of organization to the presence or absence of persecution from the outside world, the techniques and effectiveness of socialization to the sect's practices and values, the nature and types of group leadership and so on. It does not attempt what Wilhelm Windelband would have identified as nomothetic knowledge except in an indirect and inferential way, as when the author discusses in the final chapter "The Strategy of Hutterite Survival." The book, in other words, is primarily historical and ethnographic. As a monograph, it is thoroughly and carefully researched and well-written. It includes a bibliography which brings to light the very extensive literature on the group—at least a dozen books, including doctoral dissertations, specifically and exclusively devoted to the Hutterites, in addition to scores of articles and other publications which deal with various aspects of their life. Again in this book, as was evident in the case of an earlier book on the Amish, the author has gone way beyond the secondary sources to produce an account that is rich in detail.

As a group devoted to communal sharing of land and other property, including many kinds of goods, Hutterites have encountered a certain amount of waxing and waning—or waning and reaffirmation—of enthusiasm for the thorough-going communal values and economic principles which continue to prevail today. The sect has not been without its periods of testing, but it has been sustained largely by its vigorous dedication to its patterns of socialization, tempered with a kind of institutionalized wisdom in matters of conformance and non-conformance amongst its adolescent members (and with something quite different from any merely "puritanical" asceticism). There are other factors which the author cites as contributing to the maintenance of the Hutterite colonies: "vicinal isolation" as Howard Becker called it, the unwavering certainty that the "carnal nature" of human beings could be, and must be, "supplanted" not by extreme measures such as celibacy but by patient socialization, and what Hostetler describes as "the management of innovation." This latter was a kind of refusal, on calculated failure, "to acknowledge any conflict between religious beliefs and technological improvements" (p. 297) not unrelated to the kind of tolerance of deviance in adolescent Hutterians which the author speaks of as "reconciliation of the delinquents." Hostetler also cites "biological vitality"—the average size of completed families in the group is over ten children—as a factor in the group's survival. Successful and carefully planned "hiving" might appear to be another, although I do not recall Hostetler using this term.

Another of the many significant factors, one is tempted to think, might be the careful attention to explicit norms which serve to guide—but not to shackle—details of everyday life and work. Ordnungen, for example, established rules for varieties of crafts as well as for other aspects of life in the group. This, incidentally, reminds us that the Hutterites were by no means limited to agrarian pursuits from the outset. At one time, specialized crafts approached what seems to resemble industrial if not commercial scale in the sixteenth and seventeenth century order of things, although this may be somewhat of a distortion in the reviewer's reportage.

Perhaps a question of some interest to those social scientists who are willing to grant the possible efficacy of values and ideological commitments in the objective study of religious behavior is one raised, perhaps not intentionally by the author, but implicitly by the data themselves, both historical and ethnographic—namely, is there anything convincingly (i.e., scientifically) significant about the particular *content* of Hutterian beliefs and perceptions which *may* be responsible in a direct way for Hutterite "success" or at least for their duration as a group? Or is the "explanation" better kept non-ideological and not "value-oriented"? If the former, is there anything peculiarly apposite about the Hutterian "solution" of the multiple problems of human social organization?

Religion and Revolution, by GUENTER LEWY. New York: Oxford University Press, 1974. 694 pp. $17.50 cloth.

ROGER O'TOOLE
University of Toronto

In his last book, *The Catholic Church and Nazi Germany,* Professor Lewy gave an account of a "passive and accommodating" religious body rendering to Caesar (or Führer) more than his due. In the present work, he analyzes religion less as "a force upholding the *status quo,* reinforcing the stability of society and enhancing political quietism" than as "an important force facilitating radical political and social change, providing the motivation, ideological justification, and social cohesion for rebellions and revolutions" (p. 3). In examining "the general relationship of religion and revolution on a . . . cross-cultural scale and from a comparative perspective" (p. ix), he undertakes a task of avowedly Weberian proportions.

Thus, after presenting a brief historical guide to the "political traditions" of the great world religions, Professor Lewy offers seventeen case-studies under four headings "based upon types of revolutionary change" and provides six chapters of general theoretical conclusions. An indication of the dimensions of his project may be derived from the range of its case-studies: millenarian revolts in ancient China, ancient Israel, medieval Europe, seventeenth-century England, nineteenth-century Sudan, and modern Africa are analyzed alongside modern nationalistic revolts in India, Ceylon, Burma, and Egypt, and a number of chapters are devoted to the Great French Revolution, the Spanish Civil War, the Mexican Cristero revolt, and the contemporary Latin American "Theology of Revolution."

The author is to be commended for the scope and magnitude of a work which has been almost ten years in the making and which offers a readable, scholarly, and fairly comprehensive synthesis of a vast literature. He contributes both a balanced perspective on the complex relationship between religion and politics, and provides a useful source for scholars in a variety of disciplines. Yet, this is not a work of Weberian insight or originality, and scholars anticipating important, lucid, and novel theoretical formulations will be disappointed.

The book's most obvious weakness is inherent in its greatest strength. Its worth as an example of "the only truly comparative and cross-disciplinary work . . . that which is carried on . . . within the mind of one individual investigator" (p. xi) renders it less useful to a more specialized readership. This is not merely because "specialists in various historical periods or areas will undoubtedly miss one of their favourite episodes" (p. xi), but rather because such readers will find in this work little more than useful, though of necessity slightly dated, surveys of research and debate in their respective fields. The student of millenarianism will discover, for example, that while Professor Lewy devotes over two hundred pages and eight case-studies to the phenomenon, his theoretical analysis of it, though sound, is rather unprovocative. The lack of theoretical originality in this section of the work is underlined by the author's puzzling implication that his discussion is of a pioneering nature: "Millenarianism, the expectation of a lasting and final age of justice and bliss on earth, in the past has often been regarded as a totally irrational phenomenon, the preserve of crackpots and religious enthusiasts, and therefore of little interest to social scientists. I suggest that a belief that at times could embolden millions of people to attempt to overthrow the existing political and social order should not be dismissed in so cavalier a fashion and . . . I therefore undertake a detailed analysis of the political significance of revolutionary millenarianism" (p. x). Those for whom millennial movements present an unworthy object of study are not identified by Professor Lewy, but he is undoubtedly aware of their complete irrelevance to contemporary learned discussion of the topic. His competent and thorough investigation and appraisal of the relevant literature leaves no doubt that he is covering well-trodden scholarly ground rather than mapping an intellectual frontier.

The primary defect of this book, however, is its theoretical weakness, a fact of importance to specialist and general readers alike. Professor Lewy is ambivalent regarding his central aim. On the one hand, it is portrayed as involving nothing less than "the general relationship between religion and revolution" (p. ix) so that the reasons why religion "has sometimes acted as a force for social integration if not political quietism, whereas at other times it has led to rebellion" (p. 548) may be uncovered. On the other hand, more enigmatically, the main theme comprises "revolutionary upheavals in which religion is a causal variable" or in which it "has played a significant role" (p. 8). As he is aware, a *general* analysis of the relationship between religion and revolution necessitates investigation of the integrative and *anti-revolutionary* aspect of religion in much greater detail than is the case in the present work. Such an analysis requires, for example, much more than the brief treatment afforded to the debate surrounding Halévy's important thesis on Methodism as a preventative of English revolution. However, it may be inferred from the author's examination of "the role of religion in particular revolutionary episodes" (p. 9) that his precise concern is the "ways in which religion can assume a revolutionary posture" (p. 585), and it is in the context of this narrower, though by no means unambitious, theme that his theoretical contribution merits evaluation.

The book's lack of theoretical force is evident from its basic organization. Although partly chronological in character, its classification of case-studies is based, so the author asserts, "upon types of revolutionary change" (p. ix). But, no explanation is provided for the derivation of these "types" which comprise "millenarian movements," "religion and anti-colonial strife," "church and revolution," and "religion and the legitimation of revolutionary change." In the absence of such a rationale, they can only be regarded as potentially useful but essentially loose, ad hoc categories which are neither logically nor empirically distinct, as Professor Lewy recognizes. Thus, of the summary propositions derived from them, the first relates cross-culturally to millenarian movements, the second to militant religious nationalism in general, the third to "leaders of religious bodies with a developed ecclesiastical organization," and the fourth merely to "individual theologians or laymen" adhering to a particular variant of Christianity (pp. 585–586).

In his concluding overview, Professor Lewy builds his analysis "around four main variables—religious doctrine, ecclesiastical organization, leadership, and the role of situational factors" (p. 547), a strategy with utility for the generation of the "tendency statements" to which he aspires. Unfortunately, he fails to establish its superiority, within its specific mandate, to other major perspectives on revolutionary origins and processes. A short critique of Smelser's "value-added" scheme is provided, but other grand conceptualizations of revolution, mass movements, and collective unrest are accorded no detailed or extensive evaluation. Without a basis in a thorough investigation and critique of these formulations, the author's claim that the "multi-factor explanation [he has] advanced concerning the relationship of religion and revolution appears to be the best our conceptual tools and the data at hand enable us to develop at this time" (p. 589), remains unsubstantiated.

The view that religion merits analysis only in its socially integrative aspects, is as misguided as the belief that it is, always and everywhere, "the opiate of the people." Professor Lewy's book emphasizes this fact powerfully, and provides abundant demonstration of the vital significance of religion as an actual or potential revolutionary force. For this reason, despite its defects, it makes a worthwhile contribution to the literature on both religion and revolution.

Piety and Power: The Role of the Italian Parishes in the New York Metropolitan Area, 1880–1930, by SILVANO M. TOMASI. New York: Center for Migration Studies, 1975. 201 pp. $9.95 cloth.

OSCAR HANDLIN
Harvard University

Ethnic problems plagued the Catholic Church of the United States almost from its very origins. The Church was by its nature catholic—universal in doctrine and ritual—yet communion in it was ethnic insofar as it was inherited, transmitted through the family, and the community. In Europe, the territorial organization of the parish effectively permitted the Church to evade the problem. It could sustain its catholic quality, while being bound integrally into the life of the court, the village, the guild or the municipality. The parish could thus adjust to the distinctive circumstances of each environment and provide for all a framework that was both catholic and communal. True, there were significant differences among the practices and even among the beliefs of the Irish, French, Sicilian, and Polish parishes. But so long as those were confined to places clearly marked off from one another in space, the conflict between universality and particularity did not come to the surface. While the society of the Old World remained stable, the issue did not arise in this form.

In the United States, however, the peculiar conditions of migration and settlement brought the principles of catholicity and ethnicity into conflict and led to continuing crisis in parish organization. The Church was transplanted and grew from roots with origins in the most diverse soils of Europe. Every arriving group insisted upon the re-creation of its own forms and the preservation of its own language and thus threatened the unity of the Church. Furthermore, the people who carried the faith across the Atlantic were long in motion, and the society they entered was fluid and unstable—both circumstances which prevented an easy adjustment. Finally, the continuing hostility of Protestants who were long a majority in the country further complicated the course of adjustment.

Very little of this history has received the detailed attention it deserves and, even less of it has been subject to serious analysis. We know most about the earliest phases, down to 1870 or so, when the conflict involved native Americans, French and Irish Catholics. But the subsequent period which added to those groups Germans, Poles, Ruthenians, and Italians, among others, was far more complex, particularly since urbanization situated a large and growing percentage of American Catholics in great industrial cities where they were thrust in upon one another. In New York or Philadelphia or Boston no compromise was possible between the ethnic parish and the territorial parish. Only the German Catholics of the groups involved have received careful study.

Dr. Tomasi's book is therefore doubly welcome. It throws light on the experience of the Italian immigrants who have been far too long neglected, and it treats an aspect of American religious history that has long cried for attention. The book draws upon sources which have not hitherto been available to scholars and is rich in quoted material. It will interest anyone concerned with the problems of religion and ethnicity in the United States.

Two chapters on the Italian American

parish contain the core of the book. Drawing heavily upon archives, they are rich in new information. The views presented are largely those of church and other officials; the parishioners themselves rarely appear so that we learn their views only as reflected in the statements of others.

The theoretical framework within which Dr. Tomasi sets the study is both less original and less valuable than the core section. Nevertheless, his book is rich in leads which deserve further development.

Sex Roles and Sexuality

The New Women: Attitudes, Behavior, and Self-Image, by IBTIHAJ ARAFAT and BETTY YORBURG. Columbus, Ohio: Charles E. Merrill Publishing Company, 1976. 142 pp. $4.95 paper.

NONA GLAZER
Portland State University

The book with its loose theoretical concerns about changing levels of technology and women's social position, and about role conflicts; and with its substantive focus on changing gender roles, consists of three research reports, each published previously in journals. These are on: (1) women's and men's attitudes about sex equality and the sex division of labor; (2) women's drug use and sexual activity (related only loosely, theoretically); and (3) women's heterosexual "living together" experiences. The analyses of the research data tell us little. There is a good deal about the percent of this or that, and sweeping speculations about how the data might be understood. But, there is an avoidance of multi-variate analyses, no presentation of data from the research which bears directly on role conflict, and only perfunctory attempts to relate behavior, personality, and self-images. These research reports are sandwiched between three essays—one, about women's changing roles since pre-historical times; two, about sexual behavior and drug use over a considerable sweep of historical time; and three, about current characteristics of gender roles and problems related to these. The essays written presumably to integrate the research reports, miss the mark, provoking in this reviewer frustration with undocumented generalizations, a curiosity about the authors' views on the relevance of historical data to survey research data on college women and a puzzlement about the authors' intent in combining the writings into a single volume.

The Horrors of the Half-Known Life: Male Attitudes toward Women and Sexuality in Nineteenth-Century America, by G. J. BARKER-BENFIELD. New York: Harper & Row, 1976. 352 pp. $15.00 cloth.

MICHAEL GORDON
University of Connecticut

From a sociological perspective this is, in most respects, a rather unsatisfactory book. The topic it deals with, relations between the sexes in 19th century America, is one which many students of the family and sex roles will find of interest, but the author relies almost exclusively on the interpretation of literary material, and his interpretation is strongly informed by a rather fundamental brand of psychoanalytic thinking. To make matters worse, the writing is rather turgid and various sections of the book are not well integrated. Such problems notwithstanding, the thesis is a provocative one.

With an acknowledged debt to Tocqueville, Barker-Benfield argues that the attitudes of American men, during the nineteenth century, toward their own sexuality and their relations with women were in large part an outgrowth of the pressures placed on them as a result of their involvement in the enormous geographic and industrial growth of that century. The end result was a strong, silent, and sexually repressed creature who kept his woman under his thumb:

> Industrial growth and the phenomenal shaping of American history in the nineteenth century were inalienable from the male attitude that demanded not only that the two styles of life, male and female, be separate, but that women should remain subordinate, and in the home (pp. 20–21).

These same pressures not only produced brittle, stereotypical, and nonempathic heterosexual relations but also made insanity an ever present threat. At first men, because of their striving for progress, were thought to be especially vulnerable, but as the century progressed women were seen as the prime victims and the cause, more often than not, was found in their sex if not their sexual organs.

Women, because of their instability and their sexual allure, thus become transformed into dangerous creatures, threatening the order of the home, if not of the nation, and radical steps become necessary. Barker-Benfield tells us that the response frequently, though just how frequently we are never told, took the form of gynecological surgery. In point of fact, he suggests that the pioneering and prominent role played by American surgeons in this field during the nineteenth century must be understood as a reflection of national anxieties over female sexuality. Which brings me to the second half of the book.

Having set out his thesis, the author then proceeds to provide us with psycho-biographies of three men whose work is seen as having molded nineteenth century male attitudes towards relations between the sexes. The first, Marion Sims, an important nineteenth century surgeon, developed various procedures including a cure for vesico-vaginal fistulas, an unpleasant and uncomfortable condition suffered by many women; yet, Barker-Benfield seems to feel that his fame is more than outweighed by the infamy that resides in his cavalier use of "castration" as a cure for feminine ills. The second, the Rev. John Todd, was an author of several successful books, at least one of which contributed to the nineteenth century masturbation phobia. Todd's writings were informed with the kind of thinking about human sexuality in general and seminal conservation in particular that Barker-Benfield characterizes as reflecting the "spermatic economy" of the era. Sturdy manhood required that semen, like all other resources, be carefully conserved and only expended when absolutely necessary, since the energy lost in ejaculation could be more profitably used elsewhere. This reflects the concept of "protosublimation" (an earlier conceptualization of what Freud discussed as "sublimation") which the author sees as an important theme in nineteenth century America. The last of the three, Augustus Kinsley Gardner, was a gynecologist like Sims, but one whose pen appears to have gained more notoriety for him than his scalpel. His books dealt with the broad social and political significance of marriage, but he supposedly shared the male supremism and paranoia of Sims and Todd.

This book should leave the readers troubled irrespective of their sympathies. The charges are so wide-ranging, the conclusions so damning that one feels starved for evidence. The Haller's *The Physician and Sexuality in Victorian America* offers a much more benign, though hardly uncritical view of the medical profession during this period, suggesting that Barker-Benfield's interpretation is a controversial one. Data from several recent studies have questioned the picture of repressed nineteenth century sexuality here offered as historical reality. The problem may also be compounded by time and class. The nineteenth century covers a long period and the more we know about it the more change we see occurring within it. Moreover, this change was experienced differently by various groups within American society. My discomfort with Barker-Benfield's conclusion, then, rests not with any lack of sympathy for his thesis, but rather with an uneasiness over his evidence. We just do not know enough about the sexual lives of men and women in nineteenth century America to say this is the way things were.

Being Different: The Autobiography of Jane Fry, by ROBERT BOGDAN. New York: John Wiley & Sons, 1974. 235 pp. No price listed, cloth.

IMOGENE L. SIMMONS
Old Dominion University

In *Being Different: The Autobiography of Jane Fry,* Bogdan suggests that the "personal document" may be utilized as a methodological tool of the social sciences. He states that the autobiography enables the sociologist to develop an understanding of the subjective nature of reality. Thus, the student, professional, and layperson in the medical and social science fields may gain from this autobiography insight and understanding concerning: (1) the experiences and viewpoints of a transsexual, (2) the process whereby a person is defined and labeled as different and eventually as mentally ill, and (3) the organizational structure of mental hospitals from the perspective of those who pass through these institutions.

This autobiography is based on a series of unstructured, tape-recorded interviews by Bogdan with a transsexual during 1972. A major strength of the book is the researcher's efforts to verify the facts of the autobiography by examining medical records and by personal contacts with important persons in the life of the subject.

Although the author references social theorists such as Becker, Goffman, and Blumer, there is only a minimal attempt to theoretically interpret the autobiography. The book would be more useful for academicians if the last section were expanded into an in-depth theoretical examination of the autobiography. Throughout the book there are typographical errors that may disturb some readers.

The Inevitability of Patriarchy, by STEVEN GOLDBERG. New York: William Morrow & Company, 1974. 318 pp. $2.95 paper.

RAYNA RAPP REITER
New School for Social Research

In her post-revolutionary fantasy world, The Feminist (to whom Goldberg's book is querulously and condescendingly addressed) will have no trouble categorizing this book. She will look it up in *The Portable Phallus: Guide to Scientistic Explanation of Sexual Inequality,* in which Goldberg's work will be mentioned as a mere footnote to more salient biologicians. The Feminist will discover that her academic ancestors did battle with theories that presented more interesting challenges: the realm of the playful primate, childhood uterine constructions with building blocks, the symbolic logic of bisexual mythemes. Goldberg's "thesis" is derivative of more complex and thoughtful analyses of the nature/nurture interaction. He took the concept of "hormone," insisted it was directly responsible for "human emotion," which then was alleged to trigger "behaviors" that produced the knee-jerk responses labeled "institutions," which stacked up into societies that were universally patriarchal. That the careful, processual studies now under way to discover the biological underpinnings of sex and gender should all be reduced to accord testosterone the status of elixir of civilization is ridiculous (cf. Ramey, 1973; Sherman, 1971; Parlee, 1975 for better summaries). That testosterone should then be held accountable for a crude "CNS imperative" (p. 118) from which patriarchy, male dominance, and male attainment of all prestigious roles beyond maternal flow is reductive. That all the cross-cultural data of anthropology should be mustered to support the notion of a holy triumverate (patriarchy, male dominance, male need-achievement) as universally present and equally important is simply wrong. As an anthropologist, I could quibble with Goldberg's citation of certain sections of Morgan and Richards on the matrilinal Iroquois while ignoring other sections of Morgan, of Hewitt, of J. Brown. I could point out the uses and abuses of male-biased data, collected from men, by men, without asking the women of the societies under consideration what *they* thought about the rules and roles accorded them (cf. Leavitt, Weatherford & Sykes, 1975 which compares the perspectives of male and female ethnographers working in the same societies). I could refer him to ethnohistorical accounts of women in Africa (Van Allen, 1972) and North America (Leacock, forthcoming) whose status dropped when their social organizational bases were undercut by colonialism. But never mind; others with more time, space, and energy have already done so (cf. reviews by Leacock and Livingstone, 1974).

This is not a post-revolutionary fantasy world, and therefore more important work remains to be done. We who must refute the reductive myth of simplistic biologism are busy fighting on many fronts. Some of us are engaged in critical reviews of knowledge concerning gender, and the relative autonomy or subordination women exhibit cross-culturally (see collections edited by Leavitt, 1976; Matthiasson, 1974; Reiter, 1975; Rosaldo & Lamphere, 1974). Others are working on the very questions Goldberg raises concerning biosocial model building in a nonreductive way, looking at environment and genetic feedback (see Tanner & Zihlman, 1976; Slocum, 1975). Still others of us are researching societies in which male/female relations are known to have undergone significant and rapid change. This work includes both ethnohistory and documentation of societies in the throes of socialist revolutions whose goals include the liberation of women. Any of these lines of inquiry presents a challenge to *The Inevitability of Patriarchy*. Goldberg, however, is more comfortable misassessing such work as "the irrelevance of exceptions" (p. 94–99). In a rather ponderous style, he repeats for 306 pages the notion that "biology deals in inexorable probabilities to which all social systems must conform" (p. 99).

The myth of a reduced, immutable biological nature runs deep, and is deeply dangerous, in our culture. When social scientists celebrate that myth, instead of applying their critical powers to its understanding, they contribute to an ideology which glosses the status quo. To objectify social relations between the sexes as natural is conventional as well as convenient. At the present time, when sexual hierarchy is under serious assault, the arguments in this book are sure to have a certain amount of appeal. They will reach those who seek a simple, transhistorical answer to questions concerning complex phenomena. They will also give comfort to those who need to justify an essentially sexist social structure. But the comfort the book lends is false, for its arguments do not penetrate; they simply mystify. After all, "inevitability" means never having to say you're sorry.

REFERENCES

Leacock, Eleanor B.
1972 Introduction to F. Engels, *The Origin of the Family, Private Property and the State,* New York: International
1974 Review of Steven Goldberg, *The Inevitability of Patriarchy*. American Anthropologist 76:363–65.
Forthcoming "The Montagnais-Naskapi of the 17th Century: Social Relations and Values." Handbook of American Indians.

Leavitt, Ruby R., ed.
1976 *Women Cross-Culturally*. The Hague: Mouton.

Leavitt, Ruby R., Elizabeth Weatherford, and Barbara Sykes
1975 "Australian Aboriginal Women: Male and Female Anthropological Perspectives," in R. R. Reiter, ed., *Toward an Anthropology of Women*. New York: Monthly Review.

Livingstone, Frank B.
1974 Review of Steven Goldberg, *The Inevitability of Patriarchy*. American Anthropologist 76:365–67.

Matthiasson, Caroyln, ed.
1974 *Many Sisters*. New York: Free Press.

Parlee, Mary Brown
1975 "Review Essay: Psychology." Signs 1:119–138.

Ramey, Estelle R.
1973 "Sex Hormones and Executive Ability." Annals New York Academy of Sciences. (March 15) 208:237–245.

Reiter, Rayna R., ed.
1975 *Toward an Anthropology of Women*. New York: Monthly Review Press.

Rosaldo, Michele and Louise Lamphere, eds.
1974 *Women, Culture and Society*. Stanford: Stanford University Press.

Sherman, Julia
1971 *On the Psychology of Women: A Survey of Empirical Studies.* Springfield, Ill.: Charles C Thomas.

Slocum, Sally
1975 "Woman the Gatherer: Male Bias in Anthropology," in R. R. Reiter, ed., *Toward an Anthropology of Women*. New York: Monthly Review.

Tanner, Nancy and Adrienne Zihlman
1976 "Women in Evolution." Signs 1:585–608.

Van Allen, Judith
1972 "Sitting on a Man: Colonialism and the Lost Political Institutions of Igbo Women." Canadian J. African Studies 6:165–182.

Women: An Anthropological View, EVELYN S. KESSLER. New York: Holt, Rinehart, & Winston, 1976. 267 pp. No price listed, cloth.

Women Cross-Culturally: Change and Challenge, edited by RUBY ROHRLICH-LEAVITT. The Hague: Mouton & Company, 1975. 669 pp. $27.50 cloth.

JUDITH CADITZ
Immaculate Heart College

Is the women's movement a "white middle class" movement? Certainly, most books and articles on the subject represent information on the status of white middle class women in American Society. The two books reviewed here offer a major contribution to the social science approach to women's studies by concentrating on cross cultural materials; this offers us the possibility of expanding our descriptive materials, testing our assumptions, and elaborating our application of theory to issues of sex role differentiation.

Women Cross-Culturally challenges the reader with thirty-one essays presented by professional women at the session on women's status and women's movements at the Ninth International Congress of Anthropological and Ethnological Sciences in 1973. This authoritative volume is an outstanding contribution to the social sciences with its main focus on the interrelationships of sex, class, ethnicity, and religion in an international perspective. Women's status is evaluated in capitalist and socialist countries, agricultural chiefdoms, fishing and peasant societies, and hunting and gathering bands. Women's various occupational roles are described, including professionals, servants, traders, weavers, industrial workers, and union organizers. The research reports on women in Islam, Africa, Latin America, the United States, the Soviet Union, China, and other countries. In addition, professional women in the traditionally male-dominated field of anthropology are critically evaluated.

In contrast to the popularly held notion that women are and have been subordinated to men in most societies, Rohrlich-Leavitt demonstrates support for the thesis that equality of sex roles existed before the emergence of Western capitalist social structures. For example, in gathering and hunting cultures, the process of fission resolved conflicts and people valued cooperation, egalitarianism, and individual freedoms; women and men interacted as equal social partners. Further, in some indigenous peasant communities, traditional values of egalitarianism are maintained if the community remains relatively isolated from the dominant social structure. In Africa, sex roles showed interdependence. As Leacock writes, "Everywhere in Africa that one scrapes the surface, one finds ethnohistorical data on the authority once shared by women but later lost." In sum, there is evidence that women shared in the political decision-making of some societies. However, women's status under Islam exhibits the most subordination, dependency, and inferiority.

Rohrlich-Leavitt suggests that the nuclear family plays an important role in isolating women from one another and in making women and children dependent on men. The family hierarchy reflects inherent antagonisms, since it is a mirror-image of the class hierarchy.

The first part of Kessler's book, *Women: An Anthropological View,* deals with the status of women in many different cultures. In contrast to the Rohrlich-Leavitt collection, Kessler accepts the postulate that it is universally true that women occupy a secondary status in the social structure. However, in analyzing this thesis, she evaluates the importance of factors such as the technoenvironmental and sociopolitical subsystems, rules of residence and inheritance, power and authority, and the function of belief systems, particularly that of ritual.

The second part of the book focuses on silhouettes, or case studies, of women in different types of cultures: indigenous societies, peasant societies, the culture of poverty, and modern societies. These intensive cases analyses draw upon ethnographies and anthropological field work; they give the reader insight into the individual-in-culture. The woman's role is clearly portrayed in depth throughout her life cycle and in various segments of social life. Further, the cultural setting is witnessable for the reader through the portrayal of these life events.

The first portion of the Kessler book is at times modest in its presentation of anthropological concepts. Fuller elaboration of research studies to substantiate hypotheses and more detailed documentation of examples to demonstrate various concepts would enhance the work.

The Rohrlich-Leavitt collection of cross-cultural research is excellent for undergraduate and graduate courses in anthropology, sociology, psychology, and women's studies; it is a good resource for professionals. The Kessler book would serve as a good text in undergraduate introductory courses in sociology and anthropology and would be excellent at the junior college level. Both works provide sociologists with refreshing information and methods well-developed in the field of anthropology.

Women and Achievement: Social and Motivational Analyses, by Martha Tamara Shuch Mednick, Sandra Schwartz Tangri, and Lois Wladis Hoffman. New York: Halsted Press, 1975. 431 pp. $19.95 cloth.

Sandra Harley Carey
University of Texas, San Antonio

One of the most striking findings of early female achievement motivation studies was that females seemed neither to achieve nor to be motivated to achieve in the traditional sense. Yet, "Achievement . . . is one of the most significant, visible facets of the lives of people in industrialized societies." It is not surprising that McClelland described the area of female achievement as "totally puzzling."

This book contributes greatly to the solution of this puzzle. The volume includes a thorough examination of sociological, cultural, and psychological factors relevant to women's achievement motivation and an investigation of the interaction of these factors. Composed primarily of research literature, the work also includes theoretical sections and some excellent literature reviews. It deals primarily with "out of home" achievement, but important aspects of traditional forms of female achievement and their implications are also considered. Research by both male and female authors and by Europeans as well as Americans is included. (Also included are some of the small errors in style peculiar to the non-native speaker of English and some references to "next chapters" which are not in this book. The former are charming; the latter distracting and confusing.)

The core of the volume is a series of articles reprinted from a special 1972 issue of the *Journal of Social Issues.* Most are important statements and some may even be considered classics. Several are worth mentioning.

The Broverman study elaborates upon the finding that one cannot—by definition—be both a normal female and a normal, mentally healthy adult. Stein and Bailey, and Veroff et al. investigate the possibility that females may have as much achievement motivation as males but merely manifest it differently. Levitin et al., Cross, and Simon et al., examine opportunities for females to achieve once they have the motivation. Safilios-Rothschild's study attacks the myth that a society that allows women into non-traditional jobs is a liberated society while Haavio-Mannila searches for determinants of the liberated society. Mednick shows us that the Kibbutz wasn't it.

Hoffman looks at early childhood experience and achievement motivation. Chapters by Horner and others focus on adolescent and adult "fear of success." Helson examines the influence of attitudes toward career women on the design and interpretation of psychological research while Tangri investigates those women who escape these influences and become role innovators.

The book leads the reader to suspect that "achievement" as it has been studied is an incomplete and misleading concept and that a better understanding of women and achievement will add to a better understanding of the achievement motivation of *people*. The book also lays the foundation for this understanding.

Social Psychology

Process and Outcome of Negotiations, by OTOMAR J. BARTOS. New York: Columbia University Press, 1974. 451 pp. $15.00 cloth.

BERNARD P. COHEN
Stanford Univeristy

Bartos reports on more than a decade of research on negotiation. His research program involved thirty-four distinct experimental studies, the formulation of several mathematical models, and the analysis of his experimental data to evaluate these models. That a research program of such diversity and complexity can be described in one book is remarkable. That the book is coherent is even more remarkable.

The presentation has two main foci, the investigation of models of process and models of outcome. In examining negotiation Bartos is concerned with describing both how negotiation proceeds and how negotiators should behave, with both predictive and normative objectives. He has decided to consider simple models of process as predictive models and simple models of outcome as normative models. His eventual aim, however, is to break down the distinction between predicting how negotiators do behave and giving them advice as to how they should behave, to develop a model that deals with both predictive and normative concerns. But one conclusion of his work is that simple models are inadequate to this objective and that we will require more complex models in order to both predict and advise.

Bartos examines three simple models to describe the process of negotiation: Richardson's model, a version of the Bush-Mosteller model, and a Markov chain model. Although he does not expect these simple models with their restrictive assumptions to fit his data, his strategy is to learn from simple models in order to understand what directions to pursue in complicating the models. The strategy requires that he pick the best of the three models in terms of fit, and proceed by understanding what the model tells about the process and which of its weaknesses need to be remedied.

The game-theoretic tradition of constructing rational solutions to bargaining games represents the normative focus of his work. He draws on Nash, Shapely, Raiffa, and Braithwaite, all of whom present different normative bases for rational solutions. Since his aim is to integrate the normative and predictive focus, he asks how well each of these solutions predicts the outcomes of his experiments. In other words, he uses normative models in a predictive fashion. In the case of models of outcome he decides that the Nash solution is the best predictor of his subjects' behavior, although there are marked discrepancies between how the negotiators solve the games and Nash's rational solution.

Throughout the book Bartos's major substantive concern is with the question of *toughness*. In his analysis of the process he finds that toughness is an exploitive rather than a reciprocal relationship. If opponents are tough, the negotiator tends to be soft; and if they are soft, the negotiator tends to be tough. As he proceeds to examine models of outcome he refines his view of toughness, arguing that toughness under certain circumstances can be counterproductive. Thus, for example, toughness may be a good strategy as long as an agreement is reached, since a tough negotiator will receive a higher payoff; but toughness may seriously reduce the probability of agreement.

In addition to the models he examines,

he also formulates a simple theory of toughness which fits the data at the "tough" end of the scale but does not fit at the "soft" end.

The sheer number of ideas, technical skills employed, and the appreciation of the difficulties involved make this work impressive. It also makes the book a difficult one. Few readers, including this reviewer, have sufficient experience with models that range from path analysis to Markov chains to appreciate either the accomplishments or the problems involved in employing these models. In addition, someone with the necessary mathematical skills is unlikely to be aware of both the accomplishments and difficulties of the empirical work. The very density of presentation is a challenge to the reader. Given the nature of the research program and the desire to present its main features in one book, it is not clear that these difficulties could be avoided. Unfortunately the difficulties are compounded by a number of typographical errors.

There is, however, a larger problem, which is a problem of the strategy of the research program itself. Even though this represents more than a decade of research, this reviewer believes that the research program attempted to accomplish too much. Although Bartos rightly argues that to theorize is to simplify, he did not simplify his objectives sufficiently to maximize accomplishment and to provide a basis for clear presentation of his work. He is too concerned with generalizing from his "contrived experiments" to real-life bargaining situations, and it is that concern which leads him to deal with too many issues at once. For example, in attempting to use rational solutions to predict behavior, he could ask the question, "Under what conditions will negotiators behave according to Nash's rationality?" and design experiments to realize those conditions. Instead he utilizes all of his experiments and asks this kind of question in a post hoc manner. It is this reviewer's belief that had he conditionalized his concerns initially, and designed experiments which, although contrived, represented these conditions, he would have had a better understanding of how to proceed to gain further understanding of these factors which promote and those factors which inhibit "rational behavior." In this way he might have generated subsets of experiments for which particular models were more predictive and have more information about the scope of applicability of the restrictive assumptions of particular models.

The Drama of Social Reality, by STANFORD M. LYMAN and MARVIN B. SCOTT. New York: Oxford University Press, 1975. 180 pp. No price listed, cloth.

JAMES M. HENSLIN
Southern Illinois University, Edwardsville

Absurd. Essentially meaningless. Lyman and Scott will understand my use of this word and phrase to describe their most recent work. They will understand, for absurdity has been their central thesis for some time. But I don't think they will approve my choice of their terms to apply to their own work—although their sociological analyses demonstrate such a fine appreciation of irony that they just might.

Putting together these disconnected essays into a single volume is absurd. Since I know there is no essential meaning to such an act, I attempted to construct one. Several times I thought I had grasped such a meaning, only to have my vain attempts immediately disintegrated. For a while I thought power was the key to understanding why these essays are supposed to form a unit. Then politics. Then drama itself. But the ephemerality of each meaning-production became manifest as some following essay took an unexpected twist, tortuously disjointing itself from its predecessors.

A brief overview of this book's contents will demonstrate this problem of absurdity. The prologue (Lyman and Scott's choice of term for their introduction is significant) emphasizes that life is drama. Following this, almost two-thirds of the book is an exegesis of Shakespeare. Macbeth is first tackled, with an emphasis on alienation from roles. Then come analyses of Hamlet, Troilus and Cressida, and Antony and Cleopatra, with foci on information games, exploitation games, hierarchies of authority, Apollonianism and Dionysianism. From these highly selective aspects of Shakespearian sociology, we enter the second part of the book where the first chapter surprisingly focuses on Freud, George Herbert Mead, and Erving Goffman, respectively representing the theaters of the unconscious, the conscious, and self-presentation. Then follows a chapter listing and analyzing the various myths used by ruling groups to justify their right to rule. The next chapter covers resistance to authority by slaves, mental patients, bandits, and outlaws, while the final chapter deals with sexual adventuring. The book then concludes with a short epilogue that emphasizes power and resistance, freedom and order, meaninglessness and identity.

Thus, finding the meaning underlying this miscellany has been problematic. The quality of the writing, however, is not and the chapter on sexual adventuring is excellent and full of insight. But attempting to transcend the absurdity of Oxford University Press thinking that this was a book still leaves me shaking my head. (Granted sociological career contingencies, I do not find it absurd for Lyman and Scott to want to think of their essays as a book.) As a reviewer, however, I should inform the readers of this journal just where this book might fit into the instruction of students. Well, if you are teaching a course in the sociology of Shakespeare, the first part of the book is well suited for that purpose; if the sociology of mental illness, pp. 132–134; if the sociology of outlaws, pp. 134–146; if the sociology of sex, chapter eight; and if the sociology of deviance or social psychology, just pick and choose.

Flags through the Ages and across the World, by WHITNEY SMITH. New York: McGraw-Hill Book Company, 1975. 361 pp. $39.95 cloth.

SASHA R. WEITMAN
Tel Aviv University
and
SUNY/Stony Brook

Over twenty years ago Erving Goffman wrote his justly celebrated *The Presentation of Self in Everyday Life.* In it he deals with the ways *individuals,* acting alone or in teams, present images of themselves to their audiences in order to produce desired impressions. A few years later Gregory Stone produced a critical refinement of Goffman's approach by proposing that actors project impressions of themselves by means of *two* distinct kinds of media: their *behavior,* and their *appearance.* The focus of Goffman's work, as well as that of most symbolic interactionists, has been on the former, and Stone enjoins us to begin paying more attention to the latter. By and large, Stone's lead has not been followed, and social psychology has been the poorer for it.

The situation in sociology proper is worse still. Most sociologists profess to believe in the sui generis reality of groups, and a number of them would probably even agree to the definition of sociology as the science of groups. But you would never suspect any of this from a perusal of current modes of sociological theorizing and of doing research. Wherever you look the axiomatic individual reigns supreme. In most empirical researches it is about individuals that the sociologist gathers data, not about groups ("group properties" are operationalized by summing individuals' scores). In their theories, likewise, it is the individual who appears as the ultimate unit of action, while group structures, norms, and boundaries are derived, mathematically or logically, as "emergent properties" from the matrices of inter-individual interactions.

And yet we all know that groups exist, that they persist, and that they act, all this quite apart from the actions and inclinations of many of the individuals who comprise them. Groups seek recognition from one another, they negotiate about their differences, they form alliances, and they give each other assistance, they exchange visits and even presents, they compete in sports events, and so forth. And yet the disconcerting fact is that after nearly 100 years of scientific sociology, we have contributed precious little knowledge about any of the above. The knowledge we have produced, such as it is, is mostly social psychological: it concerns principally individuals and how their behavior, inclinations, and resources are affected by their social characteristics.

The time, then, is long past due for us to begin studying groups qua groups, especially natural groups (as opposed to laboratory experimental groups). An appropriate way to begin this task, I propose, is by focusing on the soverign territorial *nation-state.* For one thing, this type of human formation has been scandalously neglected by sociologists (perhaps because of fears of being suspected of crypto-nationalism). But few serious observers would deny that the overall historical significance of nation-states in the modern era is greater than that of social classes, ethnic groups, occupational groups, residential communities, political parties, and most any of the formations on which we have concentrated so far. For another, data on nation-states is comparatively varied, abundant, familiar, and easy to come by.

But by no means quite as easy as one might assume. Take for example, national flags (conceived here as one of the standard images projected by all nation-states). Until the publication of this book, the would-be researcher was confronted with a bewildering variety of purportedly authoritative sources (*Encyclopedia Britannica, New York Times Almanac,* specialized flag books) which, upon closer examination, would prove to be grossly inaccurate, incomplete, internally inconsistent, out-of-date and frequently in contradiction with one another. The sorting out of all this information for the purpose of creating a single, complete, and valid flag data file would require weeks, if not months, of painstaking enquiry. All this labor has now been obviated by the publication by McGraw-Hill, in glorious colors and replete with thousands of carefully selected illustrations, of the encyclopedic work by Whitney Smith, *the* world's authority on the subject which he has dubbed "vexillology." Here then, between the covers of this one book, you will find informative chapters on the history of flags, on norms of flag usage (flag "etiquette"), on the transformations undergone by some of the world's most famous flags, and most especially, you will find an entire section presenting the following data for every single nation-state in existence in May of 1975: the nation's official name, the official name of its regime, exact reproductions of the various national flags (including military flags), the flags of the territorial subdivisions into which the country is divided, and last but not least an exact reproduction of the national coat-of-arms. All these illustrations are accompanied by a lucidly written text providing the date of first adoption of the flag, the officially attributed meanings to the colors and the field design of the flag, a verbal description of the origins, form, and contents of the coat-of-arms, and more. The following section of the book, which is devoted to the symbols appearing on the flags and the coat-of-arms, even contains a raw (that is, unanalyzed) inventory of many of the symbols to be found on these flags.

There is more, much more in this book (such as flags of international organizations, of commercial enterprises, of yachting clubs, of movements of national liberation, a glossary of flag terminology) which I cannot begin to list here. If this book lacks anything, it is sociological analysis, and this is precisely what we sociologists could contribute. Such analysis *is* possible, as I proved to myself in research I did on this subject a few years ago. Now that this magnificent source book is available, we can look forward to months of rewarding research, alone or with students.

Finally, should this book be rewarded with the commercial success it deserves, it just might encourage the publication of other books, equally attractive and authoritative, on some of the other facets of national presentation of self. These might include books on national anthems, national names and regime names, national mottos, national personifications (e.g., Uncle Sam, John Bull, Marianne), national holidays, national coin and paper currency illustrations, national awards and decorations, national monuments, national pantheons of heroes, and national postage stamps. The analysis of these various facets of national self-presentation, taken singly and then together, should take us a long way, at last, toward understanding the fundamental properties of nation-states, and thence the peculiarities of their conduct.

Theory

Ideology and Social Knowledge, by HAROLD J. BERSHADY. New York: Halsted Press, 1973. 167 pp. $9.95 cloth.

BARCLAY D. JOHNSON
Carleton University

Students of Talcott Parsons's work will greet this unpretentious study with gratitude. Professor Bershady shows that at the start of his career Parsons identified certain epistemological problems which any social theory must face, and that he has consistently employed a single theoretical strategy in a lifelong effort to solve these problems.

Parsons is most explicit about such issues in *The Structure of Social Action,* from which Bershady draws leads which enable him to identify some of Parsons's intellectual forebearers and thus make his concerns intelligible. The earliest figure of importance is Isaac Newton, whose model of the solar system has been called the first successful scientific theory. It enabled the scientist to predict the future positions of the planets with an accuracy so impressive that there followed a wave of faith in the future possibilities of scientific knowledge. David Hume called this faith into question by asserting that Newton's laws, though useful in practice, rest on nothing more substantial than the observer's sense impressions, from which necessary connections between events cannot be inferred. So skeptical a view was intolerable to Kant, who maintained that there *is* scientific knowledge of nature, but that it can exist only because sense impressions are formed into experience through "categories of the understanding," such as space, time, and causality, which are not themselves generalizations from experience but contributions of the observer's mind. The categories are *a priori:* "prior" to our knowledge in an epistemological, if not a temporal sense. For Kant, human action stands in radical contrast to the physical world. It occurs in a realm of "freedom" which is not part of nature and is not scientifically knowable.

The school of German historicism, deeply influenced by Kant, espoused a skepticism about knowledge of society comparable to Hume's skepticism about knowledge of the physical world. Some historicists claimed that there are no universal categories, analogous to those of Kant, which can be used to classify societies. For this reason, observers of social life are only capable of studying unique and noncomparable cultural configurations. Historicists, and also contemporary members of what Bershady calls the "ideological delegation," have claimed that any purported knowledge of society is deeply and inevitably influenced by the biases and interests of the observer. The word "ideology" in the title of Bershady's book refers to these biases as forces which allegedly make scientific knowledge of society impossible.

Just as Kant rejected Hume's skepticism, so Parsons rejects skepticism about knowledge of social life. Just as Kant identified a priori categories which make physical science possible, so Parsons offers a priori categories which must enter into the formulation of all propositions in social science. The elementary unit of which societies are composed is the act—by analogy with the particle, the elementary unit of classical physics—and observers *must* employ the a priori categories of the means-end scheme if they are to attain scientific knowledge of action, and thus of human society.

Bershady deals more briefly with Parsons's major works since 1937. Though none of these later works is as epistemologically explicit as is his first, Parsons has persisted in his original quest. The pattern variables, the four system problems, and the evolutionary universals are *not* offered as empirical generalizations. All of them are a priori categories.

In his account of the later Parsons, Bershady is occasionally, albeit tactfully, bored or irritated. He is also skeptical about Parsons's categories, in part because a seemingly endless series of reformulations undermines Parsons's claims for them. Nonetheless, Bershady is in sympathy with Parsons's aspirations. With a few gentlemanly flicks, he sends the leftist critics tumbling. He shows as clearly as one could wish that those who have railed against Parsons's alleged conservatism have simply not comprehended his strategy as a theorist.

Bershady reminds us that, in Parsons's view, scientific knowledge of social life must satisfy yet a second requirement. A priori categories are not in themselves adequate explanations of events. They can only become so by being incorporated in testable (and tested) propositions which conform to what has been called the "covering-law" model of explanation. Various authors have observed that Parsons does not himself provide explanations which satisfy this requirement. But Bershady goes further than others have when he suggests why Parsons has not fulfilled his own aspirations. In *The Structure of Social Action,* if less clearly in his later works, Parsons holds that explanations in social science must be teleological, in the sense that they must make reference to the actor's ends: conceptions of possible future states of affairs which the actor feels morally bound to realize. A number of recent philosophers have concerned themselves with the differences between such explanations and causal explanations in natural science, which account for future events solely by reference to the present. It appears that teleological explanations may be incompatible with the predictive determinacy which the covering-law model presupposes.

It is all too common, and unfair as well, to complain that authors have not written the book which they did not set out to write in the first place. Even so, I must point out that Bershady does not speak to several issues which are central to an understanding of Parsons's philosophical assumptions, and thus of his theoretical strategy; for example, it is odd that Bershady says little about the opposed positions of positivism and voluntarism. The former, a central polemical target for Parsons in 1937, asserts that subjective states either do not exist or are mere epiphenomenal manifestations of prior physical events. The truth of voluntarism is the central claim of Parsons's first book. No one in the recent controversy in the journals about the early Parsons has succeeded in refuting John Finley Scott's demonstration that Parsons's voluntarism is an affirmation of free will in the traditional metaphysical sense. This issue is directly relevant to Bershady's concerns, for when Bershady asks whether Parsons's commitment to teleological explanations contradicts the covering-law model, he comes close to asking whether voluntarism is incompatible with positivistic determinism, a dogma which, it may be noted, many social scientists accept without careful consideration.

Insofar as these issues are philosophical, they may never admit of final resolution. But insofar as they are questions about what Parsons has been trying to say, they can be resolved empirically by close examination of what he has written. Thanks to the exegetical efforts of Scott, and Whitney Pope and his colleagues, and now of Bershady, one can no longer suppose that the central ideas of the most eminent living social theorist will never be understandably expressed or competently evaluated. If we now know that one can only comprehend Parsons after reading some philosophy, then so be it.

Theórie Sociologique, edited by PIERRE BIRNBAUM and F. CHAZEL. Paris: Presses Universitaires de France, 1975. 598 pp. No price listed, paper.

PHILLIP BOSSERMAN
Salisbury State College

This anthology on sociological theory would be useful for students at the upper college and graduate levels. Messrs. Birnbaum and Chazel have written short introductions for the volume and its three main sections. These are too brief; nevertheless, what comes through is an intriguing rationale for the selections they have chosen. For this reason the book is valuable for professionals and students alike.

The editors contend that sociological theory encompasses a great diversity of orientations and styles including such people as Goffman, Ossowski, Adorno, Gurr, Parsons, Durkheim, and Habermas. Moreover, they deem it appropriate to borrow from history and philosophy. Bloch, Althusser, and Hempel are examples.

The notion of *system* is the book's main organizing theme. These editors employ a broad use of the concept, system, to include micro as well as macro approaches to theory. They prefer no special definition. Rather, they argue, the idea of system is present explicitly or implicitly in almost every selection. Their usage of the term brings to mind Robert MacIver's terse definition of society "as a system of ordered relationships." A secondary organizing theme looks at the kinds of questions and problems each "theory" raises either directly or indirectly.

The first section examines the presence of *system* in traditional sociology. including such authors as Tarde, Simmel, Weber, Goffman, Cicourel, Mauss, Lévi-Strauss, Durkheim, Toennies, and Schmalenbach. The compilers note that system is often latent among traditional sociologists revolving around the concept of order. These selections place an emphasis on interaction processes studied by both nominalists (the individual actor is primary) and realists (the group is the ground of social life). Social control is essential to order. Conflict is constantly present. Centrifugal forces threaten stability and hasten disintegration. These are some of the problems "classical sociology" explores.

The editors next focus on structural-functionalism. Here system becomes central to such theorists as Malinowski, Radcliffe-Brown, Merton, Parsons, and Smelser. The editors at once recognize the importance of this tradition while lamenting what seems to them to be a reification of system to the neglect of conflict, history, and mutational change. They include a chapter on the critical assessment of structural-functionalism by such persons as Gouldner, Lockwood, and Nagel. Gouldner particularly appeals to them as being on the right track. They treat general systems theory through excerpts from the work of Bertalanffy, Maruyama, and W. Buckley. This leads to a chapter on cybernetic models with selections from Lazarsfeld, Deutsch, and Etzioni.

Being generally uncomfortable with a perceived a-historicism of the functionalist perspective, the editors conclude their book by "confronting the social system with history." They attempt to reconstruct from classical-traditional sociology the genesis of social change with the aid of recent theoretical models. They look first at social inequality through the perspectives of Marx, Touriane, Bourdieu, Boudon, and Chamboredon. I was particularly pleased to get acquainted with the work of Bordieu and Chamboredon. The first examines education and inequality; the latter, juvenile delinquency. Both see anomie and disintegration resulting from a lack of mobility for certain types of persons. Ideology, conflict, and the genesis of social change constitute the main themes of the two concluding chapters in this section. Althusser, Mills, Nisbet, and Tilly are among the contributors. The editors seem to agree with Nisbet and Tilly that there is no single genesis of change. The historical context is relative. The sources of change are multiple. Change produces crisis. It is mutational, and discontinuous.

This selection of readings in theory is fascinating. It would be an enjoyable book to teach, but would require considerable supplementary discussion since the editors' explanations and assessments are regrettably meagre.

Understanding Piaget, by REMY DROZ and MARYVONNE RAHMY, translated by Joyce Diamanti. New York: International Universities Press, 1976. 227 pp. $10.00 cloth.

The Origin of the Idea of Chance in Children, by JEAN PIAGET and BÄRBEL INHELDER, translated by Lowell Leake, Jr., Paul Burrell, and Harold D. Fishbein. New York: W. W. Norton & Company, 1975. 251 pp. $12.50 cloth.

KATHRYN P. MEADOW
University of California, San Francisco

The written output of Jean Piaget, alone and in combination with his students and colleagues, is enough to boggle the mind. By the end of 1964, it had reached some 20,000 pages, and dealt with the areas of Genetic Psychology, Genetic Epistemology, Philosophy, Logic, Biology, Sociology, and Education. Piaget's theories have been the subject of numerous books and discussions. Now, in the book by Droz and Rahmy, we have a Study Guide, a Reading Program, a Concordance for the Gospel according to St. Jean. The authors tell us that their effort has been "heavily influenced by Herodotus, the *Roman Itineraries* . . . the *Guides Bleus* and the *Guides Michelin*. . . . "They hope to provide something for everyone: "novice[s] will find guidelines, admonitions, advice, suggestions, . . . for initiating [themselves] into the work of Piaget. The more advanced student[s], who [know or think they know] Piaget's work . . . will find specific reading recommendations compiled for particular problems and themes, which will spare . . . much long and rather arduous bibliographic research." The book should be very useful for those who wish to become experts on Piaget. Most sociologists may find that it offers a pathway to more than they really want to know.

The Origin of the Idea of Chance in Children was published originally in France in 1951. This reflects the curious lag in the English translation of a large part of Piaget's work. He has long been considered the most important and the most original thinker in the fields of developmental psychology and cognitive processes, and it is strange that it has taken so long for the entire body of his writing to appear in English. This lag may well be related to the difficulty in both translating and comprehending Piaget's prose and his concepts. Flavell is quoted in the translators' preface as saying that this book is fairly easy to read (as Piaget's books go). This reviewer found it very difficult indeed. The level of felt difficulty is undoubtedly related to a decidedly dormant interest in mathematical education and curriculum, as well as in ideas about quantity, logic, geometry, movement, velocity, and space. Those whose interests lie in these directions, however, should not take their cue from this review.

Although some of Piaget's work is of great interest to sociologists, this book is not likely to be as useful as some others (e.g., *Play, Dreams and Imitation in Childhood, The Language and Thought of the Child*). It is a supplement to previous work on the development of thought in the child and "is the result of two preoccupations: the assimilation of ideas about experiences that cannot be grasped by deductive reasoning, 'the fortuitous or randomly mixed'; and the analysis of intellectual operations that lead to the process of induction." The authors view this work as an introduction to their investigations of intuition, where "a study of the origins of the idea of chance is unavoidable."

Engels, Manchester, and the Working Class, by STEVEN MARCUS. New York: Random House, 1974. 272 pp. $8.95 cloth. $2.95 paper.

EVAN STARK
Yale University

In 1844, just two years after he first met Marx and twenty months after he'd been sent to finish his business training in the Manchester cotton mills owned in partnership by his father, Engles returned home to write up his field notes. *The Condition of the Working Class in England* is a classic study of industrialism, occupational hygiene, urban geography, and class psychology. Why, Marcus wants to know, was Engels able to see capitalism in ways Wordsworth, Carlyle,

Dickens, and a host of minor critics could not?

Most intellectual historians put their subjects into gothic cathedrals of ideas where they balance precariously on their supposed mentors. But Marcus fully contextualizes the Engels work and provides an invaluable companion to its significant content. More important, he shows why and how sociological knowledge comes into being. The romantics, for example, tied the horrors of factory work for wages to universal moments of human suffering and dramatized, as Engels did also, the destruction in an historical instant of a generation's family life and autonomy. Engels, meanwhile, took his metaphors from within not outside the historical processes set in motion by capitalism. He invented a social theory whose categories simultaneously actualized and were dynamized by the lived antagonisms of an entire class of working men and women.

Were our methodologists less disposed to trivialize social problems to suit peculiar research techniques and instead intent on showing students how confrontations with the "big issues" can stimulate the invention of adequate research strategies, Marcus's work (and Engels's too) would be indispensible for method as well as theory courses. Marcus's book is written beautifully and stands alongside the last sections of E. P. Thompson's *The Making of the English Working Class* and Raymond Williams's *Culture and Society* as one of the few to situate the radical theory of industrialization within the class framework established by capitalism.

The Reality of Ethnomethodology, by HUGH MEHAN and HOUSTON WOOD. New York: John Wiley & Sons, 1975. 259 pp. $11.50 cloth.

BRUCE M. HACKETT
University of California, Davis

This dense and provocative essay offers a useful guide to one corner of a major contemporary "movement of thought"—the virtual collapse of the traditional boundary between "knower" and "known" in the process of inquiry. The movement extends well beyond ethnomethodology as a craft, but in the behavioral sciences at present the ethnomethodological circle probably exhibits our most concentrated gathering of investigators concerned with "meaning itself as a phenomenon" and "interaction [as] activity that accomplishes a sense of an external world." The subtleties of analysis and the philosophic refinements in *The Reality of Ethnomethodology* suggest the extensive work already done, under a canopy uneasily confining a diversity of sometimes warring methodological approaches, to render the "given" world altogether problematic in order to reveal the skills that compose it—to generate an understanding, as it were, that what appears as *datum* might better be seen as *captum*.

A central task of the book is thus to explicate a variety of researches suggesting that sights-seen, words-heard, and facts-known are neither elementary reflections of a fixed and a priori reality, nor in some sense subjective expressions, but rather the literally constructed or constituted outcomes of socially structured seeing, hearing, and knowing practices; investigation concerns itself with active nouns, e.g., realization, as opposed to reality. This turn of events implies that social realities, perhaps *any* realities, are intrinsically interactional, fragile, and permeable. The authors emphasize the sense in which reality (or realization) is a "reflective" activity, a "self preservative" process of understanding the world through procedures that simultaneously illuminate, justify, and explain away contradictions to our established assumptions regarding the nature of that world. Since studies of reflexivity have obtained a central place in the corpus of ethnomethodology—studies, e.g., of the self-justifying character of labeling and typification processes—the authors' insistence that inquiry into reflexivity has its own metaphysics, that reflexivity is a reflexively sustained notion, performs the important task of reminding the reader that ethnomethodology is caught in Zeno's paradox: the idea that all realities are self-validating is itself a self-validating idea. The point is to emphasize, in any case, that inquiry establishes only through a process of arbitrary assertion the detachment of its findings from the process of inquiry itself. If this notion is taken seriously one not only begins to experience "the reflexivity of reflexivity as a personal problem," as Mehan and Wood put it, but to understand the difficulty of avoiding the conclusion that under rigorous examination reflexivity, ethnomethodology, and indeed any inquiry become a "way of life" rather than a set of procedures for making statements *about* life.

The creative character of inquiry reduces the distinction between science and art but destroys the pretensions about science provided by the long legacy of philosophical and methodological positivism. Ethnomethodology seeks to place inquiry back into the world from which positivism sought to remove it; inquiry becomes a feature of everyday practical activity and, as a specialized activity, is now viewed as dominated by practical concerns. The current funeral oration for positivism gains an additional voice or voices here; the world exhibits a diversity of situational, opened-ended, assumption-dependent realities that have at least the semblance of a political character in being human constructions and may become imperialistic when "imposed," perhaps especially when imposed by institutions committed to the view that reality for them is truly "out there"—e.g., almost all modern public school systems.

At every point the book maintains a firm companionship between ideas and research. Six of the twelve chapters review and analyze recent studies in ethnomethodology. "The Imposition of Reality" relies on the "official distortion" of children's worlds examined by A. Cicourel and his students in *Language Use and School Performance;* it also makes use of Cicourel's Argentine fertility study; and reports at some length previously unpublished work on "naturally occurring descriptions" by Marshall Shumsky, and on Howard Schwartz's penetrating critique of formal logic. (The explication of Schwartz's unpublished work here and elsewhere in the book is a notable contribution.) "Reality as a Rules System" pursues the critique of formal logic and the "normative conception" of social action. The police-work studies reported by Bittner, Cicourel, and Emerson, the work on education by Cicourel and Kitsuse and by Mehan, D. Zimmerman's welfare agency research, and Garfinkel's studies of language "indexicality" are examined as demonstrations of the "situational" and "essentially incomplete" character of rules.

Other chapters review recent studies of controversial materials (especially the tragically estopped work of Harvey Sacks) and critique the tendency of these works to resemble abstract linguistics. They also explore reflexivity in some detail, with special reference to D. L. Wieder's study of the "convict code," Garfinkel's work on "scenic practices," the "experimental" ethnomethodology of Zimmerman and T. Wilson, and Schwartz's general critique of the use of the reflexivity concept. The book concludes with a "prospectus" for ethnomethodology, including a wise but brief discussion of ethnomethodology's "philosophical grounds" and "morality," critiques of the Parsonian and Hobbesian legacies, and a "manual of procedures" for "becoming the phenomenon"—experiencing the "mutual constitution of observer and observed."

A number of criticisms of this work are possible; my own are relatively insubstantial. The early assertion that a reality is a "coherent body of knowledge" and the later statement that within science "an organized consensus decides what is and what is not warranted as knowledge" both suggest that the inchoate character of experience and "practicality" is more primitive, less pervasive than the inquiries reported in the book seem to demonstrate. At another level, the attempt at one point to claim even Marx for ethnomethodology—to save him from the Marxists—seems something of a reach in view of Marx's own demonstrable lack of warmth toward indeterminacy and intellectual relativism. In general, the useful discussion of ethnomethodology's historic and philosophic roots, although not intended as a major undertaking, could in my view have been much improved by some reflection on the contributions of the philosophical pragmatists, especially Peirce and Dewey (Peirce does appear, briefly noted), who were examining the "practical" character of reality before the turn of the century and who of course made a major contribution to the theory of education—the focus of much of Mehan's own work.

A certain degree of indulgence, or at least largeness of spirit, may be required of the reader with regard to stylistic issues. The book, by two authors, is written in the first person singular. The prose is so thoroughly a matter of simple declarative sentences that the reading experience is akin to spending Saturday afternoon watching two promising light-heavyweights punch the heavy bag at Stillman's Gym. Finally, although the argument that one must "become the phenomenon" in order to understand it seems a necessary implication of much current research and theorizing, those who make the argument could in the future usefully employ the expository services of a good-natured academic politician.

The book has a frontispiece: M. C. Esher's *Drawing Hands*—two hands, each holding a pencil, drawing each other—"a visual display of reflexivity." One hopes that the more appropriate display would not be Ouroboros—the snake eating its own tail.

Theoretical Thinking in Sociology, by WILLIAM SKIDMORE. New York: Cambridge University Press, 1975. 277 pp. $10.95 cloth.

Sociology's Models of Man: The Relationships of Models of Man to Sociological Explanation in Three Sociological Theories, by WILLIAM L. SKIDMORE. New York: Gordon & Breach, 1975. 203 pp. $16.00 cloth.

DEENA WEINSTEIN
DePaul University

These are definitely not audacious books, but, like contemporary American politics, they attempt to appease the major and established competing interest groups. Essentially *Theoretical Thinking in Sociology* is a textbook. It presents the inoffensive conventional "wisdom" of the mid-sixties in an unsystematic manner that allows one to memorize terms, but not to recreate the theoretical visions. And like the "moderate" politicians who are basically conservatives, Skidmore's embrace of all major stances is a sham, since he generally evaluates them according to narrow positivistic criteria such as "logical purity" and the quantity of research that they have inspired.

Defining the objective of sociological theory as explaining social order, the first part of the book describes some of the meta-theoretical debates over such issues as change, function, and cause. Holding fast to the middle of the road, he advises the reader that the best plan "is to be conversant with the reasoning on both sides and be able to use whichever kind of theoretical attitude seems appropriate," and provides no standard for deciding what is appropriate. Two-thirds of the book is devoted to examining the major proponents of exchange theory, functionalism, and symbolic interactionism, which exemplify his three types of theory: deductive, pattern, and perspective, respectively. Exposition is concluded with the well-worn criticisms. A final chapter considers "emerging" movements: theory formalization and construction, and ethnomethodology.

Sociology's Models of Man is a logical analysis of the theories of Homans, Parsons, and Mead which parallels the typology of the textbook, but which is directed toward clarifying the relations between doctrines of human nature and accounts of social organization. The author's analysis is fundamentally flawed by identifying a "model of man" with a "psychological" as opposed to a "sociological" level of analysis. Hence, he guarantees at the outset of his investigation that he will conclude by showing a discontinuity between the "models" and social organization. He does not acknowledge that a "model of man" might include the proposition that human existence is intrinsically social and, therefore, he misunderstands Mead's thought, charging Mead with failing to explain "why individuals should take account of the generalized other at all." The only answer that could satisfy the author would be one in terms of individualistic motivation, which shows his bias in favor of the exchange and functionalist theories. This bias is reinforced by failure to consider any "models of man" from outside the narrow band of establishment theory.

Skidmore exposes the hidden normative assumptions (of rationality) and nonoperational features ("reward") in Homans's work, and discusses the uneasy duality between voluntarism and determinism in Parsons. The thrust of his work, as he himself proclaims, is "a contextual analysis" of "the three main sociological theories of North America," and the work's major flaw is his adherence to these self-made boundaries. Contextual analysis—which reveals the logical inconsistencies and, more importantly, the tacit presuppositions of theories—omits any consideration of validity. Revealing the presuppositions of a false theory does not make it true and, though contextual analysis may be an aid to the task of explaining social order, it is not a sufficient method for securing such explanation.

Like the author's text, this book is based on the arbitrary assumption that the "fundamental problem of sociological theory" is "to account for patterned normative behavior." This unquestioning acceptance of the centrality of the problem of order is responsible for the pervasive individualism that marks this supposed sociological treatise.

Toward a Science of Man: Essays in the History of Anthropology, edited by TIMOTHY H. H. THORESEN. Chicago: Aldine Publishing Company, 1975. 232 pp. $14.95 cloth.

LOLA ROMANUCCI-ROSS
University of California, San Diego

The purpose of this volume was to consider current problems in anthropology in historical perspective; what emerged was a globe-hopping sleight-of-time souvenir-hunt and, for the most part, proto-articles in statu nascendi. So, put in your thumb and pull out Lord Kames in eighteenth century Scotland as a personal embodiment of an epoch (Stocking) hermetically sealed from all French thought and writing. The question is (for the reader if not for its writer): "is reductionism in historical writing illuminating?"

Meanwhile, Stateside, Gallatin is busy preceding Lewis Henry Morgan's evolutionism (Bieder), fighting those who view the indigenes as fallen from civilized grace. Squier is replacing antiquarianism with scientific archaeology and even busier taking all the credit for it (Tax). Consider also a re-assessment of Bachofen in terms of symbolic structures, a hearing heretofore denied him (Heltzman). An informative analysis of social anthropology in India (Vidyartha) is followed by the undeserved fate of Croation ethnologist Radić, who wrote a century ago on inside-outside views (Belaj). Radić's obscurity is attributed to linguistic causes. If we wish to be serious about soul-loss in our discipline, I think we must consider famelessness of the worthy in the contexts of status, power, and influence as its wielders plot major beltways in the history of ideas, even within "dominant" cultures.

From under- to over-exposure (in dual-contrast thinking) we appropriately turn to the chapter on Ruth Benedict, and wonder how often Apollo and Dionysus can be revisited through *Patterns of Culture* with profit. Benedict may have worked out her female identity through anthropology (Modell). We can say with certitude, I think, that the "inadequacies Benedict discovered in *The Birth of Tragedy*" are not Nietzsche's. In the most original, then as now, contribution to the science of aesthetics, Nietzsche understood the Apollonian-Dionysian genius of the Greeks through their art-forms. Alien to his scholarly understanding is the parceling out of "appropriate" masks to American Indian tribes, introduced through poetic licence. For Nietzsche had written, "And lo!, Apollo could not live without Dionysus!"

Such re-visitation without knowledge-increment is paradigmatic of some of the other ailing chapters. Their contributors surf in on a wave, long with promise of a break followed by a long curl of innovative insights; we are left witnessing it softly wash into the beach with the riders' assurances that something completed will appear elsewhere in the future. Among "patterns of culture" assays, a central theme of this volume could have been "the mythless man remains eternally hungering in the past, and digs and grubs for roots" (Nietzsche). Nevertheless the bricoleur will find a few gems in these antique shops as Jacob Gruber organizes them into several sets illustrative of his scholarly commentary.

Urban

Urban Political Movements: The Search for Power by Minority Groups in American Cities, by Norman I. Fainstein and Susan S. Fainstein. Englewood Cliffs, N.J.: Prentice-Hall, 1974. 271 pp. $9.95 cloth. $5.95 paper.

Political Power in Poor Neighborhoods, by Curt Lamb. New York: Halsted Press, 1975. 315 pp. $9.50 cloth. $4.95 paper.

Neighborhood Organization and Interest-Group Processes, by David J. O'Brien. Princeton, N.J.: Princeton University Press, 1975. 263 pp. $13.50 cloth.

George W. Dowdall
State University College at Buffalo

These three books examine aspects of the political organization of the poor in American cities from the perspective of the early 1970s, when a decade of innovation and high mobilization had given way to federal neglect (hardly benign) and an apparently reduced level of organizational activity among minorities and the urban poor.

Lamb provides us with a portrait of the mobilization of poor neighborhoods in the late 1960s. It is based on survey findings from the Local Change Study (commissioned by the Office of Economic Opportunity) which included interviews with over 8,000 leaders and residents in 1968 and 1969 in 100 neighborhoods with OEO agencies. Individual chapters deal with the level of change in community institutions, the degree of militancy, the political attitudes and values of neighborhood residents, community leadership, the group memberships of the poor, and the political status of women in poor neighborhoods. The last chapter, "Lessons in Political Revitalization," is ironically brief.

Political revitalization among the urban poor was hardly a universal phenomenon, and political activity took many forms in the neighborhood studied. Presentation of much of the data in aggregate terms, ignoring community differences, is thus disappointing, as is the tendency to present little more than percentage distributions of particular items or scales; the exceptions are some interesting typologies. Even with these limitations, as well as the methodological ones discussed by Lamb, the survey results are a valuable resource, though their value is not exhausted by this analysis.

David O'Brien draws on the work of Mancur Olson on the "public goods dilemma" in focusing on why rational self-interested individuals should bother to participate in neighborhood organizations. O'Brien carefully examines the specific organizational problems of the poor by critically assessing the organizational strategies of the 1960s: (1) the community development approach, (2) the social action-protest strategies of New Left organizers and those influenced by Saul Alinsky, and (3) the Community Action Program of the OEO in its many local incarnations.

O'Brien's criticisms are insightful and often compelling. His solutions, however, such as neighborhood takeovers of some governmental functions, are less convincing, in part because he does not analyze in depth the central question of what the concrete short and long run class interests of the poor are. Nonetheless, his work will be useful to those concerned with building effective community organizations.

In a commendable book that deserves a wide audience, Norman Fainstein and Susan Fainstein are attentive to both the historical context and the actual behavior of participants in urban political movements, emergent groups largely composed of and acting on behalf of blacks, Latinos, and other minorities. While they argue that a social movements framework (discussed in an appendix) is useful in understanding such phenomena, they reject the often ahistorical character of that literature, instead viewing urban political movements as the outcomes of an American "urban dialectic." The demise of the political machine in the face of Progressive-era reforms left the urban poor without a way of articulating their interests —the clients of increasingly impersonal and unresponsive bureaucracies. A diverse set of movements, the subject of this book, arose in opposition.

Roughly, a third of the book consists of the authors' own observational studies. Two attempts at community control over some Manhattan schools are described in well-written and detailed chapters. A third chapter, written with Gary Redish, discusses a New Jersey organization whose success in providing services undercut its political efforts: it created clients, not cadres. The last three chapters, valuable combinations of analysis of the case studies and literature review, examine the participants, strategies and tactics, and impact of these movements.

All three books share to varying degrees a problem common to much of the recent sociological literature in this area. The existence of the poor is taken as given, and the authors show little sustained interest in the historical and structural causes of poverty. "The poor" are discussed in overly abstract terms, without sufficient attention to the variety of forms poverty takes, the social and economic system which makes poverty and wealth two sides of the same coin, or the impact of other classes on the lives of those in poverty and on their organizational initiatives. The Fainsteins' analysis is all the stronger for their efforts to examine urban political movements with these questions in mind.

Urbanization in Latin America: Approaches and Issues, edited by JORGE E. HARDOY. Garden City, N.Y.: Anchor Press, 1975. 456 pp. $4.50 paper.

The Exploding Cities, by PETER WILSHER and ROSEMARY RIGHTER. New York: Quadrangle, 1975. 238 pp. $8.95 cloth.

J. JOHN PALEN
University of Wisconsin, Milwaukee

Within the next quarter century for the first time over half the population of the globe will reside in some sort of city. In the same period, total population in cities will double its current size. The growth will be concentrated in what are commonly known as developing countries—places where problems of housing, feeding, and employing urban populations are already acute. By the year 2000 eighteen of the twenty-seven largest metropolitan complexes will be found in developing countries. Is Calcutta, where over a half a million people must sleep on the streets every night, an example of what will become a global commonplace? Can we accommodate another world on top of this one? How do we cope with the inevitability of further urbanization?

In *The Exploding Cities*, Peter Wilsher and Rosemary Righter address these questions for the concerned non-professional. The volume is loosely based on a conference of the same name, held at Oxford in 1974, sponsored by the *London Sunday Times* and the UN Fund for Population Activities. The volume, however, is not a collection of the conference papers, but rather a description of the state of the cities which draws upon the papers and additional material from other sources.

The book is divided into four sections. The first, "The Explosive Ingredients," sketches the global background of urbanization, provides the necessary demographic statistics, and makes the important distinction between growth due to migration and growth due to natural increase. These chapters are generally exceptionally well written, and the considerable variety of data and information well handled. Both authors' background as journalists is probably a factor which produces for lay readers an interesting account of the amount and consequences of population growth.

The second section, "The Crisis of Affluence," looks at the nineteenth and twentieth century cities of the developed world. The New Yorks, Londons, and Tokyos have set a pattern that rightly or wrongly is still being followed throughout the Third World. This section is less balanced than the others, with a tendency to concentrate overmuch on the problems of alienation and housing design in such cities. While not minimizing the problems, it has to be remembered that these cities, nonetheless, are the world's most successful cities. They are the model the developing world is seeking to copy.

The third section, "The Cities of the Poor," looks at the sprawling, poor, and lively new supercities of Asia, Africa, and Latin America. The expansive and balanced material on the squatter settlements, which comprise from one-third to two-thirds of the urban population, is particularly well done. Chapter 12, "The Self-help Society," written by John Turner and Bryan Roberts, particularly argues for minimum government intervention in housing schemes—that improvements in urban housing can most effectively be made by squatters upgrading their own communities.

The final short section, "Communes and Communism," considers planned urbanization in China and the Soviet Union, and the often tenuous relationship between civic policy and civic performance. The chapter on China is good but brief. The authors note that true revolutionary reorganization has not occurred in the cities—the experiment with urban communes failed and has not been followed by further radical moves to remake the cities. Still, I would tend to give greater credit to the considerable achievements of the Chinese. The permanent rural resettlement of some 20 to 25 million urban youth, and the elimination of squatter settlements are programs that have not been duplicated elsewhere.

By comparison, the Soviet cities have been less successful in achieving their urban goals—particularly in housing and pollution control. Excepting Moscow, Soviet cities have little real power to control their own destinies. In industrial towns basic services, such as housing, roads, public transport, electricity, water and sewage, are often the responsibility of industry, not the municipal government. Not surprisingly, such "nonproductive" civic elements are usually minimally budgeted by state industries.

The intended "audience" for the volume is not professionals, but the educated laity. Thus, the volume should be judged on that basis. However, several limitations of the volume will be noted. The first is the total absence of footnotes—although there is a brief annotated bibliography. Urbanologists will recognize the origin of much of the data and tables, but without footnotes the lay reader is given the unfortunate impression that all of the data presented are of roughly the same reliability and validity. A second irritant is the authors' occasional *Times* magazineish breathless prose. One only gets to the second page of the first chapter before encountering one's first "teeming hordes" and "bursting at the seams." Generally, though, the volume, as previously noted, is well written.

A final limitation is the epilogue by Barbara Ward. Unfortunately, it is of the sermonette variety and adds little but space to the volume. It begins with the inaccurate assumption that, "in devoloped lands industrialization came before . . . any population 'explosion' could take place," and ends on the note that if there were "justice" and "sharing" by the year 2000 we could have a society "in which people can be neighbors and friends." One wishes Wilsher and Righter had instead provided more of their own sophisticated analysis.

Urbanization in Latin America: Approaches and Issues, is a reader which provides a solid addition to the English language literature on Latin urbanization by dealing with the historical and potential consequences of this Latin American urbanization. In the all too frequent lumping together of developing nations, the uniqueness of the Latin American cities is often overlooked. Latin America's colonial cities were not a product of the nineteenth and twentieth centuries, but of the sixteenth century. Excepting Montevideo, all of the metropolitan areas having a population of a million plus in 1960 were founded in the sixteenth century. Nonetheless, until well into this century these primate cities remained dependent upon European and North American metropolitan areas; and often did not become industrial centers with extensive ties to their own hinterlands until well into this century.

Even today, Latin American cities are urbanizing without simultaneous industrialization, when compared to European or North American cities. Per capita income, energy consumption, and percent of the G.N.P. produced by the industrial sector are all lower. Yet Latin America demographically is more urban than Europe. Presently each year Latin American cities gain some 8.8 million new inhabitants. Between 1985 and the year 2000 this will increase to 11 to 12 million new residents.

This anthology is divided into four sections. The first, "The Background of Latin American Urbanization," provides three historical discussions of emerging patterns. Such background pieces are essential if students are to understand just how different the origin of Latin American cities was from the experiences of Asia and Africa. The second section, "The Latin American City in Transition," contains three articles which discuss the spatial structure of Latin American cities and the political, economic, and demographic forces producing such patterns. There is also a discussion of policies and programs—largely ineffective—being used to shape and regulate the growth of cities. The third section, "The Future of the Latin American City," offers three articles suggesting how the cities could be better utilized to accelerate economic growth and social development. The final section, titled "Urbanization in Selected Countries and Cities," provides case studies from different perspectives of the three most populous Latin American nations of Argentina, Mexico and Brazil (São Paulo).

The twelve essays, although well known to Latin urbanologists, are relatively unknown to English-speaking readers. The collection will be particularly welcome to scholars teaching graduate and advanced upper level urbanism courses—particularly those using a comparative or cross cultural perspective. Particular attention is paid to economic and demographic forces as shapers of urban society. Overall, the pieces are more descriptive than technical, and represent a variety of viewpoints. As such the volume is well suited for classroom use.

Quality of Life Indicators in U.S. Metropolitan Areas: A Statistical Analysis, by BEN-CHIEH LIU. New York: Praeger Publishers, 1976. 315 pp. No price listed, cloth.

KIRSTEN A. GRØNBJERG
SUNY/Stony Brook

The quality of life hase been of increasing concern in the US as basic economic needs have become at least partially fulfilled. As a result, private institutions, especially local governments, have been charged with the responsibility of improving a variety of conditions associated with the quality of life. In fact, "a good life" for all or almost all has been seen as both possible in and necessary for a modern society.

As an outgrowth of these interests, a variety of studies recently have attempted to measure the quality of life on both a national, state, and community level. The present volume by Liu presents statistical infomation on a variety of living conditions for US metropolitan areas. No attempt has been made to measure subjective evaluations of the quality of life (QOL), or the relative importance attributed by people to different aspects of the QOL. Instead, measures on about 115 (not 123 as the author claims—several are repeats) conditions are reported and combined into five major components of QOL: economic, political, environmental, health and educational, and social. The analysis consists of computing and comparing these five components of QOL separately for large, medium, and small SMSAs.

Based on this analysis Liu arrives at the following conclusions: (1) in very few cities are the five QOL components of similar magnitude, thus a single QOL index is both theoretically and empirically problematic, and economic health is not necessarily associated with high QOL in other areas; (2) there is some evidence of regional variation in the QOL, but the findings are by no means clearcut or unambiguous; and (3) the major disparities in QOL among metropolitan areas occur in the areas of health and education, environment, and social conditions. Unfortunately, Liu does not go much beyond these conclusions or present much interpretation or explanation of his findings.

Also problematic in this study is (1) the arbitrariness with which certain measures are included with one or another of the five components (and in several cases one measure is included in two different components); (2) the process by which weights are attributed to each measure when the component indexes are constructed; and (3) the quality of some of the data (i.e., measuring only the volume of books deposited in the main library in the central city, not those in other libraries in the central city or in the suburbs). In a number of cases the indexes constructed seem overly simple and possibly misleading, and several of the variables should have been adjusted for differences in the age/sex structure.

The volume does provide basic data on many conditions which presumably are related to living conditions for 243 SMSAs in 1970. As such, this volume is a valuable source of data for the urban sociologist, as long as the reader is aware of the limitations of the data. The study is a contribution to a field which until now has been characterized by a paucity of data. One hopes that subsequent studies will modify, revise, and expand both the data and theoretical formulations presented here, not simply repeat them.

The Roots of Urban Discontent: Public Policy, Municipal Institutions, and the Ghetto, by PETER H. ROSSI, RICHARD A. BERK, and BETTYE K. EIDSON. New York: John Wiley & Sons, 1974. 499 pp. $14.95 cloth.

ALBERT J. REISS, JR.
Yale University

The American public (and its government) was shaken and divided in the 1960s by events that cut deeply into its moral fabric. There developed a growing fear of victimization by crime, the spread of drug use and pornography, violence in the urban ghettos, and confrontation over the war in Viet Nam. Each set of events brought with it governmental inquiry that in turn spawned a spate of social surveys designed to answer unanswered and often unanswerable questions. The surveys for the National Advisory Commission on Civil Disorders on which this important book is based were cast in that mold. Whether they made a significant contribution to public enlightenment or social engineering is moot. Yet anyone reading *The Roots of Urban Discontent* could easily contend that major derivative or side-effects flowed from these surveys. This volume beautifully demonstrates that significant and fundamental theoretical questions can be attacked by adjusting the focus of surveys through a reanalysis.

The central question of this volume is "does the city in which one lives make a difference?" Examining that question for a segment of the American urban population —blacks living in ghettos—these authors ably demonstrate that city differences are important in determining how a local population assesses the responsiveness of local institutions to its expectations. That is not an obvious conclusion. A growing body of literature during the fifties and sixties questioned that long standing presumption by observing that city differences often are artifacts of the composition of its population and that macro-societal effects sharply reduce local effects. Studies of local community power made officials and their government appear less and less powerful as study followed upon study of local power elites. But more powerful analysis of surveys during the seventies, particularly the survey of fifteen US cities for the National Advisory Commission on Civil Disorders, attests to the power of city as an explanatory variable. Beginning with the work of Schuman and Gruenberg (*AJS*:70:213–261) on racial attitudes in these fifteen cities, we learned that the cities in which Americans live produce distinctive effects upon citizen attitudes, experiences, and perceptions of race. Yet Schuman and Gruenberg's work required speculation about the role of city government in producing differences in race attitudes, experiences, and perceptions. Drawing together this survey with surveys of political and civic elites and of institutional agents (police, welfare workers, retail merchants, major employers, educators, and political party workers) these authors explore that causal chain in greater depth. By careful and sophisticated analysis—often highly self-critical—they provide considerable evidence that "the political leadership of a city has profound effects on the actions of governmental agencies, which in turn are reflected in popular positive or negative assessments of the responsiveness of local institutions" (p. 57).

There is an additional reason, however, for reading this work. All too often reports of studies based on surveys and their analysis are a frustrating experience for the technical reader. Not so with this report since one is given an abundance of information not only on what was done but on what, unfortunately, was not done. Frequently the reader is cautioned about pitfalls in analysis or warned that the inference is shaky. This highly critical self-appraisal, I trust, is a growing sign of the maturity of our discipline and these authors are to be commended for creating one such model. To be sure, one can find occasion for disagreement about the strategies of inference and, as the authors, wish that these surveys might have been done differently. Yet, all in all, it is an admirable example of what one can do with data that are less than adequate to the problem at hand. There is here, moreover, a wealth of information for different communities of scholars.

Students of attitudes and behavior will find much that illuminates the problematic relationship between attitudes and behavior. One learns, for example, that blacks in the cities studied were more sensitive to the way the police behave toward citizens than to the attitudes police hold of citizens. Students of communities will note in turn that the police and their behavior are locally determined and those who assess the effects of public policy on practice will note that where the mayor and police chief are both sensitive and responsive to blacks, the police behave with greater restraint toward the public, and blacks in turn feel less abused by the police. There is much in store for the student of power and power elites. Issues of school quality, desegragation, and community control are quite sensitive to the characteristics of a city's political system. Moreover, as the authors note, at this juncture in our history, the local political community is much more important to blacks than to whites.

This book, then, is far more than a rich analysis of the roots of urban discontent in our cities during the late sixties or a discourse on their implications for public policy. Rich as it is in these respects, the book will stand as an important contribution to our understanding of the intricate relationship between micro- and macro-social structure and behavior.

Organizing for Agricultural Devolopment: Human Aspects in the Utilization of Science and Technology, by WILLIAM FOOTE WHYTE. New Brunswick, N.J.: Transaction Books, 1975. 60 pp. $2.95 paper.

E. A. WILKENING
University of Wisconsin, Madison

Agricultural development efforts have fallen far short of their intentions. The "green revolution" has failed to improve the lot of the small farmer meaning that the "trickle down" theory has not worked. This little book is another attempt to explore the reasons for the failure of agricultural development and to recommend some new directions.

The author brings his experience in industrial sociology to the problem of rural devolopment. Drawing from the notions of "participation management" in industry it is noted that horizontal structures which do not imply super- and sub-ordination are essential in coordinating the various programs created to help the farmer. Also the role of organized effort among the peasants in seeking information and assistance is given attention, emphasizing the need for closer exchange among farmers, and the systems created to help them. But, the tougher problems of how to deal with local and national elites to affect the allocation of resources and services needed by the small farmer are only touched upon. For example, the topic "controlling of individual interests in favor of group interests" is treated in one page.

This book gives some hints for the practitioner in agricultural development and some suggested topics for the researcher. It outlines the major organization problems within an organizational framework giving reasons for the failures of past approaches to rural development and some clues to more successful leads for the future.

Additional Reviews

The Sociology of Retirement, by ROBERT C. ATCHLEY. New York: Halsted Press, 1976. 158 pp. No price listed, cloth.

SARAH MATTHEWS
University of California, Davis

The Sociology of Retirement is designed, according to the author, to provide a conceptual framework through which retirement can be viewed as a complex and evolving social phenomenon, to summarize the research literature, and to identify conspicuous gaps in our knowledge about retirement." For the most part, the book successfully reaches its goals. Several of the chapters, including "Background and Evolution of Retirement," "The Decision to Retire," and "Retirement Income," are excellent summaries of the literature and of gaps in current knowledge, and preserve the complexity of the issues under consideration. The conceptual framework the author offers for organizing extant and future research on retirement views retirement in four ways: As a phase in the occupational cycle, as an event, as a process of transition, and as a social role. The process of transition has been the focus of the greatest amount of research, and the two chapters on consequences of and adjustment to retirement, perhaps unavoidably, reflect rather than clarify the existing confusion in the literature. The skill with which the author preserves complexity in the earlier part of the book gives way to a simplistic accounting of the findings of various studies, which because of their varied samples and research questions do not lend themselves to systemization. My major objection to the book is the author's discussion of retirement as a social role. He unsuccessfully refutes Burgess's contention that the retired are trapped in a roleless role, and in his comparison of the role of the retiree and the role of the alumnus of a school, inadvertently lends support to the "roleless role" argument. Not surprisingly, Irving Rosow's *Socialization to Old Age* does not appear in the bibliography. In short, the book, especially the earlier chapters, is a laudable discussion of the social scientific literature on retirement, and is a good introduction both for those just broaching the subject and for those trapped in the quagmire of the literature, in search of an organizing framework.

Sport and Social Order: Contributions to the Sociology of Sport, by DONALD W. BALL and JOHN W. LOY. Reading, Mass.: Addison-Wesley Publishing Company, 1975. 574 pp. $14.95 cloth.

GREGORY P. STONE
University of Minnesota, Minneapolis

This, the fifth in a series on the "Social Significance of Sport" under the general editorship of John Loy (other volumes focus on philosophy, geography, history, and the place of women in sport), is comprised of twelve chapters, ten of which are contributions written specifically for this volume. Chapters are organized in three main sections: "Sociological Analysis," "Social Organization," and "Occupational Organization." I shall not quarrel with these headings. (As a matter of fact, it is heartening to see Collective Behavior, as it is discussed in chapter 7, brought back into social *organization* [correctly interpreting that noun as a gerund] where it belongs.)

However, this review will not follow the organization of the book. Rather, I will comment first on those contributions I take to be excellent analyses; second, those I take to be suggestive, but impressionistic; third, those that provide a compilation of data sorely needed by those of us who take play seriously; and fourth, examples of inadequate sociological analysis. One of the truly important contributions of this volume is the fact that eight of the twelve chapters provide bibliographies of five pages or more with an average of somewhat more than five pages for each chapter. Thus, the volume, itself, provides a rather complete review of the field.

Three chapters impress this reviewer as being truly outstanding in that they are well grounded in theory, make good use of data, present significant questions rather than ephemerally definitive conclusions, and attempt to come to grips with problems of social process, viewed as transformations of social or social psychological arrangements, but space precludes their complete coverage. I shall focus on one chapter: Richard Gruneau's discussion of "Sport, Social Differentiation, and Social Inequality," is exemplary. Note how the title eschews the blind alleys into which sociologists have been led by the "stratification metaphor"! Gruneau begins analytically by asserting that inequality is merely one dimension of differentiation. Veblen's views are then presented and criticized before the organizing hypothesis is presented, namely that anomalous conceptions of sport and the anomalies in sport mark the persistence of two conflicting ideologies: the meritocratic which has its origins in seventeenth century bourgeois rational utilitarianism, and the egalitarian which can be referred to Marxian praxis. Although there are residues of ascriptive privilege, the ideological foundations of sport are meritocratic rather than egalitarian. In outlining Marxian theory, Gruneau demonstrates how sport contributes to the perpetuation of the classes. Records have, like money, universal currency. Athletes are alienated. Yet, the whole analysis, Gruneau insists, can not be accepted. It lacks historical and other empirical support. The middle class persists and increases on an international scale, and the power of status sentiments is seriously underestimated. What, then, of functionalism? Better we acknowledge that it is a useful analytic tool for exploring some problems, although Marx might well agree with Durkheim that sport is an integrating device. Opium, he might say; healthy, the functionalists might respond. An excellent attempt is made at some theoretical synthesis *in the dialectic sense*. Next, the problem of the relationship of transformations in sport to egalitarianism is treated. Sport recruitment does open up, as meritocracy advances, but this has little impact on egalitarianism. Finally, the emergence of the so-called "post-industrial" society is construed as providing an increasing impetus to the democratization of sport, although "stratum limits" persist, as surveys in Britain, Canada, Germany, and the United States establish. They are found in spectatorship and amateur participation in spite of the further weakening of such limits to the recruitment of those who work at play for the entertainment of others. Other chapters that deserve as extensive a commentary are "Occupational Subcultures in the World of Sport," by Alan G. Ingham, and "Coming of Age in Occupations: A Comparative Study of Career Contingencies of Musicians and Hockey Players," by Robert R. Faulkner.

Two chapters are highly suggestive contributions, but lack the data to support the kind of analysis that is suggested. "Sport and Politics," by Brian Petrie, for the most part, makes use of newspaper accounts to illustrate his points. Of course, this is necessary because so little focused research has been carried on in the area, but there are techniques of content analysis that might have been employed to carry the very worthwhile ideas in the chapter a bit below the surface of impression. Petrie immediately calls into question the notion sociologists of sport have inherited from Callois and Huizinga, namely the separateness of the world of play. Sport has mobilized such work-a-day events as riots, international boycotts, assassinations, and war. It is used to package politicians and mold political consciousness. It brings communities together as a collective representation and exacerbates community conflict by re-presenting religious and ethnic rivalries. The Olympics may be used to extend foreign policy, as "ping-pong" has been used to break through international insulations. Finally, Petrie focuses on social psychological dimensions of sport—the ideology of the coach and the jock, implications for civil and individual rights, and the "personality structure" of the athlete as it bears on ideology. Again data are in short supply, and Petrie is justifiably skeptical of the validity of personality inventories. At any rate, the struggles of the 60s may well have brought about a shift in such "personality characteristics." Rosenberg and Turowetz prefer the concept of identity as it is "worked up" in socialization to a career. Chapter 8 compares the identity work-up of physicians with that of professional wrestlers as they are recruited, trained, and certified, in their occupations, and as they perform the roles such identities mobilize. The concept is sensitizing and points up marked contrasts between those occupations. Hopefully, their lead will be taken up by others. There is little data here, and Anselm Strauss's *Mirrors and Masks* begs to be brought in.

Providing highly important data for the sociologist to exploit in some future synthetic effort, is "Sports from a Geographic Perspective," by John F. Rooney, Barry McPherson's "Sport and Consumption and the Economics of Consumerism," and "An Occupational Analysis of the Coach," by George H. Sage. Each, of course, is interpretative, but the data provided are more impressive. Rooney shows how the spatial distribution of various sports conforms to Cristallers's "central place theory." Here one initiates an inquiry with the selection of a sport and notes its dispersion. Or one can begin with an area, inventory sports within that area, and note the historical development of the important sports. Extensive data in the form of US maps are provided. Finally, he views the historical growth of sport as involving ever-widening "circles" of spatial flux, centralization, and further flux. He also notes seasonal variations and "periodic market traits," e.g., the Pro Golf Tour.

Lest doubting sociologists should still wonder about the relevance of sport as an area of significant sociological inquiry, let them peruse McPherson's work. Sport pervades the entire fabric of American life. In his view the "age of high mass consumption" has been reached in the United States, and it is nowhere more dramatically documented than in the area of sport—if consumption is writ large. The problem is no theory to apprehend and render meaningful the mass of data. Thus, conflicting findings pose perplexing and unanswered questions. Chapter 9 is an extensive presentation of research on coaches—the emergence of the occupation in the US out of the development of physical education and intercollegiate athletics; the growth of the occupational identity; personal and social characteristics of coaches (the problem here is that studies are sparse and subjects seldom include college coaches); social attitudes and value orientations (they have the middle class attitudes of mid-America!); and finally the career patterns of college coaches: origins, recruitment, socialization, mobility, contingencies, and role-conflicts. The compilation of data was a yeoman task.

Finally, let me comment on two inadequate presentations. Michael Smith's "Sport and Collective Violence" is useful, but is not a contribution to the analysis of sport and the social order. The chapter takes up thirty-eight pages with the first twenty devoted to an excellent critical summary of theory in collective behavior, but *no* mention of sport, other than a sentence on the second page (p. 282). The analysis roots violence in sport to social structural strains (ethnic, political, economic, social class, and religious conflicts) and the "deprivation gap" between performance and reward. The dynamics of sport violence is examined under the well documented rubrics of communication (rumor, stadium "milling," and the ambiguity of announcements), precipitants (the context is more important than the content), and mobilization for action (a nice analysis of the "division of labor" in a crowd). Usually the consequence of sport violence is an escalation of control measures, but Smith suggests alternatives, namely, reduce the structural strains, institute major reforms, and (who knows?) stimulate the demise of spectatorship. Rudolf Haerle attempts a sociological analysis in "Career Patterns and Career Contingencies of Professional Baseball Players: An Occupational Analysis." I assess the attempt as essentially psychologistic. For example in his analysis of career stages and contingencies, he misses the organization of baseball—one of the few contemporary sports where the farm system is not linked to the educational system. This omission persists. Moreover, he cites compelling concepts, e.g., Hughes and Mead, but misses the point. Further, I think he takes his own instrument—the BFI (Baseball Fame Index) —too seriously and psychologistically. Baseball fame seems to be a trait of personality held together by cutaneous tissue, not a dimension of identity, established, maintained, and changed in the matrix of communication. Even player-owner conflicts are individualized as conflicts of persons motivated by profit versus those motivated by desires for success and personal fulfillment in the game. Sport is, first of all, a business, and businesses are well organized, indeed.

Human Behavior in the Social Environment: A Social Systems Approach, by Ralph E. Anderson and Irl E. Carter. Chicago: Aldine Publishing Company, 1974. 183 pp. $8.50 cloth.

Gregory Williams
University of Akron

Intended as an introduction to human behavior for students of the human services not previously exposed to Introductory Sociology or Psychology, this text "maps," but does not comprehensively cover, a wide variety of ideas, terms, theories, and concepts from these disciplines relevant to the human services. Like the background of the authors, the particular focus is Social Work, but it is also aimed at Education, Nursing, Home Economics, and Child Development. The instructor will need to expand on the material and add appropriate additional readings. The discussions are interesting, lucid, readable, understandable, include many relevant examples and analogies, and are a valuable asset for an audience unfamiliar with the social sciences. The glossary and annotated bibliography are also useful.

The "Social Systems" approach as an organizing principle is the distinguishing feature of this book, the first chapter of which establishes this framework. While the authors take a basically dynamic "General Systems" view, their perspective, though not exclusively functionalist, is unfortunately firmly rooted in the structural-functionalist tradition. Furthermore, this approach all too frequently becomes an easy way to create headings for parts of chapters including a spectrum of traditional theories, concepts, and ideas. In short, the social systems framework doesn't wholly succeed; it often overlays the text rather than fully integrating the material. In spite of the size of the book, the central five chapters—"Culture and Society," "Communities and Organizations," "Groups," "Families," "The Person"—briefly cover a lot of ground. Nevertheless, much important sociological material which I would consider valuable for the human services is not included. If this book is a map of human behavior, it is a very incomplete one, not without its biases. For example, while the chapter on the person includes the theories of Freud, Skinner, Piaget, and Erikson, the focus is clearly on Erikson. It is probably impossible to distill sociology and psychology down this far without serious loss, an unfortunate consequence since the audience addressed may not be exposed to more comprehensive studies of these fields outside their respective departments. For its market, one could undoubtedly do worse than this little volume. Outside of its market . . . well, that is another story.

Television in the Corporate Interest, by RICHARD BUNCE. New York: Praeger Publishers, 1976. 141 pp. No price listed, cloth.

Television and the People: A Programme for Democratic Participation, by BRIAN GROOMBRIDGE. Baltimore, Md.: Penguin Books, 1975. 241 pp. $1.95 paper.

Television: Technology and Cultural Form, by RAYMOND WILLIAMS. New York: Schocken Books, 1975. 160 pp. $7.50 cloth. $3.45 paper.

ROBERT G. DUNN
California State University, Hayward

Taken together these books testify to the preponderant role television is playing in the integration and control of the social, economic, and political systems of advanced capitalist society. Against the view of technological determination, however, these authors show that television is not doing this of its own accord. Given the continuing struggle between commercial and public service interests, the development and use of television historically has tended to extend, strengthen, and diversify the interests of privileged groups (most notably powerful business, political, and military elites) which shape policy and practice in the telecommunications and broadcasting industries. Television, like other technologies, is part of a vast network of social forces which determine the nature of the medium; as technology, television is less a cause than an effect of social organization.

Nonetheless, in the Williams and Groombridge books, the social effect of television implicitly remains the primary concern. The major theme of these two studies, although the authors approach the problem in different ways, is the future democratization of television, i.e., the transformation of the technological and institutional forms of broadcasting in the direction of increasing the participation and public effectiveness of wider social groupings. Whereas these writers are interested in television's potential as a purposeful instrument of social change, Bunce focuses on the real economic and political barriers to such change.

Williams wages a brilliant attack on technological determinism by showing through a detailed social history of television that its development was more a response to new (political and military) needs than an automatic result of scientific discoveries. He then examines the major contemporary forms, programming patterns, and effects of television communication. Sensitive to the human purposes which govern the complex interactions between technology and cultural forms, he encourages us to consider alternative technologies and uses of telecommunications. Though sketchy, and lacking the depth and grasp of his previous work, Williams's brief study is highly suggestive and properly focused on institutional and technical arrangements.

Dealing specifically with the political and economic aspects of television, the Groombridge and Bunce books are both narrower in purpose and more provocative. Groombridge sees television as a key factor in the contemporary movement toward participatory democracy in the West and argues that television must shift from its traditional emphasis on entertainment and information to assume its primary responsibility to educate and provide a forum for public discussion and decision-making. Focusing almost exclusively on Britain, the author adopts a case study approach to these problems, calling for a "community development" model of participation. His pluralist strategy would involve more interest groups in the production of television programs and thereby the larger political process. Although Groombridge's liberal reform optimism might have some meaning in the setting of British broadcasting, it hardly comes to grips with the following issues: (1) the serious problem of the public's tastes and needs (maybe the television audience *wants* entertainment, escape, information), (2) the realities of economic and political power in highly developed capitalist countries, and (3) the relationship between the conditions postulated by mass society theory and the patterns of television communication. Bunce partially addresses these issues in his informative though poorly written study of the role of corporate power in the American broadcasting industry. Bunce shows that the history of commercial television has been marked by the almost total ineffectiveness of FCC policy (i.e., local ownership and control resulting in "business pluralism") and the concomitant triumph of centralized and monopolistic structures of corporate wealth. Reflecting the economic elite's assumption that consumer demand needs to be managed, the "communication flow" of television is now shaped by the profit system of big capitalism—broadcasting has become an extension of corporate business practice.

These books are refreshing in that they attempt to deal with the larger institutional structures impinging on television as a mass medium of communication. Unfortunately, they are too descriptive and abbreviated (curiously, like television itself) to provide genuine analytical understanding. The actual economic, political, and technological forces which shape television are only superficially examined, and their consequences (whether television induces passive psychological states, produces a false appearance of reality, etc.) are practically ignored.

Introduction of Qualitative Research Methods: A Phenomenological Approach to the Social Sciences, by ROBERT BOGDAN and STEVEN J. TAYLOR. New York: John Wiley & Sons, 1975. 266 pp. $11.95 cloth.

Beneath the Surface: An Account of Three Styles of Sociological Research, by COLIN FLETCHER. London: Routledge & Kegan Paul, 1974. 221 pp. $14.95 cloth.

KATHY CALKINS CHARMAZ
California State College, Sonoma

Each of these books provides both methodological analyses and papers by the authors intended to exemplify their discussion of methods. Bogdan and Taylor present a fine overview of central issues in qualitative research. Although much of what they have to say is not new, their explication of how to do participant observation is clear and concise. The book might be useful for classroom adoption as a single text though otherwise, its price (like the price of Fletcher's volume) is prohibitive. In any case, the book will be of interest to new students and seasoned researchers alike.

Both books devote too much attention to the articles that represent the method discussed, without providing sufficient links between the methodological discussions and the finished products that they present, although including such reports helps to create a fresh readable approach. Bogdan and Taylor's book is, however, much stronger on this point than Fletcher's as they give some important suggestions for developing the analysis and writing research reports. But, since Bogdan and Taylor emphasize a "how to do it" approach, their objective would have been more fully realized if they had provided a more extensive analysis with examples of the intermediate stages between data collection and the finished product. As yet, the analytic process in qualitative research has not been fully explicated, and Bogdan and Taylor's treatment of this phase of work remains implicit. Nonetheless, their book does show a continuity between product and method which is conspicously lacking in Fletcher's work.

Through his account of his research career, Fletcher attempts to provide an analysis of methodological approaches based upon quantitative, qualitative, and critical inquiry. His undertaking is only partially successful. The book is uneven, which suggests that the author's experience with and understanding of the different methods may also be uneven. The most useful part of the book is the section on quantitative methods, in which Fletcher is clearly well-grounded. Students will find his elucidation of the practical operations of quantitative work to be provocative and informative since he chronicles how the research process actually evolves. In contrast, his treatments of qualitative research and the method of social criticism barely scratch the surface. His scathing critique of qualitative work might be taken more seriously if he had not provided an example of his own efforts in that area. The easiness of using the method, superficially of the analysis, and trivial social significance which he attributes to qualitative work can be applied to his own example.

Fletcher apparently judges the three methods by the traditional ways in which they have been used in the past. He views them as separate entities which are supported by domain assumptions and the political stances of their protagonists. But, if we accept Fletcher's final advice to make Mills our model, then the problems we study will shape the methods we use, and thus, either quantitative or qualitative research could, conceivably, be used in conjunction with social criticism and advocacy.

Consumers in Trouble: A Study of Debtors in Default, by DAVID CAPLOVITZ. New York: Free Press, 1974. 352 pp. $10.95 cloth.

JULIUS A. ROTH
University of California, Davis

The information in this book is derived from a survey of debtors in four cities conducted by the National Opinion Research Center using a survey instrument designed and analyzed by the author. The sample was drawn from records of legal action brought against debtors alleged by the creditors to have defaulted on payments for goods they had purchased. Only the debtors were interviewed, although something was learned about the more notorious merchants, banks, and loan companies whose names appeared repeatedly in the tales of woe.

The presumed relevant variables are compared and presented to the reader in tables and discussion in chapter after chapter, e.g., the percentage of defaulters in terms of income and occupational level (no clear-cut relationship), formal schooling (defaulters more often low in schooling), age (defaulters tend to be young), ethnic status (defaulting relatively higher among ethnic minorities). Direct sales (door-to-door) more often lead to defaults than general retailers. The type of property attached by the creditor is related to the type of creditor (e.g., collection agencies usually grab real property, the direct sellers personal property). And so on for many other combinations of variables.

The information contained in these chapters is useful and the book certainly should be read by persons interested in the sociology of consumerism or in consumer protection for its own sake. However, I believe there are important limitations to an understanding of the problems of the consumer debtor as it is presented here.

For one thing, the parade of measures and interrelationships begins to pall after a time and the reader may have difficulty keeping the connections and patterns in mind. There is little effort to conceive of the acquisition of consumer debt and subsequent default as processes of decision-making or of interaction between creditors and debtors in an institutional context. The difficulty, as I see it, lies in the kind of data available. A one-shot interview survey of a population sample provides one with measures of variables to be correlated. At best, it provides frequencies or proportions of cases with given characteristics or in which given things happen. (In the case of this study, the representativeness of the sample is so defective and many of the categories so arbitrary that even this modest goal is not attained.) But surely, what a consumer protection advocate is most interested in is not so much the percentage of "types of harrassment" used by each type of creditor, but rather the step by step process by which creditors enforce payment and the kinds of counteraction available to consumers to protect their interests. And for the student of some branches of sociology, the most interesting issues are not the percentage breakdowns, but the interrelated actions of creditors and consumers in a context of laws and administrative and legal agencies. For such an analysis, the most relevant data come from detailed studies of appropriate cases.

True, the author has attempted to present a description of an ongoing process in some cases, but he has been forced to do so through inference from indirect and spotty data. Thus, he seeks to show that the bargaining between creditors and consumers is grossly unequal. But we do not need a survey of defaulting debtors to tell us that and in fact this is a particularly inefficient way to document the point. He suggests that repossession of goods which are then sold for a very low price leaving the debtor with most of the debt to be repaid is a form of collusion to defraud, but this point can be far better established with some detailed case studies. The interviews in some cities turned up repeated mention of several merchants who appeared to be in the garnishment business, but again this point should be examined by following up appropriate cases. The kind of data-collection needed here is more akin to the work of a competent detective than that of a survey interviewer. This book demonstrates what may happen when one allows one's attachment to a given data-collection method to frustrate the goals of one's research interests.

The book contains an interesting and comprehensive concluding chapter on consumer credit reform which could have been written without reference to the preceding study.

Living in Fear: A History of Horror in the Mass Media, by LES DANIELS. New York: Charles Scribner's Sons, 1975. 248 pp. $12.95 cloth.

Mass Media, Violence and Society, by DENNIS HOWITT and GUY CUMBERBATCH. New York: John Wiley & Sons, 1975. 167 pp. $12.50 cloth.

NATHAN WEINBERG
California State University, Northridge

Mass Media, Violence and Society focuses on a single question: does the portrayal of violence in the mass media, from comics to television, have a significant effect on behavior in society? The authors seek to argue that it does not.

Howitt and Cumberbatch are British psychologists; they have been associated with research on media and violence at the University of Leicester's Centre for Mass Communications. This monograph undertakes a comprehensive review of experimental and field studies on the possible effects of media violence. The discussion of the literature is both detailed and thorough. Various media effect theories—catharsis, aggression stimulation, inhibition of aggression—are raised, considered and criticized; in turn, postulated intermediary mechanisms of media effect—identification, imitation, desensitization, triggering, attitude change—are considered and criticized. The authors find ample support for their thesis of no effects in the research literature, and carefully scrutinize research findings which contradict their position. As many researchers have taken the position that fictional presentations of violence in the media do effect the viewer's tendency to behave violently, they should find reading of this contrary literature to be of interest.

In the last chapters of their discussion Howitt and Cumberbatch propose a reorientation of media violence studies to include an examination of the effect of social settings on the violence presented in the various media; as an example they review research which suggests that the cinema provides a setting for youth culture and thus delinquency and violence while the home television does not. They further propose the need to study the groups which are concerned about media violence, the differential perceptions of media violence, and the variety of forms of violence distinguished by the audience, and the institutional aspects of the media which encourage violent programming.

If the argument of Howitt and Cumberbatch is accepted, media violence does not have the effects we usually assume; nevertheless the violence is still there, and remains to be explained.

Living in Fear, a literary and pictorial encomium to the horror story, gives one an idea of the variety of ghastly, ghostly, weird, awful, morbid, often violent ways we have invented to frighten ourselves. Daniels, known for his *Comix: A History of Comic Books in America,* provides us with a literary history of horror from Walpole and Strawberry Hill to Aleister Crowley and the Golden Dawn and on to Night of the Living Dead and the Exorcist. For the novice in horror, this work will introduce you to the major horror writers and their creations; for the initiate, many minor authors are included and discussed.

Interestingly, in the history of horror literature, Daniels finds that the first active censorship was undertaken in 1954 with the Comics Code Authority, which attempted to protect children from frighteningly violent material. Horror is now back in the comics, but the movies have a rating system, and television has the children's hour (these systems of censorship are easily circumvented by children, and merely irritating to adults).

Given the argument of Howitt and Cumberbatch, and given the perverse inventiveness of horror tales, it would seem that the equation of fictional media violence with real violent behavior which is the premise of systems of media censorship is untenable. Of course, seemingly non-violent media programs, such as repetitive commercials, may, with further research, prove to be conducive to violent behavior; then a new system of censorship will have to be developed.

Youth and Society, by F. G. FRIEDMANN. New York: Humanities Press, 1971. 63 pp. $2.00 paper.

Youth: The Seventy-fourth Yearbook of the National Society for the Study of Education, Part I, edited by ROBERT J. HAVIGHURST and PHILIP H. DREYER. Chicago: University of Chicago Press, 1975. 463 pp. $10.00 cloth.

JUDITH D. HANDEL
University of Missouri, St. Louis

In recent years there has been increased recognition of the necessity for studying youth as a distinctive group in contemporary society. Youth is defined as the period between the end of adolescence and the assumption of full adult responsibilities. The writers whose works are presented in these books see youth as a social rather than a biological stage of life.

The National Society for the Study of Education has a long tradition of excellence and this yearbook is no exception. The articles cover a wide range of topics and the variety of perspectives is so diverse that no matter what type of sociology a reader prefers, one is certain to find at lease one article written from that perspective. Most of the articles include many useful and recent references and analyze, rather than merely summarize, previous research.

To accomplish the objective of providing a comprehensive treatment of youth the yearbook is divided into three sections. Section I presents theoretical and empirical background. The articles range from Keniston's discussion of the self-society relation in the tradition of Erik Erikson, to Douvan's detailing of sex differences, to a psychiatric and pediatric analysis of medical data on this stage of life. The major failing of this section is the absence of a concluding chapter pulling together the different perspectives presented.

The second section looks at the relationship between youth and social institutions. Light and Laufer present a psychohistory of the new left. Havighurst analyzes changes in education, labor force, and attitudes. Havighurst and Gottlieb discuss the meaning of work and propose ways for society to meet youth's need for jobs. Graham argues for the importance of experimental learning using a model based on Kohlberg's work. Dreyer discusses sex and marriage roles. The section ends with an article by Bengtson and Starr offering a framework for looking at youth in an historically grounded context.

Section III focuses on cultural pluralism. Taking a position that cultural pluralism is a desirable state, the authors discuss blacks, rural WASPs, Mexican-Americans, Asian-Americans, low income youth, and women. Of special interest is the article by Manning which argues that we must look at the forces that structure society if we are to understand the perceptions of its members and Cottle's case studies of poor youth are very moving.

The yearbook concludes with an epilogue by Grinder that compares this yearbook to the 1944 NSSE Yearbook, *Adolescence.* It is a well thought-out essay that provides a very good summary of the important issues raised and points made. For someone planning to read this book selectively the epilogue would be an excellent place to start.

Friedmann's book on youth is part of a series on contemporary Europe and is a very different type of endeavor from the yearbook. The author describes himself as an "essayist of liberal convictions." The book focuses on identifying the types of youth, with special emphasis on the youth movements of the sixties. Although the topic is European youth there are many examples of American incidents and references to American authors. The book is largely descriptive rather than critical.

For those interested in youth, Friedmann's book may provide a useful but somewhat sketchy introduction. The yearbook is essential reading for anyone seriously interested in the topic. It would be an excellent textbook for a course on youth, and individual chapters could be valuable reading in courses on socialization, minority groups, sex roles, work and occupations, sociology of education, family, ideology, and collective behavior.

The Soviet Soldier: Soviet Military Management at the Troop Level, by HERBERT GOLDHAMER. New York: Crane, Russak & Co., 1975. 352 pp. $17.00 cloth. $8.75 paper.

DAVID R. SEGAL
University of Maryland, College Park

This was a timely book when it appeared. Americans were beginning to realize that détente did not mean the end of tensions between the United States and the Soviet Union. The relative strength of the conscription-based Soviet Army, which mobilizes half of the military age-eligible Soviet male population, versus the all-volunteer US force, was emerging as an issue in the 1976 presidential campaign. And Marshal A. A. Grechko, the architect of the Soviet force described in this book (whose role Goldhamer underestimates) died shortly after publication of the volume.

Interestingly, many of the issues the Soviet military has confronted since the 1967 USSR Law of Universal Military Service reflect human resource problems shared by the US forces: quality of life of military families, alcoholism, relations among ethnic groups, integration of military and civilian institutions, and maintenance of civilian control of the military. Equally interesting is the fact that in a period when the US Congress has been cutting back funding for social science research in support of military personnel management, Goldhamer finds the Soviet military establishment increasingly dependent upon sociological and psychological research.

The Soviet Union has gone much further than the United States in making its military force interdependent with civilian institutions. Much military training is conducted prior to formal induction, in the context of schools, economic enterprises, voluntary associations, and summer camps. And after military service, a large proportion of veterans find they are able to use skills acquired through military training in the civilian economy.

Civilian control is maintained through the primacy of the Communist Party in Soviet society, and while the military is no more subject to such control than are other social institutions, the presence of political officers (replacing the commissars) in units of company size and above creates a dual authority structure that is problematic for the military chain of command. The presence of political officers reflects another major difference between Soviet and US military personnel resource management. Where the US seeks to build military efficiency through mastery of military skills and development of esprit de corps in combat units, the Soviet Union places far greater reliance on ideological indoctrination, and finds unit solidarity a threat to the individual soldier's loyalty to the nation-state.

In writing this book, Goldhamer was dependent upon Soviet military publications. In the United States, one would gain a different view of the military from reading *Military Review* and *Army Times* than from surveying troops, and we must assume the same holds true in the Soviet Union. Thus, the reader must be cautious in interpreting the material presented. More important, Goldhamer skims over some of the more important nuances of Soviet military organization. The reader is not told until the last chapter, for example, that Soviet military personnel estimates are inflated by the inclusion of construction troops, whose major mission is to build large-scale projects rather than to wage war. No mention is made of the railroad troops, who likewise are not primarily combat personnel. Nevertheless, this book is a worthwhile introduction to Soviet military organization.

An Introduction to Applied Sociology, by PAUL F. LAZARSFELD and JEFFREY G. REITZ. New York: Elsevier Scientific Publishing Company, 1975. 196 pp. $10.95 cloth.

MICHAEL HENNESSY
Abt Associates Inc.

In this volume the authors present a discussion of the process of utilization of social science research by planners and decision-makers. As defined here, "utilization" refers to more than simply the use of social scientific findings to inform and implement organizational and political policies but includes about all aspects of research whose ultimate aim is to define, describe, and perhaps change social or organizational structures. Therefore the major portion of the book is the presentation and elaboration of a model or sequence of the utilization process.

Of the five stages of this process, two are described and analyzed in detail. These stages (numbers 3 and 4 in the presentation) deal with the "gaps" between the existence of an empirical problem and its transformation into a research problem (step 3), and the "gaps" between the knowledge resulting from research and the practical policy recommendations which can be derived from the research (step 4 in the process).

To clarify and expand these two gaps between knowledge and practice the authors have reviewed an impressive number of studies which were conducted with the purpose of applying the results to empirical problems. These studies cover organizational, sociological, and governmental research and are presented as positive and negative exemplars of the promise and pitfalls of applied research.

I found the most interesting (and most sociological) analysis to be the discussion of the organizational determinants of social science utilization by non-social scientists in business and government. But it is exactly at this point that the book declines in clarity and quality. The purpose of the book is simply not clear. The authors refer to it as both a "text" and a "theory of utilization." It is not a text in the usual sense and most definitely not a manual for the training of applied researchers. But the authors' presentation is hardly theoretical either.

After the presentation of the sequence of utilization, the authors discuss the organizational determinants of research utilization. They acknowledge a paucity of research on these issues and yet provide no explicit perspective of their own. The book becomes a hodge-podge of research anecdotes and a jumble of interesting but unconnected ideas. The major portion of the book can best be described as a detailed agenda of future research problems in the area.

I can think of little practical purpose for this volume. It is not detailed or methodological enough to use as a text in a course on applied sociology, and practitioners will find few new insights from its recitation of the obstacles and problems in carrying out such research, issues with which they are all too familiar! It is not a theory of utilization, as the confusion within the final chapters explicitly attests. The theory of the relationship between social scientists, their products, and their clients remains to be adequately presented.

The Job Corps: A Social Experiment that Works, by SAR A. LEVITAN and BENJAMIN H. JOHNSTON. Baltimore, Md.: Johns Hopkins University Press, 1976. 117 pp. $8.00 cloth. $2.95 paper.

WILLIAM S. BENNETT
Western Michigan University

Levitan and Johnston have written one of the few inclusive descriptions of a "war on poverty" (OEO) program. The reviewer knows of no work similar to this study of the Job Corps. The book utilizes virtually every data source relevant to the confused history of the program up through 1974. In brief, their evaluation is positive, although with important qualifications.

There is no possibility here of going into a complete discussion of the Job Corps, so the reviewer will assume an understanding of the fundamentals of this important, but controversial, federal program. Its major goal was to take poor and/or disadvantaged youth and to give them a special home away from home, a kind of working-class prep school, in which they could improve their academic skills. In theory, this was to provide them with opportunities for further education or a decent job. Unfortunately, the program has been steadily cut back since its inception in 1968.

According to the authors, a few of the most meaningful results are as follows. First, general educational gains attributable to the program increased steadily through 1974. Second, gains were not evenly distributed but were greater for males and, likewise, were greater for those enrolled in rural centers rather than urban centers. Third, the findings for vocational training were similar, with the caveat that the validity of these data is not as great. Finally, there is an implication that success was especially high among the *most* disadvantaged of the enrollees.

If the book can be faulted it is that it is short on sociological analysis of the relationship of the "short happy life" of the Corps to local and national political pressure groups. This is despite a few cogent observations linking the demise of the program to its transfer to the Labor Department. (See especially page 9). In any case, the book is recommended as a fine source of descriptive data for those social scientists who may wish to do such an analysis now or in the future.

Human Systems in Extreme Environments: A Sociological Perspective, by DENNIS MILETI, THOMAS E. DRABEK, and J. EUGENE HAAS. Boulder: Institute of Behavioral Science/University of Colorado, 1975. 149 pp. No price listed, paper.

VERTA A. TAYLOR
Ohio State University, Columbus

This book, despite the somewhat more general claim made by its title, focuses specifically on how humans, individually and collectively, adapt and respond to natural disasters. Its chief virtue, for which its authors deserve much credit, is that it is the first attempt to extract, summarize, and systematically codify the wide range of empirical propositions concerning human behavior in disaster. Its chief weakness is that in neither content nor form does the book resemble what one would ordinarily take to be either a systematic or a comprehensive analysis. The authors claim to have reviewed only referred disaster research, by which they mean published research or Ph.D. dissertations, but they omit a number of significant reports and monographs whose published status is as valid as a number of the selected unreferred works they nonetheless do cite. Furthermore, although the authors state they have extracted empirical findings from several social science disciplines, the majority of these findings were derived from works in sociology and, in fact, from only six principal authors.

In reviewing disaster research, the authors' objective was not to present a system of abstract and interrelated propositions, but rather to categorize and codify empirical findings in a sociologically meaningful way. To this end, the extracted research findings were coded into a matrix derived from cross-tabulating two variables: system level and time phase of the disaster, a schema derived from Barton. One of the more important contributions of this work is that in classifying empirical findings along these two dimensions, the authors found that there is more accumulated knowledge on how the individual responds to disasters than on any other system level and that, regardless of the system level studied, over one-third of all the findings pertain to the immediate post-impact period. Having documented this, a finding of little surprise to experienced disaster researchers, the empirical findings for each time phase and system level are then presented in four chapters. Written by the three different authors, these chapters are very uneven in quality, ranging from rather well done, concise reviews of areas in some chapters to rather terse, superficial, and poorly written treatments in others.

This work is not for all sociologists. It deals with a limited range of substantive materials and offers little real sociological contribution; the reader seeking to link research findings on natural disasters with general sociological theory would do better to read Haas and Drabek's excellent book, *Complex Organizations.* Nevertheless, despite some serious flaws and perhaps inevitable omissions, this book belongs on the shelf of every disaster researcher. Although it offers nothing totally new, it summarizes the basic themes well, and points out the serious gaps in research emphasis, having as its value, therefore, a suggestion of where future disaster researchers should begin.

Children and Language: Readings in Early Language and Socialization, edited by SINCLAIR ROGERS. New York: Oxford University Press, 1975. 346 pp. $19.50 cloth.

ROBERT WILLIAMS
Goucher College

Gaining an adequate notion of the social-contextual and functional influences upon children's attainment of language requires a multidisciplinary approach. Obviously, it is unlikely that a single author would have sufficient background to do justice to this topic. Thus, Rogers has contrived this collection of twenty-one readings from previously published articles and excerpts from chapters of books representing a variety of disciplines: education, linguistics, psychology, and sociology. In selecting competent and well known authors (e.g., Robin Campbell and Roger Wales, David McNeill, Lois Bloom, M. A. K. Halliday, B. L. Whorf, Iona and Peter Opie, A. R. Luria, H. G. Furth, Eric H. Lenneberg, Heinz Werner and Edith Kaplan, Harry Osser, and Basil B. Bernstein) the editor has assured readers of informative and high quality copy.

The readings are grouped in five sections —The social contexts of language (a theoretical pro and con assessment of the role of social context in language development); The functions of language in understanding the self, the world and society; Language and the development of thinking; Language and meaning; Language and the environment (impoverished). No complaint could be made about the appropriations of the readings as assigned to the sections. I must admit that I missed Hermine Sinclair, linguist and Piagetian researcher, in the section on language and thinking. Rogers's introduction and the trite prefatory segments before the five sections and the readings are the book's previously unpublished material. The significance and value of this book might have been increased by the inclusion of some solicited original papers.

It is difficult to discern a "most" appropriate potential audience for the book. Rogers has taught linguistics and sociolinguistics and, therefore, it might not be out of order to assume that he intended the book for use as a course text. Anyone, especially the neophyte, who doesn't mind the heavy fare ($19.50) for a collection of reprints (nine of which have been published since 1969) could certainly receive some benefit from this book—particularly by way of introduction to the topic.

Urban Networks in Ch'ing China and Tokugawa Japan, by GILBERT ROZMAN. Princeton, N.J.: Princeton University Press, 1973. 355 pp. $16.50 cloth.

Urban Networks in Russia, 1750–1800, and Premodern Periodization, by GILBERT ROZMAN. Princeton, N.J.: Princeton University Press, 1976. 337 pp. $16.50 cloth.

THEDA SKOCPOL
Harvard University

These two books by Gilbert Rozman, a young sociologist at Princeton University, report results from an exciting research project in comparative history. Working with archival materials and scholarly publications in all(!)

of the relevant languages, Rozman has pulled together rich data on pre-industrial urban settlements and development for five complex and large-scale agrarian states: China, to 1900; Japan, to 1850; Russia, to 1800; France in the 1760s; and England in the 1680s. Especially for the cases of Japan, China, and Russia, a wealth of information is provided on the interrelations between urban/rural settlement patterns, on the one hand, and patterns of political administration, marketing, transportation, and class structure, on the other hand. Certainly any scholar who seeks insight into the pre-industrial social or political structures of any of these countries should be sure to consult the relevant Rozman book(s).

Yet, of course, Rozman's purpose is more ambitious than to provide aid to single-country specialists. Arguing that comparisons among premodern societies and explanations of their development are possible only in terms of an analytic framework that identifies regularities across cases, Rozman presents a basic model of seven levels of urban places. Each level represents a relative population size-category and/or a particular functional type of urban place, ranging from "national" and regional administrative capitals and inter-regional marketing centers, through provincial and local administrative seats, to intermediate and local-periodic marketing towns. This seven-level model is supposed to function *both* as the framework for comparing the urban networks of "advanced" premodern countries *and* as the key to an evolutionary scheme of "stages of development" through which all premodern societies have passed. I shall critically discuss each of these two applications of the model in turn, beginning with the latter.

Rozman claims that his approach specifies "seven stages of premodern history" and identifies "an ordered sequence of societal types," thus rendering "understandable the trend of evolutionary societal development" prior to industrialization. But it is indeed difficult for a reader to see on what evidence these hyperbolic claims are based. Rozman does not actually analyze any cases of premodern society other than the five "advanced" cases. By his own accounts, the histories of urban development of these countries were highly disparate. And each history was marked by its own pattern of zigs and zags—above all in the epochs before the achievement of stable, centralized administration of those territories now known as "France," "Russia," "China," etc. (Indeed, what exactly was "Russian society" before, say, 1500, or 1100, and was it the same entity as "Russian society" after 1700?) Moreover, when Rozman labels a premodern "stage" in terms of how many and which "levels" of urban places were present, he does not actually analyze for each stage a determinate whole pattern of organizing space. Rather, he merely retrospectively imposes definitions of levels that make sense only when all are present in one coherent network, as they are only for the final "stage." In short, Rozman does not make good his claims to reveal "seven stages of evolution in premodern countries [which] reflect seven basic patterns of organizing space. . . ."

One of Rozman's chief purposes for developing his evolutionary scheme, it must be noted, is to enable him to compare the rates of premodern development of his various cases. Thus Rozman concludes that, although Russia was "last" to advance to each successive level of urban complexity, it experienced the most rapid rate of premodern development overall, starting far "behind" the other four countries, but arriving at roughly the same stage of advanced, premodern development by 1800. Now, certainly, Rozman does make important new arguments—particularly about Russian marketing patterns and degree of commercialization in the 18th century. But full acceptance of his conclusions about rates of premodern development depends upon taking his scheme of evolutionary stages at face value. To me, the constant talk about countries being "ahead" or "behind" seems nothing short of bizarre, for I am not convinced that, for example, such diversely structured and situated countries as Sung China, feudal France, Kievan Russia, and Heian Japan were in any meaningful sense running a race—or even that they were on the same race track! Too often, Rozman forgets an important premise of fruitful comparative history: that the units to be compared and the principles of comparison should be selected and established, not once and for all in the abstract, but analysis by analysis, according to the particular explanatory problem one is attempting to solve. Tellingly, Rozman's evolutionary stage scheme is not even implicitly related to actual explanatory problems.

Where Rozman's seven-level model becomes more fruitful is where it serves as the basis for detailed comparisons of the urban hierarchies of the "advanced" premodern countries. Since England, France, Russia, Japan, and China were all, prior to the emergence of capitalism, agrarian countries that were commercially developed and administratively integrated, the seven-level model *can* be illuminating when applied across these cases. Thus, in chapter 5 of *Urban Networks in Russia,* ingeniously constructed graphs and tables, showing relative proportions of urban places and of urban population in each of the seven levels, allow us to see at a glance which countries were relatively most tightly administered (Japan, Russia), which most commercialized (England, France), which most regionally focused (France, China), and which least dichotomized between urban and rural (China). Results such as these are exciting. They constitute challenges for explanation in their own right, and they offer insights for explaining subsequent historical developments in the five countries concerned.

Nevertheless, even here, one criticism needs to be made. As ever, Rozman is so anxious to interpret all of his material in terms of his master model that he fails to notice when the model itself may be inappropriate or misleading. Thus, when it turns out that the seven-level model does not really fit late premodern England (which lacked several regional and administrative levels), Rozman resorts to an ad hoc excuse (i.e., that England is too "small in scale"—unconvincing, since Japan is also geographically small-scale and there are no reasons given for supposing that population alone should be decisive) rather than wondering whether the *distinctive* qualities of England's urban network might not help to explain why this country, as opposed to any of the other four, was the unique site of the original historical breakthroughs to capitalism in agriculture and industry.

In sum, these fascinating books should be read—by historians, area specialists, and above all, by comparative-historical sociologists—for their rich data and numerous explanatory leads. But many of the theoretical claims that Rozman makes for his urban networks approach must be regarded with skepticism and critical caution.

Handbook of Evaluation Research, vols. 1 and 2, edited by ELMER L. STRUENING and MARCIA GUTTENTAG. Beverly Hills, Calif.: Sage Publications, 1975. 1,432 pp. $25.00 each, cloth.

HOWARD E. FREEMAN
University of California, Los Angeles

In the past few years, a number of volumes of collected papers and several texts on evaluation research have been published. This spurt of publication activity is responsive both to the development of academic courses in the area and to the dramatic increase in evaluation-research support by governmental groups and private foundations. Evaluation research now is an established area of applied social research, and it is inevitable that an encyclopedia handbook would be forthcoming. The field includes investigators with a variety of academic and professional backgrounds, and thus a strong need exists for a ready source of information on the purposes, procedures, and utilization of evaluation research.

The two volumes edited by Struening and Guttentag meet the diverse needs of various participants in the field. It was undertaken with NIMH support and under the sponsorship of the Society for the Psychological Study of Social Issues. An editorial advisory committee, mostly of psychologists, provided guidance to the editors. Given the participation of NIMH and the sponsorship of SPSSI, it is not surprising that the two volumes, together totaling almost 1,500 pages, overrepresents contributions by psychologists, and emphasizes evaluation work in the mental-health field.

Although some are either reprinted articles, or modifications of papers in print, the majority of the articles have been written especially for the *Handbook*. The editors have done a fine job of piecing together the various papers so that the book flows, and the few readers sufficiently bold and energetic to read through the entire two volumes will appreciate the continuity.

There is little question of the competence of virtually all of the authors, and space does not allow a fair critique of individual chapters. I think it useful, however, to single out a few of the chapters that either provide innovative material, or are of special interest to sociologists because of their content. The chapter (by Edwards, Guttentag, and Snapper) titled "A Decision-Theoretic Approach to Evaluation Research," is a very understandable description of the Bayesian approach to evaluation research. It argues for a decision-making framework for evaluation research, rather than the experimental approach typically used by sociologists. While the chapter authors are extremely partisan in their advocacy of a Bayesian approach, it may be an attractive alternative when time, sample sizes, and data collection opportunities prevent the use of experimental and quasi-experimental approaches.

Also, there are two informative chapters on cost-benefit analysis, one by Rothenberg and a second by Levin. They provide well written expositions on the thinking of economists, and demonstrate the linkage between the evaluation research activities of sociologists (who mainly focused on impact and efficacy) and those of economists (who concern themselves with resource expenditures as well).

Evaluation researchers, particularly those distant from the policy and planning apparati, will find the Davis and Salasin chapter on utilization quite insightful. These authors have been heavily involved in the issues that surround utilization of evaluation studies, and present a codification of the concerns and issues related to the application of evaluation research. This chapter, as well as the ones by Gurel and Sjoberg, are useful commentaries on the work of evaluation researchers. Gruel considers the structural restraints and social relationships that characterize the evaluation research endeavor, while Sjoberg stresses the political and ethical issues that are relevant in evaluation research. Much of the information in these chapters is similar to the material discussed in *Social Experimentation: A Method for Planning and Evaluating Social Intervention* by Reicken and Boruch, but I suppose it is the timing of this volume's publication that accounts for a lack of references to it.

A general criticism of the *Handbook* is the tendency for some of the chapters to venture into general methodological areas. Some of the authors spend excessive time discussing standard research procedures which are used in evaluation studies without modification. A similar point could be made about the set of chapters dealing with mental health topics. Much of the material in these chapters, while interesting discussions of various orientations and approaches to the study of mental patients and treatment programs, are only by a major stretch of the imagination of special relevance to the evaluation research field.

The pages devoted to these ordinary matters might best have been saved for a more thorough treatment of issues central to evaluation research. There is a risk that every research study which has anything to do with numbers and population samples will suddenly be regarded as evaluation research. This has taken place before, as in the social indicator field, where much demographic data has been re-labeled "social indicators." Of course, there are no clear boundaries to the evaluation research field. But, simply because it is a fashionable area of activity with considerable financial support is no reason to recategorize all of the work of social research investigators as evaluations research. Doing so may deter attending to many unresolved matters of procedure and utilization in the evaluation research field.

These latter observations should by no means distract from the overall scope of the effort, and the worth of the two volumes. Editors, contributors, and the publishers merit appreciation for the timely appearance of the *Handbook of Evaluation Research.*

Aggression, 2nd ed., rev., by JOHN PAUL SCOTT. Chicago: University of Chicago Press, 1976. 233 pp. $4.95 paper.

The Making of Human Aggression: A Psychological Approach, edited by HERBERT SELG. New York: St. Martin's Press, 1976. 202 pp. $7.95 cloth.

KARL SCHONBORN
California State University, Hayward

What causes aggression? In exploring this question, Scott and Selg review the relevant empirical and theoretical knowledge from psychology, genetics, physiology, and ethology. They deal with such topics as catharsis, TV violence, psychosurgery, electrostimulation, the XYY anomaly, and the differential aggressiveness of males and females.

Scott might have entitled his book *Of Mice and Men,* had not Steinbeck beaten him to the punch. Scott describes many of his own studies of the fighting behavior of mice—as well as studies of aggression in hens, monkeys, cats, and dogs. However, he might have spent more time discussing the crucial problem of generalizing from mice to people. Humans have highly complex cultures and symbol systems which confound generalizations from nonhuman animals; and people engage in institutionalized and other kinds of aggression in which emotion and physiological arousal play little part.

Scott updates this second edition of *Aggression* with the latest studies, and he corrects a shortcoming of the first edition; he clearly acknowledges that social disorganization is an important cause of aggression. This is especially significant in the case of many studies of aggression in nonhuman animals where experiments have unwittingly disturbed social organization by altering natural sex ratios, concentrating food in certain places, or periodically adding or subtracting animals from aggregates. In this new edition, Scott also discusses how social disorganization provokes human aggression—whether the latter is externalized in crime or internalized in mental illness. Unfortunately, his discussion is incomplete since he fails to mention the work of Durkheim, Shaw, McKay, Merton, Cloward, and Ohlin. Scott does note that disorganization of genetic, physiological, and other systems can also cause aggression. His "polysystemic" theory takes this fact into account and provides a framework for understanding the interaction among the multiple factors which cause aggression.

Selg's book is actually a collection of essays by five psychologists. It attacks Freud's notion—later popularized by Lorenz, Tinbergen, Ardrey, and Morris—that human aggression is instinctive, and thus perhaps inevitable. It also attacks the frustration-aggression hypothesis of Dollard et al., which Selg claims was derived from Freud's theories concerning the accumulation and release of somatic energy. Buss, Berkowitz, Montagu, and Alland have already refuted these theories, but Selg feels that a highly polemical and "aggressive" book—such as his—is needed to clear up the misunderstandings promulgated by the widely read works of Freud, Lorenz, and others.

For Selg and Scott, social learning theory provides the best explanation of aggression. People act aggressively because they learn through imitation, identification, and instrumental conditioning that aggression can be efficient and rewarding. However, since people learn aggression through models—whether in real life or on TV—and through reinforcement, they can also *un*learn it as several behavioristic studies cited by the authors have shown.

The two books get pretty technical at times (e.g., the stimulus-response diagrams and the cross-sectional diagrams of the brain); and the authors are occasionally tedious, but this is an occupational hazard for anyone doing an extensive literature review. Nonetheless, both books are quite readable and engaging. Selg's book, however, would be improved by the inclusion of an index.

Both books should appeal to sociologists concerned with conflict, violence, or crime and of course to ethologists, biologists, psychoanalysts, and social psychologists. The books might also appeal to the sophisticated general reader or, indeed, to anyone who believes that aggression is too serious a matter to be left solely to generals—or to certain law enforcers, TV programming executives, or people given to administering severe physical punishment in the home, the school, or the playground.

Socioeconomic Methods in Educational Analysis, by WILLIAM H. WEBER, III. New York: Teachers College Press, 1975. 125 pp. $12.50 cloth. $6.50 paper.

DAVID E. DREW
The Rand Corporation

Judged either by the lofty goals set by its author, or by the more modest expectations of a reviewer interested in the subject, this book is a failure.

Weber has attempted to develop conceptual models, drawn in large part from economics, which can synthesize insights from various social science disciplines and extend them to such application areas as education. Unfortunately, the theoretical power which could make such a noble attempt succeed is missing, or, at best, well hidden in this volume.

"Socioeconomic method" is introduced early in the book. (Incidentally, "socioeconomic" as used here simply refers to this multidisciplinary technique; it does not carry the meaning sociologists usually attribute to the term.) The method consists of reducing a narrative description of a system to a series of logical or functional statements. The statements also can be, and are, presented schematically. Assumptions, drawn largely from economics, can then be made about the curves relating various concepts, and about the characteristics of the entire system of functional relationships (e.g., whether or not the system will move toward an equilibrium).

Weber has created a clever way to represent these relationships diagramatically. Essentially, he arranges four sets of coordinate axes such that each is the corner of a large rectangle. This allows him to portray not only the four bivariate relationships but also to link variables from each set with the next adjacent pair.

The technique is illustrated through a series of applications, from "macrosocietal" to "microsocietal" to "organization theoretic." It is difficult to follow the conceptual thread which guided the selection of such diverse areas as an analysis of the role of education in Plato's Republic and a model of classroom communication. The applications are not integrated substantively in this volume but simply are presented as demonstrations of the model at different levels.

The fundamental shortcoming of this work is that the model adds little or nothing to the existing statements on each of these subjects. It is essentially an outline or diagram of the concepts. For example, the reduction of

Plato's Republic to the terms required by this method does not add to the meaning of that classic.

At some points in the book, standard systems theory notions are applied to the concepts to yield predictions about a given problem area. On those occasions assumptions are made and conclusions drawn which would cause any serious student of the problem area to blanch. To illustrate from the chapters on higher education:

"Path 3 indicates a *causal* relationship between HSA (highly selective admissions) and faculty research productivity" (p. 62, emphasis added).

"Path 1 indicates that *the historical association between public higher education and non-intellectual values and orientations* serves to attract Non-Professionalized Faculty, in part due to the operation of Hypothesis 5" (p. 65, my italics).

The value of multiple objective functions in modeling the representative college or university is rejected, despite a growing literature which shows that this kind of analysis is particularly useful in studying higher education.

No serious scholar would suggest that a theorist must dutifully quote all of the relevant literature before making a genuine contribution. Nonetheless, the author overlooks major empirical and theoretical works in each application area he considers. Some of these areas have benefited from superb work in the past decade. Yet, all but a few of the references are at least ten years old.

As a result, while acronyms are created to identify every concept in a scientific-sounding manner, and while isolated studies occasionally are selected to bolster postulated relationships, the assertions made about a specific problem area simply do not ring true when compared with informed scholarly knowledge about that area.

Finally, the book could have used a thorough editing job to reduce the excessive number of tangled and turgid sentences.

The Sociology of the Arts, edited by MILDRED WEIL and DUNCAN HARTLEY. Danville, Ill.: Interstate Printers and Publishers, 1975. 179 pp. $4.40 paper.

RICHARD W. CHRISTOPHERSON
University of Redlands

This is not a remarkable collection of essays by any of the limited standards available to us for judging quality in the sociology of the arts. Perhaps its primary value is that there are so few books, of whatever quality, available in this field. The collection grew out of a college course and is suggested for use with undergraduates, but I found it to be of less value for this purpose than books previously available (including E. and T. Burns, *Sociology of Literature and Drama,* the introduction of which is cited numerous times in Weil and Hartley's introduction).

The editors include nine essays on various topics by literary persons, sociologists, philosophers, and one artist. Ben Shahn's frequently reprinted second chapter from *The Shape of Content* is perhaps the best of the lot. I also found "The Artist and the Demon," a short discussion of determinism in the arts, to be a well stated version of this perennial problem. Duncan Hartley's "Shapespeare's Living Cities," and Joseph Margolis's reprint from the *Encyclopedia Britannica,* "The Criticism of the Arts," were also well worth reading. Several of the remaining essays suffer from an annoying term paper-like quality of stating the obvious or for simply restating what has been said in more detail elsewhere. The style in some instances leaves much to be desired —I noticed one particularly intolerable sentence of over 100 words!

Computer Power and Human Reason: From Judgement to Calculation, by JOSEPH WEIZENBAUM. San Francisco: W. H. Freeman & Co., 1976. 300 pp. $9.95 cloth.

JOHN F. CROWTHER
California State University, Northridge

Weizenbaum attempts to make two simple points in this book. The first is that there are such vast differences between human beings and machines that much human thought processes can never be duplicated by computers. The second point is that there are some tasks which computers *should not* be made to do, whether or not computers *can* be made to do them.

The author develops a complex and compelling argument for his first point, in the course of which he presents the reader with an interesting parade of such things as Turing machines, compulsive programmers, artificial intelligence, and functional differences between the brain's hemispheres. He also offers his own criticisms of some of B. F. Skinner's ideas.

The author's argument for his second point is simple, moralistic, and less than compelling.

In one illustration he simply states that it is obscene even to think about producing a machine-animal symbiont in which a computer is coupled with the brain and visual system of an animal. In another illustration, he denounces as immoral any attempt to use computers in psychotherapy because they cannot provide the required human respect, understanding, and love. In still another illustration, he expresses apprehension about the potential for misuse in surveillance activities of computer systems which could recognize and understand human speech.

This book could serve as a source of some comfort for humanistic sociologists. It has little to offer, however, to sociologists who are interested in using the computer as a tool for furthering our understanding of society.

PUBLICATIONS RECEIVED

(Listing of a publication below does not assure nor preclude its subsequent review.)

ABADAN-UNAT, NERMIN. *Turkish Workers in Europe, 1960–1975: A Socio-Economic Reappraisal.* E. J. Brill, 1976. 424 pp. NPL, cloth.

ABRAMS, PHILIP, and McCULLOCH, ANDREW. *Communes, Sociology and Society.* Cambridge University Press, 1976. 239 pp. $16.95 cloth. $5.95 paper.

ADORNO, THEODOR W. *Introduction to the Sociology of Music.* Tr. E. B. Ashton. Seabury, 1976. 233 pp. $12.95 cloth.

AHMED, AKBAR S. *Millennium and Charisma among Pathans: A Critical Essay in Social Anthropology.* Routledge & Kegan Paul, 1976. 173 pp. $12.00 cloth.

ALEXANDER, HERBERT E. *Financing the 1972 Election.* Lexington Books, 1976. 771 pp. $21.95 cloth.

ANYASODO, UMUNNAKWE P. *Ebolachi: Have You Survived the Night?* Harlo, 1975. 168 pp. NPL, paper.

ASHLINE, NELSON F.; PEZZULLO, THOMAS R.; and NORRIS, CHARLES I., eds. *Education, Inequality, and National Policy.* Lexington Books, 1976. 199 pp. $14.00 cloth.

ASTIN, ALEXANDER W. *Academic Gamesmanship: Student-Oriented Change in Higher Education.* Praeger, 1976. 209 pp. $17.50 cloth.

ASTIN, HELEN S., ed. *Some Action of Her Own: The Adult Woman and Higher Education.* Lexington Books, 1976. 180 pp. $14.50 cloth.

BAKER, KEITH, et al. *Comprehensive Services to Rural Poor Families: An Evaluation of the Arizona Job Colleges Program.* Praeger, 1976. 191 pp. $17.50 cloth.

BALSIGER, DAVE, and SELLIER, CHARLES E., JR. *In Search of Noah's Ark.* Sun Classic Books, 1976. 218 pp. $1.95 paper.

BANKOWSKI, ZENON, and MUNGHAM, GEOFF. *Images of Law.* Routledge & Kegan Paul, 1976. 178 pp. $7.75 paper.

BARON, SALO W. *The Russian Jew under Tsars and Soviets,* 2nd ed., rev., enlg. Macmillan, 1976. 468 pp. $14.95 cloth.

BAUMAN, ZYGMUNT. *Towards a Critical Sociology: An Essay on Commonsense and Emancipation.* Routledge & Kegan Paul, 1976. 115 pp. $6.75 cloth.

BENN, S. I., and MORTIMORE, G. W., eds. *Rationality and the Social Sciences: Contributions to the Philosophy and Methodology of the Social Sciences.* Routledge & Kegan Paul, 1976. 416 pp. $23.50 cloth.

BLACK, MAX, ed. *The Social Theories of Talcott Parsons: A Critical Examination,* with a new afterword by Talcott Parsons. Southern Illinois University Press, 1976. 270 pp. $3.95 paper.

BLACKEY, ROBERT, and PAYNTON, CLIFFORD. *Revolution and the Revolutionary Ideal.* Schenkman, 1976. 295 pp. $9.50 cloth. $4.95 paper.

BLAXALL, MARTHA, and REAGAN, BARBARA, eds. *Women and the Workplace: The Implications of Occupational Segregation.* University of Chicago Press, 1976. 326 pp. $3.95 paper.

BLONG, CLAIR KARL, proceedings coordinator. *Systems Thinking and the Quality of Life: Proceedings of the Annual North American Meeting, 1975.* Society for General Systems Research, 1975. 627 pp. $15.00 paper.

BLUMIN, STUART M. *The Urban Threshold: Growth and Change in a Nineteenth-Century American Community.* University of Chicago Press, 1976. 298 pp. $16.50 cloth.

BOALT, GUNNAR, et al. *Communication and Communication Barriers in Sociology.* Halsted, 1976. 163 pp. $19.50 cloth.

BROW, JAMES, ed. *Population Land and Structural Change in Sri Lanka and Thailand.* E. J. Brill, 1976. 112 pp. NPL, paper.

BRUUN, KETTIL, et al. *Alcohol Control Policies in Public Health Perspective.* Finnish Foundation for Alcohol Studies/World Health Organization Regional Office for Europe/Addiction Research Foundation of Ontario, dist. by Rutgers Center of Alcohol Studies, 1975. 106 pp. $8.00 cloth.

BUDGE, IAN; CREWE, IVOR; and FARLIE, DENNIS, eds. *Party Identification and Beyond: Representations of Voting and Party Competition.* Wiley, 1976. 393 pp. $24.95 cloth.

BULLOUGH, VERN L. *Sex, Society, and History.* Science History Publications, 1976. 185 pp. $10.00 cloth. $4.95 paper.

BURNS, REX. *Success in America: The Yeoman Dream and the Industrial Revolution.* University of Massachusetts Press, 1976. 212 pp. NPL, cloth.

CAMPBELL, W. H. *The Emperor is Dying: Five Steps toward Healthy Restructuring of an Organization.* Vantage, 1976. 90 pp. $4.95 cloth.

CAPLAN, GERALD, and KILLILEA, MARIE, eds. *Support Systems and Mutual Help: Multidisciplinary Explorations.* Grune & Stratton, 1976. 325 pp. $19.50 cloth.

CARLSON, RICK J. *The Dilemmas of Corrections.* Lexington Books, 1976. 174 pp. $15.00 cloth.

CARNOY, MARTIN, and LEVIN, HENRY M. *The Limits of Educational Reform.* David McKay, 1976. 290 pp. $4.95 paper.

CARROLL, BERENICE A., ed. *Liberating Women's History: Theoretical and Critical Essays.* University of Illinois Press, 1976. 434 pp. $14.95 cloth. $5.95 paper.

CARTER, EDWARD C., II; FORSTER, ROBERT; and MOODY, JOSEPH N., eds. *Enterprise and Entrepreneurs in Nineteenth- and Twentieth-Century France.* Johns Hopkins University Press, 1976. 207 pp. NPL, cloth.

CARTER, HUGH, and GLICK, PAUL C. *Marriage and Divorce: A Social and Economic Study,* rev. ed. Harvard University Press, 1976. 508 pp. $17.50 cloth.

CARVAJAL, M. J., and GEITHMAN, DAVID T. *Family Planning and Family Size Determination: The Evidence from Seven Latin American Cities.* University of Florida Press, 1976. 96 pp. $5.00 cloth.

CASSINELLI, C. W. *Total Revolution: A Comparative Study of Germany under Hitler, the Soviet Union under Stalin, and China under Mao.* Clio Books, 1976. 252 pp. $19.75 cloth. $6.25 paper.

CASUE. *The Warbabies' Statement.* Exposition, 1976. 127 pp. $4.00 cloth.

CATER, DOUGLASS, and NYHAN, MICHAEL J., eds. *The Future of Public Broadcasting.* Praeger, 1976. 372 pp. $18.50 cloth. $6.95 paper.

CHAPLIN, DAVID, ed. *Peruvian Nationalism: A Corporatist Revolution.* Transaction Books, 1976. 494 pp. $19.95 cloth. $6.95 paper.

CHEATWOOD, DERRAL, and LINDQUIST, THEROLD. *The Human Image: Sociology and Photography.* State University College of New York, 1976. 60 pp. NPL, paper.

CLAUDE, RICHARD P., ed. *Comparative Human Rights.* Johns Hopkins University Press, 1976. 410 pp. $16.50 cloth.

COHEN, ALBERT K.; COLE, GEORGE F.; and BAILEY, ROBERT G., eds. *Prison Violence.* Lexington Books, 1976. 186 pp. $16.50 cloth.

CONZEN, KATHLEEN NEILS. *Immigrant Milwaukee, 1836–1860: Accommodation and Community in a*

Frontier City. Harvard University Press, 1976, 300 pp. $16.50 cloth.
DAVID, MYRIAM, and LÉZINE, IRÈNE. *Early Child Care in France*. Gordon & Breach, 1976. 148 pp. $10.95 cloth.
DEAN, ALFRED; KRAFT, ALAN M.; and PEPPER, BERT, eds. *The Social Setting of Mental Health*. Basic Books, 1975. 405 pp. $17.50 cloth.
DEITCH, LILLIAN, and WEINSTEIN, DAVID. *Prepaid Legal Services: Socioeconomic Impacts*. Lexington Books, 1976. 236 pp. $13.00 cloth.
DOETSCH, RAYMOND N. *Journey to the Green and Golden Lands: The Epic of Survival on the Wagon Trail*. Kennikat, 1976. 112 pp. $9.95 cloth.
DRUMMOND, DOUGLAS S. *Police Culture*. Sage, 1976. 45 pp. $3.00 paper.
DUNBAR, TONY, and KRAVITZ, LINDA. *Hard Traveling: Migrant Farm Workers in America*. Ballinger, 1976. 158 pp. $13.50 cloth.
DUNMORE, CHARLOTTE J. *Black Children and Their Families: A Bibliography*. R and E Research Associates, 1976. 103 pp. $9.00 paper.
EARLE, JOHN R.; KNUDSEN, DEAN D.; and SHRIVER, DONALD W., JR., eds. *Spinoles and Spires: A Re-Study of Religion and Social Change in Gastonia*. John Knox Press, 1976. 382 pp. $5.95 paper.
EULAU, HEINZ, and CZUDNOWSKI, MOSHE M., eds. *Elite Recruitment in Democratic Polities: Comparative Studies Across Nations*. Halsted, 1976. 299 pp. $17.50 cloth.
FABER, BERNARD LEWIS, ed. *The Social Structure of Eastern Europe: Transition and Process in Czechoslovakia, Hungary, Poland, Romania, and Yugoslavia*. Praeger, 1976. 423 pp. $25.00 cloth.
FIELD, MARK G., ed. *Social Consequences of Modernization in Communist Societies*. Johns Hopkins University Press, 1976. 277 pp. $14.50 cloth.
FRANCIS, E. K. *Interethnic Relations: An Essay in Sociological Theory*. Elsevier, 1976. 432 pp. $22.50 cloth.
FREEMAN, RICHARD B. *The Overeducated American*. Academic Press, 1976. 218 pp. $12.00 cloth.
FRIEDLANDER, WALTER A., ed. *Concepts and Methods of Social Work*, 2nd ed. Prentice-Hall, 1976. 243 pp. NPL, cloth.
GAEV, DOROTHY MEYER. *The Psychology of Loneliness*. Adams, 1976. 160 pp. $3.95 paper.
GLOCK, CHARLES, and BELLAH, ROBERT N., eds. *The New Religious Consciousness*. University of California Press, 1976. 391 pp. $14.95 cloth.
GOLDIN, CLAUDIA DALE. *Urban Slavery in the American South, 1820–1860: A Quantitative History*. University of Chicago Press, 1976. 168 pp. $12.95 cloth.
GOLDMAN, NANCY L., and SEGAL, DAVID R., eds. *The Social Psychology of Military Service*. Sage, 1976. 299 pp. $17.50 cloth. $7.50 paper.
GORDON, RICHARD L. *Coal and Canada-U.S. Energy Relations*. National Planning Association, 1976. 75 pp. $3.00 paper.
GREELEY, ANDREW M. *Ethnicity, Denomination, and Inequality*. Sage, 1976. 85 pp. $3.00 paper.
GREENE, RICHARD. *Assuring Quality in Medical Care: The State of the Art*. Ballinger, 1976. 293 pp. $17.50 cloth.
GRIMES, ORVILLE F., JR. *Housing for Low-Income Urban Families: Economics and Policy in the Developing World*. Johns Hopkins University Press, 1976. 176 pp. $11.00 cloth. $3.65 paper.
GRUNIG, JAMES E. *Decline of the Global Village: How Specialization is Changing the Mass Media*. General Hall, 1976. 297 pp. NPL, paper.
GUNARATNE, SHELTON A. *Modernisation and Knowledge: A Study of Four Ceylonese Villages*. Asian Mass Communication Research and Information Centre, 1976. 92 pp. $12.00 paper.
GUNDELACH, PETER, and REDDER, K. W. *Arbejdskraftens mobilitet 3: Omfanget* (The Scope of Labour Mobility). Danish National Institute of Social Research, 1976. 110 pp. NPL, paper.
HALLOWELL, A. IRVING. *Contributions to Anthropology: Selected Papers*. University of Chicago Press, 1976. 534 pp. $24.00 cloth.
HARRÉ, R., ed., *Life Sentences: Aspects of the Social Role of Language*. Wiley, 1976. 178 pp. $12.50 cloth. $4.95 paper.
HARRIS, WILLIAM M. *Black Community Development*. R and E Research Associates, 1976. 118 pp. $9.00 paper.
HART, DAVID MONTGOMERY. *The Aith Waryaghar of the Moroccan Rif: An Ethnography and History*. University of Arizona Press, 1976. 556 pp. $20.00 paper.
HARTZLER, H. RICHARD. *Justice, Legal Systems, and Social Structure*. Kennikat, 1976. 134 pp. $12.50 cloth.
HAZAN, BARUCH A. *Soviet Propaganda: A Case Study of the Middle East Conflict*. Transaction Books, 1976. 293 pp. $12.95 cloth.
HERZ, JOHN H. *The Nation-State and the Crisis of World Politics: Essays on International Politics in the Twentieth Century*. David McKay, 1976. 307 pp. $4.95 paper.
HICKEY, THOMAS J. *Introduction of Metascience: An Information Science Approach to Methodology of Scientific Research*, Thomas J. Hickey, 1976. 74 pp. NPL, paper.
HIESTAND, DALE L., and OSTOW, MIRIAM, eds. *Health Manpower Information for Policy Guidance: Report of a Conference Sponsored by Conservation of Human Resources, Columbia University*. Ballinger, 1976. 149 pp. $14.00 cloth.
HILTON, GORDON. *Intermediate Politometrics*. Columbia University Press, 1976. 282 pp. $15.00 cloth.
HOGE, DEAN R. *Commitment on Campus: Changes in Religion and Values over Five Decades*. Westminster, 1974. 239 pp. $10.00 cloth.
HOGE, DEAN R. *Division in the Protestant House: The Basic Reasons Behind Intra-Church Conflicts*. Westminster, 1976. 166 pp. $3.95 paper.
HOLZER, MARC, ed. *Productivity in Public Organizations*. Kennikat Press, 1976. 328 pp. $18.50 cloth. $8.95 paper.
HORNSTEIN, HARVEY A. *Cruelty and Kindness: A New Look at Aggression and Altruism*. Prentice-Hall, 1976. 154 pp. $7.95 cloth. $2.95 paper.
HORVAT, BRANKO; MARKOVIC, MIHAILO; and SUPEK, RUDI, eds. *Self-Governing Socialism: A Reader*, vols. 1 and 2. International Arts & Sciences Press, 1975. 490 and 327 pp. $21.50 and $18.50 cloth. $9.95 and $8.95 paper.
INKELES, ALEX, ed. and COLEMAN, JAMES and SMELSER, NEIL, assoc. eds. *Annual Review of Sociology*, vol. 2. Annual Reviews, 1976. 436 pp. $17.50 cloth.
ITZKOFF, SEYMOUR, W. *A New Public Education*. David McKay, 1976. 372 pp. $5.95 paper.
JACOBS, SIDNEY. *The Right to a Decent House*. Routledge & Kegan Paul, 1976. 161 pp. $9.50 paper.
JEFFERY, PATRICIA. *Migrants and Refugees: Muslim and Christian Pakistani Families in Bristol*. Cambridge University Press, 1976. 221 pp. $12.95 cloth.
JIRYIS, SABRI. *The Arabs in Israel*. Monthly Review Press, 1976. 214 pp. $12.50 cloth.
JONES, DAVID A. *The Health Risks of Imprisonment*. Lexington Books, 1976. 229 pp. $17.00 cloth.
KAHL, JOSEPH A. *Modernization, Exploitation and Dependency in Latin America: Germani, González Casanova, and Cardoso*. Transaction Books, 1976. 215 pp. $5.95 paper.
KARAN, PRADYUMNA P. *The Changing Face of Tibet: The Impact of Chinese Communist Ideology on the Landscape*. University Press of Kentucky, 1976. 114 pp. $18.50 cloth.
KASINSKY RENÉE G. *Refugees from Militarism: Draft-Age Americans in Canada*. Transaction Books, 1976. 301 pp. $14.95 cloth.
KEKES, JOHN. *A Justification of Rationality*. State University of New York Press, 1976. 275 pp. $20.00 cloth.
KENNEDY, KIERAN A., compiler. *The ESRI Research Plan 1976–80 and Background Analysis*. Economic and Social Research Institute, 1976. 72 pp. NPL, paper.
KIRSHENBLATT-GIMBLETT, BARBARA, ed. *Speech Play: Research and Resources for Studying Linguistic Creativity*. University of Pennsylvania Press, 1976. 307 pp. $15.00 cloth.
KLEIN, MALCOLM W., ed. *The Juvenile Justice System*. Sage, 1976. 287 pp. $17.50 cloth. $7.50 paper.
KOESTLER, ARTHUR. *The Thirteenth Tribe: The Khazar Empire and Its Heritage*. Random House, 1976. 255 pp. $8.95 cloth.
KRICKUS, RICHARD. *Pursuing the American Dream: White Ethnics and the New Populism*. Anchor Press, 1976. $3.95 paper.
KROGER, WILLIAM S., and FEZLER, WILLIAM D. *Hypnosis and Behavior Modification: Imagery Conditioning*. J. B. Lippincott, 1976. 426 pp. $21.00 cloth.
LAN, DEAN. *Prestige with Limitations: Realities of the Chinese-American Elite*. R and E Research Associates, 1976. 75 pp. $8.00 paper.
LAUMANN, EDWARD O., and PAPPI, FRANZ U. *Networks of Collective Action: A Perspective on Community Influence Systems*. Academic Press, 1976. 329 pp. NPL, cloth.
LELAND, JOY. *Firewater Myths: North American Indian Drinking and Alcohol Addiction*. Rutgers Center of Alcohol Studies, 1976. 158 pp. $7.50 cloth.
LENNON, JOHN J. *A Comparative Study of the Patterns of Acculturation of Selected Puerto Rican Protestant and Roman Catholic Families in an Urban Metropolitan Area*. R and E Research Associates, 1976. 148 pp. $10.00 paper.
LEVINE, ELAINE SUE. *Ethnic Esteem among Anglo, Black, and Chicano Children*. R and E Research Associates, 1976. 133 pp. $9.00 paper.

LIEBERT, ROLAND J. *Disintegration and Political Action: The Changing Functions of City Governments in America.* Academic Press, 1976. 223 pp. $12.00 cloth.
LIEBMAN, SEYMOUR B. *Exploring the Latin American Mind.* Nelson-Hall, 1976. 192 pp. $11.00 cloth.
LIN, NAN. *Foundations of Social Research.* McGraw-Hill, 1976. 458 pp. NPL, cloth.
LINDBERG, LEON N. *Politics and the Future of Industrial Society.* David McKay, 1976. 286 pp. $12.50 cloth. $6.95 paper.
LIPSET, SEYMOUR MARTIN. *Rebellion in the University,* 2nd ed. University of Chicago Press, 1976. 310 pp. $4.95 paper.
LOEHLIN, JOHN C., and NICHOLS, ROBERT C. *Heredity, Environment, and Personality: A Study of 850 Sets of Twins.* University of Texas Press, 1976. 202 pp. $8.95 cloth.
MACFARLANE, ALAN. *Resources and Population: A Study of the Gurungs of Nepal.* Cambridge University Press, 1976. 364 pp. $32.50 cloth.
MACKENZIE, KENNETH D. *A Theory of Group Structures. Volume 1: Basic Theory. Volume 2: Empirical Tests.* Gordon & Breach, 1976. 465 pp. $17.50 and $15.50 cloth ($28.00 set).
MADDEN, DENIS J., and LION, JOHN R., eds. *Rage, Hate, Assault and Other Forms of Violence.* Spectrum, dist. by Halsted, 1976. 265 pp. NPL, cloth.
MAGID, ALVIN. *Men in the Middle: Leadership and Role Conflict in a Nigerian Society.* Africana, division of Holmes & Meier, 1976. 292 pp. $25.00 cloth.
MALALGODA, KITSIRI. *Buddhism in Sinhalese Society, 1750–1900: A Study of Religious Revival and Change.* University of California Press, 1976. 300 pp. $16.50 cloth.
MALLET, SERGE. *Essays on the New Working Class.* Ed. and trans. by Dick Howard and Dean Savage. Telos Press, 1975. 224 pp. $3.50 paper.
MAMDANI, MAHMOOD. *Politics and Class Formation in Uganda.* Monthly Review Press, 1976. 339 pp. $16.50 cloth.
MARCH, JAMES G., and OLSEN, JOHAN P. *Ambiguity and Choice in Organizations.* Universitetsforlaget, 1976. 408 pp. $20.00 paper.
MARIEN, MICHAEL. *Societal Directions and Alternatives: A Critical Guide to the Literature.* Information for Policy Design, 1976. 400 pp. $16.50 paper.
MARTY, MARTIN E. *A Nation of Behavers.* University of Chicago Press, 1976. 239 pp. $8.95 cloth.
MASSERMEN, JULES H., ed. *Social Psychiatry, Volume 2: The Range of Normal in Human Behavior.* Grune & Stratton, 1976. 161 pp. $16.50 cloth.
MATTHEWS, RALPH. *"There's No Better Place Than Here": Social Change in Three Newfoundland Communities.* Peter Martin, 1976. 164 pp. $8.95 cloth. $3.95 paper.
McDONALD, LYNN. *The Sociology of Law and Order.* Westview, 1976. 340 pp. $24.75 cloth.
MEHRABIAN, ALBERT. *Public Places and Private Spaces: The Psychology of Work, Play, and Living Environments.* Basic Books, 1976. 354 pp. $15.95 cloth.
MEHROTRA, R. K., coordinator. *Mass Communication in India: An Annotated Bibliography.* Asian Mass Communication Research & Information Centre, 1976. 216 pp. $18.00 paper.
MERKIN, DONALD H. *Pregnancy as a Disease: The Pill in Society.* Kennikat, 1976. 134 pp. $9.95 cloth.
MESHACK, B. A. *Is the Baptist Church Relevant to the Black Community.* R and E Research Associates, 1976. 98 pp. NPL, paper.
MILLER, DAVID M., and WERTZ, DOROTHY C. *Hindu Monastic Life: The Monks and Monasteries of Bhubaneswar.* Queen's University Press, 1976. 228 pp. $22.00 cloth. $9.95 paper.
MONTENEGRO, MARILYN. *Chicanos and Mexican-Americans: Ethnic Self-Identification and Attitudinal Differences.* R and E Research Associates, 1976. 74 pp. $8.00 paper.
MOSCOVICI, SERGE. *Society Against Nature: The Emergence of Human Societies.* Trans. by Sacha Rabinovitch. Humanities Press, 1976. 158 pp. $16.25 cloth.
MULHEARN, JOHN, and MOMENY, GAYLE. *The Psychiatric Hospital Today: A Quality Profile.* Ballinger, 1976. 138 pp. $15.00 cloth.
MUMGHAM, GEOFF, and PEARSON, GEOFF, eds. *Working Class Youth Culture.* Routledge & Kegan Paul, 1976. 167 pp. $7.75 paper.
MURNAGHAN, JANE H., ed. *Long-Term Care Data: Report of the Conference on Long-Term Health Care Data.* J. B. Lippincott, 1976. 233 pp. NPL, paper.
NELLI, HUMBERT S. *The Business of Crime: Italians and Syndicate Crime in the United States.* Oxford University Press, 1976. 314 pp. $12.95 cloth.
NOVAK, MICHAEL. *The Joy of Sports: End Zones, Bases, Baskets, Balls, and the Consecration of the American Spirit.* Basic Books, 1976. 357 pp. $10.95 cloth.
NSPCC. *At Risk: An Account of the Work of the Battered Child Research Department, NSPCC.* Routledge & Kegan Paul, 1976. 246 pp. $10.25 paper.
NURCOMBE, BARRY. *Children of the Dispossessed: A Consideration of the Nature of Intelligence, Cultural Disadvantage, Educational Programs for Culturally Different People, and of the Development and Expression of a Profile of Competencies.* University Press of Hawaii, 1976. 270 pp. $7.75 paper.
O'CONNOR, JAMES. *The Fiscal Crisis of the State.* St. Martin's, 1973. 276 pp. $12.95 cloth.
OLDENBURG, PHILIP. *Big City Government in India: Councilor, Administrator, and Citizen in Delhi.* University of Arizona Press, 1976. 400 pp. $9.50 cloth. $4.95 paper.
ORNSTEIN, ALLAN C., and MILLER, STEVEN I., eds. *Policy Issues in Education.* Lexington Books, 1976. 159 pp. $15.00 cloth.
ORTMAYER, LOUIS L. *Conflict, Compromise, and Conciliation: West German-Polish Normalization 1966–1976.* University of Denver/Graduate School of International Studies, 1975. 162 pp. NPL, paper.
OSTHEIMER, JOHN M., and RITT, LEONARD G. *Environment, Energy, and Black Americans.* Sage, 1976. 38 pp. $3.00 paper.
OSTROM, ELINOR, ed. *The Delivery of Urban Services: Outcomes of Change.* Sage, 1976. 320 pp. $17.50 cloth. $7.50 paper.
OWEN, A. L. RIESCH. *Selig Perlman's Lectures on Capitalism and Socialism.* University of Wisconsin Press, 1976. 183 pp. $12.50 cloth.
PÉREZ, LOUIS A., JR. *Army Politics in Cuba, 1898–1958.* University of Pittsburgh Press, 1976. 240 pp. $9.95 cloth.
PERISTIANY, J. G., ed. *Mediterranean Family Structures.* Cambridge University Press, 1976. 414 pp. $32.50 cloth.
PERKINSON, HENRY J. *Two Hundred Years of American Educational Thought.* David McKay, 1976. 367 pp. $5.95 paper.
PERLMAN, HARVEY, and JASZI, PETER. *Legal Issues in Addict Diversion.* Lexington Books, 1976. 123 pp. $12.50 cloth.
PESCATELLO, ANN M. *Power and Pawn: The Female In Iberian Families, Societies, and Cultures.* Greenwood, 1976. 281 pp. $15.95 cloth.
PICKVANCE, C. G., ed. *Urban Sociology: Critical Essays.* St. Martin's, 1976. 223 pp. $14.95 cloth.
POPE, WHITNEY. *Durkheim's Suicide: A Classic Analyzed.* University of Chicago Press, 1976. 229 pp. $13.00 cloth.
REYNOLDS, DAVID K., and FAREBEROW, NORMAN L. *Suicide: Inside and Out.* University of California Press. 1976. 232 pp. $10.95 cloth.
RIPPA, S. ALEXANDER. *Education in a Free Society: An American History,* 3rd ed. David McKay, 1976. 436 pp. $6.95 paper.
ROBERTS, JOAN I., ed. *Beyond Intellectual Sexism: A New Woman, A New Reality.* David McKay, 1976. 386 pp. $14.95 cloth. $7.95 paper.
ROBERTS, JOAN I., and AKINSANYA, SHERRIE K. *Educational Patterns and Cultural Configurations: The Anthropology of Education.* David McKay, 1976. 412 pp. $7.95 paper.
ROBERTS, JOAN I., and AKINSANYA, SHERRIE K. *Schooling in the Cultural Context: Anthropological Studies of Education.* David McKay, 1976. 479 pp. $8.95 paper.
RODNITZKY, JEROME L. *Minstrels of the Dawn: The Folk-Protest Singer as a Cultural Hero.* Nelson-Hall, 1976. 192 pp. $9.95 cloth. $4.95 paper.
ROSENBAUM, JAMES E. *Making Inequality: The Hidden Curriculum of High School Tracking.* Wiley, 1976. 238 pp. $13.95 cloth.
ROSENBERG, NATHAN. *Perspectives on Technology.* Cambridge University Press, 1976. 353 pp. $24.95 cloth. $6.95 paper.
ROSENTHAL, DONALD B., ed. *The City in Indian Politics.* Thomson Press (India), 1976. 256 pp. NPL, cloth.
ROSENTHAL, JOEL T. *Nobles and the Noble Life, 1295–1500.* Barnes & Noble, 1976. 207 pp. $15.00 cloth.
ROSENTHAL, ROBERT, et al. *Different Strokes: Pathways to Maturity in the Boston Ghetto.* Westview, 1976. 358 pp. $6.50 paper.
ROSENTHAL, ROBERT. *Experimenter Effects in Behavioral Research,* enlg. ed. Halsted, 1976. 500 pp. $15.95 cloth.
ROSSI, PETER H., and LYALL, KATHARINE C. *Reforming Public Welfare: A Critique of the Negative Income Tax Experiment.* Russel Sage, 1976. 197 pp. $10.00 cloth.
ROSSMAN, PARKER. *Sexual Experience Between Men and Boys: Exploring the Pederast Underground.* Association Press, 1976. 247 pp. $10.95 cloth.
ROTHMAN, WILLIAM A. *A Bibliography of Collective Bargaining in Hospitals and Related Facilities, 1972–1974.* New York State School of Industrial & Labor Relations/Cornell University, 1976. 139 pp. $14.25 cloth. $6.00 paper.
SALERT, BARBARA. *Revolutions and Revolutionaries: Four Theories.* Elsevier, 1976. 161 pp. $9.50 cloth.

SAMUELS, FRANK G. *The Negro Tavern: A Microcosm of Slum Life.* R and E Research Associates, 1976. 115 pp. $10.00 paper.
SCHILLER, BRADLEY R. *The Economics of Poverty and Discrimination,* 2nd ed. Prentice-Hall, 1976. 241 pp. NPL, paper.
SCHNAPPER-ARNDT, GOTTLIEB. *Hoher Taunus: Eine sozialstatistische Untersuchung in fünf Dorfgemeinden.* (Originally pub. in 1888.) Verlag für Demoskopie, 1975. 249 pp. NPL, cloth.
SELIGER, M. *Ideology and Politics.* Free Press, 1976. 352 pp. $14.95 cloth.
SEWELL, WILLIAM H.; HAUSER, ROBERT M.; and FEATHERMAN, DAVID L. *Schooling and Achievement in American Society.* Academic Press, 1976. 535 pp. $24.00 cloth.
SHIPMAN, MARTEN, ed. *The Organisation and Impact of Social Research: Six Original Case Studies in Education and Behavioural Science.* Routledge & Kegan Paul, 1976. 155 pp. $8.50 paper.
SHIVJI, ISSA G. *Class Struggles in Tanzania.* Monthly Review Press, 1976. 182 pp. $9.50 cloth.
SINGH, HARJINDER. *Authority and Influence in Two Sikh Villages.* Sterling, 1976. 219 pp. NPL, cloth.
SMART, BARRY. *Sociology, Phenomenology and Marxian Analysis: A Critical Discussion of the Theory and Practice of a Science of Society* Routledge & Kegan Paul, 1976. 206 pp. $16.00 cloth. $13.25 paper.
SMELSER, NEIL J. *Comparative Methods in the Social Sciences.* Prentice-Hall, 1976. 253 pp. $7.50 paper.
SMITH, BARDWELL L., ed. *Religion and Social Conflict in South Asia.* E. J. Brill, 1976. 117 pp. NPL, cloth.
SORKIN, ALAN L. *Health Economics in Developing Countries.* Lexington Books, 1976. 200 pp. $16.00 cloth.
SPARROW, JANE. *Diary of a Delinquent Episode.* Routledge & Kegan Paul, 1976. 130 pp. $5.25 paper.
SPRING, JOEL. *The Sorting Machine: National Educational Policy since 1945.* David McKay, 1976. 309 pp. $4.95 paper.
STEPHENS, JOYCE. *Loners, Losers, and Lovers: Elderly Tenants in a Slum Hotel.* University of Washington Press, 1976. 118 pp. $8.95 cloth.
STROMAN, DUANE F. *The Medical Establishment and Social Responsibility.* Kennikat, 1976. 193 pp. $12.95 cloth.
STUBBS, MICHAEL, and DELAMONT, SARA, eds. *Explorations in Classroom Observation.* Wiley, 1976. 221 pp. $14.95 cloth.
SUDMAN, SEYMOUR. *Applied Sampling.* Academic Press, 1976. 249 pp. $11.50 cloth.
SUNG, BETTY LEE. *Chinese American Manpower and Employment.* Department of Asian Studies/CUNY, 1975. 365 pp. NPL, paper.
TAFT, JOHN. *Mayday at Yale: A Case Study in Student Radicalism.* Westview, 1976. 224 pp. $12.50 cloth.
TAMBIAH, S. J. *World Conqueror and World Renouncer: A Study of Buddhism and Polity in Thailand against a Historical Background.* Cambridge University Press, 1976. 557 pp. $37.50 cloth.
TATE, WILL D. *The New Black Urban Elites.* R and E Research Associates, 1976. 107 pp. $10.00 paper.
VASUDEVA, PROMILA. *Social Change: An Analysis of Attitudes and Personality.* Sterling, 1976. 224 pp. NPL, cloth.
VIDICH, CHARLES. *The New York Cab Driver and His Fare.* Schenkman, 1976. 186 pp. $11.25 cloth. $5.95 paper.
VOGT, EVON Z. *Tortillas for the Gods: A Symbolic Analysis of Zinacanteco Rituals.* Harvard University Press, 1976. 234 pp. $16.50 cloth.
WALROND-SKINNER, SUE. *Family Therapy: The Treatment of Natural Systems.* Routledge & Kegan Paul, 1976. 164 pp. $14.50 cloth. $7.25 paper.
WEHR, PAUL, and WASHBURN, MICHAEL. *Peace and World Order Systems: Teaching and Research.* Sage, 1976. 255 pp. $12.00 cloth. $7.00 paper.
WESTBY, DAVID L. *The Clouded Vision: The Student Movement in the United States in the 1960s.* Bucknell University Press, 1976. 291 pp. $12.00 cloth.
WHEELER, STANTON, ed. *On Record: Files and Dossiers in American Life.* Transaction Books, 1976. 449 pp. $6.95 paper.
WICKLUND, ROBERT A., and BREHM, JACK W. *Perspectives on Cognitive Dissonance.* Lawrence Erlbaum, dist. by Halsted, 1976. 349 pp. $16.50 cloth.
WIDICK, B. J., ed. *Auto Work and Its Discontents.* Johns Hopkins University Press, 1976. 112 pp. $8.00 cloth. $2.95 paper.
WIEGAND, DIETMAR. *Professioneller Status und Kontrolle über ein (symbolisches) soziales Object am Beispiel des wissenschaftrichen Bibliothekars: Ein Beitrag zur professionssoziologischen Theorie und Kasuistik.* Herbert Lang, 1976. 193 pp. NPL, paper.
WILLIE, CHARLES VERT. *A New Look at Black Families.* General Hall, 1976. 211 pp. NPL, paper.
WILSON, BRYAN. *Contemporary Transformations of Religion: The Riddell Memorial Lectures, Forty-fifth Series Delivered at the University of Newcastle upon Tyne on 2, 3, 4 December 1974.* Oxford University Press, 1976. 116 pp. $6.50 cloth.
WILSON, WILLIAM A. *Folklore and Nationalism in Modern Finland.* Indiana University Press, 1976. 272 pp. $10.00 cloth.
WING, KENNETH R. *The Law and the Public's Health.* C. V. Mosby, 1976. 167 pp. NPL, paper.
WISTRICH, ROBERT S. *Revolutionary Jews fom Marx to Trotsky.* Barnes & Noble, 1976. 254 pp. $16.00 cloth.
WOLMAN, BENJAMIN B., ed. *Psychoanalysis and Catholicism.* Gardner, dist. by Halsted, 1976. 219 pp. $19.95 cloth.
WRIGHT, JAMES D. *The Dissent of the Governed: Alienation and Democracy in America.* Academic Press, 1976. 329 pp. $16.50 cloth.
YU, TIMOTHY L. M., compiler. *Mass Communication in Hong Kong and Macao: An Annotated Bibliography.* Asian Mass Communication Research & Information Centre, 1976. 30 pp. $6.00 paper.

MARCH 1977 – VOLUME 6, NUMBER 2

ONTEMPORARY SOCIOLOGY

A JOURNAL OF REVIEWS

IN THIS ISSUE

Homage to Robert Merton; criticism of Robert Merton

Bernard Farber and Michael Gordon on the history of the family

Fred Davis reviews Peter Marris's *Loss and Change*

A survey of 3 books on creativity

John Hagan on law and order

Barry Schwartz's *Queuing and Waiting* reviewed by David Glanz

Doris Entwisle on *Causal Analysis*

Jane Mercer reviews *Adolescent Prejudice*

Syzanne Wedow on Dean MacCannell's new theory of the leisure class

Ronald Dore on the comparative sociology of education

UBLICATION OF THE AMERICAN SOCIOLOGICAL ASSOCIATION

contemporary sociology

a journal of reviews

March 1977 • Volume 6, Number 2

Concerning advertising, change of address and subscriptions, address: Executive Office, American Sociological Association, 1722 N Street, N.W., Washington, D.C. 20036.

Concerning manuscripts and book reviews, address: Editor, *Contemporary Sociology: A Journal of Reviews,* C-002, University of California, San Diego, La Jolla, California, 92093.

Contemporary Sociology: A Journal of Reviews is published at 49 Sheridan Avenue, Albany, N.Y. 12210, bi-monthly in January, March, May, July, September, and November.

Annual membership dues in the American Sociological Association, $30.00–$50.00. Student Member, $15; Associate, $20; International Associate, $12; Student Associate, $10.

Subscription rate for members, $10; non-members, $15; institutions and libraries, $20; non-member students, $10. Single issues $4.

New subscriptions and renewals will be entered on a calendar year basis only.

Change of address: Six weeks advance notice to the Executive Office, and old address as well as new, are necessary for change of subscriber's address.

Claims for undelivered copies must be made within the month following the regular month of publication. The publishers will supply missing copies when losses have been sustained in transit and when the reserve stock will permit.

Second class postage paid at Washington, D.C. and at additional mailing offices.

Book reviews from *CS* are indexed in *Book Review Index,* published by Gale Research Company.

ASA Multiple Submission Policy: Submission of a manuscript to a professional journal clearly implies commitment to publish in that journal. The competition for journal space requires a great deal of time and effort on the part of editorial readers whose main compensation for this service is the opportunity to read papers prior to publication and the gratification associated with discharge of professional obligation. For these reasons, *the American Sociological Association regards submission of a manuscript to a professional journal while that paper is under review by another journal as unacceptable.*

Cover designed by Kenneth E. Anderson, A.I.A.

TABLE OF CONTENTS

LETTERS 135

REVIEW SYMPOSIUM

Coser: *The Idea of Social Structure: Papers in Honor of Robert K. Merton* .... David Caplovitz 142
Randall Collins 150
Maurice R. Stein 154

FEATURES

Arieti: *Creativity: The Magic Synthesis;*
Stein: *Stimulating Creativity. Volume 2: Group Procedures*; and
Taylor and Getzels: *Perspectives in Creativity* .... William A. Sadler, Jr. and Sallie Green 156

Form: *Blue Collar Stratification: Autoworkers in Four Countries* .... William H. Friedland 159

Marris: *Loss and Change* .... Fred Davis 160

McDonald: *The Sociology of Law and Order* .... John Hagan 161

Pickering: *Durkheim on Religion* .... Tendzin N. Takla 163

Schwartz: *Queuing and Waiting: Studies in the Social Organization of Access and Delay* .... David Glanz 165

Shorter: *The Making of the Modern Family* and
Rosenberg: *The Family in History* .... Bernard Farber 167

Shorter: *The Making of the Modern Family* .... Michael Gordon 169

BOOK REVIEWS

COMMUNITIES

Baldwin: *Differentiation and Co-operation in an Israeli Veteran Moshav* and
Criden and Gelb: *The Kibbutz Experience: Dialogue in Kfar Blum* .... Selma Koss Brandow 172

Bernard: *The Sociology of Community* .... Philip Olson 173

Clark: *Canadian Society in Historical Perspective;*
Forcese: *The Canadian Class Structure;*
Katz: *The People of Hamilton, Canada West;* and
Tepperman: *Social Mobility in Canada* .... Jean Leonard Elliott 174

CRIME, LAW, AND DEVIANCE

Braly: *False Starts: A Memoir of San Quentin and Other Prisons* .... Peggy Ann Thoits 175

Gorecki: *Sociology and Jurisprudence of Leon Petrazycki* .... J. G. Hund 176

Hawkins: *The Prison: Policy and Practice* .... Robert Sommer 177

Hilberman: *The Rape Victim* .... Lynda Lytle Holmstrom 178

Morris and Farida: *On License: A Study of Parole* and
Waller: *Men Released from Prison* .... F. William Howton 178

Skultans: *Madness and Morals: Ideas on Insanity in the Nineteenth Century* .... Miriam Sonn 180

Wolcott: *The African Beer Gardens of Bulawayo: Integrated Drinking in a Segregated Society* .... Craig MacAndrew 180

EDUCATION

Calvert: *The Role of the Pupil* .... Rosalie Cohen 181

Clignet: *Liberty and Equality in the Educational Process: A Comparative Sociology of Education* .... Ronald P. Dore 181

Hyman, Wright, and Reed: *The Enduring Effects of Education* .... Jerry L. Fletcher 182

Rodgers: *The Black High School and Its Community* .... James P. Pitts 183

Steinberg: *The Academic Melting Pot: Catholics and Jews in American Higher Education* .... John Murray Cuddihy 184

Stub: *The Sociology of Education: A Sourcebook* .... Josephine A. Amato 185

ENVIRONMENT

Ball: *Microecology: Social Situations and Intimate Space* and
Tybout: *Environmental Quality and Society* .... Arthur H. Patterson 186

Commoner: *The Poverty of Power* .... Noman Miller 187

LANGUAGE

Chomsky: *Reflections on Language* .... William L. Raiser 188

Hymes: *Foundations in Sociolinguistics: An Ethnographic Approach* and
Sanches and Blount: *Sociocultural Dimensions of Language Use* .... Beryl L. Bellman 189

MEDICAL

Fredericks and Mundy: *The Making of a Physician: A Ten-Year Longitudinal Study of Social Class, Academic Achievement, and Changing Professional Attitudes of a Medical School Class* .... Robert H. Coombs 191

Jones: *Opening the Door: A Study of New Policies for the Mentally Handicapped* .... Morton O. Wagenfeld 192

Gubrium: *Living and Dying at Murray Manor* .... Juanita Wood 192

Robertson and Heagerty: *Medical Sociology: A General Systems Approach;*
Rossi and Filstead: *The Therapeutic Community: A Sourcebook of Readings;* and
Schulberg and Baker: *The Mental Hospital and Human Services* Judith Blackfield Cohen 193

Schoenberg et al.: *Bereavement: Its Psychosocial Aspects* .... Jeannette R. Folta 193

METHODS

Blumenthal et al.: *More About Justifying Violence: Methodological Studies of Attitudes and Behavior* .... Daniel B. McGillis 194

Heise: *Causal Analysis* .... Doris R. Entwisle 194

Hess, Riedel, and Fitzpatrick: *Probability Sampling of Hospitals and Patients* .... Coralie Farlee 195

Lave and March: *An Introduction to Models in the Social Sciences* .... David D. McFarland 196

OCCUPATIONS, WORK, AND LEISURE

Clayre: *Work and Play: Ideas and Experience of Work and Leisure* .... Andrea Fontana 197

Csikszentmihalyi: *Beyond Boredom and Anxiety: The Experience of Play in Work and Games* .... Murray S. Davis 197

French and French: *Working Communally: Patterns and Possibilities* and
Klein: *New Forms of Work Organization* .... Paul Goldman 199

MacCannell: *The Tourist: A New Theory of the Leisure Class* .... Suzanne Wedow 200

Schulzinger: *The Making of the Diplomatic Mind: The Training, Outlook, and Style of United States Foreign Service Officers, 1908–1931* .... Donald P. Warwick 202

Stein: *Work and Welfare in Britain and the USA* .... Marie Withers Osmond 202

ORGANIZATIONS

Friedlander: *The Emergence of a UAW Local, 1936–1939: A Study in Class and Culture* .... James P. Mulherin 203

Nelson: *Managers and Workers: Origins of the New Factory System in the United States, 1880–1920* .... Marshall W. Meyer 204

Vogel: *Modern Japanese Organization and Decision-Making* .... Batia Sharon 205

POLITICAL

Alberoni: *Italia in trasformazione* and
Kaufman: *Il Sistema Globale: Immagini e Modelli* .... Edith Kurzweil 206

Brown and Kaser: *The Soviet Union since the Fall of Khrushchev;*
Pipes: *Russia under the Old Regime;* and
Szamuely: *The Russian Tradition* .... Alexander Matejko 207

Carter: *Elite Politics in Rural India: Political Stratification and Political Alliances in Western Maharashtra* .... Richard P. Taub 208

Frederickson and O'Leary: *Measuring Power, Public Opinion and Policy: A Case Study of Syracuse, New York* .... Martin J. Murray 209

Higley, Field, and Grøholt: *Elite Structure and Ideology: A Theory with Applications to Norway* .... Inger J. Sagatun 210

Kasinsky: *Refugees from Militarism: Draft-Age Americans in Canada* .... John C. Leggett 211

Ladd and Hadley: *Transformations of the American Party System: Political Coalitions from the New Deal to the 1970s* .... Steven E. Deutsch 213

Moskos: *Peace Soldiers: The Sociology of a United Nations Military Force* .... Phillip Butler 214

Scott: *The Glassworkers of Carmaux: French Craftsmen and Political Action in a Nineteenth-Century City* .... Gregg Carr 214

Wheeler: *Lies, Damn Lies, and Statistics: The Manipulation of Public Opinion in America* .... David V. McQueen 215

RACE AND ETHNIC

Cross: *Blacks in White Colleges: Oklahoma's Landmark Cases* ..... Sethard Fisher 216

Dashefsky: *Ethnic Identity in Society* and
Rose: *Peoples: The Ethnic Dimension in Human Relations* ..... Douglas S. Snyder 217

Dosman: *The National Interest: The Politics of Northern Development 1968–75;*
Fumoleau: *As Long as This Land Shall Last;* and
McCullum and McCullum: *This Land Is Not for Sale* ..... Stephen O. Murray 218

Glock et al.: *Adolescent Prejudice* ..... Jane R. Mercer 219

Grace: *Domestic Slavery in West Africa: With Particular Reference to the Sierra Leone Protectorate, 1896–1927* ..... Edward Reynolds 221

Nelsen and Nelsen: *Black Church in the Sixties* ..... David O. Moberg 221

Raffaele: *System and Unsystem: An Ethnic View of Organization and Society* ..... A. Barrett Fields 222

Samuda: *Psychological Testing of American Minorities: Issues and Consequences* ..... Carl C. Jorgensen 223

Wagenheim: *A Survey of Puerto Ricans on the U.S. Mainland in the 1970's* ..... David Jess León 224

Willie: *Oreo: A Perspective on Race and Marginal Men and Women* ..... James H. Laue 225

RELIGION

Fichter: *The Catholic Cult of the Paraclete* ..... Marion Dearman 226

Morioka: *Religion in Changing Japanese Society* ..... David W. Plath 227

Smith: *Religion and Political Modernization* ..... Thomas C. Bruneau 228

Wallis: *Sectarianism: Analyses of Religious and Non-Religious Sects* ..... Harry H. Hiller 229

SEX ROLES AND BEHAVIOR

Carroll: *Liberating Women's History: Theoretical and Critical Essays* ..... Marilyn J. Boxer 230

Gross and Trask: *The Sex Factor and the Management of Schools* ..... Patricia Yancey Martin 231

Lebra, Paulsen, and Powers: *Women in Changing Japan* ..... Cornelia Butler Flora 232

Maccoby and Jacklin: *The Psychology of Sex Differences* ..... Elizabeth M. Almquist 233

Weinberg: *Sex Research: Studies from the Kinsey Institute* ..... Marjorie K. Little 234

SOCIAL CHANGE AND SOCIAL PROBLEMS

Anderson: *The Sociology of Survival: Social Problems of Growth* ..... Allan Schnaiberg 235

Honikman: *Responding to Social Change* ..... Galen Cranz 235

Nee and Peck: *China's Uninterrupted Revolution: From 1840 to the Present* ..... Ben Stavis 236

Nettler: *Social Concerns* ..... T. P. Schwartz 237

Ross: *Grass Roots in an African City: Political Behavior in Nairobi* ..... Robert Cameron Mitchell 237

Rothman: *Planning and Organizing for Social Change: Action Principles from Social Science Research* ..... Carole Joffe and Joan Mandle 238

Schur: *The Awareness Trap: Self-Absorption Instead of Social Change* ..... Louis Rowitz 239

Truzzi and Springer: *Solving Social Problems: Essays in Relevant Sociology* and
Wells: *American Society: Problems and Dilemmas* ..... Henry M. Barlow 240

SOCIAL PSYCHOLOGY

Aronson: *The Social Animal;*
Calhoun: *Persons-in-Groups: A Humanistic Social Psychology;*
Raven and Rubin: *Social Psychology: People in Groups;* and
Staats: *Social Behaviorism* ..... Morris J. Daniels 241

Block and Dworkin: *The IQ Controversy: Critical Readings* and
Lewis: *Origins of Intelligence: Infancy and Early Childhood* ..... Barbara G. Cashion 242

Couch and Hintz: *Constructing Social Life: Readings in Behavioral Sociology from the Iowa School* ..... Santo J. Tarantino 243

Fishbein and Ajzen: *Belief, Attitude, Intention and Behavior: An Introduction to Theory and Research* ..... Richard J. Hill 244

Gasson, Haller, and Sewell: *Attitudes and Facilitation in the Attainment of Status* ..... James R. Lincoln 245

Hewitt: *Self and Society: A Symbolic Interactionist Social Psychology;*
Kreilkamp: *The Corrosion of the Self: Society's Effects on People;* and
Sherif: *Orientation in Social Psychology* .... Sylvia Clavan 247

Sampson: *Social Psychology and Contemporary Society;*
Seidenberg and Snadowsky: *Social Psychology: An Introduction;*
Severy, Brigham, and Schlenker: *A Contemporary Introduction to Social Psychology;* and
Tedeschi and Lindskold: *Social Psychology: Interdependence, Interaction, and Influence* .... Mary Ann Groves 248

SPORT

Landers: *Social Problems in Athletics: Essays in the Sociology of Sport* and
Voigt: *America through Baseball* .... Carolyn R. Dexter 249

Thompson: *Retreat from Apartheid: New Zealand's Sporting Contacts with South Africa* .... Remi Clignet 250

STRATIFICATION

Duberman: *Social Inequality: Class and Caste in America* .... Joan Huber 250

Sharma: *The Changing Rural Stratification System: A Comparative Study of Six Villages in Rajasthan, India* .... Santosh Kumar Nandy 250

Westergaard and Resler: *Class in a Capitalist Society: A Study of Contemporary Britain* .... Rochelle Feldman 251

THEORY

Althusser: *Politics and History: Montesquieu, Rosseau, Hegel and Marx* and
Colletti: *Marxism and Hegel* .... Arthur W. Frank 252

Bates and Harvey: *The Structure of Social Systems* .... Richard A. Peterson 253

Benn and Mortimore: *Rationality and the Social Sciences: Contributions to the Philosophy and Methodology of the Social Sciences* .... J. David Lewis 254

Hindess and Hirst: *Pre-Capitalist Modes of Production* .... J. Craig Jenkins 254

Katz: *Structuralism in Sociology: An Approach to Knowledge* .... Ino Rossi 255

Millman and Kanter: *Another Voice: Feminist Perspectives on Social Life and Social Science* .... Myra Marx Ferree 256

Shils: *Center and Periphery: Essays in Macrosociology. Selected Papers of Edward A. Shils* .... Ellen R. Robert 257

Wolff: *Trying Sociology* .... Robert Jackall 258

URBAN

Burby and Weiss: *New Communities U.S.A.* and
Campbell: *New Towns: Another Way to Live* .... Sally S. Rogers 259

Ford: *Urban Health in America* and
Leveson and Weiss: *Analysis of Urban Health Problems* .... Jennie J. Kronenfeld 261

Hahn: *People and Politics in Urban Society, Volume 6: Urban Affairs Annual Reviews* .... John B. Williamson 261

Hawley and Rock: *Metropolitan America in Contemporary Perspective* .... Mary Donahue Stearns 262

ADDITIONAL REVIEWS

Andreasen: *The Disadvantaged Consumer* .... Susan Maizel Chambré 263

Brown and Brown: *A Survey of the Social Sciences* .... Sharon McPherron 263

Hartley: *Illegitimacy* .... Jennie J. Kronenfeld 264

Heiss: *The Case of the Black Family: A Sociological Inquiry* .... Elizabeth Higginbotham 265

Lee: *Toward Humanistic Sociology* .... David O. Arnold 266

Nauk: *Sotsiologicheskie Issledovaniya* .... Jiri Kolaja 266

Nye: *The Origins of Crowd Psychology: Gustave LeBon and the Crisis of Mass Democracy in the Third Republic* .... Maurice Jackson 268

Roby: *Child Care—Who Cares? Foreign and Domestic Infant and Early Childhood Development Policies* .... Marijean Suelzle 268

Rodnitzky: *Minstrels of the Dawn: The Folk-Protest Singer as a Cultural Hero* .... R. Serge Denisoff 269

Wakil: *Marriage, Family and Society: Canadian Perspectives* .... Marylee Stephenson 270

PUBLICATIONS RECEIVED 271

LETTERS

(Letters which comment on particular reviews are routinely sent to reviewers for a reply. Where no reply by reviewers appears in these columns, it is usually because they chose not to reply.)

To the Editor:

In a letter to *CS* (Vol. 5, No. 4) Nicholas C. Mullins states that it is clear to him that I did not read the methodological appendix to his *Theories and Theory Groups in Contemporary American Sociology*. The entire closing paragraph of my review (Vol. 4, No. 3) is based on Mullins's appendix. Mullins then attributes to me a question I never asked, about whether Don Martindale considers himself a symbolic interactionist.

While authors of books are under no obligation to read reviews of those books, letter writers are under an obligation to have read reviews that they criticize. I have read Mullins's book. I now doubt that he has read my review of his book.

My final comments are addressed to the editor. A policy statement in the letter section of *CS* states that "Letters which comment on particular reviews are routinely sent to reviewers for a reply." I never received a copy of Mullins's letter.

MARK OROMANER
Jersey City State College

To the Editor:

Marc Fried, in his review of our book, *Working Class Kinship* (*CS,* May, 1976, pp. 317–320) misrepresents our work in matters large and small.

The reader cannot learn it from the review, but the point of our book is to apply mainstream anthropological kinship theory to data on extra-familial kin interaction in order to provide a third position in the debate between those who disagree about whether the isolated nuclear family or some form of the extended family typifies American kinship structure. This debate and our contribution to it are not discussed by Fried. As it happens, we trace developments in sociological controversy about kinship over the past twenty-five years to show how they resulted in polarized views of the meaning and nature of extra-familial kin ties. We point out areas of agreement and disagreement between parties to the debate, where we think false issues are being argued, and where the arguments seem to us to have gone awry. Apparently, the existence of disagreement in the area of kinship and family structure has escaped the reviewer's attention, and our attempt to cast the problem anew has gone over his head. If we have made an original contribution to this large body of work, it is tracing the history of and applying a heretofore unutilized perspective from another field and elaborating it to coincide more closely with modern kinship structure. Thus we trace the development of kinship theory from 1924, when Rivers introduced the term *kindred* (Fried seems to think we invented it), to recent developments in and out of anthropology in the study of bilateral kinship systems, whose typical unit is the kindred. We argue that extra-familial kin ties in industrial societies with bilateral kinship systems can be examined in terms of a kindred-based system of linkages among relatives. We illustrate this with data we have on a working class population, but devote one chapter to suggesting that this may serve as a general approach to kinship in urban society. Whether this perspective on kinship is more accurate than current conceptions is an issue lost in the review.

Fried's comments on the limitations of the sample and the supposed generalizations found in our work are another major distortion. Obviously, we wrote an exploratory and theoretical essay, and [were] quite clear about it. . . . Naturally, we do not know whether our findings are generalizable. We provide an illustration to theory, not empirical confirmation.

The reviewer also makes several statements about important features of our book which are simply contrary to fact, and we would like to set the record straight. He erroneously claims that there is "no discussion anywhere in the book, either through reference to the literature or to observations, concerning social class variations in kinship behavior." We suggest he read the preface (xv) and then Chapter II, which is studded with comparisons between working and middle class, including citations to studies by Reiss, Adams, Mirande and others. We even recompute our own working class data to make it comparable to the kin categories of Winch's middle class Chicago sample so that we may directly examine middle and working class levels of availability of kin (pp. 39–40). Also, we compare a number of studies of class differentials in interaction of wives with their relatives (pp. 90–91). And in the final chapter we bring the conclusions of our analysis to bear on the issue of single-core versus plural kinship systems as a function of the class structure, discussing theorists who have made important contributions to each side of this issue. Thus, while our work has no cross-class generalizations in view, we did of course pull together what was known about relevant facets of kinship interaction at other levels than the working class as part of our effort to illustrate the empirical basis of various theoretical views of kinship.

Fried erroneously claims that "Throughout the entire volume, both in theoretical discussion and in the empirical analysis, kinship is treated without reference to other social relationships." The relationship of kinship to the economy is an important theme of the book. It is discussed in the first chapter, since the presumed impact of industrialization on family relationships is an essential part of the controversy we review as a prelude to our own contribution. We also devote over half of the final chapter to another look at kinship and economic relationships.

Fried erroneously claims that "our empirical analysis hinges on the proportions of people who see different types of kin." But this is only one of four different measures of kinship interaction employed.

And even in minor matters, Fried apparently cannot report accurately. The upper age limit of the study is 79 years (p. 23) not 75. The interviewing was not done in some "unspecified prior year" as he claims: "The field work was begun in March 1965, and was concluded at the end of May 1965" (p. 24).

Evidently, Fried has given our work only the most cursory reading. He appears to be ignorant of modern developments in kinship theory. And, to put the most charitable possible cast on it, he has been so careless in reporting our aims and results that the book we have written has not been reviewed despite the appearance of a number of lines of type in *Contemporary Sociology*.

George S. Rosenberg
Donald Anspach
Case Western Reserve University

From the Editor:

Professor Fried wrote the following in response to the Rosenberg-Anspach letter, without intending it to be published. We requested his permission to publish it and he consented.

Bennett M. Berger

"Thanks for the . . . . opportunity to reply to the Anspach and Rosenberg review. I object to replies to reviews. I think they're generally intellectually pointless and merely expressions of injured vanity. For me to reply would not only sanction the reasonableness of the process but would engage us in a circular debate. They're not going to see, any better, the extent to which their ravenous hostility blinds them to what others are saying, and encourages them to set up straw men. Nor are they likely to accept with humility my implication that they don't really know what theory is or how to use data in its service. Indeed, their reply is so much like the worst features of their book that a reply from me would have the quality of entering a hall of reflecting mirrors. And to most readers the entire argument is likely to be irrelevant."

Marc Fried
Boston College

To the Editor:

Bruce Johnson finds *Agents of Change* "an unconvincing and not particularly interesting book" (July, 1976). He proceeds to entertain himself by turning from a review of the book to speculations about the real world. At this point, his innuendos lose their sandbox quality, and become consequential.

A reviewer can have legitimate doubts about "the limits of police professionalization," but he has no right to invent documentation when talking about a real police department. Your reviewer seems to believe that police/citizen conflicts are impervious to intervention. He converts this ideological stance into the flat-out assertion that street conflict "did not decline appreciably in Oakland." Johnson happens to be mistaken about Oakland. The book tells him that he is wrong (pp. 325–330), and I could paper his walls with tables that categorically prove him wrong. Since all tangible indices of conflict in Oakland drop between 1970 and 1973 (where my data end) I suspect Johnson must look elsewhere to bolster his nihilistic preconceptions.

Johnson is cynical about human motives. And Johnson's status as reviewer may provide him the license to impugn my integrity, and that of my colleagues. But Johnson is not entitled to ascribe motives to *real life* chiefs of police or to *real life* police officers whom he does not know. Johnson cannot tell us that Chief Gain in Oakland "used" our NIMH project "as a political weapon." In fact, the chief did nothing of the kind, and was a patient and perfect host. The implication that our seven patrolmen were bribed into "abandonment of their fellow officers" is an unwarranted aspersion on the character of men whose idealism and whose professional commitment have been an inspiration to me.

I'm disturbed by Johnson's extrapolations from unexamined assumptions. I have read all the officer comments from the referendum referred to by Johnson. I remember no complaints "about, among other things, the very policies which the Toch project was designed to implement." The book (which is the ostensible subject of Johnson's review) contains data that suggest rank and file police acceptance of significant project components. Closer to home, I see no reason to assert dogmatically that "Lewin's cooperative [*sic*] model of organizational change is ineffective in highly stratified, conflict-ridden entities." The impact of participatory models in organizational change is open to inquiry. It is no one's prerogative to foreclose such inquiry because of predilections for conflict models. . . .

Finally, I have a dream. In this dream I am

introduced to a sociologist *as a psychologist,* and I let slip that I am interested in (among other things) police. In my dream—which is an ecumenical dream—the sociologist does *not* accuse me of ascribing everything to "defects of individual officers." In return (in my dream) I shall *not* accuse sociologists of seeing men as mechanistic products of situational pressures.

HANS TOCH
SUNY/Albany

To the Editor:

Professor Toch's letter, like his book, is rather overblown. I am neither ideologue nor nihilist nor cynic. My conception of people is not mechanistic; I believe in the integration of social science. I did not impugn the integrity of Professors Toch, Grant and Galvin; rather, I questioned their intellectual judgment. I have met Chief Gain and have no doubt of his integrity.

I stand by my reading of the book's very limited quantitative data. If large amounts of definitive hard data are available, why were they not included in the book? Certainly, police/citizen conflict can be ameliorated; however, the "change agent" strategy is not likely to get this job done.

My political interpretation of the course of the Toch experiment was based in small measure on my own knowledge of the OPD, gained in research carried out while I worked for the San Francisco Committee on Crime. In the main, however, this interpretation was based on information offered in the book under review (e.g., pp. 26–28, 33–36, 57–61, 67, 91, 198, 226, 263, 289–291, 316–318, 329, 336–338). These passages amply document rank and file opposition to the Gain/Toch policies. This opposition is reiterated eloquently in the news stories concerning the vote of no confidence in Gain (e.g., *Los Angeles Times,* November 25, 28, 30, 1971; December 11, 1971). I am still astonished that Toch ignored the racial dimension of that conflict.

BRUCE C. JOHNSON
University of California, San Diego

To the Editor:

I would like to comment on the review by Freeman (July, 1976) of Rosow's book, *Socialization to Old Age.* I feel that the reviewer focuses too much attention on the final chapter in which Rosow proposes what he recognizes as only one possible option to the dilemma presented in the preceding chapters. Rosow's thesis, in my reading of the book, is that socialization into a devalued role that has few proscriptive and virtually no prescriptive norms associated with it is, at best, difficult. In examining the position of the aged in terms of socialization theory rather than focusing on the problems of the aged Rosow does what few others in the field of social gerontology have done; that is, he assumes that the aged are subject to the same social forces that affect other members of society. Successful socialization into a devalued role will be difficult regardless of the age of the target group. Rosow shows not pity for the aged, but recognition that variables affecting the position of the aged in society are the same variables that affect other members of society, that the aged are social actors, too. The solution proposed, age homogeneous housing in which roles, norms, and values emerge, is based on the assumption that society will not soon become "old age oriented," but, as Rosow points out early in the book, the position of the aged is a "moral dilemma" about which we *choose* to do nothing. Rosow's carefully reasoned argument gives the reader much insight into the current position of the aged in American society and dismissing the book as justifying the status quo or condescending to the old would be a great mistake.

SARAH MATTHEWS
University of Missouri, Columbia

To the Editor:

In my review of Irving Rosow's book I used the perspectives of the sociology of knowledge and interactionism to make two points; one, that language matters and two, that power is an important element in all social relations. It is on this basis that I see as politically significant Rosow's decision to describe an age segregated option for old people, and his failure to elaborate and challenge the economic and political context in which the negative meanings of old age which countenance age segregation emerge. In fact, one of the greatest problems confronting old people is that they are studied as if economics and politics were not most significant.

Mills said it best, "vocabularies of motive arise in situated actions." The analytic preferences of Rosow and Matthews are well-suited to professional caretakers seeking to "help" categories of "them," rather than to those seeking to enable people of all ages to participate together in prestige-granting and economically rewarding activities. Rosow, and apparently Matthews, consider it legitimate to contemplate the "successful socialization to a devalued status" of others as if it were a process independent of the human experiences of enforced unemployment, social ostracism, isolation, and stigma. The recognition that we are, in part, whoever we study, leads to the question "would I like to be socialized to a devalued role?" As a woman I have experienced the answer, as a sociologist I cannot ignore the question.

MOLLY FREEMAN
University of California, Davis

To the Editor:

I want to thank Elise Boulding for her perceptive and balanced review of my book, *German Realpolitik and American Sociology* (Sept., 1976). I should like, however, to take issue with her suggestion that "Realpolitik" was a poor choice of terms to represent the tradition within which Weber, Gumplowicz, Ratzenhofer et al., and their American students wrote (namely, Ward, Small, Park, and Bentley). "The scenario out of which Simmel and Weber" (and by implication the others mentioned above), she says, was not the "liberal participatory rhetoric accompanied by ruthless suppression of minorities" which is commonly associated with "Realpolitik." What Boulding says is true, but this author did not use the term in this sense. By "Realpolitik" I meant above all, "political realism," i.e., among other things, the attempt to distinguish between the purposed ends (peace, justice, liberty) pursued in politics, and the means (anything that works) actually employed by political actors. "Realpolitik," then, stands for a definition of the preeminent political agency, the State, not in terms of the ends it presumably serves, but in terms of the means, peculiarly violence, it uses to overpower its enemies. In this respect, the tradition of Realpolitik saw the State arising and progressing less through debate and the consensus of those subject to its authority, than through forcible coercion. It can hardly be denied that Weber, Ratzenhofer, and Gumplowicz, along with their American proteges were proponents of Realpolitik in this limited sense.

A couple of points should be mentioned in order to clarify the nature of this proposition. By no means did these scholars all consider political realism to be ethically good. (Although one can indeed find throughout their writings unrestrained Machiavellian-like statements: e.g., "There can be no effective program in the state without the use of forcible means. Whatever physical force would be necessary to carry out a program in the interest of unsocialized selfishness . . . is also necessary . . . to defeat that program . . ." [Small]. "The capacity for the energetic application of force . . . which rules . . . over life and death and shrinks from no act necessary to the common good is a fundamental demand of civilization" [Ratzenhofer].) On the contrary, they were aware, if not outright appalled, by the radical Evil of politics viewed realistically. "Do we not see," asked Weber in 1918 that " 'All that take the sword shall perish by the sword' . . .?" "The science of politics," Ratzenhofer agrees, "is primarily a psychopathology of human beings. . . . For this very reason . . . the essence of politics is so repulsive." And yet by the same token they were in a sense morbidly fascinated by its somber majesty. They were simultaneously repelled by the treachery and violence of politics and yet drawn to it, attracted by its "higher ethical and spiritual significance," to paraphrase one of them. The nineteenth century German sociologists in my study viewed the power struggle as a tragic mystery. In other words they viewed it romantically, often despondently so, that is true. But after all that is one of the characteristics of the true romantic. Thus like all authentic romantics they were remarkably astute at "discovering" the ironic "dialectical" characteristics of power seeking, the "facts": e.g., that out of evil intention grows morality; out of disorder, order; out of conflict, unity; out of war, progress; out of slavery, human advancement; out of selfishness, self-denial. It is the rise of this unquestionably anti-liberal attitude toward politics that I sought in my book to explain.

In addition, and this is a point that I think is too often ignored by modern sociologists, possibly including Boulding herself: the American and German proponents of Realpolitik maintained that social progress entails increasing control over the "mindless" struggle for survival by the State. To say it in another way, all the subjects of my study were preoccupied with the Social Problem, as they called it, of maintaining social order, national unity, and strength in the face of class and racial conflict. And they all turned to the State as the prime agency of social peace. Acknowledging this as I did, does not imply that I "impute[d] totalitarian overtones" to the tradition of Realpolitik, as Boulding alleges. In fact to the extent that the German and American sociologists of conflict considered State intervention in economic and social affairs to be a consequence of class and racial conflict, they could and often did support the struggles of minorities and the proletariat for equality.

James A. Aho
Idaho State University

To the Editor:

Why is *Contemporary Sociology* perpetually replete with countless typographical (?) errors? For instance, Muriel Cantor's repeated references to "nuturing" (sick!) are most annoying (September 1976, pp. 663–664). Such illiteracy makes her superfeministic attitudes much more amusing. Long live affirmative action!

Moreover, you should have deleted Lauren Langman's inane neologism, "businesspersons" (p. 687). Obviously, like most quota quacks, or, as Robert Merton would say, "cognitive provincialists," Langman is unfamiliar with what is known as "synecdoche." At least, he should have been sufficiently consistent to write "businesspeschildren" (or is he a crypto-male chauvinist?). And his own anachronistic name should be "Langperchild"!

Seriously, when will sociologists stop being silly and start doing something useful for the taxpayers who support them? "No wonder sociology is floundering, its image nationwide deteriorating and its membership and market position eroding" (*ASA Footnotes,* August 1976, p. 8).

Panos D. Bardis
Toledo University

Reply by the Editor:

There are typographical errors in *CS* because, unlike *The New Yorker,* we are not yet perfect at reading proof.

It has been the unannounced policy of this journal to eliminate sexist language to the extent we can without distorting meaning, butchering idiom, or offending the ear (the rapid acceptance of "Ms." suggests how quickly the ear may be socialized). "Businessperson" seems to us OK; and it is, in fact, our usage, not Professor Langman's, whose original manuscript contained the more traditional usage.

We do not think our policy is silly; resistance to it is what seems silly, given the fact that it provides substantial satisfaction to a large constituency of sociologists for only small editing costs. That seems moderately useful to us.

BENNETT M. BERGER

To the Editor:

Professor Lofland, in his review of our book, *An Ethnography of a Chiropractic Clinic,* has raised several questions which, for him, are most troublesome–indeed so troublesome that he fails to see justification for our being in print. Moreover, it would seem that he would similarly banish the "continuing publication of books" which somehow fail to satisfy his demand for "refined and new analyses. . . ." Why?

It appears that the difficulty lies in some confusion over the term ethnography. We are traditionalists in our definition and for this no apology is necessary. From the Greek *ethnos* and *graphein,* the term ethnography literally means to write about peoples. According to E. A. Hoebel, sound ethnographic work is done by those trained in "participant-observer techniques calling for objective and penetrating observation and interviewing, empathetic rapport with a people, and accurate reporting." We have satisfied these ends.

We are, however, sociologists, not anthropologists, and the book was written in the language of symbolic interactionism. This frame of reference provided conceptual parameters for the understanding of everyday chiropractic life. Professor Lofland has set up a series of criticisms which, unfortunately, would only apply to the book we didn't write. In the real one, we state explicitly that our purpose is to "coherently reconstruct situationally limited social phenomena while intentionally keeping to the basic premises of symbolic interactionism. . . . The attempt [was] made to devise a situationally heuristic methodology which would meet the demands imposed by the subject matter at hand, remain faithful to the underlying premises of the interactionist tradition and contribute to the rapidly growing interest in the sociology of everyday life." The reviewer, however, would have us rewrite the work to fit his Procrustean bed.

Aside from the American Medical Association, chiropractic is the most influential of the competing health care systems in the United States. Yet, until the publication of our book, neither sociologists nor anyone else had formal access to materials on the everyday reality of the chiropractor plying his trade. Earlier work by Wardwell, Leis, Sternberg and others told us a great deal concerning the profession as a whole, training practices, and structural difficulties. Yet nothing was known (except through direct experience) about thousands of somewhat similar behavior settings throughout the United States.

We stated in the Preface that given our interactionist approach we would set forth "neither any major new point of view nor a minor theoretical twist." Ironically Professor Lofland sees our accomplishments (which he paraphrased with questionable brevity) as merely "axiomatic." *They are flatly axiomatic.* For example, the reviewer refers to our treatment of the history and philosophy of chiropractic as "lay level treatment." That is exactly what it is. Rather than present a so-called objective history of that profession (with which we were quite familiar) we chose to let the chiropractor relate history and philosophy as he saw it, thus raising the layman to the level of the professional researcher as Donald Zimmerman and Melvin Pollmer would put it. Needless to say, his presentation was quite different from what our own would have been. Yet, from the interactionist standpoint, his historical and philosophical orientation was the only one conceivably relevant in that behavior setting. Behavior is only understandable in terms of the individual's perception of the past and imaginative speculation concerning the future. For Mead, this is axiomatic.

Following this theme, we reported upon what has been termed by Justus Buchler, "methodography," a major activity on the part of the chiropractor in the study. Methodography is the professional's perception, evaluation (through training and experience) and modification of his professional method. This was accomplished by the chiropractor in terms of the philosophy of life acquired while in chiropractic training. Facing overwhelming problems in his business, the chiropractor constantly assessed and attempted to change his own professional image in the behavior setting. For Cooley and W. I. Thomas, this is axiomatic.

Through our analysis of the chiropractor's reaction to the marginally deviant label attached to him by the medical establishment, we documented the social actor's ability to respond (in a sometimes novel way) to the situation as he defined it. Labeling theorists have frequently viewed the labeled individual as a passive recipient of the label. This was clearly not the case for the professional in our study. Creative methodographic decisions were most evident on his part. Man, indeed, has the ability to adjust and modify his own behavior and thus the views others have of him.

The point is this: A sociological contribution does not have to fall into the area of methodological refinement. We stated our belief that symbolic interactionism has the potential (although too little recognized) for solid methodological explication. We sought to realize that end and no more. Professor Lofland has leveled his criticism against a phantom book rather than the one we wrote. We were not writing to answer generic questions about social movements, deviance *per se* or interaction as Lofland proposes. The thrust of his criticism remains a mystery because he is a purported symbolic interactionist. Had this review been written by a traditional structural functionalist, the authors would have understood the demand for a rigid theoretical and methodological model. Had the chiropractor in the study been adequately "dipped" in sociological theory and methodology and thus been aware of the generic questions raised by Professor Lofland, he undoubtedly would have provided the "highly strategic data" demanded.

JAMES B. COWIE
Delta State University

JULIAN ROEBUCK
Mississippi State University

To the Editor:

I understand these authors to advocate that it is sufficient for qualitative field sociologists to provide participant-framed descriptions of social life and to report yet more illustrations of ideas inherited from our sociological ancestors. For better or worse, I am among those who believe that these are the beginning rather than the end points in doing serious sociology. Already various kinds of journalists and contemporary historians routinely perform these starting tasks and they often do them better than sociologists. For this and other reasons, life is getting harder for sociologists, and more of us will now need actually to do sociology if we are to remain cogent. By doing sociology I mean we must produce advancing and generic analyses of the structures, processes, causes, functions, and strategies of social organizations, and of how people maneuver with and within social organizations.

Patently, the authors again raise a fundamental issue that already occupies a significant literature and it cannot be settled in these few inches of print. I hope, however, that the book in question and the commentary associated with it might provide an additional case among many cases that assist in future and comprehensive clarification of this on-going and agonizing conflict among qualitative field sociologists.

JOHN LOFLAND
University of California, Davis

To the Editor:

I have just read Waitzkin's review of Illich's *Medical Nemesis,* and though I agree with most of his criticisms, I think he has misplaced the book's importance. The one major positive point Waitzkin does make about the book is that it "serves a useful purpose in demystifying many of modern medicine's technical claims" (p. 402). This is no small accomplishment, and if Illich is taken seriously on this point, he has achieved his ends. The reader (after all, Illich is appealing to individuals rather than institutions) who believes that clinical iatrogenesis has created his/her health problems is unlikely to continue a medicalized routine. Isn't that discontinuance precisely what Illich wants? But like Waitzkin, as a sociologist, "policy" in the form of individual reversion is not enough for me. Therefore I can commend and appreciate Illich's work only as a *beginning*.

Medicine's dual claims of advanced technology and monopoly of expertise in medicine *and* health have created the iatrogenesis of which Illich speaks. Indeed, the dismantling of medical structures would be ineffectual in "creating" health until and unless the ideology of medical expertise is also dismantled. So long as Americans believe that medicine is the only legitimate health care institution; medical regimens (including non-regimens for individuals without diagnosed pathology) can insure health; and modern medicine, through research, is discovering "cures" for the major illnesses–the reduction of medical care facilities will not be tantamount to the development of the autonomy and self care which Illich espouses. Indeed, as Waitzkin notes, there are disadvantaged social classes in this country which have not had access to medical facilities and have not been shown to be at all better off–either less diseased or healthier. Reduction in the scope of medicine is only a partial solution to health problems. While it may reduce iatrogenesis, it in no way ensures better health.

While Waitzkin finds Illich to have fallen short on his (non) policy recommendations, I find him wanting long before he gets there. While thoroughly analyzing iatrogenesis, he neglects to note medicine's political control of health through the efforts of the American Medical Association to essentially mislead the American public by discrediting alternative health systems and promising miracle cures through research. The medicalization of society has not occurred naturally, but through the political efforts of the medical establishment. The result of this effort has been a false sense of security among Americans, the belief that health is as simple as the medical model, and that cures for the major pathologies are emanate. Meanwhile, chronic disease is still on the rise, and viral research continues to run into dead ends while social epidemiological–"life-style" studies reveal more and more about the etiology of these illnesses.

Though Illich leaves the sociologist hanging, his contribution to the demystification of medical technology is more than important–it is essential. It is the first step in debunking the assumed value of medical care itself, hopefully to be followed by first, the acknowledgment that positive health is not only an asset in and of itself, but perhaps the only insurance against chronic disease and next, the institutionalization of actual *health* care institutions to complement those of medicine, which would naturally decrease in size, scope and power.

MARSHA ROSENBAUM
University of California, San Francisco

To the Editor:

Rosenbaum notes Illich's success in demystifying modern medicine's technical claims. Illich's work was not the "first" critical appraisal of medicine's effectiveness. Research in this area spans at least two decades and includes work by René Dubos, Archibald Cochrane, and many others. Illich has served a useful purpose in popularizing, mainly through secondary analysis, this previous research.

On the other hand, like Illich, Rosenbaum chooses the medical establishment as her principal whipping boy. Few would deny, at this point, the pernicious effects of the American Medical Association and of professional dominance more broadly.

But in accepting Illich's focus, Rosenbaum downplays the importance of class structure and corporate (as opposed to professional) dominance of the health system. Recent studies by Vincente Navarro and others have shown that members of the corporate class exert major control over health-delivery institutions and medical industries. Navarro writes: ". . . the [health] industry, contrary to what Illich believes . . . is administered but not controlled by the medical profession." On deeper analysis, the same corporate groups that dominate other sectors of society also control the health sector. As I have noted elsewhere, corporate interests exploit illness in capitalist society, over and above the exploitation that occurs by the medical profession. In addition, the growing field of social epidemiology, to which Rosenbaum briefly alludes, traces many disabling chronic diseases (like occupational illnesses, hypertension, and several forms of cancer) not to individual "life-style" problems, but to the work process in capitalist industries, where profits often fall if health and safety innovations are introduced.

Because Illich de-emphasizes the class structure and organization of work in capitalist society, his aficionados have concluded that social policy should encourage "demedicalization" and "self-care." Illich himself, as Rosenbaum points out, does not clearly develop the policy implications of his work. Other critics also have noted the potentially regressive outcomes of Illich's "therapeutic nihilism." In a period of economic instability, when even the most rudimentary medical care is inaccessible to some groups in the U.S., Illich's analysis provides a rationalization for cutbacks in services. The impact of these cutbacks will fall disproportionately on the poor.

For these reasons we need to locate Illich's critique of medicine in the broader context of political-economic dominance and class structure. By placing responsibility for health care squarely on the individual, and by limiting his focus to a single institution, Illich obscures the structural conditions that transcend medicine alone. These issues deserve collective action, rather than reductionist suggestions that put the burden for change on individual modifications in life style and capacity for pain.

HOWARD WAITZKIN
University of Vermont

REVIEW SYMPOSIUM

The Idea of Social Structure: Papers in Honor of Robert K. Merton, edited by LEWIS A. COSER. New York: Harcourt Brace Jovanovich, 1975. 547 pp. $12.95 cloth.

DAVID CAPLOVITZ
Graduate School and University Center/CUNY

The book that Lewis Coser has edited in honor of Robert K. Merton consists of a collection of essays celebrating Merton the sociological theorist. All of the contributors try to show how Merton's writings on theoretical subjects have influenced their own thinking. The key to the limitations of the Coser book is provided by the word "writings" in the previous sentence. Robert Merton is most widely known for his essays on sociological theory. These essays have been read by millions and are the basis for his public reputation. But almost all the authors of the papers in the Coser volume were students of Merton, and unlike the millions who have read his essays, they know that there are other Mertons besides the theoretical essayist —Mertons that, in my opinion, far outshine the essayist. At least four other Mertons deserve acknowledgement: the teacher, the word lover or poet, the editor and the critic.* In the brief space alloted me, I shall do my best to redress the balance and evoke the flavor of these other Mertons.

Merton the Teacher

For thirty-five years, Robert K. Merton has taught what were probably the most popular courses at Columbia, Sociology 213–214 and Sociology 215–216. (These numbers predate the invasion of the computer into the world of course listings. Today the second sequence is known as Sociology 6090x and 609ly.) Apart from the 30 odd students registered in these courses, the classroom would be packed with auditors. Many of the auditors would return year after year. In 1960, some eleven years after I first took courses with Merton and at least nine years after I stopped attending his courses, he had me lecture his students—to my astonishment, I found some of my classmates in the room.

Sociology 213–214 was a brilliant course organized as a theory of social control. RKM took all the giants of the discipline and showed how the work of each complemented that of the others and how the whole constituted a theory of social control. (For reasons I am not aware of, Merton stopped giving this course in the mid-fifties and devoted his time to the second sequence, Sociology 215–216 which dealt with functional analysis.) The reason that auditors would return year after year was because these courses were living things, continually evolving. Before each lecture, Merton would spend several hours preparing his presentation for the day. He always managed to evolve new ideas and insights that gave his lectures a freshness in spite of his many years of lecturing on the same topics.

Bob's brilliance as a lecturer rested in large part on his capacity to treat the obvious in a totally new way. He was able to take common sense observations and elaborate them in ways that were not at all commonsensical. This capacity to treat the obvious seriously contributed to a strange ambiguity about his courses. Because he was so deeply involved with his own insights and developing thought, Merton managed to convey his intellectual excitement to his students. When the class would break, the students would rush out talking breathlessly to each other about what they had just heard. His favorite lecture hour was 10 a.m. and when I was in graduate school I was a notorious late sleeper and missed a number of RKM's lectures. On these occasions, I would arrive just as the class was breaking so that I could find out from my friends what I had missed. The students would burst from the room chatting excitedly, engaged in debates and arguments. I would grab my friends, interrupt their dialogues and shout, "What did he say, what did he say?" They would look at me and exclaim it was the greatest lecture they had ever heard and more impatiently, I would shake them and ask, "What did he say, what did he say?" They would look at me startled and one would finally say something like, "Oh, he said people play social roles."

This capacity to question the obvious led

* To these might be added a fifth Merton, Merton the letter writer. But that's another story that will come to light when Merton's many file cabinets of letters are examined by future historians.

to the formulation of some of Merton's richest concepts. Among the many who worked on his unpublished housing study of the mid-forties (an eight hundred page manuscript has existed in mimeograph form since 1948) was Marie Jahoda. She was given the responsibility of analyzing the friendship data that had been collected and when her analysis showed that whites chose whites as friends, blacks chose blacks, young chose young, old chose old, Protestants chose Protestants, and Catholics chose Catholics, she wrote a memorandum presenting the findings, saying, "not surprisingly, the data show that 'birds of a feather flock together.'" Merton read the memo and puzzled over the obviousness of it all. Why, he thought, was it so obvious? Didn't "opposites attract"? And then, as only he can do so well, his puzzlement translated into a theoretical question: "Under what conditions do opposites attract and under what conditions do birds of a feather flock together?" And to pinpoint the question, Merton formulated his typological concepts of "homophily" and "heterophily."

Merton's great strength as a teacher and theorist rests on his ability to conceptualize the new things he finds from pondering the ordinary. He is a master at giving exciting names to his observations of the commonplace. For example, long before Linton (the author of the terms status and role), students of society were aware that people occupied multiple positions and had multiple relationships. But it took RKM to find the terms status and role unsatisfactory because they did not capture this multiplicity of positions and roles. And from his concepts of status-set and role-set came new concepts generated by the questions dealing with role strain and status-set integration. His search for mechanisms reducing role conflict led him to the clever concepts of "visibility" and "observability," concepts that capture the all too obvious fact that role partners may be unaware of each other's role performances.

Merton the teacher is inextricably entwined with Merton the theoretician. Teaching is commonly viewed as the transmission of discovered knowledge to the initiates. But for Merton, teaching is the process of generating new knowledge. More than perhaps any other sociologist, Merton's theoretical ideas live in his lectures rather than in his writings. His writings are merely the tip of the iceberg. Like Homer, Merton belongs more to an oral than to a written tradition. This is probably so because, for all his publications, Merton has a writing block. As his friends well know, he has many more unpublished than published books.

Merton the Poet

A key to this most unusual man of sociology is the realization that he loves words, in much the same way that a poet does, that language is important to him because he understands that the highest human faculty, thought, is dependent on language and words. Bob has no tolerance for fuzzy thinking expressed in fuzzy, ambiguous language. One need only consult an index of his work of love, *On the Shoulders of Giants: A Shandean Postscript,* entitled "Places, Things and Non-Things * (* Non-things=unreified concepts)" to learn of his unabashed love for rich, colorful, concept ridden words such as "aleurophile," "anatopic syndrome," "apocope," and "aposiopesis" to cite merely some of the entries under the letter "A." In fact, let us ponder this tome, *On the Shoulders of Giants.* It is one of three empirical studies that Merton has published (the other two being his dissertation and *Mass Persuasion*) and it is by far the longest. It is the only empirical study that he has published in the past 25 years. And yet, this major effort in empirical research is not about sociology at all. Rather it is a testimonial to his love for words. In fact, the index referred to above contains the word "words" under which there are three entries as follows:

Words
    abolition of, 132, 142, 173
    long, *see* polysyllables
    short, *see* monosyllables

The second and third entries are rather self-evident, but what in the world does he mean by the abolition of words? By consulting the cited pages we learn that he is citing one of his idols, Jonathan Swift, who first hit upon a plan to "shorten discourse, by cutting polysyllables into one, and leaving out verbs and participles, because in reality, all things imaginable are nouns." Later on we learn that Swift proposed abolishing words altogether for this would have an obvious advantage "in point of health, as well as brevity. For it is plain that every word we speak is, in some degree, a diminution of our lungs by corrosion, and, consequently contributes to the shortening of our lives." As this Swiftian digression makes clear, one reason why RKM loves words is because words are fun. Why else would he write a 290 page book about an aphorism falsely attributed to Isaac Newton? A moment's thought will show that it is at the heart of what is important to him. As a student of science, Merton well understood what countless others did, that science is a cumulative endeavor, that current work is based on the work of the past, that yesterday's failures, properly understood, generate today's successes, etc. But while all the other students of science were content to live with their insight that science is cumulative, it took Robert Merton to celebrate the genius of the mentality that could so aptly express this feature of science in the immortal phrase, "If I see further than my predecessors it is because I am standing on the shoulders of giants." The wit of the phrase! The false modesty it expresses! And the truth it conveys! All this and more captured RKM's imagination. And I am convinced that much of his brilliant phraseology, e.g., "self-fulfilling prophecy," "anticipatory socialization," "compensatory consumption," "Kindle cole principle," represents his effort to be an equal of the OTSOG phrase maker.

A rather large, intimate circle of Merton fans is aware of another way in which his romance with words has been expressed: his reading of dictionaries. Whether true or not, a large number of Merton's friends think that he has read the many volumes of the Oxford English dictionary.

Merton's love for and search for words led to one of the monumental achievements of his career, his resurrection of Horace Walpole's invention, "serendipity." Until Bob published his essay, "Sociological Theory" in the *American Journal of Sociology,* 1945, Vol. 50, the rich, evocative, fun-sounding word "serendipity" had been virtually lost to the world for almost 200 years. Within a decade of Merton's essay and his elaboration of the idea in a subsequent essay entitled, "The Bearing of Empirical Research on Sociological Theory" the word "serendipity" moved into the mass media, first in quotation marks with an explanation of its meaning following its appearance, and then later, as it gained more currency, without quotation marks and without an explanation of its meaning.

It should be noted that Merton was very much aware of his achievement with respect to "serendipity" and he was prepared to honor that achievement at the same time that he would contribute to sociological knowledge regarding the diffusion of inventions. In 1952 he began, with the assistance of Elinor Barber, a book on the word "serendipity." Only three chapters of this book were ever completed and it is now one of the many unpublished books that Merton is famous for. Yet a close examination of these chapters will show the same spirit, skill, and mentality which a decade later took on the Newtonian aphorism.

Merton, the wordsmith, was enthralled by the *sound* of words. Serendipity appealed to him not only for the miraculous concept for which it stood, but for its joyous sound. It is not too much to suggest that Merton has more in common with Vladimir Nabokov and John Updike than with Marx, Weber, Durkheim, and Parsons. After all, his favorite journals are not the *ASR* or the *AJS,* but rather those eighteenth and nineteenth century literary magazines, *The Edinburgh Review, Notes and Inquiries,* and *Athenaeum.*

Merton the Editor

Of all the Mertons missing from the Coser book, the most private is Merton the editor. After all, thousands of people know of Merton the teacher and at least as many know of Merton the poet. But Merton the editor is known only to hundreds of people who have benefitted from his careful analysis of their writings.

I am convinced that if he had his life to live over, he would not be a physical scientist, as much as he loves the process of scientific discovery and glories in scientific achievements, nor would he be a sociologist, even though he is championed as the best sociologist that America has produced. I believe that Merton's first love is with the world of publishing and editing, the world of books and words. If he had his way, I believe he would be both a publisher and an editor, a combination of Alfred Knopf and Maxwell Perkins. From such a position he could generate the twentieth century equivalent of *Notes and Inquiries,* and find fulfillment by launching the careers of young geniuses that he had discovered. The sad thing is that someday the great editors of American letters will be immortalized in one or another book, but Merton's place in this Pantheon of editors will go largely unrecognized.

His love for the world of books, publishing and editing is manifested in many ways. He is a fond collector of rare books that he uncovers in out of the way second-hand bookstores. He has been, for the past 25 years, the sociological editor of the prestigious publishing house of Harcourt Brace and World (now Harcourt Brace Jovanovich). No sociology book has been published by this firm without extensive editorial input from Bob

Merton. Further evidence of his true love is that he is one of the few non-fiction or popular writers who serves on the board of the Authors Guild, a quasi-union of authors.

Editors operate on at least two levels: copy editing and rough editing. The *copy* editor changes your words into words that express your thoughts more clearly while the *rough* editor tells you how to organize your thoughts to tell your story. The rough editor helps you evolve the table of contents for your book; the copy editor helps you write the paragraphs that express your thoughts. Bob Merton is superb as both types of editors. He did copy editing by blue pencilling the texts of the manuscripts presented to him, crossing out weak words and replacing them with strong words, wiping out ambiguous language and substituting crystal clear language. The record of Bob Merton the copy editor is spread out among the hundreds of people for whom he performed this role, and unfortunately the only evidence I have is the brilliant work he did for me. But for the past thirty-five years Merton, the rough editor, has written hundreds of lengthy and detailed memos to would-be authors explaining the flaws in their manuscripts, and suggesting means of correcting them.*

As a copy editor, Merton performs at least three distinct functions. First, he has a knack for sharpening or highlighting the prose by finding a more expressive word or phrase than the word that you chose. Second, he is a firm believer in Strunk's commandment, "omit needless words." Third, Merton performs a creative function as a copy editor. The author's arguments or problems trigger his own thought processes and he offers to his client, free of charge, brilliant reformulations of and additions to the arguments that reflect falsely on the brilliance of the author.

For the purpose of this review, I carried out a study of the editing Merton did on my own book, *The Poor Pay More*. I chose five pages at random and counted the number of words on these pages that were supplied by my editor, and the number of words in my original text that he had pruned. Merton words on these pages ranged from a low of 15% to a high of 25% and the number of Merton-pruned words ranged from 10 to 39. If my manuscript is any way typical, Merton is responsible for 15 to 25% of the words that appear in the books he has edited and he saves his clients an average of 20 needless words per page.

What distinguishes Merton from the typically good copy editor, in fact what makes him a unique copy editor, is his ability to enrich the author's argument by recasting the text in totally unexpected ways. In a chapter dealing with insolvency (a classification of families according to how deeply in debt they were) I showed that insolvency was related to worry over financial affairs. To put a brave face on this hardly earth shattering finding, I wrote:

> Not surprisingly, financial worries are strongly related to family solvency. . . . This is a rather important finding from the viewpoint of an action program, for it indicates that families will be receptive to efforts to help them cope with their financial problems.

I was so unimpressed with this section of the chapter that I wrote in the margin of the copy I sent over to Merton, "Banal, no? Omit, no?" Merton wrote under my comments, "I vote for retaining this . . ." and then in blue ink between the lines of my text he wrote:

> Some of the previous findings may have left the impression that insolvent families go their way, almost as though they were totally unaware of their perilous financial state. This is, of course, possible. In more societies than one, people in chronically difficult circumstances come to take their problems for granted, and in a significant sense do not know that they are in trouble. Is this the case here? Are the insolvent families unconcerned in the sense that they take their condition as inevitable or irremediable? . . . It is of no small interest, as we see from Table 21, that the more objectively difficult their financial state, the more often they worry about it. Evidently they are not resigned to their condition. And this expressed state of concern can provide a basis for organized remedial action among those who need it most.

In such a fashion does Merton transform an obvious banality into an interesting story.

One often hears speculation as to why Merton has published so little, given the vast expectations of productivity from this man. Morton Hunt, who profiled Merton for *The New Yorker* in January of 1961, noted that Merton had a number of (still) unpublished books, and when he confronted Merton with this, he replied, "some people publish much too much." The myth has evolved that Merton has not published more because he

*In 1963, recognizing me as a fan of his editorial skill, Merton turned over to me three thick folders containing carbons of his rough editing, covering the period from 1942 to 1963. Much of what I have to say about Merton the editor comes from these materials.

is a perfectionist and the manuscripts did not live up to his expectations. I have a simpler explanation. He has not published much of his own work because he has devoted so much of his time to the work of others. I submit that Merton has spent from a third to a half of his professional life reading and commenting on the work of others. I offer in support of this proposition a memo to himself that I found among the papers he turned over to me, documenting the manuscripts he edited over a two or three month period in the winter of 1959–60.

4 February 1960

Manuscripts Read

1. Henry Lennard—Dynamics of Psychotherapy (book manuscript)—5912:06
2. Lee Benson—Critics of Beard (book manuscript)—5912:25
3. Richard Christie—sampling paper
4. Terence Hopkins—authority paper—6001:03

. . . . .

52. Michael Crozier—France and CASBS, Bureaucracy in France
53. W. J. Goode—"A Theory of Role-Strain"—6001:26
54. George Homans—Elementary Social Behavior (book)
55. 6001:19—Rose Coser—Insulation from Observability and Types of Social Conformity (2nd revision)
56. Barney Berelson—Graduate Education (400 pp.)

Space limitations prevent me from reproducing the entire memorandum. Included among the 48 missing entries are such notables as Alvin Gouldner, Bennett Berger, Donald Campbell, Lewis Coser, Paul Lazarsfeld, Daniel Bell, Charles Loomis, and Robert Weaver. The subject matter of these manuscripts includes sampling, nursing research, housing, migration, French bureaucracy, role-strain, and graduate education. It is conceivable that Merton is an expert in all these areas, but a simpler explanation is that the skills of a rough editor cut across specific areas. Regardless of the subject, there is a right way and a wrong way to tell the story, and the talented rough editor can help make this distinction. As for the authors, they include not only eminent sociologists, but obscure graduate students, and notables of other disciplines, e.g., social psychology, history, and anthropology. What greater testimony to RKM the rough editor than this universal list of clients?

Note should be taken of Merton's method of dating the documents he had read. I had always assumed that this was his invention but from a copy of a letter of his to Joshua Lederberg (they are currently collaborating on a book on science), I learn that Merton's mentor, Sarton, invented the system. Thus the Lederberg letter is dated as follows:

> Saturday, 23 September 1972
> [or, in the to-me far preferable, private dating symbolism invented by Geo. Sarton: 7209:23-mortality-rates assuring that the first two digits could be safely ignored by the likes, cohort-likes of GS & me; you, however, will have to count on bright biographers who can infer the first 2 digits from the 3rd & 4th (unless you propose to outdo the longevity of Fontenelle who having stumbled into his 101st year, almost managed to give literal meaning to his post as "perpetual secretary" of the Academie des Sciences]

Only Merton can write half a page before he begins a letter.

The full flower of Robert K. Merton, the rough editor, emerges from the vast array of commentaries he prepared on other people's manuscripts. Merton became engaged as an editor in four different ways. Early in his career, he was frequently asked by publishers to evaluate manuscripts that they were considering publishing. Second, he edited the papers of the various contributors to collections of essays that he edited, notably *Sociology Today* and *Contemporary Social Problems*; third, some twenty-five years ago he became the sociological editor for Harcourt Brace and thus evaluated all the social science books they considered publishing; and, finally, he receives each year a large number of unsolicited manuscripts from former students and colleagues for his opinions of their work.

The first publisher to consult Merton as a critic of a manuscript, according to the documents on hand, was Oxford University Press. On May 8, 1942, the trade editor of this publisher wrote the following letter to Merton:

> You have been suggested to me by Franz Neumann as the best possible person to review a manuscript on the economics of Karl Marx, which we now have under consideration. We should very much like to have your opinion of this manuscript. . . .

It may well come as a surprise to today's radical sociologists that a leading Marxist scholar, Franz Neumann, considered Merton to be an expert on Marx. And what was the manuscript that Merton was asked to evaluate? Only that classic of the left, Paul M. Sweezy's, *The Theory of Capitalist Development,* published by Oxford in 1942. Merton had high praise for the Sweezy book and wrote the trade editor a week later:

> . . . In my opinion it is eminently worth publishing. It is a painstaking, systematic, lucid, at times brilliant, exposition of Marxian economics unequalled by anything else in the literature, so far as I know. . . . I am enclosing a few comments on details of the manuscript. It is more than probable that Mr. Sweezy will reject some of these suggestions, but if you wish, you may pass these on to him.

What Merton refers to as a few comments turns out to be a nine page single-spaced document commenting on some ninety-three pages of text spread out over eighteen chapters of the Sweezy manuscript. (Whether it is symptomatic of some character quirk such as parsimony or niggardliness, almost all of Merton's commentaries are single spaced, and sometimes he types on both sides of the page.) Sweezy was so impressed that he sent Merton a lengthy memo with his comments on Merton's comments. Some idea of Merton's contribution is provided by a sampling of Sweezy's comments:

3. The contrast (alleged) between Marx and "most economists" as to genesis of interests and convictions is really irrelevant to my argument and has been eliminated. The point as it stood was quite open to the criticism you make.
5. Your distinction between *empirical* and *concrete* truth in connection with the law of the increasing misery of the proletariat is well taken. Those who have disputed endlessly about this problem have been hopelessly confused on this issue.
7. I agree that Marx's selection of the "essential" is in the nature of an hypothesis rather than an intuitive grasp of the "essence." I have tried to alter the formulation to avoid the latter implication.
15. You are correct that it was a mistake to speak at the outset about the capitalist's "desire" to accumulate. . .
20. It was an error to say that "wants are fundamentally continuous." What I meant is that consumption is fundamentally continuous.
22. I was particularly glad that you found this discussion useful. It is probably the most "original" contribution I have to make to the pure theory of capitalism.
37. The footnote on the Spanish Civil War is a good suggestion.

The role of the rough editor in making conceptual distinctions, in clarifying ambiguous, fuzzy lines of thought, in suggesting new ideas, is more than hinted at by Sweezy's comments on Merton's comments.

Merton's next major analysis of a manuscript was also done for Oxford University Press, an anthropological work by Olga Lang, entitled, *Chinese Family and Society.* Merton's blow by blow review of the text resulted in nineteen single-spaced pages. In addition to his detailed commentary, Merton wrote the author a five page memorandum in which he summarized his criticisms, and tried to soften the blow by complimenting the author on her work.

Following the Lang review, Merton moved in the mid-forties to reviewing a series of sociological classics, including James West's *Plainville, U.S.A.;* Wilbert E. Moore's *Industrial Relations and the Social Order;* Robert MacIver's *Social Causation;* and Kingsley Davis's textbook, *Human Society.* Each of these authors received from five to fourteen pages of single-spaced commentaries. Also, Merton put his imprimatur on two classics in the history of science, Dorothy Stimson's *Scientists and Amateurs: A History of the Royal Society,* and Benjamin Farrington's book on Francis Bacon. Merton's wealth of knowledge on the history of science shines through these commentaries.

In some cases the file at my disposal is extremely fragmentary. In one instance there is no carbon of the commentary, or letters from publishers, or Merton's evaluation for the publisher. The only trace of Merton's effort is a letter of gratitude from the author. On September 30, 1947, one of the founding fathers of American anthropology, 71 year old Alfred L. Kroeber, wrote to 37 year old Robert K. Merton:

> I want to thank you for your valuable string of comments on my book. In a few cases I have regretfully been obliged to lay these aside because the way the firm is crowding me on time it would be quite impossible to do any rewriting. However, usually I have been able at least to affect a little touching up and incorporate at least the essence of your point. The book consequently is going to be definitely improved as a result of your efforts. I am especially grateful to you for having picked me up on the ascription to Linton of the value-attitude relation. I was thinking of course of status and role.

From the timing of the Kroeber letter, it is obvious that the book in question is the second edition of *Anthropology,* Kroeber's classic textbook.

The second way that Merton came to comment on the writings of others was through his being the editor of two major collections of sociological essays, *Sociology Today* and *Contemporary Social Problems.* Some thirty-nine essays were prepared for these volumes and the files at my disposal contain Merton's commentaries on twenty-seven of these papers. The commentaries range from a mere half page on the essays by Bales and Hughes for *Sociology Today,* to six and seven page commentaries on the contributions of David Riesman and Robert Weiss, Scott Greer, William Goode, Seymour Lipset, and Morris Janowitz for *Contemporary Social Problems,* to a thirteen page commentary on Jack Gibbs's essay on suicide to a sixteen page commentary on James Coleman's article on community disorganization. A glance at these commentaries shows that they deal largely with the art of sociological writing. Merton politely but firmly tells these major figures how to write: how to present their ideas, how to organize their thoughts, how to communicate to the reader. He chastizes them for their obfuscations, their fuzziness, their conceptual ambiguities, and he generously praises them for the ideas that he likes.

The third way in which Merton came to comment on the work of others was through his position as the sociological editor for Harcourt Brace. Some twenty-three books have appeared in the series he has edited, ranging from textbooks to the major publications of Homans, Coser, Stinchcombe, and Kroeber. The archeological record on hand, dating to 1963, provides but four samples of his work for this firm, each one a textbook that was obviously commissioned by the publisher before the manuscripts were written. These texts are *An Introduction to the Study of Society* by Blaine Mercer, *The Principles of Organization* by Theodore Caplow, *Modern Sociology* by Alvin Gouldner and Helen Gouldner, and *Sociological Research: A Case Approach* by Matilda White Riley. Whereas Merton's evaluations of completed manuscripts ranged from three to twenty single-spaced pages, he generated this amount of criticism for each chapter of these textbooks and this labor extended over many months and even years as the authors developed and revised their manuscripts.

Although the record contains extensive documents bearing on Merton's labors on behalf of these texts, it is by no means complete. For example, I have Merton's comments on the first drafts of nine chapters of Mercer's text and his comments on second drafts of five other chapters; the file contains three sets of commentaries on the Caplow text dealing with first or second drafts of only four chapters; the Gouldners' book generated four commentaries dealing with four chapters of the first draft and a fifth commentary dealing with the entire second draft. The record of Merton's labors is most complete for the Riley textbook. This work is organized into twelve units equivalent to chapters and Merton produced lengthy commentaries on each one. The Riley text also found Merton innovating. After producing some 33 pages of single-spaced criticism on the first six units, Merton switched to dictating his comments which were then transcribed by his secretary. The dictation generated 109 double-spaced pages of comments. Matilda White Riley recently told me that Merton's criticisms exceeded the length of her manuscript, and though this may be an exaggeration, it is not a *great* exaggeration.

Some clue to Merton's input in these endeavors is provided by the contrast between his comments on the first and second drafts of the Gouldner and Gouldner book. The first four chapters of the first draft generated a total of 42 pages of single-spaced commentary. Had Merton commented on all fifteen first draft chapters, he would have produced some 160 single-spaced pages of criticism (a fair sized book's worth). His commentary on the 1,456 page second draft is only 28 pages long. This would suggest that the Gouldners were able to learn from Merton's comments on their first draft and produce a second draft more in keeping with his standards of excellence.

I happened to spend a good deal of time reading and analyzing these commentaries and I am convinced that they provide the basis for an excellent text on sociological writing. Merton's commentaries for the most part fall into two broad categories, what I call matters of substance and matters of exposition. Substance deals with the merits of the story that the author has to tell. Is it true or not? Is it complete? Does it touch all bases? Are the definitions correct? Exposition, in contrast, deals with how the story is told, that is, the art of communication. Does the author convey ideas clearly? Is the prose crisp or sloppy? Does the telling conform to time sequences or does the story spill out in all directions? Is the prose too compact or is it too loose? Does the story begin properly? Does it end properly? Occasionally

Merton's comments deal with copy editing, e.g., an appropriate word or phrase, excessive words, redundancies, etc.

I have been able to identify at least eighteen subcategories of substantive criticisms, the major ones being conceptual confusion, false generalizations, empty assertions, extreme formulations, tautologies, non sequitors, contradictions, false distinctions, overstatements, and understatements. Under the general heading of exposition are such things as faulty openings (not beginning a book or chapter properly), faulty closing (endings that are too abrupt), continuity bungling, need to define concepts, need for concrete examples, and what I call basic structural flaws, that is, faulty organization of a chapter or book.

The fourth way in which Merton came to comment on the manuscripts of others stemmed from his underground reputation as an editor. Former students and colleagues who at one time or another had been exposed to his editorial skill, would send him their unsolicited manuscripts. Apart from his contributions to the manuscript, Merton performed an extremely important function for would-be authors. If they could get their manuscripts past him, then they had nothing to worry about. They could relax in the knowledge that it would be acceptable to any journal or publisher with little or no further revisions required. Many of Merton's students have used him in this manner. People like Bernard Barber, Lewis Coser, Rose Coser, Suzanne Keller, Alvin Gouldner, Alice Rossi, Patricia Kendall, Steven Cole and myself, rarely publish their manuscripts without first soliciting Merton's comments. Sometimes, because Merton is too busy, things go awry. For example, he never found the time to read and comment on Alvin Gouldner's manuscript for *The Coming Crisis in Western Sociology*, and just as he was about to find time, he discovered to his dismay that the book was being published. The book thus appeared before Merton could register his comments and criticisms. This proved to be so frustrating for Merton that he converted his Fall seminar on functional analysis that year into a critique of that book. His students were bewildered and could not understand why he was spending so much time on this single book.

Merton the Critic

A fourth Merton unacknowledged in the Coser Festschrift is Merton the critic. Whereas the editor responds to the *unpublished* manuscript, the critic reacts to the *published* book. For my money, the most fascinating paper in the Festschrift is the Merton bibliography prepared under close supervision by his secretary, Mary Miles. For the first time we are told where articles have been reprinted (did you know that "Social Structure and Anomie" has been reprinted twenty-eight times?), and we are presented with introductions and forewords to books and commentaries by others on one's work, in all, such an innovative bibliography that it will no doubt set the standard for the next hundred years. What I find most fascinating in this fascinating document is the list of book reviews that Merton has done. In all, Merton has published some 113 book reviews, probably a record for anyone who is not a professional reviewer. While still in his twenties he published 50 reviews and in the next two years 26 more, bringing the total by age thirty-one to 76. After that Merton's output falls off sharply and by his late forties he had virtually ceased this activity. In the past two decades he has reviewed a mere 10 books. Had Merton kept up his earlier pace, he would have published more than 400 book reviews. I suspect that as he grew older Merton became more involved with the role of editor and less with the role of critic for, after all, as an editor he could put his stamp on the final product.

Merton, the critic, not only reviewed books for publication. He also wrote flattering letters to the authors of books he approved of. The Merton file at my disposal contains a number of letters of appreciation from authors whose books Merton privately reviewed and no doubt many more such letters can be found in Merton's extensive files of his correspondence. The following is a particularly apt example of such a letter of gratitude for an unsolicited private RKM review of one book:

> April 12, 1957
>
> Dear Bob Merton:
>
> Not since I won the Wabash River Swim in the summer of 1927 have I been so thrilled as I was in reading your letter. I hope you don't mind the comparison. They both involve an emotional element, appropriate to the years, I hope.
>
> Since I started on this tack I have been rather lonely. It took time to acquire the vague understanding I have of the language, concepts and techniques of social science. Then came the field work; then the book. That meant

that for ten years I scarcely produced anything in the way of scholarship. Colleagues in my own field looked at me askance for venturing out of our traditional limits. Social scientists welcomed my interest but showed that I was not really one of them, so I say it was lonely.

Now to receive a letter from the first sociologist in the country, approving of what I have done, makes me feel wonderful. I feel as though I were accepted into professional circles again.

Even many of my own colleagues in Romance Languages have said nice things about the book although some feel I have been tainted by my contact with social sciences and don't give the book a chance.

I don't mean to sound gloomy. To the contrary, my ego has never been so flattered in my life—except at the time of the Wabash River Swim, of course. I am terribly happy that you liked the book and terribly grateful to you for taking the trouble to write me about it.

Sincerely yours,
Laurence Wylie

Wylie was teaching at Haverford College when he wrote this letter. It is a measure of Merton's keen eye for spotting talent that Wylie today is the C. Douglas Dillon Professor of French Civilization at Harvard.

Wylie's tribute to RKM is a fitting close to this review of the other Mertons. You'll recall that Merton's presidential address at the 1957 ASA meetings dealt with eponymy. I wonder: is it possible to name an age after an editor?

RANDALL COLLINS
University of California, San Diego

Robert Merton was no doubt the best known figure within professional American sociology during the middle of the twentieth century. This is not to say he was the most famous in the outside world: that would probably be David Riesman. Nor the one with the greatest political impact: that would certainly be C. Wright Mills. Nor the major comprehensive theorist, which would be Talcott Parsons. And none of these, in my opinion, is the figure who contributed most to intellectual progress: that honor might well go to Erving Goffman, and also collectively to a number of theory-oriented empirical researchers in various fields. But citation studies of the sociological literature prove what we would tend to take for granted: Merton had the greatest visibility and impact in the discipline for the period that began some time around the Second World War and lasted until about 1965.

Why is he so eminent? Partly, because of the sheer number of areas in which he works, the research traditions that he began or contributed to, and the modes of analysis he labelled and popularized. In other words, Merton was the formulator of a considerable number of mini-paradigms. Or was he? This Festschrift volume is rather a good place to piece this out, for it contains not only a great many biographical encomiums, but a long section of essays "on the shoulders of Merton," which generally review the various fields in which he worked, and a couple of detailed sociology of science studies of the growth of two areas in which he made especially famous contributions. Not everything can be taken at face value, of course, since this volume consists of the Merton camp extolling their own leader. But the material is there, both in form and content, for a fairly comprehensive assessment of Merton's work and of the process that made it eminent.

The work falls by and large into five areas: (1) anomie and deviance; (2) the sociology of science; (3) various aspects of role theory, including cosmopolitans and locals, reference groups, and role sets; (4) structural ironies and dilemmas; (5) bureaucracy, and especially the bureaucratic personality. There are also his methodological essays, which add up to the reminder, once badly needed and still very pertinent, that theory and empirical research develop best in mutual interaction. This is something not specifically treated in this volume, perhaps because it is an overall strategy of analysis rather than a contribution to a particular field. It is the strategy that put him in the running for sociological eminence, though; Merton situated himself at the cross-roads of a discipline of almost mutually oblivious approaches, and thereby managed to come as near as anyone to directing traffic.

(1) Merton's paper "Social Structure and Anomie" is apparently the most cited paper in all of American sociology. According to Stephen Cole, it was the dominant theory in the area of deviance from the early 1950s until about 1970, when symbolic interactionist-labelling theory came to the fore. It proposes that deviance is engendered by the social system as a way for individuals to react to a disparity between society-wide goals (monetary success) and institutional-

ized means (mobility opportunities). If one interprets (as Cole does) Albert K. Cohen's delinquency theory as a version of Merton's, then one can make out a strong case for influence on a major line of empirical research, and one with a fair amount of explanatory power.

Yet certain questions arise. As Cole himself notes, relatively few of the papers citing Merton attempted to test the theory; even fewer presented contradicting evidence. Most simply referred to it as part of the review of the literature, or as a legitimation for the author's theories and interpretations. Cole takes this as supporting a Kuhnian view of paradigms as rising and falling not by empirical proof or disproof, but by some larger social factors. Thus labelling theory came on strong a few years ago, not because Merton was disproved, but because the fashion had shifted. If we look backwards in time, we find a similar phenomenon: a paper first published in 1938 sat dormant for about fifteen years, before enjoying a rise to phenomenal popularity in the literature. Why? Perhaps it was really Albert K. Cohen who made Merton famous in this area, and not vice versa. Or more fundamentally in the background, the great juvenile delinquency scare arose in the 1950s, which Martin Trow has nicely shown elsewhere was related to the shift to mass secondary schooling, filling up the high schools with recalcitrant working class students. So Merton's theory rode a wave which came along at the right time for it to make legitimate sociology out of topical social-problems investigations. Yet this is not entirely accidental; after all, in this rather parochial and theory-less area, he invoked the high intellectual shades of Emile Durkheim; and his typological category-constructing resonated with the contemporary grand typologizing of Talcott Parsons. And perhaps most importantly, it was a basically All-American theory; the great American creed of social mobility occupies the center of the stage, and lack of mobility opportunities (not the more fundamental structure of inequalities of distribution) is the villain of this structural drama.

(2) The sociology of science is an area which is even more uniquely Merton's own. His Ph.D. thesis was in this area, and most of his publications of the later years as well as his current work are here. Here we find Merton's application of the so-called "Weber thesis" to science, claiming that the Puritan ethos affected the scientific revolution of the seventeenth century. We find also his analysis of multiple discoveries in science, leading up to the argument that virtually all discoveries are really multiples, produced by the social structure of science rather than by individuals. There is his analysis of the norms of science, which include not only disinterestedness and intellectual communism, but the recognition of priority in scientific discoveries—Merton's claim that a disinterested element normatively governs the priority disputes that rage through the hisory of science. There is his fairly recent formulation of the "Matthew Effect," by which already famous scientists are more easily recognized for their contributions than new and obscure individuals, and which serves to integrate a science around a central focus of attention. And there is a considerable group of Merton's students, especially those of the last decade, who have developed the sociology of science as an empirical field.

As Jonathan Cole and Harriet Zuckerman (two of these students) show, Merton is far and away the most cited individual in this field since the mid-1950s. Nevertheless, one can question just what this really means. Substantively, I would suggest, Merton has done more for the sociology of science by drawing attention to the area, than in actual theoretical or empirical contributions. For the "Merton thesis" on Puritanism has almost no supporters among historians and historical sociologists of science; there were far too many Catholic scientists in the seventeenth century (an overwhelming number, outside of England), and in England itself it turns out that most of the Royal Society members, and its most eminent figures, were not real Puritans at all, but latitudinarians and backsliders. The model of multiple discoveries (put forward a good deal earlier than Merton by William F. Ogburn, among others) has turned out to go nowhere. The analysis of "norms" simply leads to a glorification of science as a perfectly tuned system, and has had little empirical application or explanatory development; in effect, it says that scientists are really disinterested, good people, and that everything happens pretty much for the best in that world. I would say that priority disputes show, much more importantly than disinterestedness, that scientists are competitive and contentious; they force other scientists to recognize yet a third scientist's priority, not because they are so disinterested, but in order to put down the pretensions of the second party with whom they are arguing. (Examine the conversations you have with your intellectual acquaintances and see if this is not so.) This kind of analysis would lead off into another direction, of course; it would point to the variations in resources that individuals have for producing intellectual work and commanding agreement, and thence to a more content-oriented explanation of what gets produced and when it gets accepted, instead of a bare formal argument that social systems are controlled by ideal norms. The same could be said about the "Matthew Effect," which really says that stratification does exist in science, but that it is basically a good thing, or at worst, an inevitable irony; it does not go on to make this an explanatory and testable model of what produces variations in stratification and hence in the types of science produced.

Looking at Merton's work in the sociology of science externally, rather than internally as I have done in the previous paragraphs, it seems apparent that his eminence in the field is not due to his having organized a workable paradigm. Again we find the lag: his Puritanism theory comes from the 1930s, republished in the late 1940s; his norms and priorities papers in the 1940s and 50s. But the literature of the field only begins to take off in the 1960s; and indeed, it is only after that that Merton himself begins to have an active research group working closely on his ideas. What happened in the early 1960s to set off the field, I would suggest, was a couple of inputs from quite different directions: Derek de Solla Price, who set off the quantitative study of scientists and citations, and above all Thomas Kuhn, with his iconoclastic theory of paradigms and paradigm-revolutions. (Ironically, one can even find evidence for this among Merton's own students; the two by and large excellent papers in this volume by the two Coles and Zuckerman, reflect much more the influence of Kuhn and Price in their methodology and theoretical reflections, than they do that of Merton.) One could even say that it was the appearance of several rival approaches that sparked Merton's revival of his own sociology of science in the latter part of the decade. In other words, one cannot explain what happens in a science by a bare analysis of some hypostatized systemic norms; nor even by the career of a particular individual or group. Rather, the conflict among rival groups may well be the feature that most strongly influences work in a given field. But this leads to a type of conflict analysis that Merton was at pains to avoid.

(3) Merton's solidest contributions, in my opinion, are in the area of role theory. I have never been overly fond of the theory of role sets; like so much of this analysis, it takes phenomena that are basically matters of stratification and disinfects them by passing them through a bath of abstractions, substituting "horizontal" categories for hierarchical ones. Yet Rose Laub Coser, in a fine paper entitled "The Complexity of Roles as a Seedbed of Individual Autonomy," uses this idea to bring together the work of Melvin Kohn and of Basil Bernstein, around the theme that differences in class cultures can be explained as products of more and less complicated role sets in people's daily encounters. Reference group theory brings us back to Merton's old favorite idea of the centrality of social mobility; Herbert Hyman's paper here gives us some potentially interesting survey data on "reference idols," but doesn't manage to bring off any theoretical interpretations. (This serves to remind us that when C. Wright Mills attacked "abstracted empiricism," he had the Columbia department in mind; Merton had an alliance with empiricists that tended to give them concepts to label their findings, but didn't necessarily generate explanations.) The theory of cosmopolitan and local roles, on the other hand, managed to set itself free from the social mobility theme. Some of the biographical materials in this volume point out that Merton initially attempted to categorize community influentials by their mobility patterns, but eventually hit on a more fruitful categorization, in terms of their structural positions. Gouldner fleshed this out empirically, and this research tradition shows up in the volume in a closely reasoned and empirically supported paper by Peter Blau which shows a number of countervailing attitudinal effects of cosmopolitan and local orientations among university faculty. Blau's main advance, interestingly enough, is to introduce the hierarchical status dimension back into role sets, and thus greatly increase the number of individual and aggregate phenomena it can explain. Here Merton has plainly engendered a considerable tradition of empirical analysis, and one that has made steady progress in explanatory refinement.

(4) Under the category of "structural ironies and dilemmas," one would include Merton's papers on manifest and latent functions; on self-fulfilling prophecies; and on the dilemmas of applied social researchers. This style of analysis has certainly had considerable appeal. But it is not an appeal to actual explanatory power: it does not tell us

what sort of conditions produce various outcomes, and hence it does not lend itself to test. What it gives instead is a kind of imagery of the world, and one with a strongly implied (but nicely disguised) political resonance. "Manifest and latent functions," after all, was a very abstract way of talking about "corrupt" political machines and why they survive. But it distracts from the struggle for power and privilege, and tells us instead that the system distributes these things, and that if our ideals seem not to be fulfilled in reality, one should look beneath the surface to where some aspect of the great self-equilibrating system does get its way. "Self-fulfilling prophesies" are introduced via the example of race relations; Merton's perspective is a liberal one, pointing out that prejudice and discrimination end up producing their own empirical justifications. But again, this ends up distracting attention from either an explanatory theory of variations in racial domination, or even from a practical effort to change the situation. Instead, the self-equilibrating image rolls gradually but inexorably into the center of attention; that's the way society is (is it really?) and the height of sociological intellect is to capture the pattern and appreciate the irony.

(5) Finally, there was the involvement of Merton in the upsurge of interest in bureaucracies as of the 1940s and 1950s. He was early into the area, and his paper on the bureaucratic personality is a fine exposition of a major idea whose origin was in Mannheim's distinction between substantive and functional rationality. Whatever impetus he gave to the organizational studies that came out of Columbia was certainly salutary, for these included major works of Blau and Gouldner (and perhaps more remotely, Selznick). But it is clear that the field owed much more of its growth to the Harvard Business School (institutional base for Mayo and Barnard), and to the Chicago school. What is apparent, though, was Merton's eye for where the action was, even though this was not a field which he entered, or legitimated, in a big way.

If there is a central theme that underlies virtually all of Merton's work, I would say it is the effort to de-fuse stratification issues. In good American style, structural inequalities are simply settings for the drama of social mobility. Instances of conflict, whether in the form of juvenile crime or scientific priority disputes, are refocused onto the claim that they really are evidence for some common values that people are upholding or striving to attain. Relationships of authority and subordination are transformed into abstract collections of roles; political conflicts and racial domination become instances of self-equilibrating systems. This kind of intellectual sleight-of-hand makes a fine stage for virtuoso performances; and given the probability that Merton's liberal biases were shared by most of his sociological audience, they drew quite a crowd. Just what the political biases of his followers have turned out to be is even more explicit in this volume: with the exception of a piece by Gouldner, these papers range from the complacent acceptance of dominant groups' definitions of reality (e.g., in Patricia Kendall's old-fashioned idealizing of the physician); to S.M. Lipset and Asoke Basu's subdued polemic (in the guise of a typology) against culturally unproductive but rabble-rousing intellectuals; to Robert Nisbet's fulminations against all modernist intellectuals, which leads him to the claim that the Renaissance produced no creative work at all (for some reason, art not being something Nisbet counts). This leads to some ironic empirical consequences, as in the piece by Charles Wright on the mass media. Wright is so concerned to show that exposure to the media leads to more information and good citizenship that he constantly fails to notice that his own data show an enormous split between the correlates of television-watching (which is related to greater political ignorance) and of the print media. He is at even greater loss to understand why it is that college-educated people who neither watch television nor read daily newspapers should have the highest level of political awareness of all. The idea that highly cosmopolitan groups might regard the media as politically biased and a relatively worthless source of information seems not to have occurred to him; nor even that television-watching is highest among the locals of the working class rather than the cosmopolitans of the upper classes. Here his blindness to class variations and a lack of any critical awareness about ideology leads to missing patterns visible on the very surface of the data.

What was weak about American sociology in the years in which Merton worked was its attempt to de-fuse stratification. In the process it ended up turning away from the very variables that are most fundamental to consider in any real explanatory theory. Those were, after all, the years of the great anti-Communist scares. Intellectuals probably did magnify the extent of the threat to themselves from the radical right, but it is clear enough that they turned against each other, conducting their own internal witch-hunts to avoid being hunted themselves. Marxism was thus driven as far away from mainstream sociology as possible. Yet it has been precisely in the times in which Marxism, and radicalism generally, has been strong, that the intellectual dialogue has had to focus on the crucial materials. In cutting off that dialogue, mid-century American sociology cut off its mainspring of development.

And yet after reading this book, I ended up appreciating Merton better than I had before. Which is not to say that this is the kind of book one is likely to enjoy reading. Even by the ordinary standards of a ritual Festschrift, it is unusually well packed with empty rhetoric, trivial reminiscence, and aging papers pulled out of the bottom of old desk drawers. But it praises Merton as much as it can and thus magnifies his intellectual achievement. Merton rose to prominence in the dark ages of American sociology, the cold war years of the 1940s and 1950s. He helped guide sociology across those mindless and repressive years, even as he helped perpetuate the darkness.

MAURICE R. STEIN
Brandeis University

Having been assured by the review editor that mine is to be one of two reviews of this book, I will use my assigned space to allow Lewis A. Coser and a few of his contributors to convey the spirit of their book in their own words. Even though I was a student at Columbia (Venice? Florence?) during the purported renaissance, it seems more appropriate to allow those whose lives were profoundly transfigured by the experience to speak for themselves.

LEWIS A. COSER

"Much the same was, of course, true for Merton's Columbia students after he moved there in the forties. Yet there was a subtle difference between Harvard and Columbia. Most of Merton's students—Gouldner, the Blaus, Selznick, Lipset, the Rossis, the Cosers, Keller, and many others—tended to be more politically engaged than the Harvard students of the thirties. The New Deal 'revolution' already belonged to the past, yet Merton had been profoundly influenced by it. These young, and predominantly Jewish, intellectuals dreamed of pushing the frontiers of American politics further toward the Left. Robert Lynd, and later C. Wright Mills, encouraged them in this respect. Merton on his part dazzled them with his profound knowledge of the Marxian canon, while attempting to defuse their ideological propensities by stressing that sociological ideas of very different ideological origins can fruitfully be combined in an effort to build systematic theories of the middle range, which in turn could inform policy-making. Theoretical gold, he often repeated, could be found in the most unlikely ideological quarries. And there was, of course, the close intellectual companionship of Lazarsfeld and Merton. At first blush this combination of European positivistic empiricism and American functionalist theory seemed most unlikely. Yet it worked. Merton's students tended to be held back from undue flights of fancy by Lazarsfeld's earthy and rigorous methodological style, and Lazarsfeld's students, in their turn, were reminded that the facts never speak for themselves" (p. 7).

HANAN C. SELVIN

"Most sociologists received their graduate education in departments that were dominated by a single person. They often describe their professional orientations by referring to this experience. They studied under Parsons, Hughes, or Park, they will say, and everyone knows what kind of sociologist each one is.

Those of us who were fortunate enough to have been graduate students at Columbia during the period from 1939 to 1970 had an altogether different experience. We were satellites, not of one sun, but of two, for Robert K. Merton and Paul F. Lazarsfeld so dominated sociology at Columbia during these three decades that no lesser figure of speech will suffice. Like a giant double star, each strengthened the other's radiance, and all of us basked in their combined illumination.

Dramatic as this metaphor is, it still does not do justice to the experience of being a graduate student under these two men. Many of us fell, sooner or later, into a regular orbit around either Merton or Lazarsfeld, with occasional showers of cosmic radiation from the other" (p. 7).

ROSE LAUB COSER

"Merton stands in a long tradition, from Vico to Hegel and Marx, that stresses conflict and contradiction in society. But he has gone further in the building of a theory because he has attempted to *specify* and *locate* disjunctions, contradictions, and conflicts within the social structure" (p. 238).

PAUL F. LAZARSFELD

"My second example involves the utilization of Merton's sensitivity to latent factors. In the tax load of a corporation, it makes a difference whether an advertisement is intended to augment the sale of a product or increase the corporation's prestige. The latter —institutional advertising—has some tax advantages. Sometimes it is not easy to make the distinction. If a company stresses the care with which it selects its raw materials, to which type of advertising does such promotion belong? I understand that Merton redefined the problem in terms of latent messages. By combining quantitative content analysis, talks with copywriters (who were not aware of the legal implications) and, I believe, some interviews with consumers, he developed criteria acceptable to the tax authorities. I am convinced that the cumulation of such cases, covering twenty-five years of experience, would greatly contribute to codifying the nature of sociological advice" (p. 60).

JAMES S. COLEMAN

"It is useful also to ask which societies are those in which bribery, graft, and other forms of corruption on the part of public officials flourish most. Generally, it is underdeveloped countries, in which the principal corporate actor of importance is, traditionally, the family and into which a modern bureaucratic form of organization has been transplanted. In such societies, there is little history of resources belonging to corporate actors of a bureaucratic form and little experience in the separation of corporate resource and personal resources. For the family, as a corporate actor whose members are permanent and whose size is small, such separation of personal and corporate resources is less important than for the modern bureaucratic corporate actor. Thus, we would expect such use of corporate resources for personal ends to be most fully pronounced in those societies that have least experience with bureaucratic bodies" (pp. 233–234).

CHARLES R. WRIGHT

"It is beyond the scope of this chapter to develop the applicability of these concepts to mass media audiences. The examples provided thus far, however, are not without relevance. We have suggested that not merely social mobility (itself possibly an abstract sociological characterization of roles), but also the intergenerational class continuity or discontinuity of lifestyles indexed by such mobility, is a useful way of classifying individuals in order to study their communications behavior. We have seen how the social role of being married can be refined by considering the homogeneity or heterogeneity of the educational statuses of the two partners and, in turn, how this relates to mass media usage. And we have speculated on the normative features of such role combinations that might account for differences in communications behavior. We have, at points, suggested the utility of such concepts as role-sets and status-sequences for analyzing media behavior: the former aiding understanding of how an individual's communications habits may be altered by the characteristics of one role partner, a spouse; the latter through consideration of movements between generations, or aging and retirement" (p. 408–409).

LEWIS A. COSER and ROBERT NISBET

"R.N. . . . . What we had, starting in the late 1930s in this country, was a distinct renaissance in sociology. I take nothing whatever away from earlier centers such as Chicago and Michigan when I say that Harvard and Columbia were in a sense the Venice and Florence of the sociological renaissance. I'm not sure which was Venice and which was Florence, but it doesn't matter. The point is, we had a couple of extremely creative centers, relatively small in size, that drew an impressive number of talented minds which, when they got there, achieved heights of excellence they just might not have achieved elsewhere.

L.C. Your Venice/Florence analogy is most apt. I am not sure either which was which. But if the art historians are right in stressing that Venetian painting excelled by its dazzling display of color whereas Florence was the home of austere structural arrangement and precise elaboration of perspective, then I would say that Columbia was Venice and Harvard Florence" (p. 6).

ALVIN W. GOULDNER

"Ordinariness and stability are the ontological requirements of security. Or, more properly, of the sense of security, and of passivity and acquience also. To construct a social world that is ordinary and solid is to quiet doubts and anxieties, to relax and tranquilize; it is to create a world in which one can be at home, or rather, at Home. Normal sociology's task, then, is to put men at their ease and to make the world homey. It is to populate it with those like ourselves, persons prepared to negotiate reasonable terms, so that each may continue to enjoy his familiar comforts. This has one small merit as a characterization of normal, academic sociology: it helps explain how it is possible to have a "science of man" that lived through continual catastrophes and people-devouring wars without speaking of war, of imperialism, of conflicts, tensions, poverty, of racism, of sexism, of hunger, of false promises, viciousness, and envy. These, after all, are scarcely the furnishing of a homey world" (p. 432).

FEATURE ESSAYS

Creativity: The Magic Synthesis, by SILVANO ARIETI. New York: Basic Books, 1976. 448 pp. $15.95 cloth.

Stimulating Creativity, Volume 2: Group Procedures, by MORRIS I. STEIN. New York: Academic Press, 1975. 360 pp. $16.50 cloth.

Perspectives in Creativity, edited by IRVING A. TAYLOR and J. W. GETZELS. Chicago: Aldine Publishing Company, 1975. 353 pp. $14.75 cloth.

WILLIAM A. SADLER, JR.
Bloomfield College
and
SALLIE GREEN
Rutgers University

The study of creativity is descended from investigations of genius and "gifted" persons, which in this half of the twentieth century have focused on creative phenomena. In America a pivotal event was the APA Presidential address in 1950 by J. P. Guilford; he called attention to the need for disciplined psychological research into creativity. There has been considerably more investigation of creativity since then; to judge from these books, the gains have been substantial.

The most disciplined as well as hotly contested research has been done by psychologists who have questioned, among other things, the relationship between creative disposition and intelligence and subsequent achievement; there have also been insightful investigations into situational determinants and into possible applications of such insights, especially in education and business. The significance of this research extends beyond psychology; it has particular relevance to sociologists.

The excellent volume by Taylor and Getzels is particularly useful. It has an original feature that both adds to and detracts from its usefulness. The chapters are freshly written contributions to a 1973 symposium on creativity research. The editors asked for autobiographical presentations that reflected both the development and present positions of leading figures in the field. Some of the autobiographical chapters are too self-serving and polemical, some too filled with trivial details. Yet the advantages of this format are great. It provides sharp insight into underlying assumptions, interests, and difficulties operative in these scientific investigations and practical experiments. Some chapters represent a summing up of a major part of one's life work, such as those by Guilford, D. W. MacKinnon, A. Roe, F. Barron, S. J. Parnes, G. M. Prince, C. W. Taylor, and E. P. Torrance. Other chapters report on and occasionally improve upon research published elsewhere by the authors. This kind of volume takes you into the life of research and brings you quickly up to date; two historical surveys by the editors nicely fill in the background.

One soon learns that there are many possible approaches to creativity. The editors stress diversity in the field; they emphasize that there is no consensus with respect to theory, definition, or method. Yet there is more agreement than at first meets the eye. The most experienced researchers seem to agree that creativity is a multifaceted phenomenon or event; it cannot be reduced to a single operation or set of factors. A four-fold structure is increasingly recognized. Creativity involves a person, a process, a product, and a situation. No satisfying answers to basic questions about creativity will be found unless they take into consideration all four dimensions. This has yet to be done adequately. However, I. A. Taylor has been concentrating for years upon developing a theoretical formulation that will yield a workable definition; and at this time he proposes that creativity be regarded as a system that "involves a transacting person who transforms generic problems into generating products."

More significant, we think, than definitions, which do not at any rate seem to have a determining influence over most of these researchers, is the emergent paradigm of human beings. As Getzels points out, much of the research into creativity operated at first on the assumption of the correctness of a homeostatic model. With this model creativity was interpreted as basically tension-reducing-problem-solving. But important features in creativity were ignored. The homeostatic model had to be questioned. Unless we dogmatically insist that creativity does not exist or assume that it is a tension reducing drive discharge, we might better view it as a *stimulus seeking activity*. Getzels argues that the creative process is often a form of *problem finding* rather than merely problem solving. A creative person often searches for a new way to make sense of material, often by constructing a problem that others have not recognized. Within this new paradigm creativity is seen to reflect a fundamental component of a human being, a desire to be open to one's world so as to make it distinctively one's own. The person-creating-a-product-that-alters-his/her-environment model opens up new ways to view common but often ignored behaviors.

Much of the research reported in this volume has itself manifested creativity. Guilford argues that clear awareness of creative components in one's personality unlocks creative output. That seems to have happened to many of these scientists and educators. In their attempts to understand creativity better they have often broken away from previous assumptions and positions. They have been open to new ideas and innovative endeavors. The majority of the writers in this volume are marvelously free of dogmatism, a trait that seems to be the antithesis of creativity. Many of these studies reflect awareness, originality, inventiveness, a searching curiosity, and perseverance, all of which are characteristics of the creative person.

The importance of creativity in scientific discovery becomes evident from these works. In so far as the persons engaged in creativity research are helping us regard old problems such as the relationship between behavior and development, person and society, motivation and achievement from new perspectives they are not only being creative, they are advancing science. Einstein's comment on science is appropriate: "The formulation of a problem is often more essential than its solution, which may be merely a matter of mathematical or experimental skill. To raise new questions, new possibilities, to regard old problems from a new angle, requires creative imagination and marks real advance in science."

While this volume indicates that there is an enormous amount of unfinished business with respect to understanding creativity, some chapters here report significant advances. For example, several studies, such as those by Guilford and F. M. Andrews, make clear that intelligence and creativity are separate although interdependent variables. Furthermore, it is apparent that creativity is much more than instantaneous originality. Spontaneity and divergent thinking (originality) may be essential primary features; but the emergence of creativity as a system of transformation that generates effective products involves other factors, such as judgment, an incubation period, productive expression, and feedback.

It seems to us that much confusion in the study and discussion of creativity stems in part from not taking seriously enough a developmental model that considers stages and levels of creativity. Getzels emphasizes the importance of sustained searching. S. R. Maddi stresses the importance of judgment and commitment in the creative enterprise. These are qualities that come later on in the creative process, and they require some degree of maturity. It seems likely that originality, spontaneity, inventiveness, and even innovative problem solving are elementary forms of creativity that can be found even in children, but the full complexity of this multi-faceted phenomenon usually occurs after a degree of maturity has been attained. Perhaps the failure to make distinctions between levels and stages is one reason why the coefficient of correlation in tests on children's creativity and later achievement is not very strong. The creativity of adults is more than an extension of childhood traits. While it may be true that all of us have creative potential, there are discernible reasons why some are more creative than others and why in some persons creativity remains an untapped source.

One clichéd opinion is that people are not creative because they were unnecessarily repressed and insufficiently reinforced in childhood. That view is challenged in this book. As D. W. MacKinnon found at the onset of his research into personality factors in creativity, large numbers of highly effective people had life histories marked by severe frustrations, deprivations, and traumatic experiences. Life history counts for something in emergent creativity, but immediate situations may count more. F. M. Andrews has conducted some highly suggestive investigations of creative sociologists involved in medical research programs. He found an insignificant correlation between creative abilities and innovative output, hence a psychological explanation for creative production had to be emended by a sociological one. He did find a strong correlation between creative output and a certain type of situation. Those settings, for example, which gave the sociologist a high degree of autonomy and security, and where the project was of limited size and scope, when combined with high motivation and extra-project activities, tended to pay off more. Under favorable conditions higher creative ability produced more innovative outputs, but in unfavorable situations the reverse was true. Where highly creative persons met unfavorable situations, they tended to produce less.

A different approach to the question of what makes people creative is presented by the eminent psychoanalyst Silvano Arieti. In his book *Creativity: the Magic Synthesis* he does little to illuminate the unfolding of the creative process and the emergence of the creative product. Much of our knowledge about creativity is so fragmented, so in need of a magic synthesis. Yet it is this very lack of integrative insight that proves to be the volume's underlying and permeating weakness. Arieti's work is inclusive and well-researched, but he presents so many competitive viewpoints and touches upon so many different topics that the reader is left confused—although somewhat more informed. The creative synthesis that he emphasized is regrettably not achieved in this book. Arieti seems to be struggling along with the rest of us—unable to filter and distill the multi-faceted viewpoints of creativity with analytic maturity, wisdom, and direction.

We believe that the phenomenon of creativity is not very receptive to or clarified by the philosophical, historical, and psychoanalytic approaches taken by Arieti. Perhaps the study of creativity is analogous to the study of the creation of life. If we are approaching the topic with a need for our questions to be answered, then a scientific method will best suit our purpose, enabling the application of more specific and conclusive knowledge to the subject, but perhaps never being able to explain fully the formation of the initial secret.

The strength of Arieti's volume is contained in four chapters dealing with the promotion and cultivation of creativity at individual and social levels. In spite of the long, confusing preparatory sections on the creative process, Arieti draws upon his own talents as a psychotherapist to elucidate the area of individual creative nurturance. He presents his ideas in these last chapters with a feeling of experience, simplistic assurance, and inspiration. He stresses a balance of seemingly opposite conditions involved in fostering creativity—those processes that require suspension of control to develop openness to effusions of internal and external stimuli and those that require great discipline, acumen, and commitment. Arieti's concept of a creativogenic society is informative, provocative, and important.

Both the above books have material that specifically considers how creativity can and has been developed. For those who want a systematic and highly informed presentation of ways to stimulate creativity the volume by Stein will be very useful. In clear, forthright language Stein reports on research into and applications of various approaches to creativity training, with detailed attention given to brain storming, Synectics, creative problem solving, and personality insight training. His objective is to increase the reader's range of possibilities for stimulating creativity. In this book he concentrates on group procedures. He believes that training programs will be differentially effective with different kinds of persons. Unlike some of the company programs that he describes, which look for quick results, Stein emphasizes the need for dedication and perseverance in the development of creativity. At the close of this volume he, too, looks forward to an emergent society that is committed to fostering creativity.

In all of these books there is clearly a call to consider factors that bear upon the development of or deterrence to creativity. It is time more sociologists heard this call. The importance of creativity research extends beyond the sociology of art, culture, and education. It pertains to our sociological perspective and the paradigm within which we operate for sociological interpretation. It relates to concerns crucial to the welfare of individuals and institutions. Bureaucracies, as Peter Blau has pointed out, pose one of the most serious problems to democracy; inherent in that problem is a threat to creativity. Is it possible to design bureaucracies that promote rather than impede creativity? Another crucial concern is apparent with respect to the growing importance of leisure. How might free time be structured so that it becomes an opportunity for creative development rather than time wasted in mindless conformity? And in this era that so needs creative leadership, how can we develop creative leaders who will stimulate the creativity of followers rather than stifle it? If these authors succeed in stimulating more of us to research perseveringly and to find new and effective answers to such crucial concerns, they will have not only advanced the causes of creativity and science but promoted social welfare.

Blue Collar Stratification: Autoworkers in Four Countries, by WILLIAM H. FORM. Princeton, N.J.: Princeton University Press, 1976. 335 pp. $17.50 cloth.

WILLIAM H. FRIEDLAND
University of California, Santa Cruz

As a former autoworker of some years, albeit a considerable number of years ago, I remain something of an autoworker literature "freak." I still "enjoy"—if that is the right word—reading about my old industry because I like to see if my sociological colleagues ever grasp that inner verstehen which I am convinced I have as a result of seven years of bucking the lines, the machines, and the foremen (and which, incidentally, I have never tried to grapple with in scholarly fashion).

By standard canons of the profession, this book is a good one. Form has provided the format of a sociological "winner" which has everything: a thorough setting out of three basic theses about comparative industrialization—the cultural, the "industrial man" (person) thesis, the evolutionary approach. There is a thorough integration of the research with a very wide and relevant body of literature. Finally, the empirical data are broad-based, utilizing materials gathered from auto workers in Lansing, Michigan; Turin, Italy; Córdoba, Argentina; and Bombay, India.

But this reader, despite the many winning features, was disappointed by the book. What one misses is the dynamics—the vital juices—of being an autoworker in a continually troublesome industry. The workers who appear in Form's pages are relatively quiet, satisfied, bourgeoisified. As with Goldthorpe's workers in Luton, the fundamental thesis of embourgeoisement rests like an environmental pall over a disappointed sociologist. The conviction grows, as one reads through this book, that Form would have liked to have found confirmation of Marxian analysis that workers are filled with alienation and class conflict but that, disappointingly, it just was not there.

The book, then, follows the critical work of many scholars who have examined class struggle notions and found them to be missing in the working classes of the world. Form reminds the reader of the Luddite (or Leninist) expectations of radical intellectuals and of their "imposition" on workers of behavioral forms which they reject, just as these workers reject the "historic mission" of Marxism.

But if this criticism is correct, at least some of the time, what Form and others fail to grasp is the richness of everyday life: the invective and bitterness of daily frustration when the line is jacked up two units per hour more than it is supposed to be; the micro-guerrilla sabotage that goes on so continually that no one even thinks about it although it raises the ire in management circles because of the sheer volume of money involved; the spontaneous songs of boredom, frustration, alienation, rejection, and hope. While I never worked in East Lansing, I am reasonably certain that the autoworkers live through these daily experiences. Ely Chinoy told us so in *Automobile Workers and the American Dream.* And while I never worked in Turin, Córdoba, or Bombay, my few days of manual labor in Tanganyika tell me that my experience in automobile factories in the United States was not culturally limited.

Workers surely do not sing "The Internationale" or "Solidarity Forever" as they gaily assemble auto engines; but events in enough factories and industries throughout the world tell us that they are not as apathetic and accepting as Form (and others) would have us believe. Perhaps the point is that there is no such thing as *the* autoworker. Let me suggest not a dichotomized auto worker but, indeed, a trichotomized one. And all three autoworkers are not "types" as much as all being present in the same individuals, e.g., the same people act differently under differing conditions.

First, there is the autoworker described by Form and a host of others: passive, accepting, finding extrinsic rewards outside of the work process through consumption. Second, there is Chinoy's autoworker: less satisfied, but unrebellious, seeking escape through myths about developing "control" over one's life. Finally, there is the autoworker of classical Marxism: riotous, rebellious, and occasionally revolutionary.

Perhaps neither Form, Chinoy, nor the Marxists are entirely correct. The first perspective, with its pluralist orientations, conveys the idea that everybody is relatively happy (except for the trouble-making intellectuals). The second conveys a passive, escapist anomie. The Marxists leap from one crisis to another and are disappointed when they fail to "mature." The Marxist viewpoint, indeed, has so inured us to the "coming crisis"—this one, the next one, or the one after that—that it has created a skepticism about the basic analysis.

Perhaps there ought to be a place for all three viewpoints: there is a tempo to life in which acceptance (e.g., pluralism), apathy, and rebellion each have their time and place. On balance, I find works such as Chinoy's more compelling than Form's. This was what autoworkers were about when I was there. That the Marxists are correct is indicated by the experience of autoworkers of the 1930s, in Lordstown and recently in Turin. Nor can I deny that there are times when the kind of analysis that Form has produced is correct. What is wrong, however, is the insistence of each view that *it* constitutes the complete reality. This results in the disappointment of Marxists when the revolution is not culminated; another result is the manner in which the pluralists handle riots, rebellions, and revolutions when they occur: not as perfectly reasonable social phenomena but as forms of irrational collective behavior, that fall into the same category as panics, crazes, and fads.

While not very engaging in an overall sense, the book is not without its merits. The closest Form came to involving this reader was in his appendices on the evolution of the study and the problems encountered in the field. While these appendices are of the variety that we used to call *bahbeh meisses bei die Eskimos* when I was growing up, they are *interesting.* It is useful to know how Bill Form evolved his ideas and the kinds of tortuous bargaining that were necessary to implement this study. If Form has not captured the vital juices of auto workers, he has at least conveyed his own.

Loss and Change, by PETER MARRIS. New York: Pantheon Books, 1974. 179 pp. $7.95 cloth.

FRED DAVIS
University of California, San Diego

Peter Marris is here concerned with what is surely a central (and quite possibly *the* central) existential issue of the modern era, namely, how people seek to sustain continuity of identity through grievous personal loss or what is its collective equivalent—disruptive social change that tears at the fabric of meaning by which they live. His inquiry into the issue displays a quality and depth fully commensurate with the profundity of the issue itself. Employing as his root metaphor the process of bereavement that nearly all of us are destined to experience at one time or another, Marris extends its processual parameters to diverse situations at first seemingly far removed from grief and mourning over a deceased loved one: to the relocation of "slum dwellers," to tribalism in newly developing African townships, to small business entrepreneurship among native Black Kenyans, and to the clash of administrators and poverty representatives in American model cities programs. In all of these examples Marris deftly delineates the subtle interplay between once firm but now tenuous identities that are no longer confirmed by changed conditions, and those emergent identities whose substance is still more a matter of gleaning than grasping, fashioning than finishing. This ambiguity is brought out most poignantly in the instance of the Kenyan small businessmen who, out of the frustrations borne of blocked mobility in a new nation, attempt with devout conviction to emulate the rationalistic and universalistic entrepreneurial styles of the West only to bog themselves down in a defensively obsessive preoccupation with the small details of retail transactions and employee behavior.

But what is it about bereavement that for Marris constitutes its archetypicality? He approaches the question from many different vantage points and at different levels of abstraction. Essentially however it is that bereavement with its phases of grief, mourning and attempts at reintegration that serves in time to reinvest with new meaning a world made suddenly meaningless through the death of someone near. More importantly this is new meaning which builds upon, takes sustenance from, and pays deference to old meaning but is not identical with it. The alteration evolves, as Marris sees it, from the inner, dialectic-like working out of:

> a profound conflict between contradictory impulses—to consolidate all that is still valuable and important in the past, and preserve it from loss; and at the same time, to re-establish a meaningful pattern of relationships, in which the loss is accepted. Each impulse checks the other, reasserting itself by painful stabs of actuality or remorse, and recalling the bereaved to face the conflict itself (pp. 31–32).

In its relative simplicity, vividness, and universality bereavement serves as the analytical fount for all and any loss or change which severely threatens the structure of meaning by which we live. Since it is precisely this kind of social change, i.e., the meaning-emptying variety, which is so widespread and has proved so troublesome in the modern world —although, as Marris is careful to point out, not all change is of this order—he believes that by closely attending to the dynamics of the bereavement process, by noting when it successfully resolves itself and when it does not, when and when not it assumes such aberrant forms as prolonged withdrawal from social involvement or aggressive displacement onto symbolic causes, we can learn how better to manage the tensions, conflicts, and identity transitions which such change inevitably entails.

And, indeed, much of the book is devoted to a knowledgeable, sympathetic, and highly literate documentation of this thesis. Thus, for example, drawing on his own research on slum clearance in Lagos and that of Herbert Gans and Marc Fried on the West End of Boston, he builds a powerful case against the *socio*logic of urban redevelopers. Despite a certain awareness by them of the social implications of their housing scheme, too often they assume mistakenly that the awareness itself, along with some suitable adjustments in basic architectural design, are sufficient to dispel the profound sense of loss and social dislocation which the disappearance of the old "slum neighborhood" can engender. Just as those who foolishly counsel the mourners to lay aside their woe because "life must go on," so do the ministrations of the urban planner fail to adequately comprehend the time, the despair, the ambivalence and the turmoil that is entailed in order to assimilate the change. And since the plan fails to do this (almost of necessity because of the essential privateness and inwardness of the experience), and yet, willy-nilly, rearranges according to some logic of its own the structure of meaning in the lives of the relocated, the natural functional outcome of the bereavement process, according to Marris, is invariably arrested or distorted. New meaning, that is, does not arise from the pained loss of the old; meaning is either destroyed altogether or old forms are clung to fetishistically. In either case, the inner life, the creative if agonized fashioning of new continuities from the dangers of discontinuity, is impoverished more than need be. Similarly, in another connection closer to recent academic experience, Marris suggests that things would have fared better had university administrators been somewhat more attentive to the *psycho*logic of identity contradiction that underlay the demands of Third World student groups in the late nineteen sixties (a logic nicely grasped in his generic formulation of the bereavement process) and payed somewhat less attention to the administrative illogic of the demands per se, (e.g., equal academic standing for their programs along with exclusive exemption from any university review or control of them). The confrontations that occurred would have been, if not fewer, than a good deal less deeply divisive in their consequences.

Doubtless there are those who will feel that the bereavement metaphor, which Marris elevates practically to the status of a ruling paradigm, is pressed too far and ceases to be felicitous or even suggestive once carried much beyond the microsocial sphere of intimate relations and acute personal loss. I myself, almost as a matter of principle, harbored such reservations and would begin a chapter deeply skeptical over how the author could possibly relate grief and mourning to the functioning of Ibo tribalism or to the emergence of a black small business class in East Africa or (more astonishingly) to revolution à la, mirabile dictu, *both* Frantz Fanon and Thomas Kuhn. Yet, with neither obfuscation nor disingenuousness, Marris succeeds every time, so finely attuned is his analytical sensibility to locating, teasing out and tracing through the quintessential condition of grievous loss and disruptive change wherever it occurs and no matter how masked, displaced, or reified it gets in the course of its symbolic transformation. All of which is perhaps just another way of saying that this is a work of great insight and imagination. I would add that it is also a work of great wisdom in that while recognizing and demonstrating, as few sociological works do, a profound intellectual respect for our attachment to and need for the familiar, it discovers in this very condition the strands whereby we can meaningfully and humanely relinquish it once it is, perforce or by choice, no longer given to us.

The Sociology of Law and Order, by LYNN MCDONALD. Boulder, Colo.: Westview Press, 1976. 340 pp. $24.75 cloth.

JOHN HAGAN
University of Toronto

This ambitious and provocative book takes as its topic the debate between consensus and conflict theories of crime. The topic is familiar, but the scope of this inquiry is uncommon. The first part of the book offers a history of the consensus and conflict traditions, from Aristotle and Plato to Parsons and Quinney. The traditions are separated on the assumption that "conflict theories are those . . . in which the factor of power is given prominence. . . . Consensus theories are those in which any other factor is dominant—social or economic conditions, psychological factors or biological" (p. 19). The resulting division, however, is neither simple nor static: while consensus theorists prior to World War I rejected the economic causes that conflict theorists embraced, following the war the consensus theorists incorporated economic variables into their explanations and the conflict theorists turned to the causal role of official agencies in "producing" crime. McDonald concludes that "Most important, for our purposes, is the contemporary debate between social and economic problems in consensus theory and the needs and resources for control in conflict" (p. 136).

Readers will find this historical discussion comprehensive in its coverage, especially of European materials. One consequence of its scope and its attention to the classics, however, is that North American theorists are considered only briefly: Richard Quinney, "the main source of conflict theory to be used in this study" (p. 124), receives just over a page; Austin Turk four sentences; and William Chambliss is not mentioned at all. On the consensus side, Jackson Toby, F. Ivan Nye, and Travis Hirschi are not considered. However, since these authors are widely known to North American readers, the emphasis on classic European figures who are now less frequently read may be judicious.

Part two of the book undertakes a competitive test of the two traditions, using cross-national, British and Canadian data. McDonald finds with the cross-national data that indicators of economic and social resources (e.g., urbanism, GNP, police force size, extent of the school system, data collection apparatus, political representation, and mass media) are most successful in explaining "ordinary" official crime rates. Indicators of various social problems (e.g., poverty, rapid population growth, large family size, and illiteracy) are less successful. There are, however, interesting exceptions: the social problem indicators are successful in explaining the "non-ordinary" (consensual!) crime of murder, while unemployment rates have a more pervasive effect. McDonald concludes that, "A revised conflict explanation would include the level of unemployment in a society as one of the factors affecting the *need* for formal control measures" (p. 175). Similar conclusions follow from British data, where school expenditures and enrollments, police force size, GNP, and unemployment are again effective predictors of official crime rates.

Although McDonald's reasons for interpreting these findings as supportive of conflict theory are clear, some additional questions can be raised. First, the influence of growing social and economic resources (schools, GNP, urbanism, media, etc.) might be explained by consensus theorists in terms of *relative* deprivation, although at the cost of making the consensus position non-falsifiable at the aggregate level. At the same time, it should be emphasized that most current claims for consensus theory are based on individual level data and self-report indicators of behavior (e.g., the work of Travis Hirschi) rather than aggregate level official data. Finally, it bears note that the relationship found between police resources and official rates is without established direction; one can hypothesize that these growth rates are reciprocally related, and a two stage least squares approach could take us the next step in determining the relative sizes of the reciprocal effects. To raise these issues, of course, is not to resolve them, and it is much of the merit of McDonald's work that they are raised at all.

A final body of Canadian data is analyzed with a rather complicated set of outcomes. Thus, McDonald compares the seriousness of crimes as evaluated by legal statutes and the public, with actual rates of incarceration. Since no control is included for offenders' prior records, no definite conclusions can be reached. Nonetheless, the point is well made that public drunkenness and other victimless offenses have little consensual base for the criminal justice resources they consume. McDonald is also able to show that the public is badly confused about the "facts" of crime, a finding made less surprising by the debates that McDonald reviews relating to some such "facts." Most interesting for its inconclusiveness, however, is a comparison of various groups' attitudes toward the sanctioning of crime. Here it is found that lawyers are nearly as different in their attitudes from businessmen as is either of the preceding from other less powerful groups. McDonald concludes from her Canadian findings that, "The predictions of conflict theory were somewhat better supported than those of consensus, but a number of findings were made in favour of consensus theory as well" (p. 251).

The concluding part of the book is a defense of its research techniques against the complaints of Quinney and others that there is a necessary connection between the objective of describing general, causal explanations and the support of consensus propositions. Evidence to the contrary is provided in the writings of Marx, Engels, Lenin, and even Weber, not to mention the findings of this book. These findings, then, stand not only as a challenge to consensus theorists, but to many conflict theorists as well.

Lynn McDonald is a brilliant sociologist, and she has written a remarkable book. Few Canadian sociologists will be surprised by this conclusion, for McDonald has often foregone wider recognition to write on Canadian topics and in Canadian journals. With this book, the issues addressed assure the broader attention her work deserves. This book is essential reading for all sociologists interested in crime, consensus, and conflict.

Durkheim on Religion: A Selection of Readings with Bibliographies and Introductory Remarks, edited by W. S. F. PICKERING. Boston: Routledge & Kegan Paul, 1975. 376 pp. $21.75 cloth.

TENDZIN N. TAKLA
University of Wyoming

This is the sixth reader or anthology and at least the tenth book devoted to Durkheim that has appeared in the past ten years, all of them in English. The immediate question is whether there is any need for yet another addition to this recent spate. The editor is well aware of the problem for he states in his introduction that the publications of Lukes's major study, which dealt with religion at length, and the Giddens reader, which made available previously untranslated pieces, partly undermined the rationale for the book. However the editor judged that there were sufficient new materials to warrant such a collection. Moreover, the present volume is to serve as the textual basis for a forthcoming book which will give detailed commentaries on Durkheim's works on religion.

Although I have some reservations about the criteria used for selection in this volume, let me mention at the outset that this is indeed a useful and valuable addition to Durkheimian studies. Nine of the twelve selections from Durkheim are new translations, most of them made available in English for the first time. Relevant materials not included in the selections are summarized in thirty-seven brief abstracts so that in one way or another the volume gives a comprehensive coverage of Durkheim's writings on religion. The book also includes three deservedly well-known critical reviews of *The Elementary Forms of Religious Life* by anthropologists (van Gennep, Goldenweiser, and Stanner) and a longish, polemical and somewhat confused critique of Durkheim's sociology of religion in general from the viewpoint of a religious believer, Gaston Richard. Since the editor felt that Richard's work was "virtually unknown in England" (and I hasten to add, likewise in this country as well), he is the subject of a short article appended to the volume. Richard, we are told, was a one-time colleague and follower of Durkheim who later fell out with him, largely it seems, on account of their divergent views about religion. For all the interesting light that the article sheds on Richard, his work, and his relationship to Durkheim and the Durkheimian school, the piece seems somewhat out of place in the book and could have better been published elsewhere as a journal article, especially since the space could have been utilized for more important materials. The bibliography of Durkheim's writings, arranged under "religion" and "totemism," follows Lukes's enumeration and adds nothing to that comprehensive compilation. The bibliography of secondary works however includes seventy-three items not mentioned in Lukes's work.

That religion was a major intellectual preoccupation for Durkheim has frequently been noted. In this respect a remark by Morton White on William James seems even more appropriate to describe Durkheim's attitude to religion: "He wanted facts but he also wanted religion" (*The Age of Analysis,* p. 138). Now although the "facts" that Durkheim saw in religion are well known and indeed have achieved the rank of a veritable classic in the sociology of religion, sociologists have not paid sufficient attention to the reasons why Durkheim "wanted" religion. Durkheim's interest in religion is generally viewed as reflecting what he felt to be the need for a normative and cohesive basis for society which only religion could provide. While this is undoubtedly the case, this view neglects another, and in my mind, a more interesting and more fundamental aspect of the question, namely the role played by this intellectual preoccupation in the structure and development of his theoretical system as a whole. In other words, while sociologists have recognized the *importance of Durkheim's theory of religion,* they have failed to realize, let alone, systematically analyze and criticize, *the theoretical importance of religion in the structure and development of Durkheim's thought.*

That there is a firm basis for the latter consideration is evident from Durkheim's own statements. In a letter to the editor of a Catholic scholarly journal he once declared that the reading of some English ethnographic and historical studies on religion, notably those by Robertson Smith and his school, brought about a "revelation," indeed a revolution—so that all his previous research had to be seen in a new light. Although this statement has often been cited or alluded to, no satisfactory explanation of the exact nature of this "revelation" has ever been given, either by Durkheim himself, or by his immediate followers, or by later commentators. Two things, however, seem clear. First, the revelation consisted of a series of insights into the central role that religion played in social life, providing not only an integrative bond, but also as the primordial source of thought, law, morality, the arts, and indeed of practically all social institutions. Second, these insights provided him with a conceptual framework which marked a dividing line in the development of his thought, so that all "my previous researches had to be taken up afresh in order to be made to harmonize with these new insights" (cited in Lukes: *Emile Durkheim,* p. 237).

A systematic investigation of this latter aspect of Durkheim's theory of religion would not only contribute to a better understanding and evaluation of his substantive theory of religion but would also provide a far better grasp of the analytical structure of his theoretical system as a whole and the metaphysical and metatheoretical presuppositions in which it is embedded. It would also greatly clarify some intriguing and sometimes confusing questions as to his position on such issues as realism vs. idealism, moralism vs. positivism, sociologism vs. psychologism, methodological strictures of strict empirical rigor vs. metaphysical speculations of the wildest sort, and on fundamental questions of epistemology and ontology. Such an investigation would also probably reveal far more unity, consistency, and comprehensiveness in the structure of Durkheim's thought than might appear from a superficial listing of his inconsistencies, or even by attempting to achieve consistency by denying or minimizing certain aspects of his theory. All of this will, of course, lead to a better critical evaluation of Durkheim. And the clue to it all lies in Durkheim's sociology of religion.

That sociology is contained in a body of varied, scattered, and numerous writings and pronouncements dating back to some of his earliest publications. Apart from three lecture courses and some public talks devoted to religion, Durkheim's several writings on the subject can be grouped under four headings: (1) sections or references to religion found in practically all his books; (2) numerous reviews of ethnographic, historical, and contemporary studies on religion; (3) a small number of articles dealing directly with religion or having important bearings on his theory of religion; and of course, (4) *The Elementary Forms.*

Faced with this large and often disparate corpus of materials, it is understandable that the editor had a hard task in selecting the pieces for the volume. The decision to reproduce complete articles, reviews, and chapters or sections from books rather than little snippets from here and there so as to avoid, the editor tells us, "a string of maxims and sayings, hardly doing justice to Durkheim's scholarship" is certainly correct and commendable. On the other hand, the brief abstracts of some of Durkheim's other writings, many of them containing much more than just passing references to religion, scarcely do justice either to Durkheim's scholarship or to their importance for our understanding of his views and theory of religion. The abstracts are certainly adequate for the book notes and shorter reviews. Sections and passages from Durkheim's major books, most of which are readily available in English, are also well served by the abstracts. The latter are particularly useful in locating the passages since the books themselves either have very poor indexes or none at all. But the relegation of some very important pieces to brief abstracts has somewhat reduced the value of this collection as a source book.

Among the abstracts of articles which should have been printed in full, the following merit special attention: (1) the review of Labriola's *Essai sur la conception matérialiste de l'histoire,* in which Durkheim, while agreeing with the basic premises of social determination of individual consciousness, argued for religion rather than the economy as the underlying structural factor; (2) the two letters to the editor of the *Revue néo-scolastique,* containing the autobiographical statements referred to earlier in this review; (3) the article on dualism which not only summarizes some of the main themes of *The Elementary Forms,* but also contains perhaps the most systematic statement of Durkheim's philosophical anthropology in which religion plays a crucial explanatory role; and (4) the third section of the original introduction to *The Elementary Forms,* which first appeared as an article in a philosophical journal and which, for whatever reason, was omitted when that book came out and was never included in subsequent editions.

The article on duality, is available in two anthologies (Wolff: *Emile Durkheim—Essays on Sociology and Philosophy,* and Bellah: *Emile Durkheim on Morality and Society*). The review of Labriola appears in the Giddens reader (*Emile Durkheim: Selected Writings*). The other two pieces are not easily accessible even in the original French, and neither, as far as I know, have been translated apart from brief extracts. Their omission from this volume which clearly aims to include all of Durkheim's major writings on religion, can only be explained by too narrow a conceptualization of Durkheim's sociology of religion on the part of the editor. One needs to approach "Durkheim on religion" with a little catholicity. In any case, their inclusion would have greatly enhanced the value of this book for students and researchers. Certainly none of the articles I have mentioned are unduly long and could easily have been substituted for Richard's critique and the editor's note on Richard.

On reflection it is surprising that while specialized monographs have been written on Durkheim as a philosopher (LaCapra), on his theory of morals (Wallwork), on the Durkheimian school (Clark), and, more recently, on *Suicide* (Pope) and on Durkheim's epistemology (Hirst), none has yet appeared on his sociology of religion. This despite the fact that it was a major inspiration for such important works on religion as those by Bellah and Swanson. If nothing else, this volume gives a good indication of the range and scope of Durkheim's approach to religion and thus deserves the attention of all sociologists. For those who might embark on further research on the topic, it is a handy and useful source book and reference. I eagerly look forward to the forthcoming companion volume of critical commentary.

Queuing and Waiting: Studies in the Social Organization of Access and Delay, by BARRY SCHWARTZ. Chicago: University of Chicago Press, 1975. 217 pp. $12.00 cloth.

DAVID GLANZ
Columbia University

Waiting might be described as one of humanity's most universal occupations. Perhaps the outstanding modern attempt to explore the meaning of waiting is Samuel Beckett's 1953 "tragicomedy" *Waiting for Godot.* Many viewers have had difficulty with this story of two clownish tramps waiting for an indefinite appointment with the mysterious Godot, whom they have never met. Report has it, however, that one audience felt it understood *Godot* perfectly—the prisoners in San Quentin. Drawing on their own experience, they saw the play quite simply as being about waiting, waiting for nothing.

As a dramatist, Beckett was concerned with the human meaning of waiting. Yet until Barry Schwartz's innovative and imaginative collection of studies in the social organization of access and delay, *Queuing and Waiting,* we have not had a sustained sociological examination of these "ordinary" social processes. In this slim, thoughtful, and wide-ranging volume, the author manages to illuminate the everyday phenomena of queuing and waiting in a series of empirical and theoretical analyses, which demonstrate both a sophisticated methodological finesse and a sociological imagination of the first order.

The central theses of Schwartz's attempt to establish a sociology of queuing and waiting are presented in the first chapter, "Waiting, Exchange, and Power: The Distribution of Time in Social Systems," (which originally appeared in *AJS,* January 1974). This seminal essay is the cornerstone of Schwartz's theory of the relationship between social structure and delay. Its key proposition is that the distribution of waiting time parallels the distribution of power, and that the social and personal costs of waiting are distributed within the social structure in accordance with identifiable principles. Here, he also tries to show how the relationship between the organized dependency of clients on servers and waiting time is not shaped solely by the ratio of the latter to the former.

Three specific issues structure the book: (1) the sources and variation of delay; (2) the internal organization, priorities, and order within queues; and (3) the meaning of waiting for servers, as well as clients. (Schwartz distinguishes between the queue, as a social structure consisting of elements organized in terms of temporal priority, and waiting, as a social-psychological orientation of the persons who are the "elements" of that structure. Thus, the book's title illustrates Schwartz's concern with both sides of the coin.) Two or more studies are devoted to each of these general problems. As the author himself notes, the unity of this volume derives from its steadfast pursuit of a single theme, working with data collected in a variety of settings via diverse methodologies. Nor does he allow himself to be locked into any particular theoretical "school," but rather draws freely on a variety of theoretical orientations.

The sources of variation in delay are examined empirically in two locales: hospital emergency departments in the Chicago area and the editorial process of the *AJS*. (The latter will, of course, be of special interest to sociologists.) In the first instance, Schwartz demonstrates that for a given level of client demand, delay is more dependent upon the organization of service than on its actual magnitude. His study of the manuscript queues and editorial organization of the *AJS* illustrates a similar principle, that "increases in the size of a work queue have distinctly different effects on the waiting time of its elements in different stages of the editorial process." In other words, there are internal subqueues of work and most of the delay in replying to authors takes place in the lowest priority stage, between the receipt of the last referee's evaluation and the date on which the journal's decision and comments are finally mailed out.

The question of how queues are orderly in the first place is explored by Schwartz in a more theoretical essay on "queue discipline," which seeks to analyze the cultural bases of the "normal rule" of "first come, first served," and "preemptive priorities," which are authorized exceptions to the principle of order of arrival. The factors related to queue disorganization and breakdown resulting from inadequate physical channelization of clientele in entry, exit, and panic situations are also discussed. An essay on "Formal and Informal Priorities in an Emergency Medical Treatment System," is an investigation of "the specific conditions under which considerations of social worth enter into client delay in a system which is officially committed to impersonal standards."

Shifting his focus from the structuring of priorities within queues to the meaning of waiting, Schwartz shows, by means of a deceptively simple study of a mortgage company waiting room, how the remedial deference the staff bestows on clients reflects the servers' valuation of a client's time, in terms of the latter's social rank. This is followed by a somewhat pedestrian and inconclusive chapter on "Religious Variation in Client Impatience," which is the book's weakest section and only disappointment. Finally, the author points out how boredom and the symbolic and degradational aspects of delay must be seen as additional costs of waiting, beyond the foregone opportunity to engage in more profitable activities.

Queuing and Waiting will undoubtedly find an eager audience among sociologists concerned with the relationship between social structure and everyday social processes. Schwartz's scholarship is impeccable and stylistically the book is exceptionally well-organized. Each of the empirical studies provides a discussion of the research setting, the problem, data collection, measurement, results, and summary conclusions. Beyond this, the author's prose is clear and uncluttered with sociological jargon. But what makes reading *Queuing and Waiting* so intellectually exciting is Schwartz's virtuoso ability in formulating problems and his skill in teasing out sociologically significant findings from the data. One only wishes the author had provided a "biographical" chapter on the origins of the book, describing the development of his interest in the sociology of queuing and waiting. Such information as to how he chose particular research questions, how he came to formulate the problems as he did, and what led to the selection of particular types of research settings, and modes of data collection, would have provided us with considerable insight into how a talented sociologist goes about developing a new special content area.

Schwartz's work, one hopes, will serve as a catalyst for further research on queuing and waiting in other contexts, including cross-cultural studies. Research sites such as airport terminals and amusement parks immediately suggest themselves as having rich potential for the study of access and delay. In addition to its intrinsic interest, Schwartz's pioneering work is relevant to such more traditional areas of sociology as formal organizations, collective behavior, exchange theory, and interactional social psychology. But the book's most significant contribution is that, by laying bare the operation and consequences, both positive and negative, of waiting, the author has given us a masterful sociological explication of the proverbial "they also serve, who stand and wait."

The Making of the Modern Family, by EDWARD SHORTER. New York: Basic Books, 1975. 400 pp. $15.00 cloth.

The Family in History, edited by CHARLES E. ROSENBERG. Philadelphia: University of Pennsylvania Press, 1975. 210 pp. $10.00 cloth.

BERNARD FARBER
Arizona State University, Tempe

To quote Edward Shorter's mother, "Nothing comes free in this world" (p. 268). And that goes as much for books on the history of family relationships as it does for a meal or anything else. The melange of fascinating description in Shorter's *The Making of the Modern Family,* which is about maternal tenderness and nurturance, keeps the reader dipping into its ingredients, but it lacks the "body" that a good intellectual meal should have. Perhaps the price of this meal is a little high.

Shorter tantalizes us with an interesting problem: something happened to family relationships in Europe around the eighteenth century, and Shorter, like many of us, is trying to "make sense" out of this event. He adopts the psychohistorical position that the eighteenth century produced a surge of sentiment in parent-child relations. Shorter suggests that the ability to establish voluntary intimate ties both within and outside marriage led to more attentive mothering, which in turn increased chances of infant survival. He attributes this change primarily to the emancipation of women from their previous subjugated position as the capitalist economy emerged. Although he adds that "other powerful factors were also at work" (p. 267), these appear almost as an afterthought—like a last-minute compensatory seasoning of the broth. Other psychohistorians, like Aries, use a reverse line of reasoning: The decline of "necessary wastage" of infants, as household crowdedness decreased, led to more attentive parenting and the development of an explicit childhood status (cf., Aries, pp. 38–39). Although, for Aries, "a new emotional relationship" between parents and children had developed earlier—by the sixteenth century—it was not until the eighteenth century that "the family began to hold society at a distance, to push it back beyond a steadily extending zone of private life" (Aries, p. 398). Presumably, for Aries, the rise in affluence led to higher survival rates and eventually to domestic privacy of the nuclear family.

This disagreement over the basis for the "sentimental revolution" evokes a series of questions: (a) Was there in fact a sentimental revolution in the eighteenth century? (b) Is Shorter accurate in attributing this revolution mainly to the freedom from traditional authority accompanying the growth of capitalist economy? (c) Are there other factors which may have played a significant role in this sentimental revolution?

As evidence of the appearance of a sentimental revolution in the eighteenth century, Shorter informs us about the rise in legitimate and illegitimate birth rates, the decline in infant mortality, and the diminished use of wet nurses in the latter half of the eighteenth century. He attributes these changes to the rise in personal freedom in marriage and courtship and in care given to children. In addition, Shorter describes the enlargement and specialization of rooms in housing, and he contrasts reports about marital relationships and parental views toward children as the eighteenth century wore on.

Much of Shorter's book is intended to counter the contention of Peter Laslett and the Cambridge group that the nuclear family had been the predominant household unit in England "for centuries before industrialization" and that there is no necessary connection between industrialization "and the small, simple, nuclear family of the contemporary world" (Laslett and Wall, 1972, pp. x and 9). Presumably if there is no necessary connection, Laslett would suggest that no "sentimental revolution" as that proposed by Shorter or Aries took place. Other writers, like Quitt, do give evidence of sentimental attachment to children even in the ninth through the thirteenth century. One might conclude that marriage and parenthood are both highly ambivalent enterprises, with indicators of both sentimental attachment and rejection in all eras. Indeed, Shorter fails to deal adequately with Laslett's major findings: Why, given the decline in infant mortality and the rise in birth rate, does mean household size tend to remain fairly constant over the centuries?

As for the second question, namely, that of attributing the change to freedom from traditional authority, Shorter's analysis presented in this book (as well as elsewhere) lacks "nutritional" ingredients. His argument is that (a) the regionalizing and nationalizing of markets, (b) the rise in the standard of living, and (c) the recruitment of an industrial proleteriat stimulated in the young people of Europe in the late eighteenth century "the sexual and emotional wish to be free" (p. 259). But his data on this matter are sparse and not convincing: the data are stronger in support of alternative interpretations. For example, Scott and Tilly in the Rosenberg volume discussed below present evidence to make a plausible case for interpreting Shorter's data as suggesting the persistence of peasant family norms in an urban setting. Similarly, Michael Anderson's work indicates extensive use of kin in centers of working class migration. The connection between the rise of capitalism and the emergence of a "sentimental revolution" in the family seems to be more tenuous or more complicated than Shorter suggests.

Non-economic factors in the "sentimental revolution" of the family are not considered by Shorter. His theme is that "contact with the marketplace gave local people a new sense of individual gratification and a corresponding unwillingness to conform to traditional community values of self-abnegation and self-denial" (p. 266). Yet, the work of Lawrence Stone, both in the Rosenberg collection and in his analysis of the English nobility, presents interesting materials on the change in social structure and the diffusion of Protestant pietistic conceptions as influences on the nucleation of the family and the decline of the authority of the kin group long before the eighteenth century. Shorter seems somehow insensitive to the dynamics of the larger social structure in his analysis.

Despite its deficiencies, however, one cannot dismiss *The Making of the Modern Family;* it is indeed the work of a "master chef." As history, the book offers much delicious detail, although as interpretation, it lacks "salt." But leaving Shorter's book and sitting down to *The Family in History,* with Charles E. Rosenberg as editor, one finds a gourmet's delight. Throughout the volume, there is a fine awareness by the "chefs" of the intricate interplay between ideological, structural, and situational factors in family experience. Beginning with a tangy essay by Lawrence Stone on the rise of the nuclear family in England, this collection is a treat of international cuisine—Chinese, German, Italian, Continental European, and finally American.

The papers in Rosenberg's *The Family in History* seem to highlight two themes. One theme is that societies tend to ooze norms and values as extensively as possible to cover doubtful situations. This theme is most explicit in Eberhard's paper on "The Upper Class Family in Traditional China," describing the "percolation process" whereby the basic values of the society are elaborated upon to justify their appropriateness to all segments of that society. The theme is also applied in the Scott and Tilly contribution on "Woman's Work and the Family in Nineteenth-Century Europe." Scott and Tilly try to show how changes in the family lives of working women, many of which have been described in Shorter's book, were not the result of a new ideology, but instead represented the extension of preindustrial values and peasant norms to an urban, industrialized setting. The normative-ooze theme appears in another guise in Zuckerman's paper, with the ironic title, "Dr. Spock: The Confidence Man." Zuckerman describes Dr. Spock's parental prescriptions as an effort to detach children from the moral authority and intensity of the nuclear family in order to fit them for life in a bureaucratic and affectively-neutral larger society. The common ingredient in these papers is the extension of family norms, developed to cover one element of social structure, to unknown situations in which their applicability may be doubtful and even distasteful.

The second theme in the Rosenberg volume is in some ways related to the first theme. It concerns the contradictory pressures on the family as a corporate entity. On the one hand, the state and community foster subordination of familial autonomy to the requirements of the larger society; on the other hand, the stability of the social structure depends, in part, upon the ability of families to organize themselves as persisting, corporate entities. Eberhard's paper consists, in fact, of a discussion of how Chinese family ideology was introduced and maintained to sustain faltering elites and how it utilized political marriage as a basis for stability. Hughes, in her analysis of family organization in medieval Genoa, describes that city as consumed by factional strife. In this setting, the merchant aristocracy organized itself into extended-family districts, with a strong emphasis upon intergenerational control and late emancipation of the young.

Perhaps as a means for escaping this factionalism, however, the artisan families were dispersed throughout the city, with less commemoration of ancestors, with a greater centrality of the nuclear family, and with early emancipation of the young. These findings are relevant to the Shorter book, for whereas the aristocratic mothers often resorted to wet nursing, in artisan families maternal nursing was generally the rule. Finally, the theme of contradictory forces is applied in the Landes article, which contrasts the destinies of two banking families, the Bleichröders and the Rothschilds. Landes shows how the Bleichröder family, intent upon integration into the German aristocracy, accomplished the assimilation of its members into the general German society, but at the cost of uprooting the family and dissipating the family firm. He indicates, however, that the corporate identity of business and family among the Rothschilds preserved continuity over a series of generations. This corporate persistence depended not only upon the utilization of family talent but also upon cousin marriages as a way of maintaining rootedness for members of the family.

It is the continual struggle between communal and factional (or segmental) forces which gives zest to the insights into the temporal and structural variations of family organization and socialization found in the Rosenberg volume. In his book, Shorter contrasts sentiment and external constraint as organizing principles of family relations (reminiscent of E. W. Burgess' distinction between the institutional and companionship family). Shorter's position leads necessarily to an opposition between freedom and constraint. But as Skinner's work suggests, people may be constrained to be "free"; the "freedom" itself is normative, the justification for a response to a set of values or other defined conditions. Presumably true freedom would imply merely considerable variation in family organization; the concept of "freedom" does not explain why family organization should take the *direction* that it did in the eighteenth century. For adequately determining this direction, one cannot avoid investigation into the communal and segmental forces, as well as the religious values, in the society. To return to the gastronomic metaphor, although Shorter's book has a wholesome, home-cooked quality, its ingredients do not seem to blend together; the Rosenberg book, however, is seasoned and simmered just right for my taste.

Michael Gordon
University of Connecticut

Edward Shorter is an historian of the new breed, as much at home in the computer center as in the library. In his most recent book he has attempted to go beyond the largely demographic work that has characterized family history since it gained impetus in the 1960s and has attempted to produce a broadly synthetic over-view of *The Making of the Modern Family*. The style and theme for that matter, are similar to that of Aries's *Centuries of Childhood,* a work that was also written by a person trained in demography who chose to go beyond the boundaries of that rigorous and conservative discipline in order to get at that big picture. The road Shorter takes us along is a harrowing one, strewn with wives infected with syphillis by their ignorant husbands, and infants dead as a result of maternal indifference. The images are vivid and presented with both erudition and flair, and one easily loses sight of where the journey is supposed to lead. When it is over, one wonders, if the billboards have obliterated the road.

It is not difficult to summarize the theme of this book. The modern family, born in the late eighteenth century, can be fundamentally distinguished from its premodern counterpart by the important role "sentiment" plays in it:

> Sentiment, I may define as the willingness to rearrange the objectives in one's life so that emotional ties to other people go to the top of the list, and the more traditional objectives get ranked further down (p. 17).

The growth of sentiment, at the expense of "calculation," is considered specifically in the contexts of courtship, marriage, and mother-infant relations. We will shortly discuss each of these in some detail, but for the moment it should suffice to say that courtship is seen as having become less exploitative, as sex is increasingly used more for "affective" than "instrumental" motives; marriage has become more companionate, though Shorter prefers to conceptualize this in terms of "domesticity"; and mother-infant relations have become more emotion-laden and supportive of the child's life. The reasons for such changes are to be found in the broad process of modernization, but Shorter focuses on the economic dimensions:

> Although any satisfactory explanation must ultimately be complex, and incorporate many

> different kinds of variables, I believe that laissez-faire marketplace organization, capitalist production, and the beginnings of proletarianization among the work force were more important than any other factors in the spread of sentiment (p. 258).

These factors make themselves felt in the development of "individualism," a phenomenon supportive of sentiment and antithetical to the domination by community and family that characterized so much of life in traditional society. This in essence is his argument; now let us consider the evidence he brings to bear on it.

Modern courtship, Shorter maintains, is characterized by a decline in parental and communal supervision and an increase in both the quantity and quality (it becomes less "exploitive" and more "affective") of premarital sex:

> The testimony we have reviewed suggests that in Europe before 1800, people seldom had sexual intercourse before it was absolutely certain they would marry, and that sex served for them larger ends of procreation and the continuation of the lineage, rather than being in itself an object of joy and delight (p. 166).

The elevation in the rates of both illegitimacy and bridal pregnancy in Western Europe from 1750 to 1850 is the foundation of Shorter's case that a "sexual revolution" occurred during this period. The fact that these rates fell during the 1850 to 1940 period is explained as the result of the increasing use of contraception; while the 1940 to 1955 explosion in illegitimacy is for him a matter of improved fecundity. Finally, in the 1960s, a "second sexual revolution" took place which he sees as doubly significant because not only were young people having more sex, but so much of the sex was truly nonmarital, i.e., involving people who would not later marry. While the growth of both illegitimacy and bridal pregnancy in the 1750–1850 interval may very well be an indicator of an increase in premarital sex it is quite another matter to infer a change in the meaning of the sex. In fact, it can be argued that Shorter makes a very unconvincing case indeed for both premarital and marital sex being the joyless experience he would have us believe it was in traditional European society. To be sure, it is extremely difficult to reconstruct the qualitative aspects of sex several centuries ago, but in view of how large this looms in Shorter's interpretation of changing behavior we are entitled to more than the impressions of a few contemporary observers. His case that contraception was at the root of the nineteenth century decline in illegitimacy has been questioned by North American scholars who see actual declines in the incidence of sexual intercourse at this time, and unlike Shorter I am not ready to dismiss their findings and interpretations. His explanation of the rapid growth in illegitimacy since 1940 being a manifestation of declining age at menarche is based on Cutright's work, which to my mind is strongly flawed by the fact that women well into their twenties as well as teenagers showed dramatic increases in illegitimacy in the 1940 to 1960 period. Certainly the older women are not having these children because the onset of first menses has declined. Interpretive problems such as these afflict the book as whole; Shorter has made up an elaborate theoretical bed and the data had damn well better fit it. Unfortunately, many readers may not find themselves very comfortable with the fit.

The growth of sentiment, we are told, also becomes more evident in the actual choice of a spouse, as romantic love becomes a more important criterion than pleasing parents by cementing family alliances or obtaining a robust helpmate. Here again we run up against problematic evidence. Shorter presents some data to show that occupational and geographic endogamy declined in the late eighteenth century and thereafter. Modernization and occupational differentiation go hand in hand, and therefore we would expect marriages to occur between people whose families were engaged in different occupations. We would also expect them to find mates from villages other than their own as the search for work led them to growing trade and industrial centers. We would, however, only expect parents to be concerned about such marriages if their children were not marrying social equals, and Shorter has no solid data to indicate that this was in fact happening. Still, in fairness to him, he does cite a study on sisters marrying out of birth order (where parents have a large input into mate choice there should be pressures for the oldest to marry first so as not to raise questions about their desirability) in Hingham, Massachusetts from the seventeenth century into the nineteenth century. Yet, when other North American data do not jibe with his theses, and more often than not they do not, we are told that the United States was "born modern" and thus is not likely to reveal the same patterns as Europe. He cannot have it both ways!

In traditional societies, once the couple was married:

> The wife's roles were all subservient. It was not merely that she occupied roles calling for her to be different from her husband. This would not have ruled out emotional equality. It was that in several important realms she was expected to be *inferior* (p. 72).

Not only was the wife's life filled with "self abnegation and personal sacrifice" it was also characterized by a rather affectionless relationship with her husband. As we intimated in our discussion of courtship, Shorter argues that marital sex was a rather perfunctory matter: a lifted night dress, a brusque entry, and a quick orgasm, for the male only; this is the sort of picture we are left with. The documentation he provides for loveless premodern marriage is rather sketchy and shows international variation that is not adequately accounted for. Similarly, when he goes on to characterize the growth of domesticity in the nineteenth century, by which he means to characterize not only the entry of affection and friendship into married life but also a special quality of parent child relations, we are offered a far from complete picture. He does not seem to appreciate the price women paid for this new found affection and more complete sexuality. To be sure, the growth of occupational opportunity outside the home strengthened womens' positions in the society at large, but for the married women the leverage her economic contribution provided in the traditional family was gone, as the new category of housewife emerged with its concomitant elevation and beatification of women, a point Alice Clark made almost sixty years ago.

Turning to parents and their children, Shorter's contention is that mothers in traditional European society were largely indifferent to the well-being of their infants:

> Impossible, says the twentieth century spirit. But in fact, among the general populace, life was that way. Mothers in villages and small towns across the continent from Cornwall to Lettland seldom departed from traditional—often hideously hurtful—infant hygiene and child rearing practices; and this is what lacking spontaniety is all about. Nor did these mothers often (some say "never") see their infants as human beings with the same capacities for joy and pain as they themselves. Parents were not, in other words, able to put themselves in their infants' tiny shoes, to imagine the world from their viewpoint, and thus to make it as agreeable and delightful a world as possible—which is what we mean by "empathy" (p. 169).

He goes on to catalog the horrors of children left with ignorant and often malevolent wet nurses, others burned to death as a result of being placed untended in front of open fires, and still others eaten by pigs while their mothers dealt with more important matters. Only deMause, hurling Freudian implications, has offered a more hideous picture of parent-child relations in past time. That modernization changed all of this is seen by Shorter in declining infant mortality in the nineteenth century, but he admits that the picture varies from country to country; mortality remained high in some, e.g., Central Europe and Italy. Yet, on balance, he maintains that the data support his interpretation of the growth in maternal care, more specifically women breast feeding their own children and in general behaving toward them in a loving manner, is what was at work here. If readers see the spector of the Spitz studies they are correct, for this research provides the empirical basis for this section of his theory. Surprisingly, what Shorter does not adequately consider is the possibility that infants died in such staggeringly high numbers in the pre-modern West not because their mothers were indifferent to them, but rather because of poverty and ignorance, and the resignation and fatalism they produce. Such an explanation is not as dramatic as Shorter's but is certainly as plausible.

There are many more arguments that I have with Shorter's interpretation of historical and contemporary data. His attribution of a vanguard role to the working class in various areas of family change seems unfounded. I am far from convinced that he is correct in his assertion that contact with friends and neighbors has dropped off in modern times, and that contact with kin has increased. His discussion of the growth of divorce, with the implicit argument that people are no longer expecting to spend their whole life with one person, even if they expect to remain married, seems to overlook the high rates of marital dissolution attributable to death that plagued the premodern world. It is only recently that marital dissolution rates have come to exceed those of 1860. I could go on and on, but there is no point in getting caught up in what nonspecialists might see as petty quibbles. When all is said and done we must acknowledge that Shorter has presented a provocative and powerful if somewhat sentimental picture of family change. One does not have to be a prophet to foresee a spate of articles and books in the years to come refining, rejecting and confirming aspects of Shorter's scholarly, audacious and eminently readable book.

BOOK REVIEWS

Communities

Differentiation and Co-operation in an Israeli Veteran Moshav, by ELAINE BALDWIN. London: Manchester University Press, 1972. 240 pp. $11.75 cloth.

The Kibbutz Experience: Dialogue in Kfar Blum, by YOSEF CRIDEN and SAADIA GELB. New York: Schocken Books, 1976. 277 pp. $3.95 paper.

SELMA KOSS BRANDOW
Trenton State College

The connection of these books lies in their presentation of the social organization of two types of cooperative communities existing in Israel. Here the similarity ends, for the experiences of the authors, the methodologies they used, and their analyses of the communities are entirely different.

Both the moshavim and the kibbutzim are imbued with the ideals that characterized their pioneer settlers, most of whom were young Russian Jews inspired by a combination of socialistic ideas and the Zionist hope of rebuilding a homeland in which Jews worked the soil without hired labor. The land for the settlements was (and is) owned by the Jewish National Fund and is leased to the kibbutz as a unit or to the individual members of the moshav. There is no private ownership of land in either case.

Both types of settlement are administered and governed by elected officers and council, and by the general assembly made up of the entire membership of each community. However, where the kibbutz has greater centralized direction and individual action is subordinated to the community, the moshav gives emphasis both to individual autonomy and to cooperation and mutual aid of the members. In the kibbutz, all aspects of social, domestic, and economic life involving both production and consumption are communally organized. No member works for his/her own benefit or for individual gain. In the moshav, more latitude is allowed to individuals. Individual members or families are allotted a parcel of land to be worked on their own initiative for benefit of self or family. At the same time, the cooperative framework exists for marketing and purchasing of supplies of goods, for municipal services, and for mutual aid of members.

In the Yishuv and the early years of the state, the interests of the national government and the settlements were concurrent. The need for agricultural production and national leadership were the top priorities. Eventually, overproduction and competition in overseas markets weakened the position of agricultural producers, creating economic difficulties for the settlements. The moshav appears to exhibit more serious conflicts arising in this context, primarily because of the paradox involving competition and struggle between members who are ideally bound together in an organization of cooperation. On the other hand, the kibbutz does not have to deal with the economic problems of individual benefits for members. Perhaps for this reason it was able to accommodate more easily to the necessary changes in agricultural production and industrialization.

As a participant-observer over a two-year period in Kfar Hefer (a fictitious name), Baldwin, a social anthropologist, describes and analyzes the organization and operation of the moshav administration and the economic relationships of its members. Through minutely detailed accounts of the meetings of the executive group, the council, the general assembly, and specialized village committees, she analyzes several special problem areas of moshav life in which members and officials attempt to cope with new situations arising within the cooperative framework.

The major problem studied was that of the continuation and prosperity of family farms. Baldwin asserts that the problems, commonly seen as a problem of generational conflict over departures from the ideals of moshav organization, arise between those families whose second generation continues on the farm, and those who do not have the second generation remaining, and between farmers and the nonfarmers who continue to maintain membership and residence in the village. She is able to show that these are actually social and economic groupings, rather than generational, and that competition for resources within the village was affected by certain demographic patterns as well as by the influence of national government decisions upon the economic activities of the members.

The central point of Baldwin's work is that the moshav cannot be understood in simple economic terms, for the relationships from all other areas of life spill over into the economic sphere. Although accounts of these relationships are often obscured by the tedious detailing of economic matters, one chapter which deals with an analysis of gossip and its effects (based upon the contrasting theories of Gluckman and Paine) clearly shows the ties between interpersonal relationships and the economic activities of the village. Here she is able to demonstrate how various categories and groups interpreted cooperation in different ways and how each attempts to have its understanding of cooperation accepted by the whole village.

The author briefly alludes to the problems of the participant-observer in a few sentences dealing with comments of villagers who repeatedly stated that she could not understand the moshav merely by collecting information and asking questions, particularly since she could not understand their spoken language, Yiddish. Although her work does not warrant this criticism, more attention by the author to her experience as participant-observer might have contributed substantially to the methodology literature, as it in fact does to general theory and to our knowledge of Israeli society.

Criden (an engineer) and Gelb (a social worker) are themselves veteran members of Kfar Blum, the kibbutz which they describe. This has both advantages and disadvantages. While they do an adequate job of describing the organization, government, economy, and socialization of children in this kibbutz, the account lacks objectivity and analysis, unlike that found in other studies of the kibbutz (*Family and Community in the Kibbutz* by Talmon; *The Kibbutz: Venture in Utopia* by Spiro; *The Kibbutz as a Way of Life in Modern Society* by Rosner). The data presented are repetitious of the majority of "studies" which superficially describe and romanticize kibbutz life. Problems, if they exist at all, are made light of or glossed over. For example, the authors insist that kibbutz men and women are completely equal and that their differential work is regarded as equally important. They assert that women, as well as men, make their individual choices about the work they wish to do, and then point out two or three women whose work is not of the domestic type. Their basic assumption seems to be similar to that of Tiger and Shepher (*Women in the Kibbutz*), i.e., that it is "natural" for women to prefer childrearing and domestic tasks, and, for the authors, this suffices to explain a particularly knotty kibbutz problem. Likewise, the problem of lack of privacy in the community is mentioned and dispensed with in one short paragraph. From my experience as a participant-observer in a kibbutz, I am aware that both of these are particularly troublesome problems and cannot be so easily dismissed.

Discussing the practice of communal life with which they are intimately associated, Criden and Gelb are highly critical of social scientists who study kibbutz life at a single point in time rather than viewing the kibbutz as a society which evolves and changes through the years as various conditions require such change. Although this appears to be a valid criticism of kibbutz studies in general, this book offers little which makes a contribution to the existing knowledge of the kibbutz, and nothing which contributes to sociological theory or method.

The Sociology of Community, by JESSIE BERNARD. Glenview, Ill.: Scott, Foresman & Company, 1973. 216 pp. $3.95 paper.

PHILIP OLSON
University of Missouri, Kansas City

Will sociologists ever stop searching for a meaningful definition of community? Will they ever stop promising to offer definitive statements on community? Will they ever stop synthesizing and summarizing what we already know about communities? Probably not. Most of the time it is the younger and newer entrants into sociology who are searching for the order amidst the chaos of community sociology. This time it is our distinguished senior colleague, Jessie Bernard. She brings to the task considerable breadth and seasoned judgment along with her own intellectual interests in social welfare, the Third World, and the Black in America.

Although this small volume is more an intellectual chart of Jessie Bernard, than a sociology of community, there is still plenty of community sociology since a good deal of the author's life work has centered on the community. She raises the familiar and yet unanswered queries: what has happened to community in modern society? and, given the dramatic changes in society, does community exist any longer? Her approach to these questions is taken from Thomas Kuhn's *Structure of Scientific Revolutions* and thus bridges the span between intellectual pursuit and the context within which that pursuit takes place: the sociology of knowledge. Sociologists are limited by the paradigms with which they work and the paradigms are shaped by the historical era in which they are devised; the sociology of community is, then, limited to the historically bounded paradigms of our era: capitalism and functional analysis. From these overarching models flow the specific community paradigms that have informed the study of community in the present century: (1) the ecological model, (2) the community class structure model, (3) the community power structure model, and (4) the evolutionary/ideal-type model.

The core of this small volume explores eclectically these four models in detail; it becomes clear that they are inadequate for understanding the Third World and the Black in American Society. Bernard asks, "Is the very concept of the community necessary for an understanding of how our society operates and, if it is, . . . is social science research guided by the classic paradigms adequate for the purpose, or are we in need of a scientific revolution . . .?" (p. 179). The questions, as she puts them, answer themselves: yes—no—yes. Unfortunately we are not offered the final solution, for she says, "While we are waiting for the revolution . . . we may have to rely on simply tinkering with the old paradigms" (p. 191).

Since this book is only a slim volume in the Scott, Foresman Introduction to Modern Society Series, perhaps it is unfair to expect answers to such a major set of questions. This work serves primarily to offer a capsule summary of community sociology à la Jessie Bernard.

Canadian Society in Historical Perspective, by S. D. CLARK. Toronto: McGraw-Hill Ryerson, 1976. 144 pp. $4.50 paper.

The Canadian Class Structure, by DENNIS FORCESE. Toronto: McGraw-Hill Ryerson, 1975. 148 pp. $4.95 paper.

The People of Hamilton, Canada West, by MICHAEL B. KATZ. Cambridge, Mass.: Harvard University Press, 1975. 381 pp. $17.50 cloth.

Social Mobility in Canada, by LORNE TEPPERMAN. Toronto: McGraw-Hill Ryerson, 1975. 220 pp. $5.95 paper.

JEAN LEONARD ELLIOTT
Dalhousie University

Katz's attempt to rebuild our sociological foundations with a reconstruction of mid-nineteenth century family and economic life in *The People of Hamilton, Canada West* is a polished, but preliminary, report. Since much of our most cherished social theory, particularly in the area of family life, is based upon mythical conceptions of the past, pre-industrial history demythologized threatens to render our assumptions meaningless. While the surface objective of this community study is an examination of the occupational structure, wealth, mobility, transiency, and the family throughout the life cycle in a commercial town of 14,000 prior to industrialization, Katz's deeper concern lies with the transition from a traditional to a modern society.

A central finding in line with Peter Laslett's English research, *Household and Family in Past Time,* establishes the nuclear family as the common family form prior to industrialization. It was expected that Hamiltonians would delay marriage until they were able to start an independent household. Women as well as men left home as adolescents to live a "semi-autonomous" life as boarders or servants. Also the distinction between manual and nonmanual work was not defined as rigidly as it is today; an individual would be likely to engage in both.

Electronic data linkages of census records permits the Hamilton story to be told. In addition Katz utilizes such data as assessment rolls, newspapers of the era, and biographical accounts. The book is dedicated, in part, to Wilson Benson, a contemporary of the period; his diary provides a human dimension to the statistical summaries.

Katz faces the question of Hamilton's representativeness compared with other cities and countries at similar stages of development. Available comparative data are cited. One finding to emerge is that the Blacks are better off than the Irish in terms of their overall distribution in the occupational structure, and the former are more advantaged at this time than their American counterparts (p. 68). Such comparative insights combined with meticulous attention to procedure and concern with larger theoretical issues contribute to making this book a work of major significance. Further reports can only round out the effort.

The volumes by Clark, Forcese, and Tepperman, part of a Series in Canadian Sociology, attempt to analyze the depth and breadth of Canadian society. This objective is achieved with varying degrees of success. There is no question that *Canadian Society in Historical Perspective,* a collection of some recent essays by S. D. Clark, a "grand old man" of Canadian sociology, is a welcome event. The nine essays, all but two previously published, achieve continuity through two recurring themes—structural changes in post-second World War II society, especially the rural/urban interface, and the development of sociology in Canada.

The relative newness of the sociological enterprise in Canada is reflected in the works of Forcese and Tepperman. Tepperman notes that the extent of his analysis is "largely defined by the limits of available data" (p. 158). Such is the case. Often Ontario data must suffice in the absence of data from the other provinces. A central Canadian bias is greatly evident. Unlike Forcese, Tepperman's perspective is not exclusively Canadian, but "cross-national." Social mobility as a social process is solidly examined in a somewhat unique fashion by taking not only the larger social structure as a referent but also formal organizations and individual career lines outside formal organizations. It is curious, though, that only one of the four deviant careers selected is Canadian. (Although sociology may be new terrain in Canada, certainly skillfully disreputable characters need not be sought elsewhere.)

The Canadian Class Structure passes the Canadian content test but Forcese's analysis seems to have some gaps when it comes to spelling out structural specifics. An advocate of minimal stratification, Forcese is careful to distinguish between what may be stated in a theoretical sense and what might be possible politically. Early in the game Forcese tells us that an ideal society of his construction would not permit inherited wealth. The implications of this ground rule for family structure are never considered; neither is the position of women. One wonders what type of family structure would mesh with Forcese's economy such that we would all start out with the same number of chips. This redistribution, though, seeks only equality of opportunity, not equality of condition.

Forcese's clearly stated value positions are definite strengths as is his critique of such establishment historians as Creighton. These features will no doubt endear him to the undergraduate students for whom this volume is intended.

Crime, Law, and Deviance

False Starts: A Memoir of San Quentin and Other Prisons, by MALCOLM BRALY. Boston: Little, Brown & Company, 1976. 375 pp. $8.95 cloth.

PEGGY ANN THOITS
Stanford University

Here is one man's autobiography, a chronicle of repeated failures and ultimate success. Malcolm Braly spent eighteen of his first forty years cycling through a succession of prisons: first for theft, then for armed robbery, again for theft, and finally for a minor parole violation. The book exerts the pull of a good novel, yet is surprisingly devoid of romanticism. Braly is honest and unflaggingly self-critical in examining his actions and his circumstances. No apologia for his behavior is offered; no appeal is made to liberal sympathies. He forces himself, and thus his reader, to grapple seriously with the problem of recidivism: how does one explain his repeated returns to prison and what reforms, if any, could have prevented them? Braly offers some interesting reflections on the problem, yet is commendably unwilling to generalize beyond his own case.

This book contains suggestive material for the anthropologist, the sociologist, and the psychologist. For the anthropologist, Braly sketches an ethnography of prison life. He casually details prison culture through its dialogue, its inmate status system, its fads and character types. For the sociologist, there is food for theoretical thought. Differential association processes appear to be crucial in recidivism. Labeling processes operate with a vengence within the prison system. Braly also deflates some myths: rapes and stabbings are much less frequent than prison lore would indicate; the ordinary inmate does not live with an everpresent sense of fear or danger; and finding a job on the outside is not so difficult—*if* one is willing to accept less pay than one is worth. For the psychologist, there are strong suggestions that the desire for approval and success and the discrepancy between aspiration and achievement may motivate stealing.

In all, Braly's account is absorbing reading. It stands testimony to the ability of individuals to learn from experience and eventually take control of their lives. And it reminds us again of the multiplicity and complexity of factors underlying both deviant and conforming behavior.

Sociology and Jurisprudence of Leon Petrazycki, edited by JAN GORECKI. Urbana: University of Illinois Press, 1976. 144 pp. $6.95 cloth.

J. G. HUND
University of California, San Diego

Leon Petrazycki (1867–1931) was a Professor at St. Petersburg and Warsaw Universities; former students include such notables as Sorokin, Timasheff, and Gurvitch. His work is barely known in English-speaking countries, and the purpose of the present volume is to draw scholars' attention to it and to provide a concise and critical presentation of his views in the context of modern scientific knowledge. The central idea underlying this collection of essays is that while there is much that is old and outmoded in Petrazycki's thought, there is also much that is relevant. The aim then is to separate the two, and to weave Petrazycki's positive and unsuperceded ideas into a coherent whole which may be used to fructify and stimulate current thinking in sociology and jurisprudence. This aim is only partially accomplished however, for Petrazycki's sociological manuscripts were lost and, as these essays show, little is really known about his sociology—and what is known seems drastically outmoded.

I will comment briefly on five of the eight essays which constitute this volume; of these five, Norman Denzin's is the most outlandish. Denzin's attempt to fit Petrazycki into the mainstream of pragmatism and interactionism seems doomed from the outset; Petrazycki's psychology was reductionist and drive-oriented, it was built on a theory of human nature modeled on a stimulus-response paradigm paralleling Pavlov's and can hardly be fit into the mold of symbolic interactionism without breaking the die which Denzin forcibly stretches to cover Petrazycki's ideas. The comparison with Mead seems strained and unconvincing, and though the quality of Denzin's paper is high and its exegetical value good, one gets the feeling that a comparison with Skinner would have been considerably more apt and instructive. Harry Johnson's attempt to argue that Petrazycki was a "kind of" structural-functionist fares no better. The paper suffers from a bad case of precursoritus, for from Johnson's premises that Petrazycki regarded the concept of function "as important" and that "he was certainly aware of the fact that courts settle disputes and thus have an integrative function" (p. 50) we cannot get the conclusion that Petrazycki's views anticipated the Parsonian model of society. Johnson does not actually go quite this far, but he comes sufficiently close to be accused of it. The third and final paper dealing with Petrazycki's sociology was written by Jerzy Lande; Lande was a former student of Petrazycki's so here at last we might have expected some substantive contribution to our understanding of Petrazycki's sociology. But, alas, the paper is embarrassingly thin. Lande admits that he knows Petrazycki's sociology in only "skeletal" form and the most he offers is a weak attempt to classify it as "evolutionary," concerned with the problem of social development. Thus, when it comes to Petrazycki's sociology we are presented with a very frail reed indeed. Happily, the same cannot be said with respect to Petrazycki's jurisprudence.

While there is by contemporary standards much that is bizzare and untenable in Petrazycki's system of jurisprudence, Alexander Peczenik's excellent paper brings to the foreground, and expertly develops, those of Petrazycki's ideas which are of current importance. Peczenik first notes Petrazycki's distinction between the doctrinal and the scientific study of law; he then finds in Petrazycki's theory of the doctrinal study of law a sound theoretical basis for steering a middle course between the vices of legal theory known as formalism and legal realism. While it is true that judges exercise a great deal of discretion in interpreting statutes and precedents, it is not the case as the realists have argued that this discretion is unfettered or completely arbitrary; rather, according to Petrazycki, there exist customary rules, standards, and criteria of interpretation, a communis opinio of lawyers with judges of the highest courts at its head, which effectively circumscribe the judges' use of discretion. Peczenik's exposition and elaboration of Petrazycki's theory of the doctrinal study of law is as fresh and new as it is exciting; its treatment of judicial discretion and criteria of recognition continues on from where the views of Hart and Dworkin leave off, and thus Petrazycki's views can be placed at the very forefront of modern jurisprudential thought. The final essay in this volume, written by Jan Gorecki, deals with Petrazycki's theory of social engineering through law; while Gorecki favorably compares Petrazycki's theory with Pound's sociological approach to jurisprudence, it could perhaps have been even more favorably compared to the currently fashionable policy-considerations approach to social engineering which has been espoused by

Chroust, Lasswell, and McDougal at Yale. Advocates of this approach will find much to their liking in Gorecki's essay and may perhaps be surprised to find that there is after all nothing new under the sun. Of the three remaining essays in this book one is an introductory chapter and the two others deal with Petrazycki's philosophy of science and his theory of law and morals.

While I would have trouble recommending this book to sociologists with no interest in jurisprudence, it is certainly the kind of book which one might buy as a gift for a sociologist friend with an interest in law. It is handsomely bound, slender and compact, has a nice heft, is printed on good paper, and there appears opposite the preface a fine old print of a bespectacled Petrazycki which is suitable for framing. On the other hand, this is a book which no serious student of jurisprudence or legal theory can afford to miss; there can be no doubt that Leon Petrazycki's posthumous appeal for jurisprudence is on the increase, and rightfully so.

The Prison: Policy and Practice, by GORDON HAWKINS. Chicago: University of Chicago Press, 1976. 217 pp. $10.95 cloth.

ROBERT SOMMER
University of California, Davis

This is an excellent, incisive, and urbane analysis of the prison system. Hawkins is blessed with a felicitous style and knows all the right aphorisms. He writes from experience that is both academic and practical. He spent seven years in administrative grades in the British penal system, including two years as head of a facility for youth offenders. Since then he has held several academic positions, including his present one in the Department of Criminology at the University of Sydney. The book was written during a research fellowship at the Center for Studies in Criminal Justice at the University of Chicago where the influence of Norval Morris, Dean of the Law School and author of *The Future of Imprisonment,* is evident.

The book begins with an elucidation of the views of prison critics whom Hawkins classifies as abolitionists, rigorists, reformists, or reductivists. Applying the customary criteria of realism and/or logical consistency, none of these critics comes out looking too well. Hawkins makes an excellent case that most writers regarded as abolitionists really are reformists. Although they want to eliminate the prison system in its present form, they do not rule out humane incarceration. Like himself, most of them believed in the necessity of some kind of imprisonment. Rigorism, or what is more commonly called the deterrent or retribution model, is rejected as unsupported by evidence and impractical, since it would provoke enormous resistence from inmates and their supporters. Reformist notions of treatment or rehabilitation have not been very effective in the past and Hawkins sees little likelihood for their success in the future. He rejects the prescription of more-of-the-same-but-better. He is somewhat more sympathetic to the reductivists desire to limit rather than expand treatment programs, and to reduce the correctional enterprise in all areas, while limiting the "deformative risk" to all those incarcerated. Hawkins is critical of the "small is beautiful" approach for its vagueness about alternatives to incarceration. Phrases such as "community treatment" are empty husks unless there is a community ready, willing, and able to handle offenders.

Hawkins questions Donald Clemmer's concept of prisonization. Defined as the process by which an inmate takes on the folkways, mores, customs, and general culture of the institution, prisonization has been of considerable heuristic value. Research has, Hawkins maintains, condemned the concept to death through a thousand qualifications. Hawkins leans towards the view that the special problems of the prison are a result of the special characteristics of the inmate. That is, they are brought in from the outside rather than existing as a special feature of the prison. Certainly there is a good deal of evidence on the role of outside gangs and outside racial animosities in creating the special climate of the prison. Yet it is the particular nature of imprisonment to bring gangs and races into forced contact that they might avoid on the outside by staying on their own turf. Not all inmates will be affected in the same way by the prison experience and the inmate society contains various sub-groupings. Any generalization about the effects of a total institution will require numerous qualifications.

Books about prisons written by social scientists often portray the guards as invisible people. Hawkins attempts to rectify this with an insightful discussion of "the other prisoners." Hawkins is favorably disposed to better selection methods for guards, including the use of objective screening tests, and better training programs. Diverging from the *Zeitgeist,* he is also sympathetic to the use of prisoners as research subjects, providing there are explicit safeguards. He feels the benefits from research outweigh the acknowledged risks and ethical problems.

As with all prison books, one is anxious to get to the end and learn the author's recommendations. This is what in other circumstances would be "the bottom line." It is easy enough to criticize what others have said but the test for many readers is what the writer personally recommends. Unfortunately, the reader interested in solutions will be disappointed since Hawkins closes the book with a chapter on impediments to change. The final section is a call not for reform but for more research. I would not describe this as a cop-out since the author never promised a prescription for change. Nor is he terribly optimistic about the likelihood of substantial change in the future. However, he does quote with approbation Shaw's maxim, "The reasonable man adapts himself to the world: the unreasonable one persists in trying to adapt the world to himself. Therefore, all progress depends on the unreasonable man." This implies that the reasoned analysis he has made will not be sufficient to produce change. Something more will be required, and this will probably be the leap of faith he describes earlier in the book. Yet we are in his debt for a thoughtful, intelligent survey and analysis of the prison system, its problems and its critics. He is not optimistic about reform, but there are no good grounds for optimism.

The Rape Victim, by ELAINE HILBERMAN. Washington, D.C.: American Psychiatric Association, 1976. 98 pp. $5.00 cloth.

LYNDA LYTLE HOLMSTROM
Boston College

In Hilberman's book, rape is viewed not from the older perspective of blame the victim, but from the newer perspective that sees an act of violence and humiliation, with the victim experiencing overwhelming fear and powerlessness. Rape is "the ultimate violation of the self" (p. x).

The author, who is a psychiatrist, aims to (1) summarize what presently is known about the needs and experiences of the female victims of forcible rape, and (2) provide a framework that will enable clinicians to provide better assistance to such victims. In carrying out these aims, she has brought together the findings of some recent studies and policy recommendations made by numerous groups.

Sociologists are not the intended audience. Nevertheless, several parts may be of interest to them. For those studying the impact of violent crime upon our citizens, the chapters on victims' reactions to rape should provide considerable food for thought. For those with an applied bent, the many guidelines and policy recommendations should be of interest; many changes are being implemented, and evaluation research needs to be done to see if such reforms, when instituted, do indeed bring about the humanistic effects that were intended. For those interested in social movements, the book is another document in the War Against Rape.

On License: A Study of Parole, by PAULINE MORRIS and BEVERLY FARIDA. New York: John Wiley & Sons, 1975. 178 pp. No price listed, cloth.

Men Released from Prison, by IRVIN WALLER. Buffalo: University of Toronto Press, 1974. 273 pp. $15.00 cloth.

F. WILLIAM HOWTON
City College/CUNY

Early release on parole of many, if not most, convicted offenders is a relatively recent and still not strongly established feature of the criminal justice system of Great Britain and Canada. Western Europe, and more particularly the United States have used parole much longer. It was not until 1968 that England and Wales used parole at all, and Canada, whose system has been roughly similar to the US did not start to release a comparably large proportion of parole eligibles (almost half) until 1971.

Now both countries are interested in assessing their new policies and procedures. Parole was established in the first place because it is cheaper than custody, and with the rapid growth of prison populations it seemed reasonable to opt for it rather than for the costly alternative of building prisons. And parole is not only cheaper, but correctionally no less effective than custody, or so it was assumed. These two books report the results of research designed to test that assumption, and not so incidentally to raise large questions about the effectiveness of the criminal justice system as a whole.

The Waller (Canadian) study follows a sample of 423 Ontario penitentiary inmates released during 1968, half on parole and half free and clear (on expiration of sentence), by means of interviews for an initial period of twelve months and for an additional twelve months by tracing information on re-arrests from police records. Since the raw figures show less recidivism for parolees than for non-parolees it would appear that parole supervision is correctionally effective. But through further analysis Waller finds this conclusion "illusory." When allowance is made for the fact that parolees are both self-selected and Board selected the tendency to recidivate cannot be shown to be affected one way or the other by the experience of having been on parole under supervision.

Morris and Farida (British study) identified and interviewed a sample of 232 parole eligible male inmates in two significantly different Midlands prisons (one "training," one "open") in 1970. Those who were granted parole (initially 100) were followed for six months after release by interviews with parolees and parole supervisors. The initial as well as the subsequent interviews were processual, and were used as the basis for constructing a typology of offenders: crime-interrupted non-criminals; impulsive offenders; non-systematic habitual offenders; professional criminals; petty persistent offenders; con men. Considering the differences among the types in relation to the differences among the four categories of subjects (parolee/non-parolee, Prison A/Prison B) yielded a qualitative analysis of the correctional effectiveness of both custody and parole. With due regard for the limitations of their data, the authors conclude that apparently neither confinement in prison nor release on parole under supervision has much effect on the convicted offender's likelihood of re-offending.

If parole does not work, as these studies seem to show, perhaps it should be abandoned. (This has been suggested recently by the US Attorney General.) If it is kept mainly because it is cheaper than building more prisons then surely it would be cheaper still simply to shorten sentences.

Morris and Farida say no, parole is indispensible; it is not working well at present for reasons—fiscal, organizational, technological—that are not inherent but contingent. While they take due note of the tide (still running high) of debunking criticism of the "medical model" and the "treatment ideology," they still keep faith in the cardinal tenet of mainstream progressive penology: rehabilitation can work and will work when truly given a chance. In Great Britain the (partial) failure of parole is due to its "tacked on" character in relation to the criminal justice system as a whole. In order to make parole an organic part of that system, which sooner or later it must be, the archaic philosophy of deterrence and retribution that continues to underly sentencing and parole decisions must find accommodation with the rehabilitationist philosophy of parole.

The position taken by the two British authors follows from their interactionist and processual conceptual orientation, their clinical and typological design of research, and, as it appears, from their doctrinal commitments. It is not surprising that their Canadian colleague's skepticism in regard to those doctrines should lead him to recommend—in effect, without quite saying so—that parole as it exists today be all but scrapped.

Waller's strategic concepts ("detached criminal," "integration," "bond," and "containment") and his affinity for statistical rather than clinical modes of getting knowledge lead him, along with his anti-"treatment" doctrinal commitment, to interpret his findings as meaning that the present criminal justice system is fraught with myths, fallacies, and sundry irrationalities because it is fundamentally misconceived. It does not and cannot deter crime nor does it rehabilitate offenders. What should be done, he suggests, is to work to remodel the whole system following a strategy of "containment" and "bonding," with specific arrangements devised for a whole range of type cases. At one extreme a small fraction (probably under 5%) should be sent to remote "limited access villages" for a long period of time. At the other extreme containment could be so mild as to be almost wholly "within the family." Within the intermediate ranges containment would imply residential facilities with varying degrees of coercive supervision of movement imposed. Rehabilitation facilities of all sorts, from metal working shops to individual psychotherapy should be available but entirely non-coercive.

Parole supervision in this scheme, what is left of it, would concentrate on one or two specialized areas (unemployment, drinking, fighting) and would be somewhat deprofessionalized—the ideal person might well be a warm, motherly, middle-aged woman who "has a certain knack" rather than the fully credentialled, trained specialist preferred at present. ("Dethrone 'The Relationship'," says Waller.)

The fact that these two monographs have much in common, reporting on aspects of criminal justice in two countries whose institutions and philosophies of practice are closely interrelated, and reporting a major failure in both—parole does not work—makes it especially poignant that the implications they see for policy are almost diametrically opposed. The debate that began (in its modern form) with Jeremy Bentham runs on as fresh and warm as ever in spite of criminology, and after all this time.

Madness and Morals: Ideas on Insanity in the Nineteenth Century, by VIEDA SKULTANS. Boston: Routledge & Kegan Paul, 1975. 260 pp. $17.25 cloth.

MIRIAM SONN
Department of Psychiatry
Massachusetts General Hospital, Boston

The state of British psychiatry in the nineteenth century is represented in this volume through the writings of some of its theoreticians and practitioners, mainly physicians and administrators of lunatic asylums. In an introductory chapter, Skultans discusses, with competence and imagination, the major themes of the book. Dividing the eighty years covered into two periods and themes, she stresses the close interrelationship between the changing approaches in psychiatry and the social, economic, and intellectual currents which surrounded them.

Dominating the first half of the nineteenth century is Psychiatric Romanticism which stresses the moral force and will of the individual to combat insanity. Psychiatric Darwinism prevails in the latter part of the century, as heredity, character, and constitution are increasingly seen as determining the etiology, course, and outcome of insanity.

Many of the selections are rich in content and philosophy. The writings of the proponents of moral management are particularly inspiring. Working before the advent of tranquilizing drugs or of swelling populations of mental patients, these writers devoted much sensitive attention toward understanding and managing those aspects of daily life which excited and soothed patients suffering from mental disorders.

The analysis is marred only by a confusing discussion of the various meanings of "moral" in nineteenth century Britain. Also, the disappearance of the author after the introductory chapter is regrettable. The appetite is whetted but never satisfied for some discussion of the relevance of the cogent issue raised for the theory and practice of contemporary psychiatry.

The African Beer Gardens of Bulawayo: Integrated Drinking in a Segregated Society, by HARRY F. WOLCOTT. New Brunswick, N.J.: Rutgers Center of Alcohol Studies, 1974. 261 pp. $12.50 cloth.

CRAIG MACANDREW
University of California, Irvine

Wolcott's stay in Rhodesia (1970–71) coincided with the brief period during which it appeared to white Rhodesians that Ian Smith just might pull it off. It had been five years since the regime issued its Unilateral Declaration of Independence from the United Kingdom, native riots of the early 1960s seemed a thing of the past, and a spirit of noblesse oblige ("Give an African his beer and his women and he'll be happy") everywhere obtained. In quest of a topic and at the behest of E. H. Ashton (the anthropologist-turned-administrator who was in charge of the Housing and Amenities Department of Rhodesia's second largest city), Wolcott elected to examine the municipality's multimillion-dollar native beer industry. Now the Housing and Amenities Department is responsible not only for the provision of housing and services for the exploding native population. It is also charged with the production, transportation, and sale of native beer within the municipality. Moreover, the Department is desirous of increasing the natives' consumption of its product, and not just because the drinking of beer is "a traditional native amenity," but because it uses the profits obtained from its sale to fund the social services it provides the natives and to partially defray the construction costs of their abodes. ("I can almost hear a critical reader questioning my morality and even my sanity. And why not? I have often done so myself," writes Ashton in his poignant introduction.)

Against this essentially Kafkaesque moral backdrop, Wolcott is at his keenly perceptive best in contrasting the exquisite care and attention the Rhodesian administration gives to all aspects of the beer trade with its seeming obliviousness to the deeper, more pressing problems that so urgently confront this troubled land. As a case study in the futility of administrative attempts—however well intentioned they might be—to solve problems by changing things without really altering them, Wolcott's report is highly recommended. However, before I would accept his conclusion that native urban drinking in Bulawayo is essentially integrative in character and does not constitute a serious social problem, I would have to be informed why I ought not take seriously the comments of the local hospital's medical staff whose duty it is to patch up as best they can some of the uglier consequences of "integrative" beer garden conviviality. ("The extent of head injury is colossal among these chaps. [When drunk] They're always bashing each other on the head." "My impression is that 75% of personal violence treated here is alcohol related." "You ought to spend a Friday evening at the hospital . . . There's blood all over, and drunks lying everywhere. It's like a casualty clearing station on a battlefield.") In a similar vein, I would want to know why I ought not take seriously the response of an official of the Housing and Amenities Department to the contention of the local police that native alcohol consumption gives rise to robberies, assaults, and the like: "They're right. That is, the increase corresponds exactly with our graphs of improved sales." Indeed, by a sufficiently judicious reckoning it would seem that one could make a case for the essentially integrative character of anything and everything from the Saint Valentine's Day massacre to our recent involvement in Viet Nam.

Education

The Role of the Pupil, by BARBARA CALVERT. Boston: Routledge & Kegan Paul, 1975. 150 pp. $9.24 cloth. $4.75 paper.

ROSALIE COHEN
Temple University

The Role of the Pupil uses a dramaturgical model of role to explain how pupils play out in the classroom their social roles, their roles as savages (to be civilized), as opponents to the teacher, as customers and clients of the school system, as products or plants (objects to be molded or nurtured), as members of peer groups and of age, stream, sex, or responsibility groups in the school, and as deviants. It includes some interesting insights into a non-American English-speaking school system; and it reflects both similarities and differences in their notions of "modernity" when compared with those in the US. However, although nicely written and potentially useful to non-specialists in sociology or education, it is a little Pollyanna-ish and much too limited in scope to be used for classroom instruction in either area.

Liberty and Equality in the Educational Process: A Comparative Sociology of Education, by REMI CLIGNET. New York: John Wiley & Sons, 1974. 418 pp. $14.95 cloth.

RONALD P. DORE
University of Sussex

Fraternity we hear less about these days, but the other two virtues of the trinity remain powerful slogan makers, two centuries after the French Revolution. Rhetorically they make a splendid pair; it is their incompatibility that concerns Remi Clignet. Equality of educational opportunity—equalizing the social as well as the physical environments of black and white children—is seen in the US to require compulsory busing. In England, it would require abolition of those nurseries of privileged life-chances, the private (prep and "public") schools; parents would have to be told: "you may spend your money on a second car or at the casino, but you may not spend it on the education of your child." "Liberty forever!" cries an Illich, fulminating against the vicious affront to the essential dignity of the individual represented by compulsory schooling and urging that our schools be replaced by networks of opportunities for individual exploration. Fine, points out Clignet, for the children of the middle class who have family backgrounds which stimulate their desire to learn and privileged connections into jobs which can give scope to their developed powers of spontaneous creativity; not so fine, if one cares about *equality* for the lower classes whose hopes of material betterment depend on being socialized into the cognitive and social norms of the middle class.

Professor Clignet's most laudable ambition was to make this theme of the tension between liberty and equality the central axis of a textbook. He has sought to provide *both* a survey, with the usual summaries of the literature, of that body of inquiry and polemic which goes under the name "the sociology of education," *and* instead of the mindlessness of most textbooks, an intelligent argument which speaks to some of the central educational issues of our day.

The enterprise was worthy, but it does not quite succeed, which is a great pity because Professor Clignet—as is evidenced by the opinions which he (albeit guardedly) expresses on busing, on the IQ controversy, on Illich, etc.—is sensible and humane, a man of generous instincts, wide personal experience and wide reading. It does not entirely succeed, partly because the central concepts are blurred in the interest of comprehensiveness. For example, a whole segment of the sociological literature—which any US textbook must cover—concerns the tension in the US and Canada between school boards, school superintendents, and teachers; bureaucratization and the problems of centralization and decentralization of administration on the one hand, professionalization, and the status and power problems of teachers on the other. What spoils Clignet's account of the matter—otherwise a reasonable summary of the literature as far as I can judge—is his insistence on hitching it up to his main theme by talking in terms of conflict between the "liberty" of the administrator and the "liberty" of the teacher—an altogether different problem from the sort of issue raised in busing or the search for educational alternatives where real conflicts between liberty and equality are involved. Of course "power" and "liberty" are closely related concepts. But it does not help to treat them as synonyms. "Liberty" should not be overworked.

Nor should "accommodation" and "assimilation," the other pair of dichotomous concepts which provide the framework for two central chapters analyzing the range of, and sources of variation in, teaching and learning styles. "Assimilation"—working *on* students, and "accommodation"—working *with* students, the one an exercise in socializing to conformity, the other a flexible response to children's needs/wishes, is altogether too crude and blurred a dichotomy either for normative analysis of the problem or for a survey of sociological determinants of the choice of teaching styles. And the problem is compounded when the chapter on teaching styles is followed by one on learning styles and one finds "assimilation" now meaning the stress on spontaneity and creativity—a natural pupil response to an *accommodation*-based teacher style. And if that is not confusing enough the last chapter then assures us that the assimilation mode, both of teaching *and* learning, belong to the liberty side of the liberty/equality equation.

That is, indeed, the most heavily elaborated side of the equation. Equality is a shadowy protagonist, and one sadly missing dimension is the lack of any discussion of egalitarian*ism*—where it comes from in history, what interest groups espouse it and why—a lack surprising in a Frenchman, heir to the tradition of Tocqueville, Guizot, and Bouglé. There *is* a developmental scheme implicit in the book, but it is nine tenths submerged and its total outline consequently blurred. Clignet seems to be saying, for instance, that industrialization ("increase in scale" presumably means industrialization) leads to greater differentiation, and *part* of differentiation (parallel to specialization of trade schools, for instance) is greater inequality of educational opportunity: a very dubious generalization. At another point the long term decline of teacher status in the US and Europe seems to be identified with the transitional Ivory Coast situation at independence when many leading teachers left what had been the best-opportunity profession under French rule for the most exciting occupations opened up by independence, and the status of teaching suffered by comparison—a very particular and local phenomenon. In general the discussion about the correlates of "development" fails to draw the basic distinction between countries where school systems grew gradually at a late stage in the process of industrialization, and late developing countries where the building of a "modern" school system is centrally planned and pushed ahead in order to provide the *foundation* for industrialization. Much of the material for such a comparison is there, however, since the wide range of African studies, quoted, combined with th mixture of European and American perspectives, is one of the original features and great strengths of the book.

The book's language is a major problem for the reader to contend with; if Professor Clignet ever possessed that mythical crisp clarity of the French he lost it in the process of learning English in a sociologese-speaking environment. It really does not help to say "exposed to the teaching activities of adult female actors" when he means "taught by women." Nevertheless, it is worth persevering: Clignet presents a useful survey of the education and mobility literature and he has some sane and shrewd things to say in the last chapter about the current American educational scene.

The Enduring Effects of Education, by HERBERT H. HYMAN, CHARLES R. WRIGHT, and JOHN SHELTON REED. Chicago: University of Chicago Press, 1975. 313 pp. $12.50 cloth.

JERRY L. FLETCHER
Department of Health, Education, and Welfare

This book is a gem. The authors have taken adult survey data from Gallup polls, the National Opinion Research Center, and the Survey Research Center, from four different time periods, and examined the degree to which the amount of education a respondent had was associated with correct answers to knowledge questions. The surveys selected allowed the authors to track a cohort over time, as they got older, as well as to make comparisons between adults of different ages and degrees of education at the time of any one survey.

The results are stunning. The amount of knowledge is consistently associated with the amount of education in such a clear and overwhelming fashion that alternate hypotheses are difficult even to postulate. Schools (years of schooling) make an awful lot of difference!

The authors very carefully describe test after test that they conducted to investigate alternative hypotheses, and none of them is tenable, given the data they have.

The book is remarkable in the clarity of *thinking* which preceded the statistical work. What a pleasure it is to read a study which does not substitute obscure and esoteric statistical manipulation for clear thought about what one could do with the data at hand to track down each possible hypothesis. I wish this book could be assigned reading in every elementary statistics class. The tables are clear; the statistical manipulations are simple and easy to understand by everyone. There are, of course, severe limits to their data, which is not unreasonable since the surveys were designed for other purposes. But the authors not only exhaust the data, they identify precisely the kinds of data that would be needed in such surveys to allow more precise testing of a number of the hypotheses. Their recommendation to piggyback these items on to future surveys seems well worth the small amount of funding needed.

The authors' methodology for examining the effects of schooling is orthogonal to that of Coleman and Jencks. While they found insufficient variation across schools at any one time to have much of an impact on the differences among children at entry, Hyman et al. use the amount of schooling (twelve years instead of six; sixteen instead of twelve). This is a major variation, and comparisons among groups with different amounts of schooling show that the amount of schooling does have massive compensatory effects.

The authors acknowledge that the data do not permit a test of the hypothesis that the more able on entry are the ones who go farthest in schooling. If this hypothesis is true instead of the one that the schools make the difference, then schools are certainly remarkable in the precision with which they filter and sort students by ability.

The authors mention at several points the possible psychic costs of the gain in knowledge from further education. While they have not attempted to find questions in the surveys which might get at this, they indicate in the concluding chapter that they hope to look at the attitude and value questions in the surveys and study the effects of increased amounts of education on changes in them. Let us hope that they can find support to be about this quickly.

The Black High School and Its Community, by FREDERICK A. RODGERS. Lexington, Mass.: Lexington Books, 1975. 127 pp. $17.50 cloth.

JAMES P. PITTS
Northwestern University

Most research and writing on the effects of desegregating black schools presume and/or attempt to verify the beneficial outcomes for black children. This book advances the rarely listened to but important argument that the actual practice of desegregation in Southern communities involves a major social cost for black teachers, students, and neighborhood institutions. Specifically, Rodgers argues that the Southern black high school is the secular focus of much black community life (civil rights and other public meetings, recreational activities, athletic competition), and the occupational base for most of the black elite. Desegregation almost always involves its dismantling as a black-run organization with little or no regard for the central role it plays in the daily life of surrounding black communities. This cry of alarm is not new. Since the late sixties, it has been expressed in more than one of the popular black publications such as Ebony magazine. Rodgers uses the format of a research monograph to bring it to the attention of a professional audience. He uses data gathered from North Carolina, records for 1963–64 and 1973 as well as interviews with school personnel and persons in the black communities of that state. Regrettably, the book has so many flaws that it is probably of limited value in stimulating the desired credibility for this perspective among professionals and policy-makers.

Rodgers begins as if he intends to use data to test a controversial proposition: that black American students learn more and develop a better self-image when they are taught in schools which are administered by blacks. He starts with the valid observation that the late sixties struggle over black community control of black schools did not allow a test of that proposition because black community control was not achieved. Rodgers argues that the closest approximation to black community control of predominantly black public schools actually occurred under the Southern system of "separate but equal." He readily acknowledges that this phrase masked the truth: that white schools were systematically and illegally subsidized by using tax money supposedly meant for the black schools, but feels that within such severe restrictions black administrators had a relatively free hand in shaping the educational experience of their pupils. This idea is worthy of serious consideration, but its credibility suffers from both lack of data and Rodger's determination to portray black administrators as uniformly self-sacrificing servants of their communities. It appears that the sole source of data used to substantiate this image was fifty-eight questionnaires from black principals and a smaller number from white supervisors of the school districts; the latter characterized by Rodgers as knowing little of what went on in the black schools.

Working with samples of data is one of the realities of doing research, but Rodgers's book shows no appreciation of how sampling biases may influence the collection of his data and the inferences he wants to make. Starting with 1963–64, the last year for which the State of North Carolina kept separate racial data on schools, he identifies the names of 187 black principals. His attempt to study them through a mail questionnaire in 1973 produced only fifty-eight respondents. Why? Rodgers apparently isn't interested in why he only received a 30% return rate. Are his respondents merely the survivors of the well-documented purge of black administrators under Southern desegregation? Similarly, a study of the effects of desegregation in a whole state should be able to produce interviews with more than nine teachers and special staff, twenty-six parents, and thirteen former high school students. The study should also tell us how these particular respondents came to be selected.

Not the least of problems with this book is the presentation of data. Summaries of interviews with teachers, parents, and students are extremely cursory, barely covering two pages. Despite the use of questionnaires for gathering information from principals, the reader is not allowed to inspect their responses in tabular form. Statistics drawn from public records to describe the demographic and organizational characteristics of North Carolina schools are presented in paragraphs that are difficult to follow. Aside from the fact that summary tables would present the data more succinctly, it is apparent that many of the data cited in prose have no significance and need not be mentioned. Finally, the author is frequently guilty of making sweeping inferences about the racial sentiments and motives of "most" white and black people living in North Carolina as many as 100 years ago while presenting little bibliographic support for those judgments. In short, it is often difficult to distinguish the data of this study from the opinions of the researcher.

The Black High School and Its Community is a disappointing book but it should not be ignored. The topic it addresses—the role of black institutions in motivating and socializing black adolescents—has major policy implications that are often overlooked by those integrationists who presume the necessity of eradicating anything not run by whites. We still lack an empirical evaluation of the topic, but perhaps persons who read this book will be inspired to try some of Rodgers's ideas and/or execute the kind of research adequate to evaluate the topic.

The Academic Melting Pot: Catholics and Jews in American Higher Education, by STEPHEN STEINBERG. New York: McGraw-Hill Book Company, 1974. 183 pp. $8.95 cloth.

JOHN MURRAY CUDDIHY
Hunter College/CUNY

Put bluntly, Jews are smart, Catholics—especially "thick micks"—are dumb, doesn't everybody know that? Refined a little, the thesis runs: Jews produce intellectuals not because of Jewish social class or Jewish genes —a "regressive theory"—but because of their culture, they are "the People of the Book." And American Catholics? Color them purple papal passive people, and check them out as "anti-intellectuals" in Richard Hofstadter's *Anti-Intellectualism in American Life* (in a coda, "A Note on American Catholicism" appended, expectably, to a chapter titled: "The Revolt Against Modernity" [pp. 136–141]). A "harsh assessment," Steinberg duly notes.

Professor Steinberg demurs from the conventional wisdom of this "scholarship theory" (held, as applied to the Jewish case, in various versions by Parsons, Wirth, Glazer, Zborowski, and Herzog). The precursor-work for this demurral is, of course, Miriam Slater's "My Son The Doctor: Aspects of Mobility Among American Jews" (*ASR,* Vol. 34, No. 3). Orthodox Talmudic "fundamentalism," she shows, is hostile to science, secular learning, and rapid social mobility. Steinberg's book on Catholics and Jews in American higher education holds that scholars, trying to explain traditional Jewish overrepresentation and Catholic underrepresentation in American higher education—as students, teachers, and scholars—reached for the culture variable rather than social class on the mistaken assumption that all the classical immigrant groups started from socio-economic scratch: all had arrived penniless. True enough, but to stop there is to opt for an impoverished idea of poverty. If we look closer, this assumption of social class parity disappears.

Jews especially, among the later immigrants, arrived with empty pockets but compared with other immigrant groups, they arrived with heads that were disproportionately literate (a "headstart" indeed) and with fingers disproportionately occupationally skilled. It was this social class capital rather than any cultural baggage that gave Jews the jump on other immigrants. Now if we add in luck (Steinberg is refreshing in ceding to chance a large role in social life) we don't need to fall back on cultural factors. As luck would have it, the great East European migration meshed perfectly with a vast expansion of higher education in the United States, the downgrading of classical languages as entrance requirements, introduction of electives, vocational-professional schooling, etc.

The third part of Steinberg's *The Academic Melting Pot* leaves historical data for the contemporary data gathered under the sponsorship of the Carnegie Commission on Higher Education in 1969. Data are analyzed on the changing religious composition of American higher education and the academic disciplines (improved Catholic class position increases their academic representation) and on the alleged incompatibility of religious commitment with scholarly productivity—the allegation is true! Jews again supply the anomaly: they do not suffer the Catholic and Protestant dilemma; perish (religiously) or publish (academically).

In an excellent book, I find only one fault. In the historical section, in "The Harvard Affair," Steinberg is too ready to accept at face the "bad faith" of Harvard President A. Lawrence Lowell on the testimony of former Harvard undergraduate, Victor Albert Kramer. Kramer and the President had met in a Pullman car on Christmas day, 1922, and had had a heated discussion of the motives for Harvard's recent introduction of religious quotas. The *New York Times* reported Kramer's version; Lowell issued a statement—part of which Steinberg calls "sanctimonious" (p. 27) charging Kramer with misrepresenting his views. Kramer's restatement of Lowell's views, disembedding them from the indexicality of the Pullman car encounter, generalized them into a kind of manifesto. It is difficult to reconstruct what actually occurred.

One thing in conclusion: we must distinguish the "cultural variable" as an etiological factor in social change (the "scholarship theory" of Jewish overrepresentation in education and in the doctor-lawyer-teacher professions) from the use made by the Jewish community—or any other community—of self- or group-enhancing cultural glosses on its socio-economic achievements. Each subculture supplies a kind of running hermeneutic on its own doings to anybody within earshot. This kind of sub-cultural public relations may not be causal explanation, but it is an enormously important component of status-enhancement or *yiches*-enhancement. "A universe of *yiches*-aspiration," Leo Rosten notes in *The Joys of Yiddish,* concluding his definition of "yiches" (prestige, status), "lies in the heartfelt cry of a Jewish woman at the seashore: 'Help! Help! My son the doctor is drowning!'" (p. 434).

The Sociology of Education: A Sourcebook, 3rd ed., edited by HOLGER R. STUB. Homewood, Ill.: Dorsey Press, 1975. 427 pp. $7.95 paper.

JOSEPHINE A. AMATO
SUNY/Brockport

This book of readings is primarily intended for sociology of education courses. Most of its sections are organized around topics standard in sociology of education readers: education and society, social class and education, the school as a social organization, the teacher, etc. The one exception is devoted to social processes and classroom interaction, an area that warrants, but seldom receives, attention in such readers.

Taken as a whole, this collection presents a perspective which is dated, limited in coverage, and suggests a low estimation of undergraduates' ability to comprehend research studies. Of twenty-four articles, thirteen appeared before 1970. The assumptions and conclusions of many selections consequently appear dated in the light of extensive subsequent research and discussion. Several significant areas receive minimal or no attention: the governance of education; structural (i.e., nonattitudinal) aspects of the relationships among social class, education, and mobility; desegregation; and sexism in the school. These gaps and the selections' datedness may be due in part to what seems to be the editor's reluctance to present students with articles utilizing analytic techniques more exotic than correlation or the presentation of means and percentages. Although the editor states his intent to "present the best rather than the easiest," his selections suggest otherwise.

Environment

Microecology: Social Situations and Intimate Space, by DONALD W. BALL. New York: Bobbs-Merrill, 1973. 38 pp. $1.50 paper.

Environmental Quality and Society, edited by RICHARD A. TYBOUT. Columbus: Ohio State University Press, 1975. 316 pp. $7.50 paper.

ARTHUR H. PATTERSON
Pennsylvania State University

In recent years there has developed a great concern for the '"environment." Environmental awareness has readily spread from the biological and physical sciences to the social sciences. This has resulted in a great outpouring of books, edited volumes, monographs, and, more recently, journal articles, from "concerned" social scientists. Unfortunately, much of this work has been rushed into print with little or no theoretical underpinnings.

Donald W. Ball's *Microecology: Social Situations and Intimate Space* does have a strong theoretical base: an attempt to cast all face-to-face social encounters into a microecological environment. However, while reading Ball's interesting (but far from comprehensive) review of the personal space, proxemics, and kinesics literature, the reader is left with a feeling of "But why microecology?"

One reason for the reader's lack of fascination with the microecology framework might be the brevity of the piece. The work is a monograph in the Bobbs-Merrill Studies in Sociology series, and was reduced from the author's doctoral dissertation. Some of the support for the framework appears to have been lost in the translation. Another, and perhaps more serious problem, is that microecology may not be an appropriate framework for this interpersonal, face-to-face literature. The author uses microecology to mean intimate spatial contexts. However, the study of human ecology is not very well established, as compared (for example) to the biologist's study of ecology. As such, social scientists are still struggling with questions such as: how does an environmental context affect behavior, and how do differences in scale (from micro to macro) matter? Thus, it seems premature to take existing and disparate literatures and attempt to integrate them because they occur in a "microecological" environment.

It is interesting to note some of the difficulties in considering scale in human environments. Ball discusses microecology as being concerned with "microspace," which he defines as the bounded limits of naturally transmitted communication. How different this is from the social psychologist's microenvironment, where large groups of people can be studied so long as the size remains controllable and measurable, or the urban planner's microenvironment, which might encompass a neighborhood as opposed to an entire city. Thus, it is indeed difficult to find satisfaction in a monograph that is based entirely on a framework of microecology.

Richard A. Tybout's *Environmental Quality and Society* is an edited volume, that, in contrast to Ball's piece, is atheoretical. The book contains various essays that are purported to deal with how one can act through social processes to achieve some balance between material and environmental needs. Unfortunately, one finds very little sociology and a great deal of technical ecology in the essays. The reader gains a better understanding of many environmental questions (e.g., ecology, meteorology, sanitation, industrial waste), but very little understanding of how our social processes relate to all this.

The explanation for this shortcoming is apparent and is a serious flaw of most edited volumes of this nature. The book is the end product of the Conference on Quality of the Environment conducted at the Ohio State University in November, 1970. As with most conferences, it appears that the various participants all had something to say, but weren't really sure how what they had to say related to the conference. This is compounded by the fact that none of the participants seemed to know what any of the other participants were going to say. The end result is a volume which contains the work of, among others, a biologist, a zoologist, a political scientist, economists, engineers, a psychologist, a sociologist, a planner, a US Senator, and the president of the Sierra Club.

It is apparent that a group with the above composition could have something to say that could aid in saving our society from environmental destruction. Or they could produce some interesting and readable essays which barely relate to environmental quality and society, let alone to one another. The result, not surprisingly, is the latter.

The editor freely (and reasonably) admits that the book's approach is "eclectic." However, the need here is not for synthesis, but for focus. No theory emerges, no framework is suggested which would facilitate a social scientist's study of (and attack upon) environmental problems. Thus, despite its title, this book does not place environmental quality in a social context.

The Poverty of Power, by BARRY COMMONER. New York: Alfred A. Knopf, 1976. 314 pp. $10.00 cloth.

NOMAN MILLER
Ursinus College, Collegeville, Pennsylvania

In this pioneer effort, *The Poverty of Power,* Barry Commoner has taken us from the environmental crisis depicted in *The Closing Circle,* to the energy crunch of the coming period. He has accomplished this by laying bare the vital connections between the eco-crisis and the economic problems of the bicentennial era. There are several strands which he weaves into a compelling thesis: one having to do with the economic system, another dealing with the production system, and a third on the ecological system. Out of this emerges a criticism of American capitalism.

Commoner makes plain that today's dominant energy sources are too frequently harnessed with the wrong technical means, or poorly harnessed, or that altogether different energy sources should be used. It looks as though we have a case of controlling insects with sledge hammers. For greater efficiency in the use of energy, he recommends use of the trolley for city travel, greater use of our railroads, more widespread use of heat pumps, and further exploration of solar energy.

The author sets out by explaining the science of energy—thermodynamics. The First Law of this science, which provides the framework most commonly adopted in analyzing energy use, is primarily directed at means for maximizing performances with a specified technology and energy source. "How can I secure better gas mileage with my Harley?" would reflect the line of questioning based on the First Law approach.

The Second Law of thermodynamics, which is considerably more complicated than the preceding law, would orient us to another set of questions. Here we would want to couple any energy source and technology to provide the least amount of work needed to complete a task. In the case of the Harley, we would want to know about the relative efficiencies of two and four-cycle engines.

In our example, with the aid of the Second Law, we want to get from here to there with the least amount of work. We might abandon the Harley for a bus or trolley. In the Second Law there are additional considerations. We might determine to use "wasted" energy from one operation, to help perform yet another. Commoner mentions how we can produce electric power by linking the braking systems of trains to generators. This would improve the Second Law efficiency ratings of a given set of operations.

From thermodynamics to case studies of energy sources, Commoner turns to the business dimensions of energy use. What is most central here is his explanation of certain developments in America's postwar economy—particularly the rates of capital and labor productivity. There appears to be a *contradictory* aspect to the manner in which capital funds are expanded: "The capability of the production system to regenerate capital at a rate sufficient to sustain itself is achieved by using less labor relative to output." The growth of capital and output hinges on improving labor productivity, among other things. However, Commoner tells us that even though output and labor productivity have been increasing in the postwar period, capital productivity has not been increasing at a rate sufficient to provide for continuation of the system in the coming 10 or more years.

The contradictory aspect of this system is rooted in a process which appears to be isomorphic with the law of diminishing returns. The process whereby output rates are increased, seems to be in conflict with the long-run goal of constantly expanding rates of capital productivity. Investments in energy-intensive, low Second Law efficiency technologies—to increase rates of labor productivity—have not been yielding sufficient increases in the rate of capital productivity to sustain the system. Commoner cites the estimates of top business and government officials which correspond to his estimate of this impending crisis.

According to Commoner, the decline in the rate of capital productivity is resulting in a decline in the rate of profit. Since World War II, the profits (before taxes) of non-financial corporations, have declined from an average of about 20% of gross output (in the years 1948–52), to about 10% by 1970. The increase in the costs of energy-intensive technologies figures prominently as a cause of this decline in capital productivity and ultimately the rate of profit.

All of this is tantamount to what the author describes as a flaw in the design of our three interrelated systems. The dominant energy sources—coal, petroleum, and nuclear power—also pose serious risks to human well-being. As in Commoner's earlier writings, we are again brought up to date on the significant findings in this sphere. The main energy sources are increasingly expensive to secure, partly because they are of limited supply in some cases, and because certain environmental safety standards must be met in their production and use.

The leading energy sources are valued for their profitability and because they can be privately owned (even while they may be publicly subsidized). In sharp contrast, there is solar power. Commoner's penetrating chapter on "The Sun" reveals that solar energy has a notable versatility in a thermodynamic sense. It can be readily coupled to low and high energy tasks. It is an inexhaustible source, and its use need not pose the hazards to the eco-sphere which routinely arise with the production and use of coal, petroleum, and nuclear power. The sun's capacity for doing work cannot be monopolized as has been the case with other energy sources. Commoner's analysis of solar power further suggests that the economic and technical challenges of its use are quite manageable.

The Poverty of Power is an immense accomplishment. It is a gift from a wide-ranging intellect. While there is a recognized need to more rigorously demonstrate some of the relationships between the economic system and the production system, a paradigm for further research and discovery has been established in Commoner's work. The facility with which Commoner bridges findings and ideas from the social, physical, and biological sciences is admirable. And it is this facility, I would submit, which makes it possible to write the "big news" we need to learn.

The next quarter century, from Commoner's perspective, has the appearance of a landscape on which a struggle over living standards and energy use will be waged. Champions of the public interest and of corporate capital will be vying with one another. The author and his colleagues command our support for outlining the scope and character of this escalating war. *The Poverty of Power* is a masterpiece of eco-anthropology—with a fierce bite.

Language

Reflections on Language, by NOAM CHOMSKY. New York: Random House, 1975. 269 pp. $3.95 paper.

WILLIAM L. RAISER
Graceland College

Noam Chomsky is a linguist, not a sociologist, but his book deals with the fundamental question of human nature and, more specifically, with the nature of the human mind. This element of his linguistic studies gives him sociological significance.

Chomsky examines the primitive assumptions of a great deal of modern social science. Because of this, many will dismiss his arguments as self-evidently false. After all, what are primitive assumptions but those aspects of life and nature which we take to be most patently self-evident? This is the very reason we should give serious attention to his arguments, for, if these assumptions are false our theoretical houses are built on sand.

Chomsky develops the case for a rationalist rather than an empiricist approach to human nature. This takes us back to the philosophical debates of the seventeenth century where the rationalists (who saw human beings as innately endowed with specific capabilities) lost to the empiricists (who saw human nature as a blank slate to be written upon by various psychological and social forces). Since the social sciences did not emerge as disciplines until considerably later, we arrived on the scene with the issue resolved. Therefore, sociology has developed as a discipline within the empiricist framework, and our research and theorizing have been guided by the assumptions of that framework.

In *Reflections on Language,* Chomsky does a good job of presenting some initial empirical (not empiricist) support for the rationalist position. He notes, for example, that we use some reasonably complex rules of grammar in our language where simpler ones can easily be imagined. Even with these complexities, however, children learn language with little difficulty. This observation causes him to posit the existence of an innate language facility in humans. Such an hypothesis receives strong support when the available evidence indicates that the complex rules noted for English are common to all known languages. Chomsky concludes that "where we have any glimmerings of understanding, we are led to theories with a distinctly rationalist character."

This exploration of basic assumptions about the nature of mind is strongly empirical. Moving from that base, Chomsky sketches what appear to him to be logical implications of opting for either the rationalist or the empiricist perspective. His work, as he appropriately recognizes, is on the shakiest ground at this point and should be seen as merely suggestive of some of the kinds of questions which need further empirical research.

Many of Chomsky's works that bear on the issues of most fundamental significance to sociology are beyond our reach because they are couched in the technical language and issues of linguistics. Some of this book moves in that direction, and understandably so, but most of it does not. Even that which does can be followed by the patient reader.

Chomsky raises a very fundamental issue, and his arguments are persuasive because of both their logic and the supporting empirical evidence. *Reflections on Language* illustrates the continual need to be aware of those on the cutting edges of disciplines other than our own. At these points, we are made most aware of the interrelatedness of all knowledge.

Foundations in Sociolinguistics: An Ethnographic Approach, by DELL HYMES. Philadelphia: University of Pennsylvania Press, 1974. 246 pp. $5.95 paper.

Sociocultural Dimensions of Language Use, edited by MARY SANCHES and BEN G. BLOUNT. New York: Academic Press, 1975. 404 pp. $22.50 cloth.

BERYL L. BELLMAN
University of California, San Diego

Dell Hymes is a major linguistic theorist who has given the word "ethnography" a renewed importance and meaning. His book is a collection of previously published essays which, even though several of them are now a little dated, provides an excellent introduction to ethnographic sociolinguistics. Hymes does recognize that the term "ethnography" has carried the negative connotation of being only descriptive and "not itself a theoretical task, but only fodder for one." Instead he redefines the *ethography of speaking* as a "description that is a theory—a theory of speech as a system of cultural behavior; a system not necessarily exotic, but necessarily concerned with the organization of diversity."

In each of his chapter-essays he characterizes sociolinguistics as inclusive of a large diversity of research interests ranging from Whorf, Sapir, Malinowski, and Firth's early linguistic concerns, the ethnolinguistic analyses which provide cultural grammars for different semantic domains by Goodenough, Lounsbury, Metzger, Gumperz, Frake, and others, the range of interests expressed by Labov, Fishman, Ervin-Tripp, Bernstein, and Goffman, the ethnomethodological positions of Garfinkel, and Cicourel, and the contributions of conversational analysts such as Sacks and Schegloff. Although he acknowledges this large plurality of interests, he does not offer a detailed analysis from any of the ethnographic perspectives he describes. However, he does give a somewhat complex, albeit elegant, presentation in his most recently written chapter, which critiques Lakeoff's essay on "Some Reasons Why There Can't Be Any Some-any Rule." He begins by considering two sets of sentences which differ only in their respective uses of "some" and "any." He demonstrates how their meanings, and by extension the meaning of any set of sentences which share a common surface structure, are dependent on their underlying speech act presuppositions (e.g., whether the given sentence is a promise or threat), key (if the sentence is to be taken at face value or as mock), and type of interpretation (e.g., whether the construction of role relationships between participants is reciprocal or reflexive). In his discussion he does not present any contextual analysis of materials. This is curious given the argument in his other chapters for a methodology concerned with actual speech acts, events, situations, and the various components of speech including message form and content, setting, scene, channel, speaker, auditor, genre, norms of interaction, and norms of interpretation.

Several ideas are repeated in different chapters. This is perhaps the fate of books whose chapters are collections of previously published work written for different purposes. Nevertheless, the importance of viewing the sociology of language as an ethnography of speaking and his critique of Chomsky's dichotomy between performance and competence structures are worth repeating. Although many of his ideas are complex, the book can be read in a sitting and for students unfamiliar with the materials it can still be read in a relatively short period. The book contains some of Hymes's most important writings and thus offers an excellent presentation of his theoretical position and a fair summary of other work being done in the field.

Where Hymes's monograph lacked specific studies, this collection, edited by Sanches and Blount, provides excellent examples of the variety of methodological and theoretical positions that characterize the ethnographic approach to sociolinguistics. Most of the essays contain either lengthy transcripts or present detailed examples recorded (video and/or audio) from naturally occurring social interactions. The data thus presented permit the reader to follow the course of each analysis and recognize adjacent phenomena to those described. The kinds of analyses used range from formal semantic analysis, structural analysis, conversational analysis, ethnomethodology, to the ethnographic description of analytic components as advocated by Hymes for the study of speech events. The contributors demonstrate that ethnography is not simply descriptive, but seriously addresses significant methodological issues and theoretical concerns.

The editors divided the book into two parts. The first, with an introduction by Blount which summarizes the history of the ethnographic approach to sociolinguistics, is on the construction of social reality. While this phrase is identified mostly with phenomenological, ethnomethodological, and symbolic interactionist oriented behavioral scientists, Blount includes two divergent studies by Selby and Frake. Frake discussed Yakan folk categories of spatiality by presenting a formal ethnosemantic analysis of different Yakan architectural styles and their significance for social interaction. Selby critiques psychological attribution theory with a content analysis of Zapotec statements of cause and effect. He concludes that the Zapotec do not use a trait-based explanation of behavior, and thus argues the inadequacy of a universal personality attribution theory.

The other five essays in the first section are more consistent with the position that the construction of social reality concerns members' methods, practices, and practical procedures for accomplishing and recognizing a sense of social structure. Agar's study is a condensed version of his monograph on the semantic structure of heroin addicts' verbal coding practices. Sacks's article, although differing from the kinds of issues and methods he used shortly before his untimely death, is a significant study in the reflexivity of meaning. In his analysis of "everyone has to lie" he introduces several of the major concepts that later became part of his more detailed conversational analysis work. The chapters by Gumperz and Hermasichuk and Gumperz-Cook respectively deal with developmental sociolinguistics. The former is a conversational analysis of a teacher-student interaction, while the latter provides data about the cognitive development of interpretive procedures or formal structures of practical reasoning (à la Garfinkel and Cicourel). Blount's own essay on the negotiation of genealogical reference terms among the Luo is an important study showing the accomplishment of a social fact.

The second section of the book as introduced by Sanches is about metacommunicative acts and events. She understands metacommunication as a concern with elements in the language code that refer to the code itself and the various signals about the message which tell us how to read or interpret talk. Although each of the essays in her section seriously deals with these issues, it can be argued that several of the chapters in the first part are also relevant to this section.

The essays in this section represent a variety of methods and theoretical interests. Rosaldo's essay on Ilongot magical spells is an analysis both of the symbolic structure of spells and the organization of their performance. Fitzgerald's study of GA ritual language takes note of Hymes's various components of speech events and their implication for analyzing participants' understanding and the efficacy of performance. Sanches's paper is on the situated interpretation of metacommunicative meanings in Japanese Rakugo theatrical performance. Brukman's chapter, although not specifically addressing ethnomethodological theory, concerns many issues shared by that approach in the analysis of the intentional interpretation of joking behavior. Stross presents an elegantly detailed musicological analysis of Tzeltal song performances showing distinctions between creative conformity and creative nonconformity and their respective relationships to cultural tradition. Mitchell-Kernan and Kernan suggest a method for understanding children's acquisition of cultural and social knowledge by comparing properties of American and Samoan children's insult talk. Finally, the chapter by Werner and his associates analyzes schizophrenic speech according to its syllogistic and metaphoric structure. Their analytic model for the path of reasoning used in problem solving admittedly needs more work, but remains highly suggestive of a methodology for analyzing logical structure.

The collection as a whole holds together well. It makes an excellent resource book for upper division or introductory graduate classes dealing with sociolinguistic/ethnographic issues.

Medical

The Making of a Physician: A Ten-Year Longitudinal Study of Social Class, Academic Achievement, and Changing Professional Attitudes of a Medical School Class, by MARCEL A. FREDERICKS and PAUL MUNDY. Chicago: Loyola University Press, 1976. 206 pp. $9.95 cloth.

ROBERT H. COOMBS
University of California, Los Angeles

As the title indicates, this research monograph is derived from a ten-year study of an entire class of eighty-one medical students/physicians who began their training in the fall of 1962 at the School of Medicine at Loyola University in Chicago. The study population, consisting mostly of male (95%) Catholics (89%), was queried primarily by means of a structured interview schedule and questionnaires. Additional data were obtained through participant observation by one of the authors, who lived for four years among medical students in a fraternity house for prospective physicians.

The objectives of this study are to examine four "empirical questions":

1. Do medical students from families of upper-class backgrounds have higher academic records in the four years of medical school than students of lower-class origin?
2. Do medical students with upper-class backgrounds have lower stress-anxiety scores and higher internalization of professional attitudes scores in medical school than students of lower-class origin?
3. What are some of the relationships (if any) between average grade in college, Medical College Admission Test scores, academic achievement, National Board scores, and stress-anxiety and internalization of professional attitudes scores for a group of medical students?
4. What are the social correlates of professional orientation? Can one distinguish clearly between the entrepreneurially oriented physicians and their socially conscious colleagues by their background characteristics, current medical practices, and the attitudes they have toward treating indigent patients and toward other related social problems?

Although these questions are cast in the form of hypotheses, it is clear that they are not derived from any theory; no common conceptual thread connects the various chapters of the book. Instead, results appear as separate bits of descriptive findings—isolated islands of data whose principal commonality is their origin.

The only aspect of this book that comes close to offering a conceptual basis is a brief discussion of social class, operationally defined as a "weighted index of father's occupations and education." Here the thesis is advanced that "a well-documented relationship exists between social class and academic achievement." Nine dated references are given as supportive evidence—one written in the 1930s, five in the 40s, and two in the 50s; the latest source is a 1960 article. References inconsistent with this thesis are omitted.

Unfortunately, the book's most interesting feature, the report by the participant observer was given only a few paragraphs. This brevity is disappointing since the investigator had a unique vantage for observing the intricacies of student culture.

Given a ten-year exposure to the same study population, one would expect a panel analysis of significant variables indicating how medical recruits evolve in their personal and professional attitudes as a result of medical training. Although this objective is suggested in the title of the book, little in the way of longitudinal analysis is actually presented. The ten-year follow-up, for instance, deals with issues altogether different than those investigated during earlier stages of the project.

The most admirable aspect of this study is the extraordinary rapport that the investigators achieved with the research subjects. Maintaining cooperative relationships with a whole class of harried medical students/physicians through an entire decade is a noteworthy achievement.

Opening the Door: A Study of New Policies for the Mentally Handicapped, by KATHLEEN JONES, with JOHN BROWN, W. J. CUNNINGHAM, JULIAN ROBERTS, and PETER WILLIAMS. Boston: Routledge & Kegan Paul, 1975. 260 pp. $21.75 cloth.

MORTON O. WAGENFELD
Western Michigan University, Kalamazoo

To those familiar with the history of health and human services in this country—most recently the community mental health movement—this volume is likely to evoke feelings of deja vu. Kathleen Jones and her interdisciplinary team of sociologists and social workers have written a very readable account of the impact of legislation on services to the mentally handicapped in Great Britain. In the United States, the deplorable conditions in state mental hospitals and the gross imbalance in our mental health care delivery system were made evident through journalistic exposes and academic research. Government-sponsored studies were undertaken, legislation was passed, and a new system of mental health care delivery was brought into being. The chronology of events for Great Britain was quite similar: public concern about the inadequate treatment of the mentally handicapped led to the issuance of a White Paper in 1971, *Better Services for the Mentally Handicapped.* It's thesis was quite simple: hospital-based care was both inadequate and counterproductive. In the future, hospitals would be used for treatment, not residential care. The door of the hospital would be opened and the bulk of services to the handicapped would be provided in community contexts and integrated into the larger context of human services.

How did this all work out? The group conducted an extensive survey in one region of England and found that, despite a great deal of goodwill and effort, little had been changed. If the door had been opened, it was only a crack. Based on the survey, Jones et al. formulated an extensive series of recommendations for the implementation of the White Paper.

This book is a felicitous combination of empirical research and policy formulation. With the growing popularity of applied sociology, *Opening the Door* could well serve as an exemplar of such efforts.

Living and Dying at Murray Manor, by JABER F. GUBRIUM. New York: St. Martin's Press, 1975. 221 pp. $8.95 cloth.

JUANITA WOOD
University of California, Davis

Living and Dying at Murray Manor is an ethnographic study of a geriatric nursing home in which Gubrium analyzes the various forms of organization within the organization. That is, the differential use made of, and meanings attached to, places within the nursing home by those who work there and those who reside there as clients.

Gubrium's main thesis is a straightforward one—that one's view of the social order depends upon where one's physical "place" is within that world. That there are worlds within worlds is not a new idea, but it is often overlooked by those who tend toward universalistic theorizing. In this sense, Professor Gubrium's study helps to understand the ways in which humans order their lives on a daily basis.

Gubrium uses his unifying theme of the importance of place to illustrate how it is possible to maintain separate social worlds within a contained physical place. For example, in referring to top staff's lack of knowledge of the clientele's daily lives, he notes, "Top staff gains 'information' about clientele and makes decisions about it in places other than those in which clientele maintain their social ties." There are certain places that are considered public and certain places that are considered private for all three categories of participants. It is, Gubrium points out, the different goals of the groups involved that also keep the social worlds apart. Top staff is concerned with the concept of total patient care, floor staff is concerned with "bed and body" work, and the clientele are concerned with making life in an institution similar to life outside the institution.

Professor Gubrium's study is interesting, but unfulfilling; he does not often enough go beyond the descriptive aspects of the study to tell us more analytically what it all means. He relies too on "letting the data speak for themselves" when, for example, he presents the reader with twelve pages of transcripts to illustrate a point. Even those discriminating critics who long for empirical verification would find this excessive. I do not mean to imply in any way that the study is superficial; Gubrium simply has not analyzed the data as fully as is warranted.

Medical Sociology: A General Systems Approach, by LEON S. ROBERTSON and MARGARET C. HEAGERTY. Chicago: Nelson Hall, 1975. 213 pp. $11.00 cloth.

The Therapeutic Community: A Sourcebook of Readings, edited by JEAN J. ROSSI and WILLIAM J. FILSTEAD. New York: Behavioral Publications, 1973. 342 pp. $16.95 cloth.

The Mental Hospital and Human Services, by HERBERT C. SCHULBERG and FRANK BAKER. New York: Behavioral Publications, 1975. 379 pp. $15.95 cloth.

JUDITH BLACKFIELD COHEN
University of California, Berkeley

These three books could lead one to believe that systems theory is the fashion in those areas of sociology concerned with physical and mental illness. Each is directed at a different reader audience and discusses different topics, yet all propose a systems perspective as the key to understanding and action.

Medical Sociology presents at a fairly elementary level, a brief, skeptical, and selective presentation of research findings and issues in medical sociology "relevant to the future health and welfare of the human race." Directed at medical students in behavioral science courses as well as at sociology students, the book presents general systems theory as an intellectual framework for understanding health and the medical care system. The various elements of a system are illustrated in a chapter discussion of social epidemiology. The critical issue, of course, is how these elements fit together in a system; here, the missing areas of knowledge are primarily at the physiological level where the role of sociologist is limited. The remainder of the book is concerned with elements in the sociology of medical care: patients, practitioners, institutions, and health and medical care programs at local to international levels.

Of course the therapeutic community is also a system, but the majority of the readings in Rossi and Filstead's book on the subject were published prior to the wide use of systems concepts. While this book was published in 1973, the average publication date for the original articles is around 1961, and little help is provided to the reader who wants to know if or how therapeutic communities have fared since these classic statements about the social environment of an institution as a therapeutic model.

The Mental Hospital and Human Services is set at a much more abstract and clinically oriented level, and is likely to be of considerable interest to professionals in the field of mental health. The authors begin by noting that major changes in the mental health programs of the last decade have been "awesome in their aspirations but still unfulfilled in their outcomes" and use their own experiences to discuss why this is still so. Their intent is to present conceptual frameworks for choosing among alternative local and national programs, and the transitions these require. One might argue that their experiences at Boston State Hospital and the United Community Planning Corporation within the Harvard aura are not typical of the environments most mental health professionals face. Nonetheless, their presentation of the issues involved at the single institutional level and the program level, while complex and detailed, is clearly generalizable to other less academic contexts. For example, the case studies of the roles of the occupational therapist and various levels of nurses in such transitions provide a framework to identify the conflicts and issues involved in changing any set of roles as part of system transitions. Their goal is to establish bases for evaluation of alternatives, using an open systems model. The relevance and utility of systems theory in this context is apparent.

Bereavement: Its Psychosocial Aspects, edited by BERNARD SCHOENBERG, IRWIN GERBER, ALFRED WIENER, AUSTIN H. KUTSCHER, DAVID PERETZ, and ARTHUR C. CARR. New York: Columbia University Press, 1975. 367 pp. $15.00 cloth.

JEANNETTE R. FOLTA
University of Vermont, Burlington

Bereavement is a crisis, a paradox, common yet unique, normal yet a peril to life, a psychological problem, a social problem, and a neglected area of study. For those who wish to understand the psychological/psychiatric aspects of bereavement, this book is a must. A compilation of thirty-one articles, it deals with some of the fundamental concepts of bereavement, its physical and psychiatric manifestations, special problems of widows, orphans and bereaved children, health workers and the bereaved, and techniques for effective therapeutic intervention.

Unlike most books of readings, all articles are original, not to be found elsewhere. While they run from excellent to so-so, none can be said to be poorly conceived or written. For the first time, hard empirical data are available on physiological and psychological manifestations of grief and on the effects of short-term therapy. Especially excellent are articles on widows, orphans, and bereaved children; essential reading for those involved in planning community services for the bereaved.

Far more psychological than social in orientation (of 31 articles approximately 80% of first authors are M.D.'s or clinical psychologists; only one article is by a sociologist), this book will benefit primarily health workers or professional thanatologists concerned with the adverse effects of grief. Those who wish to fully understand the social aspects of bereavement will have to wait for another book.

Methods

More About Justifying Violence: Methodological Studies of Attitudes and Behavior, by MONICA D. BLUMENTHAL, LETHA B. CHADIHA, GERALD A. COLE, and TOBY E. JAYARATNE. Ann Arbor, Mich.: Institute for Social Research, 1976. 401 pp. $14.00 cloth. $8.00 paper.

DANIEL B. MCGILLIS
Harvard University

Although not originally intending to illustrate the range of problems typically encountered by researchers, the authors of the present volume have effectively done so. This survey of methodological problems which occurred in the conduct of their study is perhaps the central value of this monograph, making it a potentially valuable resource for courses on research methods. The studies were intended to shed light on the reliability and validity of the measures used in the Institute of Social Research's landmark study of attitudes toward violence published in 1972 under the title *Justifying Violence: Attitudes of American Men.*

The various mini-studies have numerous limitations, however, stemming from difficulties in establishing appropriate control groups, attempts to collect data from unwilling or unavailable respondents, variations in the meaning of items over time and across different groups, perplexities in selecting appropriate criterion behaviors to assess validity, etc. The authors painstakingly provide caveats to the interpretation of the studies in light of these problems and are cautious in drawing conclusions other than that their studies unsettled more issues than they resolved. As might be expected, the writing style of the authors is challenged by the technical nature of much of the material.

Causal Analysis, by DAVID R. HEISE. New York: John Wiley & Sons, 1975. 301 pp. $15.95 cloth.

DORIS R. ENTWISLE
Johns Hopkins University

This book of modest size is ambitious. In less than 250 pages (not counting pages where answers to exercises are given) it covers the logic and ordering of causal systems, gives a fairly comprehensive treatment of the flowgraph method of solving simultaneous linear equations, presents a rapid introduction to statistics, and then covers what is commonly known as the "structural-equation approach" to system modeling with attention to the by-now classic method of path analysis. In three of its six chapters it covers, with some embellishments drawn from flowgraphs, almost all the topics covered in Duncan's recent eleven-chapter book *Introduction to Structural Equation Models.* (Despite this the books are very different and most sociologists will want to own both.) In addition there is a chapter on dynamic considerations.

The author is to be highly commended for providing many worked examples throughout the text and for providing exercises (with answers) at the end of every chapter. These allow a serious reader the opportunity to understand thoroughly what is being said. In many places major points are made in the worked examples.

What about the emphasis on the flowgraph approach? I personally enjoy it. However, I have doubts about its practical utility, at least now. All the operators one sees in sociological journals are "scalors" in engineering jargon. It will be nice for sociologists to know something about delayors (which are dynamic) and limitors (the simplest kind of non-linear operator) but the benefits of such knowledge are few at the moment. In a similar vein, flowgraph reduction as a technique for estimating models is more helpful in engineering than in sociology, precisely because, as Heise points out, in engineering the scalors are "knowns" whereas in sociology they are "unknowns" (and often stochastic to boot).

Methods of solution that depend on visual techniques such as flowgraph reduction are excellent for didactic purposes—seeing a loop instead of "two-way causation" is particularly nice, for example. Yet as one who earlier worked painstakingly through the computations in Duncan's 1966 article, setting up equations by visual inspections of figures, and also as one who has worked teaching engineering students how to solve flowgraphs, I can vouch for the ad hoc nature of the visual approach and the frustrating errors it is likely to produce as soon as systems get complicated. (It is also not easily translated into computing algorithms.) To trace all paths sounds easy, but is hard. Paths are easy to miss, especially if one does not know how many to look for. This is one serious drawback to the flowgraph approach. The algebraic approach has to win out in the long run because the same strategy can be applied to all problems and checks are easily devised.

But this clearly written book is meant to provoke thought about modeling. Despite its exercises, it is not a book to instruct readers in how to go about dealing with particular data sets, but it does a very good job of integrating a large amount of subject matter.

Probability Sampling of Hospitals and Patients, 2nd ed., by IRENE HESS, DONALD C. RIEDEL, and THOMAS B. FITZPATRICK. Ann Arbor, Mich.: Health Administration Press, 1975. $9.75 cloth.

CORALIE FARLEE
Association of American Medical Colleges

The first edition of this book was published in 1961 and consisted of the first section of the present edition. The second edition contains, in addition, (1) one chapter which describes a computer sampling algorithm which was developed to select "relatively small samples from heterogeneous populations," and (2) reprints of several articles (adding to the discussion on stratification and probability sampling) as they appeared in 1966 and 1970 in *Health Services Research* and the *Journal of the American Statistical Association.*

The authors state that their purpose in writing the original book was to demonstrate the application of probability sampling to general hospitals and patients. They also discuss the pros and cons of sampling patients or selected attributes of patients (e.g., diagnosis) as the individual sampling unit and unit for research and analysis. The issues in reviewing this book are: (1) did the authors fulfill their purpose, and (2) is their stated purpose a valid and useful one?

With regard to demonstrating the application of probability sampling to general hospitals and patients, the purpose seems well served and in great detail. However, the material seems more properly an appendix of a final project report where the reader could refer, if necessary, to the sampling methodology. It is important for users of such reports to have confidence in the methodology, thus there is ample rationale for such a detailed appendix.

But for contemporary sociologists who need to be prepared to conduct applied research in a number of human care systems (health, medical care, education, welfare, delinquency, developmental disabilities), my preference is for a general methodological approach which provides examples from many subject areas. Indeed, there were a number of such statistics and methods texts and workbooks published during the 1960s and early 1970s, none of which is cited by the authors of this book.

There are other considerations. The authors indicate that use of the *patient* (not the diagnosis) as the unit of analysis provides not only efficiency but greater methodological validity. There are no examples to illustrate the hazards of alternate approaches (as would be found in a more general text or workbook). A reference work which presents general sampling principles, with a wide variety of detailed examples from both organizations and roles-in-organizations of numerous human care systems would, in my opinion, be a more valuable contribution.

Further, if there is validity for a book on *Probability Sampling of Hospitals and Patients,* then these or other authors can be expected to generate sequels entitled *Probability Sampling of Medical Schools and Faculty,* or *Probability Sampling of Social Welfare Systems and Clients,* and *Probability Sampling of Prisons and Inmates.*

One justification does exist for this sort of book. For sociologists conducting applied research in and of human care systems, it may be of immense value for that sociologist-researcher to be able to present to a non-sociologist decision maker/administrator a compendium of "how they did it in Michigan—and as far back as the middle 1950s." The applied sociologist in alien territory may feel on firmer ground with such a specific and detailed reference work available.

An Introduction to Models in the Social Sciences, by CHARLES A. LAVE and JAMES G. MARCH. New York: Harper & Row, 1975. $6.95 paper.

DAVID D. MCFARLAND
University of California, Los Angeles

Are you a mathematical sociologist who "earns his or her way" by teaching an interdisciplinary "Introduction to the Social Sciences" course to students whose interests are not yet focused on a single discipline, such as sociology, let alone a sub-disciplinary specialty, such as mathematical sociology, and who (worse yet) have had no mathematics since ninth grade algebra? If so, the book under review is something you should consider assigning as a supplementary text. It might make the course a lot more interesting to teach without in the process scaring away most of the students.

The book has an informal, chatty style, with catchy titles and even (I kid you not!) *poems*. No college level mathematics is required at any point, and the little amount of mathematics that *is* involved is introduced at the most leisurely pace imaginable: the very *first* equation I found appears on page 91, where we are told about Sally, who cuts a class to tune up her VW, and who assigns numerical values to the probabilities that it will work much better, work the same, or blow up. (The latter, in case you are curious, is .05.) Again, still concerning the leisurely pace, the reader will be well into the final chapter (p. 361) before encountering the idea of rates of change; and even there discussion is confined to finite differences, using delta notation—no mention of derivatives.

The book begins with an eighty-four page discussion of model development and use. There are a number of such discussions in the literature, but this differs from others by its wittiness and informality, and also by its restriction to verbal models. For example, we read, "Suppose you are sitting in class when the person next to you asks a really dumb question. . . . [and] you also know that the person next to you is a football player" (page 25). The task is to produce a "model" of a process which might produce such an observation.

The discussion begins with what the authors call "a simple model," namely the verbal assertion, "Football players are dumb" (p. 25). (Many authors would object to calling that a "model.") The discussion eventually reaches the point of trying to set up critical experiments to choose among much more sophisticated (but still completely nonmathematical) "models" such as "Model 2. Everyone wants to feel successful. Achieving success in any one area, for example, athletics, is enough to make most people content" (p. 58). Interestingly, none of the "models" considered mentions the possibility that superior athletes who do not satisfy the usual admission standards are admitted anyhow.

Every page or two the reader is interrupted with a boldface upper case command to "STOP AND THINK," followed by suggestions of the lines along which thought should proceed: "What does the model leave out? Are there important factors omitted by this simplification?" (p. 30), or "What does the model predict will happen in this situation?" (p. 303), or suggestions which are specific to the model then under discussion. (These Stop and Think suggestions are in addition to exercises at the ends of the chapters, exercises whose general flavor is similar to that of the text they accompany.)

After the introductory eighty-four pages, the book contains four chapters, each devoted to consideration (in about as much depth as could be expected in a book requiring no college level mathematics) of mathematical modeling of some particular phenomenon. A seventy-one page chapter on individual decision-making, emphasizing expected utility maximization and analysis of choice within the decision tree framework, will be of more interest to psychologists and statisticians than to sociologists. A ninety page chapter on "exchange," which consists of an elementary treatment of indifference curves for supply and demand, will be of more interest to the few remaining economists who do not know calculus than to sociologists whose specialization places them within the realm of "exchange theory." The ninety-three page chapter on "adaptation," which treats some simple learning models, will be of more interest to psychologists than to sociologists.

The single chapter which bears upon sociology more than any other discipline is the seventy-seven page chapter on diffusion. This chapter's catchy titles include "Explorations of Social Diseases." Now to oldsters such as myself, "social disease" was a euphemism for VD, but several present-day students I queried claimed they had no idea what the expression "social disease" meant, so I conclude that in this case the authors' wittiness was lost on the younger generation.

Nevertheless the chapter does include serious discussions of the spread of divorce, rumors, economic development, and other objects of diffusion among undifferentiated individual units and through various kinds of social structures. The authors make the useful distinction among "birth processes," "birth processes with limits," and "broadcast processes." So despite a joke whose humor escapes contemporary college students, that chapter has something to say to students who are prospective sociologists.

In the event that you happen to be teaching "Introduction to *Mathematical Sociology,*" rather than "Introduction to Social Science," there is a much more suitable textbook available *Mathematical Sociology*, by R. K. Leik and B. F. Meeker. If, however, you are teaching an interdisciplinary social science course whose students have negligible mathematical training, and you would like to beef it up a bit, this book might be exactly what you need.

Occupations, Work, and Leisure

Work and Play: Ideas and Experience of Work and Leisure, by ALASDAIR CLAYRE. New York: Harper & Row, 1974. 217 pp. $11.00 cloth.

ANDREA FONTANA
University of Nevada, Las Vegas

In an era of trite cliches about work alienation and gratuitous attacks on the edifice of modern technological society it is refreshing to see a work which carefully examines assumptions too often taken-for-granted. This book provides a novel approach to the study of industrialization which should be carefully heeded by sociologists, economists, and other scholars interested in the study of work and its cultural implications.

The work reviewed here poses the question of whether work is the central life interest as commonly assumed or whether play is the area which provides people with fulfillment and happiness. The book is divided in two distinct parts. The first part traces the origin and the development in the nineteenth century of ideas critical of industrialization and their claim that technology has caused work to become monotonous and repetitious and thus has dehumanized it. The second part examines data to see the fit between the critical ideas and the working classes' own notions.

Rousseau, Schiller, and other early critics of machinery are examined. Marx's views on the constraining nature of work in modern societies are presented, followed by the strong ideas of William Morris against the conditions of technological work. All of the writers examined share the following assumptions: (1) if given a chance human beings would seek art and intellectual improvement, (2) it would be relatively easy to change the current state of affairs, (3) the center of life is meaningful work, and (4) the pre-industrial past was better.

Clayre points out that the assumptions of these writers do not in fact reflect the position of many pre-industrial workers. He uses Mandeville's early theory that no objective standards of measurement exist apart from the members' own expectations of a situation and he proceeds to show whatever scanty evidence of pre-industrial workers' accounts he can muster.

The data, (limited by and large to ballads and folksongs, since writing was undertaken by the rich and the clerical) indicate that culture rather than technology determines satisfaction for people. Thus, concludes the author, the philosophical critiques of industrialization reflect but the view of a particular group, "the philosophical observers of industrialization, who did not themselves for the most part work with their hands" (p. 178).

The author could have gone further in his suggestions of alternate central life interests, suggestions which are barely sketched in this volume. But to do so perhaps would have taken the writer far afield from his main point, which he drives home in a clear and succinct manner; to go on speaking of the dehumanizing effects of technology and of workers' alienation is but the perpetuation of an unsubstantiated myth created by a group of "armchair" theoreticians. Reality, as borne out by the members of the working classes themselves, is a far more complex endeavor.

Beyond Boredom and Anxiety: The Experience of Play in Work and Games, by MIHALY CSIKSZENTMIHALYI. San Francisco: Jossey-Bass, 1975. No price listed, cloth.

MURRAY S. DAVIS
University of California, San Diego

This is one of those books that makes one realize once again the inefficiency, waste, even tragedy of the current division of intellect in the academy. This book's significance for sociology might have been lost merely because its author happens to come out of the psychological tradition. Conversely, the author could have amplified his analysis advantageously by consulting more sociological and social philosophical literature.

The author sets out to examine what makes play enjoyable so that work and education might be restructured to become as enjoyable as play. He wants to learn why people engage in "autotelic" (self-purposed) activities in which they receive none of the extrinsic rewards—money, status, power—that supposedly are the only motivations operating in our society.

To discover the nature of this obscure intrinsic reward which some activities have and others don't, he studies an assortment of preoccupations done only for their own sake. Through questionnaires and interviews he asks chess players, rock climbers, rock dancers, basketball players, composers, modern dancers and, less intensively, other players and artists why they do what they do. He has provided a model study of how a topic as ephemeral as the phenomenology of play can be investigated through concrete qualitative methods. He supports his argument with both humanistic quotes and statistical tables, making it convincing to those of vastly different methodological persuasions. (Too much support, in fact, since he has more quotes than necessary and confirms his correlations with significance tests many sociologists now consider passé.)

He finds that all autotelic activities reward their participants with the "flow experience": a merging of action and awareness, ego and environment, that temporarily negates consciousness of an outside observing self.

This flow experience occurs primarily when a person's capacities are evenly matched against environmental challenges. When a person's skills are greater than the demands made on them, boredom occurs. When skills are less than demands, anxiety occurs. Two secondary conditions facilitating the flow experience are (1) limits on the stimuli field to which the person need respond, and (2) clarity of the environment's demands for future action and unambiguity of its response to past action. For example, the players in a sports event are likely to feel "flow" when they are equally matched, need react only to what the rules specify, and have clear choices for their next move as well as uncontradictory opponent responses to their last move.

Since the author does not want to restrict this flow experience to players (and artists), he also studies surgeons. For if he can find it in their work activity, the separation between work and play becomes unnecessary. Most theorists have believed this dichotomy absolute, defining play as an activity having no consequences outside itself. Yet even though surgery has life and death consequences outside itself, it still produces the flow experience: surgeons often find it fun.

Expanding his thesis by contracting its focus, the author examines "microflow activities," objectively unnecessary behaviors that occur during the interludes in everyday life, such as doodling, pacing, and light coffee break conversation. Several field experiments show that these microflow activities allow people, whose experience is not fully determined by their jobs or roles, the subjective satisfaction of structuring it themselves to maintain their personal capacities and environmental demands in equilibrium.

Surprisingly, the author ends by calling on Weber's *Protestant Ethic* to support his attempt to overcome the dichotomy between work and play. Weber, he claims, actually showed that, after Protestantism reinterpreted it as a cosmic calling, work became intrinsically rewarding rather than merely the means to external leisure rewards it had been.

Since the author feels that extrinsic rewards necessarily alienate workers and students by dividing their consciousness (à la early Marx), he wants to redesign work and education to make them intrinsically enjoyable. Unfortunately he does not specify how this might be done, except to suggest allowing workers and students to move through a series of graduated tasks to maintain the balance between their skills and challenges. But the author seems unaware of the danger in demanding that work and education become intrinsically interesting. In California, Governor Brown is attempting to make academics intrinsically interested in their work not by increasing its intrinsic rewards but by decreasing its extrinsic benefits.

Sociologists will find most provocative the author's alternative to Erving Goffman's analysis of self-consciousness. Both are mystics in the sense that they investigate the conditions causing someone to lose self-consciousness. But Goffman is what I would call a *pessimystic,* for in *Frame Analysis* (1974:378ff) he examines how the self disappears in the "negative experience" that results when situational contradictions increase its stress; Csikszentmihalyi is an *optimystic,* for he examines how the self disappears in the "flow experience" that results when situational consonances decrease its stress. (Although the book's bibliography contains Goffman's *Frame Analysis,* I could find no reference to it in either text or index. A shame, since one wonders how Csikszentmihalyi would have responded to his complete antithesis.)

One also wonders how he would have responded to other sociologists and social philosophers who anticipated or contradicted components of his thesis. What would he have made of Fredrich Schiller's remark that only when playing are people wholly themselves (rather than wholly without selves), or Charles Fourier's suggestion that work be made play, or Arthur Schopenhauer's lament that human beings oscillate between want and boredom (rather than around flow, anxiety, and boredom), or Georg Simmel's characterization of the adventure as a bounded intensification of life inextricably intermingling active and passive relations between self and circumstances, or even Erving Goffman's earlier observation in *Encounters* that the surgeon enjoys his distance from his role (rather than the role itself)? Although the book would have been richer if the author had considered these social commentators, even without them it still has enough cognitive calories to satisfy.

The book is well written, a "flow experience" (if not a joy) to read: thereby self-confirming its own thesis. I commend it strongly to sociologists of everyday life, popular culture, and work and leisure.

Working Communally: Patterns and Possibilities, by DAVID FRENCH and ELENA FRENCH. New York: Russell Sage Foundation, 1975. 269 pp. $10.50 cloth.

New Forms of Work Organization, by LISL KLEIN. New York: Cambridge University Press, 1976. 106 pp. $9.95 cloth.

PAUL GOLDMAN
American University

Recent students of the apparent trend towards greater worker participation in industry share the assumption that repetitive, highly specialized work tasks are alienating and counterproductive. Three different points of departure, however, characterize the current spate of writings on the subject. The first, typified by Lisl Klein's *New Forms of Work Organization,* sees increasing participation as an antidote to the crisis of worker motivation. The second approach, seen in David French and Elena French's *Working Communally,* focuses on the potentially rewarding nature of work itself and is sympathetic to the commune movement. A third perspective, unrepresented by the works under review, views worker control as an essential element in the struggle to establish socialism.

Klein, whose study was commissioned by a committee of the German Federal Republic, reviews dozens of experiments in participative organizational design now occurring in Denmark, Holland, and Sweden. Her book is rooted in the theories of the "modern human relations" approach to work organization and incorporates a strong critique of overrationalized production schemes including those of Frederick Taylor himself. Klein, in fact, includes, in a useful thirteen-page appendix, an edited version of R. F. Hoxie's 1915 criticisms of Taylor. The four substantive chapters deal with assumptions about work organization, new thinking, current developments, and finally the next generation of issues facing managers. While the chapters seem to run together a bit, the book's real value lies in its citations of experiments unfamiliar to most American readers. The brevity of each description, however, whets, rather than satisfies our appetites and an all too brief bibliography makes follow-up difficult.

Klein exercises scholarly caution and carefully avoids the temptation of overgeneralizing from a wide variety of cases. While she feels that the industrial democracy approach is valid in most cases, she stresses that both technology and the specific organizational climate of the firm must determine the form increased participation will take. These views conform to those taken by American proponents of planned change. Like them Klein assumes that increased worker participation generally comes from managerial initiative and that workers and managers have joint, rather than potentially conflicting, interests. The book's greatest utility is not for scholars or students but rather for practitioners in management, labor, and government who wish to be apprised of recent European developments in workplace participation.

The French book is very different from Klein's. Drawing on the traditions of the early Marx, of anarchism, and of the philosophy of Martin Buber, they present a passionate appeal for the restructuring of work as a means for greater human fulfillment. Meticulously researched and drawn from 150 years of American communalism as well as from their own experiences in contemporary communes, they present a forceful case for the potential of change. They see the contemporary workplace as deadening and dehumanizing and focus on the possibilities of establishing alternative institutions that link work and community together. Unlike many studies of counter-cultural communes, however, theirs gives primary emphasis to work organization itself and devotes much less attention to other aspects of communal life. The presentation is also more balanced and less utopian than that of other commentators, and points out the potentially alienating characteristics of many communal workplaces and tries to deal with the difficult problems of efficiency that must face many such institutions.

The contents include twelve chapters divided into three parts. The first of these includes a lengthy theoretical introduction, the second an analysis of American cooperative work experiments from the mid-nineteenth century to the present, and the third a laying-out of the possibilities for change in the near future. Their attention, however, is not limited to the American experience. The authors in two perceptive chapters deal with contemporary experiments taking place in capitalist and socialist nations abroad. They do not, unfortunately, adequately deal with the national sanction given many of these foreign workplace experiments nor compare them with the out-of-the-mainstream nature of communal work situations in this country. This reflects the one serious criticism that might be made of an otherwise outstanding book: the Frenches' analysis lacks a political dimension and fails to explain how humanistic work organization can develop in other than a voluntaristic and individualistic fashion in this country. Small work communes may serve the needs of their members, but the focus on very small production units leaves untouched the lives of the vast majority of Americans who work in large, bureaucratized factories and offices. Nor does their analysis deal with the interrelations of communal work settings and the communities in which they reside. In some cities and towns, principally those partially or fully dominated by colleges or universities, the institutionalization of work alternatives is beginning to affect community life.

Despite this reservation, French and French deserve high marks for the importance of topic, and the grace of their writing. Few works so successfully integrate philosophical issues with concrete examples. The book is ideal both for introductory sociology courses and for classes in the sociology of work and organization.

The Tourist: A New Theory of the Leisure Class, by DEAN MACCANNELL. New York: Schocken Books, 1976. 214 pp. $12.95 cloth. $5.95 paper.

SUZANNE WEDOW
SUNY/Stony Brook

Dean MacCannell's *The Tourist* rings true, at least to this reviewer crossing the continent during the Bicentennial summer of '76. Indeed the terms tourist and sociologist seem almost interchangeable in MacCannell's metaphoric commentary on the modern individual. This text, though, is more than a perceptive, entertaining discussion of tourists and tourism; it is also a skillful blend of structuralist thought, some of Marx's central tenets readdressed, semiotics, work manifesting the spirit of Erving Goffman, Veblen, and even Ethnomethodology. This synthetic approach lends a new, and I think important, tone to traditional debates about high and low culture, the impact of tourism on modern society, alienation and the workplace, the uses of leisure, and the work of genuine theorizing without pedantry.

MacCannell has set out to understand the fundamental unity or unities of modern society, a task Lévi-Strauss foreswore. Paradoxically he finds differentiation to be the key term. Structural differentiation is a systemic variable, its reality taken as a social fact. Tourism takes on the ritualistic functions of commemorating history and place. Differentiation, a key process in modernization, promotes new combinations of information and cultural products. Tourism spreads the word by dispersing individuals into settings where new understandings can occur.

The concept of the "dialectics of authenticity" is his attempt to answer a critique of structuralism's static view of society. Modernity is differentiation; but this is a process which generates alternative realities. Material and symbolic relations are constantly becoming assembled, exchanged and transformed into different realities, some of which complicate a claim he makes on behalf of tourists: that they seek more or less "authentic" experiences. The difficult issue for us all is deciding which structures are genuine, which are spurious. Differentiation produces both consensus and confusion.

Interestingly, MacCannell spends a good deal of time discussing work. His comparative analysis of guide books to Paris, for example, points to the transformation of work from a primary source of alienation to alienated leisure which makes work a type of tourist attraction. Tours of wineries, canning factories, and automobile factories are cases in point. We witness the work process but not the workers; we see the produced commodity but not the sweat of the production.

This approach to work takes up Marx's discussion of the problems of industrial society in a new way. MacCannell argues that the objects of structural differentiation are newer types of commodities, experiential in nature rather than material. When the value of a commodity is based upon promised experiences, rather than labor time invested, its usefulness, or its exchange value, the time is ripe for transforming the meaning of work settings into tourist attractions.

In the same way tourism is work and it is alienated in essence. MacCannell bases his view of "touristic consciousness" on the idea that people are now "liberated from traditional attachments into the modern world where, as tourists, they may attempt to discover or reconstruct a cultural heritage or a social identity" (p. 13). "The act of sightseeing is a kind of involvement with social appearances that helps the person to construct totalities from his disparate experiences" (p. 15). This work is discussed further in a chapter titled "Ethnomethodology of Sightseers." He considers an aspect of the tourists' authentication of their experiences or "the accomplishment of touristic certainty" (p. 135). Tourists employ sights and sight markers—all forms of information about a specific sight—in the work of producing certainty or truth about the existence and meaning of "what they've really seen." The end product is a cognitive organization of information pertinent to authenticating one's own status as a good tourist. Cliches are more than banal phrases; they are proof of one's experiences. A sense of consensus about the meaningful features of these settings, and the contemporary world, emerges from this interpretive work of viewing and conversing.

A chapter on the semiotic of attractions takes up the uses of information to construct a sense of consensus. Here he looks at the transformation of object and place into attractions, their gradual movement from a setting to a representation of a setting, e.g., a miniature Eiffel Tower. He points out there is no easy solution to the problem of what is real or not, or genuine or fake, since modernization can quickly transform the meaning of both truth and non-truth, spurious and genuine structure. The staging of authentic, or more or less apparently authentic, settings for tourists demonstrates this problem, e.g., the "staged" backstage at Paramount movie studios. MacCannell offers one possible way to distinguish the spurious from the genuine, this occurring in the operation of the commercial realm where "spurious social relations and structural elements can be bought, sold, traded and distributed throughout the world" (p. 155).

While the viability of traditional culture seems to be severely questioned today, MacCannell observes that this is an ongoing struggle between the plasticity of touristic imageries and a valid, historical past that seems less plastic, less portable. In a chapter on practical applications, he contrasts both industrial and plantation forms of tourism with "natural growth tourism." He suggests an emergent, local tourism can become one way to reinstate the best of what we think of ourselves and our histories. The weight of his argument, though, makes one less optimistic than one senses him to be.

MacCannell makes few apologies for his methodology, which combines field notes, apparently a great deal of traveling, semiotic analysis of diverse forms of memorabilia, newspapers, books, and archives. He has a clever sense of the perfect example given with a touch of amusement. He need not apologize, for his analysis is evocatively correct and well done.

Nonetheless there are a few problems with his approach. Immediately the seeker of causes will ask "why all this tourism, the plasticity of cultural forms, the hollowness of a visit to Yellowstone Park?" He doesn't truly address this issue. Social structural differentiation seems to be both cause and result of modernity. However, this criticism is more appropriate to critical discussions of structuralism itself. Since MacCannell's text is not an attempt to do such the charge is less relevant.

Some might take issue with his concept of authenticity. He is only concerned with a type of apolitical, existential authenticity. It would have made stronger political commentary (which in some sense I think MacCannell intended) had the question of political legitimacy been placed in contrast to experiential authenticity. Otherwise the fuss about the Olympic athlete's national representation, for example, would seem irrelevant or trivial. Tourism, money, and politics all affected the final packaging of that particular attraction. In another way he overvalues the term authenticity. Some tourists may not seek authentic experiences or truth. Tourists could also be cynical, amused, or altogether unconcerned with anything meaningful. Perhaps not all the tourists on this bus are pilgrims; some might be residents and indeed sociologists watching the watchers.

Overall MacCannell's book deserves praise. It is perceptive rather than pedantic, ironic (perhaps?) yet a serious commentary. Both his literary style and theoretical sophistication are genuine contributions to sociological scholarship.

The Making of the Diplomatic Mind: The Training, Outlook, and Style of United States Foreign Service Officers, 1908–1931, by ROBERT D. SCHULZINGER. Middletown, Conn.: Wesleyan University Press, 1975. 237 pp. $15.00 cloth.

DONALD P. WARWICK
Harvard University

Though diplomacy is an old profession, and has often been called a subsidiary of the oldest, it has received scant attention from the sociology of professions. Partly this is because sociology has been remarkably innocent of foreign affairs, and partly because diplomacy barely meets the sociological specifications for a profession. This short book (155 pages of text) traces the tortuous evolution of the US Foreign Service from the indolent frivolity and cookie-pushing of the nineteenth century to the serious careerism ushered in by the Rogers Act of 1924. It is largely the story of two nondescript and often warring occupations, diplomats and consuls, trying to fuse themselves, with the aid of Congress and business interests, into a coherent career service.

The prime obstacle confronting the professionalizers, and one which still plagues the Foreign Service, is a profound ambiguity about diplomacy. The Foreign Service "differed from other, more rigorous professions in its lack of a persuasive social and intellectual domain which excluded outsiders from Foreign Service work" (p. 8). Unlike medicine, architecture, and law, it had no single body of knowledge to be mastered, no sharply formulated objectives, and no explicit methods of procedure, save in the more mechanical domains of consular work. The resulting uncertainty spilled over to recruitment, training, informal professional socialization, performance evaluation, and promotion, as well as to public assessment of the diplomatic service. For obvious reasons of self-interest the diplomats tried to fill the vacuum with the well-tooled image of a gentleman generalist, while the consular service pressed for self-definition and career advancement by technical knowledge and skills. It was something of a miracle that the reformers finally did marry the two services, although the underlying divergencies in professional perspectives remain to this day.

Schulzinger tells his story well, but seems unable to break out of the aconceptual narrative exposition characterizing most diplomatic history. For the student of professions the chief merit of this book is the solid raw material which it provides for sociological analysis. The text occasionally rises to conceptualization, but for the most part it simply recounts actors, transactions, and the flow of events. Nevertheless, I would place it on my own short list for the sociology of diplomacy, along with *The Professional Diplomat* by John Ensor Harr and *Professional Diplomacy in the United States, 1779–1939,* by Warren F. Ilchman.

Work and Welfare in Britain and the USA, by BRUNO STEIN. New York: John Wiley & Sons, 1976. 112 pp. $10.95 cloth.

MARIE WITHERS OSMOND
Florida State University, Tallahassee

The welfare explosion of the 1960s generated considerable sociological interest which, however, has been expressed largely in humanitarian and reformist rhetoric. Stein's comparative study of Britain and America is politically neutral and thus offers a much needed balance. Stein (an economist) ably documents his major thesis that income maintenance policies should not, and indeed cannot, be viewed as separate from a nation's labor resources and employment policies. The results of a one-year (1972–3) study of British policies are the focal point of the book. These are supplemented with a wealth of historical and current information on the welfare systems of both countries.

The author acknowledges that he had expected to find a better developed linkage between labor and income maintenance policies in Britain than in the USA. His study revealed that, especially for the "hard to employ" population, labor programs are poorly linked to labor markets in both countries. There is a grim similarity between the "poverty trap" in England and the "welfare trap" in America. A major source of difficulty, according to Stein, is the lack of consonance between the de facto structure of "incentives and controls" and the goals of each income maintenance system. If the goal is economic independence for the client, the incentive structure should foster labor market participation. Stein sees the potential for such a structure in the British system of training services. He suggests that America would benefit by providing organized training and educational opportunities for all workers rather than the existing policy of establishing programs aimed exclusively at the "hard to employ."

Stein chooses not to deal explicitly with the obvious impact of sexism on the wage structure. The interested reader, however, will find his comparisons of America's Aid to Families with Dependent Children (AFDC) and Britain's Family Income Supplement (FIS) programs revealing. Clearly, the focus in both countries is literally on "man"-power policies. Overall this is an excellent, highly readable monograph which should become required reading for graduate students and professors concerned with work, welfare, and social policy.

Organizations

The Emergence of a UAW Local, 1936–1939: A Study in Class and Culture, by PETER FRIEDLANDER. Pittsburgh: University of Pittsburgh Press, 1975. 155 pp. $8.95 cloth.

JAMES P. MULHERIN
University of California, Berkeley

Peter Friedlander has written a very important book which will interest sociologists in a number of fields, particularly those in organizational and industrial sociology, political sociology, and the sociology of culture.

Friedlander produced his book from a "critical dialogue" with Edmund Kord, Local 229's first president and a central figure in the union's creation. Between December, 1972, and March, 1974, the two debated concepts drawn from Marx and Weber while they constructed the account of the birth and consolidation of the local. They wanted to address theoretical issues concerning the historical process of working class self-formation: cultural aids and obstacles to the process of union organization (language, ethnicity, skill level, drinking habits, marital status, fears, racism, fraternal organization and gang memberships, religiosity, etc.), the cultural roots of bureaucracy and opportunism in the labor movement, and the failure of the radical parties to generate mass socialist consciousness in the 1930s despite their key organizational roles.

The book provides a "thick description" of the contest between the new leaders and management as a dialectic between leaders and followers unfolds through the multiple social layers of the 450 workers at Detroit Parts Company, a Hamtramck supplier of the Detroit auto giants. Some of the chapter subsections include "First Efforts and the Emergence of Cadre," "Breakthrough: The Second-Generation Poles," "The Breakdown of Authority," "Applying the Pressure: The Absorption of the Fringes," and "Colonization of the Toolroom."

Friedlander's sophisticated approach to oral history generates ethnic and age data, for example, more accurate for individual departments than can be had from contemporary industrial census materials. With such data Friedlander illuminates the structural contexts in which the social movement takes place, first among the more sober and disciplined, married, second-generation, immigrant workers, and by waves among the others. No workers join without somehow being organized by the original cadre group. And always the leaders must challenge resistance from spies, authority, and cultural inhibitions.

As a case study the book casts light on the social-psychological and cultural processes largely overlooked by the institutional labor historians such as Sidney Fine and Irving Bernstein and by the anti-institutionalists represented by Jeremy Brecher and Stanley Aronowitz. The effect is like having a radical Melville Dalton in the leadership group doing participant observation during this epochal period.

Friedlander traces the roots of union bureaucratization and opportunism not to any ahistorical "iron law," but to the cultural mix constituting the labor force and to the political culture of the 1930s. Only Kord and the leadership circle immediately around him took up socialist politics, and even they tended to avoid the party intellectuals. Some of the remaining leaders not only remained aloof but later became active in the anti-socialist ACTU. In the absence of any credible alternative the bulk of the workers were swept up in the New Deal. The union incorporated large numbers of "historically inarticulate," first-generation workers who transferred their loyalties to the union but did not generate leadership from among their ranks. Likewise, the second-generation, teenage, gang members from Hamtramck could "wildcat" within the departments where they were concentrated but did not produce leaders or alliances with other segments of the shop. The more skilled WASP and old immigrant workers gave the most resistance to unionization and most often collaborated with management. In the period of consolidation they could exploit the union structure itself as a new path for mobility. While the process of unionization constituted a miniature cultural and political revolution in the shop and gave the organized workers great power over the entire process of production with the ability, for example, to establish a group incentive system making it impossible for a worker to compete against other workers, the transformation could not transcend the limits of the times by its own momentum. The very process of incorporating the "historically inarticulate" and the conservatively articulate into the same political unit which had been created through the initiative of the original leaders undermined their ability to proceed further.

In the final chapter Friedlander applies the results of his case study to the task of unraveling the factional warfare of 1938–39 within the UAW and to questions concerning the CIO and the radical parties. He argues for his own interpretation while realizing the impossibility of generalizing findings from one relatively isolated local to the giant union. To resolve the issues on a wider scale he calls for the application of his methodology to the large locals, especially Detroit's Dodge Local 3, where abundant documents would supplement and provide an additional check on the oral methods he developed.

In the theoretical introduction Friedlander argues against various positivist and Marxist historiographic assumptions about working people as historical agents. He critically constructs his own alternative approach from the works of Wittgenstein on language, the Frankfurt neo-Marxists, Piaget's structuralism, and George Lukàcs among others. While a reading of this introduction yields many flashes of insight, the language is often inaccessible and could stand improvement.

Managers and Workers: Origins of the New Factory System in the United States, 1880–1920, by DANIEL NELSON. Madison: University of Wisconsin Press, 1975. 234 pp. $15.00 cloth.

MARSHALL W. MEYER
University of California, Riverside

Sociologists usually do not turn to history for explanation of organizational phenomena, but there is some evidence that they should. Daniel Nelson's *Managers and Workers* is an account of the rise of the "new," i.e., modern, factory system in the US. Intended mainly for social historians, it holds some interest for sociologists who are concerned with the possibility that the greatest variations in organizations occur over time rather than across organizations at any one point in time. Unintentionally, perhaps, Nelson speaks to one of the central issues in organizational theory: whether bureaucratization is a contemporaneous process occurring mainly in large organizations operating in benign environments, or whether it is an historical process reflecting fundamental shifts in beliefs about ways organizations ought to be run.

Among other "variables" of interest to organizational sociologists, Nelson touches upon the following: (1) Size. Large factories were not uncommon by 1900. Some seventy factories in the US had 2,000 or more workers by the turn of the century. (2) Authority relations. The "contract system" of manufacturing was common especially in the northeast prior to World War I. Under it, "contractors" used materials, tools, power, and factory buildings owned by the manufacturer, and they agreed to produce a particular component at a designated cost. The contractor was at least partly independent, working for profit. The contract system was eventually replaced by the foreman who was a salaried employee, and the foreman's position, although initially strong, weakened greatly over time when it lost the hiring and firing prerogatives. (3) The administrative component. Specialized clerks appeared at about 1900 as more systematic information about production was sought and cost accounting became widespread. (4) The management of personnel. "Welfare work" and separate personnel departments also appeared at the turn of the century, the former perhaps to stem unionization and the latter to remove the last vestiges of the old-fashioned foreman's authority.

What, then, accounts for the rise of the modern factory system in Nelson's accounts? Size and complexity cannot be overlooked as forces stimulating "bureaucratization" of factories, but there were other causes as well. Most important among these was the doctrine of scientific management which argued that authority ought to be centralized, costs minimized, and workers selected according to their qualifications and treated humanely. The contract system disappeared not because it was inefficient—workers were "pushed" mercilessly under it—but rather because no one knew how efficient it was, least of all factory owners.

Managers and Workers, despite a title cribbed from a classic, is a useful work for students of organizations. I'm not arguing that everyone should read it, but more of us should be trying to write works which systematically take account of historical events in understanding contemporary organizational patterns.

Modern Japanese Organization and Decision-Making, edited by EZRA F. VOGEL. Berkeley: University of California Press, 1975. 340 pp. $15.00 cloth. $4.95 paper.

BATIA SHARON
University of California, Santa Cruz

This collection of papers about decision-making processes in a range of political, economic, cultural, and educational organizations in modern Japan is a product of a Japanese-American conference initiated by the Joint Committee on Japanese studies of the American Council of Learned Societies and the Social Science Research Council. It reveals a Japanese version of organizational structure and interpersonal relations, significantly different from both the European and the American.

Albert H. Craig's account of the functional and dysfunctional aspects of government bureaucracy provides the reader with a frame of reference that identifies a hierarchical structure with a direction and a locus of decision-making different from those existing in American organizations. This is the Ringi system of decision-making whereby documents are drafted at lower organizational levels and then circulated to various units for approval, keeping the various interests involved in a continuous delicate balance.

M. Y. Yoshimo's study of structural change in thirty-five large Japanese manufacturing firms that have been active in developing firms abroad, Herbert Passin's analysis of the seeming isolation of Japanese intellectuals from influential circles, Nathaniel B. Thayer's portrayal of competition and conformity in the Japanese newspaper industry, to mention only a few, give an account of the development of organizational behavior in Japan, different from that which many of us have been led to believe.

The book manifests a keen awareness of cultural relativism. Japanese organizations are compared to their counterparts in the USA and Europe in order to point out the specific meaning of structural and interactional concepts in the Japanese context. The authors deliberately avoid generalizations about Japan, and they make an effort to demystify notions and break down stereotypes, portraying the changes that have been taking place and critically questioning the effects of tradition and culture on Japanese organizational behavior.

Some papers do well to establish the congruency between Japanese cultural imperatives, and the particular way the Japanese organization functions. Excellent in depicting these issues are John C. Campbell's discussion of the principle of equitable treatment in setting up the annual Japanese budget; Taishiro Shirai's paper on decision making in the Japanese labor union; Thomas Rohlen's study of interpersonal relations in work groups at a large bank and a small manufacturing company, and George De Vos's description of paternalism, group solidarity, intergenerational vicarious identification, and the value of participation and emotional interaction in a hierarchical social structure.

Peter Drucker, on the other hand, tries to account for the seemingly low emphasis on maximization of profit in Japanese business by drawing our attention to the structure of the banking system in Japan which differs from both the European and American banking systems. The main value of this book and its potential for theoretical expansion lie in the fact that it clearly illuminates that the socio-cultural system of Japan created a modern, capitalist organizational structure which is not directly inferable from Western organizational theory. Though the majority of essays in this collection are mainly descriptive, some use a more analytical approach and implicitly suggest the necessity for new models of organizational behavior to include types and forms of such behavior not accounted for by existing models. However, the issue is not dealt with systematically by any author nor by the editor. Nevertheless, the possibilities for future major theoretical innovations are there.

For example, various papers seem to suggest that there are different conceptions of efficiency, rationality, and organizational effectiveness typical to Japan. However, these concepts are not fully defined in Japanese terms since their ontology is never explained. This is especially important for those outsiders who are bound to commit cultural fallacies each time their observations do not make sense in their foreign, sometimes alien, terms. Shirai's use of Western concepts of efficiency to discuss the seeming inefficiency of Japanese labor unions does little to convey what efficiency means in Japanese terms, although he concludes that what seem frivolous and inefficient to the Westerner is an essential cost for maintaining union solidarity in Japan.

Gerald Curtis's article on the role big business plays in government represents a challenge to C. W. Mills's elitist model. The particular pluralistic character of the Japanese power structure does not simply call for the use of the plural model dealt with by the community power structure literature. It appears to require a model which incorporates organized interests less inclined to float from one arena of influence to another than the ones we are familiar with in the US. The description of Ringi system varies slightly among the different articles dealing with it, depending on the details chosen for discussion, but the lack of systematic evaluation of possible and real consequences of this system is pervasive. The incorporation of this type of decision-making into a theory would have been a valuable contribution of this anthology.

The clarity of De Vos's analysis of the Marxist prediction of alienation and class consciousness that does not seem to have been realized in Japan, explicates the contributions this anthology, together with the works of Blauner, Lipset, Closman and Trow, Riesman and Crozier, might make toward the development of a greatly needed general theory of the socio-cultural contingencies of organizational behavior. Though some references are made to Crozier no one discussion employs any general theoretical framework.

I believe that an analytical discussion that summarizes and evaluates the findings within a general theoretical framework (and one could expect it to take place at a conference such as this) would have contributed to the definitions of Japanese style efficiency, rational behavior, organizational effectiveness, and collective decision-making and ultimately to the redefinition of such concepts within an expanded general theory of organizational behavior.

Political

Italia in trasformazione, by FRANCESCO ALBERONI. Bologna: Il Mulino, 1976. 162 pp. No price listed, paper.

Il Sistema Globale: Immagini e Modelli, by GIANNI KAUFMAN. Glorizia, Italy: Istituto di Sociologia Internazionale, 1974. 252 pp. No price listed, paper.

EDITH KURZWEIL
Montclair State College

Francesco Alberoni and Gianni Kaufman—sociologists, respectively at the Catholic University of Milan and the University of Gorizia—speak a similar Italian but a different sociology. For Kaufman "searches for a systematic empirical theory that demystifies 'literary' approaches to foreign policy and international relations" on a global level, while Alberoni "discarded such an approach" (used in his studies of social movements and Italian institutions) when writing the articles collected in this book—articles that originally appeared in the *Corriere della Sera* in 1974 and 1975. The left-Catholic Alberoni is as aware of the limits of Marxism, as Kaufman is of the limits of General Systems Theory, but the former appears to write about political practice at the edge of destruction, about chaos and conflict, while the latter's system appears to be unrelated to political practice or people, and assumes order and normative behavior. In other words, Alberoni's social criticism focuses on politics, while Kaufman's global system integrates them. Their contradictions, of course, are rooted in the dichotomy between academic and non-academic Italian sociology, and in the history and the "power-base" of the two approaches.

Kaufman's work is scholarly: his extensive bibliography and quotes range from Abbot to Zoppo. He argues, convincingly, that neither the nation-state (territoriality, military, economic, organizational, and socio-economic planning are increasingly irrelevant) nor the market any longer provides automatic social regulatory mechanisms. Thus only a General Systems Theory with a viable methodology for the understanding of our global system, that includes boundary models, that allows for "the traditional static meaning of discontinuity," and for structures dealing with the protection, support, and promotion of system performance, could organize existing reality. He chooses an "open system" (over a mechanical one, a self-regulating one, or a static structure), because it allows for dynamic societal processes (irreducible to purely conflictual or integrative factors) that can "overcome the traditional antinomies between *national-international* and *social-political*." At the root of this antithesis, he locates a *depoliticization assumption* which pretends that governmental structures are "peaceful" and tend toward self-regulation—as long as incongruencies and contradictions remain undetected in institutional structures. Hence, the *antithesis* must be played down, and politics must be discussed openly. He then anchors it all in Parsonian theory, in M. A. Kaplan's "global orders," and in many others, before tying in imperialistic relationships. Eventually, Etzioni's concept of *activation* of societal units (it subsumes collective and organizational components and political penetration) is found to be the best-suited for the construction of his seven models of political systems that could be applied to both the nation-state and global level.

Alberoni's book is political. His dialectic between politics and institutions, between private life and collective life, addresses parties, unions, religion, customs, etc. He invokes the past and the future, leaders and followers, workers and capitalists, advanced development and underdevelopment, Catholics and Communists, in order to point to social realities and trends. But his journalism is deceptive: its cutting edge is sharpened by his sociological and psychological training. Unlike Kaufman who fits Italy into the global system, he explains that system through its effect on Italy. When he talks of the corporate logic of the unions, the inefficient state bureaucracy, clientelism and bourgeois paternalism, when he links the fear of communism to the Church, to the USSR and the US, when he notes social changes since 1968, or when he points to the danger of a totalitarian turn to either the right or the left, his sharp demands for self-regulation, reform, social conscience, and political action hit home. The collapse of the international system, he argues, was expressed by the oil crisis in 1973: it "overturned" Europe, ruined relations with the US, questioned national identity and the possibility for self-determination. Its immediate effect on Italy made the unions and the communist party into the custodians of the economy, pointed to the irredeemability and paralysis of the Christian-Democrats, and encouraged the revival of anti-capitalism and anti-Americanism by the Marxist left, so that the votes of the left increased at the expense of the Catholic party. The American crisis itself, he states elsewhere, created a political and cultural vacuum for Europe. But the Europeans, afraid to fill this vacuum, allow the multinational corporations to take over. Thus, instead of a political world order based on economic planning, companies without political responsibility are able to determine the fate of countries and to create wars.

Alberoni, in the tradition of "action sociology," wants to rouse Italy and all of Europe, to assert, defend, and reform itself, and to mediate between the Third World and the US. His incisive analyses and quick conclusions lack the scholasticism of Kaufman's General Systems Theory. But given the conditions of both the Italian and the global systems, unless we listen to Alberoni, we won't be around to test Kaufman's models.

The Soviet Union since the Fall of Khrushchev, edited by ARCHIE BROWN and MICHAEL KASER. London: Macmillan Press, 1975. 294 pp. $10.00 cloth.

Russia under the Old Regime, by RICHARD PIPES. London: Weidenfeld & Nicolson, 1975. 361 pp. $6.50 cloth.

The Russian Tradition, by TIBOR SZAMUELY, edited by ROBERT CONQUEST. London: Secker & Warburg, 1974. 443 pp. No price listed.

ALEXANDER MATEJKO
University of Alberta

These three books taken together provide the best introduction to the past and the present of Russia. It is important for understanding what happens now in the Soviet Union to know that the Russian rulers claimed for centuries to own the land and its inhabitants, and that the state had a patrimonial character. All social strata heavily depended on the rulers, and this is well evidenced in the book by Pipes. Nobility, clergy, and even burghers had vested interests in supporting the patrimonial state. The total lack of any legalized personal rights prevented peasants, and, especially the serfs from fulfilling an active role, even though they numerically dominated the society.

Pipes and Szamuely both emphasize the unique historical role of the intelligentsia.

The hatred of serfdom and the hostility toward the existing imperial order were basic unifying factors of the Russian intelligentsia. A particular sense of commitment to public welfare was typical for these people, and a commitment to revolution was seen as the only way of making things better. Szamuely makes the point that there existed in no other European country such an influential social power, so totally oriented toward violence. Radicals among the intelligentsia gained the upper hand as repression by the state developed and as relationships between the ruling elite and the rest of the society deteriorated. Imperial Russia was only a prototype of a police state with many loopholes, but it was enough to radicalize the Russian society at the turn of the century.

The contemporary oppositionists in the Soviet Union are to some extent continuing the moral and intellectual tradition of the old intelligentsia. Although there are only a few of them, often better known in the West than in the Soviet Union, these dissenters create a hope of future pluralization and repoliticization of Soviet society. Peter Reddaway makes a good point in this respect in his paper included in the book edited by Brown and Kaser. It seems proper to note that working-class dissent is potentially the most dangerous factor for the ruling establishment, and the Soviet elite has good reasons to be afraid that the dissenting groups may have significant influence on blue collar workers. The example of Poland is discouraging for the Soviet regime. Three times (1956, 1970, and 1976) the Polish industrial workers have managed to arrange an effective mass resistance to the Party and state wage and price policy.

Brown, in his own essay on political developments in the Soviet Union, emphasizes the fear of chaos and disorder that permeates a large part of the Soviet society, preventing any far-reaching reforms. It is exactly this fear which provides a rationale for a very considerable conservative bias in the ruling circles. There are several internal and external factors which may potentially lead to the disintegration of the Soviet state, and the rulers must constantly keep this danger in mind. The low productivity of the Soviet agriculture is only one of many difficulties which will not be overcome without the major overhaul of the system; periodically there has been a food crisis in the Soviet Union which the rulers have not been able to prevent. The import of Western agricultural technology is very much needed in the Soviet Union, but, according to Hanson's essay, so far it constitutes only a small percent of the total Soviet equipment investment. Over-regulation and under-management are traditional weaknesses of the Russian economy, but Kaser believes that in the long run technocracy and managerialism will defeat an excessive bureaucratism.

Improvement of the living standard in the Soviet Union does not seem to be extensive enough to provide a solid basis for the political status quo defended by the conservative coalition of bureaucratic, military, and technocratic interests. The authors of papers included in the book edited by Brown and Kaser seem to differ in their diagnosis of the internal stability of the Soviet system. Under the Czarist regime the intelligentsia was relatively free in comparison with the rest of the population and Soviet bureaucracy has inherited from the old regime a problem with the intelligentsia, even though the margin of individual freedom is now much smaller, and any open mass resistance is impossible. It is now up to the rulers to determine the earnings, promotion, and even mobility of the citizens, and any dissent may be effectively suppressed. Still, the legitimacy of the rulers is based more on power than on anything else and the Leninist principles of democratic centralism are interpreted and implemented in an authoritarian manner.

The Old Regime failed in imperial Russia because of involvement in wars beyond the capacity of the system and because of the growing gap between rulers and the ruled. All three books here under review make clear that although the present Soviet Union is obviously a world power, the historical weaknesses are still there.

Elite Politics in Rural India: Political Stratification and Political Alliances in Western Maharashtra, by ANTHONY T. CARTER. New York: Cambridge University Press, 1974. 207 pp. $17.50 cloth.

RICHARD P. TAUB
University of Chicago

Authors writing about political stratification in India are faced with a problem of marginal differentiation. So much has been written in so much detail about Indian stratification in general, and rural stratification in particular, that those who are engaged in similar practice take on a peculiar stridency as they find intellectual justification for their own activities. This also leads to what might be called the narcissism of small differences. One's contributions, real or imagined, are exaggerated in a fashion which might lead a newcomer to think that the new report is really new rather than the same old stuff. This careful and painstaking book is an illustration of that point.

The author begins by counting the members in all the organizations with any political power and all the substantial landowners in a small area within the state of Maharashtra, and discovers that there is a dominant caste, *vatandar* Marathas, which controls most of the land and constitutes a substantial majority of the key positions in those organizations. Since there already exists a vast literature about "dominant castes" of a similar nature in other parts of India, one finds it difficult to discover what is distinctive about these particular findings. Carter tells us "There is a useful body of material on dominant castes, but so far it has been focused on village dominance. Little is known about regional dominance or about dominance in more inclusive, higher level political arenas" (p. 29). To increase his contribution of general knowledge, he mistakenly calls this group a "power elite." One should add, in this regard, that his general picture works much better for the rural areas than it does for the urban ones under consideration. In the one city in the area, Brahmins and Jains have disproportionate political power. The author, however, does not work out the sources of that power at the same level of detail that he does for the rural categories.

Having satisfied all of us according to the most rigorous criteria that there is a dominant caste in Satara District in Western Maharashtra, the author moves into the next subject for which there is already extensive literature, political factions. His justification for this effort is similar to the justification for identifying dominant castes: there is much data on factions at the village, state and national levels, he asserts, but much less information about this phenomenon at the level between village and district. There is also a great deal of conceptual belaboring. Instead of factional analysis, he is observing "transactional linkages or alliances which comprise political action sets" (p. 107). We are then treated again to a series of trivial findings uttered with great import. "Data on politics in rural Western Maharashtra indicate than linkages or alliances in political action sets are of two kinds, vertical and horizontal, differing in both their intrinsic and extrinsic aspects" (p. 107). Weiner, Brass, Bailey, and others too numerous to mention have gone over the same ground. Carter does document how these factions seem to work in Western Maharashtra.

In his effort to prove that he is doing something new, Carter misrepresents at least one of those who have gone before him. "This pattern consists not in irrational personal antagonisms attributable to the personality characteristics of Indian politicians (cf. Brass 1965:168–82), but rather in the relations between political action and certain antecendent structural frameworks" (p. 162). (This quote shows Carter falling into a certain kind of structuralist-functionalist trap in which all behaviors "make sense" in terms of the structural framework in which they take place.) Contrast that with what Brass actually says: "Splits and mergers, alliances and conflicts among factions are generally traceable to specific incidents involving either a loss of actual or potential power or prestige by individual faction leaders" (p. 179). This, in spirit, is very close to what Carter has in mind for his own analysis and rather far away from what he implies that Brass says. Carter also spends relatively little effort exploring the consequences of this behavior for the functioning of the system as a whole—an issue with which Brass commendably grapples. For the perplexing problem for students of India is not whether faction leaders are rational in terms of their own narrow and immediate self interest—it is hard to imagine that they would be otherwise—the question is whether this behavior results in a net gain for the society as a whole or results in stalemate: inability to make policy decisions and to carry them out over a protracted period of time.

In short, *Elite Politics in Rural India* is a careful report about "political stratification and alliances in Western Maharashtra." However, it adds little to the massive documentation which already exists about these processes in India.

Measuring Power, Public Opinion and Policy: A Case Study of Syracuse, New York, by GEORGE FREDERICKSON and LINDA SCHLUTER O'LEARY. New York: Praeger Publishers, 1973. 184 pp. $15.00 cloth.

MARTIN J. MURRAY *
SUNY/Binghamton

This book is divided into three more or less equal parts: first, the analysis of the concept

* Not the reviewer responsible for the listing in "Delinquent Reviews."

of community power and a methodology for measuring it; second, an examination of public opinion and "democracy"; and third, an evaluation of public policy-making. The first part represents the authors' efforts to study community power in Syracuse, New York, which follows and complements the work of Roscoe Martin, Frank Munger, and Linton Freeman. Frederickson and O'Leary emphasize what they consider a new dimension of community power studies: to view not only the patterns of influence among local "influentials" but also between local "influentials" and state and federal elites. The authors develop a methodology which includes the unobtrusive measure of studying the appointment calendar of each interviewee.

In the second part of their study Frederickson and O'Leary survey how public priority preferences vary widely on the basis of social, economic, and demographic circumstances. Not so surprisingly, the authors conclude here that middle and upper socio-economic groups have a "different order of public priorities than their lower socio-economic counterparts."

In the final section Frederickson and O'Leary review the decision-making process in Syracuse and how it relates to education, social services, law enforcement, and water pollution control issues. The authors conclude that their empirical findings demonstrate the existence of a democratic decision-making policy process.

However, on the whole, this book appears to be just another conventional study "proving" democratic control of the policy-making process without ever asking the question why policies are made in the first place. The simplified notion of "democracy" and the rather conventional measures cannot help but lead the reader to the same unwarranted conclusions.

Elite Structure and Ideology: A Theory with Applications to Norway, by JOHN HIGLEY, G. LOWELL FIELD, and KNUT GRØHOLT. New York: Columbia University Press, 1976. 367 pp. $17.50 cloth.

INGER J. SAGATUN
San Jose State University

This book sets out to present a general theory of elite behavior and political stability, with particular reference to political elites in developed societies. The book is divided into three poorly integrated parts. The first section develops one theoretical argument, the third section another, and sandwiched between them is a data section with questionable relationship to both. (It appears as if each author wrote one section with little collaboration.)

The first section bypasses much of the controversy surrounding the recruitment of elites, by declaring that "political elites are those who happen to be strategically placed in positions in large and complex organizations, and with power to affect political outcomes on the macro level." The main argument in this section is that the more unified the political elite, the more stable the political system. This relationship is influenced by the occupational structure of non-elites. Different occupational structures will produce different non-elite orientations to power. Developed societies are characterized by consensual elites, political stability, and a bureaucratized non-elite who views power as necessary and non-threatening.

In the second section of the book, the authors attempt to apply this theory to the Norwegian society. Using a series of interviews, surveys, and other available information, the background and structure of Norwegian elites are studied in detail.

Although the first section argues that political structures with consensual elites tend to be self-perpetuating, the major question asked in the third section is whether modern societies with consensual elites can continue to develop in a stable direction. The authors suggest that modern industrialized states may have reached the limit of their progressive development, and may now begin to experience a backlash of new and unanticipated problems. Some of these are: (1) the loss of political wisdom when the political elite no longer needs to justify its position through ideology, (2) the increased similarity between elites, which insulates them from the non-elites, (3) the inability of bureaucratic societies to employ all of their qualified members in appropriate positions, and (4) in a welfare state such as Norway, the more people are helped by the welfare system, the fewer people are in need of a welfare system, and the less support there will be for it. The authors predict that the elites will not be able to cope with these problems, and the result will be political instability.

There are major problems with the book. The first section argues that elite background is not important for understanding elite behavior; yet, the major part of the data section is devoted to studying elite background rather than the major tenets of the theory (presumably with the intent to show that background, indeed, is not important for understanding the consensual nature of elites). The data show that the Norwegian elites are predominantly upper to middle class males, from urban regions, yet the differences among groups of elites are stressed, rather than the overall similarity.

Secondly, Norway is not the best place to test a theory on the consensuality of elites. Due to the homogeneity of the Norwegian society and the small population, any elite in Norway would by the very nature of that society tend to be much more consensual than elsewhere. Thirdly, the incongruity between the first and the third sections is confusing. All the arguments in the first section lead up to the conclusion that political stability in developed societies will tend to be self-perpetuating, yet the last section argues convincingly that this may not be so. Finally, one might question the implied equations of stability and progress, or instability and an end of progress.

In summary then, this is a very uneven work. It offers a fascinating and insightful discussion of the dilemmas of modern societies brought on by the very unity and developmental level of such societies. But it also makes for very painful reading, due to the lack of integration among the three parts. Scholars in specialized areas may find parts of the book interesting, in particular the third section, but this book has no place in the classroom.

Refugees from Militarism: Draft-Age Americans in Canada, by RENÉE GOLDSMITH KASINSKY. New Brunswick, N.J.: Transaction Books, 1976. 301 pp. $14.95 cloth.

JOHN C. LEGGETT
Livingston College
Rutgers University

During the Vietnam War approximately 500,000 men deserted from all services for varying lengths of time. At the end of 1973 official statistics reported almost 29,000 deserters at large, with some 2,000 believed to be resident in foreign areas. Whatever the real number, most deserter-emigrés had fled to Canada. In crucial ways worse off than their fellow-exiles—the draft evaders—deserters have suffered inordinately due to the interlocked oppression of the State, Mom, and Dad.

Parents have been reluctant to help release their stigmatized children from the state's embrace. This study of exiles who sought refuge in Canada after 1965 illuminates this alliance between parents and the state, and how it can nonetheless be eroded through the dogged persistence of a wayward son. Witness an illustrative decline in a US mother's chauvinism expressed in a series of Toronto-bound letters, in which both she and like-kin initially supported state opposition to desertion, but later bent before the offspring's heady tenacity (pp. 160–161):

April 21

You have disgraced your family and your country. We don't know what possessed you to do what you've done, but we never want to hear from you again except to have the money back we lent you to fly back to your base. If we had known where you were headed. . . . Your Uncle Fred was in for twenty years and says he enjoyed every minute of it. You say to send your birth certificate. Well, we burned your birth certificate and your insurance policy. You are no longer a son of ours.

April 26

We got your letter and are still waiting for the money you owe us. We want nothing to do with you. Uncle Fred is sick at heart and wants to know how you could prefer a foreign country to your native land and isn't Canada the United States' ally? As far as we're concerned, you can do what you like; but whatever you do it's wrong.

May 8

Two and one half years of service is not a lifetime. If you go back now, you will lose some pay and be confined to your base for a few weeks, and that's all. If you don't believe me, why don't you write to your unit chaplain?

May 10

Jimmy, why don't you write or call? You are hurting the parents that raised you. We still have no idea what motivated you in pursuing your course of action. Uncle Fred says those Marine officers can be very mean sometimes. Maybe that was it.

May 22

We got your letter and were glad to hear you got a job. At least you won't starve. We can see in a way what you mean about that My Lai incident. Is it very cold up there this part of year?

June 3

Daddy is getting his vacation this month and

we were going to Atlantic City. Thought we might drive through Toronto on the way, and if you're not busy maybe we could stop and talk for a little while. How are the roads up that far? Uncle Fred says he might come along for the ride. He says he's heard the scenery is nice up there.

September 10

How do you like your new job? What is a "Head Shop"? We hope you like living in your new commune, but be careful getting mixed up with those political groups. The war goes on and on down here, and we, the people, have no say in stopping it. Your youngest brother says he would like to drive up and see you and talk about something. He's never driven so far before, but we guess it will be O.K. Things are so ugly here. The police seem to be going too far when they beat up people for demonstrating. We will be glad when we come up again at Thanksgiving. Daddy wants to look around at the housing situation there. Is it true that your president is a communist?

Perhaps this last remark convinced the Canada Council and hence Pierre Elliot Trudeau to subsidize this angular study of American exiles. Consciousness-raising south of the border seemed in order. To accomplish this task, the author used detailed questionnaires, taped in-depth interviews, participant observation, government and other historical materials. Together they constituted the evidential basis for a book which traced the decision to leave the US for The Northern Slope, a new permanent home for almost all of the exiles.

Unfortunately, its own findings notwithstanding, the study fails to emphasize analytically the significance of parents' social class (and hence education of exiles) in determining first, who would be drafted; second, who left the US before the call-up; third, who was slated to do the up-front fighting; fourth, who got killed in Vietnam; and fifth, who deserted. Time and again we discover from the study's data how, beginning in 1965, the US Selective Service consciously used class-occupational criteria of youngster to decide who would be channeled where: for the middle and upper classes: into the civilian and non-combat military sectors of the permanent wartime economy; for the working class; as the Vietnamese War casualties attest, it was to be a more sanguinary date with destiny. Given the brazen class bias of channelling, it is a wonder that entire Ft. Lewis, Washington platoons failed to trek to Vancouver.

Kasinsky found the on the whole less educated working class deserters more frequently unable to adjust to Canada. For deserters, there was more employer discrimination, unemployment, landed immigrancy refusal, illegal residence, dire poverty, petty crimes, Canadian public rejection, everyday RCMP harassment, illegal RCMP collusion with US military and police authorities intent on deportation of exiles back to the US, and in pursuit of this objective, RCMP *kidnappings.* Of current interest is Jimmy Carter's willingness to pardon draft evaders but not deserters. They are to be considered one case at a time. Canadian exiles must wonder whether he has patented a similar classification and selection of peanuts.

The deserter's decision to flee often followed punishment for legitimate protest against an illegitimate war (p. 187):

> Most of the men who were active in the GI movement and wrote for the GI Underground within the military deserted after the "heat" was put on them from their commanding officers. Many of the deserters who arrived in Montreal after the spring of 1969 attempted to organize within the GI ranks only to be faced with punitive reassignment or a "bust." The original editors of the GI papers *Head On, The Last Harass* and *Gig Line* were in Montreal, as were the co-editors of *Shakedown* and the *Fatigue Press.* Each of these editors had been busted on sedition charges, reassigned and ordered to Vietnam.

The book does suffer from one major weakness: a reluctance to link the successive highpoints of evader (1965–68) and deserter (1968–71) emigrations to the pulse of the Vietnam War. While the author cites 1968 as the first year of extensive deserter emigration to Canada, she fails to relate the heightened flow to the 1968 Tet Offensive. Again, her sense of history escapes her when she favorably compares the current refugees from militarism with the crusty middle and upper class United Empire Loyalists who had fled the US during the 1770s and 80s in protest against the popular fight against British colonialism. The ideological-class differences alone invite rejection of the alleged parallel. More to the point would be the tens of thousands of Great Plains farmers who seventy years ago fled bankruptcy to begin life anew on the Canadian prairies.

Despite lapses in historical conceptualization, the book is a good one rooted in research. It demonstrates both the stern determinisms of class and the laughable links between state, family, and deserter.

Transformations of the American Party System: Political Coalitions from the New Deal to the 1970s, by EVERETT CARLL LADD, JR., with CHARLES D. HADLEY. New York: W. W. Norton & Company, 1975. 371 pp. $12.50 cloth. $4.95 paper.

STEVEN E. DEUTSCH
University of Oregon

Starting with the assertion that, "It is the prime political feature of our time that the structure of conflict has been transformed" (p. xxi), the authors examine party realignments and shifts in the US electorate from the 1930s to the present time. Using primarily Gallup poll data, and some other survey data from Michigan and other sources, they examine the opposing interpretations of what has happened to American political parties and conclude that the lop-sided 1964 and 1972 Presidential elections were not aberrations.

The authors believe that most of the literature inadequately focuses on electoral behavior as an end, whereas they claim this should only be seen as symptomatic of the underlying socio-political currents of the society. However, the book relies mostly on aggregated survey data on party identification, declared party voting, election results, and measures of political ideology; the weakest part of the book is the contextual analysis of what they see happening in "post-industrial" society.

The over-all thrust of the book is important, and serious students of American political life should include this work in their libraries. Although it is somewhat drawn-out and redundant stylistically, it is not a dull presentation of survey data. The review of New Deal constituencies is interesting, and the evidence that the South was the most liberal section of the country—in support of FDR, while the Northeast was the most conservative and opposed to Roosevelt's policies, is important in light of this generation's assessments of the realities of American political behavior. The dramatic regional shifts over the subsequent decades is then spelled out, noting that the gaps widened during the 1960s as the South became the most conservative source of Republican support, while the Northeast expressed the most liberal views in the Democratic camp. They conjecture that this rising Southern conservatism has peaked, and perhaps the support for Ford over Reagan would give some credence to that argument.

I found myself bothered by several features of this book. First, the authors tend to integrate their work into the literature to a very modest degree; when they discuss religion and voting or class and voting they do not tie their work to a whole body of literature (e.g., Lenski, R. Hamilton). They seem too easily to accept the embourgeoisement thesis: that affluence means the decline of the working class (with no reflection of early works such as B. Berger's *Workingclass Suburb,* or more recent books such as A. Levison's *The Workingclass Majority,* S. Aronowitz's *False Promises*). The structural realities are ignored, as they were by the sociologists of the 1950s who saw the "end of ideology" with whom the authors are largely in agreement. The fact is that prosperity during the 1950s and 1960s did not affect all workers: black-white income gap remained, between males and females it increased, structural unemployment has remained at chronically high levels, and inflation has exceeded wage increases with a net deterioration in the economic position of workers.

This discussion is fitted into an analysis of America as a post-industrial society, in which workers become middle-class and conservative, and the massification of the intelligentsia lead them to think and act as a class. This discussion is the weakest part of the book; intellectuals are seen as critical, yet no acknowledgement is given to evidence of the role of intellectuals (see B. Miroff's new study of the Kennedy "liberal" Presidency: *Pragmatic Illusions*) as a manipulated class. The post-industrial uses of media in the formation of political culture is seen as enlightening, but the matter of whom the media serves is ignored (see C. Mueller's, *The Politics of Communication* for example). Finally, the entire discussion ignores the literature on the crisis in legitimation, the fiscal crisis, and the growth of political cynicism and apathy. For that matter, one wonders about the notion of a Nixon "landslide" in 1972 when he received the votes of only one-third of the electorate. This trend and the current projections of a declining level of participation by the electorate is not discussed by the authors.

In the context of the argument for post-industrialism, there is an interesting discussion of the impact of Vietnam, movements for racial justice, the women's movement, etc. upon the millions of college and university students of the past fifteen years and whether they were radicalized in a long-term direction. To be sure they discuss "old" vs. "new" liberals in examining these shifts, yet the discussion doesn't go beyond much material in the literature.

This book does offer some interesting analyses on the shifts in party coalitions over the past four decades, and the authors' conclusion about the immediate thrust of American electoral behavior may well be correct. They predict a push to nominate ideological candidates; yet the rejection of Reagan and Fred Harris would suggest a continuing push for centrist candidates. The 1976 election would seem to fit the more traditional mold, rather than the 1964 and 1972 elections which the authors see as a likely direction for the future. Although I offer critical comments, I think this is a useful book for understanding shifts in electoral trends and the apparent movement in party support.

Peace Soldiers: The Sociology of a United Nations Military Force, by CHARLES C. MOSKOS, JR. Chicago: University of Chicago Press, 1976. 171 pp. $11.00 cloth.

PHILLIP BUTLER
University of California, San Diego

Peace Soldiers is a concise little book which once again exhibits Charles Moskos's capacity to produce good qualitative sociology. Like his now classic study, *The American Enlisted Man,* this book tells us about the attitudes and values that bring soldiers to do, willingly or begrudgingly, efficiently or poorly, what soldiers are required to do. And as in that classic study, Moskos's report is based on his first-hand observations and interviews with soldiers on the scene. The setting for the study was with UNCIFYP, the UN Peacekeeping Forces in Cyprus, during the late sixties and early seventies. Moskos spent eight months there in 1969–1970, living with and interviewing officers and other ranks from among the British, Canadian, Finnish, Irish, Norwegian, and Swedish troop contingents that made up the peacekeeping forces.

The first part of the book reviews some major assumptions from the literature about what is required in the way of talent, attitudes, training for effective peacekeeping troops. Moskos uses these assumptions as hypotheses to be tested in the field. We also get some pertinent historical information on League of Nations and UN peacekeeping operations up to the present. The following chapter gives a slightly truncated history of Cyprus and its potentiality for military confrontation, and then a more detailed account of the formation and deployment of UNFICYP there.

Moskos's major findings are essentially reformulations of his original hypotheses. They are that: (1) soldiers other than those from middle neutral powers can adhere to peacekeeping standards; (2) peacekeeping experience in the field will yield adherence to constabulary standards of conduct; (3) participation in a UN peacekeeping role does not increase internationalist values; (4) internationalist values and the constabulary ethic do not come from the same attitudinal factor; and (5) contemporary standards of military professionalism are readily adaptable to the requirements of the peacekeeping role. Moskos has profitably tied his study into Morris Janowitz's "constabulary ethic" from *The Professional Soldier,* and is able to separate this ethic from "internationalism" to show how normal feelings of "nationalism" also prove viable in keying the individual soldier's desire to assume a peacekeeping role.

There are many bonus features of *Peace Soldiers.* Moskos is refreshingly specific about his methodology. The study dynamically traces changes in soldiers' attitudes and behaviors as they progress through their normal six month tours. There is an underlying indictment of the bungling bureaucracy called the UN and an exposé of how those working for it at the grass roots level manage to get the job done quite well—despite daily frustrations, financial handicaps, and a general lack of understanding by the parent organization. Moskos is overtly sympathetic with the lot of these soldiers and with their generally held values that peace is honorable, desirable, and worth personal sacrifice and danger to preserve.

Peace Soldiers will please readers on several accounts: the subject is important, the methodology successfully combines historical, participant observation, and interview techniques, and Moskos's style is easy and refreshing. *Peace Soldiers* is good solid sociological analysis worthy of a wide audience.

The Glassworkers of Carmaux: French Craftsmen and Political Action in a Nineteenth-Century City, by JOAN WALLACH SCOTT. Cambridge, Mass.: Harvard University Press, 1974. 239 pp. $10.00 cloth.

GREGG CARR
University of California, Santa Cruz

The argument in this fine book is that the militant socialism in the town of Carmaux in southwestern France in the years before a strike of glassworkers in 1895 was rooted in an attempt to retain control of production by the glassworkers and to defend a highly skilled, exclusive craft against the inroads of mechanization. Glassblowers had traditionally relied on the scarcity of their skill to stay employed. They formed a small, elite group whose members occasionally moved from town to town but who remained closely knit and somewhat apart from the rest of the townspeople. The craft was passed down the generations.

The strike and the glassworkers' union were broken completely because a new technique of production introduced a decade earlier had drastically lowered the level of skill required of glassblowers, shortened the apprenticeship required from fifteen years to at most five, and removed from the group its control over recruitment, training, and promotion. Wine bottles were being overproduced and wages were lowered in relation to prices and wages in other industries. The average age of glassworkers declined and recruitment became more local.

Once the term "master" had referred to the highly skilled worker; then it came to mean the employer, whose ownership of the factory permitted a mastery that had nothing to do with skill. The demands of the union's socialist leadership centered on re-establishing through the union the powers that the craft-masters once had. And as part of that struggle, the glassworkers, who now had more in common with their neighbors, the miners, allied with them to assert political control over the region. Jean Jaurès, the most famous French socialist, supported the strike and was elected to the Chamber of Deputies from the province; socialists were elected to local councils.

After their defeat, the leaders of the union left town to organize a competing cooperative glassworks nearby. Both factories, capitalist and cooperative, came to be run along similar lines, under strict management, with a new kind of work force made up of semi-skilled laborers recruited from the families of miners, peasants, and laborers, for whom technological developments created opportunities for greater material prosperity. When unionism finally reappeared some years later, it was of a different kind, and politically divided. The socialist vote had quickly declined.

Through a neat synthesis of demographic, technological, and economic history, Scott describes the experience faced by glassworkers over the last half-century of their existence as members of a craft. The implications of this work are not only that radical politics emerges in resistance to, rather than as a result of, proletarianization, but that it comes as an extension of conflicts over authority, rather than rewards, at the workplace.

Lies, Damn Lies, and Statistics: The Manipulation of Public Opinion in America, by MICHAEL WHEELER. New York: Liveright, 1976. 300 pp. $9.95 cloth.

DAVID V. MCQUEEN
Johns Hopkins University

Michael Wheeler presents the reader with an example of muckraking which reveals all the strengths and weaknesses of that genre. On the one hand he clearly, resolutely and unceasingly details the sins of the pollsters and on the other he shows a shallow understanding of the rather complicated methodological underpinnings of sound survey research. First let me address the strengths, then turn to the weaknesses, and finally to some general thoughts about "the manipulation of public opinion in America."

Wheeler's work has three major strengths. First, he provides many examples of the real fallibility of certain polling practices. In particular he attacks the practice of extensive pre-election political polling, and presents a thorough case for the pitfalls of such attempts to predict voter behavior on election day. Anyone interested in the cataloging of the major political polling disasters will find them well covered here. Similarly he makes a good case against the television ratings system, although it should be noted that his charges are probably known and accepted among most of the literate public today. Still, the Neilsen story is an entertaining one.

The second strength is that Wheeler does not attack survey research and statistics per se. Statistics in the hands of a skilled social scientist is a useful tool for empirical research. The best research utilizes statistics mainly to examine carefully thought out experimental designs and hypotheses. The unfortunate use of inferential statistics by some pollsters has often led the lay public to confuse the taking of polls with what sociologists do. Certainly some social statistical studies are sloppy methodologically and could be severely criticized, but rarely on the same grounds as the pollsters. Wheeler quite correctly identifies the major methodological problems of the pollsters.

The third strength is Wheeler's "Postscript." This section on how to read the polls is, in my view, the most succinct and careful section of his work. He offers ten questions "which a reader of polls must keep in mind in order to understand what they mean and whether they can be trusted" (p. 270). His elaboration of why these questions are important to ask is his best writing.

The weaknesses of this work are readily apparent. Wheeler engages in overkill. Worse than that, he often sacrifices his reasoned thoughts for innuendo and argument ad hominem. Schimpfen is kein Argument. For example, in describing one pollster, Pat Caddell (p. 60), Wheeler writes, "Caddell seems in good shape now, but on his desk there is a bottle of Sucaryl, a reminder of his ongoing battle with obesity." Is this useful to know? Wheeler liberally sprinkles his work with how well people are liked, e.g., "Harris is intensely disliked" (p. 48). Often one gets the feeling that these pollsters are a bunch of bad guys and usually the quotations from the bad guys are without reference, e.g., "Putting it bluntly, I elected forty-five United States senators and about twenty-three governors,"—a quotation attributed to Harris (p. 38).

The worst flaw illustrates how Wheeler is hoisted on his own petard. He reports extensively on the work of a poll-taker pseudonamed Diane. He demonstrates how haphazard her interviewing methods are and then generalizes from her to the population of poll-takers. Wheeler attacks Gallup for generalizing to the nation from a few thousand, then he generalizes from one poll-taker to all poll-takers. We simply have no way of knowing how typical Diane Bentley is and Wheeler knows that.

Given its strengths and weaknesses the Wheeler book remains as a general indictment of the "manipulation of public opinion." Is the charge valid? I don't believe there is any simple answer today. Polls are, after all, a social manifestation of the twentieth century. We exist in a mass society where the assessment of broad attitudes, beliefs and opinions is regarded as a necessity by various interest groups. How else can one know what is fashionable or politically astute without sampling some of the people? What is the alternative?

Especially in the political arena there are several myths that abound about polls: (1) issues are made too simple in polls, too black and white; (2) poll results may cause voters to change their vote; and (3) people blindly trust and put faith in polls. With respect to the first, one may simply counter that most political issues reduce to simple dichotomies and ultimately to the dichotomous choice at the polling place. With respect to the second there has been no empirical evidence demonstrating this effect. In fact recent data from the West Coast appears to show that even the knowledge of the television networks projected winner of a presidential election has no effect on voting behavior where polls are still open.

It is the third myth that is most disturbing in its perpetration because to believe it implies that the voters are simply stupid, that they will follow the pollsters anywhere. This is, simply an assertion on the part of journalists, intellectuals, and finally Wheeler himself. I frankly am more optimistic about the inherent skepticism of the body politic. In short, we should, as Wheeler clearly warns, keep our eyes on the pollsters. But, we will probably survive their simple attempts to manipulate our public opinion.

Race and Ethnic

Blacks in White Colleges: Oklahoma's Landmark Cases, by GEORGE LYNN CROSS. Norman: University of Oklahoma Press, 1975. 151 pp. $7.95 cloth. $3.95 paper.

SETHARD FISHER
University of California, Santa Barbara

This is a brief narration of some events leading up to the desegregation of the University of Oklahoma, written by the man who was president from 1944 to 1968. Cross was a dedicated servant of the institution, both during its segregationist phase and after. He was polite and cordial to the Blacks throughout. He takes some restrained pride in having been involved in this dramatic episode and in the fact that desegration was achieved. The narration is low-key, somewhat matter-of-fact, and benign.

Many of the events described by Cross seem anachronistic today. Blacks are no longer roped off in separate sections of classrooms; policemen are no longer required to escort Blacks onto college campuses; applications for admission from Black students no longer cause such extremes of anxiety, confusion, and fear among white officials as they did then. The national struggle for racial equality in the United States is reflected in microcosm in these short pages.

Some years ago Durkheim wrote of the intolerance of highly interdependent industrial systems for arbitrary, ascribed injustice. This book may interest a few sociologists seeking documentation of this assumption. Students of the history of ideas may find in the book confirmation of the tenacity of Enlightenment values in our time. These, however, are not connections made by the author himself. He has presented a simple, uninspired narration of events familiar to him, and he happened to be on the winning side.

Ethnic Identity in Society, edited by ARNOLD DASHEFSKY. Chicago: Rand McNally College Publishing Company, 1975. 251 pp. $5.95 paper.

Peoples: The Ethnic Dimension in Human Relations, by JERRY D. ROSE. Chicago: Rand McNally College Publishing Company, 1976. 201 pp. $6.95 paper.

DOUGLAS S. SNYDER
Bowie State College, Maryland

The publisher of these two undergraduate-level books on ethnicity and ethnic identity claims that they are a "related core text" and a "companion reader." Thus, the reviewer's task includes an assessment of this claim, as well as the evaluation of each book individually.

There is one clear link between the two books, inasmuch as the first chapter of *Peoples* is devoted to "Ethnic Identity." Beyond this, the different organizations and perspectives of the two books would make them difficult to use together. They are better described as somewhat complementary. *Ethnic Identity* focuses on the individual level of analysis, while *Peoples* divides its space between the intragroup ("Ethnic Groups") and intergroup ("Ethnic Relations") levels. The two books, then, do not make particularly good companions.

Having been impressed enough by Jerry Rose's pioneering introductory text to become an early adopter of it, I approached *Peoples* with high expectations, and departed slightly disappointed. Rose states that his book has three biases; it is analytic rather than descriptive, comparative and cross cultural rather than parochial, and nomothetic (theory building) rather than idiographic (case history-oriented). The first two emphases are successfully pursued, but the third one is marred by an imprecise use of key concepts. For example, at one point, Rose equates prejudice with its stereotype component and then blithely uses prejudice and social distance interchangeably.

Rose is more conscientious than most writers in reviewing the key findings that have brought us to our present, meager state of knowledge about ethnic relations. However, in his effort to stress alternative interpretations of such findings, he sometimes goes a little overboard. For instance, in citing the studies that show black college basketball players to be overrepresented among starters and underrepresented among substitutes, he has the temerity to suggest some less-talented black athletes may start ahead of better whites because of "integrationist" pressures. My first-hand, idiographic experience suggests that coaches tend to start their best players, due to the fact that the job of a losing coach is not as secure as the job of a run-of-the-mill tenured professor. Happily, lapses like the above are relatively infrequent; anyway, they tend to cultivate the critical skills of the reader.

Rose's well-organized, two-part book explicitly deals with the big questions, such as ethnic-group survival. Besides ethnic identity, major units of the "Ethnic Group" section are devoted to ethnic life styles and ethnic community; the "Ethnic Relations" section includes ethnic distance, ethnic stratification, and ethnic dynamics. I would single out for careful attention the two thorough and cogent chapters on ethnic stratification which draw upon Noel's ground-breaking article, among others. *Peoples* is well documented, but a list of selected references at the end would be a big help to the busy scholar.

This book will probably not become even the minor footnote contributing to "a single set of explanatory principles" of ethnic and non-ethnic minority relations hoped for by the author. Nevertheless, it is a reasonably well executed and relatively inexpensive ethnic relations text which lends itself to use with a more closely related book of readings than *Ethnic Identity*.

In *Ethnic Identity* Dashefsky has assembled a collection of readings and scholarly commentary on ethnicity for which he has high aspirations, as indicated by his "hard-sell" preface. Dashefsky denies his book has the faults of most readers, proclaiming the following virtues: (a) it is a text-reader because it integrates the readings with substantial "editorial text"; (b) it draws upon the experiences of diverse ethnic groups; (c) it focuses on alternative perspectives toward ethnic identity—most of the multi-disciplinary readings were selected for just this purpose; (d) it offers the student an opportunity to examine the field of ethnic relations from the viewpoint of the individual in society, rather than using structural or cultural explanations; and (e) the articles are recent and most have not appeared in other readers.

In general, the book lives up to these claims, but Dashefsky may have overachieved (a). His use of both introductions and postscripts for each article, as well as introductions, summaries, and suggested further readings for each major section is certainly commendable; but occasionally the reader feels a bit overwhelmed by the somewhat labored continuity. Also, it is often difficult to separate the articles from the commentary because one thick black line and a slightly darker, more closely-set type are sometimes the only indications of the switchover.

Because of "virtues" (c) and (d), *Ethnic Identity* is probably more suited for extensive use in an interdisciplinary, team-taught ethnic relations course than in a course taught by a lone sociologist, unless one wishes to stress the social-psychological approach.

This book has five parts: (1) society and ethnic identity, (2) the individual and ethnic identity, (3) socialization of ethnic identity, (4) the effects of ethnic identity on the individual, and (5) social movements based on ethnic identity. Well-known contributors include Pettigrew, Gordon, Newman, Fanon, Erikson, Grier and Cobbs, Allport, and Rosenberg. The theoretical and ideological range of this group is wide, and Dashefsky's commentary and tables help handle this diversity.

Although the section on social movements contains interesting "insider" articles about "liberation" programs, it does not enlighten us about the apparently ethnicity-based reactions to these movements, such as we see in the Boston conflict (see Orlando Patterson's article in March, 1975, *Change*).

These relatively minor deficiencies and limitations should not deter teachers of ethnic relations from using *Ethnic Identity* as at least a reserve reading in their undergraduate courses.

The National Interest: The Politics of Northern Development 1968–75, by EDGAR J. DOSMAN. Toronto: McClelland & Stewart, 1975. 224 pp. $4.95 paper.

As Long As This Land Shall Last, by RENÉ FUMOLEAU, Toronto: McClelland & Stewart, 1975. 415 pp. $5.95 paper.

This Land Is Not for Sale, by HUGH McCULLUM and KARMEL McCULLUM. Toronto: Anglican Book Centre, 1975. 213 pp. $3.95 paper.

STEPHEN O. MURRAY
University of Toronto

The fate of "the last frontier" and its indigenous inhabitants has become a matter of lively concern in Canada. The Berger Commission, chartered to investigate land claims of natives has embarrassed the government by focusing attention on native people's demands for justice. Its failure to defuse the issue—the latent function of Royal or Presidential Commissions—should make the conduct and impact of the Berger Commission an interesting topic of study (and comparison with those in Kommarovsky, 1975).

The books under review consider the formulation and implementation of Northern development policy, providing historical background to the Berger inquiries. Fumoleau traces the history of the last two (1899 and 1921) treaties by which native people purportedly surrendered their claims to vast tracts in the North. Since these treaties were concluded within living memory, Fumoleau was able to supplement his exhaustive scrutiny of documents, official records, and memories by interviewing surviving signatories and witnesses to the treaty signings. He is able to show that many signatures were forgeries. Every piece of evidence indicates that the native people who did sign the mysterious papers did so only after being reassured by the government negotiators and by trusted missionaries that they were not surrendering their land nor giving up their traditional mode of life. That they would have never sold out future generations is a refrain throughout the book.

It is also clear that the extensions of treaties to the far Northwest were motivated solely by the realization that there were valuable raw materials there. For years, area missionaries had petitioned for relief of a population dislocated by the incursion of prospectors, decimated by epidemics, and starved by the disruption of game. Then, suddenly, Ottawa was in a great rush to bring them under treaty.

This pattern of neglecting native people until something valuable was sighted under them continues to the present as the McCullums show. Unfortunately, their indignation and Manicheanism are so overwhelming that they devote most of their book to blundgeoning the reader. Fumoleau attempts to understand what happened, but the McCullums substitute anathema for analysis.

Dosman, who is the only one of these authors who is a professional social scientist, manages to be as atheoretical as the others. Since he proceeds as if no one had ever studied a policy decision before, one is left with no indication whether what he describes is typical of Canadian government, of liberal democracies, of governments in general, or if this is an exceptional case.

He shows that a commitment to build a McKenzie Valley pipeline preceded and outlived each rationale offered for it. Even when the rationale shifted from great reserves that needed to be exported to the famous shortage of 1974, no one in the Canadian government found it necessary to undertake independent research—to assess oil reserves, or anything else. Similarly, those affected by the pipeline were never consulted. To have done so would have limited the freedom to maneuver. The complete inability of both the Trudeau and Nixon governments to consider long-term interests, or to formulate any policy prior to a crisis is rather astounding. Even anticipating crises seems to have been beyond the capacity of the two governments.

While providing a clear, readable account of the confused politics of Northern development, Dosman obscures the bases for his judgments. Although he writes as if he knows what the policy for equitable development of the North is and what premises policy-making should be judged by, he leaves it to the reader to infer them. The flow of his journalistic prose is unimpeded by any discussions of methodology or comparability.

There is a great deal of information in these books, even if there are no generalizations or comparisons. Fumoleau's book is particularly valuable, an eloquent and definitive account of how treaties were imposed. Looking at Ottawa, Dosman's comic view seems appropriate. But Fumoleau shows the pattern of development to be tragic when it is viewed from the exploited colony itself. Since such tragedies are consequences of the comedy of errors, perhaps the McCullums' view of the buffoons as sinister is just after all.

Adolescent Prejudice, by CHARLES Y. GLOCK, ROBERT WUTHNOW, JANE ALLYN PILIAVIN, and METTA SPENCER. New York: Harper & Row, 1975. 229 pp. $12.50 cloth. $5.95 paper.

JANE R. MERCER
University of California, Riverside

Adolescent Prejudice reports findings from a study of antisemitism based on information from a questionnaire administered to eighth-, tenth-, and twelfth-grade students enrolled in 1963 in the public schools of three communities located within 200 miles of New York. Since one aim of the study was to investigate the effects of a Jewish presence on antisemitism, the selected communities varied in Jewish student population from 43% in Commutertown, to 23% in Oceanville, to .5% in Central City. The black population in all communities ranged from 14% to 16%.

Using a series of contingency table analyses, the authors concluded that there was a large amount of antisemitism expressed by non-Jewish teenagers. Contrary to the authors' expectations, the larger the Jewish presence the higher the scores of non-Jewish students on the antisemitism scale. They conclude that academic deprivation is more highly associated with prejudice than socioeconomic deprivation and that this relationship cannot be explained either by the frustration-aggression theory or the theory that the prejudiced are less socialized to "enlightened values." Instead, they argue that antisemitism results from cognitive inadequacies. Chapter 4, the most interesting analysis in the report, explores the possibility that there is some "truth" content in the perception of non-Jewish students that Jewish students are "clannish."

The study has several serious weaknesses which cast doubt on many of the conclusions reached by the authors. First, the data were collected before the civil rights movement of the 1960s, and it is impossible to estimate the extent to which the findings are still valid. More important, some of the conclusions reached by the authors do not appear to reflect the findings reported in the tables.

The authors operationalize stereotyping by presenting students with thirteen negative, five positive, and two essentially neutral statements about "Jewish teenagers" and "Jews in general." The student must respond using categories ranging from strongly agree to strongly disagree. There is no neutral category which can be used by the student who "doesn't know" or feels that rating the "selfishness," "bossiness," or "friendliness" of a group consisting of several million persons is nonsense. The authors do not look at the pattern of responses but treat each response as a separate stereotype, reporting the percentage of persons in each school who "agree" at any level with the statement. The non-Jewish white and black students ranked Jewish teenagers highest on three of the five positive characteristics: intelligence, school spirit, and ambition. Given the negative bias of the list, it is difficult to perceive how non-Jewish students could accord a more unequivocably positive ranking to Jewish teenagers, yet, the authors choose to ignore these positive results and concentrate entirely on the extent to which non-Jewish teenagers acquiesced in a forced choice situation by agreeing with the negative adjectives on the list. The authors conclude, "The sheer amount of hostility white non-Jewish teenagers express against Jews seems surprisingly large" (p. 11).

Fortunately, the authors asked Jewish as well as non-Jewish students to respond to the questions on Jews. By combining data presented in Tables 3, 6, and 63, it is possible to compare the percentage of students of each group which "agreed" with each statement. Even this simple analysis reveals remarkable similarity in the rankings given Jews by non-Jewish and Jewish teenagers. Spearman rank order correlations between Jewish ratings of Jewish teenagers and non-Jewish ratings were .703 and .784 in the two communities with sufficient Jewish students for analysis. Correlations between Jewish and black students were even higher, .788 and .901. Correlations between black and non-Jewish ranking were .864 and .830. All correlations are significant beyond the .001 level.

The students in Central City (.5 percent Jewish), who had relatively little contact with Jewish students and, presumably, were operating from hearsay, rated Jewish teenagers highest on *all five* of the five positive characteristics. The stereotype based on hearsay appears to be more favorable than the one based on knowledge, indicating that traditional stereotypes may be fading. Their data do not present a picture of "rampant bigotry" but correspond with findings from other studies which seem to indicate reduced teenage prejudice.

The measure of "prejudice" in the study, called the "antisemitism" scale, also accentuates the negative. It is based on responses to eight of the negative statements selected after a factor analysis. Apparently, the five positive descriptors did not load in any systematic way with the negative statements, indicating that students were making multidimensional judgments which included both positive and negative elements. There were probably at least three types of students: (1) those who are generally negative, (2) those generally positive, and (3) those with mixed perceptions. A scoring scheme based on the average ratings given eight negative descriptors might adequately describe the first two types of students but would grossly distort the "mixed" group since only their negative responses would be scored and they would, thus, be classified as "antisemitic." Another quirk in the scoring also probably inflated the amount of "antisemitism." A student who refused to be coerced into a forced choice response and marked *between* the two middle categories on any item was given a score of "4" for that item. A student who marked all eight items *between* the middle categories would end up with an average score of "4" and be classified as antisemitic!

The measurement of prejudice should go well beyond ascertaining the positive and negative images of the respondent. It should involve measuring the extent to which a judgment is made before the facts are known or is held in disregard of the facts. The antisemitism scale of Glock et al. is a great oversimplification of the actual attitudes of the adolescents in the study. It focuses entirely on negative images. It does not allow for the fact that perceptions may be favorable, unfavorable, or some mixture of favorable and unfavorable. Except for the analysis of "clannishness," the analysis does not examine the possibility that some of the descriptors may be based, at least in part, on the actual observed behavior of the Jewish students as experienced by non-Jewish students. The problem of disentangling fact from fantasy is, of course, the most troublesome methodological problem in the study of prejudice. Yet, it is a problem to which social scientists must address themselves if they are to add to the store of knowledge rather than perpetuate myths about group prejudices. Unless we can separate opinions held in spite of the facts from opinions held with due regard for the facts, we cannot talk in any meaningful way about "prejudgments." Attention to the problem is long overdue in the study of "prejudice."

Domestic Slavery in West Africa: With Particular Reference to the Sierra Leone Protectorate, 1896–1927, by JOHN GRACE. New York: Barnes & Noble, 1975. 294 pp. $23.50 cloth.

EDWARD REYNOLDS
University of California, San Diego

The content of this book is more accurately described by its sub-title than by its title. The general discussion of domestic slavery in Sierra Leone is preceded by a useful and competent discussion of domestic slavery in West Africa in the nineteenth century. Conditions under which slaves lived in West Africa were shaped by local considerations which varied from place to place. Slavery in the West African context is defined as ownership of some other person whose labor had economic value and whose person had commercial value. Slaves were also used for military, social and political prestige, and power. Although the initial reaction of administrators and missionaries to the institution of slavery was one of disgust and horror, they often came to the quick realization that it was difficult to abolish. Slavery as an economic institution was closely related to social and political considerations, and the inability of British authorities to isolate economic from social and political considerations led to confusion and contradictions in how to handle domestic slavery. These confusions and contradictions manifested themselves in Sierra Leone, where the slave trade was not abolished until 1928.

The introduction of legitimate trade in the nineteenth century may have encouraged the continuation of domestic slavery, but in the twentieth century in Sierra Leone it weakened the institution. It was only after the consolidation of British influence in the interior of Sierra Leone that Great Britain decided to face up to the issue of slavery. Before Great Britain could abolish the institution, it had to reshape social, economic, and political life in ways acceptable to the British conception of civilization and justice. This may explain Britain's cautious attitudes toward the institution and why it survived so long. British presence weakened the whole traditional system of economic and social organization, especially the ties which bound the slaves to the masters. Rapid development of urban centers offered the slave an alternative to a life of toil at subsistence level.

In Sierra Leone the existence of domestic slavery was used by two opposing schools of thought to justify their views. While abolitionists favored radical action to free domestic slaves, conservationists argued that the existence of domestic slavery showed how different Sierra Leone society was from British society and that it was wrong to interfere unnecessarily with the internal affairs of that nation.

Professor Grace's work is a useful study of the institution of slavery and the period 1826–1927 in Sierra Leone, but it does not go far enough. Although he has exploited contemporary accounts from former slaves and chiefs he has not made use of oral traditions. He claims that because of lack of time and money he was unable to gather much oral evidence in Sierra Leone. Given the social and economic nature of the subject, and the fact that participants of the institution would probably have been available to give accounts of the institution, it is unfortunate that it was published before he could gather this kind of information which would have given his study depth and further insights about domestic slavery in Sierra Leone.

Black Church in the Sixties, by HART M. NELSEN and ANNE KUSENER NELSEN. Lexington: University Press of Kentucky, 1975. 172 pp. $11.50 cloth.

DAVID O. MOBERG
Marquette University

This study was made primarily to determine whether Black religion in the USA is basically an otherworldly opiate which dampens civil rights militancy, or a temporal inspiration of militancy. The primary empirical sources are thirty data sets, including AIPO surveys from 1954 through 1969, Lenski's 1958 Detroit Area Study of religious participation, the 1963–64 Public Images of Mental Health Services Study in New York City, Gary Marx's 1964 research on Black political attitudes, and 1970–71 data on the Black church as a politicizing agency in Bowling Green, Kentucky. Multiple Classification Analysis is the basic data handling technique, alongside other types of statistical analysis, especially tests of the significance of observed differences. The precise techniques, rationale, and basis for selecting the various measures are specified carefully.

The debunking motif of sociology is evident here in its best form. Many ideas based upon the past and present armchair logic of theoretically or religiously biased sociologists are refuted by the carefully developed findings. This book thus is a valuable exposition of mistakes that are made when sociologists adopt a particular value perspective on the basis of a priori judgments.

Because of its basic theme, considerable attention is given to Gary T. Marx's *Protest and Prejudice*. Reanalysis of Marx's data using better controls for intervening variables along with other evidence reveals that the Black church generally has had a positive orientation toward militancy, that sectarianism apparently explains the inverse relationship of orthodox beliefs to militancy, that sectarianism is decreasing as educational levels of Blacks rise, and that orthodoxy is positively correlated with involvement in the religious organization.

The findings show that the assimilationist model of the Black church does not appear to be a valid interpretation, in spite of the general sociological bias favoring it. The compensatory model which views religious behavior and participation as compensation for deprivations, hence an opiate in regard to civil rights militancy, may be a transitional model in the church's overall life cycle. The data give greatest support to the ethnic community model which makes the Black church a prophetic instrument for social change and links Black religion with protest. The otherworldly aspects of religion are used as a basis for this-worldly social change.

Comparisons identify many contrasts and similarities to white Christians, especially Protestants. For example, in the late 1960s white Christianity (rather "churchianity"!) was declining, while there was little change or even increasing strength in the Black church. Blacks were much more likely to desire a vigorous role for their church as an instrument issuing pronouncements about civil rights and other social issues. When such factors as education, region, place of residence, age, and occupation were controlled, many differences expected from popular stereotypes of sociologists were conspicuous only by their absence.

Extensive references to other studies make this an excellent survey of literature on race, religion, and social change. It concisely summarizes the main ideas of a large number of studies. More than half of the book is devoted to explicit analyses of data; it does not constitute easy reading, but persons accustomed to statistical research will find it clear and concise.

The defects are minor. The authors do not recognize sufficiently how the monthly variations in church attendance affect time series based upon irregular samples. Each statistical table has its own footnote designations to indicate the level of significance. Items which comprise the scales and indexes ought to be in the text instead of non-indexed footnotes at the end of the book.

This is an indispensible resource for all who work in the area of race and minorities as well as in sociology of religion. It affirms the multifaceted nature of Black religion and its positive role in stimulating social change.

System and Unsystem: An Ethnic View of Organization and Society, by JOSEPH RAFFAELE. New York: John Wiley & Sons, 1974. 458 pp. $11.95 cloth. $6.95 paper.

A. BARRETT FIELDS
University of California, Santa Cruz

On the jacket of this publication the reader is informed that *System and Unsystem* is an unconventional, "ethnically oriented" view of the management and manipulation which lies at the core of dehumanization in American Society. Viewing social organization as the interrelationship between big government, big business, and big universities, the author sees dehumanization resulting from the mis-management of society. Accordingly, the management of society is not guided by a knowledge of the "actual life-experiences" of people but by the abstractions of an "intellectual elite." Decisions made by a "managerial elite," therefore, are said to impose costs upon those whose counsel is not represented in the decision making process, and which thereby deny people freedom of preference and a sense of community. As a result, the constraints which "formally" held together diverse elements of a "culturally plural" America are said to be deteriorating as cultural groups search for sources of power with which to preserve their identities and managerial elites seek to impose their values on these groups. It is this "strife" between the "traditional values" of cultural groups and the "organizational imperatives" of managing elites which is characterized by the terms System and Unsystem.

Hence, a major problem which is addressed by the author is the use and mis-use of power. Those who wield power in the System do not represent the values or preferences of those in the Unsystem. The author's central concern, then, appears to be: (1) to document the mis-management of society and the manipulative nature of those in the System; (2) to critically assess different solutions to the problems; and (3) to suggest, as a viable solution, ways in which different values and preferences can be asserted in a "civilized fashion."

The organization of the book is consistent with the author's desire to present each chapter as a "self-contained unit." It is his argument that each chapter adds to the development of his central themes but this argument is not substantiated by an actual reading of the book. Chapters and topics are introduced in a random fashion and seem to have no significance for the stated concerns of the author. For example, it is not clear how a "Mafia theory" of economics fits with the more general concerns of "power," mis-management, cultural values and preferences. Moreover, do we really need a complete chapter on "Unions and Labor Relations" to understand how negotiations can operate to reduce conflict in the larger society? I think not. And I don't believe that the author would have felt a need to include this chapter had he done a more extensive review of the literature in the area. Indeed, had this been a part of his methodology, it is possible that the many dubious assumptions and statements which he makes throughout the book would not appear so prominent. Moreover, with respect to the materials that he does use, the author sees no inconsistency in his attack upon the "Eastern News Establishment" as the propaganda tool of the System and his heavy reliance on The New York *Times* to document his many statements and assumptions.

The book adds no new knowledge to the literature on social organization and processes in American society. Even though it is directed toward the general public and not the intellectual community, the use of such terms as System and Unsystem are merely different ways of characterizing the age-old conflict between the "haves" and "have-nots." The book develops no new theses on the subject and in fact those which are presented appear somewhat "off-base." They are off base, I believe, because the author has allowed his own social policy concerns to get in the way of a truly "scientific assessment." In his desire to influence policy choices, the author seems to ignore the "hard" data. Thus the only redeeming quality of the book is in the lesson which can be drawn from it: If social scientists are to play a significant role in creating public policy, they must remain true to the canons of their science. Unfortunately, Professor Raffaele appears to have forgotten this lesson.

Psychological Testing of American Minorities: Issues and Consequences, by RONALD J. SAMUDA. New York: Dodd, Mead & Company, 1975. 211 pp. $6.95 paper.

CARL C. JORGENSEN
University of California, Davis

Certain Greek and Roman scholars thought Britons to be very dumb, as did some Moorish writers of the eleventh century. In the early part of this century a group of American psychologists returned the favor by using newly developed IQ tests to disparage the intelligence of southern Europeans. Over the past few decades, it is the mental abilities of Black Americans and the accuracy of research measuring those abilities which have been the subject of debate. Samuda's book (judging from the references,) summarizes this debate up to 1972/73. The book covers the controversy over racial bias in the construction and use of IQ tests, including court cases, hereditary and environmental effects on test performance, the educational and social consequences of the uses of the tests, and alternatives to traditional standardized tests. As is the practice these days, the book title promises more coverage than it delivers. The book's focus is the *ability* testing of *Black Americans*. Other minorities and other forms of psychological testing are hardly mentioned. The relationship between IQ scores and academic performance is described in detail; the much more tenuous relationship between scores and occupational performance is covered sparingly.

For the issues which are discussed, coverage is broad and representative. Samuda favors a "balanced" presentation, detailing pro and con arguments on each dispute, sometimes evaluating the arguments and sometimes not. Ideas are presented clearly, concisely, and accurately. The book is a pleasure to read.

There are problems. Much has happened since 1972/73. First, there have been extensive critiques of "victim-blaming" ideologies in social science research, such as Staples's *Black Sociology;* Ladner's *Death of White Sociology;* or Ryan's *Blaming the Victim.* Although Samuda is conscientious and thorough in his critique of social bias in ability testing, he extensively quotes cultural deprivationist literature without comment. Additionally, and even more importantly, the work of Sir Cyril Burt, a major basis for the assumption of the high inheritance of IQ by Jensen, Herrnstein, and others, has been thoroughly discredited by Kamin's *The Science and Politics of IQ.*

Burt's work is no longer taken seriously. Jensen has been shown to repeatedly misreport the findings of others, making his research surveys unreliable. Much of the other work in this area is under attack (cf., Block and Dworkin, *The IQ Controversy*). This makes Samuda's discussion of the inheritance of IQ erroneous and obsolete, along with that of almost all other psychological texts of the period.

Samuda's book provides the reader with a thorough coverage of the traditional debate on race and IQ testing, but it *must* be read in conjunction with recent writings on racism in traditional social science and past errors in the study of the inheritance of intelligence. To the student of race relations, analysis of the possible personal, cultural, and institutional deficiencies which have led some majority scholars to perpetuate racist ignorance in the name of science is at least as important an area of inquiry as the study of possible minority deficiencies in IQ.

A Survey of Puerto Ricans on the U.S. Mainland in the 1970s, by KAL WAGENHEIM. New York: Praeger Publishers, 1975. 133 pp. $13.50 cloth.

DAVID JESS LEÓN
University of California, Berkeley

Puerto Ricans on the US mainland remain a neglected and often misunderstood group, locked into an economic treadmill almost beyond their comprehension and control. Scholar-journalist Kal Wagenheim, in his recent and informative study of this minority, presents a clear and compellingly documented demographic picture of their grim situation.

Puerto Ricans inhabit all fifty states, though most live in New York. They form a young population, with a median age of 17.9 years, about ten years younger than the median age of Americans. This statistic indicates a high birthrate and large families: the Puerto Rican family has on the average 3.8 members, while the average US family has 3.5.

Migration is a key factor in the increase of the Puerto Rican population on the US mainland, a phenomenon which, incidentally, coincided with the growth of jet travel. Hence, the community shows a wide variation in the degree of assimilation among its members: from visitors who stay for a few days, through new migrants, US-born Puerto Ricans, to US-born Puerto Ricans married to members of other racial and ethnic groups. The Puerto Rican population on the mainland has grown rapidly, increasing 61% from 1960 to 1970. If this rate holds through the next ten years, mainland Puerto Ricans will number at least 2.3 million by 1980, approximating the island's 1970 population; thus, sometime in the 1980s, mainland Puerto Ricans would exceed insular ones, creating an odd political irony.

The author uses several SES indicators to illuminate the plight of Puerto Ricans on the mainland: lack of education, jobs, property, and low family income, to name a few.

Educational attainment of Puerto Ricans is lower than that of whites, blacks, or other Spanish-speaking groups in the US. The average Puerto Rican attends school for 8.6 years, much as the average white US citizen did in 1940. However, US-born Puerto Ricans appear to be achieving higher educational levels than their parents. For example, the migrants completed a median 8.0 school years in 1960, their children 10.8. By 1970, migrant figure had risen to 8.4, while US-born children achieved a median of 11.5 school years, an attainment just below that of all Americans (12.1 years) and higher than "Negro and other Races" (10.0 years). However, Wagenheim cautions the reader against over-emphasizing these figures, because "the adult migrant is far more representative of the community." Moreover, high dropout rates and tracking to vocational high schools still plague both groups. In either case, Puerto Ricans are assured an underrepresentation in institutions of higher education, and ultimately in the professions.

With low educational achievement, Puerto Ricans are doomed to unemployment and/or low level occupations. According to official March 1972 figures, they have one of the highest unemployment rates of all ethnic or racial groups in the US. While 6% of all US males went jobless in 1972, 8.8% of Puerto Rican men did. Among women, 6.6% overall sought work, while 17.6% of Puerto Rican women were unemployed. However, the author questions the "official" unemployment rate and adjusts it to "reflect a more realistic picture of Puerto Rican unemployment." He fixes the level at 18.7% for Puerto Rican men and 56.4% for Puerto Rican women. He concludes that about one out of every three working age Puerto Ricans in the US is without a job.

Puerto Ricans who manage to stay employed are concentrated in lower-level white-collar and mostly blue-collar and service-related occupations. Because of such jobs, the average Puerto Rican receives one of the lowest family incomes of any of the racial or ethnic groups. In 1971, median family income for Puerto Ricans was $6,185, compared to $10,672 for whites, $6,440 for blacks, and $7,548 for all Spanish-speaking people. Linked with occupation and family income is the ownership of property. Because Puerto Ricans earn less income, they can buy less property. Only 14.8% of Puerto Ricans own their own dwellings, compared to 59.1% of all Americans.

Although national statistics paint a dismal picture of Puerto Ricans on the mainland, the author uses several chapters to illuminate the situation of Puerto Ricans in specific regions. He states: "On the average Puerto Ricans living in large, urban cities often conform to the nationwide figures showing high unemployment, poverty, and low levels of education. However, a city-by-city analysis reveals small pockets of Puerto Ricans who are exceptions to the stereotypes and reveals that the population is not necessarily homogeneous."

In any case, the author argues that the Puerto Ricans' struggle for survival looks grim. Economic inequality exists in the United States, and Puerto Ricans, along with other downtrodden groups, bear the burden of it, day-by-day. He concludes that, unless the federal government delivers a guaranteed family income plan, in addition to improvements in education and job-training facilities, the future of Puerto Ricans will remain grim. This reformist approach seems inadequate to the complex, macro-level problem that creates racial and ethnic inequalities. Corporate capitalism, a sort of internalized colonialism, feeds on such relatively powerless groups as Puerto Ricans; without them, corporate capitalism could not exist. In such a situation, the reformist solution resembles an attempt to douse a fire by re-arranging the kindling.

Nevertheless, Wagenheim has provided a great service to all concerned citizens with the publication of this book. He has compiled a vast array of statistical information about a heretofore "invisible" minority group, and presented it in an easy-to-read book with numerous tables. It deserves our attention.

Oreo: A Perspective on Race and Marginal Men and Women, by CHARLES V. WILLIE. Wakefield, Mass.: Parameter Press, 1975. 95 pp. $3.95 paper.

JAMES H. LAUE
University of Missouri, St. Louis

Charles Willie is a black, interracially-married, Christian sociologist. At the 1969 Episcopal Church conference he was the object of a sign declaring: *"Dr. Willie is an Oreo cookie."*

Oreo is a short, personal, and highly readable account of Willie's efforts to deal with his own marginality, and his attempt to develop a sociological understanding of marginality. His "thesis" is that racially marginal people are "most likely to help our pluralistic society survive" (p. 25). "Identity" is the other central concept; it emerges "from knowing and being known" (p. 26). The racially-marginal person, argues Willie, is in a unique position to unite races and classes. "Unity is not enough . . . marginality . . . is an essential component in a healthy human society" (p. 40). Robert Park is cited: the marginal person has "the wider horizon, the keener intelligence, the more detached and rational viewpoint." "The marginal man is always relatively the more civilized human being" (p. 41).

Crucial to the impact of *Oreo* is Willie's understanding of the racial context in the United States. He does not take the easy out of couching his discussion of marginality in communications or encounteresque ideology. Rather the argument occurs in the realistic context of white racism and its resulting counterpart—black separatism seeking power for self-determination.

The essay is in many ways paradoxical: excellent writing juxtaposed with awkward writing and editing; sophistication together with naiveté, the sociological with the trans-sociological. At various points in reading *Oreo,* I wondered whether it was appropriate for review in a publication for sociologists. I inevitably answered yes, for Willie offers the range, erudition, and insights sorely needed by students of race, power, identity, and alienation. Moses, Martin Buber, and Martin Luther King, Jr., are his marginal heroes; he also moves among Tillich, Parsons, Merton, Pettigrew, Moynihan, Arthur Jensen, Jane Jacobs, and Richard Wright.

The audience for this unfortunately overpriced book should include students of race and change, of identity-development, of reconciliation and justice. Disciplined adult study groups should find it very useful.

Despite its shortcomings, *Oreo* leaves me wanting much more because I believe Willie is on to something important. I found it to be a provocative preamble to a serious study of the positive functions of marginality. I hope Willie will one day give us that study.

Religion

The Catholic Cult of the Paraclete, by JOSEPH H. FICHTER. New York: Sheed and Ward, 1975. 183 pp. $6.95 cloth.

MARION DEARMAN
California State University, Los Angeles

Despite the curious title, Father Fichter's book is not concerned with anything more arcane or occult than Catholic pentecostalism. The Paraclete is a fancy word for the Holy Spirit, the third person of the Trinity, from whom all charisms flow; the cult is the group (now loosely but becoming more tightly organized) which believes in and practices the charisms: glossolalia, prophecy, faith healing, and the like.

Unlike Protestant pentecostals who date from around 1900 and are mostly lower class, the cult had its beginnings with predominantly middle-class, university-educated Catholics around the universities of Duquesne, Notre Dame, and Michigan. But the Paraclete cult has been strongly influenced by Protestant pentecostals like David Wilkerson (*The Cross and the Switchblade*) and John Sherrill (*They Speak with Other Tongues*) whose books, according to Fichter, are "must" reading for cult members. Like their Protestant counterparts, too, they read the Bible—especially the New Testament, sing, and loudly "praise the Lord" in their services, emphasize love for each other, and practice the charisms. Also like other pentecostals, they oppose social activism and teach female members to submit to male authority, even though they far outnumber males in the group's membership.

The cult began as a lay movement; but it quickly drew the attention of the clergy (priests, brothers, sisters). Two years after the movement came into being "the formal bureaucracy began with the formation of a Service Committee of two priests and five laymen." Later in the same year, "an Advisory Committee was formed . . .; its membership comprised thirteen priests, ten laymen, two sisters, and one brother." Contact persons used by Fichter to choose his informants and distribute questionnaires included fifty-seven priests, twenty-seven sisters, and eleven brothers: ninety-five clergy, but only sixty-six lay persons. Since these contact persons apparently were group leaders, one is forced to conclude that a substantial percentage of the cult's leadership is composed of clergy; but Fichter insists it is a lay movement.

The 375 men and 369 women chosen by the contact persons as informants probably are not representative of the cult's membership. Because of this selection process, Fichter admits that his questionnaires probably reached the "more active and dedicated" and "relatively few of the rank-and-file membership." Hence, the data produced may well not be descriptive of the majority of the cult members.

What is more intriguing and useful than the answers Fichter's informants gave to the survey questions are the Church's and the cult's reactions to each other. Thus far, Catholic pentecostals have not demonstrated strong separatist tendencies. The cult members state their aim is that of "building a new society in the shell of the old," an apparently innocuous goal. However, there is evidence in Fichter's study that this may change. For example, sixty percent of the cult's newcomers say they would continue to hold their prayer meetings even if the bishop prohibited it. Cultists, like Protestant pentecostals, not only read the Bible, but interpret it for themselves; they also prophesy, and feel they have direct contact with God without the intercession of a priest. Many complain about being ministered to by priests who are not "spirit filled" (a latter-day Donatist heresy?).

Many Church leaders are worried and anxious about the cult. Archbishop Dwyer, for example, has this to say: "we regard it as one of the most dangerous trends in the Church in our time, closely allied in spirit with other disruptive and divisive movements; threatening grave harm to her unity and damage to countless souls." Some clergy and laity mistrust the cult because they believe it attracts the kookier elements; prelates understandably fear it because it operates outside the canonical, ecclesiastical, and educational structures of the Church.

If some are fearful of the schismatic possibilities inherent in the cult, others are cautiously optimistic. These hope the cult will lose its identity by becoming absorbed into a charismatically renewed Church. The Church itself seems to be moving discreetly toward absorption or cooptation by allowing (even encouraging?) priests, sisters, and brothers to join the cult. Whether or not they will succeed and what will happen if they don't remains an open question. Father Fichter has written a small but important book about an important subject—one which may assume increasing importance in the coming years.

Religion in Changing Japanese Society, by KIYOMI MORIOKA. Tokyo: University of Tokyo Press, 1975. 231 pp. $17.50 cloth.

DAVID W. PLATH
Konan-Illinois Center, Kobe, Japan

Japan offers a series of enigmas to the sociologist of religion. First, one learns that less than half of the people will admit to holding any religious beliefs at all. Next, when one looks into Japanese houses one finds in most of them a Shinto altar, often a Buddhist altar, and sometimes other religious objects as well. Then, when one adds up the membership rosters of religious organizations one arrives at a figure one-and-a-half to two times that of the total population.

So even if one discounts liberally for inflated membership claims one has to admit that the average Japanese somehow or other is involved in more than one kind of religious activity. And at that point one may well begin to wonder: can the usual Western styles of inquiry, which approach religion via values or via institutions, yield more than a limited understanding of Japan, perhaps at best a warped one?

Sociologists in Japan have struggled with these enigmas since the beginning of this century. But if the sociology of religion has almost as long a history in Japan as in the West, its results remain sealed off in a language read by only a small squadron of colleagues overseas. This collection of essays by Professor Morioka provides the English-reading religious sociologist with a window into the work of one of Japan's leading practitioners in the craft. And as a bonus it includes a twenty-five-page bibliography of sociological studies of Japanese religion.

In a chapter on the history of the subject Morioka points out that the sociology of religion in Japan was, in its early decades, chiefly an exercise in writing commentaries on Durkheim, Weber, and Simmel. But with Morioka and his generation, the Japanese have begun to test Western concepts directly against local conditions via field studies. They are beginning to suggest, gently, almost deferentially, that perhaps the concepts might benefit by being recalled for corrective overhaul. Or that at the very least, new paradigms are needed in order to unravel the enigmas of religious action in Japan.

Morioka's own approach is—to give it a label—a sort of ecology of religious behavior. He scans the social environment for locations (niches?) where religious actions take place. He then looks for independent variables—family role, temple affiliation, occupation, etc. —which may account for such actions. For example, whether or not one "is" a Buddhist will predict very little as to whether or not one has a Buddhist altar in the house. What matters most is one's stage in the family cycle. Few neo-marital families will have such an altar. But once there has been a death in the family (typically a death in the parental generation) there will almost always be one, even in many Christian households.

Morioka's main research technique is to follow persons through a change in social position: from role to role, from farm to city, from center city to suburb. By pinpointing changes in religious behavior that accompany changes in social position he is able to highlight the locational or contextual nature of much of Japanese religious activity. His research style is appropriately micro-social. Most chapters are built around field studies in small communities carefully selected to emphasize one or another type of positional change.

Though he uses a different vocabulary, Morioka's view of Japanese society seems consonant with that being articulated in recent years by a number of other Japanese scholars —the key concept being one of "social nexus" or "frame." The concept remains loosely defined, but it represents an attempt to break away from standard definitions of group or of institution.

The view further suggests that venerable Western notions of social class may not explain very much about Japan. For example, in Morioka's chapter on nineteenth century Japanese Christian converts he notes that the majority were of bourgeois origins. That, he says, might seem to argue for a Weberian elective affinity between Christianity and the Japanese middle class, but the case is weak. Only a tiny fraction of the bourgeoisie ever converted. And furthermore the chief opposition to Christianity in Japan has been sustained and mobilized by others in this same class.

Morioka's approach needs to be made more precise, and I see in it, the potential for a new analytic explanation of Shinto. Protean in its manifestations, Shinto has been almost impossible to explain as a set of religious beliefs or institutions, even though one can find statable beliefs and tangible institutions in it. In practice, too, no one yet has been successful in packaging Shinto for export and transplanting it overseas. It appears to be inextricably bound into local behavior niches. In the second instance, with further generalizing, the Morioka approach may prove valuable in the study of non-doctrinaire religions elsewhere.

Readers will have to exert themselves to piece together the approach from these essays. Although it threads through every chapter, Morioka never explicates it for more than a few paragraphs in any one place. But because of its latent approach, and the challenge it offers to Western traditions of religious sociology, this book will, I hope, be read widely and carefully. I am more and more dismayed by that new brand of intellectual imperialism that calls itself comparative research, and that treats the work of overseas colleagues as mere "data" to be mined for the support of one's pet hypothesis.

Religion and Political Modernization, edited by DONALD EUGENE SMITH. New Haven, Conn.: Yale University Press, 1974. 340 pp. $15.00 cloth.

THOMAS C. BRUNEAU
McGill University

Religion and Political Modernization is a collection of sixteen essays prepared for a conference held in March of 1971. By the time of publication in 1974 most of the authors had already published articles or books on similar topics and it is unlikely that the reader will find anything new here. The book is useful, however, in that it brings together a representative sample of studies on a broad range of topics by recognized scholars and might profitably be assigned in courses. While the footnotes are reasonably informative the value of the book could easily have been increased by the addition of an annotated bibliography.

The title is indicative of the general theme and is thus in line with contemporary trends in Political Science and Sociology. Religion as a phenomenon or concept is discussed on only a few pages of Smith's introduction and suffice it to say that the theme concerns the role of the four major religious systems—Buddhism, Catholicism, Hinduism, and Islam. Modernization is approached in terms of secularization, mass politicization, and the expansion of developmental capacity. The application of the concepts to the studies signifies that the essays are divided into three groups: those relating to secularization, those concerned with religion and mass politicization, and those treating the role of religion in political change. In short, the essays deal with religion and change, either as dependent or independent variables, in selected countries of the Third World. There is no integrative framework for analysis and indeed this is to be anticipated from the proceedings of a conference. What we have, then, is an introductory statement of terms and summary of findings followed by fifteen monographs or minimonographs. In this manner there is a good deal of information conveyed but no general conclusion, let alone conceptual breakthrough.

The quality of the essays seems to vary according to the level of generalization. The more interesting and insightful are the most specific. Of special mention are the following six. Daniel Crecelius provides a fascinating analysis of Islam and the state, past and present, in Egypt. He concludes that Islam has never been independently "powerful" in Egypt but does remain important even today due to the purposes of the state. Norman Zucker describes the role of Judaism in Israel and provides a good deal of information on a topic that cannot readily be integrated into the stated theme of the book. Heinz Bechert offers a solid and scholarly analysis of the role of Buddhism in Burma and Ceylon showing how it is potentially supportive of modernization. Gail Minault's study of the Indian Ulama and the Khilafat Movement is very well-researched and interesting but deserves far more space than it receives here. Also on India is the essay by Miriam and Jagdish Sharma on the Sarvodaya movement which demonstrates how Hinduism can be reinterpreted to promote social change. George Grayson's essay on the Catholic Church in Peru analyzes the evolution of the role of the Church from support of the status quo to the promotion of social change.

At the intermediate level of both generality and, in my view, utility are the essays by Razlur Rahman and Thomas G. Sanders. Rahman attempts to analyze Islamic Socialism but becomes too abstract in that he treats only intellectual themes. Sanders's essay is in fact quite good for what he attempts to do in treating all of Latin America during the past fifteen years and in highlighting the most important themes of change in the Church. His greatest strength is found in his specific treatment of the Chilean model and the emergence of the Catholic Left. His observations are generally accurate even today but covering such a large and hetergeneous continent with so many religious variations poses insurmountable difficulties.

The essay by Harry Kantor on Catholic Parties in Latin America suffers for taking on too much and lacking a specific focus. He gives a general description of Latin American Catholicism which is already covered by Smith and Sanders and consequently deals too briefly with the parties themselves. One of his themes is the pervasive anti-clericalism in the continent but as this is a very controversial topic and as he offers no new evidence the treatment is unconvincing. Rather than focusing on the parties and attributing their weakness to the anti-clericalism he might reflect back on his own work and explain the weakness of all parties by some other factor. In addition he observes that the Church is slowly being pushed out of the political areas and while this might have seemed the case in 1971 it certainly is not today. My observation concerning the quality in relationship to level of generalization can be applied as well to the two substantive essays by the editor. While Smith's essay on Gandhi offers nothing new beyond what he or others have published it is informative and useful. The same cannot be said for his essay on secularization in Latin America for not only is there no new material but the approach is so formalistic and contrived that what material he does offer becomes very confusing.

In general, then, the essays are useful for the study of religion and politics, they tend to be quite historical and institutional, but there is no integrating analysis. Smith notes on page 24 of the introduction that what evidence there is on the impact of religion on politics is impressionistic. It would seem an opportune time to leave description behind and begin analysis, using various methodologies, to evaluate the impact of religion on politics as well as other aspects of life.

Sectarianism: Analyses of Religious and Non-Religious Sects, edited by ROY WALLIS. New York: Halsted Press, 1975. 212 pp. $13.95 cloth.

HARRY H. HILLER
University of Calgary

The study of religious sectarianism is an old pre-occupation in sociology. What is of more recent interest is the application of sectarian analysis to more secular groups such as those with political and therapeutic goals. Wallis's work is a timely contribution to this discussion and research.

An interesting variety of groups are dealt with, and include the Atherius Society, Hare Krishna, Unified Family (Sun Myung Moon), Jehovah's Witnesses, Scientology, Shakers, Concept House, Internationalists (Maoists), Socialist Labour Party, Recovery, Inc., Neurotics Nomine, and short references to a host of other groups such as the Theosophical Society. In general, no attempt is made to give a comprehensive description or analysis of the groups listed; rather each contributor appears to have randomly chosen a particular aspect of the group for a more fuller discussion.

Because of the diversity of groups discussed with supposedly sectarian characteristics, it would be reasonable to expect an examination of the theoretical applicability of the sectarian motif to both religious and non-religious groups. Unfortunately, this is the weak aspect of the book. Roger O'Toole's chapter on sectarianism in two political groups (Maoists and Labour Socialists) is perhaps the most sociologically and theoretically sensitive as it relates well to the literature on sectarianism and demonstrates an awareness of the issues that are raised by transferring theory on religious sectarianism to other types of sectarianism.

It is relatively easy and quite typical of reviews of edited books to criticize them for not reading like a single-authored manuscript. While I will resist that temptation, I do feel that it is the author's responsibility to do more than just introduce the multi-authored chapters that follow. Granted that contributors frequently do not follow editor's instructions and develop their subject matter in a way that is often at odds with the thrust of the book, it is still the editor's responsibility to plug the holes by attempting to resolve unresolved issues and to raise critical points that emerge from the material presented that relates to the book's theme. For example, is the sectarian interpretive schema equally applicable to religious and non-religious groups? What advantages and limitations are there in doing so? What is the effect of this broadened application of sectarianism to our original theories of religious sectarianism? Wallis's introduction leads us to conclude that there is no sociological difference between religious and non-religious sects. Does he mean for us to draw this conclusion, and indeed is it a correct one? Perhaps a concluding chapter by the editor telling us what we have learned and where this leads us would have put the disparate contributions into some perspective and made it clearer how they relate to established theory. The editor thus leaves it to the reader to assess the significance or value of all of the interesting case studies that are presented (including his own application of Weber's mystogogue in discussing the Atherius Society). While such a practice represents one approach to handling data, it certainly blunts an obviously and potentially greater contribution to sociological theory.

In spite of the fact that the book does not turn the corner with the data that it presents and the questions that it raises, it certainly provides delightful insights (descriptive and analytic) on the groups that are examined. It is pointed out, for example, that the Hare Krishna are more likely to appeal to those who formerly used drugs because drugs have opened up to these persons an awareness of a completely different level of consciousness. Or, Jehovah's Witnesses are discussed in terms of their use of the impersonal transient salesman-customer relationship. Similarly the descriptions of the harassment of Scientology, individualist conversion themes in Maoism, or the sense of group solidarity in therapeutic communities make fascinating reading. Wallis's claim that the book should be of interest to those in social organizations and social movements as well as sociology of religion is certainly supported by the wealth of information that the book presents on a diversity of sect-like groups.

Sex Roles and Behavior

Liberating Women's History: Theoretical and Critical Essays, edited by BERENICE A. CARROLL. Urbana: University of Illinois Press, 1976. 434 pp. $14.95 cloth. $5.95 paper.

MARILYN J. BOXER
San Diego State University

Every reader who ever turned away from history bored with study of the deeds of great men should delve into the new women's history to see what has happened to the discipline in recent years. Reacting to the ethnic and women's liberation movements, influenced by Marx and Mannheim, using models and methods borrowed from social science, historians today are re-examining traditional interpretations, seeking new sources and subjects, and ultimately redefining their field. Historical change and continuity are illumined as never before by research into the domains of private as well as public, personal as well as political, sexual as well as economic life.

Borne into academe on this current of change, women's history, Clio's foundling, has recently been acknowledged as a legitimate child, and now compels attention. Freed from old constraints, historians of women are engaged in the dual task of liberating women from stereotypic definitions and of enlarging our perception of what human experience has been. This collection of twenty-three essays edited by Berenice A. Carroll is too modestly titled. As women and men are inextricably involved in life, so in history; what serves to free women frees men, and the Carroll volume serves the entire historical discipline.

Admirably conceived to demonstrate the theory and practice of women's history and to bring together some important published essays with new papers, this book offers the best single introduction to the field yet available. Essays in theory include Gerda Lerner's influential call in 1969 for development of a "new conceptual framework" for women's history and her recognition (in 1975) that no single method or model can contain the complex historical experience of women who "are and always have been at least half of humanity and most of the time have been the majority of humanity." Striking her as "a staggering flash of insight," this perception of women not as "The Other," as Simone de Beauvoir and centuries of men have told us, but as most of humanity, leads Lerner to conclude that "all history as we now know it, is merely pre-history" to a "truly universal history."

Several essays on historiography explore the extent of sexism in "pre-history" and criticize early attempts at a theory of women's history by Engels and Mary R. Beard. Hilda Smith's provocative article finds a feminist perspective essential to writing women's history. Juliet Mitchell's analysis of women's four social functions is reprinted here, complemented by Sheila Ryan Johansson's redefinition of the concept of women's "class" in terms of a complex "status pattern."

While the shape of Lerner's "universal" history remains to be drawn, its outlines emerge from the editor's selections from recent work in women's history. Covering a wide range of time and space, these are related thematically: essays on "Ideology, Sex, and History" stress traditional attitudes toward women, while those on "Class, Sex, and Social Change" emphasize economic factors. But their message belies the arbitrary classification. For example, Alice Kessler-Harris in her essay on women's work in American industry concludes that "changes in women's participation in the work force must be understood partly as a function of the ideology of the family," derived, she contends, from political economy. Similarly, connections between socio-economic structures and "women's place" are traced by Asunción Lavrin for colonial Mexico, and Renate Bridenthal and Claudia Koonz for Weimar, Germany.

Women's history may, as this anthology promises, direct us toward a more complete "future human past."

The Sex Factor and the Management of Schools, by Neal Gross and Anne E. Trask. New York: John Wiley & Sons, 1976. 279 pp. $16.95 cloth.

Patricia Yancey Martin
Florida State University

Since relatively few females occupy leadership positions, sociologists interested in comparing the organizational experiences of female versus male administrators are generally frustrated. In this respect, Gross and Trask's monograph represents a necessary and well-done first step toward documenting the consequences of gender for organizational functioning. Utilizing data from the National Principalship Study (involving a multi-stage sample survey of principals and teachers in forty-one school systems in cities of 50,000 or more in 1960–61), the authors compare the occupational experiences of ninety-one female and ninety-eight male elementary school principals. Their goal is to explore ways in which "the sex factor may influence the careers of administrators, their role performance, the functioning and productivity of their organizations, and their orientations and responses to their work" (p. 1).

Gross and Trask note the repeated failure of their findings to support typically-quoted reasons for preferring males over females for principalship positions (e.g., "neither women nor men like to work for a woman"; or "female principals are unable to maintain discipline in low socio-economic schools"). While female and male principals are observed to differ in many respects (e.g., females *enjoy* supervision of instruction more than males do; males *enjoy* routine administration more than females do), surprisingly few of these differences are associated with organizational functioning or productivity. And, where they are, a slight advantage is observed for schools headed by female principals.

Among their findings which are least consistent with conventional wisdom are the following: (1) female principals worry *less* about their work than do their male counterparts; (2) teacher morale does *not* vary according to principal gender; (3) teachers in schools with female principals rate themselves and their colleagues higher on "professional performance" (involving such things as "commitment to the job," "interest in improving the educational program of the school," "trying new methods in the classroom," etc.) than do teachers in schools headed by males; and (4) teachers with female principals rate pupils' academic performance higher than do teachers with male principals. The latter finding, furthermore, is *most* pronounced in schools with low socioeconomic pupils.

In assessing the quality of the monograph, one could complain about the age of the data (sixteen years old); the sexist wording of the questionnaire items (all pronouns referring to principals are masculine); or the basically individualistic/reductionistic perspective of the conceptual framework on the question of sexism in general (i.e., no attention is given to institutional sexism or to the concept of power as related to managerial accession or succession, etc.). Such criticisms, however, are minor in relation to the study's overall contribution.

This work is important for educators, for sociologists of organizations and occupations, and for sociologists of gender (including sex-roles, institutional sexism, stratification, etc.). The narrative of the monograph is well-written and easy to read; the methodology and data analysis are sound; and the authors provide an elaborate (if sometimes belabored) theoretical rationale for each hypothesis proposed. In short, Gross and Trask's findings dispel many of the stereotypical justifications for excluding females from organizational leadership positions and thereby highlight the necessity to seek alternative explanations for such exclusion.

Women in Changing Japan, edited by JOYCE LEBRA, JOY PAULSON, and ELIZABETH POWERS. Boulder, Colo.: Westview Press, 1976. 322 pp. $23.75 cloth.

CORNELIA BUTLER FLORA
Kansas State University, Manhattan

In the old days in Japan, there was a temple at Kamakura reserved as a refuge for women whose husbands had been mistreating them. No longer in existence, it can be seen as a symbol of the separate, unequal, but protected status of women in the old Japan. That status was undergirded by Confucian philosophy and a feudalist economic order. In 1975, when the last of the data used in this volume was gathered, capitalism had replaced feudalism, requiring a flexible and subserviant female population for profit, and the Confucian ideal of superior male, inferior female was still very much in evidence.

This is a fascinating book, begging for comparative analysis of the economic and ideological prerequisites for female equality. Two of the three editors are historians, and a welcome historical perspective infuses the book.

It is also a frustrating book because, despite the logical structuring of the chapters on women in various sectors of the economy, with interesting case history illustrations, we have no idea how those cases were selected. And in other instances, some very sweeping conclusions are based on some very small samples. For example, a sample of service workers "not based on any statistical method of selection" (p. 112), and no clue on what it was based, had a total of sixteen respondents. Their occupations varied from self-employed seamstresses and beauticians to a room service woman and two ex-stewardesses. From this small and heterogeneous sample, differences in attitudes by age and economic status are conclusively presented.

One of the most offensive in terms of sampling and use of the data is the chapter on women in the political system, where the author, a political scientist, composes a very detailed fake biography from the lives of eleven of the twelve women she interviewed. The reader is deprived of any sense of the reality of the data by this engagingly written composite fiction. In this case, we don't even know what incidents in this "past" were true of all the women, some of the women, or only one. In writing the composite, were the model life cycle activities reported? The most interesting ones? And when these are linked to opinions, we are even more in the dark. For instance, how many actually said, "Men should become more involved with their families?" (p. 248).

A golden age for Japanese women—before the Chinese influence reached the island, before feudalism took hold, and before patrilocal residence became the rule—is presented in the first chapter "Evolution of the Feminine Ideal." The historical interplay of economic, religious, and political factors over the last thousand years is alluded to in nearly all the ensuing chapters, leading to an admirable amount of continuity in the twelve topical chapters. Organization and methodology are similar in the chapters as well, making the edited volume flow like a self-contained and integrated work, rather than simply a collection of interesting papers about women in Japan. However, there is no index, which limits its usefulness.

There is a basic assumption, seemingly shared by all the authors, that the status of women will not improve until women occupy the same positions men do. Thus the various labor force chapters, covering such areas as agriculture, manufacturing, office work, family businesses, service industries, bar hostesses, teaching, the professions, the media, politics, and sports, stress a biographical approach, showing how the women in the occupations arrived—and the structural and attitudinal blockages they now face once they are in the labor force. A persuasive picture is painted of dual blockages to female occupational equality: (1) a system of tracking which leads women into domestic education, lower wages, subordinate work roles, bifurcated career patterns, and premature retirement, and (2) the dominant ideology, which stresses that those discriminatory practices are as they should be, since a woman's main—perhaps only—purpose in life is to be a good wife and mother. The judicious use of case histories shows how well this ideology has been internalized by most Japanese women in the labor force, except for a few in the male dominated areas of the professions and the media.

This emphasis on economic position means that there was no systematic examination of the largest—and increasing—section of Japanese womanhood, the housewife. Throughout, especially in the unfortunate final chapter on suicide, there is the theme of getting the women out of the home. Given the incredible pressures on males in Japanese society (never really discussed), one wonders at this goal—especially since it seems to be shared by so few of the Japanese women quoted.

The chapter "Women and Suicide," written by a nun who is also a sociologist, shows the problems of this assumption. She has two basic assumptions: suicide is always a bad thing, and being a Japanese housewife keeps one from developing a person-role (which in itself is a difficult concept to deal with, even given the author's definition, when many sociologists—feminists in particular—are questioning the viability of sex role as a concept). It is hypothesized that lack of person-roles leads to high suicide. Even though her data show housewives have the *lowest* suicide rate among Japanese women, she explains that all away with a very moving case history of the group suicide of a housewife and her husband—after her husband had "killed Kyoko Seki, the woman then pregnant with his child." That chapter is rife with problems in sampling, measurement, and terminology—perhaps because these seemed unimportant in light of the author's concern for the plight of the traditional Japanese women.

There is much of interest in this book—and there is much missing. A major question not really examined here is if the type of capitalist development in Japan helps or hinders the status of women. The trends toward the decreasing participation in the labor force and its causes are barely mentioned. Without an ideological commitment toward equality—which should include but not be exclusive to equality between the sexes—will women in changing Japan simply continue to perform the reproductive functions of procreation, household maintenance and consumption, and continuation of culture, as well as providing a cheap and expendable labor force?

The Psychology of Sex Differences, by ELEANOR EMMONS MACCOBY and CAROL NAGY JACKLIN. Stanford, Calif.: Stanford University Press, 1974. 634 pp. $18.95 cloth.

ELIZABETH M. ALMQUIST
North Texas State University

This book leaves little doubt about the thoroughness of its authors, but it does produce uneasiness about the ability of psychological researchers to capture the subtle aspects of interaction between men and women. Maccoby and Jacklin apologize for the fact that writing about sex differences almost forces them into being "trait" psychologists. They point out that sex differences appear at different ages in youngsters, remain for a short time, and then disappear, as one sex "catches up," developmentally, with the other. Sex-linked behavior shifts, it is specific to the situation, and it may escape being detected by researchers who rely on traditional psychological tests and for whom the finding of significant sex differences may be more troublesome than worthy of consideration in its own right.

The authors reviewed articles from forty journals, as well as several other sources, and they assessed research that explicitly sought sex differences as well as studies which did not. They wrote to authors to clarify findings; they even recomputed data themselves. They worked under two major assumptions: (1) findings of sex differences are more likely to be published than findings of no sex differences; and (2) results from observational studies are more reliable than results from rating scales, because inherited ideas about gender-appropriate behavior more often affect the latter than the former. These assumptions bolster their conclusion that differences in the social behavior, intellectual abilities, and motivation of the two sexes are far less prevalent than has been commonly assumed.

The results are compiled in eighty-six tables, each of which contains a brief description of several studies on a given topic, e.g., curiosity, self-disclosure, word memory, and the like. There is also a 232 page annotated bibliography which describes the methodology and findings from well over 1,600 separate studies. This particular book is intended as a sequel to *The Development of Sex Differences* (Stanford University Press, 1966) which Maccoby edited. As a sequel, it becomes a little complicated. Some crucial details included in the first volume are omitted here. In addition, Maccoby repudiates the view that sex differences in intellectual functioning stem from personality differences, an explanation she had espoused in the earlier volume.

Maccoby and Jacklin conclude that only four sex differences are well established: girls have greater verbal ability, while boys excel in visual-spatial ability, have more mathematical skill, and are more aggressive than girls. They find that the ideas that girls are more social, suggestible, responsive to auditory stimuli, and possess less achievement motivation and self-esteem are unfounded. The beliefs that boys are more analytic and better at tasks that require higher-level cognitive processing rather than rote learning are similarly not supported by the findings. There is too little evidence in current research to answer questions about sex differences in activity level; fear, timidity, and anxiety; competitiveness; dominance; compliance and nurturance.

The authors are well aware of methodological limitations both in the original research and in their own review of it. However they discuss only a few of the several hundred studies in detail. Presumably these are ones which resolve conflicts and clarify anomalies found in other work. If the authors have a bias, it is in the direction of downplaying studies which *do* indicate appreciable sex differences. Their discussion of socialization theories is a bit thin, but their suggestion that self-socialization is more important than parental reinforcement is intriguing. Self-socialization is a process in which the child observes others, somewhat haphazardly infers rules about sex-appropriate behavior, and then tries to follow them.

Maccoby and Jacklin introduce cross-species and cross-cultural evidence only sporadically, mainly to buttress the conclusion that male aggressiveness is at least partially hormonally based. If there are so few genuine sex differences in psychological traits and capacities, then we can only conclude that differential role assignment produces the marked differences in adult behavior. All in all, this book reveals more about why psychology needs sociology (and anthropology) than the other way around.

Sex Research: Studies from the Kinsey Institute, edited by MARTIN S. WEINBERG. New York: Oxford University Press, 1976. 320 pp. $12.95 cloth. $7.00 paper.

MARJORIE K. LITTLE
Ohlone College, Fremont, California

Unless one is a cultist of the Kinsey Institute, there is very little reason to read this book. Aside from passing remarks concerning Dr. Alfred Kinsey's inability to tell "sexy jokes," and some comments on a few unexpected interview experiences, the reader gains very little insight into the workings of the Institute. The introductory section basically confirms Kinsey's seriousness of intent and his struggles for funding and legitimacy.

A large portion of the book repeats the information readily available in the earlier publications, *Sexual Behavior In the Human Male* and *Sexual Behavior In the Human Female.* The selections Weinberg has included are taken verbatim from the original texts and are presented without any attempt to update or annotate them.

Although a considerable part of the book deals with current and on-going projects, the research designs are not nearly rigorous enough to allow for sufficient credibility. This is especially apparent in the sections on child molesters, rapists, and sadomasochists where conclusions are drawn almost entirely from subjects convicted of these crimes. Unfortunately for Weinberg and the general public the sample he has studied represents only a small minority of individuals actually involved in such activities.

His research on homosexuality, although more rigorous, is far less informative than alternative studies that are currently available. In addition he makes several assumptions that are never satisfactorily substantiated. One concerns the increased probability that homosexual females will develop relationships that provoke less "rancor, guilt, and jealousy" than their male counterparts but that they may be more likely to involve themselves with a "person whose sexual orientation is in an unsettled state." Even more debatable is his suggestion that Black homosexuals anticipate less sexual discrimination because of greater tolerance in the Black community. It would seem in actuality that gay Black men share with lesbians a questionable amount of tolerance in general because of their minority status. Homosexuality, use of marijuana, and other acts formerly defined as "deviant," have always been much more threatening to the general public once its presence infiltrates their community. "Deviance" among minority groups has been, if not tolerated, at least expected by dominant groups.

The remaining sections, which include articles on nudists and erotic art, are interesting but neither serve to add continuity nor to provide startling new findings in the fields of sexuality or psychology.

Social Change and Social Problems

The Sociology of Survival: Social Problems of Growth, by CHARLES H. ANDERSON. Homewood, Ill.: Dorsey Press, 1976. 299 pp. $5.95 paper.

ALLAN SCHNAIBERG
Northwestern University

That the reach of sociologists *should* exceed their grasp is attested to by this book. Despite its shortcomings, it deserves the attention of all macrosociologists, regardless of substantive area of interest or sociopolitical ideology. At minimum, it challenges many prevailing theories and policy preferences—of students and mentors alike.

Anderson systematically links problems of environmental degradation, underdevelopment, alienation, economic instability, and unemployment in the modern world-system. More than cataloguing the dual socio-ecological failures of the private and state capitalist (USSR) components of this system, he points toward an *integrated* socialist response to them. China, and to a lesser extent Cuba, are seen as the closest extant approximations to the advocated ideal type, although Anderson properly notes the revisionist strains within China. In short, Anderson has taken the best of Schumacher, Commoner, Ehrlich, and others, and merged it with a neo-Marxist perspective that attempts to rise slightly above Marx's commitment to liberating all of the anti-ecological forces of production.

There *are* some serious gaps between the grasp and the reach here. Population growth issues are treated in too unbalanced a fashion, and with far too much optimism on the prospects for population stabilization—the former is too bourgeois, and the latter too Marxist. There is too facile a treatment of "smallness" of economic and community organization as a social solution. And finally, serious radicals will find little guidance on overcoming the formidable institutional (and individual) obstacles in the path to the "new society" that the history of the capitalist world-system has cumulated.

However, the gauntlet has been well-constructed and well-flung. I strongly urge fellow social scientists to take it up, despite the intellectual pains it may cause them.

Responding to Social Change, edited by BASIL HONIKMAN. Stroudsberg, Pa.: Dowden, Hutchinson & Ross, 1975. 311 pp. $18.00 cloth.

GALEN CRANZ
University of California, Berkeley

This collection represents part of the proceedings of the Sixth Annual Environmental Design Research Association Conference. The organization is composed of both designers and social scientists who do research on theoretical models for the relationship between environmental and social life, as well as on applied issues regarding residential, work, educational, recreational, public, and stressful environments, etc.

Unfortunately, one has to know the issues already to make use of this collection. Neither the editor nor author of the preface provides an adequate introductory essay. Honikman merely mentions general issues—the relationship between the material and non-material world and the issue of causalty—and entirely overlooks other questions basic to this specialization, namely, "Is there a relationship between space and behavior in the first place? If so, what is it, and is it a significant one in terms of important social issues? Is the relationship the same for everybody?"

The book opens with three keynote essays and five commentaries. The first is a conventional demographic run-down of the world crisis in resources and gets less response from the commentators than the other two, i.e., Kevin Lynch's "Grounds for Utopia" and Constance Perin's "Social Governance and Environmental Design." Lynch, a planner from M.I.T. knows all the critiques of contemporary society: age segregation, the work-play split, land ownership and tax issues, materialism, large vs. small, over-concentration of cities, waste vs. recycling, and even overly-standardized time. His article is a collection of ideals implied by these criticisms, transposed into their spatial counterparts. Strangely, it is not as inspirational as I think was intended. For motivating environmental researchers and teachers I found four less ambitious articles more effective: Clarke on viewing environmental research as part of the humanities, Ostrander with an insightful and sympathetic analysis of the problems of designer-researcher collaboration, Archea on what interdisciplinary commitment means, and Ventre on the importance of influencing building codes and standards to affect the built environment.

Perin, urban planner turned anthropologist, looks at social conflict generically in order to place more topical concerns such as territorialty and crime prevention in a larger framework. She posits social conflict as an intrinsic process, not a problem of social life. "Social governance" is the kind of conflict resolution which is worked out informally inside a system without recourse to formal legal procedures. She sees it as "a mutual and developing system, in deliberate contrast to 'social control' which implies a top-down model in which only a few people have charge of social norms which hardly ever change." Social control was an acceptable ideology as well as analytic principle around the turn of the century, when class conflict was abhorred, and order, stability, and perfectibility revered. Today Perin's thinking is more appropriate with its acceptance of conflict and emphasis on continuous process, mutuality, and interaction (although the terminology "social governance" is probably not the most clarifying). The relationship between social governance and environmental design is not entirely clear. Once the designer-researcher has found out which elements of conflict resolutions are unavailable, under-used, exacerbating and why, one still does not know what arrangements will make "workings-out" more likely than others. Perhaps the analysis of what inhibits governance carries with it spatial implications for what could encourage it, but if this is the argument it should be made explicit.

Nearly one-third of the volume is devoted to articles which summarize the state of a particular research technique for environmental research: the semantic differential, cognitive mapping, opinion surveys through participant observation, and computer generated form. This same publisher has a better volume on the subject (*Behavioral Research Methods in Environmental Design*, Wm. Michelson, ed.).

The essays on theoretical perspectives are also covered elsewhere. Descriptions of behavior settings and understaffing appear other places; Rappoport's plug for an anthropological approach is not his best work in this area. Moos's "social ecology" is like his book—an effort to integrate biological, psychological, and social perspectives on the human environment. Broadbent's "Function and Symbolism in Architecture" is the most helpful because it covers the relatively new topic of semiotics and communication theory which has produced a lot of confusion and mystification in architectural studies. He defines the original terms (signifier and signified) and traces the evolution of further internal refinements and distinctions, leaving the reader with a simple but historically accurate and analytically clear understanding of the terminology.

With the exceptions noted, the collection offers little new in the field. In terms of writing, the introduction is weak and the set as a whole uneven. The volume, including the commentaries on the lead essays, provides no guide to the interpretation of the state of architectural research; you have to bring the analysis to it yourself. For these reasons it would not be recommended for introductory courses. The articles are best viewed as primary documents about the way contemporaries in this field think. Perhaps those collecting data on the process of professionalization would find it useful primary material.

China's Uninterrupted Revolution: From 1840 to the Present, edited by VICTOR NEE and JAMES PECK. New York: Pantheon Books, 1976. 480 pp. $15.95 cloth. $5.95 paper.

BEN STAVIS
Cornell University

China's Uninterrupted Revolution consists of five essays loosely organized around the theme that important transformations have been taking place continuously in China's culture and economic system over the past two centuries. The Communist revolution of 1949 and the unusual revolution within a revolution (the Cultural Revolution of 1966–68) thus have long antecedents. This is a valuable perspective. Observers of China, whether hostile or sympathetic often emphasize the sharp changes which occur in some particular year, and fail to acknowledge their historical roots.

The historical thesis is presented in two pieces. A lengthy introduction by Victor Nee and James Peck deftly summarizes the evolution of class relations in China as it faced the West after 1840. The emergence of a new culture and a new strategy to rebuild China is traced in the thoughts of Lu Hsün, China's great modern writer, and Mao Tse-tung. Kung Chung-wu's essay shows how China has been striving for a way of integrating the strengths of Western science and technology with the essence of China's civilization. Mao Tse-tung's attempt to combine "red" and "expert" "bears an affinity with old Confucian ideas, in this case Chang Chih-tung's *t'i-yung* [essence-utility] formulation" (p. 279).

These two essays in intellectual and cultural history are well complemented by two empirical case studies. Victor Nee shows how the theory of cultural revolution was carried out in practice in Shanghai from 1966 to 1968. The efforts to share authority and to increase participation in municipal and factory management stand as a major challenge to Weberian and Taylorist notions of bureaucracy. Unfortunately, however, Nee ends the story too early; after 1968 some of the reforms he reports were dropped, indicating the resilience of bureaucratic power. Nee captures the spirit of factional struggle: "it had grown nearly impossible to distinguish ultraleftists from leftists, conservatives from leftists, and unrepentant revisionists from revolutionary cadres" (p. 356). In Nee's essay, normal documentary sources have been supplemented with interviewing in Shanghai, and the interview material adds vitality and clarity.

Carl Riskin's (previously published) essay shows how the Chinese wage system subtly combines individual and material incentives. The Chinese system does not require a complete transformation of people's psyches, but does facilitate the development of less selfish people. Ideology has not dismissed rationality. Both Riskin's and Nee's pieces show that the construction of socialism is a long, historical process, very much shaped by past experiences and traditional culture.

Somewhat unconnected to these articles is a long essay by James Peck, which must be considered an exploration into sociology of knowledge. Peck examines the analyses of China by American and Soviet writers. He then turns the analyses inside out, and shows how they reveal the preconceptions and values of writers and their respective societies. Certainly there are better ways to probe US and Soviet systems, and the exercise reveals little about China. Nevertheless, the essay is very helpful in revealing the social and political context in which analyses of China are made. Ultimately Peck backs all China scholars into a corner by implying that all analyses of China are shaped more by the values of the reporters and their societies than by the reality of China. The other essays in the book I hope, belie Peck's view. They seem to present careful, accurate, objective accounts of China's movement through history.

Social Concerns, by GWYNN NETTLER. New York: McGraw-Hill, 1975. 360 pp. $6.95 paper.

T. P. SCHWARTZ
Crowfield, Saunderstown, Rhode Island

I like this book. I strongly recommend it if you are looking for: a highly engaging, iconoclastic, informed, free-wheeling "social problems" book in a compassionate but unsoggy personal essayistic mode suitable for mature and able students or concerned lay friends; an example of good, original textbook writing without condescension, frills, cheap thrills, or behavioral learning objectives; an interpretive refresher for yourself on problematic aspects of happiness, mental illness, loving, work, success, population, wealth, killing, crime, and lesser evils.

Nettler is correct in arguing that social concerns, "the conditions and behaviors that are the object of peoples' hopes and fears," deserve serious scholarly attention. This book delivers it. However, if not incorrect, then Nettler's arguments that social concerns should replace social problems, social disorganization, deviance, etc. as subjects of study, and that social concerns are universal and eternal, are unconvincing because of shaky logic, thin evidence (mainly Hadley Cantril's old survey data from twelve mostly Westbent nations), and an unsystematic presentation. Will we ever learn that new explanations and images, like new edifices, need not always be built from ashes over the excavations of the old ones?

Yet, once the author shifts from theoretical preliminaries to the concerns themselves, this book is worthy of one of the truest compliments because, despite my familiarity with the topics discussed, I continually found myself *reading* the book and appreciating it. It makes me want to create a course just to use the book and thereby ruminate on it further.

Grass Roots in an African City: Political Behavior in Nairobi, by MARC HOWARD ROSS. Cambridge, Mass.: MIT Press, 1975. 169 pp. $19.50 cloth.

ROBERT CAMERON MITCHELL
Resources for the Future, Washington, D.C. and *Pennsylvania State University*

This study focuses on class, life-style, ethnicity, and sex as determinants of political attitudes and participation in the fast growing city of Nairobi, capital of Kenya. After a succinct and useful summary of the social and political background of Kenya and Nairobi, the major part of this short monograph reports on a multivariate analysis of the 498 interviews conducted in late 1967, some four years after independence.

Drawing upon the literature of political participation and political attitudes, Ross formulates and tests a multitude of hypotheses using various parametric techniques with competence. Among his many findings are two quite distinct styles of political participation (which he calls the pre- and post-independance styles), the importance of social class in explaining patterns of political participation and alienation in the post independence period, the parallel importance of ethnicity (in this study, Kikuyu-Luo differences) in explaining differences in political beliefs and attitudes, and the lack of commitment on the part of the inhabitants of Nairobi to city life. Interestingly, the higher the socioeconomic status of individuals, the greater the intensity of their contact with rural areas.

Although Ross tries to use the concept of increasing scale to integrate his various hypotheses, this attempt is not very successful, and the book's merit lies in its discrete findings which are an important addition to our understanding of the political views and behavior of East African city-dwellers shortly after independence.

Planning and Organizing for Social Change: Action Principles from Social Science Research, by JACK ROTHMAN. New York: Columbia University Press, 1974. 628 pp. $20.00 cloth. $7.50 paper.

CAROLE JOFFE
Bryn Mawr College

JOAN MANDLE
Pennsylvania State University, Delaware County

Although this book presents in accessible form a host of propositions and information on planning and organizing for social change, it ultimately adds little to our knowledge of that complex and little-understood process. Rothman has organized this volume as a series of propositions—over 200 "generalizations" gleaned from the examination of academic journals between 1964 and 1970—organized into sections such as "The Practitioner-Change Agent," "The Organizational Framework," and "The Community Setting of Social Change." These summaries of empirical research are then translated into "action guidelines" for practitioners.

Rothman's motivation in presenting social science knowledge in the form of practical action-oriented statements is based on his perception of a wide gulf separating those who think about social change and those who try to bring it about. But what dooms his effort is that he provides his practitioner audience only a string of empirical statements which cannot begin to substitute for a theoretical understanding of the process of social change. Without any theoretical structure which might provide a framework of analysis, there is no way usefully to choose among or assess the effectiveness of one generalization over another in practice. Rothman, for example, discusses at length various studies of civil rights activism in the 1960s, but nowhere mentions the inadequacy of that research in predicting the ineffectiveness of this type of organizing at other places and other times (e.g., the North in the late '60s and early '70s).

In addition to the overall conceptual weakness, there is some evidence of the omission of key sociological writings in the bibliographies, which may be the result of Rothman's dependence on journal articles over a six-year period. For example, in the subsection of "Professionals and Organizations," the lack of any reference to the seminal work of Everett Hughes is particularly striking. In selecting materials and concepts, the author appears to give more weight to frequency of appearance than to an independent assessment of their quality.

The subsection of "Professionals and Organizations" also illustrates the theoretical weakness of this work. Under Generalization 5.4, for example, the author makes the following assumption: "Given that norms of 'established professions' are more coherent and crystallized than those of the 'semi-professions,' their impact on organizations will be stronger. That is, physicians and lawyers have a greater chance of affecting their employing organizations than do social workers" (p. 162). While we certainly agree that doctors and lawyers have more pull in agencies than do social workers, the point might have been more forcefully made by Rothman had he focused less on the "crystallization of norms," and more on the status of these professions outside the agency, and especially their relative degrees of political power. A consideration of the monopoly powers of various professions, in our opinion, would offer a more lucid explanation of their varying degrees of impact with an agency. Similarly, this book does not adequately confront the possible dangers associated with the professional control of services—a subject of much recent attention by activists as well as scholars such as Eliot Freidson.

This book can be criticized on several fronts—it lacks any theory of social change, its "generalizations" are subject to different interpretations, its "action guidelines" are, by the author's own admission, problematic. It is nonetheless a useful volume, as the author and his associates have abstracted and made easily accessible an enormous body of literature. While this book may or may not meet the needs of service practitioners, it should prove helpful to students in sociology, social work, urban studies, and related fields.

The Awareness Trap: Self-Absorption Instead of Social Change, by EDWIN SCHUR. New York: Quadrangle, 1976. 213 pp. $7.95 cloth.

LOUIS ROWITZ
University of Illinois Medical Center

There are a number of sociologists who are struggling with the important issue of the place of the individual in the general stream of things. There has been a tendency in much of our sociological work for the individual to be lost. The individual not only faces conflict in everyday life which creates much personal stress but also feels powerless in facing the problems of modern day society. There are a number of possible solutions to this impasse. Individuals can choose to accept all the rules of society and become social robots. They can select those parts of society with which they feel comfortable and then adopt new approaches to their lives in those areas where the fit is not right. Individuals can choose to drop out and ignore the culture completely. Individuals can adopt causes and fight the system. Finally, individuals can strive for personal freedom and understanding in the midst of the society in which they live.

The human potential movement has found adherents from this last group of individuals. In *The Awareness Trap* Edwin Schur raises many questions about the viability of this solution for people by criticizing the human potential movement from a strictly sociological perspective. He argues that self awareness may help some people, it may help generate individual change. However, a stress on self awareness leads to self absorption. When individuals become too self-centered, they become oblivious to the needs of the society in which they live. The self awareness adherent ignores society and culture as well as the realities of the social structure. Professor Schur bases his comments on an extensive review of the humanistic psychology literature, both professional and popular. There is no evidence that Schur talked directly to the people involved in the awareness movement.

The first part of the book lays the foundation for Schur's arguments by discussing the ambiguity of the major concepts of the literature. He finds *awareness, creativity, here and now, self responsibility* and the other concepts of the human potential writers confusing; each book and article defines the terms differently. Schur argues that emphasis on awareness distracts the individual from the problems of society. He believes that the awareness exponents simplify complex social relationships, are anti-intellectual, and argue for the abolition of social roles and our social history which helps us in our daily interactions with others. They ask us to return to the simple days of childhood. If we do all that the awareness preachers ask us to do, society becomes unimportant and social change becomes impossible.

The second part of the book shows applications of the awareness philosophy to a number of contemporary social movements. For example, Schur argues that the women's movement will suffer if it adopts too many of the principles of the human potential movement. Too much self-centeredness will defeat the social action needs of women. Women have interiorized themselves too much already. They need to become social activists in order to bring about change.

Schur also criticizes the new assertiveness training literature as being just another way of ignoring the realities of social structure. Schur criticizes the perspectives of open marriage advocates, transcendental meditation, the health food movement, and anything else that smacks of a stress on the individual as separate from society.

Schur criticizes the awareness writers as being too one-sided in their work: they see the development of the individual as being our most important concern in today's society; societal issues are secondary. On the other hand, Schur argues that societal issues are the most important and the development of the individual is secondary. It seems that there needs to be a meeting ground somewhere. The development of self awareness need not preclude a development of social awareness. If I have strong concern for social change in my life, then the increase in my self awareness should not stifle my interest in social change. If anything, my concern for social change will be enhanced. If I have no concern for social change, increases in my self awareness may help me even if I don't change my orientation toward society. In fact, increase in self awareness may have a synergistic effect on society anyway, although Schur does not seem to agree with this. More research needs to be done on the people participating in the movement and not just on the literature of the movement.

Another important aspect of the human potential movement that needs study is its relationship to the social environment in which it has developed. The movement has developed at a time when mass society, dehumanization, over-bureaucratization, and mass media influences predominate in our lives. A search for self reaffirmation is logical in modern day life. Some factions of the awareness movement have grown out of a discontent with traditional psychotherapy, with the medical model orientation to personal problems. This movement from a therapy orientation to a training orientation is worth investigating.

Schur argues that the awareness movement attracts the middle class predominantly. It does not seem to be worthwhile to assume that the movement is dysfunctional because of this. It may be functional for the majority (middle class) of our society.

A good book raises more questions than it answers. Schur has raised some important questions about self awareness and has opened the door to a fascinating area of research for sociologists.

Solving Social Problems: Essays in Relevant Sociology, edited by MARCELLO TRUZZI and PHILIP B. SPRINGER. Pacific Palisades, Calif.: Goodyear Publishing Company, 1976. 347 pp. No price listed, paper.

American Society: Problems and Dilemmas, edited by ALAN WELLS. Pacific Palisades, Calif.: Goodyear Publishing Company, 1976. 391 pp. No price listed, paper.

HENRY M. BARLOW
Cleveland State University

Although both of these books refer to social problems in their titles, they are very different in approach and content and must therefore be reviewed separately. Both are edited collections of previously published materials, with the exception of a few cases. Each book includes a number of well written, scholarly essays yet each volume has serious limitations.

Truzzi and Springer's title suggests a potentially major contribution to the solution of social problems, and their primary goal seems to be to demonstrate that sociology is really relevant to the solution of social problems. The book is divided into six parts which include: two introductory essays on applied sociology and social policy, five essays on socialization issues, three on patterns of social change, three on politics and power, two on law and disorder, and two on cooperation and conflict. Some students of applied sociology may find the introductory discussions of interest but those familiar with the literature will find nothing new.

On their own, the essays have much to offer; however, the editors never synthesize any of the materials by way of introductory or concluding material. Moreover, the rationale for the particular selections is not explained except that they presumably deal with important issues and demonstrate (individually) some sociologically relevant analysis.

In contrast Wells's book pays much more attention to student needs. His work is concerned with the analysis of political, economic, military, scientific, educational, and religious organizations. Wells assumes that the character of society may be derived from an analysis of its institutions. The authors of the twenty-four articles include politicians, professional writers, a number of social scientists, but very few sociologists. A virtue of the book is that students will gain an appreciation for critical perspectives on these institutional sectors and a sense of synthesis from the editor's carefully written introductions. Most important, the book provides a conflict perspective on American society and it will probably foster much student debate over issues such as the misuse of political power, capitalism and the welfare state, the concept of a military-industrial complex, the quality of health in America, the impact of education, and the civil religion in America.

When compared to leading texts on social problems, the book is much less systematic and impressive. It would appear to be most useful in courses on American society and in conjunction with a systematic text.

Social Psychology

The Social Animal, 2nd. ed., by Elliot Aronson. San Francisco: Freeman and Company, 1976. 336 pp. $12.50 cloth. $4.95 paper.

Persons-in-Groups: A Humanistic Social Psychology, by Donald W. Calhoun. New York: Harper & Row, 1976. 484 pp. $12.95 cloth.

Social Psychology: People in Groups, by Bertram H. Raven and Jeffrey Z. Rubin. New York: John Wiley & Sons, 1976. 591 pp. No price listed, cloth.

Social Behaviorism, by Arthur W. Staats. Homewood, Ill.: Dorsey Press, 1975. 655 pp. No price listed, cloth.

Morris J. Daniels
San Diego State University

If one should define the content of social psychology as social persuasion, conformity, and justification—within the theoretical posture of dissonance theory, then Aronson's book is a gem of theoretical sophistication. It is presented in good style, maintaining a tension between reader and material by using a stylistic dissonance of its own, which sets up readers to expect one thing, only to show them that their common sense expectations are misleading.

I am not myself convinced that social psychology is this limited in scope or method. Nor am I convinced that consonance is an "innate" need, as Aronson suggests. There are simply too many instances of contradiction and conflict, both logical and psychological, which reflect the diversity of group life and symbolic universes in which we participate and which generate little sensed discomfort. It would have been interesting if Aronson had presented critiques of dissonance theory other than the one offered by Bem. And it would have been even more interesting to have seen his stylistic clarity applied to the material presented by Staats in *Social Behavior*.

Calhoun expresses the hope that he can find walking room between the "cat-grin" sociologically deterministic social psychology, on the one hand, and "rat-maze" social psychology on the other. I think he is mistaken in leading the reader to infer that all social psychologists within sociology view people as simply the sum of their deterministic social roles. First, Calhoun himself has considerable material devoted to the controlling nature of norms. Second, perusal of recent books and articles by Hewitt; Blumer; Wilson; Lindesmith, Strauss, and Denzin; Manis and Meltzer, and most of those in ethnomethodology, would disabuse one of this impression. Third, the author himself acknowledges the existence of this other perspective in his referral (p. 34) to Turner's ideas on role.

Anyway, as an alternative to "cat-grin" and "rat-maze" social psychologies, Calhoun sees his objective as writing a book that affirms personhood. This means it must take into account guts, heart, creative intelligence, and self-actualization potentials à la Kurt Goldstein and Abraham Maslow. The focus upon personhood in actualization reveals an author that is quite concerned with the possibility of people being turned into objects and thereby dehumanized. He moves toward unfolding this concern by looking first at the processes and structures of norms, symbolic interaction, prejudice, etc., by which groups control the individual; second, at neuropsychological beings coping with nature, groups, and themselves; and third, at the way individuals function within varied social groups in everyday life.

In the process of working through his basic theme, Calhoun draws from a rather wide body of nonexperimental case material. Given his perspective, this is to be expected, but Calhoun is not himself above calling upon some of his own "cat-grin" deterministic variables where appropriate. With all seriousness, Calhoun has undertaken a problem of enormous proportions, namely the expression of an active concern for what people are, what they have to do in order to cope with current life, and what the probabilities are that this can be done so that personhood is maximized. For this, he needs all the data he can get. His closing epilogue, which points out the dead end assumptions of behaviorism, psychoanalysis, and exchange theory, as well as Wrong's notion of oversocialization, is quite appropriate. While instructors may at times have trouble integrating or even accepting all the material in this book, I think that they, as well as their students, will both enjoy it and learn from it. I feel that I did.

Raven and Rubin present a third orientation, one which focuses upon persons in small groups. After the first chapter on "The Person Alone," which is especially well done, the authors move on to the way in which people become aware of others and themselves, how they come to like and dislike others and themselves, the interdependence of persons, their inter-influence, etc. I mention these only to show the manner in which the authors weave a unifying theme into their work: starting with the individual and moving through involvements in various kinds of small group experiences. Naturally, they draw upon a much broader spectrum of experimentally-based material than Calhoun; their focus is on an area that has produced an abundance of this type of data. Raven and Rubin write clearly, interestingly, and with substance. Their conciseness is admirable and the visual aids are excellent.

The book by Staats is likely to be a controversial one, especially among those social psychologists of the symbolic interaction persuasion, for the ghost of the social behaviorism of Mead has reappeared under the guise of a sophisticated S-R model. Should you contemplate reading this book, I suggest that you set aside a generous amount of time, lots of cookies, and a favorite set of TV re-runs to fill in between chapters. Except in certain sections of the second half, the book is slow-going, reflecting both the nature of the material and author's style.

Staats attempts to develop what he calls an ARD (Attitudinal, Reinforcing, and Directive) scheme which presents not only the advantage of merging classical and instrumental theories of conditioning, but of rejecting the elementaristic view of the person which was depicted in earlier S-R theory. This means that Staats presumably can take into account human consciousness and ideals. He can also give a general place to the controlling effects of symbols, self, role, etc. As a tour de force, Staats manages to make bedfellows of humanists, phenomenologists, and anti-reductionists—and even comes to terms with the notion that human action is continually negotiated, emergent, and novel. Were the methodologies not so drastically different one might be tempted to ask, "Will the real Mead stand up?" Nevertheless, given the methodology within which he is working, this is an intriguing book. Among the many things that bothered me about it was the fuzziness which develops once the author begins to generalize his concepts to the broad sweep of human behaviors.

The IQ Controversy: Critical Readings, edited by N. J. BLOCK and GERALD DWORKIN. New York: Pantheon Books, 1976. 557 pp. $15.95 cloth. $6.95 paper.

Origins of Intelligence: Infancy and Early Childhood, edited by MICHAEL LEWIS. New York: Plenum Press, 1976. 413 pp. $17.50 cloth.

BARBARA G. CASHION
Wilson College
Chambersburg, Pennsylvania

These two books on intelligence and IQ deserve special attention from sociologists, whether or not they are interested in this area of sociological inquiry. The books are important because they provide a broad collection of essays which can be used to illustrate the importance of methodology to theoretical development.

The IQ Controversy is a collection of twenty-one articles, all reprints, which represents the entire history of the IQ debate. The first section of the book contains the essays of Walter Lippman and Lewis Terman debating whether intelligence is inherited and whether IQ tests measure intelligence. This debate occurred in 1922–1923, but we are reminded that the debate began with the publication of Galton's *Hereditary Genius* in 1869. The second section of the book reprints recent essays which examine inherited intelligence, and the third section deals with social and political consequences of believing that there is a genetic difference in intelligence. The book makes no explicit analysis of the 100-year-old debate, it simply records more than anyone ever wanted to know about it.

The impact of the book comes from realizing that such a thorough debate was based on such weak scientific evidence. We learn that IQ is still defined as whatever IQ tests measure. IQ tests were not designed to measure intelligence, they were designed to spot children who would benefit from special learning programs. It is assumed that the tests measure a single genetic factor, *g,* that subsumes all mental activity, although it is debated that such a factor exists. That any pencil and paper test designed to measure something else, could by coincidence measure a genetic factor that may or may not exist, is a leap of faith that even the most ardent survey researcher is normally not willing to make. Yet it is the basis of 100 years of debate, and the debate has not ended.

The reason sociologists should read this collection is because they will recognize problems inherent in their own research. Attempts to separate the effects of achieved status from those of ascribed status, for example, have much in common with attempts to separate genetic sources from environmental sources of IQ; moreover the methodological arguments in this book are sound and helpful in dealing with these and related issues. "The Analysis of Variance and the Analysis of Causes" by Richard Lewontin, a geneticist, is the clearest article on the subject that I have read. The collection as a whole covers the intricacies of the problem so well that I would recommend *The IQ Controversy* to graduate students studying methods.

The Origins of Intelligence is a collection of thirteen original essays which tries to get past the IQ debate. However, the authors of these articles are scholars in human development, and many of them are influenced by Piaget's model of development. This model implies a biological development of intelligence where the environment may have an influence, much as biological growth in height may vary because of nutrition. They do not assume a biological capacity to perform together with environmental stimulation to perform. Again, there is a basic question about the role of biology in human development, and, the assumptions used may be annoying to sociologists.

Nevertheless, the articles provide theoretical insights which sociologists might use to explore their own assumptions. For example, Robert McCall gives a profile of child development which is not unlike George Herbert Mead's, and suggests ways to study child development as transitions from simple motor skills to the perception of self and then to the meaning of objects. Jeannette Haviland describes the importance of "looking smart" even in infancy. She presents what might be a case study of the socializing of an autistic child because the child had "no affect." Marion Blank and Doris Allen present an interesting case study of various phases in learning the meaning of the word "why." It is a step toward understanding how children use nonverbal meanings as a clue to language. There is a fascinating review of cross-cultural studies in infant intelligence and a review of the literature on social class and infant intelligence, to name only a few of the subjects developed.

The common assumption in these two books that at least some of the variance in intelligence is biologically determined, is most interesting. It is apparent in *The IQ Controversy* that current methods of research cannot finally indicate whether this is a valid assumption. Nevertheless, psychologists continue to make this assumption as part of their theoretical development, and *The Origins of Intelligence* is a good example of this trend. If in the next decade we are overwhelmed with theories, research, and debate about biological causation, these two books together may help us to understand why.

Constructing Social Life: Readings in Behavioral Sociology from the Iowa School, by CARL J. COUCH and ROBERT A. HINTZ, JR. Champaign, Ill.: Stipes Publishing Company, 1975. 292 pp. $5.00 paper.

SANTO J. TARANTINO
Florida Atlantic University

This collection of seventeen papers variously authored by twelve individuals, but primarily by Couch and Hintz, generates a peculiar kind of frustration. In most of the papers one feels an elusive sense of importance that alternates with a suspicion that one is dealing with statements of a pedestrian sort in a nonvernacular language. Perhaps this is due to the astonishingly uniform style of writing characteristic of all the papers, a style that is unfortunately dull and monotonous. That, added to the confessed redundancy in the papers, makes getting through them a matter of strong determination. Nevertheless, they are worth the effort for anyone interested in a serious attempt to clarify basic concepts for the analysis of social interaction.

What appears at first to be pedestrian turns out on closer scrutiny to offer subtle and significant distinctions by which the complexities of interaction might be grasped. For example, in the section on "The Elements and Structure of Openings" concepts like "congruent functional identities," "copresent," "mutually available," "reciprocal attention," and "mutual responsiveness" are differentiated and then woven together to provide a schema for careful description. These remarks are equally applicable to the papers in the second section, which is concerned with general theory.

It is the section on general theory which contains the best papers of the book. Generally, these "attempt to outline the temporal and relational quality of human life. The attempt is to indicate those invariant qualities of social life that facilitate and constrain persons acting together and sharing each other's experiences." More specifically, these papers are all grounded in an evolutionary conception of the development of human sociality. Such groundedness necessarily leads to concern with temporal and processual thinking and the construction of social forms as a consequence of certain biological adaptations, especially the sensory systems. It is the analysis of sensory modes and their relations to social activity that most sociologists will find intriguing. The notion that locomoting organisms can participate in the negotiation of contact because they are able to detect impending contact (especially through vision) is a case in point. From such an idea one can begin to trace out the development of actions as temporal process leading to the more fully recognized concept of intention. Such analyses contribute to the shedding of the mysteriousness of concepts, like intention, that have traditionally been associated with a so called mentalistic orientation.

In the kind of analysis given in the example above one can certainly recognize the contributions of G. H. Mead who is, of course, explicitly regarded as providing the initial groundwork for these further elaborations. What may not be so readily detected in these papers is the extent to which the ideas are congruent with the thinking of B. F. Skinner, viz., concern with temporal and processual aspects of behavior within an evolutionary perspective which emphasizes the contribution of the past in the determination of future and present. There is, however, scant mention of Skinner in these papers. This is unfortunate. Skinner's kind of detailed analysis of the relationship between organism and environment (social as well as physical) and temporal processes could provide the crucial complement to an otherwise impotent conceptual schema, however clarifying it might be. These remarks are partially generated from a consideration of the last sections of the book.

These consist of eight papers under the rubrics of "Mediated Coordination," "Representation," and "Method." The first is concerned with the construction of coordinated behavior by the use of clocks, written language, and electronic devices by persons who do not share copresence. The second has to do with relationships between groups, and the third is the obvious attempt to connect ideas with strategies for empirical inquiry. Some of the papers in this section endeavor to show the usefulness if not the validity of the previously developed concepts by demonstrations that are putatively like experiments including, of course, tests of significance. These attempts leave one discouraged in that the efforts may help provide a wedge into the problem of description but there does not seem to be any potency with respect to explanation or prediction. A serious consideration of the applicability of Skinnerian formulations within this framework could provide the necessary élan and generate a behaviorism, be it social or otherwise, with significant potential for change and discovery.

Belief, Attitude, Intention and Behavior: An Introduction to Theory and Research, by MARTIN FISHBEIN and ICEK AJZEN. Reading, Mass.: Addison-Wesley Publishing Company, 1975. 578 pp. $13.95 cloth.

RICHARD J. HILL
University of Oregon, Eugene

In this volume, Fishbein and Ajzen seek to accomplish two objectives: (1) to provide a comprehensive review of a wide range of the theoretical and empirical literature devoted to attitudinal phenomena, and (2) to demonstrate that this literature can be incorporated within a unified and systematic explanatory structure. An evaluation of their efforts requires an assessment of the degree to which each of these goals has been achieved.

Given that "attitude" has been a fundamental conceptual concern of social psychology throughout the history of the discipline, no review of the available literature can be fully comprehensive. Those attempting such a task provide an important service by selecting from the total corpus of theory and research those publications that have made a meaningful contribution. Many sociologists will conclude that the selective process in this instance has introduced a disciplinary bias which favors the inclusion of work by experimentally oriented psychologists over that by those having alternative methodological orientations. Such a charge could be documented, but the criticism is overshadowed by what is achieved. Fishbein and Ajzen demonstrate an enviable command over the pertinent and significant literature. The breadth of their review may have necessitated certain stylistic decisions. Most of the chapters read as if they were written as contributions to an annual review or handbook of social psychology. The reader is confronted with detailed summaries of specific studies and a multitude of citations. As a consequence of this format, the work constitutes a valuable reference but is unacceptable as a text except for advanced and specialized seminars. Fishbein and Ajzen critically evaluate the work they consider, clearly identifying both the conceptual and methodological limitations of previous research, including their own. Their criticism of dissonance theory is particularly severe and telling. On balance, the objective of reviewing the relevant literature has been accomplished to a commendable degree, however, social psychologists working from the perspective of dissonance theory, the interpersonal attraction paradigm, or integration theory undoubtedly will object to certain criticisms and interpretations.

The second objective of the work constitutes the more serious intellectual challenge. Research on attitudes, and especially that addressed to the attitudinal-behavioral link, is characterized by definitional disagreements, methodological inconsistency, and ambiguous findings. Any scholar attempting to make sense of this disarray faces a task characterized by both high order complexity and endless tedium. In their attempt to accomplish this objective, Fishbein and Ajzen insist on the necessity of distinguishing between four classes of variables: beliefs, attitudes, intentions, and behaviors. They also make certain crucial assumptions about these variables and about the nature of human conduct. At the highest level of abstraction, Fishbein and Ajzen assume that humans are basically rational information processors whose beliefs, attitudes, intentions, and behaviors are determined by the information available to them. The theoretical structure which they advance cannot be seriously considered if one is not able to entertain such an assumption as at least an interesting hypothesis. At a somewhat lower level of abstraction, a second assumption is encountered which will be seen as problematic even by those who can entertain the possible rationality of our species. Fishbein and Ajzen define an attitude as a bipolar dimension of affect. I suspect that it is this insistence on attitudinal unidimensionality that accounts for their inadequate treatment of multi-dimensional strategies in their discussion of measurement procedures (chapter 3).

The conceptual issues introduced by the assumption of attitudinal unidimensionality are of fundamental importance. For example, Fishbein and Ajzen devote considerable attention to the analysis of prejudice, treating this concept at times as if it were what they would term a "global attitude." If attitudes are unidimensional, then logical consistency demands that this assumption must hold for all attitudes including the most global. Nevertheless, research on prejudice, including some of that cited by Fishbein and Ajzen, suggests that the phenomenon consists of a configuration of affects rather than a single evaluative continuum. I suspect that Fishbein and Ajzen would counter this criticism by claiming that I am confusing affects (attitudes) with beliefs, intentions, and behaviors. Such a rebuttal would require that the authors consistently treat prejudice as something more than a global attitude, and at least in some of their review, they do not maintain such consistency.

Given these and other assumptions, Fishbein and Ajzen proceed to construct a set of interrelated models addressing the processes of the formation and change of beliefs, attitudes, and intentions. The resulting structure has significant intellectual consequences. The system provides at least post hoc explanations for certain vexing inconsistencies in previous research. The framework facilitates the explicit statement of research strategies that are appropriate for the examination of the specific elements of which it is composed. The work moves us toward a greater integration of the existing literature. The adequacy of the theoretical system is not yet established, but the system is well grounded in past research, and a large proportion of the propositions which compose the framework are testable. Anyone who has done serious work in this area will recognize such accomplishments as being of major significance.

Attitudes and Facilitation in the Attainment of Status, by RUTH M. GASSON, ARCHIBALD O. HALLER, and WILLIAM H. SEWELL. Washington D.C.: American Sociological Association/Rose Monograph Series, 1972. 37 pp. $2.75 paper.

JAMES R. LINCOLN
University of Southern California

This brief monograph explores various nonlinear extensions of the Wisconsin status attainment model as developed in previous analyses, by these and other investigators, of a sample of Wisconsin males measured first (as high school students) in 1957 and again in 1964. The authors distinguish two sets of variables believed to affect educational and occupational attainment: (1) "attitudes," meaning educational and occupational aspirations; and (2) "facilitators," a broad term encompassing a host of background variables presumed to enhance the chances for high achievement. One hypothesis for which they readily find empirical support is that of consistency between attitudes and facilitating conditions: that is, level of aspiration is positively correlated with parental status, mental ability, and significant others' influence. The consistency hypothesis derives from attitude-behavior theory, such theory providing the main conceptual framework for the study. Its relevance to processes of stratification is suggested by Warner and DeFleur's notion of "contingent consistency": for positive attitudes to affect achievement behavior, facilitating conditions must be present. Similarly, without the requisite level of aspiration, such advantages as high parental status and intelligence will not facilitate performance. The hypothesis, then, is one of statistical interaction between attitude and environmental variables, the search for which thus becomes a prime objective of the analysis. It is hard to avoid the suspicion, however, that attitude-behavior theory is invoked largely because it offers a convenient justification for something the authors wanted to do anyway, i.e., hunt for nonlinear effects in these data.

Arguing that the finite character of educational and occupational hierarchies implies floor and ceiling effects on the relationship between achievement and its causes (such that attitudes and facilitators make less difference in the competition for positions at the extremes of these distributions than in the middle), their second key hypothesis predicts the existence of an S-shaped relation between these variables. Neither this hypothesis nor that specifying interaction finds much support in these data, however, prompting the authors to conclude that there is "no compelling evidence to abandon linear models. . . ." Varying the dependent variable and the attitude-facilitator combination produces five equations, but only two reveal positive and significant interactions. By the criterion of statistical significance, the curvilinearity hypothesis fares little better, although, when plotted, most such relations show some signs of a ceiling effect and several exhibit a floor effect as well.

In a work focused on a rather narrow set of problems, one expects a highly detailed sifting of the data, but my impression is that these data are underanalyzed. Extensive use is made of graphs to depict the form of regressions, but the tests for interaction and curvilinearity are almost cursory, making use of few of the available methods for exploring such patterns, and it is not evident that those employed yield the most precise results. For example, curvilinearity is examined by comparing the squared correlation between an attainment variable and its predictor with the correlation ratio produced for the same association by coding the predictor as a set of categories. But the categories are apparently so large and heterogeneous that a great deal of error is introduced, since five of seven comparisons of this sort yield correlation ratios which are *smaller* than the corresponding coefficients of determination. Also, I kept expecting the authors to replicate the entire Wisconsin model as presented, say, by Sewell, Haller, and Ohlendorf in 1970, but this they never do. A simple comparison of the ability of a version of this model incorporating nonlinear effects to account for variance in attainment relative to the original linear rendition of these relationships might have been the most direct and inclusive approach to the issues raised here.

The authors conclude by discussing some practical implications of the existence of nonlinear effects in status attainment models; implications which might seem more poignant had the evidence for such effects proved more substantial. If the effect of structural conditions on achievement behavior depends on aspirations, forms of policy intervention which concentrate on improving school quality or family income may have the unintended consequence of aggravating inequality, since they may be useless for low aspirers while facilitating the achievement of the ambitious.

Unfortunately, the net effect of this study will probably be to add to the already abundant literature on disconfirmed hypotheses postulating interaction. It is therefore regrettable that the subject does not receive a more thoroughgoing treatment in the present analysis. Not that what is done here is bad; the discussion of procedures and results suggests a reasonably skillful execution. But the problem deserves scrutiny from as many angles as our present repertoire of techniques permits, and in this regard I think the present study falls a bit short.

Self and Society: A Symbolic Interactionist Social Psychology, by JOHN P. HEWITT. Boston: Allyn & Bacon, 1976. 248 pp. $5.95 paper.

The Corrosion of the Self: Society's Effects on People, by THOMAS KREILKAMP. New York: New York University Press, 1976. 235 pp. $12.50 cloth.

Orientation in Social Psychology, by CAROLYN WOOD SHERIF. New York: Harper & Row, 1976. 441 pp. $8.95 paper.

SYLVIA CLAVAN
Saint Joseph's College, Philadelphia

These three books have in common only that they all deal with the broad area of social psychology. Other than that, each differs in its purpose, intended audience, main thesis, and degree of success in realizing a stated goal.

To begin, Carolyn Sherif's book is a well-written and easily understood introduction to social psychology. From the initial examination of social psychological dimensions of "interaction in brief encounters," the reader is introduced to a selection of research in the field through a potpourri of topics ranging from "becoming related to others," through the group processes, to the self system and reference groups, attitudes, communication, and finally, "social movements." Pertinent research is incorparted into informal ongoing discussion of a particular topic, and the total organization of the book is a refreshing change from standard texts. The gain by what the author refers to as a "personal approach" is offset somewhat by a loss of precision in outline, definition, and summary of material covered. Also, readers looking for some theoretical framework(s) will not find it here. On the whole, however, Sherif has succeeded well in what she set out to do—to share her interset and enthusiasm about the field and to whet the appetite of newcomers. I think that undergraduates will enjoy this book, and that in conjunction with collateral material, it would be an excellent choice for an introductory course.

In contrast to Sherif's lack of emphasis on a theoretical stance, John P. Hewitt's *Self and Society* is an ambitious effort to explain social psychological phenomena within the tradition of symbolic interactionism. Whereas Sherif's orientation could be characterized as biased toward the psychological, Hewitt's work is purely sociological, an orientation that he describes as "perspectival" (p. 3). Hewitt views the present level of psychological knowledge as inadequate to deal with the complexity of social interaction and societal structure. He feels, rather, that concepts that stress symbols and interaction such as those drawn from linguistics, anthropology, biology, philosophy, as well as from sociology, go much further in explaining human behavior. The author notes that human conduct is far less a matter of direct response to environmental stimuli than action toward, and in response to, the "meaning" of objects, the "meaning" emanating from linguistic symbols and social interaction (p. 9).

The symbolic interactionist frame of reference works well here with traditional interactionist concepts such as the "self" and "self-processes," human interaction, role, etc. The theoretical frame begins to show strain, however, when it is applied to concepts more commonly explained psychologically. In discussing cognition, for instance, the author relies more heavily on phenomonological sociology rather than interactionism (pp. 118–122). To be fair, Hewitt does caution the reader in his preface that he draws on other theoretical perspectives at times. The fact that this attempt to present a broad area of social psychology within one particular theoretical context is not consistently even, does not take away from the overall scholarship. Advanced students and those interested in these areas of inquiry will want to read this sociological social psychology book. I think that it will be referred to frequently in the future.

Kreilkamp's *The Corrosion of the Self* seemed to me to fall short of the quality of the two books commented on above. The book has far more to do with social thought, social issues, and social criticism than with rigorous, systematic analysis of the relationship of self and society. Kreilkamp attempts to use some of the work and fundamental ideas of scholars and social theorists (e.g., Kenneth Keniston, Elliot Aronson, B. F. Skinner, Ronald Laing, Erving Goffman, Carl Rogers, Thomas Schelling, and Kenneth Burke) to point to the lack of unifying theory in social psychology, to show how the field bears directly on social problems and social criticism, and to suggest ways in which social thought contributes to the understanding of the relation between man and society. This reviewer found the author's purpose and development of ideas rather obscure, and, regretfully, was left with an impression of a book somewhat erudite for a general reading public, and too descriptive for social science.

Social Psychology and Contemporary Society, 2nd ed., by EDWARD E. SAMPSON. New York: John Wiley & Sons, 1976. 567 pp. $12.95 cloth.

Social Psychology: An Introduction, edited by BERNARD SEIDENBERG and ALVIN SNADOWSKY. New York: Free Press, 1976. 561 pp. $12.95 cloth.

A Contemporary Introduction to Social Psychology, by LAWRENCE J. SEVERY, JOHN C. BRIGHAM, and BARRY R. SCHLENKER. New York: McGraw-Hill, 1976. 462 pp. $11.95 cloth.

Social Psychology: Interdependence, Interaction, and Influence, by JAMES T. TEDESCHI and SVENN LINDSKOLD. New York: John Wiley & Sons, 1976. 705 pp. $16.95 cloth.

MARY ANN GROVES
Montclair State College

The Sampson text has an interdisciplinary focus and puts greater emphasis on language and cognitive processes, and less on experimental research, than the remaining three books. Sampson uses Kurt Lewin's field theory as a model for the interactionist perspective stressed throughout the book. Especially good are the first two chapters which distinguish between the person-centered and situation-centered perspectives, illustrate the concept of statistical interaction, and stress the importance of considering the joint operation of person and situation. Other chapters include cognitive processes, attribution theory, language, identity and self, authority and the tasks of freedom, responsibility and morality, prosocial behavior, justice, and the person and modernism.

Sampson devotes ten pages to presenting symbolic interactionism as one version of an interactionist perspective, and he includes more references to symbolic interactionist sociologists than the other three books. (Severy, Brigham, and Schlenker made no references to the work of George Herbert Mead or Charles Cooley.) The Sampson text is clearly written, but more pictures and illustrations would have added to student interest.

The format of the text by Severy et al. is good, with summary statements and lists of goals for each chapter; many pictures, illustrations, and inserts illustrate the concepts; and contemporary examples (Watergate, *All in the Family* characters, the Viet Nam war, political figures) should help students relate the material to real-life situations. However, the content of the text seems to oversimplify some of the issues, and is unclear and misleading in places, especially in the sexism and socialization chapter. Some of the tables are not explained adequately, and some generalizations which I questioned are not referenced. The description of how parents socialize boys and girls and the consequences of certain socialization practices are based upon only two studies (done in 1963 and 1969), and students might infer that the material is "undisputed truth" since there is inadequate discussion of the complexity and controversy of this topic. The following quotation is from that discussion:

> The more his [the father's] interests and attitudes are masculine in nature, and the more he encourages his daughter's participation in feminine-typed activities, the more likely she is to develop "appropriate" sex-role preferences. . . . In effect, young males need one model (a father), while females need two (both a strong mother and a strong father). Apparently, since "femaleness" is not valued so highly in our culture, more effort is needed to "appropriately" sex-type females (pp. 153, 155).

The book by Tedeschi and Lindskold is a long, technical treatment of social psychology in which "social influence" is used as the central theoretical focus. (For example, aggressive behaviors are conceptualized as forms of coercive social power.) This text is more suitable for upper-division courses and as a professional reference than for an introductory course. The emphasis on theory and integration of the text around one theme is a strong point, given the profusion of experimental studies which have disconnected hypotheses, and which are published with little or no attempt to relate their results to any theoretical framework.

In spite of the note on page 1 in which

Tedeschi and Lindskold state that the terms *man* and *he* refer to both sexes and apologize for the "awkwardness of the English language," I was irritated by the frequent usage of the masculine terms in chapter subtitles and throughout the book. Also I would have preferred the insert boxes to have been more clearly differentiated from the body of the text.

The reader edited by Seidenberg and Snadowsky contains fifteen chapters written by twenty social psychologists. Chapter topics include the field of social psychology, the social psychology of the experiment, social motivation, socialization, situational determinants of hurting and helping behavior, attitudes, attitude change, person perception, interpersonal attraction (equity theory), interpersonal influence and conformity, power and bargaining, group development and structure, group processes and leadership, social movements, and applied social psychology (focused on poverty and race relations). The editors did not discuss or relate the various chapters to each other; instead they are presented as surveys of topics and discussions of research and problems in the particular areas.

In discussing the field of social psychology, the editors seem to support the usage of several research methods, but express their preference for the experimental method. Although *Sociometry* and other journals are mentioned, they state that "perhaps the best overview of social psychology would be obtained by leafing through a few volumes of the *Journal of Personality and Social Psychology*" (p. 7). Another comment which indicates the tone of the description of the field is the following:

> Although most social psychologists view their goal as establishing functional relationships among variables, the complex subject matter of social interaction may be more amenable to concepts based on emergence and field properties. *These, however, have not yet evolved to the point of usefulness* (p. 20, emphasis mine).

I would use the Seidenberg/Snadowsky book as a professional reference, but would consider using parts of it in an introductory course only in combination with more sociologically-focused references, including the symbolic interactionist perspective and discussions of *non*-experimental research.

Of the four books reviewed here, the Sampson one seems most desirable as a basic text in an introduction to social psychology course.

Sport

Social Problems in Athletics: Essays in the Sociology of Sport, edited by DANIEL M. LANDERS. Urbana: University of Illinois Press, 1976. 251 pp. $12.50 cloth.

America through Baseball, by DAVID Q. VOIGT. Chicago: Nelson-Hall, 1976. 221 pp. $9.95 cloth.

CAROLYN R. DEXTER
Pennsylvania State University, Middletown

The study of sport has become an acceptable activity for sociologists. I am reminded of Paul F. Lazarsfeld's explanation for shifting the locus of his decision-making investigations from consumer behavior to voting behavior. Consumer research, he said, was not high-faluting enough for university professors. Now that the American Sociological Association has devoted a session of its 1976 annual meeting to the sociology of sport (and will again in 1977), and two more books have recently joined the growing body of literature, sport has indeed become sufficiently high faluting to attract the attention of serious sociologists.

Voigt's *America through Baseball* is a collection of the author's articles previously published in historical and popular culture journals. In this volume he organizes a body of his work to illustrate the extent to which the sport of baseball has mirrored major themes in American historical development. In describing the reflection of nationalism, territoritorial expansion, racism, and unionism in the historical development of baseball he argues the usefulness of sport as a research site for understanding processes extant in the larger society.

Landers's *Social Problems in Athletics* is also an anthology but differs from Voigt's. It is composed of original work presented at a multidisciplinary conference on "Sport and Social Deviance" held at State University College of Brockport, New York and sponsored jointly by student clubs and the departments of Men's and Women's Physical Education, Recreation, Sociology, Psychology, and Anthropology as well as the Black Student Liberation Front. Three of the four problems selected for study cover old ground: competition, deviance, and racial discrimination. The fourth, sports as an arena for expressing alternate political values breaks new ground. Dealing with the opposite side of the coin described by Voigt, the articles in this section describe a new role for sports as a mechanism for expressing minority political values associated in the past with intellectuals rather than athletes. The problems selected for study represent the current distribution of power in academic establishments. That the woman athlete is largely ignored in spite of the sponsorship of the Women's Physical Education Department and Title IX is hardly accidental.

These two works represent the polarities in the study of sport. Voigt's book illustrates the most common model: the use of the historical approach, a concentration on a single sport, and the use of sports as a microcosm of society. The studies in Landers's work represent the other end of the continuum: use of a micro-empirical approach, generalizations across sports, and sports as an important phenomenon in itself for sociological study. Voigt's collection will interest baseball fans. Sociologists of any persuasion will find in Landers's book insights and suggestions for hypotheses to test in their own work. And I believe this is the direction in which the sociology of sports is moving.

Retreat from Apartheid: New Zealand's Sporting Contacts with South Africa, by RICHARD THOMPSON. New York: Oxford University Press, 1975. 102 pp. $3.50 paper.

REMI CLIGNET
Northwestern University

This document describes graphically the controversies generated by the rugby games between New Zealand and South Africa. More specifically it shows some *Blacks* who are not *black* (the Maoris of New Zealand have been colonized all right but does this make them black?) are dropped from a team called the *All Blacks*, whenever the team visits an almost *all black* country (i.e., South Africa). South African whites are willing to play only against the *white* players of the *All Black* team; ironically, the black audience in the almost all black country applauds the exploits of the *lily white All Black* team.

To engage in this selective segregation requires a tremendous amount of imagination and New Zealander sport administrators do it because they claim to have a "duty" toward rugby (p. 41). To make things worse, the Maoris themselves have the same "duty" and claim, therefore, to have doubts about their own blackness but no doubts whatsoever about their superiority over the African make them black?) are dropped from a blacks—as the pressures grow to stop this nonsense, so does the sophistry of the arguments offered to challenge or justify the status quo.

Stratification

Social Inequality: Class and Caste in America, by LUCILE DUBERMAN. Philadelphia: J. B. Lippincott Company, 1976. 314 pp. $4.95 paper.

JOAN HUBER
University of Illinois, Urbana-Champaign

This book, intended for undergraduates, tidily summarizes Lenski, Marx, Weber, and Pareto in the first two chapters; the rest of the book, more descriptive than analytic, is eclectic to a fault. The theoretical stance consists of apparently equal parts of functionalist, reformist, and radical thought; the research findings are unevaluated, hence good and bad research receive equal space. The attempt to rescue race, age, sex, religion, and ethnicity from neglect by treating them as castes is mostly a reporting of what some groups don't have that others do. Causal analysis is rare.

Sloppy diction and errors of scholarship occur too often, e.g., "Lenski uses the dialectic method to correlate the [functional and conflict] theories" (p. 52). The German upper classes are said to speak high German while the lower classes speak low German (p. 142) —a total confusion of geographical and social altitude.

The Changing Rural Stratification System: A Comparative Study of Six Villages in Rajasthan, India, by K. L. SHARMA. New Delhi: Orient Longman, 1974. 226 pp. No price listed, cloth.

SANTOSH KUMAR NANDY
Research Enterprise, Toronto

This revised version of the author's doctoral dissertation based on field-work in 1965-66 and updated with materials to 1971 explores the structures and processes of social stratification in six villages in three selected districts in Rajasthan, India. The villages differ in urban proximity, modes of cultivation, and types of land tenure.

The significant finding is that a process of minimization of social inequalities has started in the era of planned social development. However, traditional social bonds of caste, class, and power, still prevail, especially in ex-Zamindari settlements, which are irrigated, and dependent on agriculture. In fact, a continuum of traditional and secular elements of social ranking has emerged. Sharma indicates that widespread education and reduction of economic disparities among villagers will accelerate the emergence of the egalitarian order envisaged in the Constitution and national policies.

Sharma claims his systematic analysis of social stratification in present-day India fills a major gap in the growing literature which has been mainly holistically oriented. Sharma's study indeed corroborates and supplements recent systematic studies on stratification by Bailey, Béteille, and Mukherjee.

Class in a Capitalist Society: A Study of Contemporary Britain, by JOHN WESTERGAARD and HENRIETTA RESLER. New York: Basic Books, 1976. 432 pp. $15.00 cloth.

ROCHELLE FELDMAN
University of Connecticut

Westergaard and Resler's stated purpose is to analyze class inequality in contemporary Britain from a Marxist position. The result of the study, however, is primarily a description of the consequences of British capitalism rather than analysis of inequality. The authors themselves assume that inequality is rooted in the private ownership of capital, the ebb and flow of the labor market, and the changing role of the State. But with no explanation of the exploitive nature of the relationship between labor and capital, nor an analysis of the labor theory of value as it affects the formation and maintenance of class divisions, the authors' understanding of the roots of inequality is theoretically incomplete like the theories of Domhoff and Bottomore. While the authors document the consequences of class inequality by the critical examination of welfare, taxation, national health, and the comprehensive school, they offer little analysis of why and how accumulation and the expropriation of surplus significantly determine British class relations.

While the above criticism limits the theoretical potential of the work, there is much to be said for the authors' synthesis of important data on the British class structure. For example, in their criticism of embourgeoisement, Westergaard and Resler are quick to point out the tendency of the literature on social inequality and mobility to confuse descriptive changes, e.g., an absolute rise in the standard of living, with the erosion of class inequity. In fact, the authors document well the trend toward the increase rather than the decrease in income inequality in Britain.

In attempting to explain occupational stratification, the authors emphasize the lack of shared values, life, and voting style among salaried workers and wage workers. But this describes the articulation of a status hierarchy; it does not analyze the roots of these differences. Since one of the central assumptions of the book is the conflict between labor and capital, it is crucial to understand the development and function of the differentiation of labor in the context of its potential unity. In other words, the description of the differences within labor tends to contradict the basic premise of the book unless it is explained more clearly as a consequence of the expansion of the State and the institutionalization of class conflict. The shared interests of labor are, however, hinted at in the authors' assessment of pluralism and the extent to which the changing role of the State conditions social reform in Britain. Westergaard and Resler's analyses of the nationalization policies of the twentieth century, the real versus apparent differences between Tory and Labour, and the legislation to limit strikes and works-to-rule, give strong support to their argument that the institutionalization of class conflict, in the intrests of capital, constrains the revolutionary potential of labor.

While I have given greater emphasis to the shortcomings than to the strengths of this book, I must acknowledge it's significance in the field of stratification. It is clearly one of the better documented and comprehensive examinations of a particular class society. It avoids over-generalization and abstraction, and provides a basis for important theoretical work. It is therefore extremely useful in assessing the extent to which capitalist penetration affects all aspects of British society. If we recognize its limits as a Marxist explanation of the British class structure, this book is an important contribution to our understanding of the consequences of British capitalism and is a worthwhile addition to both undergraduate and graduate courses in stratification.

Theory

Politics and History: Montesquieu, Rousseau, Hegel and Marx, by LOUIS ALTHUSSER. Translated by BEN BREWSTER. London: NLB, 1972, 1975 (distributed by Humanities Press). 192 pp. $9.00 cloth.

Marxism and Hegel, by LUCIO COLLETTI. Translated by LAWRENCE GARNER. London: NLB, 1973 (distributed by Humanities Press). 287 pp. $15.75 cloth.

ARTHUR W. FRANK, III
University of Calgary

The editorial decision to review these works together may express the distance of both authors from North American sociology. By design and content the books have little in common. Althusser's *Politics and History* contains three unrelated pieces: a monograph on Montesquieu, published in French in 1959, comprises over half the volume; the section on Rousseau transcribes lectures from a course given by Althusser in 1965-66; the final essay, "Marx's Relation to Hegal" (French publication, 1970) is a schematic presentation given by Althusser in Jean Hyppolite's seminar on Hegal and depends on Althusser's longer writings on Marx. Colletti's book, by contrast, pursues a single theme: the philosophic basis of Marxism, with emphasis on the interpretation of idealism.

Thus each book has different aims. Althusser's collects previously published but untranslated materials, while Colletti's presents a major statement on the understanding of Marx. What the books have as their strongest commonality vis à vis North American sociology is not their Marxism, as might be expected, but rather their scholarly sense of what it is to *read*: both books are lessons in the textual analysis of social theoretical writings.

The occasional frustration caused by Althusser's self-conscious fragmentation is more than compensated for by the personal appeal, methodological clarity and interpretive suggestiveness of his writing. *Politics and History* is perhaps the best display yet to appear in English of both Althusser as a teacher and Althusserian structuralism as a method. Although *For Marx* and *Reading Capital* remain his important books, *Politics and History* may provide a better introduction to Althusser's intellectual influence.

The monograph on Montesquieu is written with an affection which does not blind the author to his subject's shortcomings, but does lead the reader to an appreciation of his achievement: "I simply hope that I have given a more living portrait of a figure familiar to us in marble or bronze" (p. 13), Althusser writes. He creates this "living portrait" by considering the structure of *The Spirit of Laws*, with his analysis demonstrating a coherent order within an apparently random chapter arrangement.

The sense which Althusser makes of Montesquieu's work may not satisfy all, but his analysis has two indisputable values: it takes Montesquieu's text seriously, refusing to dismiss its structure as accidental or inconsequential, and it focuses future scholarly dialogue on that text, since those who would refute Althusser's reading now must supply one of their own.

The same values are exemplified by the lectures on Rousseau. Althusser demonstrates the structural arrangement of the arguments in *The Social Contract* to be based on a sequence of four "discrepencies," each of which generates, by theoretical necessity, the next. Perhaps the highest achievement of Althusser's reading of Rousseau is his demonstration, based on his reading, of the textual authorization for other readings: the Kantian, the Hegelian, and, most interestingly, the Husserlian. In demonstrating these readings' authorization, Althusser himself partially mirrors Rousseau's structure to the extent to which "the solution is itself a problem" (p. 145).

In *Politics and History* Althusser stands close to the reader, as a guide and teacher, and limits his objectives. Colletti's *Marxism and Hegel* is also an invitation to study again the works it discusses, but the objectives of the more formal analysis are less restricted. Unlike Althusser, Colletti pursues his subject to whomever's work it leads, and the themes discussed barely can be suggested in this review.

"In order to understand Marx," Colletti writes, "one must reconstruct in some way the entire antecedent tradition" (p. 247). Such a reconstruction necessitates an epic, and Colletti has written an epic of the interpretation of idealism, from its beginnings in Spinoza to its most consistent expression in Hegel, its application and transformation by Marx, its misinterpretation by Engels and Lenin, and the confusions this misinterpretation causes in Lukács and Marcuse. The latter writers, Colletti demonstrates, fail to understand that for Hegel idealism is necessarily Christian; thus for Lenin to attempt to read Hegel as a philosophy of movement and change and " 'cast aside for the most part God, the Absolute, the Pure Idea, etc.' " (p. 24) could only lead to misunderstanding, not only of Hegel, but also of Marx.

Like Althusser, Colletti's strength is in his insistence on reading seriously. Confronting the texts, he maintains *both* Marx's transformation of Hegel, by which the *Logic* becomes *Capital* and idealism is rejected for materialism, *and* his continuing debt to Hegel, exemplified by his adoption of much of Hegel's logic, e.g., "If this statement [of Marx's] means anything, it means that the commodity, just like the Christian, is the unity of the finite and the infinite, the unity of opposites, *being* and *non-being* together . . . It *is* and it *is not*" (p. 278).

Colletti's work is summarized by his own critique of Lukács: ". . . *History and Class Consciousness* is the first Marxist book after Marx . . . which deals with Hegel and German classical philosophy at a European level and with a thorough knowledge of the subject; it is the first book in which philosophical Marxism ceases to be a cosmological romance and, thus, a surrogate 'religion' for the 'lower' clases" (p. 178).

Colletti's implicit demand that Marxists read not only Hegel but Kant ("the only classical German philosopher in whom it is possible to detect at least a grain of materialism" [p. 105]) will probably not lead to mass revisions in reading habits or syllabi; Colletti acknowledges that Marxists rarely read Marx. If Colletti's argument on the understanding of Marx is correct, however, the peril of such omissions is misinterpretation in theory, leading to failure in practice.

These particular works by Althusser and Colletti do not allow a comparison of their respective versions of Marxism; they do present what Colletti calls "a European level" of analysis. While such analysis—such serious reading—is hardly absent from North American sociology, its too isolated pursuit is aided significantly by the availability of *Politics and History* and *Marxism and Hegel.*

The Structure of Social Systems, by FREDERICK L. BATES and CLYDE HARVEY. New York: Gardner Press. Distributed by Halsted Press, 1975. 419 pp. $17.95 cloth.

RICHARD A. PETERSON
Vanderbilt University

Save your Tinker Toys. They are the perfect building blocks for representing the structure of social systems as conceived by Bates and Harvey. Like many standard introductory sociology text book authors, and Talcott Parsons during the *Social System* phase of his work (1948–1953), Bates and Harvey believe that society is best understood as built-up out of numerous nested role-relationships between actors occupying clearly defined positions.

The parallels with Parsons's work of a quarter of a century ago is quite compelling. Like Parsons, the authors eschew both research findings and theory building in order to develop "a single integrated set of concepts designed to enable sociologists to describe and analyze both large and small social systems" (p. 1). Bates and Harvey define eight active, and eight cognate passive social units varying from act and norm to society and culture. They define four forms of complementary social relationships and identify three forms of groups. In the first form, called "social groups" each member is directly related to all the others. In the second, called "organization," members cooperate to achieve a single purpose. In the third form, "community," each element expects exchange to take place on terms favorable to itself. Numerous social units of these three sorts are structurally articulated and functionally integrated in a way which is not specified to form a large clocklike mechanism, "society" (p. 204). Exchange theory of Gouldner, Homans, and Blau is briefly noted and dismissed. The interactionists, Goffman, Becker, and Turner, are not considered, and neither are the more recent network formulations of Harrison White and others.

Like Parsons, Bates and Harvey are not unaware that society does not always keep perfect time. They identify fourteen analytically distinct forms of stress. As in the *Social System,* questions of deviance are framed in individual psychologistic terms which do not allow for structural imbalances in power and exploitation. For example, when culture and situation are not congruent, "role frustration" is generated.

Reading this book may induce a sense of nostalgia in sociologists over forty, since it could have been written two decades ago. Appearing then, it would have been considered a useful elaboration and critique of the *Social System,* and C. Wright Mills might have cited it as a distortion of the sociological imagination. Published in 1975, it provides a variant of structuralist role theory terms but hardly lives up to the authors' assertion that they "are presenting a new sociological problematic . . . [which asks] what are the underlying principles or laws which govern the structure or form of human social systems" (p. 3).

Rationality and the Social Sciences: Contributions to the Philosophy and Methodology of the Social Sciences, edited by S. I. BENN *and* G. W. MORTIMORE. Boston: Routledge & Kegan Paul, 1976. 416 pp. $23.50 cloth.

J. DAVID LEWIS
University of Notre Dame

This reader aims to present and evaluate alternative theoretical conceptions of rationality and their applications in anthropology, social psychology, economics, political science, social philosophy, and psychiatry. There are fifteen previously unpublished papers by eleven authors. The seven chapters written by one or both of the editors fill approximately half of the volume, and provide excellent clarification of different models of rational belief and rational action. These discussions, which are philosophically technical and often require special background knowledge for full comprehension, are directed primarily to professional audiences. In particular, the paper "Technical Models of Rational Choice" should be an aid to theory construction efforts by social scientists working experimentally with decision theory, game theory, models of conflict resolution, and the like. The editors synthesize a sizable quantity of literature within a comprehensive analytical framework.

The chapters contributed by other philosophers and by social scientists examine models of rational action and belief as they relate to such diverse processes as voting, forming political coalitions, cultural rituals, psychological adjustment mechanisms, budget allocation, and psychosis. These essays are of widely varying quality and, although some may be of interest to experimental social psychologists, I doubt that many sociologists would find them intrinsically valuable. Nevertheless, they serve a useful function by suggesting possible empirical elaborations of theoretical propositions developed in a more philosophical vein by the editors.

One of the more controversial chapters is the editors' paper "Can Ends Be Rational?: The Methodological Implications." Following Kant and Aristotle, they argue for the possibility that reason alone can determine objectively and rationally the ultimate ends which humans ought to pursue. They advance this thesis in opposition to that of Hume and Weber which holds that intellect is powerless to establish ultimate values. This meta-ethical objectivism carries the following implication: "A sociologist or a social psychologist might find in it a taxonomy capable of distinguishing people with rational attitudes, and capable of sustaining an operational theory about the conditions under which persons come to have rational concerns" (pp. 270–271). While admitting reservations about Weber's value-neutrality principle, most sociologists would not assume themselves, or any group, to be expert judges of whose ultimate aims are rational and whose are not. Moreover, the editors fail to consider the potential political uses of such a "social science" research agenda.

Philosophers and social scientists studying any of the many facets of rationality will be stimulated by this book; however, its cost and narrow, but technically sophisticated, topical focus make it unsuitable as a text for most types of courses.

Pre-Capitalist Modes of Production, by BARRY HINDESS and PAUL Q. HIRST. Boston: Routledge & Kegan Paul, 1975. 345 pp. $23.50 cloth.

J. CRAIG JENKINS
University of Missouri, Columbia

Despite the current revival of Marxist thinking, there has been little effort to state a theory of the modes of production that moves beyond Marx's own vague outline in the *Grundrisse*. This work by two British Marxists is an attempt to fill this major gap, offering both a conceptual framework for the analysis of whole societies and a philosophical rationale for their program. Though primarily theoretical in concern, the framework offered is clearly intended to be useful empirically. Drawing on recent historical scholarship, the authors provide several rich case studies of particular social formations to illustrate their scheme.

Using standard Marxist terminology to delineate a mode of production (as composed of the forces and relations of production), the major departure is the delineation of modes of production in terms of the relations of production. As the authors express it, relations of production (fundamentally, the various ways in which a surplus product is appropriated) are "in dominance." Though left ambiguous, what apparently is meant is that the relations of production define the boundaries for variation in the forces of production. For example, under the capitalist mode of production the most important defining feature is the appropriation of a surplus through hiring of wage labor. Only certain forces of production (e.g., forms of work supervision, instruments of production) are compatible with capitalistic relations of production. In this way the authors escape vulgarmarxisumus while retaining the central thrust of Marxian theory.

Problems with the scheme, though, erupt in what is probably the most provocative section of the book—a challenge to Karl Wittfogel's analysis of "Oriental Despotism." Wittfogel's argument was that a distinctive Asiatic mode of production existed in the Orient in which the ruling class was coterminous with the state elite. The latter's power, and thereby ability to appropriate a surplus, depended upon the technical necessity in arid climates for extensive irrigation works that could be organized only by the state. Managerial "despotism" effectively froze development in these societies, setting them off forever from the dynamic West.

Hindess and Hirst's attack, aside from noting the well-known empirical inaccuracies that plague Wittfogel's work, is to argue that "oriental despotism" is actually a variant of feudal society in which the state apparatus has been centralized. Wittfogel leans back on technological determinism, thereby failing to specify a distinctive set of relations of production. State taxation, the only alternative, cannot be distinguished from the conventional Marxian notion of "feudal rent." Nor can the notion of exploitation through taxation be used to identify any distinctive set of productive forces that would make up a mode of production.

At this point the argument begins to weaken. Early in the book the authors claim that the asserted "correspondence" between the forces and relations of production was not that of technological determinism. Nor is it an historicist's notion of "totality." Precisely what "correspondence" did mean, though, was left vague. About the only clarification offered is the argument that the purported "Asiatic mode" lacked it. Until the notion of "correspondence" is clarified the authors' assertion that there is no Asiatic mode of production must remain an open question.

Several other sections deserve note. The authors' discussion of the slave mode of production and the American Civil War is one of the most succinct and up-to-date treatments available. In dealing with the various pre-capitalist modes of production, their handling of economic anthropologists is generally solid. Especially interesting is the treatment of the Polanyi-Arensberg school. On the one hand, Hindess and Hirst accept the notion that a "surplus" is not physiologically but socially determined; at the same time they reject the focus of the school on distribution systems, arguing like good Marxists that production is the key. The side product of arguing against technological determinism is that "class struggle" is left as the only explanation for social change. For a theory of society that most sociologists would identify as preeminently a theory of change, Hindess and Hirst's brand of Marxism is weak in its "strong suit."

The organization of the book is straightforward. Other than a few lapses into sterile polemics, the volume is quite readable. Though a technical vocabulary is employed, sufficient definitions are provided for the Marxist initiate.

Structuralism in Sociology: An Approach to Knowledge, by FRED E. KATZ. Albany: State University of New York Press, 1976. 218 pp. $15.00 cloth.

INO ROSSI
St. John's University

In the last few years, the readers of this periodical have been made aware of the challenge raised by recent French structuralism against the empiricist paradigm prevailing in contemporary social sciences. Katz is one of the first sociologists who attempts to show the "operational" usefulness of certain structuralist ideas and their advantage over the empiricist paradigm. He applies some structuralist ideas in the area of sociology of knowledge through an analysis of roles and role performance. Katz's basic idea is that both microsocial systems and macrosocial systems are not totally knowable because role expectations define ranges of acceptable behavior within which various options are possible. This degree of indeterminacy is a structural characteristic which permits a smooth functioning of the system and its adaptation to the environment (chapters one and two). Katz presents a graphic model and a locational model for the study of empirical social structures from a structuralist point of view. He claims that the locational model approximates a structuralist model of the rules of role combinations; a variety of role combinations is possible because roles are both interrelated and somewhat autonomous (chapter three). Katz argues that the process of translating knowledge into practical usage is mediated by the attitudes of various role players toward knowledge. He shows that a process of translation is present also in theory making where the scientist proceeds from the concrete to the abstract. In this context Katz counterposes the concretist mode of theorizing of empiricist sociologists to the analytic theorizing of structuralists (chapter five). In the third part of the book, Katz examines how knowledge is used in the learning of adult roles (chapter six) and in the actual performance of the role of nurses (chapter seven).

In addition to contributing to the sociology of knowledge, the book deserves special attention for presenting an alternative to the empiricist mode of theorizing. Katz stresses the notion that observable events are actualized options among many other possible outcomes of the interaction of a variety of forces. We need a *science of possibles,* that is, a science which explains why some and not other actualizations occur, and isolates the various constituents of events. The concretist theorizing of empiricist sociology explains particular events as resultants of a convergence and combination of variables. Multicausal explanation can isolate the weight of each variable, but it cannot explain which aspect of a variable is involved in the phenomenon under study. On the contrary, the analytic theorizing of structuralism can determine which "abstractly conceived aspect of reality" constitutes the unit of the system and operates within the system in question (p. 134ff).

One might find Katz's locational model (p. 58, 86ff) on the rules of possible combinations of roles to be a rather descriptive device which can offer only some tentative directions for scientific research. Part of the reason for the modest results of Katz's work, is, in my view, that he has adopted a minimalist structuralist position. Katz's perspective seems largely to fall still within the realm of empiricist structuralism since he deals with roles as sets of expected behavior rather than with their deep structure or symbolic matrix. Stated differently, Katz does not capitalize on the semiological aspect of structuralism. Secondly, he adopts a "weak" concept of structure because for him, structure enables one to single out one aspect of reality at a time (p. 137), whereas the deep structure should enable one to predict the structural tendency of the system as a system. Specific instances and events are the results of the interaction of structural tendencies with psychological and other contingent factors influencing human behavior.

No matter its limitations, the study of social structure in terms of the two structural principles of controlled behavior and structural indeterminacy seem to be a good starting point for strengthening the analytic scope of sociological theory. Katz deserves credit for having perceived the potential of these and other related ideas which have been widely applied by Lévi-Strauss and Chomsky and one hopes his work will contribute to lay the foundations of "a formal calculus of the combinability of different social structures" (p. 12) which, as Katz rightly asserts, constitutes the scientific perspective of modern natural sciences.

Another Voice: Feminist Perspectives on Social Life and Social Science, edited by MARCIA MILLMAN and ROSABETH MOSS KANTER. New York: Anchor Books, 1975. 382 pp. $3.50 paper.

MYRA MARX FERREE
University of Connecticut

This book attempts the difficult task of providing a detailed and yet sweeping feminist critique of sociology and, on the whole, succeeds admirably. Although the title seems to promise an equal emphasis on providing a critical view of society, the book actually offers little direct commentary on social life. Rather, there are nine articles which each focus on a separate substantive area of sociology (political, organizational, medical, educational, urban, cultural, industrial, deviance, and race) and two which provide a more general critique of social theory and methods respectively, capped by Daniels's summary of present and future research concerns suggested by feminism.

This emphasis is likely to disappoint those who turn to this book seeking a general undergraduate text on women or nonsexist introductory materials for one of the substantive areas covered. The book aims at a more sophisticated audience, one already familiar with both a range of sociological material and the essentials of feminism. For such readers, it is likely to provide not only critical insight into research already done but a wealth of ideas for restructuring and broadening their present studies and enticing new directions for future research.

The combination of review, critique, and theoretical resynthesis is an exceedingly difficult but also exceptionally important accomplishment. By and large, the articles succeed in providing a sufficient review of the field for the sociologist not specializing in the area to feel comfortable with the material as well as enough new theoretical insight into familiar material so as not to bore the specialist. The clear and unlabored quality of the prose in most of the articles and the generally high level of success achieved make this very tricky balancing act look almost easy. A few of the articles are comparatively weak. The review of political sociology is not as well written as most, while the industrial sociology article tends too much to be a simple census of research done and not done. The article on black women focuses too narrowly on self-esteem. On the whole, however, the articles offer a high level of insight and synthesis. Kanter's own article on the managerial model in organizations and organizational sociology, Lofland's analysis of the role of the community model in urban sociology, and Hochschild's suggestions for a sociology of conscious emotion struck me as particularly outstanding.

The basic premise of the collection—that feminism provides a perspective from which certain serious flaws in the sociological view of reality are evident—certainly appears justified. Taken together, the articles demonstrate convincingly that there are at least three ways in which the sociological world view is distorted. First, the lack of empathy ("loving empiricism") for women in qualitative studies, makes it difficult to see women as actors with a valid perspective of their own. Thus, while we "understand" the world of men, women are only understood as they appear in that world. Secondly, it is argued that the theoretical models which have guided sociology have undervalued those portions of society associated with women. These parts of social life—emotions, informal networks and ladders, maintenance and support activities—tend to sink into invisibility leaving the remaining parts an exaggerated prominence. Finally, the point is made that despite the sociologist's claim of detachment, popular stereotypes have always been readily brought into use to "explain" simple quantitative findings. Moreover, thinking in such stereotypes tends to lead researchers to use inappropriate quantitative techniques (bipolar M-F scales, for example) and to ignore or exaggerate intragroup differences.

All three of these points are well worth making and the articles, singly and together, provide a convincing array of evidence for each. But the editors make a further claim which I do not feel the book as a whole supports. Although Kanter and Millman, in their introduction, assert that the book also presents a case against the "machismo" of quantitative research, I was relieved to see that the articles themselves do not advocate any wholesale flight from quantitative to qualitative methods as a more feminist approach to sociology. As the collection shows, any area of sociology, when dominated by men, will be defined in masculine ways and thus limited in scope and understanding. Insofar as quantitative sociology is already distorted, this should be an incentive to expand and reshape it rather than abandon it. I would consider this a minor quibble, not worth airing, if it were not for the female graduate students I have heard making an equation between feminist sociology and qualitative methods. One of many strengths of this collection is that it does not stumble into this fallacy.

Center and Periphery: Essays in Macrosociology. Selected Papers of Edward Shils, Vol. 2, by EDWARD A. SHILS. Chicago: University of Chicago Press, 1975. 516 pp. $19.50 cloth.

ELLEN R. ROBERT
University of Minnesota, Morris

Every society, according to Shils, has a center, constituted by ultimate values and beliefs and the structure of roles, institutions and persons which embody them. The first essays in this second volume of Shils's collected papers focus on the forces—consensus is chief among them—which integrate a society around its center. Shils then brings his conception of centrality to bear on stratification phenomena; the results are mixed. In one thought-provoking essay, he fits Weber's notion of charisma to Durkheim's model of the sacred, contending that this charisma can exist both in concentrated form at the center and in a more attenuated form at the periphery. But in analyzing the class system solely in terms of the *deference* granted to individuals, roles and institutions he is asking the tail to wag the dog. By later defining deference as what is "sometimes called 'status' by other writers," (p. 276) class becomes status, and the conceptual distinction which Weber wisely drew between them is lost in the shuffle.

The final sections focus on the function of primary groups in integrating individuals on the periphery into the structures of the center (principally discussions of the German and American armies during World War II) and the difficulties of the new states of Asia and Africa in maintaining constitutional regimes.

Several of the essays included are imaginative and represent genuine contributions to social theory; others, such as his discussions of society and societies are good examples of careful analysis of key sociological concepts, but some problems need to be mentioned. First are weaknesses of style. While Shils in some essays writes with a certain grace and usually avoids cumbersome neologisms, some of the more traditionally analytic papers read too much like sentence outlines; others, particularly those sections on the history of ideas, suffer from a breezy superficiality.

More substantively, certain crucial quasi-empirical claims, such as the contention that adherence to central values is more complete among the elite than among other classes, are made without supporting evidence of even an anecdotal sort. Still more serious, Shils frequently postulates individual traits and their distribution at crucial points in his analysis. In a discussion of the persistence of the central value system, we are told that it rests on human beings' need to be incorporated into "something which transcends and transfigures" their existence (p. 7); this propensity "is rooted in the neural constitution of the human organism" (pp. 127–128). Later called the "need for order," it is conveniently concentrated in persons of high intelligence and moral sensitivity; most people feel the need for contact with the ordering center only occasionally and some few not at all. Charisma and sensitivity to charisma also occur in reassuringly normal distributions. Nor is Shils particularly interested in the genesis of these needs in the social order.

As Shils himself notes, the sort of sociology with which he is associated has frequently been accused of not adequately dealing with conflict and change. Critics hoping for an essay which addresses their concerns will not find it here. Nor will they be made any happier to be told that one of the reasons for social change is that "some men have a need for novelty" (p. 25). While Shils recognizes the ubiquity of change and the importance of conflict in engendering it, he conceives of conflict only negatively—as a lack of censensus. This perspective has a certain plausibility, but does not press its analysis far enough. It is likely that consensus and dissensus stand in a more dialectical relation, and that a highly integrated society with almost universal consensus on the central values would create either an irresistable press towards the center or a deadly stillness presaging disintegration.

Trying Sociology, by KURT H. WOLFF. New York: John Wiley & Sons, 1974. 662 pp. $16.95 cloth.

ROBERT JACKALL
Williams College
Williamstown, Massachusetts

This book is a collection of essays which were written and, for the most part, previously published between 1940–1973. Together with detailed introductions to each of the book's six parts, and an epilogue, the collection represents the author's attempt to define for a professional audience what he means by sociology.

That definition and Wolff's efforts to frame it are quite complicated. He starts his work with a trio of essays appreciating and criticizing the contributions of Pareto, Durkheim, and Simmel, with the kindest words for the latter, and simultaneously admonishing sociologists to extricate themselves from the notions of their intellectual ancestors. Part II is an uneven and disjointed section containing a thorough but uninspired review of the literature on social control; a seminal piece on social change where Wolff's deep historical approach to sociology begins to assert itself; a syllabus, now outdated but still interesting, for the study of the Jews; a dry, traditional population study of Jews in Dallas in 1940; and, finally, a hint of themes and tones to follow, a series of intensely personal reflections on the Jewish Holocaust, where the issue is not only Jews but all people.

It is in the third part of the book that a key aspect of Wolff's sociological style becomes evident. In reflective essays on Germany, America, and on intellectuals, he emerges as a dialectical, critical thinker, whose posture towards his subject matter, however, is always tentative and inquiring. In his studies he finds paradoxes and anomalies rather than truths. This inquiring tentativeness pervades his work and, indeed, even the premises of his thought. He embraces a human or philosophical radicalism but is puzzled by the implications of such a stance for his politics; politically, he remains a liberal, but certainly a good deal removed from what passes for liberalism today.

The meaning of Wolff's human radicalism becomes clearer in the book's last three sections. Part IV critiques the present practice of sociology, especially its ahistorical, bureaucratic and scientistic character. In Wolff's view, the remedy for such fragmented positivism can only be a historical, genuinely empirical approach to the individual and society—that is, a concern with what actually *is* and with how that came about. In our era, this necessarily implies a concern with the ethics and politics of our society, if one is to understand our social order. As one concrete proposal to express these concerns, Wolff suggests, and characteristically offers an agenda for, the development of a sociology of evil; the study of evil, as it is experienced by people, can provide sharp insights into how a social order is put together and also into what is necessary to change that order.

But a genuinely empirical, historical sociology presupposes, antecedent to the choice of critical subjects, a certain attitude on the sociologist's part. That attitude is one of "surrender," a theme which Wolff begins seriously to develop in part IV and returns to repeatedly in part V, which contains a series of essays on cultural anthropology, and in part VI, which deals with the sociology of knowledge. The idea of surrender came to Wolff during a field study of a southwest community during the 1940s; the concept has been modified several times since then and some of these changes are evident in the essays here. It is an idea which has literally obsessed Wolff, surprising even himself, as he notes in the epilogue, in the pervasiveness of its impact on his work. Surrender means complete immersion in one's data; a cognitive love for one's subjects and an identification with but not a capitulation to them; perhaps most basically it means completely suspending preconceived ideas and established theories about the people and the situations one is studying, and reporting, as fully and honestly as possible, whatever ambiguities the data hold. In surrendering, the sociologist is closest to the pure experience of the rational, and, at the same time, most completely human. From surrender comes a "catch," ideas which emerge directly out of one's reflections on data; a catch illuminates reality, but does not exhaust the experience of surrender. Wolff's radicalism is then basically an epistemological one. In his view, the real radicals—those who go to the root of things—are those students of society who open themselves up to the complex ambiguities of other people's experiences, rather than those who approach the world with politically sophisticated but already formed analyses.

For Wolff, sociology is basically a humanistic enterprise. By practicing their trade and by retrospectively analyzing their work, sociologists not only learn about other people and society, but also, and perhaps especially, about themselves. This self-learning, which Wolff presents before each section and in the somewhat enigmatic epilogue, is one of the most interesting features of *Trying Sociology*. Indeed the autobiographical quality of the book partially accounts for its several irritating aspects—especially its unnecessary length, Wolff's occasionally tortured style, and his constant returning to the notion of surrender. Puzzling out the meaning of one's life and work is at best a long, uneven, and troubling process, and one where whatever integrating concepts one has managed to fashion become critically important. On the whole, the book provides many rewarding insights into the thought of a fine sociologist.

Urban

New Communities U.S.A., by RAYMOND J. BURBY, III and SHIRLEY F. WEISS. Lexington, Mass.: Lexington Books, 1976. 593 pp. No price listed, cloth.

New Towns: Another Way to Live, by CARLOS C. CAMPBELL. Reston, Va.: Reston Publishing Company, 1976. 283 pp. $12.50 cloth.

SALLY S. ROGERS
Montgomery College
Rockville, Maryland

Since the passing of the "Great Society," evaluative research on new towns and new community development seems to have gone the way of new towns. However, Burby and Weiss's massive work revives the issues. *New Communities* has two purposes: (1) to provide a solid information base for evaluating new community development as an alternative to urban growth, and (2) to provide an indication of the critical factors affecting the new communities' success or failure in their ability to meet residents' needs. This study, the product of the two senior authors, three collaborating colleagues, a number of research associates, and a supporting research staff, amply fulfills its purpose.

The data are based upon over 6,000 resident interviews, almost 200 developer interviews and almost 600 interviews with new community professionals, such as school and health officials and community association leaders. Seventeen new communities, including thirteen developed by the private sector without federal assistance, two participating in federal new community programs, and two specifically designed for the elderly, are evaluated in detail. These communities are paired with seventeen "conventional communities" in terms of age, location, types of housing, and price range.

Research focuses upon housing, neighborhood design, community facilities, and governmental characteristics. These are considered in relation to their contribution to residents' satisfaction and quality of life. Additionally, attention is given to the decision factors leading to their production. The matched conventional communities then offer a yardstick for measuring the new communities' strengths or weaknesses.

Not too unexpectedly, the new communities succeed in some areas while failing in others. They are primarily successful in providing an improved living environment for certain target groups such as low and moderate income households, blacks, and the elderly; an enhanced community livability; and superior recreation facilities. There is better land use and planning, access to community facilities, and a reduction in auto travel. On the other hand, they are not noticeably different, at many levels, from the conventional communities in areas of governance, residents' satisfaction with the quality of life and achievement of key goals, resident participation in community life, and resident evaluation of housing and neighborhood livability.

The findings may be somewhat disillusioning for those proclaiming new communities' virtues. Chapter after chapter documents that while new community development has produced substantial benefits in many areas, the program has fallen short. If the program is to serve effectively as a solution to urban problems or as a means for improving the quality of life, the authors indicate the need for greater commitment at the local, state, and federal level. Changes in financing, revisions in state policy, and the creation of a transitional new communities authority are recommended at the state level. Suggested federal changes include a closer federal-developer relationship, and an increased public sector role in the planning and providing of high quality community services.

So what else is new? The extensive and detailed data analysis offers a substantial base from which to move. Local, state, and federal officials as well as public and private developers to whom this study is addressed should read at least the first chapter. It neatly offers not only an introduction and a summary of major findings and recommendations, but also a brief methodological essay, and a succinct chapter by chapter summary. It would behoove them, however, and the rest of us, to read on.

Campbell's slim volume offers additional support to the thesis that while new towns offer much potential, that potential has yet to be fully realized. The study is based upon his on-site visits to twenty-four new communities. Over five hundred residents, planners, staff, and developers are interviewed. Additional data are drawn from the author's six year participant observation in Reston. The study's focus is upon the residents' perception of their community, racial integration, and such social issues as drugs and divorce. Other areas of interest include citizen initiated programs, governance, community services, and housing development programs.

New towns are seen as constructive alternatives to uncontrolled growth. Optimistic that new towns can provide a greater social and economic diversity than conventional communities, Campbell suggests they can alleviate the racial and economic polarization found in many American communities. The federal government along with the planning profession are taken to task for the program's many failures. Recommendations include a federally supported national growth program, the use of private enterprise, and financial incentives.

Both works face similar limitations. Each presents basically cross-sectional views of communities caught in a time frame. That the communities are at varying stages of growth makes analysis difficult. Many recommendations, while laudable, require perhaps more implementation than can be expected. However, the dust jacket on *New Towns* claims this to be "the first comprehensive analysis of new towns based upon on-site research. . . ." That's a rather bold claim for such a lightweight book.

Urban Health in America, by AMASA B. FORD. New York: Oxford University Press, 1976. 294 pp. $10.95 cloth. $5.95 paper.

Analysis of Urban Health Problems, by IRVING LEVESON and JEFFREY WEISS. New York: John Wiley & Sons, 1975. 390 pp. $17.95 cloth.

JENNIE J. KRONENFELD
University of Alabama, Birmingham

Health, in particular urban health, is an important topic. These two books approach urban health and health care from very different perspectives. *Analysis of Urban Health Problems* deals with issues in health care delivery, politics, and organization in New York City from 1970 through 1974 by describing the experiences of the Health Services Administration (HSA). *Urban Health in America* is a more general attempt to describe the health of people living in cities in the United States as compared with people living in other parts of the country, both currently and in the past.

Leveson and Weiss, once with New York's HSA, begin by introducing the concept of analysis (really a form of evaluation research and policy analysis) and by reviewing health care politics in New York City. The bulk of this work contains over twenty-five analyses of specific problems, such as addiction, physician staffing, and long term care. The book suffers from a lack of continuity between chapters and between specific sections within chapters. One feels continual annoyance at the brevity of the selections (most are between ten and twenty pages) and at their cutting (many have editors' notes indicating the omission of tables or parts of the report due to space limitations). Overall, this work may be of use to those with a particular interest in health care issues in New York City, but it will probably leave most readers confused by the lack of organization and direction.

Ford, on the other hand, presents us with a well organized, concise book. Detailing the health consequences of the physical and social environment of the city, the work goes on to describe the current operation of the health care system in the United States, including the use of care, distribution of facilities, and health politics. Ford also incorporates a discussion of ways to humanize health care, in which he emphasizes the need to consider the merits of national health insurance and prepaid group practice not only in economic (dollar cost) terms, but also in larger social human cost terms. The book could serve as a useful introduction to the health care system and its problems for sociology undergraduates. Useful also in teaching future physicians, it provides a helpful mix of information on general social conditions and social problems, with a special emphasis on the relationship of social factors to health and health care.

People and Politics in Urban Society, Volume 6: Urban Affairs Annual Reviews, edited by HARLAN HAHN. Beverly Hills, Calif.: Sage Publications, 1972. 636 pp. $20.00 cloth.

JOHN B. WILLIAMSON
Boston College

This edited volume by a Professor of Political Science is the sixth in Sage Publications' urban affairs annual review series. As has been the case with previous volumes in the series, it consists of a collection of original essays (in this case twenty) by a number of authors (in this case thirty-two), some clearly recognizable as "experts" and others who are much less well known. As with previous volumes in the series the essays are on quite diverse topics, but all are at least indirectly relevant to the theme of the volume (in this case urban politics). Of the thirty-two authors six are identified as sociologists and twenty-one are identified as political scientists. As is typical with such collections the quality of the articles varies, but given the diversity of the topics considered, evaluations as to which of the articles are most interesting or most useful depends in large measure on the reader's areas of specific interest.

In the introductory essay Hahn argues that "as a result of research on such diverse topics as alienation, urban violence, public policy, decentralization, and race relations, a growing interest has emerged in the possibility of restructuring political institutions to encourage the enhanced participation of all segments of the population in the policy-making process." The readings in Part I deal with the "means by which people, acting as individuals, seek to express their sentiments to public office holders." Consistent with this theme is the essay by Eisinger on the characteristics of those who make contact, the type of political leader that is contacted, and the type of contact made. The essay by Thomas Pettigrew reviews his research on a series of mayoral elections (Gary, Newark, Los Angeles, and Cleveland) which involved black candidates. He argues that one source of resistance to black candidates seems to be feelings of relative deprivation which he contrasts to explanations based on the concept of white backlash.

The essays in Part II consider the efforts of organized interest groups to influence local government leaders, e.g., Lipsky and Levi consider the possible impact of community organization in poor areas, and conclude that such efforts do not assure that the poor will achieve their political objectives. The essays in Part III deal with the factors which influence how local government responds to pressure from individuals and interest groups. In one essay Terry Clark argues that the ability to influence policy is determined by such things as the socioeconomic composition of the population, the extent of centralization of political authority, and the nature of the issue. Schuman and Gruenberg survey attitudes toward the adequacy of various city services in fifteen major cities. They find that attitudes are influenced by the race of the respondent and characteristics of the neighborhood. Part IV is entitled "Emerging Issues in Urban Policy," and is basically a collection of those essays which would not fit under any of the other three sections headings. The essay by Perry and Feagin questions the stereotype of the black ghetto as a disorganized pathological place. They argue that much recent evidence suggests that there is a high level of kinship interaction, friendship, and neighboring. They find evidence that the black ghettoite is as likely as the white urbanite to participate in voluntary organizations.

Metropolitan America in Contemporary Perspective, edited by AMOS H. HAWLEY and VINCENT P. ROCK. New York: Halsted Press, 1975. 504 pp. $25.00 cloth.

MARY DONAHUE STEARNS
Transportation Systems Center
U.S. Department of Transportation

Metropolitanization may be the major social trend of the twentieth century; at this time 64% of the national population now resides in such areas. Recognizing the imperative need of the planner and policy-maker to comprehend the contours and impacts of metropolitanization, the Advisory Committee to the Department of Housing and Urban Development of the National Academy of Sciences-National Academy of Engineers requested the Assembly of Behavioral Science of the National Research Council to establish "a Panel on the Significance of Community in the Metropolitan Environment." The technical papers collected in *Metropolitan America in Combined Perspective* were commissioned by this panel to summarize the inter-disciplinary state of knowledge about metropolitanization processes.

The ten papers are organized according to three headings ("Metropolitan Context," "Quality of Life," and "Governance of Metropolitan Communities") which convey demographic trends, subjective characteristics of urban and metropolitan existence, and the evolution of and discontinuities in metropolitan political structures, respectively. The content of the papers is generally guided by Hawley's conceptualization of a community as both integrative and allocative, independent of size.

Although the quality of all the papers is consistently excellent and well focused on metropolitan issues, the variety of formulations provides a useful balance between issue identification, methodology and data analysis, and empirical description. Zimmer's discussion of metropolitan demographic trends as "centrifugal," summarizes the historical dispersion of the metropolitan area through devices such as overlaying travel time contours on a metropolitan map, monitoring historical expansion of the toll-free telephone service areas. Foley's measurement of transportation access closely replicates the individual experience and reveals sources of the distributional problem within metropolitan areas. Marans and Rodgers's methodological definition of elements of the subjective quality of life provides data on public service correlates with community satisfaction. Campbell and Dollenmayer chronicle the evolution of attempts to formulate metropolitan political structures. Their discussion of the original intent and actual effect of the Council of Governments (COG) format sheds light on reasons for typical jurisdictional and financing issues experienced in implementation of metropolitan focused programs.

Despite the rich variety of information, several caveats are necessary. Although the sponsoring effort specifically addressed the role of community within the metropolitan environment, neither the introductory material nor the papers, with the exception of Marans and Rodgers, sufficiently consider the impact of place and of neighborhood in the context of expanding personal mobility and functional geographic redistribution. Additionally, the introductory material overstates the conclusions of some of the papers. For example, the recommendation that metropolitan areas could evolve toward political unity initially through consolidated school districts is made without sufficient consideration of county school districts or of alternative, less highly charged public services more readily adaptable to larger geographic areas such as fire protection, water, or sewerage.

Overall this book will be part of the basic reference library for all social science practitioners responsible for planning and policy raphy, it will also serve as a handbook of formulation. Because of its extensive bibliog- recent reference material on metropolitanization.

Additional Reviews

The Disadvantaged Consumer, by ALAN R. ANDREASEN. New York: Free Press, 1975. 366 pp. $14.95 cloth.

SUSAN MAIZEL CHAMBRÉ
SUNY/Stony Brook

"Fly now, pay later" describes a culturally approved buying pattern in American society. *The Disadvantaged Consumer* considers the situation of those in a "fly now" society who have a limited ability to "pay later."

Disadvantaged consumers are those "handicapped in achieving adequate value for their consumer dollar in the urban marketplace because of their severely restricted incomes, their minority racial status, their old age and/or their difficulties with the language" (p. 6).

This book is an extensive review of empirical research related to the subject. Andreasen presents and explicates a model of the "Structure of Disadvantaged Consumer Problems" which is comprised of three interrelated, independent factors: characteristics of disadvantaged consumers which influence their attitudes and buying habits, the market structure in disadvantaged areas, and exploitative practices of merchants in low income areas. After examining each of these factors, he presents a number of solutions including: stimulation of business development in low income areas, consumer education, consumer cooperatives, innovative marketing practices, and legal reforms.

My initial reaction on completing the book was confusion. So much information had been presented that I found it necessary to reconstruct the key issues by skimming through the book. The author is unclear about his audience, therefore, he considers almost every issue conceivably related to the subject in detail and thus diverts attention from his central concerns.

The model clarifying the subject matter presented in the first chapter should have allayed my confusion. However, the model oversimplifies what the book actually considers. Had the antecedent conditions and the outcomes of the factors included in Andreasen's model been incorporated in a revised model at the end of the book, the massive amount of information presented would have been more comprehensible without a cursory rereading.

This is a book on an important subject which unfortunately diverts the reader from following an argument leading to two valuable conclusions. First, because the problems faced by disadvantaged consumers are due to several forces, a number of remedial strategies are warranted. Secondly, since disadvantaged consumers have problems qualitatively different from the middle class, reforms directed at all consumers would not significantly affect the disadvantaged.

A Survey of the Social Sciences, by GARY D. BROWN and DUANE BROWN. New York: McGraw-Hill Book Company, 1975. 374 pp. $7.95 paper.

SHARON MCPHERRON
Saint Louis Community College, Florissant Valley

Regardless of the title, this book is not a survey of the social sciences nor is it a very decent text for instruction about the social sciences. The book, which was designed to be a core text in an introduction to social science course, is a juxtaposition of definitions and fragments of topics most frequently listed in the table of contents of introductory texts. The promise of the book, via the preface, is that the text is uniquely designed and written to meet the needs of classrooms characterized by diversity, particularly those in community colleges. Diversity, I suppose, refers to a range of abilities or a breadth of interest or both. The preface also states that the text will help students integrate the diverse material covered in social science courses.

But nothing in either the substance or the layout of the text differs from dozens of other texts. The glossary, study questions, and suggested readings precede the chapters, but that is hardly a significant innovation or a substantive adaptation to particular needs. The writing style is barren. Simple subject/verb sentences follow one another in rapid succession. One is told, repeatedly, the "something" is "something." Definitions replace concepts and proximity replaces relationships as the text jumps from topic to topic. On page 37, for example, in a paragraph that begins with a topic sentence that refers to race and culture as one of the substantive areas of sociology, culture, value, and norm are defined. Value is then re-defined ten pages later with no reference to the first definition. The sections of the book are designed as self-contained units and the text is void of statements that relate one chapter to another or one topic to another. Thus by design, the promise of integration is defeated.

The division within chapters between what are supposed to be major problems or topics is uneven, leaving truisms for topics such as poverty, while overwhelming the student with detail on others such as drugs. Despite the authors' claim to have removed all dull sets of figures, one chapter has seven pages of tables with no summary discussion of their contents. There are no reports of research findings in the sociology portion of the text and not a single graph.

The book opens with a chapter on the study of social science which is one of the better chapters in the book. That chapter is followed by four sections, each two or three chapters long, introducing sociology, psychology, economics, and political science. The opening chapter of the sociology section defines sociology, then focuses on socialization as a process even though no discussion of process, but rather end results, follow. In rapid order, groups, institutions, stratification, ethnic and racial groups, and deviation are discussed. The second chapter introduces social change and social problems, though a link is never developed between the two, but I assume their inclusion in the same chapter indicates that change and problems are related. This chapter discusses marriage and child rearing in a section that opens with a discussion of divorce. One isn't sure whether these topics are case studies of change, or problems, or both. Discussion of women's role and population conclude the chapter. The final chapter in the sociology section continues the problem theme with a discussion of employment, drugs, crime and delinquency, and poverty. The discussion of drugs is the best technically treated of any topic in the book, but community college students certainly deserve a far better textbook than this.

Illegitimacy, by SHIRLEY FOSTER HARTLEY. Berkeley: University of California Press, 306 pp. $10.00 cloth.

JENNIE J. KRONENFELD
University of Alabama, Birmingham

Illegitimacy discusses the subject of illegitimate birth in society from demographic and sociological perspectives. The first detailed attempt to deal with the topic in fifteen years, the author uses a variety of cross national (including historical) data to test combinations of variables affecting illegtimacy. She begins by viewing illegitimate reproductions as a social fact (à la Durkheim) apart from welfare or psychological concerns. She "explains" why certain societal groups have high levels of births out of wedlock while others have extremely low levels, by viewing illegitimacy as the result of an interrelated chain of events, the combinations of which allow alternatives to births in and out of wedlock. The author believes that the normative principle of legitimacy comes as close as any social rule to being truly universal, since all societies exhibit concern for the orderly succession of generations and the socialization of children. Because the negatively-connoted label "illegitimate," is applied by the social group, Hartley feels that doing away with the word, as some have recently suggested, would not eliminate the burden on the child. The term of reference (bastard, illegitimate) is less important than the condition and its consequences.

The author begins by discussing this "ideal of legitimacy" and citing literature about the consequences of illegitimate births for the mother, the child, the father, and the society. Reviewing international trends of illegitimacy, Hartley most frequently uses the ratios of illegitimate births to total births in various countries after World War II, supplemented by limited earlier data for selected countries. This leads to problems at certain points in the analysis, since the rate and ratio sometimes provide differing results. An example is Western Europe after 1880, where illegimacy rates declined substantially while illegitimacy ratios showed little or no decline. Reviewing the four major theories proposed in earlier research as explanations of illegitimacy—physical factors such as climate, sex drive, and race; psychological factors such as personality or general socialization; structural factors such as poverty, the sex ratio, and the proportion of women in the labor force; and cultural factors such as cultural relativism—Hartley concludes that single variable theories are not as adequate in explaining illegitimacy as are multiple causation theories.

In chapter 4, Hartley presents her own theory of illegitimacy, developing its details in the remaining half of the book. This theory of illegitimacy, called "the concatenated, multi-dimensional theory," is an extension of the Kingsley Davis-Judith Blake model of the intermediate causes of fertility. Thus, Hartley presents chapters on marriage and the age structure of the unmarried; variations in the extent of pre- or nonmarital sexual intercourse; fecundity, conception, and contraception; marriage to legitimate a premarital pregnancy; and abortion. Hartley concludes that no one of these intermediate variables provides a total explanation of illegitimacy among populations over time.

In each of the chapters focusing upon intermediate variables, she lists a series of propositions to be tested, then discusses the data pertaining to the propositions. She spends a great deal of time pointing out how variables interrelate so that, for example, populations may have the same level of nonmarital intercourse but have different levels of illegitimacy because of differences in contraceptive use, frequency of abortion, or use of marriage to legitimate a preexisting pregnancy. At these times, the analysis becomes overly detailed and laborious, making minute points beyond the reader's limits of comprehension and patience.

Although the chapter on contraception provides useful description of various techniques, it includes no data from the 1965 or 1970 U.S. National Fertility Studies. Also, the reader could easily conclude that couples employing the rhythm method have failure rates equal to or less than IUD users (untrue) or that IUDs can be used with success in nulliparous women (a matter of some debate). The author further implies, mistakenly, that the cause of the decline in illegitimacy in Eastern Europe was not legalization of abortion but an increase in the proportion of women remaining unmarried.

Given Hartley's orientation and turgidly written prose, her book will be of most interest and use to those studying illegitimacy from a demographic point of view or to family sociologists. Despite criticism, it is a useful addition to previous research, which has too frequently viewed illegitimacy myopically as a welfare problem, or as a consequence of psychological problems.

The Case of the Black Family: A Sociological Inquiry, by Jerold Heiss. New York: Columbia University Press, 1975. 246 pp. $12.50 cloth.

Elizabeth Higginbotham
Brandeis University

It is certan that the experiences of Black and other Third World people in this country differ from those of dominant groups. Their stigmatization has been lengthy and severe. One can only expect Third World groups to have made cultural adaptations which are evident in an analysis of the family structure. The Black family has been seen as unique, but in a derogatory sense, because it often deviates from the norms of white middle class families in this country.

In this book, Jerold Heiss reviews the charges brought against the Black family by social scientists who see the roots of Black problems embedded in the family structure of Black people. The major value of this work is the thorough secondary analysis Heiss does of quantitative data gathered by Robert Crain and NORC in 1966. Many assumptions about traits of Black families and the consequences of these traits have been accepted as fact, without being tested as hypotheses. An example would be that larger families do contribute to the problems of the Black community, having both short and long term effects. Yet, Heiss's work shows that these effects have been exaggerated by critics, and that Black people would still be troubled by certain conditions even if their families were not as large. This makes Heiss's work a much needed piece of research. It helps to dispel myths and put certain Black family traits into their proper perspective.

The results presented here about family and nonfamily variables are comprehensive, and both critics and supporters of the Black family need to be attentive to his results. It is probably essential reading for graduate students concerned with the Black family, particularly when balanced with more descriptive presentations of Black family life. Heiss focuses on traits found in Black families, assessing how evident they are both across SES groups and in comparison with white families. Then, most importantly, he looks at how much variance in outcomes is explained by these traits. He finds many family variables correlated with each other; showing that some family traits are associated or linked with other traits. But these traits often fail to predict, in any consistent manner, outcomes such as achievement, marital stability, future family income, and so forth. The careful examination of supposed consequences of family structures which characterize parts of the Black community is revealing, and puts maternal dominance, early marriage, and the effects of a broken home into a more realistic perspective.

Although the analysis is excellent and this work fills a gap in the field, there are shortcomings in Heiss's work. At times the material is not sufficiently well organized. Lengthy statistical discussions put readers at a disadvantage in having to assess for themselves the relative importance of particular content. Yet, as one reads through the gammas and beta coefficients there is a lot to be gained. Since the original data were not set up to answer all the questions with which Heiss is concerned, he is forced to reinterpret variables. Although he demonstrates innovative ways of testing his hypotheses with the available data, because of the time lapse certain cultural assumptions have changed and the contemporary reader may find responses stereotypic and outdated, especially in the case of sex-related variables.

Heiss puts unnecessary restrictions on what he must do with his data by using the trial presentation format, which necessitates the defense of the Black family in the face of the charges brought against it. This ploy forces the readers to focus on negative aspects of Black family traits and to review the evidence to either refute or support these charges. Possibly if he were more open to recent research by Black sociologists and other exploratory work he would have had a more open format. A more dispassionate or objective approach would have allowed Heiss to draw conclusions from the data not predicated on the opening charges. By entering the framework which by inference views deviations from white norms as the source of negative social traits, his conclusions are limited to a simple refutation. Important as this might be, he could have begun from another premise which would have shed more light on antecedents and consequences of Black family structures. There is certainly a lot to be learned there about the survival of a people and their humanity.

Toward Humanistic Sociology, by Alfred McClung Lee. Englewood Cliffs, N.J.: Prentice-Hall, 1973. 224 pp. $3.95 paper.

David O. Arnold
Sonoma State College

The book reviewer's version of a Parkinson's law would read: "book reviews expand to fill the space available for them." I have been allocated 800 words for this review, but I won't use them because the book is not worth 800 words. Its publisher claims that *Toward Humanistic Sociology* is an introductory textbook. I'm not entirely sure what it is, but it is not an introductory text. Lee does say a number of things that are worth saying, but most of them were said earlier and better by C. Wright Mills in *The Sociological Imagination.*

Sotsiologicheskie Issledovaniya, by Akademiya Nauk SSR. Moscow: Institut sotsiologicheskih Issledovaniy, April-June 1976, No. 2. 240 pp. No price listed.

Jiri Kolaja
Netherlands Institute for Advanced Study, Wassenaar

This is the second number of that long-awaited Russian journal of sociology, coming two years after the appearance of the first in 1974. With the exception of the first seven (unsigned) pages and one or two articles on the relationship between the Soviet Communist Party and sociological research in Russia, it is a pleasure to report that the journal focuses more on sociological than on political argumentation.

The thirty-two articles which comprise the issue have in most cases been written by one, or sometimes two, authors; in two cases, by three authors. The introductory section tells us how sociological research can contribute to the development of communism, and there are also the usual articles pointing out the deficiences in Western ideology. The journal as a whole is the work of the Soviet Sociological Association.

The growing acceptance of sociological research in the Soviet Union is indicated by the fact that of the units of the Soviet Academy of Sciences, some forty carry out some form of sociological investigation. It is stated in this journal that there are also sociological units in 120 cities of the Soviet Union and that advisory centers have been established in some 49 towns. Moreover, one reads that the Institute publishes mimeographed information circulars which are used to coordinate and further develop sociological research. When one tries to account for this current acceptance of sociology, the most apparent reason is that sociology can also be used for political ends.

The volume is divided into several sections according to such topics as mass information, effects of ideological work, families, budgeting of time, sociolinguistic and social planning, ethno-sociological problems, work, and socio-economic issues. M. S. Kosolapov, discussing methods of classification, and V. V. Cherednichenko analyzing prognosis by experts, are worthy of attention. There are three or four lengthy discussions of problems of migration—especially to Siberia, where there is a problem of maintaining a stable population—and the effort to avoid a return-migration to European Russia or such southern Asiatic republics as Kazakhstan, Turkmenistan, and others. V. V. Bovkyn gives a short description of the Soviet Sociological Association, telling us, along with M. N. Rutkevich, that the SSA has as members some 400 organizations, as well as 1,500 individual members. He notes that regional sections exist widely, and presently there are efforts underway to develop branches in the Baltic, the Far East, Moscow, and the Caucasus. The Leningrad group is the most active, having produced seventy publications in 1975. In the Ukraine there are four sociological institutes and eighteen sociological groups; in the Ural region, sociologists participate in 170 "plans" called "social plans"; in Novosibirsk, researchers published twenty-one monographs, organized thirteen conferences and twenty-nine seminars during 1975.

V. V. Kolbanovskij offers a study of social structure and workers, while V. I. Staroverov concentrates on rural prospects, especially in regard to the future years of 1990 and 2000. F. R. Filipov discusses problems of youth; the integration of different Soviet nationalities is discussed by M. S. Dzhunusov, and the resulting problems of migration are discussed by L. L. Rybakovskij. The editor of *Sociologicheskie Issledovaniya,* A. G. Charchev, continues his earlier investigations at Leningrad University on marriage and the family.

Six Russian sociologists have edited *Work Book of a Sociologist,* which, one hopes, might guide the Soviet sociologists in developing more sophisticated methodological approaches. A history of Marxist-Leninist sociology is given by V. S. Kruzhov, and along the same lines, G. V. Osipov continues in his criticism of contemporary bourgeois sociology. Other publications criticize structural functionalism, neo-evolutionism, social existentialism, phenomenological sociology, social neo-Freudianism, critical sociology, and so forth. They are to be published under such titles as *Criticism of Bourgeois Sociology* and *Criticism of Social Philosophy as Developed by the Frankfurt School.*

It should be noted that the Soviets have established cooperative studies of a cross-cultural nature with Polish sociologists, resulting so far in several publications, the most significant of which has probably been *Social Problems of Work and Production: A Soviet-Polish Comparative Research.* It is reported that another study, titled *Problems of Changing Social Structure in the Soviet Union and Poland,* is now being published. I. V. Bestuzhev-Lada continues his study of youth, while V. D. Patrushev investigates time problems. One also should report further studies of Soviet scientists by B. Z. Kononyuk and A. A. Zvorykin, a social competition study by I. I. Changli, and territorial and social-economic planning investigation by O. I. Shkaratan.

What about the future? It is stated that at the last international sociological conferences in Toronto and Montreal in 1974, Soviet sociologists presented 130 papers, which were available not only in Russian but also in English and French. What do the Soviets think that sociologists should try to achieve in the future? They stress that sociologists should become practically involved in social problems such as planning; they should investigate various methods of planning, and develop a system of social indicators to assist them in their efforts. Sociologists should concentrate upon the integration of different social classes and ethnic groups in the Soviet Union. And they should delineate and define the image of socialistic life, therefore they must pay special attention to ideological processes and their expansion in Soviet society.

Finally, ideological opponents of the Soviet Union should be the target for massive sociological investigation.

The Origins of Crowd Psychology: Gustave LeBon and the Crisis of Mass Democracy in the Third Republic, by ROBERT A. NYE. Beverly Hills: Sage Publications, 1975. 225 pp. $13.50 cloth.

MAURICE JACKSON
University of California, Riverside

This first detailed analysis of LeBon's life by historian Nye is sociologically interesting because of LeBon's historical prominence in some specialized fields of sociology and his vast influence in Western societies. As an indication of his influence, Nye claims that LeBon "gained a reading public no other social thinker could rival," and again, "*The Crowd* has been one of the best selling scientific books in history." His influence stemmed from his thirty years of editing the Bibliotheque de Philosophie Scientifique, selling of scientific equipment from laboratories he built, leading a luncheon group of intellectuals, being a friend of famous people, and advancing certain ideas.

Trained as a physician, LeBon developed influential ideas by applying extant knowledge of medical pathology, e.g., mental contagion, and of the individual organism, e.g., the unconscious, to the study of crowds. LeBon thought crowds, epitomizing social disorganization, to be generated in democracies by substitution through imitation and suggestions from leaders of unconscious action for the conscious action of the individual.

There is more concerning influences on LeBon, e.g., scientism, evolution, affective psychology, and pragmatism; conceptions that he influenced, e.g., racism, nationalism, nonmaterialism, education, and the military; and solutions he devised to crises in democracy, including theories of crowd control.

The book is well researched and includes an extensive bibliography, but its brevity somewhat limits the amount of evidence present and restricts the explication of relationships between some of the points. It is a book which can be read by sociologists with profit.

Child Care—Who Cares? Foreign and Domestic Infant and Early Childhood Development Policies, student edition, edited by PAMELA ROBY. New York: Basic Books, 1975. 226 pp. $3.95 paper.

MARIJEAN SUELZLE
Northwestern University

Teachers of early childhood socialization courses will be delighted with the reissue of this excellent reference text in inexpensive paperback form, as will those teaching courses in the areas of the family, women's studies, social policy, sociology of education, educational administration, social work, early childhood education, and child welfare. Until the early 1970s literature on child care was not easily accessible and research in the area of early childhood was dominated by psychologists and educators. The original hardcover edition, published in 1973, was an important contribution toward redressing this imbalance. It brought together articles which evaluated diverse infant and early childhood development policies throughout the industrialized world, linking child development to the larger questions of changing family patterns and living conditions within the community. Although the articles were originally written for a professional audience—policy makers, advocates for children, early childhood educators and program directors, college teachers, and researchers—many of us found that both the perspectives represented and the clarity of presentation of the articles made the book an extremely valuable resource for our students as well. The cost of the original hardcover edition, however, limited its utility as a textbook.

The primary purpose of *Child Care—Who Cares?* was to suggest concrete guidelines and directions for developing child care policies and programs in the United States at a time when America had a "nonsystem" of services for young children. The book remains current because little change has occurred with regard to child care policies. A new introduction to the student edition does review the recent literature, organizational developments, statistics, and policy and political developments through 1975. The student edition follows the same general format as that of the original hardcover edition, covering diverse aspects of child care programming and policy in terms of: (1) discussion of who would use the service and why; (2) examination of current services, problems and issues in the United States; and (3) analysis of child-care systems in other nations. Articles by Roby within each of these major areas succinctly summarize and integrate the breadth of coverage provided.

No other single volume covers such a wide diversity of issues affecting child care as that provided by the original hardcover edition. Although the student edition contains only one-half of that material, thirteen out of the original twenty-six articles, the range of the text as a survey introduction remains relatively unaffected. Some of the depth of coverage has been omitted, suggesting that the professional will want to continue to utilize the original edition as a more comprehensive reference.

What has been retained is a realistic assessment of the large and growing need for child care because of women's increasing levels of educational attainment, the dependence of the American economy on working mothers, the rise in single-parent families, and the increasing accumulation of research findings which demonstrate the benefits for young children from early educational and group experiences. The early chapters examine the need for child care from the developmental perspective of children, including infants, and the resistance to the provision of such care which has emerged from invalid comparisons between institutionalization and group child care. Within the context of the United States, the major historical events affecting the provision of child care services over the past hundred years are examined. Uncoordinated reactions to the problems of caring for children created by family disruption, poverty, immigration, depression, and war are revealed to have resulted in a current federal funding maze of over sixty different autonomous programs for child care or development. The failure of this patchwork approach to meet the needs of special interest groups such as blacks, university populations, and feminists is examined in depth. Because the United States lags behind other highly industrialized nations with high or rising female labor force participation, child care systems in Sweden, Finland, Hungary, and Israel are described in the context of a comprehensive social policy. Child care centers in these countries are discussed in terms of the distribution of national resources, prenatal and postnatal health and nutrition programs for mothers and children, maternity-leave policies, birth allowances and other income maintenance policies, and parent education programs.

What has been omitted from the student edition are the more detailed discussions of parents' needs for child care, legislative proposals, governing childcare centers, economics, federally sponsored care, early childhood programs, industry-provided care, family day care, the black child, and child care programs in Norway, England and Wales, the Soviet Union, and Japan. As someone who has used the original edition for my own teaching and research interests over the past three years it obviously pains me to have any of this excellent material deleted. However if the trade-off for a more compact inexpensive edition means making some of the material more accessible to a wider audience, then I think the compromises entailed will have been worth the sacrifice.

Minstrels of the Dawn: The Folk-Protest Singer as a Cultural Hero, by JEROME L. RODNITZKY. Chicago: Nelson-Hall Publishers, 1976. 192 pp. $9.95 cloth. $4.95 paper.

R. SERGE DENISOFF
Bowling Green State University

Peter, Paul, and Mary once told a journalist "Do you realize the power of Peter, Paul, and Mary? We could mobilize the youth of America today in a way that nobody else could. We could conceivably travel with a presidential candidate, and maybe even sway an election." The folk trio attempted just that, failing to get either Eugene McCarthy or George McGovern into the Oval office.

Sociologists testing the propaganda power of music have almost unanimously found that "popular music is popular but not terribly persuasive." Except, perhaps for the already committed.

Despite strong empirical evidence, the thesis that "art is a weapon" is a popular one. Going back to *The Republic,* advocates of the far Right and extreme Left have promulogated the *affectivity* of music. This is Rodnitzky's basic argument.

Minstrels of the Dawn is a history of the use of "protest" music by American social movements and entertainers. Rodnitzky traces the use of message songs from the early Wobblies to the slick renditions of Joan Baez. He indicates that movement oriented songs were quite different from the more individually directed efforts of Bob Dylan and Phil Ochs. Moreover, the author dismisses "folk-rock" or "folk-rot" as Tom Paxton regretfully termed it, as crass commercialism.

Protest singers are portrayed as "cultural heroes" indicative of a historical Zeitgeist.

To illustrate his point, Rodnitzky devotes most of his book to the careers of Woody Guthrie, Phil Ochs, Joan Baez, and naturally, Bob Dylan. Combining biographical data with lyrical material the author attempts to capture the spirit of the stormy 1960s.

Perhaps borrowing from *Esquire*'s "bard of a generation" description of Dylan, *Minstrels of the Dawn* tries to use these four figures as the prophets of their time: "And the words of the prophets are written on the subway walls . . . ." However, much of this is fundamentally conventional wisdom. The author *assumes* that Guthrie et al. moved the hearts and minds of the student movement and the so-called "counter-culture." Nowhere is this thesis established. Only Dylan—after consciously entering the commercial rock field—has a gold record to his name. The rest either tragically died penniless or, as is the case with Joan Baez, are struggling to survive.

While it is true that Guthrie and Ochs were symbols to certain ideological groups, it is equally correct to say most record buyers or fans had never heard of them. Indeed, A & M did not bother to release Phil Ochs's last album in the United States and Guthrie was never with a major recording company.

Perhaps "cult hero" is a better description than "cultural hero" since all of the singers discussed rarely enjoyed a massive following even in the so-called youth movement in the 1960s. Dylan, despite music critics, was virtually unknown until he switched over to the rock genre and abandoned protest music.

There are other problems with *Minstrels of the Dawn*. The author, unfortunately, did not interview any of his subjects or their associates. Consequently, much of the material is basically interpretative. Discourses on songs as reflective of the artist's mood or ideology make poor historical cases. For example, Woody Guthrie's *Bound for Glory*, a primary biographical source, is mostly fiction, yet the author accepts it as fact. Other secondary sources are treated likewise.

More significantly, one can easily quarrel with Rodnitzky's selection of artists. Pete Seeger is without question the most important "protest singer" of this century, yet he is not featured in the book (although he is briefly discussed). Tom Paxton and several others are not mentioned, while Joan Baez, not a bonifide protest singer, receives an entire chapter.

Finally, the author misses an essential point: the protest singers of the 1960s were essentially entertainers, *not* movement oriented activists as Bob Dylan so clearly indicated in a 1964 interview with Nat Hentoff. Ochs made a similar statement to folklorist Bruce Jackson and later myself (c. 1966). Guthrie's ideological commitment was even questioned by his friends in the "progressive" movements of the 1930s and 1940s. Only Baez acted out her lyrics in the political arena.

Minstrels of the Dawn is a well documented and written book, but a reader has to accept some of the author's assumptions. Unfortunately, I do not.

Marriage, Family and Society: Canadian Perspectives, edited by S. PARVEZ WAKIL. Toronto: Butterworth & Company, 1975. 515 pp. $8.95 paper.

MARYLEE STEPHENSON
McMaster University

The family as an institution has been called severely into question by several feminists. One object of their critique has been the traditional modes of conceptualizing, describing, and analyzing the family (Oakley). The *value* of the family as we know it can be debated, but its crucial function in the maintenance of the status quo cannot be denied. That academics have often served as apologists for it seems evident.

If the reader seeks material that will help make a critical evaluation of the role of the family in our lives today, there is very little of it in this book. Except for the article by Turk there is no evidence of a critical challenge to the methodological assumptions of the sub-discipline of Marriage and the Family. Nor is there in this book any evidence of theoretical or moral challenges to the traditional approach.

As a further limitation, the book's subtitle "Canadian Perspectives" is not borne out in fact. A number of articles which describe the existing (or changing) family patterns of various ethnic groups in Canada does not present a *perspective*. It provides empirical data and analysis in terms of the concerns of the individual authors, but that is all.

What the book *does* do, and does thoroughly, is present twenty-nine articles dealing with the family through its "life cycle." The first stage is about setting up a marriage—thus, articles on dating, premarital sex, the law in relation to marriage, the demography of marriage, etc. The second segment is on the established marriage and its ending—articles on life styles, fertility, interaction patterns, an attack on the myth of egalitarian marriages, swinging couples, kinship, and finally, divorce. The final part is on change and adaptation, and exploration into the future—articles on women in the labor force, the adaptation of rural families, changes in Inuit, and Ukrainian families. The articles on the future discuss how radical change isn't really taking place. And then there is an article on future parents in Canada.

The range of description is wide, the demographic articles in particular are thorough and informative, but the collection is somehow pedestrian. And as a final note, the book is set in that photographed-from-typing format and then reduced. It is unsightly and a real strain on even healthy eyes. Very off-putting, indeed.

PUBLICATIONS RECEIVED

(Listing of a publication below does not assure nor preclude its subsequent review.)

ABEL, ERNEST L., ed. *The Scientific Study of Marihuana.* Nelson-Hall, 1976. 299 pp. $12.50 cloth.
ADAMS, J. MACK, and HADEN, DOUGLAS H. *Social Effects of Computer Use and Misuse.* Wiley, 1976. 326 pp. $11.50 paper.
ADLER, RICHARD, and CATER, DOUGLASS. *Television as a Cultural Force.* Praeger, 1976. 191 pp. $17.50 cloth.
AMERICAN HOSPITAL ASSOCIATION. *Hospital Statistics: 1976 Edition: Data from the American Hospital Association 1975 Annual Survey.* American Hospital Association, 1976. 206 pp. $7.50 paper.
ANDERSON, RODNEY D. *Outcasts in Their Own Land: Mexican Industrial Workers, 1906–1911.* Northern Illinois University Press, 1976. 407 pp. $15.00 cloth.
APPLEYARD, DONALD. *Planning a Pluralist City: Conflicting Realities in Ciudad Guayana.* MIT Press, 1976. 312 pp. $19.95 cloth.
AUSTIN, LEWIS, ed. *Japan: The Paradox of Progress.* Yale University Press, 1976. 338 pp. $20.00 cloth.
BADCOCK, C. R. *Levi-Strauss: Structuralism and Sociological Theory.* Holmes & Meier, 1976. 125 pp. $7.50 cloth.
BAHR, HOWARD M., and GARRETT, GERALD R. *Women Alone: The Disaffiliation of Urban Females.* Lexington Books, 1976. 207 pp. $17.00 cloth.
BAILEY, ROY, and BRAKE, MIKE, eds. *Radical Social Work.* Pantheon Books, 1976. 171 pp. $8.95 paper.
BALDAMUS, W. *The Structure of Sociological Inference.* Barnes & Noble Books, 1976. 238 pp. $17.50 cloth.
BELL, BILL D., ed. *Contemporary Social Gerontology: Significant Developments in the Field of Aging.* Charles C Thomas, 1976. 454 pp. $28.50 cloth.
BERLINSKI, DAVID. *On Systems Analysis: An Essay Concerning the Limitations of Some Mathematical Methods in the Social, Political, and Biological Sciences.* MIT Press, 1976. 186 pp. $15.00 cloth.
BERMANN, TAMAR. *Produktivierungs-mythen und Antisemitismus: Eine soziologische Studie.* Europaverlag, 1973. 207 pp. NPL, paper.
BERMANT, GORDON; NEMETH, CHARLAN; and VIDMAR, NEIL, eds. *Psychology and the Law: Research Frontiers.* Lexington Books, 1976. 302 pp. $15.00 cloth.
BOBO, BENJAMIN F., OSBORNE, ALFRED E., JR., eds. *Emerging Issues in Black Economic Development.* Lexington Books, 1976. 233 pp. $17.00 cloth.
BONJEAN, CHARLES M.; SCHNEIDER, LOUIS; and LINEBERRY, ROBERT L., eds. *Social Science in America: The First Two Hundred Years.* University of Texas Press, 1976. 221 pp. $10.00 cloth. $3.95 paper.
CAREY, ESKANDAR. *Orang Asli: The Aboriginal Tribes of Peninsular Malaysia.* Oxford University Press, 1976. 376 pp. $21.00 cloth.
CARNEGIE COUNCIL ON POLICY STUDIES IN HIGHER EDUCATION. *Progress and Problems in Medical and Dental Education: Federal Support Versus Federal Control.* Jossey-Bass, 1976. 178 pp. NPL, paper.
CHALMERS, HELENA. *Clothes on and off the Stage: A History of Dress from the Earliest Times to the Present Day.* Orig. pub. 1928. Gale Research, 1976. 292 pp. $15.00 cloth.
CHANCE, MICHAEL R. A., and LARSEN, RAY R., eds. *The Social Structure of Attention.* Wiley, 1976. 339 pp. $24.50 cloth.
CHICKERING, A. LAWRENCE, ed. *Public Employee Unions: A Study of the Crisis in Public Sector Labor Relations.* Institute for Contemporary Studies, 1976. 248 pp. NPL, paper.
CHIROT, DANIEL. *Social Change in a Peripheral Society: The Creation of a Balkan Colony.* Academic Press, 1976. 179 pp. $12.50 cloth.
CLAUSEWITZ, CARL VON. *On War.* Ed. and tr. Michael Howard and Peter Paret. Orig. pub. in 1832. Princeton University Press, 1976. 717 pp. $18.50 cloth.
CLIFFORD, WILLIAM. *Planning Crime Prevention.* Lexington Books, 1976. 148 pp. $13.00 cloth.
COMBS, JAMES E., and MANSFIELD, MICHAEL W., eds. *Drama in Life: The Uses of Communication in Society.* Hastings House, 1976. 444 pp. $18.50 cloth. $10.50 paper.
COMMITTEE ON NATIONAL STATISTICS. *Setting Statistical Priorities.* National Academy of Sciences, 1976. NPL, paper.
CONRAD, DAVID R. *Education for Transformation: Implications in Lewis Mumford's Ecohumanism.* ETC, 1976. 230 pp. $10.00 cloth.
COOPER, CHESTER L. *Growth in America.* Greenwood, 1976. 262 pp. $15.00 cloth.
CROSBY, JOHN F. *Illusion and Disillusion: The Self in Love and Marriage,* 2nd ed. Wadsworth, 1976. 300 pp. NPL, paper.
DAVIS, BERNARD D., and FLAHERTY, PATRICIA, eds. *Human Diversity: Its Causes and Social Significance.* Ballinger, 1976. 248 pp. $13.50 cloth.
DOUGLAS, JACK D. *Investigative Social Research: Individual and Team Field Research.* Sage, 1976. 229 pp. $11.00 cloth. $6.00 paper.
DUNHAM, VERA S. *In Stalin's Time: Middleclass Values in Soviet Fiction.* Cambridge University Press, 1976. 283 pp. $16.95 cloth.
EADINGTON, WILLIAM R., ed. *Gambling and Society: Interdisciplinary Studies on the Subject of Gambling.* Charles C Thomas, 1976. 466 pp. $34.75 cloth.
EDGE, DAVID O., and MULKAY, MICHAEL J. *Astronomy Transformed: The Emergence of Radio Astronomy in Britain.* Wiley, 1976. 482 pp. $25.00 cloth.
EISENSTADT, S. N. *The Form of Sociology: Paradigms and Crises.* Wiley, 1976. 386 pp. $17.95 cloth.
ELAZAR, DANIEL J. *Community and Polity: The Organizational Dynamics of American Jewry.* Jewish Publication Society of America, 1976. 421 pp. $12.00 cloth.
ERIKSSON, TORSTEN. *The Reformers: An Historical Survey of Pioneer Experiments in the Treatment of Criminals.* Tr. Catherine Djurklou. Elsevier, 1976. 310 pp. $17.50 cloth.
FARBER, SAMUEL. *Revolution and Reaction in Cuba, 1933–1960: A Political Sociology from Machado to Castro.* Wesleyan University Press, 1976. 283 pp. $15.95 cloth.
FARMANFARMAIAN, KHODADAD, ed. *The Social Sciences and Problems of Development.* Near Eastern Studies/Princeton University, 1976. 332 pp. $4.00 paper.
FINESTONE, HAROLD. *Victims of Change: Juvenile Delinquents in American Society.* Greenwood, 1976. 235 pp. $14.95 cloth.
FISCHER, JOEL. *The Effectiveness of Social Casework.* Charles C Thomas, 1976. 342 pp. $19.75 cloth.
FISHMAN, JOSHUA A. *Bilingual Education: An International Sociological Perspective.* Newbury House, 1976. 208 pp. $6.95 paper.
FLEW, ANTONY. *Sociology, Equality and Education: Philosophical Essays in Defense of a Variety of Differences.* Barnes & Noble, 1976. 143 pp. $13.75 cloth.
FOWLES, JIB. *Mass Advertising as Social Forecast: A Method for Futures Research.* Greenwood, 1976. 153 pp. $10.95 cloth.

FRANKLIN, JOHN HOPE. *Racial Equality in America*. University of Chicago Press, 1976. 113 pp. $7.95 cloth.
FRIEDENBERG, EDGAR Z. *The Disposal of Liberty and Other Industrial Wastes*. Anchor Books, 1976. 196 pp. $2.95 paper.
FRY, PETER. *Spirits of Protest: Spirit-Mediums and the Articulation of Consensus among the Zezuru of Southern Rhodesia (Zimbabwe)*. Cambridge University Press, 1976. $10.95 cloth.
GADAMER, HANS-GEORG. *Philosophical Hermeneutics*. Tr. and ed. David E. Linge. University of California Press, 1976. 243 pp. $12.75 cloth.
GERSTL, JOEL, and JACOBS, GLENN, eds. *Professions for the People: The Politics of Skill*. Halsted Press, 1976. 230 pp. $9.50 cloth.
GEYER, R. FELIX, and SCHWEITZER, DAVID R., eds. *Theories of Alienation: Critical Perspectives in Philosophy and the Social Sciences*. Martinus Nijhoff, 1976. 305 pp. NPL, paper.
GILLESPIE, DAVID F.; MILETI, DENNIS S.; and PERRY, RONALD W. *Organizational Response to Changing Community Systems*. Kent State University Press, 1976. 65 pp. $4.50 paper.
GLASSIE, HENRY. *All Silver and No Brass: An Irish Christmas Mumming*. Indiana University Press, 1976. 192 pp. $10.00 cloth.
GMELCH, SHARON. *Tinkers and Travellers*. McGill-Queen's University Press, 1976. 144 pp. $12.50 cloth.
GOLANY GIDEON. *New-Town Planning: Principles and Practice*. Wiley, 1976. 389 pp. NPL, cloth.
GOODIN, ROBERT E. *The Politics of Rational Man*. Wiley, 1976. 210 pp. $14.95 cloth.
GORDON, MARGARET T. *Involving Paraprofessionals in the Helping Process: The Case of Federal Probation*. Ballinger, 1976. 151 pp. $15.00 cloth.
GRIFFITHS, N. E. S. *Penelope's Web: Some Perceptions of Women in European and Canadian Society*. Oxford University Press, 1976. 249 pp. $4.95 paper.
GUDEMAN, STEPHEN. *Relationships, Residence and the Individual: A Rural Panamanian Community*. University of Minnesota Press, 1976. 274 pp. $18.75 cloth.
HABERMAS, JURGEN. *Legitimation Crisis*. Tr. Thomas McCarty. Beacon, 1975. 166 pp. $8.95 cloth.
HARRIGAN, JOHN J. *Political Change in the Metropolis*. Little, Brown & Co., 1976. 450 pp. $8.95 paper.
HARRISON, IRA E., and COSMINSKY, SHEILA. *Traditional Medicine: Implications for Ethnomedicine, Maternal and Child Health, Mental Health, and Public Health: An Annotated Bibliography of Africa, Latin America, and the Caribbean*. Garland, 1976. 229 pp. $22.00 cloth.
HAYDEN, DOLORES. *Seven American Utopias: The Architecture of Communitarian Socialism, 1790–1975*. MIT Press, 1976. 401 pp. $16.95 cloth.
HEILMAN, SAMUEL C. *Synagogue Life: A Study in Symbolic Interaction*. University of Chicago Press, 1976. 306 pp. $12.95 cloth.
HENSON, TRUDY KNICELY. *The Wedding Complex: The Social Organization af a Rite of Passage*. Park Bromwell, 1976. 83 pp. $4.50 paper.
HEYERDAHL, THOR. *Fatu-Hiva: Back to Nature*. New American Library, 1974. 293 pp. $1.95 paper.
HIRSCHOWITZ, RALPH G., and LEVY, BERNARD, eds. *The Changing Mental Health Scene*. Spectrum, dist. by Halsted Press, 1976. 382 pp. $25.00 cloth.
HOLMES, ROGER. *Legitimacy and the Politics of the Knowable*. Routledge & Kegan Paul, 1976. 191 pp. $11.50 paper.
HUNT, GAILLARD. *Life in America One Hundred Years Ago*. Orig. pub. 1914. Gale Research, 1976. 298 pp. $9.00 cloth.
INBAR, MICHAEL. *The Vulnerable Age Phenomenon*. Russell Sage, 1976. 56 pp. NPL, paper.
JONES, R. KENNETH, and JONES, PATRICIA A. *Sociology in Medicine*. Halsted, 1976. 222 pp. $9.95 cloth.
KALT, NEIL C., and ZALKIND, SHELDON S., eds. *Urban Problems: Psychological Inquiries*, readings and text. Oxford University Press, 1976. 543 pp. $13.00 cloth. $8.00 paper.
KANE, ROBERT L.; KASTELER, JOSEPHINE M.; and GRAY, ROBERT M., eds. *The Health Gap: Medical Services and the Poor*. Springer, 1976. 321 pp. $13.50 cloth. $8.95 paper.
KHATRI, A. A. *Manual of the Scale to Measure Jointness of Families in India*. B. M. Institute, 1976. 48 pp. NPL, paper.
KIPNIS, DAVID. *The Powerholders*. University of Chicago Press, 1976. 230 pp. $12.50 cloth.
KLEINMAN, ARTHUR, et al. *Medicine in Chinese Cultures: Comparative Studies of Health Care in Chinese and Other Societies*. U.S. Dept. of Health, Education, and Welfare, 1976. 803 pp. $11.00 cloth.
KNOKE, DAVID. *Change and Continuity in American Politics: The Social Bases of Political Parties*. Johns Hopkins University Press, 1976. 192 pp. $11.50 cloth.
KNOWLTON, ROBERT J. *Church Property and the Mexican Reform, 1856–1910*. Northern Illinois University Press, 1976. 265 pp. $12.50 cloth.
KOHN, ROBERT, and WHITE, KERR L., eds. *Health Care: An International Study*. Oxford University Press, 1976. 557 pp. $26.50 cloth.
LAUER, ROBERT H., ed. *Social Movements and Social Change*. Southern Illinois University Press, 1976. 292 pp. $10.00 cloth.
LEE, PHILIP R., et al. *Primary Care in a Specialized World*. Ballinger, 1976. 224 pp. $15.50 cloth.
LEFF, ARTHUR ALLEN. *Swindling and Selling*. Free Press, 1976. 194 pp. $10.95 cloth.
LEISS, WILLIAM. *The Limits of Satisfaction: An Essay on the Problem of Needs and Commodities*. University of Toronto Press, 1976. 159 pp. $12.50 cloth. $4.50 paper.
LEVIN, GILBERT, and ROBERTS, EDWARD B. *The Dynamics of Human Service Delivery*. Ballinger, 1976. 257 pp. $16.00 cloth.
LEVINSHON, FLORENCE HAMLISH, and WRIGHT, BENJAMIN DRAKE, eds. *School Desegregation: Shadow and Substance*. University of Chicago Press, 1976. 216 pp. $3.95 paper.
LEVY, SHLOMIT, and GUTTMAN, LOUIS. *Values and Attitudes of Israel High School Youth: Second Research Project*. Israel Institute of Applied Social Research, 1976. 105 pp. NPL, paper.
LEWIS, CHARLES E.; FEIN, RASHI; and MECHANIC, DAVID. *A Right to Health: The Problem of Access to Primary Medical Care*. Wiley, 1976. 367 pp. $17.95 cloth.
LITTRELL, W. BOYD, and SJOBERG, GIDEON, eds. *Current Issues in Social Policy*. Sage, 1976. 248 pp. $15.00 cloth. $6.95 paper.
MASOTTI, LOUIS H., and LINEBERRY, ROBERT L., eds. *The New Urban Politics*. Ballinger, 1976. 266 pp. $14.00 cloth.
MAYS, JOHN BARRON, ed. *The Social Treatment of Young Offenders: A Reader*. Longman, 1975. 331 pp. $15.00 cloth. $8.50 paper.
McCLELLAND, DAVID C. *The Achieving Society*. Orig. pub. 1961. Halsted, 1976. 512 pp. $17.95 cloth.
McKAY, JOHN P. *Tramways and Trolleys: The Rise of Urban Mass Transport in Europe*. Princeton University Press, 1976. 266 pp. $14.50 cloth.
MELTSNER, ARNOLD J. *Policy Analysts in the Bureaucracy*. University of California Press, 1976. 310 pp. $10.00 cloth.
MESSERSCHMIDT, DONALD A. *The Gurungs of Nepal: Conflict and Change in a Village Society*. Aris & Phillips, dist by ISBS, 1976. 151 pp. $14.50 cloth. $9.50 paper.
MILLER, JEAN BAKER. *Toward a New Psychology of Women*. Beacon, 1976. 143 pp. $9.95 cloth.
MIROFF, BRUCE. *Pragmatic Illusions: The Presidential Politics of John F. Kennedy*. David McKay, 1976. 334 pp. $9.95 cloth. $4.95 paper.
NATIONAL SCIENCE BOARD. *Science Indicators 1974: Report of the National Science Board 1975*. US Gov. Printing Office, 1975. 242 pp. $4.60 paper.
NEWMAN, GRAEME. *Comparative Deviance: Perception and Law in Six Cultures*. Elsevier, 1976. 332 pp. $12.95 cloth.
NEWTON, KENNETH. *Second City Politics: Democratic Processes and Decision-Making in Birmingham*. Oxford University Press, 1976. 270 pp. $11.00 paper.
NIEMI, RICHARD G., and WEISBERG, HERBERT F. eds. *Controversies in American Voting Behavior*. W. H. Freeman, 1976. 543 pp. $12.95 cloth. $6.95 paper.
NILLES, JACK M. *The Telecommunications-Transportation Tradeoff: Options for Tomorrow*. Wiley, 1976. 196 pp. $22.95 cloth.
NISBET, ROBERT. *Sociology as an Art Form*. Oxford University Press, 1976. 145 pp. $8.95 cloth. $2.50 paper.
NOELLE-NEUMANN, ELISABETH. *Allensbacher Jahrbuch der Demoskopie, 1974–1976*, vol. 4. Verlag Fritz Molden, 1976. 355 pp. NPL, cloth.
PARLIN, BRADLEY W. *Immigrant Professionals in the United States: Discrimination in the Scientific Labor Market*. Praeger, 1976. 97 pp. $11.00 cloth.
PARRINDER, GEOFFREY. *Introduction to Asian Religions*. Oxford University Press, 1976. 138 pp. $2.50 paper.
PEDERSEN, PAUL; LONNER, WALTER J.; and DRAGUNS, JURIS G., eds. *Counseling across Cultures*. University Press of Hawaii, 1976. 228 pp. $7.50 paper.
PEPINSKY, HAROLD E. *Crime and Conflict: A Study of Law and Society*. Academic Press, 1976. 159 pp. $14.50 cloth.
PERRY, JOHN, and PERRY, ERNA. *Face to Face: The Individual and Social Problems*. Educational Associates, 1976. 560 pp. $11.95 cloth.
PETERSON, PAUL E. *School Politics Chicago Style*. University of Chicago Press, 1976. 304 pp. $15.00 cloth.
PINE, VANDERLYN R., et al. *Acute Grief and the Funeral*. Charles C Thomas, 1976. 301 pp. $16.50 cloth.
REUBAND, KARL-HEINZ. *Rauschmittelkonsum: Soziale Abweichung und institutionelle Reaktion*. Akademische Verlagsgesellschaft, 1976. 192 pp. NPL, paper.

RICH, ADRIENNE. *Of Woman Born: Motherhood as Experience and Institution.* W. W. Norton & Co., 1976. 318 pp. $8.95 cloth.
ROSENBERG, CHAIM M., and RAYNES, ANTHONY E. *Keeping Patients in Psychiatric Treatment.* Ballinger, 1976. 167 pp. $16.00 cloth.
ROSNOW, RALPH L., and FINE, GARY ALAN. *Rumor and Gossip: The Social Psychology of Hearsay.* Elsevier, 1976. 166 pp. $9.95 cloth. $4.95 paper.
ROSS, JACK C. *An Assembly of Good Fellows: Voluntary Associations in History.* Greenwood, 1976. 325 pp. $14.95 cloth.
ROVNER-PEICZENIK, ROBERTA. *Pretrial Intervention Strategies: An Evaluation of Policy-related Research and Policy-maker Perceptions.* Lexington Books, 1976. 232 pp. $14.00 cloth.
RUBIN, VERA, and COMITAS, LAMBROS. *Ganja in Jamaica: The Effects of Marijuana Use.* Anchor Books, 1976. 217 pp. $2.95 paper.
RUMMEL, R. J. *Understanding Conflict and War, Volume 2: The Conflict Helix.* Halsted, 1976. 400 pp. $17.50 cloth.
RYNKIEWICH, MICHAEL A., and SPRADLEY, JAMES P. *Ethics and Anthropology: Dilemmas in Fieldwork.* Wiley, 1976. 186 pp. NPL, paper.
SELLIN, J. THORSTEN. *Slavery and the Penal System.* Elsevier, 1976. 202 pp. $12.50 cloth.
SELLS, S. B., ed. *The Effectiveness of Drug Abuse Treatment, Volume 3: Further Studies of Drug Users, Treatment Typologies, and Assessment of Outcomes during Treatment in DARP.* Ballinger, 1976. 463 pp. $22.50 cloth.
SELLS, S. B., ed. *The Effectiveness of Drug Abuse Treatment, Volume 4: Evaluation of Treatment Outcomes for 1971–1972 DARP Admission Cohort.* Ballinger, 1976. 483 pp. $22.50 cloth.
SHAPIRO, THEDA. *Painters and Politics: The European Avant-Garde and Society, 1900–1925.* Elsevier, 1976. 341 pp. $15.00 cloth.
SHEA, WILLIAM R., and KING-FARLOW, JOHN, eds. *Values and the Quality of Life.* Science History Publications, 1976. 181 pp. $3.95 paper.
SHONICK, WILLIAM. *Elements of Planning for Area-Wide Personal Health Services.* C. V. Mosby, 1976. 227 pp. $7.95 paper.
SHORT, JAMES F., JR., ed. *Delinquency, Crime, and Society.* University of Chicago Press, 1976. 325 pp. $15.00 cloth.
SHORT, JOHN; WILLIAMS, EDERYN; and CHRISTIE, BRUCE. *The Social Psychology of Telecommunications.* Wiley, 1976. 195 pp. $15.50 cloth.
SINGH, VIJAI P. *Caste, Class and Democracy: Changes in a Stratification System.* Schenkman, 1976. 158 pp. $12.50 cloth. $5.95 paper.
SKIRBEKK, SIGURD. *Psychoanalysis and Self-Understanding: A Critique of Naturalistic Interpretation of Man.* Duquesne University Press, dist by Humanities Press, 1976. 151 pp. $8.00 cloth.
SLATER, PATRICK, ed. *The Measurement of Intrapersonal Space by Grid Technique, Volume 1: Explorations of Intrapersonal Space.* Wiley, 1976. 258 pp. $19.95 cloth.
SMELSER, NEIL J., and WARNER, R. STEPHEN. *Sociological Theory: Historical and Formal.* General Learning Press, 1976. 284 pp. NPL, paper.
SNYDER, LOUIS L. *Varieties of Nationalism: A Comparative Study.* Rinehart & Winston, 1976. 326 pp. $12.95 cloth.
SOBEL, ROBERT. *The Manipulators: America in the Media Age.* Anchor Press, 1976. 458 pp. $9.95 cloth.
SPRAY, S. LEE, ed. *Organizational Effectiveness: Theory—Research—Utilization.* Kent State University Press, 1976. 185 pp. $12.50 cloth.
STANLEY, DAVID T. *Prisoners Among Us: The Problem of Parole.* Brookings Institution, 1976. 205 pp. $9.95 cloth. $3.95 paper.
STEIN, PETER J. Single. Prentice-Hall, 1976. 134 pp. NPL, cloth.
STEINBERG, Jonathan. *Why Switzerland?* Cambridge University Press, 1976. 214 pp. $12.95 cloth.
STEINER, STAN. *The Vanishing White Man.* Harper & Row, 1976. 309 pp. $10.95 cloth.
STEMBER, CHARLES HERBERT. *Sexual Racism: The Emotional Barrier to an Integrated Society.* Elsevier, 1976. 234 pp. $13.50 cloth.
TABAH, LÉON, ed. *Population Growth and Economic Development in the Third World.* Ordina Editions, 1976. 816 pp. NPL, cloth.
TEITELBAUM, MICHAEL S. *Sex Differences: Social and Biological Perspectives.* Anchor Books, 1976. 232 pp. $2.95 paper.
THIESSEN, D. D. *The Evolution and Chemistry of Aggression.* Charles C Thomas, 1976. 211 pp. $18.50 cloth.
THOMPSON, DENNIS F. *John Stuart Mill and Representative Government.* Princeton University Press, 1976. 241 pp. $13.50 cloth.
UKERS, WILLIAM H. *All about Coffee,* 2nd ed. First pub. 1922. Gale Research, 1976. 818 pp. $35.00 cloth.
UNION OF INTERNATIONAL ASSOCIATIONS AND MANKIND 2000, Compilers. *Year-book of World Problems and Human Potential.* Union of International Associations/Mankind 2000, 1976. 1,136 pp. NPL, $65.00 cloth.
VERMA, BAIDYA NATH, ed. *The New Social Sciences.* Greenwood, 1976. 276 pp. $15.95 cloth.
VEATCH, ROBERT M., and BRANSON, ROY eds. *Ethics and Health Policy.* Ballinger, 1976. 332 pp. $15.00 cloth.
VIANO, EMILIO C., ed. *Victims and Society.* Visage, 1976. 642 pp. $16.50 cloth. $8.95 paper.
WEAVER, JERRY L. *National Health Policy and the Underserved: Ethnic Minorities, Women, and the Elderly.* C. V. Mosby, 1976. 161 pp. $7.25 paper.
WEINER, JACK B. *Drinking.* W. W. Norton, 1976. 241 pp. $8.95 cloth.
WEINSTEIN, DEENA, and WEINSTEIN, MICHAEL A. *Choosing Sociology: An Introduction to Critical Inquiry.* David McKay, 1976. 182 pp. $3.95 paper.
WEPMAN, DENNIS; NEWMAN, RONALD B.; and BINDERMAN, MURRAY B. *The Life: The Lore and Folk Poetry of the Black Hustler.* University of Pennsylvania Press, 1976. 205 pp. $15.00 cloth.
WESSEL, ANDREW E. *The Social Use of Information: Ownership and Access.* Wiley, 1976. 244 pp. $15.95 cloth.
WHYTE, WILLIAM FOOTE, and ALBERTI, GIORGIO. *Power, Politics and Progress: Social Change in Rural Peru.* Elsevier, 1976. 307 pp. $15.00 cloth.
WILKIE, JAMES W.; MEYER, MICHAEL C.; and WILKIE, EDNA MONZÓN de. *Contemporary Mexico: Papers of the IV International Congress of Mexican History.* University of California Press, 1976. 858 pp. $27.50 cloth. $12.00 paper.
WUTHNOW, ROBERT. *The Consciousness Reformation.* University of California Press, 1976. 309 pp. $12.50 cloth.
WYNAR, LUBOMYR R., and WYNAR, ANNA T. *Encyclopedia Directory of Ethnic Newspapers and Periodicals in the United States,* 2nd ed. Libraries Unlimited, 1976. 248 pp. $15.00 cloth.
ZAEHNER, R. C. *The Teachings of the Magi: A Compendium of Zoroastrian Beliefs.* Oxford University Press, 1976. 156 pp. $2.50 paper.

MANUSCRIPTS FOR THE *ASA ROSE SOCIOLOGY SERIES*

Manuscripts (100 to 300 typed pages) are solicited for publication in the *ASA Arnold and Caroline Rose Monograph Series*. The Series welcomes a variety of types of sociological work—qualitative or quantitative empirical studies, and theoretical or methodological treatises. An author should submit three copies of a manuscript for consideration to the Series Editor, Professor Robin M. Williams, Jr., Department of Sociology, Cornell University, Ithaca, New York 14853.

lutions Manual includes detailed answers to the questions and problems in the text.

MANNY: A CRIMINAL-ADDICT'S STORY

Richard P. Rettig, Manuel J. Torres, and Gerald R. Garrett
University of Massachusetts, Boston
About 256 pages, paper. Early 1977.

Manny, the autobiography of a former criminal, lucidly describes present-day gang life, heroin addiction, and prison life. Manny Torres's vivid expression of his experiences, coupled with perspective chapters that relate them to theory, widen the scope of study.

SOCIOLOGY: Understanding Social Behavior

Alan P. Bates and Joseph Julian
both of the University of Nebraska-Lincoln
606 pages, with Instructor's Guide and Resource Manual by Patricia A. Harvey. 1975.

Students learn sociology through authentic sociological activity by means of photographs, questions, project suggestions, a wide-ranging text, and a wealth of assignments.

POPULATION: The Dynamics of Demographic Change

Charles B. Nam, Florida State University, and
Susan O. Gustavus, University of Cincinnati
320 pages. 1976.

Nam and Gustavus introduce students to the determinants and consequences of demographic change. Population trends are viewed as an integral part of broader societal trends.

AMERICAN EDUCATION
A Sociological View

David W. Swift, University of Hawaii
and eleven contributors
480 pages. 1976.

In a comprehensive analysis, twelve authors present an inside look at American education, each examining particular facets that they have experienced directly.

FAMILY STRUCTURE AND EFFECTIVE HEALTH BEHAVIOR
The Energized Family

Lois Pratt, Jersey City State College
280 pages, paper. 1976.

Pratt's interdisciplinary text connects the areas of family with those of health and illness and explores the type of family needed to function effectively in contemporary society.

THE AMERICAN CLASS SYSTEM
An Introduction to Social Stratification

Daniel W. Rossides, Bowdoin College
480 pages. 1976.

The first text to combine a thorough introduction to social stratification with an extensive analysis of an industrial system of stratification — the American class system.

SOURCEBOOK IN MARRIAGE AND THE FAMILY, Fourth Edition

Edited by Marvin B. Sussman
Case Western Reserve University
430 pages, paper. 1974.

Sussman presents an updated collection of pertinent articles covering recent trends in marriage styles and family forms, sex roles, socialization, theoretical perspectives, and empirical research.

AN INTRODUCTION TO THE SOCIOLOGY OF LEARNING

Sarane S. Boocock, Russell Sage Foundation
370 pages. 1972.

A comprehensive study, Boocock's text evaluates past research, reports on present efforts, and sets guidelines for future work.

For adoption consideration, request examination copies from your regional Houghton Mifflin sales office.

Houghton Mifflin

Atlanta, GA 30324 Dallas, TX 75235 Geneva, IL 60134
Hopewell, NJ 08525 Palo Alto, CA 94304
Boston, MA 02107

MAY 1977 – VOLUME 6, NUMBER 3

ONTEMPORARY SOCIOLOGY

A JOURNAL OF REVIEWS

IN THIS ISSUE

Irving Louis Horowitz on American Jewish Communities

Mary Ann Clawson on Early Industrial Capitalism in England

Charles Perrow reviews March and Olsen's *Ambiguity and Choice in Organizations*

A symposium on *Beyond Economic Man*

Judith Adler reviews Adorno's *Introduction to the Sociology of Music*

George H. Lewis on *The Car Culture*

Jane Scheff and Thomas Scheff on the Male Sex Role

Jerome Skolnick on Japanese and American Police

May Diaz on Women in Revolutionary China

UBLICATION OF THE AMERICAN SOCIOLOGICAL ASSOCIATION

contemporary sociology

a journal of reviews

May 1977 • Volume 6, Number 3

Concerning advertising, change of address and subscriptions, address: Executive Office, American Sociological Association, 1722 N Street, N.W., Washington, D.C. 20036.

Concerning manuscripts and book reviews, address: Editor, *Contemporary Sociology: A Journal of Reviews,* C-002, University of California, San Diego, La Jolla, California, 92093.

Contemporary Sociology: A Journal of Reviews is published at 49 Sheridan Avenue, Albany, N.Y. 12210, bi-monthly in January, March, May, July, September, and November.

Annual membership dues in the American Sociological Association, $30.00–$50.00. Student Member, $15; Associate, $20; International Associate, $12; Student Associate, $10.

Subscription rate for members, $10; non-members, $15; institutions and libraries, $20; non-member students, $10. Single issues $4.

New subscriptions and renewals will be entered on a calendar year basis only.

Change of address: Six weeks advance notice to the Executive Office, and old address as well as new, are necessary for change of subscriber's address.

Claims for undelivered copies must be made within the month following the regular month of publication. The publishers will supply missing copies when losses have been sustained in transit and when the reserve stock will permit.

ISSN 0094–3061

Second class postage paid at Washington, D.C. and at additional mailing offices.

Book reviews from *CS* are indexed in *Book Review Index,* published by Gale Research Company.

ASA Multiple Submission Policy: Submission of a manuscript to a professional journal clearly implies commitment to publish in that journal. The competition for journal space requires a great deal of time and effort on the part of editorial readers whose main compensation for this service is the opportunity to read papers prior to publication and the gratification associated with discharge of professional obligation. For these reasons, *the American Sociological Association regards submission of a manuscript to a professional journal while that paper is under review by another journal as unacceptable.*

Cover designed by Kenneth E. Anderson, A.I.A.

TABLE OF CONTENTS

LETTERS 279

FEATURE ESSAYS

Elazar: *Community and Polity: The Organizational Dynamics of American Jewry* .... Irving Louis Horowitz 287
Foster: *Class Struggle and the Industrial Revolution: Early Industrial Capitalism in Three English Towns* .... Mary Ann Clawson 289
March and Olsen: *Ambiguity and Choice in Organizations* .... Charles Perrow 294

REVIEW SYMPOSIUM

Leibenstein: *Beyond Economic Man: A New Framework for Microeconomics* .... Duncan MacRae, Jr. 298
Samuel H. Preston 300

BOOK REVIEWS

ART AND MUSIC
Adorno: *Introduction to the Sociology of Music* .... Judith Adler 301
Cheatwood and Linquist: *The Human Image: Sociology and Photography* .... Philip H. Ennis 302
Hess and Baker: *Art and Sexual Politics: Why Have There Been No Great Women Artists?* .... Robert D. Leighninger, Jr. 303
Wolff: *Hermeneutic Philosophy and the Sociology of Art: An Approach to Some of the Epistemological Problems of the Sociology of Knowledge and the Sociology of Art and Literature* .... Batia Sharon 304

CRIME, LAW, AND DEVIANCE
Cahalan and Room: *Problem Drinking among American Men* .... Howard M. Bahr 305
Claude: *Comparative Human Rights* .... Harry M. Johnson 306
Frazier: *Theoretical Approaches to Deviance: An Evaluation* .... Lee Ellis 307
Friedman: *The Legal System: A Social Science Perspective*;
Nelson: *Americanization of the Common Law: The Impact of Legal Change on Massachusetts Society, 1760–1830;* and
Unger: *Law in Modern Society: Toward a Criticism of Social Theory* .... Allan Horwitz 308
Hartzler: *Justice, Legal Systems, and Social Structure* .... A. J. Bergesen 310
McIntosh: *The Organisation of Crime* .... John L. McMullan 310
Rosett and Cressey: *Justice by Consent: Plea Bargains in the American Courthouse* .... Jerald W. Cloyd 311
Shoham: *Social Deviance* .... Nanette J. Davis 312

DEVELOPMENT/MODERNIZATION
Bailey: *Debate and Compromise: The Politics of Innovation* .... Michael Lewis 313
Griffin: *The Political Economy of Agrarian Change: An Essay on the Green Revolution* .... William L. Flinn 313
Inkeles and Holsinger: *Education and Individual Modernity in Developing Countries* .... Scott Christopher Wren 314
Berg, Scrimshaw, and Call: *Nutrition, National Development and Planning* .... Roy Wehrle 315

METHODS
Bennett and Lumsdaine: *Evaluation and Experiment: Some Critical Issues in Assessing Social Programs* and
Bernstein: *Validity Issues in Evaluation Research* .... Lynne G. Zucker 316
Blalock et al.: *Quantitative Sociology: International Perspectives on Mathematical and Statistical Modeling* .... Nancy Brandon Tuma 317
Carlsmith, Ellsworth, and Aronson: *Methods of Research in Social Psychology* .... Royce Singleton, Jr. 319
Cohen and Cohen: *Applied Multiple Regression/Correlational Analysis for the Behavioral Sciences* .... Neil W. Henry 320
de Neufville: *Social Indicators and Public Policy: Interactive Processes of Design and Application* .... Brian Vargus 320
Golden: *The Research Experience* and
Riley and Nelson: *Sociological Observation: A Strategy for New Social Knowledge* .... Norman K. Denzin 321
Isaacson and Madsen: *Markov Chains Theory and Applications* .... Robert McGinnis 322

Nachmias and Nachmias: *Research Methods in Social Sciences* .. S. Padmini Ravindhran 323
Norlén: *Stimulation Model Building: A Statistical Approach to Modelling in the Social Sciences with the Simulation Method* .... Theodore L. Reed 323

MILITARY

Fidel: *Militarism in Developing Countries* and
Schiffrin: *Military and State in Modern Asia* .... Stephen P. Cohen 324
Goldman and Segal: *The Social Psychology of Military Service* .... Scott G. McNall 325
Harries-Jenkins and van Doorn: *The Military and the Problem of Legitimacy* and
Vayda: *War in Ecological Perspective* .... Richard Machalek 326
McCubbin, Dahl, and Hunter: *Families in the Military System* .... Athena Theodore 327
Pérez: *Army Politics in Cuba, 1898–1958* .... George A. Kourvetaris 328

POLITICAL

Blackey and Paynton: *Revolution and the Revolutionary Ideal* .... Ronald Y. L. Cheng 329
Bloch: *Political Language and Oratory in Traditional Society* .... Lloyd Etheredge 330
Crozier: *Où va l'administration française* .... Ezra N. Suleiman 331
Graber: *Verbal Behavior and Politics* .... M. Glenn Newkirk 332
Lindberg et al.: *Stress and Contradiction in Modern Capitalism: Public Policy and the Theory of the State* .... Michael Useem 333
Mandel: *Late Capitalism* .... E. K. Hunt 335
Miller: *The Modern Corporate State: Private Governments and the American Constitution* .... Stephen J. McNamee 337
Pomper: *Voter's Choice: Varieties of American Electoral Behavior* .... Carl A. Sheingold 337
Rosenbaum and Sederberg: *Vigilante Politics* .... Harold A. Nelson 338
Tillion: *Ravensbrück: An Eyewitness Account of a Women's Concentration Camp* .... Nancy R. Chiswick 339

POPULATION AND FERTILITY

Arnold et al.: *The Value of Children: A Cross-National Study. Volume 1: Introduction and Comparative Analysis*;
Bulatao: *The Value of Children: A Cross-National Study. Volume 2: Philippines;* and
Arnold and Fawcett: *The Value of Children: A Cross-National Study. Volume 3: Hawaii* .... Moni Nag 339
Malthus: *An Essay on the Principle of Population: Text Sources and Background Criticism* .... Etienne van de Walle 340
Overbeek: *History of Population Theories* .... G. Edward Ebanks 341
Presser: *Sterilization and Fertility Decline in Puerto Rico* .... John J. Macisco, Jr. 342

RACE AND ETHNIC

Braroe: *Indian and White: Self-Image and Interaction in a Canadian Plains Community* .... Philip A. May 342
Dworkin and Dworkin: *The Minority Report: An Introduction to Racial, Ethnic, and Gender Relations* .... Joseph S. Roucek 343
McCaffrey: *The Irish Diaspora in America* .... John Murray Cuddihy 344
Hundley: *The Asian Americans: The Historical Experience* .... Rawlein G. Soberano 345

SOCIAL MOVEMENTS

Flink: *The Car Culture* .... George H. Lewis 345
Isaac: *Israel Divided: Ideological Politics in the Jewish State* .... Rita J. Simon 346
Pinkney: *Red, Black, and Green: Black Nationalism in the United States* .... Paul T. Murray 347
Rosen: *Political Ideology and the Chicano Movement: A Study of the Political Ideology of Activists in the Chicano Movement* .... Lionel A. Maldonado 348
Westby: *The Clouded Vision: The Student Movement in the United States in the 1960s* .... Peter K. Manning 348

THEORY

Hondrich: *Demokratisierung und Leistungsgesellschaft*;
Hondrich: *Theorie der Herrschaft*; and
Hondrich: *Menschliche Bedürfnisse und soziale Steuerung* .... Gianfranco Poggi 350
Lenzer: *Auguste Comte and Positivism: The Essential Writings* .... Donald N. Levine 352
Matter: *Love, Altruism, and World Crisis: The Challenge of Pitirim A. Sorokin* and
Zimmerman: *Sociological Theories of Pitirim A. Sorokin* .... Don Martindale 353
Nisbet: *Sociology as an Art Form* .... Frederick R. Lynch 354
Stub: *Status Communities in Modern Society: Alternatives to Class Analysis* .... James Murtha 356

THIRD WORLD STUDIES

Béteille: *Six Essays in Comparative Sociology* .... Joseph R. Gusfield 357
Bozeman: *Conflict in Africa: Concepts and Realities* .... David D. Laitin 359

Cornelius: *Politics and the Migrant Poor in Mexico City* .... Bruce Harris 360
Hirschman: *Ethnic and Social Stratification in Peninsular Malaysia* .... John A. Lent 361
Liu: *Political Culture and Group Conflict in Communist China* .... Martin K. Whyte 361
Pak: *China and the West: Myths and Realities in History* .... Francis L. K. Hsu 362
Pescatello: *Power and Pawn: The Female in Iberian Families, Societies, and Cultures* .... Marta Tienda 363
Mernissi: *Beyond the Veil: Male-Female Dynamics in a Modern Muslim Society* .... Janet Abu-Lughod 364
Oldenburg: *Big City Government in India: Councilor, Administrator and Citizen in Delhi* .... Mark Spevak 366
Sharma: *The Indian Industrial Worker: Issues in Perspective* .... Rudi Volti 368
Smock and Smock: *The Politics of Pluralism: A Comparative Study of Lebanon and Ghana* .... Paul D. Starr 368
Smith: *The Race between Population and Food Supply in Latin America* .... William E. Bertrand 369
Wiebe: *Social Life in an Indian Slum* .... Jay Weinstein 370

URBAN
Gorham and Glazer: *The Urban Predicament* .... Joseph M. Conforti 372
Liebert: *Disintegration and Political Action: The Changing Functions of City Governments in America* .... Warner Bloomberg, Jr. 373
Lojkine: *La politique urbaine dans la region lyonnaise, 1945–1972* .... Edith Kurzweil 374

WORK/OCCUPATIONS
Alex: *New York Cops Talk Back: A Study of a Beleaguered Minority* .... Michael Williams 375
Bayley: *Forces of Order: Police Behavior in Japan and the United States* .... Jerome H. Skolnick 375
Blaxall and Reagan: *Women and the Workplace: The Implications of Occupational Segregation* .... Virginia Olesen 376
Davin: *Woman-Work: Women and the Party in Revolutionary China* .... May N. Diaz 377
Sacks: *Women's Work in Soviet Russia: Continuity in the Midst of Change* .... Marilyn Power Goldberg 378

ADDITIONAL REVIEWS
Barnlund: *Public and Private Self in Japan and the United States* .... Minako K. Maykovich 378
David and Brannon: *The Forty-Nine Percent Majority: The Male Sex Role* .... Jane H. Scheff and Thomas J. Scheff 379
Elkana: *The Discovery of the Conservation of Energy* and
Newman and Day: *The American Energy Consumer* .... Robert Cameron Mitchell 379
Faber: *The Social Structure of Eastern Europe: Transition Process in Czechoslovakia, Hungary, Poland, Romania, and Yugoslavia* .... Zoltán Tar 381
Forman: *"Physics circa 1900: Personnel, Funding, and Productivity of the Academic Establishment"* .... David A. Woodrow 382
Kaufman: *Are Government Organizations Immortal?* .... Marshall W. Meyer 382
Jones and Jones: *Sociology in Medicine* .... Thomas J. Sullivan 383
Montagu: *The Nature of Human Aggression* and
Moscovici: *Society against Nature: The Emergence of Human Societies* .... Richard McClintock 384
Needham: *Belief, Language and Experience* .... Beryl L. Bellman 385
Niemi: *How Family Members Perceive Each Other: Political and Social Attitudes in Two Generations* and
Raush et al.: *Communication, Conflict and Marriage* .... Suzanne K. Steinmetz 387
Nixon: *Sport and Social Organization* .... Barry D. McPherson 388
Noble and Thomas: *The Rising South: Volume 1: Changes and Issues* and
McKenzie: *The Rising South. Volume 2: Southern Universities and the South* .... Alvin L. Bertrand 389
Sanders and Morawska: *Polish American Community Life: A Survey of Research* .... Eugene E. Obidinski 390
Stephens: *Loners, Losers, and Lovers: Elderly Tenants in a Slum Hotel* .... Andrea Fontana 391
Szasz: *Heresies* .... Robert S. Broadhead 391
Thompson: *Bureaucracy and the Modern World* .... Robert N. Stern 391
Zimmerman, Wieder, and Zimmerman: *Understanding Social Problems* .... Malcolm Spector 392

PUBLICATIONS RECEIVED 393

LETTERS

(Letters which comment on particular reviews are routinely sent to reviewers for a reply. Where no reply by reviewers appears in these columns, it is usually because they chose not to reply.)

To the Editor:

I wish to protest strongly the insult to my professional competence contained in the review of *Catholic Schools in a Declining Church* and to demand an apology from the three reviewers and from *Contemporary Sociology*.

I cite the offensive paragraph.

> . . . "Those familiar with the numerous works of the main investigator, Greeley, know that one head wears two hats—that of a social scientist and that of an individual whose interest in the future of the Catholic Church is passionate. With his double concern, Greeley is not only attempting an assessment of the causes of declining religiosity among American Catholics, he is also attempting a critique of the Catholic hierarchy for its insensitivity and rather blatant disregard of demographic facts. The authors' polemical defense of the encyclical hypothesis is best viewed within this context" [p. 806].

You will note, incidentally, the slippery and intellectually dishonest jump the reviewers make from "my passionate interest" to the "authors" polemical intent. Apparently I am such a passionate soul that I have carried my colleagues along with me. But more about that point later.

Now I would submit that there are one of two possibilities. Either my commitment is such that it does not interfere with unbiased and impartial research and hence is irrevelant to the review or it does interfere and my professional competence and objectivity is the victim of this commitment. If the latter be the case—the authors clearly imply that it is—then I am an incompetent, unobjective and dishonest sociologist. This I take to be the substance of their innuendo. I demand either proof or a retraction.

Consider, sir, if a reviewer wrote the same paragraph about a committed black radical or a committed woman militant? I doubt that the paragraph would have been printed. But if it were the outrage would be heard around the land. Apparently passionate interest can co-exist with objectivity and competence for blacks and women but not for Catholic priests.

Or suppose that in response to the reviewers I would say that they are wearing two hats—that of committed social scientists and that of faculty members of Notre Dame who have passionate interest in criticizing anything that comes out of the pluralism program at NORC because of longstanding animosity toward that program on the part of the Notre Dame faculty, and that their review must be judged in that context. They would quite properly be outraged and you yourself would call foul. Why then can they do the same thing to me—and through guilt by association, my colleagues?

As it happens, we state categorically in the introduction that we did not begin with an "encyclical explanation" and were forced to it by the data. Indeed, we say that even in the NIE proposal leading to the project we did not mention the encyclical. Now either the reviewers did not read that part of the introduction—which, given the ineptitude of much of their review, seems very likely—or they did and assumed that my "passionate interest" has led to quite simply lying about the facts.

Fortunately, we have the original proposal and I submit with this letter as proof a copy of it. I am humiliated that I must do this, but when a charge of bias is aimed at a Catholic priest in the sociological profession, he is guilty until he is proven innocent. I must ask you to verify for your readers the fact that the purpose of the research was not an "anti-encyclical" polemic.

I will not comment on the substance of their review until an apology is forthcoming. I do not dialogue with those who accuse me by implication of rigging the data—and I note in passing that their response to the book is exactly the same as that of the leadership of the Catholic hierarchy—strange bedfellows indeed!

However, I cannot resist commenting that their suggestion that reaction to Father Groppi's marches is one of the causes of Catholic decline is ludicrous even from the University of Notre Dame. For what it is worth, however, about half the Catholics in the country approve of clerical activism (and half disapprove) and there is no correlation between religious devotion and this approval.

One final note of personal protest: I am used to such treatment from the faculties of Catholic universities. My principal anger is aimed at the implication that my two colleagues supinely permitted themselves to be swept along by my "passionate interest." To smear two other scholars in such fashion is outrageous.

Or as Mr. Welch said to the late Senator McCarthy when he went after a junior member of his staff, "Sir, have you no honor in you at all?"

ANDREW M. GREELEY
NORC, University of Chicago

To the Editor:

We regret that Father Greeley has taken such offense to our reference to his two hats without attempting to refute the evidence offered. We would have preferred to discuss the merits of our substantive criticisms of the book, but his reply renders intellectual exchange impossible. We remain convinced that the book is flawed by the interspersion of policy interests with scholarly analysis. Greeley grossly misinterprets the paragraph he quotes in several ways. First, we made no claim that Greeley *et al.* began with a premeditated bias in favor of the encyclical hypothesis. However, it is clear that at some stage of the research Greeley *et al.* became persuaded by the encyclical model to the extent that other plausible explanations (indicated in our review) were too readily discarded.

Throughout Chapter 5, the authors insert statements informing the reader that their case for the encyclical model is virtually airtight. To wit: "No one is likely to come up with better evidence" (p. 105). Few sociologists would direct such statements toward other professional sociologists. This leads us to suspect that they are, instead, directed toward other audiences, especially church policy-makers. This suspicion is confirmed by the last three pages of the chapter in which the authors make a direct pitch to church policy-makers. "To fulfill their responsibility, it would seem, they must view the encyclical explanation as practically certain and make policies accordingly."

Given such clear evidence of policy interest, we attributed Greeley's neglect of alternative models to his second hat rather than to incompetence or dishonesty. We made no implication that Greeley falsified the data, and we are at a loss to understand how he could impute such an implication to our review. However, couching the analysis in terms of an either-or choice between the council model or the encyclical model has the effect of giving the encyclical model far more credibility in the eyes of non-sociologists (e.g., the "church hierarchy") than if the findings are clouded by the usual caveats and misgivings sociologists express about their research results. Such qualifications are difficult for non-sociologists to evaluate and, therefore, tend to diminish the impact of the findings upon these audiences. Greeley's interest in presenting the encyclical model to these audiences as *undeniable* is apparent in numerous passages.

Second, we are puzzled by Greeley's charge that we have "smeared" his colleagues. The authors of a text, it seems to us, are collectively responsible for its tone and content, even though they may not have shared equally in its production. Thus, we might just as well have begun the offending sentence with the words "the book's" rather than "the authors'." The sentence would then read: The book's polemical defense of the encyclical hyphothesis is best viewed within this (Greeley's wearing two hats) context.

Greeley's perception of us as "bedfellows" of the Catholic hierarchy may account for his misinterpretation of our reference to Father Groppi. We made no suggestion that Father Groppi's marches were a major cause of Catholic decline or that Catholics disapprove of clerical activism. If read in the context in which it was presented, the reference to Groppi only suggests that his marches symbolize the fact that there were other significant social issues besides the encyclical which concerned Catholics during the 1960s period. This is the primary theme of the paragraph in which the Groppi reference is imbedded.

Greeley (p. 316) appears to concede that the reader "will have to judge for himself whether I am a competent enough sociologist and an honest enough human being to prevent my predispositions from distorting the data or the analysis." We trust interested readers will judge for themselves and indeed they may wish to accept the offer by Greeley *et al.* to provide their data tapes for alternative analysis.

C. LINCOLN JOHNSON
J. DAVID LEWIS
JAIME SENA-RIVERA
University of Notre Dame

From the Editor:

As an author who has been bloodied (unjustly, in my opinion) by a reviewer, I can appreciate Father Greeley's anger. But as an editor, I must say that implications or outright allegations of bias against an author are very common in book reviews in virtually all media I know of. I would not expect authors to be pleased by such allegations, but it is a long way between an understandable disappointment or displeasure at a negative review and feelings of insult or outrage. Reviewers impugn the competence of authors whenever they write a negative review, and *CS* cannot apologize for that. What we can do is let Father Greeley be heard in rebuttal, and we regard it as a privilege to do that.

BENNETT M. BERGER

To the Editor:

Years ago I strongly attacked Professor Skolnick's *The Policies of Protest* at a public debate. He took it badly and promised retaliation. If he neglected to tell the editor about his rancor, he acted unethically in accepting my *Punishing Criminals* for review.

Skolnick attributes to me the view that "punishment is a sacred obligation, a fundamental promise of society to those of its members who do transgress its rules. From this perspective it is unfair not to punish." I explicitly repudiated this view, held by Kant and Hegel, and stated mine (p. 17): "But a promise need not be kept if both parties consent. And a threat, unlike a promise, can be withdrawn unilaterally by the party that made it." Skolnick adds: "[van den Haag] loves punishment." No evidence is presented. I do not. I did indicate why punishment is required, but requirements do not depend on loving or hating.[1]

I argue explicitly that the threat of punishment of crime is a promise, not to offenders, but to non-offenders. The promise must be honored (1) because promises are moral obligations, and (2) because, if it is not, the threat becomes incredible and therefore ineffective, a bluff. (Wherefore punishment is independent of motivations such as revenge or "love.")

Skolnick paraphrases my view that the legal order, including the criminal law, enforces the social order. Here Skolnick misleads only by omitting that I theorized about *any* legal and social order, capitalist, socialist, democratic, or totalitarian. But Skolnick also states that I believe that "drastic punishments, like mutilation and flogging should seriously be reconsidered [for reinstitution]." This is a lie. I explain that such punishments have become repulsive to the modern conscience, in part for quite rational reasons (which I suggest)—here I explicitly mention mutiliation—in part because of unconscious identifications (which I also try to suggest). Sixty lashes may be preferred by some offenders to e.g., two years in prison (and may be as deterrent). Nonetheless, corporal punishment, I explain, is not acceptable to the modern conscience, and therefore *cannot* "seriously be reconsidered."[2] I do not approve of corporal punishment. I approve even less of Skolnick's lying.[3]

Skolnick continues, "Professors must be responsible for crime according to van den Haag since current economic gains of blacks do not otherwise 'justify the current high rate of black crime.'" The phrase Skolnick places in quotes to attribute it to me does not occur in my book. The illogical inference is Skolnick's too: if "economic gains do not justify [does he mean 'explain'?] the current high rate of black crime" how would it follow that "professors must be responsible for crime"? I did write (p. 99): "Crime becomes less odious if moral disapproval of poverty, slums, or ghettos becomes intense, pervasive, and exculpatory enough to suggest to the 'underprivileged' that they are entitled to take revenge through crime, and when they do, to be spared punishment.[4] Those inclined to offenses will perceive the reduced certainty and severity of punishment in such a moral climate as a failure of society to defend its social order," and (p. 93): "In many minds this [social] injustice legitimizes offenses the poor commit, absolves them from responsibility, and makes deterrent measures unjust and somehow also ineffective." I also wrote that economic factors do not satisfactorily account for the black crime rate. The "professors" are the product of Skolnick's (quite understandable) guilt feelings: they do not occur in my book. "The liberal-professor crime-causation theory" Skolnick attributes to me is his invention. Skolnick actually reversed the burden of what I wrote about black crime rates. To wit (p. 100): "The age specific crime rates of blacks are only slightly higher than those of whites on the same socio-economic level," and (p. 100): "the difference in crime rates should not come as a surprise. Blacks have been oppressed for a long time . . . their access to the labor market . . . still is limited because of lack of training due to past discrimination . . ." and (p. 102): "it is quite likely that . . . poverty produces high crime rates probably by affecting motivations and temptations." Skolnick asserts ". . . In [van den Haag's] view poverty and deprivation—relative or absolute—are not properly interpreted as causes of crime." Neither kind of poverty is necessary or sufficient and both are "causes" (of the variance). *Punishing Criminals* is quite clear on the matter.

Skolnick's misunderstanding of my economic data may charitably be blamed on deficient reading comprehension. Describing the relative improvement in the economic position of blacks 1951–1971, I stated (p. 101), "the figures used are in dollars of constant purchasing power, i.e., they exclude the effects of inflation." Yet Skolnick asserts, "[inflation] could easily account for the whole 20 year rise." Skolnick goes on to complain that "inflation effects aside," my data, indicating that 3% of black families earned more than $10,000 in 1951, while 13% did in 1971, still show that "87% of black families earned less than $10,00 in 1971, and 97% in 1951." Yes. Wherein would that be relevant to my contention that (a) black economic improvement has occurred, and (b) has not resulted in a decrease in the crime rate any more than (p. 90) general economic improvement led to a decrease of the general crime rate? Skolnick adds, "van den Haag never discusses the economic opportunities of black youth who account for most of the black crime rate." I wrote (p. 101), "for teenagers the economic picture is

1 Nor does one, if "loathe to employ [punishment]," "rob society of its inalienable rights" as Skolnick alleges I believe. (I do not.) Disliking, or wishing to avoid (being loathe), need not lead one to reject what is required: if Skolnick were loathe to have a surgical operation, would he deny the need for it? If he does not deny the need, would this indicate that he is not "loathe," or "loves" surgery?

2 My chapter "The Decline of Corporal Punishment" describes the change in public attitude in the 18th and 19th centuries. The beginning of that change in the 17th century is most competently described in *The Decline of Hell*, by D. P. Walker (University of Chicago Press, 1964).

3 Skolnick reformulates his lie later on to attribute the idea to me that "citizens . . . are supposed to appreciate corporal punishment administered for their own good" [or] "ought to be dealt with more severely." There is no basis in my book for Skolnick's fantasy.

4 I do not believe either that "the major cause of crime is disinclination to punish," though I believe that the rise of the latter is *one* cause of the rise of the former.

much darker . . . one third were unemployed in 1971 against 15% of white teenagers" and go on to discuss the matters that Skolnick asserts "van den Haag never discusses."

Skolnick accuses me of "essential lack of interest in the relationship between social deprivation and crime." Several chapters of *Punishing Criminals* are devoted to that relationship. I do not see it as Skolnick does. He might have pointed out wherein I'm wrong. Instead, he accuses me "of essential lack of interest": if you don't agree with me you are not interested. Nor am I "unconcerned with social justice" as charged, even though as Skolnick notes, I reject Rawls's notion that "justice is the first virtue of social institutions." Matters, such as survival and social welfare, rank with social and with legal justice and may be in conflict with either. "Justice, Order, Charity" (Chapter IV) is devoted to such conflicts–in which I am more interested than any criminologist I know.

Skolnick notes that I stress the deterrent effect of certainty of punishment and writes, "Even if we were to suspend civil liberties entirely, we would not achieve certainty . . . certainty is a practical illusion." In criminology, "certainty" is a term of art (derived from expected psychological effects) which refers to the *degree* of probability of punishment, i.e., its frequency. That degree varies, and I referred to that variation on which deterrent effects largely depend.

Skolnick mentions that I oppose the exclusionary rule, "but unlike Justice Burger who proposes a tort remedy . . . he offers no deterrent remedy." I don't propose tort remedies because they already are available, though rarely deterrent. I did write, "Unlawful conduct by the police should be punished," but "recruitment, training and discipline of the police force" are probably as important in restraining it. Since the exclusionary rule does nothing to restrain police, we lose nothing by doing without. The courts which instituted it should give up the failed experiment. Something effective is needed to restrain police, but the exclusionary rule failed, not because, as Skolnick has it, "the deterrence theory did not work in this context either," but because inadmissibility of evidence cannot deter policemen. Demotions, more effective damage claims, and punishments might.

Skolnick opposes my view that credible threats of punishments deter. Ignoring the statistical and experimental evidence presented in *Punishing Criminals,* he points out that people are not deterred from smoking, despite threats to health. *Ergo* deterrence does not work. Indeed, some threats do not deter people from continuing socially approved habits. How does Skolnick infer therefrom that other threats in other situations won't deter people from socially disapproved acts? People are deterred from jumping from the 60th floor by the threat to their health. If many are not deterred from smoking, shooting heroin, drinking, overeating, etc., it is because the felt advantages of these, often socially supported, activities outweigh the felt dangers, perhaps because the dangers (unlike those of jumping or of crime) arise not from one act but from the continuation of a habit, which leads to the discounting of danger. Indeed, this discounting may also help explain why professional criminals are seldom deterred–I offered this explanation. It does not invalidate the deterrence theory, but helps clarify it.

Skolnick concludes his vendetta (I noted only some documentable highlights): "Although [van den Haag] does not actually advocate a totalitarian state, his . . . stance . . . and . . . arguments point to a totalitarian direction, not communism surely, but thinly disguised fascism. . . ." It is a well worn device of Fascists to call anyone they disagree with "communist," and of Communists to call anyone they disagree with "fascist." That Skolnick resorts to this device tells more about his personality and his intellectual affinities than about *Punishing Criminals.* Had I presented a Rohrschach blot, his projections would be relevant. But I wrote a book. Skolnick made up stupid ideas, attributed them to me, and refuted them.[5] The practice is common in political propaganda, but this is the first time I encountered it in an academic journal. I hope it will be the last.

ERNEST VAN DEN HAAG

To the Editor:

Dr. van den Haag's letter fairly exemplifies his wit, perspicacity, and charm. His deductions about my motives reflect his usual standards of inferential accuracy. He also misnames my report. It is *The Politics of Protest.* I agree that the ideas I criticized are "stupid," although I would not, and did not, choose precisely that word to describe them. Moreover, whether or not I imagined these ideas to be the ones in Dr. van den Haag's book or merely conjured them to settle an old score is–you should pardon the expression–empirically verifiable, should anyone care to bother.

JEROME H. SKOLNICK
University of California, Berkeley

To the Editor:

Although E. O. Wilson's *Sociobiology* may not warrant more space in *Contemporary Sociology*

[5] I need not discuss sado-masochistic feelings Skolnick attributes to me, such as "For van den Haag punishment, and love are indistinguishable. Punishment is love." I do distinguish acts from motivations. And the motivation for punishment need not be love. Thus Skolnick deserves punishment not because I love him, or punishment, but because any person writing unfair reviews does. The *motivation* of a person punishing a child may be love (or hostility), just as the motivation of a person failing to punish a child may be hostility (or love). That leaves punishment and love quite distinct.

than was granted to it in November,[1] I still beg for a few additional comments.

Wilson contrasts individual and groups forms of natural selection and tells us that the theory of group selection is still rudimentary (p. 129). To understand how it works he posits (chapter 4) a gene for altruism, defined as "self-destructive behavior performed for the benefit of others" (p. 578). Its operation is traced through sub-human populations under specifications set up in several models [2] and four hypotheses are offered (pp.123–124).

While we are playing around with genetic models for altruism may I throw another one into the hopper? It states that among human beings the gene for altruism is, if not sex-linked, at least more frequent among females than among males, that human females are like the "individuals [sex not specified] referred to by entomologists as the elites [who] are unusually active, perform more than their share of lifetime work, and incite others to work through facilitation" (p. 549).[3] Women, like such individuals, have usually performed more than their share of work (Elise Boulding, "Familial Constraints on Women's Roles," *Signs*, Vol. 1, No. 3, 1976, pp. 95–117; Theodore Szalai et al., *The Use of Time,* The Hague, Mouton, 1973), and are well recognized as facilitators.[4] Everyone is shocked and outraged when or if they refuse to sacrifice or ask merely to have others share the sacrifices even if they don't have the gene for it. Consider how much this model explains. Consider the implications. Consider how it complements and supports the male-dominance biogram.

As a sociologist I am not prejudiced against sociobiology. At least I have no objection to genes. Provided they fit well and appear only in appropriate places.

JESSIE BERNARD

[1] Wilson foresees the demise of sociology as it merges with cultural anthropology, social psychology, and economics even before it has advanced beyond the natural-history stage (p. 574).

[2] Viz.: R. Levins: "the more altruistic genes . . . the lower the extinction rate" (p. 110); S. A. Boorman-P. R. Levitt: "extinction of a severe and peculiar form is required to elevate the frequencies of altruist genes significantly . . ." (p. 113). In the R. L. Trivers model the concept of reciprocal altruism—limited almost wholly to human beings—is introduced. This is not a gingham-dog-and-calico-cat kind of mutually self-destructive behavior but coalition and exchange behavior (p. 120).

[3] Wilson's theoretical models deal largely with "brothers" (pp. 118–119) though many of the examples given of the gene for altruism are among females (pp. 122–135). He includes defense also as altruistic (pp. 121–125).

[4] All this and more, too. I was taught that women invented digging-stick agriculture. I now deduce that it must also have been women who led the human species to become bipeds. Wilson tells us that "because the early pre-men . . . were the largest primates depending on grain, a premium was set on the ability to manipulate objects of very small size relative to the hands. Man, in short, became bipedal in order to pick seeds . . ." (pp. 568–569). It must have been women who picked up the small seeds because their hands were even smaller than the males'. Men became not only bipeds but also paragons of manly virtues. Under sexual selection, Wilson tells us, men became, quoting Robin Fox, "controlled, cunning, cooperative, attractive to the ladies, good with children, relaxed, tough, eloquent, skillful, knowledgeable and proficient in self-defense and hunting" (Alliance and Constraint: Sexual Selection in the Evolution of Human Kinship Systems," 1972. Present reference, Wilson, p. 569). Chalk up another contribution by women.

To the Editor:

A basic policy issue is raised by several reviews appearing in recent issues of *Contemporary Sociology*. Stated in the most general way, the issue is: Should books be reviewed by individuals known to have a very strong personal commitment, pro or con, on the subject matter of the book being reviewed?

The issue can be phrased another way. Is it reasonable to: set foxes to guarding chickens? or, ask a lover to pass judgment on a manifestation of his/her love object?

An immediate case in point is Pierre L. van den Berghe's review of Edward Wilson's *Sociobiology: The New Synthesis* (*CS*, November 1976). Another example is provided by Edward Sagarin's (with Fred Montanino) review of books on deviance (*CS*, May 1976). Still another is Ernest van den Haag's (with Robert Martinson) review of Zimring and Hawkins' *Deterrence: The Legal Threat in Crime Control* (*CS*, September 1974). One would have to be a hermit not to know that each of these reviewers has taken a strong, personalized stand on the subject matter of the books they review and would therefore have to be almost inhuman to be an objective observer.

At the same time, Im sure it is tempting, even logical, for the editor of *CS* to send books for review to people known to be particularly interested in the subject matter of a given volume. The difficulty is that there are interests and interests. Some reflect professional specialization; others are more in the nature of emotional crusades. I'm not in principle opposed to such crusades. But I am concerned about their implications for book reviewing.

Perhaps there is no good solution to this problem. I know I have no magic formula to apply. But I would suggest this: if a book is going to be reviewed by an individual known to be strongly partisan on the subject matter of the book, then it ought also be reviewed by an individual who is partisan on the other side of the issue in question. For example, when the Edward Wilson volume was sent to van den Berghe (or when his review of it was accepted), another review should have been solicited from a person known to oppose strongly the sociobiological thesis—anthropologist Alexander Alland, Jr., perhaps, or biologist Richard Lewontin, or the undersigned sociologist. Van den Berghe's companion in review, Marion Blute, seemed to try to be reasonably objective, but for that very reason was unable to provide a needed balance to the lover's paean of van den Berghe.

Please note that I am *not* saying we should refrain from taking a stand on ideological and philosophical issues; indeed, I am convinced we cannot and should not avoid such stands. But this is quite another issue from the problems posed by the book review question presented above.

THOMAS FORD HOULT
Arizona State University

From the Editor:

I entirely agree with Professor Hoult, and if that makes me a hermit, well, so be it. It is probable that there are controversies within subfields of sociology which are well-known to people in that field but unknown to me, and it is even likely that my ignorance has increased over the last few years when I have read far fewer books than in the years before I became Editor of this journal. Nevertheless, we do not knowingly send books to reviewers from whom we expect strictly partisan reviews, except when we are deliberately soliciting opposing views (as we sometimes do in review symposia). And when we make a mistake, we expect to hear about it, do hear about it, and let others know we've heard about it by printing letters like this one from Professor Hoult.

BENNETT M. BERGER

To the Editor:

Being an avid reader of the "Letters" section of *Contemporary Sociology* and *Science*,–a section which is the most spontaneous part of any periodical–we suspect that this letter will be disappointing to the reader because of its lack of the customary gibing polemics with the reviewer. Indeed, the reviewer presented very fairly the main corpus of our *Sociologues Allemands: Etudes de Cas en Socioligie Historique et Non-historique avec le Dictionnaire de "L'Ethique Protestante et l'Esprit du Capitalisme" de Max Weber* (September 1976, Vol 5, No. 5) but as far as his treatment of the second, apparently more compact part of the book–which is an "elaborate (computer-assisted) multiphased analysis" of Weber's work–is concerned, some closer inspection is called for.

Why did we chose to embark upon the *first* transcription of a *whole* sociological work (104,444 words and 3,749 sentences) in machine-readable form? (See "Epistemometrics: A Case Study in Epistemological Sociology," in: *Computers and the Humanities*, May 1970, Vol. 4, No. 5, pp. 351–352.)

An intensive methodical critique applying systematic criteriology (A. Lalande) developed fully on all three levels of Morris's semiotics (namely logico-syntactic, empirico-semantic and pragmatic) is not possible for a lengthy work without the necessary transparency created by a well programmed transcription.

In order to give an initial illustration of the possibilities which are offered by a computer-aided critique (viz. scientific review essays) understood as epistemological praxis, we transscribed Weber's *Ethic*. The choice of text was not made lightly, in order that the software and other preparatory investments might be profitable: Weber is *the* classical author par excellence but one whose importance may be overestimated. His name is mentioned in symposia time and again often with only fragmentary reference to his work (cf. our interview in short transcription: "Computer Against Max Weber: The Three Levels of Semiotics," in: *Literary Gazette,* February 1974, pp. I-IV). And to be fair to Weber we chose this particular sociological work which was surprisingly the only one that he completed in book form (see Bongras's Preface, p. 8).

As regards the service rendered by the computer, the reader only sees the tip of the "dry" iceberg, namely Weber's wordstock. Compared to the service which the computer has offered and can offer in the future (see our interview) for the epistemological analysis by indexing, by epistometrics and by partial book review simulation especially on the logico-syntactical field, simply counting the wordstock is not impressive, but on the one hand we mentioned on page 150 that the interested person can address the publisher for the whole supportive computerized material, and on the other hand evidently this vocabulary providing each word with 6 characteristics supplied and will supply at every stage of our research or that of others all addresses, viz. with *exhaustive reference* (e.g., the critical edition of the work gave locations for "capitalism," whereas we used 139). We think this taking into account of all references is itself a sine qua non to any definitive progress towards well-founded, more unbiased (less arbitrary) epistemological analysis. This was the "first aid" which the computer provided in analyzing this lengthy work.

Concerning the substantive side, we could now definitely say that the hypothesis that Weber had the intention to prove empirically was formulated in sentences which were sometimes confusing sometimes even contradictory (pp. 139–144). We compared *all* these variations and found also that he followed a deceptive polemical strategy: where he will situate the historical signficance of his work he expressly promises to invert the causal relation produced by the historical materialism (p. 142), but elsewhere, where he develops the empirical proofs, his intentions become surprisingly more modest and insufficient to enable him to succeed in replacing the Marxian general theory of history (p. 140). The contradictions, apparent already on the level of formulation, mean that it is not a question of proving or disproving the hypothesis, because the latter is itself unverifiable, in the strictly scientific sense "indisputable," and therefore relegate it to the historian's intuitive or erudite approach. However, out of respect for Weber's imposing work, we looked for a defendable relation between the protestant ethic and capitalism, in order to prove that variant of his hypothesis which, on the one hand does not seem too insignificant, and on the other does not demand too heavy a burden of empirical evidence (pp. 123–124). This chosen variant was in symbolic terms $\exists_{(p)} \forall_{(c)}$ where "p" is the protestant ethic and "c" capitalism (p. 143). So that he might know why we were unable to find, after all this meticulous treatment, enough empirical proof, the reader must read the book.

A final point which must be made concerns the present and future scientific usefulness of a *computational epistemology* of which you find the blue print in this book. We discuss this question on pages 277–290.

As is the case in all linguistic-oriented analyses, the lexical "dissection of organic unity of a book" does not damage the unity of meaning irreparably, because the lexical dissection is only one facet with its own scientific output, the remaining being, the dissection of sentences, an extremely complicated operation.

From the first by comparing wordstocks, richness of vocabulary, e.g., between historical and experimental sociological works, we can expect to produce an epistemological preclassification of sociological works, as so determine the "epistemological genre." We can also formulate particular epistemometric *hypo*theses, e.g., such as the negative correlation between richness of vocabulary and direct and (in axiomatized systems) "indirect" experimental control. Naturally we did not state this as a thesis (p. 281), because we have not yet transcribed in machine-readible form an experimental sociological work for comparison.

The use of the computer in analysing a whole work as a sentence system is an attempt to extend by analogy the problem-solving methods of extremely *numerous* simultaneous equation and inequation systems, where there could be more unknowns than propositions. (For the logical control of a limited number of sentences see Roland Maris in: *American Sociological Review*, 1970, Vol. 35, No. 6, pp. 1069–1081.) The results are amongst others that the new analytical form of presentation brings to light the connection of all contradictory propositions. The juxtaposition of all occurrences of a term in a work reveals whether the author had or had not always implicitly a correct scientific definition of a term in mind irrespective of whether he offered an explicit definition or not. The further perspective of this computational analysis is to make semi-automatic the book critique on the logico-syntactical level of semiotics.

We take the liberty of finishing this letter addressed to the sole Journal of Reviews for our profession with the last sentences of our book:

> this intensive critique is extremely onerous. It is clear that no journal can apply such a systematic procedure to all the works that it treats now in its review but the problem is this: has a *specialized* review any reason to analyze semiscientific and popular works? The most important pragmatic contribution of such systematic critique is its exemplary and preventive nature; it discourages the scholars and publishers from entertaining the illusion that any work can be at the same time truly profitable for specialists and for the public at large.

GUY G. ANKERL
M.I.T.

To the Editor:

While I may not have done justice to all the details of the latter part of his book—the computerized lexical analysis of Weber's *Protestant Ethic*—my personal evaluation of his methodology remains unaltered after his elaborate letter attempting to clarify his work.

Ankerl writes that Weber "followed a deceptively polemical strategy: where he will situate the historical significance of his work he expressly promises to invert the causal relation produced by historical materialism, but elsewhere, where he develops the empirical proofs, his intentions become surprisingly more modest and insufficient to enable him to succeed in replacing the Marxian general theory of history." Now this single paragraph, it seems to me, conveys Ankerl's criticism of the *Protestant Ethic* better than the 128 pages of computer analysis.

Near the end of his letter, Prof. Ankerl restates the desirability of lexical (and syntactic) dissection of text. My reaction to such methodology is not one of total rejection, for that would be foolish in view of the enormous and valid work done by linguists, semanticists, ethnomethodologists, etc. However, Ankerl and I may simply not share the same "paradigmatic definitions": While I, too, believe in canons of consistency, logic, definitions, conceptual precision, etc., my conception of meaning is based on a humanistic-interactionist orientation. The meaning of a phenomenon is found in its totality, its gestalt, its larger (socio-historical) context, not in its atomized components. Perhaps this makes me pre-scientific (along with Mead, Blumer and two thousand others). . . .

The last paragraph, about "automatic" book reviewing? Perhaps an ideal, for the distant future. Today, thank God, reviews are still written by fallible humans who use judgment, imagination and, yes, error.

I hope that this reaction serves its purpose.

I still feel, as I stated in my review, that Ankerl's book has much to recommend it, particularly its discussion of Simmel and Von Wiese.

THOMAS M. KANDO
California State University, Sacramento

To the Editor:

James Beha's review (September 1976, Vol. 5, No. 5) unfairly attacks my book, *The Impact of Crime*, as "depressingly dated." He complains about the absence of bibliographic references to work published after early 1973 (actually there are a number of references in the book to material from that entire year); however, he fails to show that the incorporation of that material would have altered my conclusions. Since the manuscript was sent to the publisher in February 1974 and the book was published in January 1975, there was no way to include this more recent material. Perhaps now that Beha has had his book review published, he can understand the difficulty of keeping published material up-to-date; his review appeared a full 21 months after my book was published.

Beha is dissatisfied with my treatment of certain empirical relationships. My findings were not "often inconsistent" with my general arguments, as he claims, but where they were I examined possible reasons. This may not have yielded as neat a presentation as Beha wished, but it was an honest presentation of the results of my research. Because one major audience for the book was undergraduate criminology students, most tests of statistical significance were omitted. Beha incorrectly chooses to assume that this means that the results were not statistically significant, a rather unusual inference. I thought, perhaps mistakenly, that an interested reader could consult the original papers presenting my research for tests of significance; those papers are cited throughout the book. Indeed, Beha's review suggests that he himself was familiar with those papers and thus knew that most results were statistically significant.

Beha accuses me of confusing individual respondents with their neighborhoods as units of analysis. However, his treatment of this issue reveals his own misunderstanding about methodology. My comparisons of the two communities employed data gathered from respondents in those communities, *not* data on the communities as units of analysis. Beha shows his confusion here in the very example he selects from the book: "the inverse relationship that exists between criminal environment and support for the law at the community level." Both variables in that relationship are based on measures carried out at the individual respondent level; they are not structural variables for communities as units of analysis. It is proper to control for respondents' characteristics and to compare the two samples' responses to questions when dealing with data gathered from individual respondents.

Beha apparently disagrees with the goals I had in mind in writing the book. I sought to discuss and synthesize material from a number of sources, including my own research, which dealt with the effects of crime on the community and the ways in which community reaction exacerbates the crime problem. Although I may not have met whatever goals Beha had in mind for my book, I am satisfied that I achieved the goals that I had in mind.

JOHN E. CONKLIN
Tufts University

To the Editor:

Professor Conklin apparently considers my unfavorable review of his book an unfavorable review of *him*. This is doubly unfortunate. First, a fair reading of the review should confirm that it is not remotely *ad hominem*. Moreover, I am much impressed by *other* work Conklin has done, most particulary *Robbery and the Criminal Justice System*. But a book review is properly addressed to the present utility of the book, and not to the author's bona fides.

(1) The topic areas of victimization and of citizen attitudes toward crime have advanced enormously since Conklin's field research (in 1969) and literature review (1973). I do not know whether such advances would alter Conklin's conclusions; their inclusion *would* alter the quality of the book. The book is depressingly dated precisely because recent literature largely eclipsed it before Professor Conklin's efforts completed the trip from his research to my reading. By the time my review was published, the eclipse was total.

(2) Professor Conklin effectively admits that a significant portion of the data he gathered was inconsistent with his general theory. Attempting to explain why this might be due to faulty data collection does not contribute to the reconciliation of theory and results, nor does it increase one's confidence in the accuracy of those data which do appear to be consistent with his theory.

(3) I did not assume that some of Conklin's results were not statistically significant. I *tested* his results against the sample sizes he reports, and found that some of his results were not significant. I also found that he reasoned from his results whether they were statistically significant or not. It is that approach which I thought improper.

(4) Much of Professor Conklin's book concerns the different attitudes which citizens in two communities had; he discusses the variation between the two communities, and attributes much of this variation to differences between the

two communties. This *is* reasoning from a sample of two.

I hope that these comments provide the necessary clarification.

JAMES A. BEHA II
Harvard University

To the Editor:

John C. Alston's brief descriptive review of my book *The Functions of Prejudice* (September 1976) contains the apparently racist (but unattributed) remark: "Blacks must be kept in their place, a place beneath the lowest-class white." Several of my colleagues have suggested that it is not clear whether this remark represents a personal opinion of the reviewer or an interpretation of the self-esteem function that prejudice performs for lower-class whites.

One of my reasons for writing *The Functions of Prejudice* was to move away from the benign prejudice or "blaming the victim" viewpoint and to provide a framework for understanding and reducing the level of prejudice in our society. In no way does Professor Alston's statement reflect my own point of view or the viewpoint set forth in my book.

JACK LEVIN
Northeastern University

Editor's Note: We have not received a reply from Professor Alston.

To the Editor:

An elliptical error was made in the printing of my review of Jack Douglas' *Defining America's Social Problems* (November 1976). The omission significantly alters the concept of the book that should be conveyed. As printed, the sentence reads, "the entire book is devoted to a study of the complex social problems . . ."; it should have read, "the entire book is devoted to a study of the complex *process of defining* social problems. . . ." It is precisely this emphasis on the definitional process that sets this book apart from most others and should be clearly noted.

DON H. SHAMBLIN
Ohio University

FEATURE ESSAYS

Community and Polity: The Organizational Dynamics of American Jewry, by DANIEL J. ELAZAR. Philadelphia: The Jewish Publication Society of America, 1976. 421 pp. $12.00 cloth.

IRVING LOUIS HOROWITZ
Rutgers University

Community and Polity is a thorough account of the organizational dynamics of American Jewry. The book helps to explain the factors in Jewish organizational life that give it internal coherence as well as national impact. As a result, this book deserves and should receive the attention of all social scientists concerned with ethnic, racial, and sexual politics. The ability of Jews to articulate their goals has led to a powerful literature delineating ideological and theological aspects of Jewish life. But precious little of the more mundane aspects have been dealt with, such as fund-raising mechanisms, social welfare networks, religious structures, or institutional impacts through cultural instruments such as the Young Men's and Women's Hebrew Associations, or the Council of Jewish Federations. In this work, Daniel J. Elazar joins the ranks of people who have made major contributions in this area, such as David Sidorsky, Marshall Sklare, and Nathan Glazer. On the other hand, this is no *World of Our Fathers*. Elazar has neither the literary flair nor the concern with the strictly secular exhibited by Irving Howe in his recent masterpiece. But this comparison does not in any way deprive this work of its own integrity and worth.

In framing the problem of the American Jewish community in terms of assimilation versus authenticity, Elazar displays genuine appreciation for the special circumstances of Jewish life in America, which in organizational terms is probably better cast as local organization versus cosmopolitan ideology. The treatment of American Jewry as a "state" serves as a vehicle to understand the dialectic between political assimiliation and personal authenticity. At the very least, this formulation allows the author to account for the emergence of federalism, or what might better be called "federationism." But whether or not there really has been a move from congregationalism to federalism in religious terms is not made entirely clear, since the synagogue's importance, rather than being diminished by the rise of suburbia, has actually been enhanced. In spite of the fact that the neighborhood settlements and federations of relatively nonregligious activities are very extensive, Elazar claims the organic links provided by the synagogue, rather than the functional ties provided by the federations, remain very much intact.

The great strength of the book is its emphasis on organizational forms and community contexts. The various tables outlining American Jewish occupational patterns, stages of acculturation and assimilation, the Jewish population as a percentage of state and city populations, and in general, the state-by-state analyses, are of great value to the researcher and a model to others interested in placing ethnic and racial patterns within a larger national framework. The tabular material on distribution of federation allocations, the data on the finances of national Jewish agencies in domestic and overseas programs, and the simple review of Jewish community studies, all illustrate the great value of the book as a statistical mine of information pulling together in one place what not even the *American Jewish Yearbook* offers in this regard. The tables, for example, are integrated into the narrative rather than simply left as a series of appendices that have little relationship to the empirical questions under consideration.

Another strength of Elazar's approach is his keen historical sense. Many of the chapters, such as "Jewish Adaptations to American Life," provide excellent historical summaries of Jewish participation and the impact of such factors as sectionalism, regionalism, and American individualism on patterns of Jewish participation in the New World. The successful adaptation pattern leads Elazar to conclude that organizationally, the American Jewish community has never been in better condition, and that Jews may well have developed a pattern that can provide for communal governance within a free society. But as he well appreciates, organizational advances by themselves do not come to terms with the question of who is or who is not "seriously Jewish." Elazar understands that institutions facilitate decisions but do not exactly account for the quality of that organizational activity. Indeed, one gets the distinct impression that the pattern of adaptation he describes is not unlike that of many Protestant sects, from Congregationalism to Unitarianism, that have emphasized communal bases of religious life. The trouble is that Jews have special problems of a universal, international, and national sort that do not permit the same set of outcomes to occur despite similar organizational devices.

A final strength of the book is the careful operational definitions given to Jewish leadership types and how these dialectical divisions between religious and secular, public and private, cosmopolitan and local, professionals and volunteers, all calibrate in various ways, particularly in Jewish communities. Here, too, the book is realistic as well as provocative, outlining the strengths and weaknesses of Jewish ethnicity in New York, its fragmentation in places like Washington and New Jersey, and segmentation in metropolitan environments such as Boston, Philadelphia, Chicago, and Miami. It makes those sections of the book on "The Major Communities" and "Institutions and Decision Makers" particularly worthwhile. There is careful concern for smaller communities and how they fit the larger patterns through a series of organizational linkages, all of which underscore the author's belief in a Jewish mosaic that seems to afford maximum autonomy, while at the same time insuring large-scale interpenetration in terms of leadership, decision-making, and cultural unity.

This said, I find myself not quite satisfied with the treatment on various levels. Elazar provides no real analysis of Jewish organizational life as part of a larger political network. The notion of a Jewish community exists as a closed monad without any window on the larger world of the American political system. Perhaps the author took too seriously his fronticepiece in which Richard Hooker declared: "Nor is it possible that any form of politie, much less politie ecclesiasticall should be good, unless God himselfe bee the authour of it," and not seriously enough the distinction between that which belongs to Providence and those secular obligations due to the State. The manner in which Jewish administrative affairs feeds into the larger political networks clearly helps make sense of Jewish organizational life in general. As a result, in his fine appendix on the American Jewish community's response to the Yom Kippur War, Elazar is driven to introduce, albeit peripherally, some of these larger political networks, from the federal apparatus at one level to organized labor at the other.

Elazar has mandated his organizational analysis in strict terms, without much sense of ideology: as a result, there is a flattening out instead of an enrichment of a sense of Jewish life. For example, he sees the Jewish press in terms of four components: weekly newspapers, monthly house organs of Jewish organizations, independent publications, and quality magazines. Yet his concept of the Jewish press has nothing to do with the *Jewish* press, but rather with that portion of American society that writes about Jewish topics in the *English* press. So there is absolutely no discussion of such major vehicles as the *Forward, Morning Journal, The Day,* and the *Morning Freiheit.* While only the *Forward* remains as a general Jewish newspaper, the real organizational messages for nearly forty years were carried by these papers. Here, as in many other parts of the book, Elazar betrays a strong bias toward third generation Jews, who are removed from the world of their fathers by language, culture, and tradition. He also displays a peculiar second echelon sense of organizational linkages. It is not only that the author is at Temple University, but also that he is clearly a Philadelphian in his choice of examples and illustrations. The disadvantage is that in Philadelphia, the secular sense of Judaism is perhaps weaker than it is in many other cities of comparable size, and certainly far less so than in New York.

This leads to a penultimate problem: the book offers a welter of organizational forms over time and space, but its portrait of communal life is curiously a world without people. Elazar's communities lack individuals—the linkages are not fleshed out, and we are left with a variety of carefully tabulated organizational forms but not much sense of the spirited, innovating framework of American Jewish life.

Toward the conclusion, Elazar indicates that contemporary Jewish life is beginning to overcome the fragmentation produced by socialism on one hand and Protestantism on the other. The difficulty with this formulation is that socialism was ingrained in and intrinsic to Jewish experience in America. Protestantism was something quite extrinsic and alien to that life. Here, the dialectic of assimilation and authenticity fails Elazar entirely, since the equation of socialism and Protestantism as fragmenting devices betrays an ideological standpoint; not so much a failure of nerve as a lack of insight into the Jewish "mosaic."

Elazar's concept of Jews living in a modern and post-modern environment is cloudy and, for this reader at least, confusing. It is hard to decide from the text itself, whether local federations, public and community relations organizations, organized Zionism, or community synagogue life are all on the ascent or descent; and which, if any, represents the modern or post-modern eras. Nor am I entirely certain that discussing the issue in terms of an increase in the commitment to different kinds of local organizations rather than to global aspects of Jewish existence, is anything other than a mystification of the problem posed by modernism. To speak of a new pluralism in Jewish life which "leads to federalism" does not quite address the question of Jewish survival. In short, this is a book whose parts remain significantly greater than the whole. As a clustering of data, information, and insight into Jewish community life in America and how it is organized over time and space, this is a superb contribution. However, as a work seeking to situate Jewish community life in the context of American political life as a whole, it is far less successful. But we have every right to anticipate, on the basis of Elazar's achievement, further research that would move toward a resolution of the current Jewish dialectic of survivalism as an ideology and triumphalism as an organized style.

Class Struggle and the Industrial Revolution: Early Industrial Capitalism in Three English Towns, by JOHN FOSTER. New York: St. Martin's Press, 1974. 346 pp. $16.95 cloth.

MARY ANN CLAWSON
SUNY/Stony Brook

Since the publication of Stephen Thernstrom's pioneering work on Newburyport, Massachusetts, a dozen years ago, historians have increasingly used quantitative methods and non-narrative sources such as the census in order to study nineteenth century social structure. The new urban historians have produced many valuable studies of local communities and have made great advances in solving the difficult methodological problems which exist in using this type of data. But theoretically these studies are disappointing. Basically they have restricted themselves to answering the questions traditionally asked by stratification researchers in sociology—questions pertaining to the occupational careers, status attributes, and mobility patterns of individuals and groups. In this not only have they neglected many of the subjective concerns that marked the older narrative history; they have failed to achieve a critical relationship to the sociological theory that is the source for many of their questions.

John Foster's work on nineteenth century English working-class movements, which has been much discussed (and debated) in Great Britain, deserves to be better known in the United States by both historians and sociologists. His pronounced Marxist-Leninist perspective may enrage some, but his attempts to develop historically based theory from that perspective, and his original attempts to test and concretize it using quantitative analysis and comparisons of local social structures, should prove challenging to all who read it. It is not only that Foster has extended the range of theoretical questions we can fruitfully ask of demographic sources, offering us examples of imaginative attempts to use "objective" data to come a little closer to an understanding of the generally unrecorded "subjectivity" of working-class communities. In addition, his attempts to develop and actually use theoretical concepts such as class and class consciousness in a concrete historical situation represent an important contribution to Marxist theory and a sophisticated Marxist critique of stratification theory.

The book is concerned with political and industrial struggles in Oldham, an important British textile center, during the period 1790 to 1850. From its origins in the rural putting-out system of the seventeenth century, the Oldham textile industry was dominated by a small group of families who became large landowners and capitalists with extensive investment in coal as well as in textiles. United by financial, political, social, and familial ties, these factory-owners formed a close-knit local bourgeoisie remarkable for its visibility, stability, and coherence.

Out of this process of industrial growth an equally remarkable working class was created. It produced a political movement that controlled Oldham politics for over twenty years. The enormity of this achievement can be appreciated only if we recall that it occurred at a time of limited suffrage, when no factory worker could vote. Instead, workers managed to control the votes of the small shopkeepers, publicans, and tradesmen who comprised the bulk of the Oldham electorate (and whose votes were publically recorded since the ballot was not then secret). This was accomplished through vigorous campaigns of boycott, selective buying, picketing, and outright physical intimidation when necessary—it meant that to be successful the working class of Oldham had to be organized for action not just in the factory but in the community as well.

Through these tactics, the working class of Oldham was able to elect radicals to parliament such as William Cobbett and John Fielden against employer backed candidates. A majority of vestrymen, responsible for poor relief, were usually radicals from the 1810s on, and when the new poor law was enacted in 1834, it proved to be unenforceable in Oldham (as in many other areas) for at least twelve years. But most important in Foster's view was Oldham labor's control of the police and its ability to frustrate all the employers' attempts at take-over and reform. Control of the police meant, of course, that the Combination Acts and other laws making trade-union activities illegal could not be enforced, strikes could not be broken by state power, and the various tactics of extra-legal intimidation aimed at the shopkeeper electorate could not be prevented. So secure was this working class veto on the power of the state that the militia could not be called in from Manchester because the military commanders believed Oldham to be unsafe for their troops.

Not until the late 1840s was the Oldham bourgeoisie able to regain control of these strategic institutions, amidst the collapse of the working-class movement. The obvious question of how the workers of Oldham were able to organize themselves in such an effective and self-conscious way for so many years, and how, despite this, the bourgeoisie was finally able to regain dominance, suggest the theoretical concern which dominates this book: an attempt to characterize class consciousness and to relate its appearance or absence to the social structure. This goal prompts Foster to look at factors such as the economy, technology, the organization of work, the social composition of local elites, and the formation of working-class sub-cultures.

The main theoretical concepts Foster uses to do this are those of class consciousness, at one end of a spectrum, and status systems (also discussed in terms of sub-groupings, authority systems, and labor fragmentation) at the other. These concepts are used to characterize the variety of responses made by the working-class to the problem of living in a capitalist society. Foster's stress on the *reasonableness* of a wide range of responses, ranging from accommodation to militancy (revolution) forces us to consider the entire political and economic context surrounding the development of class consciousness and constitutes a useful alternative to the "what went wrong with the working class?" type of inquiry engaged in by many leftist intellectuals.

The concept of labor fragmentation represents Foster's attempt to give a structural as well as an ideological meaning to the much abused notion of false consciousness. Ideologically, in Foster's terms, a class conscious movement involves a critique of capitalism as a system (as opposed to an attack on unfair privilege, for example, or a Populist critique). But if such a critique has any meaning beyond the rhetoric of its leaders, then it will have a structural expression in the movement that advances it. This movement will be acting to overcome the ethnic, racial, and occupational divisions that so often divide the working class and prevent a sense of total working-class identification. In the same way, an ideology of false consciousness has its structural expression in the perpetuation of such divisions.

Foster goes on to define "status systems" as the chief mechanism of labor fragmentation and here particularly addresses existing sociological theory. Extending Engels's description of "the social division of society into innumerable gradations, each recognised without question, each with its own pride but also its inborn respect for its 'betters' and 'superiors,'" Foster describes the ways in which people construct status systems or sub-groups in order to protect themselves from inequality and lack of control over their lives and what they produce. By restricting their social contacts to those with similar jobs, incomes, consumption patterns, and life-chances, people

> recreated the conditions for a meaningful "social" existence . . . . The result is a series of sectional groupings which—by possessing an approximate equality of consumption—serve to cancel out the most immediate expression of people's larger social irrelevance and, within these limits, allow them to find some measure of social fulfillment (p. 4).

The existence of these status groups is an important aspect of the continuing creation of a "false consciousness" because they represent, not just an ideological accommodation to the existing order, but the structural isolation of one section of the labor force from another. These groups define themselves in opposition to other such status groups, rather than as part of a more inclusive working class (which would be defined in opposition to a ruling class), thus effectively blocking the development of any collective class consciousness.

In my view Foster's discussion of "status systems" is an important step toward a more sophisticated Marxist critique of stratification theory. Many theoretical discussions of stratification (a term which, for want of a better one, I continue to use, despite its theoretical/ideological connotations) take the form of a contest between what are seen as the rival notions of class and status. Each seeks to supplant the other as the sole reality-defining term: the stratification theorists hold that class can't be defined or measured and so doesn't "exist" (certainly not in the United States!), while Marxists and assorted other leftists, wishing to reject Satan and all his works, argue that class differences are what really count and that status represents a kind of illusion imposed on reality by bourgeois social scientists at the behest of the ruling class. Implicit in both these views, at least in their vulgarized forms, is an extremely positivistic view of class as a measurable and unchanging entity, rather than as a dynamic historical relationship, something that "happens," to quote E.P. Thompson's suggestive characterization.

Foster's advance lies in his rejection of both these oversimplified views along with his acceptance of some parts of each. Unlike many Marxists, he accords the notion of status a reality, within the terms of capitalist society. But Foster approaches the concept of status in a way that is quite different from most contemporary stratification theorists, although in a way that is consistent with Weber's initial formulation. Foster sees status as a quality of group life and membership, as a social and historical reality, which people create through their social institutions, their relationships with one another, and their attempts to preserve and defend certain life styles and privileges. Status is not, in this view, an attribute, a passive characteristic which is either possessed or not possessed by particular isolated individuals. The alternative term for status that Foster often uses is "the sub-grouping process," and perhaps this better expresses his insight that people construct these sub-groups for themselves, that they have a concrete, historical reality, and that they serve as systems of self-defense as well as of outright accommodation. By rejecting the notion of status as either an individual attribute or as the product of bourgeois manipulation, Foster escapes the individualism of the stratification theories and the elitism of many left analyses. Status groups represent false consciousness in social relationships; false consciousness now becomes not simply an incorrect ideology but a part of the way people structure their lives, organizing their social and cultural reality. Here Foster makes a significant contribution to Marxist theory by recognizing and reworking a useful analytic concept from within bourgeois sociology.

Foster's treatment of "status" is typical of his concern to reconcile an awareness of the subjective, relational aspects of class with a commitment to structural, social-scientific explanation. This is further exemplified in his comparison of Oldham with two other towns of equivalent size and dependence on industry. Politically these towns provide an interesting contrast to Oldham: one of them, South Shields, had an active trade union movement which never extended its activities to the political sphere, while the other, Northampton, possessed a visible contingent of political radicals who never established connections to the working class, which was itself quiescent. These towns represent different types of consciousness which can be related to structural influences such as living standards, workforce characteristics, types of industry and property, and character of each town's political and economic elite.

Probably the most ingenuous of these comparisons is an attempt to gauge the strength of status groups among the workers of the three towns. In Foster's conception, the existence of status groups is an indication of labor fragmentation and false consciousness; class consciousness occurs when ethnic, racial, and occupational differences within the working class are transcended, a sense of total working-class identification and unity is created, and therefore a critique of capitalism as a system emerges. The labor movement in Oldham was the most militant and successful of the three towns studied. Can this class consciousness be seen in the social relations of its working class? Here Foster's goal is to find an objective measure which can approximate the subjective reality of class consciousness. He does this by looking at residence and marriage as the two most important indicators of social distance among sectors of the working class.

Marriage is an especially crucial relationship, since there is such strong pressure on people at all levels to marry only their status equals. Therefore by looking at whom people marry, we can gain some idea of whom they consider to be part of their social universe. Foster reasons that if we find marriages to be more common between children of craftsmen and laborers, or English and Irish, in one town than in another, we can assume some breakdown of the traditional hierarchies of occupational and ethnic status and (presumably) an increasing identification as part of a common class. Foster provides interesting indications that this was the case; there were more marriages across occupational and ethnic lines in Oldham than in the other two towns. He also shows that ethnic residential segregation was minimal in Oldham during the thirties and forties, the period of greatest labor militancy, but increased during the quiescent fifties, when distinctive Irish neighborhoods began to emerge. The differences are not that great and the evidence is necessarily fragmentary. This attempt is unquestionably of value, however, in the possibilities for research it suggests: Foster has made an original effort to use non-narrative types of evidence to reach an understanding of the subjective dimension of class and status relationships.

An equally important aspect of the book is Foster's careful attention to the social and cultural institutions of the working class, the bourgeoisie, and intermediate groups. These are, of course, the concrete institutional expression of status groups as Foster conceives them. Looking at their pastimes and characteristic social forms in different periods contributes to his analysis of how the ruling class exercises authority in a particular time and place, how social and leisure pastimes "fit" the particular problem set by the nature of capitalist production at that time.

For example, in the early days of the Oldham area textile industry, when most production occurred in mill villages or on an outwork basis, the model of authority and class relationships was a patriarchal one. It was a system organized around the moral discipline of the parish church, touching all members of the rural community, a paternalistic relationship between worker and employer, who still met personally in this small scale, localized system of production. "The essence of the solution seems to have been an attempt to gloss over the class split by binding the worker into the larger household of the employer and then asserting the moral priority of the overall group" (p. 27).

This cultural "solution," however, became more and more implausible as production became large-scale, the workforce larger and more urban, and the differences between workers and capitalists harder to ignore. The growing urban working-class detached itself from the patriarchal claims of the employer to form its own social and cultural institutions, chiefly the pub and the friendly society. Now if the ruling class wanted to maintain its influence over these potentially autonomous institutions, it would have to do so by co-opting or coercing the indigenous leadership, rather than by relying on its traditional authority. By this time, for example, the pubs had become the place where working-class men spent their leisure time, and where meetings of lodges, clubs, and political societies took place. Consequently, the authorities instituted a strict system of licensing as a means of control over the publicans who occupied such a strategic place in the working-class community.

Foster's analysis of these institutions is particularly valuable because he stresses their potential to go either way, to become politically and culturally tied to bourgeois authority, or to become autonomous institutions contributing to working-class solidarity. The friendly society, for example, was the one social organization that included nearly half the working population. In addition to its convivial functions, its system of benefits served an important financial purpose, handling "four of the situations in which working people might otherwise be forced to seek help outside their immediate circle: unemployment, sick pay, medical attention and death" (p. 217). Potentially such a self-help organization could be a source of strength and autonomy. Foster's research indicates that this was probably the case in Oldham. The Oldham friendly societies were exclusively working-class organizations: they never resorted to outside financial help, nor did they contain middle- or upper-class members. Moreover, their membership was recruited on a neighborhood basis rather than by trade, so that the friendly societies would presumably serve to overcome, rather than accentuate, skill differentiations. But this same type of organization could just as easily be a source of bourgeois dominance and labor fragmentation were these factors to be reversed, as they seem to have been in the equally influential lodges and friendly societies of the United States.

This conflicting potential can be seen in Foster's analysis of a later type of working-class self-help organization which included the temperance society, the cooperative and the workers' education institutes. Unlike the friendly societies, these groups were overwhelmingly composed of skilled workers, and their emergence, in Foster's view, coincides with the reassertion of bourgeois power within Oldham and with the related use of skilled workers to exercise authority and enforce discipline within the factory. Structurally these new institutions helped insulate the skilled workers from the social pressures they might encounter from their supposed subordinates in the more inclusive world of pub and friendly society. Ideologically they expressed a new commitment by these elite workers to individual advancement, self-improvement, and bourgeois culture.

This analysis is valuable for a number of reasons. It extends the definition of political relevance to institutions and activities often seen as trivial by academic researchers. This is done concretely and historically, by looking at the meaning and composition of specific groups and activities, rather than by just paying lip service to the concepts of culture, hegemony, social control, etc. And in its historic specificity and insistence on the two-sided nature of such institutions, it gives us a more dialectical view of social control, which emphasizes that these cultural and social systems of authority are themselves objects of struggle which have to be periodically rebuilt, in response to both the systemic contradictions of capital and the self-activity of the working-class.

In my zeal to interest sociologists in the questions raised by this book, I don't want to overlook the many serious problems with it. One is the difficulty of reading it satisfactorily. Its organization is analytic rather than chronological, so that readers will have to reconstruct much of the sequence of events for themselves, and this is frequently hard to do without a specialist's knowledge. Had the book been written for specialists, this might be excusable, but Foster's theoretical and political arguments are clearly meant to reach a broader public than historians studying early nineteenth-century Britain. In addition to depriving us of a basic knowledge of and feel for the period, the lack of narrative detail makes it much harder to evaluate the success or failure of the arguments. This is most serious in Foster's failure to delineate the ideological content of the Oldham labor movement, when a fuller understanding of this is absolutely crucial for considering the contention that the labor movement of Oldham had developed a genuine working-class consciousness.

A much more serious theoretical flaw is Foster's inattention to the role of women. The early textile industry was of course notable for a workforce having large numbers of women, adolescents, and children, yet Foster gives us almost no information on their role within the labor force or in the political movement outside the factory. He does comment that during the period of the ruling class restoration of power in Oldham, women and juveniles constituted the most militant, dissatisfied portion of the workforce, chafing under the domination of the adult male spinners who were enforcing the piece-work system. But he has no interest in how this might relate to the more general problem of women's position within the family and society.

Indeed, in the few instances that Foster does mention women, he reveals that he stands in that particular Marxist tradition which has, whether naively or willfully, refused to consider the idea that the oppression of women might constitute a special problem for a working-class movement, even an otherwise revolutionary movement. A prime example of this attitude is when Foster remarks on the curious fact that there were no women in the working-class leadership of Oldham, and then attributes this to the one-sidedness of the industrial base. In other words, says this Marxist-Leninist, we don't even need a revolution to free women—it will come automatically with capitalist development!

This attitude is all the more pitiful because Foster actually has something to offer a feminist analysis (just as it obviously has something to offer him). His work on status groups constitutes an imaginative effort to incorporate ethnic, racial, and occupational identities into a Marxist theory of class, and to see them as factors which must be overcome, not just in ideology but in the world of real social relationships, as part of the achievement of a genuinely class conscious struggle. A similar analysis of male identity and domination as another instance of this sub-grouping process begs to be made.

Ambiguity and Choice in Organizations, by JAMES G. MARCH and JOHAN P. OLSEN. Oslo, Norway: Universitet Sforlaget, 1976. 408 pp. $20.00 paper.

CHARLES PERROW
SUNY/Stony Brook

This is an important book, and I will explain why directly. But first I should warn you about the minor annoyances you will experience if you follow my advice and get hold of it. First, I don't know how one would get hold of it without writing directly to Norway (the address for your friendly campus book store, is Universitet Sforlaget, Box 7508–Skillebekk, Oslo 2/Norway). It suffers from numerous printing and spelling errors. Part of one paragraph is printed upside down. One or more lines are omitted in another key place. The footnotes for one chapter do not appear in the book. Chapters dealing with the same case study are widely separated entailing loss of continuity and much repetition. Most of the theoretical chapters have appeared elsewhere. Finally, for all this poor editing and printing, one must pay $20.00. I am tempted to recommend that you simply read the Cohen, March, and Olsen article "A Garbage Can Model of Organizational Choice" in the *Administrative Science Quarterly* of March, 1972 and save a lot of money. However, you would miss the elaboration and an extension of that argument and some brilliant sections and case studies. So, at the very least give the address to your friendly librarian.

When organizational theory first got underway again after World War II one of the major preoccupations was with the "informal organization." There was a discrepancy between what really went on in organizations and what our rational and bureaucratic theories told us to expect. The problem was handled through invocations of the whole person, higher needs, small group processes, organic studies, leadership theories and so on.

The image of the organizational actor as a rational calculating being was criticized, and a sentient, affective, self-realizing actor was invoked to explain the discrepancy. The rational structure was opposed to the distinctively human actor caught in its net. An alternative interpretation of the supposed duality of formal and informal, rational and sentient, has been slow to emerge, but receives a significant push in this volume. It is hard to formulate it, but it builds upon the idea of cognitive limits on rationality, found in the early work of Herbert Simon and James March, wherein people are only intentionally rational and severely limited in their ability to formulate goals and understand processes; also in the work of Lindblom where organizations muddle through because of the proliferation of preference orderings and complexity of cause-effect relations; and in the work of E.E. Schnattschneider and Murray Edelman which stresses the manipulative role of symbols; and most recently, in the striking reformulations of conventional wisdom put forth by Karl Weick in extended aphorisms which more or less make organizations run backwards—the deed is father to the thought, a goal is an imaginative reconstruction of past performances, disorder is the recreation that permits invention.

What we have here is less a theory of organizations than of human behavior (though its proponents have failed to confront more explicit and compatible theories of behavior found in the work of cognitive psychologists such as Walter Mischels or—yes—the ethnomethodologists). It is a theory of behavior because the "organization" is dependent upon the nature of behavior, whereas in conventional theories human nature either takes its form from theories of rational organization, or is a constraint on the organization, limiting efficiency. In one formulation, if only management would take into account the human qualities of personnel we could reduce conflict and increase the efficient use of these human resources in the service of organizational goals. We would increase rationality. But, assert March and Olsen and their collaborators, everywhere we find non-rationality. One does not have to be a close observer of organizations to find daily events that would have to be labeled as pathological from the point of view of the theories of organizations we espouse and laboriously test. Decisions are taken with great effort and then not implemented; major decisions are made casually with only minor participation by key personnel; hard-won rights to participate in decisions are indifferently exercized if at all; the past is reinterpreted and fictionalized to justify sharp changes in present direction; planning is conducted to explain away past mistakes; solutions wander about looking for problems that will actualize them.

The authors are not disposed to explain these organizational peculiarities in terms of faulty structures, poor control, lack of leadership, insufficient indoctrination, or some fracture of the structure into formal and informal parts. They are "explained," if we can use that term, by a series of ambiguities rooted in the cognitive and affective characteristics of participants as interacting human beings. Though they do not put it this way, we simply expect far too much of organizations; it is a wonder they work at all, and our conventional theories are designed to reassure us that they are not pathological and do work well. The unreflecting managers know far better, even as they invoke the theories to preserve their sanity. What if they seriously believed that organizations really run backwards?

The argument by March and Olsen, joined by Michael Cohen for one chapter, is laid out in the first five chapters, and illustrated in eight case studies with seven additional authors in the remaining 12 chapters. Their concern is with decision-making or "organizational choice." There is no concern, it should be noted, with several contemporary preoccupations such as administrative intensity, size and structure, technology and structure, or comparative analysis. Some concerns, such as efficiency, environment, power and control, and change do enter in but only through a theory of organizational choice. The case studies are limited to universities or exotic organizations or situations (severely limiting the generalizations possible, though they assert these are merely extreme examples of a general phenomenon). Finally, they are rarely concerned with the routine aspects of organizations, which they imply are limited to housekeeping details, nor with macro power issues, such as university complicity in the social problems of racism, sexism, and war, or the recent erosions of academic freedoms.

Given choice situations in universities and exotic organizations, we find substantial ambiguity regarding intentions like preference orderings, or objectives and goals; we find ambiguity even in self-interest itself. There is the ambiguity of cause-effect relations and techniques; of what can be learned from past events and experience (an "ambiguity of history" but more exactly, of experience). Finally, there is an ambiguity of organized patterns of participation since attention varies, participation varies, time as a resource fluctuates, making patterns of effort and participation highly uncertain.

In addition to these pervasive ambiguities, much organizational action that is conducted in a framework of rational choice—e.g., a new dean has to be selected, so let us set up a search committee; or that a new policy must be formulated since the old one doesn't seem to work, so let's call a meeting—is really organizational action shaped and permeated by concerns of allocation of status among participants, friendship processes, conceptions of virtue or loyalty and so on. Thus, the action can only be understood in these terms, with the rational issue being merely a container for the really important processes.

In addition to the ambiguities and the problem-as-context, the actors, and especially the observers and theorists like ourselves, are under a further handicap. All impose a reality on events that produces a satisfying order which may be only a fiction. There are three aspects of this. We assume that what appeared to happen did actually happen (though there may be no consensus later, or even a manipulated consensus that reconstructs the action). We assume that what actually happened or appeared to happen was intended to happen (if something happened, someone must have wanted it to happen, whereas the flow of behavior may produce outcomes no one imagined or desired, or external forces might override all intentions but not be acknowledged). Finally, we assume that what happened had to happen, whereas in fact unpredictable and even minor random events can determine an outcome that is then treated as predictable because it in fact occurred.

To activate these characteristics of decision making, the authors use a central metaphor: opportunities for choices occur in "garbage cans" into which three things have been thrown. First, problems are deposited there. They arise from nowhere and everywhere. They may be programmed formal requirements such as replacing people whose term has ended, allocating budgets, or establishing new universities in Norway, or exceptional events such as a court-ordered plan for integrating schools in San Francisco, or what to do about tenured professors of speech or architecture when these programs are being phased out. Other problems get dumped into the container, such as problems with group relations, status distributions, or frustrations of family life or careers. Since there are generally several cans available one important aspect of the process is where a problem gets dumped or more exactly, into which stream of decision-making it gets located, since decision-making is not seen as an event, but a stream with many tributaries and inputs.

Second, solutions get tossed in too. A computer is a solution looking for problems. Problems get formulated in the can because there is a solution there that would benefit somebody, even to the extent of simply amusing the proposer. (How often have you thought of a reorganization of your department or school that would be fun to try, and then tried to think of problems that it might solve and thus justify it? If your answer is never, you are not an inveterate organizational theorist).

Finally, participants jump into the can. But they jump from other places, perhaps other cans, changing the mix in those. (As we hear at least three times, basso profundo, "every entrance is an exit some place else.") They are frequently distracted by other streams, and in and out of a can as well, have limited attention spans, and competing demands. Decisions are made by those with nothing better to occupy them.

The choice, then, is highly contextual, depending upon the problems, solutions, participants, and cans that interact. The metaphor is designed to distinguish this view from the conventional one wherein a problem "arises," is noted by someone, the proper participants analyze it, and a decision is made about how to handle it, and they or others implement that decision. Now of course the conventional view admits that time is limited, solutions are often hard to come by, and problems cannot always be clearly defined—for that we pay managers high salaries. But it sees these as limitations on an otherwise purposive and rational process. In the sanitary disposal method (I can't bear their incessant use of "garbage can"; their inventiveness dried up there) these are basic characteristics of the model; the limitation is the attempt to play at rational decision making, not the other way around. For example, in this view problems and decisions can be readily decoupled. Take the Physics Department at Oslo (chapter 14): a decision is required regarding the problem of retaining a departmental secretary when there is no place for her in the table of organization commensurate with her duties and skills. A can is set up, and the junior faculty see a chance to reorganize the department so as to have more say in decisions, and other groups have other solutions looking for choice opportunities. The problem and the decision is readily decoupled. Eventually, a series of decisions result in an extensive change in departmental and divisional structure independent of the original problem, changes not forseen nor necessarily desired. After it is all over, the process is reinterpreted by the faculty as one of democratization of feudal structures, something going on in many universities in Europe. Since there was originally no discontent with the structure, it was not what was intended to happen, in a sense it didn't really happen, and it certainly did not have to happen and didn't in other departments. This is a far cry from saying, sure, things do not always work out and decisions are hard to make, but more rational planning and criteria will improve the choice.

None of us in academic life should be surprised by this fascinating case presented by Olsen, but the point is that our theories should be surprised, and our favored research techniques do not accommodate it. More generally, in a point that March and Olsen do not make, when we observe such a process and outcome from afar, say from another part of the university, we are likely to construct power theories, or conspiracy theories, or invoke leadership factors, or bureaucratic elaboration or increases in administrative intensity, and so on. We like or dislike the result and pick rational explanations that assume what we think did happen was intended, inevitable, and actual. We use conventional theories when we do not have one leg in the can, even as we use them in our research and publications. Thus, in cameo, we also sustain myths about human behavior and organizational behavior that have tenuous validity.

It is now time for the "on the other hand" section of a rationally structured review. The cases should validate the theory's importance, by showing how the theory illuminates where other theories would not. Too few do. Unless one is prepared to believe that whenever things are untidy and goals not pristine and action not maximizing intent that the refuse impactor theory is validated, the repeated invocation of the superiority of the garbage can theory is unsubstantiated. For some cases the analysis is quite unexceptional; no one is enlightened to learn, for example, that in the battle over busing in San Francisco those who put in the most effort were able to shape the terms best. It is an interesting case in it's own right, but could comfortably appear in a book edited by any number of the unenlightened. More seriously, in some cases the theory is fortuitously bent, even warped. For a theory that evokes accidents, ambiguity, exogenous events, "the world of the absurd," the independence of action and response, the importance of context, the "technology of foolishness," and play (there is, incidently, no gritty Terkel-like work in these pages!), for a theory with these evocations, it comes as a surprise to find that one chapter by Cohen and March attempts "to identify the stable underlying logic of some major classes of decisions within American higher education" (p. 175). Stable, underlying logic among refuse bins? It is a good chapter, and we are on familiar grounds as we learn of the limited but substantial power of university presidents, the decisions they rather uniformly attend to, and by implication, the rather clear objectives they have. But throughout the book, the connection between the stable, the routine, or the channeling effects that rules have on behavior (e.g., p. 52) and the world of the absurd is uneasy, tenuous, and not perceived as a problem. It is claimed as a trophy that "the garbage can view of decision making in an organized anarchy" suggests "how the logic of decision in four key areas of university action provides a stability that is significantly independent of the detailed timing in flows of problems, solutions, choices, and participants" (p. 203). Why, then, all the fuss about the flows of problems, etc.? It is one of the best chapters; the section dealing with legitimate actual power and perceived power (pp. 196–200) is quite brilliant. But the chapter's affirmation of garbage can theory applied to an "organized anarchy" is less than clear.

There is a basic problem here, dramatically presented by an excellent, even exciting thirteen page chapter complete with a computer program examining the decision to locate six new district colleges in Norway. The author (Per Stava, University of Bergen) tests alternative theories of public policy formulation, and finds that legal-bureaucratic theories, emphasizing equity and justice, fare much better than power, interest group, democratic or decision-process theories (and one might add, sanitation receptacle theories). "Our analysis indicates a case for treating decisions as explainable in terms of stable, structural elements in the situation, rather than in actions defining the apparent process of decisions" (p. 217). It poses the dilemma the reader has; if Stava had been witness to the daily processes that went on, we might have had another complex, tedious case proclaiming the ambiguity of problems, solutions, choices, and participants. Instead, he used population, economic and geographical distance variables—and that is all.

So, in one sense, it doesn't quite come off. The familiar dynamics of messy organizational actions that we find in our daily life and ethnographic accounts (such as Melville Dalton's) are dressed up in aphorisms that parade as concepts and elevated to the status of a (non falsifiable) theory. They name things that may not be worth the effort of naming, and distort others in an effort to be sensational, and create an ugly jargon (try this: "energy deficit calculations appear to be essential elements of the garbage ejection process under deadline conditions" p. 246). The cases are hardly representative (the free school non-decision case, about which so much is made, for example, or the selection of a new dean at Irvine where March resigned his deanship, has disposable sanitary liners largely because the dean refused to be decisive), or when they are representative, the theory is tortuously invoked. And the book itself is a pastiche of jumbled chapters, perhaps appropriately misprinted and unattainable.

But it doesn't matter. We have enough of well printed accessible books, of standard, representative cases, of bloodless accounts of organizational linkages and school districts. These people are struggling more overtly and consciously than anyone else I know of, save the ethnomethodologists in their contentious way, with something that has a long underground history, and if I can find no neat way to plug it in, if I can't for the life of me understand what they mean by "flight" (one of three decision modes in the GC theory, elliptically "explained" on page 33), if it outrageously ignores what I know about the power of top management and boards and university presidents, it is still something I must come to terms with. They do not provide satisfying terms, but they come closer than anyone else, and though their aphorisms, repetitions and cleverness make me impatient, I know I should join them. Too much of it rings true here and is muffled or never sounds at all within the conventional theories I used.

We should make contact with two other disturbing developments, in cognitive psychology and ethnomethodology, that will deepen and extend the septic tank theory with a more explicit consideration of what my colleague at Stony Brook, John Gagnon, refers to as a "low coherence model of social action." If we take their developments seriously in two or three years organizational theory might be due for an even ruder shock than is outlined by March, Olsen, and their co-conspirators.

REVIEW SYMPOSIUM

Beyond Economic Man: A New Framework for Microeconomics, by HARVEY LEIBENSTEIN. Cambridge, Mass.: Harvard University Press, 1976. 297 pp. $15.00 cloth.

DUNCAN MACRAE, JR.
University of North Carolina, Chapel Hill

The potential cooperation between economics and sociology can be furthered by a critical examination of microeconomics. This field centers about an elegant theory of equilibria in market systems, attained through maximizing behavior on the part of independent units such as firms and households. This book is a significant and far-reaching critique of the basic assumptions of microeconomics.

Leibenstein's basic criticism is directed toward the conventional assumption of microeconomics that the firm and the household are rational maximizing units. Once this assumption is made, the problem of "efficiency" becomes a problem of allocation of factors of production to firms, and of the satisfaction of consumer preferences through the market. But in a 1966 article, Leibenstein coined the term "X-efficiency," referring to the efficiency with which the firm transforms its inputs (factors of production) into outputs. This simpler and more nearly commonsense concept had been defined out of existence by microeconomic theory. Real variations in productive efficiency, however, may be much greater because of X-inefficiency than because of the allocative inefficiency that governs the inputs and outputs of the firm.

To account for variations in the efficiency of firms, Leibenstein asks that economists look at the behavior of the *individuals* within the firm and the household. He thus proposes a "micro-micro" economics in which the unit examined is strictly the individual. Such an approach for the firm would seem to lead to a social psychology of the behavior of individuals in organizations; but any approach that aims to explain organizations' external activities through study of their internal processes should be consistent with his proposals.

A key concept in Leibenstein's scheme is "selective rationality." Instead of an economic man engaging in continual maximization with regard to goods, services, and income, he postulates an individual who is simultaneously engaging in this sort of of behavior to some degree, and also engaging in more impulsive or less calculating behavior. The individual is thus seen as making a prior choice as to the mix of these two ingredients in his behavior. Components of personality such as the id and superego may enter into this choice. The individual may thus choose sometimes to be less concerned with the constraints expected from the environment, to act somewhat more spontaneously, and to accept willingly the later pressure that the environment may impose on him as a result of his lack of calculation. In this sense the chooser might make "rational" choices from the standpoint of his own economy of effort and information, while at the same time departing from the model of economic man in his activities of production or consumption. Because effort is required to maximize carefully, or to change an existing situation, he may thus find himself in "inert areas" of his supply or demand curves, in which he will not easily move to adjacent points under the influence of prices or wages. Within the firm, behavior of this sort resembles the "satisficing" that Simon and his co-workers have described. Norms may also be set among co-workers as well as by larger social systems (e.g., occupational roles), leading to an even greater resistance to change than would be expected for a single individual. Further departures from rationality in the firm may result from slack in the agent-principal relation, in which higher-level personnel act as only imperfect representatives of those below.

These features of human behavior, Leibenstein points out, may not only contribute to low "X-efficiency" in the firm, but also affect the market behavior of the firm. Managers who behave in this way may be less than perfect competitors in the market. The bargaining among firms may itself involve "inert areas."

Leibenstein's approach to the household as a consuming unit is to look both outside it—at the relation between its consumption and that of other households—and within it, at the relations among its members. He analyzed relations among consumers in a 1950 article on "bandwagon, snob, and Veblen effects" whereby the demand of one consumer can affect that of others. These interdependencies, which depart from the microeconomic model, are social phenomena. Noting that man is a "standard-creating species," Leibenstein advances a notion similar to that of normatively governed behavior. And in noting that households may consume in accordance with their membership in "socioeconomic influence groups," he advances a concept akin to that of reference groups. Such norms or group phenomena may lead consumers to place special value on the attainment of a particular quantity of consumption (e.g., four years of college), rather than having monotonically decreasing marginal utilities for the goods in question.

In calling attention to these normative standards, Leibenstein explains to his fellow economists why noneconomists often deal with target quantities of goods or services corresponding to "needs." Norms may thus give rise to consumer preferences, or preferences about social policy, that attach special importance to the provision of these target quantities. Economists may still ask whether some provision should be made for tradeoffs in value between various types of need; but Leibenstein's approach reminds us that in some such tradeoffs the elasticity of demand for certain goods will be very low in the vicinity of their normatively defined "proper" quantities.

Within the household, Leibenstein considers the degree of possible interdependence among family members, including the division of resources among members, the possible interdependences among their utilities, and intrahousehold conflict. His line of reasoning is parallel to that of the "new home economics" developed by Gary S. Becker and others; but his theory is laid out more as a conceptual scheme than a series of rigorous deductions confronted with empirical evidence.

Economists may resist Leibenstein's proposals because they lead to diverse and ramifying empirical studies rather than to a neat model of general equilibrium. The paradigm of microeconomics has been so successful that its practitioners may prefer to adhere to it firmly and extend it into nonmarket domains rather than to move to the empirical level and measure degrees of "constraint concern," the prevalence of "inert areas," or even "X-efficiency." But sociologists may be more willing to carry out such empirical studies, if they can relate the concepts to their own theories of behavior of groups, organizations, and social systems. The behavior of individuals in markets has conventionally been the province of economists, but it can be studied by sociologists as well.

Leibenstein's criticism of the foundations of microeconomics deserves careful study by sociologists. This study will require effort (one of Leibenstein's variables) because the author makes little reference to the sociological literature. It will require confidence in the ultimate value of this interdisciplinary cooperation, because he provides few examples of new empirical research findings. But the opportunities for translation of Leibenstein's criticisms into the language of empirical sociological research are considerable. Especially in the study of organizational outputs, but also more generally for the examination of the relations between norm-oriented behavior and maximizing action, an important interface between the two disciplines deserves to be explored by both together.

SAMUEL H. PRESTON
University of Washington

This book might more appropriately be titled "Back to Economic Man." Leibenstein argues that conventional microeconomic theory is mistaken in neglecting personal motivations and interpersonal relations and focusing instead on the larger units of firm and household. That theory assumes firms to be profit maximizers and households to be utility maximizers. But Leibenstein suggests that the competing and sometimes incompatible goals of the members of those units will usually prevent the units from behaving in the assumed way. In effect, individuals who are members of the units play games against one another, with each game player maximizing self-interest. It is a well known result from game theory that many games in which individuals may plausibly be assumed to engage fail to maximize the total rewards accruing to the participants as a unit.

Game indulgence is only one of many postulated mechanisms that produce nonmaximizing behavior of the economic units. Individuals are assumed to attach negative utility to any movement to a new equilibrium position. Unless the advantages of movement outweigh this cost, the individual's position is fixed through time. The result is that individuals may have large "inert areas" within which activities are inflexible with respect to changes in environmental parameters, contrary to the automatic equilibrating adjustments presumed in naive versions of microtheory. Reliance on agents in interfirm transactions creates still another likely inefficiency, since agents concerned with job retention can be expected to be more risk aversive in their dealings than the firm itself should be. These and other mechanisms, elaborately labeled, are illustrated with very extensive graphs and abundant hypothetical examples. Interested readers are advised to create a companion dictionary of new terms and phrases as they proceed. The amount of jargon invented in the book would make many sociologists blush.

Although an attempt to make economic theory more realistic, the book is uncontaminated by evidence on behavior that would permit one to judge the realism of the newly-postulated relations. Social psychologists and sociologists of organizations may be justifiably dismayed by the virtually complete neglect of their efforts. However, data do underlie the book. Brief but fascinating evidence is presented in chapter 3 that firm inefficiencies in the aggregate are enormous, far greater than the allocative inefficiencies resulting from monopoly or barriers to trade on which most microtheory is focused. Simply put, firms in general come no where near maximizing output with given physical units of inputs. Reorganization of workers and especially revision of workers' incentive schemes can radically alter output, largely (it is assumed) by eliciting greater work effort. Leibenstein has labeled the shortfall in production that results from suboptimal organization "X-inefficiency." It is a powerful organizing concept and the original version of chapter 3, published in 1966, has received a great deal of attention and acclaim.

An important question that the theory fails to address is how massive amounts of inefficiency can persist in the face of competition from other firms in the same industry. Capital flows should be disproportionately directed to those firms who by chance or design happen upon an organization of production that is unusually efficient, and these firms should drive out the inefficient. It seems that Leibenstein has left us primarily with a theory of the firm in immature industries or those characterized by a high degree of monopoly power, but this qualification is never made explicit. Leibenstein's theory of intrafirm relations is rather seriously incomplete without a theory of interfirm relations.

His theory of household behavior has a grab bag quality. He lists a very large number of effects that seem inconsistent with conventional precepts—including "snob," "Veblen," and "bandwagon" effects, empathy utility, target doses—and shows that these violations do not require one to sacrifice the rigor of microtheory and its graphical and mathematical trappings. The examples are amusing, but there are no clues regarding the prevalance of the hypothesized behaviors. The work here, though more eclectic, is somewhat less compelling than that of Gary Becker and his school of sociological economists, who have offered important economic insights into the nature of marital and household decisions and who have systematically tested their predictions. But there are relatively few economists in recent decades who have chosen to recognize the social bases of economic performance. Leibenstein deserves much credit as one of the most persistent and innovative of these much-needed revisionists.

BOOK REVIEWS

Art and Music

Introduction to the Sociology of Music, by THEODOR W. ADORNO. New York: Seabury Press, 1976. 233 pp. $12.95 cloth.

JUDITH ADLER
Memorial University, Newfoundland

Given the paucity of studies in the sociology of art it is unfortunate that this English translation of a book by one of the major figures of the Frankfurt Institute for Social Research does not redeem the promise of its title. Originally formulated as a series of lectures delivered at the University of Frankfurt in 1961–62 and subsequently published with little revision, the book offers some sensitive and erudite reflections on Western music, but no systematic examination of theory and method in the sociology of music nor any detailed analysis of empirical research in that field. Instead, the author provides a collection of essays like those which a sociologically insightful art critic might write on topics such as: types of listening behavior, the ideological functions of popular music, the occupational consciousness of orchestral musicians, and the social role of the music critic.

Adorno polemicizes against any attempt to distinguish the sociology of music from either social criticism or music criticism and this position is both his strength and his weakness. A composer himself, he risks overidentification with his subject, regarding the professional relationship to music as the only fully adequate one and condemning popular music as "objectively untrue" (p. 38). Adorno regards the sociology of music as a branch of the critique of ideology, and therefore responsible for deciphering the truth value of musical compositions. But he remains vague about the procedures for doing so. In practice, the links he draws between social structure and musical structure seem at times to consist only of his own idiosyncratic associations—as when a static quality of avant-garde compositions is said to reflect political resignation. Once made, such judgments become prescriptive and music which fails to hold a mirror up to society in the manner expected is dismissed as a form of false consciousness. On the other hand, while Adorno's commitment to a comprehensive critical theory of society leads at times to a forced search for musical illustrations of social sermons, it also gives his thought a bold and often rewarding historical sweep—as when he draws parallels between the development of chamber music and the flowering of Liberalism, or Berlioz's treatment of the orchestra and the spirit of industrial capitalism.

Adorno's prose style is always demanding, and this translation leaves a few of his passages completely incomprehensible. Therefore I would recommend this book primarily to readers who need no introduction to either the sociology of music nor the critical theory of the Frankfurt School because they already feel at home with both. After some labor, readers such as these will be rewarded by many passages of agile sociological insight into the history of Western music.

The Human Image: Sociology and Photography, edited by DERRAL CHEATWOOD and THEROLD LINQUIST. Fredonia, New York: State University College of New York, 1976. 60 pp. $2.00 paper.

PHILIP H. ENNIS
Wesleyan University

This slim book of 42 black and white photographs is a challenge to those sociologists and photographers who think their two fields have something useful jointly to venture and exchange. The challenge is, of course, to create a continuing forum for those ventures and exchanges. It is also a challenge to those sociologists who believe in the primacy of perception over sanction in the shaping of conduct. That challenge is to develop the theory and empirical generalizations which can connect a set of sociologically relevant visual images (still or moving) to the linguistic labels attached to them. Heretofore only the linguistic labels have been treated as data, not their visualizations.

Still photography is on the rise as an art form, as an independent mode of social inquiry, and as a research instrument for some of the social sciences. If it is now sociology's turn to embrace the visual image as part of its research and theorizing, then it has a formidable history of mutual indifference to overcome. To the best of my knowledge there has not been a single photograph in the *ASR* since its founding in 1936. The *AJS*'s practice of including photographs, mainly in the documentary tradition of showing poverty and the disgrace of the American city, ended in 1915. The major monographs in our field have rarely contained photographs, not to speak of *using* them. It was the cosmetic hand of publishers after WWII that sprinkled pictures mindlessly in undergraduate sociology texts.

This book is the published version of an exhibition (which I did not see) of over 100 prints by twenty-eight sociologists and photographers organized around the theme, The Human Image. It was shown at the second annual Sociology and the Arts meeting at SUNY/Fredonia in 1975. A third version (which I did see) is two full carousel trays (160 slides) of all the pictures submitted. There are, thus, three quite different presentational forms of these photographs.

What is the sociology promised in the book's sub-title? It is difficult to summarize, not so much because the content is so diverse, but more because the language of translation from photograph to sociological concept is too underdeveloped. Yet it is not difficult, paradoxically, to code the pictures thematically. Four subject matters dominate, each related to an established sociological specialty. The most frequent theme deals with the assemblage or dissolution of the visual surface of the individual, emphasizing thereby, the conscious and concerted social actions which make, remake, or unmake the images of ourselves. Phyllis Ewen's picture illustrates this type. It shows a sagging and plain middle aged woman in the beauty parlor, hair in curlers, sitting under the dryer, staring at the camera. Behind her, on the wall, is a photograph of a young elegantly coiffured model, also staring at the camera. This, like many of the type, is a comment in the ironic mode.

A second theme, sparsely represented, explores the boundaries of humanness. These include our border zone with animals, our transition states at birth and death, our mid-journey negotiations with freaks, cripples, and foreigners. A third theme is "emblematics," the photographic equivalent of history painting and portraiture exemplified by Flip Schulke's "March on Washington, D.C. —August 23, 1963." The fourth theme is the capturing of consequential action in its revealing moment, e.g., Judith Erickson's "On Being Nearly Five: Randy," in which the kid, adult baseball glove on hand, is planted to receive the ball, shouting to the thrower to throw it.

The single picture "illustrating" a sociological concept, however, is not the only way this book works. The format of showing two pictures at once, on facing pages, strongly constrains the reader/viewer to consider the pair. How is the one on the left related to the one on the right? One way is *narrative,* as Therold Linquist's sequence of two successive moments in the subway are shown in separate pictures. A second and more highly conceptualized way is *metaphor*; this is like that. The very first two pictures in the book by Bruce Jackson and Howard S. Becker execute this two case comparison cunningly. The left hand picture shows a young black person, naked from the waist up in a jail cell. He or she—a stunning sexual ambiguity for a moment—stares through the bars. In the center of the cell door is a steel lock plate, at the corner of which is coiled a chain and padlock. A third of the prisoner's torso is obscured by the plate which becomes the focal and controlling point of the picture's frontal plane. This plane is the barred door separating the viewer from the subject.

The picture on the right shows seven Catholic altar boys in their religious garb caught informally grouped at San Francisco's Fisherman's Wharf. In the bottom center of the picture is the face and shoulders of an adult woman with dark glasses. As the eye (which is part of the brain) works back and forth between the two pictures, this metaphor emerges: prisoners all! The altar boys are also in jail. Their sexually inverting dress signals back to the first picture's sexual confusion. The boys' jailer is the lady whose head is the same size as the cell door's lock plate and in the equivalent frontal interceding plane. Thus the pair of pictures invites this generalization. The human image is made in constraint by other people, by mothers and other jailers, who in turn, are shaped and distorted by their constraining actions.

Not the deepest insight perhaps, not even the interpretation the editors intended. Neither is it the generalization the two photographers intended. When Jackson's and Becker's full sets of pictures, some of which are scattered throughout the book, are collected and seen successively, as in the slide carousels, it is clear that both had further and different ideas. The presentational form of the photographs shapes their content.

The book is a promising beginning for those who are willing to work at it. As Stravinsky once said, "The only answer to a piece of music is another piece of music."

Art and Sexual Politics: Why Have There Been No Great Women Artists? edited by THOMAS B. HESS and ELIZABETH C. BAKER. New York: Collier Books, 1973. 150 pp. $1.95 paper.

ROBERT D. LEIGHNINGER, JR.
SUNY/Oswego

An informal symposium which originally appeared in *Art News* has been bound with seventy-three black-and-white reproductions in this relatively inexpensive book. The participants are all artists, critics, or art historians. All except the senior editor are women.

The lead articles argue for a sociological perspective on the processes and structures which have confined women to subordinate positions in the art world. Linda Nochlin, an art historian, describes access to art training, noting, among other things, that in eras when figure drawing was the backbone of composition, women were forbidden to sketch nude models of either sex. Hess adds the ironic point that the lack of "great women artists" is a phenomenon occurring despite the existence of great paintings by women. He is referring to a number of highly praised works attributed to various Masters and later discovered to be the work of their women students. These include a "David" costing the modern equivalent of $2 million.

A number of artists responding to these issues exhibit the stereotypic resistance to sociological generalizations. An interesting dialogue between Rosalyn Drexler and Elaine DeKooning contains the statement by Drexler: "I don't want to create any new institutions. I don't want to be *in* any institutions" (p. 70). Other artist respondents are quite comfortable with an institutional analysis. Both camps, and particularly Drexler and DeKooning, provide ample evidence of institutionalized discrimination and other grist for the sociologist's mill. Among the fringe benefits of this volume is a piece of Marjorie Strider which should disturb those who think a dialectical analysis is always a clumsy ideological imposition inappropriate to art.

Overall, while the text is not noted for sustained analysis or copious data, it raises issues and allows artists to describe their work dilemmas as they see them. Its modest price and wide range of reproductions make it a possible adjunct to an Art and Society course.

Hermeneutic Philosophy and the Sociology of Art: An Approach to Some of the Epistemological Problems of the Sociology of Knowledge and the Sociology of Art and Literature, by Janet Wolff. Boston: Routledge & Kegan Paul, 1975. 138 pp. $12.25 cloth.

Batia Sharon
University of California, Santa Cruz

Wolff thinks that the apparent inability of sociology to study the nature of artistic creativity and styles, as manifestations of artistic consciousness, stems from the lack of a comprehensive theory of knowledge. Not only is there no consensus among philosophers and sociologists about the nature of knowledge, neither do they have a well integrated methodology to guide a sociologically meaningful study of it. Wolff's book is devoted to the construction and evaluation of a comprehensive theory of knowledge and its relevance to the sociology of art.

The basic concern of this book is the legitimization of *verstehen* sociology. An elaborate review of the various approaches to the study of knowledge leads Wolff to conclude that while phenomenological sociology accounts for the constitution of knowledge and its origin in experience, language, and social interaction, it fails to account for what structuralists have attempted: an examination of the social unit to which a totality of social and cognitive experience can be attributed. Furthermore, phenomenology appears to ignore the temporal aspects of the socio-experiential determination of knowledge.

Wolff's central thesis is that the inquiry into the nature of knowledge and its origins in its creators' life-world should integrate the phenomenological, structural, and historicist perspectives. She finds such integration in Gadamer's and Habermas's hermeneutic philosophies which provide both theoretical ground and a methodology to expand the range of social facts to which systems of knowledge should be related.

In focusing on sociology of art as a branch of sociology of knowledge, Wolff maintains that both the subjective meaning of the work of art held by its creator(s), and the ways in which the work is related to the subjective and objective realities that constitute the life experience of both creator(s) and audiences, are essential in establishing the role the arts play in society.

To hail the heuristic value of hermeneutic philosophy for the sociological study of knowledge in general and of art in particular is one thing, but to explore the actual transformation of philosophical guidelines into meaningful sociological concepts and categories so that the heuristic value will bear sociological substance, is another. This is where Wolff's book is wanting. Although she is well aware that her work is not more than a foundation for a fully developed theory and method, the reader who is seeking to do sociological research would be hard put to use the envisioned hermeneutic philosophy for such a purpose. The discussion is heavily philosophical, the central concept of the totality of culture is not at all clear, and the offering of hermeneutic philosophy is laden with what it *can* do rather than *how*.

Her call for an integrated theory and methodology is convincing, and the use of the concept of world view to analyze temporal and contextual expressive manifestations is undoubtedly essential. She promises that (a) hermeneutic philosophy is not confined to one level of association or to coincidental structural boundaries, i.e., it can refer simultaneously to natural, religious, political, and other affiliations of individuals; (b) this philosophy assumes the relativity of knowledge; and (c) it is capable of incorporating both the individual's subjective and the group's relatively objective epistemology. Such promises are not a guarantee that all this is empirically feasible. The example of modern dance and her suggestive comments on it are too short and sketchy to offer any particular answer to the inevitable question that Wolff's able critique of phenomenological sociology and her recommendation of hermeneutic philosophy lead to—how can it be done sociologically?

Crime, Law, and Deviance

Problem Drinking among American Men, by DON CAHALAN and ROBIN ROOM. New Brunswick, N.J.: Rutgers Center of Alcohol Studies, 1974. 269 pp. $12.50 cloth.

HOWARD M. BAHR
Brigham Young University

The findings reported in this technical monograph deserve a wider audience than the graduate students, researchers, and scholars who are likely to read it. But the work has its share of jargon, and the painstaking correlation analysis which makes up the bulk of the book, typically multiple regression followed by Automatic Interaction Detector (AID) analysis, will put off many accustomed to more literary approaches.

The authors concede that persons concerned with policy and treatment may not like the book. It further erodes the already weakened Jellinek model of stages of alcoholism, but offers no more certain model to replace it. Persons who need clear-cut answers for immediate application, say the authors, "are likely to have small patience with our desire to disaggregate and complexify." In the earlier research literature on problem drinking a primary flaw was that firm conclusions were based on limited evidence. In this book the conclusions are most tentative, but there is more evidence that the reader may appreciate.

The dependent variable is "problem drinking," broken into three broad areas: drinking behavior, psychological involvement, and physiological and social consequences. Summary measures are constructed from self-reports, and the book consists of analyses of how personal and neighborhood characteristics are related to these summary measures. The subjects are men aged 21 to 59 in two national samples and a sample of white males in San Francisco. The data are cross-sectional, but many of the questions were retrospective, allowing the authors to compare past or lifetime with present experience.

Among the most striking findings about the patterning of drinking problems is that most males have had a drinking "problem" at some time in their lives: almost three-fourths of the subjects had achieved a level of drinking-related problem which the authors considered "noticeable." But at the time of interview only about 5% had loss of control of drinking severe enough to be considered alcoholics under the classic disease concept.

Twice as many men reported ever having a given problem related to their drinking as reported having the problem currently, suggesting a high degree of fluctuation in incidence of drinking problems in the general population, far more than could be attributed to the effects of formal agencies of intervention. These findings cast serious doubt on the widely accepted notion that drinking careers take an irreversible progression or snowball effect. Furthermore, the overlap among the various indicators of alcohol problems is not nearly so great as has been suggested by studies among populations of institutionalized drinkers.

The prevalence of current drinking problems is highest among men in the youngest age group (21–24), and there is a rapid decline in drinking problems as age increases. It is the habits acquired during early adulthood, rather than after age 40, that set the stage for long-term serious drinking. And despite the sociological truism that the best predictor of future behavior is past behavior, the authors find that measures of drinking problems in the past provide only moderately good prediction of present problems. Drinking problems, at least the thirteen types of problems considered in this volume, are loosely associated once persons in the population who have never had any of the problems are excluded.

The primary predictors of tangible negative consequences of drinking are those denoting or correlated with low status: the poor have higher rates of drinking problems and get into trouble far out of proportion to their frequency of heavy drinking. People living in the "wetter" regions of the country (in terms of historical acceptance of alcohol use) have higher rates of drinking problems, and so do people living in cities. Fairly high correlations between problem drinking and age, socioeconomic status, urbanization, ethnic origin, and religion are interpreted as evidence that the development of drinking problems is "heavily environmental" in character.

The effects of four classes of childhood variables—childhood unhappiness, hardship, family disruption, and youthful rashness—are explored. None of them are in themselves necessary or sufficient conditions for the development of adult drinking problems. Analysis of the combined effects of personality, demographic, and childhood variables supports a two-stage model where social differentiation (demographic) variables are primary predictors of heavy drinking per se, but personality variables are the best predictors of tangible consequences of drinking among those who put themselves "at risk" by heavy drinking.

An unusual and welcome contribution is a chapter assessing the effects of neighborhood characteristics, measured by pooling information from respondents in a given neighborhood cluster. Heavy intake is shown to be most common in a "culture of wetness," and tangible consequences of heavy drinking seem particularly associated with heavy drinking in a supportive close environment located in a community generally hostile to drinking. In fact, it is in the "dry" areas, those having a strong abstinence tradition, that explosive drinking patterns predominate among those who drink heavily. Not only the rates but also the forms which alcohol problems take seem to vary as a result of sociocultural pressures.

Results of administration of the surveys in San Francisco prior to the national surveys produced results congruent with the latter. Among the more interesting findings of these pilot studies is that friendship patterns are important determinants of cultural vulnerability to drinking problems: having Scandinavian friends is at least as important as being Scandinavian in predicting problem drinking.

At the end there is an appeal for more longitudinal studies to resolve developmental issues, and for much more work on processes of habituation to tobacco, alcohol, and even calories. There is also a plea for more coordination of research from general population surveys with results from evaluations of treatment programs. The authors promise future follow-up surveys from their ongoing program of research; one hopes that they will continue the technical soundness of the present volume and at the same time pay more attention to readability.

Comparative Human Rights, edited by RICHARD P. CLAUDE. Baltimore: Johns Hopkins University Press, 1976. 410 pp. $16.50 cloth.

HARRY M. JOHNSON
University of Illinois, Urbana

This is a solid book on an important subject. It should interest readers in comparative law, the sociology of law, and social problems. Of the sixteen authors, eight are political scientists, six are lawyers, one is a sociologist, and one, a psychologist. Thirteen of the authors received all their degrees in the United States, and two of the other three (all Indians) were partly American-trained. The book is limited to the liberal democracies. The countries given most attention are the United States, Canada, the Scandinavian countries, England, and France. Somewhat less attention is given to Japan, India, West Germany, Mexico, Uganda, Switzerland, and a few other countries. The book is divided into three unequal parts: political-legal development, policy problems in comparative perspective, and new directions in behavioral research.

The comparative method is potentially important for at least five reasons. (1) If the researcher is interested in a particular case, only comparison with at least one other case will sensitize him or her to the importance of factors that might otherwise be ignored. (2) Comparison reveals functional alternatives. (3) Comparison can bring out the relative importance of different variables. (4) Structural and functional comparison is necessary for the construction and testing of evolutionary theory. (5) Comparison may sensitize the policy-maker to social defects and structural remedies he or she might otherwise be unaware of. All these advantages are illustrated in *Comparative Human Rights*, but not equally well. As several of the contributors in effect point out, the theoretical framework for good comparative institutional analysis would have to be rather complex; and of course for maximum effectiveness it would have to be shared by all the researchers, who would thus constitute a team. It is oversimplified but perhaps not too far wrong to say that the closest to agreement these authors come, at the level of a general theory, is implicit agreement on something like the assumptions of legal realism.

Consequently, part 2, on policy problems in comparative perspective, is to my mind the most satisfactory. Fortunately, it is also the longest; it contains eight fairly detailed, often extremely informative studies, each comparing two or three countries with respect to a particular type of human right. (Part 2 also contains a valuable essay called "Research Resources on Comparative Rights Policies.")

Among the legal areas studied in these comparative essays on policy are constitutional limitations on government, privacy, unequal justice for rich and poor, linguistic minorities, racial discrimination, the status of women, and the welfare of children. Taken together, these essays illustrate some of the more important factors affecting the existence and stability of "human rights." Among these factors we might mention the fundamental emphases of the societal value system apart from the legal constitution (written or unwritten) and apart from the formal law as a whole; the degree of consensus at the value level and (closely related) the conflicts, or breaks in solidarity, in the societal community; the degree of political stability; the type of government, whether centralized or decentralized; variation in the legal system itself, e. g., whether and to what extent it is independent of the executive branch of government, and the relative reliance on legislation and judicial review (or reliance on a one-party system representative of broad segments of the population, as in Mexico); and the stage of technological and economic development. As one might expect, some of the best comparisons are between societies fairly similar in equalitarian, democratic values and political stability, such as the United States and the Scandinavian countries. But Lawrence W. Beer's beautiful study of two rather different societies, "Freedom of Expression in Japan with Comparative Reference to the United States," equally well brings out the fact that fruitful comparison must focus explicitly on the *same* functional problems and structural dilemmas. These better-focused and more detailed essays are also the best-organized and most readable. Even a layman like myself had little difficulty following them.

The book as a whole might well serve as a stimulating introduction to the field of human rights and the literature about it. At the same time, I imagine that most of the essays would be of interest to specialists. For example, the two essays in a subfield I know something about, minority problems, are outstanding. One is Manfred W. Wenner's essay on "The Politics of Equality among European Linguistic Minorities." The other, by Ved P. Nanda, is called "Racial Discrimination and the Law: Recent Legislation in Great Britain, Canada, and the United States." However, of the total fourteen essays, none is really poor. I rated four as "good" and five as "very good to excellent."

Unfortunately, there is no index.

Theoretical Approaches to Deviance: An Evaluation, by Charles E. Frazier. Columbus, Ohio: Charles E. Merrill Publishing Company, 1976. 256 pp. $5.95 paper.

LEE ELLIS
Minot State College

Frazier's book is divided into two parts. The first part deals with problems in defining *deviance*—which for Frazier is essentially any violation of an "important standard"—and contains a separate chapter devoted to each of what Frazier considers the three approaches to understanding deviance: socialization, societal reaction, and control. The first is fairly well epitomized by the notion of "cultural transmission"; the second, by "labeling"; and the third, by "incomplete socialization." The distinction Frazier draws between the first and the third is somewhat confusing in that *anomie* is considered with respect to each (pp. 14 & 50). The particular form of deviance (e.g., criminality, mental illness, drug addiction, homosexuality, alcoholism) is unimportant to Frazier with regard to understanding how such behavior "emerges, stabilizes and changes" (p. 7). This proposition is not elaborately defended, and would have to be abandoned if Frazier attempted to consider it in light of the enormous number of studies suggesting somewhat different physiological factors that may predispose persons to each of these behavioral aberrations. In any case, it is the basis upon which Frazier justifies generalizing about deviant behavior using only case histories of prisoners.

Frazier entitles the second, and most lengthy, part of his book "An Empirical Evaluation." Those who associate the word *empirical* with statistics and scientific rigor will be totally misled by the title. It consists of an entirely narrative description of excerpted criminal case histories that Frazier compiled, tape recorded, and later had typed. Between the passages, Frazier inserted his impressions of the degree to which each seems to mesh with his three postulated approaches to deviancy. Regarding the tendency for deviancy to persist in a given individual, Frazier concludes that the socialization approach seems to have the least explanatory power; whereas the control approach was judged most "applicable," in Frazier's words, "probably because it is the least explicit" (p. 170).

The type of reader to which Frazier's book

might appeal would be one with a holistic, symbolic interactionist type of orientation, and/or one who feels more can be learned about the causes of behavior by reading interview transcripts than by any statistical analyses. From my own rather rigid "scientific perspective," the book seemed neither to advance nor bring up to date knowledge regarding any significant factors responsible for human normative conduct.

The Legal System: A Social Science Perspective, by LAWRENCE M. FRIEDMAN. New York: Russell Sage Foundation, 1975. 352 pp. $12.50 cloth.

Americanization of the Common Law: The Impact of Legal Change on Massachusetts Society, 1760–1830, by WILLIAM E. NELSON. Cambridge, Mass.: Harvard University Press, 1975. 269 pp. $14.00 cloth.

Law in Modern Society: Toward a Criticism of Social Theory, by ROBERTO MANGABEIRA UNGER. New York: Free Press, 1976. 309 pp. $12.95 cloth.

ALLAN HORWITZ
Rutgers College/SUNJ

Sociologists have long expressed concern over the lack of good theoretical and empirical studies in the sociology of law. The major issues, raised but neglected by the classical sociologists of law, have been the relationship between the legal and the economic, political, and moral orders of society, the law and social change, and legal variation across societies and across time; the field has been dominated by studies of the contemporary American criminal justice system. The three books under review here go a long way to restore the sociology of law to a central place in sociological inquiry. It is perhaps relevant that none of these books is written by a professional sociologist. Nelson, Friedman, and Unger are are legally-trained scholars at Pennsylvania, Stanford, and Harvard law schools, respectively.

William Nelson's, *The Americanization of the Common Law*, provides an exemplary model for historical research in the sociology of law. Using Massachusetts court records over the period 1760–1830, he shows how changes in the economy, community, and morality of the colony transformed the legal system from one which enforced the Puritan morality of a tightly-knit community to one more suited to meet the needs of a developing capitalist economy. In the pre-revolutionary period, juries had the power to determine law as well as fact, insuring that case outcomes would reflect community sentiment. Property and contract law restricted the pursuit of wealth and speculation and the criminal law focused on upholding religious and moral values. State power was strictly limited and the legal system served to reinforce community values. However, the changing nature of post-revolutionary American society rendered this type of legal system obsolete. Competing economic, political, and religious factions and the emergent capitalist economy undermined the social stability of the formerly homogeneous colony. Economic entrepreneurs could not rely on the unpredictable verdicts of juries which made economic planning impossible and property rights insecure. Changes in property and contract law abolished restrictions which prevented economic speculation and new entrepreneurs from entering the market system. The criminal law no longer served to uphold morality but came to focus on the protection of private property.

Nelson's analysis shows how a total transformation of the legal system both reflected the changing nature of American society and facilitated the breakup of community and the establishment of entrepreneurial interests. Deprived of the consensus which had formed the basis of the pre-revolutionary legal system, the post-revolutionary legal system responded to the needs of competing interest groups and aided in the development of the capitalist system. In addressing itself to the major questions raised by the classical sociologists of law, in particular, the relationship between the development of the capitalist economy and rational legal systems, the growth of a legal system dominant over society from one controlled by the community, and the interplay between law and custom, Nelson's study is of major importance for an historically oriented sociology of law. It is a model of historical scholarship and should considerably raise the level of discourse in the field.

Lawrence Friedman's, *The Legal System*, is a text-type book oriented toward upper-level undergraduate and graduate courses in the sociology of law. The bulk of the book focuses on empirical sociological and social-psychological studies of law and the author generally avoids theorizing. Friedman gives most attention to the topic of legal effectiveness: the conditions under which law will have the desired impact in changing behavior. Some other topics he covers are the development of laws, law and power, legal culture, and the law and social change. Much of the book is devoted to creating typologies and to classification: of types of legal acts, types of legal systems, types of legal reasoning, factors affecting legal impact, and so forth.

The Legal System reflects both the strengths and weaknesses of contemporary mainstream sociology of law. The book's strong points are its careful specification of terms, presentation of empirical studies, and codification of a wide body of literature. In sum, the book presents a good descriptive picture of the current state of the sociology of law. The book's weaknesses represent the weaknesses of the field itself. Friedman rarely goes beyond the classification of empirical material and his approach lacks any theory of society and of the state. The book focuses on law in contemporary American society and lacks a consistent comparative and historical perspective. The excellent studies in the anthropology of law are almost completely neglected. The absence of a historical perspective is particularly surprising since Friedman has done some of the most outstanding work in the historical sociology of American law. Not until the final chapter, on the law and social change, does Friedman begin to generalize from a range of empirical materials, and this chapter is the most satisfying in the book. Despite the flaws in Friedman's approach, *The Legal System* is the only text on the sociology of law which does not focus on the criminal law and it provides a useful overview of the current state of the discipline.

Dramatically different in focus from Friedman's work is Roberto Mangabeira Unger's *Law in Modern Society*. Unger revives the sweeping scope of Max Weber's sociology of law and places the development of rational legal systems in Western societies within a broad historical and comparative framework. Unger locates the study of law within the major questions of social theory in general: the conflicts between individual and social interests, between legitimacy and coercion, and between the state and society. His main thesis is that the development of the rule of law, law which is committed to general and autonomous legal norms, could only take place when competing groups struggle for control of the legal system and when there are universal standards which can justify the law of the state. Unger contrasts the development of the rule of law in Western societies with its failure to emerge in other civilizations. The unique historical conditions in European societies created a situation where while none of the competing groups of the middle class, the aristocracy, and the monarchic bureaucracy wanted an autonomous legal system, all settled for one as a compromise solution.

Much of Unger's work examines the tensions inherent in rational legal systems such as their appearance of impartiality which masks a system of domination by powerful groups, their need both to draw upon consensus and to satisfy the interests of special groups, and their legitimation by reference to universal norms in societies pervaded by moral skepticism. The central paradox of rational legal systems is that the same condition which brought about the rule of law in society, the struggle between competing social groups, also deprives the legal order of its basic condition of self-legitimating consensus. Finally, Unger develops the thesis that in the absence of consensus, modern societies are increasingly turning away from the rule of law toward a law which is less autonomous and more oriented to the achievement of substantive goals. Unger clearly relocates the sociology of law within the mainstream of social theory and his book is one which cannot be ignored by anyone interested in the field. It should provide the basis for the generation of numerous empirical studies for some time to come.

Despite the great dissimilarities between these three books, all take what can loosely be characterized as a "pluralist" perspective toward the legal system. Friedman's metaphor of the legal system as a rope in the game of "tug of war," one which is in itself neutral but which serves as the necessary basis for the struggle between competing social groups, also fits, with some differences, Nelson and Unger's general view of the legal system. As such, these books represent the reemergence of a pluralist view of law in opposition to the Marxian-conflict model which has dominated theorizing in the sociology of law for the past few years. These three books breathe new life into a model of the legal system which has been dormant for some time and provide a healthy theoretical contrast to the conflict model of law.

The sociology of law, while still in its infancy, is growing into a healthy adolescence and scholars in the field can take heart from Nelson, Friedman, and Unger's efforts. Clearly, sociologists in the field have much to learn from their legally-trained colleagues.

Justice, Legal Systems, and Social Structure, by H. RICHARD HARTZLER. Port Washington, N. Y.: Kennikat Press, 1976. 134 pp. $12.50 cloth.

A. J. BERGESEN
University of Arizona

H. Richard Hartzler intends to define the interrelationship of justice, legal systems, and social structure. He states at the outset that his ideas are based on reading Lasswell, Smelser, Pound, Lewellyn, Hoebel, Weber, Dahl, and Lindblom. From his reading he concludes that there are some general social goals we all possess with the usual problems in attaining them. Law serves as a means for resolving these difficulties. In some general sense this is probably true, but hardly worth the effort of wading through 128 pages of garbled prose and incomprehensible diagrams. There are, though, some short bursts of coherence and a sense of logical progression. Consider the following argument: "no group functions for long . . . without the presence of some authority. Authority is therefore necessary to a group's continued survival. The elements of authority are the identical conditions of a legal system. Therefore, no group long survives without a legal system. Legal systems are necessary" (p. 40). Well, that's the gist of it, and on it goes for 128 pages. The only suggestion I have for those who might share Hartzler's interest in law and social structure is to do as he did and read Lasswell et al. and compose your own synthesis.

The Organisation of Crime, by MARY MCINTOSH. London: MacMillan Press, 1975. 80 pp. No price listed.

JOHN L. MCMULLAN
London School of Economic and Political Science

The Organisation of Crime is a brief, stimulating, and substantial contribution toward a theoretical understanding of professional crime. The focus is on the *pattern of relationships* which constitutes organized crime in different historical periods. Professional criminals are defined as those who practice crime as their major occupational role. It is their full-time job whereby they labor and make a living. Built up around this basis of criminal labor is a structure of work and personal relationships. Professional crime, according to McIntosh, is an autonomous reality, differentiated *organizationally* from other institutions. It has its own uniformities, its routinized patterns, sets of meanings, and a tradition of work practices.

By utilizing a perspective that stresses the "rationality of an organisational structure as an explanation of its existence," McIntosh, like Cressey, directs our attention to the historical contexts of specific social control structures. In doing so, she demonstrates the subtle intermeshings of the *internal* organization of criminal work groups with the *external* conditions for crime. Criminal organizations are perceived as being anchored in a larger social totality involving the State, the judiciary system, the police, the criminal underworld, opportunities for crime, the criminal's victims and customers, etc. The autonomy of organized professional crime is relative, a reflection in part of the social control apparatus of society. Variation in the conditions of social control invoke changes in the type of professional criminal organization. Thus the configurations of social relations which constitute criminal organizations are built up interactively over time. So, for example, the organization of different kinds of thieving can be best understood in terms of the forms of protection that have been developed by property owners and the State. As protection has shifted from personal defense of property, to banks and armored cars, to a constantly improving technology of safes and alarms, so the organization of thieving has evolved from a small urban craft form of crime to a well planned project crime involving advanced planning, high risk, and large networks of information, communication, and personnel. The *rationality* of criminal organizations varies in order to cope with crime protection, to meet new criminal markets, and to avoid legal detection and apprehension.

In exploring the historical conditions for the emergence of stable patterns of professional crime, McIntosh defines four types of organized crime. They are: the *picaresque*—typical of banditry and brigandage; the *craft*—exemplary of routine small scale urban thievery and confidence cheating; the *project* organization—typical of certain forms of robbery, smuggling, and fraud where crimes are large scale and technically difficult; and the *business* variety—represented by extortion and racketeering that has obtained immunity from the law. Her focus is on elucidating the social characteristics of each organizational form, stressing the importance of criminal "technique" in confronting, neutralizing, and circumventing the agencies of social control.

McIntosh concludes by arguing that no one type of criminal organization is dominant. Various organizational configurations can co-exist at certain historical junctures. There is no discernible tendency toward a centralized *business* form of crime.

There are a number of difficulties with McIntosh's formulations. First, her approach, primarily one of developing a conceptual framework is sketchy and her attention to historical specifics is minimal. The categories of her analysis lack historical content. The etiology and relationship between organizational types is not clearly articulated. Second, the defining features of the organizational types are ambiguous and much too general. *Project* crime for example, appears as a supra-historical type operating in almost any kind of society. Third, there is an unresolved tension between the alleged autonomy of professional crime and the parallel character of criminal organization. The *separateness* of criminal organization is made problematic. Forms of criminal organization may be but patterns of existing historical forms of social organization. *Craft* crime may be more a patterned variation of trades and fraternity organization rather than a collective social reaction to social control. Fourth, her formulation of the relationship between social control and professional criminal organization is one-sided. She does not analyze the effects which criminal organizations have on the maintenance of social order. Finally, and paradoxically, the source materials for her theory of rational criminal organizations are based on failed, jailed, reformed, or exaggerated criminal accounts. There is a clear need to study the crimes of the powerful.

Despite these reservations, McIntosh has ordered a diverse array of ideas into a perspective that merits attention. It is a valuable working guide toward making sense of professional crime and a necessary body of thought to bring to bear on historical research.

Justice by Consent: Plea Bargains in the American Courthouse, by ARTHUR ROSETT and DONALD R. CRESSEY. Philadelphia: J. B. Lippincott, 1976. 227 pp. $10.00 cloth. $3.95 paper.

JERALD W. CLOYD
SUNY College/Geneseo

In *Justice by Consent,* Rosett and Cressey attempt both to integrate the relatively atomized literature on plea bargaining and to present it to scholars and laity alike in a readible and easy-to-understand manner, and they seem to be successful on both counts. Prior to this book, most of the research on plea bargaining has been scattered throughout various legal, political science, and sociological journals, not to mention specifically authorized commission reports and private research projects. Given the recent public awareness of plea bargaining due to the Watergate and related political scandals, there has been a need for a volume that can cut through the more technical legal language and give a working knowledge of the process, points of tension, and possible modes of reform within present plea bargaining practices. These authors present this knowledge without undermining the actual complexity of the social and legal factors recognized in past research by both lawyers and sociologists as affecting the plea bargaining process.

The book is structured around a hypothetical burglary, "The Odyssey of Peter Randolph," and relates the ways in which the arresting officer, public defender, prosecuting attorney, and judge perceive the case, interact with each other and with the defendant, and "negotiate" a conclusion. Each chapter centers around a different member of the court, focusing on the legal and organizational responsibilities facing him/her. Prosecutors often are concerned with efficiently processing large case loads within the general confines of legal rules and community norms. Public defenders are usually caught between clients who are often seen as "unattractive," superiors who want the cases moved through the courts efficiently, and their own ideal of protecting the rights and interests of each client. Judges are presented with cases in which guilt has been decided (through plea bargaining), where the only information available is often exclusively that on the arrest and probation officer's report, and where there may be pressure by police and the two attorneys to hand down a particular sentence; from these factors the judge is required to give a "just" sentence.

The crucial issue therefore involves the tension between the ideal of objective procedural standards (i.e., equal cases being treated equally) and the need of members of the court to have and use discretionary power to fit the law to each particular and unique case. As the authors put it, "Procedurally, the officials' first task is to decide whether a defendant is guilty of a specific crime; if he is, the second task is to decide what, if anything, shall be done to him. To avoid becoming deadlocked in unanswered questions, the professionals ask the second question first" (p. 101). That is, the authors argue that there exists among the members of the court a set of informal norms for plea bargaining cases which is based more heavily on subjective notions of justice (i.e., what should be done to the defendant) than on strictly statutory or procedural law. This represents an organic resolution that is flexible enough to fit the unique aspects of each case, and uniform enough to maintain equality before the law.

On the whole, the authors are optimistic in their evaluation of the compatibility of the plea bargaining process with the ideal of justice. Although the last chapter of the book outlines some possibilities for structural reform, they assume that each member, in his/her own way, is concerned with maintaining justice, and that therefore the end result of the plea bargaining process is just. In my own research on the judicial system, I would agree with this conclusion; however, many researchers do not (Blumberg, Alschuler, and Schur). The ultimate motives of each member of the courts (whether they be justice, organizational efficiency, or personal motives) are, of course, difficult to ascertain. Nevertheless, the authors integrate the literature currently available on plea bargaining cogently to support their conclusions.

Finally, the book is designed for a specific audience: the non-specialist interested in the basic process of plea bargaining. In this capacity, the book could be useful to laity with an interest in the area, to professors for assignment in undergraduate courses in criminology, and to lawyers interested in an overview of sociological research on plea bargaining. The rather complete annotated footnotes provide a very helpful bibliography for the sociologist interested in the various debates surrounding the issue of plea bargaining.

Social Deviance, by S. GIORA SHOHAM. New York: Gardner Press, 1976. Distributed by Halsted Press. 162 pp. $13.95 cloth.

NANETTE J. DAVIS
Portland State University

For a field which has elicited almost as many critical exposés as serious theoretical works, S. Giora Shoham's *Social Deviance* joins the handful of scholarly attempts to elucidate the nature of deviant phenomena. Unlike the "nuts, sluts, and perverts" (Liakos) school of deviance, Shoham synthesizes history, sociology, literature, and psychology, proposing a unique (and, at certain points, debatable) model based on phenomenology and Durkheim's structuralism.

Five additive components comprise the model: self-concept + value deviance + deviant behavior + social stigma + transcendental conviction → social deviance. Becoming a social deviant initially involves persistent identification with group-imposed negative identities and self images. This creates the detachment from conventional values and groups, the deviant behavior, subsequent social reaction and exclusion, and an oppositional belief system confronting the group's mundane realities. The deviance process is enhanced by anomie—conditions of social and economic turmoil that undermine traditional solidarities. As anti-hero in a classic morality play, the deviant is both sinner and saint; hero and victim, offering group salvation through pollution, collective unity through individual separateness.

Not recommended for beginners, sophisticated audiences will delight in Shoham's ironic sensibilities and mastery of literary allusions. Alas, the critical perspective is not evident. The personal fate of underdogs subjected to often oppressive social machinery of stigma and expiation is ignored. Siding with the functionalist, Shoham leaves unexamined the concept of community as a class differentiated entity. The quiet desperation of the silently detached (rather than those who openly flout rules) is also given little attention. Neither the risk-taker nor situational deviant are adequately considered. Shoham's book remains an insightful, often imaginative, but incomplete theory of social deviance.

Development/Modernization

Debate and Compromise: The Politics of Innovation, edited by F. G. BAILEY. Totowa, N. J.: Rowman & Littlefield, 1973. 343 pp. $16.00 cloth.

MICHAEL LEWIS
University of Massachusetts, Amherst

In eleven ethnographic essays the editor and contributors whose work this volume encompasses would have us understand the following with regard to technological and economic innovation in small communities, primarily located in Western Europe:

(1) Such innovation always occurs in political context.

(2) Resistance to such innovation is maximized when a community's basic values are threatened by its introduction.

(3) The response of given individuals to a proposed innovation is likely to be a function of their attitudes and interests. When they perceive an advantage to themselves in the adoption of a proposed innovation, they favor it; when they perceive disadvantage to themselves in the adoption of a proposed innovation, they oppose it.

(4) Changes in the environment—both social and natural—of a community are likely to be predisposing toward innovation within the community; but such changes do not of themselves guarantee successful innovation.

(5) Social structure and extant rules of interaction within a community can either maximize or minimize the probabilities for successful innovation.

(6) Successful innovation is, in the last analysis, the result of successful moral entrepreneurship, wherein the innovators are able to gain acceptance for a definition of the situation which favors their proposal.

There isn't much that is particularly wrong with this book, but there isn't much that is instructive about it either. The ethnographies will, on the descriptive level, perhaps be helpful to those scholars who are interested in small communities, but as far as theory and interpretation are concerned we've "heard it all before." So, Professor Bailey, what else is new?

The Political Economy of Agrarian Change: An Essay on the Green Revolution, by KEITH GRIFFIN. Cambridge, Mass.: Harvard University Press, 1974. 264 pp. $11.00 cloth.

WILLIAM L. FLINN
Ohio State University

Green Revolution—the process of introducing new super seed varieties along with their accompanying pack of inputs—has produced a myth that this peaceful transformation is the solution to feeding the world's hungry while promoting economic progress for all people. Griffin investigates the contributions to date of high yielding varieties of foodgrains. His data indicate that while some regions or countries may have increased production, the underdeveloped countries as a whole have not experienced a revolution in agricultural output. He concludes that the direct quantitative effects of green revolution technology have been rather modest at the aggregate level. While one may quarrel with the reliability of data from underdeveloped countries, Griffin's argument is sound and plausible.

In focusing on the more significant indirect effects of green revolution in specific "successful" regions and localities, Griffin uses a conflict approach which examines the class interest of landlords and peasants. The former have greater access to factors of production than the latter. These market "imperfections" represent different opportunity costs for each group and mean that present green revolution technology is usually "landlord biased." This has accelerated the development of a capitalist, market-oriented agriculture with resulting changes in cropping patterns and methods of production—mechanization. The consequence for rural areas is greater specialization, division of labor, and greater social differentiation. This differentiation gives greater power to landlords and encourages growth of agricultural laborer sectors. Not only is class conflict increased between landlords and peasantry but within the peasantry—middle peasant, small peasant, and agricultural laborers. Thus, green revolution generally accentuated class distinctions, class conflict, and increased inequalities. Inequalities are caused not by differences in attitudes of landlords and peasants toward change but by monopolistic exploitation and/or governmental policies. Most governments represent the interests of the landlords and urban elite with a resulting policy devoted to raising exportable output and are not concerned with the welfare of the rural population or with improving the distribution of income and wealth.

Griffin does see a positive potential for technology to produce economic and social development, if used properly, but with the exception of Taiwan it hasn't occurred. The reason for this, he feels, lies not so much in inadequate technology but in inappropriate institutions and poor policy. The latter is due to the powerlessness of the governed.

Some may not agree with the theoretical perspective employed but Griffin synthesizes a mass of literature and data to support the conclusions. The book is an important contribution to the literature questioning the consequences of green revolution. Some parts of the text seem redundant, perhaps due to its earlier printing as progress reports of the United Nations Research Institute. The points are important enough, however, to warrant repeating.

Education and Individual Modernity in Developing Countries, edited by ALEX INKELES and DONALD B. HOLSINGER. Leiden, The Netherlands: E. J. Brill, 1974. 136 pp. No price listed, cloth.

SCOTT CHRISTOPHER WREN
University of California, Davis

This collection of quantitatively oriented research reports argues, not altogether persuasively, that education has an independent role in developing countries as the prime determinant of individual modernity. The collection is often tedious and lacks a cogent synthesis of the results of the diverse projects, including studies in Brazil, Puerto Rico, Tunisia, and one of a "negro" section of Boston.

In all the studies "modernity" was measured by the OM scale developed by Smith and Inkeles. The scale purports to measure a complex set of attitudes, values, and behavioral tendencies which are distinctively modern. Unfortunately the reader who is not already familiar with the nuances of the scale is left wondering what exactly "modernity" is, other than an ethnocentric perspective on American society. If the US is "modern" then are the values embodied by its dominant culture the ones which should be used in accessing the degree of modernity of individuals in other cultures? One of the only clear indications of what the authors mean by modernity is presented by Holsinger in his article on Brazil. Two out of the fifteen questions asked of third through fifth grade school children were to identify a picture of a camera as a camera, as a tape-recorder, or as a radio and to indicate the number of organizations to which they belonged. While one could legitimately ask what these questions have to do with modernity (e.g., how many people have never seen a camera or how many organizations do any third graders belong to?) one also wonders what they have to do with schooling as opposed to other factors such as tourism or urbanization.

The lead article, by Inkeles, discusses the results of a six-nation study by the Harvard Project on the Social and Cultural Aspects of Economic Development and suffers from some measurement ambiguity. In presenting evidence for his assertion that modernity increases with the length of formal education, he includes data from Argentina which show that only 16% of the sample with less education were "modern" compared to 32% of those with more education. However, "modern" only indicates a score in the top one-third of the frequency distribution on the OM scale. In actuality the differences between mean scores for those with less education and those with more was only four points (50 and 54 on a scale that ranges from zero to one-hundred). What Professor Inkeles has done is to select arbitrary and rather misleading cutting points in the distribution.

Furthermore, these are only relative rankings of individuals, scored only in relation to other respondents in a particular national sample. No standardization of scores on the OM scale across countries was attempted, which accounts for the fact that only 2% of those in the Argentina sample with three years of education had a high modernity score, as compared to 43% in East Pakistan with the same amount of education.

As to the assertion that education is *the prime* determinant of modernity, Professor Inkeles finally admits that "of course since we tested individuals only after they reached adulthood we cannot say for certain that the modernity to which education evidently contributed was already manifest in them at the time the better educated men left school. . . . We are equally comfortable with the assumption that . . . schooling merely laid the groundwork. . . ." The reader is assured, however, that the Holsinger study in Brazil is conclusive in this regard.

The critical issue in the Holsinger study finally boils down to a comparison of OM scores for children in school and scores for children of the same age who had not attended school. He presents data showing that the mean score for children in the fifth grade is ten points higher than that of the third graders', whereas the mean score for children of the same ages not in school remains constant. On this basis Holsinger argues that education is the prime cause of modernity.

There are several problems with this conclusion. First, it is empirically impossible to demonstrate that the non-school children "do not grow more modern" for the simple reason that the data are cross-sectional and not longitudinal. Secondly, no statistical tests of significance are reported to indicate that the difference could not have been found by chance. In addition, most of the increase in the mean OM score for school children occurred between the fourth and fifth grades. But as the author points out elsewhere, "fifth graders are a very high achieving group by definition, since four years of elementary schooling are all that traditionally have been expected for an elementary education." One would expect, then, that fifth graders would have higher OM scores, not because of the influence of education, but because most fifth graders were "high achievers."

Holsinger also shows, however, that at each grade level the school children had higher OM scores than did the non-school children of the same ages. The comparison was only made between children from low SES family backgrounds because no children from middle and upper SES families could be found who were not attending school! More importantly, no non-school children, regardless of SES, could be found in the major urban area of Brazilia. But it was not revealed what proportion of the low SES school children were from Brazilia, thus leaving open the possibility that controlling for the "urban experience" factor would account for the higher mean OM scores of the school children. This possibility is further strengthened by other data presented by Holsinger which show that the mean OM score of third graders with high "urban experience" is actually higher than that of fifth graders with low "urban experience."

No one would argue that formal education and modernity are related in some fashion. But it is impossible to conclude from the evidence presented in this collection that education is the prime cause of modernity, however measured. An equally plausible explanation would be that education is only a symptom of increasing modernity in these societies. Put another way, it may be that to be "modern," that is, to attend school, is to be modern.

Nutrition, National Development, and Planning: Proceedings of an International Conference Held at Cambridge, Mass., Oct. 19–21, 1971, edited by ALAN BERG, NEVIN S. SCRIMSHAW, and DAVID L. CALL. Cambridge, Mass.: MIT Press, 1973. 401 pp. No price listed, cloth.

ROY WEHRLE
Sangamon State University

Unreason and anger are increasingly the currency exchanged between the Northern and Southern nations of our globe as they confront compounding problems of population, economic growth, and environment. For the last ten years (or so) Alan Berg, formerly with the US Agency for International Development, and others, have sought to bring attention, knowledge, and development planning to the improvement of one strand of this tangled web: human nutrition in the developing countries. An international conference was held in Cambridge, Massachusetts in 1971 to consider this objective by bringing together from around the world over 300 experts and practitioners in economic development and nutrition. *Nutrition, National Development and Planning*, an edited manuscript of the conference, provides a wealth of information, and is a delight to read. The volume sparkles with ideas, experience, controversy, and insights. The presented papers are of high quality as are the commentaries and the short discussion sections. The editing is crisp. How seldom we read conference discussions where the ideas shine forth as they do here.

Top thinkers in development and nutrition are included: Joaquin Craviota, V. Ramalingaswami, John Mellor, Mohamed Nour, David Call, James Levinson, Alan Berg, J. M. Bengoa, Robert Muscat, Toshio Oiso, Robert Nathan, Nevin Scrimshaw, Asok Mitra and Carl Taylor, among others.

There are essays on the complex nutritional interactions between food, society, and the family and the individual. Studies show that specialization of land use for cash crops may reduce the variety of foods available to local residents and thus decrease their nutritional status. The failures and the limited success of selected and mass feeding and fortification programs are described in stark terms, as are the difficulties of improving the nutrition levels of the very poor.

The major thrust of the conference, however, is improving nutrition by improving national planning and policy in developing countries. The essays on this subject assume that nutrition comes from food, conditioned by a given level of health. Most articles assume an implicit model of nutrition as an output produced by inputs, with national planning given the task of producing and staging the right inputs.

I end this review in a skeptical vein. I suspect that nutrition is, to the contrary, best viewed as an organic concept embedded in, and determined by and determining of, health and well-being. Society nourishes or fails to nourish the individual as surely as food does, with the well-being of the mind and body influencing how effectively nutrients and calories are utilized. This circular and organic model of nutrition would call for a very different plan of nutrition improvement than does the linear model; in addition to food production and availability, it would focus attention on indigenous institutions, small-scale technology, participatory and village level programs (in addition to production of more or different food) in order to improve, not nutrition alone, but the composite of nutrition, well-being, and health.

Methods

Evaluation and Experiment: Some Critical Issues in Assessing Social Programs, edited by Carl A. Bennett and Arthur A. Lumsdaine. New York: Academic Press, 1975. 553 pp. $17.50 cloth.

Validity Issues in Evaluation Research, edited by Ilene N. Bernstein. Beverly Hills: Sage Publications, 1976. 134 pp. No price listed, paper.

Lynne G. Zucker
University of California, Los Angeles

Both books address important issues in evaluation research, though overall the much longer Bennett and Lumsdaine book suffers in comparison with the Bernstein volume. Bernstein's collection appeared as a special issue of *Sociological Methods and Research* (August 1975) and the articles are focused, succinct, and clearly organized. In contrast, the essays in Bennett and Lumsdaine are uneven in quality; they cover diverse topics; and are not well integrated by the introductory and summary chapters written by the editors. Many of the essays are too long and discursive, appearing to be unchanged from their conference format (all but one are the product of a 1973 symposium at Battelle Institute).

The most intriguing and innovative essays deal with the problems faced whenever a true experiment is not feasible. Rather than resurrecting the old arguments about experimental research, these essays contribute techniques for handling problems in design and analysis when true experiments are not practical. Boruch (in Bernstein) outlines possible combinations of true experiments and quasi-experiments (or even non-experiments). These combinations are designed to increase reliability of inference from data collected in approximations to experiments and to speed up the verification process by combining results obtained using different designs. Though Boruch's essay is the most outstanding, other essays provide valuable suggestions for overcoming some of the problems inherent in approximations to experiments. The Alwin and Sullivan article (in Bernstein) explores and suggests different kinds of correction for nonrandom assignment, carefully specifying conditions under which they are appropriate. Cain (in Bennett and Lumsdaine) also deals with selection problems, but in a much less comprehensive or satisfactory way.

True experimental designs are the principal focus of the two books. On the whole, the essays discussing true experiments add less to the available knowledge than those discussing approximations to experiments, repeating many of the earlier arguments. However, two are outstanding: the Gilbert, Light, and Mosteller essay (in Bennett and Lumsdaine) and the Lyall essay (in Bernstein). The Gilbert et al. essay makes a powerful argument for randomized trials, demonstrating that treatment effects are generally small and difficult to interpret. Non-randomized studies in medicine frequently produced results that did not hold up in later randomized studies. The detailed data they report are presented poorly, and in a misleading manner because they take at face value the reported results of the studies. For example, Gilbert et al. ignore the controversies regarding the New Jersey negative income tax experiment—controversies which are presented in several of the essays in Bernstein. In fact, most questions of method—other than true experiment or not—are put aside. In contrast, Lyall's essay (in Bernstein) deals with fundamental methodological problems faced by large-scale experiments. She focuses on the process by which a given sample is allocated to a specified number of treatments, providing a clear discussion of the Watts-Conlisk model used in the New Jersey Experiment and the problems involved in optimal designs. Since experimental designs comparing different treatments, rather than one treatment and a control, are being encouraged (e.g., Lumsdaine and Bennett's summary) Lyall's essay is particularly timely.

There are several other essays in the two books which are focused on interesting problems, but which fail to make significant additions to the evaluation literature. The Bernstein, Bohrnstedt, and Borgatta article on external validity problems touches on too many issues to be able to deal in depth with any of them. A graduate level introductory course could, however, make good use of this overview. The Edwards and Guttentag essay in Bennett and Lumsdaine also might prove useful in such a course. Their review of problems in using evaluation research is good, if not complete. Their discussion of the use of decision analysis is suggestive, but poorly developed, and their condemnation of experimental evaluations is not at all persuasive. Which experiments in particular do they condemn? This is not at all clear. Katz (also in Bennett and Lumsdaine) provides a clearer and more original discussion of the use of evaluative information, but again rehashes many of the old issues in a somewhat new framework.

Some of the essays I have not explicitly reviewed generally repeat (or to some extent extend) work available in other places. For example, Campbell and Boruch's excellent essay (in Bennett and Lumsdaine) addresses basic issues already raised in Campbell and Erlebacher (in Hellmuth, J., ed., *Disadvantaged Child,* Vol. 3, 1970, pp. 185–210), though substantially extended beyond regression artifacts. Other essays were so detailed and difficult to follow (e.g., Hilton and Lumsdaine on the impact of fertility planning programs) that only those directly interested in the subject matter would be willing to examine them further. Issues of general interest are not presented clearly.

Both books are significant sources of information on new developments in evaluation research, especially on experiments and approximations to experiments. Both would be improved by the addition of a good index. When reading the books, similar themes or references are often made, and the reader must hunt through the other material to make comparisons.

Quantitative Sociology: International Perspectives on Mathematical and Statistical Modeling, edited by H. M. Blalock, A. Aganbegian, F. M. Borodkin, Raymond Boudon, and Vittorio Capecchi. New York: Academic Press, 1975. 643 pp. $18.50 cloth.

Nancy Brandon Tuma
Stanford University

Quantitative Sociology (*QS*) contains twenty-two chapters by European, Soviet, and US social scientists. The common element connecting the chapters is the use of "quantitative" methods, i.e., mathematics and statistics, to deal with sociological (more accurately, social scientific) problems. The chapters vary greatly in breadth of appeal and in the kind and extent of mathematical knowledge required for comprehension. Many sociologists will find some chapters in *QS* of interest. Very few will find most of them interesting. I will first discuss the stated purpose of *QS* and the degree to which it meets this purpose, and then give a highly selective overview of its contents.

According to the preface, the main purpose

of *QS* is to increase cross-national communication among social scientists on quantitative topics. To achieve this goal the editors might have collected international surveys on a series of special topics or overviews of quantitative approaches to social science in various countries. They chose neither format; instead they collected research contributions from distinguished quantitative social scientists in many nations. Consequently, *QS* resembles an issue of an international journal of quantitative sociology. (In fact, a third of the chapters are revisions of previously published articles, and several others contain ideas that their authors have developed more fully in other books.)

The journal-type format has both advantages and disadvantages. A major virtue is that new things can be learned even when reading chapters by co-nationals writing on one's own specialty. But I found it less than ideal for increasing cross-national communication.

In reading chapters by authors with an American orientation (those who publish in American journals or cite a high proportion of American authors), I usually knew the work's context: the background literature, the relevant problem areas, the pertinent mathematical techniques, etc. As a result, my gain in information from these chapters (when the ideas were new to me) was relatively high and mainly varied with the work's quality.

On the other hand, the context of chapters by many non-American authors was unfamiliar, and therefore I found it difficult to understand their substance and to appreciate their significance. This was especially true of the five chapters by Soviet authors, most of whom use highly sophisticated mathematics to tackle very abstract problems. Thus, I usually learned less from these chapters than from those by American-oriented authors, but this is attributable more to my ignorance of their context than to their intrinsic value.

The above remarks have a two-fold purpose. They give my evaluation of *QS*'s attainment of the editors' stated purpose. They are also intended to explain why my references to specific chapters in the following overview of *QS*'s contents give disproportionate attention to American authors. Most readers of reviews of edited books want to know which chapters will interest them most. This depends as much on the reader's prior knowledge and concerns as on the merit of the particular chapters.

QS is divided into three parts. Part I, "Causal Analysis, Structure and Change," contains the most abstract and some of the most mathematically demanding chapters. Four of the eight chapters in part I deal with causality. I especially recommend Suppes's "A Probabilistic Analysis of Causality" for useful remarks, clearly and briefly stated. S. Nowak's "Causal Interpretations of Statistical Relationships in Social Research" is lengthy, but clear, and will be appreciated by those interested in causal modeling. Two of the eight chapters deal with structure. I particularly liked Høivik and Gleditsch's discussion of graph-theoretic measures of structural properties (integration, centralization, polarization, etc.) because of its potential applicability to empirical research. Only one chapter in part I deals with change. Galtung establishes some typologies for longitudinal analysis and considers designs for following one variable over several time points and a few units and for comparing two variables on a single unit over several points in time. This chapter, originally published in 1970, has largely been superceded by recent work on pooling cross-sections over time. Charvát and Kučera's chapter, "On the Theory of Social Dependence," is not on the meta-methodological level of the other chapters in part I and, in my opinion, would be better placed in part III of the book.

Part II, called "Design, Measurement and Classification," deals with what American sociologists call Methodology. Kish convincingly argues that experiments, surveys, and controlled observations differ in their strengths so that each can be the most appropriate design in certain circumstances. Duncan explores several linear models with two unobservable variables, each with a single indicator on which there are measurements at two points in time. He considers the relationship between observed correlations and parameters of the models and uses exemplary data to illustrate that the range of an unidentified parameter in a model can sometimes be established and that a model can sometimes be ruled out because it leads to parameter estimates that violate assumptions. In "Indirect Measurement in Social Sciences: Some Nonadditive Models," a chapter with a particularly wide appeal, Blalock considers several linear models in which the effect of one independent variable on some dependent variable is a linear function of other independent variables. Given the revived interest in analysis of data on nominal variables, many readers will want to read Möller and

Capecchi's "The Role of Entropy in Nominal Classification." These authors use concepts from information theory to choose a minimal set of variables that classify the position of units on some dependent nominal variable, to distinguish typical response patterns on the basis of the smallest possible number of independent variables, and to evaluate the "distance" between members of different classes. Zagoruiko and Zaslavskaia's "Pattern Recognition Methods in Sociological Research," the least mathematically-demanding chapter by a Soviet author, uses a method called random search with adaptation to tackle very similar problems; it may give a clue about the nature of Soviet social research, as well as suggesting an alternative approach to the problem of classification.

Part III, "Social Models: Some Applications," contains seven chapters on specific substantive topics: Land on the use of the differential calculus to derive a theory of organizational growth and differentiation; Boudon on incorporating movers and stayers into the analysis of mobility tables; Coleman on modeling behavior in systems with perfect exchange (so that power is transitive); Rainio on formalizing theories of choice behavior and social interaction; Keyfitz on consequences of various measures of population regulation; Malm, Olsson and Wärneryd on simulation models of urban growth. Appreciation of these chapters will depend highly on the reader's concern for the specific topic.

As this overview indicates, the chapters in *QS* are highly diverse. While I suspect that many American sociologists will share my disappointment in having learned less about the quantitative approaches of their European and Soviet counterparts than they would have hoped, perhaps *QS* will whet appetites for further cross-national exchange of ideas. In the meantime, readers may decide, as I have, to read the European journal *Quality and Quantity,* the source for over one-third of the chapters in *QS*.

Methods of Research in Social Psychology, by J. Merrill Carlsmith, Phoebe C. Ellsworth, and Elliot Aronson. Reading, Mass.: Addison-Wesley, 1976. 326 pp. No price listed, cloth.

Royce Singleton, Jr.
University of California, Riverside

This book is an expansion of the Aronson and Carlsmith chapter "Experimentation in Social Psychology" in *The Handbook of Social Psychology*. Despite the promise of the title, the reader expecting a full and equal treatment of *non*experimental methods will be disappointed. Nonexperimental research is mentioned only briefly, while building a case for the advantages of experimentation which is seen as the most efficient method currently available in social science for providing information about causal relationships. Even within this context, the book has a still more specific bias toward the predominant research paradigm in contemporary social psychology —*between-subject* designs, in the *laboratory,* that involve *deception*.

Given their narrow focus, Carlsmith, Ellsworth, and Aronson do offer a comprehensive and lucid discussion of techniques, guidelines, and inherent problems pertinent to conducting laboratory experiments on social psychological issues. Indeed, this is probably the best book available on the practical problems involved in actually doing experiments, and the interested reader will find many useful techniques for minimizing error and bias.

The first third of the book introduces key terms, outlines major problems in experimentation (e.g., control versus impact and relevance, experimental versus mundane realism), and presents a thoughtful, balanced discussion of the ethical and methodological problems of deception. The remainder of the book discusses, in turn: the "empirical realization" of the independent variable (an excellent discussion of this neglected topic); verbal and behavioral measures of the dependent variable; characteristics of effective experimental settings; experimental design problems and alternatives; techniques for minimizing demand characteristics and experimenter effects; and debriefing. All of these topics are thoroughly covered, with varied research examples drawn chiefly from the authors' own work carefully interwoven into the discussions.

Although alternative techniques are discussed under each of the topics mentioned above, the authors' preferences are usually quite clear. For example, they prefer laboratory manipulational experiments—role playing and simulation studies are dismissed as uninterpretable, and field experiments are seen as presenting greater ethical and control problems. They prefer impact and direct experimenter control over standardized procedures and instructions which may standardize the external stimulus but not the subject's response that it is intended to produce. And they prefer behavior and behavioroid (subjects' commitment to perform the behavior) measures to rating scales because the latter have been overused and are subject to more systematic sources of error.

While the authors do not indicate for whom the book is intended, its narrow focus will certainly limit its use and appeal. Graduate students and practicing social psychologists will probably find it most useful, indeed, essential. But since the book ignores the beginning and end of the research process—no attention is paid to the origin of the ideas behind experiments or to data analysis—undergraduate instructors are likely to find it incomplete for most purposes. Also, the technical language and generally sophisticated treatment of most subjects will probably make it difficult reading for undergraduates without some prior knowledge of social psychology, general research methods, and statistics.

Applied Multiple Regression/Correlation Analysis for the Behavioral Sciences, by JACOB COHEN and PATRICIA COHEN. Hillsdale, N.J.: Lawrence Erlbaum Associates, 1975. Distributed by Halsted Press. 490 pp. $19.95 cloth.

NEIL W. HENRY
Virginia Commonwealth University

Although it is promoted as a textbook for students in any discipline related to behavioral or social science, this book is most appropriate for persons who have gone through a psychological statistics course. It is intended to be an alternative to the usual followup course in statistical methods which emphasizes analysis of variance and experimental design. The message is that analysis of variance and covariance can, and should, be studied as special cases of regression analysis. The great advantage of this approach is that it puts the analysis of experimental and non-experimental data within the same framework.

Despite my approval of the aims of the Cohens I cannot recommend their book as a text. It is far too long, given the topics covered, and uses quite a lot of idiosyncratic notation and jargon. Chapters 5 and 7 are thorough discussions of dummy variable coding and missing data, respectively, and could be read profitably by experienced social researchers who have already been introduced to regression analysis by, e.g., Cooley and Lohnes.

Social Indicators and Public Policy: Interactive Processes of Design and Application, by JUDITH INNES DE NEUFVILLE. New York: Elsivier, 1975. 311 pp. $13.75 cloth.

BRIAN VARGUS
Indiana University-Purdue University, Indianapolis

Most work in the area of social indicators has tended to be either an elaborate (sometimes uninformative) technical exercise or a review of existing data that might somehow be used by policy makers. Few writers have attempted to treat the development and utilization of social indicators within a sociological framework. This book fills the gap and fills it well.

Social Indicators and Public Policy addresses two issues: how to design indicators that can be used in policy formulation, and how to design mechanisms to provide for the better use of such information. The author is acutely aware of the complex relationships between theory and measurement and provides a textbook review of the problems of measurement with careful attention to the special difficulties relating to policy formulation. De Neufville demonstrates that measures without a theoretical basis are at a distinct disadvantage. This position is based on a careful review of the social indicators movement and a most impressive history of three indicators with differing impacts upon policy: the unemployment rate, standard family budgets, and the crime rate. In particular, de Neufville demonstrates the relative successes of each of these indicators within particular organizational contexts based upon their respective strong or weak links between theory, concept, and indicator.

The later sections of the book present a blueprint for the institutionalization of the design of indicators for both the purpose and the theory of public problems. The final portion of the book contains a good review of many of the key methodological questions in indicator design. The author makes a strong case—through the historical reviews—for her position that the design of indicators cannot be solely a technical exercise; nor can it ignore prevailing public conceptions of issues. Tables are included showing the historical development of each of the indicators used as case studies and illustrating the main components and alternative conceptions of each.

In general, this is useful book—particularly as an introduction to the problems of measurement that pertain to social indicators. It will sensitize readers to the interactive nature of social indicators. The work could serve as a text for advanced undergraduates or beginning graduate students interested in social indicators. The author successfully explicates the ways in which social indicators can be developed and used—rather than concentrating upon elaborate techniques that tax all but those highly trained in applied mathematics. The case histories of the three well known indicators alone are worth the purchase price of the book.

The Research Experience, edited by M. PATRICIA GOLDEN. Itasca, Ill.: F. E. Peacock Publishers, 1976. 528 pp. $6.95 paper.

Sociological Observation: A Strategy for New Social Knowledge, edited by MATILDA WHITE RILEY and EDWARD E. NELSON. New York: Basic Books, 1974. 320 pp. $10.95 cloth.

NORMAN K. DENZIN
University of Illinois, Urbana

Sociological methods are in a state of change, drift, and disorganization. Quantitative methodologists debate the various virtues of path analysis, log linear analysis, sociometrics, and borrowed techniques from econometrics. Qualitative methodologists quarrel over the uses of the historical-comparative method. Participant observers debate field strategy. Ethnographers dispute methods of reporting field data. Historical sociologists argue that sociological methods are not suited to the problems they confront. Theory and substance, central elements in the research enterprise, seldom touch these methodological controversies. As a consequence the sociological imagination tears at itself and the student of sociological affairs is given little direction, other than current fad and fashion, when a serious, scholarly research project is undertaken.

The two collections under review do not capture this methodological unrest. This is largely due to the journals and authors they draw from. Garfinkel, Circourel, Blalock, Goodman, Duncan, Hamblin, Selvin, Hirschi, Lofland, Strauss, and Schuessler, to name but a few, are absent.

The Riley-Nelson collection is a volume in the now discontinued *Issues and Trends* series of the American Sociological Association. In keeping with the original theme of that series, which was to draw together under one heading articles presented in the Association's periodical publications, seventeen of its twenty-eight articles are taken from ASA sponsored journals. (Thirteen are taken from the *ASR*, four from *Sociometry* and seven from research monographs, including Gans's *Levittowners,* Whyte's *Street Corner Society* and Goffman's *Asylums.*) The nineteen selections in Golden's collection range across such journals as *Sociometry*, *AJS*, *Rural Sociology*, *Journal of Social Psychology*, *Journal of Personality and Social Psychology*, *and Journal of Marriage and the Family*. These journals have not succeeded in capturing the current methodological controversy. Such topics as serious mathematical sociology, experimental design, ethnomethodological procedures, and interactionist field methods are not discussed. This is not to slight either collection; it is a comment on the state of the field.

The Riley-Nelson reader stresses sociological observation and charges researchers to return to their original calling which is the study of what people do when they interact with one another. The editors note that since the early 1930s there has been a distinct trend *away* from observational studies and a clear movement toward ahistorical cross-section surveys, social indicators and other trend data.

Their collection is organized into six sections: (1) Dynamic Studies of Interaction, (2) Interpretation of Data, (3) Data Gathering, (4) Systematic Control over the Observed Action, (5) Measurement and Analysis, (6) Sampling. Representative substantive materials are presented in each section and the work of Bales, Whyte, Gans, Rose Coser, Becker and Geer, Berger, Cohen and Zelditch, the Langs, L. Humphreys, Goffman, Dalton, Strodbeck, S. M. Miller, Roy, Roth, Short, Back and Le Play is presented. Each section is preceded by a thoughtful introduction which fits the readings to one another, while stressing strengths and weaknesses in each author's approach.

One can dispute their organization of sociological methods into the above listed six categories. But it is time that sociologists begin to take first-hand field observations seriously. This volume offers an important challenge in that direction and certainly captures some of the very best research and theory that has appeared in ASA-sponsored publications since the inception of the *ASR* and the ASA in 1936.

Golden's collection stresses the research experience as well as the problems of choice and constraint in the observational process. Slightly more psychological in nature, her volume has the strength of presenting personal remarks by the included authors on their own research experience. These personal statements are quite useful and will benefit students as well as practicing sociologists for they show that the links between attitude and research act are often less than clear-cut, and most certainly problematic. Representative authors include Gans, Moskos, Haney, Banks and Zimbardo, Weldon Johnson, Howard Suchman, and John Kasarda.

Her book is organized into six chapters. Chapter one is a detailed and well grounded statement on research strategies, including surveys, field studies, simulation, experiments, and the analysis of secondary data. It reviews the entire research experience from problem formulation, to selection of topic, research unit, research method, data collection, measurement, analysis, and ethical considerations. Subsequent chapters report research utilizing field studies, experiments, surveys, and available data. The last chapter presents papers by Doob and Gross and Zick Rubin which bear on the measurement problem.

This is a useful collection of readings and could well serve as a supplement in an undergraduate methods course, as could the Riley and Nelson volume. Golden's decision to seek or select authors who would reflect on their research experiences is to be applauded. Schuman's reflections on his study of antiwar sentiments during the Viet Nam period, for instance, is but one of several telling statements in this volume which link the private with the public side of scientific activity.

These two collections, drawing as they do on diverse sources, provide a useful guide to contemporary sociological methodology. They do not reflect cutting edge controversy for such controversy seldom appears on the pages of the sampled journals. Qualitative sociologists turn to their research monographs and quantitative sociologists turn to *Sociological Methodology*, (ASA sponsored) or any of a number of Sage Publications. This suggests two proposals. Serious quantitative methodology needs an airing in our major journals, as does serious discussion of qualitative innovations, developments, and elaborations. The American Sociological Association might well consider the sponsorship of a quarterly, or annual, devoted to the publication of strictly non-quantitave materials. But more importantly, method ought not to be thought of as a set of activities which is separate from theory and substance. The Riley-Nelson and Golden collection suggest that the time has come to seriously consider where sociological methodology is going.

Markov Chains Theory and Applications, by DEAN L. ISAACSON and RICHARD W. MADSEN. New York: John Wiley & Sons, 1976. 256 pp. $18.95 cloth.

ROBERT MCGINNIS
Cornell University

The non-trivial purchase price will get you a copy of this latest entry in the distinguished Wiley Interscience Series in Probability and Mathematical Statistics, whose stable of authors includes Doob, Feller, Kendall, Lehmann and Wilks, among others. A solid grounding in probability theory, matrix algebra—a bit more than the ability "to multiply vectors and matrices" (p. viii), that the authors suggest—analysis (of sequences and series) and a dabble of the calculus (of real variables) will let you read it. This done, you will probably be reasonably satisfied with your purchase, but a bit let down on some scores.

The publishers, on the dust jacket, and the authors, both in their preface and subtitle, emphasize the "practical" nature of the book "balanced between theory and applications." About twelve pages are given over to abbreviated summaries of six empirical applications of Markov models. The rest is pretty much theorems, proofs, remarks (sometimes cloyingly cute) and illustrations (often enlightening and useful).

The first half of the book takes us through the "classical" development of Markov Chains, in discrete tune and countable state space (if you don't dig these words, don't buy this book). The second half provides a good introduction to the "Algebraic approach," stressing eigenvector analysis and the "ergodic coefficient" that was new to me and rather interesting, a device for studying the erogodic properties of non-stationary metrices. The emphasis on non-stationarity is welcome.

While this review may not ensure that the book will move like a prairie-fire in the sociological community, I am not certain that it should. It is a text, but far less useful for the typical sociology major than is a Bartholomew or a Keneny and Snell. It is worth the price as a reference work, particularly with its numerical examples and introduction to what should be new and reasonably useful topics to many of us. Although less faddish today than a few years ago, the tool of Markov chains remains a basic and powerful one for the analysis of sociological dynamics.

Research Methods in Social Sciences, by DAVID NACHMIAS and CHAVA NACHMIAS. New York: St. Martin's Press, 1976. 335 pp. $12.95 cloth.

S. PADMINI RAVINDHRAN
University of Texas, Arlington

This book presents in a comprehensive way, the various procedures involved in scientific research in the social sciences. The authors' objective is to view scientific research as a process involving seven interrelated steps—generating researchable problems, constructing hypotheses, formulating the research design, measuring, collecting data, analyzing the data, and generalizing.

The book is divided into four parts. Part I, which includes the first four chapters, deals with the foundations of empirical research, examining the aims of science in social sciences. The various research designs for evaluating hypotheses and significance of measurement are also discussed. Part II discusses methods of data collection. Data processing and analysis, including various statistical methods of control and interpretation, are discussed in part III. Part IV adequately discusses methods of statistical inference, hypothesis testing, and sampling designs.

The study suggestions at the end of most of the chapters are very useful. A summary at the end of each chapter helps clarify the contents of the chapter. The book gives empirical examples of various research designs which are very valuable. The style is clear, which makes the book interesting to read. Information about coding of data and computer analysis of data will be valuable for people who do not know much about computers.

The qualitative techniques of case study and historical analysis could have been discussed in greater detail. The ideas of conceptualization and its problems should have been emphasized to a greater extent in the discussion of "concepts," in chapter 2. The authors' emphasis is on quantitative research, and the role of statistics in research is very well treated. But the level of discussion of statistical methods is beyond the comprehension of a beginner in research methods. This book can be used as a reference for beginners in graduate school, who already have some basic knowledge of statistics. It is also a good reference book for teaching research methods at the introductory level.

Simulation Model Building: A Statistical Approach to Modelling in the Social Sciences with the Simulation Method, by URBAN NORLÉN. New York: Halsted Press, 1976. 172 pp. $14.95 cloth.

THEODORE L. REED
Temple University

Simulation Model Building, the revision of a doctoral thesis in statistics at the University of Uppsala, makes two major contributions to the literature on computer simulation in sociology. Norlén's principal objective is the presentation of a highly technical application of statistical theory to the fields of parameter estimation and model testing to the development of simulation models. Although the monograph is intended for those familiar with simulation in econometrics, many of the statistical techniques he employs are already familiar to sociologists.

Several introductory chapters also discuss the structure and utility of computer simulations. Abstract and formalized computer simulations are seen as valuable strategies for the study of complicated general systems. As in modern econometrics, Norlén expects that the structure of the model system can be used as a substitute or prototype for the structure of real (modelled) systems. Instead of carrying out experiments or surveys in the real world, outputs obtained through simulation with the model are used to generate further knowledge about system processes. From his illustrative simulations, the difficulties of this strategy become obvious. The utility of any model as a research instrument depends on an accurate description of the modelled system. Numerical analysis, such as that included in the sample "model of general education," requires a level of knowledge about the real world currently unavailable in our descriptions of any but the most simple or most abstract social systems.

Sociologists who are well trained in techniques of numerical analysis and who seek to understand the application of statistical theory to the practical problems of simulation parameter estimation and validation may find this a useful monograph.

Military

Militarism in Developing Countries, edited by KENNETH FIDEL. New Brunswick, N.J.: Transaction Books, 1975. 319 pp. $12.95 cloth. $4.95 paper.

Military and State in Modern Asia, edited by HAROLD Z. SCHIFFRIN. Jerusalem: Jerusalem Academic Press for the Hebrew University, 1976. 309 pp. No price listed, cloth.

STEPHEN P. COHEN
University of Illinois, Urbana

Two fair-sized collections of papers, with twenty-five chapters between them constitute an almost indigestible hodge-podge of case studies, pure theory, polemic, and insight. In the Schiffrin volume "Asia" is represented by three papers on Japan, three on China and Maoism, three on Indonesia, and three on the Middle East, with one paper covering both Thailand and Burma and two devoted to general or theoretical considerations. Fidel's book is as narrow in scope, despite its claim to the "Third World." Every country paper except his own deals with Latin America, with two papers on Peru, and two on Guatemala. One chapter covers Latin American coups, while two general chapters rely very heavily upon Latin American data, and only Fidel's introduction and two survey or theory-oriented chapters can be said to apply themselves to the Third World. The analytic utility of *that* concept—which, like "militarism," seems to breed more confusion than anything else—is not effectively questioned by a number of authors, although it should be. Let us try to place these books in the context of the literature on the subject, and then discuss some of the more rewarding and infuriating contributions.

Were graduate students to enter the mini-field of military-in-politics/society through these volumes they would conclude that it is a field in which there is no precision of terminology, no theoretical framework of any importance, and a peculiar lack of contact between scholars who are concerned with the particular and those who are concerned with the general. Fidel's volume is seriously mistitled: Only one chapter (Irving Louis Horowitz's stimulating reconsideration of the civilianizing-of-the-military thesis) discusses "militarism," and it does not define it. The work of Mosca, let alone the insights of Andreski (in his *Military Organization and Society*) are simply ignored. So many of these papers reinvent the wheel, or present "insights" which can be traced back to any number of classical theorists that one wonders what goes on in graduate education these days.

The conceptual weaknesses are particularly strong in the country chapters, many of which are simple narrative history with no attempt to link military institutions to their supportive societies and political systems. One surmises that both collections were put together on a very casual basis without any effort to impose a common framework, test common hypotheses, or even summarize and integrate the individual studies. This is particularly noticeable in Schiffrin's collection, when S. N. Eisenstadt's attack on those who assume there is a natural or proper dominance of military by civilians is followed by a number of papers dealing with Japan which make that very assumption.

Despite their narrow focus, some of the case studies of particular military regimes are excellent. This is particularly true of chapters in Schiffrin's book on Indonesia (by Ulf Sundhaussen, Martin Rudner and Reuven Kahane), and Luigi Eiunadi's summary of his work on Peru and Fidel's own study of Turkish military conspiratorial behavior. Two papers on the Guatamalan military, in Fidel, tell us more than we probably want or need to know about that state, and a group of papers (by Israeli scholars) cover the military in Egypt, Iraq, and Syria.

A very few chapters attempt to combine middle-range theory with a country-focus. Moshe Lissak does this in Schiffrin's volume with some skill in a chapter which compares Burma and Thailand and develops his ideas on the role expansion of the military (this chapter is an abbreviated version of a book published by Sage); in a contribution to Fidel, Lissak explores more fully the theoretical dimensions of military involvement in societies at dissimilar levels of development. Miles Wolpin begins with a promising idea (the influence of foreign military training on the political behavior of military elites) but quickly falls to the level of his subject, relying upon a flimsy data base.

One finishes these volumes with a suggestion. Let there be a moratorium on such collections, unless they meet some minimal tests. Let them look at aspects of the role of the military in politics that have not been carefully examined (such as the interaction of military elites with their foreign counterparts), or as Horowitz suggests in a fine chapter in Fidel, the ways in which the military (and, I would add civilian groups) have "militarized" their societies in order to increase economic growth in sectors that are critical to national prestige and defense (roads, heavy industry, modern agricultural systems); or, let such volumes be truly comparative in methodology or coverage. That this can be done was shown by Claude Welch, Jr., who has edited a volume of studies which deal with successful instances of civilian control over the military in a number of developing states (*Civilian Control of the Military*, SUNY Press, 1976) and which follow a common framework of analysis. We have passed the point where anything was better than nothing, and editors, publishers, and the scholarly community might well begin to practice some of the restraint that they so often urge upon the military.

The Social Psychology of Military Service, edited by NANCY L. GOLDMAN and DAVID R. SEGAL. Beverly Hills: Sage Publications, 1976. 299 pp. $17.50 cloth. $7.50 paper.

SCOTT G. MCNALL
University of Kansas

The Inter-University on Armed Forces and Society (IUS) has now provided us with the sixth volume in their ongoing series on war, revolution, and peacekeeping. After six volumes from the IUS we still do not have one that consciously tries to develop a critical perspective on the military. (The only volume that remotely approaches this is Sarkesian's, *The Military-Industrial Complex*.) I personally feel there ought to be a moratorium on studies of the all-volunteer army, whether or not it's going to be isolated from civilian society, and so forth. Military sociology must move beyond Janowitz and Moskos if it is to continue to be viable. Their contributions are clearly outstanding, so that they continue to shape the nature and direction of most of the work being done and the articles being published. We need new perspectives, and this collection doesn't provide it. With two exceptions, the papers in this volume were first presented at a 1975 meeting on the social psychology of military service. Like most such papers, they run the gamut from simple-minded to competent. The papers based on data from the Survey Research Center at Michigan, or from people who've been connected with it, are the best. These authors have taken their subject matter seriously, if uncritically.

The contents are divided into six sections; in the first Faris tells us that, contrary to what we might have thought, recruits really like their drill sergeants, who in the all-volunteer army can help integrate them into the organization. The second section of the book is made up of the contributions of two psychiatrists, Borus and Lifton. Borus, confirming some of my worst ideas about psychiatrists, notes that a soldier has trouble returning to civilian society. One observation, deserving elaboration was that many veterans were confronted by friends and relatives who explained to them what the war was *really* like—they'd seen it on TV. Lifton's article, following his work, *Home from the War*, stresses the need for advocacy research, and points out that there is corruption in the healing professions.

In the third section, which deals with reactions to the military as an organization, Gunderson, another psychiatrist, points out that it is noisy, hot, crowded, and dirty on ships. Nelson, another member of the health professions, tells us that some people cope with stress better than others, and maybe we can make up scales to determine who'll get along best in the military. Bower's article is a good, straight-forward study of differential feelings about the quality of organizational life; how navy personnel and civilians differ, and what the implications are for the volunteer army.

The fourth section deals with the military family, a subject that has only recently received the attention it deserves. Goldman provides us with the data to see that more service personnel are married now then at the turn of the century, and that the big shift came with WWII, when a large number of married men were drafted. Stanton, in his analysis of the military family in an all-volunteer setting, argues that the family unit, rather than the individual, should serve as the basis for management decisions. One of the most interesting articles in the volume is that of Stoddard and Cabanillas, who analyze the sources of stress for officers' wives, and also suggest that the decision to retire is very often made by the officer's wife.

The articles on transition to civilian life, Section V, also present some intriguing conclusions. Jennings and Markus examine the political participation of Vietnam veterans and find that there really is no clear and discernable pattern of involvement that distinguishes them from those who didn't serve. This is echoed in the Segals' comparison of Detroiters who served in Vietnam and those who didn't. They found no meaningful attitudinal differences.

The final section contains three good articles. The first, by Blair and Bachman, makes the important distinction that, though the public was generally dissatisfied with the Vietnam War, it was not dissatisfied with the military. There were, of course, variations in attitudes toward the military by age and socioeconomic status. The ideology of younger people is treated in the next article, by Bachman and Blair, in which they express concern for an all-volunteer force made up of extremely pro-military types, and suggest ways to recruit a broader segment of the population. Inglehart, in the final selection, distinguishes between what he calls materialist and postmaterialist value systems, and posits that if people become increasingly postmaterialistic, e.g., think truth, beauty, and equality are primary goals in life, then support for military institutions will be eroded.

Though there are some good pieces in the volume, I don't think it tells us much about the social psychology of military service.

The Military and the Problem of Legitimacy, by GWYN HARRIES-JENKINS and JACQUES VAN DOORN. Beverly Hills: Sage Publications, 1976. 217 pp. $12.00 cloth. $6.00 paper.

War in Ecological Perspective, by ANDREW P. VAYDA. New York: Plenum Publishing Corporation, 1976. 129 pp. $14.95 cloth.

RICHARD MACHALEK
Trinity University

Andrew P. Vayda has written an enviable book, it is scrupulously researched, theoretically provocative, and engaging. This slim volume deserves the careful attention of any scholar interested in the large issue of armed conflict as a response to societal "perturbations" (Vayda's term) of various sorts and armed conflict itself as a perturbation.

The book is based on case studies of three Oceanian societies: the Maring of eastern New Guinea, the Iban of the Malaysian State of Sarawak in Borneo, and the Maoris of New Zealand. Vayda's analysis is built around a dominant organizing principle: war is not to be viewed in dichotomous opposition to peace, but rather, as a multiphasic process. War as a process is seen to have important variable dimensions such as magnitude, duration, intensity of involvement of the respective parties, and reversibility. Furthermore, the war process can be adaptive or disruptive. In the face of demographic and ecological pressure, the institutionalized multiphasic war process enabled Maring and Iban societies to respond adaptively. During its lower intensity, earlier phases, the war process was not prohibitively expensive in lives and productive power for either the Maring or the Iban. For instance, the "nothing" and "true" fights among the Maring allowed them to vindicate an insult or injury and, simultaneously, assess the fighting strength of their adversaries. The discovery of a weakened enemy could encourage attempts to relieve population pressure by territorial annexation. Similarly, the vengeful headhunting of the Maories reduced tension, provided prestige and relaxation, and occasionally resulted in the redistribution of land. In both Maring and Iban societies, the multiphasic war process tended to persist.

Conversely, the multiphasic war process broke down with catastrophic results among the Maoris. The introduction of European muskets to Maoris warfare yielded efficient and apocalyptic results. Prohibitive costs made *all* warfare disruptive and maladaptive. Consequently, the process was terminated.

Students of conflict, particularly those operating from the "conflict functionalist" orientation of Georg Simmel and Lewis Coser should feel an enthusiastic affinity for the valuable work of Andrew Vayda.

The Military and the Problem of Legitimacy is a collection of ten essays and research reports spanning at least seven socio-cultural contexts. Van Doorn's lead essay locates the topic in theoretical context and describes the "crisis of the military" in the modern world. Harries-Jenkins discusses the legitimacy of the military as it pertains to the maintenance of social order by employing "militocratic, democratic, and anarchist" models of state-military relations. The remainder of the papers consider specific aspects of the legitimacy problems in various societies. Understandably publishing under a pseudonym, "John Brown" effectively portrays the legitimacy crisis confronted by Latin European countries which rely upon the military as an internal security force. Morris Janowitz convincingly develops the thesis that armed service became coterminous with citizenship during the nation-building processes in the U.S. and western Europe. Two of the most clearly conceived and interesting selections pertain to Israel and the Netherlands. Yoram Peri and Moshe Lissak provide evidence that retired senior officers in Israel may crystallize into a new elite which will intervene significantly in public and political life. While Peri and Lissak suggest a possible "militarization" of the civil life, Ger Teitler documents the "civilianization" of the Dutch military. Teitler's essay is an informative and suggestive account of the organizational crisis accompanying the emergence of a union of Dutch conscripts.

The overall quality of the selections is somewhat inconsistent. Emil Nagy's report displays methodological vulnerability, and Mieczyslav Michalik's essay contains a few passages that are simply incomprehensible. Unfortunately, there are enough typographical and related errors to be annoying. Nevertheless, read selectively, the book is quite useful for students of the military considering this very important and timely topic.

Families in the Military System, edited by Hamilton I. McCubbin, Barbara B. Dahl, and Edna J. Hunter. Beverly Hills: Sage Publications, 1976. 400 pp. $20.00 cloth.

Athena Theodore
Simmons College

A surprisingly substantial amount of social-psychological research, much of it quite recent, has been accumulating in the area of the military family even as sociologists have been preoccupied with studying military institutions mainly from the perspective of the male military role in its occupational, organizational, and combat settings. The three editors/authors/psychologists of this book—a project sponsored by the Inter-University Seminar on Armed Forces—have brought together ten articles of sound empirical content and have included in separate chapters their own excellent summary of research on the military family along with a comprehensive bibliography.

The book's major contribution to our knowledge of the military family relates to the effects of the missing father/husband's role on the remaining members of his family under varying conditions of residential location, branch of service, and military rank and career pattern, with retirement and divorce status also receiving attention. Despite some redundancy, the studies all contain well-documented data to substantiate the theoretical formulations put forth. (Nine of the studies were originally doctoral dissertations; however, the authors write mainly from first-hand professional experience working with military families.) Perhaps to no one's surprise, the military family is viewed largely as a social problem of considerable proportion.

Two points may be noted. The first is that, in whatever context, it is the wife of the military officer or enlisted man (most of the studies deal with officer ranks) who exacts the costs for our society's need to defend itself. In the ultimate dependency role, it is she who bears the brunt of the prolonged separations, the frequent mobility, the risks and tortures of sudden life loss or POW uncertainties during war periods and afterwards, the role-juggling dilemmas and role discontinuities, the alienation and the rootlessness.

The second point derives from the first: the military family (and the military man) now needs to be studied with respect to recent changes taking place in the society: the climbing divorce rate, alternative life styles with marriage as one option, resistance to war, and especially the women's movement, including female entry into the military academies and female insistence on full and equitable occupational status separate from the spouse's occupational identity. These are sociological gaps which must be confronted irrespective of whether or not the Department of Defense subsidizes research not dealing specifically with winning wars. In the process it may be possible to come up with some creative alternatives to the present organization of military life—and to war itself—which will ameliorate the stresses endured by hundreds of thousands of people throughout the world who are members of military families.

Army Politics in Cuba, 1898–1958, by LOUIS A. PÉREZ, JR. Pittsburgh: University of Pittsburgh Press, 1976. 240 pp. $9.95 cloth.

GEORGE A. KOURVETARIS
Northern Illinois University

Louis A. Pérez traces in *Army Politics in Cuba*, the genesis, pre-eminence, and the fall of the Cuban army. This much needed book is as much a historical analysis of "nation building" as it is a case study of army politics in Cuba. The author shows how political order can fail if it rests on a narrow base of social support. Using the army as leverage to maintain internal stability and societal control, the politicians brought the army into national politics. The Cuban army, a US sponsored institution, grew increasingly estranged from the people and became the tool of a clique of political leaders. Quite often the Cuban army served foreign interests rather than those of Cuba. There are similarities with other emerging nations where the army played a prominent role in national politics and the country then turned to communism, e.g., Vietnam, Angola.

The book can also be seen as an indictment of American diplomacy, political intrigue, and American involvement in the internal affairs. It tells the story of how US diplomacy failed to understand the rise of Cuban nationalism and the search of the Cuban people for nationhood and national identity. The US took a paternalistic attitude and adopted a neo-colonial policy when Cuba gained independence following the Spanish-American War. The frequent American intervention under the Platt Amendment proved shortsighted for the Cuban people and US foreign policy. Indeed one can't help but think that US foreign policy has not changed much.

The book consists of fourteen chapters or 240 pages; more than one-third or 77 pages include notes for each chapter, bibliography (published and unpublished sources in both English and Spanish), and an index. In the first four chapters, the author details the beginnings of the Cuban army. He shows how instrumental US policy was in the creation of the Cuban army. The Americans helped to establish the Rural Guard which served the US and other foreign interests in Cuba and maintained order in the rural provinces. The author feels that through the symbiotic relationship between the Rural Guard and the American occupying forces, the US carried out a colonial experiment. The Rural Guard gave way to the Cuban regular army which the Americans did not particularly want but the Liberals in Cuba sought to establish.

The author examines the establishment of the regular Cuban army during the first quarter of the century, the formative years of Cuban nationhood, its role in national politics through the Machado regime, the bizzare seizure of power by the NCO in 1933, and the relationship of the Cuban army and the US. The 1933 revolt of lumpenproletariat in uniform shattered the American hegemony in Cuba and upset the institutionalized racism between white and non-white military personnel. Most of the officers were white and were linked to the political and other social elites while a large number of the NCO came from non-white backgrounds.

The rest of the book covers the period between 1934–1959. In these pages the author details the rise of Batista, the consolidation of army hegemony, the Batista incumbency, the restoration of army pre-eminence, patterns of resistance and opposition to the Batista regime, the emergence of Fidel Castro and the guerrilla movement, and the eclipse of the Batista politico-military order. This period was as turbulent as the early formative years. Conspiracies, corruption, and disorder permeated the entire body politic including the military. The rise of

Batista to power was facilitated by US support, other foreign powers and the Cuban economic and military elites. Gradually, resistance and opposition to Batista's authoritarian rule came not only from his political foes but from students, labor unions, and the ranks of the army itself.

By the mid-1950s widespread dissention and conspiracy in all three branches of the Cuban armed forces were evident. These developments, coupled with a grass roots guerrilla movement spearheaded by Fidel Castro and his followers, made the Batista government precarious. Indeed, the final confrontation and the eclipse of the Batista rule came when the government forces failed to crush the guerrilla movement and Castro's forces in the Sierra Maestra region. A counter-offensive launched by the guerrillas against the government forces proved successful and meant the end of Batista's government and US hegemony over Cuba.

The author's scholarship and his impresssive list of sources amply support the thesis of the book. The volume can be used for courses in comparative analyses of civil-military relations, international relations, military institutions and politics in Latin America, and diplomatic history and politics.

Political

Revolution and the Revolutionary Ideal, by ROBERT BLACKEY and CLIFFORD PAYNTON. Cambridge, Mass.: Schenkman Publishing Company, 1976. 295 pp. $9.50 cloth. $4.95 paper.

RONALD Y. L. CHENG
University of Colorado, Boulder

Revolution and the Revolutionary Ideal is divided into two parts. The first part (chs. 1–5) is written from a sociological perspective and includes analysis of such social phenomena as violence and strategy, social institutions, social-psychological factors, and urbanization and the parts they play in revolution. The second part (chs. 6–21) is written from an historical perspective and includes accounts of the changing nature of the revolutionary ideal from the ancient Greeks to the twentieth century.

The brief treatments of both parts make the book useful for an undergraduate survey course but rather inadequate for graduate courses, although the selected bibliography at the end of the book will be useful at both levels. Since cost consideration dictated that the book must not be too long, I wish that the authors had dispensed with the first part and had dealt more extensively with the second part. After all, the main purpose of the book is the study of the changing nature of the revolutionary ideal. If the authors wanted to include both the historical and sociological orientations, they could have studied the interrelationship between social conditions and the changing nature of the revolutionary ideal and analyzed the influence through time upon the revolutionary ideal of such factors as violence and strategy, social institutions, social-psychological factors, and urbanization. But probably the publisher's desire for wider adoption decided the issue. As it is, the book adds nothing which is not already known.

The authors define revolution as "a political and/or social and/or economic and/or cultural upheaval which calls for a fundamental change in the existing order . . ." (p. 8). It is perfectly all right for them to use a very broad definition of revolution, but they they should have included as examples a few social, economic, and cultural upheavals, such as the rise of Islam, the Reformation, the Industrial Revolution, and the Cultural Revolution in China, instead of concentrating on political revolutions, so as to achieve a relative balance of social phenomena included in their definition of revolution.

The authors have dealt with a large number of political revolutions. But there are notable omissions, such as the Meiji Restoration of 1868, the Turkish Revolution of 1922, and the Egyptian Revolution of 1952. There are already a number of books of similar nature such as the reprint of P. J. Proudhon's 1923 book, *General Idea of the Revolution in the 19th Century*, *Revolution* by P. Calvert, *The Nature of Revolution* by C. Beals, *Modern Revolutions* by John Dunn, and *New Theories of Revolution* by Jack Woddis. Therefore I think future publications should be devoted to either more specialized studies such as *Rebellion, Revolution, and Armed Force* by D. E. H. Rusell, *Religion and Revolution* by Guenter Lewy, and *Agrarian Revolution* by Jeffrey M. Paige or more systematic studies of theories of revolution. Although there are a number of works dealing with theories of revolution such as *Revolutionary Change* by Chalmers Johnson, *Why Men Rebel* by Ted Gurr, *A Study of Revolution* by Peter Calvert, and *The Phenomenon of Revolution* by Mark N. Hagopian, a systematic theory is still to be developed.

Political Language and Oratory in Traditional Society, edited by MAURICE BLOCH. New York: Academic Press, 1975. 240 pp. $18.25 cloth.

LLOYD ETHEREDGE
Massachusetts Institute of Technology

This edited collection, originating with a University of London Intercollegiate seminar in 1972 devoted to Oratory and Traditional Society, seeks to advance the interdisciplinary understanding of the types and functions of different verbal styles used for political persuasion in traditional societies and in the 1968 civil disturbances in France. A thoughtful theoretical essay by Bloch seeks to draw together case material and conceptual distinctions advanced by the contributors who report their participant observation experiences with the Tikopia, Maori, Balinese, Tswana, Mursi, inhabitants of the plateau area of Madagascar, of a Kenya farming area, and Melpa speakers of Papua New Guinea; a final case deals with French political tracts issued in May, 1968.

Remarkably, these case studies converge in finding a continuum between two types of rhetorical styles: a formalized style through which traditional authority, social structure, and norms are maintained and invoked, and a more specific, flexible, and rich language code for pragmatic political interchange.

How does formalization of language enhance the authority of the speaker, coerce and socially control another person? It seems that one aspect is the device of portraying the immediate case within a hierarchical structure where it is "revealed" as a specific instance of a general cosmology. Hence the audience is symbolically engulfed within "a comforting sensation of union within a common heritage." One cannot help but think of the analogous "power" of scientific theories, the fascination of even the contemporary social scientist's mind with symbolic formalization that rhethorically expresses the specific as the child of the general.

Why should this symbolic strategy be so powerful? It "removes the authority and the event from the speaker himself so that he speaks when using formalization less and less for himself and more and more for his role," and behind this the image is invoked of a state and social order which is acting impersonally, "a state which has always existed and is therefore of the same kind as the order or nature" (pp. 16–17). In short, there is the attraction of collective unity, of encompassment within a natural and powerful canopy which is both impersonal yet deeply owned and merged with by an audience. And this seems to work to shape action, inviting willing obedience at the same time that it subliminally threatens chaos, deprivation, insecurity to anyone who might be tempted to assert autonomy from traditional authority. There is a hypnotic quality at work here, hints of an opportunity for an interdisciplinary social psychology of authority. For example, the authority of science (the specific seen as a function of the general, impersonal symbolic theoretical forms merging with the private actions and motives of individuals, the quest to state a unifying order of nature) would, as suggested above, be a plausible extension. Bloch and his coworkers seem to have clarified rhetorical patterns which may generalize broadly, and it is a useful conceptualization.

There is, of course, a cost to traditional authority, namely that its code, to become unifying, necessarily becomes ambiguous. It lacks the power, within itself, to deal pragmatically or creatively with political problems. Thus different actors, or the same actors on different occasions or in different phases of their persuasive communications shift to different "codes" which are less filled with high-sounding generalities or homilies, and less ritualized. The genius of a stable political system—to retain order while dealing with change, adjusting and retaining a common equilibrium in the face of inevitable pluralism, personal disagreements, and conflict in social life thus appears as a result of the skillful use of language codes which have a specialized psychological function. Bloch and his co-workers are contributing here to the new, emerging, sociolinguistic model of order, an exciting and potentially powerful addition to the conceptual repertoire of social science.

This is not to say, however, that a sociolinguistic model is fully explicated here. One would like to know how much individuals are fully taken-in and absorbed by the linguistic strategies and styles of traditional authority. Even in hypnosis Freud felt the subject might retain, at some level, an awareness that what was transpiring was only a game. And divine kings have faced death or dethronement at the hands of their subjects if they failed to make the crops grow. We do not know the boundary conditions of linguistic techniques for system maintenance. But if there is a sociolinguistics of traditional authority and order, there also appears to be a systematic sociolinguistics of the revolutionary left. Seidel's study of political tracts in France during May, 1968 gives an opening to understanding the sociolinguistic strategy of revolution, an effort by dissidents to establish "nous" that defines and seeks to create a viable unity of a sub-group in opposition to the traditional "nous" of the state. The early concerns of Lasswell and his co-workers and the RADIR studies appear to be alive and well, albeit rediscovered here by researchers apparently unaware of the earlier conceptual apparatus and methodological sophistication of the "symbol and society" tradition of content analysis in political science.

Despite the labors of the writers presented here, they are only partially interdisciplinary. The great bodies of work summarized in Graber's *Verbal Behavior and Politics*, Nimmo's *Popular Images of Politics*, the psychological sensitivity of Edelman's *Symbolic Uses of Politics* go virtually unnoticed, and one cannot help but feel a sense of loss, that the case studies here could have been richer, the pay-off from doing them still more stimulating, if the varied theoretical equipment and insight of previous work in neighboring disciplines had been incorporated at an early stage in the inquiry.

Oú va l'administration française, by MICHEL CROZIER et al. Paris: Les editions d'organisation, 1974. 223 pp. No price listed, paper.

EZRA N. SULEIMAN
University of California, Los Angeles

The French administration has long been recognized for the important role it plays in French political and social life. Some (particularly foreigners) have tended to look with great admiration on an institution that is supposed to attract the cream of the educational system, be relatively efficient, and place a high priority on technical expertise. Others (mostly the French themselves) have looked on the administration as being undemocratic, autocratic, and inefficient. Reality, however, conforms to neither view.

It is one of the major merits of this volume that it has no particular ax to grind. The complexity of the French administration, as well as the difficulties involved in interpreting its structure and its impact on the society, are evidenced in this collective work by members of the Groupe de Sociologie des Organisations, headed by Michel Crozier. This team of sociologists has, over the past ten years, produced a series of enlightening works on French local and central administration. In its earlier years, the work of this team took its impetus from, and was heavily influenced by, the model developed in Crozier's own pioneering work, *The Bureaucratic Phenomenon.*

This volume of essays shows the extent to which these sociologists working under Crozier have remained attached to his model, the extent to which they have found it necessary to elaborate on it, and the extent to which they have been forced to incorporate important elements not previously included in the model. The opening and closing essays by Crozier are a lucid exposition of his views on the French administrative structure. Readers familiar with his previous writings will recognize his insistence on the centralization of the state apparatus. According to Crozier, it is the phenomenon of centralization which inhibits the free flow of information, distorts the decision-making process and, ultimately, prevents the introduction of badly needed reforms.

Crozier's views are perhaps most closely shared by Worms, Thoenig, and Catherine Grémion. Worms's essay, "La découverte du politique," puts a heavy emphasis on the extensive role of the administration in French society. Like Crozier, he views the administration as incapable of responding to society's demand and sees "crises" on the horizon. Thoenig's contribution on "La Stratification" argues that the French administration is not only highly centralized; it is also highly stratified. He shows, in a succinct manner, how the Grands Corps form the apex of the administrative hierarchy, a hierarchy of which they are the chief beneficiaries and which has profoundly adverse effects on the system as a whole. Using material from his fine book, *L'Ere des technocrates*, Thoenig analyzes the strategy by which the corps manage to maintain their prestige and to dominate the entire administrative structure. What he implies is that what is good for the corps is good for neither the administration nor the society. Catherine Grémion's essay compliments Thoenig's analysis, showing how important the corps phenomenon—that is personal contact—is in the actual decision-making process.

Because the book does not have a single thesis to propound, one notes a welcome diversity in the contributions in the volume. The essays by Friedberg and Pierre Grémion show that there have been important changes in the administrative structure occasioned by the changing relationship between the administration and the society. Grémion is concerned with the relationship between the center and the periphery, a periphery that is by no means uniform and static. Friedberg's essay is the only one in the volume to consider the interaction of the administration and the outside world (in this case, the industrial sector). This is a commendable move, for hitherto this team has tended to consider the administration as a closed system. Friedberg's essay shows that the former role of the state, which consisted merely in regulating and maintaining an equilibrium among the various economic forces, has given way to a new role in which the state has an important "entrepreneurial" function. Consequently, the interdependence of the private and public sectors has helped to change the administrative structure and the role of the administration.

This is not a theoretical work, nor is it comparative in any sense. In fact, most of the references in the essays are to works done by one or another of the authors. However, the essays are serious, well-written, and make a welcome contribution to the study of the French administration.

Verbal Behavior and Politics, by DORIS A. GRABER. Urbana: University of Illinois Press, 1976. 377 pp. $12.95 cloth.

M. GLENN NEWKIRK
University of Denver

Political scientists are generally a self-effacing lot when their concepts are pitted against the concepts of sociologists, psychologists, and economists. Professor Graber begins *Verbal Behavior and Politics* in just such a self-effacing manner when she states in the preface that "political science has neglected linguistic studies more than other social sciences." According to Graber, who has worked widely in the area of verbal behavior research, this shortcoming is manifest in political science's lack of a "disciplinary subfield of political linguistics which focuses on verbal behavior as an important aspect of politics." After reading the 331 pages of text and going through the 30-page bibliographic essay (which discusses over 300 studies of verbal behavior and politics), I was not convinced of her original premise. The fact that many of the studies in Graber's book were undertaken by non-political scientists is irrevelant, since they address some aspect of political behavior.

Apart from this quibble, I found little to criticize. The first five chapters present a brief, textbook-like introduction to the essential concepts of verbal behavior and are absolutely laden with examples of linguistic analyses of political life. The treatment of these concepts follows a sensible progression from a statement of the importance of examining verbal behavior in political settings, through the theoretical problems confronted while studying verbal behavior, to the techniques for measuring and analyzing verbal behavior. Surely someone will criticize Graber for the brief and almost superficial treatments given to some concepts in this first section. However, the author was fully aware of this characteristic of the book and made the decision to use numerous theoretical approaches, instead of discussing a few theories, to point out the difficulties and rewards of studying the verbal components of political behavior. If Graber had attempted to present a more thorough, exhaustive, and unified theory of political linguistics, she would have deviated from her original goal of showing "how and why knowledge of verbal behavior is important to an understanding of politics." I also suspect that any theoretical superficiality which is attributed to the book is actually a reflection of the field of political linguistics. After all, as Graber points out with a quotation from Bernard Berelson, most theories of verbal behavior and politics have only been able to tell us that "some kinds of communication on some kinds of issues, brought to the attention of some kinds of people under some kinds of conditions, have some kinds of effects."

The second half of the book continues the use of research examples. However, the second half, is even less concerned with broad theories of verbal behavior and politics than was the first half. The examples in the second half are grouped together in substantive chapters to demonstrate how to study verbal behavior in political settings—the mass media, decision-making bodies, public assemblies, and small bargaining groups. The substantive scope of these chapters is quite amazing since they include verbal analyses of newspaper coverage, election campaigns, political speeches, legislative debates, crisis decision-making, and international negotiations. The research techniques which are covered in these chapters are equally numerous and diverse: surveys, participant observation, sociometric analyses, and content analyses, to name only a few. Unfortunately, the final chapter of this section is curiously out of place since it is a potpourri of uses of condensation symbols (also known as "catch phrases") in an unfocused variety of political settings.

The conceptual nature of the book's first section and the encyclopedic scope of the second section will give a potentially wide market for the book in upper division/graduate courses on political behavior, political sociology, and research methodology. Furthermore, some researchers will find the book useful since it presents suggestions for a wide range of verbal behavior studies. Unfortunately, the scholarly nature of the book and the writing style, which is clearly aimed at academics, will probably limit the use of the book to the classroom. Political wags who are trying to make sense out of the verbosity of semanticists and ambassadors who go to Congress will probably not be attracted to the book due to its academic approach. This is unfortunate because concepts in the first section and the practical applications in the second section are a potential gold mine for serious political journalists and practitioners—a gold mine that is likely to remain unmined. Regardless of its eventual use outside academe, the book contains an epilogue which presents several intriguing possibilities for practical research into what Graber calls the field of applied political linguistics.

I suppose that I will have a long wait before seeing a successor volume on the body language of politics—a volume which simply must have a dust jacket picture of Nelson Rockefeller's famous salute to a crowd during the 1976 campaign season. Until such a volume appears, I recommend *Verbal Behavior and Politics* to teachers of political behavior, political sociology, or specialized courses in research methodology. Other persons might simply want to use the book as a resource guide if they are interested in pursuing studies of the varying relationships between words and politics.

Stress and Contradiction in Modern Capitalism: Public Policy and the Theory of the State, edited by LEON N. LINDBERG, ROBERT ALFORD, COLIN CROUCH, and CLAUS OFFE. Lexington, Mass.: D. C. Heath & Company, 1975. 450 pp. $23.00 cloth.

MICHAEL USEEM
Boston University

Few major institutions of advanced capitalist democracies have demonstrated more rapid expansion in recent decades than the state. Even in relative terms, government expenditures and public employment have soared, and state agencies now routinely intervene in nominally private domains ranging from aircraft production to scientific research and artistic work. While solving immediate problems, this growth has exacerbated other strains, including the government's own inherent instability—manifest most recently in what economist James O' Connor has labeled the "fiscal crisis of the state," an insolvency produced by an inadequately financed effort to simultaneously ensure both corporate profitablility and political stability.

State expansion has different implications for classes with contradictory interests and, as Alvin Gouldner and Göran Therborn would remind us, this divergence will surely be mirrored in opposing social scientific analyses. In the disciplines most centrally preoccupied with matters political—economics, political science, and sociology—public policies have indeed been dissected from radically different paradigms. A sampling of the best contemporary work from several of these perspectives has been assembled in *Stress and Contradiction in Modern Capitalism: Public Policy and the Theory of the State*.

The seventeen collected papers originated in a 1973 conference on "Change in Advanced Industrial Society." The self-conscious shift from the conference's concern with "industrial" society to the book's focus on "capitalist" society is indicative of the participants' agreement that social theory would best be served if analytic attention were directed at the distinctive economic and political features of advanced capitalism. Neo-Marxists, of course, have always preferred this focus, but even liberal analysts have of late fixed on the special problems of modern capitalism, agreeing that differences between capitalist and socialist societies overshadow their similarities.

The present volume contains both neo-Marxist and liberal treatments of the capitalist state. The neo-Marxist concern with "contradiction" and the "theory of the state" and the liberal focus on "stress" and "public policy" are joined in the book's title and contents, perhaps most effectively in the editors' long introductions to the book's four major sections. Fortunately, the editors and authors avoid the appealing but vacuous effort, evident elsewhere, to synthesize these opposing paradigms. They also avoid the equally pernicious tendency of refusing to draw on the theoretical insights and empirical materials of one or the other perspective. The volume's writers are also notably successful in overcoming the usual barriers between the social science disciplines, between abstract theory and concrete research, and between scientific inquiry and practical politics. As a result, this collection contains a number of theoretically informed and penetrating essays on critical issues in contemporary capitalism and the capitalist state.

The articles are organized around four dilemmas: state planning versus the private market, where the social and economic roles of the capitalist state are examined; inequality versus opportunity, where the government's role in reproducing or eliminating inequality is discussed; efficiency versus legitimacy, where the state's contradictory functions of facilitating capital accumulation and maintaining public order are examined; and dominance versus vulnerability, where the impact of the international economy and multinational corporations on national political systems is explored.

The state planning/private market dilemma can only be examined within a general theory of political economy. The conceptual thicket surrounding the many theories of political economy is nicely cleared by Robert Alford in an essay on three major approaches to state-society relations. Alford lucidly demonstrates that the pluralist, elite, and class paradigms focus on different contexts of action, identify the origins of state policies in sharply different factors, and draw opposing conclusions on the functions of the capitalist state. In what is perhaps the most valuable theoretical essay of the volume, Claus Offe extends the class analysis by offering a compact definition of the state as consisting of those institutions which facilitate business activity but eschew production themselves. Yet state power, he asserts, ultimately resides on, and is therefore limited by, corporate power; as a consequence, the government underwrites business activity without fully controlling either the means of doing so or the resulting profits which are, of course, privately appropriated. An elaborte ruse is necessary, Offe concludes, to disguise the non-public purposes of public funding, giving rise to the government's obsession with the maintenance of legitimacy. Offe's structural-functionalism shows analytic parallels with another structural-functionalist school of some repute, but the contents and implications are radically different. His essay demonstrates that structural-functionalism is not, and should not be, the exclusive monopoly of pluralist analysts.

If the state's operations are limited by the massive power reserved by the corporations, is it possible for a government to adopt policies which serve any interests other than those of the capitalist class? Robert Solo and Theodore Lowi, in separate essays, contend efficient, enlightened political elites could crack corporate resistance. But detailed historical analysis of movements to reform social services in France, by Stephen Cohen and Charles Goldfinger, and of the record of labor-oriented parties in Britain, Sweden, and the US by Andrek Martin, suggest the opposite. The relative powerlessness of the state nearly always frustrates efforts to reform welfare and reorient the economy.

In the section on the inequality/opportunity dilemma, Manuel Castells provides further argument that the government's record is one of actually reinforcing rather than mitigating inequalities. Yet Martin Rein, Peter Marris, and Colin Crouch contend that the government's growing intervention in areas traditionally considered the domain of the market, such as wage determination in private industry, can facilitate the rise of progressive political movements. These authors note that though the state may initially control industrial wages to avert public disorder, wage controls can in the end heighten dissent by stripping the mystique of impersonal market forces from existing inequalities in income.

The book's third section turns to the efficiency/legitimacy dilemma, where Murray Edelman and Isaac Balbus catalog the government's arsenal of legitimizing symbols for disguising its class bias. While James O'Connor, Jürgen Habermas, and Claus Offe have elevated the maintenance of legitimacy to a primary state function, without which chaos may ensue, Renate Mayntz and Michael Mann pointedly challenge this assumption by arguing that political stability is not necessarily threatened by a legitimacy crisis. Mayntz suggests that government authority can be equally well imposed through other means, such as material incentives; Mann takes the critique to its logical extreme by contending that abstract symbol systems are rarely if ever a source of mass stability.

The book's final section on the dominance/vulnerability dilemma includes essays on the domestic and international impact of multinational firms and a world economy, by Stephen Hymer, James Kurth, and Pierre Hassner, and a particularly provocative piece by Alberto Martinelli. Among the consequences cited are a strengthened and increasingly international capitalist class, a deteriorating economic position of labor, and a growing tendency of national governments, especially that of the US, to promote the welfare of their own multinational firms through diplomatic pressure, subversion, and military intervention.

This collection includes a few articles whose ratio of rhetoric to social fact is distressingly high; theoretical certitude is occasionally substituted for what should remain problematic; little attention is given to many specific areas of state activity, such as education; and the process by which class and corporate interests are translated into concrete public policies is barely examined. Nonetheless, the book "is intended to be a general call for comparative research on advanced capitalist societies," according to its general editor and, although few articles set forth an explicit research agenda, nearly all bristle with the powerful theoretical insights necessary to ensure that comparative research will be undertaken. And it will be undertaken since the contradictions of advanced capitalist societies guarantee an increasing supply of analysts whose guiding purpose, clearly facilitated by this volume, is the unraveling of the structural secrets of capitalist democracies.

Late Capitalism, by ERNEST MANDEL. New York: Humanities Press, 1975. 599 pp. $25.00 cloth.

E. K. HUNT
University of California, Riverside

Mandel's most recent book, *Late Capitalism*, is very difficult to adequately review within the constraints of a short journal review. Its scope is massive: it attempts to provide an analysis of the totality of post World War II capitalism within the context of an historical-theoretical discussion of the entire capitalist mode of production. The book is an eclectic effort to synthesize a wide variety of Marxist ideas, theories, and empirical assertions which have appeared over the last thirty years with many ideas or conclusions of liberal academic scholars about the nature of contemporary capitalism. Mandel attempts to use selected ideas, theories, and assertions of Marx and Trotsky as a framework which, after suitable revisions, appears to be intended to provide the unifying connections among the numerous and diverse theoretical assertions and empirical observations which make up the book.

The comprehensive and eclectic nature of the book partially accounts for many of its strengths and, simultaneously, many of its weaknesses, and gives the writer of a short review a difficult task to adequately describe either the strengths or the weaknesses.

Mandel sees capitalism as having passed through two distinct historical phases (competitive capitalism which lasted from the onset of the industrial revolution until about 1880 and imperialism which lasted from that point until World War II). He believes that, since the war, a third, distinctively new phase, which he calls "late capitalism," has characterized capitalist development.

While he gives some attention to the peculiar or differentiating aspects of each phase, he is most interested in showing that revolutions in technology, long waves of economic expansion and contraction, and cyclical crises of over-accumulation are common to all three phases. More particularly he is concerned with explaining the nature and significance of these recurring phenomena in the present phase of late capitalism.

The strengths of the book are: first, it has a comprehensiveness that at times strikes a reader, who is accustomed to the intellectual products of this age of academic specialization, as a communication of almost intellectual grandeur; second, it contains innumerable statements, suggestions, and hypotheses, any one of which offer potential for extensive research, development, and writing that could be of great importance in understanding contemporary capitalism.

The most critical weakness of the book is foreshadowed in Mandel's discussion of methodology in the first chapter. Here Mandel expresses an opinion which is widely held among Marxists and which seems to this reviewer to be utterly mistaken. In the time-honored debates in epistomology between rationalists and empiricists each side has unquestionably evolved certain strengths and weaknesses. An historical look at both bourgeois and Marxist writings shows that this division does not coincide with ideological divisions. Rationalism and empiricism each has its devotees in the bourgeois tradition and the Marxist tradition. And within either tradition, both epistomological approaches have strengths and weaknesses. Unfortunately, the issues raised in these methodological debates are real and important. In their zeal to equate Marxism with "true science" many Marxists, including Mandel, have been unwilling to accept either rationalism or empiricism. Rather they argue that the dialectical method transcends both approaches by incorporating them both in a manner that retains the strengths of each while eliminating the shortcomings of each. But given the historical length of this epistomological debate and the seriousness of the issues involved, such a claim would require a major effort to convince a critical reader that this age-old dilemma has been resolved. Unfortunately, Mandel, like all other Marxists who take this position, is totally unconvincing. His methodological discussion combines certain commonplace statements taken from both the empiricist and rationalist traditions with a good deal of "dialectical" jargon (some of which was not comprehensible to this reviewer) without ever really attempting to come to grips with the real issues dividing these two approaches to epistomology.

This methodological indecisiveness is clearly reflected throughout the book. The many suggestive interpretations of data and theoretical hypotheses contained in the book do not cohere into any definite theoretical structure. While most of them have a plausibility when considered separately, this reviewer searched in vain for an integrating, cohesive theory. Several theoretical assertations are made but not defended, which is exasperating. For example, Mandel asserts that "no real synthesis is possible between Neo-Ricardianism and Marxism." First, there are many who question the very existence of anything that could accurately be labeled a neo-Ricardian school of economists. Second, Mandel fails to give any evidence that he is aware of what theoretical considerations led such eminent Marxist economists as the late Maurice Dobb to consider the work of Sraffa and the so-called neo-Ricardians to be important for Marxist economic theory. He simply makes this undefended assertion.

Moreover, as a work of empiricism the book has a number of serious weaknesses. Mandel gives very little indication that he is aware of the severity of the difficulties in using the statistics compiled and published by capitalist governments within the framework of Marx's theoretical categories. Furthermore, Mandel's usual method is to make an assertion, buttress the assertion with several verbal statements, and then use available statistics only sporadically and naively. For example, in the chapter on the "Permanent Arms Economy," five empirical tables are presented, about which there is no serious discussion nor attempt to integrate the numbers into a theoretical framework. Similarly, his analysis of the state makes only the most feeble attempt to substantiate any assertion by an assemblage of available data.

In conclusion, this reviewer recommends the book for the grandeur of its vision, and for its innumerable, suggestive hypotheses which might lead future investigators toward fruitful research in many areas. As a scientific investigation of capitalism, however, the book leaves much to be desired. This reviewer believes that carefully delineating the epistomological foundation of Marxism should be a starting point for scientific investigation. In this endeavor Mandel's treatment of methodology seems most inadequate.

The Modern Corporate State: Private Governments and the American Constitution, by ARTHUR SELWYN MILLER. Westport, Conn.: Greenwood Press, 1976. 269 pp. $15.00 cloth.

STEPHEN J. MCNAMEE
University of Illinois, Urbana

This book describes the development of a new constitutional order in the United States, the modern "corporate state," which is the product of a fusion of private (corporate) and public (state) governments. The new order lacks both legitimacy and accountability. It serves the interests of the wealthy, removes the individual qua individual from the decision-making process, and takes on a life of its own—larger and more threatening than the sum of its constituent parts.

Miller traces the development of the corporate state in the context of Constitutional law. His findings are disturbing. Since the Supreme Court recognizes corporations as juristic persons and not as governing bodies, corporate policy decisions of national consequence manage largely to escape judicial scrutiny. The problem is even more acute at the international level, where multinational corporations set economic and political policy with almost no legal regulation whatever.

Miller's basic thesis is that big business and big government have entered into a symbiotic union, aided and abetted by both the mainstream intellectual and cultural establishments.

Emphasizing clandestine forms of control, organization-based centers of power, and domination by a limited circle of rotating elites, Miller's analysis comes closest to the elitist tradition of political scholarship. While sympathetic with Marx, particularly with respect to Miller's portrayal of the law and the media as carefully orchestrated cover-ups, Miller's corporate-state fusion is one of dual rather than one-way causality; each group needs and desires the other, although corporations tend to reap the greater share of benefits.

Many of these themes are repeated from Miller's earlier book, *The Supreme Court and American Capitalism;* consequently, not much new is presented in this recent volume. But it is nevertheless a cogent macrotheoretical analysis of interinstitutional relations, with an especially good critique of Galbraith's technocratic theory of corporate growth.

Voter's Choice: Varieties of American Electoral Behavior, by GERALD M. POMPER. New York: Dodd, Mead & Company, 1975. 259 pp. $5.95 paper.

CARL A. SHEINGOLD
Cornell University

Gerald Pomper's *Voter's Choice: Varieties of American Electoral Behavior* provides a review of survey data on voting in presidential elections from 1960 to 1972. The data were collected by the University of Michigan's Survey Research Center and are here employed to support two major arguments. First, that the portrait of voters which emerged from the pioneering studies of the 1940s and 1950s—voting as habitual behavior determined by fixed social characteristics and partisan loyalties—was time-bound. In recent presidential elections the dynamics of voting seemed to change with each election. Since 1960 most voters have been highly responsive to campaign issues and have often responded to them in ideological terms.

The author also argues that we may be at a decisive turning point in American politics. The electorate has become "modernized." "The public is participating more broadly in public life; traditional constraints have been loosened; national integration has proceeded; and politics has become more ideological." Yet, according to Pomper, our political institutions, particularly our political parties, remain underdeveloped. The author seems to be arguing that the people are ready to participate in a responsive democratic process. They await the construction of political institutions "that are both capable and democratically responsible."

As a compilation and review of survey data on voting, the book succeeds admirably. Pomper's contention that portraits of the American voter must be sensitive to changes in historical circumstances—as sensitive as the voters apparently are—though hardly a new point, is an important one which is effectively supported in this book.

Pomper is less successful in his more ambitious discussion of the future and meaning of democracy in America. The theoretical and philosophical bases of Pomper's concept of political modernization—and, even more, the normative implications of political modernization for democratic processes—are not sufficiently developed. Nor does he consider alternative ways of conceptualizing these issues.

A more fundamental problem is Pomper's failure to consider alternative historical interpretations of the data. He makes a convincing case that the dynamics of voting in the last two decades were fundamentally different from that of the preceding two decades. But it seems premature to conclude that the American electorate has, therefore, acquired political maturity—or, at least, a political scientist's conceptualization of it.

It is equally plausible to suppose that the kind of flexible, issue-oriented voting of the 1960s and 1970s has always emerged in periods of crisis and change in American politics; that habitual voting rooted in fixed partisan affiliations has always, and perhaps appropriately, characterized periods of stability such as the 1940s and 1950s and may once again characterize voting in America in the near future. This alternative hypothesis is not considered by Pomper.

The greatest strength of this book is in the convincing case it makes for *historical* interpretations of survey data. It is, thus, ironical that its greatest weakness derives from Pomper's unwillingness to inform his analysis with data, albeit of a different kind, from periods of American political history before the advent of large-scale survey research.

Vigilante Politics, edited by H. JON ROSENBAUM and PETER C. SEDERBERG. Philadelphia: University of Pennsylvania Press, 1976. 292 pp. $10.00 cloth.

HAROLD A. NELSON
University of Houston

The intent of this volume is to provide a useful starting point for the systematic consideration of Establishment violence. Thirteen essays by social scientists, eleven of which are published for the first time, focus on issues attendant to the defense of established order by means which violate law. Distributed among three perspectives, theoretical, American, and comparative, the essays' themes range from the vigilante personality and vigilantism and political theory to consideration of the House UnAmerican Activities Committee, community police patrols, spontaneous and police vigilantism, and an historical treatment of the phenomenon in the United States. Also included are a comparison between its operations in the United States and South Africa and instances in Africa, Northern Ireland, and "pariah" communities in Asia and Africa. The editors' introductory chapter includes useful conceptual material, both as a guide for analysis and as a loose format which informs the essays which follow. The concluding chapter, again by the editors, includes a partial reconsideration of their position set forth in the first chapter in light of the essays, a statement on ethical issues involved both in research and participation in vigilante activities, and thoughts on the future course of vigilante action.

The editors' assertion that the subject of vigilantism is too little explored is a correct one. Their contention that it is too little understood is at least as correct if not more so, hence their brief comments on the ethics of research and participation in vigilantism have a special merit. Rather than attempting to understand the phenomenon, there has been a tendency to issue blanket denunciations of it. One may not embrace the KKK, IRA, or Minutemen and still give thoughtful consideration to the perceptions of some populations that the law is both inadequate and ineffective protection for social order. And one may, as well, give some thought to the possibility that these perceptions are correct. No informed thinking on the subject of vigilantism may proceed until we free ourselves from the spirit of denunciation which appears to pervade so much thinking on the subject. By and large, these essays will assist in so doing and will direct the reader into productive areas of inquiry. Marx and Archer's "Community Police Patrols and Vigilantism," may even stimulate researchers to move into the "field," where there is firm belief that the security of order and the safety of human beings can only be achieved by extra legal means.

Consistent with the aim of the volume the essays do provide a place to begin a systematic examination of vigilantism. Students should find the material intriguing (and highly "readable") and sociologists will find that it explicitly or implicitly raises a host of valuable (and researchable) questions. In an era when many books promise much more than they deliver, it is a pleasure to find one which delivers on its promise.

Ravensbrück: An Eyewitness Account of a Women's Concentration Camp, by GERMAINE TILLION. Translated by Gerald Sotterwhite. New York: Anchor Press, 1975. 280 pp. $2.95 paper.

NANCY R. CHISWICK
Pennsylvania State University

Tillion's *Ravensbrück* provides us not only a reminder of what horrors the human race is capable of, but also demonstrates the effect of time on Tillion's own historical perspective in this look at the sociology of a Nazi concentration camp.

The book is a composite of writings done during three different periods of the author's life: first, a 1945 documentation of the immediately preceding years of war and incarceration; second, a painstakingly detailed comparison of eyewitness accounts and of official documents written from 1947 to 1953; and third, a 1972 review of her own writings, which is most notable because of the effect which the Algerian War had on her perspective of her own earlier wartime experience. The idea is interesting; however, the pieces alternate with each other in a way that makes one feel lost both as to the chronology of events as well as to the feelings attached to them. This reader wishes that she had kept each part a whole, allowing for comparison.

Perhaps the greatest disappointment is due the reader wishing to know how Tillion views women, and what special interpretations she makes of their concentration camp experience—she offers only a few tidbits on this subject. It is as if Tillion bends too far in her attempt to provide a model sociological work, and in the process neglects the intimate side that the book promises at first, in the section describing her and her mother's arrest and incarceration.

All in all, it makes its contribution because its author experienced the things of which she writes and as an example of sociological method.

Population and Fertility

The Value of Children: A Cross-National Study. Volume 1: Introduction and Comparative Analysis, by FRED ARNOLD, RODOLFO A. BULATAO, CHALIO BURIPAKDI, BETTY JAMIE CHUNG, JAMES T. FAWCETT, TOSHIO IRITANI, SUNG JIN LEE, TSONG-SHIEN WU. 251 pp. $2.75 paper. *Volume 2: Philippines,* by RODOLFO A. BULATAO. 222 pp. $3.00 paper. *Volume 3: Hawaii,* by FRED ARNOLD and JAMES T. FAWCETT. 152 pp. $3.00 paper. Honolulu: University Press of Hawaii, 1976.

MONI NAG
Population Council, New York

The value of children to human societies is obvious: the continuity of societies—both biological and social—is assured by birth and survival of children. But what is the value of children to parents? How is the social imperative reflected in the thoughts, feelings, and behavior of parents? These questions are being asked in a serious manner only now since sex increasingly is being divorced from reproduction, and since many societies are interested in regulating birth rates either positively or negatively. These three volumes address these questions. They form a part of a prospective series of seven volumes containing basic findings from the Value of Children (VOC) project conducted in six countries: the Republic of China (Taiwan), Japan, the Republic of Korea, the Philippines, Thailand, and the US (Hawaii). Volume 1 presents the whole project and selected results from all six countries in comparative form. Other volumes are country-specific.

One important finding in the study is the existence of distinctive profiles of perceived satisfactions and costs of children to the parents of the three socioeconomic groups in each country: urban middle class, urban lower class, and rural. For example, in the urban middle-class group, psychological advantages of having children are emphasized whereas for the rural group, the economic advantages of children are more salient. The study also brings out clearly the differences between the responses of developed countries (US and Japan) and less-developed ones. The parents in the former, for example, are more concerned about the opportunity costs (particularly relating to mother's time) of having children.

The responses of both husbands and wives

in the samples for each country were obtained through interviews containing structured and open core items as well as country-specific items. A prolonged process of conceptualization, preparation of questionnaires, and training of investigators was necessary for a comparative study of such magnitude. It represents the first attempt to quantify and analyze the responses regarding various dimensions of the value and cost of children from a wide variety of perspectives. The findings have been used effectively to revise the framework for the study so that future investigations can benefit.

How valid are the attitudinal responses obtained through interviews? The investigators took several measures such as the application of multi-item attitude scales to provide internal evidence of validity but these are not sufficient to satisfy the critics who would give more importance to actual behavior than verbal responses.

The theoretical contribution of the project in terms of new concepts, framework, and hypothesis regarding perceived value and cost of children is highly significant. What about its contribution toward formulating policies and programs to influence the perceived value of children and therefore fertility? Findings of the study have been analyzed in these terms, but it is doubtful whether policymakers will be able to use the present level of analysis for purposes other than broadening their general understanding of the relevant issues. The detailed findings of the country-specific volumes may be more useful for policy-making purposes.

Two important aspects of the study should be mentioned. First, it is a genuinely collaborative effort of investigators from more-developed and less-developed countries. Second, it is claimed as an exploratory study intended to provide guidance for a more definitive study which is already under way.

An Essay on the Principle of Population: Text Sources and Background Criticism, by THOMAS ROBERT MALTHUS. Edited by Philip Appleman. New York: W. W. Norton, 1976. 260 pp. $10.00 cloth. $2.95 paper.

ETIENNE VAN DE WALLE
University of Pennsylvania

The true emphasis of Malthus's 1798 Essay—given here in its entirety—is provided by its full title: *An Essay on the Principle of Population, as It Affects the Future Improvement of Society*. The so-called "First Essay" centers on the detailed refutation of William Godwin and Condorcet's visions of unending progress for human society, and even for individual human life. In later statements of the principle of population, Malthus's emphasis was to shift considerably. Eight chapters are devoted to Condorcet and Godwin in the First Essay, but their names do not even apear in the text of "A Summary View of the Principle of Population" published in 1830.

The gist of the argument is as follows. The potential for population growth is infinitely greater than earth's potential to produce food; and population can only be checked by misery and vice. (Virtuous celibacy at this stage of Malthus's thinking is classified under the heading of misery.) Nature has ordained growth as a result of abundance, and thus imposes perverse consequences on attempts at improving the institutions of society and at securing happiness for the masses. This forbidding logical construct starts, however, from one premise which is either wrong, or irrelevant, namely "that the passion between the sexes is necessary and will remain nearly in its present state" (p. 19). If "passion between the sexes" is a euphemism for unrestricted exposure to conception within sexual unions, the postulate is wrong; but if we are to take the phrase at face value, it is irrelevant, since contraception need not interfere with passion. Malthus failed to understand Condorcet's veiled allusions to birth control as a way out of the quandry of over-population.

Malthus's pamphlet of 1798 is a dead classic, however fascinating for its place in the history of ideas. It lacks the intellectual coherence of the 1830 statement; compared to later versions of the Essay, it lacks the massive evidence and the systematic application of the principle of population as a guide to social policy. As a masterpiece of the English language, it belongs to a collection that provides critical editions of the classics, from Austen to Whitman. But although interesting enough as a reader on population, this text fails as a critical edition.

The coverage of the Malthusian controvery is perfunctory. Godwin and Condorcet are never given a fair hearing. Their own version of progress and perfectibility is not presented, and we have to take Malthus's word that they claimed, for example, that man would some day attain immortality on earth. The two pages that are given to *The Future Progress of the Human Mind* would not seem to deserve Malthus's scorn for Condorcet's work "which will amuse, if it does not convince" the reader (p. 58). In the debate presented here, Condorcet appears right, since he recognized the probability of wide scale fertility control.

The critical apparatus consists, however, mostly of texts by writers debating the world's population problems. The guiding principle seems to sample the literature of Malthusianism; but in the broad sense adopted by this book, Malthus was hardly a Malthusian. The editor, in his introductory essay, claims that "pollution and resource-depletion effects" of technological progress vindicate Malthus's vision of the limits to growth—an anachronism. The authors cited are represented by considerably abbreviated pieces, classified in an arbitrary matter. Thus an excerpt from Pope Paul VI's encyclical *Humanae Vitae* is given in a section devoted to "Some Contemporary Anti-Malthusians"; but in its concern for responsible parenthood and its condemnation of contraception, it appears highly compatible with Malthus's own concerns.

Finally, the book will prove mostly useful to English instructors who will want to enliven their course about the Enlightenment with half-truths about contemporary population problems.

History of Population Theories, by J. OVERBEEK. The Netherlands: Rotterdam University Press, 1974. 232 pp. No price listed, cloth.

G. EDWARD EBANKS
University of Western Ontario

The book claims to review population theories from Aristotle and Plato to the present time, and in part, this has been accomplished. The claim is not wholly true since the emphasis is upon theories of population as these relate to economic situations. In fact, the book is a review of economic theories of population from Plato and Aristotle to the present time. Neglected are theories involving population parameters and the sociocultural aspects of the population. Psychological theories of population are also omitted. Even though this "History of Population Theories" deals mainly with population theories from an economic viewpoint, the scholars whose writings are reviewed come from a variety of academic disciplines.

Many of the theories and theorists reviewed and presented are little known. However, their contributions are worthwhile and their inclusion has made this book one-of-a-kind. This is a very comprehensive coverage of the population theories of such well-known scholars as Malthus, Ricardo, Mill, Marx, Keynes, Carr-Saunders, Darwin, Hansen, Myrdal, Coale, Spengler, Leibenstein, Becker, Kuznets, Hirschman, Boserup, and Davis. There is, perhaps, a list of equal length of lesser known scholars from both developing and developed societies. The inclusion of scholars from the developing societies adds a dimension generally excluded from books of this type. In addition to the works of the thirty-six scholars individually reviewed, the author points out influences of theorists and theories upon each other as well as overlaps among theories. Also treated are theories not specifically associated with any one name: among these being "mercantilism, physiocracy and population theory." Theories "before mercantilism" are also presented.

Although the author covers the history of population theories in a very comprehensive manner, the present is not so well treated. Neither demographic transition theory nor the works of such scholars as W. Arthur Lewis and Richard Easterlin are treated. The contributions of Leibenstein, Coale, Spengler, and Davis are not well covered and represented. The weakness in this book is the inadequacy of the treatment of modern theorists.

The author is fair in his presentation of the various viewpoints, although his emphasis upon condensing these works perhaps detracts from the book in many parts—some scholars are given less than a page of coverage. Readers not already familiar with these works will find it difficult to obtain a clear idea of the salient components of these theories.

The concerns and opposing views expressed at the World Population Conference in Bucharest in 1973 are not presented. The Club of Rome presentations are not given.

This small, very readable book should be extremely useful to demographers, sociologists, and economists alike, and for that matter to all those interested in the relationships between population and the economy. It is a good review book for courses in population and economic development.

Sterilization and Fertility Decline in Puerto Rico, by HARRIET B. PRESSER. Berkeley: Population Monograph Series, Institute of International Studies, University of California, 1973. 211 pp. $3.25 paper.

JOHN J. MACISCO, JR.
Fordham University

This is a thoughtful and careful study of voluntary sterilization in Puerto Rico. The techniques of secondary analysis when placed in the hands of a skillful researcher can illuminate complex sociological and demographic relationships. In this revision of her doctoral dissertation, Presser has brilliantly analyzed unused survey data and hospital records together with published surveys and vital statistics to assess the impact of voluntary sterilization on the decline in the birth rate in Puerto Rico.

According to Professor Presser, this monograph is designed to describe and analyze the practice of sterilization in Puerto Rico. She began her study with the following analytic problems: "Why Puerto Rican women have been so highly motivated to control their fertility and why so many have chosen sterilization as a means of achieving this end . . ." (p. 1).

Presser undertakes the empirical analysis of the decline in fertility and the role played by sterilization. She finds that about one-third of all Puerto Rican mothers aged 20–49 in 1965 were sterilized, and speculates that, "as a result of sterilization, an average of about two births per mother may have been averted for the cohort of women in their forties and perhaps more than two births per mother for younger cohorts" (p. 92). Presser also demonstrates that the prevalence of sterilization varies by parity, marriage duration, and age. She shows that more than half the sterilized women had borne only two or three children before *"la operación,"* and that sterilization, on the average, occurs in the first seven years of marriage and that the average age of women securing sterilization has declined slightly.

By using the classic sociological method of ruling out alternative explanations, Presser concludes that, between 1950 and 1960 the decline in marital and total fertility for women aged 25 to 39 was chiefly attributed to increasing prevalence of sterilization. An increase in marital instability was seen as a factor of secondary importance.

The interpretation of history as presented in chapter 5 needs comment. I find it difficult to agree with the interpretation of the "grass roots" support for voluntary sterilization without some attention being paid to the linkages at work in the mid 1930s between US governmental, medical, and social science elites and their counterparts on the island. This could be the subject of another monograph.

Does the research serve the purposes intended by the author? Yes, Presser has made a significant contribution to our understanding of sterilization and the role it plays in fertility decline. It is a good example of what a competent researcher can do with secondary analysis of data and as such can serve as a model to all of us who clamor for our own survey. This well written, technically precise, and carefully documented monograph goes beyond the Puerto Rican experience and helps us to see the demographic impact of sterilization.

Race and Ethnic

Indian and White: Self-Image and Interaction in a Canadian Plains Community, by NIELS WINTHER BRAROE. Stanford, Calif.: Stanford University Press, 1975. 205 pp. $8.50 cloth.

PHILIP A. MAY
Navajo Health Authority

Niels Braroe has done an excellent job in both researching and writing *Indian and White.* Gaining rapport and the confidence of both Indians and Whites is such a difficult task that a book of this sort has never before been published. Living and working on a reservation or in a border town, one becomes easily perplexed by the confusing and complex web of norms and values at play. Given this complexity and the ongoing prejudice, an understanding or logical analysis is not easy to develop. Since Indian and border town communities are predominantly Gemeinschaftan, it is difficult for an outside researcher to gain the confidence of one group, let alone both groups, so that meaningful sociological research can be accomplished. In spite of such obstacles, Braroe has accomplished this task, and this book represents a well written and easily understandable analysis of Cree Indians and Whites interacting on the Plains of Canada.

The major accomplishment is that through a symbolic interactionist perspective, the values of both groups are examined. Throughout the book, numerous situations and incidents are described in such a manner that the behavior and reactions of the Indians or Whites are illustrative of their values and world view. Whites see Indians as lazy, unreliable, and unworthy of any trust. Indians in turn see Whites as stingy, prejudiced, and as being "not as smart as they think they are." But the full range of values of each group is represented. Stereotypes and overgeneralizations are not apparent, but generalizable patterns are a result of the numerous illustrative instances described. Individuals, both White and Indian, receive objective, just treatment in a manner which fully depicts the range of opinions, values, and behaviors present in many reservation border areas. Neither group is championed; rather, individuals in both groups are realistically described as living, breathing, individuals acting upon their beliefs as best as they can.

The significance of this book is wider than a first impression might indicate. First of all, there are slightly under 300 Indian reservations in the continental United States alone, with many reserves and settlements in Canada and Alaska. Thus, the study of Indian-White interaction has relevance to a large number of communities and people. Most books on race relations deal with interaction between Blacks and Whites; with this book, colleges and universities in the western United States and Canada have a book which is more appropriate to their needs. Second, this book does an extremely good job of describing the conflicting values and opinions of two ethnic groups and demonstrates very clearly how individuals of these two groups maintain their self-identity while interacting in a bi-cultural situation. In other words, it has relevance to other bi-ethnic situations. Third, whereas many books are concerned with either self-report or the structural concomitants of prejudice, this book explores a middle ground between the other approaches. Sociological concepts are explored through a variety of examples, structural and personal.

Many sociologists involved in Native American studies and the sociology of the West have long complained about the lack of well-done, topical literature. *Indian and White* is a book which will help to fill the need for books of this type.

The Minority Report: An Introduction to Racial, Ethnic, and Gender Relations, edited by Anthony Gary Dworkin and Rosalind J. Dworkin. New York: Praeger Publishers, 1976. 410 pp. $12.50 cloth.

Joseph S. Roucek
CUNY (Retired)

Claiming to be "the first text for courses in minorities and race relations to combine a survey of sociological findings and theories on minority relations with the personal views of sociologists who themselves are minority-group members," *The Minority Report* has its ten authors stress two central themes: (1) that race, ethnicity, and gender relations are social variables subject to social definition and consequences; and (2) that sociology can provide several heuristic orientations toward such social data, definitions, and consequences.

Part One, "Theoretical Perspectives," presents a sociological paradigm for studying minorities that introduces the concept of the minority group, and examines several theoretical models for explaining the diversity of minority-group life and the resolution of minority-group status. Part Two, "The Reports," comprises the individual case studies authored by sociologists who are members of the minorities they discuss both in the light of personal experience and with scientific objectivity.

Since the editors admit frankly that the publication is basically only a textbook, we cannot be too critical of part one, whose seven chapters are quite readable and whose "Notes" are pretty inclusive, but whose "Suggested Readings" are too meager and fail to notice some excellent studies available in this field.

The reports in part two (on Afro-Americans, Mexican-Americans, Puerto Rican Americans, Indian Americans, Japanese Americans, Chinese Americans, Jewish Americans, Irish Americans, and "Women") are the better part of the symposium, somewhat more carefully prepared, although their "Suggested Readings" tend to suffer from the same "exclusiveness" as those in part one.

Strangely enough, and on balance, the symposium cannot be criticized so much for what it contains as for what it omits. With the possible exception of the American Jews, no chapter has been assigned to cover the more than 30 million immigrants between 1880 and 1924—coming primarily from Central-Eastern-Balkan Europe—the largest migration in the history of the world. Although these white, ethnic Americans are not today well organized politically, the rebirth of their ethnic awareness in the US is already being felt dramatically at the polls. This major weakness makes this compilation an acceptable textbook instead of a very good one.

The Irish Diaspora in America, by LAWRENCE J. MCCAFFREY. Bloomington: Indiana University Press, 1976. 214 pp. $8.50 cloth.

JOHN MURRAY CUDDIHY
Hunter College/CUNY

This book by an historian tells the story of the Irish from their earliest encounter with English imperialism (in 1169) to their latest defeat at the hands of American suburbia (post World War II). The history is competent—Penal Laws, Repeal, Catholic Emancipation, Union, The Great Famine, Irish America—though it is starved for sociology; the writing is only passable, but McCaffrey's ideas and findings are exciting and frequently subvert the conventional wisdom.

For instance he argues: (1) against Daniel Patrick Moynihan (in *Beyond the Melting Pot*), that it was not the protestant middle-class with its moralism and individualism, but the "corrupt" Irish urban machine with its Catholic sense of Gemeinschaft, that was the precursor of welfare state liberalism in the United States. (New York's 1920s governor, Al Smith, was F.D.R.'s "scene of instruction" for the New Deal 1930s.)

(2) Against Michael Novak, that the Irish were the only possible ethnic candidates for leading the American Catholic Church. Their Irish political experience—under O'Connell—had socialized them into a de facto acceptance of church-state separation unknown or unacceptable to the French, Italian, Polish, or German groups. There was the language problem but, more importantly, the Irish experience had legitimated democratic politics. To this day, as NORC findings show (p. 171), the Irish commitment to civil liberties is wider and deeper than any other Catholic ethnic group.

(3) Against Oscar Handlin, that the Irish stayed in the cities instead of going West to farms, not through lack of money but through lack of agrarian skills. The Irish immigrants weren't peasants, on the European model; British occupation had reduced them to serfs (p. 63). The Irish were England's blacks.

One theme runs through McCaffrey's book: the Irish "diaspora" pioneered for all the later ethnic immigrants. They were the earliest targets of American Nativism (they "created" nativism). Maria Monk's *Aweful Disclosures* prefigured the *Protocols of the Elders of Zion* (p. 93). Irish pioneered the urban ethnic ghetto. They were the first ethnic diaspora to sponsor an "old country" nationalism and "to use ethnicity as a tool to manipulate American foreign policy" (p. 113). It is here that McCaffrey could have used sociology. He shows how the interest politics of overseas Irish nationalism functioned, for the Irish Americans, as a quest for domestic respectability for themselves (chapter 7). Gusfield could have instructed him in the status politics of this "symbolic crusade" issuing from status anxiety and seeking the conferral of respect.

The Irish were also the first to run through another ethnic scenario: they pioneered the "ostjuden" problem. The earlier, prefamine (pre-1840s) Irish were just about "making it"—as early as 1818, 3,000 Irish were digging the Erie Canal—when the "famine Irish" masses poured out of steerage and, thanks to their insistent visibility, threatened to pull down the entire Irish-American community "from the modest heights of respectability that it had worked so hard and so long to achieve" (p. 67). The Irish were also the first ethnics to succeed in inserting their social vices into the American lexicon: "hooligan," "paddy wagon," "malarkey," "shenanigan," "phony," etc. (I often think that there may be more authentic ethnic history fossilized in the words in our dictionaries than is dreamed of in all the ethnic-studies programs in our academies.) The Irish pioneered, finally, in moving up the social ladder "normally," more or less, from unskilled labor as navvies and pugilists, through domestic servants and civil service "servants," to the middle class arts, business, and professions (from John L. Sullivan, boxer, to Annie Sullivan—Helen Keller's "eyes and ears"—to Louis Sullivan, architect, Harry Stack Sullivan, psychiatrist, Mark and Frank Sullivan, writers, Ed Sullivan of TV, and Walter Sullivan, *New York Times* science editor).

The experience of the American Irish has been paradigmatic. Even that "brief residency in that very famous mansion on Pennsylvania Avenue in Washington, D.C." (p. 151) may be viewed as just the latest case of Irish ethnic pioneering for other latecomer ethnic groups. This general American acceptance of the Irish makes all the more puzzling for McCaffrey what he takes to be the bias of many academic intellectuals against the Catholic Irish. He wonders out loud (pp. 5, 188), together with Andrew Greeley, whether anti-Catholicism may not be "the anti-Semitism of the intellectuals."

The Asian Americans: The Historical Experience, edited by NORRIS HUNDLEY, JR. Santa Barbara, Calif.: Clio Press, 1976. 186 pp. $15.75 cloth. $5.75 paper.

RAWLEIN G. SOBERANO
OLHCC, New Orleans

This is an excellent socio-historical presentation, by various authors, of the Asian-American experience of five major groups of Oriental immigrants: Chinese, Japanese, Filipinos, Koreans, and East Indians. R. Daniels's article alone provides substantial material for a deeper study of the first three, while S. Lyman deals comprehensively with the Chinese ghetto framework and operations, an area scarcely touched by past scholars. The contribution of S. Ts'ai supplies the reader with valuable insights on the Chinese Communist exploitation of the discrimination leveled against early immigrants from China to the United States, a topic superficially treated by academicians.

J. Modell and H. Kitano depict the Japanese experience as an ultimate success story achieved through painful physical abuse and national dishonor. The latter's analysis of the Japanese "middleman" is superb. The Filipinos, the third arrival from Asia, have received the least attention from the academic community as indicated by H. Melendy who provides a general background for a future more detailed study of them. The Korean experience is a historical scene of twenty-one years (1903–1924) of struggle against the Japanese occupation of their homeland and for American recognition of their efforts. Although the East Indians are latecomers to the United States, it is projected that the great number of professionals among them will enhance their contribution to the Asian-American millieu. Truly a great picture of the American pluralistic structure, precious to both students and laity!

Social Movements

The Car Culture, by JAMES J. FLINK. Cambridge, Mass.: MIT Press, 1975. 260 pp. $14.95 cloth.

GEORGE H. LEWIS
University of the Pacific

Flink, in this social history of the automobile, openly suggests that the reader seeking an objective study had best look elsewhere, as his intention in this volume is to be "suggestive, partisan, and controversial" (p. 4). This fine book succeeds on all three counts as it identifies what Flink labels "automobility" as the most significant force to have shaped twentieth century American history.

The rise of the "car culture" is analyzed within the context of mass movements. According to Flink, given the technology and social problems of the late 1800s, it was more a question of who would gain credit for inventing the automobile, than it was whether it would be invented. His early chapters present the ideology of the times —on both sides of the Atlantic—and trace the parallel technological developments that produced several independent and nearly simultaneous versions of the motor car.

The climate was right for the motor car in America because of the social problems the car was thought to be able to solve. Pollution in New York City at the time consisted partially of the 2.5 million pounds of horse manure and 60,000 gallons of horse urine that daily had to be removed from the streets (in addition to 15,000 dead horses per year). The motor car could alleviate this problem (with the disease it produced) as well as solving other urban problems by allowing people to leave the cities. According to Henry Ford, when everyone could commute, urban problems would be solved. Furthermore, transportation would open up rural areas and possibly even reverse the rural-urban migration of young people of the time. Flink does a grand job in showing how the car culture was seen at the turn of the century as a positive reform movement.

In a strong chapter on Henry Ford, Flink identifies him as the mythical leader of the car culture, a cynical elite paternalist who was reflected as an American populist in the minds of the American people. "The idolization of Henry Ford as a symbol of differing national aspirations reflected the universal human tendency to personify the impersonal forces of history" (p. 72). Clearly according to Flink, if Henry hadn't done it, somebody would.

Probably the most controversial portion of the book is Flink's interpretation of The Great Depression, which he attributes to the automobile. His account of market saturation and the over-extension of time sales by the auto industry in the late 1920s makes for an intriguing, but ultimately unconvincing argument. Clearly, the automobile industry (and Wall Street leaders such as General Motors' Will Durant) were important factors in the collapse—but scarcely the whole story. What is important, though, is calling attention to the part the auto industry did play in American life in general and The Great Collapse in specific, an analysis both fresh and challenging for others to follow through on.

Flink's final chapter, in which he sounds the death knell for the car culture, may seem a bit premature for some. The automobile has been replaced by television and the computer as the important technologies of social change. The world market for cars is nearing saturation, the environmental concerns of the 1960s and the oil shortage combine in Flink's analysis to sound the final horn for automobility. Created in the form of a mass movement for positive social reform, the car culture is doomed as it is seen increasingly by the public as the problem, not the solution.

Clearly things are changing, car-wise, in America. But this reviewer suggests the rise and fall of mass movements is not quite as logically progressive and inevitable as Flink's analysis suggests. As someone once said, cars are important to Americans because so many were conceived in them—and so many will die in them. To the extent one or both of the above remain true, I suspect automobility, in one form or another, will remain an integral part of American life and culture.

Israel Divided: Ideological Politics in the Jewish State, by RAEL JEAN ISAAC. Baltimore: Johns Hopkins University Press, 1976. 227 pp. $10.95 cloth.

RITA J. SIMON
University of Illinois, Urbana

Israel Divided offers a clearly written description of two politcal movements that made their formal debut in Israel following the Six Day War: the Land of Israel Movement, and the Peace Movement. The author spends much more time on the Land of Israel Movement, which is the more important of the two. Both movements were provoked and effected by the June 1967 and the October 1973 Wars. Both movements have roots in traditional Zionist ideology. The Land of Israel Movement traces its ideological and intellectual support to chapter 15, verse 18, of Genesis, in which Abraham receives a divine promise "Unto thy seed have I given this land, from the river of Egypt unto the great river, the river Euphrates." Elsewhere in the Bible (Numbers, Ezekiel) other boundaries are described, usually of a more limited nature. But essentially the Land of Israel Movement, which according to the author is composed of a conglomerate of people including poets, generals, intellectuals, kibbutz dwelling labor Zionists, religious Zionists, and former members of the Irgun and Stern Gang, is seeking to establish Jewish settlements in all of those regions of Israel that were included in the kingdom of Israel and Judah during the reign of David and Solomon, and in practical terms is opposed to returning any of the territories occupied by the Israeli Army as a result of their victory in the June 1967 War. The territories of present day Samaria and Judea, which include the cities of Jerusalem, Bethlehem, Hebron, and Nablus that had been part of the Kingdom of Jordan prior to the 1967 War, are viewed by the Land of Israel Movement as especially significant, and indeed the current Gush Emmunum Movement (which is an outgrowth of the Land of Israel Movement) has sought to establish settlements in those areas, and in some instances has succeeded.

The Land of Israel Movement, while small in numbers (and it is one of the weaknesses of this work, that the author does not deal in any systematic manner with the number of people involved, with the roles performed or indeed with the infrastructure of either of the movements) has strong and widespread symbolic-expressive appeal. It recalls the continuity of the contemporary Jewish state with its Biblical and Talmudic Ancestry. It also relates directly to the modern Nineteenth and Twentieth Century Zionist appeal of the right of the Jewish people to their traditional homeland. Thus, even though representatives of the Land of Israel Movement do not comprise a majority of the Parliament, nevertheless its position about the Jewish right to settle in Samaria and Judea and Israel's right to retain all of the territories (except for the Sinai) occupied since June 1967 is reflected in all of the public opinion polls conducted between 1967 and the end of 1972.

In discussing the Peace Movement in Israel, the author correctly points out that it is composed of several smaller groups that are mostly identified with the Left (old and new), with the rights of Israeli and Palestinian Arabs, and with non-Zionist Canaanite symbols. But I think that the author does not emphasize sufficiently that it is these groups who have monopolized the Peace appeal in Israel between 1967 and 1973. Because that point it not sufficiently elaborated the fact that only about 5% of the Israeli public support representatives of the "Peace Movement" might seem odd to readers who have been exposed only to the popular media in which they have read about the Israeli government's consistent and determined desire for peace with its Arab neighbors.

In sum, I think that for readers who know quite a lot about politics in Israel this book will seem superficial. For readers who are not well informed, the analysis is inadequate for them to assess the importance and the impact of these two movements on Israeli society.

Red, Black, and Green: Black Nationalism in the United States, by ALPHONSO PINKNEY. New York: Cambridge University Press, 1976. 258 pp. $13.95 cloth.

PAUL T. MURRAY
Millsaps College

Black nationalism has been a recurrent response by Afro-Americans to their ambiguous status in American society. It has taken a variety of forms including the "back to Africa" movements of Martin Delany and Marcus Garvey, the religious and commercial enterprises of the Nation of Islam, and the gun-toting militance of the Black Panthers. One aspect of the most recent resurgence of nationalism has been an interest in its earlier manifestations. This book is one product of the revival of scholarly interest in black nationalism.

Pinkney presents a comprehensive review of past and present nationalist movements. He uses the characteristics of racial solidarity, cultural pride, and desire for autonomy to define black nationalism. Leaders and organizations are identified as being nationalistic if they reject the goal of assimilation in the larger (white) American society and seek to create or preserve distinctive black values, customs, and institutions.

The first chapters of the book review the programs and accomplishments of outstanding nationalists including Paul Cuffee, Delany, Bishop Henry Turner, Garvey, and Malcolm X. Pinkney then traces the impact of modern nationalism on the arts, law enforcement, the military, the professions, and politics. The final chapters of the book explore the four main varieties of contemporary nationalism: Revolutionary Nationalism (the Black Panthers), Cultural Nationalism (Amiri Baraka and Ron Karenga), Religious Nationalism (the Nation of Islam and the Council of Black Churchmen), and Educational Nationalism (black studies programs and alternative institutions).

Although the book bears a 1976 copyright, major portions appear to have been written in 1972. Of course, this has little effect on the historical chapters, but it renders the sections on the Black Panthers, Baraka, and the Black Muslims sadly out of date. Indeed, any current book on black nationalism should explain its rapid decline and disintegration, as well as lasting contributions, but these topics are mentioned only in a brief epilogue.

This book cannot be considered original in the sense that it presents information which is not available elsewhere or develops a new interpretation of these facts. Rather, Pinkney draws together and summarizes a large body of knowledge from the work of other scholars, the popular press, and the works of the leading nationalists themselves. This information is presented in a concise and coherent form which will be valuable as reference for future students. Readers who are familiar with black history and follow the activities of black leaders in the national press, however, will find little new here.

The major weakness of this book is its lack of systematic sociological analysis. In discussing the causes of nationalism, for example, Pinkney relies upon the concept of internal colonialism, but since this form of racial exploitation has been relatively constant for the past 100 years, it cannot explain why nationalism flourishes in some periods and is dormant in others. He describes the rise and fall of various movements, but offers no theoretical explanation of their fates. He offers no comparisons with other nationalist movements (Zionism, for example) which might yield meaningful generalizations. Pinkney is generally sympathetic to the nationalist impulse and spends more energy defending various nationalist leaders and programs than developing a critical analysis of his own.

Political Ideology and the Chicano Movement: A Study of the Political Ideology of Activists in the Chicano Movement, by GERALD PAUL ROSEN. San Francisco: R & E Research Associates, 1975. 140 pp. No price listed, paper.

LIONEL A. MALDONADO
University of Utah

Rosen's monograph sets out to describe the Chicano movement in order to use it as a context for understanding the political ideology of Chicano activists and as a means of showing the relationships among the movement, the Chicano community, and the general sociopolitical system.

The data were collected through a series of extensive interviews with thirty-one Chicano activists in East Los Angeles during the period of March 1968 to June 1969. The means of selecting the sample is not clearly spelled out, except that they were judged to be influentials of the movement in East Los Angeles.

The qualitative nature of the data is a significant strength of the monograph. The reader is treated to the activists' descriptions of terms used for self-identification: Chicano, Mexican-American, Mexicano, etc. The mode of presenting this information allows valuable insight into ethnic pride believed by Rosen to differ significantly from other eras.

The failure to follow suggestions in the data, however, is a weakness of the monograph. Much of the data are rich with historical references. Respondents recall early personal experiences and those of friends and family; these recollections could be used to portray the development of Chicano ideology in East Los Angeles. It is clear, for example, that long-standing social conditions spanning generations produced an ideology characterized by typical features of internal colonialism. It is regrettable that this theme from the interviews is not developed, although it is inherent in the respondents' discussions of education, the justice system, the employment situation, and the political arena. This is a regrettable shortcoming to an otherwise informative piece of research.

There is an unusually large number of typographical errors and some awkward syntax in parts of the monograph. These present an unnecessary burden to the reader.

The Clouded Vision: The Student Movement in the United States in the 1960s, by DAVID L. WESTBY. Cranbury, N.J.: Bucknell University Press, 1976. 291 pp. $12.00 cloth.

PETER K. MANNING
Michigan State University

"Youth," a never analytically defined category wandering in and out of recent (and very American) "theories," is a Rorschach that reads as we have wanted it to read. The path to a "sociology of youth" is strewn with toppled once great clay-footed idylls —where are the Reichs, the Flacks, the straw-chasers of the 1970s? Much as momentary illumination is shed in a prison yard by a rotating searchlight, theories of youth blink, retreat, and disappear. It is precisely the ad hoc nature of much of this theorizing that surrounds it with such a glorious aura of half-light. Pretension will ever attend a popular and symbolically tumescent field. In the past twenty years or so, books espousing, developing, or otherwise asserting a theory of youth with these sociologically colored foci have appeared: psychoanalytical and neo-psychoanalytical (Lipton, Erikson, Keniston, Blos); social-psychological (Newcomb, Flacks); demographic-historical (Moller, Feuer [who also has psychoanalytic sympathies]); structural-functional (Eisenstadt, Parsons), and existential-situational (Douglas). With some exceptions, they are largely ahistorical, ethnocentric, time-bound, and advance individualistic, reductionistic, and psychologistic explanations. That is, they tend to analyze American student attitudes toward this or that in the sixties. Only Feuer, Eisenstadt, and Moller draw upon historical and comparative non-individual data, e.g., structural characteristics of societies in other periods and associated youth-based movements, masses and publics as well as social psychological characteristics of participants. None, except these last named and Douglas's profoundly American and situational analysis seem to take into account the sorry history of clichéd theories of youth—the "silent generation" theory which was superceded by the "bohemian-beatnik" theory only to be cast away in favor of more dramatic "student radical-activist" theories. (The weakness of such faddish "generational" theories is nicely revealed by Bennett Berger's superb essay, "How Long Is a Generation?" in *Looking for America* [Prentice-Hall, 1971].)

Only against this background of failure does Westby's book seem ambitious. It is a solid, unambitious project which adheres very closely to a well-articulated aim: describing and analyzing the American collegiate student movements of the 1960s. It seems to leap over the background alluded to above (and too many of the most critical works in the field in which it claims a niche), and moves directly to petit pointe attitudinal data. But perhaps a few cautionary desiderata might properly introduce his exercise and this review.

(1) It is possible that there was no single student "movement" in this country, nor many movements, but many masses of semi-coordinated taste groups whose interests were, in fact, expressive politics (See Douglas, J., *Youth in Turmoil*, U.S.G.P.O., 1970; and Lyman, S. and M. Scott, *Students in Revolt,* Appleton-Century-Crofts, 1970).

(2) The entire panoply of ideologies, rationales, and symbols were, in fact, conflicting, contradictory, highly expedient, pragmatic, semi-articulated, and situationally defined tools (contrast the petulant bourgeois radicalism of the early SDS with the leftish early Berkeley and Columbia demonstrations and with the threat-guerrilla tactics employed at Cornell). What holds them together is not class, age, or sex, but rather situationally defined attempts to protect the perquisites of the upper middle mass (education, freedom from the draft, the comfortable right to demonstrate for whatever, etc.).

(3) The core of students leading and participating in, as opposed to thinking about, activism, is small, limited, elitist; those who at one time or another get involved is indeed large. But so are the numbers of people who watch Monday night football games on television.

(4) Given the moribund state of the mass, any theory which cannot account for the "death" of the mass is perhaps explaining too much.

(5) Analyses based on attitudinal data cannot and do not adequately reveal the invisible infrastructure of social control and the effects of imperative coordination.

(6) Attitudinal theories, since they posit person-centered value/attitudinal clusters in-the-person, can hardly explain the time-bound expression of such posited "motivations." Where are the bank-burners? Why, running the banks!

(7) A theory accounting for youth movements must ask how it is that structure absorbs, swallows, transmogrifies, and reconstitutes "radicals."

This book seizes rather well on the data at hand, but trips on gaps in the literature. On balance, it is a very interesting undertaking. Its concern is with four dimensions of the student movement in the sixties: the social origins of participants, the academic context, the dynamics of campus confrontations, and the societal course of the movement. The chapters on these subjects are clear, useful, and on the whole present a balanced treatment of the material discussed. Two concluding theoretical chapters outline a critique of selected theories of youth movements and "The Theory of the Student Movement." The author's good sense and restraint make that pretentious title misleading. His focus on attitudinal data, ahistorical interest (at least in this book), and focus on "the" movement make his extrapolation of individual aggregated survey data into characterizations of social structure somewhat strained. Westby's notion is that student activism is nurtured in settings (and among departmental majors) that are *least* closely tied to or coordinated by central economic institutions. His interpretations of the extant data support this generalization, but it is at least surprising that the book contains no mention of important theoretic books articulating a parallel conceptual approach to macro-sociological analysis (Shils on center and periphery); a similar interpretation of the student movement (the above-mentioned Douglas book) and two of the most significant sociological works on youth movements and activism (H.P. Becker's *German Youth: Bond or Free* and Max Heirich's *The Spiral of Conflict*).

The claim to having developed *the* theory of *the* student movement is premature. Westby does shed some half-light on the importance of *contradictions* between developing individuals and developing mass-produced production units; between education and certification; between maintaining a surplus labor pool and producing eager laborers; between liberal democracy and imperative and sometimes repressive force. The most engaging line in the book, after all this data presentation, "model building," and theoretic posturing, is, "There seems to be no reason in particular to expect either quiet or turmoil among students in the immediate future. Whatever happens will depend on the specific configuration of historical forces" (p. 263). It is possible, but difficult to imagine a structural theory that posits outcomes based upon situational factors. It may be that if one develops an elaborate explanation for a nonexistent or at least shadowy figure one does not explain very much. That is to say, if there was no single movement, but a mass with a variety of very different centers and taste aggregates, if there was no movement at all (in the usual meaning that "movement" has in collective behavior literature—goals, means, tactics, and ideologies shared in common), then it is unlikely that a theory based on data collected by questionnaires, and lacking an historical or comparative dimension, can adequately "explain" a movement.

Theory

Demokratisierung und Leistungsgesellschaft, by KARL OTTO HONDRICH. Stuttgart: Kohlhammer, 1972. 156 pp. No price listed, paper.

Theorie der Herrschaft, by KARL OTTO HONDRICH. Frankfurt: Suhrkamp, 1973. 220 pp. No price listed, paper.

Menschliche Bedürfnisse und soziale Steuerung, by KARL OTTO HONDRICH. Reinbek: Rowohlt, 1975. 272 pp. No price listed, paper.

GIANFRANCO POGGI
University of Edinburgh

The author of these works was born in 1937; he studied economics, sociology, and political science at Frankfurt, Cologne, Paris, and Berkeley. In the mid-sixties he conducted research and taught in Afghanistan; in 1969 became *Privatdozent* in sociology at Cologne; and in 1972 was called to a sociology chair at Frankfurt University.

His publication record is impressive, comprising, besides the three books being reviewed, three earlier books and several essays. His writings show a remarkable continuity in their themes, and homogeneity in intellectual style. The latter is characterised by plain and sober (and colorless) writing, and by a preference for stating in limine operis a complex argument and then developing it carefully while proceeding step by step through a painstakingly organized, well-designed set of headings and subheadings. Mostly, Hondrich's treatment of his topics is at the conceptual level; but he is careful to separate definitions from propositions (or "theses") and among the latter those derived axiomatically from those of a contingent nature. These last are formulated in such a way as to make them in principle amenable to empirical verification (though Hondrich himself generally illustrates them rather than verifying them).

On these counts, it might be noted, Hondrich distances himself from what might be called the Frankfurt tradition; he does not share, for instance, the tradition's perchant for essayistic and aphoristic statement, its speculative cast of mind, or its Hegelian insistence on trying to say everything at the same time. On other counts, too, Hondrich is a new-and-different Frankfurt sociologist. He proudly declares his theoretical eclecticism, and draws inspiration freely from Marxism *and* functionalism *and* other varieties of "positivistic" theory. He does not indulge in *Kulturkritik;* his attitude toward contemporary Western society is, at bottom, an affirmative one (and reminds me of Theodore Geiger's). However, Hondrich holds that affirmative attitude because he expects that Western society will ultimately satisfy value demands of a progressive nature: increasing dispersion of power; increasing equalization of life chances and opportunity; increasing mastery of the society as a whole over its own destiny. Besides, Hondrich is not overly confident that these demands *will* be realized; and he expects their realization to require sustained and bitter socio-political conflict. He intends his own writings as a contribution to public awareness and political debate, not just to academic discussion. Finally, he shares with the Frankfurt tradition a commitment to the *societal* level of analysis.

Having thus characterized what I have called Hondrich's intellectual style, let us consider briefly his substantive concerns. In the first of his books known to me (*Oekonomische Entwicklung, soziale Konflikte und politische Freiheiten,* 1970) he dealt with the relationship between "economic development, social conflicts, and political freedoms." In the three books here under review, he remains concerned with that broad theme; but he formulates it more abstractly, and explores in depth some of the resultant re-conceptualizations of its terms. Below, I shall merely illiustrate the range of the problems he raises, rather than try to synthesize or assess his treatment of them.

Hondrich's key move consists in conceptualizing the master trend in contemporary societies not as (just) economic development, but as "increase in societal performance": "At the present state in the development of productive forces and in the corresponding societal complexity and sociological strategy, the concept of performance [Leistung], understood as the elaboration [Bereitstellung] of means to the satisfaction of needs, addresses the social phenomenon that can best account for current societal conditions."

Those means to the satisfaction of needs consist either in material resources, or in facilities for coercion, or in symbolic and normative resources. Typically, they are unequally distributed, and thus unequally guarantee the "need satisfaction" of those who hold (or lack) them. But the differential control over resources of each type can also be employed, rather than directly to satisfy one's (or other people's) needs, as a base for the (respectively) economic, political, or normative power (Macht) of one part of society over others. What, then, is the relationship between, on the one hand, the societal trends (differentiation, system formation, emergence of new resources, etc.) which increase the society's total performance capacity and broadly equalize that of its parts, *and* the power differentials between them? Also—power becomes domination (Herrschaft) by becoming attached to structured positions with privileged faculties for forming and enforcing collective decisions; how far does this allow the powerful to maintain their power (qua domination) even once their original superiority in performance capacity has been attenuated by increasing societal differentiation, and the attendant equalizing effects?

These are among the problems addressed in the first two books under review. *Democratization and the Performance Society* discusses them at length also, with reference to industrial settings, showing the tension between the equalization of performance capacity due to technological progress, and the internal structures of domination. In a later chapter Hondrich also discusses (enlighteningly) German universities and *their* political tensions. He explicitly addresses a theme—democratization—which was arousing considerable public and scholarly controversy in Germany at the time this book was written.

The same theme is at the centre of *Theory of Domination.* Hondrich, however, after making explicit the political impulses underlying the writing of this book, has made it into a fairly traditional scholarly treatise, with some rather heavy-going sections. I found chapters 4 and 5, which discuss long-term trends in power relations and in socialization patterns, the best in this book. In the earlier, more exclusively conceptual chapters, I missed something for which Hondrich has apparently little taste or patience: an explicit discussion of discrepancies between his own usage of basic terms and the usage of other major theorists. In particular, it is not clear how he reconciles his concept of power (a modification of Weber's) with Parsons's. Yet reconcile them he must, since he treats power as having both distributive and aggregative aspects, and the latter presupposes an understanding of power different from Weber's and thus from Hondrich's own. Also, important questions concerning the relations between economic, political, and normative power are not confronted.

The third book, *Human Needs and Social Control,* examines other implications of the concept of performance, and especially its reference to needs. This last book is intended as a general introduction to sociology for undergraduates and the general public, and the last 190 pages of it contain selections from various authors, from Marx to Lenski. Hondrich's presentation of the intellectual and pragmatic significance of the discipline culminates in the discussion of that which is seen as the central contemporary social issue: ours being, in Tom Burns's phrasing, "a system-ridden world," can the autonomy of individuals, and the significance of their needs as an the ultimate standard for the operations of those systems, be preserved? Hondrich formulates and discusses this problem, in spite of its undertones of "cultural pessimism," in the pathos-free manner which the reader of his books will learn to recognize as characteristically his.

Auguste Comte and Positivism: The Essential Writings, edited by GERTRUD LENZER. New York: Harper & Row, 1975. 505 pp. $7.25 paper.

DONALD N. LEVINE
University of Chicago

Strict empiricism; mathematical methodology; study of behavior, not meanings; explaining acts through self-interest; avoiding value judgments—such are the signals for social research commonly linked with the label of positivism; and such were notions which Auguste Comte, founding expositor of positivism, viewed as ill conceived if not dangerous.

Commonly credited for grounding a theoretical natural science of society, Durkheim and Radcliffe-Brown (as Evans-Pritchard observed some years ago) wrote little of general theoretical or methodological significance that was not as clearly and cogently enunciated by Comte.

Commonly devoted to the analysis of a single society or smaller social units, sociology has been offered a novel agenda by some recent practitioners: study of the modern world system; yet the man who coined the term 140 years ago thought the main task for sociology would be to study the emergence of a universal human community.

Faced by such anomalies in the historical self-consciousness of sociologists, I have long searched for an anthology adequate to introduce students to Comte's work. For this purpose, Gertrud Lenzer's edition is clearly the best of the four published in the last decade. It has the advantage, over Simpson, of including substantial excerpts; over Fletcher and Andreski, of including selections from all three phases of Comte's work—two of the *Opuscules,* including most of the famous "third essay" of 1822; eighteen chapters from the *Cours de philosophie positive,* including six from the book on sociology; and fourteen chapters from the *Système de politique positive.* If one were to take issue with the selections, it might only be that nearly all the sociological chapters are from Comte's social statics, whereas most of his own work dealt with social dynamics, or historical development.

Although the *Cours* chapters are taken from the archaic condensed translation by Harriet Martineau, at least they have been modernized in punctuation and spelling, and some of the most poorly translated passages have been left out in this edition. It contains, in addition, a fine bibliography, omitting, in a list of more than seventy secondary sources, only a handful (Bernard, Engels, Fletcher, Marvin, Nisbet, Salomon) with distinctive glosses on the man's thought.

The value of the selections is not quite matched by the introductory essay. Although Lenzer insightfully discusses Comte's efforts to reorganize society, his philosophy of science, and his relationship with J. S. Mill, she fails to discuss his substantive sociology. In what she does write, moreover, her stance is palpably tendentious (described on the jacket as "delightfully wicked"). She transcends early Marxist views of Comte as hopelessly derivative and philistine only to label, rather than read him by calling Comte "the theoretical exponent *par excellence* of modern capitalism" and going on thereby to implicate him in a plot to secure the " 'voluntary' acquiescence" of those who "drew the blank lottery tickets in the 'free' competitive struggle for profit and accumulation" (p. xliii). So oriented, she distorts Comte's argument in several respects.

Lenzer accuses Comte of advocating a social science that secures dumb compliance with the status quo—ignoring the critical thrust inherent in any sociology that distinguishes between social normality and pathology and forgetting that Comte advocated that sociologists should play the role of being moral critics of captains of industry. She implies that Comte wished to advance sociology by the application of mathematics, ignoring his extended strictures against this on grounds that it would either plunge the study of social phenomena back into the domain of metaphysical abstractions or else restate, without adding anything interesting, what sound observation had already established. She indicts Comte as a precocious apologist for the scientistic-technocratic society of late capitalism, a man who viewed objectified science as the highest human achievement—apparently oblivious to Comte's resurrection of what he called the "subjective method" and his prophetic advocacy of the time when industrial production would satisfy basic material needs and people would turn their energies away from science and technology toward artistic expression and fraternal affection.

It is, however, to Gertrud Lenzer's credit, not to mention Comte's, that many of his passages which scarcely fit her slanted interpretations are to be found in the volume under review.

Love, Altruism, and World Crisis: The Challenge of Pitirim Sorokin, by JOSEPH ALLEN MATTER. Chicago: Nelson-Hall, 1974. 313 pp. $9.95 cloth.

Sociological Theories of Pitirim A. Sorokin, by CARLE C. ZIMMERMAN. Edited by T. K. N. Unnithan. Atlantic Highlands, N.J.: Humanities Press, 1974. 88 pp. $4.00 cloth.

DON MARTINDALE
University of Minnesota

If one accepts the conventional position which, whatever its antecedents, dates sociology's origin from Comte's *Cours de philosophie positive*, it is not unfair to ask how far our discipline has come as of 1977, 147 years after the appearance of the first volume of Comte's system of sociology. Comte founded the positivistic program of the unity of science, conceptualized progress in terms of the stages in the intellectual development of mankind, promoted history as supplying the factual foundation for all programs of social reform, and advocated universal education. All of these proposals and programs were preparatory to the socio-political reorganization of human society which, in his *System de politique positive* (1851–1854), Comte proposed to achieve through establishment of the Religion of Humanity (the Great Being), complete with women safely returned to the home and placed in charge of domestic morality, sociologists, in charge of public morality, and the liturgical year organized into holy days in which scientists and other benefactors of mankind had been substituted for the saints.

Many of Comte's contemporaries who had eagerly heralded the development of his theoretical system were embarrassed by his program of social reform and attributed it to mental collapse induced by his unhappy affair with Clotilde de Vaux and her death a year later (in 1847). However, such critics of nineteenth century thought as Tolstoy and Nietzsche, insisted upon seeing Comte's theoretical and reformist thought as one piece, and Nietzsche described him as the cleverest of the Jesuits who was undertaking to lead the West back to the Church by the devious route of science.

Whatever else is said of Pitirim Sorokin, he is the last of the pioneering sociologists, who promoted an historically based, global program of social theory and social reconstruction similar in many essentials to that of Comte. His personal odyssey was to carry him from the status of an itinerant workman on the Russian frontier to a professorship at Harvard and presidency of the International and American Sociological Associations. On the way he was to be twice imprisoned by Czarist forces and twice by the Communists and eventually exiled to the West in lieu of the death sentence. He was to found revolutionary newspapers and serve as secretary to the head of the provisional revolutionary government. He was destined to found sociology departments at Petersburg, the stronghold of Communism, and at Harvard, the Delphi of Capitalism. His writing career stretched over 55 years during which he authored more than 40 books, 400 essays, and saw some 41 translations of his books into all of the major languages of the world. Along the way he founded half a dozen sub-fields of sociology.

Carle Zimmerman, Sorokin's associate at Minnesota and at Harvard, and his friend for 44 years, describes Sorokin as the World's Greatest Sociologist and compares him to Aristotle. He reviews Sorokin's concern for social and cultural dynamics, his theory of the centrality of value systems and the alteration of historical periods between sensate and ideate types. He traces the gradual emergence in Sorokin's later career of the notion that the fulfillment of history is possible in an intergralist system of culture with corresponding types of society and personality. The method appropriate for the analysis of such a socio-cultural synthesis is an integralist methodology which will unite in one procedure whatever is of value in rational, empirical and intuitional methods. Zimmerman provides a solid workman-like review of Sorokin's social and cultural theories and the new areas he established in the course of their elaboration. However, he turns aside without comment from Sorokin's theories of love, altruism, and social reconstruction in a manner strongly reminiscent of the way in which Comte's contemporaries ignored the founder's religion of humanity.

In the 1940s the Young Turks at Harvard (who numbered Talcott Parsons in their ranks) established the Department of Social Relations to by-pass the old guard in the traditional social science departments. Sorokin in the Sociology Department found himself shorn of power and without graduate students; after 12 years as chairman he resigned. By happenstance at this very time Ely Lilly made a grant of first $20,000; later an additional $100,000. to Sorokin to set up and direct the Harvard Research Center for Creative Altruism. Joseph Allen Matter, formerly of the law firm of Chapman and Cutter of Chicago, member of the Arizona State Investment Council, trustee of Hastings College, and founder of the Sedona Community Center has undertaken to synthesize ideas on how, through love and altruism, to resolve the world crisis—ideas deriving from this phase of Sorokin's work. Among the publications in which Sorokin's ideas for social reconstruction were developed and which were made possible by the Center are: *Altruistic Love*, 1950; *Social Philosophises of an Age of Crisis*, 1951; *S. O. S.: The Meaning of Our Crisis*, 1951; *The Ways of Power and Love*, 1954; and *Forms and Techniques of Altruistic and Spiritual Growth*, 1954. There were numerous others.

This is not the place to examine in depth either Sorokin's views nor the presentation of them by Zimmerman and Matter. It is, however, quite appropriate to note the striking parallels between Comte's positivistic organicism and Sorokin's integratism in both their theoretical and social reformist aspects. Both Comte and Sorokin were working in the tradtion of the Christian Church Fathers: Comte secularized this tradition and relocated it in a framework of secular progress; Sorokin first relativised these traditions and visualized them as manifest in historical cycles, but eventually adopted the position that the pendulum of historical development would eventually come to rest in an integralist synthesis. Both Comte and Sorokin eventually turned their talents to the moral regeneration of mankind. Both lost much of their support from contemporary social scientists in the process, but began to gain adherents from a new audience.

It is to the credit of American sociologists that in the mid-1960s they started a grass roots campaign to set aside the judgment of the professional clique that had long excluded Sorokin from consideration for president of the American Sociological Association. When the membership of the society elected him the old man responded gallantly and ran a memorable program, one of the high points of the society in the post war period. But the field has yet to come to terms with the remarkable similarities between the intellectual outlook of the founder of sociology and the man who in the 1970s is still, in some quarters, viewed as the World's Greatest Sociologist. Have we advanced so little in the nearly 150 years since the first volume of Comte's positive philosophy, that most of the same problems, potentialities, tensions, and polarities are still with us?

Sociology as an Art Form, by ROBERT NISBET. New York: Oxford University Press, 1976. 145 pp. $8.95 cloth. $2.50 paper.

FREDERICK R. LYNCH
Pitzer College

In the 1960s an increasing number of young social scientists, many of whom had just been forced-marched through an ever-lengthening sequence of methodology and theory construction courses, began to rebel against their assigned role as the intellectual janitors of the sociological community. That is, in the lexicon of Thomas Kuhn's *The Structure of Scientific Revolutions*, they had been dutifully trained to perform the dreary "mopping up" work of the discipline, testing and re-testing hypotheses deduced from the conventional paradigms of the day. Alienation and revolt were, and still are, the products of such preparation and a literature of liberation, sociology's own counterculture, evolved.

Interestingly, several established scholars authored the major intellectual statements for the counterculture, including C. Wright Mills, Alvin W. Gouldner, and Robert A. Nisbet. *Robert A. Nisbet a leader of the counterculture?* Yes, indeed. Nisbet earned his status as a revolutionary heretic with his 1962 essay, "Sociology as an Art Form," in which he called for an end of the artificial distinctions that had separated art and science since the nineteenth century. Instead, he urged the recognition of the basic similarities in the mental processes underpinning both artistic and scientific enterprises, especially that of disciplined, individual creativity. Attacking the pretensions of contemporary positivism, Nisbet wryly observed that not one of the great ideas of classical sociology came about as "the result of what we are today pleased to call the scientific method." Then, forever endearing himself to the disgruntled army of intellectual janitors, he angrily declared: "How many mute, inglorious Simmels, how many village Cooleys lie today buried in required sequences of curriculum and in the computer rooms, their talents occupied not by development of ideas and insights but the adaptation of trivial or well worn ideas to the language of the machine or the endless replication of studies that often shouldn't have been done in the first place." As many of us said in the '60s: Right on!

The themes in the essay "Sociology as an Art Form" are carried forward and considerably expanded in Nisbet's new book by the same title. Indeed, the contents and title of the first chapter on "The Sources of Imagination" also echo those of C. Wright Mills in *The Sociological Imagination*. Nisbet steps up his attack on the "consecration of method" and the tyranny of systems-theory, hammering home his message that the more subjective and intuitive logic of discovery in scientific work should not be sacrificed to the more mechanical logic of verification.

Having disposed of methodolotry, Nisbet devotes the rest of the book to furthering his inquiries into the social and cultural bases of sociological thought, particularly the classical perspectives of his beloved "Titans": Tocqueville, Marx, Weber, Durkheim, and Simmel. Assuming that "what is common to art and science is vastly more important than what is different" (p. 10), Nisbet sets out to demonstrate that the central themes of sociology (community, authority, status, the sacred, and alienation) have been inextricably interwoven with the four great concerns of Western thought as a whole (the individual, order, freedom, and change).

Nisbet maintains that the same shared conceptual imagery has been drawn upon by social scientists and artists alike in rendering such "sociological landscapes" as: (1) the rise of *the masses* and the eclipse of community, (2) the advent of *power* with the French and Industrial Revolutions coupled with the waning of older forms of authority, (3) the nature of the *factory system* and its accompanying social form, (4) the *metropolis*. Artists (particularly novelists and essayists) and sociologists have also constructed similar "sociological portraits" or ideal role-types, individual representations of various groups or classes. Here, for example, we find writers ranging from Edmund Burke to Charles Dickens to (especially) Karl Marx all constructing similar portraits of the *bourgeois capitalist*. So, too, was Marx instrumental in furnishing us with another portrait, *the worker*, though the rediscovery of the idea of poverty by many intellectuals of that period produced other portraits of the proletariat in literature and in art. *The bureaucrat* and *the intellectual* are two more portraits singled out by Nisbet as similarly sketched in both the artistic and scientific communities.

The final two chapters on "The Problem of Motion" and "The Rust of Progress" are vintage Nisbet and contain many of the criticisms and insights in his previous writings on sociologists' proclivities and problems in dealing with change. New, however, is his use of the term "diorama" in dealing with small-scale social motion. For example, "Marx's *Capital* is a diorama, complete with figures called workers and capitalists and with constructs called factories and offices; and out of his diorama comes a sense of movement, of becoming just as surely as the same sense is given to us by the sculptor working with a block of marble or the painter with brushes and oils on canvas" (p. 106). We watch the motion and conflict in capitalism, of course, against the broader, panoramic background of the entire history of class struggle, just as Weber's diorama of bureaucracy is merely a part of the more sweeping, long-term process of rationalization.

Nisbet's reverence for the Titans is all well and good, but I suspect that many readers will be disappointed that Nisbet did not advance his analysis of the relationship between art and sociology beyond the early twentieth century. For example, what is the relationship between contemporary cultural and social currents and the works of *any* of the following major sociologists: Becker, Berger, Blau, Blumer, Cicourel, Coleman, Collins, Coser, Garfinkel, Goffman, Gouldner, Homans, Lyman and Scott, Shibutani, to name but a few. Indeed, how has and how is *Nisbet* reflecting or responding to fluctuations in the contemporary societal and cultural milieux? Nisbet drops a hint or two about his thoughts on such topics, but a chapter or two on these matters would have been more welcome. One final, perhaps minor, criticism: although there are a fair number of direct quotations in this book, there are no footnotes.

The paperback version of the book is most attractively priced, which should encourage its use in a wide variety of courses —especially those in methodology and theory construction.

Status Communities in Modern Society: Alternatives to Class Analysis, by HOLGER R. STUB. Hinsdale, Ill.: Dryden Press, 1972. 326 pp. No price listed, paper.

JAMES MURTHA
Columbia Univeristy

The debate between advocates of class and status models of social stratification now spans several generations. Theorists working from a class orientation focus on economic characteristics (not usually limited to Marx's relations to the means of production) in order to locate individuals in the social structure. The status approach, which has occupied a strong position in American sociology since the early (1925) prestige studies, focuses on shared evaluation as the basis of hierarchical differentiation between social actors. Holger Stub's volume is, primarily, an example of the latter tradition.

A status community is a group which shares similar prestige or "social honor" and, around this shared estimation, develops a shared life style. Stub argues that this concept can serve as a more or less neutral research tool, one which avoids the rhetoric of class analysis.

The first part of the book offers several "theoretical" (Weber, Schumpeter, Nisbet, Hodges) and "contemporary" (Mayer, Wrong, Wilensky, Stub) perspectives on stratification. Each of these selections, in one way or another, suggests that stratification is a multi-dimensional phenomenon which cannot be adequately explained by class analysis alone. Stub's concluding piece in this section draws heavily on Weber's short discussion "Class, Status and Party," which is included in the volume. According to Stub, Weber's status dimension is crucial for explaining differences in the dynamic middle levels of society. Stub's view is bolstered by Mayer's argument that class is a pertinent analytic tool only at the uppermost and lowest economic levels where positions tend to be inherited from one generation to the next. The author also draws on Wrong's assertion that inequalities based on occupation, income, education, etc. have become more salient bases of inequailty than class (defined in terms of class consciousness) in modern society.

The remaining sections of the text include articles about middle, lower, and upper status groups (chapters 3–6), and the final three chapters are devoted to discussions of status symbols, elites, and social mobility.

As far as Stub's organizing principle is concerned, I have one major reservation: the author offers little evidence for the claim that "the Weberian dimension of class may decline from its preeminent position" to be replaced by status. An undue emphasis on status is no less polemical than over-emphasizing class. Notwithstanding this criticism, however, the status community concept leads Stub to include several interesting and important selections in his volume.

Given the consistently high quality of the selections, let me comment briefly on several articles which seem of particular relevance to stratification students. Joseph Bensman's discussion of the urban musical community is particularly interesting, both as an example of the status approach and as an important illustration of the sociology of art. In "The Crawfords: Life at the Bottom" Jack L. Roach uses an indepth interview format to describe the everyday life of a family that is characterized by the husband's irregular employment and a constant struggle to make ends meet.

In his section on social mobility, Stub includes "The Chronology of Aspirations," a chapter from Chinoy's *Automobile Workers and the American Dream.* In this piece Chinoy describes the response of workers to limited opportunity for social advancement. A (re)reading of this chapter sensitizes the reader to a basic dilemma of American society—the unceasing striving of many for a relatively few desirable positions—and demonstrates how Chinoy copes with the methodological problems of small sample size and retrospection in an instructive manner.

Many of the other selections—Domhoff and Baltzell on the higher circles, Bottomore on elites, Wilensky on career patterns, an early piece by Blau on social mobility—are similarily of high interest and quality. Even the brief selection from Gerth and Mills's *Character and Social Structure* will send many back to the original.

As can be seen from my comments, I think that the selections in this reader are valuable and, in general, stand on their own. I would not, however, recommend Stub's volume as a text for an undergraduate course. Rather, it seems to me that this volume would serve students best if presented along with material oriented toward Weber's other dimensions (class and party). For graduate students, Stub's orientation will probably elicit valuable discussion; the collected articles are certain to be a useful resource.

Third World Studies

Six Essays in Comparative Sociology, by ANDRÉ BÉTEILLE. New York: Oxford University Press, 1976. 113 pp. $4.00 cloth.

JOSEPH R. GUSFIELD
University of California, San Diego

If a diamond is an object that sparkles and gives off light, then this is indeed a gem of a book. Reading it is an experience of intellectual pleasure and excitement in contemplating old ideas critically assessed and new ones generated and illustrated. Over the past decade André Béteille, Professor of Sociology at the University of Delhi, has produced a stream of studies and essays on Indian society that has achieved a major position in the sociology of new nations and contemporary social change. Here, in 113 pages, he has given us a work of major significance, not only for specialists in Indian studies or in comparative social change, but for all sociologists with a concern for the basic orientations of their discipline.

This long essay originated in the National Lectures in Sociology which Béteille gave in September, 1972 under the sponsorship of the Indian University Grants Commission. These constitute the first three of six chapters, two others are new, and the final chapter (on "Marxism and Modern Sociology") is, as the author tells us, a lecture he has sometimes given to his students. What holds these essays together is the general theme of "peasant societies" and the author's critical stance toward dominant concepts of the "peasant" currently in use. A second theme, or leitmotif, is the nature of academic disciplines and their approaches to this subject matter.

What Béteille has achieved in these essays is a major revision of the concept of peasant and peasant studies. It is for this reason that he begins his analysis with a splendid discussion of the academic split between sociology and social anthropology. It was a separation which reinforced the theoretical distinction between primitive and advanced societies; tribe, peasantry, and urbanites; kinship and class as foci of social study. Indian society, Béteille argues, provides no factual basis for this distinction, either as a present or an evolutionary reality. Such distinctions posit a peasantry which is homogeneous and primarily in conflict with an outside non-peasant or non-tribal society.

Béteille is both mindful and appreciative of the work of Robert Redfield and later anthropologists in developing and accentuating this view of peasants in the trichotomy of tribe-peasant-city communities. While they turned anthropology toward the study of contemporary developing nations, the emphasis on culture-values, religion, and symbol systems neglected the material basis of social structure and thus ignored significant heterogeneities and conflicts in the Indian village. Here the studies of the institutional bases of Chinese rural economy in the 1930s undertaken by Fei Hsiao-Tung ("Earthbound China") and others present a better model for him than does the overly caste-concentrated models of many Indian anthropologists and sociologists.

Professor Béteille argues that failure to attend to elements of the economic, technical, and material structure has prevented the recognition of the Indian village as a differentiated, stratified community in which economic units present a face of conflict among themselves. To tack the label of "peasant" on agrarian communities distorts and hides such vital issues of social stratification. The peasant must be viewed as one group, albeit significant, in a stratified community. "No understanding of [peasants] can be complete unless we see them in relation to non-working land owners on the one hand and landless workers on the other" (p. 22). In this respect, the distinction between tribe and peasant loses its value in India, where the only major difference between "tribe" and "peasant" villages lies in religion. Both appear similar in their social structures and have done so for too long to see tribal villages as in "transition" to peasantry.

Modern India, as Béteille recognizes, presents much overlap in its agrarian classes. The peasant household, in which men and women till the land which they themselves control, has many exceptions of partial ownership, partial non-cultivation, or partial hiring out. In fact, in an important analysis of Chinese and Indian peasantry, the author points out that mobility in Chinese agrarian life was expressed by exempting men from labor but in India by exempting women. The matter is important because it may be a source of demand for hiring of field labor by more prosperous peasants. For a variety of reasons agricultural labor in India is becoming contractual, thereby creating, in some parts of India, conditions of organization which carry it into conflict with peasants.

These reassessments of the peasant concept are a welcome relief to the undeniably romantic perspectives of those who see the peasant as overrun by an urban world destroying a pleasant harmony, or those who see a peasantry united in political opposition to an intrusive capitalism. In his final chapter, Béteille pays great tribute to Marx for pointing to the nature of social conflicts and their origin in the division of labor. However, he sees the value of Marx in developing a method for studying conflict, rather than in producing laws or theories. He is critical and even contemptuous of those Indian and European Marxists who, seeing sociology as "bourgeois" and Marxism as Truth turn away from empirical description and analysis of the realities of Indian life as unnecessary academic ideology.

In my judgment Béteille leaves many questions unanswered. What he throws out with the bath at the back door, he allows in with the baby at the front door. Caste and cuture emerge again in Béteille's analysis of the peasant household and the meaning of women's farm work and still again in his discussion of the impediments to political and economic organization of agricultural workers in West Bengal. The relation of culture to social structure needs more illumination than he has given us here. Having won his war against social anthropology, Béteille must still define the terms of peace.

So too, the value of the Redfieldian concept is too easily dismissed. It is both possible and probable in the Indian context that there are sources of both unity and diversity; cooperation and conflict. Marriott's perspective of great and little traditions in India is also mirrored in the "centre-periphery" distinction and its relation to political and social conflicts between city and village. George Rosen's analysis of the differential productivity and economic returns of urban and rural India also suggests that, for some problems, the village community is usefully seen as homogenous and in opposition to the urban. There are interests that unite and interests that divide. To continue my tiring metaphor, armies fight against enemies and within themselves.

But I am asking for too much illumination from a bright but very small candle. Hopefully Professor Béteille will take these issues up again. Until he does, this book will stand as a major achievement. I hope that its title and small size will not keep many sociologists from reading a wise and exciting book.

Conflict in Africa: Concepts and Realities, by ADDA B. BOZEMAN. Princeton, N.J.: Princeton University Press, 1976. 429 pp. $27.50 cloth. $12.50 paper.

DAVID D. LAITIN
University of California, San Diego

Professor Bozeman claims that because traditional African societies are nonliterate, Africa has never been and will never be peaceful. In nonliterate societies, she proclaims, speech and action are rarely held to be distinct, and so words do not have the power, as they seem to in the West, to provide a substitute for violent conflict. Latent conflict, without a clear distinction between words and actions, all too often spills over, without any moral restrictions, into its manifest form.

Without writing, furthermore, political communities cannot easily grow in size. Bozeman suggests that "space transcendent" ideas, such as "world peace," do not easily develop when there are no large scale territorial communities. Also, because nonliterate societies tend to merge past and present into undifferentiated time, with almost no vision of a future, there is as well an absence of "time-transcendent" ideas in Africa.

Finally, Bozeman suggests that nonliteracy makes intellectual pursuits impossible. With no unambiguous written records, fact and fiction merge into one. Mythmakers and magicians abound when there are no written records, and any political structure which relies on a commitment to recorded truth, such as a treaty, is of dubious value. Without any restraint on latent conflict, or commitment to truth, or great ideas, Africa is seen in this study as a continent trapped, by its past and future, in a Hobbesian state of nature.

Bozeman's theory rests on a rigid dichotomy between literacy and nonliteracy. In nonliterate societies, she argues, since the spoken word "is apt to be remembered differently by different listeners" (p. 73) and to change meaning over generations, there can be no objective criteria of truth. Bozeman does not consider, however, the rather well-known evidence that written languages are also subject to "drift," their words changing meaning over generations, and their speakers unaware of the differential connotations of the same word to different people. Nor does she consider the fact that written records, including treaties, are usually rife with ambiguities. Her argument, therefore, that a (written) treaty is unequivocally more sacred than a (oral) promise, is unfounded.

Even if a rigid dichotomy between literacy and nonliteracy were tenable, Professor Bozeman does not seem to recognize the theoretical consequence of using the concept of nonliteracy as an explanatory variable. She includes a practice of the Amharic people, for example, as evidence for one of her arguments, even though they have a long and rich literature tradition. And in her general conclusion, Bozeman admits that while literacy is now widespread in Africa, it "can be achieved without dramatically altering traditional beliefs" (p. 369). Bozeman does not seem to understand that this observation vitiates her whole theoretical construct. If she hopes to explain Africa's level of conflict by focusing on the lack of literacy on the continent, she cannot marshall evidence in her support from a literate African society, nor can she claim that if literacy were to come to Africa, it would make little difference.

Not only is the theory deficient, but so is the evidence. That Bozeman can collect countless examples from Africa in which treaties are broken and in which conflict easily became manifest is, for lack of standards of comparison, unconvincing. Only by developing carefully controlled comparative studies would it be possible to give evidence to support a conclusion that Africa is more or less conflict-ridden than the Occident.

Bozeman not only did not compare, but she seemed to ignore any examples of peace- or treaty-keeping in Africa. The record of the OAU, for example, in mitigating interstate conflicts can be compared favorably with that of other regional bodies (see J. Nye, *Peace in Parts*, 1971). The intense conflict among Somalia, Ethiopia, and Kenya has been kept latent through brilliant diplomatic efforts by Africans. And even in the case of the Nigerian civil war, the record of the Aburi Conference months before the outbreak suggests that the participants in the imminent war were men of their word, who understood clearly the difference between truth and falsity. The rather considerable evidence of successful conflict avoidance in Africa has been virtually ignored by Bozeman.

Finally, despite voluminous references, when Bozeman's citations crossed this reviewer's area of expertise, they were often found to be misinterpretations. She speaks, for instance, of "the tribal hatreds of the remote pre-colonial past" (p. 34) but most contemporary social science research demonstrates that tribalism is a function not of past hatreds, but rather of the social mobilization induced by colonialism. Elsewhere she suggests that the Mau Mau were Kikuyu who fell "prey to moral chaos" (p. 163) ignoring all the recent evidence on the Mau Mau movement to the contrary. At another point she instances Richard Rosecrance's work as teaching "that states are stable when there is no major war" (p. 50). In fact, Rosecrance argues just the reverse, viz., that major wars are less likely to occur when states are stable. And critics of Rosecrance's work have noted that the data in his work do not support even that conclusion. Bozeman has simply misread Rosecrance's conclusion and has accepted it too uncritically. Other errors of fact and interpretation could also be cited, but the point is made already.

This book has all the accoutrements of serious scholarship: extensive bibliographic support, a complex set of arguments, and a polished writing style. Unfortunately, it lacks the minimal requisites of good scholarship: theoretical rigor, a careful weighing of evidence, and an abiding concern to represent other scholarly traditions faithfully.

Politics and the Migrant Poor in Mexico City, by WAYNE A. CORNELIUS. Stanford, Calif.: Stanford University Press, 1975. 319 pp. $12.50 cloth.

BRUCE HARRIS
University of California, San Diego

This book will impact variously on the branches of social science. The statistically oriented must consider the validity of Cornelius's "stratified proportional sample" and the inferences one may be allowed from it, as well as the relevance and coding of a voluminous questionnaire of 600 to 700 items arranged into 134 "summative indexes," themselves selectively combined to form "overall indexes." Political scientists will carefully consider Cornelius's conceptualization and operationalization of political involvement (which he divides into a typology from "complete non-participant" to "complete activist"), political attitudes (divided generally, à la Easton, into specific and diffuse support), and sense of community. But the enduring value of this book is in the nature, rather than the content, of its conceptualizations and the promise of approaching an encompassing theory of urbanization which it, along with Gans's *Urban Villagers* and Ross's *Political Integration of Urban Squatters*, appears to hold.

Six colonia proletaria (squatter settlements) are analyzed and compared along a number of political dimensions, and each is embedded in an historical context. The "profiles" along these dimensions are compared and explanations given for the variances (generally hinging on differences in origins and historical experience with the larger system). Though the colonia are all basically squatter settlements it becomes clear that poverty has many faces and may be the expression of a number of different processes with different results.

Cornelius admits his sample of six is much too small to be conclusive regarding the most important sources of political socialization, but he rightly concludes that he has shown the local community to be of crucial importance in such processes. While the content here is political we have a conceptual approach which encourages the use of the comparative method *within* rather than only between cities. In concentrating on the community and seeing previously unitary concepts (especially poverty and migration, but also urbanization in general) as situationally and historically relative individual urban areas may be more finely characterized thus allowing for more precise interurban comparison. The historical perspective encourages a view of the city as a number of co-occurring processes which alter one another over time and argues against any absolute definitions of the components of urbanization.

The community, as Cornelius clearly perceives, is the most suitable vehicle for the next step in the development of urban "theory." It is a meaningful context for the individual; often provides structure for interaction with noncoresidents in the form of stereotypic expectations; permits a manageable study of urban process(es); and when integrated with the other communities in the urban ambit, can be the basis of a more finely tuned comparison among urban areas in general.

Ethnic and Social Stratification in Peninsular Malaysia, by CHARLES HIRSCHMAN. Washington, D.C.: American Sociological Association/Arnold and Caroline Rose Monograph Series, 1975. 115 pp. $5.00 paper.

JOHN A. LENT
Temple University

The aim of this monograph is to describe and explain the socioeconomic inequalities among the ethnic communities of Peninsular Malaysia. As such, it fits neatly with the growing literature on Malaysia pluralism, most recent examples being the edited works by J. A. Nagata, *Pluralism in Malaysia—Myth and Reality: A Symposium on Singapore and Malaysia,* and John A. Lent, *Cultural Pluralism in Malaysia: Polity, Military, Mass Media, Education, Religion and Social Class.*

Hirschman examines in his own words, "the magnitude and persistence of ethnic occupational differentials in Peninsular Malaysia and attempts to account for ethnic differentials in terms of differing social backgrounds." Chapters 3 through 6 are made up of the important analytical substance of the study, measuring the trend in structural assimilation; using occupational differentials from several censuses and a survey from 1931–1967; analyzing data from the 1966–67 West Malaysia Family Survey; and examining patterns of ethnic inequality in educational, occupational, and income attainment.

Among his findings: all ethnic groups are moving out of agricultural employment; white-collar occupations are increasing in all ethnic communities; in several occupations (sales and crafts) very little movement toward equality between Malays and non-Malays is occurring. Intergenerational occupational mobility patterns show "substantial occupational inheritance of all occupations in all ethnic groups but clear differences, as well." For example, the Chinese are more apt to follow their fathers' non-agricultural occupations and thus stay out of farming; the Malays are still concentrated in agriculture, and the Indians are intermediate between the patterns of Chinese and Malays.

Because this monograph is a revision of the author's 1972 doctoral dissertation, it is somewhat dated, as well as statistically and methodologically oriented. The appeal lies more in the methods and models Hirschman attempts to build than in the content regarding inter-ethnic relations in Malaysia. The author builds a good case for socio-economic and historical factors affecting ethnic and social stratification but generally ignores the political factors. Despite these shortcomings, the work adds a needed dimension to Malaysian studies and is welcomed.

Political Culture and Group Conflict in Communist China, by ALAN P. L. LIU. Santa Barbara, Calif.: Clio Press, 1976. 205 pp. $17.95 cloth. $5.75 paper.

MARTIN K. WHYTE
University of Michigan, Ann Arbor

Many studies of contemporary China suffer from an esoterica complex. Perhaps because the obstacles to gaining reliable information about social processes in China are so formidable, the unusual scholars who make the effort tend to become so involved in the intricate mysteries of China that they are unable to relate their findings to issues of general concern to other social scientists. Nowhere is this more true than in studies of the Chinese Cultural Revolution of 1966–1969. One would think that an event in which a charismatic leader (Mao Tse-tung) mobilized a massive rebellion against the instruments of power he himself had created would provide a fascinating test case for theories of collective action. Instead, most accounts of the Cultural Revolution have been byzantine tales of intrigue and violence, without much analysis. In this light the study by Liu is especially refreshing. He attempts to examine the Chinese Cultural Revolution using Western theories of collective action and social protest, to see whether those theories help to explain what went on. For good measure he adds ideas drawn from the work he did earlier on political culture and mass communications. We have, then, an earnest attempt to treat the Chinese events as something other than bizarre.

There are two parts to Liu's study. In the first part (and concluding chapter) he treats the Cultural Revolution chronologically, attempting to explain the process by which the rebellion was mobilized and then escalated into mass violence. In the second part he focuses on the major social groups involved (youths, workers, peasants, and army veterans, although curiously omitting officials) attempting to explain how and why they responded to the Cultural Revolution in different ways. The results are often illuminating but also quite uneven. At times the confrontation of Western theory and Chinese reality leads to new insights about why the Red Guards or some other groups acted as they did. At other times the effort seems much more mechanical; terms and labels drawn from Western theories are tacked on to a Chinese event without adding to our understanding of that event. In a few cases a generalization drawn from a Western work is even used to explain a Chinese phenomenon to which it clearly does not apply. For this reader the result was alternative phases of illumination and frustration.

Professor Liu is eclectic in his approach to Western theories, relying on the likes of Smelser, Obserschall, Lipset, E. Erikson, and many others. He does not recognize that some of the theories he is dealing with are in disagreement about how best to explain collective action. Everything goes into the pot in this book, and we see both groups using resources to protect their interests, and "marginal men" playing prominent roles. Liu's goal is to illuminate Chinese events rather than to "test" Western theories, and, as a result, conflicting interpretations are de-emphasized.

The eclecticism used does have its advantages in dealing with something as complex as the Cultural Revolution. No doubt there is no single theory that could adequately explain its many events and the wide variety of individuals and groups who got involved at one time or another. But Liu's approach has drawbacks as well. After reading about the many ways in which the accumulating strains, grievances, and cultural propensities existing in China prior to 1966 reflect those mentioned in Western works as conducive to collective action, the Cultural Revolution becomes "overdetermined." We wonder why it did not break out sooner, rather than why when it occurred it astounded observers, Western and Chinese alike, the way it did. We also get no sense of the relative importance of the many sources of social conflict involved. Major and minor forces and events are touched upon and noted to parallel things observed in collective action elsewhere, but no sense of the central and peripheral emerges. Finally, we get no clear idea of what aspects of the Cultural Revolution contradict that which particular theories of collective action would have led us to expect.

There are many useful ideas in this study, and even if it is not totally successful, Liu should be commended for breaking out of the Chinese esoterica complex, leaving a path which other scholars will hopefully follow.

China and the West: Myths and Realities in History, by HYOBOM B. PAK. Leiden, The Netherlands: E. J. Brill, 1974. 120 pp. No price listed, cloth.

FRANCIS L. K. HSU
Northwestern University

This book intends to show that China and the industrialized Western nations have "converged culturally to the point where China today has been at last modernized or christianized in social organization" (book jacket). In arriving at this thesis the author lumps religion with political ideology, such as Fascism, Nazism, and Marxism (p. 7), declares monotheism to be "an expression of the tribal segregationist outlook of a weak people in order to seek spiritual protection from a self-righteous, omnipotent god" (p. 13), diagnoses that the failure of reform in China in response to Western challenge before 1949 is due to lack of "the kind of organized faith so effectively institutionalized by the Christian religion" (p. 103), and finally, concludes that "Christian thought of our modern times and Confucian thought of classical times share the common ideals of man at moral relativity of human values, humanism, social democracy as well as human harmony, all of which are the dominant trends of thought of the Confucian tradition" (p. 112).

The reviewer cannot agree that religion be identified with political ideology. It is true that they are both matters of faith, but one involves the supernatural while the other does not. Turnip and cabbage are both vegetables, their consumers may find both equally satisfying, but students of plants must differentiate between them.

The idea that monotheism comes from "the tribal segregationist outlook of a weak people . . ." is ridiculous. Many tribes and most Asian societies including China believe in some supreme deity but the latter only lords it over numerous other deities held equally true. They are polytheists, in sharp contrast to real monotheists who hold only one *God* is true, and all others are false. Hence they alone will tend to eliminate other religious faiths by proselytization. In the whole of human history there are only three monotheistic religions: Judaism, Christianity, and Islam. Judaism could not proselytize because of the minority status of Jews everywhere since the sacking of the Second Temple. Islamic proselytization was largely coterminous with Moslem military and political conquest. Western Christianity is truly the most proselytizing of all monotheistic religions. The scholarly community has yet to appreciate the significance that all or nearly all the world's missionaries are Westerners.

As to the author's link between industrial advances and "organized faith so effectively institutionalized by the Christian religion," has he thought of the paradox that the Industrial Revolution emerged in northern Europe, where the church is Protestant and not so unified and well organized, but not in southern Europe where the church is Catholic and far more unified and well organized? Does the author not know that the same contrast can be made between North and South America with reference to industrial progress?

Finally it must be appealing to quite a few one worlders to see, as the author does, convergence between classical Confucianism and modern Christianity. For that matter, the author can find certain affinities among diverse creeds and ideologies; but the ways these creeds and ideologies have manifested themselves in concrete behavior patterns among different peoples are greatly different. For example, Christianity is essentially intolerant, regardless of what modern church-related writers, such as Jerald C. Brauer (on whose authority the author relies), say. Apart from the Inquisition and the Crusades and other acts of outright persecution and aggression in the name of protection or spread of Christianity, religion continues to be a barrier to marriage, residence, political office, occupation, and even social intercourse. Nothing remotely comparable to these existed in China before or after contact with the West.

That China today has changed greatly as a society and a nation since the century of 1840–1949, no one can deny. China has made impressive advances industrially, politically, and militarily, and is one of the leading powers of the world. That all or most of these gains have something to do with a newer type organization also cannot be denied. Max Weber and R. H. Tawney promoted the thesis that the Protestant spirit was the source of European enterprise. Now Pak insists Christian-type organization is responsible for Chinese industrial development. The fact that industrialization and political modernization can be achieved via other psychological organizational patterns (such as the case of Japan) is a lesson that most social scientists and humanist scholars have yet to learn.

Power and Pawn: The Female in Iberian Families, Societies, and Cultures, by ANN M. PESCATELLO. Westport, Conn.: Greenwood Press, 1976. 281 pp. $15.95 cloth.

MARTA TIENDA
University of Wisconsin, Madison

In the introduction to her 1973 anthology, *Female and Male in Latin America,* Pescatello signaled the need to study the position of women in society in a historical framework. *Power and Pawn* is such a study. It is a commendable undertaking for there are few studies about women which share the broad temporal and geographical scope of this work. This cross-cultural and multidisciplinary study is a fascinating historical account of women's social position in Iberian cultures. Not only does it deepen understanding about the impact of Iberian civilization on other cultures, but it shows how present social structures and practices are vestiges of the past. As a whole, this study is a benchmark for future investigations of women in Iberian-influenced societies, but its relevance is not confined to this geographical and cultural arena.

Pescatello is fundamentally concerned with the dual interpretation of women's place in society as reflected in the appearances and realities of their condition over time. The title conveys this dualism quite nicely. The power notion is consistent with theses about women as agents of social change whereas the pawn side conveys the idea that as a group, women have played passive roles in sociocultural evolution by transmitting instead of forging social structure in a male-dominated world. The paradox of this dualism can be reconciled by tracing changes in the activity domains of men and women across time and cultures. Whereas men have predominated in public domains, women's activities have been generally confined to the private spheres of social life. But this is not necessarily the same as being powerless. The distinction between private and public activity domains allows for a more systematic analysis of the overt and covert social influences exercised by women over time and thereby permits an elaboration of the power-pawn thesis. Also, by exposing the visible and invisible as well as the real and ideal aspects of women's position in society, we can appreciate how changing female roles reflect shifts in the activity domains from private to public spheres.

Pescatello's case is that the discrepancy between the ideal and the real historical positions occupied by Iberian women can be better understood by focusing on the family. This is, after all, the most important social institution cross culturally. Those who argue adamantly that women must be studied in their own right and not in comparison to men or vis à vis their family roles may not find this suggestion compelling. Pescatello's evidence is convincing and illustrates that the family is vital for both reconstructing the way of life for most societies which have previously existed and for making generalizations about similarities and differences among contemporary societies. However, this does not mean that it is not possible or worthwhile to study women in their own right. The message is simply that social scientists determined to learn more about women's role in social change should carefully examine the linkages with the institutional configurations which molded women's micro and macro environments through the ages.

Another noteworthy and forceful message Pescatello makes is that the division of cultures into socioeconomic strata is vital for understanding variations on the power-pawn theme. Not only is this the most fundamental qualification for generalizing about women's history across cultures, but it will advance the reconciliation of the seemingly paradoxical role of women as wellsprings of power and pawns in male-dominated worlds.

Despite the historical strengths of this book, Pescatello's chapter about Iberian women in the twentieth century is cluttered with statistics and chopped with unnecessary subheadings which fail to organize the content. Why "education" and "society" or "civil rights" and "politics" are parallel subheadings is unclear. Even more disturbing is the fact that the economics section, which is tedious reading, needs updating. A study published in 1976 should draw upon 1970 census and statistical abstracts to portray the economic opportunities available to women.

There are, admittedly, advantages to be had from being specific, but Pescatello does not exploit these in the choice of information about the twentieth century. Because the focus on contemporary Latin America fluctuates between the region and individual countries, the content of chapters eight and nine (especially the former) is not as forceful as it should be. A more general regional synthesis with "hard data" used strategically for emphasis would be more appropriate.

On the other hand, generalizations made from comparatve historical analyses do not obviate the need for further study to determine how women in a constantly changing society accommodate new social stresses and role strains. Pescatello is sensitive to this need and therefore calls for "more specific monographic analyses of the structrual implications of sex, race and class phenomena" to highlight the "observed reality biased by a consistent male view and . . . the coexistence of seemingly polar values of female power and male authority" (p. 159).

Beyond the Veil: Male-Female Dynamics in a Modern Muslim Society, by Fatima Mernissi. New York: Halsted Press, 1975. 132 pp. No price listed, paper.

Janet Abu-Lughod
Northwestern University

More accurately entitled "Contradictions in Male-Female Relations in Changing

Morocco: Building a New Modus Vivendi," this book (originally a Brandeis University doctoral dissertation) by Morocco's first woman sociologist is profound, original, and courageous. These qualities are obscured on first reading, since one is distracted by the contentious tone, the incompleteness of certain lines of argument, the tangential and often suspect quality of much of the evidence ("devil-quoting-scripture" problem), and the breadth of the issues, each covered in a mere handful of pages. During a second and more careful reading, I realized that these flaws are inevitable concomitants of the author's deep conviction and pained understanding, of the originality of her insights which often leap well beyond available evidence, and of the synthetic sweep of a too ambitious mind seeking to probe *the* relationships between religious ideology, economic organization, *and* sexuality in Arab culture from pre-Islamic times to the present.

Mernissi's argument is complex and subtle. In summarizing it I shall do an injustice which can only be undone by consulting the book itself. The simplest way to proceed is to begin with the conclusions and work back to the argument and evidence, for not until the final chapter is it evident *why* the earlier chapters contain the strange assortment of items they do.

Post-independence Morocco has a legal code of family law (derivative from Islamic shari 'a) which institutionalizes two customs intrinsically incompatible with an egalitarian relationship between the sexes: (1) the husband is held completely responsible for the support of his wife and children; and (2) wives presumably must have their husbands' permission to enter "male space," i.e., go to work, walk in the streets, enter public places, etc. (The law requires only that a husband not prevent his wife from visiting her family.)

This family law is in direct conflict with the economic and social realities of contemporary Moroccan society in several important ways. First, due to economic stagnation, many men cannot find work. Their inability to support their families thus becomes not only an economic but a sexual failure; unemployment impugns their manhood, encouraging them to deflect toward women hostilities which rather should be directed against the system which denies them a livelihood. Second, the state has taken over many of the functions previously provided by the male household head and has thus undermined his authority, despite the assurance of male supremacy given in the law. Third, nationalist ideology encouraged unveiling and the education of females, and now these facts, plus the currently expanding work opportunities for urban women as well as the heightened impecuniousness which requires their contribution to household support, have brought many women into "male space" where they are viewed as threatening invaders and/or (unrespectable) fair game for sexual advances. These changes have completely and irreversibly undermined the complexly integrated modus vivendi which Arabo-Islamic culture evolved to handle the relationship between men and women, a modus vivendi which depended upon two chief "mechanisms": spatial segregation and a devaluation of the conjugal bond.

Using quotations from the Qur'an, various "lives" of the Prophet, a medieval collection of biographies of early female converts to Islam, reflections on sexuality by one of Islam's most noted philosophers, al-Ghazali, and the early researchers into marriage and family among the semites by Robertson Smith (each source suspect in itself and used selectively to support her case), Mernissi builds up an uncomplimentary (and often angry) image of sexism in Islam, one which many Muslim males will defensively deny. She finds Western culture equally sexist, but points to a number of fundamental differences between Arab and Western sexism which she believes will aid Arab society in resolving its sexual conflict. She argues that whereas the West tends to dismiss women as inferior, Arabs view women as potentially powerful and threatening. Second, whereas Christianity sought to denigrate and suppress sexuality, Islam accepted it, seeking only to regularize and contain it. But third, whereas the West tried to regulate licentiousness through internalized restraints, Islam sought to achieve regulation through rigid spatial segregation—hence veiling, seclusion, sexual division of labor, etc.

That such spatial segregation has broken down irretrievably in urban Morocco she substantiates by her depth interviewing of a small sample of bourgeois women. And that the breakdown of such segregation has left young Moroccan males and females in an anomic (deregulated) state she substantiates by a content analysis of over 400 letters written by perplexed Moroccans to a respected religious leader who offers advice to a wide radio audience.

The devaluation of the conjugal bond between sexual partners she identifies as the second basic mechanism of the old modus vivendi. She contends that the Islamic Umma (religious community) was primarily for males. Females, whose potential power to distract men from their religious duties and relationship to God was feared, had not only to be secluded, chiefly to protect *men* from temptation, but (within the limits of marriage) also to be made interchangeable (i.e., into sex objects) in order to neutralize their power. She argues that polygamy (particularly its rules governing unvarying order of sexual rotation regardless of preference) and the institution of repudiation (incontestable divorce by the husband by triple repetition of a simple verbal formula) both served to defuse the potential intensity of the conjugal bond, as did the deep and unbreakable attachment between mother and son which took precedence over mere marriage. Concerning the latter, the older generation "traditional" women she interviewed all reported that the most significant person throughout their married life had been not their spouse but their mother-in-law. In contrast and as evidence that the conjugal bond has now, by default, become central in Morocco, among the younger women she interviewed it was the spouse who was of central importance. Most extended families were breaking up, due to urban employment patterns, job-related mobility, etc. Mernissi argues that Moroccan husbands and wives now find themselves thrown together in a conjugal situation of confrontation for which their early socialization in aversion and their religious training have ill-prepared them.

The tensions generated by the breakdown of these two mechanisms which "handled" male-female dynamics in the past have left Moroccan men and women with a critical need to restructure their relationships with one another. But there are as yet no viable models for how this can be done. The two models at hand are both suspect. One is the model of female liberation from the *Jahaliyah* (pre-Islamic period of "ignorance"), a model of matrilineal, female self-determination which Islam defined as licentious and which it outlawed by institutionalizing the *patria potestas*. The second is the model of female liberation observed in the West, tainted by its association with the colonizer and hardly relevant, given the basically different "hang-ups" of the two cultures. Mernissi hints at a third model, that of China, as offering a true revolutionary reorganization of male-female relations, but she does not pursue this.

Even if Mernissi is wrong in some, or even most, of the particulars in this study, she has written a powerful and seminal book whose theoretical insights deserve a careful reading and much further testing.

Big City Government in India: Councilor, Administrator and Citizen in Delhi, by PHILIP OLDENBURG. Tucson: University of Arizona Press, 1976. 400 pp. $9.50 cloth. $4.95 paper.

MARK SPEVAK
University of Delhi

As a long-time resident of Delhi, I was looking forward to going through the above work (based on the author's doctoral thesis), in view of its avowed aim to examine Delhi government and politics. I felt that a clear analysis of these processes might contribute much to understanding this city and its problems, and, by extension, urban India in general, since politics (in both its electoral and sociological senses) is a significant factor in Indian city life.

I was further encouraged by the author's analytical frame, described in the promotional blurb at the back of my copy, which credits the author with "a discerning study of municipal government in Delhi" which "deftly describes and analyzes the roles of councilor, administrator, and citizen at three levels of government—the municipal ward, the zone, and the Municipal Corporation as a whole."

There is a wealth of accurately presented thoroughgoing historical, city-structural, and sociocultural detail, and these areas are indeed vital in understanding Delhi government:

(1) The historical context of the city is very important, owing to its complex transitions from a (half-mythical) Hindu capital to a Moghul administrative center,

then to a subsidiary British town, and again to the capital of independent India. In addition, its recent administration has gone through many forms, each with a different equation of power vis-à-vis the central government. It began with the more or less powerless Metropolitan Council (which still enjoys a vestigial status) and reached the stage (before the declaration of emergency) of democratic decentralized rule under the Old and New Delhi Municipal Corporations. These latter adiminstrations formed the subjects of Oldenburg's study especially the Old Delhi Corporation.

(2) The structure of the city in terms of its political subunits is also significant, and is presented ably by Oldenburg. Commencing at the level of the politically important *katra* dwelling complexes, which control a large number of votes, the author progresses to the street (*gali*), neighborhood (*mohalla*), ward (his area of main analysis, here with the pseudonym of "Kucha Khirkiwala"), zone, and finally reaches the highest level of Old and New Delhi. Each of these has attached political significance, most significantly from the ward on up, which contain specific administrative organs: the councilor is attached to the ward, and is the author's main focus of attention.

(3) Sociocultural patterns in the population under study are also well-documented, as the author well recognizes their significance for possible political activity. Indeed, the electoral competition of the Congress, Muslim League, and Jana Sangh parties attests amply to this. Class cleavages were found of little moment, since the ward was relatively homogeneous.

The problem comes when the writer attempts to utilize all this effective background material in understanding the political processes described in the beginning; this part of the book does not, in my opinion, live up to the promise in earlier pages.

The fault is methological. Oldenburg relies here almost exclusively on interviews with the councilor-actors involved, as well as the use of participant-observation—he accompanied them on their "rounds" of the ward. There are no independent checks made on this material outside the system under investigation.

Resulting data provide the impression of the municipal councilor as a tireless ombudsman between the citizen and the complex maze of the Old Delhi Town Hall (housing the Corporation). For example, we read that: "The councilor felt that going on rounds was not only necessary but also a duty" (p. 91). And there are many such commendations throughout the book.

Even the informal conflict between civil service employees and the councilor at various levels of government is only presented in one dimension, that of differences over delimitation of authority. Here, the lower level civil servant is more under the control of the councilor in the ward, with a gradual tilting of the balance on higher planes of administration. Yet, though he admits the possibility that a councilor can exceed the purely "deliberative" role and infringe on the "executive" powers of the ward civil officers, there is hardly any mention of corruption: "There was only one instance where this [stretching of rules] could be interpreted as an attempt to get something done for a party follower" (p. 79). No partisanship, no favors! Would that all governments be that way. But of course, even Delhi isn't.

Such a record anywhere would be found enviable, and, if true, would have made declaring the emergency lack rationale. Yet it was on the basis of actual massive corruption (to no small extent in Delhi) that gave the Indian government its excuse to end freedom.

Getting the ethnographic "goods" is difficult in any study; this is compounded in such work as just described, where the actors often have an interest in presenting themselves in the best possible light. Unfortunately, it seems that Oldenburg allowed them to do just that, both through their self-serving statements and the great show of honesty and competence on ward rounds (probably put on in part for the benefit of the investigator). With no independent checks, we can never know for sure. It's not that all Delhi politicians are corrupt and lazy (though many were at least before the emergency), but neither can they be as consistently ideal as the author describes.

It is admittedly a trying task to collect data in a foreign context and I can understand the problems that can lead to pitfalls such as the one above. Nevertheless, I am disappointed that a work so fine in detail and so ambitious in effort should suffer from weak technique, especially in view of the obvious need for such studies.

The Indian Industrial Worker: Issues in Perspective, by BALDEV RAJ SHARMA. Delhi: Vikas Publishing House, 1974. 205 pp. No price listed, cloth.

RUDI VOLTI
Pitzer College

Most industrial sociologists now realize that automobile workers have received disproportionate attention and although this book deals with automobile workers in a country which is barely on the threshold of industrialization, it takes little notice of this special environment. Firmly placed in the Western sociological mold it employs the basic theories and methodologies which have informed studies of factory work in the industrialized world. Through the administration of an extensive questionnaire to 262 automobile workers in Bombay, Sharma investigates some of the standard topics of industrial work-life such as occupational aspirations, absenteeism, union involvement, and alienation. These are statistically cross-tabulated with attributes of individual workers such as religion, caste, rural-urban background, seniority, and education.

Very little that is surprising emerges from the analysis. Perhaps the most interesting finding is that workers with rural origins differ little from those born in the city. The chapter on alienation is thoughtfully done, if inconclusive. In sum, Bombay automobile workers seem indistinguishable from their Detroit counterparts. Yet this may be due to the rather mechanical fashion in which the survey and data analysis are carried out, resulting in the distinctive elements of Indian social structure and culture being reduced to questionnaire items. Sharma seems more than willing to accept technological determinism, and his analysis of the data indicates that the technical demands of factory work overshadow sociocultural factors. The narrow scope of the inquiry and the lack of any extended treatment of the distinctive conditions of Indian industrialization render this judgement questionable at best. The reader cannot help but wonder if the Indian industrial worker can be so easily captured by the social methodologies employed in the West.

The Politics of Pluralism: A Comparative Study of Lebanon and Ghana, by DAVID R. SMOCK and AUDREY C. SMOCK. New York: Elsevier, 1975. 396 pp. $12.50 cloth.

PAUL D. STARR
Auburn University

This is a useful study for students of comparative politics and ethnic relations as well as for Middle Eastern and African area specialists. It has become an even more interesting work since it was published, however, in ways not intended by the authors.

The basic question dealt with in this book—the ways in which nation-states composed of two or more ethnic groups can attempt to prevent conflict or dissolution within a democratic political structure—is not only a crucial one to most Third World societies but is also of growing significance to industrialized countries. In dealing with this question, the Smocks have provided a detailed comparative study of how two quite different societies have used divergent approaches in attempting to deal with serious internal cleavages. Ghana has tried to minimize ethnic distinctions to achieve a more unified society while Lebanon has openly recognized the importance of primordial allegiances and created a political structure based upon the many different religious interest groups which compose its population.

The treatment of the basic question and the analysis of the two societies is accomplished with a thoroughness which could serve as a model for other comparative studies. Existing historical, ethnographic, and other data are used with the Smocks' original qualitative and survey research to treat a complex phenomenon with a sophistication and depth often lacking in cross-national research. Too often, comparative studies have entailed the simplistic examination of a particular question in a number of societies in a manner which minimizes important idiosyncratic elements found in each.

Those with an interest in Middle Eastern societies will find the description of pre-civil war Lebanon to be the best documented available and useful in describing those many factors which helped to bring about the bloody conflict. The treatment of Ghana is also thorough and insightful.

In spite of the impressive scholarship that went into this work, events have proven the authors to be dead wrong in their positive and optimistic assessment of the future of quasi-democratic pluralism in Lebanon. Seldom have the conclusions of social scientists been so vividly disproved by subsequent events. Monday morning quarterbacks may relish the book's discussion of converging Christian and Moslem political attitudes and the description of the dedication of many members of the same groups to democratic pluralism, but it should be pointed out that the Smocks are only the most recent of many scholars, both Lebanese and Western, who have not only found much to praise in the "Lebanese formula" but have also suggested that it could be exported to Northern Ireland, Cyprus, parts of Africa, and other areas troubled by ethnic or religious conflict. There is no doubt that the larger Arab-Israeli conflict has had much to do with the widespread violence in the country, but it is also extremely likely that any society with Lebanon's social structure, even if it were largely isolated from international political dynamics, would experience significant internal conflict.

Much of the information provided in this volume could be used to demonstrate the point that multi-ethnic states cannot long survive without authoritarian controls when a significant proportion of their members come to occupy a cluster of characteristics, based on a combination of economic, physical, religious, ideological, or geographical similarities, which places them in competition for scarce rewards with a substantial number of other persons sharing another rather distinct set of homogeneous characteristics. In the absence of an effective stabilizing or intervening force, such as that provided by a government or an influential third party, conflict will occur. It can be facilitated by the practice of allowing political factions to maintain armed forces and, given the intensification of differences, may be triggered off by minor disputes or even accidents involving members of opposing sides. The practice of ignoring or minimizing differences and small disputes between factions allows minor conflicts to escalate into more destructive ones. A series of unresolved small conflicts promotes further polarization and permits the antagonists to establish a greater internal unity and to better prepare and equip themselves for fighting on a larger scale. The results are predictable.

Given the circumstances in Lebanon, to achieve a workable form of pluralism or at least prevent open conflict between component groups may have been beyond the capacity of any democratic or quasi-democratic type of political system. This failure offers no consolation to other multi-ethnic societies, particularly in the Third World, attempting to develop pluralistic societies within a democratic framework.

The Race between Population and Food Supply in Latin America, by T. LYNN SMITH. Albuquerque: University of New Mexico Press, 1976. 194 pp. $12.50 cloth.

WILLIAM E. BERTRAND
Tulane University

At the time of his death in the spring of 1976, T. Lynn Smith could easily lay claim to the title of Dean of Latin Americanists who direct their writing towards socio-demographic phenomena. His work and that of his students, from Colombia's Orlando Fals Borda to Harold Clements of the United States, spans a broad political and content range which has contributed immensely to our knowledge of South and Central America.

The current volume holds little that will come as a surprise to those who have followed Smith's work. It is essentially a compilation of previously published pieces on the interrelationships of agricultural production and social systems in two major Latin American countries: Brazil, the emergent population and production giant of the continent, and Colombia, whose tremendous regional differences mirror development problems throughout Latin America.

The rapid growth of Brazil as the emerging dominant force in South America makes this book, with its unique historical perspective, an important contribution. Smith's observations of the massive changes that have characterized Brazil from the 1930s to the present is singular in that he has been a participant observer. Particularly cogent are his comments about the colonization process and changes in farm techniques as the country expanded toward unsettled lands.

In his discussion of Colombia, Smith again provides a good overview of the path of agricultural development over a forty year period. With regard to demographic questions the author accurately predicts the significant decrease in the crude birth rate as well as the national growth rate that have been recently documented in the results of the 1973 Colombian census. The recent publication of the results of the 4% sample for that census however makes most of the data presented in the book obsolete and the reader should be forewarned.

Smith's continued insistence on the value of the corn, beef, and bacon hog chain as a single major solution to Colombia's and other Latin American nations' agricultural problems seems to be overemphasized. In the extremely fertile Cauca valley, for example, the production of high protein grains and other cash crops is possible year round. The few cases of attempts to establish feed lot operations have fared poorly due to the high price of grain. I must question the appropriateness of this solution in an environment where humans are competing with animals for increasingly scarce grain protein. In minifundia operations capital intensive techniques such as suggested here have met with little success.

An important section for all of us who deal with demography and its application to problems is Smith's sage commentary on the use of population projections and other techniques for planning purposes. It is a sound and needed reminder for all who use the methods and resultant data referred to. This section of the book is also very useful as a historical treatment of census taking in all of Latin America, one of the only summaries available in the English language.

In this time of controversy and speculation about the human potential to produce sufficient foodstuffs, the role of Latin America in the global process has often been neglected. This compilation of writings from a pioneer among US scholars who have looked to the south is an important contribution to those beginning to study this area. While I am aware of and sympathetic to, some of the critiques of Smith's work in Latin America, his importance, as one of the first to realize the potential of that area cannot be minimized. The contents of this short collection can only serve to remind us of the loss in experience and humanistic wisdom represented in the death of T. Lynn Smith.

Social Life in an Indian Slum, by PAUL D. WIEBE. Delhi: Vikas Publishing House, 1975. Distributed by Carolina Academic Press, 1976. 179 pp. $6.75 cloth.

JAY WEINSTEIN
University of Iowa

Approximately one third of the population of Madras, India's fourth largest city, lives in slums. According to Census of India estimates, the proportion of slum dwellers in urban populations has been increasing steadily for decades. In Bombay, slum dwellers constitute well over one half of the population. The demographic situation is much the same in other third world countries: where one finds urbanization at peripheral areas of the modern world-system, one finds settlements crowded with poor people who live in makeshift housing (huts, tents, shanties) and who have only quasi-legal rights to the land that they occupy.

The physical contrasts between slums and other, "formal," urban settlements are striking; and they are markedly so in Madras, and other Indian cities, where slums occur in the midst of middle- and upper-income neighborhoods of bungalows and multistory apartment buildings. The physical similarities among slums in Indian cities and throughout the third world—the mudwalls, lack of infrastructure, and high areal and in-dwelling densities—are equally striking. These and other physical parameters can easily inspire the conclusion that slum dwellers share a culture which reflects their environment and which contrasts sharply with that of higher-income groups.

Such a conclusion has, in fact, been drawn by urban planners, for whom the classification "slum dweller" is especially meaningful. Census and survey research data support the view that the slum dweller occupies a distinct and inferior niche in the ecology of third world cities. But, what is meaningful for planners and statisticians may not always be meaningful for social scientists. The physical and ecological characteristics of slum settlements tell us very little directly about the social life and culture of their inhabitants. In light of this, and in light of the rapid growth (a growth that has characteristically been termed "cancerous") in the number of slums, it is surprising that so little attention has been paid to their actual social life and culture.

Perhaps the best-known attempt to come to an understanding of cultural and behavioral aspects of slum life is Oscar Lewis's culture of poverty thesis. The fact that slum dwellers are urban, poor, and subject to modern economic conditions would, according to Lewis, suggest that their social life is deficient in three principal ways: (1) little social organization exists beyond the immediate (extended) family; (2) attitudes toward society-at-large are fatalistic and negative; (3) the transition from child to adult status is unclear and often incomplete—children perform adult roles and adults are poorly socialized.

Despite the fact that sociological studies of poor urban neighborhoods in the US have, for decades, been fairly consistent in showing that Lewis's formulation is inadequate, and despite theoretical weaknesses that have been indicated by Charles Valentine and others, the culture of poverty thesis is widely believed to hold for Indian slums. Indeed, a culture of poverty thesis still guides policy formulation and implementation to a significant degree, in India and elsewhere.

Paul D. Wiebe's *Social Life in an Indian Slum* is the first published report of a systematic test of Lewis's thesis in an Indian urban context. Wiebe's approach and conclusions deserve the careful attention of social scientists and planners in a variety of disciplines, including those who may have no particular interest in India. For, like Milton Singer, André Béteille, and Jan Breman, Wiebe has managed to gain general insight into theoretical issues by focusing on the complexities of Indian society. Although the book reports a single case study, it presents a well-supported counter-argument to the culture of poverty thesis. The study takes an important first step toward dispelling ignorance in an area vital to social policy; and it contains a significant empirical challenge to the view that social relations in a third-world slum are as "deficient" as the housing and infrastructure.

The subject of the study is "Chennanagar," a squatter settlement of about three hundred families in the northern industrial section of Madras City (1971 population c. 2.5 million). The research design is based upon a test of the extent to which Lewis's three aspects of a culture of poverty can be attributed to the residents of Chennanagar. Data were gathered via participant-observation, informant, structured interview, and case history techniques. The study is an exemplary piece of social anthropological research, one that continues the tradition of sympathetic community studies mastered by Murray Wax, Wiebe's teacher.

Indeed, Wiebe's methodology is adapted from that of the more common village study, of which his own earlier work in Andhra Pradesh is an example. Yet, while the data point decisively away from a culture of poverty and to what the author tentatively calls "politics of scarcity," the book avoids the somewhat hackneyed position that Chennanagar is a literal urban village. Throughout we find detailed evidence that the community is deeply involved in *urban* and *modern* institutions. The culture of this slum community and the biographies of its members, many of whom are second- and third-generation Madrasis, are as thoroughly urban as any can be in contemporary India.

Information about attitudes, aspirations, community organization, and economic and social activity in Chennanagar argues significantly against Lewis's expectations. Instead, a highly organized network of secondary relations appears to permeate social life within the settlement and to orient members of the community to the city as a whole. Caste, patronage, the *Jajmani* system and the village *panchayat* have, for some time, served as extra-familial bases of affiliation for India's rural poor. Wiebe's study indicates that a recognizable functional alternative to each of these exists and plays an active part in the social life of Chennanagar. We find, rather than fatalism and antagonism toward society-at-large, a worldview that is mildly optimistic, continually resourceful in the face of scarcity, and receptive to the general values and goals of non-slum Madras. Rather than a deficient social maturation process, we find a clear understanding of the differences between child and adult roles, a common sense of responsibility on the part of parents for the well-being of their children, and careful ritual observance of puberty, marriage, and birth ceremonies (ritual that reflects the general adaptation of village ways to the urban milieu).

Patronage, in a multitude of forms, deeply affects social relations in rural India. In discussing the manner in which village patronage has been transformed in Chennanagar,

Wiebe has provided some very important (and, I believe, unique) information about Madras's highly effective political machine. Chennanagar's land—formerly a refuse dump—was "sold" to the residents and a neat grid of (unpaved) roads and some access to infrastructure were provided by the Dravidian Nationalist (DMK) Party (a party which, until the declaration of emergency in June, 1975, ruled the city *and* the state of Tamil Nadu with an "iron mandate"). In exchange for these services, the residents of this and other slums promised and (until the early 1970s at least) delivered their votes to the DMK on election day. This process, a highly integrative one, parallels that in US cities in many respects. Its existence and the participation of the poor in it constitute substantial evidence against a culture of poverty thesis. The implications of a widespread and well functioning pattern of urban party patronage in India's future are profound. One of the most disappointing aspects of *Social Life in an Indian Slum* is that its author did not choose to look more closely at Madras's political machine.

The book has weaknesses in other, related respects. Data are left in a relatively raw form where extended interpretation is necessary; Wiebe is perhaps overly-cautious in the face of enormous complexity. Controlled comparison with other Madras slum and non-slum communities is lacking, as is exact comparison with the author's own village studies. The book is also rather poorly edited.

But Paul Wiebe has a keen and sensitive understanding of South Indian Society. He is competent with an uncommonly wide range of research techniques and he can employ a variety of them in a single, problem-oriented research design. He has, in addition, a clear position on the issues surrounding culture of poverty type explanations of urban poverty. For these reasons, *Social Life in an Indian Slum,* Wiebe's first book, constitutes an important addition to the large, but often fragmentary, body of literature on contemporary India.

The book is as much about urban community, the third world, and social stratification as it is about India. It can be used as supplementary reading in various undergraduate and graduate courses in sociology and anthropology. Moreover, it contains useful data relevant to the test of hypotheses which have, heretofore, generated little more than speculation.

Urban

The Urban Predicament, edited by WILLIAM GORHAM and NATHAN GLAZER. Washington, D.C.: The Urban Institute, 1976. 364 pp. $10.00 cloth. $4.95 paper.

JOSEPH M. CONFORTI
SUNY/Old Westbury

"The urban crisis" came into vogue as a term during the 1950s, largely as a summation of the physical deterioration of American cities that served as the focus for urban renewal, the solution in which hope was then placed. As the promise of urban renewal faded, so did concern with the urban crisis, until rioting and rebellion set the cities ablaze in the late 1960s. It again faded in benign neglect, but has been resurrected once again as insolvency confronts American cities. As the co-editors of this volume state in their first sentence, "In 1975 the financial crisis in New York City brought the city back into public view."

From the vantage point of 1976 the editors are able, in the introduction, both to review the factors to which the urban crisis has been attributed over the past twenty-five years as well as the various programs instituted to combat them. The several programs, including forty years of housing acts, experiments in planning, metropolitan government proposals, anti-poverty and income maintenance programs, and revenue sharing, are all examined in the perspective of federal initiatives. That these programs have failed while spending billions of dollars in pursuit of these solutions, underlies the editors' conceptualization of the situation as a predicament.

They then go on to explore several dimensions of the predicament that, if not newly discovered, have become sufficiently exacerbated in recent years to take on new significance. These include the microscopic and macroscopic demographic and economic trends affecting the northeast and northcentral regions, in particular the continuing suburbanization of the white middle class and the westward and southward shift of population and economic activity. These two trends have combined to make the older cities vast ghettos for poor blacks, cities that keep losing ground trying to match declining revenue with increasing service demands and whose leaders have almost given up hope in the viability of rebuilding or redevelopment for the future. The editors view the recent economic recession as responsible for bringing the slow deterioration dramatically to public attention in terms of the fiscal insolvency threatening several cities.

While they do not offer any new explanations or resolutions, the editors are fairly certain that the cities no longer contain the resources their revitalization requires, that the various federal programs instituted over the past twenty-five years promise little more, and that only the federal government has the necessary resources. The glimmer of hope they express is that perhaps federal revenue sharing and the local initiative of emerging young black political leaders will combine unencumbered resources with first hand knowledge of how they might most effectively be deployed.

The five chapters that follow propose no solutions either. At most, they share as a theme the implicit explanation that the basic problem is a shortage of money. The several authors tend to focus on dimensions for which hard data are available, and have particularly striven to include 1975 or 1976 data.

In chapter 2, George E. Peterson delineates the financial crisis with unusual clarity, if dismal cynicism. The author stresses that federal assistance had blunted the full impact of the crisis, but that federal assistance has been diminishing since 1974, bringing the fiscal crisis to a head, particularly in New York City, where efforts to avoid confronting fiscal reality took the form of kiting loans and misrepresentation. The predicament is that any attempts by financially strapped cities to rectify the situation, such as through payroll taxes or a reduction in services, tend to contribute to a further erosion of the cities' viability.

Chapter 3 informs us that housing segregation has increased, in spite of anti-discrimination laws and more tolerant attitudes. As whites continue to move to the suburbs, black ghettos expand in their wake; blacks thus acquire better housing at lower cost (filtering) and in turn their former housing in the center of the ghetto is abandoned in the absence of any demand for it.

In chapter 4, James Q. Wilson and Barbara Boland explore many possible solutions to the crime problem, find them wanting, and conclude that removing offenders from the streets and keeping them imprisoned for long periods of time may be the only course of action available at this time.

Chapter 5, on education, is of greatest interest for the opportunity it affords the author, James Coleman, to explicate his much publicized disenchantment with busing. He documents in detail the increasing segregation between central cities and their suburbs as a concomitant to desegregation in the city, together with a lack of evidence that integration enhances academic achievement.

Chapter 6 is an elongated, if accurate, delineation of transportation issues by Michael A. Kemp and Melvyn D. Cheslow. Like most other exhaustive reviews of transportation issues, it arrives at the not so new conclusion that people want to drive cars on freeways at sixty miles an hour, in preference to any other mode of transportation.

As a book written by a committee, there is little integration of the chapters. It is most useful for the reader who wants current information on select dimensions of the urban crisis that is still very much with us. It is, finally, useful as a prolegomenon for the next decade of urban problems.

Disintegration and Political Action: The Changing Functions of City Governments in America, by ROLAND J. LIEBERT. New York: Academic Press, 1976. 223 pp. $12.00 cloth.

WARNER BLOOMBERG, JR.
San Diego State University

Specifically stipulated as an undertaking in "pure" research, Liebert's study brings concepts and propositions from interorganization theory to bear on municipal government, seeking to explain variations from one municipality to another in citizen participation, innovativeness, accountability, and fiscal performance. A recent addition to a variety of works under the heading of "Quantitative Studies in Social Relations," it should be very useful in seminars for advanced graduate students concerned with the potentialities and limitations of such efforts to obtain a secure statistical purchase on the complex and slippery realities of local political organization and process, as well as with the theoretical ideas which Liebert struggles commendably, though not always successfully, to test. Indeed, the latter seemed far more lucid and exciting to me than many of his exercises in counting inadequate indicators and trying to discern by sophisticated calculation what reality might lie behind the often vague shapes and outlines suggested by his computerized manipulations of "hard" data.

Central to the theoretical argument is the proposition that the greater the range of functions performed by a municipal government, the broader will be the range of interests and power groups involved in what goes on at city hall and what it accomplishes. The more extensive and intensive such involvement, the more resources will be mobilized, the more the citizenry will be involved in determining allocations and assessments of results, and the more dynamic will be the local political culture. There is a fruitful sense of history underlying this thesis. Older cities in the US have functional and cultural roots in the colonial and early post-colonial periods when the national government was both weak and distant and the states chartered municipal corporations to carry out much of the governance that local citizenry in urban communities actually experienced. Continuing urbanization, industrialization, and especially rapid advances in transportation and communications were conducive to state centralization and most recently to a substantial nationalization of policies and projects for localities. As a result, the theory argues, newer municipalities have fewer functions and thus (hypothetically) less mobilization of both citizenry and resources. We would expect them to be more concerned with bureaucratic efficiency than with participation and innovation. Indeed, age of city proves to be Liebert's most potent variable. "Scope" comes in a very poor second, in spite of the author's valiant statistical and rhetorical efforts to rescue that part of his thesis. Not only do "functionally limited" municipalities show unexpected behavior, at least as "measured" by Liebert's indicators, but so much of the variation in dependent variables remains unexplained in "successful" tests of most of his hypotheses that the uninvolved bystander must be forgiven for not fully sharing the author's admiration for his handiwork, even given a sample of 668 cities.

Except for that altogether normal bias, Liebert is painfully honest; and in encouraging those with appropriate interests to read and use this volume, I must with equal honesty warn that he shares the pain with the reader. "Prolix prose" describes his writing throughout. He tediously recounts the shortcomings of his measures and the unavoidable compromises that produced them. Each disappointing test is buried under pages of subsequent, post facto interpretation and speculation about where the truth may be hiding. He has painstakingly searched the literature—190 references—without finding it. Perhaps it is hiding somewhere between all those contrived quantities and the realistic but non-comparable case studies which once were in vogue. The cover jacket, appropriately, displays a stylized urban skyline which looks as if it had been cut out of punched IBM cards.

La politique urbaine dans la region lyonnaise, 1945–1972, by JEAN LOJKINE. Paris: Mouton & Company, 1974. 294 pp. No price listed, cloth.

EDITH KURZWEIL
Montclair State College

Jean Lojkine—university professor and senior researcher at the Centre Nationale de Recherches Scientifiques—is not only a skilled demographer and systems theorist, but manages to combine his technical and sociological expertise with a historical and class analysis. His sixty-five detailed maps and tables indicate, for example, economic, administrative, and political breakdown of territories, financial resources, investments, and actual expenses by local, regional, and state agencies, for every year of this study; they show the increase in highways, tunnels, airports, subways, commercial and residential buildings; they describe the impact of the four new towns in the regional territory created in 1966, the changes in salaries and in voting patterns; and patterns of migration, of consumption and of political influence by communists, socialists, and the "reactionary center"—whose composition itself changed—supplys us with an extraordinarily detailed and comprehensive picture of the ramifications of industrialization around France's second-largest city.

But Lojkine's empirical data also confirm his hypotheses that "local power" is a myth, and that the recent class alliance between monopoly capital and the salaried middle class against the old urban middle class of small industrialists, artisans, and merchants (now located in the more rural communities of the new "region") grew out of traditional values and beliefs. Thus, in Lyon at least, people vote against their class interest, because they unite against anarchic urban development, the destruction of fertile land, the pollution of vineyards and fields, and against housing projects, poor transportation, the arrival of promoters, speculators in land, etc. In other words, discontent with the very modernization they had approved when government funds were to stimulate business and to create jobs, is expressed in votes. Hence, traditional values—Peter Berger's forces of demodernization—even upset the current coalition between communists and socialists, since in recent years the socialists (primarily reformist) have voted with the radicals (left of the communists and mostly anti-Moscow) and the parties of the right, while the communists, of course, represent the industrial working class.

In such a short review it is impossible even to touch on the many insights the author provides, on his analyses of the complex politics, without becoming reductive. But this study could provide an excellent model for sociologists interested in urbanization. For it is an application of demographic analysis to the understanding of the relationships between local and national politics, between voters and politicians, between modernization and mobility, multinational corporations and policy, that examines class in relation to government policy.

Work/Occupations

New York Cops Talk Back: A Study of a Beleaguered Minority, by NICHOLAS ALEX. New York: John Wiley & Sons, 1976. 225 pp. $12.50 cloth. $5.95 paper.

MICHAEL WILLIAMS
University of Maine, Portland-Gorham

New York Cops is "about the crisis experienced by the police." Toward this end, "the disintegration under pressure of police methods, prerogatives, autonomy, standards, and codes are described and analyzed."

Alex's effort is, at once disappointing and exciting. It is disappointing because the weakness of his methodology taints the sometimes insightful, sometimes controversial, but always interesting conclusions.

The data would be much more credible if Alex had employed participant observation techniques as well as conducting one to three hour interviews of his forty-two police officer informants.

Chapter titles such as "Motives for Choosing Policework," "The White Policeman as Victim of His Occupational World," "The Division Between White and Black Policemen," and "The Police Counter Attack" imply that the reader will learn something about patterns of police behavior in New York. The question remains: does the data presented allow the reader to draw any conclusions about police behavior?

Despite a negative reaction to the methodology I feel compelled to stress the positive. The positive is that reading *New York Cops* made me reflect on issues which I had considered resolved. More importantly, *New York Cops* suggests the importance of verbalizations for the sustaining of patterns of social action. For example, Alex suggests that the police engage in a "counter-attack" against the public and politicians who (the police perceive) frequently demand protection from the ravages of criminals yet simultaneously place inordinately restrictive procedural limitations on the police.

The police argue that these limitations necessitate the violation of procedural law in order to enforce the substantive law. Because the police lump criticisms of their transgressions of the law into one class of violations, i.e., violations of procedural law, they avoid dealing with the problem of violation of substantive law which the Knapp Commission has indicated is endemic to New York Police. Through this "neutralization process" the police are, at least temporarily, able to resist demands for change.

One can, in fact, view the entire set of interview responses as rhetorical attempts by New York police officers to sustain their traditional perspectives and methods in the face of a rapidly changing environment. If one is interested in the forms and functions of verbalizations as related to social action in general and criminal behavior in particular then *New York Cops* will provide interesting reading.

Forces of Order: Police Behavior in Japan and the United States, by DAVID H. BAYLEY. Berkeley: University of California Press. 1976. 217 pp. $10.95 cloth.

JEROME H. SKOLNICK
University of California, Berkeley

Japan is "heaven for a cop": that is the theme of this well-written, craftsmanlike and insightful study of Japanese patrolmen. The study was conducted as an unusual form of participant-observation. David Bayley, a political scientist, employed a translator while the two of them—like Don Quixote and Sancho Panza—rode in patrol cars, hung around a *koban*, a uniquely Japanese neighborhood police house, or interviewed the superior officers of the patrolmen. The result is a fascinating and important book.

A policeman's lot, Bayley argues, ultimately depends upon the social and cultural conditions of the society being policed. That generalization, baldly stated, is scarcely earth-shaking or novel; when fleshed out to provide comparison with the police in the United States, it comes alive. Some highlights: the Japanese population is remarkably homogeneous and its police are neighborhood oriented. They are deployed primarily in fixed posts, rather than in patrol cars. Twice a year uniformed patrolmen survey the neighborhood and ask questions about the people living there. "To the Japanese," writes Bayley, "the residential survey is as natural as rain."

In the United States, contempt of cop is a serious street crime, frequently committed. Urban court records are littered with charges of resisting arrest and assaulting an officer, the escalated results of undeferential conduct. By contrast, when cited by police, Japanese are polite and respectful. The police are paternalistic. A citizen can be required to write a letter of apology instead of paying a fine. The act of contrition is meted out on the spot, in the *koban*. The police are not the enemy; they are moral authorities. Moreover, the Japanese citizenry are not permitted weapons, the tradition of a disarmed society going back almost 400 years. The police carry guns, but rarely use them. Instead, they work at staying in physical condition and are experts in martial arts. In those instances where force is required, deadly force is avoided. On the whole the police rely on moral force rather than firepower and technology to accomplish their goals.

American police seek compliance with law; Japanese police seek acceptance of the community's moral values. It would be impossible to transfer the Japanese system to the United States point-for-point. We are a pluralistic and morally fragmented society. Moral values are a point of contention, as apt to tear us apart as bring us together. A society as heterogeneous and conflictful as ours cannot be heaven for a cop. Nevertheless, this book convinces us that we have much to learn about the possibilities of law and discretionary enforcement from the Japanese system, even if only our differences. It is commended to every serious student of the police.

Women and the Workplace: The Implications of Occupational Segregation, edited by MARTHA BLAXALL and BARBARA REAGAN. Chicago: University of Chicago Press, 1976. 326 pp. $12.50 cloth. $3.95 paper.

VIRGINIA OLESEN
University of California, San Francisco

This book is a collection of papers presented at a conference on women in the workplace at the Center for Research on Women in Higher Education and the Professions at Wellsley College, May, 1975. The papers were first published as the Spring, 1976 issue of *Signs* and now appear as a book. This transformation serves the admirable goal of disseminating conference papers, and rather quickly, too. It must be noted, however, that little cutting has been done; hence some of the book is more fulsome than necessary. The index is regrettably skimpy, a crucial shortcoming in a volume where there are so many diverse contributions.

The volume builds on substantial documentation from Reagan and Blaxall and Griffiths on occupational segregation; presents four institutional analyses of this problem (Lipman-Blumen, Laws, Safilios-Rothschild, Gates); offers four interpretations of historical roots (Bernard, Boulding, Lapidus, Hartman); introduces the reader to economic dimensions in a section which is very useful for readers not acquainted with economic theory (Blau and Jusenius, Sawhill, Ferber and Lowry); concludes with policy analyses and a summary statement. Throughout there are comments, some of which (Tangri, K. Boulding, Gordon) contain ideas as provocative as those in the papers.

Because social institutions and circumstances change even as materials such as these are aborning, the most useful contributions of these papers are in conceptualizations which open fresh perspectives on the moment at hand and the circumstances to come. (Subsequent to this conference the controversial Bakke decision regarding affirmative action and higher education in California was announced; the Supreme Court review and decision on that matter may well alter the configuration of problems discussed in this volume.)

Some of these perspectives are Lipman-Blumen's "Homosocial Theory of Sex Roles," which, taken to the extreme, explains segregation but invokes a "caste" system of sex roles; Laws's methodological caveat that "the fundamental validity of linear-prediction models based on current statistical methodology is questionable" (p. 40) in understanding women's motivations for work and her useful reminder of Leona Tyler's mandate that, "Instead of trying to trace continuous variables, we must analyze successive states of organization" (p. 40); Kenneth Boulding's invocation of a new science of dimorphics.

In spite of these and other conceptualizations, there are no bold challenges to taken-for-granted assumptions or conceptualizations in the social science repertoire as applied to these or other women's issues, such as, for example, the journal *Catalyst* (Trent University Sociology Department, Peterboro, Ontario) is undertaking early in 1977 wherein "patriarchy," "universal oppression," and "equality," among other concepts, will be critically analyzed. Moreover, only one issue (Lapidus) deals with cross-cultural matters, hence the collection is short on the anthropological perspectives, though Lapidus's essay is in political science. Finally, only two (Blau and Jusenius, Ferber and Lowry) concern poverty, race, *and* sexual occupational segregation.

These disclaimers notwithstanding, the collection is useful as text or resource, and, in addition, valuable in that it comprehends a multidisciplinary perspective, including policy recommendations, something all too often neglected in such volumes.

Woman-Work: Women and the Party in Revolutionary China, by Delia Davin. New York: Oxford University Press, 1976. 244 pp. $10.95 cloth.

May N. Diaz
University of California, Santa Cruz

This is an excellent book, in which the author explores the changing status of women in China from the early days of the Jiangxi Soviet before the Revolution to the 1960s. The "woman-work" of the title, though awkward in English, is a direct translation of a term in Chinese that unites in one single category women's labor, campaigns directed toward changing women's roles, and women's participation in community affairs. The content of the book is therefore broader than the title might suggest. Davin gives us an understanding of both why and how the position of women has changed.

The book is a solid, scholarly work, drawing on a wide variety of sources: official Chinese publications, Party statements, writings by public figures, published life histories and interviews, the works of foreign scholars both on traditional culture and contemporary life, and the author's own experiences as a resident of Peking for two years.

As she examines the history of the women's movement, the efforts to revolutionize marriage and the family, and the position of women in town and country, Davin traces the interplay of economy, administrative action, and daily life. It is a pleasure to read a book which takes Marxist theoretical structure seriously and applies it to examine social action informed by that theory. I found chapters 4 and 5 particularly illuminating. They gave me a direct look at some aspects of women's experience. They also analyze the differing impact of the rise in unemployment of the 1950s, accompanied by a temporary re-emphasis on the "feminine mystique," on women workers and intellectuals in the cities, and women in the countryside.

The conclusion one comes to is that when faced by the pragmatic considerations of the economy, decision-makers temporarily sacrificed women's liberation. Or perhaps they modified their views of the dynamics of the historical process, for previously (and subsequently) they emphasize, as did Engels, the direct relationship between women's roles in commodity production and their liberation.

Considering women's role in production as well as their community and political work, Davin concludes that equality is still far from complete. However, she believes that "inequality and discrimination will not become rigidly institutionalized so long as a critical consciousness of them exists."

Women's Work in Soviet Russia: Continuity in the Midst of Change, by MICHAEL PAUL SACKS. New York: Praeger Publishers, 1976. 221 pp. $17.50 cloth.

MARILYN POWER GOLDBERG
University of California, Berkeley

This book is an ambitious venture: an evaluation of the role and status of women in the Soviet Union through their work, both in the workplace and in the home. Sacks is attempting to determine whether the high labor force participation of Russian women indicates a change in ideology from the pre-Soviet period, or whether it reflects merely a reaction of pre-industrial ideology to a new situation (a juxtaposition which is weak because it is over simplified and non-dialectical).

Sacks is to be commended for understanding the need to look at all aspects of women's work experience, both their paid and their unpaid work (something academics have often failed to do in the past). However, neither his facts nor his conclusions are altogether new (although some of his statistics are quite recent), therefore this book should be seen largely as a survey, a compilation of previously existing information.

Sacks concludes that Soviet women's experience does not reflect a commitment to equality, but rather a response of old values to a new situation: women had contributed to the economic survival of the pre-industrial family through home production; with industrialization, they merely moved the center of their economic activity to the factory. What change in values has occurred has been recent, due to rising prosperity and a decrease in the shortage of adult males. This change has been in the direction of an increased emphasis on the domestic role of women, and has been reflected in such factors as a growing emphasis on women staying home to take care of their own children.

Sacks's book is taken from his doctoral dissertation, and it reads like a thesis, dry and impersonal, and also at points almost written in code, assuming an audience familiar with the issues and writers he cites. At the same time, because his topic is so broad, the book is essentially a survey, lacking depth on specific points. For example, Sacks spends a little over three pages on the quality of housing and availability of household appliances. There is a problem of audience for this book; it seems appropriate for neither undergraduate nor graduate teaching, although it would be a useful reference work.

Additional Reviews

Public and Private Self in Japan and the United States, by DEAN C. BARNLUND. Tokyo, Japan: The Simul Press, 1975. 201 pp. $12.00 paper.

MINAKO K. MAYKOVICH
California State University, Sacramento

To compare the communicative styles of two cultures, those of Japan and the United States, is the central purpose of this book. The effort is commendable because so many books on national characteristics in the past have been either (1) speculative without empirical validation, or (2) too narrowly focused on specific hypotheses testing without a systematic theoretical framework.

Barnlund develops the notion of a "public self" (the portion of the self known to others) and a "private self" (the portion of the personality known to the self) in exploring cultural differences. These concepts sound profound as basic components of complex psychological, philosophical, and/or sociological theories; however, the model is quite simplistic. The author assumes that the minimal exposure of the self is the unconscious motive of the Japanese and hypothesizes interpersonal behavior patterns accordingly. Motives are given without any raison d'etre, and cause-effect relations are uncertain. Whether or not motive manifests itself in behaviors, exactly which behaviors have led the author to speculate on motive is not clarified. Methodologically, deductive or inductive approaches are sound so long as they are not confused in the logical presentation of the issue.

The instruments used yield quantification and standardized comparison of two cultural styles. However, verbal disclosure of the private self to a stranger out of social context is not the same as non-verbal, non-tactile telepathic revelation of the private self to a fellow Japanese. Psychoanalytic methods, such as TAT, Rorschach, or a depth interview, might have been more suitable for delving into the private self than precoded questionnaires dealing with generalized, hypothetical interaction situations.

The relative infrequency of talking or physical gestures, as found in his research, does not preclude communication of the inner self. There are other factors, such as ethnic homogeneity, group integration, emphasis on harmony, and the structure of language, which facilitate communication of the private self. The author recognizes this fact but does not incorporate it into his research. Otherwise, how could he have postulated that the Japanese inner self is "not known to others"?

In style the author seeks a compromise between a collection of speculations and a detailed summary of research data. For a specific audience, possibly defined by the publishing company (i.e., general public with interest in intercultural relations), the book is in a good readable form with a flash of scholarship; for readers of *Contemporary Sociology,* the book may be unsatisfactory. These readers will be faced with lengthy elementary discussions of culture and society instead of an ingenious theoretical scheme, and with simple research designs likely to be found in MA theses.

Be that as it may, the book is one of few in the field which attempts to bridge the gap between the specialists and the generalists.

The Forty-Nine Percent Majority: The Male Sex Role, edited by DEBORAH S. DAVID and ROBERT BRANNON. Reading, Mass.: Addison-Wesley, 1976. 338 pp. $5.95 paper.

JANE H. SCHEFF and THOMAS J. SCHEFF
University of California, Santa Barbara

This collection of thirty-six articles begins with a lengthy introduction which presents the editors' model of the male sex role. Their model has four components: anti-femininity ("No Sissy Stuff"), competition for status, The Sturdy Oak ("A Manly Air of Toughness, Confidence, and Self-Reliance") and, finally, the emphasis on violence and aggression. Much of the book is devoted to articles which illustrate each of these components. The book ends with two short sections, one on socialization, the other on changing the male role.

Most of the selections are quite familiar. Many of the articles are taken from recent books on males and the male role: three by James Farrell, two each by Marc Fasteau and by Michael Korda, and one each by Jack Sawyer and by Joseph Pleck. However, there is also a new article on homophobia, published here for the first time, which carefully explores some of the ways which prejudice against homosexuals helps to maintain the traditional male role for heterosexual men.

This book should be extremely useful for a course in the sociology of sex roles. The introduction is well written. It takes the concept of social role seriously, providing a simple but serviceable definition which the reader can use to integrate much of the material found in the articles. The articles themselves are of varying quality. Several are standard scholarly treatments, such as Short and Strodbeck on why gangs fight, and Hartley on socialization of the male child. Of interest in academics will be the article on academic gamesmanship by van den Berghe, and the elegant analysis of competition among scientists by Reif, both of which well illustrate the role component of competition for status. Some of the articles, on the other hand, are little more than personal impressions. This variability is not the fault of the editors, but a shortcoming of social science, as they point out. In the absence of a body of scholarly work, they have had to extract relevant materials wherever they could find them. In the process, they have done well, virtually defining a new and vitally important area of study. We hope that this book will serve not only as a teaching resource but a signpost, pointing to new areas of research in psychology and social science.

The Discovery of the Conservation of Energy, by YEHUDA ELKANA. Cambridge, Mass.: Harvard University Press, 1974. 213 pp. $8.50 cloth.

The American Energy Consumer, by DOROTHY K. NEWMAN and DAWN DAY. Cambridge, Mass.: Ballinger Publishing Company, 1975. 308 pp. $15.00 cloth. $5.95 paper.

ROBERT CAMERON MITCHELL
Pennsylvania State University

A major scientific achievement of the nineteenth century was the realization that energy is subject to a conservation law. From this has developed the modern expression of the laws of thermodynamics. The two books under review, one a study in the history of science and the other a survey of American consumers' direct household energy use, are strikingly dissimilar in their purpose, methodology, and intellectual style. Nevertheless, they both focus on these laws and both use the word "conservation," albeit in different senses. Elkana describes the circumstances which led to the precise formulation of the first law of thermodynamics—the law of the conservation of energy (that energy in a closed system is constant, irrespective of changes of form). Newman and Day, however, deal with conservation in the popular sense of "preserving from loss" and in their proposals for public policy ignore the inexorable reality of the second law of thermodynamics (that any system plus its surroundings tends spontaneously toward increasing entropy).

Elkana's monograph focuses on the achievement of Herman von Helmholtz who, in 1847, first made the general mathematical demonstration of the conservation of energy. To answer the question, why von Helmholtz?, Elkana considers three interacting factors which, he argues, affect the growth of knowledge: the scientific metaphysics, the social image of science, and the social and political context of the era. His sophisticated, wide ranging analysis of these factors is outstanding, especially his extended consideration of the inherent assumptions about the nature of the world (scientific metaphysics) which characterized the prevailing scientific schools of thought. Much of this analysis consists of a painstaking exegesis of the pre-1847 use of such words as Kraft, force, and energie and demonstrates the rich conceptual confusion existent at the time. Helmholtz fully shared in this confusion which was only resolved *after* 1847 as the full implications of his demonstration, that the basic entity which is being conserved in nature must be equivalent in dimension and form to mechanical energy, became understood.

Elkana's book could have benefited from greater editorial attention. At times it is unnecessarily difficult to follow its argument. This is regrettable because not only is it an important case study, but it also exemplifies an approach to the study of the growth of knowledge which attempts to overcome the so-called internalist-externalist controversy.

The *American Energy Consumer* is one of a series of special studies commissioned by the Ford Foundation Energy Project. The Project's controversial 1974 final report, *A Time to Choose,* synthesized the results of the various special studies and the studies themselves have been published subsequently as monographs.

Although American households consume about one third of the nation's energy in their homes and cars, there have been relatively few studies of this phenomenon and none of this magnitude. Based on interviews with a national sample of 1,455 households in May 1973 and a second survey of actual utility data for the sample households, the monograph describes the patterns of direct, primary energy use. The major results are presented in two chapters which treat energy use in the home and on the road, and in two chapters which look at energy use and cost by socio-economic status and race. Another chapter, based on data from metropolitan Washington, D.C., discusses the experience of air pollution (a side-effect of energy use) by socio-economic group and race.

Among the study's conclusions are the following (holding various factors constant, including climate): the more money you have, the more energy you use at home and in your automobile; paradoxically, the more money you have the more likely you are to have equipment (such as insulation) that saves energy; the more money you have the less you pay per unit for electricity and natural gas (because the more you buy, the less you pay). The chapter on black households' energy use shows that blacks use less electricity and natural gas per household than others, spend less money for it, but pay more per unit (even holding incomes constant). Using census tract data and map overlays, the air pollution chapter concludes that disadvantaged people are disproportionately subjected to air pollution. Since energy use is inversely related to income this makes them the victims of middle and upper class pollution.

In general, the study is a competent benchmark for future studies of household energy use. Despite its many recommendations for policies to conserve household energy use, its usefulness in this regard is limited for three reasons. The first reason, which the study emphasizes, is that consumers have relatively little choice about what type of house they live in and what mode of transportation they use. The second is that the policy recommendations tend to be ad hoc lists and lack calculations of the magnitude of energy savings they would produce. Finally, while the study recognizes the effect of the second law of thermodynamics by calculating electric energy use in terms of the energy expended in making and transmitting the electricity (two thirds is lost before it reaches the consumer), its policy recommendations ignore the energy waste involved in the growing trend towards electric space and water heating in new single-family homes.

The Social Structure of Eastern Europe: Transition and Process in Czechoslovakia, Hungary, Poland, Romania, and Yugoslavia, edited by BERNARD LEWIS FABER. New York: Praeger Publishers, 1976. 423 pp. $25.00 cloth.

ZOLTÁN TAR
City College/CUNY

Before World War II, Eastern Europe was a unique mosaic of social structures at different levels of economic and social development ranging from underdeveloped Romania to modern-industrial Czechoslovakia. Even within a country, the contrast could be striking. In Hungary, for example, a backward, semi-feudal, rural social structure contrasted with the high level intellectual, artistic, and scientific achievements of the Budapest intelligentsia.

By 1945, the process of political and economic Gleichschaltung was set in motion, aiming at uniformity and leveling. After three eventful decades the balance sheet can be drawn. *The Social Structure of Eastern Europe* is a serious, scholarly attempt to assess the process of modernization in five Eastern European countries. Of the articles selected—all related to "the system of social stratification as a critical factor in the process of societal transformation"—only three are theoretical. It is interesting to note that thirteen empirical studies deal with Hungary, Poland, Romania, and Yugoslavia—and only one with the most advanced industrialized country of the area, Czechoslovakia.

First, stratification and social mobility are discussed. One theoretical article deals with the problems of strata and class in socialist societies. The other empirical articles deal with stratification in Yugoslavia and with social mobility in Hungary and in Poland. Strata rather than class is the more useful conceptual-analytical tool, we are told. Instead of ownership, deliberate political (governmental) decision-making has become the major mechanism for stratification and restratification. A "new class" (Djilas) with rights over poverty has appeared all over Eastern Europe. The editor claims that members of the new class lack the power to transmit inheritance to such rights—a naive assertion that the late Isaac Deutscher made about the Soviet "new class." It becomes questionable in light of the fact that education is the main avenue for social mobility and that there is a differential access to higher education. It is further damaged by the startling conclusion reached by the Hungarian sociologist, R. Andorka, who states that "the chances of a son of a skilled, semi-skilled and unskilled worker to enter the group of intellectuals and executives (professionals, managers) are higher in the United States and lower in England than in Hungary" (p. 67).

Under the heading "Social Groups and the Polity," conformity and dissent of the intelligentsia in Czechoslovakia and Poland are discussed. One article assesses the situation of minorities (Hungarians, Jews, Germans, and gypsies) in Romania. Although minorities benefitted somewhat from urbanization and modernization, basic inequalities persist: Hungarians and Germans are underrepresented in higher education, assimiliation is forced, and the gypsies are almost completely excluded from the benefits of modernization. The section on rural and urban life includes studies on the non-collectivized Polish peasant way of life and on the life of a collectivized Romanian village, including family change. The "peasant-worker" of Yugoslavia, a social type unique to Eastern Europe and the result of underurbanization in Hungary, is analyzed in some detail. Furthermore, the process of urbanization in Belgrade is described.

Finally, studies on the economy and industrial work are presented. There is a very informative essay on the role of the Party and industrial sociologists in factories in several countries of the area. One article assesses the relationship between stepped-up economic activity of women and fertility in Hungary. Workers' self-management as concomitant to industrial decentralization in Yugoslavia is discussed in the last article.

In sum, one basic conclusion stands out: that in spite of leveling efforts, national traditions and inequalities have reasserted themselves in every sphere of social life. The volume, an invaluable reader, pulls together seventeen articles scattered throughout a dozen professional journals. The editor succeeded in both of his announced aims: the contributions are all of high calibre and they demonstrate the nature and thrust of sociological research in Eastern Europe. This collection should be useful for professors and students alike. The lack of an index, however, in a book priced at $25.00 is an unforgivable omission.

"Physics circa 1900: Personnel, Funding, and Productivity of the Academic Establishment," by PAUL FORMAN, JOHN HEILBRON, and SPENCER WEART, (Volume 5 of *Historical Studies in the Physical Sciences*. Russell McCormmach, editor). Princeton University Press, 1975. 138 pp.

DAVID A. WOODROW
SUNY/Stony Brook

Reviewing a volume of an annual publication may seem, at first, an unusual undertaking. However, as is apparent from the title, the volume contains only one piece. In a very real sense it seems appropriate to treat this publication as one would treat any monograph or book.

The bulk of the commentary in this piece is devoted to explaining the composition of tables which report information on the worldwide investment in academic physics in 1900 and its rate of change in the following decade. Data have been culled from a wide range of sources to show the number of academic posts, the number of students and degrees granted, personal income, laboratory expenditures, and some indication of scientific productivity. In fact, the extraordinarily diverse scope of sources makes this study a worthwhile example of scholarly perserverance and ingenuity. The sources extend from official publications of yearbooks to personal accounts to national archives.

The data were gathered for a dozen European nations, but the major focus is on the Big Four; France, Germany, the United States, and the United Kingdom. Throughout the narrative the authors point out special cases where they have had to estimate, and what kinds of errors these estimations might incur. Because of the inclusion of only certain academic posts, chairs in mathematics, electrotechnology, astrophysics, and other specialties are omitted. The consequence is that individuals in these positions who made contributions to basic physics are left out. It seems obvious that the occupant of Technical Expert, Third Class at the Swiss Patent Office would also be excluded.

In other places, the authors bring to light logistic problems including estimations, multiplication by constants, and comparisons of the levels of different national hierarchies. Monies have been standardized to the German Mark of 1900 and used throughout the time period without taking into account fluctuations.

The authors made no attempt to test hypotheses systematically or even to supply ad hoc explanatory schemes. But they have succeeded in producing a rich data base which has a variety of uses in conjunction with other data. However, while the data base holds great promise, it will take much work and a large amount of additional material to reach any meaningful sociological conclusions. While this study is of primary interest to sociologists of science, those interested in comparative national studies and the examination of institutional life certainly may find it useful.

A study which could use the data supplied might take many forms. Sociologists interested in the growth of higher education might use these data and some supplements to arrive at an idea of national differences in terms of the money spent for science, the amount spent on classical curriculum (a very pertinent comparison in the reforms of American higher education at this time), and the amounts spent on administration. Using a thesis of change in industrializing countries, the institution of education could be used as an example of major structural re-arrangements.

In general, this research monograph sets the stage for a more productive working relationship among investigators of science as an institution. It helps to clarify some of the problems in the historiography of the area and presents an excellent opportunity for historians and sociologists to collaborate on an area of mutual interest and challenge.

Are Government Organizations Immortal?, by HERBERT KAUFMAN. Washington, D.C.: Brookings Institution, 1976. 79 pp. $2.50 paper.

MARSHALL W. MEYER
University of California, Riverside

Yes, maybe. Herbert Kaufman's pilot investigation of ten of the eleven executive departments existing in 1973 and the Executive Office of the President suggests that the mortality of government agencies is relatively low and their birth rate high compared to the private sector. Altogether, some 421 departmental headquarters units and sub-units of departments—bureaus and groups of bureaus—were considered by Kaufman. Of 175 agencies in existence in 1923, 148 survived. There were 27 deaths and 246 births during the fifty-year interval. The mortality rate of government organizations, Kaufman surmises, is about half that of businesses, and their rate of formation has increased exponentially.

Some subsidiary results of Kaufman's analysis are equally intriguing. Staff organizations proliferated more rapidly than line units. From 1923 to 1973, the proportion of line units dropped from 64% to 58%, and the proportion of staff grew from 28% to 38%. (The remaining organizations were of mixed character.) This shift occurred largely because a substantial number of new units, 42%, were staff. Births and deaths occurred in spurts rather than steadily and were often haphazard. Organizations created by statute were not much more durable than those created by executive orders.

Despite these findings, any conclusions drawn from Kaufman's work must be viewed skeptically for two reasons. First of all, as Kaufman notes, his sample did not include agencies which were born and died between 1923 and 1973. Their number is probably small, but some effort to identify them should have been made. Second, the comparison of government with business mortality may have been misleading. Most business failures are *small* business failures, and I believe that the government organizations studied by Herbert Kaufman were somewhat larger than small businesses.

In sum, we have an interesting little book that would have been a good journal article had the author tried harder to make his data on business and government organizations more comparable. *Are Government Organizations Immortal?* is a first step, but only a first step, toward answering the question.

Sociology in Medicine, by R. KENNETH JONES and PATRICIA A. JONES. New York: Halsted Press, 1976. 222 pp. $9.95 cloth.

THOMAS J. SULLIVAN
Northern Michigan University

For sociologists involved in teaching health care practitioners, the search for books that adequately elaborate sociological concepts and perspectives in a manner that is useful and interesting to practitioners is never-ending and too often futile. This text by Jones and Jones, written primarily for nurses, will probably be of limited utility in filling this need. Their work is an introduction to sociology with an emphasis on the medical field. (It is not as the title might imply, a text in medical sociology). The authors cover the major concepts and topics that are normally found in an introductory text. Roughly half of the fourteen chapters are primarily concerned with presenting sociological material (in some chapters there is only brief mention of the health field). The remaining chapters are more directly concerned with the contribution of sociology to medicine.

In a work such as this—which is intended to introduce, rather than be comprehensive—any author is confronted with the problem of selecting those aspects of the field which would be most useful to the intended audience. Jones and Jones have chosen topics that effectively sensitize novices to the contributions that sociology can make to the health field. For example, among the areas given extensive treatment are: social factors contributing to illness and illness behavior, mental illness (discussed within the context of deviant behavior), hospitals as bureaucratic organizations, and health care professions as interest groups. There are many other traditional areas touched on, but the main thrust of the book is to introduce nurses to the social forces that shape both their own and their patients' behavior and to aid them in understanding the commonly stereotyped forms of human behavior (such as alcoholism, sexual deviation, etc.) that they will encounter as practitioners.

Despite a commendable effort, there are some problems with this text that will limit its usefulness—especially to those teaching health care practitioners in the United States. The primary resource material and the majority of examples are drawn from the British health care system. For example, they discuss English health agencies, professional organizations, and the National Health Service. Although some problems in the health field are cross-national and one can certainly learn from the experiences of other countries, this is still a severe limitation since the many financing problems, professional conflicts and innovations, and so on, that are relevant to practitioners in the United States are simply not analyzed. Another characteristic that some will find troublesome is that Jones and Jones do not use any particular sociological perspective in their analysis. The text heavily emphasizes concepts with little attempt at any theoretical linkage between them. The final chapter entitled "Some Well-Known Sociologists and Their Theories" contains a listing of eleven schools in sociology along with a brief (i.e., one to five-sentence) description of each. However, these descriptions are not adequate to train the student in the use of any theoretical approach to analyze problems.

While the book is generally an adequate presentation of sociological material, there are areas where the pedagogy suffers—seemingly for the sake of brevity. Some concepts (such as reference groups, or exact vs. descriptive science) are introduced with little or no definition, discussion, or examples. In other areas, opportunities to link theoretical materials with current developments are passed over. For example, while discussing the stratification theories of Marx and Weber, the authors miss the opportunity to use these theories to analyze the position of various professional groups in the health field. They also present occupational ranking scales in various countries—but with no mention of the position of nurses who are the primary audience of the book. Finally, in discussing the health professions, there is no discussion of developing health roles (such as nurse practitioners and physician's assistants), and little consideration of the changes in the status and power of the various professions.

In summary, if the limitations of the book are not a hindrance, it might be useful for nursing students who have had no other exposure to sociology. However, students who have had an introductory course in sociology will not benefit a great deal from this book.

The Nature of Human Aggression, by ASHLEY MONTAGU. New York: Oxford University Press, 1976. 381 pp. $9.95 cloth.
Society against Nature: The Emergence of Human Societies, by SERGE MOSCOVICI. Atlantic Highlands, N.J.: Humanities Press, 1976. 158 pp. $16.25 cloth.

RICHARD MCCLINTOCK
University of California, San Diego

Anthropologist Ashley Montagu endeavors, as he states in the first sentence of the first chapter, "to refute the conclusions . . . presented to an enormous public in recent years by a group of popular writers who state that human beings are inescapably killers. . . ." Montagu especially attacks Konrad Lorenz's *On Aggression,* and also attacks writings by Ardrey, Tinbergen, Morris, Dart, Storr, and certain other writers.

Montagu is grossly unfair to Lorenz and the others. In contrast to Montagu's assertions about the contents of *On Aggression,* Lorenz states in the book that although people have a drive that can motivate violence, this same drive can motivate peaceful achievements in art, science, and medicine. He further states that violence can be eliminated through love, humor, and other means. In the last paragraph of the book he states, "The obvious conclusion is that love and friendship should embrace all humanity. . . ." He does state, pessimistically, that humanity has been powerless to avoid violence, but he also states that "this powerlessness is entirely the consequence of the lack of human insight into the causation of human behavior." He contends that people who, like Montagu, reject ethological knowledge are contributing to the continuation of this deadly lack of insight.

Blurbs on the covers of some copies of *On Aggression* do mention a "killer instinct," but these blurbs are meant to attract attention and sell books; *On Aggression,* like *The Nature of Human Aggression,* is popularized to sell to an educated general audience. Inside the book, Lorenz states that people *do* have free will, and he does *not* try to show that people's instincts cause them to be unable to control their own destinies. Montague is correct that Lorenz uses the words *instinct* and *innate* in his discussions of aggression, but he does not define these words the way that Montague does. On page 257 Montagu rebukes Ardrey for describing innate patterns that incorporate learning, which, Montagu asserts, "is wholly opposed to the customarily accepted definition of an instinct as a fixed action pattern which causes the organism to react to a given stimulus with a predetermined behavior." Although in Lorenz's earlier writings he casually refers to learning and instinct as though they were mutually exclusive, in more recent writings he explains that learning is not the opposite of instinct, but instead *is* instinctive and innate, because (here we will see that his definition is vastly different from Montagu's definition) learning does not have an astronomically low probability of allowing DNA to continue replicating through geological time.

Not only does Montagu misrepresent Lorenz's opinions on issues that Montagu considers to be paradigmatically important, but he also misrepresents Lorenz's entire paradigm. In stark contrast to the naive conceptions that Montagu attributes to the paradigm, Lorenz contends that his theories center on adaptation and natural selection, which he justifiably views as central to biology as a whole. Like Comte, Lorenz incorporates into his theories the conception of the hierarchy of the sciences, but he recognizes also that if biological negative entropy is not explained, then either the conception of the hierarchy of the sciences or the second law of thermodynamics must be rejected. He explains biological negative entropy in terms of adaptation resulting from natural selection.

The lack of understanding is not one-sided, however; Montagu is misunderstood by Lorenz and other ethologists. Montagu is not just an impractical dreamer whose idyllic fantasies blind him to reality and prevent him from taking action to solve the problem of violence. He *is* taking action by endeavoring to demonstrate that human beings are not inalterably violent. He takes action with respect to the self-fulfilling prophecy and tries to prevent violence from being justified by the belief that it is natural.

In contrast to Montagu's and Lorenz's attacks against each other's paradigms, diverse paradigms are combined in *Society against Nature*. Moscovici is especially concerned with combining perspectives of human society as part of nature and as different from nature. In this English translation of his French, he does not present empirical research conducted by himself, but instead describes his interpretations of literature that is mainly anthropological, including cultural anthropology and anthropological primatology. He concludes that hunting with tools has been crucial for the development of human society. I think that the book is seriously flawed by many misconceptions involving incongruous combinations of biology and the view that humanity is above nature. For example, in the introduction he states that humanity departed from nature when "a virtually stabilized organism" underwent a "sudden, all-or-nothing cortical transformation (comparable to the quantum jump of an electron to a higher orbit)" that "provoked a rupture in the process of evolution." Still, he can be commended for attempting to understand diverse perspectives.

Perhaps if Montague had attempted to better understand Lorenz and the others before attacking them, Montagu might have been able to contribute valid criticisms instead of attacks against theories that exist only in his imagination. In addition to his attacks on the theories of Lorenz and the others, Montagu also attacks other perspectives, including psychological behaviorism. He implies that the perspectives he attacks are as incompatible with his perspective as Evil is incompatible with Good. Nevertheless, I do not think that we need to accept only one of these perspectives as legitimate and reject the rest. First, I think that these diverse perspectives yield to synthesis. Violence and peacefulness are learned through social interaction in which the probability of future occurrence of a behavioral configuration increases if the configuration precedes ritualized displays representing an increase in dominance for the individual or if it precedes stimulus configurations that have been paired with increased dominance, and decreases if it precedes ritualized displays representing a decrease in dominance or if it precedes stimulus configurations that have been paired with decreased dominance. Second, I think that even if the perspectives could not be synthesized, each perspective should still be retained because each is a major perspective with its own unique contributions to offer. The study of societies can advantageously tolerate the coexistence of multiple paradigms that have not yet yielded to complete synthesis, as physics has advantageously tolerated the coexistence of Einsteinian field theory and quantum theory, which also have not yet yielded to complete synthesis. The perspective of the self-fulfilling prophecy in violence and the perspective of phylogenetic adaptation in violence are both valuable contributions toward reduction of a threat to humanity.

Belief, Language, and Experience, by RODNEY NEEDHAM. Chicago: University of Chicago Press, 1972. 269 pp. No price listed, cloth.

BERYL L. BELLMAN
University of California, San Diego

The study of belief systems has long been a recognized field of inquiry in philosophy and across the social science disciplines. In this monograph Rodney Needham, a major British social anthropologist and a leading figure in the Structuralist movement, questions the very concept of belief, and argues that its empirical grounds are highly problematic. If his reflections are considered valid, the phenomenon discussed with that rubric must seriously be looked at anew.

Needham wrote this monograph after

realizing that he could not think of any word for belief among the Penan of Borneo, a cultural group he did extensive research on and frequently used as an ethnographic resource in advancing his structuralist theories. He then shows that his discovery is not unique to the Penan; as Evans-Pritchard likewise argued that the Nuer, a Nilotic people in the Sudan, have no single word which stands for belief either. Yet, according to various missionary linguists who translated the bible into the Nuer language, there was a list of Nuer words they transliterated as "belief." However, Needham demonstrates the evasive nature for those terms, and supports Evans-Pritchard's assertion. Next, he argues that there is also a lack of empirical grounds for "belief" in numerous other languages including English. For the latter, he asserts as well that "the grounds for difficulty in understanding and translating the English verbal concept of belief can readily be seen to be very numerous and bewildering."

Needham then searches for criteria to analyze the concept of belief. He attends to various philosophical positions including those of Kant, Hume, Hampshire, Griffith, Lichtenberg, and Wittgenstein. He maintains that in spite of their various investigations, there exists no real criteria for belief. Next, using Wittgenstein's methodology concerning grammars of use and the idea of a family of objects he examines what classifitory principles, if any, constitute the class of uses for belief. Here he summarizes both Vygotsky and Wittgenstein's theories about classes of ideas, and discusses the potential analyzability of other concepts such as comparing, wishing, and the like. He shows that instead of a feature which all members of a class share there exist overlapping similarities which together constitute it. With this method he explores the possibility that belief may be a Whorfian cryptotype or latent notion which has subtle meanings. He finds this is not the case; rather, he finds that the phenomenon of belief "consists of no more than the custom of making statements about belief." The various uses of "belief" can be rendered away by other words such that the grammar of use for belief "tells us that there is no such object." He then compares the phenomenon of imagination to belief and argues that "imagination is real, belief is not."

Needham then discusses concepts related to belief and searches for behavioral demonstrations of the concept. Again he concludes that not only is it not a discriminable mode of consciousness, neither is it the recognition of a bodily phenomenon, nor does it belong to a universal psychological vocabulary, nor is it a necessary institution for the conduct of social life.

Needham next addresses the history of investigations on primitive classification. He examines Durkheim and Mauss's work, and presents a detailed examination of Levy Bruhl's theory and its development concerning the relationship of belief and experience. He shows how Levy Bruhl's invalidation of "experience" as a term of universal application supports the position that belief cannot be regarded as a natural resemblance among humans, and is not to be expected to be among their collective representations.

In the final and longest chapter of his monograph, Needham addresses the question of cross-cultural comparison of cognition. He shows how a comparative study of different forms of knowledge becomes transformed into a comparative theory of knowledge. He challenges the taken-for-granted assumption of most cross-cultural researchers that all humans will have certain "well-known logical and psychic capacities that they share with the observer," and argues that the objective of his monograph is primarily to show that this notion is not well founded and that the "essential capacities of man have yet to be empirically determined by comparative research." He then discusses the position necessary to undertake such an enterprise drawing again from Wittgenstein, Hampshire, Waismann, etc. This leads him into the nature of language and its relationship to thought.

Needham's investigation is quite impressive, albeit onesided. It is curious that he does not even give mention to the number of phenomenological, existential, and hermeneutical philosophies which have seriously examined the structures of belief. For example, Husserl in advocating the phenomenological epoche presented a methodology for bracketing "belief" in the investigation of lived experience. Again, Schutz, an early advocate of the phenomenological method for the social sciences, analyzes what he refers to as multiple orders of reality (the world of dreams, everyday life, phantasy, science, and the like) in terms of layers of belief and the nature of their bracketing. The various analysts using the different versions of the phenomenological method likewise have much to say about classification of ideas and concepts, the relationship of language to thought, and the nature of experience. Perhaps Needham's ignoring their work was unintentional. Yet, given his rigorous treatment of other philosophies I must assume that he at least knew of their existence. Indeed, the concepts of natural language philosophy and phenomenology (especially existential phenomenology) have much in common. One need not accept the eidetic reduction as the crucial step in the phenomenological method. Such theorists as Merleau-Ponty, Gurvitch, Gusdorf, Heidegger, and Gadamer have themselves rejected it as originally argued by Husserl. Yet, taken together there is a communality of method which goes beyond natural language philosophy in the investigation of the phenomenon of lived experience. In the limited space of a book review I cannot offer a comparison of methodologies but can only point the reader to another philosophical tradition that may lead to different conclusions than those arrived at in this otherwise excellent book.

How Family Members Perceive Each Other: Political and Social Attitudes in Two Generations, by RICHARD G. NIEMI. New Haven: Yale University Press, 1974. 214 pp. $10.00 cloth.

Communication, Conflict and Marriage, by HAROLD L. RAUSH, WILLIAM A. BARRY, RICHARD K. HERTEL, and MARY ANN SWAIN. San Francisco: Jossey-Bass, 1974. 250 pp. $10.75 cloth.

SUZANNE K. STEINMETZ
University of Delaware

Both these studies are attempts to provide a fuller explanation of family interaction processes. In *Communication, Conflict and Marriage*, the authors attempt to manipulate couples in a series of role improvisations aimed at presenting a more accurate picture of marital interaction during the resolution of a conflict. In *How Family Members Perceive Each Other*, the data obtained from both parents and the child are analyzed revealing how each member biases his or her portrait of family in a slightly different, but not a socially desirable way.

Rausch et al., noting the limitations of a single variable explanation of marital conflict resolution, utilize an adaptive probabilistic model. This model, based on methods used in communication theory, has as a basic assumption the dependence of a given act on other events in which it is embedded. The methodology presented in *Communication, Conflict and Marriage* attempts to assess the extent to which one spouse's statements increases or decreases the likelihood of certain statements by the other spouse. Forty-six newly married couples were followed through marriage, pregnancy, and childbirth. The couples were interviewed, completed questionnaires, and participated in four improvisation scenes designed to force the couples to resolve a conflict. Participation occurred during the fourth month of marriage, seventh month of pregnancy, and fourth month after childbirth. Couples expecting a child were matched with couples married a similar length of time who were still childless. These data, submitted to informational analysis, resulted in the identification of six categories of husband-wife interaction: cognitive, resolving, reconciling, appealing, rejecting, coercing. The liability of this methodology noted by the authors is the lack of experimental design. However, this is also an asset since it offers a greater range of legitimate generalization about the phenomena.

The book suffers from a lack of cohesiveness; it switches from applied to theoretical to methodological concerns with no warning or rationale provided. The unevenness, possibly resulting from insufficient collaboration among the four authors, could have been improved by the inclusion of a more comprehensive plan of the book and introductions in each section to provide the needed linkage for ease of transition.

One persistent methodological concern is the bias resulting from obtaining data about families from only one member, usually the wife. Niemi's study *How Family Members Perceive Each Other*, represents an attempt to compare different family members' reports of the same phenomenon. The goal of this research was to assess the effect of biases which occur when one family member reports the behavior of all other members. While it is reassuring to discover that at least in the area of political attitudes and behavior there is little evidence of systematic bias toward socially desirable answers, Niemi did note a tendency for children's and parents' description of other family members' attributes to be more congruent with one's own preference or feelings— a self-directed bias. For example, since students assumed that if their parents were well educated they would be highly interested in politics, and less interested if poorly educated, they based their report of their parents' political interest on their parents' educational level. Similarly, reports of party loyalty, by race, show the influence of students' expectations. Black students were more accurate reporters of Democratic parents and less accurate reporters of non-Democratic parents than white students. Black students *assumed* that their parents would be Democrats, while white students did not automatically make that assumption. Students also consistently overestimated the amount of agreement between their mothers' and fathers' political attitudes. Self-directed bias apparently influenced parents' reports of students more significantly than it influences youth's reports about parents. Utilizing students' reports, no differences were observed between bias for mother or father. However, mothers' reports of students' behavior exhibited a higher degree of self-directed bias than fathers' reports. The effect of social desirability does not appear to be a factor in student-parent differences, and although mothers tend to describe family members in a manner which is congruent with their own attitudes and beliefs, the degree of bias is slight and "poses a much less serious threat to family descriptions than originally suspected" (p. 25). This book provides much insight into a variety of methodological problems associated with family research.

Sport and Social Organization, by HOWARD L. NIXON, II. Indianapolis, Ind.: Bobbs-Merrill Company, 1976. 75 pp. $2.95 paper.

BARRY D. MCPHERSON
University of Waterloo

While other monographs in this series present "important statements" about their field by "critically reviewing the most significant research and writing on central theoretical and methodological issues," this book consists of a pot pourri of unrelated mini-chapters which seek to depict sport as a social organization related to culture, socialization, deviance, group behavior, social stratification, racial and sexual discrimination, big business, and social change. In each section the author sets out to clarify the key sociological concepts, apply these concepts to the study of sport, and review and discuss what is known about sport in an effort to show how the sociological perspective can be applied to sport. Unfortunately the goal is not realized in that the concepts are superficially treated and illustrated with elementary descriptive examples such as "helmet wearers in professional hockey today violate an informal norm" (p. 17). Furthermore, the review and discussion of research findings tend to be highly selective and descriptive, rather than explanatory, and no alternative explanations are proposed. Further weaknesses in the text result from the failure to utilize one or more theoretical perspectives in the presentation of topics, from an over-emphasis upon one piece of work (H. Edwards, *Sociology of Sport*, 1973), and from an over-emphasis in some sections on journalistic rather than empirically-based findings. For example, other than three papers briefly cited in the text, the seminal work on the economics of sport presented at the Brookings Conference in 1971 is ignored. Space limitations prevent citing other major theoretical or empirical papers not included in specific topics.

Although the book lacks substantive breadth and depth, the material is presented clearly and succinctly, especially in the sections where the author reviews the literature and avoids imposing his own view of the world of sport. It is in these sections that the objectives of the series' editors come closest to being realized.

Since this book represents a narrow, incomplete, and in some cases, dated (e.g., the section on the athletic revolution) view of the field, the appropriate audience would not be university students in either an introductory sociology or a sociology of sport class. For both groups, the concepts are not well enough developed to be useful in any meaningful analysis, no theoretical perspectives or methodological issues are introduced or discussed and the substantive material is not representative of the current state of the art. If a general overview of this subdiscipline is needed, review articles by Page (in J. Talamini and C. Page, eds., *Sport and Society*, 1973) or Snyder and Spreitzer (in D. Ball and J. Loy, eds., *Sport and Social Order*, 1976), or reference to one of the many readers on the subject, would prove more fruitful in understanding the significance, structure, processes, and problems of institutionalized sport in a number of industrialized and developing societies.

The Rising South. Volume 1: Changes and Issues, edited by DONALD R. NOBLE and JACOB L. THOMAS. University: University of Alabama Press, 1976. 124 pp. $6.95 cloth.

The Rising South. Volume 2: Southern Universities and the South, edited by ROBERT H. MCKENZIE. University: University of Alabama Press, 1976. 195 pp. $8.95 cloth.

ALVIN L. BERTRAND
Louisiana State University, Baton Rouge

To one who has devoted a considerable part of his life to teaching and doing research in the American South and who has a great deal of "native son" concern for the region, there is an irresistible urge to plunge into materials and documents which promise a new and fresh interpretation of regional phenomena. This was the mood which launched my perusal of *The Rising South*. This two volume work includes contributions from some 22 different authors. These authors range in status and accomplishments from the President of a major state university and the Dean of a law school to the President of a local labor council and an undergraduate student. In each instance the intensity and sincerity of the writer is apparent, even if the theme of the volume seems, on occasion, to be forgotten.

Volume 1 of *The Rising South* is subtitled "Changes and Issues." This volume is introduced by one of the co-editors, Donald R. Noble, who does a superb job of setting the tone for still another edited work "on the 'new' or the 'changing' or, indeed, the 'rising' south. . . ." The first selection is by a renowned historian, George B. Tindall, who sees the South as having a great opportunity to profit by the mistakes of other regions as it is launched into the mainstream of an emerging mass society, but who is pessimistic about Southerners making the most of this opportunity. The second article, by the President of the Alabama Labor Council, AFL-CIO (Barney Weeks) is in sharp contrast—almost a union "pitch"—but does highlight the major labor issues and trends in the South. Another quite different chord is sounded in the third article, written by a life-long conservationist (Verda Horne), although it is a bit difficult to reconcile the title "The South's Threatened Landscapes" with the limited Alabama scene depicted. The fourth article is, in reality, the testimony and life philosophy of Tom Gilmore—the black sheriff of a county in Alabama recently featured in a TV documentary. This article captures a side of southern life and attitudes not too well understood outside the region. The fifth article in volume 1 is written by an ardent civil libertarian (Pat Derian), one who has been active in the Women's Movement. The article is hard hitting in an attempt to show that the Southern woman is shedding her "non-liberated" stereotype, but is a little less than convincing to one who has reviewed recent survey data which shows the conservatism persisting among Southern females. The next article is devoted to an assessment of the question, "Is the Southern Literary Renascence Over?" The author (Louis D. Rubin, Jr.) in effect says, "No," and bluntly states that present day middle-aged critics just do not understand the modern breed of Southern literary commentators. The seventh article is the product of no less a man than David Matthews—a historian, who is President of University of Alabama, and has been Secretary of the Department of Health, Education, and Welfare among other things. Matthews writes skillfully about the presence of strong regional identification and of the bright future of the South. The next to last article in volume 1 was written by a non-Southerner. After spending only a short time in the South, the author, Peter Schrag (a widely known commentator on the American scene), feels that something special is going on in the South in the way of change and cautions against the region being "hoodwinked" into trying to become something it can't become. The final article in volume 1 is by Joseph B. Doughty, Jr., an ex-student at the University of Alabama, attracted to the state from his home in Minnesota by a football scholarship. For him, the rising South has been a revelation of the role and destiny of a people.

The second volume of *The Rising South* is sub-titled "Southern Universities and the South." Robert H. McKenzie, the editor of this volume, provides an insightful perspective for contemplating the South as a region filled with external hope for progress but hampered in the quest for this goal by an inherent moderation and caution. The author of the first article in volume 2 is James F. Doster, a historian. Doster contrasts the old South with the new South, which he sees as bombarded by a flood of federally legislated programs, many with welfare implications. The second article is by an economist, Arthur A. Thompson, and is concerned with what he calls Alabama's five economies. The emphasis of the article is the uneven rate of economic development and the need for sustaining a trend toward industrial and economic expansion. The third article is written by the Dean of the University of Alabama Law School, Thomas W. Christopher. It is addressed to the "Role of Leadership" and is one of the most profound statements on the subject this writer has seen. Dean Christopher boldly denounces the poor leaders and leadership tactics of the past and challenges Southerners to rise to their potential. The fourth article is by a political scientist, Donald S. Strong, who sees the South as basically conservative but becoming increasingly aware of the fact that its political future is tied to developments outside the region. Stan Murphy, a law student, is the author of the fifth article. He tells a cogent story of the drama and facts of the changing political scene in a predominantly black Alabama county. A theme heard more frequently within recent years is highlighted in the sixth article, authored by a black dentist and community leader. This is that the South, whatever its problems, represents a home and a heritage which cannot be foresaken lightly by the blacks born and reared in the region. The seventh article reflects the view of O. B. Emerson on emerging literary trends in the South. Emerson, a specialist on Faulkner and Southern literature, feels that contemporary Southern writers have succeeded in catching the mood of the changing South. Ray Jenkins, a newspaper editor and author of the eighth article, addresses the mass media changes in the South since WWII. Pointing out some rather drastic changes in reporting and editorial policies among Southern papers, Jenkins feels there still remains a curious mixture of Southern realism and Southern romanticism among newspapers in the region. The ninth article in volume 2 is by Ester J. Swenson, a professional educator. She sees definite signs of progress in Southern schools and charges Southern universities to take the responsibility for even greater improvement. The last article is by Neal R. Beste, Vice President for Educational Devolopment and Dean of the University of Alabama New College. He provides exciting evidence of long needed educational reforms in Southern universities.

Overall, I must note that my sense of something new and exciting vacillated as I moved from one author to the next in this work. The unevenness in the style and objectives of the authors is a bit bothersome, although it lends a definite aura of authenticity. As I moved through the two volumes the overall impression of a worthy contribution to an already quite comprehensive literature gradually crystallized. My greatest difficulty was in reconciling the several narrowly parochial contributions, i.e., those limited to one community, county, or to Alabama, to the title of the volume. The hazard of generalizing to the whole Southern region is self-evident. Yet, even in these instances, one cannot help but catch the drama in the volume of confrontation and response to massive social forces which is characteristic of the "rising South." Sometimes the response of Southerners to this change is depicted as gracious and sometimes it is described as not so gracious. However, on the whole, the authors paint a positive picture. All in all, *The Rising South* is a very creditable and timely contribution to the understanding of perhaps one of the greatest regional developmental experiences in the history of the United States.

Polish American Community Life: A Survey of Research, by IRWIN T. SANDERS and EWA T. MORAWSKA. New York: Polish Institute of Arts and Sciences in America, 1975. 300 pp. $6.50 paper.

EUGENE E. OBIDINSKI
SUNY College/Oneonta

This extremely helpful guide to diverse studies of Polonia is essentially a review of a body of literature that is as eclectic as it is extensive. Although the monograph is among several bibliographic works published during the current period of renewed ethnic consciousness, it is more systematic and sophisticated than similar lists of assorted, sometimes annotated, references to Polonian topics.

Analyzed within a conceptual framework of the community as an ethnic-ecological phenomenon, sixty-one studies (section 1) are basic units of analysis. Of these, thirty-six are "contemporary studies" and the remainder are "historical" or "classical local studies." The majority are obviously relevant analyses of Polonian subcommunity life; however, *Elmtown's Youth* and two of the volumes from the *Yankee City* series are less appropriate listings. No doubt, the authors cast an even wider net (sections 2 and 3) in a commendable effort to include any remotely relevant research. The result is a "mixed bag" of studies ranging from carefully prepared dissertations and journal articles to impressionistic interpretations of historical records. Data of these studies are cited in fourteen well-organized chapters which describe structural, relational, and psychological elements of various Polonian settlements.

Any review of the literature gives a selective, concise, and sometimes irrevelant perspective to on-going research and *Polish-American Community Life* is no exception.

Loners, Losers, and Lovers: Elderly Tenants in a Slum Hotel, by JOYCE STEPHENS. Seattle: University of Washington Press, 1976. 118 pp. $8.95 cloth.

ANDREA FONTANA
University of Nevada, Las Vegas

Joyce Stephens belongs to that rare breed of sociologists who dare study human beings in their natural setting, even if the setting is, as in this case, a decaying single-room-occupancy hotel for old people. Stephens lived in the hotel and was able to penetrate the walls of isolation and suspicion built by the elderly tenants around themselves. What results is an informative and sensitive book about the life of a group of forgotten human beings, old people in hotels which in terms of the wear and tear of age, compete with the tenants themselves.

Stephens's book is a "symbolic interactionist" ethnography of the hotel. It describes accurately the setting, the people in it, the strategies employed by the tenants to survive in the hotel (where to eat, when to pay the rent, etc.), the small ways in which the old folks "hustle" some money, and the relations between the men and women in the hotel.

The book portrays the hotel tenants as loners fighting to survive in the urban jungle of the slum. The old people do not passively wither away but create a world of aloneness which provides them with a buffer necessary to operate within their harsh environment.

Loners, Losers, and Lovers does not provide theoretical insight into old age; it is not meant to do so. What it provides is a first-hand look at old people. The book is aimed at a general audience beyond the sociological one, but serious students of aging and social problems would do well to read this book and learn about this subculture of the alone in our midst.

Heresies, by THOMAS SZASZ. New York: Anchor Press, 1976. 183 pp. $2.95 paper.

ROBERT S. BROADHEAD
University of California, San Francisco

Although Szasz is an important intellectual figure, this particular book is definitely not important, especially sociologically. Szasz offers here a series of brief observations, "one-liners," and pot shots in a number of relatively disparate areas. Having cut up the pie of anti-psychiatry into as many pieces as it will go, what is left is Szasz's fury unleashed, but without a clear object left to cut. There is only one developed idea in the book, and this is in the introduction. Nor are the remainder of his comments really heretical; one finds a few cynical jokes, some old chic radicalism, some nonsense, and some insights, for sure, but dated ones.

In short, the book goes nowhere; indeed, it hardly warrants a review in the already inundated pages of *Contemporary Sociology.*

Bureaucracy and the Modern World, by VICTOR A. THOMPSON. Morristown, N.J.: General Learning Press, 1976. 141 pp. $5.95 paper.

ROBERT N. STERN
Cornell University

Five essays in search of integration comprise this new text designed for courses in organization theory and administration. All five papers have appeared in print before: three are previously published essays and two are condensations of other works. These essays cover the evolution of bureaucracy and decision theory, as well as bureaucracies as systems, innovators, and potential failures. They provide some insightful analysis and a basic understanding of a systems theory approach to organizations, but suffer as a text in being bound but untied. Though Thompson apologizes for overlap in the content of the works, students may be unwilling to forgive the repetition of theoretical points, illustrations and phrases in the introduction and three essays.

Thompson develops a useful didactic device by breaking with current styles of analysis. He conceptualizes organizations as the interplay of two interacting systems. The artificial system is the tool of the organization's owner and consists of roles, tasks, and technologies. Its concern is efficiency in accomplishing the goal of the owner and its roles are filled by functionaries who are to do nothing but meet role prescriptions. Interacting with the artificial system is a natural system which consists of all the people who fill the roles and give organizations a "spontaneous, unplanned emergent quality" (p. 3). The goal of this system is survival which produces an inherent conflict with the owner's organizational design.

The distinction will lead students to notice the traditional formal-informal organization dichotomy, an antagonism between formal structure and human interaction, and the relative use of extrinsic and intrinsic rewards. The artificial system inhibits innovation, attempts to elicit ever more effort from role incumbents and utilizes principles of hierarchy (from administrative science) for control. He argues that the natural system in turn, tries to thwart the accomplishment of goals through politics, conflict, particularism, and other human "frailties."

Though the linkages between the systems are specified, the text presents a number of critical weaknesses. Thompson, as a systems theorist, leaves the message that organizations would be fine if they did not rely on people. The system would work but for human failings of judgment, desire for security and compassion. Public administration would be efficient if interest group advocacy was eliminated and government officials followed organizational prescriptions rather than seeking equality in the distribution of goods. Bureaucratic functionaries who deviate from the owner's plan are described as thieves. While Thompson's position on public administration raises fundamental questions, its dependence upon the fulfillment of the heroic assumptions underlying the two-system dichotomy gives the argument an air of unreality.

Technically, there are other difficulties. Exchange theories of power are used to describe control systems, but most recent literature and theoretical development in the area are not included. The organization is defined as a tool designed to meet the owner's goal, but in commenting extensively on public administration there is no discussion of who the owner of government might be or how collective goals are established. The artificial system is in itself an efficient instrument, but it is designed by a human being who is part of the natural system. So much for perfection.

While there is some value in using this text as a supplement in providing a systems perspective on organizations, problems of coverage and ideology are such that I would not leave my class with it unattended.

Understanding Social Problems, edited by DON H. ZIMMERMAN, D. LAWRENCE WIEDER and SIU ZIMMERMAN. New York: Praeger Publishers, 1976. 438 pp. No price listed, paper.

MALCOLM SPECTOR
McGill University

The previous writings of Don Zimmerman and the introductory chapter, which sparkles with references to Garfinkel, Cicourel, et al., would seem to promise that this reader might be a good teaching tool for those with an ethnomethodological bent. Indeed, Hadden and Lester begin, in the theory chapter, by distinguishing between social problems as *resource* and as *topic*. "The first treats social problems as given. That is, common-sense conceptions (which create our perceptions of social problems) are left unexamined as the researcher endeavors to explain the causes of drug abuse, juvenile delinquency and the like, all of which are simply taken as problems 'out there.' The second approach takes the opposite tack and considers the social creation of social problems per se as the topic for research" (p. 6).

However, not one of the thirteen chapters, all written for this volume, follows this very interesting recommendation, to treat social problems as topic not as a resource. All treat the objective extent and causes of the problematic condition. All grind through the historical background without considering the possibility that what is currently regarded as the history of a social problem is also a socially constructed members' accomplishment. Sporadic, half-hearted, and sadly incomplete discussions of recent legislation or reform attempts are the sole hints of "social problems as topic."

The editor explains it all in the preface: "no editorial control was exercised over an author's approach, nor was any attempt made to define 'appropriate' problems according to some theoretical prejudice. Thus concern for the consistency of the treatment accorded topics in the book was secondary to encouraging the autonomy and creativity of its contributors" (p. v). With the single exception of the chapter by Enos, the writing is heavy and turgid, poorly edited, and uneven in scope and content. Three chapters seem to treat poverty and are redundant to the point where exactly the same "poverty cycle" diagram is reprinted both on page 62 and on page 168. Neither the publisher, the authors, nor the editors (who strangely, have not written either an introductory nor concluding chapter) seem to have put any effort into this book, and it shows.

PUBLICATIONS RECEIVED

(Listing of a publication below does not assure nor preclude its subsequent review.)

APPLEBAUM, RICHARD P., et al. *The Effects of Urban Growth: A Population Impact Analysis.* Praeger, 1976. 330 pp. $20.00 cloth.

ARNOTT, MARGARET L., ed. *Gastronomy: The Anthropology of Food Habits.* Mouton, 1975. Dist. by Aldine. 354 pp. $19.50 cloth.

ASHCRAFT, NORMAN, and SCHEFLEN, ALBERT E. *People Space: The Making and Breaking of Human Boundaries.* Anchor Press, 1976. 185 pp. $2.50 paper.

ASHER, HERBERT B. *Causal Modeling.* Sage, 1976. 80 pp. $3.00 paper.

BACHRACH, LEONA L. *Deinstitutionalization: An Analytical Review and Sociological Perspective.* DHEW #76–351. Washington, D.C., 1976. 43 pp. $1.10 paper.

BAINBRIDGE, WILLIAM SIMS. *The Spaceflight Revolution: A Sociological Study.* Wiley, 1976. 294 pp. $16.95 cloth.

BANE, MARY JO. *Here to Stay: American Families in the Twentieth Century.* Basic Books, 1976. 195 pp. $11.50 cloth.

BANKS, OLIVE. *The Sociology of Education,* rev. ed. Schocken Books, 1976. 294 pp. $13.75 cloth. $4.95 paper.

BARBEAU, ARTHUR E. and HENRI, FLORETTE. *The Unknown Soldiers: Black American Troops in World War I.* Temple University Press, 1974. 279 pp. NPL. cloth.

BARBER, THEODORE X., ed. *Advances in Altered States of Consciousness and Human Potentialities, Volume 1: A PDI Research Reference Work.* Psychological Dimensions, 1976. 698 pp. $20.00 cloth.

BARBER, THEODORE XENOPHON. *Pitfalls in Human Research: Ten Pivotal Points.* Pergamon, 1976. 117 pp. $6.95 cloth.

BARON, SALO W., KAHAN, ARCADIUS, and others. NACHUM GROSS, ed. *Economic History of the Jews.* Schocken Books, 1975. 304 pp. $5.50 paper.

BATESON, P. P. G., and HINDE, R. A., eds. *Growing Points in Ethology: Based on a Conference Sponsored by St. John's College and King's College, Cambridge.* Cambridge University Press, 1976. 548 pp. NPL, cloth.

BELL, QUENTIN. *On Human Finery,* 2nd ed., rev. & enlg. Schocken Books, 1976. 239 pp. $14.95 cloth.

BENNETT, SPENCER, and BOWERS, DAVID. *An Introduction to Multivariate Techniques for Social and Behavioural Sciences.* Halsted, 1976. 156 pp. $14.95 cloth.

BEREANO, PHILIP L. *Technology as a Social and Political Phenomenon.* Wiley, 1976. 544 pp. $13.95 cloth.

BETTELHEIM, CHARLES. *Class Struggles in the USSR: First Period 1917–1923.* Tr. Brian Pearce. Monthly Review Press, 1976. 567 pp. $18.95 cloth.

BHARATI, AGEHANANDA, ed. *The Realm of the Extra-Human: Volume 1, Agents and Audiences. Volume 2, Ideas and Actions.* Mouton, 1976. Dist. by Aldine. 556 & 521 pp. $27.50 & $24.50 cloth.

BLANKENSHIP, RALPH L., ed. *Colleagues in Organization: The Social Construction of Professional Work.* Wiley, 1977. 426 pp. $10.95 paper.

BLOOR, DAVID. *Knowledge and Social Imagery.* Routledge & Kegan Paul, 1976. 156 pp. $7.50 paper.

BRAIN, ROBERT. *Friends and Lovers.* Basic Books, 1976. 287 pp. $10.95 cloth.

BRUNING, JAMES L., and KINTZ, B. L. *Computational Handbook of Statistics,* 2nd ed. Scott, Foresman, 1977. 308 pp. $8.95 paper.

BÜHL, WALTER L. *Theorien Sozialer Konflikte.* Wissenschaftliche Buchgesellschaft, 1976. 178 pp. NPL. paper.

BUTLER, EDGAR W. *Urban Sociology: A Systematic Approach.* Harper & Row, 1976. 526 pp. $13.95 cloth.

CALHOUN, CRAIG J., and IANNI, FRANCIS A. J., eds. *The Anthropological Study of Education.* Mouton, 1976. Dist. by Aldine. 360 pp. $18.50 cloth.

CAPLAN, ROBERT D. et al. *Adhering to Medical Regimens: Pilot Experiments in Patient Education and Social Support.* Institute for Social Research/University of Michigan, 1976. 284 pp. $10.00 paper.

CHEEK, NEIL H., JR., and BURCH, WILLIAM R. JR. *The Social Organization of Leisure in Human Society.* Harper & Row, 1976. 283 pp. $10.95 cloth.

CHENG, RONALD YE-LIN, ed. *The Sociology of Revolution: Readings on Political Upheaval and Popular Unrest.* Henry Regnery, 1973. 334 pp. $4.95 paper.

CLARK, NORMAN H. *Deliver Us from Evil: An Interpretation of American Prohibition.* W. W. Norton, 1976. 246 pp. $10.95 cloth.

CLIGNET, REMI. *The Africanization of the Labor Market: Educational and Occupational Segmentation in the Cameroun.* University of California Press, 1976. 230 pp. $12.75 cloth.

COOK, RAMSAY, and MITCHINSON, WENDY, eds. *The Proper Sphere: Woman's Place in Canadian Society.* Oxford University Press, 1976. 334 pp. $6.75 paper.

COTTLE, THOMAS J. *Perceiving Time: A Psychological Investigation with Men and Women.* Wiley, 1976. 267 pp. $14.95 cloth.

CRAIG, JOHN G. *Multinational Co-operatives: An Alternative for World Development.* Western Producer Prairie Books, 1976. 135 pp. NPL, paper

CRAWFORD, ELISABETH, and PERRY, NORMAN, eds. *Demands for Social Knowledge: The Role of Research Organisations.* Sage 1976. 276 pp. $15.00 cloth.

CULYER, A. J. *Need and the National Health Service: Economics and Social Choice.* Rowman & Littlefield, 1976. 163 pp. $11.50 cloth.

DANIELSON, MICHAEL N. *The Politics of Exclusion.* Columbia University Press, 1976. 443 pp. $17.50 cloth. $6.95 paper.

DAVIES, DUNCAN; BANFIELD, TOM; and SHEAHAN, RAY. *The Humane Technologist.* Oxford University Press, 1976. 180 pp. $10.50 cloth.

DAWKINS, RICHARD. *The Selfish Gene*. Oxford University Press, 1976. 224 pp. $8.95 cloth.
DEAN, THOMAS. *Post-Theistic Thinking: The Marxist-Christian Dialogue in Radical Perspective*. Temple University Press, 1975. 300 pp. NPL, cloth.
DEDRING, JUERGEN. *Recent Advances in Peace and Conflict Research: A Critical Survey*. Sage, 1976. 249 pp. $12.00 cloth. $6.00 paper.
DEFLEUR, MELVIN L.; D'ANTONIO, WILLIAM V.; and NELSON, LOIS DEFLEUR. *Sociology: Human Society*, 2nd brief ed. Scott, Foresman, 1977. 461 pp. $9.95 cloth.
DEMERATH NICHOLAS J. *Birth Control and Foreign Policy: The Alternatives to Family Planning*. Harper & Row, 1976. 228 pp. $6.95 paper.
DEVOL, KENNETH S. *Mass Media and the Supreme Court: The Legacy of the Warren Years*, rev. 2nd ed. Hastings House, 1976. 400 pp. $14.50 cloth. $8.50 paper.
DION, LÉON. *Québec: The Unfinished Revolution*. McGill-Queen's University Press, 1976. 218 pp. $15.00 cloth. $7.50 paper.
DOBYNS, HENRY F., and DOUGHTY, PAUL L. *Peru: A Cultural History*. Oxford University Press, 1976. 336 pp. $12.50 cloth. $3.95 paper.
DOLCE, PHILIP C. *Suburbia: The American Dream*. Anchor Press, 1976. $2.95 paper.
DORE, RONALD. *The Diploma Disease: Education, Qualification and Development*. University of California Press, 1976. 214 pp. $15.00 cloth. $5.50 paper.
DOWNS, GEORGE W., JR. *Bureaucracy, Innovation, and Public Policy*. Lexington Books, 1976. 150 pp. $15.50 cloth.
DUBB, ALLIE A. *Community of the Saved: An African Revivalist Church in the East Cape*. Witwatersrand University Press, 1976. 175 pp. NPL, cloth.
DUBRIN, ANDREW J. *The New Husbands: And How to Become One*. Nelson-Hall, 1976. 213 pp. $8.95 cloth.
EASTWOOD, GERRY. *Skilled Labour Shortages in the United Kingdom: With Particular Reference to the Engineering Industry*. National Planning Association, 1976. 37 pp. $3.00 paper.
ELKINS, STANLEY M. *Slavery: A Problem in American Institutional and Intellectual Life*, 3rd ed., rev. University of Chicago Press, 1976. 320 pp. $12.50 cloth. $3.95 paper.
ENGLISH, JOHN; MADIGAN, RUTH; and NORMAN, PETER. *Slum Clearance: The Social and Administrative Context in England and Wales*. Holmes & Meier, 1976. 223 pp. $16.50 cloth
EVANS, SPOFFORD LEWIS. *Marriage and the Family*. Vantage, 1976. 51 pp. $4.50 cloth.
EYSENCK, H. J. *Sex and Personality*. University of Texas Press, 1976. 256 pp. $13.95 cloth.
FALK, RANDOLPH. *Lelooska*. Celestial Arts, 1976. 144 pp. $7.95 paper.
FELICE, RENZO DE. *Fascism: An Informal Introduction to Its Theory and Practice*. Transaction Books, 1976. 128 pp. $5.95 cloth.
FILSTEAD, WILLIAM J.; ROSSI, JEAN J.; and KELLER, MARK, eds. *Alcohol and Alcohol Problems: New Thinking and New Directions*. Ballinger, 1976. 304 pp. $15.00 cloth.
FITZPATRICK, BLANCHE. *Women's Inferior Education: An Economic Analysis*. Praeger, 1976. 189 pp. $16.50 cloth.
FLORA, CORNELIA BUTLER. *Pentecostalism in Colombia: Baptism by Fire and Spirit*. Fairleigh Dickinson University Press, 1976. 288 pp. $13.50 cloth.
FREEDMAN, MARCIA K. *Labor Markets: Segments and Shelters*. Allanheld, Osmun, 1976. 202 pp. $18.50 cloth.
FREIDHEIM, ELIZABETH A. *Sociological Theory in Research Practice*. Schenkman, 1976. 325 pp. $7.95 paper.
FUCHS, ESTELLE, ed. *Youth in a Changing World: Cross-Cultural Perspectives on Adolescence*. Mouton, 1976. Dist. by Aldine. 346 pp. $22.50 cloth.
GALT, ANTHONY H., and SMITH, LARRY J. *Models and the Study of Social Change*. Halsted, 1976. 180 pp. $10.00 cloth. $5.95 paper.
GAYLIN, WILLARD. *Caring*. Alfred A. Knopf, 1976. 199 pp. $7.95 cloth.
GELLA, ALEKSANDER, ed. *The Intellegentsia and the Intellectuals: Theory, Method and Case Study*. Sage, 1976. 235 pp. $12.00 cloth. $6.00 paper.
GETMAN, JULIUS G.; GOLDBERG, STEPHEN B.; and HERMAN, JEANNE B. *Union Representation Elections: Law and Reality*. Russell Sage, 1976. 218 pp. $7.50 cloth.
GETZELS, JACOB W., and GSIKSZENTMIHALYI, MIHALY. *The Creative Vision: A Longitudinal Study of Problem Finding in Art*. Wiley, 1976. 293 pp. $17.50 cloth.
GIBBONS, ROBERT J., et al. *Research Advances in Alcohol and Drug Problems*, vol. 3. Wiley, 1976. 476 pp. $29.00 cloth.
GIDDENS, ANTHONY. *New Rules of Sociological Method: A Positive Critique of Interpretative Sociologies*. Basic Books, 1976. 192 pp. $10.95 cloth.
GLASS, GENE V. *Evaluation Studies: Review Annual*, vol. 1. Sage, 1976. 672 pp. $29.95 cloth.
GOLDMAN, RALPH M. *Contemporary Perspectives on Politics*. Transaction Books, 1976. 454 pp. $14.95 cloth.
GOLDSMITH, JACK, and GOLDSMITH, SHARON S., eds. *Crime and the Elderly: Challenge and Response*. Lexington Books, 1976. 177 pp. $15.00 cloth.
GRAY, DOROTHY. *Women of the West*. Les Femmes, 1976. 179 pp. $5.95 paper.
GREENBLATT, SIDNEY L., ed. *The People of Taihang: An Anthropology of Family Histories*, 3rd ed. International Arts & Sciences Press, 1976. 305 pp. $15.00 cloth.
GROLLIG, FRANCIS X., and HALEY, HAROLD B., eds. *Medical Anthropology*. Mouton, 1976. Dist. by Aldine. 485 pp. $27.50 cloth.
GUINTHER, JOHN. *Moralists and Managers: Public Interest Movements in America*. Anchor, 1976. 262 pp. $2.95 paper.
HAARGAARD, JYTTE, et al. *Arbejdskraftens Mobilitet 5: Konsekvenser. (The Consequences of Mobility*. With English Summary.) Danish Institute of Social Research, 1976. 95 pp. NPL, paper.
HALEBSKY, SANDOR. *Mass Society and Political Conflict: Toward a Reconstruction of Theory*. Cambridge University Press, 1976. 309 pp. $19.95 cloth. $6.95 paper.
HARDESTY, DONALD L. *Ecological Anthropology*. Wiley, 1977. 310 pp. $12.95 cloth.
HAWKES, JACQUETTA. *The Atlas of Early Man*. St. Martin's Press, 1976. 255 pp. $15.00 cloth.
HELFER, RAY E., and KEMPE, C. HENRY, eds. *Child Abuse and Neglect: The Family and the Community*. Ballinger, 1976. 438 pp. NPL, cloth.
HENKEL, RAMON E. *Tests of Significance*. Sage, 1976. 92 pp. $3.00 paper.
HERMAN, ROBERT D. *Gamblers and Gambling: Motives, Institutions, and Controls*. Lexington Books, 1976. 142 pp. $12.00 cloth.
HILBERMAN, ELAINE. *The Rape Victim*. Basic Books, 1976. 105 pp. $7.95 cloth.
HILLESTROM, KARSTEN. *Arbejdskraftens mobilitet 4: Processen. (The Mobility Process*. With English Summary.) Danish National Institute of Social Research, 1976. 117 pp. NPL, paper.
HILOWITZ, JANE. *Economic Development and Social Change in Sicily*. Schenkman, 1976. 204 pp. $11.95 cloth.
HIRST, PAUL Q. *Social Evolution and Sociological Categories*. Holmes & Meier, 1976. 135 pp. $15.00 cloth.
HOROWITZ, IRVING LOUIS. *Genocide: State Power and Mass Murder*. Transaction Books, 1976. 80 pp. $5.95 cloth.
HOROWITZ, IRVING LOUIS. *Ideology and Utopia in the United States 1956–1976*. Oxford University Press, 1977. 464 pp. $17.95 cloth. $5.95 paper.
HOWE, IRVING, ed. *The Basic Writings of Trotsky*. Schocken Books, 1976. $6.95 paper.
HUANG, AL-CHUNG-LIANG, and KO, SI CHI. *Living Tao: Still Visions and Dancing Brushes*. Celestial Arts, 1976. 120 pp. $5.95 paper.
HUTCHESON, JOHN D., JR., and SHEVIN, JANN. *Citizen Groups in Local Politics: A Bibliographic Review*. Clio Books, 1976. 275 pp. $19.75 cloth.
IANNI, FRANCIS A. J., and REUSS-IANNI, ELIZABETH. *The Crime Society: Organized Crime and Corruption in America*. New American Library, 1976. 377 pp. $5.95 paper.
IVERSEN, GUDMUND R., and NORPOTH, HELMUT. *Analysis of Variance*. Sage, 1976. 95 pp. $3.00 paper.
JACKSON, ANTHONY. *A Place Called Home: A History of Low-Cost Housing in Manhattan*. MIT Press, 1976. 359 pp. $15.00 cloth.
JAMBREK, PETER. *Development and Social Change in Yugoslavia: Crisis and Perspectives of Building a Nation*. Lexington Books, 1975. 280 pp. $19.50 cloth.
JAMES, WILLIAM. *Essays in Radical Empiricism*. Harvard University Press, 1976. 318 pp $16.50 cloth.
JOHNSON, ELIZABETH, and JOHNSON, GRAHAM. *Walking on Two Legs: Rural Development in South China*. International Development Research Centre, 1976. 72 pp. $5.00 paper.
JOHNSON, ROBERT. *Culture and Crisis in Confinement*. Lexington Books, 1976. 179 pp. $16.00 cloth.
JOHNSTONE, JOHN W. C.; SLAWSKI, EDWARD J., and BOWMAN, WILLIAM W. *The News People: A Sociological Portrait of American Journalists and Their Work. University of Illinois Press*, 1976. 257 pp. $9.95 cloth.
JONES, DOROTHY M. *Aleuts in Transition: A Comparison of Two Villages*. University of Washington Press, 1976. 125 pp $9.95 cloth.

KATZ, ROBERT N., ed. *Protecting the Consumer Interest: Private Initiative and Public Response*. Ballinger, 1976. 277 pp. $15.00 cloth.
KERSHAW, DAVID, and FAIR, JERILYN. *The New Jersey Income-Maintenance Experiment, Volume 1: Operations, Surveys and Administration*. Academic Press, 1976. 232 pp. $15.00 cloth.
KINTON, JACK, ed. *American Ethnic Revival: Group Pluralism Entering America's Third Century*. Social Science and Sociological Resources, 1977. 203 pp. $9.95 cloth $6.95 paper.
KIRKPATRICK, JEANE. *The New Presidential Elite: Men and Women in National Politics*. Russell Sage and Twentieth Century Fund, 1976. 605 pp. $20.00 cloth.
KLEIN, JOHN F. *Let's Make a Deal: Negotiating Justice*. Lexington Books, 1976 160 pp. $14.00 cloth.
KLEIN, LISL. *A Social Scientist in Industry*. Halsted, 1976. 257 pp. $16.50 cloth.
KNAPP, HERBERT, and KNAPP, MARY. *One Potato, Two Potato . . .: The Secret Education of American Children*. W. W. Norton, 1976. 274 pp. $9.95 cloth.
KORNBERG, ALLAN, and MISHLER, WILLIAM *Influence in Parliament: Canada*. Duke University Press, 1976. 403 pp. $14.75 cloth.
LANDER, PATRICIA SLADE. *In the Shadow of the Factory: Social Change in a Finnish Community*. Halsted, 1976. 191 pp. $12.50 cloth. $5.95 paper.
LASAGNA, LOUIS. *The VD Epidemic: How It Started, Where It's Going, and What to Do about It*. Temple University Press, 1975. 160 pp. NPL, cloth.
LEBRA, TAKIE SUGIYAMA. *Japanese Patterns of Behavior*. University Press of Hawaii, 1976 295 pp. $5.95 paper.
LEBRA, WILLIAM P., ed. *Cutlture-Bound Syndromes, Ethnopsychiatry, and Alternate Therapies, Volume IV of Mental Health Research in Asia and the Pacific*. University Press of Hawaii, 1976. 305 pp. $16.00 cloth
LEE, RICHARD B., and DEVORE, IRVEN, eds. *Kalahari Hunter-Gatherers: Studies of the !Kung San and Their Neighbors*. Harvard University Press, 1976. 408 pp. $18.50 cloth
LESLIE, GERALD R., and LESLIE, ELIZABETH McLAUGHLIN. *Marriage in a Changing World*. With student guide prepared by Margaret DiCario. Wiley, 1977. 451 pp. $12.95 cloth.
LEVIN, LOWELL S.; KATZ, ALFRED H.; and HOLST, ERIK. *Self-Care: Lay Initiatives in Health*. Prodist, 1976. 133 pp. $8.95 cloth $3.95 paper.
LEWIS, JUDITH A., and LEWIS, MICHAEL D. *Community Counseling: A Human Services Approach*. Wiley, 1977. 382 pp. $12.50 cloth
LOFLAND, JOHN. *Doing Social Life: The Qualitative Study of Human Interaction in Natural Settings*. Wiley, 1976. 328 pp. $14.95 cloth.
LOUBSER, JAN J et al., eds. *Explorations in General Theory in Social Science: Essays in Honor of Talcott Parsons*, vols. 1 & 2. Free Press, 1976. 909 pp. $32.50 ea. $60.00 set, cloth.
LUNDSGAARDE, HENRY P. *Murder in Space City: A Cultural Analysis of Houston Homicide Patterns*. Oxford University Press, 1977. 269 pp. $10.95 cloth.
LURIA, A. R. *Cognitive Development: Its Cultural and Social Foundations*. Harvard University Press, 1976. 175 pp. $12 50 cloth.
MAESTRO, MARCELLO. *Gaetano Filangieri and His "Science of Legislation."* American Philosophical Society, 1976. 76 pp. $6.00 paper.
MAHONEY, MICHAEL J. *Scientist as Subject: The Psychological Imperative*. Ballinger, 1976. 248 pp. $13.50 cloth.
MANNING, PETER K. *The Sociology of Mental Health and Illness*. Bobbs-Merrill, 1976. 115 pp. $3.95 paper.
MARSHALL, LORNA *The !Kung of Nyae Nyae*. Harvard University Press, 1976. 433 pp. $20.00 cloth.
MARTIN, HAROLD P., ed. *The Abused Child: A Multidisciplinary Approach to Developmental Issues and Treatment*. Ballinger, 1976. 304 pp. NPL, cloth
MARTINEZ, TOMÁS. *The Human Marketplace: An Examination of Private Employment Agencies*. Transaction Books, 1976. 159 pp. $8.95 cloth.
MARX, EMANUEL *The Social Context of Violent Behavior: A Social Anthropological Study in an Israeli Immigrant Town*. Routledge & Kegan Paul, 1976. 130 pp. $8.25 paper.
MAY, ANTOINETTE. *Different Drummers: They Did What They Wanted*. Les Femmes, 1976. 156 pp. $4.95 paper.
McCORMACK, WILLIAM C., and WURM, STEPHEN A., eds. *Language and Man: Anthropological Issues*. Mouton, 1976 Dist. by Aldine. $24.50 cloth.
McDONALD, WILLIAM F., ed. *Criminal Justice and the Victim*. Sage, 1976. 288 pp. $17.50 cloth. $7.50 paper.
MILOFSKY, CARL. *Special Education: A Sociological Study of California Programs*. Praeger, 1976. 177 pp. $17.50 cloth.
MONTEIRO, LOIS A. *Monitoring Health Status and Medical Care*. Ballinger, 1976. 221 pp. $17.50 cloth.
MORODAMAS, *The Call of the Purpose: A Selected Chapter*. Exposition, 1976. 79 pp. $4.50 cloth.
MORROW, CAROL KLAPERMAN *Health Care Guidance: Commercial Health Insurance and National Health Policy*. Praeger, 1976. 140 pp. $15.00 cloth.
NAGEL, STUART S., and NEEF, MARIAN. *Operations Research Methods: As Applied to Political Science and the Legal Process*. Sage, 1976. 76 pp. $3.00 paper.
NASH, JUNE; DANDLER, JORGE; and HOPKINS, NICHOLAS S. eds. *Popular Participation in Social Change: Cooperatives, Collectives, and Nationalized Industry*. Mouton, 1976. Dist. by Aldine. 621 pp. $34.50 cloth.
NEAL, ARTHUR G., ed. *Violence in Animal and Human Societies*. Nelson-Hall, 1976. 229 pp. $11.00 cloth.
NEWELL WILLIAM H., ed. *Ancestors*. Mouton, 1976. Dist. by Aldine. 403 pp. $26.50 cloth.
NEWMARK, GERALD. *This School Belongs to You and Me*. Hart, 1976. 431 pp. $10.95 cloth. $5.95 paper.
O'NEILL, JOHN, ed. *On Critical Theory*. Seabury, 1976. 265 pp. $12.95 cloth.
ORLOSKI, RICHARD J. *Criminal Law: An Indictment*. Nelson-Hall, 1976. 146 pp. $8.95 cloth.
ORNAUER, H., et al. *Images of the World in the Year 2000: A Comparative Ten Nation Study*. Humanities, 1976. 729 pp. $45.00 cloth.
ØSTERBERG, DAG. *Meta-sociological Essay*. Tr. Patricia Shaw. Duquesne University Press, 1976. Dist. by Humanities. 96 pp. $5.50 paper.
OVERBEEK, JOHANNES, *The Population Challenge: A Handbook for Nonspecialists*. Greenwood, 1976. 214 pp. $13.95 cloth.
öZBUDUN, ERGUN. *Social Changes and Political Participation in Turkey*. Princeton University Press, 1976. 253 pp. $13.50 cloth.
PARKES, ALAN S. *Patterns of Sexuality and Reproduction*. Oxford University Press, 1976. 148 pp. $3.75 paper.
PELZ, DONALD C., and ANDREWS, FRANK M. *Scientists in Organizations: Productive Climates for Research and Development*, rev. ed. Institute for Social Research/University of Michigan, 1976. 401 pp. NPL, cloth.
PETTIT, PHILIP. *The Concept of Structuralism: A Critical Analysis*. University of California Press, 1975. 117 pp. $8.50 cloth.
POST, JAMES E. *Risk and Response: Management and Social Change in the American Insurance Industry*. Lexington Books, 1976. 206 pp. $17.00 cloth.
POWER, EILEEN. *Medieval Women*. Ed. by M. M. Postan. Cambridge University Press, 1975. 112 pp. $12.95 cloth. $4.45 paper.
PUSEY, MICHAEL. *Dynamics of Bureaucracy: A Case Analysis in Education*. Wiley, 1976. 160 pp. $19.50 cloth.
RANDALL, JOHN HERMAN, JR. *The Making of the Modern Mind*, 50th anniversary ed. Columbia University Press, 1976. 696 pp. $20.00 cloth. $7.00 paper.
RAYNOR, HENRY. *Music and Society since 1815*. Schocken Books, 1976. 213 pp. $15.00 cloth.
REED, JOHN SHELTON. *The Enduring South: Subcultural Persistence in Mass Society*. University of North Carolina Press, 1974. 135 pp. $13.95 cloth. $4.95 papers.
REICHEL-DOLMATOFF, G. *The Shaman and the Jaguar: A Study of Narcotic Drugs among the Indians of Colombia*. Temple University Press, 1975. 280 pp. NPL, cloth.
REIN, MARTIN. *Social Science and Public Policy*. Penquin Books, 1976. 272 pp. $2.95 paper.
RODGERS, HARRELL R., JR., and BULLOCK, CHARLES S. III. *Coercion to Compliance: Or How Great Expectations in Washington Are Actually Realized at the Local Level, This Being the Saga of School Desegration in the South as Told by Two Sympathetic Observers—Lessons on Getting Things Done*. Lexington Books, 1976. 189 pp. $16.00 paper.
ROSENHEIM, MARGARET K., ed. *Pursuing Justice for the Child*. University of Chicago Press, 1976. 361 pp. $12.95 cloth.
RUBIN, LILLIAN BRESLOW. *Words of Pain/Life in the Working Class Family*. Basic Books, 1976. 268 pp. $11.95 cloth.
RUSSELL, DIANA E. H., and VAN DE VEN, NICOLE, comps. and eds. *Crimes against Women: Proceedings of the International Tribunal*. Les Femmes, 1976. 298 pp. $5.95 paper.
SAID, ABDUL, and SIMMONS, LUIZ R., eds. *Ethnicity in an International Context*. Transaction Books, 1976. 241 pp. $12.95 cloth.
SAMUELS, FREDERICK. *The Durable Group: Thoughts on Human Identity*. University Press of America, 1976. 118 pp. NPL, paper.

SANSOM, ROBERT L. *The New American Dream Machine: Toward a Simpler Lifestyle in an Environmental Age.* Anchor Press, 1976. 251 pp. $8.95 cloth.
SANWAL, R. D. *Social Stratification in Rural Kumaon.* Oxford University Press, 1976. 213 pp. $7.25 cloth.
SARGENT, ALICE G. *Beyond Sex Roles.* West, 1977. 489 pp. NPL, paper.
SARRI, ROSEMARY, and HASENFELD, YEHESKEL, eds. *Brought to Justice: Juveniles, the Courts, and the Law.* University of Michigan, 1976. 252 pp. NPL, paper.
SCHRAN, PETER. *Guerrilla Economy: The Development of the Shensi-Kansu-Ninghsia Border Region, 1937–1945.* SUNY Press, 1976. 323 pp. $25.00 cloth.
SCHWARTZ, THEODORE, ed. *Socialization as Cultural Communication: Development of a Theme in the Work of Margaret Mead.* University of California Press. 1976. 250 pp. $15.00 cloth.
SCHWIRIAN, KENT P., et al. *Contemporary Topics in Urban Sociology.* General Learning Press, 1977. 660 pp. NPL, cloth.
SCOTT, JAMES C. *The Moral Economy of the Peasant: Rebellion and Subsistence in Southeast Asia.* Yale University Press, 1976. 246 pp. $15.00 cloth.
SCOTT, JOSEPH W. *Woman, Know Thyself.* Charles B. Slack, 1976. 399 pp. $12.50 cloth.
SEIFER, NANCY. *Nobody Speaks for Me!: Self-Portraits of American Working Class Women.* Simon & Schuster, 1976. 477 pp. $10.95 cloth.
SELLS, S. B., and SIMPSON, D. DWAYNE, eds. *Studies of the Effectiveness of Treatments for Drug Abuse Volume V: Evaluation of Treatment Outcomes for 1972–1973 DARP Admission Cohort.* Ballinger, 1976. 522 pp. $25.00 cloth.
SENNETT, RICHARD. *The Fall of Public Man.* Alfred A. Knopf, 1977. 373 pp. $15.00 cloth.
SHOTLAND, R. LANCE. *University Communication Networks: The Small World Method.* Wiley, 1976. 179 pp. $6.95 paper.
SHYROCK, HENRY S.; SIEGAL, JACOB S.; and ASSOCIATES. *The Methods and Materials of Demography,* condensed ed. by Edward G. Stockwell. Academic Press, 1976. 577 pp. $16.50 cloth.
SILK, LEONARD, and VOGEL, DAVID. *Ethics and Profits: The Crisis of Confidence in American Business.* Simon and Schuster, 1976. 250 pp. $8.95 cloth.
SIU, BOBBY. *Fifty Years of Struggle: The Development of the Women's Movements in China (1900–1949).* Revomen, 1975. 283 pp. NPL, paper.
SIU, BOBBY C. Y. *A Sociology of American Feminism: The Rise of Women's Consciousness in Nineteenth Century America.* Revoment, 1976. 103 pp. NPL, paper.
SLUZKI, CARLOS E., and RANSOM DONALD C., eds. *Double Bind: The Foundation of the Communicational Approach to the Family.* Grune & Stratton, 1976. 359 pp. $19.75 cloth.
SOLZHENITSYN, ALEKSANDR. *Détente: Prospects for Democracy and Dictatorship.* Transaction Books, 1976. 112 pp. $5.95 cloth.
STAPLETON, JEAN, and BRIGHT, RICHARD. *Equal Marriage.* Abingdon, 1976. 144 pp. $5.95 cloth.
STEWART, PATRICIA R. *Children in Distress: American and English Perspectives.* Sage, 1976. 285 pp. $12.00 cloth. $7.00 paper.
STONE, CLARENCE N. *Economic Growth and Neighborhood Discontent: System Bias in the Urban Renewal Program of Atlanta.* University of North Carolina Press, 1976. 256 pp. NPL, cloth.
TERRELL, PAUL. *The Social Impact of Revenue Sharing: Planning, Participation, and the Purchase of Service.* Praeger 1976. 114 pp. $12.50 cloth.
TIMMS, NOEL, and WATSON, DAVID eds. *Talking about Welfare: Readings in Philosophy and Social Policy.* Routledge & Kegan Paul 1976. 306 pp. $13.75 cloth. $6.75 paper.
TORBERT, WILLIAM R. *Creating a Community of Inquiry: Conflict, Collaboration, Transformation.* Wiley, 1976. 184 pp. $14.50 cloth.
TURNER JONATHAN H. *American Society: Problems of Structure,* 2nd ed. Harper & Row, 1976. $8.95 paper.
TUZIN, DONALD F. *The Ilahita Arapesh: Dimensions of Unity.* University of California Press, 1976. 376 pp. $16.50 cloth.
VALLIANATOS, E. G. *Fear in the Countryside: The Control of Agricultural Resources in the Poor Countries by Nonpeasant Elites.* Ballinger, 1976. 180 pp. NPL, cloth.
VAN GEEL, TYLL. *Authority to Control the School Program.* Lexington Books 1976. 249 pp. $15.50 cloth.
VANSITTART, JANE, ed. *Lifelines: The Stacey Letters, 1836–1858.* Taplinger, 1976. 180 pp. $8.95 cloth.
VEATCH, ROBERT M. *Death, Dying and the Biological Revolution: Our Last Quest for Responsibility.* Yale University Press, 1976. 323 pp. $12.95 cloth.
WAMSLEY, GARY L., and ZALD, MAYER N. *The Political Economy of Public Organizations: A Critique and Approach to the Study of Public Administration.* Indiana University Press 1976. 110 pp. $3.50 paper.
WARFIELD, JOHN N. *Societal Systems: Planning, Policy and Complexity.* Wiley, 1976. 490 pp. $29.95 cloth.
WASBY, STEPHEN L. *Small Town Police and the Supreme Court: Hearing the Word.* Lexington Books, 1976. 264 pp. $18.00 cloth.
WATTENBERG, BEN J., ed. *The Statistical History of the United States: From Colonial Times to the Present.* Basic Books, 1976. 1,235 pp. $24.00 cloth.
WEEKS, JOHN R. *Teenage Marriages: A Demographic Analysis.* Greenwood, 1976. 171 pp. $13.75 cloth.
WEINER, NORMAN L. *The Role of the Police in Urban Society: Conflicts and Consequences.* Bobbs-Merrill, 1976. 51 pp. $2.50 paper.
WELCH, CLAUDE E., JR. ed. *Civilian Control of the Military: Theory and Cases from Developing Countries.* SUNY Press, 1976. 337 pp. $20.00 cloth.
WHITEFORD, MICHAEL B. *The Forgotten Ones: Colombian Countrymen in an Urban Setting.* University Presses of Florida, 1976. 143 pp. $8.50 cloth.
WIGGINTON, ELIOT, ed. *"I Wish I Could Give My Son a Wild Raccoon."* Doubleday, 1976. 366 pp. $10.00 cloth. $4.95 paper.
WILKERSON, ALBERT E., ed. *The Rights of Children: Emergent Concepts in Law and Society.* Temple University Press, 1973. 313 pp. NPL, cloth.
WILKINSON, DORIS Y. ed. *Social Structure and Assassination Behavior: The Sociology of Political Murder.* Schenkman 1976. 226 pp. $9.50 cloth.
WILLIAMS, JOHN E., and MORLAND, J. KENNETH. *Race, Color and the Young Child.* University of North Carolina Press, 1976. 360 pp. $12.95 cloth.
WILLIAMS, WALTER, and ELMORE, RICHARD F., eds. *Social Program Implementation.* Academic Press, 1976. 299 pp. $14.50 cloth.
WRONG DENNIS H. *Skeptical Sociology.* Columbia University Press, 1976. 322 pp. $14.95 cloth.

JULY 1977 – VOLUME 6, NUMBER 4

ONTEMPORARY SOCIOLOGY

A JOURNAL OF REVIEWS

IN THIS ISSUE

The Crises and Contradictions of Capitalism: Jonathan Rieder and Norbert Wiley review work by Daniel Bell, Jürgen Habermas, and James O'Connor

Roy Austin surveys recent books on juvenile delinquency

S.D. Berkowitz on Eric Hobsbawm's *The Age of Capital*

Daniel Kegan on education and society

Roy Wallis and Zelda Gamson on religious change

Louis Schneider reviews *Adam Smith's Sociological Economics*

H.C. Greisman on *The Sociology of Karl Mannheim*

Peter Singleton on South American peasants

UBLICATION OF THE AMERICAN SOCIOLOGICAL ASSOCIATION

contemporary sociology

a journal of reviews

July 1977 • Volume 6, Number 4

Concerning advertising, change of address and subscriptions, address: Executive Office, American Sociological Association, 1722 N Street, N.W., Washington, D.C. 20036.

Concerning manuscripts and book reviews, address: Editor, *Contemporary Sociology: A Journal of Reviews,* C-002, University of California, San Diego, La Jolla, California, 92093.

Contemporary Sociology: A Journal of Reviews is published at 49 Sheridan Avenue, Albany, N.Y. 12210, bi-monthly in January, March, May, July, September, and November.

Annual membership dues in the American Sociological Association, $30.00–$50.00. Student Member, $15; Associate, $20; International Associate, $12; Student Associate, $10.

Subscription rate for members, $10; non-members, $15; institutions and libraries, $20; non-member students, $10. Single issues $4.

New subscriptions and renewals will be entered on a calendar year basis only.

Change of address: Six weeks advance notice to the Executive Office, and old address as well as new, are necessary for change of subscriber's address.

Claims for undelivered copies must be made within the month following the regular month of publication. The publishers will supply missing copies when losses have been sustained in transit and when the reserve stock will permit.

ISSN 0094–3061

Second class postage paid at Washington, D.C. and at additional mailing offices.

Book reviews from *CS* are indexed in *Book Review Index,* published by Gale Research Company.

ASA Multiple Submission Policy: Submission of a manuscript to a professional journal clearly implies commitment to publish in that journal. The competition for journal space requires a great deal of time and effort on the part of editorial readers whose main compensation for this service is the opportunity to read papers prior to publication and the gratification associated with discharge of professional obligation. For these reasons, *the American Sociological Association regards submission of a manuscript to a professional journal while that paper is under review by another journal as unacceptable.*

Cover designed by Kenneth E. Anderson, A.I.A.

TABLE OF CONTENTS

LETTERS 400

REVIEW SYMPOSIUM

Bell: *The Cultural Contradictions of Capitalism;*
Habermas: *Legitimation Crisis;* and
O'Connor: *The Fiscal Crisis of the State* .... Jonathan Rieder 411
Norbert Wiley 416

FEATURES

Bauer: *Chilean Rural Society from the Spanish Conquest to 1930* and
Forman: *The Brazilian Peasantry* .... Peter Singelmann 425
Hobsbawm: *The Age of Capital, 1848–1875* .... S. D. Berkowitz 428

SURVEY REVIEWS

Bartollas, Miller, and Dinitz: *Juvenile Victimization: The Institutional Paradox;*
Carter and Klein: *Back on the Street: The Diversion of Juvenile Offenders;*
Klein: *The Juvenile Justice System;*
Mays: *The Social Treatment of Young Offenders;* and
Sanders: *Juvenile Delinquency* .... Roy L. Austin 430
Black: *Comparative Modernization: A Reader;*
Goldthorpe: *The Sociology of the Third World: Disparity and Involvement;* and
Turner: *Industrialism* .... Randall G. Stokes 432
Clark: *The Problems of American Education;*
Robischon, Rabow, and Schmidt: *Cracks in the Classroom Wall;*
Shimahara and Scrupski: *Social Forces and Schooling: An Anthropological and Sociological Perspective;* and
Wilson: *Education, Equality, and Society* .... Daniel L. Kegan 434

BOOK REVIEWS

Culture

Bascom: *African Dilemma Tales* .... Steven S. Jones 436
Glassie: *All Silver and No Brass: An Irish Christmas Mumming* .... Roger Abrahams 437
Liebman: *Exploring the Latin American Mind* .... Edgar G. Nesman 438
Schelsky: *Die Arbeit tun die anderen: Klassenkampf und Priesterherrschaft der Intellektuellen* .... Gerd Schroeter 438

Development/Modernization

Austin: *Japan: The Paradox of Progress* .... Brian S. Vargus 439
de Kadt and Williams: *Sociology and Development* and
Farmanfarmaian: *The Social Sciences and Problems of Development* .... J. Bernard Murphy 441
Golde: *Catholics and Protestants: Agricultural Modernization in Two German Villages* .... Eleanor Meyer Rogg 441
Kahl: *Modernization, Exploitation and Dependency in Latin America* .... Ira Studin 442
Karan: *The Changing Face of Tibet: The Impact of Chinese Communist Ideology on the Landscape* .... Mario D. Zamora 444

Environment

Bell: *Strategies for Human Settlements: Habitat and Environment* .... Howard M. Hammerman 445
Cooper: *Growth in America* .... Albert J. Mayer 445
Steiner: *The Vanishing White Man* .... Joe T. Darden 446

Family and Intimate Lifestyles

Brain: *Friends and Lovers* .... Craig Calhoun 447
Myers and Leggitt: *Adultery and Other Private Matters* .... Louis Rowitz 448
Nickell, Rice and Tucker: *Management in Family Living* and
Schulz: *The Changing Family: Its Function and Future* .... Rela Geffen Monson 449

Methods

Lin: *Foundations of Social Research* .... Roger Spielmann 449
Michelson: *Behavioral Research Methods in Environment Design* .... William R. Burch, Jr. 450
Platt: *Realties of Social Research* .... Bob Hinings 451

Occupations

Angrist and Almquist: *Careers and Contingencies: How College Women Juggle with Gender* .... Bettina J. Huber 452
Dunbar and Kravitz: *Hard Traveling: Migrant Farm Workers in America* .... David Harvey 453
Dunkerley: *The Foreman: Aspects of Task and Structure* .... Richard K. Brown 454

Political

Eckstein and Gurr: *Patterns of Authority: A Structural Basis for Political Inquiry* .... Anthony Orum 455
Engelmann and Schwartz: *Canadian Political Parties: Origin, Character, Impact* .... Paul Lamy 457
Ericson: *Radicals in the University* .... Henry Pachter 457
Pipes: *Soviet Strategy in Europe* .... Paul Hollander 459
Taft: *Mayday at Yale: A Case Study in Student Radicalism* and
Wood: *The Sources of American Student Activism* .... Richard G. Braungart 461

Race and Ethnic

Baron: *The Russian Jew under Tsars and Soviets;*
Baron: *A Social and Religious History of the Jews, Volume XVI: Late Middle Ages and Era of European Expansion;* and
Greenberg: *The Jews in Russia: The Struggle for Emancipation* .... Francesco Cordasco 463
Brewer and Campbell: *Ethnocentrism and Intergroup Attitudes: East African Evidence* .... Stanley J. Morse 465
Cox: *Race Relations: Elements and Social Dynamics* .... Don O. Watkins 466
Francis: *Interethnic Relations: An Essay in Sociological Theory* .... Richard T. Schaefer 466
Franklin: *Racial Equality in America* .... William P. Nye 467
Kitano: *Japanese Americans: The Evolution of a Subculture* .... Darrel Montero 467
Martin: *Race First: The Ideological and Organizational Struggles of Marcus Garvey and the Universal Negro Improvement Association* .... Douglas S. Snyder 468
Michelman: *The Black Sash of South Africa* .... Linda Stoneall 469
Moore: *Mexican Americans* .... Audrey W. Forrest 470
van den Berghe: *Race and Ethnicity in Africa* .... Sharon Stichter 470

Religion

Fry: *Spirits of Protest: Spirit-Mediums and the Articulation of Consensus amongst the Zezuru of Southern Rhodesia* .... Bennetta Jules-Rosette 471
Glock and Bellah: *The New Religious Consciousness* .... Roy Wallis 472
Hoge: *Commitment on Campus: Changes in Religion and Values over Five Decades* .... Zelda F. Gamson 474
Jules-Rosette: *African Apostles: Ritual and Conversion in the Church of John Maranke* .... Daniel J. Crowley 475

Sex Roles and Behavior

Dinnerstein: *The Mermaid and the Minotaur* .... Miriam M. Johnson 476
Iglitzin and Ross: *Women in the World: A Comparative Study* .... Janet Zollinger Giele 478
Miller: *Toward a New Psychology of Women* .... Nancy Chodorow 479
Rich: *Of Woman Born* .... Nona Glazer 480
Roberts: *Beyond Intellectual Sexism: A New Woman, A New Reality* .... Athena Theodore 482
Russell and Van de Ven: *Crimes against Women: Proceedings of the International Tribunal* .... Teresa D. Marciano 483
Wertmuller: *Swept Away* .... Chandra Mukerji 483

Social Change

Matejko: *Social Change and Stratification in Eastern Europe: An Interpretive Analysis of Poland and Her Neighbors* .... Szymon Chodak 486
Rotstein: *Beyond Industrial Growth* .... Irene Taviss Thomson 487
Singh: *Caste, Class and Democracy: Changes in a Stratification System* .... Baidya Nath Varma 488

Social Psychology

Campbell, Converse, and Rodgers: *The Quality of American Life: Perceptions, Evaluations, and Satisfactions* .... Richard M. Cohn 489
Gaev: *The Psychology of Loneliness* .... Robert A. Stebbins 490
Sheehy: *Passages: Predictable Crises of Adult Life* .... Michael S. Kimmel 490

Theory

Craib: *Existentialism and Sociology: A Study of Jean-Paul Sartre* .... Dean MacCannell 493
Emery and Trist: *Towards a Social Ecology: Contextual Appreciations of the Future in the Present* .... Richard O. Mason 494
Krader: *The Asiatic Mode of Production: Sources, Development and Critique in the Writings of Karl Marx* .... Gail Omvedt 495
Leach: *Culture and Communication: The Logic by Which Symbols Are Connected* .... Robert D. Leighninger, Jr. 496
Pettit: *The Concept of Structuralism: A Critical Analysis* .... Ino Rossi 497
Reisman: *Adam Smith's Sociological Economics* .... Louis Schneider 497
Remmling: *The Sociology of Karl Mannheim* .... H. C. Greisman 499

Additional Reviews

Rogers and Agarwala-Rogers: *Communication in Organizations* .... Rita Braito 500
Bragg: *Speak for England* .... Joan Gilbert 500
Conzen: *Immigrant Milwaukee, 1836–1860: Accommodation and Community in a Frontier City* .... Eric H. Monkkonen 501
Deitchman: *The Best-Laid Schemes: A Tale of Social Research and Bureaucracy* .... David R. Segal 502
Etzioni: *A Comparative Analysis of Complex Organizations: On Power, Involvement, and Their Correlates* .... Paul M. Hirsch 503
Parker: *The Sociology of Leisure* .... Worth C. Summers 506
Robinson: *From Drinking to Alcoholism: A Sociological Commentary* .... Walter Davis 507
Rynkiewich and Spradley: *Ethics and Anthropology: Dilemmas in Field Work* .... Elvi Whittaker 508
Shapiro: *Painters and Politics: The European Avante-Garde Society, 1900–1925* .... Barbara Rosenblum 509
Schneidman: *Suicidology: Contemporary Developments* .... James F. Short, Jr. 511
Tulloch: *A Home Is Not a Home: Life within a Nursing Home* .... Thomas J. Cottle 512

PUBLICATIONS RECEIVED 513

LETTERS

(Letters which comment on particular reviews are routinely sent to reviewers for a reply. Where no reply by reviewers appears in these columns, it is usually because they chose not to reply.)

From the Editor:

Several of the letters in this and other issues contain implicit or explicit criticism of *CS* for printing reviews which the letter writers regard as in one way or another unworthy of appearing in a scholarly journal. That, of course, is a matter of opinion, and there is room for more than one. Particularly with negative, harsh, even caustic reviews, the line between printable and unprintable reviews is often hard to draw, and errors of judgment are probable now and then. This editor prefers to err by printing rather than by censoring; an error is at least remediable that way, as the vitality of our letters columns suggests.

CS, for example, has received twenty-four letters in recent weeks protesting the very brief and very harsh review which Al Lee's book, *Toward Humanist Sociology*, received in these pages. We replied directly to the writers of the first three or four letters, before realizing that there was an organized campaign of protest under way which would produce more.

Well and good. The letters tell us, at least, that the journal is read and that its readers have energy and vigor enough to speak up when something displeases them. Now the question is what to do about these letters. In general, they demand from *CS* (1) an apology for having printed the review, and (2) the reassignment of the book to another reviewer.

The apology is demanded on the grounds that the review in question is "unprofessional," "irresponsible," "unethical," "dishonest," "vulgar," and so on. What is it that the review says? That the book is not worth the 800 words we assigned the reviewer; that there's little worthwhile in it not said earlier and better by C. Wright Mills. These are certainly harsh judgments, but not, it seems to us "dishonest," "vulgar," or "unprofessional," etc. We could have taken the reviewer to mean that the book was really not worth reviewing, and thus not printed his (or any) review (we have done that several times before, when reviewers have recommended against devoting space to a book). But then there would have been protests that the book was not reviewed (we get many letters from authors protesting their books' not having been reviewed). We knew that the brevity and harshness of the review would evoke strong response; we even wrote Dr. Arnold, long before the review was published, asking him if he wished to reconsider committing it to print. He replied that he wanted it printed because he regarded it as his obligation to warn readers away from bad books as well as to praise good ones.

To have rejected the review and sought another reviewer would have exposed *CS* to allegations of censorship or suppression, for we have never, repeat never, rejected a review because of the opinions expressed in it (although more than a few of these opinions have offended me personally), and under the present Editorship, *CS* never will. Nor do we seek more than one review except when in our judgment a book is likely to be unusually important or controversial. In short, we knew there would be protest if *CS* printed the Arnold review, and we knew there would be protest if we didn't. We chose to print the review (and would do so again), expecting that there would be Letters to the Editor quarreling with the reviewer's judgments and otherwise defending the book—which we also expected to print, for that is our routine procedure.

The most regrettable thing about this whole episode is that not a single one of the twenty-four letters we received bothered to attempt a substantive rebuttal to Arnold's review or to defend the intellectual achievement of Lee's book. That, it seems to us, would have been the most dignified and professionally effective way of countering Arnold's judgment: in effect providing that "other" review which the protesters demand. But instead of defending Lee's book, surely a "professional" and "responsible" thing to do (if that is their opinion), the letter writers chose to demand an apology from *CS* for having printed the review, hence applying pressure to future Editors of this journal to avoid offending authors with a constituency sufficient to organize a protest in his or her behalf. We will mount no soapbox in lofty affirmation of intellectual freedom, but it is our view that the publication of honest opinion (however harsh) does not do a disservice to the profession; demands for an apology do.

Therefore, there will be no apology from *CS* for having printed the review. We do apologize, however, for the proofreading error in the printed title of Dr. Lee's book. Nor will we seek another review. We are, however, printing the following letters. The first letter of protest we received was from Flynn, and we replied to him suggesting that a substantive rebuttal to the Arnold review would be more effective for publication as a Letter-to-the-Editor than a simple letter of protest. His solicited response appears below. The writers of the three additional letters which follow specifically requested that their letters be printed.

Dr. Arnold chose not to reply publicly.

BENNETT M. BERGER

To the Editor:

When is a "review" not a review? There is no question of the right, and even responsibility, of a reviewer who finds the book he/she is evaluating to be of inferior quality, to express this opinion strongly and even castigate its author, if such seems warranted. But if a strong opinion, either positive or negative, is set forth, some sort of reasons should be given in support of the opinion, not only out of respect for the author but, more importantly, so that the readers of the review can have some basis for knowing how and why the reviewer came to his/her strong perspectives on the book.

Professor David O. Arnold's so-called "review" of Albert McClung Lee's *Toward Humanist Sociology* (the title of which is not even correctly reported) is not a review, but a curt, unsubstantiated dismissal. Arnold spends about sixty words saying, in effect, that the book "is not worth" an eight hundred word review, stating that he "is not sure" what the book is. *Toward Humanist Sociology* is a closely reasoned plea for a type of sociology that is ethically and morally committed to the achievement of betterment of the human condition, rather than a province of elitists who like to conceive of themselves as "above" their subject "matter," i.e., other human beings. It has been enthusiastically reviewed in a wide variety of American and international journals as an important statement of how sociology can and should be committed to humane values. Arnold is correct when he states (in his only genuine, albiet perfunctory, comment about the contents of the book) that *Toward Humanist Sociology* bears some semblance to another, earlier classic, C. Wright Mill's *The Sociological Imagination*. Certainly, such a comparison should, one would think, render Lee's opus at the least a genuine review. But Arnold evidently does not agree. Had he cared to carry out the responsibilty he was assigned, Arnold would have seen, and perhaps mentioned, that rather than being a mere rehash of Mills's points, Lee's book not only extends some of Mills's perspectives into areas of concern with which Mills did not deal, but also disagrees with some central aspects of Mills's argument. If, using Arnold's words, Lee has "some worthwhile things" to say, why not summarize some of these things? If they are worthwhile, they certainly deserve some sort of discussion.

Any book, especially (though not at all exclusively) by immediate former A.S.A. presidents, or indeed by anyone of whatever stature in the discipline and however distasteful his/her views might be, deserves more than the summary dismissal accorded *Toward Humanist Sociology*. *Contemporary Sociology*, as the leading review journal in the discipline, has a responsibility not only to the authors of books reviewed, but to its readers, to provide something more than a statement that says, in effect, "this book is not worth reviewing," especially a book as important and even profound as *Toward Humanist Sociology*.

CHARLES P. FLYNN
Miami University

To the Editor:

I want to strongly express my disappointment in the "non-review" given to Alfred McClung Lee's book *Toward Humanistic* [sic] *Sociology* written by David O. Arnold in *CS* (Vol. 6, No. 2, March 1977). If for no *other* reason, it shows the utmost disrespect for our recent past president to have been treated in such a cavalier manner. Sociologists read *CS* to find out about new books, not cute little disclaimers about Parkinson's Law. I hope that either a new review will be written or that Arnold will answer this letter and respond with a short review: what Lee has written, what C. Wright Mills wrote, and why and how Mills said it "earlier and better." That may be true, that Mills said it better, but it is a conclusion that the reader must make, not just the reviewer. I am sure there are many others out there who feel as I do.

JACK NUSAN PORTER
Boston

To the Editor:

I am writing to you to protest the review in *CS* of Al Lee's *Toward Humanistic* [sic] *Sociology* in the March 1977 issue.

I would classify it as a "non-review." What particularly disturbs me is the fact that Arnold, the reviewer, says: "Its publisher claims that *Toward Humanistic* [sic] *Sociology* is an *introductory textbook*" [my emphasis]. Actually, the description of the publisher on the back of Lee's book states, *"Toward Humanist Sociology* . . . is a comprehensive introduction to issues and problems of our society. It takes an activist view and offers perspectives on the relevance of sociology to contemporary struggles . . . *Toward Humanist Sociology* is the culmination of his concern about society's *problems* [my emphasis], what can be done about them, and what can be learned about them."

This is a very accurate description of the book, and nowhere on the back of this paperback book is there the slightest indication that the book was intended as an introductory textbook.

I have used this book in my Social Problems courses, and I have also used it as collateral reading in other courses, all with good effect.

Perhaps your reviewer does not understand action-oriented sociology. If this is the case, then it would seem that the editor should be obliged to assign this book, written by the immediate past president of ASA, to some reviewer capable of making an authoritative critique of Lee's viewpoint.

Arnold's review comes across as a "demolition" job. It is extremely irresponsible on the part of a reviewer-scholar and the editor of an academic journal to criticize a book without examining the substance.

James Young
Wilmington College

To the Editor:

I have read with much interest the review of Alfred McClung Lee's *Toward Humanist Sociology* in the March 1977 issue of *Contemporary Sociology*. David O. Arnold's review of Lee's book does not come as any surprise to me. I have been noting with deep regret the decline in professional scholarly standards of journals officially supported by the American Sociological Association in the past few years; David Arnold's frivolous, incoherent and ill-informed utterance (for the caricature he offers of Lee's work is too brief and intellectually dishonest to be called a "review" in any meaningful sense) in the aforementioned issue is only a vivid and graphic example of the drift of the official journals in general and *Contemporary Sociology* in particular. The fact that in some issues of your journal there are one or two reasonably well-written and sometimes incisive review articles does not, in my judgment, offset the deteriorating scholarship of which Arnold's article is an extreme example.

I do not know whether other members of the Association and subscribers to *Contemporary Sociology* have been forming the same impression as mine in recent years, but I do think you and your associate editors should be held answerable for the integrity of articles that you have decided to publish. Will the current trend toward mediocrity, superficiality and "gut-feeling" reviews be allowed to continue? Will MacIver Awards, Sorokin Awards, C. Wright Mills Awards and the taking of editorships become a new means of celebrating this new style of professionalism? Will David Arnold be adding to his *vitae* the fact that he published a book review in a prestigious journal of sociology and be on his way to bigger and better things?

I would like an opportunity to review critically Lee's *Toward Humanist Sociology* or, if you prefer, to see some other prospective reviewer undertake an informed analysis of this work. I would appreciate knowing whether you are prepared to consider a new review of it, because the one you saw fit to publish reveals much more about the author of the review and the editors deciding to publish it than about *Humanist Sociology*.

Irwin Sperber
SUNY/College at New Paltz

To the Editor:

In the May 1976 *CS* Bruce C. Johnson reviewed *Opinion-Making Elites in Yugoslavia*. We are delighted that he liked the chapters by our Yugoslav collaborators, but feel that the review was fundamentally inaccurate in its criticisms of the chapters in which we analyzed data from the elite survey.

(1) Johnson says, ". . . major weight was given to items which asked legislators to rank the relative importance, from a prepared list of: informing their constituents, representing their constituents, working for socialist humanism, etc. Such flat and stale attitudinal indicators pre-limit and trivialize the issues at hand in very basic ways. They helped cheapen a magnificent research opportunity."

The item quoted (a "legislator's role" question repeated from previous political elite studies)—indeed turned out not very useful and *was not in fact used* in the chapters he criticizes. Attitude items actually used included such "flat and stale" issues as: what should be the relative salaries of unskilled, skilled and white-collar workers, engineers, managers, and high officials; the priority of economic growth versus equality; whether the mass media criticized government and economic officials too much; and how satisfied the elites believed the public was with the economic reform, foreign policy, living standards, and nationality policies.

(2) "The basic strategy of all three essays is brutally simple: run lots of cross-tabulations, designate any fairly strong correlation a major finding, and then offer ad hoc interpretations of the correlation."

The chapter by Barton starts with an explicit set of propositions linked in a model (pp. 224–229) at the level of "general orientations"—relationships between classes of variables; this model guided the specific relationships to be examined, and results are related back to the model. The "major finding" reported (p. 229) is not "any strong correlation" but a pattern of controlled relationships showing that the most important determinant of policy attitudes (such as listed above) among Yugoslav elites is their occupational function, and not their class background or early political career. This is a general relationship also found in surveys in many capitalist countries (Edinger, Searing, Schleth, Barton) and has important implications for the theoretical model. The Kadushin and Abrams chapters likewise use explicit causal models, not random search.

(3) "Many of the latter [interpretations] are clichés not specifically rooted in Yugoslav life. (Example: why are intellectuals in favor of more wage egalitarianism? Because they never had to meet a payroll, p. 236.)"

The finding that intellectuals express more egalitarian sentiments than economic managers and state bureaucrats is not specifically rooted in Yugoslav experience because it occurs also in the Soviet Union and Mao's China, to say nothing of capitalist societies (Ladd & Lipset, Kadushin). One test of the explanation (structural pressure for productivity on managers versus intellectuals' specialization in producing social criticism) is the fact that intellectuals and politicians who *have* held economic administrative jobs ("meet a payroll") are less egalitarian (Table 8.10) and more devoted to economic growth as a national goal (Table 8.9), their resemblance to a cliché notwithstanding.

(4) "The time order of variables is decided by fiat."

The issue of time order is dealt with specifically. Some variables have an obvious order: father's occupation before son's, wartime experience before post-war jobs, past party activity before present policy influence. The analysis tests whether some clearly prior factors (social origin, early political experience) explain attitude differences between elites in different institutions. It examines possible socializing experiences which intervene between type of job and attitude (e.g., the relation between exposure to types of communications media and attitudes, which turns out to be spurious when job is controlled). Not *all* time order questions are resolved; there remains the question of whether there was selection to past and present jobs on the basis of prior attitudes which were *not* related to the measures of social origin and early political affiliation which we did control. This alternative hypothesis should have been explicitly noted along with the need for longitudinal data to test it against our explanation of "occupational determination" of attitudes.

(5) "Perceived influence is confounded with actual influence."

The Kadushin-Abrams chapters examine four measures of influence: *reputation* for general influence; being mentioned by respondents as *influencing them* on important problems in their own fields ("opinion leadership"); being mentioned as a *discussion partner* on both general and specific problems; and *participation* in policy-making through advisory commissions and drafting proposals. Far from confounding perceived and "actual" influence, the chapters analyze the relations between different indicators of influence of which reputation is only one.

The reviewer concluded his discussion of these chapters with the comment: "This is little more than science fiction." We invite the reader to look at the chapters themselves to see who is writing the science and who the fiction.

Allen H. Barton
Bogdan Denitch
Charles Kadushin
Bureau of Applied Social Research
Columbia University

To the Editor:

I shall respond to the five points made by Professors Barton, Denitch, and Kadushin in order, and close with some more general remarks..

One. I did not object to the topics analyzed in this book, but rather to the indicators, the measures, thereof which were used. The legislator item seemed particularly silly. Since Barton et al. agree that it was not useful, I probably should have chosen a different example. In fact, the items Barton et al. mention here were also generally unsatisfactory, as were questions 21 and 23–35 in the schedule. The schedule's best items were the open-ended ones (especially 12–16 and 51); these were unaccountably left aside in the analysis. However, both the close-ended and the open-ended items could have been much improved. In the general and hypothetical form in which they were cast, these questions greatly oversimplified the phenomena under study. It would have been more productive to use questions which were embedded in specific historical, policy, and situational contexts, particularly since the respondents were articulate and informed elite persons. Many such contextual possibilities for questions were mentioned by Lenard Cohen and by Rudi Supek in their essays in the book under review. To the constellation there outlined, one should add the endemic conflicts among Serbs, Croatians and other national groupings within Yugoslavia, and also Tito's Economic Reform of 1965; both were and are very important in Yugoslav life. *Union Democracy* is an example of a survey study which does contextually ground itself; a survey of this sort of Yugoslav elites could easily have met with my approval.

Two. The models to which Barton et al. refer are loose and vague. Rather than limit or direct investigation in any strong way, they actually permit a nearly random search within a general set of parameters. At the outset of chapter 8, Barton states that his initial propositions there "specify neither the particular variables nor the direction of relationships but say only that there probably are some relationships between certain types of variables that are worth investigating" (p. 225). In fact, this chapter's model proposed that occupational function *and* class background *and* early career all influence attitudes. Almost any correlation which turned up could have been fit into such a framework. The two Kadushin/Abrams chapters have still less in the way of models. At the outset of chapter 7, several bodies of scholarly literature are mentioned incidently, whence it is concluded that they offer few clues for direction of the investigation (p. 192). Reference to these literatures is then dropped, and a variety of empirical findings simply summarized. The "social circles" notion which underlies chapter 6 is not a model, but an empirical phenomenon. At the outset of this chapter, no propositions about how cohesive, extensive, etc. these circles might be among Yugoslav elites are offered; again, the chapter mainly summarizes particular findings. Since the models which inform these chapters specify neither what relationships to expect in the data nor how to explain those relationships, all three chapters are suffused with ad hoc interpretations of particular findings. These interpretations are rooted in common sense notions, not specific to the models in use, of how occupational mind sets, working relations among experts, reward structures, and so on, seem to function in social life generally.

Three. Barton et al. agree with me that the claim that intellectuals are egalitarian because they are impractical is not specifically rooted in Yugoslav life; we disagree over whether this claim is a cliché. Their analysis assumes that economic growth and egalitarianism are conflicting goals. This silently reifies a defective theory of stratification, the functional one. Barton et al. ask, in effect, why intellectuals have fantasies of egalitarianism. Since equality would benefit the less privileged in any society, a more neutral and pertinent way to put this question is to ask why intellectuals tend to identify with the less privileged. I agree with Barton et al. that people often learn their politics in occupational positions. However, I read the literature on the politics of intellectuals as telling us that the extent to which intellectuals identify with the less privileged, and the reasons for their doing so, vary considerably in the first, second, and third worlds, not to speak of particular nations, and eras. This is in part a question of judgment. Barton et al. stress the commonalities; I stress the contrasts.

Four. I should have said that the time order of *many* variables is decided by fiat. Even among the background variables, which Barton et al. stress in their rebuttal, there are some problems. For instance, many Yugoslavs retrospectively invented a personal history of partisan activity (p. 105); it is certainly conceivable that proletarian or peasant backgrounds have also been concocted on occasion to further career advancement. The study's major time order problem lies in the fact that respondent attitudes were measured at but a single point in time. There are no data at all on prior attitudes: no panel data, no retrospective self-reports, no controlling for occupational tenure, and precious little controlling for age. In other words, the crucial assumption of these chapters (that attitudes are subsequent in time order to most other variables used) remains arbitrary and undemonstrated. In these circumstances, the examination of attitude variation by occupational sector is a descriptive, not a causal, endeavor. A causal chain leading from current political roles to current formal influence to current informal influence is declared by fiat on pages 201 and 208. A causal chain leading from social context to communications exposure to opinions is declared by fiat on pages 226–227, though not without some hedging of bets. Often, it should be said, the authors of these three chapters simply give up on the time order problem and retreat to mere description of the variation uncovered.

Five. The best way to study actual influence is to directly observe people at work—to do qualitative case studies in a decision-making mode. Sociometric analysis is an inadequate surrogate for such case studies, the claims of Professors Kadushin and Abrams to the contrary notwithstanding. Barton et al. mention six survey items. The first two measure perceived influence. Kadushin and Abrams recognize this, though they also systematically imply that actual influence is being tapped by these items, as when they refer to them as measures of informal influence and as evidence of the existence of social circles. The second two (discussion partner) items might well have gotten close to actual influence. However, since they neglected to inquire into the content of the interaction in question, we are left not knowing whether, during the reported interactions, respondents were influencing, being influenced, or both or neither. The last two items cited, which Kadushin and Abrams misleading term measures of formal influence, are actually measures of authority. Throughout these two chapters, "influence" is treated as an umbrella concept which can subsume power, authority, manipulation, prestige and information gathering. This creates a conceptual swamp.

In sum, I remain convinced that chapters 6 through 8 of this book are distinctly flawed, even though the "science fiction" remark probably should have been blue-penciled. I was disappointed that Barton et al. remained silent on other major questions concerning *Opinion-Making Elites in Yugoslavia* raised in my review. In my judgment, one half of this book criticizes the other half. Was there indeed (as Professor Denitch suggests on page 21) a lack of genuine intellectual collaboration within the book's research team? In my judgment, the book's data cannot tell us whether Yugoslavia's elite is a maker, a shaper, or merely a conduit for mass public opinion. Has a major undocumented conclusion been bootlegged into the book's title? Nonetheless, I thank Professors Barton, Denitch and Kadushin for seriously addressing a number of the scholarly issues which separate us. Our common goal is intellectual clarity, even in disputation.

BRUCE C. JOHNSON
University of California, San Diego

To the Editor:

It is a pity that Gwynne Peirson, having concluded that *Violence, Race, and Culture* by Lynn A. Curtis was not a book he could review objectively, decided to write the review nonetheless, thereby depriving us of the opportunity to read a more balanced assessment.

Peirson takes issue with the author's attempt to explain racial differences in participation in conventionally defined crimes of violence by raising the familiar argument that official data on offenders may be biased. This is not unlikely; but evidence that differences are not *entirely* an artifact of differential enforcement is overwhelming. It comes from victimization surveys, self-reporting participation studies, and from careful internal examination of arrest data as well. In the face of this evidence, those who insist on denying racial differences choose to live in a world of fantasy.

Peirson expresses the fear that for most readers the book will reinforce widely held beliefs about racial inferiority. Leaving aside the dubious proposition that most of the book's readers, who will be sociologists, actually hold such views, this is improbable, as the book consists of an attempt to explain crimes of violence as a normal response to externally imposed oppression. Peirson's attempt to make crime the crucial test of racial equality is bound to backfire, because the racial differences are there. Given the differences in life circumstances between most blacks and most whites in our society, it would be incredible if they weren't.

DAVID F. GREENBERG
New York University

To the Editor:

A low level in book reviewing was reached in the November 1976 issue of *Contemporary Sociology* in Gwynne Peirson's discussion of *Violence, Race, and Culture* by Lynn A. Curtis. I am not writing to defend the book which I have not yet read, but I would like to point out that Peirson's review is a calumny on thousands of sociologists. Thus Peirson says, "We seem to be living through a decade during which white sociologists are either attempting to 'prove' that Blacks are different ('different' in most instances meaning inferior), or attempting to 'prove' that white racism does not pervade our society." Elsewhere there is another sweeping and unwarranted generalization about white sociologists exhibiting "a particular interest in the alleged sexual prowess of Black men, and more particularly the question of Black men raping white women."

The last thing we need in the profession is censorship of book reviews by the Book Review Editor, but doesn't every reviewer have the responsibility to deal with the work of fellow scholars on its strengths and weaknesses rather than in terms of personal prejudices?

ELLIOTT RUDWICK
Kent State University
Fellow, Center for Advanced Study in the Behavioral Sciences

To the Editor:

David Greenberg of New York University, and Elliott Rudwick of Kent State have responded to my review of *Violence, Race, and Culture* in a predictable and not unexpected manner. Both of these men take issue with my position that whites exhibit an inordinate interest in attempting to "prove" that racial differences exist between blacks and whites that contribute to criminality and deviance among blacks. Rudwick found these statements to constitute a "sweeping and unwarranted generalization about white sociologists," and Greenberg termed it a "dubious proposition" that sociologists hold such views.

My statement was not, as Rudwick stated, a generalization of (white) sociologists. It was a generalization of white society, which, as much as Professor Rudwick might like to deny it, white sociologists are a part of. There is an abundance of evidence that white sociologists reflect the attitudes, values, and prejudices of that larger society. Lerone Bennett, in *The Challenge of Blackness,* stated that:

> It is necessary for us to develop a new frame of reference which transcends the limits of white concepts. It is necessary for us to develop and maintain a total intellectual offensive against the false universality of white concepts, whether they are expressed by William Styron or Daniel Patrick Moynihan . . . We must say to the white world that there are things in the world that are not dreamt of in your history and in your sociology and your philosophy.

I would not expect whites, including sociologists, who benefit from the institutional racism of our dominant society to agree with my position. I would hope that when faced with positions on race that differ from theirs, they would, over a period of time, become sensitized to the fact that there are legitimate views, that differ from theirs, on the causes of violence and crime. The claim that because a person is a sociologist he does not believe in, or have a vested interest in policies and practices that have the intent *or the result* of perpetuating racism may tend to soothe the guilt feelings of whites, but it cannot change the documented past and present history of this country which details the many ways in which white society benefits by the perpetuation of racism in all its forms.

GWYNNE PEIRSON
Howard University

To the Editor:

I have no way of knowing on what wave length Ms. Henrika Kuklick usually broadcasts her opinions, but from the style and content of her review of *Prominent Sociologists Since World War II* in the September 1976 issue of *Contemporary Sociology,* I infer that her antenna is located between the windmill and the outhouse.

DON MARTINDALE
University of Minnesota, Minneapolis

To the Editor:

You run a classy journal for the most part and I guess you can't win them all. The review of Don Martindale's *Prominent Sociologists Since World War II* is a case in point. While Ms. Kuklick can neither read nor write, she certainly can sell books! When anyone sums up a Martindale book in Ms. Kuklick's manner, one is compelled to rush out and read it to see what truth might lie in the allegations. Sloppy style! Phony philosophy! Indeed not.

To paraphrase Max Reger's response to a bad review: I'm sitting in the smallest room in my house with your review before me. Soon it will be behind me. But, Don Martindale's book will stand in my library and proudly.

Ms. Kuklick's review has gone the way of all flush. However, as I recall, she did not like any part of the book. The introductory summation of philosophy seemed to me to be written by a man who reads and knows philosophy and not at all a slick tertiary account derived from secondary sources. The parallels between Parsons and Mills are refreshing as an analytic framework. Martindale has incorporated the oral as well as written traditions among sociologists in discussing these two men. The 'book-end' sections on Weber and Sorokin clarify the thematic distinction between school founders and non-school founders in sociology.

In closing, I would like to thank you for reading this and to remind Ms. Kuklick that to separate a thinker from his life and times goes rather against the sociological grain, does it not?

MARY MILAM
Texas Woman's University

To the Editor:

Had Don Martindale not attained some eminence as the author of earlier, useful works on sociological theory, his effort to distill his material for an unsophisticated audience might have gone entirely unremarked. Certainly, it does not merit the level of recognition effected by this exchange of letters. As for the letters themselves, they raise no substantive issues for debate. Readers who wish to know what provoked these inarticulate howls may read my review; if my argument is unpersuasive, they may consult the book itself.

HENRIKA KUKLICK
University of Pennsylvania

To the Editor:

In the 1950s the patterns of discrimination enforced against blacks by whites in the United States varied sufficiently with geographic region as to make possible a study of the effects on the personality structures of blacks and of whites of living within varying systems of structured discrimination. The original version of the book *Black Scars* reported only the data on blacks. The revised edition adds data on whites. It was possible to show in a rigorous scientific way that the patterns of discrimination were destructive and what the nature of the destructive effects were on personality functioning. The new edition shows that those people that were the supposed beneficiaries of the system also were subjected to pressures which increased the frequency of certain personality problems, albeit different ones from those produced in blacks.

Dr. Henderson says "The design of the experiment and test results are meticulous and easy to comprehend. Unfortunately, the results taken from the late 1950s are at best questionable." What Dr. Henderson seems to mean by this is that the results from the 50s are not reflective of the 70s. But at no point in the book do I claim that the data were gathered in the 70s, and only data gathered in the 70s could reflect the intervening developments in a scientific experiment. As Dr. Henderson notes, both the social structure and the personality problems in functioning of the North and the South are no longer so distinct geographically. The differences between local areas in a single city may be greater than the general regional differences. This would make a similar study more complex, and it would probably be interpretable only against the findings of an earlier era.

Dr. Henderson says disapprovingly "[Karon] rejects the notion that there is little qualitative difference in being black in the North as opposed to the South." Karon empirically demonstrates that there was a qualitative difference as of the 50s. Whether there is a qualitative difference in the 70s is an empirical matter. My patients in psychotherapy seem still to show differences, but one can never be sure that this is a general finding unless someone does an empirical study of a more extensive sort.

Finally, Henderson says, "Karon would have his readers erroneously believe that the personality of black Americans is based primarily on anger and aggression." Karon would not have his readers believe there is any such thing as the personality of black Americans, but rather a widely varying set of personalities to be found among black Americans; in so far as black Americans are more frequently hurt unfairly by the social system there would be more problems based on anger and aggression just as with any human being subjected to unfair hurt.

In short, *Black Scars* is a rigorous contribution to our understanding of what caste-like societies do to the human beings who live in those societies. This should permit us to predict more accurately what will happen to human beings in our society, or any society, as it moves toward or away from becoming caste-like.

BERTRAM P. KARON
Michigan State University, East Lansing

To the Editor:

Dr. Karon's letter places *Black Scars* within a perspective that does indeed give the book both historical and social scientific significance. Were his comments more explicitly woven into the text, my reservations would have been non-existent. If the reason for an exchange such as this is to facilitate communication and possibly alter opinions, then I would now say that *Black Scars* is, as Dr. Karon points out, "a rigorous contribution to our understanding of what caste-like societies do to the human beings who live in those societies."

GEORGE HENDERSON
University of Oklahoma

To the Editor:

Michael Useem's review of Zollschan and Hirsch, *Social Change: Explorations, Diagnoses, and Conjectures* in the November 1976 issue begins with the bald statement that "this is not a volume on social change." It is difficult to see how anyone who has perused the volume if only superficially, can come to such a conclusion. Useem then proceeds to comment on Zollschan's and his associates' theoretical framework that is developed in eight of the thirty-four assembled articles and asserts that "the remainder of the volume is given over to papers that implicitly elaborate, illustrate or confirm the scheme and its elements."

This is simply not the case. Few of the authors of the chapters were aware of the Zollschan scheme at the time their chapters were commissioned. Each author made his contribution in terms of his own frame of reference—ranging from Kenneth Boulding through William Evan and Bert Hoselitz to Louis Schneider to Benjamin Zablocki, to mention only some of the contributors whose work the reviewer did not deign to mention.

Useem is entitled to his estimation of the Zollschan scheme, but his failure even to describe the contents of the rest of the volume indicates that his judgment on this matter also ought to be put to the test by readers of the review before it is accepted. He has not fulfilled his obligation to review the book, which *is* a volume on social change.

WALTER HIRSCH
Purdue University

To the Editor:

In 1976 a collection of readings in social change was published, edited by myself and Professor Walter Hirsch. In that volume of nearly 1,000 pages I and some associates contributed around 230 pages pertinent to my general theory of goal formation and its application to the analysis of social change processes. Among other things, these pages contained a deliberate, careful, effort to move beyond Max Weber's attempted—and not entirely successful—solution to the taxing theoretical problems of the *Methodenstreit* which still underlie the conceptual difficulties of most contemporary sociological theory.

Would the review by Michael Useem (in the issue of November 1976) of a volume—*Social Change,* edited by Zollschan and Hirsch—possibly bear any relation to the above? Given the astonishing parallel of title and names I really feel that Useem should grasp the opportunity to read *our* work.

I have considered, with some incredulity, the possibility that the book Walter Hirsch and I edited and the book reviewed (or supposedly reviewed) by Useem might be one and the same. This justifies my present letter to you.

If, indeed, they are identical it would not be possible, within the confines of a letter, to correct the distortions of such a grotesque non-review. I take this opportunity, therefore, of requesting that an actual review of Zollschan and Hirsch, *Social Change,* appear in your esteemed journal in the near future.

GEORGE K. ZOLLSCHAN
Center for Policy Research

To the Editor:

I wish to take issue with Michael Useem's review (Nov. 1976) of Zollschan and Hirsch (eds.) *Social Change: Explorations, Diagnoses, and Conjectures.* It is both inaccurate and misleading.

Plainly, Useem was much taken with the work of Zollschan and his associates; the entire review is given over to a discussion of their eight chapters. As a co-author of two of these, I am inclined to be as much impressed; but I really must insist that the book is actually about social change, and ¾ of it has nothing at all to do with Zollschan's "exigentialism." The volume is not simply "an ambitious effort by . . . Zollschan to promote his own encompassing theoretical framework," nor do the other 26 chapters "implicitly elaborate, illustrate, or confirm the scheme's elements." They have nothing to do with it: the purity of their innocence is unsullied by a single reference to Zollschan's work.

Moreover, Useem misleads readers about "exigentialism." I am by no means a convinced advocate of Zollschan's position; yet his theoretical framework is far from the systematically naive individualism, thoughtless of other viewpoints, that Useem suggests. Zollschan's individualism is methodological in character and its roots in Weber, Freud and Popper are variously traced in Chapters 4 and 9. Indeed, a careful reading of these (and other chapters) would indicate that he is quite self-consciously working on the problems of analysing social action that bedeviled Weber. In effect, he wants to show that a solution to these difficulties may be available in a theory of goal formation wherein the conditions under which goals are articulated and activated may be treated as both the causes of *and* the reasons for action. From the "causal voluntarism" of individual goal formation Zollschan displays the possibility of building up (on methodic grounds) a general theory of action that interrelates concepts like culture, social structure, power, authority, personality, economic exchange *and* social change without reification or appeal to the social structuralist's *deus ex machina,* "social forces." Such an approach is not to everyone's taste, but the issues and Zollschan's proposed solution will be of considerable interest to many sociologists.

Further, Useem's claim that Zollschan's work is isolated "from other theoretical and empirical currents" and exhibits no attempt to build on fields such as symbolic interactionism, ethnomethodology and phenomenology with which he "claims kinship" is insupportable. The only kin that he claims with these fields (kissing cousins?) is to note that he will also stress the "problematic nature of interpersonal systems of meaning" (p. 192). More serious, is Useem's charge that his work is isolated. Any work with some claim to originality is open to such a charge, of course. Yet Chapter 9 reveals a clear, painstakingly developed, set of systematic relationships between important dimensions of his framework and major schemes in sociological theory. To be different is not necessarily to be isolated.

Finally, on a personal note, I was disappointed that the review made no mention of the careful scholarship of Zollschan's contributions. Whether or not one has a taste for his efforts to reformulate the major bases of our discipline, the erudition of his work is a striking contrast to what today passes as "theory." Yes, it is a little old fashioned to be erudite; but I think no harm done to encourage sociologists in a preference for solid wood over plastic veneer. Even if a base is a little shaky, wood can be reworked and put back together; plastic is fit only for discard.

MICHAEL A. OVERINGTON
St. Mary's University

To the Editor:

In their remarks above, Walter Hirsch and George Zollschan imply that I failed to properly digest, or perhaps even read, their volume, *Social Change: Explorations, Diagnoses, and Conjectures.* Alas, this is not the case. Their charge is a familiar device for obscuring the thrust of a critical assessment of their book; namely, that Zollschan's own theoretical scheme (occupying nearly a quarter of the volume) is largely uninformed by contemporary research and theory on social change and offers little or no promise for explaining important forms of change. The remaining articles, though often valuable in themselves, appear to have been selected primarily for their utility in illustrating Zollschan's theory. They certainly do not illustrate the classical or contemporary literatures which touch on social change. I say this with much regret, for the subject is an important one and the authors have clearly devoted considerable time to the compilation of this volume.

Zollschan and Hirsch also castigate me for not more fully describing the contents of their collection. On initially receiving the volume I was troubled by *Contemporary Sociology's* 200-word limit for the review. However, following the principle that review space should be allocated according to a book's significance, after reading the volume I agreed that 200 words was adequate for the task at hand. Ultimately, of course, it is for the reader to decide, and I would direct the reader to the book were it not likely that its acquisition would prove of little value to most readers beyond resolving this dispute.

MICHAEL USEEM
Boston University

To the Editor:

Any author defending his book from a reviewer's criticisms is bound to appear self-serving. Nevertheless, I feel compelled to respond to Anne Abler's opinions of my book, *Social Structure and Social Personality,* included in the November issue of *CS*. Reading that review may be the closest experience I'll have to receiving an obscene phone call. Like an obscene phone call, you know you aren't supposed to take it personally, but you still can't help but feel implicated. Unfortunately, unlike an obscene caller, Prof. Abler has been granted access to a major professional journal read by many of my friends, colleagues, students and employers.

Professor Abler's criticisms are of such a general and vituperative nature that to attempt to address each one would be to give them more credence than they deserve. Besides, she contradicts herself so often that most of my defense already is inadvertently revealed in her own criticisms. However, I feel that a few points are in order. She claims that "the articles are not only, without exception, old reprints or cannibalized sections of books easily available elsewhere, they are, in the main, out of date and often out of place."

The thirty-one articles reprinted in *Social Structure and Social Personality* represent fifteen journals, five books, and the proceedings of a conference on aging and retirement. The journals serve the disciplines of Sociology, Anthropology, Psychology, Psychiatry and Political Science and also include such lesser read publications as *The Black Scholar, Personnel Journal,* and *Journal of Health and Social Behavior.* Twenty-two of the thirty-one articles were originally published within ten years of the date of publication of my book. Apparently, Prof. Abler's conception of the rate of progress of social science is more optimistic than mine. If any of the publishers or authors, all of whom had to grant me permission to reprint their material, felt that their books had been "cannibalized," they didn't say so.

Social Structure and Social Personality was designed as a text-reader; a different concept for a classroom book. In addition to a general introduction, there are thirteen section introductions which review much of the important literature in the various research areas and discuss the major theoretical and social issues involved. The introductory essays, which comprise over a fourth of the book and summarize hundreds of relevant studies, are followed by two or three journal reprints or book excerpts which serve as examples of the typical mode of analysis or explore theoretical dimensions which have not been operationalized adequately.

Since this was a book on social structure and personality and not just on the family or race (to refer to the two sections Abler picks out for special abuse), I was restricted with respect to the number of essays which could be included in any one of the thirteen sections. In original draft, the section on the family had four articles, but the publisher's insistence on cutting the length of the book from 600 pages to under 450 necessitated the reduction. I'm not sure the book suffered for it. Prof. Abler neglects to mention that the ten-page essays introducing each section summarized twenty-six works on the family and thirty-eight on race.

Is Prof. Abler seriously suggesting that the book should have contained "genuine articles" based on the "notions" of Marx, Weber, Durkheim, Mills, Merton, Blumer or Goffman (whom she would have her readers seek in vain in the Anthropology department at Penn) rather than reviewing the relevant ideas of at least all but the last two as I did? Would such re-publication meet her criteria of inaccessibility and recency?

In her conclusive harangue, Abler imputes a variety of unseemingly motives to the publisher and myself. In this context, I wish only to point out that, if any "old boys" were to look for "up and coming sociologists in training" in my "acknowledgements section," they would be disappointed to find only the names of six former undergraduates at Penn (none of whom would meet this criteria) along with those of the series editor, Alex Inkeles, three Little, Brown editors and two of my former colleagues at Penn. Unfortunately, there are no "captive audiences in mandatory courses" for a subject like social structure and personality (even at the "finest eastern schools"), so there will not be the "second edition" which Abler tells readers they can "count on."

What disturbs me most about this nasty business is that the editors of *CS* should see fit to promote it. One would think that just their sense of responsibility to inform their readers about relevant books would dissaude them from publishing a review which told one so little about the book and so much about the petty resentments and fantasies of the reviewer.

Basic professional standards alone should preclude publishing a review riddled with caustic phrases enclosed in quotation marks without making it clear that the phrases belong to the reviewer and not the author. This is the official journal of scholarly reviews for a major professional association and it would seem that common decency would require a civil discourse, some presentation of the author's intentions and efforts, and some reasonable documentation of those criticisms which are made.

JEROLD M. STARR
West Virginia University

To the Editor:

Anne R. Abler's caustic review of *Social Structure and Social Personality* by Jerold M. Starr (*CS*, Vol. 5, No. 6, p. 821) does *CS* readers a disservice.

In a four-paragraph review, Abler devotes her first and last paragraphs to comments on anthologies as a genre rather than on the book under review. Such discussions may be appropriate to review essays and symposia but not to shorter reviews. Paragraph three tells us what is not in the book—Marx, Weber, Durkheim, Mills. Starr has discussed their ideas, Abler admits, but she says nothing of the substance of Starr's essays, save that they use clichés.

Only paragraph two is somewhat informative. Here Abler takes Starr to task for not including other articles—this in a book of thirteen sections, 2 or 3 articles per section, 461 pages. She also assails his omitting to criticize the articles he did include, but she fails to tell us anything about what Starr does say in his 4 to 16 page introductory essays.

Finally, paragraph 4, devoted entirely to the attribution of venal motives (to those who would edit or read anthologies), is both irrelevant and uninformative. The *CS* reader finishes the review knowing almost nothing about the book itself. Certainly the editors and reviewers owe us better than this.

JAY LIVINGSTON
Montclair State College

To the Editor:

Professor Starr's letter is, I think, a fair example of the kind of writing he employed in the review and discussion sections of his 1974 book. While his conceptualizations and expressions are merely insipid, his use of the English language is egregious. I stand by my review.

ANNE R. ABLER

To the Editor:

Hackett's review of Mehan and Wood's *The Reality of Ethnomethodology* in the January issue is as clever and provocative as the work it scrutinizes, however, one aspect has been left out of this review which being added now may make the review of this work more comprehensive. One of the essential aspects of the Mehan and Wood book is their analysis of the ethnomethodological contribution of McHugh, Raffel, Foss and Blum in *On the Beginning of Social Inquiry*. This analysis occupies an ample amount of physical space in their book (pp. 166–176), but much more importantly the analysis provides a kind of cognitive format for the last portion of their book (the last four chapters).

The subject of reflexivity, as Hackett notes in his review, is a dominant theme of this book as it is with the work of McHugh *et al.*; but the orientation that Mehan and Wood take with regard to the subject of reflexivity is by their own admission less "metaphysical." Mehan and Wood state that they do not criticize this orientation, but rather use it as ". . . an occasion for exploring their own grounds." Though the authors may take this sanguine view of McHugh *et al.*, I believe that it is at this theoretical point where ethnomethodology meets with somewhat of a *bete noire* whose ugly head is not easily disguised. McHugh *et al.* maintain that ethnomethodology continues to adhere to a "descriptivist form of life," and they offer an alternative method, "that does not assume that language describes any phenomena beyond itself." McHugh *et al.* rather than having an interest in everyday life *per se*—the arena of ethnomethodology—use the phenomenon of everyday life as a "point of departure" for their inquiries, and in this manner invoke the phantasma of "deep structure" and "grammar" in the sense of Wittgenstein.

Due to the fact that Mehan and Wood strive to incorporate such antithetical material into the "establishment" of ethnomethodology is only further justification for commending their work. Hackett closes his review with a remark on the frontispiece chosen by Mehan and Wood to illustrate reflexivity: Escher's *Drawing Hands*—two hands, each holding a pencil, drawing each other—"a visual display of reflexivity." Hackett forebodingly "hopes that the more appropriate display would not be Ouroboros—the snake eating its own tail." There are no grounds for this fear. I've thought about this image a good deal since I first saw it many years ago, and I have decided, though the metaphor may be extended a bit, that the snake's repast must logically end for there are limits to even a viper's versatility. As a result of its efforts it *is* truncated, but it is nourished too, and what better energy conservation can we find than this? Mehan and Wood though they've not resolved the McHugh *et al.* schism have none the less provided us energy to grow once again.

STANFORD W. GREGORY, JR.
Kent State University

To the Editor:

Professor Robert Bierstedt's review of P. Q. Hirst's book, *Durkheim, Bernard, and Epistemology* (*Contemporary Sociology*, Vol. 5, November, 1976, p. 828), may lead your readers to perpetuate a serious error regarding the intellectual relationship between Emile Durkheim and Claude Bernard. Bierstedt states that, to his knowledge, there is no reference to Claude Bernard in any of Durkheim's writing, thus supporting Hirst's assertion that "Durkheim, to our knowledge, does not mention Bernard nor does he refer to any of his works" (Hirst, p. 13).

The intellectual relationship between Durkheim and Bernard was much closer than Professors Hirst and Bierstedt suggest. Emile Durkheim was a self-styled scientific rationalist. He defined his principal objective as a sociologist as the extension of scientific rationalism to human behavior (Durkheim, E., *The Rules of Sociological Method*, 1938, p. xxxix). The method of the social sciences, in his view, must rest on the principles of scientific rationalism as they were successfully used in the natural sciences and as they were systematically set forth by Claude Bernard in his *An Introduction to the Study of Experimental Medicine* (See Aimard, G., *Durkheim, et la science économique*, 1962, p. 115).

It is not surprising, therefore, to find that Durkheim did, indeed, refer to Bernard. Two examples should suffice. In his review of Schaeffle's *"Bau und Leben des sozialen Körpers: Erster Band,"* which appeared in the *Revue Philosophique* in 1885, Durkheim, arguing against the type of reductionism that sees in sociology only a new application of biological principles, noted that "the great service that Claude Bernard rendered to physiology was precisely to liberate it from this yoke, from that of physics and chemistry as from that of metaphysics, putting off to some distant future the time for generalizations" (Durkheim, E., *Textes*, Vol. 1, 1975, p. 373. See also Lukes, S., *Emile Durkheim: His Life and Work*, 1972, p. 73, footnote 41).

Three years later, in his "Introduction to the Sociology of the Family," the opening lecture of his course on the family given in 1888 at the Faculty of Letters of the University of Bordeaux, Durkheim, after presenting an analytical table of family relations, was moved to observe: "But an analysis is not an explanation. In the natural sciences one discovers causes through experimentation. Here we obviously are unable to do experiments properly so-called. But, as Claude Bernard said a long time ago, the essential element in experimentation is not the production by the experimenter of artificial phenomena. The artifice is only a means whose aim is to subject the thing studied to different circumstances and forms in order that useful comparisons can be instituted." (Durkheim, E. *Textes*, Vol. 3, 1975, p. 13).

The Durkheim-Bernard connection is significant because of the extensive reliance in Durkheim's early works on methods, metaphors and analogies borrowed from biology and medicine: functional analysis, internal milieu, health, the normal and the pathological, as well as numerous organismic figures of speech. It is also important because Durkheim's views on the nature of science were derived, in part, from Bernard.

HARRY ALPERT
University of Virginia

REVIEW SYMPOSIUM

The Cultural Contradictions of Capitalism, by DANIEL BELL. New York: Basic Books, 1976. 301 pp. $12.95 cloth.

Legitimation Crisis, by JURGEN HABERMAS. Translated by THOMAS McCARTHY. Boston: Beacon Press, 1975. 166 pp. $8.95 cloth.

The Fiscal Crisis of the State, by JAMES O'CONNOR. New York: St. Martin's Press, 1973. 276 pp. $12.95 cloth.

JONATHAN RIEDER
Yale University

The recent tribulations of the West have diminished the exultant promise of postwar growth. Elegies for the ebb of a majestic global era can invoke North-South debates, resource cartels, or a weak "Mediterranean flank." The same diversity is manifest over a wide spectrum of resilience and vulnerability. After all, the mark is not the lira, French indicative planning outstrips the American employment act of 1946, and unsavory teamster scheming lags behind German co-determination. Intriguingly, though, Bell, Habermas, and O'Connor shun these "accidental" features and detect a more immanent flaw in the logic of capitalism.

If recent social science tends to be less than grandiose in its endeavor, these authors show the same proclivity for embracing synthesis as the classical theorists. The search of a Marx or a Durkheim for underlying unities was partially a response to a feeling of personal dislocation. These books are also personal works, suffused with biting indictment and confessions of faith. Bell, Habermas, and O'Connor resort to bankers' parlance to evoke the "bankruptcy" of a social stage: they depict an overdraw of fiscal, cultural, and political accounts; they discern deficits of loyalty, reason, community—and even money. The imagery owes much to a fractious business civilization which they find lacking an integrative ethos of justice. To the moral void each opposes the image of universalism, O'Connor's community struggling together, Bell's community sacrificing together, Habermas's community speaking together.

The sundry accents on community stamp the formative visions. O'Connor's demon is monopoly capitalism; his goal is simply socialism. Bell's adversary is rampant hedonism; his ideal is a chastened political liberalism humanized by the caress of community. Habermas's nemesis is a technocracy which would liquidate individual dignity in the name of efficiency. His doctrine is the blazing eschatology of reason that he associates with Enlightenment. If the force of these hopes can scant the messy variety of social life, they prove that the amalgam of vision and social science remains a vital force in intellectual life.

James O'Connor's *The Fiscal Crisis of the State* deciphers the tendency in state capitalism for government expenses to outpace revenue. The budget is a kind of code for the political economy of the society: allotments of money "reflect . . . social and economic conflicts between classes and groups." How does the drab budget attain a stellar presence at center conceptual stage? In O'Connor's coherent if inelegant Marxian scheme, "monopoly capitalism is in part a self-correcting system." An agile state deftly promotes investment, productivity, and social harmony in order to guarantee *accumulation* and *legitimization*. Paradoxically, such expensive tasks create a new drift toward crisis.

Why not another dose of self-correction?

Prudent spokesmen for big corporations desire more economic direction and have allies in the executive branch "eager to transform the budget into an instrument of national planning." But O'Connor eschews a superficial account of the state as executive committee for united capital. The key impediment to systematic steering of the economy is the triumph of the Broker State. The mighty multinationals have reduced influence in congress, the statehouses, and city halls. Small capitalists, charismatic leaders, and ethnic machines weave a tangled thicket of competing claims in a labyrinthine federal system. The parochial politics of interest are "inconsistent with the survival . . . of capitalism." Meanwhile, the crisis rages on.

O'Connor catalogues the pressures to spend. *Social investment* does not trigger the capital shortage that incites trembling executives to proselytize on Op Ed pages; research and development and highway construction advance "the growth of the monopoly sector." *Social consumption* like social security is required to "reproduce" the workforce. O'Connor here evinces the neat functionalist thrust of his revisionism. Social security reinforces morale and discipline. "Seen in this way, it is a kind of insurance for capitalists and corporations." Finally, burgeoning *social expenses* graphically testify that state spending is the concomitant of capitalism as well as its catalyst: growth creates victims and bounty. Victims compel an ample welfare state to provision and to pacify the volatile underclasses. Bounty calls for a bellicose warfare state to secure the markets and investments that "monopolistic producers need and seek." Model Cities programs and Northrop cost overruns drain faster than state enterprise, debt, or taxation can replenish the coffers of the treasury.

Having charted the course of collapse, O'Connor wonders if the state can regenerate capitalism through job-creating investments in housing and mass-transit. He pronounces the political parties unlikely champions for such a reform—realignment seems to him hardly headed for An Emerging Social Industrial Majority. Myriad forces sabotage planning and aggravate crisis. Feisty welfare activists, spur of O'Connor's socialist desire, resist bureaucratic professionalism. Tax revolts presage retrenchment rather than munificence. Robust public employee unions make for chaotic labor relations.

With passion breaking through solemn analysis, O'Connor vacillates between extravagant hopes for revolutionary alliance and disappointment. Taxpayer against civil servant, white craftsman against black dependent, the disheartening spectre of fiscal factionalism violates the pledge of socialist unity. "The fiscal crisis will continue to divide all these groups and strata that today fight in dismal isolation for a greater share of the budget or a smaller share of the tax burden." Justice founders on a polarized, riven polity.

O'Connor has inventively gathered insight and research under his Marxist mantle. In the best tradition of revisionism, he highlights those wily capitalists ready to jettison economic homiles to smooth out kinks in the economy. In the main he is sensitive to the fine nuances of planning and politics which defy sectarian analysis. But the pitfalls will be familiar to students of the revisionist genre. He slips into raw shibboleths—imperialism is inherent in capitalism—which becloud serious study of American world hegemony and slight the geopolitical and historical factors which mold foreign policy. Most damaging, he never confirms the ineluctable crisis, even conceding "there is no iron law that expenditures must always rise more rapidly than revenues." The system is elastic—witness tranquil barrios and ghettos, delphic gubernatorial ideologues of abstemiousness, and the penitential moderation of AFSCME at the present bargaining table.

Many of these flaws flow from the style of Marxian functionalism, its drive to derive every flutter in the part from movement in the whole. This conceptual parsimony can confuse design and consequence. The Office of Management and Budget *has* stimulated Northeast disinvestment and Southwest bullishness; it was also a Nixonian device to consolidate political power. Social welfare programs *did* stabilize the dangerous classes; the aim was often to secure local constituencies (e.g., Lindsay) or the Democratic national electoral coalition.

These reflections on the autonomy of politics suggest the autonomy of tradition. O'Connor obliquely distinguishes the American from the European experience yet never follows up the promising lead of "exceptionalism." Many elements of crisis are more American than capitalist, from Tudor polity to "liberal tradition," from mercurial shifts to party alignments to an unparalleled international status, from short-term demographic movements to the legacy of ethnic and racial quandaries. This pastiche underscores the need for more modest studies of the subjective, historical, and national meaning of crisis.

Daniel Bell elevates the argument from the earthly austerities of fiscal crisis to the exalted plane of *The Cultural Contradictions of Capitalism*. The language of deficit gives way to Bell's more precious literary style —"instauration"—and flashy subheadings—"The Dionysiac Pack." The grandiloquent manner augurs Bell's conceptual ambitiousness and the tone of apocalypse that haunts this collection of diverse essays.

While preoccupied with sublime matters, Bell is not unmindful of the disorder of state finances. He traces spiraling fiscal demands to more basic—and exorbitant—psychological claims. The enemy is not Monopoly but Modernism, whose credo of unfettered self corrodes the religious, cognitive, and communal restraints that sustain identity. Hence the plaintive existential mood, the nostalgic feeling of homelessness.

Ever the pluralist, Bell eclectically insists that change can originate in any of the three societal realms—economic, cultural, political —each obeying its own axial principle. Functionalism and Marxism hallow the idea of totality in their "holistic" view of society, but Bell is struck by the "radical disjunction" between an efficient, rational social structure and a culture that is prodigal, promiscuous, and passionately devoted to self-fulfillment.

Bell furnishes a grand narrative to pinpoint the source of disjunction. It is a familiar story. The energy of the rising bourgeoisie was tempered by sobriety and a Protestant Ethic propitious for accumulation. The shattering of cultural tradition unleashed the rebellious forces of Modernism, personified by movements like Surrealism and affirming the "absolute imperiousness of the self." The narcissism dictates stylistic innovations like stream of consciousness which dissolve the formal syntax of culture into privatized, almost autistic expression. "The disruption of mimesis," Modernism "denies the primacy of an outside world."

A cocksure culture eventually triumphed over the social structure. The highpriests of Bohemia were joined by lusty voluptuaries itching to translate avant-garde doxology into life-style. The coupe de grace was the victory of mass-consumption hedonism, encouraged by installment buying and flamboyantly rendered by Bell as the move "From the Protestant Ethic to the Psychedelic Bazaar." In his whimsically simple tale of modernization, a righteous and hidebound accent on frugality yielded to indulgence. This evolution climaxed in America during the 1960s, that licentious decade, with its sexual convulsions and hip-rock-drug culture. Bell interprets these frenzies not as the fortuitous events of history but as the ordained end of a teleological double play—Adam Smith to Andre Breton to Andy Warhol. The unholy marriage of elite Modernism and mass hedonism strikes at "the motivational and psychic-reward system which has sustained capitalism."

Bell deems the idolatry of self no less dangerous for the polity: the state directs economic growth and social policy, "the basic allocative power is now political, rather than economic." Petitioning the state to gratify private and group wants transforms the polity into a crowded forum of barking claimants and overloads the capacity to manage, mediate, and finance. Bell admits "O'Connor is half-right." Legitimacy and accumulation are vexing for capitalism. Bell shrewdly adds that they are irritants as well to Algeria, the Soviet Union, or any economically engaged state. Revolts against inflated prices have razed more than one Polish regime.

The dialectic of voracity and discipline has more ominous reverberations: the religion of growth fuels unbridled inflation which could undo capitalism. Bell's economics etherize concrete price-administering corporations into the *spirit* of appetite, and gloss over responsible unions in America and Europe. He claims that restraint is now unpalatable to "irreversible" expectations of abundance. The instabilities which ensue from insatiable desire erode respectful compromise, the linchpin of liberalism. Here is where Bell judges O'Connor misguided. The pivotal problem is less Marxian than Weberian, not a debacle of capitalism but of democracy: "consensual agreement on the normative issues of distributive justice."

Bell's measured remedy endorses political liberalism with its valuable emphasis on the sanctity of the individual. A contributor to *Fortune Magazine* often facilely pigeonholed with the prophets of neo-conservativism, he surprisingly disputes that "a social decision is best served by the sum of individual decisions, especially when a few individuals hold a disproportionate amount of the resources." The trick is to civilize economic individualism with a social-economic bill of rights which disciplines acquisitiveness and generates bonds of collective purpose.

A prolific, erudite, and imaginative presence in American letters, Bell is always stimulating. He has ventured provocatively into aesthetic realms that many sociologists have neither the humanistic inclination to fathom nor the sensibility to illuminate with grace. But Bell's speculations on culture cascade over a dazzling wealth of topics unimpeded by precise method. He gambols from "pivotal tendency" to "singular trend" as if emphasis substitutes for evidence. He has a penchant for stark antinomies which devour subtlety. For example, Bell sees *the* central concern of novelists in the 1960s as madness. Quite plausibly *a* concern. How about Salinger, Updike, Malamud—surely no mean list? Bell dismisses them with a footnote and presumption. "Given my own sociological reading of the apocalyptic temper of the times, I feel that the novelists I have chosen are the ones making the distinctive statements about the sensibility of the decade." Sociological? *The* sensibility? *Whose* sensibility?

The critical flaw is Bell's partiality to high culture, the sway of Cassirer rather than Geertz. "I mean by culture . . . the realm of symbolic forms" like painting and fiction. Yet capitalism can dispense with justifications from a hermetic high culture, can endure the barbs or indifference of a Jackson Pollack. Bell talks as if a single-minded, etherial culture (he rarely grounds sensibility in tangible strata) is all Baudelaire and not Bauhaus functionalism, all Heideggerean angst and not positivism. He excludes "cognitive modes" like science and philosophy which surely reveal tenaciously rational strains. He dismisses those who consider technocracy dominant and so disregards at least vigorous currents of behaviorism and structuralism. The drive for distinct patterns forces him to depreciate historical fluctuation. Even during the 1960s classical ballet flourished, but many of Bell's insights now seem especially dated in a period when "the fundamental conservatism of middle-class taste has regained its confidence," as Hilton Kramer puts it, and academic painting and Broadway revivals of the well-made play are prominent features of the cultural scene. Lastly, the lofty perspective of high culture neglects the profusion of everyday cultures which *are* crucial to the vigor of capitalism—from the ethnic to the evangelical, in Subdivision and Sunbelt, where they do not fret about Randall Jarrell.

Bell lacks a feel for the rhythms of ordinary cultural life. He sterilely caricatures mass culture and rock and roll. He *deduces* a crisis of motivation by reading themes in cultural works, not from the phenomenological data of disoriented people, leaping perilously from art object to human consciousness. Human behavior is ambivalent enough that a person can appreciate Salvador Dali and run a corporation. When Bell shifts in midstream to assimilate mass hedonism to his modernism argument, he assumes hedonism subverts capitalism. More likely hedonism increases its longevity by quickening the flow of gratifications. Capitalism might well thrive because the philistine masses wear platform heels as they do the Latin Hustle.

For all his considerable astuteness, Bell has perpetrated a mythic theory of development unsupported by adequate social history from below. He romanticizes prior transcendence and overstates present disorientation. The sharp dichotomies seem to project the malaise of the West Side and Cambridge onto the whole of American society. The Manhattanization of perspective might derive from the trauma inflicted on the self-esteem of various cultural interpreters by the turmoil of the 1960s. Ironically, the apocalypse those elites confer on the outside world may in part mirror an inner world of unsettlement.

Habermas infuses Bell's cultural fascination with O'Connor's class concerns. *Legitimation Crisis* is ostensibly a recital of crisis tendencies in late capitalism. It is simultaneously a metaphor for Habermas's faith in the freedom and truth with which he endows the demotic speech community. Forsaking what he glibly dubs "a retreat to a Marxistically embellished orthodoxy," Habermas ardently advances his idea of Enlightment with the idealism he has previously embodied in a hopeful critical theory and a glorified conception of the bourgeois public. He accomplishes this in typically recondite Germanic prose, with masterful command of assorted disciplines, and one gargantuan appetite for abstraction.

A weighty meta-theoretical preamble portends the crisis argument to follow. Habermas aims to revamp Marxism and systems theory to restore critical reason to its rightful place in development theory. If societies evolve through technical learning typified by the growth of the forces of production, they also develop through communicative learning symbolized by the conquest of myth and superstition by rational discourse. The keystone of this luminous future is the accession of an ethical, skeptical, and spunky citizen who refuses to take the claims of authorities at face value and who challenges the smooth self-adjustment of societies. Habermas glimpses "no guarantee that a development in the forces of production and an increase in steering capacity will release those normative orientations that correspond to the steering imperatives of the social system." This arcane sorcery means that norms of criticism might impose unbearable strains on the integuments of a society. "The institution of general practical discourse would introduce a new stage of learning." The forces of cognition and not production might topple capitalism and bring Enlightenment to fruition.

Habermas descends from these olympian heights to sketch a model of late capitalism reminiscent of O'Connor's. A latent class structure is still a class structure, while Keynsean tinkering does not mean democratic control of investment. Inequitably supplying private corporations with risk capital and price supports, the obliging state needs additional rationales for its partisanship. The solution is privatism: a tight fit between formal democracy, political abstinence, and personal indulgence. A heretical disclaimer of dogmatism—collapse might be "permanently avoided"—indicates the fearless exploration of crisis ahead.

Habermas does not assume the economic ruin of capitalism; knowledge-intensive production compensates for the falling rate of profit and obviates the classical theory of value. He does not foresee a crisis of rational administration; regulation is compatible with freedom of investment, and there is no sharply etched definition of failure in social planning as in bankruptcy. Nor can he divine the immediate source of collapse in a languishing of legitimations; state activity in behalf of private capital might prompt "a questioning, rich in practical consequences," but a moderately effective welfare state can compensate for transgressions of equity with rewards which curb mobilization.

A crisis would originate in a failure of "motivations necessary to the system." The decline of forces which nurture privatism—religion and achievement—coincides with the rise of subversive cultural tendencies—modern art, scientism, universal morality. This rich account of culture enhances Bell's preoccupation with the irrational. Habermas echoes Bell that modern art corrodes the values of polity and economy. The canons of science stimulate an analytic spirit which undermines the claims of the state. Habermas's perception of the growth of universal morality demonstrates an almost mystical confidence in the progress of reason. Against Bell's stress on the recurring *existential* dilemmas of culture, Habermas portrays a cumulative *cognitive* development. "The evolution of morality, like the evolution of science, is dependent on truth." Moral universalism is antagonistic to the unfair particularism of class societies.

Habermas has sanguinely presumed that ornery, lucid citizens would overwhelm an unjustifiable capitalism with demands for justification. But Habermas yields to a lingering pessimism. Has the species succumbed to gullibility? Is the need for legitimation an anachronism? It is as if the enemies of Enlightment had turned the weapon of critique on Habermas! After his incantations of discursive reason, they demand that *Habermas* rationally argue *his* assertion that "norms admit of truth."

Sociology cannot answer these questions, so Habermas draws on ethics to rebut the "Weberian pluralism of value systems, gods, and demons." Weber holds that norms are basically arbitrary: a social order legitimates itself when people merely believe its allegations. This catholicity says nothing about the truth of the allegations. Duplicity or cant will suffice if it induces consent. Habermas retorts that every norm contains the supposition that it could be defended through reasonable argument. In his happy consensus theory of truth, discourse "guarantees" the democractic debate and agreement on "generalizeable interests" which inhere in the "structure of intersubjectivity." For "in taking up a practical discourse, we unavoidably suppose an ideal speech situation."

Despite the rhapsodizing of ordinary language, *Legitimation Crisis* ends on a melancholy note. Habermas observes cynical suspicions of truth. Theorists of democratic elites like Lipset view democracy as a mere device for choosing leaders rather than realizing the collective will. Systems theorists see political dialogue as useless bickering which hinders "rational preference selection by technocrats and administrators." Habermas is left with his "partiality for reason" and a fervent determination to fight "the stabilization of a nature-like social system over the heads of its citizens, that is, at the price of—so be it!—old European dignity."

Wading through Habermas's prose demands heroic stamina for even the most zealous Frankfurt School devotee. It is rewarding effort. *Legitimation Crisis* is an impressive summary of crisis theory. It is an exemplary expression of critical theory's probe of ideology and culture as founts of capitalist debility. There is refreshing humility in the caveats that the results are provisional. Nevertheless, Arthur Vidich has craftily reiterated the simple point that modern bureaucratic societies can forego the loyalty of significant sectors of the population. Moveover, the targets of legitimacy challenges are more often parties, policies, or leaders than the foundation of the social system. The sources of stability are incredibly varied: inertia and coercion maintain an ongoing social order, as do irony, grumbling, and gallows humor. Habermas's infelicitous formalism gravely magnifies the power of the technocrats, reifies the "old European dignity" of the autonomous subjects his theory aims to consecrate, and converts the polity and culture into pale emanations of system requirements. In Bell's canny critique of Habermas, "the recalcitrances of individual societies, the character of people or traditions, disappear under the monolithic weight of the term 'system'. . . . The strength of democracy derives from an autonomous tradition of liberty, not the 'needs' of the capitalist system."

The exotic feature of *Legitimation Crisis* is the postulate of a redemptive general will, the premise that "constraint-free consensus permits only what all can want." The notion of freedom indelibly congealed in ordinary speech is a leap into linguistic idealism from a history rife with conflict and domination. Habermas's ruminations form an abstruse patois which transposes an ambiguous reality into signs of hope for the failed revolutions. But this is a sleight of language, not the verdict of history. Without methodical, potentially grim studies of social change, critical theorists are left to perform "simulated dialogues"—a curious kind of politics.

So we come full circle. Bell, Habermas, and O'Connor elucidate an array of instabilities in advanced capitalism. The bite and verve of these works is a function of their bold scope. They foreswear the diffident sociology of the middle range that has entranced social science for so long. Yet each succumbs to intellectual hubris and reaches beyond his means. The attempt to appropriate history ends with its abolition.

NORBERT WILEY
University of Illinois, Urbana

Here are three books in search of the crisis in capitalism. All three authors see a crisis, but they disagree on how it's happening, where it's happening, and what's bringing it about. There was a simpler time when we all knew that depression and mass unemployment was the crisis. And there was a good twenty years after World War II when many of us thought the crisis had been permanently overcome by Keynesian economic controls. But the protests of the sixties and the stagflation of the seventies have renewed a sense of crisis and contradiction, and the question now is how and why the thing is popping out again after the high hopes of those twenty some workable years.

Each author locates the crisis in a different place. Bell has it coming from the modernist culture into the state and economy; O'Connor has it going from the economy into the fiscal state; and Habermas takes O'Connor from the state into the personality and culture. These authors know each other's works, they cite specific points of agreement and disagreement, and they conciously build in relation to each other's ideas. This cross-reading was possible because each book appeared earlier in article form, and, except for O'Connor, each author cites the other two's earlier works. The result is an interactive intellectual process in which you can almost see the three of them lobbing the crisis back and forth like a volleyball, or maybe more appropriately a hand grenade.

Bell's book is a compilation of essays he wrote in the late sixties and early seventies, introduced with a new theoretical essay that gives some conceptual order to the rather disparate themes of the six reprinted essays that follow. His overall conclusion is that we need a return to moral standards, the sacred, a sense of shame, religion, delayed gratification, a public philosophy, and some sense of cultural values that will allow us to live within the limits of what the economy and state can deliver. Bell places the blame for the capitalist crisis squarely on a culture that's gone berserk in the search for individual self realization, no matter what the cost for the society.

His introductory essay frames his argument by providing a structural picture of society in which the key tensions can be located. While most of the book leans heavily on the case of the United States, his division of contemporary capitalist social structure into three parts is of broader applicability. His three parts are the (a) "techno-economy," (b) "polity," and (c) "culture," and he grants some internal autonomy to each sector.

The economy is *by definition* functional, efficient, economizing, rational, bureaucratic, and hierarchical. The state or polity is by definition democratic, pluralistic, and reasonably fair. And the culture, by which Bell means only the core values and symbols, and which is our response to existential crises, is the only sector not defined in a functional way, though this will become his whole point. His culture gradually narrows down to religion and the fine arts, especially the arts.

There are difficulties with this division. It is not clear, for example, where the class system comes in or whether it is produced by the technical logic of the economy or the bargaining methods of the polity, but on the whole it is a theoretically useful division. Leftist scholars, including both Habermas and, implicitly, O'Connor, are also working with a similar three-part division, and it appears to be a case where both the left and right are paying more attention to the state. The left is uncoupling it from the economy and examining it as a semi-autonomous force, and the right is freeing it from the value system and looking at political legitimation as a process unto itself.

While Bell credits some causal autonomy to each of the three areas, he also sees each influencing the other, and it is in these influences that he finds tension and conflict. The major contradiction is between the contemporary culture, with its modernist orientation toward the exploration of the self, and the economy, with its sets of roles and specializations. The two realms are in collision, with each wanting to re-make the other on its own terms. He also sees a contradiction between the equalitarian norms of citizenship and the hierarchical norms of the economy. The latter is a material contradiction over who is to get what, while the former is a contradiction between two ways of defining the meaning of life, though Bell thinks that the conflict in meaning is a partial cause of the conflict over equality. The book, then, is primarily about the cultural contradiction, and the equality question is given fewer pages, a less profound analytic dissection, and a certain amount of subordination.

Bell begins his history of the cultural conflict with the sixteenth century, which marks the Reformation and the rise of individualism in the economy and the arts as well. The entrepreneur and the artist both break out of traditional restrictions by finding freedom on the market. The innovating entrepreneur seeks profit and the artist seeks meaning, and they both do so with a new dynamism and self direction. So far so good. Two aspects of modern individualism are both being themselves and responding to the principle of individuality proper to their activity. But by the early nineteenth century, typified for Bell by Byron in England and Baudelaire in France, the artist and entrepreneur had come to stand for mutually contradictory values. Art had taken a self-absorbed, "modernist" turn, which denigrated the business values of the bourgeoisie, while the latter had adopted a comfortable stolidity, for which the artist's pursuit of self realization was simple nonsense.

The adversary relation between business and the artistic culture went on in a state of reasonably healthy tension for some hundred years, but as the twentieth century progressed, the two realms started crowding each other and there was a fight for hegemony. The conflict was over the future of the Protestant Ethic, that new value system which slowly grew with business after the Reformation, and which expressed a softening of strict Calvinistic predestination. In the nineteenth century this ethic became a major regulative principle in the socialization institutions of family and schools, and we might say the bourgeoisie developed their own working moral culture, taking it in a quite different direction from the searching self exploration of the early existentialists and modernists.

But by the early twentieth century, the Protestant Ethic of thrift, hard work, and self discipline was being whittled away for a number of reasons. Not only were modern painters, writers, and esthetic thinkers constructing symbols and living lives that flouted the staid virtues of this ethic. In addition, and this is one of the most confusing points in Bell's book, *business was destroying its own ethic.* The auto complex, for example, created and thrived on a new freedom to get out of town and escape the watchful eyes of the local community. Behind the new technology, marketing and sales sought new targets in the areas of luxury and self indulgence. Advertising assisted by creating wants where they did not exist. And the new industry of consumer credit demolished the traditional virtue of thrift with the seductive suggestion that you buy now and pay later.

So the cultural conflict between art and business has the following peculiarity: art detests the protestant virtues and it is out to destroy them, while business is *ambivalent*, as it simultaneously undercuts them to maximize demand and consumption, while still needing and begging for them in the areas of production and bureaucratic organization. The contradiction Bell is talking about could just as well have been located, not between art and business, but within business itself, but this would not have allowed Bell to make the interpretation he wanted to make of the American sixties and the counter culture.

The most heartfelt concern of Bell's book is with the sixties' hippie culture and the moral effect he thinks this culture has had on people's attitudes, family life, and schools. The counter culture, of course, was seen in different places and looked at in different ways by different people. Bell has a New York view of it, with a heavy reliance on the unique qualities of that city, particularly its art colonies, and on the more headline-catching, sensationalized aspects of the counter culture. What he sees is a kind of moral monster, born in avant garde art and carried to a depraved extreme in the themes of sex, nihilism, violence, and contempt for all authority. In particular the business virtues, or what was left of them, were attacked by the counter culture, for these qualities would keep people from fully being themselves.

At this point Bell hooks together the two contradictions—of culture and equality—by suggesting that the unleashing of limitless appetites, which he sees coming from the counter culture, fanned the flames of minority and underclass protest and induced these two groups to demand more social services than the state could provide. The point is made obliquely, but it is important to the outraged tone of this book, and it allows Bell to connect the counter culture of the sixties with the fiscal crisis of the seventies.

Bell's cure for the cultural contradiction is a return to religion and the sacred. He likes to draw from Durkheim on the importance of the sacred, and he contrasts Durkheim's ritualized tribal society with today's "self-infinitization" and the "idolatry of the self." Bell thinks a return to something resembling traditional religion is necessary to save capitalism from collapse and possible revolution.

The same point is returned to in the later section of the book, in which he confronts the conflict over equality. There he calls for the moral sense of a "public household," in which each group making claims on the state will get what it needs, not what it wants. This new moral theory, which is intended to be imposed on the fiscal overload, is to be specified by the "principle of relevant differences," which will determine which groups are to get what. This crucial principle is not spelled out well, and he seems to be trying to extend the Davis-Moore theory of occupational stratification to the new, fiscal trough, but the atmosphere of religion is also on these pages as he calls for "normative commitments," "non-rational allegiance," a sense of "shame," and a "transcendent tie." Religion seems to be the cure for both crises, just as irreligion was party to their having both been produced in the first place.

The book has a great many secondary arguments, but the line of logic is about as I presented it. Much of the exposition is ingenious, rich with insights, and written with grace, but it's an awfully shaky argument at both ends, and he doesn't make it at all clear who killed the Protestant Ethic or whether religion can bring it back to life. Protestantism was a self-liquidating religion, according to Max Weber, for it led to the science that destroyed the Old Testament, and it led to the mass consumption society that had to slice away at its own morality to avoid running short of markets and collapsing into mass unemployment.

I don't suppose we can give Protestantism all the credit, but the thesis of the self-destroying Reformation is present in other

Weberian ideas that Bell adopts, and he almost comes out and says it himself at times. But if Protestantism did itself in, and, within that frame, business systematically destroyed thrift and restraint to sell its product, why blame the thing on modern art? The more interesting question is why business is destroying itself in the first place. Why there is, in Bell's words,

> an extraordinary contradiction within the social structure itself. On the one hand, the business corporation wants an individual to work hard, pursue a career, accept delayed gratification–to be, in the crude sense, an organization man. And yet, in its products and its advertisements, the corporation promotes pleasure, instant joy, relaxing and letting go. One is to be "straight" by day and a "swinger" at night. This is self-fulfillment and self-realization! (pp. 71–72).

If we add the point that the Protestant Ethic, viewed as a theory of meritocracy, is still alive in the explanation of social inequality —implying that the poor just didn't work at it hard enough and that the rich got there by effort and thrift—we can see that business continues to have selective use for this ethic, even as it must be rejected in principle at the point of consumer morality.

This intriguing contradition is one that was not theoretically highlighted by Bell's framework, for he dealt with only three major realms, and he did not develop the analytic tools to deal with conflicts within the techno-economic sphere itself. But if the search for the killer of the Protestant Ethic is inconclusive, the proposal for a religious revival is even more unconvincing.

Business and science destroyed religion in the first place. These institutions gobbled up the very foundations on which they rested, and now they want new foundations. To put this in the language of Durkheim, the division of labor, which is the organizational heart of organic or modern solidarity, grew by forcing the pre-existing collective conscience to shrink. This did not happen all at once, as Durkheim's ahistorical categories almost imply, but it went on over centuries in a slow, corrosive "disenchantment," which, by Durkheim's generation, had resulted in a moral solidarity that was scarcely based on public rituals and beliefs at all, but on the rights of individuals and the sacredness of the person. Durkheim's modern collective conscience does have other sources than the sacredness of the individual. There are professional societies and codes of occupational ethics, rituals of punishment, nationalistic loyalties, and organized religions. But the anchor point is in the very "cult of the individual" (Durkheim's words) that Bell abhors. Bell did not mention the Durkheim who observed that the populations of complex societies have little in common but their humanity. Commenting on the moral confusion in France at the turn of the century, Durkheim went on to say:

> This is why man has become a god for man and is why he can no longer turn to other gods without being untrue to himself. And just as each of us embodies something of humanity, so each individual mind has within it something of the divine, and thereby finds itself marked by a characteristic which renders it sacred and inviolable to others. The whole of individualism lies here. That is what makes it into the doctrine that is currently necessary. For, should we wish to hold back its progress, we would have to prevent men from becoming increasingly differentiated from one-another, reduce their personalities to a single level, bring them back to the old conformism of former times and arrest, in consequence, the tendency of societies to become ever more extended and centralized and stem the unceasing growth of the division of labor. Such an undertaking, whether desireable or not, *infinitely surpasses all human powers* (my emphasis) (*Selected Writings,* Anthony Giddens, ed., 1972, pp. 23–24).

Another disclaimer I have about calling for a religious revival is in Bell's purpose. His purpose is not to praise God, but to shore up the stratification system. This is something of an insult to the integrity of religion itself, and in this day and age it won't work anyway. Too many people read books, and you can't spread religion by giving social arguments for it.

In sum, we have a book which is often brilliant, but whose major arguments don't stand fast. Blaming the moral drift of the twentieth century on modern art and the hippies may sound convincing in New York but it doesn't square with economic history, as Bell himself paradoxically admits. And we are most unlikely to solve the fiscal crisis by sitting around like cargo cultists, waiting for the return of traditional religion.

James O'Connor is a working Marxist economist, and *The Fiscal Crisis of the State* is a firm display of scholarship as well as political economic theorizing. It is one of the most influential pieces of radical research coming out of the sixties, originally appearing as a two-part journal article in 1969, and it is striking that both Bell and Habermas rely rather strongly on O'Connor's categories and findings, though in quite different ways. His major argument is that the classic economic crisis of mass unemployment has now been transferred to the state, and that it comes as a political rather than as an economic crisis. The fiscal crisis of the state, with its unbalanced budgets and inflation, is the contemporary version of thirties' unemployment, and if we did not have the former we would have the latter.

O'Connor's originality is not only in the boldness of his general argument, but in the way he systematizes it, presents data for it, and relates it to other political economic theories. Some of his predictions were off the mark, but the general design of his argument still looks impressive in 1977.

O'Connor has the contemporary fiscal crisis coming from causes that trace back to the rise of oligopolies in the early twentieth century. Two economic changes were occurring at that time: the railroads, infra structure, and physical plant had been built and the economy was making a critical switch from producers' to consumers' goods, and second, the major areas of industry were forming themselves into concentrations of price-fixing oligopolies. The two changes worked together—the oligopolies made the consumers' goods, most notably those of the auto complex—but each change brought its own problems to the economy. The shift to mass consumption meant that income would have to be redistributed to the mass consumer or there would be a chronic shortage of demand, and the rise of oligopolies decreased the flexibility of the market and introduced rigidities and gaps that could be solved only by government intervention.

Keynes was most concerned with the first change, and his theory of counter-cyclical government fiscal intervention envisioned a budget that would be balanced, not on an annual basis but over a decade or so, for it would run a deficit during bad times and a surplus during good. He was ambivalent about redistribution, and he sometimes said it didn't matter where the public money was actually spent, just so the atmosphere was changed and investors were cajoled into making investment decisions.

In contrast to Keynes, O'Connor is the more impressed with the second, turn-of-the-century change—the shift from the market to oligopoly. He points out that in addition to the expenses of maintaining raw aggregate demand and manipulating the nerve of investors, the government must also spend large sums to rectify imbalances and gaps that derive from the rigidity and bulkiness of oligopoly. These latter expenses are constant and rising—they do not go away during good times—and the state may never be able to return to balanced budgets. Government borrowing, along with oligopolistic price and wage setting, leads to an inflation which is the political counterpart of depression. Thus the same economic processes that led the optimistic Keynes to say that "mankind is solving its economic problem," lead the pessimistic O'Connor, some years later, to see a fiscal crisis of the state.

To make his argument, O'Connor uses two sets of concepts to explain how oligopoly has led to the fiscal crisis. These are the "three sector" or "triple labor market" theory of the economy and the distinction between the state's roles in "accumulation" and "legitimation."

The three sectors are the oligopolistic or monopolistic, the competitive, and the public or state, with each employing about a third of the labor force. The monopolistic sector is the area of large corporations, strong profits, a predominantly white, male labor force, high wages, and strong trade unions. The competitive sector is the area of small business, service, and most of farming. Technology is low, profits and wages are low, and the labor force is heavy with minorities, females, students, and the aged as it gradually merges with poverty, unemployment, and welfare. The state sector includes state operated agencies, such as the various health, education, and welfare units, and also private contractors, such as the space and military firms that work for the state. The state labor force and that of its contractors is relatively well paid, generally maintaining parity with the monopoly labor force, but tending to slide behind during inflation.

The intriguing aspect of the three-sector approach is that it divides the class system along a new axis. The old Marxian axis was the relation to property and to place in the productive process. O'Connor still works with that axis, but he superimposes on it the three sector division, which cuts the pie on the basis of vulnerability to market forces: the competitive sector being totally vulnerable, the oligopolistic only partially, and the state sector not directly vulnerable at all. This new axis is not only theoretically revealing; it also highlights certain horizontal conflicts in the class system—within labor and within capital—that are not disclosed by purely hierarchical theories of stratification. O'Connor presents the three sectors as a source of structural rigidity which prevents normal market processes, favors the monopolistic sector over the competitive, and requires that the state both expand and spend more money than it can afford.

Turning to his other set of concepts, he distinguishes two general areas of state spending: those of "accumulation" or economic growth, and those of legitimation or the pacification of the poor with welfare and other benefits in kind. Accumulation includes a variety of industrial services, research programs, subsidies and guarantees, transportation systems, communication systems, and innumerable programs that go mainly for business. It also includes expenses for the employed labor force, especially the various forms of social insurance; for the assistance or "reproduction" of this labor force has a bearing on how much they need to be paid at work and on how fit they are to work. Most of O'Connor's book consists of data showing how government expenses are rising in these areas, how the existence of the three sectors, itself a result of oligopoly, complicates and increases the spending problem, and how there is no workable way out of the ensuing deficits and inflation.

More formally, O'Connor argues that the accumulation and legitimation functions of government are in contradiction. For the expenses of accumulation maintain a triple labor market which generates poverty. And when the government, to maintain legitimacy and loyalty from the poor, distributes welfare and other benefits, it runs short of money for the expenses of accumulation.

The only way out O'Connor sees for American capitalism, and even this will be temporary, is that big business create a "social industrial complex" of problem-solving corporations that serve the needs of the poor for a guaranteed profit from the state. This complex, which was talked about by liberal democrats and business persons in the late sixties, would provide a new industrial outlet for business capital, hire many of the unemployed and low-paid competitive sector workers, and create an alliance between big business and the competitive labor force, adding up to something like Marx's "feudal socialism." This complex, which would work against the interests of the other two labor forces and the employers of competitive labor, did not come about, and it is unlikely to appear in the future, but it is interesting that O'Connor was of two minds about it when it was still a possibility. On the one hand he sees it as a humane, worthwhile set of services, possibly leading as a bridge to socialism. On the other he sees it as reactionary, buying off discontent and merely postponing the big collapse. But what he did not see is that a set of corporate social programs could also slide toward having a repressive effect by controlling the private lives of the poor, including supplementary schooling, family life, mental health services, and community organizations.

More generally much of O'Connor's analysis seems compatible with a non-Marxist and even a conservative view. He gives a detailed picture of how the government is over-spending, and he gives a convincing argument that present trends will get worse. He thinks the spending is indispensible and that there is no way out but tax strikes, crippling inflation, discontent, and a move to the left. But some of the people who read his book will conclude that expenses must still somehow be cut and that the ripest areas are in the social services. O'Connor thinks, for example, that the present level of higher education—the level that existed a few years ago when he wrote this book—is required by the economy and military. But other industrial countries get along with a far lower percent of people going to college, and it is unlikely that the American economy would run short of trained technicians and trained workers if education expenses were lowered, though other serious problems might be introduced. O'Connor was of the opinion that the sixties' protest would continue and that it would somehow combine with the conservative protest of the anti-tax groups. This did not happen, though we are experiencing the very cutbacks in social services O'Connor thought impossible.

The great strength of O'Connor's book is that he predicted the fiscal crisis quite early, and when others on the left were seeing an end to scarcity and a constantly enlarging public sector, he showed we would be smashing into a brick wall any minute. O'Connor was right, though the crisis has come, not with a bang but a whimper. On the other hand, O'Connor is something of a socialist technocrat, and he sees more technical necessity in the budget, particularly in the social and educational services, than may actually be there. What he does not seem to see is that the state can legitimize itself, not only by passing out welfare and material goods, but by creating programs that "manage" the private social and cultural life of the low paid population. This is the insight of critical theory, and it points to a psychological or epistemological dimension of state control which goes well beyond the influence of the cash flows and budgetry that O'Connor handles so well.

Habermas's *Legitimation Crisis* assumes some familiarity with the author's general approach, which is probably best encountered by reading "Technology and Science as 'Ideology,'" the last essay in *Toward A Rational Society*. The center of Habermas's thought, in this book as well as his others, is the distinction between two kinds of knowledge: the technical and the practical, deriving from the Greek philosophical distinction between "techne" and "praxis." The technical is the area of work, science, the economy, linearity, and the narrowly rational processes by which we fit material means to material ends. The practical, in contrast, is the sphere of fully human activity. This kind of knowledge can be reached only by open human discourse, in which subjectivity and reflexivity are constitutive ingredients. Culture, morality, and the normal human personality are formed by practical discourse.

The technical is programmed knowledge, for the conclusions are based on premises that must remain unexamined within the system. The practical or "symbolically interactive" is a self-programming process, for the premises and conclusions are under constant revision, and reflexity replaces the linearity of technical discourse.

The former is the realm of facts, formal rationality, artificial language, and positivistic theories of truth, including both the correspondence theory of empirical truth and the coherence theory of deductive truth. The latter is the area of values, substantive rationality, natural language, and the consensus theory of truth, which describes the rational grounding or validation of morality and culture.

Armed with this distinction, Habermas has staked out a theoretical position that is unique in modern social theory. He is not a traditional Marxist because he does not make the economy the foundation or infra structure, he does not make human labor the central human process, and he does not think the proletariat is necessarily a revolutionary force. Instead he insists on the radical duality of the technical and the practical, of work and interaction, of infra and super structure. Neither pole is central nor foundational for Habermas, though he does locate work within the overall defining context of interaction, and in that sense the technical is a subordinate but internally autonomous realm. And he is not a liberal, for he does not see the market as foundational, nor does he accept the value-free, procedural approach to morality and culture. Nor is he an idealist, for his realm of inter-subjective, interpretive culture is not the whole of reality. The technical and the material are very much with us, even though they can never be humanly interpreted and contextualized except with reflexive symbols. And he is not a technocratic communist, for such a society can do even more violence to the subtle process of moral or symbolic interaction than capitalism is doing.

Against all monistic theories and ideologies, Habermas is an epistemological dualist, and this dualism gives his thought a pincers quality that tends to surround a problem and solve it in a flash of contextualization. *Legitimation Crisis* is an attempt to deal with the crisis question by surrounding it historically and theoretically. The first of the three chapters is historical, or rather evolutionary, and it presents a stage theory of society, going from primitive to traditional to liberal capitalist to late capitalist. Societies face a crisis when they have a problem whose solution lies outside the adaptive range of their organizing principles and structures, requiring that they either change structures—which can move them ahead in Habermas's evolutionary scheme—or suffer destruction from the unsolved problem.

In Habermas's second chapter he gives his theory of crisis displacement, arguing that the economic crisis has not only shifted to the political sphere, as O'Connor argues, but that there is still another displacement from the political to the sphere of motivation and culture. The economic and the public administrative are both in Habermas's technical realm, while the culture is in his practical or symbolic realm. Thus he is arguing that the capitalist crisis, originating in the technical realm of the political economy, is displacing or externalizing itself by consuming the moral capital of the culture and imposing its own technical epistemology on the realm of practical human discourse.

In a way, this is Bell backward, for Bell had the crisis coming from the culture into the political economy, while Habermas has it going in the opposite direction, though they do differ in what they dislike in the culture itself, Bell being morally outraged and Habermas epistemologically threatened. Yet these two theorists are working in much the same groove, and some of what Bell says can be pushed left, just as some of what Habermas says sounds compatible with classical conservatism of the libertarian variety.

Habermas's notion of crisis displacement is the key idea of this book, and, while it comes in a sketchy, almost off-handed way, it is a gripping line of thought. The initial crisis displacement is the transfer of the economic problem into the state administration. This is a straight case of borrowing from Peter to pay Paul, for the taxing power and finances of the state are used to buy off problems that come from the oligopolistic economy. But Habermas, following O'Connor, thinks this displacement has been a failure, and that still another attempt is being made to go from Peter to Paul. This time the crisis is in the state itself, and this institution wants to be bailed out by borrowing something from the culture and motivational system. What does it want to borrow, and what will allow it to displace or transfer its crisis in a manner analagous to the way the economy displaces its own crisis onto the state?

Habermas answers this question in two ways: first by discussing the legitimation crisis and then, its psychological counterpart, the motivational crisis. The legitimation crisis is a condition in which significant sections of the population do not support the activities of the state. The state of early, liberal capitalism needed less legitimation, for it was a smaller state, it touched on fewer areas of social life, and it could rely on the market itself, with its principle of equal opportunity and fair exchange, to give basic legitimation to all social institutions. The corresponding bourgeois culture and personality systems of the time were reasonably congruent with the legitimation needs of the state, for they combined an occupational achievement ethic with a low emphasis on political participation.

But the contemporary capitalist state is running short on legitimation, for its interventionist activities have weakened the market that once gave it justice, and its expansion into the areas of family, community, and personal life all require new justification. The state is also having problems legitimizing what it will *not* do, for the expansion of social services has created something of a "rising expectations" problem, and many of the new groups making claims on the state must go away empty handed. In addition, the bourgeois culture of political privatism and occupational achievement is eroding in many quarters, being replaced by more participatory and equalitarian tendencies.

Yet the state needs more legitimation, not less, and the only way to increase it is to directly confront the refractory motivational system, i.e., the people who ask questions and refuse automatic loyalty, and somehow neutralize or change this system and these people. Habermas thinks the advanced capitalist societies, especially the United States, are edging toward the control of motivational systems by a kind of methological or epistemological coup in which technical truth will become the only publicly acceptable truth, and practical truth will become relegated to the private and inconsequential level. He refers to this as the "uncoupling of truth from culture," and he has in mind a society in which you can believe anything you want, but you will have to socialize your children, at home and in school, into symbol systems that are purely technical, and from which the moral elements of intersubjective human interaction will have been gradually removed.

This is the blank check that the state needs—to be empowered to do anything required by the technical logic of systems theory, and to be able to convince people that the technical has replaced the moral and that the state is thereby self-legitimizing. In other words, to get back to the question of displacement, the state wants to export its crisis into the culture by diminishing the autonomous power of morality, and by gaining strength for itself at the expense of what can only be called the natural and normal consciousness of human beings. Habermas does not use the phrase, "1984," since that despotism was based on mechanical surveillance, not epistemology, though the phrase would not be far off the mark. The 1984 state manipulated truth as state imperatives required, and while George Orwell's dictatorship did not bother to give technical arguments for its policy changes, the potential was always there.

So the raw crisis, which began as class conflict, became formalized into the business cycle, and then oozed into the fiscal crisis of the state, is now reaching the end of the line. Either the motivational system becomes compliant to the imperatives of the technical state, and human beings become robots, or the ideals of the culture hold fast and the state becomes structured into some form of socialism. Those are the two alternatives Habermas sees.

I will not discuss his concept of socialism, for it is linguistic rather than economic, and it is both interesting and full of problems. But there is the question of whether his extraordinary charge of incipient totalitarianism can be taken seriously. Note, the despotism he sees coming is not a matter of police, propaganda, and jails. It is a cognitive despotism in which the very intellectual resources by which people grant or withhold legitimation will have been replaced by a scientism that is self legitimating. It is tests for everything, cost-benefit ratios across the board, quantification without limit, programs where we've never dreamt of them before, feedback loops that supply their own evidence, the denigration of all other forms of discourse, and a widespread feeling that you'd better join up or get crushed.

Of course the existing communist countries are by no means untainted by this technocratic nightmare, and one of Habermas's problems is to explain why countries that do *not* have a capitalist crisis are also manipulating their cultures and motivational systems. But this answer does not escape the question, and Habermas is making a valid point. The capitalist countries are in an economic crisis and their governments are looking for support wherever they can get it, including the fast and loose use of statistics, research designs, and technical analyses where they cannot be epistemologically justified.

Habermas's crisis, then, is largely a crisis of the social sciences, for it is these disciplines that will be asked (and paid) to do the job for the legitimation-hungry state. If the social sciences collapse under this pressure and become uniformly, if unofficially, logical positivist, as the present trend has it, the technical will gradually replace the practical. For Habermas, human freedom is grounded in a kind of pluralism or check-and-balance in the tension between the technical and the practical. This is also an epistemological pluralism, and to stay alive it will have to operate within the institutions and process of social science as well as in the society at large. If social science loses its epistemological pluralism and becomes a technically monolithic instrument, Habermas's point will have been made and the crisis may be over, but the patient will never look quite the same again.

Returning now to the other two books, what do these three treatments of crisis add up to? The authors contradict each other, both in specific findings and in the theoretical structures that lead to these findings, and the three don't add up at all in any simple sense. There is a certain minimal convergence among them, for they all indict the economy in some way and they all lean toward decentralization at times, but the divergencies are the more striking. I found Habermas to be the most intellectually exciting, but the dominant impression of the three together is one of confusion and pessimism. Imagine three doctors all agreeing that the patient is gravely ill, but disagreeing on the nature of the illness, the prognosis, and the proper means of cure. Such a patient would have good reason to be worried. That's the human message of these books.

Turning to their implications for sociology, they add up to something more. All three authors are unabashedly theoretical, in the sense of being free-swinging thinkers who create categories as they need them and don't hesitate to take on the biggest questions. Whether or not any of them has accurately analyzed the crisis, they have all shown where the roots of social theory lie. They lie in the no-holds-barred examination of the biggest questions, with special attention to the sources and directions of change. Reading these authors, you realize that theory has no fixed rules, for it examines the processes that make the rules, and this entails a reflexivity that is open to premises as well as to data. The authors did not intend to make this point, but it may be just as important as the one they did intend.

FEATURE ESSAYS

Chilean Rural Society from the Spanish Conquest to 1930, by ARNOLD J. BAUER. New York: Cambridge University Press, 1975. 265 pp. $18.95 cloth.

The Brazilian Peasantry, by SHEPARD FORMAN. New York: Columbia University Press, 1975. 319 pp. $13.50 cloth.

PETER SINGELMANN
University of Missouri, Kansas City

One of the most critical problems faced by contemporary Latin American societies is the transformation of their agrarian economies and social structures into sectors which are capable of sustaining increasingly urban populations while at the same time resolving the progressively more accentuated contradictions in their class structures. While scholars and political practitioners disagree on the origin of the crisis and the most feasible alternatives for solving it in different countries, recent academic debates have focused on a number of centrally important issues.

A first issue centers around the nature of the socio-economic formations which have developed out of colonial society on the subcontinent. Some scholars dispute whether the colonial societies were originally "feudal" or "capitalist" and whether accordingly the classical hacienda should be considered as an archaic form of production or whether it was the forerunner of modern agricultural enterprise.

A second issue concerns the nature of the current transformations in rural agrarian structures. Given the capitalist nature of development in all countries but Cuba, will the movement be toward increasingly large-scale and mechanized production with a concomitant proletarianization of the rural labor force? Is peasant production on the verge of disappearing or does it continue to fulfill supportive functions in an underdeveloped capitalist economy?

The answers to such questions require both a further development of our theoretical instrumentarium and its separate application to the historical context of each country. These studies under review, on Chile and Brazil, have in different ways contributed to advancing our knowledge in both respects.

Forman's *The Brazilian Peasantry* is a provocative attempt to explain the history, functions, and prospects of Brazilian peasants within the context of the larger society. Going beyond the general notion that peasant communities are "part-societies" which are related to other segments of the social order through a system of "linkages" but which can nevertheless be analyzed separately, Forman argues that the Brazilian peasants cannot be understood apart from the larger system into which they are integrated as one of the constituent elements. His focus is, therefore, on analyzing the integrative processes which connect the local peasant community with the region and the nation along social, cultural, economic, and political dimensions. The integration and contradictions in this larger system are thus crucial elements in understanding the peasantry from a class perspective.

An anthropologist by profession, Forman bases his analysis on statistical information, published studies, and his own extensive field work in several parts of the country. His documentation is conscientious and the writing is not only clear but thoroughly enjoyable; in fact, Forman not only keeps the reader interested but also manages to convey a feeling for the flair of rural Brazil.

Forman begins by depicting the historical panorama of export-oriented, commercial agriculture practiced on the large estates, and which received its impetus from the demand for sugar in the incipient capitalist world-economic system. In this context, peasants have almost from the beginning served a triple function: to produce food for their own subsistence and for sustaining the population employed in the export sector; to produce commercial crops for the export sector via the marketing monopoly of the large estates (independent smallholders, sharecroppers); and to provide labor services to the large estates as a rent for the utilization of subsistence plots. Peasant labor and peasant production were thus of a precapitalist nature which served precisely the function of raising the profits in the incipient capitalist sector of production. The socio-economic formation of the early colonial period thus defies the simplified feudal-capitalist scheme of classification. Peasant economy and the sort of capitalism developing in Brazil were not antagonistic but to an extent supportive of one another within a larger integrated system. Forman illustrates this point with some highly instructive descriptions of different labor and tenancy systems and the integration of local peasant markets with a national capitalist market structure.

While the relative abundance of land and the limited national demand for food products permitted, for a while, an extended period of relatively stable equilibrium in the rural class structure and the persistence of low-productivity subsistence agriculture, increased population pressures, urbanization, and industrialization changed the demand structure for agricultural products in the twentieth century. The large estates responded to increasing international demands for cash crops by extending production to land previously given to peasant-laborers and by demanding increasing amounts of labor service from their service tenants. By the same token, less land was dedicated to the production of food crops, peasants were increasingly obliged to pay for their means of subsistence in cash without receiving commensurate incomes, and the traditional peasant production became increasingly insufficient to supply a growing non-agricultural population with food crops. In response to the new demands, agriculture became increasingly commercialized and expansive. While the rural economy became increasingly monetarized, the peasants' relative self-sufficiency, derived from their precapitalist form of production, broke down. It is against this background of an increasingly untenable economic situation that the large scale mobilizations of peasants and rural laborers in the 1950s and 1960s are analyzed.

While Forman examines a number of mechanisms whereby peasant producers and peasant market middlemen become progressively decapitalized in the face of increasing concentration of land and capital, the reader may have some reservations about the extent to which the proletarianization of the rural masses may go. Forman himself points out how in a number of ways the traditional peasant modes of production have been reinforced in the 1960s: laborers continue to receive small garden plots to supplement their low wages in the sugar mills or on the large estates; and absentee owners act as central collecting agents for wholesalers buying peasant products, a pattern which has strengthened traditional forms of sharecropping. While Forman does not elaborate the implications of such phenomena, his analysis suggests that precapitalist forms of peasant production may contribute to greater capitalist exploitation in underdeveloped countries by reducing the amount of cash outlay necessary to remunerate rural "proletarians."

I can only point out briefly some of the excellent chapters discussing the break-down of traditional patron-dependency relations and its political consequences in rural Brazil; the perceptive analysis of changes in the local power structures over the last two centuries; and the finely differentiated last chapter on some cultural dimensions underlying the paradoxical mixture of conservatism and rebellion (messianism, banditry) of the peasant. I do have some minor criticisms. For example, the suggestion that sharecroppers may be viewed as salaried workers misses the crucial distinction between the capitalist cash nexus and precapitalist remuneration in kind; a sharecropper is not the recipient of a wage but rather the payer of a land rent in the form of an agricultural surplus. But reservations of this kind are really minor in comparison with the overall contributions of the book.

Bauer's *Chilean Rural Society* is an economic historian's contribution to understanding the transitional phase between the relatively slow development of colonial rural structures in central Chile and the political explosions resulting from rapidly expanding international markets, urbanization, and industrialization. While tracing his analysis back to the development of colonial society and projecting its implications for the turbulent years to come after the 1930s, Bauer centers his study around the effects which growing international markets, commerce, and mining had on Chile's rural class structure between the 1850s and the first decade of the twentieth century. Like Forman, Bauer examines the place of landowners, peasants, and rural labor, in their interconnections with one another and within a larger societal system. In addition, Bauer systematically traces the consequences of developments in the Atlantic capitalist economy for the constraints which central Chilean agriculture faced during that period. His meticulous analysis of relatively unaccessible archival data is enriched by his skillful use of literary and travelers' accounts. The volume is superbly written and makes not only a scientific contribution but also leaves the reader "involved" with the country and its people.

Due to peculiar historical circumstances in Chile, independent Indian settlements disappeared soon after the conquest in the central region, as the vast land grants de facto came to entail the rights to exploit the Indian labor residing on the estates. Production on the estates was geared to supply European cereals to Santiago and Peru; plows and draft animals were used in this market-oriented production, in contrast to the hoe which was still the predominant tool of the natural economy whereby the resident labor force produced its means of subsistence. Apart from slave and drafted labor, there began to develop a system of service tenancy (*inquilinaje*) which became most prominent during the nineteenth century. As in Brazil, we find in Chile rural enterprises feeding agricultural products into an incipient capitalist world market. Within the estate, profits were derived from labor remunerated with land to plant subsistence crops. Peasant production was thus an early complement to a developing capitalist system. Bauer stresses, however, that well into the nineteenth century markets were rather small, thus providing no incentive for expanding agricultural production or modifying the relatively stable equilibrium in rural class relations. As long as markets were limited and land abundant, the perquisites of the *inquilinos* were relatively generous and even enabled a fortunate few to accumulate some land and capital.

In the 1850s there was a brief period of high demand for Chilean wheat in overseas markets. Chilean landowners did not perceive this as a long-range opportunity and were hesitant to intensify production. They rather chose to increase the areas under cultivation and the number of laborers. After the brief boom, Chilean agriculture benefited from the gradual opening of new markets due to the emerging mining sector and the concomitant proliferation of an urban and industrial population. Moreover, Bauer shows how land values increased both for economic and non-economic reasons and mortgage loans became easily accessible to the landowners who also constituted the political elite of the country. Most owners lived in Santiago and rented their land. The rent was frequently used to service interests on mortgage loans which in turn were diverted to underwrite a sumptuous life style and investments in non-agricultural enterprises. During the second half of the nineteenth century, the gradually increasing demands for agricultural products could, in the face of abundant land and labor, again most easily be met by increasing the amount of land under cultivation and adding labor. Capital improvements were mostly restricted to irrigation works (precisely to increase the amount of cultivable land). This and the demand for increasingly diversified agricultural products made it possible to subdivide the vast colonial estates into a number of smaller but still large *fundos*. As a result, we find that the number of large estates increased, but that their average size declined, with the landed elite increasing in size.

The opportunities offered by expanding markets thus did not give rise to the development of modernized and capital-intensive productive units but rather tended to intensify traditional pre-capitalist labor and production systems on the large estates. As the market pressures increased, the perquisites of the *inquilinos* declined, and there is evidence of their increasing decapitalization during the latter part of the nineteenth century. It was only in the twentieth century that the contradictions between an unproductive agriculture and the rapidly increasing food needs of the exploding urban populations fully unfolded.

Bauer explores this theme in the context of the larger societal structure that was evolving in nineteenth century Chile. In separate chapters he analyzes Chile's landholders as a cohesive social group and political elite; the interpenetration of this elite with the nouveaux riches of the mining and commercial sectors; the development of a rural subproletariat; and the foreign domination of the most dynamic sectors of the economy which caused native Chilean capital to retreat into increasingly anachronistic rural estates. Bauer's analysis is perceptive, competent, and occasionally provocative. Some readers might wonder whether he over-emphasizes the sentimental value attached to landownership. Others may suspect (as he does himself) that he understated the significance of direct coercion in attaching rural labor to the estates (this may be due to the nature of the records he examined). But none of these questions detract from the outstanding contribution Bauer's book has made to the study of Chilean development.

This essay has focused on the treatment of peasants and the development of rural class relations in the two monographs under review. While studying diverse historical and cultural contexts, both authors present similar conclusions about the issues raised at the beginning of this essay. First, both reject the capitalism/feudalism dichotomy as inappropriate for the Latin American historical realities. Agricultural production in Latin America has to be interpreted in the context of the incipient capitalist world economy. But while the large estates have been oriented to the market and to production for profit, the degree of their expansion has always been a function of the size of the markets. Internally, the estate system has exploited labor through a variety of precapitalist patterns; its profits were derived from low or inexistent cash outlays required for the remuneration of peasant labor or the appropriation of peasant commercial crops. Pre-capitalist peasant production was thus not a relic of the past but an essential element within a larger system of capitalist production. Second, both authors note that nineteenth and twentieth century developments have strained this exploitative symbiotic relationship between landlord and peasant and point to the increasing proletarianization of the rural population. At the same time, both note that traditional forms of peasant production not only persist but appear to be strengthened by the very onslaught of commercialization and the cash economy. Neither one of them attempts to resolve that paradox, both seem to think that peasants are in the process of being displaced by the imposition of capitalism. Yet neither Brazil nor Chile has industries capable of absorbing the displaced rural populations. In fact, if we reinterpret some of the pieces of evidence offered in both books, we might entertain the thesis that peasant production persists precisely because of the particular nature of dependent capitalist development. While it is possible on the one hand that peasant production continues to exist simply for lack of other alternatives, there continues to be, on the other, the undeniable "advantage" peasant production entails for subsidizing industrial development and agrarian capitalism in dependent nations. Peasant production takes important segments of the population out of the commercial food market and thus contributes to maintaining low food prices; this, in turn, reduces the minimum wages required for sustaining the industrial and urban labor forces. And in a more direct way, assigning subsistence plots to rural laborers today still reduces to a minimum the amount of cash payment they need to receive as remuneration (Forman, pp. 62, 195). As long as peasant production is required to subsidize capitalist wages, we can by no means take for granted that the peasantry is about to be eliminated from the Latin American scene.

The Age of Capital, 1848–1875, by E. J. Hobsbawm. New York: Charles Scribner's Sons, 1975. 354 pp. $17.50 cloth.

S. D. Berkowitz
University of Toronto

The great strengths of this book arise from the author's thorough and powerful command of the sources and literature on the social forces, movements, ideologies, and personalities which shaped the latter part of the 18th and first half of the 19th centuries in Europe. In this sense, Hobsbawm skillfully paints the backdrop against which his period, the great era of the consolidation of industrial capitalism, took place. These same strengths, however, are also the principal sources of weaknesses in his account. As Hobsbawm, himself, points out, the dynamics of the period from the revolutions of 1848 until 1875 are really quite different from those of the era which preceded it: 1848–75 was pre-eminently an era dominated by worldwide capitalism and international capitalists; by new forms and institutions for directing the flow of capital; and by new ways of applying capital goods in production. As a result, the later epoch would seem to demand, at the very least, different foci and emphases in interpretation from those of the earlier period: away from a piecemeal, nation-state oriented view of production and towards a global view; away from a view of money as a medium of exchange to a tool for control and direction; and away from the economics of simple production and consumption to the economics of accumulation. Hobsbawm does not fully succeed in making these transformations in perspective, and his work suffers as a result.

The Age of Capital is divided into three parts. The first consists of a brief (17 page) chapter on the revolutionary ferment of the period around 1848. It serves to introduce the reader to the central political and social issues, important personages, and key alliances of the day. To this extent, though brief, it is quite adequate.

It does not, however, prepare the reader

for the second part, "Developments," which consists of eight chapters on changes in the structure of international capital. Whereas both the introduction and the first chapter discuss, in general terms, the *social* and *political* results of economic transformations which preceded those which occurred between 1848 and 1875, they do not describe the state of the organization of the world economy, *itself,* prior to that time. Thus the reader is left unprepared when a wave of legal-judicial facts, trade policies, and production statistics bursts over him/her in the second chapter. The changes that these data signal are not adequately summarized in theoretical terms, so their relationship to one another is not always clear.

The key theoretical concept around which Hobsbawm seeks to organize this second part is the notion of a *global economy*. Before the triumph of industrialism, he tells us, economies were *relatively* localized. While there was extensive trade before this, it had the character of an *adjunct* to the central dynamics of production and consumption. "The forging of the globe into a single interacting economy was in many ways the most far-reaching and certainly the most spectacular aspect of industrialization" (p. 40). But Hobsbawm does not *demonstrate* this case, nor does he produce the sorts of evidence which would lead us to *infer* it, inter alia, from his account: simple increases in trade or production do not demonstrate the relationship between parts of a single interacting system. *Interdependency* among these parts —as, for instance, the dependence of one country's textile manufacturing on another's machinery—would be evidence of this. Similarly, one might examine the dependence of one country's export sector on financing provided by foreign capitalists. Astonishingly, Hobsbawm does not even attempt to describe changes in the structure of financial markets or institutions in an era which was, preeminently, the era of finance capitalism.

Not surprisingly, then, much of the data which Hobsbawm brings forth to illustrate his case is either not relevant theoretically, or is difficult to interpret. For instance, in chapter 2, "The Great Boom," Hobsbawm speaks of the 1848 to 1875 period as "an age of unexampled economic advance" (p. 30). In order to elaborate this point, he cites a number of promiscuously selected sets of statistics on cotton exports from one country (Britain) between 1850 and 1860; cotton operatives from the same country in the 1850s; iron exports from another country (Belgium) between 1851 and 1857; and the number and total capitalization of joint stock companies established in yet a third country (Prussia) between 1851 and 1857. *Each* datum is compared, in turn, to a different base period—except for those in Belgian iron exports, for which we are given no base at all.

Perhaps it is asking too much for social historians—as opposed to sociologists and economists—to be sensitive to the importance of common standards of measurement. And perhaps the purpose of historical glosses such as this is to convey a sense or aura of the period to the reader—and, as such, do not lend themselves to close and systematic assessment. The problem is that Hobsbawm frequently gets himself into *theoretical* trouble by doing this. For instance, Hobsbawm compares, as an example of this "unexampled economic advance," the growth in the number and capital value of Prussian joint stock companies in the period from 1825 to 1850 (67 companies with a "total capital" [authorized? paid in? of 45 million Thaler] with that between 1851 and 1857 (115 companies with 114.5 millions). But since we reckon "capital value" at date of creation, the average simple increase in the *average* value of these companies during the 15.5 year period from the mid-point of the first interval to the mid-point of the second was only slightly more than three percent—or less than inflation. Coupled with (a) the realization that there are a number of different forms of investment—joint stock companies being only one; and (b) the observation that much of the capital in this period is in the form of *private* ventures, we can only really be sure from his datum that the average size of joint stock companies *declined* in real terms in Prussia during the second period.

One is left with the distinct impression, from all of this, that Hobsbawm is not as comfortable as he might be when talking about the development of *capital structures,* per se, as opposed to their *consequences*. His chapters on the expansion of capitalism into peripheral areas (chapter 7, "Losers" and chapter 8, "Winners") give excellent, though brief, images of the impact of industrial capitalism on all aspects of local societies. But even these chapters, and the summary chapter for this part (chapter 9, "Changing Society") suffer from the absence of a single overarching framework to explain the developments in financial and industrial structure from which these changes flow. True, Hobsbawm tells us, in chapters 4, 5, and 6, of the impact of the globalization of capitalism on international relations ("Conflicts and War"), the formation of new national entities or the consolidation of old ones ("Building Nations"), and class relations ("The Forces of Democracy"), and he does this well—straightforwardly, lucidly, and elegantly. But without a clear picture of *why* these changes are occurring, *where* they are, *when* they are, and through *what* means—a picture which Hobsbawm should have provided in chapters 2 and 3—there is a tendency for his account to degenerate into the old style of history as names/dates/battles/events.

This is unfortunate because the third part of *The Age of Capital* (chapters 10 through 16 inclusive) is vintage Hobsbawm at his best. Here he examines, in turn, changes brought about by this extension of industrial capitalism in land economy, patterns of international migration, class and community structure, lifestyles, and ideology—all, appropriately, at a global level. This part is extremely well done, and, given the force and elegance with which these changes are summarized, would, itself, justify the purchase of the book.

While *The Age of Capital,* then, is not likely to cause a wave of uncontrolled excitement among economic historians—particularly those interested in financial structures and mechanisms—it is good, readable social history. It lacks a coherent and detailed theoretical framework for the economic changes it describes, but it makes up for this in its scope and depth of presentation of the *consequences* of the extension and consolidation of modern industrial capitalism.

SURVEY REVIEWS

Juvenile Victimization: The Institutional Paradox, by CLEMENS BARTOLLAS, STUART J. MILLER, and SIMON DINITZ. New York: John Wiley & Sons, 1976. 324 pp. $17.50 cloth.

Back on the Street: The Diversion of Juvenile Offenders, edited by ROBERT M. CARTER and MALCOLM W. KLEIN. Englewood Cliffs, N.J.: Prentice-Hall, 1976. 368 pp. $8.95 cloth.

The Juvenile Justice System, edited by MALCOLM W. KLEIN. Beverly Hills, Calif.: Sage Publications, 1976. 287 pp. $17.50 cloth. $7.50 paper.

The Social Treatment of Young Offenders, edited by J. B. MAYS. New York: Longman, 1975. 331 pp. $15.00 cloth. $8.50 paper.

Juvenile Delinquency, by WILLIAM B. SANDERS. New York: Praeger Publishers, 1976. 238 pp. $10.00 cloth. $4.95 paper.

ROY L. AUSTIN
Pennsylvania State University, University Park

These books reflect many of the disagreements existing over the explanation and control of delinquency. There is even disagreement on the nature of the phenomenon that should receive attention. Sanders emphasizing the *characterization* of acts or persons as delinquent while other scholars stress *involvement* in acts characterized as delinquent. But there is agreement that the system established to control delinquency has failed dismally. Furthermore, all of the books show some concern with the claim that this system exacerbates delinquency by stigmatizing youths.

Back on the Street is a timely collection of papers on the controversial subject of diversion, a direct response to the hypothesized harmful effects of processing by criminal justice agencies. Selections are included on the theoretical foundation of diversion (labelling theory and differential association) and the support for this practice from government sponsored investigations. But it is easy to accept the editors' contention that diversion comes close to being a fad, especially given one reported finding that official labelling seemed to reduce recidivism (p. 98).

The most serious problem in the book is the limitation on generalizability of conclusions due to the emphasis on California programs. In addition, the reader might be bothered by the redundant occurrence of the widely reported findings by Black and Reiss,

Wilson, and Briar and Piliavin on characteristics associated with police disposition of offenders.

Of the twenty-six papers, the seven journal articles are particularly strong, as might be expected. However, even those papers that may have undergone less rigorous review contribute valuable insights into, for example, rules police are expected to follow in making diversion decisions. Readers should also find useful the distinction between institutions controlling "legitimate identities" and those controlling "illegitimate identities." The book is a convenient and reliable reference source on diversion.

Institutionalization is regarded as especially stigmatizing; and the authors of *Juvenile Victimization* see juvenile inmates in the institution studied as labelled through institutional records, cottage assignment, psychiatric designations (which serve no useful purpose), and by staff and other inmates. The labels are said to force most of the boys into harmful careers which they carry over to outside life. The *potential* harm and benefits of labelling are well argued.

But the primary concern of this book is the exploitation of weaker inmates by stronger. With the aid of an institution staff member/researcher, staff and inmate questionnaires, and psychological instruments it was found that boys from impoverished outside environments or boys who had previous institutional experience functioned best in the deprived institutional environment. The psychological tests produced little of value but suggested that boys able to adjust best in the outside world are most likely to be exploited in the institutions.

The authors' goal of dissecting, digesting, and organizing is achieved in this exploratory study. However, the goal of understanding proved elusive. The rich descriptions may contain some of the answers but they may emerge only after systematic comparison of the institutional environment with other environments. Persons who intend to work in institutions should make this book a part of their preparation.

In *The Juvenile Justice System* comments by a former juvenile court judge and by several police officers in two selections reassure the reader that the problems of this system are not manufactured by academicians. Judges do disregard Supreme Court decisions and render politically expedient judgments. The police are annoyed with interference in their work by citizens and judges, and Klein et al. show that police attempts to control diversion programs often distort the ideal of diversion.

Gordon's eighty-three page paper on prevalence rates ("proportion of an age-specific cohort that have become delinquent by a given age") contains a number of defects. For example, small differences in official prevalence rates for data from different cities and countries are difficult to interpret with no stated assumptions about class distributions. Further, arguments based on the high heritability and heavy biological basis of I.Q. should refer to the literature rejecting these claims about I.Q.

The seven selections preceding Gordon's are, however, logically and empirically strong and presented in a manner that allows easy appreciation by undergraduates. More advanced students of juvenile justice will also find much of interest in a history of attitudes toward childhood, findings from the National Assessment of Juvenile Corrections, and the recommendations for reform of the system that emerged from a conference of eleven scholars.

In England as in America there is dissatisfaction with delinquency control methods. The twenty-eight selections in *The Social Treatment of Offenders* describe English approaches, provide some reasons for changes, and include thoughts on punishment. The theoretical basis of the strategies is rarely stated and claims about effectiveness are mostly impressionistic.

Like many textbooks, *Juvenile Delinquency* surveys major theories in the field. Sanders regards differential association, Goffman's theory of moral character development, and labelling theory as philosophically and theoretically compatible and as answering the important questions in delinquency. These theories are clearly stated and the presentation of Goffman justifies its inclusion among delinquency theories. However, none of the theories discussed (social deprivation, delinquent subculture, and value conflict are included) receive adequate empirical assessment.

Sanders's arguments for limiting the study of delinquent gangs and delinquents to those so regarded by the community as such, are not convincing. Also, this restriction is inconsistent with his use of self-reports to estimate the number of juveniles involved in delinquency. Further, it is contradictory to claim that self-reports show greater lower-class criminality and also assert that labelling accounts for lower-class over-representation in official statistics.

The chapters on separate offense types, gangs, and the police are well grounded empirically but not systematically related to the favored theories. Nevertheless, the clear writing style and the contents of this portion of the book make it suitable for introductory delinquency courses.

Comparative Modernization: A Reader, edited by CYRIL E. BLACK. New York: Free Press, 1976. 441 pp. $12.95 cloth.

The Sociology of the Third World: Disparity and Involvement, by J. E. GOLDTHORPE. New York: Cambridge University Press, 1975. 325 pp. $19.50 cloth. $6.95 paper.

Industrialism, by BARRY A. TURNER. New York: Longman, 1975. 126 pp. $7.50 cloth.

RANDALL G. STOKES
University of Massachusetts, Amherst

Each of these works was apparently intended to serve the same purpose, that of providing classroom materials for courses in "modernization," social change, and comparative sociology. They differ significantly, however, in the way this task was approached.

The collection of articles edited by C. E. Black is a quintessentially (North) American work. Its introduction and twenty-one articles manage to summarize much of what American social scientists know, believe, and assume about social change in the underdeveloped nations of the world. There is a diverse mixture of conceptual pieces, historical case studies, and cross-national empirical analyses. Topics range from Arthur Wilson's comparison between the developmental thought of the eighteenth century *philosophes* and contemporary theories of modernization, to Judith Blake's excellent essay on the relationship of development to the status of women. There are familiar stops along the way, for example, Alex Inkeles's model of "modern man" and Samuel Huntington's systems view of political development. And there are less well-known issues raised, such as Knight Biggerstaff's survey of modernization in late nineteenth century and early twentieth century China, and Bernard Brown's application of the modernization perspective to the development of contemporary France. In contrast to many other works on modernization, there are also several contributions which take an introspective look at the concept of modernization. These include, among others, Ian Weinberg's discussion of the problematic assumption that industrial societies are converging toward the same end state, and A. R. Desai's attempt to distinguish between capitalist and socialist routes to development.

Despite such critical discussions and the determined effort by Black to avoid the more ethnocentric excesses of much previous work in this area, the book is badly marred by weaknesses which I believe are endemic to the American view of modernization. The very term "modernization," and the assumptions which it represents, are one major root of these weaknesses. Above all, the term begs questions which the book does not successfully answer, the most important being the criteria by which one can determine relative degrees of modernity. Black explicitly disavows any intent to equate modernization with Westernization—the implicit model behind most rationales for the concept of modernization—so the developed nations can not serve as the yardstick, and nowhere else in the book is there a convincing alternative justification for the use of this essentially evaluative term. Black's agenda for "comparative modernization" is to "contribute to an understanding of how the advancement of knowledge—the scientific and technological revolution—affects societal development." In less evaluative terms, the task is simply to investigate the social impact of scientific and technological change (i.e., industrialization). Granting that this is indeed an area worthy of investigation, and assuming for the moment that the underdeveloped world is experiencing scientific and technological change, there seems no earthly reason to apply the irrelevant term "modernization" to the process.

The second major weakness of the book is that it virtually ignores the growing body of theory and research on the "world system" as a barrier to economic development. That the underdevelopment of the poor nations may be a dynamic and integrated part of the international economy is, aside from a brief note in Simon Kuznet's contribution, not considered. Rather, the dominant perspective is that the poor countries are in a traditional state, waiting to be transformed *if* they can overcome *internal* social and psychological barriers to such a transformation. In light of the ample evidence now available which suggests that the current condition of the Third World is as recent as the development of the West, the failure to even consider this viewpoint can not be easily excused.

Because of this failure to look at the international base of underdevelopment, many of the contributions fall into using what Becker has called the "ficticious we," in regard to social scientific approaches to American social problems. As with many social scientists concerned with solving problems of inequality in American society, the assertion that "we" must and "we" will do something about the terrible fix the poor nations are in is made in oblivious disregard of the fact that many of "us" earn our bread and butter from this very fix. Indeed the parallels between the 1960s conception of American poverty and the conception of underdevelopment apparent in this work are striking. There is, for example, a reliance on cultural handicaps to explain lack of development, which is very similar to the culture of poverty perspective William Ryan has tellingly called "blaming the victim." Huntington describes the traditional person as "passive and acquiescent; he expects continuity in nature and society and does not believe in the capacity of man to change or control either." The implication that this psychological syndrome is somehow the cause of underdevelopment is a disquieting echo of the false assumptions which underlaid the war on poverty.

There is, finally, the same dazed and goofy goodwill which marked the 1960s crusade against poverty—goodwill which was so pervasive it blinded most social scientists to the economic and political bedrock of inequality. In the first article in the collection James O'Connell says "only through . . . intelligent goodwill can the peoples of the world avoid blowing themselves to pieces with the terrible power they now command *and instead join their resources.*" Let us hope these are not the only two alternatives.

Barry Turner's short work on industrialization will not have much appeal for the American reader. It concentrates most of its energy on reviewing theoretical approaches which have either been left by the wayside by American sociologists or incorporated into background assumptions. Saint Simon, Comte, Marx, Weber, and the pattern-variables consume fully half the book. The remainder is a survey of relatively well known contemporary theories of development (i.e., Hoselitz and McClelland) and general descriptive summaries of major processes of change in the underdeveloped world. It is worth noting, however, that even a brief overview of this nature finds space for a look at dependency theory, while the longer and more ambitious work by Black does not. It is not incidental that Turner is English and thus writing from a perspectivc less circumscribed than that which prevails in American sociology.

J. E. Goldthorpe's *Sociology of the Third World* is potentially the most useful of the three as a teaching resource. The book's title provides a concise statement of why this is so. Like the other two, the primary intent of the work is to provide an overview of the problems and prospects of the underdeveloped nations, but Goldthorpe manages to accomplish this task with admirable fidelity to the empirical world and without falling into the conceptual pitfalls that Black, for example, leaps eagerly into. His success rests on his approach to the subject as the sociology of the Third World, rather than as an attempt to illuminate processes, such as "modernization" or "industrialization," the reality of which remain doubtful. Guided by his stance toward the subject, Goldthorpe is led to consider issues of vital import which are neglected elsewhere. There are, for example, excellent chapters on the racist legacy of colonial administrations and on the very real problems posed for development by resource conditioned "limits to growth." There is also a very good chapter which considers theories of development, including those which have been articulated by Third World social scientists. While the book does not attempt to make an original contribution to the sociology of underdevelopment, it is one of the better summaries available, and is thus a good text for courses in this area.

The Problems of American Education, by BURTON R. CLARK. New York: New Viewpoints, 1975. 342 pp. $5.95 paper.

Cracks in the Classroom Wall, edited by THOMAS G. ROBISCHON, JEROME RABOW, and JANET SCHMIDT. Pacific Palisades, Calif.: Goodyear Publishing Company, 1975. 424 pp. No price listed, paper.

Social Forces and Schooling: An Anthropological and Sociological Perspective, by NOBUO KENNETH SHIMAHARA and ADAM SCRUPSKI. New York: David McKay Company, 1975. 368 pp. $4.95 paper.

Education, Equality, and Society, edited by BRYAN R. WILSON. New York: Harper & Row Publishers, 1975. 207 pp. $15.00 cloth.

DANIEL L. KEGAN
Hampshire College

When I approach an unknown edited volume, I generally assume that the editor(s) has tried to save instructors and students the effort of running to the local library and various journals to obtain a selection of the best writing on the subject. However, I found myself surprised as I read each of these four edited volumes concerning contemporary sociological views of schooling: one book captured me in its adventure, another tore me between its provocative readings and its ponderous editorial comments, a third fed me the tantalizingly enriched demi-ersatz menu of partial analyses of the newspapers, and the fourth reminded me that a commitment to nonelitist and nonsexist values is by no means yet universal—even among sociologists.

Social Forces and Schooling held my interest like a good mystery novel! Its eight coauthors have successfully collaborated within a single conceptual framework of the dialectic of convergent and divergent forces to view schooling within the larger context of social and cultural systems. A central theoretical theme of the book is the role of technology in the evolution of culture. Technology is broadly defined as "the socially organized capacity for activity controlling and altering objects of the physical environment in the interest of some human want or need" (p. 16). In this view, culture is seen as a process of energy transformations; it "captures energy from nature and transforms it into people and their social and political systems."

Social Forces begins its analysis of schooling in the Neolithic period some eight thousand years ago, and finds that it is not the modern Industrial Revolution or American capitalism that creates stress between the individual and the state, between education and schooling; it is an inherent tension of civilization.

In an outstanding chapter, Donald Oliver explores and critiques the ideology of innovative education, and offers hope. He sees most educational innovation as a process of "improving the efficiency, the order, and the morale of those who inhabit schools" (p. 251). This is an outgrowth of the ideology of utilitarian perfectionism—"the belief that the purpose for which the planet was created is the comfort, convenience, and perfection of the human species and that man's maximal comfort and convenience can be attained through large, highly differentiated social organizations" (p. 257). This is seen as a dangerous ideology because it discounts people's nonrational sides.

A contrasting and more promising view does not place humans at the very center of the universe, but places the initial unit of moral consideration as "the universal space and immense time in which energy, matter, and life exist and have existed on this planet" (p. 259). This evolutionist or communitarian belief is a basis of much of the current radical school criticism, but modern schools generally do not permit communitarian cultures. In our highly segregated and fragmented society, Oliver continues, much of the work is invisible to those not actually doing it; the only shared life is abstract and complex. Schools transmit this common, abstract culture, but only to those oriented to think abstractly. Others who tend to think more visually, kinesthetically, or concretely have no common culture but only transitory fragments such as TV ads and popular songs. Without the sense of common life, education is seen as losing its internal motivation, and the culture and schooling thus exist only with coercion and extrinsic rewards.

Oliver suggests that "schools no more have the potential for fulfilling man's basic communitarian needs than businesses or factories" (p. 278). His suggestion is that "the most productive role for the teacher is in teaching an evolutionist or communitarian ideology as a basis for an alternate vision of society as well as creating opportunities for students to have positive experiences which would reinforce and be consistent with this vision" (p. 279).

Cracks in the Classroom Wall is a mixed, inconsistent volume; it has a good selection of readings, but its editorial writing is weak. Selections from Aristophanes, Xenophon, Plato, Aristotle, Quintilian, St. Thomas Aquinas, and the editors' writings to fill the gaps between them and to continue the history to Dewey, well indicate our Greek heritage: the belief in the supremacy of Reason, the permanency of reality, the use of education for the formation of an elite class, and the meeting of individual goals through the objectives of the State. Many current educational reform books seem to start their analyses of the ills of American education somewhere between the American Revolution and the Civil War. I found it refreshing to go back a bit further with *Cracks* and see just how immense is the cultural tradition of our contemporary schools.

The now traditional radical view of schools as not ivory towers but integral institutions of a racist, sexist, classist society is well presented by the readings in the sections on the school and politics, the school and the economy, and schools and socialization. But the first and last sections of the book are weak. "The need for a new analysis" is a neo-Marxist critique of capitalism. Capitalism does have its problems, but the use of schools to promote the ideology of the state is not limited to current capitalistic cultures. *Crack's* own historical section clearly indicates that. And if someday a classless society is formed, I'd tend to agree with Karl Mannheim (*Ideology and Utopia*) that schools will still be used by the state to promote its ideology. There are differences between schooling and education, but those differences are likely to exist in any society.

Half the readings in the final section, "What Is to Be Done?," present alternatives: on being a radical substitute teacher, on organizing a group of radical teachers for activist programs and personal support, and on establishing alternative schools within and free schools outside the public school system. These are some of the things that can be done, but they sidestep awareness of a fundamental tension: the contradiction between the divergent forces of education and the convergent forces of schooling and society.

The editorial sections do a disservice to the quality of content and writing of most of the readings. Even a devout believer of the editors' conclusions should reject the logic of many of their arguments; many are just too simplistic and omit consideration of any plausible rival hypotheses. If one knew and believed Marxist analysis, then what is presented as simple causality, often involving the "changing means of production." would be less of an issue and one could accept as example what one may be reluctant to accept as complete logic. But I doubt many undergraduate or graduate readers of *Cracks* will begin the book as believing neo-Marxists. Thus the editors are caught in their own contradiction: while condemning the indoctrinating forces of schooling in service of a capitalistic ideology they present their own unacknowledged ideology. They also inconsistently address the reader in the third or second person, and sporadically use a few "his/her" replacements for their usual masculine third person pronoun: minor but distracting faults.

The Problems of American Education contains seventeen articles drawn from the New York *Times*, reflecting, in the editor's opinion, "much of the best public thought about education in the last two decades" (p. 15). He's probably right—a sad judgment of public thought and journalism. The articles do read like the newspaper columns they originally were: easily, but without much depth or comprehensive logical or empirical support for many conclusions. This could be an asset, for a student could use the provocative articles as a collection of observations from which to derive a framework, selecting important variables and concepts, developing theories of generalizations and limiting conditions, and searching for other empirical bases supporting or disconfirming the conclusions of the authors.

The articles focus strongly on New York City, but I wonder how concerned about that city's problems students in Iowa, Mississippi, or even Chicago would be. The editor adds a few explanatory notes to remove the mystery of olden household words that no longer are. President Johnson is amended to read "former," but Rhody McCoy is left unexplained (pp. 201, 95). Most of such meanings can be roughly inferred from context, but the editor's choice of what needed explanation is a bit mystifying.

Twenty-three suggested readings are listed after the *Times* articles and before the index. I suppose that may be helpful, but I would suspect that a student would be more apt to pursue another source if it were directly tied to a stimulating paragraph in the text, or in consideration of the original nonreferenced format of newspaper articles, tied to a specific article.

The five sections in *Problems* do cover many of the issues of educational criticism: the search for excellence, the black and the poor, the adolescent meets the bureaucracy, reform in the public schools, and the crisis of purpose and identity in higher education. For some purposes that may be enough, but while the reader gets a good feel for the continuity of problems in American education, there is no systematic framework of what might be done to break the cycle.

Education, Equality, and Society is a bad book. At least I found its conservative apology for elitism and sexism disagreeable. The British authors present to their British audience an argument that all individuals are not equal, that inequality is necessary for the continuation and advancement of culture, and that the schools should recognize and promote elitism. They present extreme statements as representing the liberal position, and anecdotes, not representative data, are used as strong support for logical arguments—arguments which I found too often overgeneralizations and false dichotomizations. Even their scientific chapter on the inheritance of mental differences is flawed. Noting that a fifteenth century villain had grandchildren related to Queen Elizabeth I and that the majority of the descendents of King Edward III belonged to the trading or laboring class does not prove free social mobility as much as statistical regression artifacts and the "small world" phenomena (p. 105).

The editors see coeducation as a "way in which human relationships are coarsened by treating manifestly different people as if they were the same" (p. 32). They warn of:

> the destructive process at work that is changing the female to being the very opposite of her natural self. Present-day secondary education is the denial of every adolescent girl's due rights and needs—respect for her physiology, protection from the excitements of the opposite sex, time and peace in which to dream in preparation for her important womanly role, restfulness and relaxation of the body, mind and spirit to accustom her to her femininity, preservation of her innocence and natural modesty, and opportunity to use and extend her gifts of intuition and sympathetic understanding.

Their view of men's and women's natures is not mine.

BOOK REVIEWS

Culture

African Dilemma Tales, by WILLIAM R. BASCOM. Chicago: Aldine Publishing Company, 1975. 162 pp. $12.50 cloth.

STEVEN S. JONES
University of California, Davis

William Bascom's *African Dilemma Tales* is a compilation of 168 different types (in 449 separate versions) of a special kind of folktale that asks its listener a problematical or puzzling question. Bascom calls these folktales "dilemma tales" (they are also known as riddle stories or problem stories) and describes them as oral prose narratives that ask the listener to make an evaluative choice between given alternatives. For example, in one tale a hunter kills a pig, another builds a fire, and a third cooks the meat. A decision is required as to who owns the food. In these dilemma tales the choice usually involves either an evaluative decision as to which character is the most skillful, greatest, or the like, or a moral judgment as to which character is the most deserving or worthy. Both kinds of choices involve discrimination based on practical, ethical, or legal grounds.

In his introduction Bascom discusses the reasons why he considers dilemma tales to be a separate category of folk narrative and reviews the previous attempts to classify and study them. He suggests that although some dilemma tales are told without posing a question and some dilemma tales are simply versions of other folk narratives with a dilemma added to them, the fact that a large number of tales can be consistently identified as posing a dilemma to their audience justifies regarding them as a separate class of folktales. With regard to the classification of dilemma tales, Bascom points out that few have been typed in Aarne-Thompson's

Types of the Folktale; the few exceptions, such as "The Rarest Thing in the World" Type 653A, have little or no African references. This reveals a strong justification for Bascom's book: African tales have not been well collected or classified, and his work is an initial and praiseworthy attempt to identify and organize one special category of African folk narrative.

By way of criticism we should note that for the purposes of intensive study we are obviously hampered by the fact that these tales are presented only in translation. This is especially bothersome in a few tales where Bascom has had to rely on a translator who has retold the tale more in his own words than in those of a folk narrator. However, there is no way around this (given the extensive linguistic barriers), and we must content ourselves with the knowledge that Bascom has identified and assembled for us a group of previously overlooked, indigenous African folk narratives. Since the dilemma tales by the kinds of questions they pose tend to reveal the mores, morals, and mind set of their audience, this collection should prove to be a treasure trove for other humanists in the future who are interested in studying the philosophical and sociological concerns of African peoples.

All Silver and No Brass: An Irish Christmas Mumming, by HENRY GLASSIE. Bloomington: Indiana University Press, 1975. 192 pp. $10.00 cloth.

ROGER ABRAHAMS
Univeristy of Texas, Austin

This lovely book, ostensibly an ethnographic account of Christmas countryside amusements of the generation just passed, is really an essay on what folklorists are up to these days. Self-consciously caught between the more elegant (and sometimes parsimonious) techniques of sociological and anthropological collection and analysis of socio-cultural data, and the more powerfully (if often sentimental) metaphoric renderings of symbolic systems employed by humanists when faced with the same data, the folklorist here is concerned with investing description and analysis with the liveliness of the people and their creative concoctions.

Sociologists are liable to say of this book, "a nice little community study." Well it is that, an exploration of one little social network and one tiny swatch of cultural fabric, textured throughout with the actual words of those involved. In this case, the swatch is a little Christmas custom in which a group of youngsters in an Irish horticultural community mark the passage of the year with a folkplay that couldn't take more than a minute or two to reenact. But this book is more than that, much more than that. For it is written about people who live in County Fermagh, up against Northern Ireland, who have been in the midst of "the troubles" all their lives. Furthemore, the mumming which Glassie discusses with his friends around their turf-fires, hasn't been played in twenty-five years and those who discuss it are superannuated, often in ill health, and in few ways representative of the cultural life of the countries they are caught between. Yet, it becomes clear as we talk (through Glassie) with these men and women that they know exactly what is going on around them, and exactly what has been gained and lost as a result of the troubles. If they exhibit sentimentality at the loss of this one tradition among many, they also continue to rest securely on the ways of measuring life, judging behavior, and maintaining their sense of resigned joy in continuing creativity. These are the musicians and singers, the story-tellers and historians of the race. Through them we enjoy not only a glimpse of the simple profundities of enduring agrarian experience, but come to understand more fully how nature (and human nature) continues to provide some people with an enduring sense of continuity —and with it the possibility of celebration.

The author renders explicit for us what the organization of life is as it operates in this play in this community. He describes the centrality of tradition with such people, exploring along the way why we must continue to study such oldfashioned and unfashionable things—if only because these people themselves continue to find the subject important.

A nice little community study, then, but one which demonstrates that, as social scientists, we misjudge the intelligences of our informants—that they often have a profound and complexly textured understanding not only of what life is always about but what brings about social change and what social changes bring about. Sentimental? Trivial? Perhaps. But the troubles continue for sentimental reasons, and somehow the social scientist in us discounts such motives, even in these times in which the United States elects a self-styled peanut-farmer to its highest office. For those looking for qualitative insights into the workings of society and community through expressive behavior and performance, this book is an excellent way to get a purchase on the literature, not only because Glassie surveys and depicts so nicely, but because he provides, in his notes, an excellent survey of the related literatures.

Exploring the Latin American Mind, by SEYMOUR B. LIEBMAN. Chicago: Nelson-Hall Publishers, 1976. 192 pp. $11.00 cloth.

EDGAR G. NESMAN
University of South Florida

This book gives a general view of Latin America and is written in an attempt to bridge the understanding gap between the Anglo cultures in North America and the Latin cultures to the South. The writing style is more journalistic than academic. It is the kind of book that is easy to read and can be done in a few hours with pleasure.

The content is not unlike others that have appeared in the last twenty years. The chapters deal with topics such as geography, personality, religion, the family, education, social class, government, and international relations. The information used is amazingly up to date. Professor Liebman is well acquainted with the literature, including the current news events. Although he writes as a North American interpreter of Latin America, he demonstrates his knowledge of the outstanding Latin American authors and their insights.

This book furnishes an overview of Latin American thought but does little to dispel the common myth that Professor Liebman himself points out, that "all of Latin America is the same." This book would not serve well for a person who wanted to do a comparative study of the different Latin American republics. It would be a good book to initiate a general study of Latin America but other sources would be necessary to find the specific characteristics of each country.

The book is pleasant reading, the impressions are accurate (although Jose Figueres was president of Costa Rica and not Guatemala; see p. 79) and it serves well in its goal to introduce Latin America to the North American reader.

Die Arbeit tun die anderen: Klassenkampf und Priesterherrschaft der Intellektuellen, by HELMUT SCHELSKY. Opladen: Westdeutscher Verlag, 1975. 376 pp. No price listed.

GERD SCHROETER
Lakehead University

This is not just another predictable book about intellectuals. It draws no inspiration from such cardinal analyses as Max Weber's essay "Wissenschaft als Beruf" or Theodor Geiger's *Aufgaben und Stellung der Intelligenz in der Gesellschaft*; nor does it have anything in common with definitions advanced by Parsons: that intellectuals always put cultural interests above societal ones, or by Dahrendorf: that they are our modern equivalent of the court jester or "fool" (both in *On Intellectuals*, edited by Philip Rieff).

Instead, Schelsky goes back as far as Veblen and even Sorel to buttress his central thesis that the producers of meaning (*Sinn-Produzenten*) have gradually come to dominate and exploit the producers of commodities (*Güter-Produzenten*)—this is the significance of the title. The axial premise of the book is that the Marxian bi-polar model of industrial society is outdated, and that the classes now vying for power and legitimacy are those who define and interpret the modern world, on the one hand, and those who produce material goods or provide vital services, on the other. Schelsky reverses Marx's claim that the ideological superstructure is a reflection of "ruling" class interests, to insist that whichever class can control the superstructure will, ipso facto, become the ruling class; thus, teaching of, caring for, and planning for (*"Belehrung, Betreuung, Beplanung"*) always involve domination (p. 367ff).

The author is focusing on a much narrower segment of activities than has traditionally been included under the rubric "intellectual." His vitriol is directed against the following: teachers and professors, theologians, journalists, artists, recreational organizers, and particularly students, all of whom he identifies with the New Left. He specifically excludes from his definition most professionals (such as lawyers, physicians, accountants), politicians, and all natural scientists. Schelsky thus conveys a very different message from those analyses which derive the status of "the new class" from its influence within organizations (e.g., David Bazelon's *Power in America*); what he maintains, instead, is that a traditional segment of the educated population (the reflexive elite) has, in fact, become a new *class*.

The book consists of only four chapters. Schelsky begins by elaborating the dimensions of domination spelled out by Max Weber and he proceeds to identify intellectuals as the contemporary equivalent of priests, who practice what Weber had called "hierocratic coercion": the use of psychic (rather than physical) coercion through the distribution or denial of religious benefits (*Helisgüter*). These religious benefits include a theoretical explanation of the world as well as ways of transcending the sense of powerlessness.

The second and third chapters deal with the increasing power of the reflexive elite and its exploitation of those doing so-called productive work. Particular emphasis is given here to monopolies over socialization, information-flow and the creation of new words. The brunt of Schelsky's anger is reserved for the final chapter where he lays the blame for these conditions squarely on the discipline of sociology; he goes so far as to claim that sociology and socialism have become identical.

In a sense, Schelsky aligns himself with the burgeoning literature on the "crisis of sociology," but he insists that what none of the other writers seems to understand is that sociology cannot be reformed, it must be eradicated; for this reason, the fourth chapter is entitled "Anti-Sociology." In its place Schelsky urges a return to the recognition of individual responsibility. He pays particular attention to what he claims are the subversive effects of focusing on groups, roles, and norms to explain human behavior. Such emphasis becomes inevitably transformed into a social gospel dispensed by teachers, social workers, and journalists with the result that teaching has to become domination and the person who is "cared for" must act submissively. He castigates all attempts at social criticism. In short, Schelsky believes that those who have made themselves indispensible because they address the metaphysical needs of people, shape their personalities and control information, are now the dominant class, prepared to exploit and live off the producers of commodities.

At first the reader may not be sure whether Schelsky's purpose is only to depict the contemporary German situation as he sees it, but there are enough references to Western society throughout the book (pp. 192, 222, 256, 367) to indicate that he intends to analyze all Western industrialized countries. His range of quotations bears this out as well: from Veblen to Riesman, from G. K. Chesterton to Ivan Illich. However, he never marshals any concrete evidence to support his contention that the intellectuals are making the "others" do all the work, that they define their lives or dominate their leisure. Nor does Schelsky convince the reader that the majority of intellectuals, even those within his narrow definition, are adherents of the New Left.

If we focus on North America, it becomes clear that the "producers and conveyors of meaning" who influence our lives are not inside the universities or schools but in the public relations departments of multinational corporations. The recent trend among academics to form collective bargaining units is surely an admission of a decrease in their influence and prestige as well as a sign of identification with the labor force. On the other hand, several of the occupations which Schelsky intentionally omits from the new "priesthood," such as lawyers and psychiatrists, have great influence far beyond their areas of expertise.

This book was intended for a general audience and was actually on *Der Spiegel*'s bestseller list for seventeen weeks in the summer of 1975, despite the fact that it is poorly organized and quite repetitive. Having waded through it, however, one may well marvel at Norman Birnbaum's reference to Schelsky as "one of the most significant of European post-war sociologists" (Foreword to Robert Friedrich's *A Sociology of Sociology*); the ideas advanced here undermine any such claim.

Development/Modernization

Japan: The Paradox of Progress, by LEWIS AUSTIN with ADRIENNE SUDDARD and NANCY REMINGTON. New Haven: Yale University Press, 1976. 338 pp. $20.00 cloth.

BRIAN S. VARGUS
Indiana University-Purdue University, Indianapolis

Though this book is about Japan, its consideration of social change and post-industrial society takes it far beyond the average book which considers only one society. The outgrowth of a conference on the future of Japan held at Yale under the direction of Lewis Austin and Hugh Patrick, the book brings together several important articles concerned with the choices facing Japan in the near future. None of the contributors denies that Japan must change but the issue is, of course, the degree to which Japan can develop as an industrial power and yet maintain traditional values. As the editor emphasizes, the heart of the problem of social change in the industrial world is this paradoxical relationship between tradition and modernity. Japan becomes a very useful case study, both because experts disagree as to the applicability of the convergence hypothesis, i.e., all industrial societies develop along the same path, and because Japan faces an immediate problem soon to be faced by others—rich human potential but a lack of natural resources. This second factor will force major value decisions.

Skillfully edited by a person who sees a cultural uniqueness to Japan, this book, in contrast to similar collections, portrays both sides of the uniqueness issue. Austin arranges and comments on articles about the politics, the economics, and the social life of modern Japan. These give the reader views which range from the liberal-optimistic conclusions of Robert Cole—who sees Japan developing fairly well as an industrial power though having to deal with a progressively unhappy labor force due to demographic changes and changes in industrial organization—to the more pessimistic and more conservative conclusions of Austin—who sees Japan as changing but finding itself in great difficulties due to the slowness of its changes relative to the West and thus, the ever greater separation of neo-traditional Japanese culture from that exemplified by Western industrial powers.

The important thing about this book is that it not only deals with Japan but it presents in several areas the evidence necessary to assess what modernization and social change mean for post-industrial societies. One of the most interesting judgments suggested by the selections is that the methodology used by different investigators seems to profoundly affect their conclusions. Those who deal with the cold hard facts of economic life such as Patrick, Cole, and others seem able to fit the evidence of Japan into a Western mold. Those who deal with more qualitative data such as observations of daily living, etc. seem more able to turn their data to support the argument for the cultural uniqueness of Japan. In one of the most insightful articles, Frager and Rohlen footnote their feelings that many people have faced the problem of finding their living experience in Japan vastly different from the kinds of experiences reported in survey research. They hypothesize that the method itself may be too modern to catch the essence of Japanese culture.

While one does not get any definitive answers from this book, one does gain an important understanding of some of the choices facing Japan and the rest of the post-industrial world. Selections of particular interest include MacDougall's careful and provocative discussion of the development of political opposition through local politics in Japan; Patrick's discussion of Japanese plans for growth under alternative world economic conditions; and Cole's predictions of what changing labor force characteristics will mean for Japanese industrial relations. All these writers seem to agree on the greater convergence of Japan with the West. Aligned against them are Austin's comparisons of responses to psychological tests of two different generations in the US and Japan; Frager and Rohlen's discussion of the Japanese spirit (*seishin*) in the 1980s; Kiefer's discussion of accelerated urban life in high rise suburban housing (*danchi*); and Pharr's consideration of the changing importance of Japanese women. Each of these writers finds evidence for a continued uniqueness to Japanese culture.

This book has an excellent introduction by Lewis Austin. Each of the articles also begins with a commentary by the editor which seems to be balanced and worthy of careful attention. The selections will provide ammunition for both sides of the continuing debate among Japanologists about the degree to which Japan can maintain its uniqueness. Of greater importance, the book succeeds in its intentions to delineate the multifaceted paradoxes of modernity and tradition that are evident in all post-industrial societies, and to show that the paradoxes involve serious value choices forced by external social pressures. The volume will find a broad audience among those interested in modernization theory, social change, and certainly among everyone who is a student of modern Japan.

Sociology and Development, edited by EMANUEL DE KADT and GAVIN WILLIAMS. London: Tavistock Publications, 1974. 374 pp. $19.00 cloth. $6.95 paper.

The Social Sciences and Problems of Development, edited by KHODADAD FARMAN-FARMAIAN. Princeton, N.J.: Near Eastern Studies/Princeton University, 1976. 332 pp. $4.00 paper.

J. BERNARD MURPHY
Old Dominion University

Sociology and Development may be an inappropriately promising title for this disjointed series of commentaries about selected cases and aspects of international development. The thinking is too tired for a 1970s book published "under the auspices of The British Sociological Association," and the mode of presentation is wearisome. Part of the disappointment stems from introductory promises of "change of mood" (p. 1), "new outlook" and "shift of focus" (p. 2), and "change of emphasis" (p. 3). The fact is that most of the case studies and essays come across as old-fashioned Marxist polemics.

Part one has its merits. Papers about development in Soviet Russia and Mao Tse-Tung's China are handled in relatively even-handed fashion, leaving the reader mildly enlightened and interested in what may follow. Aidan Foster-Carter then presents a useful, straightforward summary of sociological Marxism and Neo-Marxism. From here on, however, the bulk of the book—seven essays out of twelve—is a tiresome exposé (here we go again . . .) of the good-for-nothing, damned-if-they-do-and-damned-if-they-don't development efforts of the Capitalist-Colonialist West. This part of the book suffers so mightily from ideological bias that it is virtually useless to the social scientist.

There are other major flaws as well. The editors have been too ambitious in scope: The diverse bits and pieces of evidence that they offer are gathered from China, Argentina, Zaire, South Africa, Zambia, Nigeria, Peru, the Soviet Union, Scotland, India, Java, and elsewhere. The range of topics is also exceedingly broad and diverse: poverty, health care, Gay Liberation, housing quality, class conflict, multi-national business corporations, mass communications, unionism, and on and on. The net result is superficiality, confusion, and reader overload. On top of all this, the thinking is naive. For example, one paper recalls how African mass communications were initiated, fostered, trained, and equipped by Europeans, and then seems shocked to find that they exhibit marked European characteristics. Ho hum.

The Social Sciences and Problems of Development runs some of the same risks. Here again, you have an edited volume, with papers of differing styles, covering a wide range of topics, based on diverse bits and pieces of research evidence. This book, however, manages to rise above the risks. One of the saving graces is the fact that it focuses roughly half of its space upon a single nation: Iran. More importantly, success rests upon a brilliance of thought and expression. Suzanne Keller's opening essay generates enough light itself to keep the whole book glowing. Keller reviews the changing nature and meaning of work, changes in family, fertility, and sex roles, and concludes with a simple, thought-provoking synthesis of ideas which bears upon the future of modernized societies. John Galtung follows fast with an equally tight review and synthesis of general development theory. Then Nikki Keddie provides impressive historical insights on economic development. The reader is brought up-to-date in matters of regional development, roles of the peasantry, demographic transition, and realities of dualism and inequality—in brief, pointed, non-polemical presentations. This first section skillfully weaves a theoretical context, and the second section provides pertinent empirical examples from Iran.

If this review seems unbalanced, with relatively too much space devoted to a book which it damns, consider this an invitation to explore for yourself the rewarding intricacies of substance and thought which the Princeton compendium offers. It is useful for professionals as well as for students of modernization.

Catholics and Protestants: Agricultural Modernization in Two German Villages, by GÜNTER GOLDE. New York: Academic Press, 1975. 198 pp. $12.95 cloth.

ELEANOR MEYER ROGG
Wagner College

This book examines the adaptation to socioeconomic change of farm families in two small communities in Southwestern Germany, one predominantly Roman Catholic and the other Evangelical Lutheran. Golde attempts to trace the process of change from "traditional" to rational "modernized" type farm families over a period of 150 years.

The study tests Weber's hypothesis that particular differences in the economic behavior of Catholics and Protestants result primarily from differences in religious beliefs and not simply from external political and historical influences.

Golde chooses to study two neighboring villages because they are ecologically, historically, and structurally similar. He concludes that the one and only important difference between the two villages is religious affiliation. From this position, Golde contends that differences in value orientations between the Catholic and Protestant villagers in his study stem from their religious beliefs. He shows that the rate of modernization in these two villages is distinctly different with the Protestant community consistently demonstrating a somewhat faster rate of adaptation.

Golde measures modernization by studying changes in demographic patterns, land tenure and inheritance patterns, land use and production patterns, ownership and usage of tractors and other mechanical equipment, and social interaction. Golde's attempt at operationalizing the concept "modernization" is problematic and open to criticism.

Golde, who is an anthropologist, lived in the study area for one year of fieldwork from November, 1970 to November, 1971. His methods of investigation were extensive. Foremost was Golde's detailed observation of life in the two villages. He collected quantifiable data from community and church records. Furthermore, Golde surveyed all the farms in the area itemizing their agricultural equipment as well as the dates the equipment was acquired. Finally, he conducted structured interviews with 112 respondents. One of the strengths of this study was the use of several research gathering techniques. Golde's fieldwork and research instruments were thorough and precise, carefully focusing on his intended goal, a test of Weber's hypothesis.

This fine study should be of special interest to sociologists and anthropologists interested in modernization and change in communities.

Modernization, Exploitation and Dependency in Latin America, by JOSEPH A. KAHL. New Brunswick, N.J.: Transaction Books, 1976. 215 pp. $5.95 paper.

IRA STUDIN
University of California, San Diego

Over the past few decades a growing number of North American social scientists have written extensively on the political economy, society, and history of Latin America. This volume is an attempt by one North American social scientist to let three influential Latin American scholars speak for themselves: Gino Germani, from the perspective of structural functionalism and *modernization;* Pablo González Casanova, in terms of Marxist theory and *exploitation;* and Fernando Henrique Cardoso, in terms of neo-Marxist theory and *dependency.* Drawing from personal interviews, plus a careful review of their written work (much of which is not in English), Joseph Kahl has presented a lucid, evenhanded, and thorough account of three major contributors to a body of thought many have come to know as the "new sociology" of Latin America.

In his introduction, the author suggests that this reference to a "new sociology" stems from the "relative neglect by economics of certain essential themes concerning the process of development" (p. 2). Following the depression and the Second World War many Latin American governments made a concerted effort to industrialize rapidly. Abandoning the century-old tradition of laissez-faire they undertook a deliberate import-substitution policy of industrialization. Unfortunately, the optimism underlying this strategy, much of which was subsidized by North American capital, was overshadowed by a litany of problems: growing reduction in rates of industrial expansion; contracting domestic markets; and increasing unemployment, illiteracy, marginality, class polarization, etc. Neither North American economics, nor sociology, was especially prepared to explain the sudden stagnation of Latin American economies immediately after their now infamous and much heralded "take off." (One exception being the then maligned Paul Baran in *The Political Economy of Growth,* 1957.) The relevance of Kahl's book is precisely in its bringing to light some of the major statements Latin Americans have made in their struggle (some more than others) to provide such an explanation.

For Germani, much of the "social tension in Latin America stemmed from the great speed with which it was modernizing combined with uneven rates in different spheres, which produced disjointed results" (p. 11). Theoretically, Germani's acquaintance with Durkheim, Tonnies, and, in particular, Parsons led him to explain Latin America's economic problems in terms of assorted "noneconomic concommitants" within a framework which sees it as passing from a "traditional" to a "mass" or "modern" society. Problems are seen as "disequilibria" produced by the "demonstration" and "fusion" effects; "noneconomic concommitants" refer to the social processes of urbanization: secularization, migration, and mobility. The perspective is evolutionary; the method relies on scientific and "culture free" indicators; and, for Germani, an Italian emigré spending much of his life in Argentina, perhaps the major issue revolves around the rise of working class authoritarian movements.

Unlike the latter, Casanova and Cardoso are Latin Americans whose analyses are thoroughly informed by the Marxist tradition. Among other things, they reject the ideology of empiricism which sees development as a "progress of averages." Unlike European Marxists, they focus on the internal structures within their own countries which all too often have tended to be ignored. Casanova, a Mexican, sees his country "as existing at an early-capitalist stage strongly influenced by external imperialism and suffering from internal colonialism" (p. 80). "Internal colonialism" represents Casanova's attempt to integrate the categories of imperialism and class with *region* in an attempt to explain development of underdevelopment in Latin America. In this sense, exploitation of *inquilinos* and the attendant transfer of wealth from the peripheral regions to the central cities enriches not only the bourgeoisie and some sectors of the working classes there, but those in the advanced capitalist nations as well.

Cardoso, a Brazilian, is primarily noted for having been the major, and one of the earliest, proponents of dependency theory. Dependency may be understood as a polemic against Weber, Schumpeter, and others who, in constructing a general model of development based on the role of the entrepreneur, have "failed to specify the concrete circumstances in which that entrepreneur was operating" (p. 155). In the concrete circumstances of Latin America, Cardoso notes that as firms grew bigger while technology became more complex and markets appeared more profitable, industrialists increasingly turned to foreign capital. National interests in Latin America were, and continue to be, conditioned by the internationalization of capital. Dependency is, therefore, the other side of imperialism—that is, from the bottom up.

With that said, I must commend this book to the general student of Latin American political economy and society, and to those who might be in search of a good secondary theoretical work for a course in development. Nevertheless, there are certain matters of a critical nature I feel obliged to raise.

First, the author's penchant for "case studies of specific political decisions" (p. 188) belies the very tenor of the arguments he presented. At one point he even goes so far as to suggest that "an ideal project for cooperation with North American scholars" (p. 206) would be a detailed study of decision-making in multinationals since their home offices are in New York with ample access to Washington, D.C. Aside from naively taking for granted a certain autonomy on the part of decision-makers, not to the process itself, this approach begs the question of why the conditioning effect of dependency or (to use a Poulantzian term) the "objective coordinates" which determine an actor's/class's dependency to begin with. It is as if a study of decision-makers going through the motions could explain statistically, structurally, qualitatively, or otherwise, why misery and wealth along with stagnation and inflation have persisted for so long in Latin America. Besides, who ever heard of the corridors of power being open to anyone, least of all sociologists!

Secondarily, while I found the time lapse between the completion of the book in June of 1973 and its publication in 1976 peculiar but not in itself a problem, I found the absence of any discussion of the coup in Chile a serious omission. Certainly, if its purpose was to present to the English-speaking reader the perspectives of three important

Latin American scholars, then their opinions, reflections, etc. on that conjuncture demanded a hearing.

Finally, since as the saying goes, "you can't have it both ways," the author might have been better advised to entitle his volume "Modernization, *or* Exploitation and Dependency in Latin America?"

The Changing Face of Tibet: The Impact of Chinese Communist Ideology on the Landscape, by PRADYUMNA P. KARAN. Lexington: University Press of Kentucky, 1976. 114 pp. $18.50 cloth.

MARIO D. ZAMORA
College of William and Mary

One of the serious problems encountered by researchers from the West and the "free" third world is the ban imposed by authoritarian regimes on scholars, especially those attempting to reseach sensitive political issues. Despite this barrier, Karan has succeeded in organizing and analyzing his data on Tibet based on what anthropologists call "the study of culture from a distance."

The author's major purpose in writing this book, *The Changing Face of Tibet*, was to evaluate "the ways in which the particular configuration of Chinese communist ideological attitudes has been shaping spatial processes and structures in Tibet." His main sources of information were varied. They range from the author's claim of "intimate association with Tibet . . . for over twenty five years" to the use of official news releases, radio broadcasts, and Tibetan refugees' eyewitness accounts. The published materials are reinforced by unpublished maps, air photographs, and other data that reflect Tibet's changing landscape.

Karan presents basic data on the historical sociocultural, political, and economic conditions of the country before 1951 as perspective for his analysis of change after occupation. The author's findings are instructive. The reader is told that the techniques of governance by the new Chinese communist rulers have been "ruthless, devious, and destructive of traditional human values." He is told that despite the ruthlessness, the communists have made remarkable progress in advancing the material well-being of the Tibetan masses. For example, Tibet currently produces steel and mines coal; factories produce varied products for an industrialized economy; road mileage has multiplied since 1951; communications (e.g., airlines and telephones) now enhance national unity; and the Chinese have likewise made impressive gains in the fields of education, welfare, housing, health, production, and social reform. Karan concludes that the Chinese have had limited success in reshaping the Tibetan mind; while they have remarkably succeeded in remolding the face of Tibet. According to the author the ancient Tibet that "fascinated the world for centuries has ceased to exist."

Karan almost has attained his stated objective of relating the impact of ideology on the landscape. His extensive documentation and incisive analysis of the basic reforms by the Chinese communists more than compensate for the inadequacy of data on his research methodology. However, despite his assertion of long term acquaintance with Tibet, this reviewer is not satisfied with the author's brief account of his sources. Who are Karan's informants? How did he choose them? How many are they? How did he conduct his interviews? What problems did the author encounter in the research process? These and more questions can be raised regarding his techniques. The reliability and validity of his data and conclusion greatly depend on the rigor and integrity of his methodology. His critical bibliography, maps, illustrations, pictures, and index are, however, very useful and substantive.

The author explains his unsuccessful attempt to do field work in Tibet under the Chinese regime. Yet he castigates the same regime for being "ruthless" and "devious" in their mode of operations. How does the author know the regime is brutal and repressive? From the refugees' verbal accounts? From Western propagandists? From his own subjective assessment? Karan enumerates a long list of far-reaching achievements of the Chinese communists supposed to benefit the masses, notwithstanding their "ruthlessness" and "deviousness." Does forced or directed change dignify or degrade the human being? To what extent are authoritarian regimes (both of the left and the right) justified in using ruthless methods to enhance the general welfare of their constituents? What are the ethical problems involved in revolutionary change? These are moot questions that Karan and other social scientists have not so far satisfactorily answered.

Environment

Strategies for Human Settlements: Habitat and Environment, edited by GWENN BELL. Honolulu: University Press of Hawaii, 1976. 172 pp. $9.95 cloth. $3.95 paper.

HOWARD M. HAMMERMAN
Cornell University

During the past decade authors such as Barry Commoner, Kenneth Boulding, Dennis Meadows, and E. F. Schumacher (to name just a few) have been reminding us that our entire civilization has been built on a technology which is (in turn) dependent upon a limited and vanishing set of resources. The continuing energy crisis has reminded urbanists of the city's dependence on the hinterland for food and fuel.

Gwen Bell's edited volume goes a litttle beyond the consciousness-raising of the initial doom-sayers, but not far enough. The majority of the twenty contributed articles are from participants in the University of Hawaii's East-West Center. As such they are progress reports on pilot projects and demonstrations in Hawaii and other parts of the Pacific in which various forms of "alternative technology" were used to make a particular village agriculturally self-sufficient (using aqua-culture) or energy independent (using solar collectors), etc. Other articles report on the need to be sensitive to the cultural definition of space when designing new villages and caution the planner to improve upon, but not to seek to replace, native technologies, designs, and materials.

Some of the innovations are fascinating and anyone who enjoys leafing through *Popular Science* in the dentist's office will find these chapters easy reading. The larger questions, however, are only touched upon. Certainly, as Bell states in her introduction to part one, we have to go beyond the traditional distinction between natural and social systems. These systems can be separated analytically, but they do interact, and the nature of their interaction is crucial. Likewise, the reminder that waste is only misplaced resources is welcome. But all this merely begs the question: Can alternative technologies be adapted to complex urban settlements?

After several chapters which demonstrate that labor intensive technologies can conserve natural resources, Bell asks why have these technologies not been adapted? She answers, "Because each one, to be incorporated into an urban plan, calls for reform in the established ways of doing things" (p. 104).

Very gratifying for sociologists to hear, but we knew that already. It is time to direct scholarly attention away from the alternative technology hardware and toward the difficult questions of changing lifestyles to accept decreased mobility, more labor intensive processes, less privacy, and less individual freedom.

For someone interested in a brief overview of the technologies presently available which can feed, house, and transport a populace using the sun, wind, and what are now called "waste products," I suggest this book as a very readable primer. Those already familiar with the problems of scale and continued dependence on fossil fuel technologies, will find the book frustrating. The key problems concerning human settlements in the Northern industrial countries have not been addressed.

Growth in America, edited by CHESTER L. COOPER. Westport, Conn.: Greenwood Press, 1976. 262 pp. $15.00 cloth.

ALBERT J. MAYER
Arizona State University

Growth in America is a collection of brief essays edited by Chester L. Cooper and published under the auspices of the Woodrow Wilson International Center for Scholars. The essays question growth as a concept, as a value, as a way of life which is built into America's institutional framework in the same way "as steel girders are built into the World Trade Center" (p. 27). Indeed, growth may be considered an American religion, perhaps the American religion, and the essays all re-emphasize this view.

Although the volume is titled *Growth in America*, most essayists ignore the geographic confinement and discuss the worldwide impact of a philosophy of growth.

Perhaps the worldwide scope is due to the fact that the *Growth in America* was a response or a further exploration of the problems brought into focus by the Club of Rome study.

The essayists: historians, economists, technologists, philosophers, and others represent a broad spectrum of disciplines. Literally hundreds of ideas are flung at your reeling brain as you read and reflect on implications, both immediate and long range. As the editor freely admits, the book lacks precise organization, but this is a small matter in view of the fundamental nature of the issue and the necessity for our society first to face, and then to understand the enormous consequences of the exponential growth of nearly every aspect of human groups and their impact on the environment.

As might be expected, none of the essayists offered any panacea or global cures for the ills accompanying rampant growth and associated problems of shortages, pollution, destruction of the environment. Yet as Cooper points out "The growth concept has become so dominant an American value that the no-growth option, whatever its merits or demerits, would be a difficult course for Americans to follow" (p. 214). Cooper is talking at the societal level, but at the individual level Wallich makes a great and telling point which I believe needs far more emphasis than he or any of the other essayists accorded to it. Wallich says "it always remains open to single individuals to drop out of the growth race. A person who wants to conserve less can do so without others doing the same and without government compelling him. . . . Anyone not satisfied with the prevalent growth scene need not limit himself to protesting it. He can do something about it" (p. 65). Perhaps this is the key to the retreat from the tyranny of the exponential curve soaring ever upward to destruction.

The Vanishing White Man, by STAN STEINER. New York: Harper & Row Publishers, 1976. 309 pp. $10.95 cloth.

JOE T. DARDEN
Michigan State University, East Lansing

This book deals with the controversy over the energy companies' search for energy resources in the Western United States in the midst of the desert and isolated mountain areas among the Indian reservations. Steiner's major thesis is that such ever-expanding searches for energy resources are having a destructive impact on the environment of the conservation oriented Navajo, Hopi, Pueblo, and Cheyenne tribes. Furthermore, Steiner predicts that if the warnings of the Indians are not heard, the fossil fuels of the West, America's last unspoiled wilderness, will be used up; the land will be hollow, the air and water will be polluted, and the Indian way of life will be destroyed. But this time, history will not repeat itself; the white race is on a collision course with the earth. It is committing suicide by its ever expanding development. This time, it will destroy itself. It will vanish.

Stan Steiner gathered data for his book by traveling throughout the West and interviewing fifteen selected individuals including the vice-chairman of the Hopi Tribe, a former manager of the Atomic Energy Commission's operations at Los Alamos, a foreman of a Montana coal mine, a former governor of Alaska, the Secretary of the All-Indian Pueblo Council, a Wyoming newspaper publisher, a South Dakota lawyer, a Montana Area Director of the Bureau of Indian Affairs, a New Mexico store owner, the Director of the All-Indian Inter-Tribal Ceremonial, a US senator, a Montana rancher, and the Director of the National Indian Youth Council. How or why these *particular* individuals were chosen for interviews is not stated by Steiner.

The book is written in Stan Steiner's typical novelistic style although the characters are quite real. He has written a dramatic work which appeals to the reader's emotions as the Indian and white characters' dispositions and temperments are revealed (through interviews) in the development of the ultimate plot—the inevitable destruction of the West and the vanishing of the white race.

A basic weakness of the book is its poor organization. There is no preface or introduction. The chapters appear to be randomly organized and some chapters appear to be totally unrelated to the thesis of the book.

Thus, this book cannot be read with ease by the average student. Its audience must be strongly motivated by a combined interest in the "energy crisis," Indian-white relations, and the environment of the American West. Nevertheless, this polemic work should be read by anyone involved in the environmentalist movement.

Family and Intimate Lifestyles

Friends and Lovers, by ROBERT BRAIN. New York: Basic Books, 1976. $10.95 cloth.

CRAIG CALHOUN
St. Antony's College
Oxford University

Sociologists do not give much credit to friendship. For most it seems to have become a residual category, something to be quantified in simple aggregation (one friend is as good as another) and/or analyzed in terms of immediate instrumental value. We are virtually obsessed, on the other hand, with marriage and the family. Hardly any department fails to offer an undergraduate survey course, and indeed the students register for it. The lifelong love of friends and the more often fleeting sexual relationships of lovers seem to have fallen into the interstices of conventional definitions of sociological subject matters. The great virtue of Robert Brain's book is to show the ethnocentricity which has led to this, and by systematic comparison to show how this may be to our personal and social as well as our professional misfortune.

Brain's method is to look in detail at six societies on which fairly extensive information concerning friendship has been gathered by social anthropologists. He contrasts these with each other, adds notes on several other peoples and throughout considers the implications his comparative data may have for understanding intimate relationships in Western society. Such pointed, even polemical, exercises in comparative sociology are an old tradition in anthropology, and have flourished in the last ten years after a period of unfashionableness. Sociologists would do well to take account of and participate in such efforts. Among other things, they help to define more clearly the nature of phenomena under investigation, and they offer a running critique of our naive assumptions. Our assumptions concerning the fundamental importance of the nuclear family and the marriage relationship have been the subject of such critiques for at least a century, with moderate success at best. We now pay lip service to kinship systems in tribal societies and extended families in peasant ones. But we don't go very far in drawing conclusions about what we see as a natural delimitation of subject matter. If I get married next year to someone I don't even know yet, most sociologists, like the rest of our society, will assume that that fact makes more difference in understanding me, as a social individual, than my entire accumulaiton of friendships during the past twenty-five years.

The underlying reason for this seems to be that we regard marriage as a *formal* relationship, friendship as an *informal* one. Both the content and the very existence of friendship we take to be far more optional and malleable than marriage. We invest marriage with great emotional weight and passion; we protect it with legal and ritual sanctions, yet as sociologists we often argue that the reason marriages endure is to be found in the supports of their immediate social contexts. The irony is that we persist in studying these social groups and networks as contexts more often than as part of the same phenomenon of intimate relationships. Even a recent textbook trying to break out of the tradition added only unmarried couples living together and communes to the nuclear family. In society after society Brain shows us that friendships are given equal or greater stress than marriages and "loverships." More importantly, perhaps, he demonstrates that friendships are formal, often ascribed (but no less "meaningful" for that) relationships, that they are ordered by norms and conventions which are generally clear to all concerned, and that they are enduring.

Brain goes on to argue that friendships are inherently more likely to endure and maintain satisfaction than sexual relationships with their pressure of passion. "Friendship," he maintains, "must be taken as seriously as sex, aggression, and marriage. We come into the world programmed to need love—but not to marry. And since the need for love between two persons—rather than passion— is as real and basic as the need to satisfy our bodily wants, the whole subculture of the lonely should be seen as a deprived group, and something done about it" (p. 264). Brain makes also a strong argument for friendship in the particular, rather than in its democratized mass-brotherhood sense. In passages often reminiscent of early Christian communalism he suggests that only as we identify with, have secure relationships with other members of our social groups, societies or indeed species, can we really come to act as part of the whole.

Friends and Lovers is strikingly well-written and entertaining. The fact that it continually reminds the reader of additional information or analysis that he might have included is only an indication of how stimulating it is. The reader should remember, however, to take it as a serious claim for formal friendships with both ritual and commitment (neither universally fashionable today). He should not be misled, as was the writer of the jacket notes, into thinking it a plea for some sort of freedom from the bonds of marriage. The freedom for which Brain argues is from the bonds of an *idea* of marriage that allows one relationship to try to eat up the whole person and increasingly often leads to a little passion and a lot of disillusionment. Students will enjoy the book. I hope their teachers will be made to feel a bit uneasy when they think of their neglect of the claims of friendship to be studied *as an institution*. We sociologists take institutions seriously; the rest of life we are apt to explain away with interaction rates and instrumentality.

Adultery and Other Private Matters, by LONNY MYERS and HUNTER LEGGITT. Chicago: Nelson-Hall, 1975. 209 pp. $8.95 cloth.

LOUIS ROWITZ
University of Illinois Medical Center

Since the end of World War II, there have been a number of social science "best-sellers" that have had a major influence on both social science in general and on certain segments of American society specifically. These books have not always represented the best of our sociological research efforts. They have often been ideological interpretations of a number of contemporay social happenings. They have often been criticized severely in journals and the press. And yet, these books have had an impact, garnered large audiences, and remain known long after many other excellent studies have been forgotten. Some books that come to mind include *The Lonely Crowd, Hidden Persuaders, The Greening of America, Future Shock*, and *Open Marriage*. As with successful television shows, these books have had a number of "spin-offs."

The interest in alternate life styles has mushroomed during the 1970s. *Open Marriage* by Nena and George O'Neill was a financial bestseller a few years ago. Articles by the O'Neills are reprinted in many new Marriage and the Family readers. Building upon and also criticizing the O'Neill book, this new spin-off by Myers and Leggitt looks at open relationships in some detail. Early in the book, the authors argue that the book is written for sophisticated and affluent middle-class people living in a mobile society who want extramarital relationships and do not want to destroy their marriage relationship. They argue that the O'Neills' stress on total honesty will often restrict the possibility of real openness in the marriage relationship.

Myers and Leggitt point out that the important decision to be made in a marriage is to respect each other's need for privacy. They discuss the need for a special compartment for each individual in a marriage which they call "Compartment Four." If individuals have a Compartment Four, they have a place and time to develop themselves in whatever way they deem appropriate without the necessity of getting spousal agreement for every extramarital activity, sexual or otherwise. Individuals do not need to tell their spouses what they do in Compartment Four unless they want to. This is where Myers and Leggitt differ from the O'Neills' discussion on disclosure of extramarital relationships. Compartment One is the time individuals spend with their spouses. Compartment Two is the time the couple spend away from each other in activities that relate to the marriage. Compartment Three is the time that the couple is doing things (jobs, community responsibilities) that have no direct relationship to the marriage relationship but for which the individual is accountable. As stated above, Compartment Four refers to the free time for independent activities for which individuals are accountable only to themselves.

Myers and Leggitt state that the reason that more couples do not have marriages that allow for personal freedom is that marriage is seen in terms of a number of myths. These myths include the myth of the scarcity of love, a conception that the resources of love are limited, and the belief that the exclusive male-female relationship is the sole source of adult love and sex. Our society stresses the sanctity of marriage by giving financial benefits to these relationships and positive personal status to married people in the community relative to single people.

This book will prove most interesting to people who are already interested in pursuing ways to change the traditional nuclear marriage situation. It is fun to read, with drawings, parables, and interesting case histories. Aside from the concept of Compartment Four, the book does not offer the sociologist interested in alternate life styles much that is new. The problems which were inherent in *Open Marriage* are still with us in this new book. What appears to be needed is specific research with people who are choosing open marriage relationships. This research should be concerned not only with the selection of an open marriage orientation but also with the factors that make for a successful or unsuccessful alternate marriage style.

Management in Family Living, 5th ed., by PAULENA NICKELL, ANN SMITH RICE, and SUZANNE P. TUCKER. New York: John Wiley & Sons, 1976. 475 pp. $13.95 cloth.

The Changing Family: Its Function and Future, 2nd ed., by DAVID A. SCHULZ. Englewood Cliffs, N.J.: Prentice-Hall, 1976. 418 pp. $11.95 cloth.

RELA GEFFEN MONSON
Gratz College

It is difficult to write a textbook which is comprehensive, clear, sophisticated, and, at the same time, interesting for the student to read. David A. Schulz, in the second edition of *The Changing Family: Its Function and Future* has made an admirable attempt to fulfill these somewhat contradictory demands. New chapters are included on conflict and violence, disorganization and divorce, the women's movement, and alternative family lifestyles. More than the inclusion of these topics, it is the excellent manner of their treatment which engages the reader in serious consideration of the family as a dynamic institution. The author has included analyses of the human potential movement and Jessie Bernard's shared-role pattern for marriage as well as classical approaches to the division of labor in marriage. The effort to be comprehensive without being pedantic sometimes leaves the reader breathless with the effort required to leap from theory to theory and quote to quote within a few pages. For example, structure-functionalism, role theory, and the utility of analytic models are all covered in four pages! While attention is given to the feminist movement and alternative lifestyles, sexist language within the text has been retained in this revision, i.e., men is used consistently instead of people or persons. Nevertheless, as textbooks go, this one is exciting at its best while being thorough and true to the original sources. Moreover, its format and graphics are very attractive.

Management in Family Living, in contrast to *The Changing Family* is a textbook designed for courses specifically oriented to planning and managing one's own life. Although the technical terminology of management and business approaches is used, there are frequent references to familiar sociological literature about the family of a general theoretical nature. Findings, however, often appear as cumbersome lists or graphs which are difficult to follow. Material is not effectively synthesized for the student and sometimes the generalizations are just plain silly. In justifying their own book for the reader the authors state:

> Unfortunately the non-business use of management has been linked so often to home management and to middle-class standards for homekeeping that any other approach is slowly and reluctantly understood. . . . Contrary to this belief, personal management is the key to successful and satisfying living and is a strong tool for regenerating society and bringing about a more harmonious world population. Management is far from "how to clean the parlor" or "organize the linens." Most modern houses don't even have parlors (p. 32).

The apologetics evident in this paragraph, exemplify the problems with this revision which is aimed at "heightening the interest of readers through controversy and a sense of inquiry, by raising questions rather than providing 'pat' answers. Unfortunately, the authors have not succeeded in their aim.

Methods

Foundations of Social Research, by NAN LIN. New York: McGraw-Hill Book Company, 1976. 458 pp. No price listed, cloth.

ROGER SPIELMANN
University of Texas, Arlington

The avowed intention of this book is stated explicitly in the introduction: to acquaint the beginning student with the basic tenets of social research and to supplement the background of the practitioner who has had limited training in research methodology. Both of these ambitions have been quite realistically attained in this introductory-level volume.

Nan Lin belongs to the progressive school

of social researchers who believe in preserving the context of the methodological perspective. In this vein the book offers a heretofore unique approach in textbook design. It varies from other existing social research texts in that equal treatment has been given to three topics which are traditionally either treated separately or given different amounts of consideration: theory construction, the use of statistics, and the procedures of social research.

The text is comprised of six major sections: (1) Conceptualization and Verification, (2) Use of Statistics in Social Research, (3) Research Initiation, Sampling, and Measurement, (4) Data Collection, (5) Data Analysis, and (6) Presentation and Use of Social Research. Each of the nineteen chapters concludes with a summary/discussion.

The fundamentals of field research, content analysis, documentary-historical methodology, and statistical analysis are incorporated into the mainstream of the text, while research design, conceptualization, and verification, measurement, survey construction, and a thorough discussion of research presentation and usage completes the corpus of material. There is an extensive index, several data analysis tables, a flexible teaching plan, and appendices on sample items and response categories.

Statistical analysis is central to this text in marked contrast to most methodological texts. Most methodology texts fail to distinguish between the two functions of statistics in social research—description and inference—if statistics is discussed at all. This book plows full bore into the statistical arena by explaining the essential phases of social research, such as measurement (scaling, reliability and validity) and sampling in terms of the basic statistical notions of description and inference. Descriptive statistics and the aspect of statistical inference are introduced before sampling and measurement in order to develop the linkage between statistical estimations and hypothesis testing with theory construction.

The last chapter of the book is devoted exclusively to the issues and problems of policy research. Lin makes it a point to deal with the benefits of social research in solving social problems. The student is urged to use this text in conjunction with *Conducting Social Research*, by Nan Lin, Ronald S. Burt, and John Vaughn, which was prepared simultaneously with this text.

Lin's concern in the offering of a new social research textbook is that the total context of social research will be reinstated intact. The matter of subject relevance for the undergraduate is prominent. The author writes with a lucid style and a conceptual clarity while maintaining a well-organized format.

Beginning students involved in social science research could hardly hope to find a more amicable text. It deserves a strong recommendation.

Behavioral Research Methods in Environmental Design, edited by WILLIAM MICHELSON. Stroudsburg, Pa.: Dowden, Hutchinson & Ross, 1975. 307 pp. No price listed, cloth.

WILLIAM R. BURCH, JR.
Yale University

William Michelson seems determined to save sociology. He believes that sociology can and should be useful. His prose is spare and clean. His earlier book on urban environments neatly summarized findings from a wide range of studies and related them to the pressing issues of urban design and survival. The present volume is a natural successor to his earlier book. I doubt if sociology will heed this quiet pioneer.

Usefulness has not been a mainstream concern of sociology. The discipline seems to dote upon arcane theories, abstruse points of methodology, or the regular conversion of personal ideology into a scientific principle. The glamour of crime and medicine seem to have been our major ventures into utility. By contrast, Michelson and his colleagues are dull. They want to deal with the regular, recurring, mundane dailiness in which most of us live most of our lives. They look at the thousand and one ways in which design helps or fouls up our attempts to cross streets, use escalators, handle baggage in airports, maintain security in our apartments, and organize to make our air cleaner and our journey to work shorter and more pleasant.

Michelson and colleagues do not have the drama of the six o'clock news. Yet, in carefully building techniques for measuring the regularities of daily life, they are truly building the necessary steps for a genuine science of society. Several of the papers in this volume create new and unique techniques for measuring major dimensions of social life.

Lindberg and Hellberg have an important discussion on the useful role aerial photography could play in social analysis. Robinson et al. illustrate how trade-off games can get at non-economic social values. Michelson and Reed use time budget analyses to develop unique maps of behavioral space. Davis and Ayers provide a thorough and exciting discussion on the potential of photography for many kinds of social analyses. In short, while the mainstream is draining into a desert of thought, these environmental design upstarts are flooding with ideas on how to better and more accurately understand the regularities of social life.

Further new life is given to old techniques. Bechtel has a detailed and well balanced treatment of pencil and paper techniques. He gives an excellent summary of the various types of tests, identifies nine problems in their use, happily points out the liabilities of the Rorschach and similar tests, and provides excellent examples of "good" paper and pencil tests well fitted to a particular research problem. Robert Marans does an equally excellent job in outlining the strengths and weaknesses of survey research. His paper is a superior short manual on "how to do it" that both the amateur and the professional can gain much from. The only real let-down is the paper on observation which took a long time to say very little that was new.

The book has some peculiar defects of detail. Marans's chapter has an entire interview schedule reprinted, yet the schedule has only minor relationship to the text. Michelson and Reed have endless pages of a computer printout but only a few items are referred to in the text. Bechtel has complete tests when he merely needs to cite one or two instances to give the flavor of the test. The articles on photography, both aerial and land based, seem to have pictures that are included simply because the authors found them in their files. I have a difficult time knowing what I gained from a picture of a Digitizer table. Indeed, many of the illustrations, tables, and graphs seemed like the kodachromes of the returned vacationer whose quantity attempts to substitute for quality.

Further there is an irritating lack of attention to proof reading. Michelson and Reed make much use of a 1972 study by Robinson and Converse yet it appears nowhere in the references. Marans's fine article has sentences scrambled on page 142. Similar editing problems are found in other chapters.

I imagine some of the detail problems stem from a confusion about the intended audience. There is an obvious interest in having the environmental design professions appreciate the usefulness of social science. At the same time there is an interest in having one's own discipline approve your work. So the design professionals may gain more than they wish and the sociologists may not find enough.

These dual interests are always a problem. I am not certain they are worth resolving. This volume is a major contribution to developing the means for measuring and understanding human social life. And since design, whether the grand one of nature or that of the planner and architect is a condition of all social life, the affected professions should find their own level of value. More importantly, unlike other methodological studies, I had a feeling that the authors were concerned that their science help people to gain a better control on the shape of their lives. The methods were not just designed for the specialist to objectively and neutrally manipulate "subjects." Rather there was a strong and continuous concern with the ethics of research and the discovery of means for enhancing public participation.

For all these many reasons the book deserves a wide audience. It is not just for design professionals and environmental sociologists. It is for all of us looking for vital signs in our discipline.

Realities of Social Research, by JENNIFER PLATT. New York: Halsted Press, 1976. 223 pp. $17.50 cloth.

BOB HININGS
University of Birmingham, England

As the first sentence in chapter 1 says "this is a book about the sociology of the social research process." The study deals with fifty-five research projects, some individually based, some large groups, some in between, covering all of the main fields of sociology, different institutional settings, and different theoretical and methodological concerns. Platt, from her data on these projects, deals with the process of obtaining research grants, the impacts of university and non-university settings on research, the nature of team organization, research careers (and their impossibility in Britain), and the relationship between research work and private life.

The chapters of description certainly accord with many of my experiences in carrying out sociological research. The problems of integrating research and teaching, keeping teams together, lack of institutional support, and development of research hierarchies are all well documented, as are many others. But somehow the book lacks the cutting edge that it ought to have. This is because this research project encountered some of the problems that are documented for the projects which are the actual objects of study. The original idea came from a suggestion for a British version of Hammond's *Sociologists at Work*. After a start in this direction a stronger editorial and comparative perspective was injected. (Most research projects at some time or other change direction, it's just that the researchers never formally admit it in their writings.) This gradual change of direction is not reflected in the development of an adequate comparative, analytic framework to support the kind of data being collected. The author admits to a tension between "ethnographic responsibility" and "theoretical implications." Dealing with this and the other tensions examined in this book is the researcher's constant dilemma; Platt's inability to satisfactorily deal with the problem is an ample illustration of the problems she so ably describes.

Occupations

Careers and Contingencies: How College Women Juggle with Gender, by SHIRLEY S. ANGRIST and ELIZABETH M. ALMQUIST. New York: Dunellen, 1975. 269 pp. $15.00 cloth.

BETTINA J. HUBER
University of California, Santa Barbara

With the aid of data derived from a longitudinal study at a small women's college, this book presents a critical review and extension of the literature on occupational choices. The authors argue that the predilection for considering occupational aspirations and decisions in a vacuum has given rise to narrow explanations, perhaps applicable to men, but certainly not to women. Their critical evaluation of previous work represents one of the strengths of the book, as does their combination of interview and questionnaire material in dealing with the evolution of college women's aspirations and plans.

The book examines two separate bodies of research: occupational choice and occupational aspirations among college students. The first half of the book deals with the latter. Most studies of occupational aspirations focus on single item measures of career commitment and ignore the possible constraining influence of other factors. To remedy such narrowness, the authors view occupational hopes as one aspect of a complex set of life style aspirations. Similarly, they are critical of prevailing theories of occupational choice for focusing only on choice of occupation rather than broader life style. Since these theories were formulated in the context of the male work world, where occupation is a primary determinant of life style, they do not apply to women. By the time women enter college they have already learned that their lives are to be geared to marriage and motherhood, and they formulate their occupational plans accordingly. Thus, it is the constraints imposed by familial obligations that are key to explaining women's career choices rather than their inclinations or abilities.

The authors derive their own explanation of women's career thinking using data from a four-wave panel study of one class of women attending a college affiliated with a technically-oriented university. The sample consists of eighty-seven predominantly white, middle class, Northeastern women who were members of the class of 1968. The panel approach yielded unusually extensive data on the evolution of plans and preferences.

Almost all respondents consistently planned for marriage and children, viewing their life patterns in terms of family considerations. Their work plans were dependent on general life circumstances. The authors focus much of their analysis on the nature of these occupational plans and try to isolate factors leading to career orientation. It is this focus which makes the sample's mid-sixties origin of limited significance. Although the frequency of career commitment may have increased in the intervening years, due to the impact of the Woman's Movement, major types of life style orientation are probably unchanged. These orientations are delineated with the aid of the "Life Style Index," which the authors claim is a composite measure of career aspirations and encompasses several aspects of adult life. It may be more accurate, however, to view it as a measure of women's willingness to be employed, since eight of the eleven items deal with respondents' willingness to *work* under given family conditions.

In the first half of the book, Life Style scores serve as the basis for a discussion of how occupational aspirations change. About one fifth of the respondents are Careerists, having high index scores all four years, while another third are consistent Non-Careerists. The remaining half of the sample exhibits a major shift in orientation; some develop career orientations (Converts), others abandon them (Defectors), and some are Shifters. The authors present qualitative portraits of each type to highlight the differences and similarities. Most students, even the consistent ones, are quite uncertain and changeable. Their future is an unpredictable one offering little control over family situations. Thus, they have difficulty formulating specific career plans and adopt a vague "contingency" orientation, leaving them flexible and uncommitted.

Although the contingency approach has advantages, the authors stress its uncertainty and lack of specific occupational commitment. In doing so, they may present an exaggerated picture, arising in part from the absence of a male comparison group. The women studied belong to the sixties generation characterized by student unrest, questioning, and rejection of conventional patterns. Thus, their uncertainty may be generational rather than feminine. Even if it is not, one need not conclude that they are ambivalent. Perhaps the data simply reflect women's differing priorities. In our society women develop a primary commitment to the family. Everything else may appear secondary, leading to disinterest in other aspects of adulthood, such as having a career. The women's uncertainty may, therefore, reflect perplexity about college's career emphasis rather than their perception that career aspirations are unrealizable. Perhaps the authors gave women's familial orientation insufficient weight in interpreting the data, even though they clearly point to its importance in their theoretical discussion.

In the second half of the book, the focus shifts from the evolution of career aspirations to the background factors fostering them. The discussion covers a variety of pertinent determinants of career choice (maternal employment; lack of sorority membership, male peers with similar career interests; exposure to occupational role models; extensive, and varied, work experience; and a natural science major), but they are not explored in as much depth as they might have been. Assessing their relative importance would have been facilitated by a multivariate approach. Although not stated very explicitly, career commitment is operationalized differently in the second part of the book. Rather than being articulated as a pattern of scores, the dependent variable is based on the seniors' Life Style Index scores, which makes for an unfortunate discontinuity. Overall, career-oriented respondents seem to be exposed to a broader range of people and experiences, leading them to aspire to more than the typical home and family; they want a career in addition. This "enrichment view" of occupational commitment is more in keeping with the authors' data than the usual deviance view.

In sum, this book presents an informative discussion of various factors impinging on college women's career aspirations and should be of interest to everyone concerned with occupational plans or choices. Only its price might prevent its widespread use in undergraduate courses.

Hard Traveling: Migrant Farm Workers in America, by Tony Dunbar and Linda Kravitz. Cambridge, Mass.: Ballinger Publishing Co., 1976. 158 pp. $13.50 cloth.

David Harvey
University of Nevada, Reno

There is no area in modern social life so cursed with the irony of uneven development as that of agriculture in contemporary America. It stands with one foot in the board rooms of America's largest corporations, and with the other in the squalor of rural labor. This schism has historical roots in that it was as much a presence in Marx's day as it is in ours. From Steinbeck's *The Grapes of Wrath*, to Edward R. Murrow's *Harvest of Shame*, to the present legal phase of the struggle as it is now unfolding in California, agricultural labor's plight has been a continuous refutation of business's claim to represent ultimately the universal best interests of society.

Dunbar and Kravitz in their fine small book have provided us with an introductory and updated survey of agricultural labor in America. Their work is largely descriptive and non-analytic—perhaps the work's major shortcoming. In the early sections of the book they set out their major theme when they argue that migrant labor is not a purely economic category but, equally, a political one. Page after page is filled with fact and reminder that agricultural laborers are kept in a degrading state of economic and cultural peonage by a systematic, legal exclusion from rights which have already been granted to most other industrial workers in America. Furthermore, the roles of the state and federal bureaucracies do not stop there. Agencies, when not excluding the workers from equal protection, inadvertently contribute to the workers' degradation by legally acting to facilitate the employers' profit. Finally, they cite case after case of protective laws having been written and then discretely ignored by understaffed or indifferent agencies that are seldom an equal match for wealthy agricultural lobbies at the state and national level.

Under the rubric of agricultural labor, Dunbar and Kravitz show a diversity of political economic contingencies, ethnic composition of the work force, international complications, and historical conditions which effect the migrants' life chances. These life chances and life styles vary, depending on the part of the country being worked. The authors bring out this fact by effectively contrasting and comparing the structure and development of migrant labor as it occurs in the context of what they call four major labor "streams." These streams are major routes of labor migration in America. They have their beginnings in Texas, California, Florida, and the North Eastern section of the United States. Each of these streams then spreads, with the developing season, into almost every state in this country. Each stream varies in the role which state governments play in helping farmers find and organize their workers. They vary in the ethnic composition and labor history of the geographical sector. Finally, they vary in terms of the degree of success which labor has had in organizing the worker in the field.

The last part of the book discusses various aspects and problems of migrant living in America. There are the problems of health and safety in their living arrangements and in the laboring conditions (pesticide poisoning cases are an outrageous example of this form of neglect). The migrants' problems with the law are discussed. Migrants are, as the objects of persecution, the unwarranted recipients of legal attention in some sectors, while their rights are totally ignored or suppressed in others. The education of migrant children is a chronic problem for which there are as yet few good solutions. Finally, Dunbar and Kravitz touch briefly on the dominant role which non-agricultural monopolistic corporations play in exacerbating the problems of the agricultural worker. The list of subjects that Dunbar and Kravitz treat are broad, and often they do not provide the completeness of detail that some readers might want.

If the book has one major weakness, it is that it lacks any coherent analytic framework within which to discuss the facts. They document the disgraceful poverty of men and women who are on the edge of society and who are daily threatened with extinction as socially located beings. Yet, they do not explain why this is happening; why it is necessary, if it is necessary, for a system to systematically destroy humans in the process of creating such wealth.

While this work has its weaknesses, and its ideological rough edges, the limitations of the book are relatively minor. Such flaws as it has do not keep it from being a valuable primer on the problems of migrant labor in the 1970s.

The Foreman: Aspects of Task and Structure, by DAVID DUNKERLY. Boston: Routledge & Kegan Paul, 1975. 192 pp. $18.50 cloth.

RICHARD K. BROWN
University of Durham, England

The role of the foreman was one of the fashionable topics in industrial sociology in Britain for a decade or more after the Second World War, but it has recently attracted relatively little interest, though valuable comments and insights have been made in the course of research on other problems. This book reviews some of the older and the more recent research findings, and therefore may be useful as a statement of the "state of the art." Certainly a lot of work has been considered and summarized, revealing some obvious strengths and weaknesses. For example, there appears to be an almost complete absence of any British or continental European contributions to the general area of "foreman as a group member," in contrast to the individual characteristics of foremen, or organizational variables.

From a European point of view, however, a better review of this sort exists in Thurley and Wirdenhuis, *Supervision: a Reappraisal*, published in 1973, and that book is also likely to be of more use to practicing managers. Certainly Dunkerley's coverage of the literature is far from complete even for British material (*Supervision* is not in his bibliography), and his treatment of it leaves something to be desired. Can conventional definitions of a "profession," for example, still be used uncritically (p. 72)? Can leadership be seen so straightforwardly as both "a personal quality" and "a relational concept" (pp. 97–98)? Do research findings really justify thinking in terms of a single continuum with two polar types of foremen, "working class" and "middle class," distinguished in terms of "class consciousness" (pp.170–172)?

This book, however, asks to be judged by more demanding criteria as an attempt "to integrate the findings relating to foremen into a coherent framework" using "an adaptive open systems model" (pp. 6, 7). The wisdom of such an enterprise may be doubted, but doubts or not it has not succeeded. Clearly the "role" of foreman "is an integrated part of a larger system" (p. 25); discussion of it can usefully be arranged in terms of the relevance of research for organizational, group, and individual factors (though in view of the many areas of overlap, more and more precise, internal cross references would have been helpful); but the value of trying to regard each of these levels as a "system" involving "inputs, conversions and outputs" remains hidden from me, and indeed frequently gets lost in the discussion. The theoretical approach used appears inappropriate; it may be helpful to think in terms of "a supervisory system" but surely not "a system model of the foreman role" (p. 165). And it has been applied in an arbitrary way; power is treated as a "conversion variable" in "the organizational subsystem," but could equally well be placed in almost any other slot. The development of theory demands more rigorous thinking than this.

Political

Patterns of Authority: A Structural Basis for Political Inquiry, by HARRY ECKSTEIN and TED ROBERT GURR. New York: John Wiley & Sons, 1975. 488 pp $19.95 cloth.

ANTHONY ORUM
University of Texas, Austin

There are few people who would dispute the claim that authority is one of the most central and critical features of social life. Social scientists long have been aware of this fact. Among sociologists, Max Weber was the first to alert us to the special significance of authority, to its different bases and forms throughout history. Political philosophers as well as political scientists long have been interested in authority, dating at least from the writings of Plato, and have involved themselves specifically in studying the nature and form of rulership, particularly those qualities that distinguish good from bad rulership, or, in the case of Machiavelli, effective from ineffective. Lately we have had even further testimony to the significance of authority in society: little more than a decade ago, Stanley Milgram, a social psychologist, showed that even on matters of fundamental moral importance—whether to inflict injury, perhaps even death, on another human being —a surprisingly large number of people freely will choose to commit a heinous act, simply because they are submissive in the face of authority. For all these reasons and more, a book which undertakes to elaborate an empirical theory of authority, in all realms of social life, must be granted special consideration. As it happens, this particular book, by Harry Eckstein and Ted Robert Gurr, must be given more than its categorical due, for it is done very well—so well, in fact, that any future scientific work on authority, whether in the firm or in the State, may neglect this work only at serious costs to its own merit.

A Workshop in Comparative Politics, under the direction of Eckstein and Gurr, took place at Princeton between 1966 and 1971, and this book represents the most important intellectual outgrowth of that endeavor. The basic inspiration for the project, it appears, was Eckstein's, who for a number of years has devoted himself to creating a science of politics in which authority is the fundamental notion—as fundamental, we might say, as social class and the theory of value were to Karl Marx's science of society. Throughout the book the authors refer to various pieces of graduate student research that helped to test and to refine the theory and instruments created by the Workshop; and it appears, from the number of citations and considerable praise heaped upon them, that the works of Robert Friedman, Ronald Rogowski, William R. Schonfeld, and Lois Wasserspring were particularly important to the manufacture of this product.

There are three fundamental parts to the book. In the first the authors lay out a definition of authority (asymmetric relations among the hierarchically ordered elements of a social unit in which higher positions [superordinates] direct the activities of lower positions [subordinates]) and then, based on this definition, proceed to identify the various dimensions and sub-dimensions that must be studied in order to elicit a complete and full description of the nature of authority in any social setting. They write, for instance, of the directiveness of authority relations, referring to the directives (commands) of the superordinates, or, for another, of the distance of those relations, speaking of subjective perceptions of superordinates, alike. In this section of the book, which is as significant for its lucid demonstration of how to construct a theory as for the product, itself, the concepts are given substance through references to assorted works of fiction and non-fiction as well as to the specific empirical undertakings of Workshop members. The second part of the book then discusses the critical decisions that moved the ideas from theory to research, many of the problems raised in the reader's mind by the highly abstract discussion of the first part being sufficiently put to rest. One of the more important and useful aspects of this portion of the book is that large sections are devoted to an explicit demonstration of the sorts of strategies and methodological designs that Workshop participants employed as guides to their own research: the authors hope that readers, interested in the study of authority, might draw upon such demonstrations for their own research, and I can see why.

And, in the last part of the book we are presented with the synthetic lessons on authority, the authors drawing upon the results of their students' research as well as on great ideas (notably some of Durkheim's) and from other disciplines to show how one can go about creating some imaginative generalizations about authority relations, both their causes and consequences. Books on theory usually only present us with this last section skipping the other two; while such a strategy often leaves readers astounded with the intuitive brilliance of the theorist, say a Tocqueville on America, Eckstein and Gurr have done us and themselves the rare honor of candidly showing how they got there. I, for one, found it considerably instructive, and students of theory would do well to follow the lessons of this book closely.

If there is but a single adjective which this book merits, it is that of systematic. From beginning to end, the authors follow a meticulous and disciplined strategy: they identify the basic notions they have in mind, discuss the weaknesses and strengths of them, and then, depending on whether they are engaged in theory construction or methodological implementation, show what must logically follow from these notions. It is not an easy course for readers to follow; it often becomes a tedious one; but for the wisdom and instruction it conveys it is far superior to the sweeps of imagination that often blow in like a gale only later to show themselves as really a trifling gust.

As one would guess, I have few arguments with the book. Their own protests notwithstanding, it seems that the authors might have enriched their own work by drawing more on related writings in other fields (and from universities other than that of Princeton), though perhaps this is one of several items on their agenda for future works. There are only a few spots where the reasoning seems faulty, notably some tendentious passages on why the Eckstein-Gurr conception of the legitimacy of authority is preferable to that of Weber; while the authors' final conceptions are, indeed, perhaps better than those of Weber, the reasons they give for their preference are less than compelling. And, I was struck by the fact that the authors' explanation of significant regularities in societies, even those in certain patterns of authority, often had to resort to the use of some very broad ideas, resembling those of "egalitarianism" or "individualism," for example. The implication, of course, is that contrary to the authors' wishes dimensions of authority are subsidiary in the explanation of social stability to what Parsonians call values, and Marxists identify as ideology.

Others will locate additional weaknesses, I suspect. But for me these are greatly overshadowed by the strengths of this work—by its invaluable demonstration of how to construct systematic social theory, its concern with a critical element in social relations, its effort to connect theory to empirical research, its success in coming up with intriguing theoretical generalizations. I thus end where I began: this is a book that must be consulted by all who are interested in patterns of authority; to ignore it is to risk the impoverishment of one's own scholarship.

Canadian Political Parties: Origin, Character, Impact, by F. C. ENGELMANN and M. A. SCHWARTZ. Scarborough, Ontario: Prentice-Hall of Canada, 1975. 358 pp. $6.95 paper.

PAUL LAMY
University of Ottawa

This text is the revised version of an earlier one which appeared under a different title. While much new content has been added, the same basic set of topics is covered; changes have also been made in the organization and presentation of material. It is doubtful whether these changes, substantial though they are, warrant a change of title and a new review. One of the major reasons for revising the text was simply to update it. By the time the revised version appeared in print, another federal election had already been held, and yet another one will be held between now and the end of 1978. Meanwhile, an independentist party has come to power in Quebec, in the light of which treatment given this party (le Parti Québecois) is already obsolescent. Since the text is "analytic-descriptive" in style, the authors will be forever trying to stuff an ever-changing reality into their rather static theoretical categories (and they will not, it is to be hoped, keep changing titles as they go along).

As a second or third year text, however, this book appears quite satisfactory. It opens with a discussion of the role of political parties in democratic states, then proceeds to deal with Canadian political parties in historical context at both the federal and provincial levels, with the parliamentary, electoral, and federal systems, the influence of elites, mass media, and interest groups, party organization, support, and programs, the electoral process, the operations of government, the mobilization of the electorate, and party influences on society. The book covers a lot of ground and chapter by chapter bibliographies are adequate for undergraduate students. The authors' intuitive grasp of provincial politics east of Ontario leaves something to be desired and most instructors will find it necessary to supplement the text with material on political parties at the provincial level. While this text "does the job" it is not intellectually stimulating—turgid prose, abundant truisms, and the feeling that information has been poured like concrete into pre-determined castings quickly strangles intellectual curiosity.

Radicals in the University, by EDWARD E. ERICSON. Stanford, Calif.: Hoover Institution Press, 1975. 281 pp. $11.00 cloth.

HENRY PACHTER
Rutgers University

Professor Ericson's objective in the book under review is to prove that the student movement suffered from a basic dichotomy, to which it eventually succumbed: between its goal of political liberation for all, and the pursuit of personal liberation by its various followers. This is, of course, the easiest thing in the world to show for any movement be it religious, political or generational; it is even valid for those sects that expect salvation from a particular choice of food or from some kind of calisthenics. The moment people start promising that their special taste in happiness will make others holy and sane too, a conflict is bound to arise. Trade unionists have not been able to persuade consumers that higher costs for services are good for their children; nor have students succeeded in translating their beefs about university administrations into demands for a general reform of society. Elementary, especially when the biographies of various SDS, Yippie, and Panther leaders can be shown to have ended, for the time being at least, in various forms of renunciation or privatistic cults.

What did Professor Ericson expect of nineteen year olds? That they continue expressing their impotent rage in gestures of symbolic protest? He does not, in fact. Having satisfied himself that the kids of 1968 misunderstood their undertaking, he adds the pertinent question: What do grown-up radicals do at the university? Have they restructured it? Can they function in the framework of a world they still have not made (although it feeds them rather well)? Do they bring a radical attitude to their fields? Or are they simply—to use the half-cynical, half-heroic term of the German SDS—"marching through the institutions"? Do they subvert, not only their students, but their fields of study too?

In the two-thirds of his investigation that are not petti-fogging righteousness vis à vis minors (how I would hate to have Ericson as a teacher!), the author describes the tergiversations of the New University, of the radicals in the Professions Conferences, and the confusions of the Radical Caucus in the Modern Languages Association. The value of the book here is in its numerous quotations. They suggest that radicals are roughly divided into three groups: those who would not burn a library under any conditions; those who think it a revolutionary act to proclaim that they would; those who would add to the library a wing containing radical literature. The first group wisely directs its activism to the society outside the academy; though collecting money or signatures for worthy causes on the campus and occasional demonstrations are not excluded, its members see no fundamental difference between an experiment on color-blindness in frogs and a new interpretation of "The Ancient Mariner" in the light of Coleridge's reading of Schiller. The second group, of course, holds this to be a deliberate, vile and corrupt diversion of the proletariat from its true task. The third group's magazine would take the author of such an interpretation to task for neglecting to mention that the mariner, after all, is a proletarian; then they would indulge in a lengthy discussion of the use of albatrosses by Marx, or of Schiller by Marcuse. In a subsequent issue of the magazine, a reader would warn of the danger that albatrosses have by now been co-opted by the system. On this ever-present danger, Mr. Ericson quotes a New Left symposium to the effect that "the toleration of radical academics is actually advantageous to the System since it allows the perpetuation of the myth of the university as a marketplace of ideas." Radicals are shown to suffer pangs of conscience about their inevitable role in supporting, implementing, or masking the educational goals of society. To be dysfunctional in the university, they would have to adopt an elitist attitude in flagrant conflict with their professed love of the masses.

Amusing as Mr. Ericson is, he is shallow and cheap even where his information is useful. It is one thing—and an easy thing at that—to show that radicals are against the myth of objective science, on the one hand, and against relativism on the other; or to cite one of our foremost critics of foreign policy who draws his salary from a defense-related grant to MIT, where he teaches linguistics; or to quote Marcuse's advocacy of intolerance against rightist propaganda and add: "There it stands in all its grotesque nakedness." It is, however, quite another thing to analyze the relationship between schools and society, between ideas and established truths, and between professionalism and political philosophies. A medical student may be interested either in biological research or in healing patients; in either case may be led to the conclusion that there is a political side to the job and that his/her purposes would be better served in a different type of society. Depending on his boiling point, s/he may devote more or less of his/her spare time to saying so in public. In fact, s/he may even get disgusted enough to exchange his/her profession for that of a medical lobbyist or politician—there are at least three famous economists who came from medicine—but s/he wouldn't be so foolish as to ask all doctors to stop practicing medicine.

Professor Ericson understands Louis Kampf, who apparently has hated literature since his political awakening or who may never have loved it, but he wonders what people like Jesse Lemish (or Georg Lukács), who obviously never stopped loving literature, are doing among the radicals. He fails to understand that scientific honesty, curiosity about things worth knowing and even about things not yet thought to be worth knowing, love of things beautiful, and being radical may flow from the same source. The dialectics of the idea of the University is not discussed; neither Veblen nor Benda is quoted as a *point de repair* from which radicals digress. Instead, Ericson takes refuge in that catch-all alibi, "the existential dilemma": Is she (Ellen Cantarov, quoted from Kampf and Lauter's *The Politics of Literature*) a teacher of literature or a woman revolutionary socialist using literature to act out her political fantasies? He quotes, not without relish, Kampf as regretting that the Movement failed "to harass Lincoln Center . . . without interruption." But, for every academic Luddite there must be hundreds whose radicalism began with the genuine pursuit of science, or aesthetics, or philosophy, and who still teach because they want to make students sensitive to values and alert them to the pleasures of the mind before they teach them specific values or particular radical thoughts. Radical militants may have a limited horizon, but their critic accepts their limitations along with their Manichean world view. One can be either for or against conventional wisdom in the same way.

Ericson falls into the trap of thinking that a revolutionary movement can be understood only by a radical theory; he thinks a radical cannot remain a humanist. If the Movement collapsed because it lacked the right ideology, Ericson agrees that happily it is over because its devotees have returned to their private religious retreats. His book concludes with an attempt to show that the Movement was basically religious. This does not need proof. It was characteristic of the Movement that its people invested politics with the power to provide salvation. They looked at political action as a way to get immersed in the general, the communal. Their action was the proclamation of a this-worldly religion. Following Kopkind, Professor Ericson asserts the contrary—that people of the Movement later withdrew into transcendental religion because the Movement itself had been religious to begin with. His double use of the term "religion" is a measure of the inadequacy of his analysis. He therefore cannot understand—despite some avuncular gesture of respect—the legacy, or perhaps the time bomb which the Movement left in the University. Young professors are much more aware than their elders of the philosophical and sociological problems which affect the study of various disciplines. The questions they ask, the books they read and assign are totally different from those of the pre-Vietnam, pre- 1968, period. So are their attitudes to students on the one hand, and institutions on the other. The mere fact that the Movement collapsed, as did other revolutions elsewhere, is not tantamount to saying that it was intellectually sterile. Admittedly, it is difficult to put one's finger on any proof of fertility; some of the ideas which the kids of 1968 were so proud of inventing are in fact rather old. It just so happened that, as I was writing this review, someone sent me from Germany the republication of Georg Herwegh's *Literature as Politics;* Herwegh, a minor poet, was a friend of Karl Marx, who participated in the revolution of 1848 and, who in his collected essays, gave a thrashing to sterile professors, worshippers of Goethe, and romantic youths who didn't know what their revolution was about. It is fair to say that the abortive revolutions of 1848 determined history for the rest of the century, though its ideas were recast. As a warning, I recommend Herwegh's little volume to Professor Ericson.

Soviet Strategy in Europe, edited by RICHARD PIPES. New York: Crane, Russak & Company, 1976. 316 pp. $14.50 cloth. $7.50 paper.

PAUL HOLLANDER
University of Massachusetts, Amherst

I was pleasantly surprised when I was asked to review the above volume. Neither *Contemporary Sociology,* nor other sociological journals are in the habit of reviewing books on international relations or foreign affairs. Moreover, American journals of sociology also tend to stay away from books not self consciously or professionally sociological, even if they possess sociological significance. At last I was surprised to see a book concerned with the Soviet Union selected for review since, again, such items get scant attention in our journals—not that there are many of them.

It is of course hardly a mystery why American liberal intellectuals, including, I presume most sociologists, do not lose many nights of sleep over the activities of the Soviet Union, domestic or foreign. Understandably enough they are fixated on the deeds, and misdeeds, of their own country, at home and abroad. Not that the Soviet Union is popular in liberal circles, or among social scientists. Nonetheless I would hazard the guess that the vast majority of American sociologists know little about Soviet society and in part for this reason their attitudes toward it range from benefit of doubt, indifferent neutrality (or neutral indifference) to some degree of distaste. I am of course not suggesting that knowing little about a country determines one's attitude toward it one way or another. Quite to the contrary: massive ignorance about a society is compatible with both its fanatical hatred and fervent adulation. In any event, I believe it is safe to say that most American social scientists are disinclined to pay much attention to the activities of the Soviet Union around the globe, let alone entertain the idea that they may not be altogether harmless or inconsequential.

In the light of these observations it may not be surprising that I found this a most welcome collection of essays. Though edited by a historian, Richard Pipes, and written mainly by English, French and German political scientists and economists, the book has much to say that is, or could be, of interest to American sociologists. And while focused on Soviet policy in Europe, it also enlightens us about the US and Western Europe. Specific topics include the Soviet view of detente, Soviet decision making processes, Soviet and East and West European relations, Soviet economic policies toward Western Europe and Soviet military policies, capabilities and intentions in Europe. Besides Pipes, the contributors probably best known in this country are Michel Tatu, a French specialist on Soviet affairs, and Thomas Wolfe, an American student of the Soviet military establishment. Unlike many more conventional—one might say, less sociological, or socio-historical—treatments of foreign policy, this volume, and especially the lead essay by Pipes, analyzes Soviet foreign policy as a product of Soviet (and Russian) history, culture, norms and values, political institutions and traditions. And although it is something of a cliché to point out that foreign and domestic policies and politics of nations are always interrelated, rarely is this so illuminatingly brought home as in Pipes's essay.

Two major themes can be discerned in this volume. One is the integration of foreign and domestic political practices in the USSR, or, "the application to other countries of habits acquired at home, in dealing with one's own subjects" (p. 6). The other is an inventory of the disadvantages of detente as practiced so far, for the West. Many of the Soviet policies in Europe, and especially their ideological and attitudinal underpinnings can be projected onto a global scale.

In the introductory paper Pipes scrutinizes various American illusions and misconceptions which have contributed to the origin and character of detente. Americans, he suggests, have great trouble understanding or accepting that there can be *fundamental,* and not only ephemeral or transient, differences between nations, cultures and polities: "It is probably true that only those theories of international relations that postulate a fundamental convergence of all human aspirations with the American ideal have any chance of acceptance in the United States." Hence detente (from the American standpoint) rests "on nothing more substantial than a vaguely and poorly articulated faith that the march of human events follows the script written by the Founding Fathers and that if one can only avoid general war long enough all will be well" (p. 5). Here, one may note, Pipes fails to do justice to the recent decline of optimism in America, some of it deriving from cultural or value problems, much of it related to the apprehensions of the ecologists. To be sure the environmental pessimists have yet to influence our foreign policy-makers.

A closer examination of the nature of the Soviet political elite—rarely engaged in these days—will also deflate expectations tied to detente. In the heyday of detente it would have been bad form to be reminded, as this volume does, that the present Soviet leaders "rose to positions of power in the 1930s, in the turmoil of Stalin's purges and massacres—that is, under conditions of the most ruthless political infighting known in modern history. . . . This elite is the product of a process of natural selection under which the fittest proved to be those who knew best how to suppress within themselves everything normally regarded as human . . ." (p. 10).

Pipes also believes that the peasant background of these leaders influences their outlook in ways which are, once more, not particularly helpful for the spirit of give and take, compromise and at least rudimentary fair play, which good relations with other countries must entail. While cultural traditions are hardly infallible guides for an understanding of the foreign policies of those partaking of this culture, it is refreshing to be reminded through proverbs what this tradition was like. For example: "The basic thrust of these [Russian] proverbs is that life is hard and that to survive one must learn to take care of oneself and one's own without wasting much thought on others ('the tears of others is water'). Force is one of the surest means of getting one's way ('. . . beat a Russian and he will make you a watch'). In personal relations the Russian peasant always was . . . one of the kindest creatures on earth . . . . But these qualities of decency and empathy have never been successfully institutionalized. . . . They tend to vanish the instant the Russian peasant leaves the familiar environment of personal contacts" (pp. 11–12). Moreover the unfortunate fact remains that "all the great national experiences, especially since 1917, happened to reinforce the illiberal and antidemocratic impulses . . ." of the Soviet masses and elites (p. 12). Pipes concludes by recommending that "Detente ought to be global and all-inclusive. One should not tolerate the Soviet Union, while ostensibly engaging in 'peaceful coexistence with us,' inciting its own population to 'ideological struggle' against us, . . . or arming the Arabs to wage war against a small country to the survival of which we have a deep commitment. . . . In particular detente is not compatible with an unabated Soviet military effort for which no reasonable military justification exists" (p. 44).

The latter theme is also taken up in another chapter written by John Ericson who is a British expert on Soviet military history. He also concludes his assessment of "Soviet military posture and policy" by observing that "allowing for almost any conceivable rationale—the expansion of Soviet military capability in Europe seems to defy the strictly rational. . . . In sum, whichever way the military statistics are argued, the 'military threat' has grown substantially . . ." (pp. 206, 205).

The idea that there is more to the "Soviet threat" than the propaganda of our military-industrial complex forever seeking lucrative defense contracts is not congenial to many Americans, especially liberal academics. Since the Kissinger-Nixon foreign policy we have been increasingly presented with an image of an inward looking, pragmatic Soviet leadership, responding to the material needs of its people, anxious to avoid confrontation abroad and scaling down its foreign ambitions altogether.

Responding to such analyses of the Soviet threat and viewing it as credible is also problematic for the American liberal because of the association of such discussions and warnings with the cold war years, in turn associated with McCarthy and the anti-communism of some of the most unappealing segments of the American political spectrum.

Reflecting on such and other issues raised by this book, and speculating about its hypothetical reception among American sociologists I felt it to be unfortunate that students and critics of American and Soviet society respectively tend to be arrayed in rigidly separated scholarly grouping. Were they more familiar with each other's work and concerns the appearance of such a volume would be less of an event and its contents less likely to be a controversial novelty for the readers of this journal.

Mayday at Yale: A Case Study in Student Radicalism, by JOHN TAFT. Boulder, Colo.: Westview Press, 1976. 224 pp. $12.50 cloth.

The Sources of American Activism, by JAMES L. WOOD. Lexington, Mass.: D. C. Heath & Company, 1974. 187 pp. $15.00 cloth.

*RICHARD G. BRAUNGART
Syracuse University

It is difficult to understand and predict historical change, and sociology is perpetually haunted by its inability to develop propositions and theories that explain human group behavior. Who expected that ten years ago the Vietnam War, civil rights movement, and student movement would give way so quickly to Watergate, "CBers," the Moon movement, and sports riots? Who would have foreseen the outward, expressive, and critical generation of young people in this country replaced by an introspective, privatist, and cynical generation? Other historic anomalies include the recent published confessions and near total ideological reversals of Jerry Rubin and Eldridge Cleaver. One of the original founders of the anti-establishment SDS, Tom Hayden, recently ran, albeit unsuccessfully, in the California primary for the United States Senate; while his political antagonist, S. I. Hayakawa was elected Republican Senator from California. The radical black politics of Rap Brown was replaced in the evening news by the new politics of Jerry Brown; the Free Speech Movement and Mario Savio supplanted by the Right-to-Life movement and Karen Anne Quinlan, and so on. Only through hindsight are we able to perceive, much less comprehend, such dramatic historical shifts, occurring within the period of a single decade.

Wood's *The Sources of American Student Activism,* and Taft's *Mayday at Yale* are books written about the student movement in the late 1960s and represent products of that historical period. They are echoes of another time and place, neither telling us why the student movement dissipated nor explaining the present mood of quietism and apathy on college campuses. The authors share several characteristics: they were both students when they wrote their books—Wood was a graduate student in sociology at Berkeley, Taft was an undergraduate philosophy major at Yale; both witnessed student politics first-hand at their respective institutions and have

* Editor's Note: Not the reviewer responsible for the listing in "Delinquent Reviews."

something important to say on the subject. However, that is as far as the similarities go, with each author taking a markedly different approach to the study of student politics.

The purpose of *The Sources of American Student Activism* is to test empirically the major theories explaining student protest in the 1960s. Toward this end, Wood employs secondary survey research data from two Berkeley samples originally collected by Robert Somers and Jeanne Block in 1968. This is a case study of Berkeley students and their parents, using the "elaboration" technique to test a variety of theories of student activism. Wood's approach is highly quantitative, employing numerous tables, statistical tests, and causal inferences. Theories tested include family socialization, generational conflict, alienation, class politics, youth idealism, impulsiveness, and permissiveness as they relate to student activism. From this desultory list, two theories emerge which partially explain the Berkeley data. The first consists of a "middle-range" theory of generational conflict, which suggests that activists, as opposed to nonactivists, appear to be acting out parental values. These same activist youth perceive their parents as failing to live up to their espoused beliefs and standards. The second theory is essentially a truncated version of Smelser's theory of collective behavior. Here, Wood argues that structural strains and conduciveness provide the "necessary and sufficient" conditions for student political mobilization. Unfortunately, this latter theory is not tested or confirmed by the empirical data. On the face of it, Wood's monograph appears to be a hard-hitting methodological treatise on student activism. It is a well-balanced and objective study, except for the unsuccessful attempt to couch his argument within Smelser's theoretical framework.

An entirely different approach to student politics is offered by Taft. This is a historical account of student radicalism set in the context of a Yale campus strike. Taft and four of his undergraduate colleagues participated, observed, and recorded the events which took place between March and May of 1970. Together these young scholars interviewed 74 administrators, faculty, students, and New Haven police, all of whom were involved in some way with the strike. In addition, information was gathered from numerous books, articles, newspaper reports, letters, leaflets, minutes, personal notes, and other memoranda. In this highly original case study, Taft captures the human drama and unfolding dynamics of a unique period in Yale history with painstaking reconstruction of facts, organizations, and participants. The chronology of events can be classified into five stages.

(1) The initial controversy started in in Spring 1969, when members of the New Haven Black Panther party were arrested for the brutal murder of Alex Rackley, a local chapter member. Bobby Seale was arrested in Berkeley, charged with masterminding the murder and extradited to New Haven to stand trial in the County Courthouse, located less than a block away from the Yale University campus. In retaliation, the national Black Panther party sent organizers to reconstruct the decimated New Haven chapter and to enlist Yale University students and faculty in their cause. The newly formed New Haven Panther Defense Committee (NHPDC) moved on the Yale campus and announced plans for protest rallies to be held on behalf of the "New Haven Nine."

(2) The jailing episode was dramatized and the NHPDC successfully polarized the Yale University community. Eschatological rhetoric ("destroy society," "kill the pigs," "burn Yale" for what "they" are doing to Bobby Seale) escalated and the ideological sides were drawn into at least four camps: (a) the *radicals,* including the Panthers, campus radicals, New Haven blacks; (b) *liberals,* including Yale President Kingman Brewster, William Sloan Coffin, Kenneth Keniston, Cyrus Vance, and others; (c) the majority of *moderate* Yale students and faculty; and (d) *conservatives,* including Police Chief James Ahern, the mayor of New Haven, and local community citizens.

(3) The blurring of issues, appeals to guilt, and ensuing confusion led to an entente between the "Black Panthers and Yale Bulldogs." Students voted to strike, and faculty and administrators agreed to modify academic regulations.

(4) In spite of his early concessions to the radicals, President Brewster remained in control of the entire incident with a series of brilliant maneuvers, grounded in a web of personal communication, which provided the framework for defusing the potentially explosive uprising. Brewster, Coffin, and Ahern allowed the campus conflict to run its natural course without over-reacting. In this way, they were able to ameliorate a volatile situation without serious violence.

(5) No major reforms resulted from the

Mayday strike. Some critics argued that Yale benefited from the strike by opening itself up to society's problems; others conceded that Yale survived the trying ordeal with its usual dignity.

What is ironic about these two studies is that each one manages to accomplish what the other set out to do. Wood's intentions are to test a number of theories of student activism, only to discover an imperfect fit between fact and theory. Taft's objectives are to document the series of events that led up to, and transpired during the Mayday strike. Surprisingly, the sequence of events, as outlined in his study, conforms to Coleman's theory of community conflict which proposes five stages of conflict (issue identification, crystallization and polarization at the extremes, cooptation of moderates, attempt at amelioration, and resolution of conflict).

Wood's book can be commended for its methodological rigor and disciplined interpretation of data. This is one of the few attempts at theory construction on this topic. Taft's careful treatment of the Mayday strike awakens memories and emotions of the turbulent 1960s and represents a fascinating original piece of historical research. I would recommend both books to scholars searching for a more thorough understanding of the student movement. The wider merit of these works may well lie in their unique quantitative and qualitative approaches to sociology. Despite these accomplishments, neither book is able to explain attitudes and behavior of college youth in the 1970s, and this is the agendum at hand.

Race and Ethnic

The Russian Jews under Tsars and Soviets, 2nd ed. by SALO W. BARON. New York: Macmillan Publishing Company, 1976. 468 pp. $14.95 cloth.

A Social and Religious History of the Jews, 2nd ed. *Volume XVI: Late Middle Ages and Era of European Expansion*, by SALO W. BARON. New York: Columbia University Press, 1976. 460 pp. $17.50 cloth.

The Jews in Russia: The Struggle for Emancipation, by LOUIS GREENBERG. New York: Schocken Books, 1976. 448 pp. $6.50 paper.

FRANCESCO CORDASCO
Montclair State College

In an era of turbulently frenetic ethnicity, whose *disjecta membra* lie strewn across the American intellectual landscape, the Jews have a unique status: unlike other American ethnics, the Jews have always known who they were and, for them, the rediscovery of ethnicity has been unnecessary, if not superfluous (and one need not be reminded that Irving Howe's nostalgic *World of Our Fathers* and its pursuit of a lost *Yiddishkeit* are essentially incongruent with the doleful lamentations of Richard Gambino and Michael Novak who have sought to recreate an ideological infused Italian *campanilismo* and new Polonia in an otherwise indifferent America); and the unique status of the Jews in the contexts of the new ethnicity is further attested by the embarrassing enquiries of a WASP historian (i.e., John Higham in *Send These to Me: Jews and Other Immigrants in Urban America*, 1975) who seeks to endow American Jews with the mantle of a resurgent ethnicity.

The books under review make clear two facts which dramatically differentiate the Jewish experience from that of other ethnic groups in America: (1) the existence of a Jewish past, unbroken in an evolving continuum wherein the American components are, at best, part of a Diaspora; and (2) the zealously treasured archives out of which a Jewish identity can, given appropriate diligence, be rearticulated, examined, and defined. An illustration of the point is in order: an American Jew would entertain small difficulty in relating the volumes by Louis Greenberg and Salo W. Baron (on Jewish experience in Russia, Poland, Lithuania) to the *theologia pectoris* which animates an otherwise disembodied ethnicity; for an American Pole much of what is in Florian Znaniecki's classic *The Polish Peasant in Europe and America* would be unintelligible, and as "foreign" as the encounter of an American Italian with Giuseppe Pitrè's voluminously encyclopedic *Biblioteca delle Tradizioni Popolari Siciliane*.

The decision to reissue Louis Greenberg's *The Jews in Russia* is not unrelated to contemporary events, and the work's subtitle (i.e., *The Struggle for Emancipation*) is poignantly appropriate. Louis Greenberg (1894–1946) took his doctorate at Yale, and these volumes were originally published by Yale University Press (Volume I in 1944 and Volume II posthumously in 1951). In a strict sense, the Jewish struggle for emancipation had its origin outside Russia, in the Russian piece-meal absorption of the Polish-Lithuanian state beginning in the mid-seventeenth century; and Professor Greenberg's narrative deals "with the rise and development of the movement for civic rights carried on by Russian Jewry during the second half of the nineteenth century" (Volume I), a period which closes with the death of Alexander II in 1881; and his work, left unfinished at his death, carries the story of the Jews in Russia down to the Bolshevik revolution in 1917. (Volume II, 1881–1917, was edited and prepared for publication by Mark Wischnitzer.)

Above all, the significance of Louis Greenberg's study lies in his formulation of the "Jewish question" in Russia, with all its basic ingredients carefully studied in an historical matrix which makes them and the realities which accompanied them intelligible: from the study one can derive a valid image of Jewish society on the eve of the 1917 revolution, illuminating the background against which contemporary Jewish life under the Soviets is to be understood. Out of the elaborate historical narrative which Professor Greenberg fashions, two significant themes are sketched: (1) Russian Jews began a quest for civic rights a century later than their Western brethren simply because the thought of the enlightenment had made no progress in the land of the Tsars until the mid-nineteenth century. (2) Beyond the period of the Great Reforms initiated during the reign of Alexander II, the Jews, encouraged by the spirit of the new liberalism, asserted claims to civic equality (removal of the Pale, the right to own land, eligibility for government service), and out of this new hope evolved the movement for secular education known by the Hebrew name of *Haskalah,* and the strides toward Russification, assimilation, and religious reforms.

It ended disastrously for Jews: Russia's basic attitudes in the nineteenth century continued into the twentieth century and tenaciously viewed the Jew as a dangerous economic and social pariah. In a perspicacious foreword to this new edition of Professor Greenberg's study, Alfred Levin trenchantly concludes: "Dr. Louis Greenberg saw all of these events through the eyes of a scholar and an American Jew professionally dedicated to the propagation and preservation of his faith. Some of his judgments may emerge as too harsh for the tastes of the practiced historian. But the realities of Jewish life in the last century of the old regime were themselves harsh."

Salo Wittmayer Baron, the doyen of Jewish historians, Professor Emeritus of Jewish History, Literature, and Institutions at Columbia University, has chosen a propitious time to reissue his *The Russian Jew under Tsars and Soviets.* Originally published in 1964, Professor Baron has now chosen to revise the work, taking note of "revolutionary transformations" which "have shown many similarities with those which had taken place in certain periods of the tsarist regime." And echoing Professor Greenberg's earlier themes, Professor Baron somberly observes: "It has long been recognized that, despite the far reaching impact of the great Communist Revolution, the basic continuity of Russian life, from tsarist to Soviet times has been maintained." In revising the work, Professor Baron has added an entirely new chapter "devoted to an analysis of the transformations which took place during the last decade"; and it is sadly disquieting to note his observation: "Nonetheless, the prospects for the coming years have remained so constant that the final chapter, looking into the future, has required little alteration": the story remains, as he observed in 1964, "sad and heroic."

There are important differences between the earlier work of Louis Greenberg and that of Professor Baron; it is not only a difference in timeframes (Baron's chronicles extend from the time of Vladimer of Kiev, c.980 A.D., to Leonid Brezhnev). Professor Baron's work is not primarily political history encapsulated within the contexts of continuing prejudice. In a fuller sense, it is a social kaleidoscope incorporating vivid portraits of life in Russian Jewish communities, and it is in these portraits that Professor Baron's great powers lie: e.g., the *Kahal,* the traditional council which had jurisdiction over almost every aspect of community life; the growth and destruction of Jewish economic power; dissent between wealthy Jews and the less affluent; the acrimonious debate between Zionists and assimilationists, between *Hasidim* and *Mitnagdim*; the influence of Jewish writers and poets, and the strange ambivalence of loyalties to Jewish tradition and Mother Russia.

Salo W. Baron's monumental *A Social and Religious History of the Jews* continues to evolve into one of the great panoramic histories of our time. Organized into broad socio-historical tableaux (Ancient Times; High Middle Ages; Late Middle Ages and Era of European Expansion), sixteen volumes have been thus far published with six more projected. Volume 16 (the concluding volume of the third tableau which extends from 1200–1650) deals with *Poland-Lithuania, 1500–1650,* the "Golden Age" of Polish and Lithuanian Jewry: and it epitomizes Professor Baron's interdisciplinary approach to Judaism which is the legacy which Baron leaves as the most impressive contribution to Judaica in modern times and which has done so much to make Columbia University an international center of Jewish studies.

As the work of a single scholar, *A Social and Religious History of the Jews*, has no modern counterparts, and in the canons of social historiography, it can be compared, in scope and comprehensive design, to the labors of William E. H. Lecky, and without presumption to those of Edward Gibbon; and it is hardly fortuitous that *A History of England in the 18th Century*, and *The Decline and Fall of the Roman Empire* are (not unlike Baron's *A Social and Religious History of the Jews*) the social histories of a people whose chronicles are delineated in lucidly sharp and muted chiarascuro portraits of institutions and events, all interrelated over vast periods of time. Baron's sixteenth volume of his history is a vivid attestation of the fact: the history of Polish and Lithuanian Jewry is caught up in this chronicle in that extraordinary creative élan of the sixteenth century, eventually impeded by the onset of the Polish Counter Reformation, but whose momentum carried the Jews through a golden period in which a Jewish communal structure, unprecedented in the annals of Christian Europe, evolved and prospered; and basic to the design of his narrative, Professor Baron's assertion that "By the end of the sixteenth century, the dual Commonwealth of Poland-Lithuania achieved the hegemony of all Ashkenazic, in fact, of all the world, Jewry" is unchallengeable.

If this golden age was to come to an end, and its termination remain unforeseen, still (in Professor Baron's words) "at the moment of great crises, the people's inherent vitality, resourcefulness, and vigor reasserted themselves, and before long it resumed the earlier rhythm of life with sufficient élan to face all subsequent adversities with a measure of equanimity." And this cannot but have meaning for the Jew's present anguish defined out of contemporary fragile social contexts.

Ethnocentrism and Intergroup Attitudes: East African Evidence, by MARILYNN B. BREWER and DONALD T. CAMPBELL. New York: Halsted Press, 1976. 218 pp. $15.95 cloth.

STANLEY J. MORSE
The Flinders University of South Australia

William Graham Sumner's classic conceptualization of ethnocentrism, with which this book begins and ends, is obviously too simplistic. This study analyzes data collected in 1965 from 1,500 members of thirty tribes in Kenya, Uganda, and Tanzania, most of whom were males living in urban areas. Using single-response item formats, respondents indicated their perceptions of their own group and of thirteen other groups as well as the nature of their contacts with members of each group. This is a major, highly sophisticated contribution to the study of ethnocentrism. It is particularly useful because it not only deals with non-US samples living in a relatively restricted geographical area but because the groups studied vary along such key dimensions as level of economic development and degree of urbanization. Chapters deal, in perhaps too much detail and with too many subtle statistical qualifications, with such topics as the role of cultural-linguistic similarity, geographical proximity, and self-regard on ethnic attitudes. The book ends with ten succinct summary propositions.

A number of theoretical ideas derived from social psychological and psychological theories formulated initially to account for dyadic interaction are extrapolated and successfuly tested at the intergroup level. This book will therefore probably be of most interest to social psychologists. Sociologists and especially students of African studies may be disappointed. Not only are structural and political considerations usually overlooked, but the authors purposely refrain from discussing in concrete terms how the particular tribes studied are perceived by others and how they see themselves. More such studies, using what Campbell has called the "multiple-ethnography paradigm," are nevertheless sorely needed.

Race Relations: Elements and Social Dynamics, by OLIVER C. COX. Detroit: Wayne State University Press, 1976. 337 pp. $17.50 cloth.

DON O. WATKINS
Medgar Evers College/CUNY

Race Relations, utilizing much significant recent and historical data, considers the categories surveyed in traditional texts on race. However, it is Cox's theses, not the data, that are of interest:

(1) Capitalism, requiring subordinate classes, is the genesis of racism. Through capitalist expansion, Europeans gained absolute control over Africans.

(2) Capitalist urbanization extends racism. In cities, Negroes (Cox, late recipient of the DuBois-Johnson-Frazier Award, uses this term) have been isolated from the dominant culture. White ruling elites ghettoized Negroes by implementing repressive, degrading policies. Consequently, lower class culture is the norm in Negro communities.

(3) Black racists—separatists, nationalists, militants—support capitalist exploitation and exclusion of Negroes by advocating their separation, thereby exacerbating weaknesses and preventing effective participation in the dominant culture.

(4) Assimilation and integration of Negroes into the mainstream is essential, achieved only through full employment via the dissolution of capitalism and the transition to socialism.

Through his book, Cox emphasizes social pathologies. He ignores the work of scholars such as Professor James Comer, Andrew Brimmer, and John Scanzoni who have highlighted the range of culture and strengths in black communities without glossing over the tragic consequences life in racist America bears. They seem more relevant for contemporary policy-making.

Interethnic Relations: An Essay in Sociological Theory, by EMERICH K. FRANCIS. New York: Elsevier Scientific Publishing Company, 1976. 432 pp. $22.50 cloth.

RICHARD T. SCHAEFER
Western Illinois University

For too long, race relations specialists who are unable to read German have had to settle for the few but excellent articles available in English by E. K. Francis, now professor emeritus at the University of Munich. This has been especially frustrating given the many favorable secondary accounts of Francis's *Ethnos und Demos* which appeared in 1965. In *Interethnic Relations,* the author has presented himself a formidable challenge—the construction of a theory of ethnicity applicable across a range of societies stretching from tribes without rulers to the multinational Hapsburg Empire. The result is successful and deserves a careful reading.

Francis employs the case study method from which emerges inductively a series of theoretical constructs summarized in the final chapter. The propositions are at the level that political scientist David Easton terms "narrow-gauge theories." Francis synthesizes the cases to produce one hundred and three interrelated propositions that are applicable to any group that share a sense of identity, solidarity, and belief in a common ancestry. The dependence on previously published studies to produce a theory is not unlike Blalock's *Toward A Theory of Minority Group Relations.* It would, however, be a mistake to interpret the present effort as either repeating or replacing that work. Unlike Blalock, Francis does not become preoccupied with micro-level Black-White relationships, but emphasizes instead the process of nation-building.

The breadth of Francis's treatise is both the book's strength and weakness. Few sociologists will be equally knowledgeable of the Moravian Compromise of 1905 and the Hispanos of New Mexico, and thus many will benefit by the exposure to such a bountiful assortment of cross-cultural materials. With the possible exceptions of Lieberson, Shibutani, and Kwan, no theoretical approach to ethnic relations has depended so heavily on a historical approach as Francis's. Future work in the field can take a lead from Francis in this respect. Unfortunately some of the case studies are rather superficial and all have minimal documentation. The reliance on pre-1960 accounts is at times annoying. Similarly, despite his concern for imprecise language, Francis occasionally chooses to coin terms (such as "'little' and 'big' Apartheid") when more insightful terminology is commonly in use (van den Berghe's distinguishing among macro-, micro-, and meso-segregation).

The weakness in supporting detail does not necessarily mitigate the usefulness of the theory. The author admits in the preface that the book is best suited as a reference work, not as a textbook. The initial reading is difficult as one struggles through the deduction of the theoretical framework. In a footnote, Francis chides that the "impatient" reader may wish to start with the final outline of the theoretical propositions. In this instance "impatience" may be rewarded.

The utility of this work rests with the willingness of the student or scholar to apply the propositions and not just read them passively. Like most other theoretical approaches to race and ethnic relations, some may question the empirical testability of the propositions, but they can be applied constructively to a variety of ethnic situations. The publication of this book should signal the end of pronouncements that the field of ethnic relations has a dearth of well-grounded theory and initiate the application of the available approaches.

Racial Equality in America, by JOHN HOPE FRANKLIN. Chicago: University of Chicago Press, 1976. 123 pp. $7.95 cloth.

WILLIAM P. NYE
Hollins College

John Hope Franklin's latest contribution to the study of American race relations consists of a three part essay composed and delivered as the 1976 Jefferson Lecture, an event supported by the National Endowment for the Humanities. As might be expected under these circumstances, the essays are more polemic than scholarly. The author restrains his acknowledged historical erudition in order to deliver a concise, eloquent, and morally compelling message to the effect that racial inequality has been a pronounced and persistent component of American social structure since the seventeenth century.

Part one of the book focuses on racial inequality in colonial times, paying extended attention to the ambiguous position and influence of Jefferson. The second part centers on the latter half of the nineteenth century and documents the fact that the life situation of the newly emancipated Negro was little different from that which was endured under slavery. The third essay traces the history of racial inequality from World War I forward and demonstrates that no real and significant reduction in inequality occurred until after the formation of the Truman Committee on Civil Rights in 1947. Considered together, the essays contribute little that is new to our knowledge of its subject matter. It is also devoid of references, footnotes, and index, which restricts its utility for serious research. Still, the book deserves a wide, popular audience and should be particularly effective in undergraduate sociology courses. Franklin's Jefferson Lecture combines a devastating moral indictment of more than three centuries of American hypocrisy with an impassioned and reasoned plea to extend equality across the color line. His artful blending of historical fact, black poetry, and ethical reflection leads the reader to the inescapable conclusion that the time for concerted and direct action on all levels is long overdue.

Japanese Americans: The Evolution of a Subculture, 2nd ed., by HARRY H. L. KITANO. Englewood Cliffs, N.J.: Prentice-Hall, 1976. 231 pp. $8.95 cloth. $3.95 paper.

DARREL MONTERO
University of Maryland, College Park

Since the late 1960s teachers of race and ethnic relations have observed a dramatic change in the attitudes of students. For example, Robert Blauner in *Racial Oppression in America,* observed that "In the late 1960s the white scholar who persisted in the sociology of race had his back up against the wall. Or, to shift metaphors, he was at least caught between the priorities and perspectives of subordinated groups—including his or her own students—and those of the academic community" (p. viii).

In 1969 when Kitano brought out the first edition of his volume, *Japanese Americans,* he did the students of race and ethnic relations a considerable service. At the time no other comparable volume was available for classroom use. Kitano's volume forms part of Prentice-Hall's well received series, "Ethnic Groups in American Life." Other volumes in the series include Anderson's *White Protestant Americans,* Fitzpatrick's *Puerto Rican Americans,* Moore's *Mexican Americans* (2nd ed.), Wax's *Indian Americans,* and most recently Lopata's *Polish Americans.*

As in all successful commercial enterprises, Random House followed Prentice-Hall with their own series on ethnic Americans. Demographer William Petersen penned his volume by the same title, *Japanese Ameri-*

cans. Whereas Petersen relies heavily on historical accounts of the Japanese Americans drawn from a very thorough culling of historical sources and the use of experts, Kitano borrows less heavily from historical sources and more heavily from a set of taped interviews with Issei, Nisei, and Sansei (i.e., first, second, and third generation Japanese Americans) respondents largely residing in Los Angeles. Although these interviews were not intended to be representative of the larger Japanese American community, they provide a very personal view of both the experiences of immigration and socio-economic adaptation of the Japanese. In the second edition, the author retains the basic format of his earlier volume while expanding upon selected sections, up-dating historical and census data, expanding the bibliography from three pages in the first edition to some nine pages in the present edition, and developing a stronger theoretical cast to the volume. Kitano employs Gordon's assimilation paradigm, as well as Edna Bonacich's theory of middleman minorities as an explanation of the Japanese adaptation into American society.

The volume's first chapter begins with a brief discussion of the Japanese immigrant experience in the United States. Chapters two through four cover the period up to World War II, wherein Kitano discusses the structure of the family and community. Chapter five addresses the question of wartime evacuation; while chapter six explores the conditions after the war. Chapter seven turns to an examination of the current relations of the Japanese family and community; chapters eight and nine discuss culture and social deviance. Chapter ten represents a new chapter in this edition. It addresses the large population of Japanese Americans residing in Hawaii. The final chapter represents much more than a conclusion, rather Kitano addresses some of the central issues of the volume: the question of assimilation by generation and area of residence; the concept of middleman minority; and cultural and structural pluralism.

Although the volume is presented in a very informal, descriptive style (in some spots it is totally anecdotal), it is interesting and generally well written for an undergraduate audience.

It is clear that I find Kitano's revision a successful one. However, I do have some suggestions for a third edition. The volume presents twelve tables which represent generally useful demographic data regarding such topics as marriage and divorce rates and occupational distribution. Unfortunately, these are presented with little discussion or interpretation in the text. The tables would be more instructive if they were placed in the text with some interpretation regarding the relatively low rates of mental illness and poverty among the Japanese. Although these rates are considerably lower than those for the total US population, many Sansei argue that it does their community a disservice to imply that the Japanese are a "Model Minority." Overplaying their economic success serves to work against a sizeable minority of poor Japanese who are being ignored by the federal and state service agencies.

In short, Kitano's slim volume has accomplished its apparent task. It is a readable, interesting volume which in some 200 pages captures many of the salient factors of the Japanese experience in America.

Race First: The Ideological and Organizational Struggles of Marcus Garvey and the Universal Negro Improvement Association, by TONY MARTIN. Westport, Conn.: Greenwood Press, 1976. 448 pp. $17.50 cloth.

DOUGLAS S. SNYDER
Bowie State College

This book is the nineteenth volume in a varied and valuable series of multi-disciplinary studies titled "Contributions in Afro-American and African Studies." It particularly complements Weisbord's *Ebony Kinship* (#14) which is a comprehensive study of back-to-Africa movements.

It is always a challenge for a sociologist to review a work by a historian because the historian focuses on peculiar causes and unique sequences of events; the sociologist, on broader causal factors, uniformities, and generalizations. For a work by a historian to be seen as valuable by sociologists, it needs to include some higher-order abstractions and theoretical interpretations.

Race First, coming shortly after books by Vincent and by Clarke, sheds light on the reasons for Garvey's and the Universal Negro Improvement Association's (UNIA) successes and failures (Garvey was eventually deported) as they relate to ideological components, organizational efforts, and inter-organizational relations. The book is well documented, and has an extensive bibliography of primary and secondary sources; the former include the holdings of the National Archives and the British Public Records Office, in addition to those of the Garvey family and the New York Public Library's Schomburg Center.

The early chapters deal with the key ideological elements of racial separatism, self-reliance, Black nationhood, Black religion, and Black history. After a chapter, "Propaganda," about a major Garvey tactic, a chapter on Africa concerns itself with the mostly negative reactions by the governors and political leaders of various African colonies and countries to Garvey's program.

Following an informative chapter on the major means for African resettlement, the ill-fated Black Star Line steamships, the final four chapters focus on inter-organizational relationships between the UNIA and these entities: the United States Government (Justice, Post Office, Treasury, and State Departments), the NAACP, the Communists, and white supremacists. It is these chapters which will probably be of most interest to sociologists because they trace common interests and resulting contacts of the UNIA with such unlikely groups as the Ku Klux Klan, and they point out the conflict relations with "allies" such as other Black organizations and the Communist party. These chapters provide convincing evidence that Garvey was taken seriously by several national groups and leaders during his lifetime. A concluding chapter which would draw the themes of the earlier chapters together into a meaningful conceptual pattern is sorely missed; what we get is a one-page "Afterword."

Martin goes to some length to construct an argument for Garvey's being taken seriously as not only the most important forerunner of Black nationalism in the 1960s but one who "has as good a claim as anyone to the distinction of being the greatest black figure of the twentieth century" (p. 359). At times this argument gets a little pedantic and detracts from the telling of a fascinating saga.

The Black Sash of South Africa, by CHERRY MICHELMAN. New York: Oxford University Press, 1975. 198 pp. $18.75 cloth.

LINDA STONEALL
Michigan State University

South Africa has become a dirty word because of its increasingly totalitarian policy of apartheid. The importance of Michelman's book appears in its effort to point out that some people—in particular, white, middle-class, English-speaking, liberal women—in South Africa protest these policies. Though we are not told when, where, and why this study was done and there is no introduction or conclusion to provide any thesis to the study, the apparent purpose of the book is to provide an understanding of dissenters against apartheid through documenting the history of a particular case, the Black Sash. It was formed as a reaction against the Senate Act in 1955 extending the powers of the National Party and, however ineffectual, has continued its silent protests. Black Sash members will not break the law and they will not admit non-whites to their group, yet they have become a kind of gadfly to South Africa, creating an uncomfortable embarrassment. Using data based on interviews with Black Sash members and their records, Michelman presents the Black Sash in different phases corresponding to reactions to different governmental policies and to crises of its goals and structure of its membership. Moreover, she relates the Black Sash to other liberal groups in South Africa and provides some information on what they are protesting. However, her information is at times inadequate for a reader who does not know the society (for example, what are Pass Laws?). The closest Michelman comes to making an analysis is in chapter 7, "Conclusion to the Early Years," which is more or less an apology for the liberalism of the Black Sash, answering possible criticism from conservatives and radicals.

However, Michelman has collected enough material for sociological analyses, among other things, of women's groups and social movements. For example, though the Black Sash's main purpose is silent protests and the League of Women Voters image as the ideal, they also at times engage in such womanly activities as raising funds through bake sales and acting as social workers to non-whites. How are other women's groups similar to the Black Sash? What are the affinities to feminist groups? Two suggestions are that the Black Sash was particularly instrumental in considering the plight of non-white women and also that the Black Sash bears a likeness to the Women's Movement in either being ignored or ridiculed by the press. Another consideration is how does the Black Sash work as a social movement? Is it another of the "when-prophecy-fails" syndrome where activity is intensified in the face of failure?

One important piece of information is missing in the book: how does the non-white community feel about the Black Sash? Michelman has fallen into the same liberal trap as the Black Sash in not considering how it feels to be on the receiver's end of the charity. Does the Black Sash generate as much hatred as the members of the Black Movement in this country feel toward white liberals? After all, the Black Sash position is that the conditions of non-whites be improved, but they are not willing to give the non-whites power. Thus, Black Sash women, as part of the middle class, are dependent on non-whites being kept down.

Mexican Americans, 2nd ed., by JOAN W. MOORE with HARRY PACHON. Englewood Cliffs, N.J.: Prentice-Hall, 1976. 173 pp. No price listed, cloth.

AUDREY W. FORREST
Drake University

Readers interested in the "ethnic experience" will find Moore and Pachon's *Mexican Americans* a suitable selection. As the authors indicate, the book is a compact description of the second largest minority in the United States. Even though the primary focus is on the various stresses and strains occurring across the whole spectrum of social participation, another major concern is to emphasize the variation or heterogeneity of this large population. The reader is reminded of the wide range of diversity among Mexican Americans from the peons of Ozona, Texas, to the aristocratic Canary Islanders of San Antonio. Further, the authors contend that although La Raza is concentrated in the Southwest region of the country, vast differences of life chances exist from state to state and from city to city.

The authors want to familiarize the reader with the group's historical, economic, educational, and political development; and feel that its American experience is unique enough to merit greater attention than it has been getting. The current research data contribute to the book's value as an adequate resource.

Some of the trends and prospects for the group's future are viewed in terms of circumstances peculiar to it. For instance, the proximity of Mexico and the continual legal and illegal influx of Mexicans into this country help to hinder accuracy of predictions about them.

With the possible exception of the last chapter, the tone of the book is too defensive. The "spirit of protest" is too obvious; it figuratively strikes one in the face. Indeed, this writer is intellectually offended when the "compare-the-scars" game (to use Kitano's expression) is zealously overplayed. Being more traditionally oriented, I plead that sociologists writing in this area return to a more "scientific spirit" and attempt to soften if not eliminate the emotional involvement in research and to accentuate sociological analysis.

Despite the above comments, I agree with the purpose of the Ethnic Groups in American Life series, and believe that Moore and Pachon have made some contribution to it.

Race and Ethnicity in Africa, edited by PIERRE L. VAN DEN BERGHE. Nairobi, Kenya: East African Publishing House, 1975. 357 pp. No price listed, paper.

SHARON STICHTER
University of Massachusetts, Boston

Given Pierre van den Berghe's outstanding contributions to the comparative study of racism, one would expect this new volume of readings on race and ethnicity in Africa to be of the same high quality. As a reader, however, it has some limitations. Despite them, it will probably stand for some time as the best thing of its kind available.

Conceived as a textbook for students in African universities, the book fills a major gap in that it places the seemingly unique African phenomenon of "tribalism" squarely within the corpus of sociological theory on ethnic relations. The chief issue here is the same as that posed in the American context: how to explain the persistence and even increase of ethnic consciousness in an environment of modernization and economic growth? To this question the volume does not provide a clear answer, nor does it juxtapose the competing approaches.

The introduction tells us that the problem in post-independence Africa of the 1960s was that the "real nations," the meaningful units, were not the weak and artificial new states but rather the old African tribes. And, in the absence of a crystallized class structure, ethnic affiliation persisted as a natural substitute. This picture does not really sufficiently explain the fierce ethnic competition detailed in subsequent chapters. A more adequate view is that the fifty-odd years of colonial rule wrought massive social changes affecting all Africans, that the post-colonial states are quite real sources of power and privilege, that class structures have already begun to form, and that the new "tribalism" is precisely a response to these changes. Ethnicity may facilitate individual adjustment to the new society, but it also functions as a disruptive tool of competition for scarce rewards and top positions.

The theoretical section of the book does not confront these issues directly. One exception is Immanuel Wallerstein's classic discussion of ethnicity and national integration in West Africa, but Max Gluckman's equally seminal interpretation of tribalism in Central Africa is unfortunately omitted. Good articles by Robert (mistakenly listed as Paul) LeVine on ethnic groups' mutual perceptions and Leo Kuper on religion and racial structure use African data to illuminate other theoretical concerns: Kuper's piece, for example, questions the applicability of Weberian and Durkheimian theories of religion to southern Africa.

The section on modern societies has a broad topical and geographical range and many worthy papers. Among the best are Leon Carl Brown on North African attitudes to Black Africa, Stephen Imoagene on causes of the Nigerian Civil War, Lionel Cliffe on Tanzania's low level of ethnic hostility, and Pierre van den Berghe on South Africa. Two papers on Kenya illustrate divergent approaches: Marc Howard Ross argues that since higher class and income levels in Nairobi have not led to any decrease in ethnic identification, there is therefore no necessary relationship between changes in the socio-political sphere and in the cultural one. But he does not recognize that the ethnicity is in fact "new," in part stemming from the socio-economic inequalities. John Okumu's detailed analysis makes this point, showing how uneven growth of social differentiation among Kenya's tribes led to an elite-based ethnic resentment. Most—but not all—of the papers were published elsewhere during the 1960s, but this does not diminish the overall usefulness and relevance of this volume as a text and reference work.

Religion

Spirits of Protest: Spirit-Mediums and the Articulation of Consensus amongst the Zezuru of Southern Rhodesia, by PETER FRY. New York: Cambridge University Press, 1976. 145 pp. $10.95 cloth.

BENNETTA JULES-ROSETTE
University of California, San Diego

Peter Fry has made a significant ethnographic and conceptual contribution to the literature on charismatic religion and political protest. His book combines a micropolitical study of apprenticeship among spirit mediums with a broader analysis of the relationship of spirit mediumship to cultural nationalism and change in Zimbabwe. A British social anthropologist, Fry declares the necessity for a more situational approach to ethnographic description as exemplified by Turner's 1957 work on social drama and Mitchell's 1969 approach to social networks. From this perspective, he describes both village factional struggles and the larger political currents expressed through the expanding importance of spirit mediums.

Fry openly admits that he came upon the topic serendipitously. While attempting to study political organization, he became increasingly impressed by the extent and vigor of contemporary spirit mediumship. When his research assistant announced his intention of becoming a medium, Fry recorded the process as a case study in village factional politics. His larger scale political analysis was put aside, only to resurface in the study of mediumship on the national scene. More discussion of Fry's personal involvement in the data collection process could only have strengthened the ethnographic orientation of the volume.

The study introduces kinship and village political structure among the Zezuru, one of the four Shona-speaking groups of Zimbabwe. The author shows the importance of Zezuru spirit beliefs in the interpretation of illness and in the rise of individual charismatic practitioners. Their reputations rest not only on demonstrated spiritual powers but also on political skills in formulating and solving local disputes. Mobilization of popular support requires the "articulation of consensus," the ability to strike a common chord in a local and, eventually, a broader constituency.

This argument, familiar in its general outlines, is then applied to the case study of his research assistant Thomas's initiation as a medium. Fry, however, does not take advantage of the richness of his own materials. He tends to reduce mediumship to political opportunism, when he might also have treated the mastery of mediumship as a form of knowledge in its own right, involving trance communication and personal innovations in ritual practice. Here, a consideration of comparative studies of Shona religion, including both traditional and newer syncretic groups (cf., Murphree, 1969, 1971; Daneel, 1970, 1971; Jules-Rosette, 1975) would have enabled him to expand the study of contrasting world views and to place the description of spirit mediumship in the context of other spiritual expressions.

Instead, Fry's analysis shifts to the larger political scene as the background for the cultural ramifications of mediumship. He describes mediums as politically autonomous cultural spokesmen, not constrained by the Rhodesian regime as are the traditional chiefs and the Christian missions. He suggests that mediums, drawing on nationalistic currents in Shona culture, can engender wide-scale political protest, as in the 1896 Shona Rebellion that spirit mediums led.

There is much of interest in this argument. Certainly, the history of African religious movements includes several cases in which revitalistic faith and nationalistic action were combined. The rise of Kimbanguism and the revolt of John Chilembwe are two well-known examples. Fry's implication that indirect and symbolic protest may be as important as its more explicit varieties is also sound. This section of the book offers important insights into the popular mood of the country in the mid-sixties, when a forced retrenchment from direct political action contributed to the rise of indirect expressions of protest.

If Fry's argument encounters difficulties, it is primarily through the lack of comparative material. His narrow focus on spirit mediumship is understandable from a methodological perspective, but it would have been helpful to include some larger theoretical discussions of the context of cultural and political change in Southern Africa. Both ideologies and utopias vary. Spirit mediumship as one possible combination can be compared with other ideological responses to political stress and cultural ambiguity. These range from the nativistic to the syncretic and millenarian and from the spiritual to the secular. However, the rise of indigenous or independent churches and modern political movements in Zimbabwe is ignored. The contemporary Zimbabwean scene offers the complex ideological and cultural mixture of a plural society in transition. Fry's analysis provides a poignant portrayal of one aspect of this scene. The task of integrating his description with the broader comparative study of cultural change in Zimbabwe today still remains. *Spirits of Protest* is, nevertheless, an important book that introduces an informative descriptive component to the overall picture of religion and politics in Southern Africa.

The New Religious Consciousness, edited by CHARLES Y. GLOCK and ROBERT N. BELLAH. Berkeley: University of California Press, 1976. 391 pp. $14.95 cloth.

ROY WALLIS
University of Stirling, Scotland

Sociology, perhaps even more than history, is often a child of its times. Conceived in the context of current euphorias and preoccupations, a research enterprise may survive the vagaries of parturition only to succumb to the later chill winds of infancy. The nuptual union of Berkeley sociology and the counter culture has produced such a progeny.

Glock and Bellah began their enterprise with noble purpose. The new religious and quasi-religious phenomena that breached the citadel in the middle and late 1960s were not at all respectable. Academic sociology paid scant attention until well into the 70s. But Glock and Bellah, perhaps more secure in scholarly esteem than the neophytes, had the courage to brave the scorn of polite intellectual society and take seriously the advances of phenomena of dubious academic virtue. I acknowledge the courage of the union, but have nonetheless to challenge the legitimacy of its issue. The basic mistake was to view the mixture of commitment and frivolity that formed the counter culture as a unitary phenomenon. Like so many marriages, doubtless not only in America, the spouse one thought one married was not really like that at all.

Had there been a new religious consciousness to study, this book could have been a success. But no *evidence* for its existence makes any appearance in this work and hence the commitment of Glock and Bellah to the validity of the notion in their theoretical essays is rather puzzling. While, on the one hand, Glock and Bellah are acutely aware of the heterogeneity that was the counter culture, they somehow became committed to the view that underlying this diversity lay the unity of a new mode of consciousness, a new cognitive and experiential orientation to the world. This they sought to explore through studies of a somewhat diverse range of new religious and quasi-religious groups and the adaptations of more traditional religious facilities, and through a survey of Bay Area inhabitants. The diversity of the groups selected for study suggests a certain arbitrariness because, while tiny groups, like the Healthy-Happy-Holy organization (3HO) and the Church of Satan, are explored in depth, the numerically much more significant group, Scientology, which flourished in the late 1960s merits no more than passing mention; the Children of God (by far the most dynamic of the groups to survive the decline of the Jesus people), Transcendental Meditation, and the Unified Family likewise; and the Divine Light Mission seems to have been included solely as an afterthought. Doubtless this had more to do with where the researchers wanted to spend their time than with any explicit decision rule.

To what extent, though, do these groups exhibit a shared form of consciousness unique to the 1960s? The Church of Satan is a theatrical version of magical and occult orders like the Ordo Templi Orientis, the Order of the Golden Dawn, etc. which stretch back well into the eighteenth century. The aim of its initiates of improving their worldly powers or success by supernatural means is also scarcely new and as Randall Alfred, the author of this chapter shows, its appeal is principally to those approaching or into middle age.

Indeed one can draw a broad division among the new religious and quasi-religious movements between those which reject the world as it is currently structured, seeking to create a new world in its interstices (3HO, Iskcon, Children of God, for example) and appealing primarily to late adolescents/early adults; and those which largely accept the world as it is but aim to equip their adherents with increased competence to negotiate that world and enhanced "self-realization" within it (Scientology, Transcendental Meditation, the Human Potential Movement) appealing far less exclusively to the young. That these two broad aggregates share a common "consciousness" seems to me a somewhat shaky proposition. Unfortunately Glock and Bellah also seek to draw into the same cognitive orientation political developments such as student and civil rights movements, and Anti-Vietnam War protests (much of the support for which was drawn from individuals with a thoroughly reformist and amelioristic orientation); and revolutionary groups like SDS, the Weathermen, etc. The fact that in a few notable cases individuals made the transition from revolutionary to religious devotees does not convince me that revolutionaries and religious devotees shared the same "mode of consciousness" (although I remain uncertain about how that concept is to be understood). The developments of the middle and late 1960s were a rag bag, and while they doubtless shared many causal antecedents, personnel, and even items of rhetoric, we do not get any closer to understanding them by extravagantly labeling this potpourri as informed by a new form of consciousness.

As a unified endeavour then, this volume is disappointing. It lacks focus and direction as a body of research. The generalizing essays of the editors stumble around in the dark trying to grapple with an opponent who isn't there anyway. Bellah engages in a curious guessing game about future developments having secured little analytical purchase on the origins of the crisis of meaning he describes. Glock, in an essay which I find difficult to take seriously, seems to locate the "scientific worldview" as both cause and content of the "new consciousness." This is not to say that these essays don't contain useful insights on occasion, but that as a whole they are analytically and theoretically very weak, and lack any clear definition of such terms as "new religious consciousness," clear specification of the domain to which they refer, or clear distinctions within it. Analytical and theoretical weakness is a problem throughout the book.

Most of the individual studies are of good descriptive quality, and therefore certainly a valuable addition to the available literature, but except for those by Stone (Human Potential), Ofshe (Synanon), Heinz (Christian World Liberation Front), and Alfred (Church of Satan), they fail to rise above the level of description, lacking any analytical insight. There seems to be an inordinate resistance to conceptualization, and only the editors attempt to utilize the data to some theoretical purpose. The individual studies range from the sociologically acute (Stone) to the theologically apologetic (Messer on Divine Light

Mission). Many of them seem to lack any extensive acquaintance with the relevant extant literature. Alfred, for example, could have benefited from some acquaintance with the historical literature on witchcraft before introducing his chapter with a discussion of the topic. Most of the authors could have benefited from a greater familiarity with the literature on new religious movements of earlier periods.

As a source of descriptive understanding of particular new religious and quasi-religious developments of the 1960s, this volume will undoubtedly find a place, but only a few of the essays justify any greater expectations.

Commitment on Campus: Changes in Religion and Values over Five Decades, by DEAN R. HOGE. Philadelphia: Westminster Press, 1974. 239 pp. $10.00 cloth.

ZELDA F. GAMSON
University of Michigan, Ann Arbor

In Robert Bellah's preface, it is clear immediately that the modest title of this book underplays the scope of the questions it addresses. Although the heart of the book is in a series of surveys of college students' religious beliefs, practices, and other values between the 1920s and the 1960s, the findings lead to an examination of the way historical events and cultural shifts affect personal commitments. In reaching to this level of analysis, Hoge supplements his college surveys with data from national sample surveys, newspaper and magazine accounts from each decade, and interviews with campus ministers.

Starting in 1966 with a reading course with Gordon Allport at Harvard, Dean Hoge began to look for early surveys of religious attitudes and practices among college students. He ended up with data collected at different points between the 1920s and 1950s at thirteen institutions: Harvard, Radcliffe, Dartmouth, Haverford, Bryn Mawr, Williams, Ripon, Clark University, Northwestern, the University of Wisconsin, the University of Michigan, the University of Denver, Syracuse University, and Los Angeles City College.

Hoge worked with researchers on each of these campuses and, between 1966 and 1969, he replicated the earlier studies, using identical questionnaire items with student samples drawn to match the earlier samples as closely as possible. Note that the institutions are not representative of colleges and universities in the United States, even in the 1920s. The author deliberately excluded those that would be likely to have high levels of religious orthodoxy—Southern and denominational colleges and universities. The sample, with the exception of Los Angeles City College (a community college with an open-door admissions policy), is skewed toward selective, intellectually demanding, almost exclusively residential campuses. Thus generalizing, even to the population of college students, is a problem. The author covers himself by saying the findings are "probably generalizable" to Eastern colleges and Midwestern universities. Since these institutions have disproportionately produced the intellectual, political, and business elites in the US and draw their students disproportionately from these elites, it is fair to say that Hoge has a study of the changes in and formation of values among these groups at a particularly crucial time in their lives. Whether and how these values are maintained and expressed after college cannot be answered by this study. Nor can we really understand value changes among students in less favored circumstances.

Hoge reports on many different religious and non-religious values and behaviors across the five decades. His major interest, however, is in changes in religious orthodoxy. I will, therefore, summarize the main findings in that area only. "Orthodoxy" is measured by a variety of items in the thirteen replication studies, all of which attempt to get at belief systems close to those of evangelical churches: belief in a personal God, in immortality, in the church as an infallible foundation for life, in the Bible as literal truth. Over all thirteen campuses, Hoge finds a long-term decline in religious orthodoxy. From the late 1940s to the late 1960s orthodoxy decreased by 13 to 23 percent, with the more prestigious colleges showing the greatest declines. That Los Angeles City College students showed a much smaller decline in orthodoxy (9 percent over the twenty-year span *vs.* 18 to 22 percent at Harvard, Radcliffe, and Williams in the same period) indicates the danger in generalizing from elite institutions.

There are striking short-term fluctuations within the overall trend: Orthodoxy began declining rapidly in the late 20s until it reached a low point in the late 30s. In 1940, the level of orthodoxy began to rise and continued to a high point around 1952–1955. After about 1956 it fell rapidly throughout the 60s. The middle 20s, then, resembled the early 50s and the late 30s resembled the late 60s.

Hoge quite correctly seizes on these shifts as indicating the effects of other forces. He empirically rules out demographic factors and shifts in college admission practices, differences between freshmen and seniors, large-scale economic indicators, family generation in the United States, urbanization, and rate of social change. While I am not convinced that Hoge's measures adequately tap some of these factors (job market shifts, for example), he does an honest, systematic job of relating them to his measures of religious change.

Other changes accompanied religious change. Shifts in the birth rate paralleled the shifts in religious orthodoxy; so did fear of Communist subversion, conformity to collegiate norms, commitment to military duty, and patriotism. Political activism for social change and criticism of college education went in the opposite direction. Thus, the middle 20s and early 50s were characterized by higher levels of traditional religion, fear of Communist subversion, conformity to college social norms, commitment to family life and patriotism, while political activism was at low levels. The 30s and 60s showed the reverse pattern. Regrettably, Hoge's painstaking efforts flag at this point and he does little more than sketch an explanatory model. How do historical events affect personal values? Following Durkheim, Hoge suggests that historical events affect ideas and sentiments directly and indirectly through their impact on the social integration of groups. Times of perceived danger—wars, fear of external forces (e.g., Communism)—raise social integration. High social integration increases religious commitment. Ergo, the orthodoxy of the 50s.

Hoge also offers a social psychological model—the "personal investment model"—to account for shifts in religious orthodoxy. Individuals have a fixed quantity of energy to give to institutions, ideologies, and leaders. For middle-class Americans, potential objects of investment include family, career, community participation, political participation, religion, friends. Commitments can shift, depending on the "returns" to the individual; since the total amount of energy available for investment is limited, strong commitment in one area reduces commitments in others. Involvement in larger social and political spheres shifts an individual's total package of personal commitments away from immersion in "private" concerns, including traditional religion. (This would be particularly true in the 30s and the 60s when student political activism was liberal or left, skeptical if not downright hostile to religion.) Lack of involvement in these larger arenas is "privatism," an exclusive focus on family, occupation, consumption, and friendships. At least in the 50s (if not in the 70s), privatism went along with religious orthodoxy and political conservatism.

I have smoothed over some rather rough ground. Hoge's book leaves many unanswered questions. The personal investment model is an interesting and perhaps useful heuristic for understanding how people shift their attention from public to private concerns. But it does not explain why these shifts occur across large groups at certain times. And it does not bring us any closer to understanding how historical and cultural shifts affect values, even in a group as susceptible as students at good colleges.

African Apostles: Ritual and Conversion in the Church of John Maranke, by BENNETTA JULES-ROSETTE. Ithaca, N.Y.: Cornell University Press, 1975. 302 pp. $17.50 cloth. $4.95 paper.

DANIEL J. CROWLEY
University of California, Davis

The conversion of a scholar to the values and beliefs of the people studied is a commonplace of field research. One thinks of Nimuendajú, Driberg, and perhaps Castañeda, but to a degree every anthropologist qualifies. When an upper-class Radcliffe and Harvard educated Black American woman with a Ph.D. in Sociology and a first rate mind converts to an obscure pseudo-Christian sect in Central Africa, the phenomenon is as significant as it is poignant. This monograph of conversion is a long, humorless, diffuse field report of research carried on, during three trips between 1969 and 1972, at Kananga (formerly Luluabourg), Zaîre (formerly Congo Kinshasa) and neighboring countries.

The Apostolic Church of John Maranke, also known as the Bapostolo (Luba) or Vapostori (Shona), claims over 150,000 members in Rhodesia, Zambia, Malawi, Zaîre, and neighboring countries, and is often confused with the better-known Kimbanguists and Kitawala among the 300 or more such "independency" sects in the area. One of a number of Shona prophets, Maranke founded the Church in 1932 on orders from spirits believed to have been angels who appeared to him in visions, and it is run after his death by his two eldest sons, Abel and Makebi Sithole, from their headquarters at Bocha in eastern Rhodesia (Zimbabwe). Maranke is believed to descend from one Chakazunkano, the host of the Holy Family in Egypt, whose son was healed by washing in the Christ Child's bathwater. In spite of international borders, linguistic and cultural differences, and the opposition of both the former colonial powers and the present independent governments, the cult has slowly grown and spread.

As one volume of a series on "comparative symbology" edited by Victor Turner, this tripartite work first describes the author's conversion through exposure to Apostolic ritual and belief system, then the expression of these beliefs through the rituals, and finally her concept of change by means of Christian imagery being grafted onto traditional religious beliefs and assumptions. The method of reporting through edited interviews with various church leaders, members, and ex-members, is oblique at best and often inconsequential, especially since the investigator resists any straightforward summary or formal analysis. Although sometimes poetic, her writing style is also maddeningly vague and imprecise. In attempting to describe the ritual and symbolism, and the beliefs and assumptions they represent, as they appear to the believers, Jules-Rosette specifically eschews any search for the "causal" factors behind culture change because she feels they freeze "the view of traditional culture and its diversity and assume that the member-valid reasons may either be reduced to a set of primary variables or ignored." Since for many scholars, that reduction is the primary duty of the social scientist, this book contains an element of controversy, but then all Apostles hope to die a martyr's death. Certainly gross simplistic explanations have done more harm to the progress of the social sciences than all the tomes of unanalyzed ethnography now moldering on our library shelves.

The appeal, of the sect for Africans is not hard to understand: all active members receive "gifts" of prophecy, exorcism, or healing, and all responsibility for worldly actions rests with God who communicates through dreams and visions. Men shave their heads, wear beards and long white robes, and carry long staffs, while women wear white robes and turban-like headties, but no jewelry. No medicines, neither traditional nor Western, are permitted, witchcraft and divination are forbidden but polygyny is not, and "inspired singing," trance, and even firewalking are practiced. The celebration of Christmas is forbidden as "pagan," and indeed Christ is mentioned only occasionally as "the great doctor." Tightly organized small communities of believers, mostly craftsmen, farmers, and small traders, practice a "biblical utopianism" that frees them from involvement in the political and economic turmoil around them. They are superior, "chosen," infinitely disdainful both of their own cultural past and of Western materialistic values, a dour and self-righteous bourgeoisie bent on edifying and converting the world.

In a classic academic "cop out," the most interesting aspect of this research, the appeal of this strange syncretic faith for the author is never explained beyond the fact that "the experiences that were central to my eventual understanding of ceremony were the most ineffable." As it happens, the symbolic system she describes turns out to be somewhat familiar, not unlike millenary sects in America and the Caribbean, and alas, not strikingly revelatory of the nature and processes of Central African culture change. As an earnest and painstaking ethnography of religion, this monograph makes a contribution, but it does not pretend to be a psychologically-informed symbolic analysis in the manner of Turner, the series editor. As a sequel, Professor Jules-Rosette owes us an explication of how, from her knowledge of science, she came to believe in immediate divine revelation, faith healing, and firewalking, that "impossible" feat reported around the world but never yet satisfactorily explained.

Sex Roles and Behavior

The Mermaid and the Minotaur: Sexual Arrangements and Human Malaise, by DOROTHY DINNERSTEIN. New York: Harper & Row, 1976. 288 pp. $10.95 cloth.

MIRIAM M. JOHNSON
University of Oregon

This is a tedious, repetitious, and labored book that nevertheless may be important for those of us who are concerned with the origin and perpetuation of male dominance over women. It represents one of a growing number of works which utilize psychoanalytic theory not to justify male dominance, but to explain its roots in order to put an end to it. These roots, according to Dinnerstein, a psychology teacher at Rutgers, lie in the fact that mothers (or female mother substitutes) have been the primary caretakers of infants of both sexes throughout the ages. While Dinnerstein is a feminist, she does not blame male dominance on men, but rather sees men and women actively collaborating with each other to allow masculine power to prevail in the world. Male hegemony must be ended, according to Dinnerstein, not so much because it oppresses women as because masculine "achievements" threaten to destroy the world.

Beginning with chapter 4 and in each succeeding chapter, Dinnerstein deals with some facet of male dominance and shows how the mother's being the central figure in the infant's life is related. She sees all of the following: (1) the double standard and men's propensity for jealousy, (2) men's fear and hatred for women, (3) men's associating women with both death and carnality, and (4) men's formal authority and history making propensity as being related to the early primacy of the mother. While it is not always clear what the crucial mechanisms are that intervene between early child care by women and male dominance, the central theme is this: Both males and females allow males to have power because it appears to be less of a psychological threat than the primitive and all encompassing power the mother had over us as infants. The mother is perceived by the infant to be not only the source of life and love, but also, in the very nature of the case, she also must appear to the infant to be ungenerous, capricious, restricting, enveloping, etc. In each of her arguments she assumes that female and male children react differently to the centrality of the mother because they are either the same sex as she is or different than she is. It is never explicit in her account, however, when or how it is that children learn about gender differences; neither does she deal explicitly with how heterosexuality is established. She mentions both of these issues in asides and footnotes, but they remain basically outside of her central argument.

Throughout the book, Dinnerstein describes the negative consequences that result from the raging needs of infants being focused exclusively on women, but she avoids spelling out just how fathers becoming child rearers can put an end to these consequences. Her failure to grapple with this question is a cop-out, but an understandable one, since it raises all of the theoretical problems which her analysis manages to sidestep. For example, it is not clear whether she is picturing a male and female parent nurturing an infant exactly equally or whether she is suggesting that males nurture male infants and females nurture female infants. Merely posing these questions points up a major difficulty with Dinnerstein's analysis—she consistently ignores the question of how sex identity comes about, while assuming that it does.

Dinnerstein, of course, is far from being alone in having speculated on the psychological consequences of the primacy of the mother in early child care. Apparently she is aware that much has been written on this subject and declares that she did not survey the literature "on principle" preferring to let her instincts be her guide. Almost all of the writing which Dinnerstein ignores has involved the idea that the primacy of the mother creates "identity problems" for the male: Robert Stoller, a psychiatrist, for example, has recently argued that the core gender identity of males is considerably shakier than that of females because the male's first experience is one of primitive oneness with a female. This is why male transsexuals (men who feel deeply that they are female) are so much more common than female transsexuals. David Lynn, an academic psychologist, has argued that the primacy of the mother means that females are able to identify with their own particular mothers while males must identify with an impersonal abstract conception of the masculine role. Talcott Parsons, has described the "bad boy pattern" as being the result of the boy's effort to become "masculine" in the relative absence of the father from early childrearing. Ruth Hartley has suggested that boys learn what they must *not* be before they learn what they are supposed to be. None of the above mentioned people, however, were explicitly concerned with explaining *male dominance* itself in terms of the primacy of the mother. This is where Dinnerstein has the important edge.

More recently, however, there have been attempts to make a psychological link between male identity problems and male dominance. Nancy Chodorow has argued that in denying the femininity in themselves, males must devalue women in general. Males need power authority and prestige to shore up their tenuous masculinity. In our own work, a group at The Center for the Sociological Study of Women have tried to carry this a bit further to argue that male dominance itself is a mechanism used by males to reinforce males' *commitment* to masculinity. This mechanism by which males come to shore up their masculinity by denigrating femininity, is called the "devaluation dynamic."

While Dinnerstein's failure to see the possibilities of the identity issue constitutes a problem for me, I am nevertheless glad she wrote the book the way she did, because it does open up some further possibilities concerning the psychological underpinnings of sexism. Readers who cannot accept the Freudian notion that there are vestiges of the outrageous infant in all of us will have trouble with the book. Those who feel that psychological explanations are mere rationalizations for economic explanations will find it impossible. It is steadfastly and unerringly psychological, but it does link up with a structural arrangement that can be changed. What if men did become childrearers?

Women in the World: A Comparative Study, edited by LYNNE B. IGLITZIN and RUTH ROSS. Santa Barbara, Calif.: Clio Press, 1976. 427 pp. $19.75 cloth. $6.50 paper.

JANET ZOLLINGER GIELE
Brandeis University

International Women's Year, 1975, so designated by the United Nations, lent significance to comparative studies of women already in progress and undoubtedly helped spur others yet to be reported. This book consists of twenty-four chapters on different aspects of women's status in almost as many countries. The result of a conference in the spring of 1974, jointly sponsored by the Department of Political Science at University of California, Santa Barbara, and the Center for Study of Democratic Institutions, it captures in still form a moving stream of thought that is still developing. Much of it projects useful lines for future research by suggesting in what different types of society and in what different aspects women's status may be measured.

One of the strongest features of the book is the implicit conceptual framework underlying it. The editors arranged their materials according to three major types of society: Western Europe and the United States, the developing countries, and the socialist nations (Eastern Europe, Russia, China, Scandinavia). The lazy explanation of women's status as due to universal "patriarchy" crops up in a few places. But in general the more sophisticated message of the book predominates: variations in the structure of societies account for the major differences in the treatment of women. Muslim societies restrict women more. Socialist societies are committed to liberation and give official support to subsidized child care and liberal maternity leaves. Women in Western Europe and the United States appear to stand somewhere between these two extremes. Perhaps as a result their situation is presented less clearly.

Women in the developing countries occupy a somewhat anomalous position. On the one hand, expansion of education and factory and clerical jobs opens opportunities to them even in Muslim countries as Youssef shows. On the other hand, the modernization of agriculture frequently eliminates women from traditional farming roles in such African countries as Ghana and contributes to the adverse impact of development on women.

If there is a single thread running throughout the book it is interest in the political status or power of women. But this may mean economic, legal, domestic, or religious status as well as office-holding or voting. Some authors define the issue broadly, others in narrow political terms. A major shortcoming of the book is that its comparison of women's status across societies is unsystematic, focusing on different dimensions in each country. Nevertheless, the resulting chapters provide useful background for the systematic work that will eventually come.

Particularly useful for reference are chapters by Lapidus on women in Russia, Means on Scandinavia, Van Allen on Africa. Rae Lesser Blumberg's analysis of women's changing status in the Kibbutz is the single most useful chapter for giving a comprehensive view of the interplay between demographic, economic, and ideological factors in the position of women. Salaff's documentary on Hong Kong factory girls provides an engaging glimpse at the industrial revolution as it occurs today. Other chapters deal with Colombia, Mexico, Italy and Ireland, France,

West Germany, Great Britain, the United States, Iran, Algeria, Yugoslavia, mainland China, and Sweden.

Toward a New Psychology of Women, by JEAN BAKER MILLER. Boston: Beacon Press, 1976. 143 pp. $9.95 cloth.

NANCY CHODOROW
University of California, Santa Cruz

Jean Baker Miller's *Toward a New Psychology of Women* will be a popular, widely read book. It is written in a moral, hortatory tone, and advocates what we all believe in—the reevaluation of emotions, caring for others, and cooperation. It also advocates collective struggle and conflict, but in such muted, gentle tones that it is more likely to be understood as suggesting individual and humanist solutions to fundamental, socially-generated problems of sexual inequality.

Despite her title, Miller's main argument is not new. Drawing on her clinical experience, Miller argues that our culture creates women as repositories for a myriad of devalued and denied psychological qualities: emotionality, connection to others, capacity to serve others, dependence, vulnerability, weakness, cooperation, and connection to one's inner life. These qualities are double-edged. They are a liability (women, for instance, are trained to be dependent on men, and therefore feel extremely depressed and empty when alone), but they are also the "strengths" we need to rescue our destructive, distorted world.

Because they embody needed strengths, even in repressed and distorted form, women are thus a psychological and cultural vanguard that can rescue us from our destructive society and attack sexual inequality. Miller wants to encourage women to recognize their strengths and to engage collectively in conflict, a practice that has been denied them. Miller here echoes those nineteenth century feminists and reformers who argued for the importance of women's special maternal and spiritual qualities for humanizing society and maintaining morality outside the home.

Miller explicitly advocates conflict and argues that women are exposing conflict, not creating it. (This latter argument hardly seems necessary today.) More strongly, she argues that conflict is a necessary and desirable part of the human condition. She draws from psychoanalysis to point out that conflict (in psychoanalytic terms, frustration, anxiety, and ambivalence) is necessary, and the very stuff of human growth.

Miller frames her argument in Neo-Freudian (or psychoanalytic "cultural school") terms. Women's psyche is a product of the "dominant culture," which trains women for certain qualities and teaches them at the same time that these qualities are bad. Women, for instance, are trained to tolerate feelings of helplessness, while the "dominant culture" is against such toleration. But her account bypasses those specific social arrangements and processes by which these qualities, and the feminine psyche more generally, are created. She gives us instead an implicit model of intended socialization similar to most feminist and social-psychological accounts. Thus, Miller omits the uniquely Freudian contribution to our understanding of psychic life: the interaction of conscious and unconscious; the ways that development does not proceed according to consciously held values and intentions; aspects of emotional life that we cannot describe or explain in everyday terms, because they have been repressed, or have become part of a psychic structure that is unconscious.

Miller couches her account of women's qualities in a stage theory of the development of psychoanalysis. Psychoanalysis has focused successively on two necessities to human life: first, sexuality (Freud), and second, the fundamental need for emotional connectedness and the centrality of vulnerability, dependence, and feelings of helplessness (Sullivan, Fairbairn, Fromm-Reichman, Kernberg, Guntrip). According to Miller, both these needs have been assigned exclusively to women. Miller suggests the necessity and probable arrival of a third stage, one that recognizes the human need for cooperation and personal creativity. (She defines creativity here as the ability to have an inner concept of personhood and to work internally with one's emotions.) Once again, she suggests, these qualities have been heretofore relegated to women.

One could argue with aspects of this model. I read with great surprise, as a fan of Freud's *Studies on Hysteria*, that society had accorded women the sphere of sexuality. But the problem is more general. Miller tells us explicitly on numerous occasions, that she "won't discuss subjects in the usual psychoanalytic terms" (p. 28). Now, it is one thing to avoid jargon and to refuse to hide behind technical terms. But in translating psychoanalytic terms to their everyday counterparts, Miller turns therapeutic insights into moralizing, and implies that simply explaining their problems to them helps women. I do not doubt that it does, but the therapy that Miller is then describing does not seem to differ much from feminist consciousness-raising, or from the help of your insightful best friend. It does not confront those psychic qualities and intrapsychic conflicts that are repressed and built structurally into development at an early age.

Miller's everyday language also flattens multilevel, contradictory intrapsychic and interpersonal phenomena and confounds description with explanation. For example, she points out that issues of vulnerability and helplessness are central to early human experience and talks of the terror of psychic annihiliation and threats to selfhood that result from feeling vulnerable in infancy and later. She then claims in everyday terms that women are allowed greater feelings of dependence and weakness while men must deny these. This claim is certainly true, but training for openness to or denial of vulnerability bears no relationship to the paralyzing anxiety that feelings of overwhelming vulnerability and dependence generate.

To take another example, Miller argues that traditional psychoanalytic ego and superego merely "represent" the culture, and give persons the right to act and judge their own actions according to criteria that benefit them. Since women serve others and experience their actions as mediated through others, they have no ego or superego. Her definition of the ego here is a totally conscious self-concept. It has no structural nor dynamic aspects, as ego-psychologists describe it, nor is it embedded in an unconscious inner object world as object-relations theoretists would claim. It is not even a Sullivanian defensive self-system. In any of these traditional formulations, one could make meaningful claims about gender differences in ego development, ego structure, intrapsychic ego, and object worlds, or the ego's particular choice of defenses. But Miller leaves us with the assertion that women are without psychic structure.

Miller's Neo-Freudian approach simplifies both psychological and sociological understanding. In opposition to Freud's biological determinism, she has substituted an equally simplistic model of direct internalization. Her model implies that culture is directly transmitted to the psyche, and substitutes cultural transmission for an account of the ways people appropriate and internally transform actual social structures and social experiences, through conflict, symbolization, defense, and fantasy. Sociologically, this same framework leads Miller to employ an unanalyzed, holistic notion of culture. Rather than discussing how specific social arrangements and institutions embody and perpetuate inequality between the sexes, Miller refers continually to "culture" or the "dominant culture" acting on women.

The looseness of Miller's formulations defeats her political purpose. Miller's case examples suggest that she is a skillful and supportive therapist, and has astute insight into the kinds of interpersonal problems women face. But if the book jacket comments are any indication, she fails to convince even her admirers that we need anything more than goodwill to overcome sexual inequality. None of these comments mentions politics or inequality, though these form the subject of two-thirds of the book. All depoliticize Miller's message, frame it in terms of personal male-female relationships, and wax utopian about possibilties for change. If we are to engage in political conflict, and successfully confront systemically generated structures of sexual inequality, we must forcefully return structure and conflict to the center of our analysis of the psychic and social world.

Of Woman Born, by ADRIENNE RICH. New York: W. W. Norton & Company, 1976. 318 pp. $8.95 cloth.

NONA GLAZER
Portland State University

A book by a poet is an unusual one to be asked to review for a sociology journal. But, it is of interest to sociologists because of its content, and because a book by Adrienne Rich, respected as a poet by many who are sympathetic or active in the women's liberation movement is likely to have a large readership.

Rich writes about motherhood as a social institution, especially but not only, as it is organized in the United States today. The mother of three sons, and now a feminist, she mingles historical analysis, and sociological and psychological insights with important bits and pieces of her own life. Basically, deromanticizing motherhood, she sees the feelings and preferences that contemporary American women were taught to accept as unwomanly and unmotherly (anger at incessant demands of small children, the absence of "unconditional" love, the resentment at being robbed of time of one's own) as human responses to the burden of parenting being assigned mainly to mothers. Rich's work is, in a sense, an easily understood statement which converges with themes being developed in several social sciences: she explicitly draws from anthropologist Sherry Ortner's thesis that patriarchical ideology sees woman as "nature" and man as the more valued "culture," while related statements on how the world needs viewing now from the perspective of women can be found in other writings—in Jean Baker Miller's essay on psychology of women, and in Dorothy Smith's essay on developing a sociology *for* women. A wide range of topics is examined: the normative view that women's sense of social and self-worth depend on childbearing and childrearing; how men control contraceptives as developers and dispensers as well as definers of the "right" methods, and how men control childbirth by defining it as a medical crisis; men's fear of women's capacity to bring forth life and the virtual suppression of the recognition of that fear until recently. After all, Freud's widely read essay on penis envy was followed, quite literally in the same edition of the journal, by Horney's long neglected essay on men's dread of women and womb envy.

Few sociological studies of motherhood depart so sharply from the conventional sociological wisdom which sees reproduction as the mainspring of satisfaction for women, and motherhood as a social practice which, in the United States, satisfied women while compensating children, at least implicitly, for deficiencies of society. (Bart and Bernard are exceptions.) Rich examines: mythologies of creation, including the prominence given to women's reproductive capacities, and the loss of such prominence and replacement by the cult of the phallus; men's gradual exclusion of women as midwives and as active mothers from the birth process; the monopoly by men on forceps; the organization of childbirth as an event to suit medical workers rather than delivering women (e.g., the prone position enforced in hospitals in this country). She also explores the relationship between mothers and their children as it is shaped by patriarchy which, devaluing women, teaches sons to devalue their mothers, and is the basis for a good deal of the lifelong ambivalence which men may feel about women, and which women may feel about the worth of being female. Rich also addresses the issue of how women may free their sons from patriarchical violence toward women, from acceding to war, from subjugation to the work ethic, and how women may free themselves from perennial mothering meant broadly to include not just a lifetime commitment to childcare, but to the at-least-as-burdensome, "giving, assenting, maternalistic relationship to men." Rich observes that the great themes of both Western literature and social science have been about fathers and sons, mothers and sons, and even, fathers and daughters, but never about mothers and daughters—a measure of women's low estate without a man. Finally, Rich explores women's violence against their own children. She closes with deserved skepticism about the solutions to motherhood as it is now organized which call for avoidance of present organization of childcare or of present science, or which see the solutions as resting in some special purported quality of females, or the rejection by women of their physical beings.

Many sociologists may not like this book. The scientific model is absent while the underside of sacred institutions—motherhood, patriarchy, heterosexuality, the antagonism of men toward woman—is exposed. To me, these need Rich's pithy examination. However, my sociological questions, such as about the continuing source of the battle of the sexes and the domination of patriarchy, are not answered to my satisfaction by her analyses. She does not explore adequately the social as distinct from the psychological context of men's fear and urge to subjugate women. I value the book, however, as a stimulus, as contributing to the sociological endeavor by raising issues quite forthrightly about the taken-for-granted. Thus, the book would be useful for educating sociologists and students in sociology courses considering the sociology of knowledge as well the courses which directly consider gender roles, sex stratification, childhood, and motherhood. I must also add that fewer men than women are likely to appreciate Rich's book not only because of the general nature of her analyses, but because she stays away from the dominant theme of the men's liberation movement—that men must be allowed the full dimensions of humanness by accepting the female in themselves—to concentrate on how women have been and continue to be deprived of authority and power in patriarchial structures. Read it: at the very least, it may raise your ire; perhaps, it may raise your sociological awareness about some of the unexamined dimensions of a major social activity.

Beyond Intellectual Sexism: A New Woman, A New Reality, edited by JOAN I. ROBERTS. New York: David McKay Company, 1976. 386 pp. $14.95 cloth. $7.95 paper.

ATHENA THEODORE
Simmons College

This anthology evolved from the first women's studies course offered at the University of Wisconsin at Madison in 1970 by author/editor Joan Roberts. Twenty-one women, most of whom were on the faculty at that time, representing various basic and applied disciplines—biology, zoology, sociology, psychology, political science, humanities, medicine, and education—comprise the contributors to a volume which is intended to be more "a survey of knowledge" than "a set of theoretical discourses on limited topics." In a real sense, as intended by the author, the book also documents the development of women's studies at the University of Wisconsin within an additional supportive network called the Association of Faculty Women, an organization which Roberts herself helped found. Attempts to raise consciousness in terms of both disciplinary perspective and political activism are apparent to a considerable degree in this original collection, but the autobiographical notes also tell us something of the politicization process as these contributors individually confront sexism and sex discrimination in the university and in the society.

Both undergraduate and graduate women's studies courses should find plentiful use for this book, whether the course deals with a specific discipline or a combination of disciplines. Virtually no repetition occurs in content from one article to the next, and readers should find no difficulty understanding the specialized language of any one discipline. Several of the articles present an overview of women's status in a particular area—in law, social work, politics, physical education, and home economics. There are also several cross-cultural views of women in Israel, China, Sweden, and Mexico (the last depicted mainly through literature); especially to be noted is Kay Ann Johnson's comprehensive view of women in China within the context of the Cultural Revolution and Rae Lesser Blumberg's proposal of a model of unequal sexual division of labor in the kibbutz based on a "push" rather than a "pull" explanation. New research data on female participation in mixed-set discussion groups are also offered by Jane Allyn Piliavin; and Ruth H. Bleier, Annis V. Pratt, and Germaine Brée present feminist critiques of theoretical, conceptual, and methodological problems relative to their own fields. While most of the remaining authors do not move in any particularly new or challenging directions with respect to both theory and content, they all offer factual information which saves the reader from searching for it elsewhere. Julia A. Sherman's summary of psychological facts about women and Hania W. Ris's assessment of the control of reproduction may be especially noted as useful summaries. Not unexpectedly, throughout all the writings is the message, either implied or outwardly stated, that things can be made better for women and here is how to do it. Together, these articles also present opportunities to evalute both the authors and the content of their writings on a scale of feminism and feminist thought, given some prior conceptualization. For example, with respect to use of language, here is Annis Pratt making deliberate non-gendered reference to women as "heroes," while Bonnie Cook Freeman makes recurring reference to women scholars as "he" and "his."

Roberts's contribution as author-editor of this collection cannot be ignored. Her own involvement in challenging discriminatory practices on her campus permeates her reaction to the articles in the book in the two beginning chapters. She presents a personal synthesis of power and powerlessness (she is a social psychologist) explained in the past through a "masculist cultural screen." Some may find such expression of her own individual convictions an unacceptable base for the theoretical framework she presents, especially in a book which professes to be a scholarly work and contains the undeniably scholarly work of eminent women. To such criticism Roberts would be the first to respond that she is challenging existing modes of action as well as modes of thinking, that she does not impose her own conceptions of cultural and political alternatives on any of the authors in the collection, and that the whole point of women's studies courses is to raise feminist consciousness and how better to do this than to provide food for polemical thought.

The book speaks strongly for the interdisciplinary approach to women's studies, an approach which advocates of this burgeoning field should encourage on their campuses, especially if only one course can be offered. The practicalities of size of institution, costs, and general resistance to equality for women makes such an approach almost mandatory.

Crimes against Women: Proceedings of the International Tribunal, compiled and edited by DIANA E. H. RUSSELL and NICOLE VAN DE VEN. Millbrae, Calif.: Les Femmes, 1975. 298 pp. $5.95 paper.

TERESA D. MARCIANO
Fairleigh Dickinson University

If in a religious age suffering was believed to hold the possibility of redemption, in a secular age it holds the possibility of revolution. Classic Marxian preconditions for the latter would in fact appear to be revealed in part 3 of this book, wherein the herstory of the International Tribunal is traced from its origins: discussions in the Redstockings Camp at Femø (Denmark), through the 1974 International Feminist Conference in Frankfurt, to the Tribunal hearings at which more than 2,000 women, from forty countries, participated. Having come together, face-to-face, and sharing their common grievances against patriarchy, the question now is whether (and indeed, how) the contradictions between consciousness and oppression will lead to overturning the old order.

The bulk of evidence at the hearings was offered through the narrations (in person or by letter) of individual women, a characteristic for which the Tribunal was criticized. The critics contended that the personal testimonies obscured the larger political analysis necessary to galvanize women against their worldwide oppression. The critique, and the responses to it by the editors, reflect the problems of those who will wish to continue the work of the Tribunal: how *will* women who are frightened, isolated, and poor, be encouraged to link their fates to a larger feminist movement? The individual testimonies were often the first chance the witnesses had to speak openly of their experiences. Analyses at impersonal levels could not have had the impact of the individual testimony. Yet, organized action on a large scale is the necessary next step to halting crimes against women. The proposals for change (part 2 of the book) assume this necessity for collective action to remedy documented injustice. Thus the question arises for this, as for any movement, of how organizational structures can be shaped which will crystallize and channel individual consciousness and energies, shaping them into a collective force, without muting the cause for which the structures were created. One answer may lie in the new form of collectivity which seemed to be evolving at the Tribunal, and which one observer described as "organized anarchy" that worked. What was called "anarchy" may well have been a novel, nonhierarchical form, of collective action.

Whatever the objections to personal testimony as a mode of raising consciousness, however, that testimony has stunning impact upon the reader. The queasy of stomach will find much to disturb them in the accounts of clitoridectomy, rape, wifebeating, femicide, forced sterilization, and torture. These accounts are not presented sensationally; their power lies in the steady continuity of the narrations, so that among all the crimes against women, these most physically brutal further assault sensibilities already outraged.

This book also places in better perspective the supposedly great strides women have made of late, toward achieving equality. By these testimonies from all over the world, women's progress is analogous to the great leap from the caves into the Iron Age. It leaves rather a long way to go before they reach this height of male achievement, the Atomic Era.

Swept Away. Producer: ROMANO CORDARELLI. Director: LINA WERTMULLER. Distributor: Cinema 5 (Los Angeles). 116 minutes.

CHANDRA MUKERJI
University of California, San Diego

Swept Away, a film directed by Lina Wertmuller, has become an object of controversy in feminist circles. A woman filmmaker has brought to the screen images of a man who beats and almost rapes a women as a way of subjugating her. The object of this sexual domination seems to deserve it. She is an upperclass bitch, demanding, critical, arrogant, self-satisfied, and apparently independent. The man who uses his physical strength to dominant her is a working class Communist. Given the chance, he uses his dominance to give her a taste of what the upper class has routinely dished out to the poor. The filmmaker is apparently condoning his behavior by giving it a logic that is hard to refute. This makes some feminists very nervous.

Swept Away is also a love story. The two major characters have a passionate affair once the woman has accepted her domination. As if it were not offensive enough that her domination is apparently condoned, the film also shows her loving her oppressor. It is a painful film for women to watch because this unpleasant woman only seems human once she has been thoroughly subjugated. But a careful exploration of her character reveals the logic of her bitchiness, her acceptance of male domination, and her love for the man who beats her. Though the painful process of examining this behavior and its sources, we can learn more about the film and its portrayal of the position of woman than we can by simply condemning the film as sexist.

As the story goes, a group of prosperous Italians are out on a yacht in the Mediterranean for a vacation. One woman, Raffaela, appears to be the hostess for this trip. She and her husband are an amusing, if difficult, couple. He is a politician who has some high post in the Italian Communist Party. She is an avid anti-Communist who is always arguing with him about his politics. She is exuberantly expressive, often funny, and very contentious. He humors her to some extent, allowing her to express her ideas, but he often ends their arguments exasperated, by walking away and ignoring her.

Gennarino, a leader in a local branch of the Communist Party, who is working on the yacht, gives Raffaela a dirty look during one of these loud discussions. That is all she needs. She vents all her hostility toward the Communists on this one man. Everything he does is wrong. He, as expressive among his peers as she is among hers, hates her arrogance and recognizes the political meaning of her criticisms of him. She is the main object of his class hatred just as he is the main object of her hostility.

Late one afternoon, Raffaela wakes from a nap, hungover, to find that most of her friends are off swimming. She wants to join them and orders the dinghy. It's almost dark, the wind is up, and the current is strong, but she wants to go anyway; Gennarino reluctantly takes her. The motor breaks down, and they are swept away.

Raffaela and Gennarino are as hostile on the dinghy as they have been on the boat; she constantly derides him for not being able to fix the motor. She is annoyed and inconvenienced; he warns her that they are in trouble; she is angry with him for frightening her. They drift for a few days. They spot an island and row to it, puncturing the rubber dinghy on the rocks; she wants coffee. He walks to the top of the rocks to see if there is anyone on the island, there isn't; she tells him she doesn't believe him. He refuses her order to climb the rocks and look again; she insults him. He dives for lobster, collects salt from the rocks, sticks for a fire, and cooks himself a good dinner. She demands that he share the food. He replies that since rich people don't have to share he doesn't either. He can try out being rich now. She unsucessfully looks for food, then proposes to buy the food from him. He says it's not for sale, but she can work for it by washing his clothes. She does. He gives her only a little food, and on it goes. In the successive scenes, he derides her for all the ways the ruling class has made other people suffer. He beats her, starts to rape her, but when she says she wants him to fuck her, he stops and demands her love before sex. She sits alone, stunned, looking at an ocean heavy with seaweed swirling against the rocks; she notices him kill, skin, and skewer a rabbit; she goes to him saying she feels like the rabbit and kisses his feet. They argue a little more and make love.

Later he finds himself lying on the ground with a ring of flowers around his groin. He is shocked, looks up, and sees her grinning with flowers in her hair. They continue to live affectionately, playfully, with him still in charge, until the day she sees a boat. She starts to wave at it, but she stops and hides. She tells him. He's angry and hits her, saying she should tell him when a boat comes. It's his decision to signal it or not. More lovemaking. She learns to sew. She says he looks bored with her. Another boat comes and he signals it. She is worried and afraid to leave. He wants to test her words of love. They are "saved."

They are picked up by a French yacht. He goes below with the workers. They asked how he survived with that "ball-breaker." He says nothing. Her husband arrives, and she says nothing. They get back to shore and his buxom wife is there to meet him. She has accepted a bribe from Raffaela's husband. Gennarino takes the money, buys Raffaela a ring, calls her up, asks her to meet him at a boat which can take them back to the island; he forgives her for not saying what has happened; he sends her the ring; she cries; he waits by the boat; she doesn't come.

The film is shot in five different settings—on the boat, in the dinghy, on the island, on the rescue boat, and on shore. These settings represent different political situations that constrain the behaviors of all the characters. When the characters are on the boat at the beginning of the film, they are acting out their class roles, either ruling class or working class. These two classes live separately on the boat. The ruling class does not ask the workers to join them in any capacity other than to serve them.

Adrift in the dinghy, Raffaela and Gennarino maintain the previous class distinctions, but they are forced to share the same lifestyle. Raffaela complains, still gives the orders, and demands that Gennarino do the work to save them. Gennarino still resents taking orders, but he accepts them.

On the island, the relationship changes. Stratification by class is replaced by sexual stratification. Using his dominance Gennarino demands that Raffaela give up her class characteristics. He successfully gets her to work according to his desires and needs.

Picked up by the rescue boat, Raffaela and Gennarino are separated, as they were on the vacation yacht. On shore, they communicate to each other only indirectly and in private because their class differences do not provide for public meetings. They are back in the class system, and they do not leave it.

These five settings contain the two major themes in this film. The first is the expression, destruction, and revival of the class system as Raffaela and Gennarino embody it. The second is the creation and destruction of a system of sexual domination. If we look more closely at how the characters are affected by these two types of stratification, we can begin to see the complex character of Raffaela's oppression.

While most critics of this film assume that life on the island is presented as a garden of Eden, the political message of the film is both more complex and more interesting if we do not interpret it so naively. If we take life on the island as utopian, then Gennarino is the only important character in the film; but if we take the class and sex stratification systems as two oppressive ways of organizing social life, then Raffaela emerges as an important character. She recognizes the limits of life on the island and her subjugation in both systems of stratification.

Raffaela suffers all the disabilities of oppression that feminists claim most women suffer. She is the wife of a politician who ignores her political opinions. She is the lovely, laughable fool that fluffy-headed women are meant to be when they try to understand and present their thoughts on any serious subject. She is also the prototypical bourgeois woman. She makes sure that everything in their life is done with "good taste." She is the family consumer who must be a critical observer of what is produced so she can make sure that the family gets only the best goods and services. However, all of these "qualities" do not make her a personal success. She seems like a bitch. The rented yacht provides the best in food and entertainment only because she continually complains when things are not up to her expectations. She takes both her social class and her role in it seriously. Because she is expressive, her failings are obvious. Because her role is unattractive, she seems to be a thoroughly nasty person.

But in the dinghy, she begins to show her dependence and helplessness. She does not question her dependence on others. She only bemoans her fate—being dependent on others who do not provide her with what she wants. Raffaela's subjugation on the island is the result of her helplessness. The only obstacle to Gennarino's control over Raffaela is her sense of class and he beats that out of her. Had she been able to gather her own food and provide her own shelter, there would have been no reason for her to return to Gennarino after he had insulted her. He was able to give her the taste of lower-class life because she had to turn to him for help.

Not only must she come to terms with her own dependence, Gennarino insists that she must *want* her dependence on him and love him for it. She does, abandoning her role as upper-class woman in favor of her role as subjugated lover because that is the rule of his game and she is dependent on him for her survival. She obeys orders. She is more attractive because her new role demands sexual charm, rather than consumer-competence.

When they are rescued, she knows that Gennarino expects her to express her love for him to her middle-class friends; it is up to her to maintain their relationship. What Gennarino fails to realize is that she has never made her own decisions or expressed feelings that were contrary to expectations. Back in the class system, she is still the docile woman. Throughout the film, she has remained compliant to the major roles imposed upon her (even with her complaints and her bitchiness).

Once we begin to understand Raffaela, Gennarino's character takes on new dimensions. We can begin to see the limits placed on him by his sexism. He does not understand how upperclass men can put up with the bitchiness of "their" women. At the same time, he is as vociferiously discontent with his class oppression as Raffaela is with her sexual oppression. Their frustrations provide a bond between them long before they are forced to recognize it.

Gennarino loses Raffaela not because she wanted to leave the island, but because he wanted to act as an upper-class man. He tries to show his affection by sending her an expensive ring, failing to realize that her husband could always give her jewelry.

It is difficult to watch this film and not hope that Raffaela and Gennarino will overcome "the odds" and "the situation" and in the end, make love, not order. But class and sex as bases for domination limit their actions even when they are removed from the social system that has taught them these social forms.

The strange circumstances that allowed them to care for one another were not of their own choosing; nor was it their choice to end the relationship. The end seems inevitable because they could not erase "social reality" from their consciousnesses. While the audience may hope that acts of faith and will can overcome social control, Lina Wertmuller makes it clear she does not think that possible. As long as people think in terms of domination, only fate can disturb social reality, creating occasional moments in which people can isolate and confront the contradictions in their social selves.

Social Change

Social Change and Stratification in Eastern Europe: An Interpretive Analysis of Poland and Her Neighbors, by ALEXANDER MATEJKO. New York: Praeger Publishers, 1974. 325 pp. $18.50 cloth.

SZYMON CHODAK
Concordia University

This book serves three purposes: (1) it is informative as to the history and social change of Poland, particularly that of the post-war period; (2) it reviews the large body of sociological research implemented by Polish sociologists; (3) it introduces several new insights on sociological stratification in Eastern European societies.

Albeit that certain of the approaches developed in this book might be more generally applied to studies of Eastern Europe, this work is essentially an analysis of Poland, as indicated in the subtitle, and not of Eastern Europe as the title suggests. Societies other than the Polish are discussed only in comparative context. Of the 514 publications quoted by the author, the majority are either Polish or otherwise related to Poland, and only 21, chiefly statistical manuals, pertain to Eastern Europe. The content is equally disproportionate.

In an interesting manner Matejko confronts his personal experience and opinion, cited reports on sociological research, official governmental data and declarations. Although it would appear that this was not the deliberate intention of the author, the three interpretations also exhibit a conflicting portrayal of social change and social structure. The official data quoted by Matejko demonstrate that Polish society is more or less egalitarian and conflict-free and developing at a steadily progressing rate, whereas the sociological data indicate that the society is not entirely egalitarian, and that, despite the common preference for socialism in general, the members of divergent groups differ in their expectations concerning most of the ideological and practical matters.

Despite an admittedly negative attitude toward the regime in Poland, Matejko nevertheless perceives Polish society as becoming not only more industrialized, but increasingly prosperous—a society in which workers and peasants have acquired higher social status and greater opportunities than ever before. Yet he also portrays the society as one of a disenchanted and frustrated people, and largely ascribes this state of affairs to their common experience of acute crisis of expectation. Matejko believes that under the "authoritarian rule" of the Party and state bureaucracy, the intelligentsia and the working class "enjoy the freedom of asking for more without taking responsibility for delivery" (p. 26, also 42, 86–88). This constitutes the main theme of the book. From Matejko's perspective, the major issue confronting Communist Eastern Europe, and Poland in particular, does not concern the degree of equality attained, but rather the extent to which the Party is able to fulfill the expectations of the workers and intelligentsia. He repeatedly tells us that all achievements are less than those claimed by the Party, and that they are not substantial enough to satisfy the needs and expectations of the population.

In addition to criticizing numerous aspects of social life, the writer discusses a number of conflicts inherent in the socio-economic structure of Poland, such as: (a) the need for greater economic efficiency which is prevented by the rigidity of the bureaucratic management; (b) the high social status accorded to workers contrasted with their poor standard of living; (c) the general declarative commitment to equality clashing with the elitist aspirations of individuals, whether members of the Party or of the intelligentsia. Matejko asserts that, despite the Marxist egalitarianism exhibited in ideological declarations, the Party has in many respects become an elite body, and that this is resented by other groups. He shows that the official data demonstrate, on the other hand, that the incomes of the highly-placed individuals and those of the average white and blue collar workers do not differ substantially (p. 19). In Poland most people spend more than they officially earn; some have two jobs which are not recorded in official statistics, and many have illegal incomes. Even more significant are the consequences of fringe benefits enjoyed by those in high positions, they can, for example, obtain goods in special stores, where commodities are much cheaper. Their *zloty* buys more than that of the average citizen's. Matejko is aware of this state of affairs and even occasionally alludes to it. Yet he nevertheless accepts the official statistics at their face value.

Neither the Marxist, the Weberian, nor the functionalist theories of social stratification are employed in this book. Instead, Matejko prefers to describe Polish society as essentially structured by occupation and encompassed by larger clusters of blue collar and white collar employees, managers, and intelligentsia. This could perhaps be transformed into a new theory of social stratification delineating a society encompassed by a hierarchical order of ranks. Although undeveloped, elements of such stratification theory are certainly evident in the book. The writer fails also to discuss the power elite as a separate group. Nor does he include in his analysis the military, the security forces and the police, which total approximately 400,000 or more and constitute an important part of the social structure. The still highly influential, albeit less numerous (about 18,000) clergy is also not included in his discussion. Hence the portrayal of the ranking order is incomplete. Even in view of this deficiency, I consider Matejko's book an important contribution to the analysis of social stratification within East European Communist societies, as exemplified by Poland. The book is of interest primarily for students of Eastern Europe.

Beyond Industrial Growth, edited by ABRAHAM ROTSTEIN. Buffalo: University of Toronto Press, 1976. 131 pp. $12.50 cloth. $4.95 paper.

IRENE TAVISS THOMSON
Fairleigh Dickinson University

The six essays in this slender volume address themselves to various facets of the transition to a "no-growth" or "steady state" society. While a few of the essays do contain some provocative ideas, this is not a particularly illuminating book.

Many of the arguments seem all too familiar. Thus, the opening essay by Maurice Lamontagne restates the arguments about "the limits to growth" and suggests that the institutions which have seen us through an era of exponential growth are not adequate either to handle the problems caused by growth or to effect a new steady state. What we need is a "new anticipatory institution" to study "alternative futures." Since issues like population growth and the rate of use of resources entail non-economic as well as economic values, and since their resolution will not be accomplished by market mechanisms alone, A. W. Johnson urges economists to abandon their devotion to the market model and to become more interdisciplinary.

Claude Castonguay and George Grant criticize the values of our technological society. Castonguay calls for "a reordering of priorities" that would have a reduced rate of growth as one of its consequences, rather than as an end in itself. Grant suggests that it is foolish to ask how we can construct a society "beyond industrial growth" while preserving and extending human values, because this way of formulating the question obscures the fact that our values and ideals "have come forth from within industrial growth." To think "beyond industrial growth" must mean to assess "the virtue of these concepts" (p. 119).

Vivian Rakoff attacks the images of a "new man" portrayed by Herbert Marcuse, Norman O. Brown, and others. He contends that psychologically, a society that has renounced growth will not differ radically from "the conditions which social man in some way or other has always had to endure" (p. 112).

In the richest essay in the collection, Charles Taylor analyzes our "addiction" to growth and explores the political problems that would be entailed if we were to overcome it. He points out that "the justifying image of ourselves as a vast interdependent enterprise of production is part of the essential rationale for social differentiation, one of the main underpinnings of social discipline" (p. 53). To achieve the steady state without losing democracy would require both decentralization and a strong sense of purpose.

Perhaps the problem with this book lies in the subject matter: it is hard to be both intelligent and original in dealing with an important and much discussed topic that nevertheless remains speculative. The difficulty in thinking about the future is made evident by the reminder that a scant fifteen years ago books similar to this one were addressed to the question of how we would distribute the wealth in an affluent, fully automated society.

Caste, Class and Democracy: Changes in a Stratification System, by Vijai P. Singh. Cambridge, Mass.: Schenkman Publishing Company, 1976. 158 pp. $12.50 cloth. $5.95 paper.

Baidya Nath Varma
Graduate School/CUNY

This book is a promising beginning in the study of the changing stratification system of rural India. Most Indian village studies are in the social anthropological tradition which emphasize holistic analysis of the caste system. When change in the stratification system is discussed, it is more impressionistic than theoretically confirmed. Singh has gathered data from three adjoining villages in Uttar Pradesh and has shown through quantitative analysis what kinds of shifts have occurred in the village social structure in a period of thirty-five years. His field work was done from March 1964 to May 1965, during which period he compiled statistics on all families of the three villages. Only the data on the stratification system have been reported in this book; he has more data which will presumably be analyzed later on.

Let me report some of his crucial findings. He makes a comparison between two time periods, one, 1930–1947, and the other, 1947–1965. During this time, ritual distinctions of the caste system were increasingly rejected in all three villages. The establishment of elected panchayats and cooperative societies helped in this process by opening up more opportunities to the lower caste. Factionalism continued to grow. The mean level of education increased in all villages, partly because of increased facilities and partly because of the elimination of barriers for lower caste children to attend school with upper caste members. Inequalities in the spheres of ritual, economic status, and power declined, but educational and occupational inequalities increased. The lower castes used their members and governmental programs to improve themselves, but the upper castes used education and higher occupations to bolster their strength. As a result the emerging stratification system became "more ordered and probably more rigid than the previous ones." The quantitative documentation of various facets of the emerging stratification system is convincing.

Some criticism is in order. The concept of "community influentials" used by Singh is fuzzy and needs to be refined. He either makes it synonymous with "power elite" or thinks of it as an amalgam of leaders identified for the period of 1947–65 by the reputational method. Neither Marx nor Weber, whom he reviewed extensively in the first chapter, can be of much help in this enterprise. (By the way, the first two chapters of the book are simple summaries of the stratification literature, but the last chapter, especially the theoretical application part, is rather superficial.) If he is interested in the power dimension of stratification or social change in rural India, the concept of "rural elite" will help. Similarly for an analysis of the role of panchayats, he should scan carefully the literature on its various modes of functioning throughout India. We hope that he publishes the rest of his data soon.

Dr. Singh deserves commendation for making even simple background data on caste speak so eloquently about the changing scene of rural India.

Social Psychology

The Quality of American Life: Perceptions, Evaluations, and Satisfactions, by ANGUS CAMPBELL, PHILIP E. CONVERSE, and WILLARD L. RODGERS. New York: Russell Sage, 1976. 583 pp. $15.00 cloth.

RICHARD M. COHN
Duke University

It is a refreshing break from journal articles dealing with the minutiae of human behavior to read a book whose goal is no less than to explain variation in human happiness. With such a goal the reader must expect some gap between intent and performance. This gap is evident throughout the book; however, the authors are sensitive to it and generally honest in noting the limitations of the empirical analysis.

Despite a few diagrammatic models and references to Lewinian "life spaces," the study is atheoretical and largely descriptive. Theory rears its ugly head only when the data run out, as the reference to "relative deprivation" and "adaptation" theories to account for the increased satisfaction with many aspects of life among the old. Yet, the empiricism is not "mindless" in any sense and the authors can not be faulted for not going as far as the data will take them.

The data are from a survey of over 2,000 adult Americans interviewed in 1971 (approximately 300 were reinterviewed in 1972). The interview covered no less than seventeen "life domains," ranging from "life in the U.S." to "friendships." Although the authors admit that the choice of areas was somewhat arbitrary, with the exception of explicit sex, they cover a wide range of experiences. The first section of the book presents analysis of the interrelationships of satisfactions among the "life domains" and their relations to a composite index of well being. The second section includes analyses of five of the domains (neighborhood and housing, the nation, work, family life, and the self). The final section includes chapters on the experiences of women and blacks, and in perhaps the best chapter of the volume, excellent discussions of: (1) the relation of objective conditions to measured subjective evaluations, and (2) the implications of this type of research for social indicators and social policy.

As noted above, the authors are honest with the reader concerning the problems of measuring the quality of life. An indication of this honesty is that the discussion of measurement error is an entire chapter early in the book; it is not relegated to an appendix. In addition to measurement problems (social desirability of responses, broadly-defined attitude objects, ordinal level measurement), the inability to "explain" variation in satisfaction in many of the "life domains" results from a general satisfaction of Americans with their lives. There doesn't appear to be that much unhappiness and what there is is only weakly related to poor objective conditions. The introduction of aspirations and expectations has only scattered success in linking experience with satisfaction.

This study is conceived of as a baseline to which future surveys may be compared. For purposes of monitoring the social welfare of the nation, such dynamic analyses are, of course, necessary. However, we can hope that future studies concentrate on improving (not necessarily making more complex) the measurement of subjective evaluations and do not replicate the measures used in this study solely for comparative purposes.

The importance of this book to social policy must be inferred from some of the "negative" findings. The weak relationships between objective conditions and subjective evaluations suggest a limited impact of social welfare programs on increasing Gross National Happiness. Furthermore, the authors note that those areas of life which are most important to overall happiness are not directly manipulable by governmental policy, e.g., interaction with spouse and the weather (p. 507). However given the current rates of divorce and migration to the Sunbelt, it appears the American population is capable of seeking its own solutions.

The Psychology of Loneliness, by DOROTHY MEYER GAEV. Philadelphia: Dorothy M. Gaev, P.O. Box 27291, Philadelphia, Pa. 19118, 1976. 160 pp. $3.95 paper.

ROBERT A. STEBBINS
The University of Calgary

This book treats us to a readable review of, and scattered new observations on, the psychiatry and psychology of the problem of loneliness in America. Its central thesis is that pathological loneliness plays a major role in most mental disorders and that mental health is achieved to the degree that pathological loneliness is overcome.

There are four parts to the book. The first, on loneliness and the inner self, covers loneliness and anxiety, relationships with our inner selves, and acquiring personal integration. The second centers on communication, particularly its role in love, and the effect of loneliness in such emotional disorders as depression, alcoholism, and obesity. In the third, and most sociological part, various forms of social isolation are considered, including loneliness among adolescents, women, and the aged. The final part deals with spiritual loneliness (the meaning of life established through our sense of destiny) as it relates to our fundamental personal values. The book concludes with the subject of loneliness and death and the provocative idea that we can transcend our time on earth by various means and thus prevent the sort of loneliness that typically attends the ultimate crisis. Suggestions for alleviating or avoiding loneliness are made throughout, which often contrast with the conventional psychotherapeutic procedure encountered here.

The only raw data in the book are clinical, being letters to the author from practitioners. Consequently, when an occasional assertion is implausible, no systematically collected data are available to back them up. For example, it is stated that the compulsive talker tries to overcome loneliness in an ineffective way (p. 59). Why compulsive talk should spring from loneliness is unclear. But there are also credible observations such as the one that self-actualization (a key concept in the book), when tied to a commitment to people, things, or ideas, leads to participation and reduction in or prevention of loneliness (p. 137).

Altogether, the book is a contribution to the field and an asset in undergraduate education. Symbolic interactionists will also find the heavy reliance on H. S. Sullivan compatible with their framework.

Passages: Predictable Crises of Adult Life, by GAIL SHEEHY. New York: E. P. Dutton, 1976. 393 pp. $10.95 cloth.

MICHAEL S. KIMMEL
University of California, Berkeley

It is often a difficult affair for a social scientist to write a review of a book which has dominated the non-fiction best-seller lists. Our predisposition may be to over-criticize the book for its over-generalizations and scholarly misconceptions. We may seek to belittle the book because it waters down serious scholarly research, and a writer (not an academic scholar) has rendered that research accessible to a mass market. The temptation to discredit may be inspired by academic elitism—guarding of scholarly knowledge and protection from accessibility —or from a sense that the work over-simplifies matters to such a degree as to render them vacuous, if not totally incorrect.

I think it is this last motivation which informs my reading of Gail Sheehy's *Passages: Predictable Crises of Adult Life*. Sheehy has attempted to rectify the great imbalance in the studies of the life-course, and do for adult life what psychologists have already done in their studies of childhood and adolescence: that is, to demystify the confusing and painful stages of adulthood.

Sheehy's version of post-pubescent passages has gained her a wide and devoted readership. Hordes of people are reading her book, and discussing it with mates, and friends; it has become a hot cocktail party topic. It is suddenly very fashionable to be caught in the throes of a mid-life crisis; many Americans are "relating" to both the premises and the conclusions of the book. Consequently, before turning to a discussion of the value of this book to social scientists, it seems important to examine the reasons that *Passages* has become such a popular book, and why particularly in the late seventies.

Sheehy undertakes to: (1) "locate the individual's *inner* changes in a world in which most of us are preoccupied with externals . . ."; (2) "compare the developmental rhythms of men and women"; and (3) "examine the predictable crises for couples" (p. 15). To accomplish this, Sheehy posits four stages of post-adolescent growth through which each individual must pass on his or her way to healthy ego functioning. Her argument is essentially that each individual must pass successively through a stage of "pulling up roots" (ages 18–22) during which the individual attempts to balance off the polls of the "seeker" and the "merger" selves, all the while admonished by the moral voice of an "inner custodian." (If "merger self," "seeker self," and "inner custodian" sound suspiciously like Freud's id, ego, and superego, do not be misled. Sheehy rejects the identity, although she acknowledges the similarity. But Sheehy's terms gain nothing in the translation to clever journalistic prose; what they lose is their analytical clarity.) Our roots pulled, we enter the "trying twenties" (22–28), task of which is to "shape a dream" and "prepare a lifework" (p. 85). But following the twenties, the individual is caught, wondering if the life-direction chosen will prove itself capable of blossoming into a successful mission and retain the emotional security of intimate relationships. This is "Catch-30," an interregnum during which we try to catch up with ourselves. Coming to terms with the painful decisions and indecisions of Catch-30 prepares the individual for the last of Sheehy's passages, the "deadline decade" (35–45) when the individual passes (if he or she is lucky) through a "mid-life crisis," a stage when the accomplishments of the preceding decades are suddenly less important and time seems to close in as one confronts concretely one's mortality. At the very moment in which the individual has made his or her greatest mark on the world, a large portion of the glamour fades.

Sheehy's second level of argument is that men and women experience these passages differentially both in their timing and in their effects. For men, the trying twenties are filled with career ambition at the expense of their spouses who may still attempt to attach themselves to a "stronger one." By Catch-30, women experience themselves as being left behind and through the "deadline decade" begin to assert themselves in constructing their own life work. By the mid-40s, then, the roles have reversed; the women have passed right by the men, who are now, themselves, caught in an anxious squeeze of time and age. Just at the moment when men feel most lost, the women are finally finding themselves. The consequences for heterosexual couples are obvious to Sheehy, who writes that, "Growing in tandem is virtually impossible in a patriarchal society . . ." (p. 90).

This, then, is the basic outline of Sheehy's passages and their differential occurrences and effects on men, women, and couples. But underneath this structure lies an important moral: in order to become a healthily integrated human being, one *must* experience these crises in their proper sequence. Early in the book she writes that, "Times of crisis, of disruption or constructive change, are not only predictable but desirable. They mean growth" (p 21). She reasserts this point in her conclusion, stating that, "the willingness to move through each passage is equivalent to the willingness to live abundantly. If we don't change, we don't grow. If we don't grow, we are not really living. Growth demands a temporary surrender of security" (p. 353).

For Sheehy, growth is a purely internal, individual phenomenon. Her central thesis is that "it is our view of ourselves that determines the richness or paucity of our middle years" (p. 345) and her last sentence reads: "The power to animate all of life's seasons is a power that resides within us" (p. 354). This thesis becomes acutely evident for Sheehy in her descriptions of the individuals she interviewed. One young man described himself as a political activist. About him, she writes "He is still at pains to describe himself as part of a political movement rather than as part of the humbler process of growing up" (p. 179).

From this perspective, it is not difficult to understand why *Passages* is as popular as it is. It speaks to people who are somewhat less than satisfied with their present lives (which, I suppose, includes just about everyone) and informs them that their pain, anxiety, and confusions are not only predictable but desirable; they are the necessary growing pains that are perquisite to advancing to a higher stage of emotional development. The sources of our problems are not to be sought in the organization of work, in impersonal interpersonal relations, or in a repressive social structure. The source of our unhappiness is internal and the pain is temporary. The story, after all, has a happy ending. Sheehy states, "One of the great rewards of moving through the disassembling periods to renewal is coming to approve of oneself ethically and morally and quite independent of other people's standards and agenda" (p. 351). The anxiety we experience is simply symptomatic of the larger "passage" in which we find ourselves; thus reduced, it isn't fully real.

As a best-seller, then, Sheehy has written a most American book, in which the rainbow always appears after the storm and clouds still have silver linings. But instead of writing "non-fiction," Gail Sheehy has written a book of what Philip Roth has called "useful fictions." But it is only when we examine the theoretical and methodological components of *Passages* that we come to understand both how fictitious and how useful her argument is.

Sheehy has based her theory of specific passages and the "mid-life crisis" on a selective reading of the literature on human development and an even more selective sample of 115 individuals who were interviewed at length. Nearly all interviewees were acquaintances or friends, and all belonged to what she calls "America's 'pacesetter group'—healthy, motivated people who either began or have entered into the middle class . . ." (p. 16). (For Sheehy, this "middle class" is populated by lawyers, doctors, advertising executives, and publishing house editors. It is hard to imagine who is left for the "upper class.") All but one is white and the one black man studied is hardly representative; he went to Hotchkiss (one of the leading prep schools in the East). From this sample, however, Sheehy has drawn her two substantive insights: that all adults pass through all the stages on their way to healthy, integrated lives, and that especially, a mid-life crisis is universal and essential.

The class and racial biases in such a sample are obvious. But these biases not only skew the responses; they permeate the entire structure of the book. Throughout, she punctuates her points with slick journalistic phrases that unmistakably reveal her sentiments. She writes of young men in their "Bolshevik jeans" (p. 67), and the political impact of the student movement as "commonplace violence" (p. 75). Sheehy implies that the demands of welfare recipients are symptomatic of the "systemic disease in America": dependency (p. 102). But most important here are the ways in which Sheehy's class biases inform the entire structure of her argument.

She argues that risk-taking is a necessary prerequisite for growth, but that "The willingness to risk is based on a history of accomplishment" (p. 142) and that "It costs money to have a mid-life crisis" (p. 284). She asserts flatly that "middle age is the time of maximum influence" (p. 342). What emerges here is that these "universal passages" are universal only to a well circumscribed group of Americans, and that others *i.e.*, all but upper middle class whites are systematically excluded from passing through these stages, and, by extension, of achieving a full and meaningful life.

But if the source of all growth and change is our individual selves, who can the working class man and woman blame for the structural preclusion from having a mid-life crisis (assuming, of course, that they would want one)? Nobody but themselves. Thus very subtly, Sheehy has replicated the ideology of "blaming the victim."

But it is not only Sheehy's methodology which is suspect, nor simply the ideological biases that underlie her work. The empirical inferences that she draws from her research can hardly be taken as givens. Her thesis centers around the most critical of passages: the mid-life crisis. Yet the research from the longitudinal study at the Institute of Human Development at the University of California, Berkeley (which she cites a number of times in the book) has found no evidence of a mid-life crisis as a predictable passage of adult life. Moreover, the data from the study categorically reject the very notion of a mid-life crisis. Without this critical juncture in adult development, Sheehy's entire argument collapses internally.

Gail Sheehy has not sought to explain the pain and frustration of adult life in the United States in structural terms; terms that would allow her to locate the sources of strains on individuals as part of larger social forces. The paradox she observes (that just at the moment in one's life when things seem to be falling into place, they also begin to fall apart) is reduced entirely to an individual focus. Family dynamics are reduced to the interactions among individuals experiencing different crises resulting from different ages. (She can be said to offer the mid-life crisis ridden parent the opportunity to say to a child, "Don't bother me with your adolescent acting out. This is *my* crisis!") She has removed social structural explanation as a mode of analysis of the behavior of individuals.

What the reader gains from *Passages* is not, therefore, an analysis of the individual attempting to understand the structural underpinnings of alienation. Rather we are presented with a solipsistic vision of individual dynamics. Rather than an understanding of our adult passages, Sheehy has delivered a palliative to the upper middle class; a well-written assurance that we are not alone in our pain and fear. That misery seems still to require the company of a book which tells us that basically we're all O.K.

Theory

Existentialism and Sociology: A Study of Jean-Paul Sartre, by Ian Craib. New York: Cambridge University Press, 1976. 242 pp. $18.50 cloth.

Dean MacCannell
University of California, Davis

The most recent generation of British sociologists is fascinated by the idea of combining French and American social theory in a new synthesis, a humanist structuralism. Toward this end, a surprising volume of secondary interpretations of theory has been produced including Steven Lukes's admirable *Emile Durkheim*. J. Maxwell's (forthcoming) analysis of theories of suicide, and Ian Craib's *Existentialism and Sociology*. Craib's book contains a close reading of Sartre and, based on that reading, an underinterpretation of Goffman's work, an overinterpretation of Gouldner's, and a nicely balanced section on Garfinkel.

Craib is at his best re-working philosophical terms and issues so as to make them useful for sociologists. There is a good discussion of causality (pp. 28–29) and an excellent critique of the ethnomethodologists' notion of "shared assumptions" as a mode of consciousness (p. 78 ff.).

Craib aims to establish a Sartrean, existential version of sociology. He believes that this can be accomplished by pure intellectual force, unsupported by research findings. The foundation of his claim is a relatively unproblematical theory of the self as "pure negativity" and "pure possibility." Craib's and Sartre's argument runs into real difficulty, however, at the moment this mutable self is displaced from their philosophical systems into the everyday world. Everyday life, jammed with objects, accidents, and willful others, negates the negativity of the self and turns it into a thing. In everyday situations, that is, the self appears to have identity, personality, and a status in the hierarchy of things. Craib is not sensitive to, nor aware of, the recent progress in deciphering the problematic of the self made by students working in post-phenomenological modes: semiotics, criticism, and ethnographic studies of familiar settings. Even when he confronts the published findings of others which have been placed at his disposal, for example Goffman's study of hospital underlife or Garfinkel's work on suicide prevention, Craib belittles their observations. He seems to want to interpret the empirical social world out of existence.

The motivations for writing such a book are very complex. Like much of Sartre's non-fiction, what is passed off as theoretical and methodological discussion is, on close examination, a thinly disguised political pamphlet, an effort to re-direct social change into bourgeois-idealist channels. Craib wants to claim that "existential freedom" operates in empirical social situations. He wants prison and asylum inmates (the examples are his) to deny their bonds. This is possible, of course, but it requires more than Craib believes, more than an act of consciousness. It requires (socially) organized, revolutionary struggle. Craib has not merely failed to comprehend social life on other than naive psychological grounds, he has made it his mission to establish these grounds as the only possible ones.

There are numerous and important sociological studies based on Sartre's work including, if only by indirect influence, Sudnow's study of the glance and Goffman's study of normal appearances-for-others. But these studies only develop interesting Sartrean concepts, they are not conceived as crucial tests of his "existentialism." Craib follows Sartre too closely, reproducing his errors and weaknesses as well as his strengths.

The issues here are old and worn out. An early materialist, Feuerbach, was criticized by Marx for seeing change as a kind of individual restlessness, for failure to comprehend structure and order in the ensemble of social relationships, for an inability to understand consciousness in other than psychological terms, to understand class consciousness, for example. In the early 1960s Claude Lévi-Strauss attacked Sartre's system in terms which precisely parallel Marx's critique of Feuerbach. Unfortunately, for reasons which should by now be evident, the same criticism applies to Craib's book. Sociology should transcend the terms of this fusty debate.

Towards a Social Ecology: Contextual Appreciations of the Future in the Present, F. E. EMERY and E. L. TRIST. New York: Plenum Publishing Corporation, 1975. 239 pp. $5.95 paper.

RICHARD O. MASON
University of California, Los Angeles

This is a book for the contemplative social scientist. Occasionally, a social scientist ought to reconsider his or her discipline, one's role and career in it, and the future of the social entities one studies. If you are in this kind of reflective mood, Emery and Trist provide considerable food for thought.

The first question to ask about a discipline is whether its basic assumptions are fruitful and defensible. The authors argue that a new root metaphor is needed for social sciences, one which stems by analogy from biology. A social entity is to be studied as an open system—a set of interrelated elements which has exchanges with its environment. Social entities are not to be viewed as mechanistic cause and effect machines. Rather social entities are to be viewed as living systems whose most fundamental, genotypical characteristics are the system/environment relations that determine survival. Consequently, "ecology" is the operative word in the book's title. Vitalism replaces mechanism as social science's fundamental assumption.

The living systems metaphor implies that a social entity not only must satisfy the basic need for maintenance of the integrity and continuity of the system itself; but also, it must create new structures and functions to cope with the changing dimensions of its environment. That is, it must be adaptive. A fourfold, hierarchical taxonomy of social environments is developed based on the complexity of an environment's *causal texture* —the degree to which relevant external, independent variables are causally related or interwoven with each other. The most complex environment and most challenging for adaptive behavior is the "turbulent field." In the turbulent environment a system is affected by processes which emerge dynamically as an unplanned consequence of the system's own actions.

The use of a biological metaphor is not new. It has been around in sociology since the social Darwinism of William Graham Sumner in the late 1800s. Emery and Trist, however, break new ground by applying it to the analysis of environments, the trends in environments and the implications for contemporary social systems.

The authors argue that many social organizations are currently in, or moving toward a turbulent environment. In the first part of the book, Emery anticipates some of the effects of the turbulent environment during the next thirty years. He develops open systems concepts and methods for dealing with society's transition to the turbulent environment. In the second part, Trist presents a series of analyses of the implications of this transition. The objects of his inquiry include science policy, technical innovation, social change, welfare, insurance, new personal values, and other contemporary social issues.

Much of Emery and Trist's argument rests on a subtle, but fundamental concept of livings systems—the notion of "directive correlation," as first formalized by Sommerhof. Highly rigorous definitions exist; but the main idea may be stated simply. A system is directively correlated with its environment if (a) its initial response R_{t0} at time t_0 produces both an environmental state E_{t1} and a response R_{t1} at time t_1, and (b) R_{t1} and E_{t1} further interact to co-produce a desired goal state at time t_2. Directive correlation is not just a theoretical postulate for Emery and Trist, it is the basis of a manifesto for social science and social scientists: "The survival and growth of social science presupposes a role in which it [social science] enhances the range and degree of directive correlations that men can form between themselves and their environment" (p. 9).

The concept of directive correlation implies that a scientist's research findings are also a part of the response array which help give rise to future environments. Science is a part of (and perhaps a partial source of) the turbulent environment the authors see encroaching upon us now. This has implications for the personal decisions scientists make concerning the kind of research to untake and their roles, qua scientists, in society.

Emery and Trist present guidelines for making these decisions. They believe that more social science should be problem-oriented or "domain based." Research should link a group of sciences to a major sector of social concern. This, of course, is an issue of current political focus. In chapter 8, Trist anticipates much of the present controversy in Washington concerning the role of science in society, and the relative social value of applied research versus basic research. The authors' position in this debate is clear: "the social sciences can play an active role in the next decades, not simply a passive one—they can seek to modify their social environment so that men can better pursue the ends they desire and not be left to adapt blindly to whatever emerges" (p. 5).

For some readers the book represents a substantial departure from their own paradigm of research. They may abhor both the theoretical and practical implications of the book. Some readers will take exception to the lack of rigorous empirical support for some of the statements. However, many will be excited by its direction and vision. No reader should be unaffected.

The book is essentially a collection of essays, many of which are emerging for the first time from a very effective "xerox underground" among organizational theorists and socio-technical systems analysts. It suffers from occasional voids, redundancies, and slips in integration. As the authors acknowledge, this book is not intended as the definitive work but, rather, a step *Towards A Social Ecology*. The step is timely and provocative.

The Asiatic Mode of Production: Sources, Development and Critique in the Writings of Karl Marx, by LAWRENCE KRADER. Assen, The Netherlands: Van Gorcum & Company, 1975. Distributed by Humanities Press. 454 pp. $39.75 cloth.

GAIL OMVEDT
University of California, San Diego

A recent resurgence of interest in Marxist theory as well as the growing sophistication of studies of nonwestern societies have led to a revival of interest in Marx's own attempts at analyzing pre-capitalist systems. It is natural that the concept of the Asiatic Mode of Production (AMP), historically one of the most controversial of his theories, should be reassessed. The attraction of the concept was to provide a useful theoretical tool to understand differences between European feudalism and nonwestern societies with no stable landlord class between the peasantry and the state, where the state itself gains power from directly organizing productive forces, especially irrigation (but other forms of labor as well). The idea seemed appropriate not only for "Asia" (an unnecessary geographical reference) but for many early state systems in Mesopotamia, Egypt, and America.

However, there have been important ideological problems in the development of the concept. Ideas of "oriental society" and then of the "asiatic mode" arose largely as a way in which the West explained the "East" to itself as something inherently different and unique, emphasizing first despotic power and then the unchanging nature of the underlying village society. Even Marx himself, though sometimes viewing the AMP as the first form of development of a class society out of primitive communism, also often used it to imply a dead end to development, and most of his data on India came from its British conquerors, concerned with justifying their own replacement of the Mughals' "despotic" power. Thus, the idea was conveyed that a society with an AMP, because of the unchanging quality of its communal villages, had no inherent dynamism of its own, and that therefore Western imperialism was justified in forcibly breaking up the system to lay the way for future development of productive forces. For these reasons, the concept was not only rejected by the Comintern under Stalin, but also by Asian Communists themselves, including the Chinese in debates in the 1920s and later by Indian Marxists such as D. D. Kosambi. Conversely, when Karl Wittfogel developed his own version of the theory of "Oriental despotism," it was intended to reveal Russia and Chinese Communist societies as the inheritors of this state despotism.

It is only recently, in fact, that the AMP has come in for more serious scholarly examination. British and French scholars (many of them students of Louis Althusser), including third world scholars, have been re-examining this and other pre-capitalist modes, asking whether the AMP is *theoretically consistent* as a Marxist concept, or examining its *validity* and reinterpreting and developing it. No longer is the governing question why capitalism developed in Europe rather than someplace else (many reject the question as such), but rather what were the specific characteristics and dynamics of development of varying societies.

In this context, Lawrence Krader's massive study of the historical development of the concept, and Marx and Engels's use of it, would appear welcome. In part, Krader reveals some of the ideological factors mentioned above. But Krader claims to do more than this: he claims to "develop the theory in a systematic form and examine both the theory and its sources critically" (p. xii). This is precisely what he fails to do. He does not try to assess the logical consistency of the theory; he does not ask whether it is empirically valid; he does not try to develop or revise it; and he seems unaware of the work of those who are making these attempts. The book is thus not a work in sociology at all (certainly not Marxist sociology) but a study in the history of ideas. Even as such, its awkwardness in style of writing and organization make it less than useful.

Finally, Krader tends throughout the book to forget the difference between concept and reality and to refer to "Asiatic society" as if he were describing not an idea but the actual societies (India, China) themselves. The result is a confusion between concept and reality and a substitution of unchecked speculation for serious examination of a theoretical concept.

Culture and Communication: The Logic by Which Symbols Are Connected, by EDMUND LEACH. New York: Cambridge University Press, 1976. 105 pp. No price listed, cloth.

ROBERT D. LEIGHNINGER, JR.
SUNY/Oswego

Those struggling to domesticate the vigorous and protean manifestations of French Structuralism have found British anthropologist Edmund Leach a welcome intermediary. His small book on Lévi-Strauss for Viking's Modern Masters series was a lucid introduction to a complex and jargon-filled world. *Culture & Communication* is a primer of structuralist method that may appeal to those sociologists of science, religion, or the arts who are beginning to look beyond their institutional areas to a general sociology of culture.

In a very short space Leach introduces what he frankly calls a "jargon apparatus," a lattice of language characteristics, and weaves around it a variety of standard cultural phenomena: magic, religious ritual, hierarchy, mating rules, etc. The jargon is justified by its ability to decode the highly condensed messages that Leach believes are communicated within a culture by ritual. These multi-level, "symphonic," ritual communications have sufficient detail and complexity to necessitate this kind of treatment, he argues. Leach provides one full-scale application to illustrate the merits of his apparatus, an analysis of sacrifice using the Bible as ethnography.

Whether or not the results are worth the effort will probably depend on whether one accepts the many assumptions underlying the approach. Leach is open about these assumptions, though they pop up throughout the book rather than at the outset. They include an avowedly rationalist epistemology (though Leach sees this as a dialectical complement to empiricism rather than a competitor), a functionalist belief that "everything is meshed with everything else" (p. 5), a conviction of the existence of a symbolic alphabet with grammar and syntax that constitutes all verbal and non-verbal culture, and the traditional structuralist insistence that symbols come in binary sets. Other definitions and distinctions, while admitted to be arbitrary or tentative or convenient, are nonetheless held to with a simplemindedness that belies the supposed subtlety of the approach. An important example is a distinction between technical and expressive actions upon which quite a lot of the argument depends.

If one can tolerate all of this, the resultant perspective is both intriguing and disturbing. Some of Leach's explanation of boundary-making in space and time seems beautifully apt. His recurrent portrayal of non-scientific thought processes as a "mistake" of metaphor for metonymy raises some interesting questions about religion and art as well as about Leach's positivist biases. The appeal and the peril of Leach's structuralism is perhaps best expressed in the observation that

> the whole process of carving up the external world into named categories and then arranging the categories to suit our social convenience depends upon the fact that, although our ability to alter the external environment is very limited, we have virtually unrestricted capacity for playing games with the internal-

ized version of the environment we carry in in our heads (p. 36).

The Concept of Structuralism: A Critical Analysis, by PHILIP PETTIT. Berkeley: University of California Press, 1975. 117 pp. $8.50 cloth.

INO ROSSI
St. John's University, New York

Pettit offers a brief and clear exposition of the linguistic foundations and main types of structural analysis derived from the linguistic model. He discusses Lévi-Strauss's development of the linguistic model and the scientific value of the linguistic model for semiology in general. The overall thesis of the author is that the "scientific" framework of structuralism is useful to organize data and formulate analyses in homegenous categories but it cannot produce testable and cumulative scientific theory (p. 114 ff).

I do not find Pettit's argument always relevant nor do I find his argument conclusive. To begin with, the author restricts the term "structuralism" only to semiotic, that is linguistically based, structuralism with the exclusion of other important forms of structuralism, such as those of Piaget and Dumezil. Secondly, his discussion of the linguistic model does not extend to Hjelsmev who has influenced a large segment of the semiotic movement. Thirdly, the author arbitrarily selects two linguistic principles as the bases for his critique. He considers the sentence as the unit of linguistic model and argues that most forms of structuralism cannot produce a language in relationship to which a given text can be considered as a sentence. But one does not see how this criticism applies, for instance, to Lévi-Strauss's analysis based on the notion of distinctive features. Moreover, Pettit argues that linguistic analysis has to be based on an "intuitive" judgement of the grammaticality of a sentence, a criterion on which all forms of structuralism fail (pp. 47, 72, 97, 114). Whereas, this notion may fit the author's phenomenological orientation, it does not seem appropriate to evaluate Chomsky's and Lévi-Strauss's quest for deep (unconscious) structures.

According to Pettit, structural analysis as practiced by Lévi-Strauss has the merit of producing a "language" and using a hypothetico-deductive model, but it does not fully qualify as a "science" because it produces unfalsifiable hypotheses, operates transformations without contraints, and uses too abstract descriptive units. The end result is that Lévi-Strauss (and all other proponents of structuralism) raise interesting questions but do not produce answers which can be subsumed within a system of scientific laws and permit the deduction of particulars (pp. 114–115). Obviously, this criticism is based on a neopositivist (Popperian) conception of science and a failure to draw appropriate conclusions from the thesis, i.e., that understanding of how humans produce meaning may be different from the understanding of how natural systems work (see p. 117). Lévi-Strauss has repeatedly stated that he applies linguistic and mathematical notions in an analagous and tentative fashion since he tries to map the logical structure of symbolic systems, a pioneer task previously held impossible or not relevant. Considerations on the importance and necessarily tentative nature of this task seems totally absent from the thrust of Pettit's argument.

All in all, the book may prove a useful introduction to the assumptions of semiotic structuralism and its main varieties with the provision that the reader becomes aware of the author's restricted conception of modern structuralism and its underlying linguistic model as well as of the phenomenological and positivistic bases of his criticisms.

Adam Smith's Sociological Economics, by DAVID A. REISMAN. New York: Barnes & Noble, 1976. 274 pp. $21.50 cloth.

LOUIS SCHNEIDER
University of Texas, Austin

This book has many valuable features. Its author knows Adam Smith well and he has provided a kind of near-encyclopedic survey of Smith's work which can be used as a handy guide by any student: the concise subheadings of the seven chapters will quickly lead one to wanted material. There are, however, certain shortcomings which it seems to the reviewer should be kept in view as one works with this generally very fine volume.

There are obviously social or cultural "influences" in economic life, just as there are economic "influences" in social life. Adam Smith was well aware of such influences. His economics, in any case, emerged from a larger matrix of moral philosophy and natural law and bears plain traces of the generous scope this might well suggest. Numerous earlier commentators have stressed that his economics should be seen in a wider sociological context. But Reisman in the end leaves us rather in the dark about the phrase, "Smith's sociological economics." There is a sort of small foray into sociology here; another, there. And there are important matters too: consumption patterns have evident "sociological" backgrounds; Smith's conception of social evolution has evident "economic" backgrounds. (Reisman himself draws adroitly on sociological literature to illumine or expand various positions of Smith's.) Precisely, what is *in* "sociological economics," at least of the Smithian variety? A statement on this, pulling together Smith's (and Reisman's) relevant views, might have been most helpful. Such a statement is lacking.

Reisman is insufficiently alert to Smith's sense of dealing with an economic system, to his "detailed and elaborate application to the wilderness of economic phenomena of the unifying concept of a co-ordinated and mutually interdependent system of cause-and-effect relationships," in Jacob Viner's words (from his "Adam Smith and Laissez Faire"). More explicit treatment of system would have improved Reisman's understanding of Smith as a "functionalist." Somewhat related to this is what appears to the reviewer to be another insufficiency. Reisman conceives this study as one in the history of ideas, but he barely alludes to certain significant tones in Smith which remind us of a Hegel, a Vico, or a Mandeville, and which are sounded in the *Moral Sentiments* and (briefly but quite clearly) in the *Wealth of Nations*—tones whose character Reisman himself does intimate when he writes (p. 65) that "the rational businessman takes on for Smith the dimensions of a Hegelian world-historical individual, the unwitting contributor to the realization of philosophy on earth." Smith quite explicitly suggested the construction of social systems with a considerable "unwitting" base (which might easily take in all social systems). And the tones referred to have been well captured once more in a quite recent work largely concerned with Smith which apparently escaped Reisman's generally wide-ranging attention, namely Hans Medick's 1973 *Naturzustand und Naturgeschichte der burgerlichen Gesellschaft.*

No "definitive" treatment of Smith's views of morality and the impartial spectator exists, although there are some good ones (including T. D. Campbell's *Adam Smith's Science of Morals,* on which Reisman draws). It would be too much to ask of Reisman that he provide the definitive treatment, particularly since he already has the major self-assigned task of dealing with Smith's economics. But it is interesting to note the indecisive struggle Reisman goes through in the matter of Smith on morality. Smith is aware of the need to accommodate moral standards to particular circumstances and in this sense wishes to avoid "absolutism." Yet it is by no means easy to make him out simply as a moral "relativist." There appears to be something like an "impartial spectator" who does not merely reflect norms or values that represent a factual group consensus. Perhaps the fairest general statement Reisman has on the matter is this, which appears in a footnote on p. 237: "Smith . . . sought in both his ethics and in his economics, to steer a middle course between total relativism and absolute, immutable, eternal standards. His approach seems to postulate a sort of moving absolute, unique for the moment but still delimited by time and place." Yet on page 86 Smith is represented as holding that the moral code is "not based on absolute . . . rules . . . but *simply* on observed standards of propriety in a given place at a given time . . ." (emphasis mine). At the least, there is some unclarity here. (It is by no means impossible that it resided in Adam Smith himself.)

One could quarrel with the author about other things. Barely to mention one more, I am not at all confident that he has handled well Adam Smith's complex and ambivalent attitude toward luxury and the various contrivances of the rich for their own comfort. But, given the general competence and really gratifying range over Smith's social science that this book exhibits, it is only fair to repeat for stress what was said of it in the beginning: it is a very fine book. Its price nevertheless seems inordinately high for what is evidently a rather cheaply produced volume. In a note on page 259 Reisman says of a passage in the *Wealth of Nations* that it suggests Smith was "aware both of price-elasticity and income-elasticity of demand." Presumably no huge number of people will be interested in buying a book on the subject of this one. But will those who are interested hang on, even if reluctantly, up to $21.50, for a book that presents the modest physical reality we have here? The Adam

Smith thought to be aware of elasticity—or inelasticity—of demand might well shake his head sadly at the price tag for *Adam Smith's Sociological Economics.*

The Sociology of Karl Mannheim, by GUNTER W. REMMLING. Atlantic Highlands, N.J.: Humanities Press, 1975. 255 pp. $15.00 cloth.

H. C. GREISMAN
University of Maryland, College Park

Remmling's book on Mannheim is one of the more important contributions to sociological theory to appear in the last decade. This is because it is a truly definitive treatment of the subject, and shows a protracted commitment to scholarship that is often missing in the frenetic publishing tempo of contemporary academic life. *The Sociology of Karl Mannheim* is also one of the very few books that discuss Mannheim's development as an intellectual figure. There is some attention to this in Kurt Wolff's edited collection, and there have been some articles published that deal with the subject; but to date Remmling's book is the sole authoritative source, and as such its appearance should be welcomed.

With a few notable exceptions, sociologists have tended to ignore historical and biographical factors in their treatments of sociological theory. Remmling's work is a pleasant departure from this pattern since he ties most every aspect of Mannheim's thought to concrete and personal happenings. The brief flourishing of the Soviet Republic in Hungary, the pathetic gleam of Weimar Germany, and the intellectual migration to England are all connected to what Remmling outlines as basic stages in Mannheim's development. Tying all this together is demanding, and apart from Coser, Zeitlin, and a few others, few have attempted it on a grand scale. Remmling's grounding of Mannheim's thought in his existential situation is generally successful.

In a funny letter to *Footnotes, ASR* editor Zelditch said he was unable to read many of the articles in the journal for which he himself is responsible. The rather uncomfortable irony of this situation can be forgotten when the reader picks up Remmling's book—it is highly readable. The style is brisk, engaging, and approachable. There are some instances where rather ponderous Teutonicisms creep in, such as discourses about the "immizerization of the masses," but most of these are more quaint than annoying. Remmling has a talent for bringing abstract ideas into the realm of concrete situations, and this book might serve as a model for sociologists who have failed in this for years.

The Sociology of Karl Mannheim is the most recent of several books by Remmling in the sociology of knowledge. The most familiar of these is *Road to Suspicion,* which appeared in 1967. It was preceded by several works in German, and followed by a reader, *Towards the Sociology of Knowledge.* His most recent book can be said to conclude a successful attempt to explain and interpret Mannheim's sociology. After reading Remmling's exegesis of Mannheim, one gets the impression that Remmling himself may have a contribution to make that is equal to, if not greater than, the man whose life and work he has so painstakingly researched. Remmling removes much of the obsequious lingo that has come to surround Mannheim since his death, and what emerges is a picture of a confused if well-intentioned man who never quite figured out what he was all about. Even today, a full forty years after the first English edition of *Ideology and Utopia*, Mannheim's notion of a "relatively unattached intelligensia" provokes a sardonic grin amidst the superheated factory atmosphere of today's university. Remmling correctly sees that Mannheim was wavering on the brink of nihilism, but lacked the resolve to plunge into the abyss. In a world that clamors for "answers," Mannheim's sociology of knowledge is sadly wanting.

There is a great deal to be said for relationships between intellectuals that produce valuable information about a great figure in history. Johnson had his Boswell, and Goethe his Eckermann, but Remmling might be well-advised to cap his reseach on Mannheim with his current achievement. It is a book that creates a fascinating interlock of sociological theory, intellectual history, and personal biography. Some of the sections should be expanded, like the pages that treat the "cult of the proletariat" to which so many romantic intellectuals fell victim, but on the whole the book is a superior account of hopelessly antiquated relativism that cannot exist in a world which refuses intellectuals the luxury of gazing at events through the periscope of a sociology of knowledge.

Additional Reviews

Communication in Organizations, by EVERETT M. ROGERS and REKHA AGARWALA-ROGERS. New York: Free Press, 1976. 209 pp. $10.95 cloth. $4.95 paper.

RITA BRAITO
University of Denver

The authors' intend to provide a textbook that focuses on communication in complex organizations, that cuts across disciplinary lines, and that presents a concise synthesis of conclusions drawn "from hundreds of available research reports, articles, dissertations and monographs" (p. xxii) dealing with the topic. Key concepts in communication are focused on in chapter 1. Criticisms of communication research presented are (1) lack of process orientation; (2) the ignoring of mutual causality among the elements in the communication process, and; (3) predominance of a psychological orientation. In chapter 2, three schools of organizational behavior are reviewed: the scientific management school, the human relations school, and general systems theory school. General systems theory is advocated as the context within which organizational research should be conducted as it gives the understanding of communication a high priority, causes shift from individual to relational variables, and influences organizational scholars to consider organizational boundary issues and external environments (chapter 3).

Organizational structure (formal and informal) and bureaucracy are the concerns of chapter 4. Chapter 5 focuses on networks analysis such as (1) personal networks consisting of radial and interlocking types; (2) clique analysis, involving isolates, bridge, and liasons, and; (3) the roles of gatekeeper, opinion leader, and cosmopolite played by individuals in organizations.

In chapter 6 the authors discuss innovation in organizations. The key to this problem definition which involves specification of performance gaps—"perceptions of discrepancies between the organization's expectations and its actualities" (p. 157). Such a gap may create a search for innovations. They contend that four factors affect the nature and direction of the innovative process: (1) knowledge of innovation; (2) external accountablity; (3) slack resources; and (4) organizational structure.

Different organizational characteristics (complexity, formalization, and centralization) are suggested to have a differential impact upon innovation depending upon the stage of the innovation process.

The last chapter, six pages, presents fifty-two propositions summarizing the book.

To attempt, in 209 pages, to synthesize relevant research in diverse fields, introduce one's own model, and present fifty-two propositions, in addition present sufficient textbook information about communication and complex organizations, is very ambitious. All three aspects require more attention. Support for most of the propositions is very skimpy, and in many instances not provided.

A state of the field textbook on communication in complex organizations is much needed. Readers should not expect this book to be that. On the other hand, a number of interesting issues are raised, some research not readily available is presented, and needed research areas are suggested throughout the book. The authors' model focusing on the innovation process in complex organizations will probably be subject to much future research.

Speak for England, by MELVYN BRAGG. New York: Alfred A. Knopf, 1977. 512 pp. $15.00.

JOAN GILBERT
Staten Island

"If we want a new start, we must look to the past. The present is too occupied, the future too obscure." So begins Melvyn Bragg's oral history, *Speak for England*. As the people of his birthplace Wigton, a small market town nestled at the foot of the Cumbrian fells, are turned into the voice of a nation, reminiscences and experiences are woven into a social history designed to reveal change in Britain from the beginning of the century to the present.

Bragg's Wigtonians reflect the social structure of what is essentially a working-class town. They are of all ages; come from all classes and walks of life in fair proportion to these breakdowns. (From Barbara Wilson, a foxhunting member of the horsey set to Mary Reeves, transplanted from Water Street, Wigton's pre-World War II "ghetto" to a new Utopia at Brindlefield, to Bragg's own hard-worked, poor-but-honest grandmother, Elizabeth Armstrong; from educationally deprived Tom Jackson, window cleaner turned writer and painter, to Norman

Fell and Edwin Routledge, rivals in a power struggle at the local factory, to such assorted figures as religionists, doctors, lawyers, schoolmasters, war heroes, housewives, businessman and town characters, they afford a comprehensive insight into life as lived in the town and its environs). The collective voice tells of poverty and hardship; of servitude in "big house," field or coal pit; of depression years when extending an upturned palm at the local dole office was a shameful act; of opportunities missed when poverty intruded; of wars and valor; politics and labor; migration and return; of faith, achievements and simple pleasures; of affluence, horses and cruel blood sports.

As Britain's post-World War II "Welfare State" produces social and economic change, "place" in the seventies is no longer the "knowable" thing it was in the past. Bragg's own family is proof of this phenomenon. "When I was young, you would have thought that they were better than you," says his grandmother of her one-time neighbors, the Misses Barnes, one, a music teacher at the grammar school, "and you wouldn't like to have spoken to them or anything of that sort unless they spoke first. You just felt you weren't on the same level. But you see, as we grew older and grew better as regards the sort of work we did and everything—farm work's very degrading for an ordinary farm labourer—it was in them days. . . ." Although Mrs. Armstrong got sidetracked, her meaning is clear. A new assurance is hers with improved social status. Bragg, himself, sums it up. "Her [Elizabeth Armstrong's] grandchildren have forged ahead on the back of the social and economic progress made by the working classes—scholarships, grants, apprenticeships, travel—and one of them wrote this book."

With real names backing up voices, and voices, feelings and facts, the spoken word if at times, discursive, is unquestionably authentic. I know. I am a Wigtonian. Bragg's people are my people; the voices, those of my friends and acquaintances.

The tone is stoic: the acceptance of one's "fate" as opposed to the nineteenth century "lot"; the ethos, the Protestant ethic: "It was crime if you were lazy in them days"; and the pervading mood a perverse kind of security as, through peace and war, adversity, deprivation, and prosperity, Wigton, to its inhabitants, will always be "The Throstles, [Thrushes] Nest."

As all phases of life are examined through the voices, with the possible bias of informant selection counteracted by alternating, researched accounts of eras, events, and phenomena, the book is a social document which presents a fair and honest picture of the town and its residents.

But does the microcosm speak for the macrocosm? Can Wigtonians, the inhabitants of a snug, practically self-sufficient, relatively stagnant secure racially-pure community, which totally escaped Nazi bombing, speak for the bombed-out, post-war millions who still live in endless streets of rebuilt, wall-to-wall houses in England's industrial Midlands? Or for the teeming population of the vast London megalopolis? Or for the multi-ethnic cultures of these urban areas?

While the same events touch the lives of all Britons and social progress and practices reach down to even the smallest hamlet, nationwide, the effects are staggeringly different as problems compound themselves in proportion to population and cosmopolitanism. In essence, war, lifestyle, friction, slum clearance, and education in Wigton are not war, lifestyle, friction, slum clearance, and education in the great metropolises. Even Bragg's own assurance on this score is tinged with hesitancy: "I would claim that Wigton is a representative town or, *RATHER*, that out of it I have been able to gather as representative a sample as is consistent with the resources of an essay such as this."

Immigrant Milwaukee, 1836–1860: Accommodation and Community in a Frontier City, by KATHLEEN NEILS CONZEN. Cambridge, Mass.: Harvard University Press, 1976. 300 pp. $16.50 cloth.

ERIC H. MONKKONEN
University of California, Los Angeles

This book, the most recent in the Harvard Studies in Urban History series, edited by Stephen Thernstrom and Charles Tilly, is important both for its own sake and for showing us what directions the no longer so "new" urban history is taking. Thirteen years ago, the publication of Thernstrom's *Poverty and Progress* spurred a kind of historical analysis which has come to be known as the "new urban history." Using the manuscript federal census as his central data source, he looked at the occupational mobility, or lack of it, of ordinary, and mainly Irish, laborers in Newburyport, Massachusetts.

Times have changed: Kathleen Conzen doesn't even ask if the German or Irish immigrants in Milwaukee showed differential occupational mobility as compared to native born whites; presumably she knows that we know they did. Instead the substantive focus of her study is the nature of ethnic communities and the means by which these communities structured and were structured by the lives of immigrants. In large part the book deals with German immigrants, not only because they dominated Milwaukee, but because their prolific community building activities left evidence for an historian to work with.

A complex picture of the German community emerges, showing a social structure which had room for wide diversity and even conflict of political practices, religious affiliation, occupational and economic class interests. This very diversity, Conzen maintains, allowed the German community to create its own self identity within the larger city, giving German ethnics the ability to learn Yankee business skills as apprentices or clerks, for instance, with the express intent of returning to a life based in the German community. The Irish, in stark contrast, developed little of such diversity and depended upon individual adaptation to the social system of the city's Yankees.

The Irish and German differences had contrasting short and long run consequences, the Germans experiencing less short run but more complete long run assimilation into the dominant culture. Paradoxically, Conzen observes, the very success of the German community encouraged its ultimate dissolution, its early stability and richness a product of its flexibility and diversity.

One of the book's main strengths lies in its blending of traditional historical sources and methods with the methods of sociology, geography, and political science. It begins and concludes with a model which predicts both the speed and degree of ethnic acculturation and assimilation, a model important for its emphasis on the ethnic community, not the host society. The maps add strength and understanding to the arguments, with only the appendix giving a sense of the difficulty with which their seeming ease has been achieved. And the underlying structure of the work tests an if/then set of hypotheses, derived in the introduction, hypotheses which are rejected and with them the conventional wisdom which attributes the existence of ethnic communities to deprivation.

The major weakness of the book lies in paths not taken. For example, in a brilliant analysis of the informal activities centered about the taverns, Conzen claims that such interactions "lay at the base of the social structure" (p. 156). But we want to know more, and there is a suggestion in an all too brief comparison of German, Irish, and native marriage patterns (pp. 227, 288) that marriage decisions could have been used as an index of informal relationships. Another unfollowed path comes in the conclusion, where the strong implication is that incomplete community structure and acculturation of the Irish led to a strong ethnic/class identification: this extremely intriguing notion remains unexplored.

Clearly the directions of the "new urban history" are changing. Conzen demonstrates that the new urbanists, while staying interested in ordinary people, have now begun the challenging task of understanding these people within their own social structures. None of the "new" urbanists would claim that the definitive answers (or even questions) are in, but such works as this show the increasing subtlety of our analyses of the process of urbanization in nineteenth century America.

The Best-Laid Schemes: A Tale of Social Research and Bureaucracy, by SEYMOUR J. DEITCHMAN. Cambridge, Mass.: MIT Press, 1976. 483 pp. $14.95 cloth.

DAVID R. SEGAL
University of Maryland

Reading this book was a deja vu experience. Deitchman, an engineer, was Special Assistant to the Director of Defense Research and Engineering in the mid-1960s. Would that I had read his book before I moved to Washington some ten years later to help the Army establish a sociological research program on issues related to soldier morale and performance.

Deitchman shares with the reader keen insights regarding the nature of the Federal reseach planning and budgeting cycle. These should be read by any academic social scientist contemplating joining the ranks of the federal civil service. Taking the lessons learned to heart will convince some not to make such a change, and will save those who do several months of on the job training. This information will also be useful to social scientists conducting contract research for federal agencies.

The book also presents an inside view of Project Camelot and related Defense Department research on counter-insurgency during the 1960s. Deitchman's presentation here is neither dispassionate nor disinterested: he played a major role in the development of these programs. He does a far more thorough job of placing the events related to Camelot in a historical perspective than do other analyses I have read, and he paints a picture of a research debacle rooted in inter-agency rivalry and misinformation, rather than in attempts by the Defense Department to play an expanded role in the formulation of foreign policy. At the same time, the presentation is far from a whitewash. Deitchman recognizes that in the planning of Camelot and related research, issues ranging from ethics to methodology that should have been raised and addressed were overlooked, and that errors of judgment were committed.

Deitchman's analysis is most useful, I think, as a case study in the sociology of applied social science. He touches on most of the important issues involved in the social organization of social science, and the utilization (or lack thereof) of social science research by policy-makers. He notes the problems engendered by the clash in values and priorities between the culture of the policy-maker, who wants to define problems narrowly, maintain a low profile, particularly in sensitive areas, and needs an answer yesterday, and the culture of the academic scientist, who wants flexibility in problem definition, wants sufficient time to do the research properly, and wants to be able to publish results widely. One of the results of this value clash has been the increased dependence of federal agencies on commercial social science research organizations, despite the fact that until very recently, the best social research talent was found in universities. Also involved here was the estrangement of university based social scientists from the government because of the Vietnam War. The result was that the government bought less than the best talent for its research.

If I read Deitchman correctly, I find myself in disagreement with him on the issue of publication. He seems to feel that there are times when it is not in the national interest to publish scientific results. In my view, the sharing of information within the scientific community is one of the definitive characteristics, and the major quality control mechanism, of science. If information cannot be published, it may be thought of as intelligence, it may be something else, but it is not science.

I also disagree with Deitchman's conclusion that because of the clash in values, the ethical and technical issues raised, and other constraints, the government should sponsor less research on how societies work. I think more such sponsorship is needed. I also think that the social science community needs to educate policy-makers about what social science is and to educate its own students about the policy implications of research. Neither of these tasks has been adequately addressed to date.

A Comparative Analysis of Complex Organizations: On Power, Involvement, and Their Correlates, revised and enlarged edition, by AMITAI ETZIONI. New York: Free Press, 1975. 584 pp. $11.95 cloth. $5.95 paper.

PAUL M. HIRSCH
University of Chicago

Growing subfields need incisive, analytical, and integrative stocktakings of their own literature every ten or fifteen years. When an author, in addition, shows a clear command of implications, traditions, links to related areas, and alternative perspectives, as well as providing a personal point of view, such works are properly hailed as major contributions to the discipline. Etzioni's *A Comparative Analysis of Complex Organizations* (hereafter *CACO*) clearly fit this description when it first appeared in 1961. It tied together an impressive assortment of disconnected studies and substantive areas, providing the conceptual umbrella of an analytical typology incorporating many types of organizations. The framework of utilitarian, normative, and coercive forms of power, and correlary forms of members' motivational involvement comprise a relationship Etzioni has termed the organization's compliance structure. *CACO* exhibited a superlative grasp of sociological theory, of studies in industrial sociology, group dynamics, formal organization, professional and other occupational roles, and also of research in many substantive areas, including prisons, educational institutions, corporations, combat armies, and religious orders. It continues to sensitize new cohorts of sociologists to the value of thinking comparatively, to possible organizational roles for non-members, organizational limits on the value of charisma, forms of organization staffed by professionals, and to the hazards of inferring causal relations among social organizational variables from correlations found in small group research and programs in human relations.

CACO also related the compliance typology to other organizational variables, suggesting hypotheses and propositions for future testing. Although the book was loosely organized around an incipient theory of relationships surrounding the concept of compliance, the widespread admiration it still commands is very likely based as much on Etzioni's many insights, interpretations of the literature, and analytical typology, as on his espousal of a tentative, albeit empirically derived theory of organizational relationships. In this "revised and enlarged" edition of *CACO*, however, Etzioni makes clear that the primary value *he* places on the original work is its presentation of compliance theory.

The 1975 edition combines a virtually unchanged reprinting of the original volume with 200 pages of new chapters devoted entirely to describing the findings of every sociologist (about forty) who has tested any aspect of "the theory." Etzioni concludes that expectations generated by compliance theory receive full or partial confirmation from most of these studies. Missing from the "revision" are (1) the concluding chapter from the original book, which had carefully set out suggestions on how to go about testing its ideas, and pointed out several important limitations of the theory; (2) any discussion, revision, or clarification based on work that was not designed explicitly to test the theory; and (3) any significant discussion or incorporation of developments in the field of complex organization—a field whose growth was stimulated by, and which still owes a substantial debt to *CACO*— since its original publication.

These editorial inclusions and omissions are straightforwardly announced in the preface to the new edition. Consequently, it should be assessed not only in terms of the pros and cons of the decisions they represent, but also in terms of how well the book succeeds in accomplishing the task Etzioni set himself. A disjunction between the clear policy and macrosociological orientations of his work between 1961 and 1975, and the absence of either in both editions of *CACO* also should be addressed, for here the striking dualism exhibited in Etzioni's own intellectual career reflects a mode of adaptation to a larger problem characterizing sociology in general: the traditional and rather short-sighted segregation of theory and research about industrial society, on the one hand, from the complex organizations which generate or administer activities and policies that influence the nature of society, on the other.

Between the first and second editions of *CACO*, the field of organizational analysis has taken significant steps to reduce the distance between these poles. Its concern with open systems and information-processing models, interorganizational relations, and the influential works of James Thompson and Lawrence and Lorsch, for example, represent strong efforts to bring organizational analysis and macrosociology closer together. In his work dealing with organizations, however, Etzioni appears headed in the opposite direction. While he applauds a study by Skinner and Winckler applying the compliance typology to as largescale a topic as political changes in Chinese history, it is jarring to find much recent "closer-to-home" work in organizational analysis— by Thompson (*Organizations in Action*), Evan, Blau, and Schoenherr, Katz and Kahn, Dornbusch and Scott, Graham Allison, Stinchcomb (*On Creating Efficient Industrial Administration*), and others ignored simply because they have not chosen to rely on or explicitly test Etzioni's theory of compliance. Why haven't they? Should they have? One might expect some efforts to incorporate their work, and to build a bridge from compliance theory to these and other influential contributors since 1961 if Etzioni is to continue being viewed as one of the prime spokespersons for this subfield. Out of admiration for his talents, I am reluctant to dismiss the added sections in the enlarged edition as comprising "just another" of the many works on organization which appear with relatively little impact. That Etzioni himself is concerned with some of the very issues now current in organization theory (missing in this work) is obvious from both his own work and a statement in the now-deleted concluding chapter of the original volume: "we chose in this book to focus on compliance relationships within organizations, and on their association with other organizational variables. Obviously, the next step is to extend the study of compliance and its correlates to environmental factors" (p. 310). In fact, it is a reasonable guess that one reason for his extended absence from this subfield follows from dissatisfaction with the narrow (closed-system) boundaries created or reinforced for it partly by his own formulation.

Certainly this judgment reflects an admitted bias in favor of the broader scope and analytical and integrative contribution of the original book, rather than toward an emphasis on the validation of compliance theory which is the hallmark of the revision. The original version, for example, contained approximately 1,000 citations in 313 pages, while the enlarged edition adds only about 150 references despite the addition of nearly 200 pages of text. On the other hand, as he points out, the present edition does provide a comparative review of efforts to operationalize the same set of variables and organizational properties, and represents an attempt to provide continuity of work, codify findings, and relate them to a theory. Etzioni is determined to marshal empirical support for the independence of the elements in his compliance theory. He chides Perrow and others for suggesting it is tautological, arguing one cannot logically derive the direction of empirical correlations among organizational variables from a simple knowledge of the typology alone. Unfortunately, even though some of the findings discussed are interesting and impressive, most of the evidence adduced will fail to excite or convince doubters of the original formulation. Rather, it will reinforce those who already believe, and may persuade some indifferents (like me) who admire the typology for its intellectual value and face validity, irrespective of its more controversial status as an empirical predictor.

From the enlarged edition, we learn that students of normative organizations (where goals, motives, and criteria for assessment can be quite hazy) have found the typology especially useful, while researchers of utilitarian and coercive organizations (where these can be operationalized more easily) have apparently found other theories more suitable. But all organizations falling into a single large category will not necessarily exhibit identical internal structures just because their goals or compliance relations are codeable as utilitarian, coercive, or normative. Acknowledging this in the (now-deleted) last chapter of the original edition, Etzioni suggested ordering organizations *within* each category, relative to each other, on the same set of dimensions. His disciples have not done so, however, and these categories remain nominal, more gross and descriptive than productive for locating variance within each category, and therefore refer mainly to the modal organization within each of the cells on the diagonals of the typology. This problem, addressed within a different vocabulary in Thompson's *Organizations in Action* (also a useful tool for coding what Etzioni delineates as "secondary patterns of primacy") is simply ignored in the revised edition. The omission is unfortunate, as it then provides few additional guideposts to test such dynamic hypotheses as whether universities and their faculties have adopted a more utilitarian orientation toward each other over the last decade; or if employees of utilitarian organizations now seek more (normative) opportunities for "self-actualization" to avoid becoming alienated from their work; or for studying how organizations have adapted their compliance structures to incorporate programs of affirmative action, or improved technologies in cost accounting. Organizational analysis, as it develops, should be positioning itself to take into account greater variability within gross categories, rather than to rigidify them. Since Etzioni, as policy analyst (in his other works), is clearly interested in these very issues, the 1975 edition of this book poses a challenge by implicitly suggesting that others working in the area of organizational analysis are unable to contribute to a better understanding of such topics and policy issues.

The added chapters assessing every study inspired by the first edition are, by virtue of Etzioni's editorial strategy, structured and constrained by those which have been conducted. For example, a full chapter is concerned with describing and explicating a series of studies conducted by a team of sociologists at Iowa State University. Based on research into college fraternities, farmers' cooperatives, and civil defense programs (where local organizations could apparently consist of the person filling out the questionnaire, the discussion is ambiguous), compliance theory is tested and causal models, based on the last two organizations, are presented. One might argue (as these studies' authors and Etzioni also note) these hardly constitute a representative sample of organizations from which to reach any firm conclusions. But the studies were conducted, and he apparently feels obliged, here and with others as well, to critique, explicate, make sense of, and then advocate these efforts as "proof" of compliance theory. On balance, it seems a tedious exercise, unnecessary for the theory and somewhat demeaning to the author, who occasionally uses the vehicle of this "revision" to criticize others' methods and operationalizations (e.g., Hall, Haas and Johnson) wherever their results constitute a departure from expectations drawn from the theory. In my view, this approach adds little to the immense value of the first edition (mostly reprinted within the second), other than to show Etzioni in the less flattering position of being his own advocate. Most of the newer studies could have been discussed in just one or two review articles for journal publication.

In the next edition, I hope Etzioni will choose to: incorporate into the text an updated, critical, and integrative review of the field whose growth he helped foster; discuss at length only the best of the many studies which have found the theory and typology of value (such as Z. Gamson's or E. Lehman's), since most readers probably are more impressed by their contribution and utility than Etzioni appears to believe; and add a new chapter on how those of us concerned with research useful for guiding an active society, and in better understanding the organizations needed to do it, can (and should) pursue both interests simultaneously rather than ad seriatim.

The Sociology of Leisure, by STANLEY PARKER. New York: International Publications Service, 1976. 157 pp. $11.25 cloth.

WORTH C. SUMMERS
California State University, Sacramento

This book seems intended primarily to acquaint those concerned with planning and administering leisure with the sociology of leisure. Though chiefly sociological in its overall orientation, it uses material from a variety of disciplines including anthropology, psychology, history, geography, and economics. Parker draws upon a good deal of the best North American and Continental writing, but the focus, examples, and sources are preponderantly British, a fact which will seriously limit the usefulness of the book for North American undergraduates or practitioners.

The book is divided into three rather disparate sections. The first, most general and most interesting section, is a good but quite condensed introduction to problems of defining leisure, contrasting leisure in industrial society with historical and cross cultural examples, and has a discussion of leisure and the life cycle. The second section is a survey of research and theory on the relation between leisure and work, family, education, and religion. The third, and most applied, section deals with issues in the demand and supply of leisure facilities. A concluding chapter attempts to tie together the three separate sections by summarizing some recurrent themes: future trends in the growth of leisure, changes in the meaning of leisure, the proper role of leisure for individuals and society, and the "paradox of planning for freedom in leisure" (p. 149). This last chapter also contains an intelligent summary of value questions that are necessarily confronted in leisure planning. The role of values in leisure is an issue to which Parker is sensitive throughout the book.

The major weakness of this book is one to which all "surveys-of-the-field" are prone: the lack of an overall theoretical perspective or orientation which makes them hang together as something greater than the sum of their numerous parts. In the present instance, the inherent limitation of this genre is heightened not only by the rather non-theoretical and descriptive character of the subject itself, but also by brevity: 152 pages of text and references divided among 12 chapters do not permit much more than the most scanty discussion of topics which are often of considerable complexity. Consequently, the book comes perilously close (especially in section two) to reading like a catalog of findings.

However, given the inherent limitations of the form within which he has chosen to work, Parker handles his subject well, with generally good—if rather short—summaries of a wide range of materials in a compact, clear prose. Given its brevity, readers will find the book most useful as an introduction to issues and as a guide to the literature, which the ample footnoting and a good index will facilitate.

Let us hope that having written this survey, Parker will now turn his attention once again to developing the theory and synthesis so badly needed in the sociology of leisure.

From Drinking to Alcoholism: A Sociological Commentary, by DAVID ROBINSON. New York: John Wiley & Sons, 1976. 187 pp. $16.95 cloth. $7.50 paper.

WALTER DAVIS
Boston University School of Medicine

"Yet another book on alcoholism!" is likely to be the initial reaction of any potential reader—lay or professional—to David Robinson's new book on a subject that many feel has been over-investigated with all too few meaningful results. Such an attitude is not completely without basis, as Robinson would be the first to attest, for the scholarly study of alcoholism is shared (or contested) by at least six established disciplines. In terms of delineating an etiology, the combined track record of these disciplines is the hardly revealing finding that alcoholism results from the interaction of physiological, psychological, and sociological factors.

Robinson's aim is not to register yet another theory of alcoholism, but to offer us a sociological perspective on a subject he feels has not been seriously looked at by sociologists, in spite of the obvious widespread social significance of alcoholism. While not discounting the role of biochemical and physiological processes in the onset of alcoholism, Robinson's point of departure is the inescapable fact that such processes are identified in specific social contexts, and it is here that the sociologist should have much to say.

The unique contribution of the present volume to the literature on alcoholism, then, is that it offers us a perspective on the social *meaning* of drinking and alcoholism, "to describe and indicate the social and medical implications of people's differences in their assessment of what counts as alcoholism, problem drinking, treatment, and so on." The central question he tackles is "how do some people get into the position in which they are defined, by themselves or by others, as alcoholics?"

He addresses this question in two related ways: (1) a first portion of the book is epidemiological. He presents findings from a survey on drinking patterns in a general population (who drinks what, when, and where) and discusses the intricate question of how these patterns may relate to the development of "problem" drinking, especially in particular demographic categories of the population. Here we learn, for example, that "for each level of alcohol consumption younger people of both sexes reported more alcohol effects and alcoholism indicators than their elders, and that males reported more than females." (2) The above provides the background for the sociological core of the book, in which Robinson is concerned with meaning and definition. Thus, rather than inundating us with one more theory of alcoholism, he looks instead at the causal theories used by various professionals, helping agencies, and the laity who come into contact with problem drinkers, as well as those theories espoused by problem drinkers themselves. Here we learn, perhaps surprisingly, that professionals as a group tend to operate in terms of social causes of alcoholism, as opposed to biochemical or psychodynamic ones, but that physicians in particular tend to view individual weaknesses and susceptibilities as causative.

Then, instead of looking at the kinds of help made available by various agencies, he looks at the kinds of help potential consumers of services find most and least appropriate and why. Similarly, rather than mull over *the* most reliable clue or sign of the onset of alcoholism, he looks at how those in the helping profession actually perceive and act upon their perceptions of problem drinking and drinkers. Finally, he skips the usual comparison of the effectiveness of various treatment methods and deals instead with the hard questions of what "success" should be and what do various helpers and the general public consider success to be.

The interview data which Robinson uses to address the above issues emanated from a general population survey conducted in South London (N=286). While the inferences he makes based on the analysis of this data are insightful and raise a number of questions for further study, this reviewer kept wishing that he would tackle the problem of cross-national representativeness more consistently, as was done with the comparison of consumption patterns. It would have been instructive to the American reader, for example, to indicate the extent to which the findings on the professionals' attitudes might differ from those in the US. Additionally, placing a copy of the interview protocol in the appendix would have assisted the careful reader in following the analysis of the data.

For those familiar with Straus's familiar paradigm, the book may be seen as representing a "sociology of alcoholism" perspective, rather than the more prevalent "sociology in alcolohism" one. That is, Robinson is more concerned with the social contruction of reality centered around the role of alcohol and drinking in modern society than he is with certain assumptions about the nature of alcoholism.

This book has many strengths, one of its major ones being the skillful and interesting way the previous literature has been interwoven into each question. Its contents are well-integrated and it is extremely well written. *From Drinking to Alcoholism* would be invaluable as a text in advanced undergraduate sociology courses as well as graduate courses in the sociologies of alcoholism, deviance (especially the labelling theory variety), and knowledge.

Ethics and Anthropology: Dilemmas in Field Work, by MICHAEL A. RYNKIEWICH and JAMES P. SPRADLEY. New York: John Wiley & Sons, 1976. 186 pp. No price listed, paper.

ELVI WHITTAKER
University of British Columbia

A collection such as Rynkiewich and Spradley have compiled could be commended on several counts. Firstly, by bringing together the experiences of twelve fieldworkers, the book is a much needed step toward systematizing, and making public, experiences which have been largely in the province of professional folklore and oral tradition. Secondly, it contributes toward the debate of the last decade on anthropological imperialism, the myth of value-freeness, and the relationship of the discipline and its findings to outside powers. Thirdly, together with a few other works, it could be seen as making a beginning toward what is urgently needed in the profession—an anthropology of anthropology. The implications of the collection are made more potent by an appendix of the formal directives of the American Anthropological Association's Statement of Ethics.

The book evokes some very old themes, occasionally found in the literature, but certainly familiar to both anthropologists and sociologists. All fieldworkers will recognize here the friendship dilemma, the guilt associated with professionalized voyeurism, the probably unavoidable Machiavellian manipulation of respondents, the problems of dealing with damaging data and with the possible uses to which published materials could be put, the "contamination" issue, the responsibilities of reciprocity, and the stresses of working with institutional or governmental funding. The essays by Spradley, Pierce-Colfer, Cohen, Mann, Harrell-Bond, Hansen and Chrisman mainly fall within this province.

Perhaps an inherent problem in such a collection is that full appreciation by necessity is denied the reader in that the research plans, ideological stances and methodological taken-for-granteds of each contributor are not supplied. Occasionally one is aware of ideological commitments to "doing anthropology" in some predefined way which does not permit adjusting more fruitfully to ethical dilemmas. Perhaps the anthropological dicta of the early sixties did not permit plans to be changed to study instead the roles thrust upon the researcher or the very dilemma itself. Along this line the essay by Nader considers the problems raised by epistemic decisions.

Special mention should be made of the contributions of Rynkiewich, Kiste, Nash, and Spradley. They allude directly to the responsibility of the anthropologist to the people studied and to the emerging considerations of action anthropology. Quite clearly they reveal some of the themes which have endured from the discussions about the Vietnamese war and Cambodia when the traditional claims to value-freeness were effectively challenged. Further, while anthropology and sociology have produced innumerable ethnographies and studies, no researchers have explored the ramifications of their finished efforts. Yet professional lore and selected interactional networks carry such information.

Underlying the contributions seems to be a hidden assumption that if certain recurrent ethical issues could be solved, dilemmas would be eradicated and moral precepts satisfied. This is endearing innocence indeed. Does not a more realistic perspective suggest that field work may never be free of the ethical demands anthropologists would impose upon themselves and the conditions of their work? Hence, will field work endure in its present form?

Painters and Politics: The European Avant-Garde and Society, 1900–1925, by THEDA SHAPIRO. New York: Elsevier, 1976. 341 pp. $15.00 cloth.

BARBARA ROSENBLUM
Stanford University

Theda Shapiro is a professor of French and Italian who has entered an intellectual domain usually claimed by other specialists, chiefly art historians. Well equipped to undertake a social history of art, she has written an interesting book. In it, Shapiro posits several relationships between French, German, and Italian avant-garde painters and the political milieu of their times. Her intention is to "describe and explain the early social attitudes and, whenever possible, more explicit political opinions and activities of a generation of painters who wrought a revolution in the arts and who witnessed technological change, social unrest and world conflict on a unprecedented scale" (p. xii). To do this, she creates a sample of eighty-three avant-garde painters and includes, in addition to the text itself, excellent and concise biographical sketches in an appendix. She begins her study with a historical sketch of the art worlds in each of the three countries, thus providing the social and historical background for the study.

The book traces these artists from 1900 to just after WWII. To find out their backgrounds, attitudes, and both political and artistic activities, Shapiro went through voluminous and diverse materials such as memoirs, published and unpublished letters, public records, documents, articles printed in small, short-lived avant-garde journals (what the French charmingly call "les revues éphémères") and reviews in major newspapers. All the translations from French, German, and Italian are the author's own, an impressive feat, in and of itself. Even more impressive is that the translations are superb and successfully capture the emotions of artists's writing about their own painting. The translations are sensitive to individual differences between persons and differences between the languages. The touches of modernism, in both syntactical construction and vocabulary, make the translation smooth for the contemporary reader. Compare her translation of a few lines from the 1910 Manifesto of the Futurist Painters with another translation:

> To other peoples Italy is still a land of the dead, an immense Pompeii whitened by tombs. On the contrary, Italy is reawakening and an intellectual rebirth is following its political rebirth.
>
> (Translated by Theda Shapiro)

> In the eyes of other countries, Italy is still a land of the dead, a vast Pompeii, white with sepulchres. But Italy is being reborn. Its political resurgence will be followed by a cultural resurgence.
>
> (Translated by Robert Brian)

While both passages capture the larger meaning, I prefer Shapiro's translation for its greater intensity and for the energy that is achieved through the use of the present, rather than the future tense. Her intensity, I believe, successfully captures the nationalistic passion (and, for some, the later Fascism) of the Italian Futurists.

To study the relationships between painters and politics, Shapiro performs three major types of "analysis," without calling them such. The first type is what sociologists would call a cohort analysis. She treats all the avant-garde painters as an ideological cohort and traces their collective career, by country, over the years. This provides a natural historical framework around which the book is organized. In France, she begins with the pre-Cubists, in Germany with the pre-Expressionists, and in Italy with the pre-Futurists.

The second type of analysis is what we would call a network analysis. Within each chapter, Shapiro studies in greater detail, the avant-garde painters within their own countries. She traces out who knew whom, who exhibited where, who frequented the cafés together and so on. Shapiro includes all sorts of wonderful anecdotal materials and good gossip about the artists. For instance, she includes Picasso's expenses for rent and food for three months, as well as the budget expenses of other artists (p. 73). In another place (p. 57), there is a hilarious excerpt from a satirical piece written by the art dealer and Expressionist propagandist, Herwarth Walden, who mimics the "ordinary citizen's" reaction to the avant-garde clientele at the Café Megalomania:

> Timid and fearful, the ordinary citizen hastens past this pit of hell . . . Cold Shivers run down their normal limbs, through their healthy blood. For inside they have glimpsed demonic figures sitting. Men with long hair, serpentine, curly locks, flowing ties, Sezessionistic socks and teetotaling trousers are tasting life to the full.

The analysis of paintings and other illustrated materials comprise the third type of analysis. One of Shapiro's major theses is that the avant-garde painters' chief means of expressing their antibourgois sentiment was through their painting. Thus, she interprets the rise of avant-garde painting as the product of a self-conscious political movement rather than the crystallization of artistic developments which had already been set in motion years earlier, as argued by some art historians. The graphic materials are organized well and are analyzed intelligently. Shapiro is at her best in this type of analysis. Her interpretations of the paintings are simultaneously scholarly and humanly sensitive. On this level of analysis, she skillfully weaves together the political biographies of painters with their art. She also shows how political commitments shaped painters' choices of imagery, such as the selection of scenes from everyday working-class life rather than, for example, the recreational activities of the bourgeoisie, as the Impressionists were wont to do. Though I am familiar with paintings of the period Shapiro studies, her comments opened my eyes and taught me to see in new and better ways, which makes me feel that her command of the visual materials is as fine as any art historian I have ever read.

The book is fun to read. It's a good, juicy story that intertwines historical narrative, social commentary and biography. She succeeds in creating the ambience of the time, which results in delightful reading when compared to dry, pedantic exegeses on the subject. Her writing is lovely and she tells the story with wit, charm, empathy, and intelligence. For lay readers, for art students, and possibly for professional art historians, this is an interesting book that offers an unconventional interpretation of a slice of art history. However, for sociologists interested in studying art sociologically, the book's shortcomings exemplify the necessity for trained sociologists to bring their skills to this domain. I do not fault Shapiro for not being a sociologist but, by her use of the rhetoric of social analysis, combined with her attempt to marshall evidence systematically, she opens herself to sociological criticism.

The book's basic flaw is the absence of theory. There is no guiding conceptual scheme which helps make sense out of the entire empirical enterprise. As a consequence, the book is full of empirical difficulties. Sampling, for instance, is problematic, for there are no meaningful criteria for the selection of the sample. Why Shapiro picked these eighty-three artists—and not others—from the thousands who flocked to Paris, Rome, Milan, Dresden, Munich, and Berlin is not clear. In short, the definition of "avant-garde" is problematic by virtue of the absence of criteria for inclusion.

Once having selected her sample, Shapiro does not manage it as systematically as the text would lead us to believe. Out of eighty-three painters, only about thirty names keep coming up again and again. For instance, while Paula Modersohn-Becker is among the eighty-three painters, Shapiro refers to her only twice in the text, whereas such notables as Klee, Kandinsky, Picasso, Matisse, and Boccioni are referred to often and quoted throughout the text. Shapiro has distorted the larger sample by differentially weighing the painters so that, in effect, she drew a biased sub-sample and based her interpretations on the lives of perhaps thirty and not eighty-three painters, as she claims.

Another problem concerns her use of evidence. Her stance towards evidence is not selective but rather exhaustive, which is the historian's main strategy for marshalling evidence. But where the historian evaluates varieties of evidence by assigning differential importance, Shapiro does not. As a result, she treats everything as evidence, without explicating her logic of selection and inclusion. Another problem is that the meaning of the evidence is sometimes not clear. For instance, she stratifies her sample by residential (urban-rural) and class background (pp. 20–25) but that particular operation is meaningless, not only because the sample size is small but because it seems to have been done for the sake of "looking sociological," rather than for the sake of supporting a larger point. Similarly, she inventories the "other" occupations the painters had, noting that Matisse studied law and that Emil Nolde worked in a furniture factory. She makes the inference from these data that many painters "opted for the artist's life rather late" because they were unwilling to buck parental opposition. While this psychological interpretation may be valid, an alternative and more historically accurate interpretation would be that artists during that era had to have second, extra-artistic careers simply to make enough money to survive.

Finally, while Shapiro has painstakingly

assembled and translated a wealth of data, for which she is to be thanked and congratulated, her management of the data and her interpretations show that her lack of training in historical and sociological methods is a serious handicap. Where the evidence clearly shows diversity and heterogeneity, Shapiro strains towards uniformity by forcing her sample to appear more homogenous than the data indicate. Consequently, she blurs the national differences between the countries in her attempt to make global statements about a "European" avant-garde. For instance, one of her major claims is that painters used their art as a vehicle for their political expression. The case is clearly true for the Italian Futurists, and somewhat true for the German Expressionists but her own data show that the French case is quite different. Yet, Shapiro would have us believe that such differences are minimal. The analysis which works so well for the Italian case is rendered suspect when misapplied to the other two countries. What is missing here is a historian's sensitivity to time and to place. What is also missing is an awareness of the grounds for generalization and an understanding of the types of evidence that permit generalization.

In sum, Shapiro's major contribution is that she brings life into the materials she has assembled. She brings her knowledge of the times, knowledge of the artists' lives and, most important, knowledge of their cultures and languages. But she does not bring with her other skills that a study such as this one demands. The book's shortcomings have convinced me, once again, that a sociological approach to such materials as these can help avoid evidentiary and interpretive errors and, furthermore, furnish insights that other approaches do not seem to yield.

Suicidology: Contemporary Developments, edited by EDWIN S. SHNEIDMAN. New York: Grune & Stratton, 1976. 571 pp. No price listed, cloth.

JAMES F. SHORT, JR.
Washington State University

This is one of a series of Seminars in Psychiatry under the general editorship of Dr. Milton Greenblatt, Chief of Psychiatry at the Veterans Administration Hospital in Sepulveda, California, and Professor of Psychiatry at UCLA. The editor of this volume is Director of the Laboratory for the Study of Life-Threatening Behavior, also at UCLA, and the world's first Professor of Thanatology. A dedication page pictures Editor Shneidman with the three "scholars and gentlemen who personified all the best contemporary developments in suicidology" to whom the book is dedicated—Jacques Choron, Louis Dublin, and Erwin Stengal. The role of sociology in contemporary suicidology is perhaps symbolized in that picture, in the disciplinary representation of contributors, and the placement of chapters.

Only three of twenty contributors are identified as sociologists (Warren Breed and two of his collaborators, Leonard Linden and William Swanson). Their chapters are placed with psychologist James Diggory's examination of recent trends in US suicide rates, in part 1 of the book, on "Demography of Suicide." Neither here nor in remaining sections of the book, in which methodological developments in suicidology, logical, cognitive, clinical, philosophic, and legal aspects of suicide, and responses to suicide are examined, are sociological theories of suicide systematically tested or developed. Provocative findings and speculations of relevance to those theories can be found, however, e.g., the age, race, and sex-specific suicide rates presented by Diggory for the years, 1933–1968; the finding by psychologist J. William Worden that life-threatening behavior was associated with lower levels of lethality among a group of suicide attempters admitted to Massachusetts General Hospital (consistent with psychiatrist Michael Simpson's findings that wrist-cutting self-mutilators are not attempting to die but to gain "reintegration, repersonalization," and "reality").

The relevance of sociology to suicide prevention is made explicit in Litman and Wold's description of a "Continued Relationship Maintenance" experiment, in which the theory that external constraints involved in interpersonal relationships lower suicidal risk is employed as a basis for treatment. The idea is applied also in the program of the Samaritans in Britain, described and evaluated by psychiatrist Richard Fox.

Editor Shneidman enlivens the book by including at the beginning of each chapter an excerpt from a "classic" piece from the literature of suicidology. One guesses that if sociologists are to be taken seriously in the field we had best lay claim to our relevance, and participate in development of implications of both theory and empirical research.

A Home Is Not a Home: Life within a Nursing Home, by G. JANET TULLOCH. New York: Seabury Press, 1975. 122 pp. $6.95 cloth.

THOMAS J. COTTLE
Tavistock Clinic, London

It has always been the case that certain people among us are able to write about the conditions of their lives in such a way that we come to know our own conditions that much better. We read these writers and feel perhaps enriched, renewed, perhaps more intrigued by the nature of our being on the earth, less afraid of the moment of departure and of the months and years of decaying and dissolution that often terrify us far more than the eventual conclusion of life. The gift of these special writers will never be wholly defined, but surely part of it is the capacity and willingness to look at their reality with an unfailing eye and to portray or report that reality in a precise prose that sparkles with clarity and truth on the page before us. Another part of their talent is the ability to keep out the sounds of a driving capitalism that seeks to transform all human experience no matter how intimate or profound into some sort of marketable commodity. The artist knows that the commodity will inevitably substitute for the reality of the experience being described, thereby taking man and woman long steps away from the truth of their conditions.

In one of the most unbelievable ironic turns of our culture and century, dying and death have become commodities. They're just two more of what the British call "trendy topics." In the false art of the commodity makers, dying and death, even old age, are portrayed in such fashion that we no longer are able to see that our confrontations with them are merely elaborate denials. We are turned away from them, even as we acknowledge their existence, for there are other commodities to chose from, other realities to be distorted. And besides, we say, life's too short, and each of us knows too much pain.

A Home Is Not a Home is a book of such rare beauty and honesty, such artistic honesty, that one not only treasures every word of it, but begins to question the substance of so much literature that precedes it. It is a work of fiction with stories and characters based on the world of a nursing home, presumably the one in which the author lives. In the brief stories of Essie, Susan, Cecile, Rachel, Blanche, Dubois and Joady, we are made to feel the feelings of aging and illness, of dying. The scenes, pitiful in their comedy, bitter in their portrayals of indignity and unrelenting anger, hurt and humiliation, tells us more about the final moments, what Shakespeare called the "right hour," of life than we ever dared to know. Tulloch's rare gift for vision and language and of course, her day by day experiences yield a veritable painting of that special time in the life cycle. How masterfully she shows the return in old age of the dependencies, frustrations, forgetfullness, even purity of childhood. How wondrously she makes us feel the passage of time, the crystalline sharpness of the immediate moment, the slow disappearance of all we have been taught to call the present and the past. And always the humaneness and that special sting and warmth of the novelist.

The ninteen episodes of *A Home Is Not a Home* play hard on one's sensibilities and emotions. One woman in the home has lost her dentures somewhere in her food. A woman soils herself and is distressed about the slime on her treasured yellow sweater. A woman looks forward to a visit from her family. She circles the date on her calendar, prepares herself yet, when her daughter fails to come, seems to have forgotten the visit entirely. But that night in her dreams, she remembers, and she weeps. Joady watches as a bimonthly devotional magazine is passed out to residents of the house. It is called, "Come Ye Apart." She resents a doctor's patronizing and incidious manner. Should he not tell her that a drug designed to relieve the tensions of her spasticity has been shown to be carcinogenic in animals. The women's privacy and sense of dignity are constantly assaulted. "Blanche DuBois was pushed in and out of the bathroom somewhat as a terrier is let out the back door. . . ." Undone by the frustrations of the treatment shown her and by the recognition of what she has become, a woman becomes furious at the dinner table, a three year old child in the midst of an ugly tantrum. And then, moments later, an apology is offered, one that carries remembrances of motherhood and the times when one comforted one's own screaming child. A woman dies, but the other residents are not informed. Instead, a fire drill is called to get the survivors out of the home while the deceased is taken away. So the women are left to hallucinate about the death of their friend, and then wonder who now might receive her transistor radio and the few personal articles her own family has left behind. Rachel says: "Why didn't they simply tell us? We should be old enough to face death by now. A fire alarm is so much scarier."

Everyday Joady watches the comings and goings, the inadequate staff, the stealing, the mismanagement of people, deaths before deaths. "A psyche which has persevered being for eighty two years has no alarm clock to stop itself spontaneously. It wrestles its own resistance while knowing the time to forfeit personality has come. Ambivalently, it accepts oblivion on the one hand, while protesting it on another. . . . Death and birth ignore seasons and days as they struggle in the coming of their own timing."

I read this book and I ask the questions now so trite and commonplace. What has happened in our culture that we deal with our friends and relatives of other generations so? Why are we still surprised to learn that young ill people are in nursing homes along with the aged? How is it possible that people grow rich in the nursing home rackets? How is it possible that we have let ourselves be deceived by those commodity makers so that we have actually lost touch with our present lives and our lives as they most assuredly will be when we reach our own right hours? And how is it that human beings can survive so much and produce such beauty and wisdom, such truth about life that our very souls are touched?

A diabetic, Cecile was not allowed to have sweets, but for a special celebration a lady visitor had kindly left her a chocolate cupcake: "Licking her fingers (Cecile) threw the incriminating evidence into her trash basket and returned to her chair. Her eyes burnt with the dryness of wasted tears. Only a small sigh indicated that she knew she had just celebrated her last birthday."

PUBLICATIONS RECEIVED

(Listing of a publication below does not assure nor preclude its subsequent review.)

ABERCROMBIE, CLARENCE L., III. *The Military Chaplain*. Sage, 1977. 191 pp. $11.00 cloth. $6.00 paper.

ANDERSEN, RONALD; LION, JOANNA; and ANDERSON, ODIN W. *Two Decades of Health Services: Social Survey Trends in Use and Expenditure*. Ballinger, 1976. 387 pp. $16.50 cloth.

BARASH, DAVID P. *Sociobiology and Behavior*. Elsevier, 1977. 378 pp. $9.95 cloth. $4.95 paper.

BARKER, DIANA LEONARD, and ALLEN, SHEILA. *Dependence and Exploitation in Work and Marriage*. Longman, 1976. 265 pp. $15.50 cloth.

BARKER, PAUL, ed. *The Social Sciences Today*. Littlefield, Adams, 1977. 118 pp. $1.50 paper.

BARTH, HANS. *Truth and Ideology*. Tr. Frederic Lilge. University of California Press, 1976. 201 pp. $12.75 cloth.

BASU, ASOKE. *Elementary Statistical Theory in Sociology*. E. J. Brill, 1976. 98 pp. NPL, cloth.

BECK, DOROTHY FAHS. *Marriage and the Family under Challenge: An Outline of Issues, Trends, and Alternatives*, 2nd ed. Family Service Association of America, 1976. 101 pp. NPL, paper.

BECKER, HOWARD S. *Sociology Work: Methods and Substance*. Transaction Books, 1977. Orig. pub. in 1966. 358 pp. $5.95 paper.

BELOTTI, ELENA GIANINI. *What Are Little Girls Made Of? The Roots of Feminine Stereotypes*. Schocken Books, 1976. 158 pp. $7.95 cloth.

BEN-DAVID, JOSEPH, and CLARK, TERRY NICHOLS, eds. *Culture and Its Creators: Essays in Honor of Edward Shils*. University of Chicago Press, 1977. 325 pp. $15.00 cloth.

BENDIX, REINHARD. *Nation-Building and Citizenship: Studies of Our Changing Social Order*, new enlg. ed. University of California Press, 1977. Orig. pub. in 1964. 449 pp. $18.75 cloth. $5.95 paper.

BENVENISTE, GUY and BENSON, CHARLES. *From Mass to Universal Education: The Experience of the State of California and Its Relevance to European Education in the Year 2000*. Martinus Nijhoff, 1976. 123 pp. NPL, paper.

BERGER, JOSEPH, et al. *Status Characteristics and Social Interaction: An Expectation-States Approach*. Elsevier, 1977. 196 pp. $14.50 cloth.

BERNSTEIN, PAUL. *Workplace Democratization: Its Internal Dynamics*. Kent State University Press, 1976. 127 pp. $12.50 cloth.

BERRY, BRIAN J. L., ed. *Urbanization and Counter-Urbanization*. Sage, 1976. 329 pp. $17.50 cloth. $7.50 paper.

BEUF, ANN H. *Red Children in White America*. University of Pennsylvania Press, 1977. 155 pp. $9.00 cloth.

BIRCH, CHARLES, and ABRECHT, PAUL, eds. *Genetics and the Quality of Life*. Pergamon Press, 1975. 232 pp. $16.00 cloth. $10.50 paper.

BLACK, DONALD. *The Behavior of Law*. Academic Press, 1976. 175 pp. $12.50 cloth.

BLANCHARD, KENDALL A. *The Economics of Sainthood: Religious Change among the Rimrock Navajos*. Fairleigh Dickinson University Press, 1977. 240 pp. $12.00 cloth.

BLAXTER, MILDRED. *The Meaning of Disability: A Sociological Study of Impairment*. Neale Watson, 1976. 258 pp. $10.00 cloth.

BOULDING, ELISE, et al. *Handbook of International Data on Women*. Halsted, 1976. 468 pp. $25.00 cloth.

BREMER, STUART A. *Simulated Worlds: A Computer Model of National Decision-Making*. Princeton University Press, 1977. 249 pp. $15.50 cloth.

BRIGGS, VERNON M., Jr.; FOGEL, WALTER; and SCHMIDT, FRED H. *The Chicano Worker*. University of Texas Press, 1977. 129 pp. $9.50 cloth.

BRIGHT, WILLIAM. *Variation and Change in Language*. Stanford University Press, 1976. 283 pp. $10.95 cloth.

BRIGHTBILL, CHARLES K., and MOBLEY, TONY A. *Educating for Leisure-Centered Living*. 2nd ed. Wiley, 1977. Orig. pub. 1966. 128 pp. $5.95 paper.

BRODSKY, CARROLL M. *The Harassed Worker*. Lexington Books, 1976. 174 pp. $15.00 cloth.
BROOM, LEONARD, and JONES, F. LANCASTER. *Opportunity and Attainment in Australia*. Stanford University Press, 1977. 154 pp. $12.50 cloth.
BROWN, D. E. *Principles of Social Structure: South Asia*. Duckworth & Westview, 1976. 248 pp. $18.75 cloth.
BROWN, RAY, ed. *Children and Television*. Sage, 1976. 368 pp. $17.50 cloth. $7.50 paper.
BRUCE, JAMES B. *The Politics of Soviet Policy Formation: Khrushchev's Innovative Policies in Education and Agriculture*. University of Denver/Graduate School of International Studies, 1976. 138 pp. NPL, paper.
BURBANK, GARIN. *When Farmers Voted Red: The Gospel of Socialism in the Oklahoma Countryside, 1910–1924*. Greenwood, 1976. 224 pp. $13.95 cloth.
BURBY, RAYMOND J., III. *Recreation and Leisure in New Communities*. Ballinger, 1976. 366 pp. $17.50 cloth.
BURKOLTER, VERENA. *The Patronage System: Theoretical Remarks*. Social Strategies Publishers Co-operative Society, 1976. 53 pp. NPL, paper.
BURNS, TOM R., and BUCKLEY, WALTER, eds. *Power and Control: Social Structures and Their Transformation*. Sage, 1976. 290 pp. $12.00 cloth. $6.00 paper.
BUTT, DORCAS SUSAN. *Psychology of Sport: The Behavior, Motivation, Personality, and Performance of Athletes*. Van Nostrand Reinhold, 1976. 196 pp. $12.95 cloth. $6.95 paper.
CADITZ, JUDITH. *White Liberals in Transition: Current Dilemmas of Ethnic Integration*. Spectrum, dist. by Halsted, 1976. 187 pp. $12.50 cloth.
CAFFERTY, PASTORA SAN JUAN, and CHESTANG, LEON, eds. *The Diverse Society: Implications for Social Policy*. National Association of Social Workers, 1976. 176 pp. NPL, paper.
CANFIELD, ROBERT LeROY. *Faction and Conversion in a Plural Society: Religious Alignments in the Hindu Kush*. University of Michigan, 1973. 142 pp. $3.00 paper.
CARDINAL, HAROLD. *The Rebirth of Canada's Indians*. Hurtig, 1977. 222 pp. $9.95 cloth. $4.95 paper.
CARMICHAEL, JOEL. *Arabs Today*. Anchor, 1977, 216 pp. $2.95 paper.
CARNEY, LOUIS P. *Corrections and the Community*. Prentice-Hall, 1977. 342 pp. $13.95 cloth.
CARTER, ROBERT M.; GLASER, DANIEL; and WILKINS, LESLIE T., eds. *Correctional Institutions*, 2nd ed. J. B. Lippincott, 1977. 571 pp. $7.95 paper
CHADWICK-JONES, J. K. *Social Exchange Theory: Its Structure and Influence in Social Psychology*. Academic Press, 1976. 431 pp. $29.25 cloth.
CHANGE MAGAZINE PRESS, eds. *The Third Century: Twenty-Six Prominent Americans Speculate on the Educational Future*. Change Magazine Press, 1977. 194 pp. $9.95 cloth.
CHAO, YUEN REN. *Aspects of Chinese Sociolinguistics*. Stanford University Press, 1976. 415 pp. $13.50 cloth.
CHISMAN, FORREST P. *Attitude Psychology and the Study of Public Opinion*. Pennsylvania State University Press, 1976. 253 pp. $13.50 cloth.
CLANTON, GORDON, and SMITH, LYNN G., eds. *Jealousy*. Prentice-Hall, 1977. 244 pp. $8.95 cloth. $3.95 paper.
CLARK, ROBERT S. *Fundamentals of Criminal Justice Research*. Lexington Books, 1977. 181 pp. NPL, cloth.
CLEVERLEY, GRAHAM. *The Fleet Street Disaster: British National Newspapers as a Case Study in Mismanagement*. Sage, 1976. 175 pp. $12.95 cloth.
CLYNES, MANFRED. *Sentics: The Touch of Emotions*. Anchor, 1977. 249 pp. $7.95 cloth.
COHEN, ROBERT. *"New Careers" Grows Older: A Perspective on the Paraprofessional Experience, 1965–1975*. Johns Hopkins University Press, 1976. 132 pp. $9.50 cloth. $3.50 paper.
CONNELL, R. W. *Ruling Class, Ruling Culture: Studies of Conflict, Power and Hegemony in Australian Life*. Cambridge University Press, 1977. 250 pp. $19.95 cloth. $5.95 paper.
CONRAD, PETER. *Identifying Hyperactive Children: The Medicalization of Deviant Behavior*. Lexington Books, 1976. 122 pp. NPL, cloth.
CONVERSE, PHILIP E. *The Dynamics of Party Support: Cohort-Analyzing Party Identification*. Sage, 1976. 175 pp. $11.00 cloth. $6.00 paper.
CRAPANZANO, VINCENT, and GARRISON, VIVIAN, eds. *Case Studies in Spirit Possession*. Wiley, 1977. 457 pp. NPL, cloth.
CRITES, LAURA, ed. *The Female Offender*. Lexington Books, 1976. 230 pp. $18.00 cloth.
DAVIS, J. *People of the Mediterranean: An Essay in Comparative Social Anthropology*. Routledge & Kegan Paul, 1977. 288 pp. $14.00 cloth.
DE JESUS, EMILINDA V., comp. *Mass Communication in the Philippines: An Annotated Bibliography*. Asian Communication Research and Information Centre, 1976. 335 pp. NPL, paper.
DINNERSTEIN, LEONARD, and JAHER, FREDERIC COLE, eds. *Uncertain Americans: Readings in Ethnic History*. Oxford University Press, 1977. 325 pp. $4.00 paper.
DOLGIN, JANET L. *Jewish Identity and the JDL*. Princeton University Press, 1977. 189 pp. $12.50 cloth.
DOREIAN, PATRICK, and HUMMON, NORMAN P. *Modeling Social Processes*. Elsevier, 1976. 172 pp. $10.50 cloth.
DOWNES, D. M., et al. *Gambling, Work and Leisure: A Study across Three Areas*. Routledge & Kegan Paul, 1976. 260 pp. $22.00 cloth.
DRAPER, HAL. *Karl Marx's Theory of Revolution: Part 1: State and Bureaucracy*, in two volumes. Monthly Review Press, 1977. 728 pp. $28.50 set, cloth.
DREYER, JUNE TEUFEL. *China's Forty Millions: Minority Nationalities and National Integration in the People's Republic of China*. Harvard University Press, 1976. 333 pp. $14.00 cloth.
EASTMAN, GEORGE D., and CHAPMAN, SAMUEL G. *Short of Merger: Country Wide Police Resource Pooling*. Lexington Books, 1976. 159 pp. $14.00 cloth.
EDISON ELECTRIC INSTITUTE. *Economic Growth in the Future: The Growth Debate in National and Global Perspective*. McGraw-Hill, 1976. 423 pp. $19.50 cloth.
ELLIS, ALBERT. *Sex and the Liberated Man*. Lyle Stuart, 1976. 347 pp. $12.95 cloth.
EMBER, CAROL R. and EMBER, MELVIN. *Cultural Anthropology*, 2nd ed. Prentice-Hall, 1977. Orig. pub. 1973. 361 pp. $9.95 paper.
ERIKSON, ERIK H. *Toys and Reasons: Stages in the Ritualization of Experience*. W. W. Norton, 1977. 182 pp. $8.95 cloth.
ERIKSON, KAI T. *Everything in Its Path: Destruction of Community in the Buffalo Creek Flood*. Simon & Schuster, 1976. 284 pp. $8.95 cloth.
EVAN, WILLIAM M. *Organization Theory: Structures, Systems, and Environments*. Wiley, 1976. 312 pp. $14.95 cloth.
EVANS, ROBERT H. *Life and Politics in a Venetian Community*. University of Notre Dame Press, 1976. 228 pp. $15.95 cloth.
FEATHER, NORMAN T. *Values in Education and Society*. Free Press, 1975. 350 pp. $14.95 cloth.
FLOYD, MARY K., comp. *Abortion Bibliography for 1975*. Whitston, 1976. 295 pp. $12.00 cloth.
FLYNN, CHARLES P. *Insult and Society: Patterns of Comparative Interaction*. National University Publications/Kennikat Press, 1977. 131 pp. $9.95 cloth.
FOX, RICHARD G. *Urban Anthropology: Cities in Their Cultural Settings*. Prentice-Hall, 1977. 176 pp. $5.95 paper.
FRANCOEUR, ROBERT T., and FRANCOEUR, ANNA K. *Hot and Cool Sex: Cultures in Conflict*. A. S. Barnes, 1976. 220 pp. $3.95 paper.
FRANK, HAROLD H. *Women in the Organization*. University of Pennsylvania Press, 1977. 308 pp. $12.00 paper.
FRIEDMAN, KENNETH M., and RAKOFF, STUART H., eds. *Toward a National Health Policy: Public Policy and the Control of Health-Care Costs*. Lexington Books, 1977. 257 pp. $14.50 cloth.
FRIEDMAN, LAWRENCE M., and MACAULAY, STEWART. *Law and the Behavioral Sciences*, 2nd ed. Bobbs-Merrill, 1977. Orig. pub. 1969. 1,076 pp. NPL, cloth.
GANS, HERBERT J. *Popular Culture and High Culture: An Analysis and Evaluation of Taste*. Basic Books, 1974. 179 pp. $10.00 cloth. $3.95 paper.
GARSON, BARBARA. *All the Livelong Day: The Meaning and Demeaning of Routine Work*. Penguin 1977. 221 pp. $1.95 paper.
GATH, DENNIS, et al. *Child Guidance and Delinquency in a London Borough*. Oxford University Press, 1977. 189 pp. $15.75 cloth.
GEE, EMMA, ed. *Counterpoint: Perspectives on Asian America*. Asian American Stduies Center/UCLA, 1976. 595 pp. $8.95 paper.
GILCHRIST, WARREN. *Statistical Forecasting*. Wiley, 1976. 308 pp. $19.95 cloth. $10.50 paper.
GINER, SALVADOR, *Mass Society*. Academic Press, 1976. 288 pp. $14.50 cloth.
GLIDEWELL, JOHN C., ed. *The Social Context of Learning and Development*. Gardner, dist. by Halsted, 1977. 239 pp. $18.95 cloth.
GLOCK, CHARLES, and BELLAH, ROBERT N., eds. *The New Religious Consciousness*. University of California Press, 1976. 391 pp. $14.95 cloth.
GOLD, ALICE ROSS; CHRISTIE, RICHARD; and FRIEDMAN, LUCY NORMAN. *Fists and Flowers:*

A Social Psychological Interpretation of Student Dissent. Academic Press, 1976. 204 pp. $11.50 cloth.

GOLDBERG, JOSEPH P. et al. *Federal Policies and Worker Status since the Thirties*. Industrial Relations Research Association, 1976. 269 pp. $7.50 paper.

GORMAN, ROBERT A. *The Dual Vision: Alfred Schutz and the Myth of Phenomenological Social Science*. Routledge & Kegan Paul, 1977. 234 pp. $8.75 cloth.

GRATHOFF, RICHARD, and SPRONDEL, WALTER, eds. *Maurice. Merleau-Ponty und das Problem der Struktur in den Sozialwissenschaften*. Ferdinand Enke, 1976. 193 pp. NPL, paper.

GREELEY, ANDREW M. *The American Catholic: A Social Portrait*. Basic Books, 1977. 280 pp. $15.00 cloth.

GREENWOOD, GEORGE. *Love and Lawgic: Territorialisticism Exposed*. Vantage, 1975. 193 pp. $5.95 cloth.

GREEP, ROY O.; KOBLINSKY, MARGORIE A.; and JAFFE, FREDERICK S. *Reproduction and Human Welfare: A Challenge to Research: A Review of the Reproductive Sciences and Contraceptive Development*. MIT Press, 1976. 622 pp. $16.95 cloth.

GREW, RAYMOND, and STENECK, NICHOLAS, eds. *Society and History: Essays by Sylvia L, Thrupp*. University of Michigan Press, 1977. 363 pp. $18.50 cloth.

GRINSPOON, LESTER, and BAKALAR, JAMES B. *Cocaine: A Drug and Its Social Evolution*. Basic Books, 1976. 308 pp. $15.00 cloth.

GROUP FOR THE ADVANCEMENT OF PSYCHIATRY. *Mysticism: Spiritual Quest or Psychic Disorder?* Group for the Advancement of Psychiatry, 1976. 117 pp. $4.00 paper.

GUILLET, DAVID, and UZZELL, eds. *New Approaches to the Study of Migration*. William Marsh Rice University, 1976. 181 pp. NPL, paper.

GUTMAN, HERBERT G. *The Black Family in Slavery and Freedom, 1750–1925*. Pantheon Books, 1976. 664 pp. $15.95 cloth.

HACKER, FREDERICK F. *Crusaders, Criminals, Crazies: Terror and Terrorism in Our Time*. W. W. Norton, 1976. 353 pp. $9.95 cloth.

HALE, JULIAN. *Radio Power: Propaganda and International Broadcasting*. Temple University Press, 1975. 196 pp. NPL, cloth.

HALEVY, ZSI. *Jewish Schools under Czarism and Communism: A Struggle for Cultural Identity*. Springer, 1976. 298 pp. $14.50 cloth.

HALL, EDWARD T. *Beyond Culture*. Anchor, 1977. 298 pp. $2.95 paper.

HALL, STUART, and JEFFERSON, TONY, eds. *Resistance through Rituals: Youth Subcultures in Post-War Britain*. Holmes & Meier, 1976. 287 pp. NPL, cloth.

HALLS, W. D. *Education, Culture and Politics in Modern France*. Pergamon Press, 1976. 276 pp. $12.50 cloth. $6.50 paper.

HANUSHEK, ERIC A., and JACKSON, JOHN E. *Statistical Methods for Social Scientists*. Academic Press, 1977. 374 pp. $19.00 cloth.

HARRINGTON, ALAN. *The Immortalist*. Celestial Arts, 1977. Orig. pub. 1969. 313 pp. $5.95 paper.

HARRISON, G. A., and GIBSON, J. B., eds. *Man in Urban Environments*. Oxford University Press, 1977. 367 pp. $15.75 cloth.

HARTMAN, MARY S. *Victorian Murderesses: A True History of Thirteen Respectable French and English Women Accused of Unspeakable Crimes*. Schocken Books, 1977. 318 pp. $15.00 cloth.

HARVEY, JOHN H., and SMITH, WILLIAM P. *Social Psychology: An Attributional Approach*, with instructor's manual. C. V. Mosby, 1977. 426 pp. NPL, paper.

HAWTHORN, GEOFFREY, *Enlightenment and Despair: A History of Sociology*. Cambridge University Press, 1976. 295 pp. $17.95 cloth. $5.95 paper.

HEARNDEN, ARTHUR. *Education, Culture, and Politics in West Germany*. Pergamon, 1976. 164 pp. $12.50 cloth. $6.50 paper.

HELLER, CELIA S. *On the Edge of Destruction: Jews of Poland between the Two World Wars*. Columbia University Press, 1977. 369 pp. $14.95 cloth.

HENRY, LOUIS. *Population: Analysis and Models*. Academic Press, 1976. 301 pp. $19.50 cloth.

HENSHEL, RICHARD L. *Reacting to Social Problems*. Longman Canada, 1976. 191 pp. NPL, paper.

HERBERT, D. T., and JOHNSTON, R. J., eds. *Social Areas in Cities. Volume I: Spatial Processes and Form. Volume II: Spatial Perspectives on Problems and Policies*. Wiley, 1976. 281 & 243 pp. $19.50 & $18.95 cloth.

HILL, LARRY B. *The Model Ombudsman: Institutionalizing New Zealand's Democratic Experiment*. Princeton University Press, 1976. 411 pp. $18.50 cloth.

HINDELANG, MICHAEL J. *Criminal Victimization in Eight American Cities: A Descriptive Analysis of Common Theft and Assault*. Ballinger, 1976. 499 pp. $22.50 cloth.

HÖRNING, KARL H. *Gesellschaftliche Entwicklung und soziale Schichtung: Vergleichende Analyse gesellschaftlichen Strukturwandels*. Verlag Dokumentation, 1976. 208 pp. NPL, paper.

HÖRNING, KARL H., ed. *Soziale Ungleichheit: Strukturen und Prozesse sozialer Schichtung*. Hermann Luchterhand, 1976. 260 pp. NPL, paper.

HOROWITZ, DONALD L. *The Courts and Social Policy*. Brookings Institution, 1977. 309 pp. $11.95 cloth. $4.95 paper.

HUDSON, JOE, and GALAWAY, BURT, eds. *Restitution in Criminal Justice: A Critical Assessment of Sanctions*. Lexington Books, 1977. 180 pp. $17.00 cloth.

JINDEL, RAJENDRA. *Culture of a Sacred Town: A Sociological Study of Nathdwara*. Popular Prakashan, 1976. 233 pp. NPL, cloth.

JONES, GRACE A. *The Political Structure*, 2nd ed. Longman, 1976. Orig. pub. 1969. 125 pp. $4.75 paper.

JONES, HARDIN B., and JONES, HELEN C. *Sensual Drugs: Deprivation and Rehabilitation of the Mind*. Cambridge University Press, 1977. 373 pp. $15.95 cloth. $3.95 paper.

JONES, KENNETH L.; SHAINBERG, LOUIS W.; and BYER, CURTIS O. *Sex and People*. Harper & Row, 1977. 365 pp. $12.95 cloth.

KAISER, EDWARD J. *Residential Mobility in New Communities: An Analysis of Recent In-movers and Prospective Out-movers*. Ballinger, 1976. 188 pp. $15.00 cloth.

KAMARCK, ANDREW M. *The Tropics and Economic Development: A Provocative Inquiry into the Poverty of Nations*. Johns Hopkins University Press, 1977. 113 pp. $7.50 cloth. $3.00 paper.

KARDINER, A. *My Analysis with Freud*. W. W. Norton, 1977. 123 pp. $6.95 cloth.

KARP, LAURENCE E. *Genetic Engineering: Threat or Promise?* Nelson-Hall, 1976. 235 pp. NPL, cloth.

KÄSLER, DIRK, ed. *Klassiker des Soziologischen Denkens: Erster Band von Comte bis Durkheim*. C. H. Beck, 1976. 530 pp. NPL, cloth.

KESSNER, THOMAS. *The Golden Door: Italian and Jewish Immigrant Mobility in New York City 1880–1915*. Oxford University Press, 1977. 224 pp. $12.95 cloth. $3.50 paper.

KIELL, NORMAN. *Varieties of Sexual Experience: Psychosexuality in Literature*. International Universities Press, 1976. 753 pp. $25.00 cloth.

KING, F. P., ed. *Oceania and Beyond: Essays on the Pacific since 1945*. Greenwood, 1976. 265 pp. $22.50 cloth.

KOBAYASHI, TETSUYA. *Society, Schools, and Progress in Japan*. Pergamon, 1976. 185 pp. $12.50 cloth. $6.50 paper.

KOSOLAPOV, V. *Mankind and the Year 2000*. Progress, dist. by Imported Publications, 1976. 236 pp. $2.50 cloth.

KRAMER-GREENE, JUDITH, comp. *Venereal Disease Bibliography for 1974*. Whitston, 1976. 446 pp. $15.00 cloth.

KURTZ, JOHN W. *John Frederic Oberlin*. Westview, 1976. 341 pp. $15.00 cloth.

L'ABATE, LUCIANO. *Understanding and Helping the Individual in the Family*. Grune & Stratton, 1976. 261 pp. $16.50 cloth.

LACONTE, P., ed. in chief. *The Environment of Human Settlements: Human Well-being in Cities: Proceedings of the Conference held in Brussels, Belgium, April 1976*, vol. 1. Pergamon, 1976. 311 pp. $22.50 cloth.

LANSIPURO, YRJO; SHAHZADEH, IBRAHIM; and ANG, LUKE. *Television News Exchange in Asia*. Asian Mass Communication Research & Information Centre, 1976. 77 pp. $6.00 paper.

LEPSIUS, M. RAINER., ed. *Zwischenbilanz der Soziologie*. Ferdinand Enke, 1976. 455 pp. NPL, paper.

LERNER, ALLAN W. *The Politics of Decision-Making: Strategy, Cooperation, and Conflict*. Sage, 1976. 215 pp. $11.00 cloth. $6.00 paper.

LEVI, MARGARET. *Bureaucratic Insurgency: The Case of Police Unions*. Lexington Books, 1977. 165 pp. $15.00 cloth.

LIBBY, ROGER W., and WHITEHURST, ROBERT N. *Marriage and Alternatives: Exploring Intimate Relationships*. Scott, Foresman, 1977. 412 pp. $6.95 paper.

LIPSITZ, JOAN. *Growing Up Forgotten: A Review of Research and Programs Concerning Early Adolescence*. Lexington Books, 1977. 267 pp. $16.00 cloth.

LIPTON, MICHAEL. *Why Poor People Stay Poor: Urban Bias in World Development*. Harvard University, Press, 1976. 467 pp. $15.00 cloth.

LOEWENBERG, BERT JAMES, and BOGIN, RUTH. *Black Women in Nineteenth-Century American Life: Their Words, Their Thoughts, Their Feelings*. Pennsylvania State University Press, 1976. 355 pp. $16.95 cloth. $7.95 paper.

LOEWENBERG, F. M. *Fundamentals of Social Intervention: Core Concepts and Skills for Social Work Practice*. Columbia University Press, 1977. 374 pp. $12.50 cloth.
LOUDON, J. B., ed. *Social Anthropology and Medicine: A.S.A. Monograph 13*. Academic Press, 1976. 600 pp. NPL, cloth.
LUCAS, STEPHEN E. *Portents of Rebellion: Rhetoric and Revolution in Philadelphia, 1765–76*. Temple University Press, 1976. 333 pp. NPL, cloth.
LÜSCHEN, GÜNTHER, and WIES, KURT, eds. *Die Soziologie des Sports*. Hermann Luchterhand, 1976. 339 pp. NPL, paper.
MACCOBY, MICHAEL. *The Gamesman: The New Corporate Leaders*. Simon & Schuster, 1976. 285 pp. $8.95 cloth.
MALEC, MICHAEL A. *Essential Statistics for Social Research*. J. B. Lippencott, 1977. 235 pp. $7.95 paper.
MARTIN, B. G. *Muslim Brotherhoods in Nineteenth-Century Africa*. Cambridge University Press, 1976. 267 pp. $19.95 cloth.
MARTZ, JOHN D., and BALOYRA, ENRIQUE A. *Electoral Mobilization and Public Opinion: The Venezuelan Campaign of 1973*. University of North Carolina Press, 1976. 339 pp. $17.95 cloth.
McCORD, ARLINE, and McCORD, WILLIAM. *Urban Social Conflict*. C. V. Mosby, 1977. 201 pp. NPL, paper.
McCORD, WILLIAM, and McCORD, ARLINE. *American Social Problems: Challenges to Existence*, with instructor's guide. C. V. Mosby, 1977. 291 pp. NPL, paper.
MILLER, WILBUR R. *Cops and Bobbies: Police Authority in New York and London, 1830–1870*. University of Chicago Press, 1977. 233 pp. $16.00 cloth.
MILLMAN, MARCIA. *The Unkindest Cut: Life in the Backrooms of Medicine*. William Morrow, 1977. 252 pp. $8.95 cloth.
MITCHELL, DOUGLAS D. *Amaeru: The Expression of Reciprocal Dependency Needs in Japanese Politics and Law*. Westview, 1976. 288 pp. NPL, cloth.
MOLLENKOTT, VIRGINIA RAMEY. *Women, Men, and the Bible*. Abingdon, 1977. 144 pp. $3.95 paper.
MONTAGNA, PAUL D. *Occupations and Society: Toward a Sociology of the Labor Market*. Wiley, 1977. 456 pp. $12.95 cloth.
MOOR, CHRISTINE H. *From School to Work: Effective Counseling and Guidance*. Sage, 1976. 191 pp. $13.50 cloth. NPL, paper.
MOORE, KENNETH. *Those of the Street: The Catholic-Jews of Mallorca*. University of Notre Dame Press, 1976. 218 pp. $11.95 cloth.
MORONEY, ROBERT M. *The Family and the State: Consideration for Social Policy*. Longman, 1976. 142 pp. $6.50 paper.
MORRIS, MONICA B. *An Excursion into Creative Sociology*. Columbia University Press, 1977. 212 pp. $10.00 cloth.
NEFELSKI, PAUL, ed. *Social Research in Conflict with Law and Ethics*. Ballinger, 1976. 197 pp. $15.00 cloth.
NEWMAN, CHARLES L., and PRICE, BARBARA R. *Jails and Drug Treatment*. Sage, 1977. 223 pp. $11.00 cloth. $6.00 paper.
O'NEIL, DANIEL J. *Three Perennial Themes of Anti-Colonialism: The Irish Case*. University of Denver/Graduate School of International Studies, 1976. 131 pp. NPL, paper.
ORGANISATION FOR ECONOMIC CO-OPERATION AND DEVELOPMENT. *Measuring Social Well-Being: A Progress Report on the Development of Social Indicators*. OECD, 1976. 213 pp. $8.50 paper.
O'TOOLE, JAMES, and THE UNIVERSITY OF SOUTHERN CALIFORNIA CENTER FOR FUTURES RESEARCH. *Energy and Social Change*. MIT Press, 1976. 184 pp. $9.95 cloth.
OWEN, A. L. RIESCH. *Selig Perlman's Lectures on Capitalism and Socialism*. University of Wisconsin Press, 1976. 183 pp. $12.50 cloth.
PATRICK, HUGH, ed. *Japanese Industrialization and Its Social Consequences*. University of California Press, 1976. 505 pp. $6.95 paper.
PERRY, JOHN, and PERRY, ERNA. *Pairing and Parenthood: An Introduction to Marriage and the Family*. Canfield, 1976. 400 pp. $11.95 cloth.
POTEET, G. HOWARD. *Death and Dying: A Bibliography (1950–1974)*. Whitston, 1976. 192 pp. $12.50 cloth.
POTHOLM, CHRISTIAN P., and MORGAN, RICHARD E. *Focus on Police: Police in American Society*. Halsted, 1976. 412 pp. $16.95 cloth. $6.95 paper.
PRATT, HENRY J. *The Gray Lobby*. University of Chicago Press, 1976. 250 pp. $15.00 cloth.
PRESTON, SAMUEL H. *Mortality Patterns in National Populations: With Special Reference to Recorded Causes of Death*. Academic Press, 1976. 201 pp. $16.50 cloth.
PROGER, SAMUEL, and WILLIAMS, GREER. *A Career in Primary Care*. Ballinger, 1976. 190 pp. $15.00 cloth.
PUROLA, TAPAI; KALIMO, ESKO; and NYMAN, KAUKO. *Health Services Use and Health Status under National Sickness Insurance: An Evaluative Resurvey of Finland*. Social Insurance Institution, Finland, 1974. 317 pp. NPL, paper.
QUINNEY, RICHARD, and WILDEMAN, JOHN. *The Problem of Crime: A Critical Introduction to Criminology*, 2nd ed. Harper & Row, 1977. 198 pp. $8.50 paper.
RABINOWITCH, ALEXANDER. *The Bolsheviks Come to Power: The Revolution of 1917 in Petrograd*. W. W. Norton, 1976. 393 pp. $14.95 cloth.
READ, WILLIAM H. *America's Mass Media Merchants*. Johns Hopkins University Press, 1977. 209 pp. $10.95 cloth.
REECK, DARRELL. *Deep Mende: Religious Interactions in a Changing African Rural Society*. E. J. Brill, 1976. 102 pp. NPL, cloth.
RHODES, ROBERT P. *The Insoluable Problems of Crime*. Wiley, 1977. 269 pp. $7.95 paper.
RIDKER, RONALD G., ed. *Population and Development: The Search for Selective Interventions*. Johns Hopkins University Press, 1976. 467 pp. $22.50 cloth.
RIEDEL, MARC, and VALES, PEDRO A., eds. *Treating the Offender: Problems and Issues*. Praeger, 1977. 177 pp. NPL, cloth.
RIVERA, ANGEL QUINTERO. *Workers' Struggle in Puerto Rico: A Documentary History* Tr. Cedric Belfrage. Monthly Review Press, 1976. 236 pp. $11.95 cloth.
ROEMER, MILTON I. *Health Care Systems in World Perspective*. Health Administration Press, 1976. 289 pp. NPL, cloth.
ROSE, HAROLD M. *Black Suburbanization: Access to Improved Quality of Life or Maintenance of the Status Quo?* Ballinger, 1976. 288 pp. $16.00 cloth.
ROSE, PETER I; GLAZER, MYRON; and GLAZER, PENINA MIGDAL. *Sociology: Inquiring into Society*. Canfield, 1977. 605 pp. $13.95 cloth.
RUBINGTON, EARL, and WEINBERG, MARTIN S. *The Study of Social Problems: Five Perspectives*, 2nd ed. Oxford Press, 1977. 253 pp. $5.00 paper.
RUGINA, ANGHEL N. *American Capitalism at a Crossroads! Where Do We Go from Here?: A Chronicle of How Three United States Presidents Missed Sound Economic Advice to Resolve the Problems of Inflation, Unemployment,. Poverty and Deficits in the Balance of Payments*. Exposition Press, 1976. 269 pp. $9.50 cloth.
RUNYON, RICHARD P. *Winning with Statistics: A Painless First Look at Numbers, Ratios, Percentages, Means, and Inference*. Addison-Wesley, 1977. 210 pp. $5.95 paper.
SAHLINS, MARSHALL. *Culture and Practical Reason*. University of Chicago Press, 1976. 252 pp. $17.50 cloth.
SALT, JOHN, and CLOUT, HUGH, eds. *Migration in Post-War Europe: Geographical Essays*. Oxford University Press, 1976. 228 pp. $12.50 cloth.
SAWARD, ERNEST W. ed. *The Regionalization of Personal Health Services*, rev. ed. Prodist, 1976. 305 pp. $15.00 cloth. $6.95 paper.
SCHRAMM, WILBUR, and LERNER, DANIEL, eds. *Communication and Change: The Last Ten Years—and the Next*. University Press of Hawaii, 1976. 372 pp. $16.00 cloth.
SCHWARTZ, MICHAEL. *Radical Protest and Social Structure: The Southern Farmers' Alliance and Cotton Tenancy. 1880–1890*. Academic Press, 1976. 302 pp. $17.50 cloth.
SCHWARTZ, PUSHPA NAND, ed. *Confrontation or Cooperation? Proceedings of the 14th World Conference of the Society for International Development held in Abidjan, Ivory Coast, August 12–16, 1974*. Pergamon, 1976. 104 pp. $10.00 paper.
SCIMECCA, JOSEPH A. *The Sociological Theory of C. Wright Mills*. National University Publications/Kennikat Press, 1977. 148 pp. $9.95 cloth.
SCULL, ANDREW T. *Decarceration: Community Treatment and the Deviant: A Radical View*. Prentice-Hall, 1977. 184 pp. $8.95 cloth. $3.95 paper.
SHAPIRO-BERTOLINI, ETHEL. *Through the Wall: Prison Correspondence*. Peace Press, 1976. 353 pp. $5.95 paper.
SHOLEVAR, G. PIROOZ, ed. *Changing Sexual Values and the Family*. Charles C Thomas, 1977. 179 pp. $11.95 cloth.
SHOUP, LAURENCE H., and MINTER, WILLIAM. *Imperial Brain Trust: The Council on Foreign Relations and United States Foreign Policy*. Monthly Review Press, 1977. 344 pp. $17.50 cloth.
SHOVER, JOHN L. *First Majority-Last Minority: The Transforming of Rural Life in America*. Northern Illinois University Press, 1976. 338 pp. NPL, cloth.
SICARD, GERALD L., and WEINBERGER, PHILIP. *Sociology of Our Times*. Scott, Foresman, 1977. 329 pp. $5.95 paper.

SIMÕES, ANTÓNIO, JR., ed. *The Bilingual Child: Research and Analysis of Existing Educational Themes.* Academic Press, 1976. 272 pp. $16.50 cloth.
SIMPSON, RUTH. *From the Closet to the Courts: The Lesbian Transition.* Penguin Books, 1977. 180 pp. $2.25 paper.
SINGER, JUNE. *Androgyny: Toward a New Theory of Sexuality.* Anchor Press, 1976. 375 pp. $8.95 cloth.
SINHA, P. R. R., ed. *Communcation and Rural Change.* Asian Mass Communication Research and Information Centre, 1976. 232 pp. $21.00 paper.
SLATER, PHIL. *Origin and Significance of the Frankfurt School: A Marxist Perspective.* Routledge & Kegan Paul, 1977. 185 pp. $13.75 cloth.
SMART, CAROL. *Women, Crime and Criminology: A Feminist Critique.* Routledge & Kegan Paul, 1976. 208 pp. $10.50 cloth.
SMITH, RONALD W., and PRESTON, FREDERICK W. *Sociology: An Introduction,* with instructor's manual. St. Martin's Press, 1977. 575 pp. NPL, cloth.
SMOOKLER, HELENE V. *Economic Integration in New Communities: An Evaluation of Factors Affecting Policies and Implementation.* Ballinger, 1976. 236 pp. $15.50 cloth.
SPERBER, MICHAEL A., and JARVIK, LISSY F., eds. *Psychiatry and Genetics: Psychosocial, Ethical, and Legal Considerations.* Basic Books, 1977. 204 pp. $10.95 cloth.
STARK, WERNER. *The Social Bond: An Investigation into the Bases of Law-abidingness, Volume One: Antecedents of the Social Bond, The Phylogeny of Sociality.* Fordham University Press, 1976. 229 pp. $15.00 cloth. $7.50 paper.
STEARNS, PETER N. *Old Age in European Society: The Case of France.* Holmes & Meier, 1976. 163 pp. $16.00 cloth.
STIVERS, RICHARD. *A Hair of the Dog: Irish Drinking and American Stereotype.* Pennsylvania State University Press, 1976. 197 pp. $13.50 cloth.
STOHL, MICHAEL. *War and Domestic Political Violence: The American Capacity for Repression and Reaction.* Sage, 1976. 153 pp. $11.00 cloth. $6.00 paper.
SUTTON, S. B. *Cambridge Reconsidered: Three and a Half Centuries on the Charles.* MIT Press, 1976. 134 pp. $4.50 paper.
SWEETS, JOHN F. *The Politics of Resistance in France, 1940-1944: A History of the Mouvements Unis de la Resistance.* Northern Illinois University Press, 1976. 260 pp. NPL, cloth.
TANNENBAUM, EDWARD R. *1900: The Generation before the Great War.* Anchor Press, 1976. 463 pp. $10.00 cloth.
TAX, SOL, and FREEMAN, LESLIE G., eds. *Horizons of Anthropology,* 2nd ed. Aldine, 1977. 391 pp. $14.95 cloth.
THURSZ, DANIEL, and VIGILANTE, JOSEPH L., eds. *Meeting Human Needs 2: Additional Perspectives from Thirteen Countries.* Sage, 1976. 286 pp. $17.50 cloth. $7.50 paper.
TIMASHEFF, NICHOLAS S., and THEODORSON, GEORGE A. *Sociological Theory: Its Nature and Growth,* 4t ed. Random House, 1976. 403 pp. NPL, cloth.
TOMPKINS, MARGARET, and SHIRLEY, NORMA. *Serials in Psychology and Allied Fields,* 2nd ed. rev. & enlg. Whitston, 1976. 472 pp. $22.50 cloth.
TOURAINE, ALAIN. *La Société Invisible: Regards 1974–1976.* Éditions du Seuil, 1977. 285 pp. NPL, paper.
TRICHE, CHARLES W., III, and TRICHE, DIANE SAMSON, comps. *Drug Abuse Bibliography for 1974.* Whitston, 1976. 450 pp. $18.00 cloth.
TRICHE, CHARLES W., III, and TRICHE, DIANE SAMSON. *The Euthanasia Controversy 1812–1974: A Bibliography with Select Annotations.* Whitston, 1975. 242 pp. NPL, cloth.
TRIPODI, TONY, et al. *Social Workers at Work: An Introduction to Social Work Practice,* 2nd ed. F. E. Peacock, 1977. 259 pp. $5.95 paper.
VAN DEN BERGHE, PIERRE L., and PRIMOV, GEORGE P. *Inequality in the Peruvian Andes: Class and Ethnicity in Cuzco.* University of Missouri Press, 1977. 324 pp. $17.50 cloth.
VAN DER POST, LAURENS. *Jung and the Story of Our Times.* Vintage Books, 1975. 275 pp. $3.95 paper.
VASIL'EVA, EVELINA KARLOVNA. *The Young People of Leningrad: School and Work Options and Attitudes.* International Arts and Sciences Press, 1975,6. 177 pp. $15.00 cloth.
VERGHESE, GEORGE. *Project Chhatera: An Experiment in Development Journalism.* Asian Mass Communication Research and Information Centre, 1976. 14 pp. $3.00 paper.
VREE, DALE. *On Synthesizing Marxism and Christianity.* Wiley, 1976. 206 pp. $14.95 cloth.
WACHTEL, PAUL L. *Psychoanalysis and Behavior Therapy: Toward an Intergration.* Basic Books, 1977. 315 pp. $15.00 cloth.
WARREN, CAROL A. B. *Sociology: Change and Continuity.* Dorsey, 1977. 427 pp. $12.95 cloth.
WATZLAWICK, PAUL. *How Real Is Real?: Confusion, Disinformation, Communication.* Vintage, 1976. 265 pp. $2.95 paper.
WATZLAWICK, PAUL, and WEAKLAND, JOHN H., eds. *The Interactional View: Studies at the Mental Research Institute, Palo Alto, 1965–1974.* W. W. Norton, 1977. 405 pp. $12.50 cloth.
WEBB, RODMAN B. *The Presence of the Past: John Dewey and Alfred Schutz on the Genesis and Organization of Experience.* University Presses of Florida, 1976. 133 pp. $4.50 paper.
WEINBERG, MARTHA WAGNER. *Managing the State.* MIT Press, 1977. 244 pp. $5.95 paper.
WEINSTEIN, MICHAEL A. *The Polarity of Mexican Thought: Instrumentalism and Finalism.* Pennsylvania State University Press, 1976. 128 pp. $11.95 cloth.
WHITE, RONALD C. JR., and HOPKINS, C. HOWARD. *The Social Gospel: Religion and Reform in Changing America.* Temple University Press, 1976. 306 pp. NPL, paper.
WHITEHURST, CAROL A. *Women in America: The Oppressed Majority.* Goodyear, 1977. 164 pp. $8.95 cloth.
WILLENER, ALFRED; MILLIARD, GUY; and GANTY, ALEX, *Videology and Utopia: Explorations in a New Medium.* Tr. & ed. Diana Burfield. Routledge & Kegan Paul, 1976. 171 pp. $10.50 paper.
WILLIAMS, ELIZABETH FRIAR. *Notes of a Feminist Therapist.* Dell, 1976. 219 pp. $1.50 paper.
WILLIAMSON, NANCY E. *Sons or Daughters: A Cross-Cultural Survey of Parental Preferences.* Sage, 1976. 207 pp. $11.00 cloth. $6.00 paper.
WILSON, FLORENCE A., and NEUHAUSER, DUNCAN. *Health Services in the United States,* rev. & enlg. 1st ed. Ballinger, 1976. 283 pp. $10.00 cloth.
WINNER, LANGDON. *Autonomous Technology: Technics-out-of-Control as a Theme in Political Thought.* MIT Press, 1977. 386 pp. $17.50 cloth.
WORKS, JOHN A., JR. *Pilgrims in a Strange Land: Hausa Communities in Chad.* Columbia University Press, 1976. 280 pp. $15.00 cloth.
ZALTMAN, GERALD, and DUNCAN, ROBERT. *Strategies for Planned Change.* Wiley, 1977. 404 pp. $19.95 cloth.

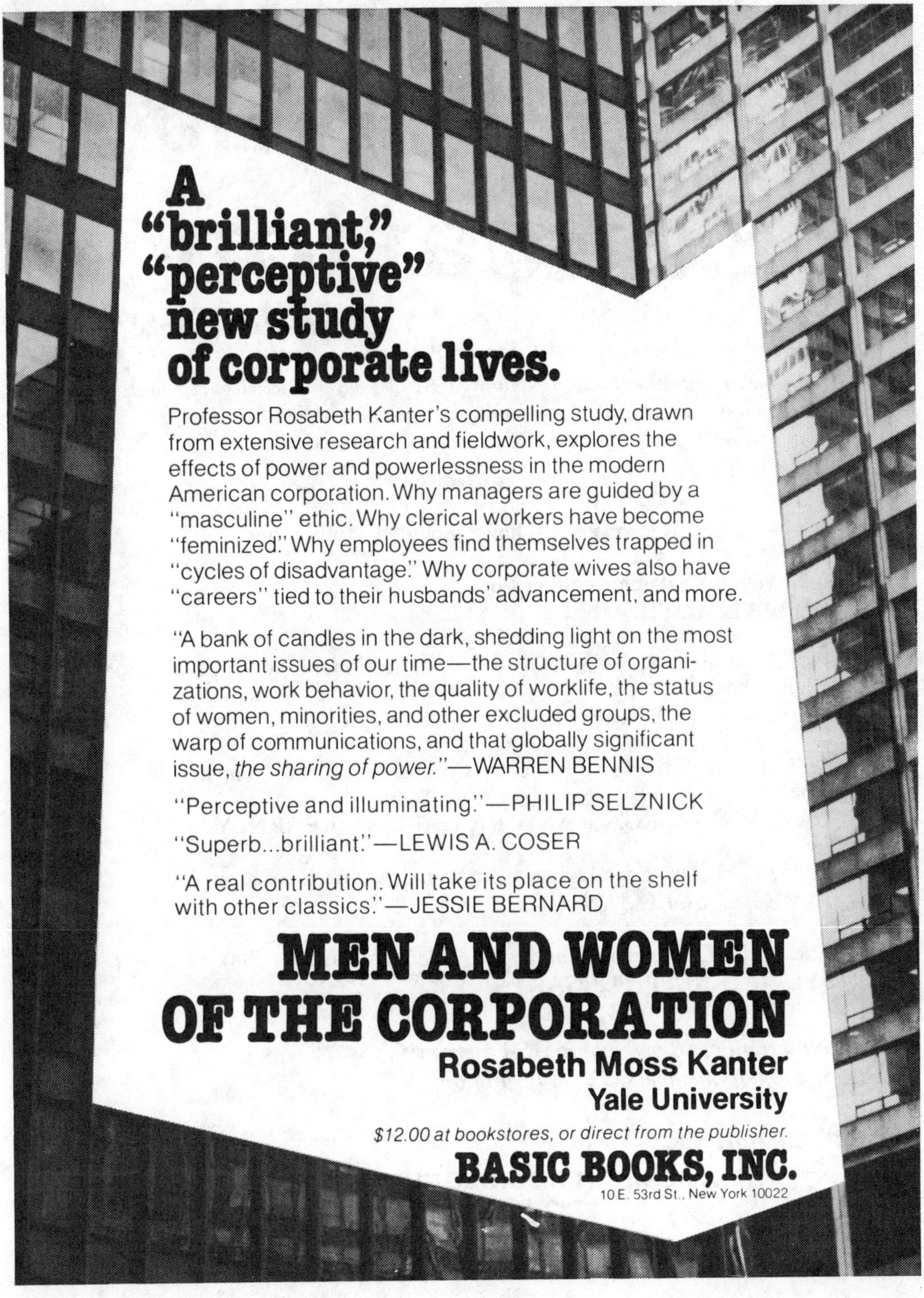
A "brilliant," "perceptive" new study of corporate lives.
Professor Rosabeth Kanter's compelling study, drawn from extensive research and fieldwork, explores the effects of power and powerlessness in the modern American corporation. Why managers are guided by a "masculine" ethic. Why clerical workers have become "feminized." Why employees find themselves trapped in "cycles of disadvantage." Why corporate wives also have "careers" tied to their husbands' advancement, and more.
"A bank of candles in the dark, shedding light on the most important issues of our time—the structure of organizations, work behavior, the quality of worklife, the status of women, minorities, and other excluded groups, the warp of communications, and that globally significant issue, the sharing of power."—WARREN BENNIS
"Perceptive and illuminating."—PHILIP SELZNICK
"Superb...brilliant."—LEWIS A. COSER
"A real contribution. Will take its place on the shelf with other classics."—JESSIE BERNARD
MEN AND WOMEN OF THE CORPORATION
Rosabeth Moss Kanter
Yale University
$12.00 at bookstores, or direct from the publisher.
BASIC BOOKS, INC.
10 E. 53rd St., New York 10022

SEPTEMBER 1977 – VOLUME 6, NUMBER 5

ONTEMPORARY SOCIOLOGY

A JOURNAL OF REVIEWS

IN THIS ISSUE

Symposia on

Robert Alford	*Health Care Politics*
Anthony Giddens	*New Rules of Sociological Method*
Nathan Glazer	*Affirmative Discrimination*
Rene Thom	*Structural Stability and Morphogenesis*

Alfred McClung Lee on *Insult and Society*
Shirley Hartley on the demographic transition
Robert Cole on the Japanese factory
Diana Russell on violent spouses
Kristin Luker reviews Komarovsky's *Dilemmas of Masculinity*
Armand Mauss surveys recent Social Problems textbooks
Reyes Ramos on Black sociology
Lloyd Raines on *The Twilight of Capitalism*

Letters

Steven Goldberg on patriarchy
Stephen Murray on the Collins review of Merton
More on the Socio-Biology issue.

BLICATION OF THE AMERICAN SOCIOLOGICAL ASSOCIATION

contemporary sociology

a journal of reviews

September 1977 • Volume 6, Number 5

Concerning advertising, change of address and subscriptions, address: Executive Office, American Sociological Association, 1722 N Street, N.W., Washington, D.C. 20036.

Concerning manuscripts and book reviews, address: Editor, *Contemporary Sociology: A Journal of Reviews,* C-002, University of California, San Diego, La Jolla, California, 92093.

Contemporary Sociology: A Journal of Reviews is published at 49 Sheridan Avenue, Albany, N.Y. 12210, bi-monthly in January, March, May, July, September, and November.

Annual membership dues in the American Sociological Association, $30.00–$50.00. Student Member, $15; Associate, $20; International Associate, $12; Student Associate, $10.

Subscription rate for members, $10; non-members, $15; institutions and libraries, $20; non-member students, $10. Single issues $4.

New subscriptions and renewals will be entered on a calendar year basis only.

Change of address: Six weeks advance notice to the Executive Office, and old address as well as new, are necessary for change of subscriber's address.

Claims for undelivered copies must be made within the month following the regular month of publication. The publishers will supply missing copies when losses have been sustained in transit and when the reserve stock will permit.

ISSN 0094–3061

Second class postage paid at Washington, D.C. and at additional mailing offices.

Book reviews from *CS* are indexed in *Book Review Index,* published by Gale Research Company.

ASA Multiple Submission Policy: Submission of a manuscript to a professional journal clearly implies commitment to publish in that journal. The competition for journal space requires a great deal of time and effort on the part of editorial readers whose main compensation for this service is the opportunity to read papers prior to publication and the gratification associated with discharge of professional obligation. For these reasons, *the American Sociological Association regards submission of a manuscript to a professional journal while that paper is under review by another journal as unacceptable.*

Cover designed by Kenneth E. Anderson, A.I.A.

TABLE OF CONTENTS

LETTERS 523

Review Symposia

Alford: *Health Care Politics: Ideological and Interest Group Barriers to Reform* ....Scotty Embree 529
Rosemary C.R. Taylor 530

Giddens: *New Rules of Sociological Method: A Positive Critique of Interpretative Sociologies* ....Aaron V. Cicourel 533
Thomas F. Gieryn 535

Glazer: *Affirmative Discrimination: Ethnic Identity and Public Policy* ...Andrew Billingsley 537
Jack D. Douglas 539
Joan W. Moore 542

Thom: *Structural Stability and Morphogenesis: An Outline of a General Theory of Models* ....Timothy W. Collins 543
Hector J. Sussman 544

Book Reviews

Communications

Adler and Cater: *Television as a Cultural Force* ....Paul Dimaggio 545
Altheide: *Creating Reality: How TV News Distorts Events* ..........M.G. Dunn 546
Davison, Boylan, and Yu: *Mass Media: Systems and Effects* ....Herbert I. Schiller 548

Crime, Law, and Deviance

Clark: *Deliver Us from Evil: An Interpretation of American Prohibition* and
Filstead, Rossi, and Keller: *Alcohol and Alcohol Problems: New Thinking and New Directions* ....Marston M. McCluggage 549
Gurr, Grabosky, and Hula: *The Politics of Crime and Conflict: A Comparative History of Four Cities* and
Gurr: *Rogues, Rebels, and Reformers: A Political History of Urban Crime and Conflict* ....Michael Polen 550
Kaplan and Kessler: *An Economic Analysis of Crime: Selected Readings* ....Herman Schwendinger 551
Miller: *Cops and Bobbies: Police Authority in New York and London, 1830–1870* ....Eric H. Monkkonen 552

Culture

Arens and Montague: *The American Dimension: Cultural Myths and Social Realities* ....Lester R. Kurtz 552
Douglas: *Implicit Meanings: Essays in Anthropology* ....Bennetta Jules-Rosette 554
Hanson: *Meaning in Culture* ....Robert A. Paul 555

Demography, Population, and Migration

Beaver: *Demographic Transition Theory Reinterpreted: An Application to Recent Natality Trends in Latin America* and
Weinstein: *Demographic Transition and Social Change* ....Shirley Foster Hartley 556
Cantrelle et al.: *Population in African Development* ....Karol J. Krótki 558
Abadan-Unat: *Turkish Workers in Europe, 1960–1975: A Socio-Economic Reappraisal* ....Jonathan Matthew Schwartz 559
Jeffrey: *Migrants and Refugees: Muslim and Christian Pakistani Families in Bristol* ....Sharlene J. Hesse 560
Lewis, Rowland, and Clem: *Nationality and Population Change in Russia and the USSR: An Evaluation of Census Data, 1897–1970* ....D. Peter Mazur 561
Overbeek: *The Population Challenge: A Handbook for Nonspecialists* ....Paul R. Williams 562
Viel: *The Demographic Explosion: The Latin American Experience* ......Barry Edmonston 563
Yaukey: *Marriage Reduction and Fertility* ....Ruth B. Dixon 563

Education

Boyd: *Community Status and Conflict in Suburban School Politics* ....Regina H. Kenen 564
Lewis: *Scaling the Ivory Tower: Merit and Its Limits in Academic Careers* ...Gerald Grant 564
Milofsky: *Special Education: A Sociological Study of California Programs* ....Gelestino Fernández 567
Seabury: *Universities in the Western World* ....Philip G. Altbach 567
Smelser: *Public Higher Education in California* ....Walter Phillips 568
Vasil'eva: *The Young People of Leningrad: School and Work Options and Attitudes* ....Jiri Kolaja 569

Family and Intimate Lifestyles

Bane: *Here to Stay: American Families in the Twentieth Century* .... Roger W. Libby 570
Cromwell and Olson: *Power in Families* .... Mirra Komarovsky 571
Gelles: *The Violent Home: A Study of Physical Aggression between Husbands and Wives* .... Diana E.H. Russell 572
Heiss: *Family Roles and Interaction: An Anthology* .... Irwin Kantor 573

Medical

Dean, Kraft, and Pepper: *The Social Setting of Mental Health* and
Hirschowitz and Levy: *The Changing Mental Health Scene* .... Muriel W. Pumphrey 574
Parry and Parry: *The Rise of the Medical Profession* .... Dorothy Douglas 575
Stroman: *The Medical Establishment and Social Responsibility* .... Thomas J. Sullivan 575

Methods

Adams and Haden: *Social Effects of Computer Use and Misuse* and
Wessel: *The Social Use of Information: Ownership and Access* .... Harvey E. Rich 576
Erdos: *Professional Mail Surveys* .... David Bills 577
Herzon and Hooper: *Introduction to Statistics for the Social Sciences;*
Hilton: *Intermediate Politometrics;*
Lehmann: *Nonparametrics: Statistical Methods Based on Ranks*;
Olson: *Ideas and Data: The Process and Practice of Social Research*; and
Runyon and Haber: *Fundamentals of Behavioral Statistics* .... Charles E. Starnes 577
Smelser: *Comparative Methods in the Social Sciences* .... Henry Teune 579

Organizations

Bowen: *Social Control in Industrial Organisations: Industrial Relations and Industrial Sociology: A Strategic and Occupational Study of British Steelmaking;*
Bowers: *Systems of Organization: Management of the Human Resource;*
Harvey: *Industrial Society: Structures, Roles, and Relations;* and
Susman: *Autonomy at Work: A Sociotechnical Analysis of Participative Management* .... George H. Westacott 580
Marsh and Mannari: *Modernization and the Japanese Factory* .... Robert E. Cole 582

Policy

Freidson: *Doctoring Together: A Study of Professional Social Control* .. Nancy R. Chiswick 585
Komorovsky: *Sociology and Public Policy: The Case of Presidential Commissions* .... Richard Rosenfeld 585
Demerath: *Birth Control and Foreign Policy: The Alternatives to Family Planning* .... Charles F. Hohm 584

Political

Burbank: *When Farmers Voted Red: The Gospel of Socialism in the Oklahoma Countryside, 1910–1924* .... Ellen Rosen 587
Harrington: *The Twilight of Capitalism* .... Lloyd Davis Raines 587
Horvat, Marković, and Supek: *Self-Governing Socialism: A Reader* and
Vanek: *Self-Management: Economic Liberation of Man: Selected Readings* .... George Fischer 589
Janowitz: *Social Control of the Welfare State* .... Gosta Esping-Andersen 590
Silk and Vogel: *Ethics and Profits: The Crisis of Confidence in American Business* .... Michael Useem 592

Race and Ethnic

Bowker and Carrier: *Race and Ethnic Relations: Sociological Readings* .... John W. Martin 593
Greeley: *Ethnicity, Denomination, and Inequality* .... Dorothy Wertz 594
Miller: *A Comprehensive Bibliography for the Study of American Minorities* .... Francesco Cordasco 594
Peach: *Urban Social Segregation* and
Triandis: *Variations in Black and White Perceptions of the Social Environment* .... Richard S. Sterne 595
Staples: *Introduction to Black Sociology* .... Reyes Ramos 596
Stember: *Sexual Racism: The Emotional Barrier to an Integrated Society* .... Paul D. Starr 597

Sex Roles and Behavior

Bahr and Garrett: *Women Alone: The Disaffiliation of Urban Females* .... Helena Znaniecki Lopata 597
Belotti: *What Are Little Girls Made of? The Roots of Feminine Stereotypes*. .Karen M. Jennison 598
Cook and Mitchinson: *The Proper Sphere: Woman's Place in Canadian Society* .... Susan Mann Trofimenkoff 599
Komarovsky: *Dilemmas of Masculinity: A Study of College Youth* .... Kristin Luker 600

Teitelbaum: *Sex Differences: Social and Biological Perspectives* .... Janet Saltzman Chafetz 601
Wiseman: *The Social Psychology of Sex* .... Jetse Sprey 601

Social Problems

Etzioni: *Social Problems;*
Henslin and Reynolds: *Social Problems in American Society;*
Manis: *Analyzing Social Problems;*
Shepard and Stewart: *Sociology and Social Problems: A Conceptual Approach;* and
Tallman: *Passion, Action, and Politics: A Perspective on Social Problems and Social-Problem Solving* .... Armand L. Mauss 602
Rubington and Weinberg: *The Study of Social Problems: Five Perspectives* .... James D. Orcutt 606

Urban and Rural

Chudacoff: *The Evolution of American Urban Society* .... Matthew Edel 606
Cornelius and Trueblood: *Latin American Urban Research, Volume V: Urbanization and Inequality: The Political Economy of Urban and Rural Development in Latin America* .... William L. Flinn 607
Hawley et al.: *Theoretical Perspectives on Urban Politics* and
Young: *Essays on the Study of Urban Politics* .... Ellan Odiorne Derow 608
Loomis and Beegle: *A Strategy for Rural Change* .... Gene F. Summers 609
Meier: *Planning for an Urban World: The Design of Resource Conserving Cities* .... John D. Kasarda 610
Whyte and Alberti: *Power, Politics and Progress: Social Change in Rural Peru* .... William L. Canak 611

Additional Reviews

Cook et al.: *"Sesame Street" Revisited* .... Glady Engel Lang 612
deMause: *The New Psychohistory* .... Lloyd S. Etheredge 614
Flynn: *Insult and Society: Patterns of Comparative Interaction* .... Alfred McClung Lee 615
Franklin and Thrasher: *An Introduction to Program Evaluation* .... Dan S. Green 616
Glick: *The Comparative Reception of Darwinism* .... Nicholas C. Mullins 617
Krauss: *Stratification, Class, and Conflict* .... Paul Blumberg 618
Osgood: *The Chinese: A Study of a Hong Kong Community* .... Chong-chor Lau 618
Seyfarth and Schmidt: *Max Weber Bibliographie: Eine Dokumentation der Sekundarliteratur* and
Weber: *Wirtschaft und Gesellschaft* .... Guenther Roth 619
Wilson: *Contemporary Transformations of Religion* .... Thomas Robbins 620
Vulliamy and Lee: *Pop Music in School* .... Peter Hesbacher 621
Yablonsky: *Psychodrama: Resolving Emotional Problems through Role-Playing* .... Kurt W. Back 622

PUBLICATIONS RECEIVED 623

LETTERS

(Letters which comment on particular reviews are routinely sent to reviewers for a reply. Where no reply by reviewers appears in these columns, it is usually because they chose not to reply.)

To the Editor:

It was, I suppose, quixotic to hope that a sociological journal would assign a book on the psychophysiological roots of sexual differentiation to a reviewer who was not an irredeemable prisoner of the faith of pure environmentalism. Such a reviewer, knowing that all physiological explanations must be incorrect, finds no need to deal with such explanations, no matter how much more parsimonious or concordant with the empirical evidence. It does not take a discerning reader to see that the reviewer of my *The Inevitability of Patriarchy,* Rayna Rapp Reiter (Jan., 1977), is one of those who is less interested in truth than in flaying the infidel. This outburst is typical: "We who must refute the reductive myth of simplistic biologism are busy fighting on many fronts."

Reiter goes further than most in ignoring explanations she finds unpleasant. She does not even find it necessary to present a summary of the argument she is asserting away. But it is not this that I wish to consider here. Readers who would like to see my own summary might want to look at *American Anthropologist* (March, 1975) and those who are interested in my response to critics might consult the revised British edition of *Patriarchy* (Maurice Temple Smith, 1977).

For my purposes here, the reader need merely know that *Patriarchy* attempts to document and explain the universality, the presence in every society without exception, of patriarchy (male attainment of the overwhelming number of upper hierarchical positions) and male dominance (the psychological association of dominance and the social association of authority in male-female relationships with the male).[1] The hypothesis at the core of the theory I present states simply that there are neuroendocrinological differences between men and women that engender different male and female "motivational" responses to the environment. These differences—specifically those responsible for the male's lower threshhold for dominance behavior in a hierarchical or dyadic setting, his greater "aggressiveness" or "competitiveness"—set limits on social institutions.

Here I wish merely to consider a criticism that is as ubiquitous in sociological reviews of *Patriarchy* as it is fallacious. This is the criticism that my argument is inherently "simplistic" (or "reductionist"). Simplism is, by definition, always undesirable; it is an attempt to explain varying empirical facts in terms of unvarying causal factors that are incapable of explaining the variation. Simplicity, a parsimony of explanation, is always desirable.

Were I attempting to explain social variation (such as various societies' different values relevant to patriarchy, different social populations' attitudes towards patriarchy, or cross-cultural differences in the sexual division of labor), then an explanation stressing psychophysiological differentiation would, in most cases, be simplistic indeed.

This is why I devoted so much of *Patriarchy* to documenting the universality for which I was attempting to offer a *sufficient* explanation. I took such pains to demonstrate that the upper positions of the hierarchies of every society are attained overwhelmingly by males in order to make clear that there is no variation significant enough to demand social hypotheses. None of this, of course, denies the relevance of environment (the necessity of a hierarchy to act as a cue to elicit male behavior) or socialization; indeed, much of the book is devoted to demonstrating how socialization increases the sexual behavioral differentiation by making qualitative a differentiation that is, on a psychophysiological-behavioral level, quantitative. (Thus the statistical reality of the male's lower dominance threshhold becomes the stereotype "men are aggressive; women are passive.") The book does not argue that sexually-differentiated social factors are unimportant, but that they are given their direction primarily by the psychophysiological differentiation. Reiter invokes non-existent variation in order to explain patriarchy in social terms. This is, at best, to beg the question: *why* does no society associate dominance with females and socialize them accordingly?

Since I attempt to explain only universal limits and not the insignificant (to my thesis) variation, one can not invoke variation in attitudes, values, rights or any other irrelevant variable as refutation. But this is precisely what Reiter does when she provides a list of references that allegedly offer counter-evidence, when, in fact, they address variation that *Patriarchy* does not deny. The very point of *Patriarchy* is that such factors are irrelevant to a sufficient causal ex-

[1] Reiter simply asserts that male dominance is not universal, invoking Morgan. Since Morgan wrote that the Iroquois "regarded the woman as the inferior, the dependent, and the servant of man," one would, I think, be hard put to deny male dominance in Morgan's Iroquois. It took much of a book to document the universality of male dominance and I can not do so here. This does not pose a problem. For even Reiter can not deny the universality of patriarchy and for my purposes here this is sufficient empirical underpinning. I might, however, make the point that even one who offers social explanations should find it unlikely (once acknowledging that patriarchy is universal) that a society in which suprafamilial authority is associated with the male would fail to associate dominance and authority in male-female relationships with the male. If one found empirically that this was the case, then, of course, one would have to account for the fact that male hierarchical authority was not reflected in dyadic situations. But there is no empirical exception to warrant doing this.

planation of patriarchy. This is worth stressing because, obvious as is the distinction between attitudes towards patriarchy and the fact of patriarchy, virtually every sociological reviewer invokes technological change, Reiter's "socialist revolutions," and other social variants. They do so despite the fact that none of these changes have had more than a peripheral effect on patriarchy. The sixty-seven heads of General ministries of China are all headed by men; well over ninety percent of the Israeli Parliament is male; the Central Committee of the Communist Party of the U.S.S.R. is over ninety-five percent male. These all espouse egalitarian values and all serve to support the thesis that, whatever a society's values and attitudes, differentiated motivation is far more relevant to patriarchy than are values, attitudes, and ideologies; they also support the thesis that such differentiated motivation is far more a cause of differentiated socialization than its effect.

It is worth noting that even most feminists do not deny the decisive importance of the differentiation of motivation; they provide us with endless examples of parents telling boys that dominance is masculine and girls that nurturance is feminine. Rarely do they consider that parents tell children these things because they are true; rarely do they consider the possibility that these things are true for primarily psychophysiological reasons.

As has virtually every other sociological reviewer, Reiter invokes the predictable *ad hominem* and *ad consequentium* attempts at refutation and objects to my use of "inevitability." There is no point in responding to the *ad hominem* criticisms; those who accept pure environmentalism can not conceive of non-political motivations and, in any case, explaining my motivations to Reiter is not to the point. It seems, however, that it is worthwhile to state the obvious fact that the consequences of a theory are irrelevant to the truth of that theory. Even if *Patriarchy* did "[justify] an essentially sexist social structure," this would be no evidence against it. Finally, I use the word "inevitability" to specify conditions of falsification (a single society that had hierarchy in which males did not attain the upper positions). This, and not the question begging that typifies so much that is written on the subject, is what a scientific theory is *supposed* to do.

I can not offhand think of a single other non-trivial and non-obvious hypothesis in all sociology that has at its call both anthropological universality and direct neuroendocrinological evidence. Is there not something a bit absurd about the penchant of sex-role sociology for asserting away an hypothesis so well-supported, while accepting as received truth assertions grounded in dubious little studies whose inadequacy is apparent at a glance or, even more often, in wish alone?

Steven Goldberg
City College/CUNY

To the Editor:

I'm sorry that Steven Goldberg found my response to his book inadequate. I found his response to the complexities of modern evolutionary theory inadequate as well, which is what motivated the review. To assert as Goldberg does that neuroendocrinological differences (themselves a matter of controversy in current research) are responsible not only for gender-linked psyches, but for universal social structures as well distorts all the findings of contemporary anthropology, both biological and cultural. The meaning of the theory of biological evolution is that genotypes change only as phenotypes are selected or deselected under constantly changing sets of environmental conditions. Biological traits are the outcome of the process in which both organism and environment interact and change. The point of the theory is precisely that *nothing* is inevitable, in evolutionary terms. Anthropologists use the concept of culture to describe the process in which shared meanings among human beings are constituted, reproduced and changed. Such shared meanings both grow out of, and in turn intervene in the processes we gloss as "sex roles" and "social institutions," among many others. Polemicizing ponderously about the male-dominant character of the Israeli parliament misses the point: That men carry out certain roles at the present time tells us nothing about the "inevitability" that they will do so in the future either biologically, or in terms of the potential cultural meanings of "men," "women," or "parliament" (in Israel or elsewhere). To understand the potential for change and stability in human biology and culture is to ask precisely the kinds of critical questions of evolutionary theory and cultural anthropology that Goldberg dismisses as "dubious little studies." Had he acknowledged the epistomological issues underlying both the theory of evolution and the meaning of culture, Goldberg would not have written such a grossly misleading and simplistic (not simplifying, but simplistic) book. Nothing in his response alerts me to any change in his essentially anti-evolutionary and non-culturalogical position. The review therefore stands as written.

Rayna Rapp Reiter
New School for Social Research

To the Editor:

Prescriptive Misuses of Sociology of Science Indicators

In his review of the Merton *Festschrift,* Randall Collins rightly criticizes the prescriptivist and Panglossic readings of the norms of science. If we confuse ideal norms with actual behavior—as many users of Merton's typology of the norms of science have certainly done—the result is self-congratulation and "a glorification of science as a perfectly tuned system"(p. 151). But does Merton himself confuse the two? His ASA presidential address on priority disputes, after all, focused on the divergence from one of those norms, that of disinterestedness. Much of his work has focused on conflict within science.

Instead of Merton, it seems to me, it is Collins who uses findings and indicators from the sociology of science prescriptively and uncritically. First in reference to "Social Structure and Anomie," and then in reference to Merton's work in the sociology of science, Collins notes scornfully that Merton's work did not have a great immediate impact. Apparently, Professor Collins believes that good work is always immediately recognized. If work isn't built on within five years, we can presume it wasn't very good, he seems to say, since a research front follows automatically upon revelation of Truth. This view is, of course, naive. Scientific research is socially organized, and good ideas are not a sufficient cause of a research tradition (cf. Mullins, 1973). The posthumous impacts of Copernicus and Mendel are two well-known cases in point. Or, to look back at the impact of the giants in our own discipline, the impact of Marx's *Capital* (let alone the Paris Manuscripts!), Durkheim's *Division of Labor* or Weber's *Protestant Ethic* was in each case miniscule five years after initial publication. Each required decades to generate sustained attention from social scientists. Derek Price proposed using percentage of citations within five years after publication as an indicator of consolidation of physical science research fronts. It is *not* a standard for evaluating a particular work. Price himself noted that five years is an arbitrary figure: there is certainly nothing sacrosanct about it. Although it is somewhat surprising to find the author of *Conflict Sociology* using the failure to generate immediate consensus as a criticism, it is not exactly news that the recency coefficients in sociology journals are (a) considerably lower than in physical science journals and (b) diminishing. Within the sociology of science, however, as Cole and Zuckerman show in their contribution to the book under review, the recency coefficient has been rising, and it is Merton's more recent papers concerned with stratification that are most cited among his papers (p. 156).

In regard to Merton's "Priorities" paper, Cole and Zuckerman noted that half the citations to the paper were made after more than a decade had elapsed. Collins ignores their quite plausible explanation, which is: "It now seems obvious that Merton's early papers (and, we think, those of any founder) had limited initial impact because they had no audience specifically attuned to publication on this subject" (p. 156). There was no sociology of science in 1957. Merton's work helped stimulate one. Although he was not the sole intellectual leader of the sociology of science that emerged in the 60s—Collins correctly adds Kuhn and Price—Merton certainly was one. Furthermore, as both Caplovitz's review and Cole and Zuckerman's paper remind us, Merton's impact as a teacher, an editor, and an organizational leader may be greater even than the impact of his writings. Merton's role in encouraging and legitimating Kuhn's work, incidentally is detailed in the book (p. 159).

As for *Science, Technology and Society in 17th Century England,* it was published in Europe just in time to be lost in the Second World War. Collins's contention that it was "republished in the late 1940s" (*CS*, p. 152) will come as a surprise to all those who attempted to find copies prior to its reissue in 1970. That the work has no supporters among historians of science will come as a surprise to Kuhn who devoted a major portion of his general article on science in the *International Encyclopedia of Social Science* to it. It may come as a surprise to Collins that only a third of the book dealt with the relationship to Puritanism: less than what discussed economic and military influences on science (Merton, 1970:xii).

The work of Merton and his disciples in the sociology of science has been centrally concerned with stratification. Professor Collins is entitled to regard this work as attempting to "defuse" stratification, but it is impossible to interpret it as ignoring stratification. It seems to me that the empirical work of Merton and his followers can be interpreted in ways other than those in which they interpret them. Those of us who do reinterpret the findings, however, should recognize that their work has made ours possible, just as Marx acknowledged his indebtedness to his predecessors.

STEPHEN O. MURRAY
University of Toronto

To the Editor:

Given the controversy surrounding Edward O. Wilson's *Sociobiology: The New Synthesis*, it is particularly unfortunate that the "Review Symposium" did not contain a truly critical review. There are numerous objections which social scientists should be raising concerning Wilson's book and the various spinoffs from it (including the film, "Doing What Comes Naturally" aimed at high school students).

It is odd that sociologists like Blute and van den Berghe should welcome the demise of their own profession. Wilson's aim, as Blute notes, is to have sociology become one of the branches of biology. Criticizing Wilson is not, however, just a matter of self-preservation. Biological frames of reference such as Wilson's have been used consistently to establish an ideological justification for the status-quo. There is not very much that is new in Wilson's basic outlook. It is merely the latest restatement of the scientifically erroneous and politically reactionary conception that the world we live in is caused by our genes, not our social institutions.

Wilson believes that I.Q., creativity, mental stamina, drive, entrepreneurship, homosexuality, and various other personality characteristics are hereditary. Class structures are to be explained then by physiology, not by an examination of such variables as property relationships and the structure of power. It should be noted that Wilson presents no evidence for this and many of his other assertions, except to argue from analogy. Is our understanding of war really enhanced by Wilson's pointing to an alleged parallel between Moses's instructions to the Israelites and "aggression and genetic usurpation by male langur monkeys" (p. 573).

Among the most biased (and offensive) parts of Wilson's book is his repeated insistence on the inevitability of male dominance. It is a widespread feature of primate social groupings, he asserts, ignoring much contradictory evidence. He then goes on to claim that "primitive man lived in small territorial groups, within which males were dominant over females" (p. 567). In all societies it is typical for "the women and children [to] remain in the residential area while the men forage for game or its symbolic equivalent in the form of barter and money" (p. 553). Not only is a thoroughly false picture given of sex-roles and the labor force but the implication is that sexual equality is forbidden by our genetic heritage: so much for women's liberation. It is really a new notion that women's place is in the home as Wilson postulates?

I think it is incumbant upon the editors of *Contemporary Sociology* to solicit some reviews which are critical of Wilson's book, that will analyze the flaws in his methodology and the erroneousness of many of his statements. In the meantime, an excellent critical review has been written by scientists from several disciplines and can be obtained by writing to Science for the People, 897 Main St., Cambridge, Mass. 02139.

BARBARA CHASIN
Harvard University

To the Editor:

Seldom is one taken to task for having written a favorable review. The anomaly is doubly surprising when the writer of the review finds himself in numerous and distinguished company. Of the twenty-odd reviews of Wilson's book I read, I have yet to find one that says it is a bad book. The great majority say it is a brilliant book; a few raise legitimate questions about its applicability to human behavior but still acknowledge the outstanding intellectual status of the work. The sample of reviews in *Contemporary Sociology* is thus representative of the reception Wilson's book has received in other media, including other leading sociology journals such as *Social Forces* and *The American Journal of Sociology*.

In contrast to this general acclaim, a small Harvard-based group calling itself "Science for the People," and with which Chasin is clearly associated, has mounted a campaign of political innuendo against E.O. Wilson, Robert Trivers et al., accusing them of a sweeping array of ideological heresies. My guess is that their strident protests will make as much of a contribution to the history of science as the objections of religious fundamentalists to natural selection, or the doctrines of Lysenko in Stalinist Russia. Whether they like it or not, Darwinian evolutionary theory is alive and well, and 1977 seems a bit late to reopen the Scopes monkey trial.

PIERRE L. VAN DEN BERGHE
University of Washington

To the Editor:

A Problem for Sociobiology

Having browsed the social-scientific menu for a cannibal feast, Wilson (*Sociobiology*) has chosen Homans's (*Social Behavior*) analysis of social behavior as a first course in an anticipated incorporation of sociology into the projected "new synthesis" of sociobiology. However, Wilson's voracious appetite is unlikely to be appeased by hors d'oeuvres, which is all he will be served by Homans and other sociologists. This metaphor harbors a problem—overlooked by Wilson and *CS* reviewers Blute and van den Berghe (November, 1976) but readily apprehended by putting metaphors aside and briefly reexamining Wilson's synthetic program, allowing some latent issues to surface.

In the millennium of Wilson's synthesis, sociobiology will describe and explain the overt, directly observable social behavior of organisms, whether human or not. Though Wilson (rightly) consigns this millennium to the distant future, he presumes that its coming may be hastened by systematic efforts to incorporate existing findings of sociology—a science which has supposedly been intensely engaged all along in the study of the overt social behavior of human organisms. Viewing Homans's work as an exemplar of sociological concerns, Wilson recommends Homans's thoroughly Skinnerian-behaviorist analysis as a starting point for the incorporation efforts. However, Homans's analysis is not representative of sociological analysis to date; nor has sociology been intensely engaged in the analysis of overt, human social behavior—a desideratum of Wilson's sociobiology.

At least since Comte, the mentalistic bias of most sociologists has prompted a response of "Watch out! Dangerous! Avoid!" to behaviorist analyses (Marwell, *CS*, 1972:1:1:19). Such negative reactions (to any work stressing overt behavior vis-à-vis "subjective conceptualizations") are typical in sociology, a discipline which suffers from what Tarter has aptly labeled the "cognitive affliction." Representing "an error common in the early stages of a science" (Tarter, *American Sociologist,* 1973:8:155), this disability stems from the pervasive assumption of sociologists that their discipline's subject matter must ultimately be conceived mentalistically, via the imputation of covert cognitive (and other subjective) "contents" to the still impenetrable "black box" of the human "actor," whose "behavior" and concomitant social "phenomena" are viewed as being qualitatively different from those of nonhuman organisms. As Skinner (*Science and Behavior*) has argued:

> So long as external variables go unnoticed or are ignored, their function is assigned to an originating agent within the organism. If we cannot show what is responsible for man's behavior, we say that he is responsible for it. The precursors of physical science once followed the same practice, but the wind is no longer blown by Aeolus, nor the rain cast down by Jupiter Pluvius (p. 283).

Such reasoning remains prevalent in sociology, despite correlative (albeit occasional) recognition that sociological claims that individuals "engage in subjective behavior and that this unobserved behavior is connected to observed behavior. . . are only inferences" (Wallace, *Sociological Theory*). Nevertheless, overt behavior and social phenomena have received very little attention from sociologists—who carry their predilection for the subjective even into their not very numerous "observational" studies, which generally focus on "subjective phenomena." Most sociologists have been unwilling even to begin to deal conceptually and empirically with social *behavior*. Indeed, sociology has not yet "developed a technology for observing, ordering, analyzing, and interpreting overt behavior" (Deutscher, *Social Problems,* 1966:13:243). Studies have been concerned largely with what people *say* about what they *do,* often under the blithe assumption that the two correspond; or energies have been spent trying to penetrate the so-far impregnable "black box," by "studying" norms, values, situational definitions, and other "mentalisms" (Deutscher, *What We Say/What We Do*).

As Wilson suggests, Homans's extrapolation of Skinnerian behaviorism to the study of social *behavior* may provide a first course, or starting point—though I think it provides a starting point for the sociological analysis of social behavior, rather than for the cannibalistic incorporation of sociology by sociobiology. In short, efforts at such incorporation seem premature. What *is* needed is the study of human social *behavior*. Homans has pointed the way, for sociologists and others; and such work will undoubtedly get under way, once attention has begun to be directed toward the complex philosophical, theoretical, methodological, and empirical issues surrounding the study of such behavior. Whether or not Wilson's "new synthesis" is ever fully realized (an empirical question, to which time holds the answer), the anticipation of his sociobiological millennium supplies a valuable corrective for the focus of contemporary sociology. If sociologists do not "heed Skinner's call," others almost certainly will.

HENRY J. TRAVERS
James Madison University

To the Editor:

Prior to the publication of *Academic and Entrepreneurial Research,* no empirically based information was available on who gets evaluation funding, what sorts of budgets are allocated, what types of awards are made, what are the organizational affiliations of evaluation researchers, what sorts of working arrangements they have with the programs to be evaluated, what sort of scientific methods they use. Bernstein and Freeman provide, in their book, the first broad picture of the evaluation field.

They also open an essential debate over the proper relations between evaluation research and academic institutions, scientific theory building and program development. Not only has Kenneth Tremblay, in his review of *Academic and Entrepreneurial Research,* misrepresented Bernstein and Freeman's theoretical background, research methods and conclusions, which I find quite adequate, but his review has also functioned to stifle this debate.

The authors present evidence that evaluation research done by individuals or corporations without university affiliation was less rigorous, often failing to meet basic standards of scientific method, than that done by those with university affiliation. Should, therefore, the universities accept a responsibility to carry on evaluation research, and should national policy encourage the universities to do it?

The issue questions the purpose of the university. No one doubts that the university is the instructor of researchers. But the tradition of independence carried by the university conflicts with the imposition of the duty of evaluating human service programs.

The experience of medical schools, which for centuries have been closely associated with hospitals and clinics, highlights the difficulty. On the one hand, clinical services have sometimes become more important to medical faculty than research and teaching. Medical care institutions and facilities have sometimes outlasted their academic uses but continued to exist, diverting effort and money. Hospitals are an enormous drain on funding, especially in the early obsolescence of many tools and techniques.

On the other hand, control over a clinical service has allowed medical researchers to carry out experiments ranging from large scale clinical studies to the most basic microcellular investigations. The sample of patients available in a particular clinical setting has produced specializations of interest at each institution. As a result, we see medicine as an experimental science, and have seen it so at least since Rudolph Virchow and Claude Bernard.

I think that medical schools have found their alliances to hospitals and clinics indisputably beneficial. Sociology would similarly improve from opportunities to structure theoretically important alternative interventions and evaluate their outcomes. Evaluation research is an opportunity to do experiments which are not only useful to human service program development, but basic to theory building.

Evaluation research is of primary importance to the social, behavioral, and health sciences, whose fountainheads are in the universities. Evaluators must be trained by the universities, and the universities must interest and involve themselves in evaluation research.

However, the independence of the university-based evaluator must be protected, as he moves to give his theory construction a base in current empirical investigation. There are major new mutual interests now present among service, training and research functions which should not go unaddressed. New organizational problems will be faced, but we must protect the university as an institution whose primary job is the generation of knowledge. We can thank Bernstein and Freeman for providing us a systematic base of knowledge for this important debate.

SHEPPARD G. KELLAM
University of Chicago

To the Editor:

In responding to Kellam's comments, I would first like to address a point to which he allocates only superficial treatment. Specifically, Kellam attempts to discount my review in one sentence, but fails to supply the necessary evidence to support his contention. I maintain that my review of Bernstein and Freeman's *Academic and Entrepreneurial Research* is quite representative of the book. However, I should add that my criticisms leveled at the book were intended to be directed more at the current state of evaluation research than at Bernstein and Freeman per se. Indeed, these two sociologists are eminent scholars who command much respect within the field of evaluation research. The fact that Bernstein and Freeman fail to meet their own prescribed standards of evaluation research in their study seems to be reflective of an area of research in great need of further development. Although I stand by my opinion that the book contains some serious drawbacks, I agree with Kellam that it effectively depicts the current status of the field of evaluation research. Thus, I recommend that if someone is interested in evaluation research they should pick up the book and arrive at their own assessment of its merits.

The second point I wish to make pertains to my general impression of Kellam's letter. It seems to me that Kellam is quite perceptive in addressing the issue concerning the relation between evaluation research and academic institutions. I agree with him that academic sociologists should become involved in evaluation research, inasmuch as such research allows ample opportunity for sociologists to test theory and provide inputs to program development. His example of medical schools is useful for illustrating this notion. However, I would proceed one step further and suggest that sociology *must* become involved in evaluation research for survival purposes if for nothing else. It seems inevitable that due to declining college enrollments, waning interest in the social sciences among college students, and the effects of recessionary pressures, the sociology profession must carve out a more diversified niche than it has held in the past. Rather than producing only teachers and basic researchers, academic sociology programs need to turn out applied sociologists as well. These applied sociologists might work in either academic or nonacademic situations and would be trained, among other things, to conduct evaluation research, implement survey research or experiments with social policy implications, and effectively work with governmental or research agencies as well as with scholars from other disciplines. If this was the case, the distinction between academic and entrepreneurial research that Bernstein and Freeman and Kellam feel is so important would become meaningless, as sociologists in nonacademic positions would be adequately prepared to conduct high quality research. However, such a diversification demands that at least some sociologists obtain a working knowledge of social policy formulation, the fundamentals of evaluation research, and how to utilize theory to guide research efforts. Unfortunately, most undergraduate and graduate university programs in sociology do not presently offer the essential applied experience or coursework, and do not have the contacts with the proper nonacademic agencies which could result in jobs for graduates.

It is my position that the sociology profession is encountering a period of relative hard times, times which may not improve in the near future. The academic market seems to be drying up for recent recipients of the doctorate degree, and the employment prospects for those with a bachelor's or master's degree in sociology appear to be bleak. I feel that only through a concerted effort to make sociology relevant in the eyes of students (i.e., a high extant correlation between a degree and a job) will the field attract the desired quantity and quality of students. The development of a bonafide applied sociology which encompasses evaluation research, and social policy research in general, may be one road to travel in providing such relevance. Thus, I feel that Bernstein and Freeman's book, Kellam's letter, and my own comments are useful insofar as they may open up sociologists' eyes concerning the relevance of evaluation research for the sociology profession and the future development that the profession might follow.

KENNETH R. TREMBLAY, JR.
Washington State University

To the Editor:

James Veney's November 1976 review of Ingman and Thomas's collection of readings, *Topias and Utopias in Health,* requires at least one correction: The material on Cuba has *not* been published elsewhere.

Until my own book, *Cuban Medicine,* is published later this year by Transaction Books, the article which appears in the Ingman and Thomas collection will likely continue to be the only source for detailed analysis of the structures and processes of Cuban health care organization in the first five years of the revolution. The only possible exception in this regard is another article by me (*Inquiry,* Supplement, June 1975) which treats the second five years and includes a brief summary of the earlier period.

On other matters (by the way): Is the world really moving so fast—or have we become sufficiently complacent—as to render a truly "antique quality" to the editors' reference to Spiro Agnew? And if the Ingman and Thomas collection has maintained a "somewhat other worldly quality," this is at least consistent with the title!

ROSS DANIELSON
University of Oregon

To the Editor:

It has occurred to me that it would be of benefit to readers of *Contemporary Sociology* if a "Forthcoming Book Reviews" listing were included regularly, much as other scholarly journals list manuscripts accepted for future publication.

Several times during the past year it would have been quite useful to me to have known that a particular book was going to be reviewed in a forthcoming issue. Since such a list could be in a format similar to the one for "Publications Received," very little journal space would be used each issue. Immediately following (or preceding) the "Publications Received" section would seem to be an appropriate placement for such a listing.

The reviews each issue are very well done, and I find some of them particularly helpful in my work. Knowing which books will be reviewed in advance could only make the review service performed by *Contemporary Sociology* even more valuable.

JON D. SWARTZ
University of Texas, Permian Basin

SYMPOSIA

Health Care Politics: Ideological and Interest Group Barriers to Reform, by ROBERT R. ALFORD. Chicago: University of Chicago Press, 1975. 294 pp. $12.50 cloth.

SCOTTY EMBREE
Brooklyn College/CUNY

Robert Alford's *Health Care Politics* is particularly disappointing in light of its great promise. What at first glance appears to be a book which offers hope by tackling the major forces blocking real change in the field of health care ultimately turns out to be a conglomeration of vague and contradictory terminology and inauspicious methodology which at best confuse and at worst anesthetize the reader's creative thinking.

In brief, Alford presents an analysis of the chronic crisis in health care based on a model of interest groups rooted structurally in the existing political economy. He argues that any organizational solution to the current health care crisis within a market economy is impossible. The barriers to such reform are both ideological and structural. Ideologically, the barrier to change is that the image of a reformed, integrated delivery system incorporates the two contradictory principles of professional and bureaucratic modes of organizing and performing work. The structural barrier to change is that the groups which currently control medical care are deeply rooted in the institutional structure of society.

The book is neither an integrated analysis nor a series of chapter essays, as its structure might suggest, but a collection of three monographs and several short essays. One monograph is a case study of commissions of investigation of the New York City health system between 1950 and 1970; another is a case study of ambulatory care centers in New York during the late 1960s; and the third is a conceptual model of structural interests in health care. In addition, there is a short chapter on crises in other policy areas at the state and national level; one on the difficulties of researching documents in the health field; and one briefly reviewing three different models of interpreting the health care crisis.

The two case study monographs do not particularly flesh out the theory expressed in the third monograph, nor does the model explain the case studies. Most disturbing is Alford's refusal to take a clear stance. He takes great pains to point out that his case studies provide no "data" but rather merely maintain "consistency" with his theory. These first two monographs are extremely weak theoretically and methodologically. Theoretically, his formal categories of market and bureaucratic reform perspectives are inadequately developed. They remain as categories rather than becoming concepts having sufficient explanatory power to encompass such diverse phenomena as commission reports, affiliation contracts, and neighborhood clinics. One result is that his points become as repetitive as the material he describes. The complexity of these types of organization requires an elegant paradigm to identify the most important facts and variables and to explain why certain variables are more important than others. From Alford's book, we don't know if we are getting the most important facts and we are not given any criteria for evaluating the facts presented.

Alford's lack of methodological discussion interferes with an understanding of the material presented. He does not bother to explain his choice of the two decades for study, nor does he explain his selection of only particular commissions, affiliation contracts, and clinics. The omission of Lincoln Hospital, for example, is striking in a discussion of New York ambulatory program development and community control. As a means of describing the chosen two decades, Alford presents five pages of historical material drawn from the

New York Times on developments in health policy. To ignore the major economic and political developments at the federal and local level in an analysis of a period of turmoil in the health arena borders on the ludicrous. The chapters on crises in other policy areas and on general data collection do not explicitly deal with his own data; they are sketchy and therefore extremely disappointing. He does touch on the difficulty of acquiring even fundamental data in the field of medical care; however, had his discussion been more in depth, he would have made a genuine contribution.

In his last monograph, Alford presents an interest group model to interpret policy making in the health field. He offers the concept of structural interest as a tool by which the analyst can go beyond the premises of interest group theory and the market economy. To summarize his argument, interest groups, rather than facilitating change, constitute the barriers to change in the health arena. The concept of structural interest provides the link between groups and the state by categorizing otherwise diverse groups in terms of their common, objective roots in the political economy. Such interests may be dominant, challenging, or repressed depending upon which social institutions and political mechanisms in the society ensure their existence.

In analyzing health policy, he describes professional monopoly or dominant interests as those physicians, biomedical researchers, voluntary hospitals, and others who benefit from the autonomy, independence, and control over work conditions incurred under the present system. Technological innovations, scientific management, the division of labor, and the increasingly social character of medicine have created structural interests which challenge these dominant interests. Alford calls the challenging groups "corporate rationalizers." This group is composed of administrators and planners who control hospitals, medical schools, and government agencies. He defines repressed structural interests as those groups—consumers, community people, minorities—which are marginal to the system, which occasionally organize around a specific need, and which tend to be easily co-opted.

The dynamics of this model are limited. While detailing many examples of the corporate rationalizers' attempts to gain control over the medical system, both Alford and the model he uses pay too little attention to the roles played by the professional monopolists and the repressed interests. His model is closed and ahistorical.

The major weaknesses in this analysis are common to many current political economic explanations. Concepts from political economy and interest group analyses are used as analogies and metaphors rather than as integral parts of the analysis. The meanings of such central concepts as public and private sectors, class, contradiction, political economy, and even pluralism remain fuzzy and distract from the monograph in two ways. First, the terminology creates a mood of false promise that a new level of insight into the causes and possible cures of health care inadequacies is about to begin. Second, the terms are used in contradictory contexts, so that the reader formulates a variety of interpretations all of which can be supported textually. Although Alford has attempted to undertake a much needed task of integrating a class analysis with an institutional one, his lack of clarity both in vision and the expression of the vision leaves the reader with the feeling of having eaten thick soup with a fork.

ROSEMARY C. R. TAYLOR
Harvard University

America's health care "crisis" has been hitting the headlines for the last decade. The sixties' crisis of equity and access has become, in *Newsweek's* terms, the "health-cost crisis" of the seventies. Economists who have watched the national health bill soar over $100 billion annually fight in vain to control costs; contemporary seers like Ivan Illich claim that health care has little to do with health and lament the insidious effects of professional control over medicine. But sociologists have been curiously reticent to apply their insights to the nation's fastest growing industry and systematically consider its effects on society.

Medical sociology, as the subfield concerned with analyzing the interrelationships among medicine, health care, and society has, unfortunately, contented itself with a much narrower range of issues. Reviewing the contributions of sociology to medicine five years ago in the *Handbook of Sociology*, Kendall and Reader asserted that the principal contributions of sociology *in* medicine have been to explore the social factors which affect attitudes and behavior regarding illness and its incidence. The sociology *of* medicine has produced an impressive body of research on the socialization and organization of the medical profession. Yet the burgeoning literature in medical sociology rarely situates the health care sector in a broader social and political context which might explain its present chaos or predict its future development.

In this context a book like Robert Alford's *Health Care Politics* seems both timely and welcome. Cataloguing the drawbacks of existing research in the field of health care, Alford affirms that there has been "no full theoretical revision which treats the health system as a whole in more than a rhetorical sense" (p.10). Politics, he asserts, plays no role in "analyses of health care hoping to produce change via consensus" (p.9). The most glaring fault of previous studies has been their inability to "touch the core problem of the structure of *producing* institutions" (p.247). An appropriate focus of analysis and a realistic agenda for reform will emerge only with the recognition that "the principal barriers to health care reform lie in the powers of strategically structured interests" (p.xiii). Alford proposes to employ precisely such a theoretical perspective to illuminate the question of "the links of hospitals and clinics with overarching funding, regulating, and planning agencies, both governmental and private" (p.xiii).

To summarize his argument briefly: Alford views the developments in the health care system in the last twenty years as "a rapid increase in almost every index of growth—dollars, human resources, programs—except those pertaining to quality, distribution, accessibility, and reasonable cost to the consumer" (p.181). The explanation for these "dynamics without change" can be found in the symbiotic relationship between two sets of "structural interests": the "dominant" structural interest of "professional monopoly" (private physicians and voluntary hospitals), and the "challenging" structural interest of "corporate rationalization" (represented by "persons in top positions in 'health organizations' ") (p.204). Both have a stake in maintaining "their respective positions of power and privilege which depend upon the continuation of market institutions" (p.193) and therefore resist the development of any meaningful mechanisms of public control. The losers in this quiet tug-of-war are the "repressed" structural interests of the "community population" (p.15), a heterogeneous group which includes "ghetto blacks, . . . the lower middle class just above the Medicaid income maximum . . . and those occupations affected by job-related diseases" (p.15). Their interests are repressed because "no social institutions or political mechanisms in the society insure that these interests are served" (p.15). Their efforts to obtain more accessible health institutions, better insurance coverage, and quality care are doomed to failure because of the iron grip maintained by the dominant and challenging structural interests over the health care system. Even improvements proposed by the less radical "market reformers" who want to revive the system with an injection of "market competition and pluralism," or by "bureaucratic reformers" who call for increased coordination and more government control of health care will rarely achieve more than cosmetic changes which maintain the status quo. "Every reform proposal becomes trapped in the pluralist political process which safeguards all existing professional and organizational interests" (p.261). Plus ça change. . . .

Alford devotes the bulk of his empirical chapters to a careful analysis of how this process is played out at the local level in New York City. Chapter two consists of a thorough review of eight reports published between 1950 and 1971 by commissions appointed to investigate the city's health services. Alford concludes that few of their recommendations were implemented, and that the handful of ameliorative measures designed to integrate health services brought about further fragmentation. New York City, he argues, suffers not from a crisis in its medical care system but from a chronic disease. Periodic announcements of "crisis" are manufactured as political weapons to be used in the ongoing battle between dominant and challenging structural interests. Similarly, commissions are not expected to improve anything; they are so much shadow boxing on the part of a temporary coalition of corporate rationalizers designed to lull the fears of an increasingly restive public. Chapter three describes the history of New York City's effort to establish neighborhood family care centers. Only one of seventeen projected centers was actually established, a predictable outcome since the New York Health and Hospital Planning Council, which was supposed to "coordinate" care at the community level, fell victim to the same entrenched interests that paralyze investigative commissions.

To assess Alford's book as a whole is difficult because the links between the theoretical and empirical materials are weak. They are tied together by a transitional chapter devoted to the thesis that "the observations of New York City hospitals, the commissions of investigation, and the attempts to coordinate health care are not atypical of other cities, other policy areas, and higher levels of government" (p.xiii). Alford wishes to make the case not only that propositions about the underlying causes of one city's health crisis will apply to the American health care system as a whole, but also that the problems and processes he describes are unique neither to health care nor to New York but "endemic to the structure of society and political system as a whole" (p. 261). Thus explanations for the failure of efforts to coordinate the planning of neighborhood health centers which put the onus on administrative bungling, lack of funding and errors of judgment are not enough; "an ultimate explanation is probably to be found in fundamental features of the political economy of health care in the United States" (p.167). Alford's theoretical essays are designed to elaborate those fundamental features yet they are not grounded in his case studies. The latter, he claims, do not provide supporting data but are "consistent with the theory" (p.190). Rather than try to consider the two, this review will concentrate on Alford's theoretical endeavour since it appears to offer such a promising challenge to existing perspectives on the American health care system.

In a 1972 *Politics and Society* article in which Alford first proposed his argument about the dynamics of the health care sector, the principal actors in the system were described as "major interest groups." In *Health Care Politics* Alford has introduced a major conceptual change. He is now careful to distinguish between *structural interests,* which "are served by the way they 'fit' into the basic logic and principles by which the institutions of a society operate" (p.14), and an *interest group,* or "the organized action of a group to represent its interests" (pp.13–14). By drawing this distinction Alford joins the protracted debate between pluralists and Marxists on the nature of political struggle and social reality. For pluralists, interest groups operating within a consensus on the rules of the game constitute the central political actors and the main agents of social change in society. For Marxists, the political struggles between interest groups are the surface manifestations of an underlying reality grounded in the social relations of production. Alford attempts to take insights from both traditions and merge them, but the resulting analysis falls awkwardly between the two. He describes in detail the strategies, motives and achievements of political actors, but he refuses to accept the maneuverings of interest groups as exhaustive of political reality. At the root of the health care sector's paralysis, he argues, lie entrenched structural interests. But when we look more closely at those entities we confront a number of conceptual problems.

The very term "structural interest" is confusing. As Anthony Giddens has pointed out, the term "structure," has two essential meanings in current social science: in structural functionalism it has come to mean a discernible pattern in social relations; in structuralism the word is used in the sense that underlying or deep structures are held to explain surface appearances. In neither usage can "structure" be reconciled satisfactorily with "agency"; the actor often vanishes, together with motivations, intentions, purposes—and interests. The concept structural interest at first seems an interesting attempt to escape this problem. But Alford is caught in a second, related dilemma when he moves from conceptualization to explanation. The notion of structure drops out. His structural interests are defined ultimately not by objective conditions but by goals and motivations. Even though he asserts that challenging structural interests are being created "by the changing structure of society" (p.14) and, specifically, by changes in the technology, costs, and social organization of health care, *corporate rationalization* is, in essence, an "ideology and a vision" (p.15) of planning and coordination. Corporate rationalizers are defined simply by what they want—to vest control over health services in the hospital. It is an ideology "linked to concrete structural interests within a market economy" (p.15), but the substance of those structural interests is never clarified.

This conceptual confusion in Alford's exposition may account for a certain ambiguity at the descriptive level about the nature and composition of his structural interests. Voluntary hospitals, for example, are usually included with the medical profession at the core of the structural interest of professional monopoly, but they also appear to support the cause of corporate rationalization through the participation of their directors in New York City's investigative commissions. The distinction between structural interests and interest groups tends to break down for the same reason. The structural interest of professional monopoly is anthropomorphised into the "professional monopolist," fighting with colleagues against the threat of the corporate rationalizers to maintain control over the distribution and cost of services. The distinction collapses yet again when Alford asserts that the same individual, an academic sociologist for example, can play the role at different times of market reformer, professional monopolist, corporate rationalizer, and bureaucratic reformer. This is the familiar territory of pluralism: individuals can play multiple and even contradictory roles, thus preventing irreconcilable polarization in society. What has happened to *structural* interests?

The notion of an underlying reality has evaporated. This suggests the fundamental problem with Alford's theoretical approach. He cannot clarify the role of voluntary hospitals because he does not spell out the objective socio-economic forces which constrain them; he cannot explicate the underlying reality behind the strategies of interest groups because his perspective on the health care system is not rooted in a theory of society. Caught between pluralism and Marxism, with no unifying perspective for assimilating discrete social phenomena into a coherent theoretical framework, Alford derives his categories of professional monopoly and corporate rationalization from the empirical reality of a chaotic medical care system. Then later he attempts to extend this ad hoc analysis to society as a whole: "the processes and forces I have described are endemic to the structure of the society and political system as a whole and must be understood at that level, not within the context of a particular institution or the particular interests of doctors and hospitals" (pp.261–262). The contention remains unconvincing because the laws for generalizing from the particular are never clearly enunciated.

It is therefore not surprising that Alford is pessimistic about the potential for change in the health care sector. There is no theoretical basis for such a hope. All policies and programs to reform the medical care system in the last twenty years lead to the same stalemate created by the contending structural interests. "Contradictions" abound in Alford's analysis but they lead nowhere. Some, like the "contradiction" between the interests of corporate rationalizers and professional monopolists, could be more fruitfully conceptualized as conflicting pressures and demands. Others, such as the "contradiction" between the expectations of consumers for quality care and the inability of the private sector to provide it for everyone (p.255) or between the character of health care technology and the private appropriation of power and resources (p.251) approach the idea of contradiction in the Marxist sense—the tendency inherent to a specific mode of production to destroy the conditions on which it depends for survival. But in Alford's analysis conflict and contradiction only reaffirm stasis. He offers no historical perspective on the health care system and no account of the relationship between the health sector and broader developments in the American economy. We are left with no sense of what specific contradictions in the present might generate change in the future. Alford's method dictates his conclusion—temporary historical conditions become permanent structural attributes.

In his final chapter Alford sketches out the beginnings of an alternative perspective, a "class or institutional perspective." Once again Alford's analysis reflects his uncertainty of the theoretical terrain and an unwillingness to choose between two distinct methodological orientations. The dynamics without change, he argues, can be attributed to the "dominance of the private sector and the upper middle class" (p.254). Classes, however, remain essentially spectators to the power struggle between contending structural interests. It is not the relationship between classes that will generate political struggle and change but the deus ex machina of a "social movement and political leadership which is not yet visible" (p.266). An institutional perspective, on the other hand, (and Alford has separated them in his more recent work) must surely take into account the role of the state. But the state is a shadowy entity in *Health Care Politics*, with little autonomy. It is not "an independent power standing above and beyond the competing interest groups, but represents changing coalitions of elements drawn from various structural interests" (p.251). Alford therefore ignores what is perhaps the fundamental source of future struggle in the health care sector—the changing modes of intervention by the state in health care.

Health Care Politics has exposed the failures of the pluralist approach to the politics of health care and it should encourage sociologists to pursue an understanding of the health care sector as a whole. Alford promises to broaden that understanding with an elaboration of his class perspective into a theory of state-society relationships in a forthcoming work on political sociology. This is an important transitional step which may take us beyond dynamics without change to an analysis of the health care crisis as part of the broader fiscal crisis of the state in late capitalism.

New Rules of Sociological Method: A Positive Critique of Interpretative Sociologies, by ANTHONY GIDDENS. New York: Basic Books, 1976. 192 pp. $10.95 cloth.

AARON V. CICOUREL
University of California, San Diego

The book under review is a sympathetic critique and evaluation of sociological theories concerned with "meaningful action," "action as rationalized conduct ordered reflexively by human agents," and of the way language helps to make meaningful action possible. The notion of self-reflection as mediated linguistically is an organizing theme of the book. The title refers to "method" in the tradition of European social philosophers, not in the sense of how research is done in a substantive, empirical context.

The introductory chapter reveals Giddens's sympathies for key aspects of what he calls "interpretive sociologies," particularly ideas associated with Schutz and Garfinkel. For example, Giddens describes the production of society as "a skilled performance" that depends on the encounters or activities of human beings acting as practical theorists. Members of a group are said to utilize their practical resources or "mutual knowledge" to generate social interaction, and this knowledge is also routinely shared and used by social scientists for understanding their own activities and the activities of members whom they study. Reflexive understanding and the social context of language as a sign-system that mediates practical social life are also discussed briefly in the introduction. These ideas are incorporated into the "new rules" in the closing pages of the book.

In chapter one Giddens again emphasizes the point that the schools of thought he discusses are all concerned with "problems of language and meaning in relation to the 'interpretive understanding' of human action" (p.23). He lists three such schools: "hermeneutic philosophy," "ordinary language philosophy" combined with the later Wittgenstein, and "phenomenology." Phenomenology is viewed as having acted as a broker between hermeneutic philosophy and ordinary language philosophy and the later Wittgenstein. I am not aware of work by Garfinkel to establish this link as claimed by Giddens, but others associated with the term ethnomethodology have attempted to connect ideas from Schutz to ideas in Austin and Wittgenstein.

In chapter one Giddens provides the reader with a useful description of Schutz's writings, and then discusses several issues from the writings of Winch and Garfinkel. He challenges the indifference of ethnomethodology to sociology, noting how they both clearly share an interest in the same issues. There is a useful description of problems associated with the term "indexical expressions," but Giddens is not very clear when talking about the regress problem. His discussion of the regress problem suffers from a reliance on the narrow views of Hindess and an inadequate appreciation of various empirical studies ignored by this book.

Giddens embraces many key concepts (pp. 52–53) from the interpretive sociologies while criticizing the authors cited for failing to deal with action as praxis instead of only with action as meaning. He faults the interpretive view for not recognizing the central role that power occupies in social life, for failing to recognize that social norms or rules can be differentially interpreted, and finally he sees a failure to address problems of institutional transformation and history. All of these criticisms carry some truth. One problem here is the selective review of the literature conducted by Giddens. This selectivity leads him to ignore empirical issues, particularly as they derive from differences within what is called ethnomethodology.

The theme of language and understanding is pursued when addressing authors like Gadamer, Apel, and Habermas. The issues of "living in" a language, meanings-in-context, and ordinary language, are presumed to be relevant to how these ideas can contribute to a study of institutional structures. Issues like the domination of men and women and the progress of human self-understanding are tied to the role of language in everyday life and the problem of meanings-in-context.

In chapter two there is a discussion of action or agency and its relation to intention, the reflexive monitoring of conduct that leads to some kind of principled account of completed action, and the separation of meaning in interaction from meaning in non-communicative acts. The person or acting self is seen as the basis for an analysis of action. Much of this chapter deals with theoretical issues that straddle philosophy and sociology. Here Giddens strikes out on his own to define and explain some basic concepts that he feels are foundational elements of sociological theory. The issues raised in chapter one are again found in chapter two when he discusses how "lay actors" participate in, monitor, and produce social life. He continues this line of discussion by reference to the role of commonsense understandings, and how social scientists' studies of such activities can become part of the subject-matter being researched.

In chapter three limitations in the work of Durkheim and Parsons are discussed briefly. Marxism is examined as an alternative to Durkheim and Parsons. But we are then brought back to what is now a familiar theme; the reflexive monitoring by humans of their place in their environment, and how this is made possible by language. He uses language as a convenient way to exemplify some central features of social life. The key aspects of the production of interaction are described as its negotiated meaningful constitution, its constitution as a moral order, and how relations of power are established. Power is viewed as a general feature of social interaction, whereby actors can alter the course of a series of events by the resources or facilities they can mobilize in the pursuit of practical activities.

In his concluding remarks Giddens outlines his "new rules." They include the idea of a sociology concerned with a social world produced by "the active doings of subjects." The skilled activities of members are seen as necessary to produce and reproduce society. Social actors are always historically bounded in pursuing action, but we must distinguish between intentional action and behavior that can be seen as a set of "occurrences." Structure is seen both as constraining and as enabling conditions. Ideas about intentional action and structure presuppose three primitive terms in social science: meanings, norms, and power. The study of social life requires observers to make use of their own knowledge as members when a topic is chosen for investigation. Researchers must be participants to generate their sociological characterizations, but they do not have to "go native" to do successful research. Finally, a "double hermeneutic" governs sociological concepts in that on the one hand theoretical schemes in all of the sciences are like self-contained concepts, and are also a form of practical activity. But these schemes must be understood "from within." In sociology the study of social life occurs within frames of meaning and interpretation generated by those being studied such that a reinterpretation occurs that mediates between ordinary and technical language. Sociologists must use metalanguages of social science to follow "the hermeneutic explication and mediation" of diverse forms of life, and they must see "the production and reproduction of society" as a human accomplishment.

There are several aspects of this book that I like. Giddens is not afraid to tackle complex theoretical issues that many others have described inadequately. He reveals a strong grasp of theoretical issues that have not proven very popular with other contemporary theorists. The abstract theme he proposes between language and meanings and the production and the reproduction of society is one that I believe is central to sociology. However, I do not believe he has always done his homework in tracing out the implications of this thesis. He fails to discuss the symbolic interactionists, except for a few passing remarks about Goffman's work. He does not realize how important the work of Searle and Grice has been for contemporary linguists and psychologists concerned with pragmatics and information processing, and virtually ignores the important work of anthropological linguists and the ethnographic semanticists. (There is one reference to a paper by Hymes.) The references to linguists and psycholinguists are sparse and not always relevant to his general theme, while many works that are quite relevant to his thesis are not cited. He does not cover the empirical works associated with the term ethnomethodology, and ignores many important differences within this area that go beyond the abstract theoretical issues he discusses. Finally, the arguments of the book are stated too abstractly to have much impact on most empirically-minded American sociologists.

But despite the drawbacks I think it is a valuable book. It provides us with a sympathetic but detached view of issues that should be incorporated into mainstream theory.

THOMAS F. GIERYN
Columbia University

The New York Review of Books is for many scholars the *Vogue* of the intellectual world. So it is that the Nobel Laureate in Medicine, P. B. Medawar, sought its pages to parade the currently fashionable sins of sociologists. Social scientists, it is said, chase after chimerical images of natural science, believing that precise measurement is intrinsically praiseworthy, that facts are prior to beliefs, and that computer processed statistical formulas provide the shortest route to understanding. Never mind the practicing natural scientists who have not relegated such ideas to the bargain basement, and never mind the social scientists who never even tried them on. Fashionable tastes in intellectual debates have an objective force no matter how poorly they fit the reality of the case, and Medawar is not alone in this view.

Anthony Giddens is decidedly au courant. This latest book in his series on sociological theory begins with an echo of Medawar's indictment. Sociology, it seems, suffers from cognitive lag: sets of ideas become popular here even as they become obsolete in other intellectual domains. If positivism no longer describes natural science, we are told that sociologists are still working away in often tacit accord with its principles. If phenomenology has begun its eclipse in philosophy, as Giddens suggests, more sociologists find it congenial. Happily, Giddens does not stop with mechanical recitation of the view that sociology is a collective anachronism: he provides a fresh conceptualization that at once enlightens our reading of other theorists and breaks through to a promising synthesis.

Giddens's agenda has three parts. First, he provides a detached, informed critique of several schools of meta-sociology. Functional analysis, symbolic interactionism, and structural analysis are given just a glance as Giddens surveys three kinds of interpretative sociology: Schutz's existential phenomenology, ethnomethodology, and the post-Wittgensteinian philosophy of Peter Winch. The author then turns to hermeneutic theory, unknown to many American sociologists though it has a long tradition drawing on the works of Herder, Schleiermacher, Dilthey, Heidegger, and more recently Hans-Georg Gadamer and Karl-Otto Apel. In a word, hermeneutics in the study of society emphasizes that "all understanding demands some measure of preunderstanding" and that "no type of enquiry, from the most casual conversation to the apparatus of natural science, . . . is free from presuppositions which express the framework of tradition within which alone thought is possible." Similarities to selected concepts in recent philosophy of science such as Polanyi's tacit knowledge, Holton's themata, and Kuhn's paradigmatic assumptions are hard to miss. Giddens concludes with Habermas's critical theory, more familiar than hermeneutics to the American audience if only because of greater availability in English.

Second, Giddens offers a catalog of aspects of social life that must be included in any comprehensive theory of society. The Giddensian social world pivots on a duality of *production* and *reproduction* of social structure. Society is not a "pre-given" universe of objects, but rather is one produced by subjectively constituted activities of individuals. These activities must be thought of as taking place within structural contexts that constrain and enable human "agency." Individual actions reproduce (and occasionally alter) shared objective structures of meanings, norms, and power relations. Plainly, Giddens takes off from the joint inadequacy of interpretative sociologies that ignore the objective reality of social structure, and structural sociologies that ignore the subjective interpretation, creation, and transformation of these structures. He is not the first nor, probably, will he be the last to attempt the tour de force of reconciling these two traditions.

Third, Giddens provides a paradigm for sociological research, and here he stumbles a bit from the pace set in the rest of the book. His image of social life stipulates that social theories account for actors' construction of the social world and for durable social structures as well. The nine rules which in a synoptic way end the book will not satisfy those seeking articulated strategies for investigating this structural or that phenomenological problem. Sociology is said to obey a double hermeneutic: its theoretical scheme is itself a frame of reference, a kind of preunderstanding used to understand the frames of reference of individuals who use their own sort of preunderstanding to make their way in the world. All this says that individuals use various tacit and explicit sets of assumptions to determine the nature of things. The idea has been set forth for decades, and one might ask how much more dirt must be shoveled on the kind of naive empiricism that Giddens opposes before those critics are willing to pronounce it dead.

The stickiest problem in admitting that things look different to those with distinct frames of reference is the epistemological relativism that tags along. How can one decide the better of two allegedly scientific accounts of social life that are grounded in different frames of meaning? For Giddens, one cannot. He insists that sociologists "respect the authenticity of mediated frames of meaning"; greater validity of this or that proposition can be determined within but not between frames of meaning. The cognitive superiority of Western rational science cannot be defended against such potent rivals as Zande witchcraft by using criteria that are themselves part of the Western scientific method. Giddens may have subverted his own effort to redirect sociology, for the sociologist who disagrees with his recommendations could plead a disjunction of frames of reference and end all further debate.

Giddens is part of a modest crowd of scholars trying to find a better way to do sociology; for several reasons he stands a leg up on his rivals. He is an informed eclectic, selectively making use of existing theoretical orientations while refusing to fall in love with only one of them. For example, much of Alfred Schutz finds its way into Giddens's synthesis, but he is quick to note that Schutz was never able to "reconstitute the social reality as an object world." To balance this omission, Giddens weaves into his own scheme a bit of Marx, a bit of Durkheim.

Perhaps this eclecticism has roots in Giddens's refreshing reminder that within a single theoretical perspective, not all works are of one piece. Ethnomethodology is of varying utility since its advocates have addressed themselves to distinct problems of rationality in action, the relation between lay and technical terms, and indexicality in communication.

Finally, Giddens resists the temptation to claim universality for his or any other explanation of social life. Hermeneutics is insufficient for interpreting some situations as positivism is insufficient for others, and we are best off in Giddens's mind with both.

Giddens's *New Rules* will get a different reception from the sociological community than the one given Durkheim's *Rules,* all apart from the substance of the two works. In retrospect, Durkheim's *Rules* seems better integrated with empirical studies, say, of suicide or the division of labor than Giddens's work is integrated with contemporary empirical sociology. The pursuit of meta-sociology today has begun to acquire a fetishistic quality, and some practitioners seem unbothered by their work having less and less to do with the substantive science they seek to rearrange. Nevertheless, to substantive sociologists wanting to track the largely independent courses charted by philosophers of social science, Giddens's book extends a cordial invitation.

Affirmative Discrimination: Ethnic Identity and Public Policy, by NATHAN GLAZER. New York: Basic Books, 1976. 248 pp. $10.95 cloth.

ANDREW BILLINGSLEY
Morgan State University

Affirmative Discrimination, by Nathan Glazer, carries the subtitle "Ethnic Inequality and Public Policy." Both the title and the subtitle are fairly accurate descriptions of the points of view being expressed by the author.

He sets forth his view that affirmative action programs designed or enforced by public policies which have the aim of bringing about a greater measure of equality, particularly for Blacks and other disadvantaged minorities and for women, have been misinterpreted by enforcement agencies and now result in affirmative discrimination against white Americans in general and white males in particular.

In order to appreciate this central thesis of the book, it may be helpful first to make some observations about Nathan Glazer as a person and then some comments on the social and political context in which his book is written. Then we will look more closely at his central argument.

As a sociologist, Glazer writes out of a particular intellectual, academic, and social tradition. At the present time, he is Professor of Education and Social Structure in the Graduate School of Education at Harvard. Prior to his present appointment, he was a professor of sociology at Berkeley. He and I were colleagues on the faculty there in the early 1960s when some of the programs he discusses in his book were being developed with both his and my active support. Glazer is also a very distinguished author. He collaborated with David Riesman on the prize-winning book *The Lonely Crowd,* and later a follow-up book entitled *Faces in the Crowd.*

Glazer is also an outstanding Jewish scholar with strong intellectual and social commitments to his ethnic heritage. In this connection, he is author of a book on American Judaism and is editor and frequent contributor to *Commentary* magazine.

As a sociologist, Glazer has developed a strong interest in inter-ethnic relations and has done some highly acclaimed studies on ethnic pluralism in America. Thus, he collaborated with Daniel Patrick Moynihan on the highly acclaimed *Beyond the Melting Pot,* which was a study of the major ethnic groups in New York City. He has also edited with Moynihan a book entitled *Ethnicity, Theory and Experience.*

Glazer is a prodigious writer and these cited works are only examples of the many books and essays he has produced. They show, however, his continuing professional and intellectual interests in the subject matter he deals with in the book under review today, *Affirmative Discrimination.*

It might also be observed that Nathan Glazer is a prominent member of the so-called Eastern Intellectual Liberal Establishment. He was an early and persistent supporter of efforts to combat racial segregation and discrimination in the South. It is also fair to say, however, that he and others of his colleagues associated with *Commentary, The Public Interest,* and centering especially around New York City, New Haven, and Boston, have withdrawn their support for efforts to combat segregation and discrimination in recent years as these efforts have moved further North. Thus, Nathan Glazer, Daniel Moynihan, Lee Rainwater, S.M. Lipset and Edward Banfield, Ben Wattenburg, Christopher Jencks are some of the principal social scientists providing the intellectual rationale for contemporary efforts to slow down, withdraw, and rethink affirmative action programs designed to assist Blacks, disadvantaged minorities, and women to reach equality and equity with the more privileged white American males in all aspects of society.

Let us come then to the central feature of Glazer's new book. The book is divided into six chapters. In the first chapter, Glazer sets forth his idea of American history, in which prior to the 1960s American society had evolved a consensus in favor of the inclusion of minorities and ethnic groups into American society. The major feature of this consensus was the view that persons should not be given special consideration positive or negative because of group identity. Thus, Glazer describes and endorses what has generally been considered a color-blind attitude and philosophy in America. He cites on page 31, for example: "That in 1964, we declared that no account should be taken of race, color, national origin, or religion in the spheres of voting, jobs, and education (in 1968, we added housing)." What he and some others of his colleagues are opposed to, however, are special efforts to bring minorities up to the level of equality shared by the majority and special efforts designed to bring women into standards of equality with men. He argues that after 1964, the national government and major sections of public opinion supported these efforts to deal with segregation and discrimination. These positive efforts, however, he argues, were misguided and unnecessary. The American society was in the process of correcting whatever inequity existed on the basis of race, color, and sex.

In chapter two, Glazer focuses on affirmative action in employment. In this chapter he makes a strong argument against special efforts to set up time tables for the equal inclusion of Blacks and other minorities into the work force. He argues that equal employment is a proper policy, but special efforts to produce equality of results are inappropriate and are in fact discriminatory against the white male majority. He is particularly critical of the use of statistics, numbers, and percentages of employment as measures of whether equality is being achieved. He does not, however, provide an effective substitute for measuring the progress of equality. He quarrels with whether segregation and discrimination really exist. To the extent that it does exist, it could be corrected by the voluntary action of the marketplace. Preferential treatment, preferential hiring, and promotion of minorities, previously excluded, are objected to by Glazer on three grounds:

First, he holds that these special efforts are unnecessary. He observes on page 69, that these measures were developed at a time when "very substantial progress had been made and was being made, in the upgrading of black employment and income, a progress that had, oddly enough, taken place without benefit of such extreme measures."

Second, he argues that it is questionable whether these affirmative action measures in employment actually helped Black people with problems of employment.

Third, he argues that such affirmative action measures violate what he considered a pattern of employment in society which has been evolving for the past 100 years.

What this analysis shows clearly is Glazer's commitment to the more privileged white male sector of society and the withdrawing of his commitment to social justice on behalf of the disadvantaged.

The essence of his view in this chapter is that equal opportunity is all right. That is to say that policies designed to start the advantaged and the disadvantaged at the same place in the starting line are appropriate, but measures designed to ensure that the disadvantaged keep pace with the advantaged are in his view unfair to the advantaged. This is a curious argument for a trained advocate of equality and social justice.

In chapter three, Glazer takes up the issue of busing. In this chapter, he joins forces with another prominent sociologist, James Coleman. Professor Coleman, as you know, has recently disavowed his famous Coleman Report, which was an argument for racial integration and the use of transportation as a means of accomplishing this goal. Coleman now argues that busing Black children to predominantly white schools has more negative consequences, than positive ones. The major negative consequence is that it causes middle-class white families to leave the cities and move to the suburbs, thereby producing even further racial segregation. Glazer takes a similar view of busing. He does not take issue with the Brown Decision of 1954 nor the Civil Rights Act of 1964, but he holds that the enforcement of these policies by professionals and bureaucrats, urged on by liberals and social reformers and the Civil Rights Movement, has gotten out of hand. Busing Black children into predominantly white schools is offensive to the rights of whites, he argues. Glazer would remove all enforcement measures from the courts and leave it to the Congress. He argues that it would be more consistent with the American character and to the rights of the majority.

In chapter four, Glazer deals with discrimination in housing. Here he applauds the national government, the housing industry, and others for not establishing quotas and statistical means of evaluating the progress of desegregation. He applauds the movement of Blacks into the suburbs and he questions the enforcement of non-discriminatory measures. He says on page 152, "It is clear, however, that enforcement of laws against discrimination, no matter how stringent, will have only a modest effect on residential distribution." He considers enforcement measures, therefore, too high a price to pay for a change. And again the price is too high because it infringes on what he considers the rights of the majority. He says that substantial progress is being made without special efforts toward enforcement.

In chapter five, Glazer deals with the reactions of white ethnic groups toward measures to bring about equality for minorities. Here he deals with what has been called the back-lash on the part of more privileged white citizens. His basic quarrel again is with measures to ensure equality and social justice. He says on page 201, "Compensation for the past is a dangerous principle. It can be extended indefinitely and make for endless trouble. Who is to determine what is proper compensation for the American Indian, the black, the Mexican American, the Chinese or Japanese American?"

Then Glazer states, perhaps in a positive way, the essence of his own new policy and philosophy, "When it is established that the full status of equality is *extended* to every individual, regardless of race, color, or national origin, and that special opportunity is also available to any *individual* on the basis of *individual need,* again *regardless* of race, color, or national origin, one has done all that justice and equity call for and that is consistent with a harmonious multigroup society." Glazer doesn't face squarely the question of what should the government and society do if his prescription does not result in any substantial degree of equality. Indeed, it may be argued that this aspect of Glazer's book and his new philosophy is the most irresponsible of all.

In his concluding chapter, "Morality, Politics, and the Future of Affirmative Action," Glazer returns to his introductory theme. The history of America, he says, has produced distinct progress toward equality and parity. That progress has deemphasized ethnic and racial categories. That policy has led us toward a just and good society. For the past ten years now, he argues, we have drifted away from that policy. We have decided to quote numbers and divide people into their appropriate racial and ethnic groups and let equality prevail between them and the others. What Glazer fails to say is that individuals who are already privileged, in part because of the nation and in part because of their race and sex, are not the best keepers of liberty of those who are less privileged. Glazer fails to point out the necessity for social policy and measures of enforcement which stand outside the domination of the privileged majority in embracing the whole of the nation and society.

Moreover, absent altogether from Glazer's book and his new philosophy and new intellectual movement is a concern for the elevation of the disprivileged in our society.

In an address at the inauguration of Samuel DuBois Cook as President of Dillard University, Mr. Harold Howe, II, Vice President of the Ford Foundation, observed the following about *Affirmative Discrimination:*

> He [Glazer] argues that minority groups should not seek statistical parity in all classifications of education and employment. In making his case, I think he ignores the issue of the degree of disparity in comparing minorities with the main body of the population. When statistics show that a racially identified group of 25 million people is as far behind whites as America's Blacks apparently are, they become a powerful argument for special efforts to enhance both the opportunities and success of Blacks, perhaps not to the point of absolute statistical parity but at least well beyond the current status.

JACK D. DOUGLAS
University of California, San Diego

The conflicts over racial and ethnic equality involve most of the great moral passions of the American people—equality versus inequality; freedom versus slavery; justice versus injustice; humanity versus inhumanity; good versus evil; godliness versus sinfulness. Little wonder that these conflicts so easily become melodramas of moralistic self-presentation and recriminatory denunciation that sweep aside the whisper of reason that would remind us that unconstrained moralistic passions produce human catastrophes. Anyone who has watched them unfold, especially in the increasingly bitter clashes from about 1840 that led to our terrible civil war and from about 1960 to the present, would be tempted to believe that Americans are Zoroastrians enacting the universal drama of good struggling against evil.

In the social minefields of passionate conflict the mines are red-hot political labels (like "racist," "fascist," "sexist," "hippie," "nigger-lover," etc.). The shrapnel consists of expressions of hatred and contempt, social isolation, job discrimination, and sometimes violence. In an era when such passions are unleashed most people, while feeling some of the passions themselves, become primarily concerned with avoiding the minefields and the bursts of shrapnel. They are anxious *not* to get involved, and thus, *not* to have publicly visible beliefs other than vague homilies like "All victory to the righteous" or "Down with evil." What sociologist today has not sat through seemingly endless committee and departmental meetings in which the things everyone knew were the "really important things" could not be talked about because . . . well, you know. . . . What sociologist today has not felt the fear of being "mislabeled"? Or struggled unbelievingly to read the language of New-speak in our current letters of recommendation? Or, far worse, struggled desperately in one's own letters to tell half-untruths without being dishonest? Because of all the political passions that have embroiled our academic lives in recent years we have unintentionally built up complex forms of community censorship and some cunning ways of talking around our collegial censors.

Nathan Glazer is one of the now endangered species of courageous (or foolhardy?) sociologists who insist on invading our American minefield of racial and ethnic conflicts. He brings to the task his great knowledge of and empathy for ethnicity in American society and a wonderfully subtle understanding of the complexity of situated ethnic identities and their effects in our pluralistic political arenas; but in this work he brings all of this knowledge and wisdom to bear mainly on the urgent practical task of arousing educated Americans to the dangers of our present path. While many other sociologists are furiously fanning the passions with moralistic labels, he insists on *publishing* (not simply whispering) the things we all know, at least subconsciously, but hope we never have to face up to, admit, or, perish the thought, actually *say* in public. Naturally, he tries to protect himself by denouncing traditional Southern values as "vicious" (cultural relativism stops short of Satan and the Mason-Dixon line) and even leaving open the possibility that he is a "traditional liberal" (rather than a dreaded American "conservative" who believes in individual freedoms). But surely he knows that will not save him from professional immolation. Our young colleagues will easily see the "really-real truth" that he is a "racistconservativeelitist" and he will not escape the quick justice of social shrapnel. Why, then, does he do this monstrous thing?

Does he do this thing because he believes we educated people, the only possible audience for the book, believe those silly statistical arguments about lower black (brown, yellow, red) statistical representations "proving" discrimination? But why should we believe such a thing? We don't for one minute believe that the vast "overrepresentation" of blacks in the elitist ranks of vastly "overpaid" football, basketball, and baseball players proves discrimination against whites who are struggling to take their places. Nor do we believe that the vast "overrepresentation" of the Japanese and Chinese among the rich, professional, and highly educated proves there was discrimination *for* them or *against* whites. Nor do we believe that the vast "overrepresentation" of Jews in our greatest universities, especially in sociology, proves they are involved in a "clannish conspiracy." Nor do we believe the almost total lack of non-Jewish Poles in the elite universities proves discrimination against them. Nor do we ever believe correlation proves causality. We know a *statistical con-game* when we see one.

Does he do this thing because he believes we believe busing will improve the educational achievements of blacks (etc.) or make friends out of erstwhile opponents? But why should we believe such things? Almost all of us know, both from personal experience and from the work of James Coleman and others, that personal motivation, basic skills, and family life are the crucial determinants of educational effort and achievement, and, thus, we know that educated parents generally have children who do well in school and uneducated parents don't, regardless of what the schools are like or who is in them. We also know that throwing poor and largely unmotivated children in with better off and already more advanced learners is of questionable value in achieving anything other than isolation, self-doubt, resentment, and fights. If we are sociologists, we know the evidence that busing generally increases taxes and "white flight," not integration and equality of achievement. And, of course, we know from the papers in our classes that "compensatory education" is just another political con job. We know political and judicial silliness when we see it.

Does he do this thing because he believes his tremulous voice of reason can still the irrational screams of the impassioned? But why would he believe that? He surely knows that nothing can deter the John Browns in our midst, nor any true believers, once their passions are fully aroused, as they seem to be now. Has he some unrevealed reason to believe that passion can be stilled by anything other than greater passion or by dissipating itself through innumerable frustrations?

Though he never explicitly says so, I suspect from what he does say that he believes his work can arouse a countervailing passion in those of us who would prefer to hide from those issues and, thereby, lead us to break through our community censorship. This countervailing passion is fear.

Glazer gives ample reason for any reasonable person to fear the consequences of the affirmative discrimination being pursued by many of our judges, government bureaucrats, journalists, and academics. He argues that such preferential treatment for a few minorities inevitably arouses great resentment and anger ("backlash") against those minorities by the great majority of the many minorities that make up our pluralistic society. He argues that preferential treatment also arouses and inflames passions of resentment and ethnic identity all around, so that our society becomes more fragmented and conflict-ridden, precisely as it has done since the 1960s. (If anti-WASP feelings are inflamed today, can anti-black, anti-semite, and omni-anti feelings be long in coming? Does not the growth of English-Canadian nationalism inflame French-Canadian nationalism—and vice versa?) This would be reason enough to fear the consequences of affirmative discrimination in a mass pluralistic society that is already torn with many conflicts, that is anxious, moralistic, and possibly groping for some panacea to embrace psssionately.

But it seems to me that Glazer almost unintentionally presents an even more fearsome picture of our current situation, yet fails to draw out its implications. Given, as I have argued, that we educated Americans already know most of the facts he is presenting about the failures and dishonesties of affirmative discrimination, and given the overwhelming opposition (80%) of Americans to such silly things as busing, to achieve school desegregation, how can such extremist things happen in a highly democratic society? Here (especially in chapter six) Glazer gives one of the finest and most balanced pressure-group theories of American politics I have seen. Much of the power of the theory is in the systematic, complex details, but the fearful implications are found in a few of the parts. His argument that the news media, especially the big-prestige media, help to inflame the passions against the "conservatives" (or "traditional liberals") by biased and, worse, ignorant reporting will arouse concern only in those who do not already know how the media-types work. His argument that many judges around the country are making a travesty (my word) of the law by blatantly allowing their passions to determine their interpretations of the law has fearful implications, but our society has lived with that before.

The truly fearsome part of the argument is his detailed evidence of the way in which a handful of federal (and, I would add, state) agencies have not only grossly over-interpreted the laws, but have willfully *mis*interpreted them and covered-up their illegal activities behind ludicrous frontwork—all in spite of the massive opposition of the public and of their elected presidents and congressmen. Though he does not use the term and hardly seems to see it as the most important problem he is considering, he presents a fearsome picture of *bureaucratic tyranny,* a conspiracy to usurp power from legitimate authorities and to cover-up the usurpations. It is a massive conspiracy that has been immensely successful in working its illegal will, but even in the post-Watergate era there has not been one indictment, presumably because it is the enforcers themselves who are guilty. Though this is not the only reason, surely this is one *good* reason why ever more Americans are furious at "The Government."

But, then, we come back to what I have already said. We educated people already knew about this bureaucratic tyranny, though not in all the lurid detail Glazer presents. We have known for years about the iron law of bureaucratic non-quota-quotas, and we know they are illegal on the simplest prima facie grounds, yet even when we were opposed to them most of us, like "good Germans," have silently gone along with the bureaucratic tyrants—for "practical" reasons. It seems to me that this betrayal of reason by the educated is the most fearsome, if unwritten, message of this book. But, while it should inspire fear in all who are reasonable, it need not inspire despair. After all, Glazer and a few others have spoken up.

Is it too much—or, perhaps, too late—to hope that this book will help to rally educated Americans against the fanatics who are willing to burn the foundations of freedom and justice in a vain attempt to rectify instantaneously the racial tragedy of American history? After our many years of bitter experience in what we once thought of as the home of reason, the bulwark against fanatic passions—the academy, we have grave reasons to doubt that reason can prevail in the growing struggles. We also must doubt because we know that racial ("ethnic") conflict is only one of many others, because we know most major nations of the Western World today are torn by similar and often worse conflicts, and because historical perspective arouses our suspicions that we have entered another time of troubles from which the most powerful forces of fanaticism will emerge victorious and repress all the others. But we also know historically that the few nations with centuries-long traditions (naughty word!) of democracy have negotiated their ways through other times of trouble. On balance, we do not have sufficient reason to despair—yet. And Glazer's latest work of scholarship and impassioned reason adds, if only so slightly, to our faltering hopes. But will it effectively arouse the educated against the bureaucratic tyrants and our label-mongers who enforce our community censorship? I am not undespairing enough to believe so.

JOAN W. MOORE
University of Wisconsin, Milwaukee

A thorough sociological analysis of affirmative action is long overdue. As Nathan Glazer suggests, it is an interesting social phenomenon and we have little understanding of its sources, its characteristics, and complex ramifications, or of its actual and potential impact in changing the status of minorities and women in jobs, education, and housing (three areas emphasized by Glazer). Nor do we understand how it modifies the meaning of race and ethnicity in the American polity. Such an analysis would be useful in clarifying controversies both in sociology and society.

It is unfortunate, therefore, that this book gives us a relatively unsophisticated, topical, and personal polemic.

It is unsophisticated because Glazer generally oversimplifies the issues and the evidence. He makes, for example, the unsociological decision to discuss only Blacks and to ignore Chicanos, Puerto Ricans, Native Americans, and women. Thus he compounds the oversimplification of affirmative action in employment and education, in particular.

It is topical because his use of history is tendentiously selective rather than systematic, and because agencies and institutions are evaluated with neither clear specification of their immediate context nor any sense of historical perspective. Courts are condemned, for example, in the following: "the way judges work for the most part these days . . . becomes not what is the constitutional principle but what is good for society" (p. 219). A recent series of decisions more supportive of the status quo would seem to allay Glazer's concern about the role of the courts.

It is personal polemic because his ultimate point of reference is his own judgment and his purpose is to condemn current policy. He is careful to make this clear and consistent.

Glazer's basic theme is that affirmative action is a drastic departure from the "inclusionist" course of American history. This premise rests on his view of American history defined in terms of European ethnic groups, a view in which a logic of social action in the vague "then" is supposed to be completely appropriate to the totally undefined "now." He sees us as taking a path to the Nuremberg Laws (p. 200). Worse yet, we are being led on that path by a predominantly Black cadre of activists entrenched in Federal civil rights agencies, supported by the courts and by a manipulated, moralistic, and pluralistically ignorant "liberal" public opinion.

He views the drastic departure from normality as particularly unfortunate in the light of Black progress. Glazer insists on this "progress" and its controversial nature is glibly glossed over. One particularly irritating bit of reasoning is borrowed from Kantrowitz, who argues that the index of residential dissimilarity between Northern and Southern European foreign born in New York (of 51.6) represents the " 'lower/possible/bound' " for Black-white segregation, and therefore that the *observed* Black-white index—of 81—is "realistically" "20 points lower" (pp. 154–55). And besides, the index of residential dissimilarity between Blacks and whites declined between 1960 and 1970 anyway.

One of the sorriest consequences of Glazer's topicality is the imputation of great power, wielded unremittingly, to the proponents of affirmative action. The EEOC is portrayed as a veritable octopus, strangling employers' efforts at maintaining standards. But to Glazer, EEOC, along with other "federal civil rights enforcement agencies," is "*requiring* all major employing institutions in the country to employ minorities in rough proportion to their presence in the population" (p. 66, emphasis added). "Requirement" and "enforcement" are strong words, never operationalized except for one or two cases (AT&T) and "ominous" citations from EEOC reports. In fact, half the work force is not affected by Federal compliance issues. Impact and outcome are glossed over, and actual indicators of this power are never provided. A list of actual penalties is not even attempted. This is the familiar litany of complaint at Federal incursions on private domains. Similarly, Glazer holds forth the spectre of a major revival of white ethnic identity to form a backlash effect which will permanently modify all party politics: the recent Carter-Ford campaign makes much of this chapter look like the topical rhetoric it is.

A complete review of this book as a work of sociology would take an amount of space that is incommensurate with its value as sociology. The book, however, should interest sociologists concerned with their own profession. There are more sophisticated works in the conservative tradition, and equally meretricious polemics from both liberal and radical sociologists. The literature of "pop-soc polemic" is increasingly the public face of sociology, and serious review in a journal addressed to professional sociologists has little effect on either its authors or its intended audience. *Within* the discipline we continue to be able to take a measured approach to similar controversies: the success of the recent ASA Plenary Session on School Busing is evidence that sociology is not subverted either by the passion of personal conviction or the glamour of public visibility. I would welcome a serious study of the effect of this kind of undisciplined pop-soc rhetoric on political decision-makers.

A final perspective. Academic sociologists are affected occupationally by affirmative action in hiring, promotion and tenure, recruitment and retention of students, and curriculum. Many of us establish and defend our personal biases with even less craft than Glazer. The amazing debate on affirmative action, published in a series of articles in *Footnotes* and *The American Sociologist,* is summarized in the forthcoming report of the ASA Committee on the Status of Racial and Ethnic Minorities in Sociology. In this document, *both* sides of the debate are amply quoted, but more important, the issue is viewed both in the context of our own profession's tradition of exclusion and of our current efforts at change. Glazer gives us neither context nor balance and no guidance in our occupational stake.

Structural Stability and Morphogenesis: An Outline of a General Theory of Models, by RENE THOM. Translated by D. H. Fowler. Reading, Mass.: W. A. Benjamin, 1975. 348 pp. $13.50 paper.

TIMOTHY W. COLLINS
University of Denver

Dr. Thom shares the dissatisfaction many sociologists feel when they are forced to choose between intelligible qualitative explanations which are shallow and naive, and quantitative explanations which although coherent are so abstract as to be completely unintuitive if not unintelligible. His response, contained in this book, is to attempt to demonstrate how qualitative analysis could be conducted and presented in a thoroughly rigorous way to provide satisfactory representations of partial phenomenon.

This is the seminal work on catastrophe theory by its originator. Catastrophe theory comprises the effort of theoretical mathematicians to illustrate that classical scientific models based upon continuous functions in two or three dimensions are restrictive special cases which should be generalized to consider discontinuities in N-dimensions.

Catastrophe theory is derived from topology, the branch of mathematics which investigates the properties of geometric configurations. Topology becomes crucial to sociology when one realizes that all intellectualization consists of interpreting a process geometrically (p. 5). At first glance this looks like disciplinary imperialism from the perspective of a topologist, but when one considers all of the circles, squares, triangles, diamonds, etc. which litter the pages of theory books, Thom's contention appears much more justified. The problem with the qualitative theories of the enlightenment was that they were too simple—their geometry was based upon "the experience of bodies in three-dimensional Euclidean space" (p. 6). The problem with all quantitative theories since Newton has been that they are impossible to interprete geometrically. Consider one's frustrations with the flow charts constructed out of boxes and arrows which cannot explain because they lack a geometry. Yet, as everyone who has ever constructed a flow chart agrees, it does help to see what you are talking about. Dr. Thom discusses this problem:

> In the situation where man is deprived of all possibility of intellectualization, that is, of interpreting geometrically a given process, either he will seek to create, despite everything, through suitable interpretations, an intuitive justification of the process, or he will sink into resigned incomprehension which habit will change to indifference. In the case of gravitation there is no doubt that the second attitude has prevaled, for we have not in 1975 less reason to be astonished at the fall of the apple than had Newton. The dilemma posed all scientific explanation is this: magic or geometry (p. 5).

Thom's task then becomes one of expanding our basic geometric intuition, of disseminating the recent advances in topology and differential analysis which make it possible to define a form and to determine whether or not two functions have or have not the same topological type.

Much of catastophe theory's significance for sociology lies in its particular emphasis upon the geometry of discontinuity, or catastophes. This results from the form some of our cherished concepts exhibit when represented mathematically. Systems in equilibrium produce smooth surfaces or continuous mathematical functions. System disintegration, upheaval, revolution, rapid and violent change result in surface discontinuities when they are expressed mathematically. Dr. Thom echos conflict theorists when he argues that the most distinguishing characteristics of different forms are their boundaries, the interruptions in the smooth forms, the disequilibriums, in short, their catastrophes. Thom's method of model building classifies models on the basis of the differences between their catastrophe sets. Sociologists should not jump to conclusions and believe that catastrophe theory is the grand synthesis between functional and conflict theory we have all been hoping for, only a sociologist can provide that. Catastrophe theory is however, a mathematics which permits both facets of social life to be taken into account. Now rigorous conflict theorists can express themselves mathematically and mathematical sociologists can explore conflict theoretically; neither of these options has been readily available in the past.

Although catastrophe theory is vitally important to every sociologist, this book is not equally accessible to all sociologists. The mathematics presented in the book are profound both in their originality and implications. Most of the book will be difficult reading for the average sociologist. (To the untrained in topology I recommend E. D. Zeeman's article on "Catastrophe Theory" in the April, 1976 issue of *Scientific American*.)

In this book, Thom has begun building a bridge between theoretical mathematics and the types of theoretically productive applications sociologists will want to make of them. It is fair to say that his brief sections on society are inadequate at best. Their inadequacy is the result of Thom's lack of sociological training, not in any mathematical shortcoming. Catastrophe theory provides a method for making theoretical descriptions of the phenomena under consideration which are mathematically rigorous and useful. Large numbers of mathematically trained sociologists exist today and it is to them I recommend this book. By combining our special knowledge of society with Thom's mathematical insights we can greatly shorten the time it will take for catastrophe theory to enrich our discipline.

HECTOR J. SUSSMAN
Rutgers/SUNJ

Thom is a great mathematician, and his book contains beautiful mathematics. The applications that he proposes, however, are either vague analogies, or incomprehensible, or meaningless. In particular, what he writes about society is completely unrelated to his mathematics. "Catastrophe Theory" is a precise mathematical theory which involves certain mathematical concepts that Thom *chose* to call "catastrophes." It is *not* a theory of natural or social "catastrophes." A revolution may be "catastrophic," but this does not establish any relationship between revolutions and catastrophe theory. Of course, it is not impossible that there might be such a relationship, but this would have to be shown by the proponents of Catastrophe Theory on the basis of stronger evidence than the mere fact that they made a certain choice of words. (Otherwise, I could decide to call a polynomial a "social structure," then study polynomials and claim that I am doing sociology.) Thom's speculations on aging, sex, death, dreaming, predators and preys, fortune-telling, and societies are probably questionable. For example, when he writes that "there are two kinds of society, the military society and the fluid society," or that "money . . . tends to move away from consumers and accumulate at the producers. But as it must follow a closed path in the social body, it is necessary for an artificial mechanism to carry it in the opposite direction. Such a mechanism can depend only on the structure of society, on authority, in this way money is imbued with the gradient of authority (grad u) by the process of taxes. When it arrives at the summit, it is divided up by the chief, who can, in a permanent catastrophe, share out the portions where necessary." But I am only a mathematician, and should not pass judgment. The one thing that is clear to me, as a mathematician, is that those statements have nothing to do with the mathematics of "Catastrophe Theory."

Having said all this, why I cannot write a review of Thom's book should be clear. What would my review say? I could write all the things I have just written, but then the review would look like a diatribe. The only alternative would be to explain why I make all these assertions. But this would require an explanation of Thom's theory, which cannot be given in a few pages.

I think it is regrettable that *Contemporary Sociology* will publish a favorable review of Thom's book. As a consequence of such a review, I am afraid that many young sociologists will waste a lot of their time trying to learn Catastrophe Theory. I wish I had found a way to tell them not to do it.

BOOK REVIEWS

Communications

Television as a Cultural Force, edited by RICHARD ADLER and DOUGLASS CATER. New York: Praeger Publishers, 1976. 184 pp. $17.50 cloth.

PAUL DIMAGGIO
Harvard University

This collection is a product of the Aspen Institute Program on Communications and Society, a generously funded effort to encourage scholarly communication about the media's social and cultural effects. In 1974 and 1975, the Program's Television Workshop sponsored a series of conferences at which academic luminaries, television critics, and industry professionals viewed episodes of high-quality, prime-time fare and then attempted collectively "to practice the best sort of criticism possible" (p. 2). The result is a rather slim volume, scandalously overpriced, of nine essays on television criticism and interpretation.

The contributions, which vary in quality, deal from several humanistic perspectives with the issue of meaning in television, an area where sociologists can use some guidance. It becomes clear early on, however, that the contributors have two agenda, unfortunately confused. On the one hand they are concerned with developing an aesthetic for television criticism in a formal, almost literary, sense. On the other, they attempt to interpret television content, in its social setting, as a cultural force. Most authors do neither very well. The book should be read for scattered insights, not cohesive arguments or answers.

The essays that deal most explicitly with criticism make some worthwhile points. Richard Adler, in the introduction, describes the formal elements that shape the television viewing experience and, given current technology, influence the kind of material presented. David Thorburn discusses televised drama as melodrama in literary historical perspective, arguing convincingly that video producers can artistically transcend the medium's technical (if not its sociopolitical) limitations.

Unfortunately, however, many of the authors' points are stale. Adler's treatment of program flow is good, but not so good as Raymond Williams's in *Television: Technology and Cultural Form*. Sharon Lynn Sperry's analysis of the narrative form in televised news stories was done first (and better) by Epstein in *News from Nowhere*. Much of the writing on criticism consists of hand-wringing about the sorry state of the enterprise and assertions that if only critics adopted the author's perspective (be it historical, literary, Kohlbergian, or psychoanalytic) matters would improve greatly; one senses, perhaps unfairly, a school of disciplinary sharks scenting a new body of work on which to cut their teeth.

As David Littlejohn's useful concluding essay illustrates, although most newspaper TV critics are too beset by daily repertorial chores to really criticize, the field is not completely moribund. While television has had neither the core of enthusiasts nor the need for an advertising medium (like *Rolling Stone*) that facilitated the brief efflorescence of a vital rock criticism, TV does have its Leonards, Arlens, and, in Harlan Ellison, even its own Lester Bangs. At their best, the volume's contributors acknowledge their predecessors and demonstrate that good television criticism must develop its own aesthetic; at their worst, they try to jam it into established critical molds.

Turning to interpretation, the authors vacillate between unusual sophistication and efforts to squeeze semiotic blood out of artistic turnips. Although a couple prattle about television as a collective unconscious, most are firmly aware that television programming is created by real people, working in real organizations under economic and political constraints. Paula Fass's discussion of the use of television as an historical document is especially perceptive.

When it comes down to actually explicating the social meaning of the programs they discuss, the contributors tend to flounder. The most successful fly on the strength of their intuitions more than on any solid analytic methodology. In this they are not so different from sociologists, who may be inspired by their serendipitous insights and their mistakes to develop the kind of specified models of relationships between cultural products and social organization that the book's contributors seem to be groping toward.

Creating Reality: How TV News Distorts Events, by DAVID L. ALTHEIDE. Beverly Hills: Sage Publications, 1976. 220 pp. $11.00 cloth. $6.00 paper.

M. G. DUNN
Virginia Commonwealth University

Since World War II, television has emerged as the dominant news medium in our society. Surveys have consistently revealed that televised news accounts are the most frequently relied upon and the most trusted sources of information about current events. However, despite these and other indications of its power and pervasiveness, TV news has not been a topic which has stimulated the type of scholarly interest that several sociologists have applied to the study of news production on the American newspaper. David Altheide, then, is something of a pioneer. He has apparently devoted more time to studying the creation of television news than any other sociologist. Unfortunately, if we are to judge from *Creating Reality,* Altheide has very little to contribute to substantive work in the sociology of mass communications—or, for that matter, to any area of sociological inquiry.

Altheide is concerned chiefly with castigating the news media, not with advancing sociological knowledge. A foreshadowing of the accusatory tone and content of *Creating Reality* is provided in the introduction when Arthur Vidich accurately describes the author's purpose of exposing television news as "a rotten egg that is growing bigger and bigger." Another book telling us about the tension between "the responsible citizen" and "the irresponsible media" is well and good, but readers should not be misled by Vidich's claim that Altheide's polemic "follows the sociological tradition of news analysis in a direct line from the work of Robert E. Park and Helen MacGill Hughes." For unlike Park and Hughes, Altheide has attempted to mask careless and value-laden speculation in the disguise of empirical research.

He would have us believe that his "findings" were derived principally from participant observation. At first blush, this is indeed believable. Altheide spent hundreds of hours observing the process of creating news programs at a local network-affiliated TV station in "Western City." In addition, he paid brief visits to a "network-owned and operated" local station in "Northern City" and to a couple of network affiliates in the state of Washington. But the conjectures which comprise the bulk of *Creating Reality* could not have possibly been drawn from Altheide's participant-observation research. He collected information at *local* television stations, yet his major conclusions pertain to the production of *network* news, and to the "irresponsibility" of American journalism in general. He does this, curiously enough, in spite of frequent references to fundamental differences between local TV news organizations, the networks, and other news media.

From time to time during his three-year research effort, Altheide proved to be an aggressive seeker of information (even to the point, on one occasion, of stealing a document which a news director had forbidden him from photocopying). This aggressiveness produced a splattering of insights into the inner workings of local TV news operations. However, Altheide's zeal for accumulating anecdotal data was not matched by a corresponding enthusiasm for proposing testable hypotheses. He chose instead to wander from one vague assumption to another, conveniently neglecting to operationalize such key concepts as "bias" and "distortion." The closest thing to a specific proposition in the book is Altheide's "central thesis" that "events become news when transformed by the news perspective, and not because of their objective characteristics" (p. 173). The "news perspective," is never defined explicitly, yet Altheide frequently concludes that his anecdotes confirm the existence and function of this perspective. Moreover, Altheide has no reliable way of determining the relative influence of "objective characteristics" of events on the process of news production because his research design did not allow for exact assessments of any events which were subsequently covered by the media. This is a major flaw throughout the entire study. Since he was unable to identify the objective characteristics of an event, Altheide could not adequately describe the media's "bias" or "distortion" in covering that event. It is a simple matter to charge that a news report is inaccurate or subjective; it is much more difficult to define precise standards of media accuracy and objectivity, or to measure deviations from these guidelines. Problems of definitions and measurement, on the other hand, were the least of Altheide's concerns.

The conjectural rather than empirical character of *Creating Reality* is magnified in the chapter on "The Eagleton and Watergate Stories." Altheide accuses the news media (not just local TV stations) of—you guessed it—"bias" and "distortion" in their coverage of these controversies. "Media overkill," we are told, contributed substantially to Eagleton's removal from the 1972 Democratic ticket: "The news media not only publicized aspects of the Eagleton case, but the meaning of certain events was fundamentally altered to tell a story" (p. 154). As might be expected, Altheide does not specify exactly what kinds of meanings were "altered" in the Eagleton story. Perhaps the author knows more about the whole affair than McGovern and the reporters who investigated the case. If he does, he should share this information with his readers. If he doesn't, perhaps he should refrain from accusing the media of irresponsible coverage.

Regarding Watergate, Altheide makes more serious charges of media irresponsibility. He argues that "Nixon fell from power because the news perspective transformed the series of events known as Watergate into a whole, which was then used as evidence of corruption and immorality"(p. 154). Naturally, Altheide never explains why this should not have been the media's reaction. In a revealing attempt to discount the notion that the commission of illegal deeds and political mistakes might have been major causes of Nixon's downfall, Altheide recites the familiar litany that the actions of previous presidents were equally contemptible: "The now public and sordid use of the FBI, IRS, and other government agencies by President Johnson and Kennedy to bug and harass members of 'suspicious' groups was known by legislators and journalists alike, but no indictments were brought, no articles of impeachment written, and no administration destroyed" (p. 158). Therefore, Nixon, like Eagleton, was unfairly victimized by the media—that is, if we are to trust the wisdom of David Altheide.

But why should we trust Altheide? His conclusions have nothing to do with his research on *local* TV news production; the Eagleton case and Watergate were *national* news events covered primarily by *national* news media. Having no data to support his argument, Altheide is forced to rely on popular literature and his own opinions. In his treatment of the Eagleton story, he cites accounts from mass-audience magazines and newspapers, while ignoring scholarly research which does not support his blanket indictment. For example, no mention was made of Edna Einsiedel's study (*Journal Quarterly,* Spring, 1975) which found significant differences between the three networks in their coverage of the Eagleton case. To augment his "observations" on Watergate, Altheide seeks support from best-selling author and long-time Nixon advocate Theodore H. White, frequently leading us into long quotations from White's recent books. (White "is correct about" this, "cautions against" that, "corroborates" this, "accurately describes" that, ect., etc.) And in the final analysis, Altheide falls back on his own personal sense of ethics and political reality. He concludes that "the net effect" of the media's Watergate coverage "was to greatly exaggerate the crimes of Nixon while downplaying . . . the negotiated and conflictful nature of everyday political life" (p. 171).

Sociologists, of course, should be extremely skeptical of this kind of media criticism, especially when it is packaged as scientific research. Altheide obviously has an ax to grind. More importantly, whether or not television news is a "rotten egg" simply isn't an intriguing sociological question. Even if Altheide is correct in his judgment that Eagleton and Nixon were treated unfairly by the media, what do we learn from this? Many US citizens prefer news which makes public life as insecure as possible for political leaders. According to this view, the media should be tireless adversaries rather than impartial observers. Thus, Altheide could not have provided a scientific solution to the problem of assessing media responsibility even if he had seriously aspired to do so.

This is not meant to imply that media topics such as how TV news is created should be off-limits to sociological researchers. We can certainly learn more about patterns of mass information transmission by examining this important social process. Altheide may have performed a useful service by focusing more attention on a potentially rewarding research topic. For this potential to be realized, however, we need researchers who are dedicated to producing testable propositions, who are willing to confine their analyses to the data they collect, and who are capable of suppressing their own desires to become referees in popular debates.

Mass Media: Systems and Effects, by W. PHILIPPS DAVISON, JAMES BOYLAN, and FREDERICK T. C. YU. New York: Praeger Publishers, 1976. 245 pp. No price listed, paper.

HERBERT I. SCHILLER
University of California, San Diego

The proliferation of communications, journalism, and media courses across the country has produced an expanded market for texts. Naturally, publishers have not been slow to seize the opportunity offered. Recent years have seen an increasing stream of books designed to take advantage of the *classroom* communications revolution.

But textbooks written in anticipation of substantial national sales cannot be expected to wander far from the bounds of orthodoxy. And so it is with *Mass Media: Systems and Effects,* a joint product of Professors Davison, Boylan, and Yu, all affiliated with the Graduate School of Journalism at Columbia University. Their book offers few surprises and makes even fewer, if any, waves.

Actually, the volume, well-written and up-to-date in its examples and references, tends to the "all is basically well" overview, while observing that the few problems or abuses presented are capable of correction or rectification. In a word, the tone is definitely optimistic and the word "fortunately" puts in a frequent appearance in the text.

Does the communications scene warrant so sanguine an outlook? It depends! If it is accurate that American society is genuinely pluralistic, as the authors contend, and no sector exercises undue influence on the polity/economy, there is room for confidence. But is this the true state of affairs, especially in the informational area?

Take, for example, the matter of concentration of ownership in the mass media. Concentration of press and broadcasting facilities has proceeded almost, but not quite, to the outer limits. Now, chains gobble up other chains. Is this a threat to the public's informational health or a matter that is counter-balanced by some saving factor? The authors remain untroubled because, as they interpret it, "members of the same chain may support different presidential candidates" (p. 98).

No matter if the flow of news/information/entertainment is irrelevant, trivialized, lopsided, and honeycombed with PR and advertising. Because, "fortunately, we are equipped to make a selection from the stream of messages to which we are exposed" (p. 131). And how will that choice be made? Either, according to the authors, a message consistent with already existing beliefs and attitudes—where did they come from, one wonders—or, "we will attend, perceive, and remember information that is pleasurable, or that will help in some way to satisfy our needs" (p. 139). This, the "uses and gratifications" explanation of the media, fits nicely with the overall functionalist approach of the book; whatever exists serves some need and has some useful function.

With this perspective, developments in the media, or wherever, tend to be removed from a historical context and withdrawn from critical scrutiny. When functionalism is combined with confidence in the pluralist character of American institutions, there seems to be nothing left to worry about. All flash points are defused and serious social issues are reduced to questions of individual problem-solving. Balance and well-being inevitably are restored with an upbeat appraisal of the individual's capacity to deal with large, organizational forces. Accordingly, much of the book's advice is to the individual "consumer" of the media; how to sample media offerings selectively! Actually, this is probably realistic because the producers of messages, the real decision makers, are paying attention to other advisors, mostly concerned with the bottom line.

Sensitive to the charge that the media are devoted to the maintenance of the status quo, the authors argue that if this is so, "they are doing a poor job of it. . . . social change has never been so rapid as in the past generation" (p. 148). But this change is not necessarily all, or even partly, attributable to the communications system. Larger socio-historical forces have been at work for a very long time.

According to Davison, Boylan, and Yu, the aim of their book is to provide an introduction to the history of American mass media, to provide a brief review of the media's functioning and its effects, and to offer some comparison of media systems overall. Considered formally, these matters are examined. Yet, in the larger sense, it is disquieting to realize that the fundamental character and condition of our information situation has been left mostly unexplored. Individuals today face a massively concentrated, privately-owned and directed media industry that ranges across the entire information spectrum—from hard to software, from books and records, to film and TV. This industry operates both as a profitmaking sector and as a consciousness-producing machine. Its environment is a world organized by a few hundred super-corporations.

Unfortunately, these themes remain largely unaddressed in *Mass Media: Systems and Effects.*

Crime, Law, and Deviance

Deliver Us from Evil: An Interpretation of American Prohibition, by NORMAN H. CLARK. New York: W.W. Norton & Company, 1976. 246 pp. $10.95 cloth.

Alcohol and Alcohol Problems: New Thinking and New Directions, edited by WILLIAM J. FILSTEAD, JEAN J. ROSSI, and MARK KELLER. Cambridge, Mass.: Ballinger Publishing Company, 1976. 304 pp. $15.00 cloth.

MARSTON M. MCCLUGGAGE
University of Kansas, Lawrence

These are very different kinds of books. Professor Clark has written an historical study in which he traces the social forces bringing about the social movements of temperance, the Anti-Saloon League, the passage of the Eighteenth Amendment and its ultimate repeal. *Alcohol and Alcohol Problems* is a series of eight papers based on a conference in the Alcoholism Rehabilitation Center of Lutheran General Hospital held in the spring of 1973. Twenty-four prominent scholars in the alcohol field were invited to participate. The book reflects the current state of knowledge in this field. It is written from a scientific point of view, rather than a moralistic one. It is a critical analysis of what has been done and what has not been done and carries suggestions as to what could be done to meet the problems associated with the use of alcohol.

While Clark discusses the contributions of major figures in the prohibition movement such as Frances Willard, Carry Nation, W. J. Bryan, and Wayne Wheeler, his major emphasis is upon the relationship of the movement to other social movements such as the women's movement, women's suffrage, urbanization, political reform, and religious pietism. Similarly he describes the social forces leading to repeal such as the automobile and social mobility, decline of the family, emphasis on individual freedom, and cultural pluralism. Symbolism of the drinking man such as Gable and Bogart in motion picures and novelists like Hemingway is emphasized. Thus repeal of prohibition was the mark of new social forces in a new society. *Deliver Us from Evil,* is an interesting social history, well written and well documented, and is another useful case for students of social movements.

The symposium on alcohol problems begins with an historical perspective on the state of knowledge in the alcohol field. It was written by Mark Keller, who was affiliated with the Center of Alcohol Studies, Yale University from 1941 to 1961. Since 1962, he has been with the Center at Rutgers University as editor of the *Journal of Studies on Alcohol*. The entire volume depends heavily upon the studies conducted under the auspices of these Centers with their emphasis upon research, education, treatment, and prevention. Most of the chapters use a medical model for consideration of alcoholism. A notable exception to this is Joseph R. Gusfield's final chapter on prevention, where he emphasizes situational rather than individualistic approaches to the field of alcohol studies.

There is a chapter on changing conceptions of definition and treatment of alcoholism across time, mostly in the United States. In the early period there was a moralistic approach. Only since 1940 have a few universities and professional organizations regarded the field as one for scientific analysis. In spite of the title of the monograph, Selden Bacon argues for a phenomenalistic rather than a problem oriented approach. He describes seven different historic programs to do something about alcohol. He argues for conceptual redefinition of the field of alcohol studies as a means to improving research in the field.

There is a chapter on the origin of alcoholism with discussion of pharmacological effects, theories of physical dependence, and social cultural, psycho-social factors affecting drinking patterns. The biology of alcoholism and the various diseases related to alcohol use are discussed.

Issues in the treatment of alcoholism are identified: the effect of the labelling process on the client and the problem, how the societal power structure conceives of the clientele and their problems, the physical setting of the environment of treatment, the biases of health care providers, and the tendencies of treatment organizations for self-preservation. Thus the client's condition is only one of a number of contingencies that affect the treatment process, and the fate of the individual. Policy makers and administrators in the treatment aspects need to recognize that there are alternative forms of intervention and that there is a need to consider the setting and the multiple publics in the community as well as the individual client.

There is detailed discussion of guidelines for the evaluation of treatment processes, from the perspective of client outcome. There is particular need to guard against the placebo effect of treatment. The theme of this chapter is "It ain't so much the things we don't know that get us into trouble. It is the things we know that ain't so'' (p. 230).

In the final chapter on prevention Gusfield casts doubt upon the effectiveness of individualistic policies as effectual prevention mechanisms. ''Appeals to punishment and to rational thought have not proved to be very useful means to decrease drinking or aclohol misuse'' (p. 283). He argues instead to rely on measures that change the environmental surroundings of behavior, and to consider alcohol misuse as part of wider problems.

Each chapter in this book is documented by an extensive bibliography, in some cases running over one hundred references. Consequently it contains an admirable survey and review of what is known thus far about alcohol and alcohol problems.

The Politics of Crime and Conflict: A Comparative History of Four Cities, by TED ROBERT GURR, PETER N. GRABOSKY, and RICHARD C. HULA. Beverly Hills: Sage Publications, 1977. 792 pp. $25.00 cloth.

Rogues, Rebels, and Reformers: A Political History of Urban Crime and Conflict, by TED ROBERT GURR. Beverly Hills: Sage Publications, 1976. 192 pp. $10.00 cloth.

MICHAEL POLEN
University of Michigan, Ann Arbor

In these studies, Gurr and his collaborators eschew the cross-national analyses of inferred psychological states that typified his earlier work (e.g., *Why Men Rebel*). They seek to document the courses and determine the causes of public disorder in London, Stockholm, Sydney, and Calcutta since about 1800, by asking how and to what extent socioeconomic changes and developments in the institutions of order (legal codes, police, courts, prisons) affect fluctuations and long-term patterns in various types of crime and collective conflict.

What are the major conclusions? (1) In all cases but Calcutta, crimes against property and persons declined throughout the late nineteenth and early twentieth centuries, then began to reverse upwards from about the 1930s. No similar trend appears in magnitudes of civil strife, although there may be some increase since about 1950. (2) Policies and institutions of public order—by altering the ways illicit behavior was defined, detected, punished, and recorded—account for some short-term variations, but provide no explanation for the long-term trends in crime or major fluctuations in strife (p. 6). (3) ''Societal strain'' may be connected to high levels of disorder in Calcutta, but secular social and economic improvements in the Western cities that coincided with increasing public order in the past have not declined as disorder has risen (p. 7). Subsidiary findings are sprinkled throughout. For example, there appears to be some connection in time between the incidence of ''crime waves'' and strife (p. 674).

The authors set an impressive research agenda, one that holds promise of illuminating our understanding of crime and punishment, protest and repression, change and disorder. But they fail, ultimately, to inform us about these issues in any coherent way, and the substantiations of their conclusions are unconvincing. This unhappy result can be blamed on their lack of adherence to an orienting theory of disorder, and from rather feckless data handling.

Lack of theory produces considerable ambiguity surrounding the interpretations of concepts and indicators of disorder. For example, the measures of crime include officially recorded numbers of known offenses, arrests, convictions, etc., usually expressed as rates per 100,000 population. In most analyses of the Western cities, these series are taken to be rough indicators of the extent of unlawful behavior. For Calcutta, in contrast, we are told they represent elites' efforts at control, a ''political variable quite distinct from the 'true' crime rate'' (p. 596). And at one point, Gurr cautions when graphing ''offenses known'' and ''convictions'' for theft that the ''meanings conveyed differ greatly'' (p. 621). Yet a graph of ''Trends in Theft, 1820–1972'' for London plots conviction rates (which are declining) for different segments of the period up to the 1930s, and reported offenses (which are rising) thereafter. In the absence of some evidence or strong argument that these series indicate the same thing, we must be skeptical of an interpretation of the long-term trend in ''theft.''

Although the other component of disorder, civil strife, is defined broadly to include violent and non-violent, political and non-political collective conflict, there is a discernible bias toward more violent, more drastic conflicts. (As opposed, say, to legal protest demonstrations.) This may be related to the fact that since nearly all the evidence of strife is anecodotal, there simply may be more information available for the more serious events. Sporadically, strike frequencies or officially recorded "offenses against public order" are employed as strife indicators. An index for Sydney and Calcutta of violent conflict appears but we are not told how it was produced in either case, and it is inexplicably omitted from the London, Stockholm, and comparative analyses.

As to data handling, the city studies often include analyses amounting to little more than the pursuit of large R^2s. Inattention to data sources, scant rationale for variable selection, and a tendency to minimize or ignore the effects of trend and serial correlation typify the regression analyses. The authors' interpretations of such analyses, especially for Stockholm and Sydney, may safely be ignored.

A final complaint: the format of *Politics* restricts it to those scoring high on *Sitzfleisch*. It is more a loosely edited compilation of case studies than a co-authored work. Gurr wrote the conceptual and comparative analysis chapters, which are reproduced—identically—as *Rogues*. The remaining three-fourths of *Politics* is devoted to the city studies (written by various combinations of authors), each of which doggedly surveys developments in crime, conflict, criminal law, police, courts, and penal systems over the last two centuries. The book's length might easily have been halved, with slight information loss.

The tone of my displeasure with these books stems largely from disappointment. The authors made little attempt to exploit the conceptual agenda Gurr buries in the books' last chapters. In this frame work, the proximate causes of public disorder include the legal definitions that bound illegitimate behavior, the policies of police and courts, and the "real" extent of social disorder. These relationships are nested within macro-level structures, including constraints set by the economy, social scale and cultural heterogeneity, and elite goals and interests. The careful examination of large scale social and political change, collective conflict, and individual level crime in four cities over two centuries would be quite an achievement. But these books fall far short of that mark.

Politics is obese and rather incoherent. I'd like to be able to recommend *Roques* in its stead. Unfortunately, the chapters appearing in both books seem uncomfortable in each. In *Politics*, this results from redundancy and inconsistency vis-à-vis the city studies; in *Rogues*, from insufficient connection to them.

An Economic Analysis of Crime: Selected Readings, edited by LAWRENCE J. KAPLAN AND DENNIS KESSLER. Springfield, Ill.: Charles C Thomas, 1975. 410 pp. $17.50 cloth. $12.95 paper.

HERMAN SCHWENDINGER
University of Nevada, Las Vegas

The study of criminal organizations in recent years has split wide open empirically and theoretically. The received wisdom in the field, represented by the writings of Donald Cressey, Thomas Schelling, Daniel Bell, and others, is being repeatedly contradicted or superseded. Eric Hobsbawm, Francis Ianni, William Chambliss, and others are establishing different analytic reference points. Even a comprehensive Marxist alternative by Frank Pearce has now appeared.

Hobsbawm delineates the political and class foundations of the early Mafia in Italy. Ianni denies the existence of a structured empire of Mafia families operating on a national level. Chambliss documents the support given by European and American governments to the narcotics trade. Earlier, Frank Pearce emphasized crimes by corporations. Now, he notes that criminal organizations expanded as corporate tools for suppressing working-class movements. Organized crime, he adds, disappeared after socialism was established in a number of cities (e.g., Havana).

Although these and other writers introduce significantly new analyses of criminal organizations, they are not represented at all in Kaplan and Kessler's reader. The reader being reviewed, therefore, appears to be a collection of artifacts from a bygone era. It contains extremely conventional articles describing loan sharking, gambling, narcotics traffic, etc. A few of the selections are by noted academics. However, Cressey's chapter on corruption and crime in labor unions does not provide a sophisticated theoretical view of the social class and corporate relations underlying such crimes. There are no critiques of the prosaic economics in Schelling's article or in other parts of the book. No chapters nor even fragments of chapters deal theoretically with the relations between the captialist state and economic crimes. But, as one might expect, the work does inform us about the "empire" of organized crime that threatens the nation and it refers endlessly to the costs of this crime to legitimate business, the state, and private citizens.

The title of the book belies its contents. It is

not primarily a collection of analytic articles. It chiefly contains descriptive essays. Even the introductory sections by the authors are almost devoid of theory. Brief theoretical references usually involve opportunity structure theory and the tireless miracle worker: Homo Economicus. Individual choice is the dynamic unit of analysis and no questions are asked about the vast chasm that lies between such choice-making behavior and the structures of irregular economic relationships.

Finally, the book is full of apologetic statements. Thus, from the beginning, the reader is told that our criminal justice system receives less money than it should; that this system is overburdened because of the lack of funds; that President Nixon gave the fight against organized narcotics traffic "the highest priority"; and that despite criticism "it is difficult at present to fault the Administration's strategy in trying to make heroin unavailable" (pp. 7–9).

Cops and Bobbies: Police Authority in New York and London, 1830—1870, by WILBUR R. MILLER. Chicago: University of Chicago Press, 1977. 248 pp. $16.00 cloth.

ERIC H. MONKKONEN
University of California, Los Angeles

Wilbur Miller's comparative study of the early years of the New York and London Metropolitan police is a challenging analysis of the differences between policing in the two cities, unfortunately hampered by methodological and conceptual problems. Miller argues that the London police avoided personal discretion in their street behavior, emphasizing impartiality and the rule of law, in order to create and maintain their own legitimacy during a period of conflict. The New York police, on the other hand, relied heavily on personal force and discretion, partly because of police/court conflict, and partly because of a rough and ready democratic ethos. Ironically, in New York City, the police could be brutal and oppressive because of their ultimate accountability to popularly elected officials, while the more hierarchal police of London had to encourage an image of moral and legal uprightness.

Beginning with a nod toward the Weberian notion of legitimacy, Miller never clarifies how political legitimacy relates to public image, and the latter is his main concern. Nor does he clarify the relationship of police image to police behavior, leaving the impression that image exists independent of behavior. Somehow, one suspects, "style" and "image" are quite different from "legitimacy" and behavior.

The book also has methodological weaknesses: while manuscript sources and internal orders for the London police survive, Miller is forced to rely upon non-comparable published reports and newspaper accounts for New York. This means that his concern with image making can focus on the intentions of the commissioners of the London police, but must be limited to more public observations of the New York police efforts. Thus, Miller's analysis rings true, but must remain speculative. Further methodological problems appear in his use of quantitive data; for example, he implies that the New York police were more Irish than the London police, but his data show that while true absolutely, the Irish of London were slightly over-represented on the police force, the Irish of New York slightly under-represented. (On the other hand, he presents data which suggest that as far as differential arrest behavior, police ethnicity did not matter anyway!)

In spite of these and other confusions, the book has value: it clearly analyzes police reactions to Sunday closing laws; it cleverly suggests a parallel between policing and prison reform in the United States; and the discussion of arrest procedures and rights for both cities is an outstanding contribution to the literature. As it stands, this book should be read as an interesting essay, showing how two styles of policing, one derived from the other, evolved as responses to somewhat different socio-political milieus. And though it suffers serious weaknesses, it should be seen as an important attempt to raise the conceptual level of police history.

Culture

The American Dimension: Cultural Myths and Social Realties, edited by W. ARENS and SUSAN P. MONTAGUE. New York: Alfred Publishing Company, 1976, 221 pp. $5.95 paper.

LESTER R. KURTZ
University of Chicago

Montesquieu's 1721 *Persian Letters* created quite a stir by detailing and criticizing French life and culture in what amounted to an early ethnographic study of his own culture. In that work a Persian, visiting France, comments that in one of the public houses in Paris the coffee is believed to make one witty; or, "at least everyone leaving the place believes himself four times wittier than when he entered." Similarly, coffee in America is believed to impart neighborliness when served according to custom. The serving and drinking of coffee is a symbolic expression of neighborliness in American culture, according to Lawrence Taylor, in one of the several insightful articles in this volume compiled by W. Arens and Susan P. Montague. Like Montesquieu, Arens and Montague are searching for "the symbolic underpinnings of their own culture" (p. xvi).

In their introduction, Arens and Montague isolate two major difficulties which American social scientists encounter while studying their own society. One difficulty arises from the idea "that in order to see any phenomenon clearly it is necessary to first stand at a distance from it" (p. xiv). It is difficult for natives to be detached observers.

The factor of "magnitude" raises a second difficulty. Because of the size and complexity of the American society, the holistic approaches and research techniques of traditional anthropology are not always applicable. Problems of distance and magnitude (and the attraction of exotic cultures?) have resulted in a reluctance on the part of American anthropologists to examine their own culture.

Renewed interest in cultural analysis has led to the study of basic cultural symbols in order to see how they are combined to create ideological systems, including those in the researcher's own culture. Distinctions between the disciplines of sociology and anthropology on the basis of subject matter may become less certain as such research progresses, and the resulting diaglogue could benefit both disciplines. Arens and Montague have contributed to the development of research on American culture by compiling a volume which applies some tentative solutions to the problems of distance and magnitude.

Montesquieu established distance between himself and his subject matter by taking on the attitude of a foreigner who was visiting Paris and writing letters which described French society. Arens and Montaque suggest that contributors to their volume used theoretical frameworks developed through fieldwork in other societies as mechanisms for creating detachment in the analysis of their own society.

Consistent concern with theoretical issues is a major asset of the volume. Each article states a central problem in the analysis of culture and social structure, and then proceeds to examine that problem within the context of a particular empirical case. Susan Bean's chapter, "Soap Operas: Sagas of American Kinship," for example, explicates the principles on which the American family is based, as revealed in day time television serials.

Changes in the role of women in the American occupational system provide another set of theoretical issues addressed by this volume. How those changes are reflected in American models of success form the analytical discussion in Montague's "How Nancy Gets Her Man: An Investigation of Success Models in American Adolescent Pulp Literature." Participation in "anti-structural" rituals which confront the constraining nature of social structure receives attention in Ivan Karp's "Good Marx for the Anthropologist: Structure and Anti-Structure in 'Duck Soup.' "

Lévi-Strauss's structural analysis as applied by Peter J. Claus, in "A Structuralist Appreciation of 'Star Trek,' " examines how mythology provides a symbolic mediation of conflict. Stanley Regelson addresses issues of assimilation and ethnic identity in "The Bagel: Symbol and Ritual at the Breakfast Table." Although the sociologist might sometimes feel uncomfortable in the anthropological world of archetypes, anti-structure, and liminality, most of the chapters in *The American Dimension* provide enticing, if not always convincing, treatments of cultural myths and social realities in American life.

In addition to theoretical frameworks, the authors employ a second mechanism for the creation of an analytical distance between the observer and the observed: *humor*. Implicit in several articles is a slight embarrassment about taking one's own culture so seriously. Humor arises out of the recognition of the difference between appearances and reality. It reminds the researcher to be critical and objective, and suggests to the reader that the anthropologist is not completely taken in by "folk superstitions."

A final mechanism for creating distance is an informality of style in carrying out the analysis. Most of the chapters are suggestive, rather than definitive, and are generally more sophisticated in their discussion of theoretical issues than in the actual examination of the empirical cases in question. Arens prefaces his insightful remarks in "Professional Football: An American Symbol and Ritual" by revealing that after years of watching football on television, "out of a feeling of guilt, I began to muse in a more academic fashion about this game. . . " (p. 4). Informal observations provide a good beginning for the study of American culture, and will hopefully precipitate more systematic and rigorous analyses.

The problem of *magitude* in the study of American society was more successfully resolved in the volume than was the problem of distance. The authors first examined aspects of American entertainment media, which offered a readily-available context for analyzing models of the society's most basic social situations. Second, they examined social strategies in various social contexts. In both the study of entertainment and of social strategies, Arens and Montague et al. tried to focus on "distinctively American" phenomena. Poker embodies the American dream of gaining wealth through individual effort. Football reveals group coordination through a complex division of labor, a particular form of disciplined violence, and male domination, all characteristic of American society. Although not providing a systematic view of American culture, such approaches did result in tapping significant expressions of the American dimension in everyday life in the United States.

Sociologists will find Arens and Montague's work theoretically competent, substantively interesting, and a source of sociological imagination. Furthermore, selections make excellent reading for undergraduate sociology courses, or the work can be read a chapter at a time at night while one's husband or wife is watching "Mary Hartman" or the late movie.

Implicit Meanings: Essays in Anthropology, by MARY DOUGLAS. Boston: Routledge & Kegan Paul, 1975. 325 pp. $23.50 cloth.

BENNETTA JULES-ROSETTE
University of California, San Diego

This rich collection of essays spans the past two decades of Mary Douglas's work. In looking back over the history of these essays, she relates them to a central theme from Durkheim: the relationship between symbolism and social experience. Douglas is concerned with the implicit understandings that form the social background of myth, ritual, and other forms of communication. She is equally interested in a reflexive "turn" to the preconceptions that the researcher brings to data and the study of one's own cultural assumptions. Although the two aspects of her synthesis may not be as well integrated as she intended them, the author levels an unsettling critique on the present state of the social sciences. She has combined the insights of British empiricist ethnography, structuralism, and phenomenology in a penetrating treatment of meaning in communication.

Basic to her argument is the revitalization of Durkheim's sacred/profane dichotomy in a new epistemological context. Durkheim, she states, failed to realize the revolutionary potential of his own insights because he exempted his own scientific enterprise from the examination of the social basis of symbolic thought. Non-Western groups were seen as constrained by cultural insulation, while Western science remained immune to it. Douglas suggests an innovative, more relativistic epistemology based on an ongoing social reality, whose goal is a unified theory of consciousness. The outlines ot this theory are found largely in her cross-cultural comparisons in the concluding portion of the book. Perhaps they should be read as statements of intention for further work. However, her concern with uncovering the grounding assumptions of the researcher appears throughout these essays. Many of them are already well-known, nevertheless they appear in a new light when their reflexive orientation is stressed.

The book's collected essays are gathered under three topical sections: "The Implicit" (1955–1971), "Critical Essays" (1967–1973), and "The *a priori* in Nature" (1970–1972). Each section is preceded by a critical introduction that relates the individual essays to the study of the relationship between symbolic form and social action, between explicit cosmology and an implicit motivational domain that she terms the "pre-cosmological."

"The Implicit" contains Douglas's earlier descriptive treatment of pollution and taboo, including the classic "Animals in Lele Religious Symbolism" and "Pollution," prepared contemporaneously with *Purity and Danger*. Many of her later concerns grew out of the Lele ethnographic experience in Zaire, and she notes with hindsight that she might have asked very different questions. Those essays that discuss the pangolin cult, jokes and joking relationships, and the cross-cultural study of body symbolism, raise the issues of categorical and implicit meaning that appear throughout the work.

The second portion, "Critical Essays," focuses on implicit understandings in the researcher's work. Data are structured by the researcher in the course of study, and it is necessary to examine this process. In "If the Dogon . . ." and "The Healing Rite," she lucidly shows the contrasting assumptions of French structuralism and British social anthropology. These produced radically different descriptions of similar fields of study. Her reviews of Basil Bernstein and Louis Dumont more closely combine the two aspects of her synthesis. They stress both the hidden assumptions conveyed in speech that are linked with the social production of social hierarchy, and the structural symmetries in the authors' perspectives that make their analyses appear more compelling.

Her examination of Castaneda manifests the transformation of the relationship between the seen and the unseen from an intuition to a crucial philosophical problem. Castaneda is considered not only an epistemological challenger to conventional social science but a representative of a growing cultural concern that extends beyond academic disciplines. In each essay, the central approach of the researcher is held up for comparison with its cultural milieu—an audience, an intellectual trend, or a scholarly debate—that forms a background to a work and places it in perspective.

"The *a priori* in Nature" returns to link her earlier treatments of ritual classification with the broader study of social meaning. The widely read "Deciphering a Meal" is reprinted here. In this new context, it serves as an example of Douglas's revision of structuralism based on praxis or everyday activity. It also demonstrates a return from the exotic to one's own culture and experience as a source of social science theorizing. "In the Nature of Things" also applies structuralist methods to the distinction of human and nonhuman communication. Her theory of expressive freedom in the social and individual body, explored in *Natural Symbols,* is applied here on a broader scale. The most explicitly comparative of the essays, "Self-Evidence," uses differing conceptions of the anomalous as a key to the relationship of each group with outsiders. She concludes that it is this symbolic congruity in each culture that forms the basis of intuitive truth. This self-evidence, in turn, provides the moral force of cognitive categories.

Having thus returned to the hermeneutical circle involved in the study of symbol and society, Douglas had difficulty going further. The reflexive study of the researcher that figures so eloquently throughout the book does not proceed into a final synthesis. It is, however, through this study of the logical and sociological basis of the self-evident that she sees the possibility for increased sociological relativism and for a more interpretive freedom in the social sciences. Her strong emphasis on the underlying perspective and cultural background of the researcher is used to explain the influence of symbolic expression upon social action in a variety of communicational settings. For anyone who would reflect on the relationship of ethnography, structuralism, and new epistemological alternatives for the social sciences, this book is required reading.

Meaning in Culture, by F. Allan Hanson. Boston: Routledge & Kegan Paul, 1975. 127 pp. $12.25 cloth.

Robert A. Paul
Queens College/CUNY

This modest book is a contribution to the current effort by several anthropologists to give precision to the concept of cultural meaning, which has informed American anthropology since its inception, but has often come under attack for its apparent lack of specificity. Recently, anthropology has returned to the problem armed with new sophistication derived from greater acquaintance with broader philosophical streams of thought treating similar problems.

The particular philosophical tradition within which Hanson locates his discussion is largely British. This somewhat lessens the book's impact on this side of the Atlantic—Hanson is American but wrote the book while in England—since Americans are less likely to use the vocabulary of Collingwood, Ryle, Ayer, Carnap, and so on to frame the issues, and may thus find themselves trying to make sense of refutations of positions they would never have thought of otherwise.

Hanson's approach to meaning rests on a distinction between individual and institutional meaning, the former referring to meaning as personal motivation, the latter to meaning as the ways a particular concept is logically related to other cultural concepts, without reference to individuals or motivation. Hanson then defends the study of institutional meaning as an independent field appropriate for anthropologists.

This would all be well and good, were it not for the fact that most anthropologists have known this all along; whereas others would require a powerful lot of convincing. For a book such as this one to be of major importance, therefore, it would either have to develop a theoretical argument with compelling force and originality, or else present some dazzling pieces of cultural analysis to demonstrate the effectiveness of the proposed theories. Hanson presents practically no ethnographic analysis at all, which considerably weakens his argument.

More important, however, beyond stating

quite clearly and distinctly what his position is, Hanson does not take his ideas very far at all. This leaves the reader somewhat puzzled as to who the intended audience could be, since those who already agree with Hanson's premises are likely to be far beyond where this book leads; while opponents of his position will find no new and forceful arguments to reckon with. For example, I very much doubt whether confirmed believers in the dualism of mind and body are going to be persuaded to abandon their views on the basis of Hanson's three-page summary of Ryle's position on the matter.

But if the book lacks major status as a new conceptual statement, it has many virtues which recommended it as a good introduction to the views which Hanson represents. It is well-written and unpretentious, and the major arguments are laid out with fine clarity, and then summarized and synopsized, so that the points at issue can be easily grasped. The discussions of cultural relativism, the possibility of cross-cultural understanding, and the scientific status of functionalism, while hardly definitive or original solutions, are quite excellent opening statements for discussion or further study by undergraduates, beginning graduate students, or others first finding their way in these areas.

The book is well organized until the end, when it sputters to a very unsatisfying conclusion, consisting of brief resumes and evaluations of the work of David Schneider, Victor Turner, and Roy Rappaport. Why these, one wonders, and certainly, given the author's interests, why not also Mary Douglas, Geertz, and Lévi-Strauss? I don't understand how one can write a book claiming to locate meaning in the logic of the relations of ideas to one another and not include a discussion of structuralism.

Demography, Population, and Migration

Demographic Transition Theory Reinterpreted: An Application to Recent Natality Trends in Latin America, by STEVEN E. BEAVER. Lexington, Mass.: Lexington Books, 1975. 152 pp. $15.50 cloth.

Demographic Transition and Social Change, by JAY A. WEINSTEIN. Morristown, N.J.: General Learning Press, 1976. 115 pp. $4.20 paper.

SHIRLEY FOSTER HARTLEY
California State University, Hayward

There are those who suggest that, unlike broad-based sociology, the study of population is really devoid of "theory." Yet these two new books are ready to challenge that notion. Although Steven Beaver and Jay Weinstein take contrasting means of analysis, both are interested in linking the theory of the demographic transition to a general sociological theory of social change in the tradition of Max Weber's Protestant Ethic, Durkheim's functional vs. normative integration, and Parsons's pattern variables. Indeed, it would appear that the study of population not only involves theoretical systems, but that the striking difference between population and some other sociological theories, is that those related to population are more open to *testing* than most of the speculation and ideology that frequently pass for theory.

Beaver's work is the more tightly conceived and executed examination of the theory that with socioeconomic development, societies move from (1) conditions of high birth and death rates with consequent low rates of natural increase through (2) a transitional period during which mortality declines precede fertility declines producing high rates of population increase, and finally (3) a period of relative stability is reached in which both fertility and mortality are balanced at low levels. As an empirical generalization of what *has* happened in Europe over the last 150 years, it is seldom faulted, and as a typology of various stages of socio-demographic change, it is extremely useful. It is only as a predictive theory of what *will happen* in the less developed countries of the world that the theory produces controversy and contradictions. It must be obvious to all "true observers" that the European transition cannot be exactly reproduced in the less developed countries, since their mortality declines have already occurred more rapidly than ever before and independently of economic development producing an unprecedented "explosion" in numbers. "True believers" however, still point to signs of zero population growth. Although examination of the young age structure of the less developed countries does not allow much hope for an early transition, the theory, Beaver reminds us, does not predict *when* the stages will occur, only that the same relationships will hold.

It is the relationship among variables, their potential measurement, their specification in interconnected hypotheses, and their testing for the countries of Latin America that concern Beaver. Whether the reader has or has not had prior exposure to the theory of the demographic transition, a study of Beaver's respecification will be rewarding. He produces an excellent overview of previous theoretical and empirical work, specifies his own assumptions, hypotheses, and operational measures, and follows them through a rigorous testing and experimental process. He is cautious and critical in evaluating the evidence for his own hypotheses, but there remains the gnawing feeling that the deck may have been stacked by the choice of only twelve (of thirty or more Latin-Caribbean) nations with adequate information *and* current natality declines. Sociological analysis typically benefits from examining where and why something has *not* happened as well as where it has. Thus, the cases of Brazil, Mexico, and Venezuela require more than a prediction that natality decline is expected soon. Why do these largest countries of the area, with similar levels of urbanization, education, and per capita GNP have such a different pattern than Costa Rica, Jamaica, and Puerto Rico? It is somewhat comforting to learn that the more recent the decline in mortality and fertility the more rapid the drop. Again however, fertility declines are highly unlikely to continue to the depths of mortality decline, and whether there are three or four or five times as many births as deaths, the transition to "balance" is nowhere in sight.

The fact that urbanization, enrollment, per capita GNP, life expectancy, crude death rates, land availability, and economic expansion are able to explain 65% to 81% of the variance in birth rates for the countries Beaver does include implies that the study is not only worth reading but also worth replicating. It would really be a service to the profession if the analysis were repeated for other cultural areas of the world, and updated from time to time. The longer time lags that Beaver experimented with produced ever-improved correlations. Updating the longer time series data now available, with longer time lags, might again indicate the greater predictive capacity of some variables (such as school enrollment) and continue to reduce the variance formerly attributed to economic expansion and urbanization. Although Latin America is not the best test of educational effects, I would prefer to see female or total literacy used (since it implies a built-in time lag) rather than school enrollment, which with a five or ten year time lag is less likely to affect natality. Although it would take a statistician to evaluate the problems of multicollinearity, autocorrelation, and the magnitude of residuals, it appears that each problem is discussed and dealt with according to the limits of available data and technology. The work is a contribution to both theoretical and methodological issues and deserves to be widely read by professionals and by serious graduate students. It would not be appropriate as an undergraduate text.

Jay Weinstein has clearly hoped to reach a wider audience with his more general examination for the *Demographic Transition and Social change*. He appears to hold an action orientation suggesting that "action to promote survival cannot be based on the conviction that destruction either is impossible or imminent." Certainly those who believe that birth rates will naturally decline with lower mortality or economic development are less interested in the question of what might stimulate birth declines. By the same token, however, Weinstein's belief that "when, and if, the riddle of the European transition is solved, the population crisis as a social and a sociological problem will dissolve" is overly simplistic. There is a review of a great number of variables that have some potential for explaining the riddle, but thoughtful sociologists do not suppose that *understanding* the contribution of education, or urbanization, or women's roles would necessarily lead to the change required to dissolve the population crisis.

Although Weinstein examines the theorizing and the correlational analyses of a variety of sociologists, demographers, and economists in the field, he does not add anything new to the study. Indeed, his sometimes sloppy and/or misleading use of terminology could be a serious impediment to real understanding. For instance, any population change is called a demographic transition, by which process the book title becomes redundant; the repeated reference to various numbers of children "per fertile woman" is without a clear referent: we do not know whether he is indicating the entire childbearing age group of women (typically ages 15 to 44 or 49), whether the intention is to include women at the end of the childbearing period (aged 45 to 49), or whether the reference is only to women who are actually mothers at any age or at specific ages.

While both of these books provide sociologists with a virtual smorgasbord of variables for the ongoing study of social change in general and the demographic transition in particular, these variables have been organized, critically examined and evaluated, and rigorously tested by Steven Beaver. It is up to the profession to extend the project and to test its predictive utility.

Population in African Development, Vols. 1 & 2, edited by PIERRE CANTRELLE, AHMED MALEK BAHRI, JOHN BLACKER, ROBERT BLANC, WILLIAM BRASS, KWEKU T. DE GRAFT-JOHNSTON, JAMES GREIG, LÉON TABAH, AND BRUNO REMICHE. Dolhain, Belgium: Ordina Editions, 1974. 551 pp. & 349 pp. No price listed, cloth.

KAROL J. KRÓTKI
University of Alberta

The theme of the First African Regional Population Conference in Accra, Ghana, held in December 1971, gave these two volumes their title; a theme general enough to include any virtue and sin that may have arisen. The volumes contain 74 papers out of the 144 presented to the conference; a substantially smaller proportion of the total number of papers presented than the "around one hundred" which the chief editor claims. The volumes are part of nearly a dozen titles issued by the International Union for the Scientific Study of Population in recent years. Although dated 1974, the volumes did not become available for general circulation until 1976, and have thus been superseded by several other publications in the area, such as the three volumes from the general conference (Accra was a regional conference) of the Union in Liége, or the massive volume issued by the Population Council (the latter reviewed in *Contemporary Sociology*, November 1976), or other mature and complete publications of which some of the Accra papers are only early and preliminary indicators. Tough times have come upon demographers, if they want to keep ahead of this avalanche, and gone is the comfortable feeling one could have, when it was still possible to master *all* the relevant literature in the area.

The first African conference was the fourth regional conference, following meetings in New Delhi (1963), Sydney (1967), and Mexico (1970). It is illuminating to trace the divergent increase in the quantity as against quality production from report to report. The Accra conference consisted of twelve substantive sessions, five methodological sessions, and one additional informal session. The one paper presented at this last session reads strangely subdued, when one recalls the prevailing atmosphere in Accra at that time, of conspiracy and excitement, both arising together, almost like a pre-riot stage at a North American university campus in the late sixties. Briefly, Western social scientists, but particularly proponents of the narrowly defined family planning that was foisted upon less developed societies after WWII, were being accused at best of sociological ignorance, and at worst of planned genocide. The thought arises that the motive behind the narrowly defined and mechanistic family planning campaigns may not have been wickedness and ignorance alone, but also the endearing, if naive, American feeling (call it belief, faith, subconscious reaction) that problems, including social problems, are solvable. On the other hand, the organizers of the session ignored, for ten years, writings questioning the relevance, feasibility, and effectiveness of family planning, when the social conditions are not right.

The concepts of over- and under-population are not recent inventions of Western protagonists of genocide. Malthus would not be a respectable antecedent in this context, but Kautsky's *Der Einfluss des Volksvermehrung auf den Fortschritt der Gesellschaft* could be mentioned, given its serious discussion in Engels's celebrated letter to Kautsky of February 1, 1881. Nor is the recognition of the importance of economic variables and of the mode of production an exclusively Marxist prerogative. Many, and some earlier, writers are in this category, and it is generally recognized that social scientists who abstract from economics and demography (the usual cop-out is to take them as independent "givens") miss the elegance and realism of Marxism.

The twelve substantive sessions took stock of the current knowledge of demographic parameters in Africa; some permitted themselves a peek into the future. The severe data limitations on stock taking and forecasting required a session on data collection with conclusions: forget about vital registration, hold censuses as regularly as possible; with hindsight it is possible to detect the first emergence of the later belief, that all the fancy modeling, though often more convincing and possibly closer to reality than shaky data, is no real substitute for good data. The session has also shown how very much more congenial to most people it is to write elegantly and analyze other people's data, than to collect reliable data. The needs of planners and administrators were considered in the light of social and economic development. In particular, these concerns were reflected in considerations of the labor force, resettlement, urbanization, spatial distribution, housing, and community development. Family planning was discussed in social and healthy contexts. It is useful to be reminded, and it will be an eye-opener to some, of the immense and pioneering work done in Africa by French demographers and survey statisticians, but could it be that none of the very extensive field work was representative in the statistical sense? The need for demographic training and research seems somewhat hollow today, now that there is a surfeit of trained demographers and an avalanche of research reports (difficult to digest in quantity) but still no decent data for all these highly trained people to play with and for all the new learned journals to publish. Some of the products of the concern with demographic training merely fed the brain drain (piously regretted by contributors to these volumes) and made no contribution to their own countries. Even though unintended, however, on balance the resulting internationalization of professional labor markets was probably a good thing. The methodological sessions were left behind by more recent achievements, except perhaps the paper on estimating adult mortality from the survivorship of parents, which is still useful and promising. Some of the contributions are competent summaries of practices long with us and well documented throughout the literature, but apparently still required by some clients.

The two volumes lack the minimum scientific equipment: there is no list of tables, no list of figures, no subject index, no bibliography, not even a list of references cited. The editorial blue pencil seems to have been applied too gently and sparingly, in spite of the nine editors. Some tables are numbered, titled, and easy to refer to, understand, and read. Some are not, and can be understood only by going back several pages into the text. The translations from French were done neither by professional demographers nor checked afterwards by them. Often by frowning, reflecting, and going back over the text it is possible to discern the meaning, but a general reader will be left puzzled. Even at the easiest and most simplistic editorial level there was no one to ensure that superfluous footnotes be dropped ("This paper has been prepared for. . ."), that similar ratios be used (per 100 or per 1000, but not both), that "data are" and not "data is," that a paper with more than one writer does not use the first person singular, and so on.

The question arises for whom such publications are intended. The coverage of the subject matter is neither comprehensive nor systematic. It is a collection of case studies that happened to have been available. Some of the case studies attempt generalizations that conceal the fact that there is no such thing as "Africa" as a meaningful social science entity. Some others bring out quite clearly the fact that even within quite small territories the variability of any given characteristic among peoples is greater than among European societies. It is useful to realize how severe were the data problems in Nigeria even before the 1973 census had to be abandoned. This type of publication seems most akin to a learned journal with a ratio of acceptance of papers submitted several times higher than that of an average learned journal. It also performs a useful souvenir function.

For patient diggers who are not easily discouraged the volumes will provide some interesting findings, some unexpected, some delightful in their exoticism, some impressive with wide erudition, some logically presented, and obvious outcomes of rigorous reasoning.

But on the whole one is reminded of a recent review in another journal where the book under review, even though a much more modest compendium than these two volumes, was compared to a bad and expensive Chinese dinner: one eats a lot of different dishes but is still hungry *and* suffers from indigestion to boot.

Turkish Workers in Europe, 1960—1975: A Socio-Economic Reappraisal, by NERMIN ABADAN-UNAT and contributors. Leiden, The Netherlands: E.J. Brill, 1976. 424 pp. No price listed, cloth.

JONATHAN MATTHEW SCHWARTZ
University of Copenhagen

Most of the essays in this volume take their point of departure in the policy sciences. The authors, a Turkish majority, anticipate the eventual "integration" of Turkey into the European Economic Community, and their studies would appraise the function of emigrant labor in the modernization and integration process. With more comprehensive planning and coordination, the Turkish government and society could benefit from the export (and re-import) of Turkish labor power to Western European industrial societies.

Until the 1960s Turkey had relatively little emigration. The rapid economic expansion in the 1960s, particularly in West Germany, required willing and able workers. Between 1961 and 1973 Turkish governmental agencies sent about 790,000 workers to Europe, 80% of whom went to Western Germany (p.7). The so-called "oil crisis" in the Autumn of 1973 suddenly halted the importation of guest workers. Unemployment set in, and its end is not yet in sight. The foreign workers tend to remain in the "host" societies, knowing that unemployment also awaits them in their homelands. The foreign workers and their families thus seem to live in a kind of sociological limbo.

Turkish society in the 1960s was already faced with what one author calls "structural unemployment" (p. 50). Modernization of agriculture and increase in population created an immense labor reserve in Turkey, and the Turkish state came to depend on the export of young laborers to Western Europe and the large remittances which they sent home from their earnings. 1973 and the years following have had repercussions in Turkish planning and development. Bermin Abadan-Unat and her co-authors imply that the Western European officials ought to have consulted with the Turkish counterparts before unilaterally cutting off the import of Turkish workers. This advice, though well-meant, appears to have vastly underestimated the acuteness of the economic crisis in the Western European societies.

The Abadan-Unat volume—perhaps reflecting its policy science orientation—seldom takes up the issues of critical sociology. Empirical description and interpretation are exclusively in terms of a macro-theory of modernization, not in terms of social class interest and conflict. One finds in *Turkish Workers in Europe* a scanty treatment of working conditions, labor market, and the foreign workers' relationship to the native workers.

At least one of the chapters of the book, however, provides a rich empirical discussion. That is Mubeccel B. Kiray's, "The Family of the Immigrant Worker" (pp. 210–234). The transformation of family structure under the impact of labor migration is amply documented both in the segments of families which remain in the Turkish countryside and those segments which emigrate to European towns. The chapter sketches out as well the erosion of traditional sex-roles in patriarchal family structure.

Otherwise, the book was generally disappointing. More comprehensive—and polemical—is the study of S. Castles and G. Kosack, *Immigrant Workers and Class Structure in Western Europe*. I might also refer the reader to a study by Suzanne Paine, *Exporting Workers: The Turkish Case*.

A final note: the Abadan-Unat volume would have benefited by a thorough proofreading. Many of the awkward, repetitive, and vague sentences could have been eliminated or altered.

Migrants and Refugees: Muslim and Christian Pakistani Families in Bristol, by PATRICIA JEFFERY. New York: Cambridge University Press, 1976. 211 pp. $12.95 cloth.

SHARLENE J. HESSE
Boston College

Social and economic life conditions in Pakistan are important to consider when analyzing the differences in adaptation of Muslim and Christian Pakistanis to Bristol. This theme underlies Jeffery's analysis of twenty Muslim and ten Christian households in Bristol, England.

Rashid, a typical Muslim informant, arrived in Britain in 1962 hoping for economic advancement but fully intending an eventual return to Pakistan. He is representative of those who see a chance of knocking down barriers to social mobility in Pakistan. Rashid spent several years in Bristol working at different jobs before making enough money to send for his wife, Ruxsana and their children. Jeffery shows how the expectation of returning to Pakistan has an impact on several spheres of their lives. In Bristol, one only relates to those within the kin group. The network, then, of their private lives—kinship, friendship, leisure, and religion—did not include Britons. While Rashid had contact with Britons at work, he maintained no contact outside the work sphere. Rashid's children did not see British friends in their free time; only Urdu was spoken at home; this family's roots were in the homeland. Rashid and Ruxsana sought inexpensive housing in Britain in order to save for a newly built home in Pakistan. Such a home will bring honor to their kin group and may even bring Rashid a better match when he arranges marriages for his children. Failure to send money or maintain contact with relatives at home threatens the honor of his kinship group and relatives may refuse to care for investments in property Rashid has made. Muslims, in effect, consider themselves migrants, who intend to return to their homeland when they have accumulated enough money for the higher-status life in Pakistan.

Christian Pakistanis differ from their close cultural compatriots. They view themselves as refugees. Migration to Britain enables them to escape discrimination in the political, religious, and economic spheres felt by Christians in a Muslim country. Adaptation to British society is only understood by taking into account this historical perspective on life in Pakistan. Christians seldom send remittances back home, instead they invest their savings in Britain and elsewhere. Personal networks extend into the new community, British workmates are seen in leisure time, intermarriages take place between Britons and Christians, and young children have British school friends.

The author argues that for both these groups, differences in their linkages with Pakistan explain their differential adjustment to life in Britain. Little attention is devoted to alternative explanations of adjustment. Jeffery overextends her thesis by relying too much on migrants' orientation to Pakistan as the primary explanation, to the detriment of an examination of British reaction to the migrant. Christian and Muslim informants often comment on the difficulties they face in establishing network ties with the British, and many Christians are leaving Britain for Canada. Other explanations are also relevant in this context. Christians have been in Britain for a longer time than Muslims, many come with a knowledge of English. In order to assert that these factors are unimportant, as does Jeffery, a more representative sample of the population needs to be taken into account to control for these factors.

The author filters the picture of migrant life in Britain through retrospective accounts, and in some cases recall of events is over a ten or twenty year period. These accounts may be subject to bias with the passage of time. By focusing so closely on first arrival migrants, she neglects the social changes taking place among the children of migrants, many of whom were born in Britain and consider it their home. Short shrift is also given to female migrants, since the bulk of analysis is primarily based on case studies of four male informants. Women and children are lumped together as "dependents." Certainly complex decisions concerning migration must be made by females.

Despite some methodological weaknesses, such as a non-representative sample of migrants, Jeffery does make an important contribution to the literature on migrant adaptation and assimilation by documenting the importance of studying network linkages which extend beyond the host society. Professionals in the field of migration should find it a welcome addition to the literature.

Nationality and Population Change in Russia and the USSR: An Evaluation of Census Data, 1897—1970, by Robert A. Lewis, Richard H. Rowland, and Ralph S. Clem. New York: Praeger Publishers, 1976. 456 pp. No price listed, cloth.

D. Peter Mazur
Western Washington State College

By means of factor analysis based on rank correlations, the authors focus primarily on two factors: (1) modernization, and (2) Turkic-Moslem fertility. Knowledge of population change, they claim, is essential to the understanding of contemporary modernization in the USSR. Russians are the most susceptible to modernization while the Turkic-Moslems of Central Asia and the Caucasus regions, in spite of the progress made, are still to be considered relatively backward. Since urbanization happens to be the best predictor of modernization, and Jews and Tatars live predominantly in the heavily industrialized areas, the two groups also show a certain measure of affinity for modernization although, as the authors elaborate in the course of their arguments, this is more in evidence when rank correlations are used rather than factor analysis. The latter takes on something like dinosaurian proportions. There are only 19 units of observation, but the number of variables ranges between 50 and 100 each for the urban, the rural, and the total population for each of the three census years examined, 1897, 1926, and 1959, and for the intercensal years including rates of change, altogether 18 matrices. There is little concern with the significance of the results and little apprehension about the loss of too many statistical degrees of freedom.

On the other hand, the authors try hard to stress the *scientific* approach by frequently disassociating themselves from other approaches to the study of the Soviet populations, like the historical, the qualitative, or the institutional. Lewis, Rowland, and Clem are unfortunately not too careful about the accuracy of their data. Since the 1970 Soviet census does not provide information by age for ethnic groups for males and females separately, the authors "generate" the data for females by assuming that all nationalities have 52% women aged 20–49. The numbers of children aged 0–10 in 36 ethnic groups are simply multiplied by the constant 0.9 to obtain the population of 0–9 years of age, thereby making up a rather dubious version of the child-woman ratio for 1970 (p. 290). Segments of the population are forced into the boundaries of 19 economic regions in the same proportion as are the land areas—redistributed so that the territorial units may be held constant according to the 1959 standard. There is apparently no attempt made to use the more innovative methods geared specifically to incomplete Soviet data that have been developed recently and published in the literature. Where descriptive material is discussed, the monograph is quite informative, but the method of the statistical analysis is less than imaginative. The style of the writing is somewhat chatty, and it would have been better if the authors had dispensed with the numerous digressions to the philosophy of science.

The Population Challenge: A Handbook for Nonspecialists, by JOHANNES OVERBEEK. Westport, Conn.: Greenwood Press, 1976. 214 pp. $13.95 cloth.

PAUL R. WILLIAMS
American Sociological Association

In his preface, the author refers to the "mediocre coverage in the American press" received by the United Nations World Population Conference held in Bucharest in 1974. He takes the position that the reactions of the press and of the general public to the conclusions reached at the conference were due to poor understanding of population matters and sets out to remedy the situation.

The author approaches this task of educating the press and public by presenting, in what he describes as simple terms, basic facts about what the world population situation is, how and why things got this way, and what we can anticipate if current trends continue. Specifically, this involves sixteen chapters of varying length and detail on population-related topics and a very brief conclusion.

Somewhat predictably, most of the discussion deals with the consequences of continued population growth and excessive density. After a very brief discussion of world population growth, and why individuals have children and special interest groups promote growth, the author moves on to the serious business. Ten chapters follow dealing with many of the consequences of size, growth, and maldistribution about which much has been written. These include some traditional concerns, e.g., population and economics, population and political stability, and some more recent ones, e.g., population and pollution. Chapter thirteen, "The Threat of Planetary Disaster," wraps things up with a generally favorable discussion of the highly publicized 1972 Club of Rome report, *The Limits to Growth*. The last three chapters deal with what is being done or can be done about the existing situation. They include the arguments for discontinuing foreign aid to low income countries that maintain high fertility rates, statements of the inadequacy of existing policies and fertility reduction programs, and an evaluation of past, present, and future methods of contraception.

Although some persons question the exact nature of the relationship between population variables and many of the consequences discussed in this book, it is inappropriate to attempt to restate the various arguments here. Undoubtedly, something needs to be done fairly quickly about the many problems that exist, and a deceleration of population growth could not make matters worse. I do question the logic of some of the author's proposed solutions to the problem of growth and what seem to be the assumptions that led him to write the book in the first place.

Throughout, the author adheres rather strictly to a cost-benefit explanation of contraceptive use and fertility. In what seems to be a rational, though not always conscious way, people go on having children as long as the perceived advantages exceed the inconveniences and stop when the situation is reversed. The obvious solution to the problem of excess fertility is to somehow reduce benefits and increase costs. Almost invariably, the means advocated for altering the cost-benefit ratio amount to some kind of positive or negative monetary incentives. Nowhere does it seem to be recognized that since the perceived costs and benefits are not always monetary ones, the substitution of such incentives might or might not work. Also, while the author recognizes that there are social supports for fertility, the means for reducing it are largely individual ones requiring enforcement by the social system.

Finally, it is questionable whether the nature of public and press response to the population situation is indeed a result of poor understanding. Although the author does not say so specifically, it is assumed that his dissatisfaction has to do with a lack of attention to the problem or a tendency toward its understatement. There is an equally convincing argument that, if anything, press reaction errs in the direction of overstatement with relatively little attention being given to the views of the "optimists." Similarly, although the author cautions against alarmists' publications, paragraph one of chapter one refers to that situation some 8,000 years from now when given current rates of growth, "the whole astronomical universe will be packed solid with human flesh." Statements such as these, even when clearly presented as hypothetical, should be carefully examined, not in terms of the extent to which they create paralysis, but in terms of their capacity to cause people simply to tune out.

The Demographic Explosion: The Latin American Experience, by BENJAMIN VIEL. New York: Halsted Press, 1976. 249 pp. $14.95 cloth.

BARRY EDMONSTON
Cornell University

Benjamin Viel's book, *The Demographic Explosion,* is about the need for family planning programs in Latin America. It is a search and a demand, a book of criticism and suggestion. It deals not with a specific empirical investigation of the need, management, and evaluation of family planning programs; rather it is a book speaking in favor of effective, organized birth control programs for every nation of Latin America. Those readers interested in Latin American population and health problems will want to read this book since it offers an engaging advocacy of family planning programs by a Latin American physician who has debated the merits of these programs for many years.

Viel has been Dean of the University of Chile Medical School and is now Executive Director of the Western Hemisphere Region of International Planned Parenthood Federation. The book was originally published in Spanish, entitled *La expolsión demográfica: ¿cuantos son demasiados?*, in 1966; reprinted in Spanish in 1970; and translated, updated, and published in the present form reviewed here.

In Chile, Viel first directed public focus to the high incidence of induced abortion (illegal by Chilean law) and, in raising attention to the abortion problem, he has become one of Latin America's most respected and persuasive proponents of family planning programs. In the past decade, he and others have stimulated the Latin American medical community to regard family planning as a crucial component of general health care; this effort has not been a complete success although a number of Latin American countries now have medical associations actively supporting family planning services.

Viel favors immediate public programs to achieve replacement level fertility in Latin America. These programs are required, he argues, because: (a) the general prevalence of induced abortions presents an important medical problem as well as an indication of women's desperate motivation for birth control; (b) rapid population growth poses a severe obstacle to economic development (although economic development is more complex than pictured in his book and the capital-intensive requirements for economic growth are overly-emphasized); and, (c) population growth threatens to reach limits in excess of potential food production. His book is a humanitarian examination of the individual and social elements supporting high fertility. But while his probing leads him to cite a variety of findings on the determinants of Latin American fertility, sociologists will find a patchwork argument more often than contributions to current research.

The most useful sections of the book are on induced abortion, contraceptive methods, and Catholicism. Viel draws heavily on his own data from Santiago, Chile to detail the use of abortion, with its associated high levels of maternal mortality, and how increased use of effective contraception has decreased maternal deaths. Some specific statistical procedures in the section are objectionable, however, particularly the approximation that the difference between the actual crude birth rate and a theoretical upper level of 50 per thousand is due to induced abortion (this was certainly not the case for Latin American populations in 1975).

The section on contraceptive methods offers a comprehensive, non-technical evaluation of the particular advantages and limitations of specific methods for mass family planning programs. Readers concerned with integrated health programs will especially want to note pages dealing with the benefits of locating family planning projects within broader public health programs.

A third interesting discussion in the book concerns the role of Catholicism in affecting fertility patterns. Viel makes the crucial distinction between the organizational and ideological aspects of Catholicism. He argues convincingly that Church teaching on birth control has had only slight influence on individual contraceptive use but that the Church has affected governmental policy to a moderate degree in several countries. It is not accurate, however, to characterize Catholicism as "standing alone" in opposition to contraceptive methods (p. 179). Other major world religions, such as Hinduism, Eastern Orthodox, and Islam, also stress various pronatalist doctrines.

Marriage Reduction and Fertility, by DAVID YAUKEY. Lexington, Mass.: D. C. Heath & Company, 1973. 115 pp. $10.00 cloth.

RUTH B. DIXON*
University of California, Davis

This tantalizing short book (98 pages of text) presents an analytic framework for viewing the

* Not the reviewer responsible for the listing in "Delinquent Reviews."

relation between marriage patterns and fertility. Beginning with period fertility rates as the ultimate dependent variable, each chapter examines a particular link in the causal chain, moving backward through cohort fertility rates to female patterns of age at first marriage, divorce, widowhood, and remarriage. The author modifies the Davis and Blake scheme of variables intervening between social structure and fertility so that the status of being married (defined as any union in which coitus and reproduction are socially sanctioned) becomes a determinant of the intercourse, conception, and gestation variables that directly affect fertility. A separate chapter addresses the question of fertility among the unmarried. The book culminates in a discussion of strategies for reducing birth rates through facilitating delayed marriage, nonmarriage, and divorce while discouraging remarriage and births to single women.

The book ends just when the going gets interesting. Social and economic motives underlying decisions about the timing of marriage and divorce are barely touched upon, but in their absence it is difficult to evaluate the potential for success of policies designed to "reduce" marriage. Is it possible for women to delay or avoid marriage in significant numbers in a society that provides few opportunities for female employment, for example? Nor are we offered evidence of what fertility rates would look like in a variety of populations if certain changes in marriage patterns were instituted. One longs for simulations that would permit comparisons of the relative effects of similar approaches on different populations, or of different approaches on the same population. In an early-marrying population such as India's, for example, what would be the impact on fertility (other things equal) of, say, a shift from sixteen to nineteen years in the average age at first marriage of females vs. eliminating all marriages to women under the age of eighteen vs. raising the proportion of women who stay single throughout their childbearing years to five percent, among other possibilities? Strategies with the greatest demographic potential may not be the most feasible socially or politically, but at least it would be helpful to know the range of possible outcomes.

Yaukey's book does offer some promising insights and ideas in the still generally neglected area of demography relating to the determinants and consequences of variations in nuptiality. But I wish he had gone farther. In the absence of a more substantive contribution, the book remains largely an introductory framework in search of a thesis.

Education

Community Status and Conflict in Suburban School Politics, by William L. Boyd. Beverly Hills: Sage Publications, 1976. 41 pp. $3.00 paper.

Regina H. Kenen
Trenton State College

Community Status and Conflict in Suburban School Politics is a research report dressed in book's clothing and pretentiously called "A Sage Professional Paper" (no pun intended). It is an article, not only in length, but also in approach, format, and exposition, containing little elaboration which would add insight, color, and flavor to the presentation. The paper is aimed at a narrow professional audience conducting research in the field and also would be useful to graduate students in search of a dissertation topic.

Using well-documented arguments, Boyd discusses factors affecting the incidence and intensity of conflict in high- and low-status school districts. He attributes his findings that high-status districts tend to be low on conflict and low-status districts tend to be high on conflict to differences in political culture as well as to differences in the level of management resource available. He cites relevant research in the field, particularly building on a prior study by Minar, and carefully explains the rationale behind the indices he uses to measure the independent and dependent variables.

However, anyone ever attending a heated school board meeting knows that conflict resulting from "intense controversy" involves passions, deeply cherished beliefs, and even occasional violence. Yet, Boyd writes about conflict in the passive tense, arousing about as much emotion as tepid bath water. Boyd's work is thoughtful, thorough, and dull—typical of many current journal articles. In the attempt to be scientific, must social scientists cease to be interesting?

Scaling the Ivory Tower: Merit and Its Limits in Academic Careers, by Lionel S. Lewis. Baltimore: Johns Hopkins University Press, 1975. 238 pp. $12.50 cloth.

Gerald Grant
Syracuse University

Lionel Lewis has written a witty essay—elegant and cynical by turns—in which he argues that academic men (and occasionally women) scale the ivory tower by charm and obsequiousness as much as, if not more than, by intellectual merit. The quality of Lewis's prose does honor to the profession, if not always his logic. The book, in the tradition of Caplow and McGee's *Academic Marketplace,* exhibits the debunking quality characteristic of any dry-eyed examination of an ideal. The academic system is not a pure meritocracy he finds (horrors!). People actually get hired on the basis of their human qualities and compatibility just as some people marry for reasons other than pure love.

Lewis argues that academics are frequently hired (and sometimes promoted) with only cursory examination of both teaching and research, that letters of recommendation pay more attention to social than intellectual qualities, and that dismissals investigated by the AAUP reveal that professors who bring their grievances to the Association are fired more often for personality squabbles than for incompetence. All of this may be true, but it does not quite add up to the indictment that Lewis wishes us to believe.

Lewis is most amusing in discussing letters of recommendation that academics spend perhaps one-fifth of their lives writing and another fifth reading. No one who has served on a search committee will be surprised by the appalling examples that Lewis cites. Here are two of my favorites:

> ''I haven't read anything that he has written; but if he writes as well as he speaks, he may have ahead of him a distinguished career as a scholar and critic.''
>
> ''As a person he is . . . a bit stiff and self-conscious perhaps. But as a colleague, whom one needn't enjoy on a social basis, I would suspect he would be most pleasant and helpful.''

If Lewis were content with a scolding (which, upon the evidence given here, professors of English and chemists deserve as much as sociologists), the book would be less subject to criticism. There *is* too much cant and hyperbole in academic life (could it be that too many of us attempt to atone for a stingy past by excessive generosity in letters about our advisees?). But Lewis intends a more general critique of the erosion of the principle of merit. Yet it seems highly probable to me that things have gotten better, not worse, since A.B. Hollingshead published his 1938 study showing that four-fifths of all appointments at Indiana University in the years 1886 to 1937 went to an alumnus, a faculty friend, or faculty relative.

The evidence that Lewis draws upon to sketch his dark portrait is not so much wrong as incomplete. For example, he tells us that only 40% of 160 letters written by as many sociologists on behalf of graduate school applicants mentioned intellectual ability. This would seem damaging to a lay reader who might not know that admissions committees routinely have transcripts, graduate record exams, SAT scores, and Miller analogies tests to consult in addition to letters, but Lewis writes as if letters were the only data bearing on the question of merit.

Lewis believes that the discussion of a candidate's personal qualities (which he terms the ''social ethic'') have a proper place as instrumental considerations bearing on an academic's ability to work in groups or to persist in a task. But he fears that the social ethic has degenerated ''most of the time'' into an end itself. Yet he provides no convincing evidence that senior common rooms are more clubby or faculty more indolent than they were fifty years ago. Just the opposite seems more likely to be the case.

A minor theme of the work is Lewis's recurring nostalgia for eccentricity. He is concerned that ''there is no indication that eccentricity, no matter how harmless, is valued'' (p. 94). But why should it be? He cites Bernice Eiduson's study recounting ''the craziness or eccentricity that sometimes accompanies the genius. . . .'' Yet the correlation is certainly not the proof, an illogical leap characteristic of the modern age.

Lewis makes a better case that the academy has not always honored achieved over ascribed statuses. Those of upper class origin are more likely to win first appointments at more prestigious universities, and until recently the university was not noticeably more free of sexual discrimination than other institutions in the society. Lewis repeats Caplow and McGee's by now commonplace observation that high prestige departments are more likely to consider candidates from high prestige institutions, and reports (p. 118) Berelson's data that 85% of the faculty in the top twelve research universities received their highest degrees from one of these institutions and 47% earned their highest degree from the institution where they were teaching. The implication of the author's discussion is that this reflects selection by ascribed status, but that assumption rests in turn on the belief that there is no correlation between achievement and earning a degree from one of those institutions. Presumably achievement criteria do operate in the selection of graduate students to those institutions, although Lewis's own discussion of letters of recommendation indicates that other factors are taken into account, too.

Lewis's examination of dismissals investigated by the AAUP is interesting, and he is on safe ground in arguing that most of these had little to do with a candidate's scholarly qualities or competence—that is why the cases were contested in the first place. A better way to evaluate the issue of merit in promotion would be to follow Leonard Rubin's ("Reactions to Negative Tenure Decisions in Chemistry and Sociology." Paper delivered at the American Sociological Association; Montreal, 1974) lead and interview faculty who were not granted tenure, or to seek evidence that those who occupy the most prestigious positions in a discipline do not merit them.

The growth of both unions and bureaucracy on campus are two other significant themes of the work. I would agree with Lewis's conclusion about unions: namely, that unions will lead to increasing centralization and bureaucratization of the university, that they are inimical to excellence, and that in the end faculty who are union members will be seen as partisans of an organized interest group within the state and hence will put their claims to academic freedom in jeopardy. But Lewis overestimates the degree to which unionism has spread. The growth of unions stops at the timberline of academic quality. But even here one should note that unionization has been a means of greater faculty control precisely on the most heavily bureaucratized campuses, particularly in the community college and state college level. In those cases, it has probably resulted in real increases of authority for faculty, although at the expense of a counter-bureaucracy.

Lewis is convinced that the expanding bureaucracy in institutions of higher education means that "faculty resemble civil-service employees, an ambitious class of functionaries thrive to hold them on course, and careers have come to depend as much on service, longevity, and age as on merit" (p. 181). He goes on: "To the degree that the time and interest to concentrate on teaching and research are curtailed by the infinite horizons occasioned by a university which has taken on a vast repertoire of obligations, the principle of merit is weakened." Certainly this is true but it is also true that faculty today are probably better teachers and researchers than they were fifty years ago and that many of the obligations are not unequivocally detractions to teaching and research but sometimes enriching. The American university has risen to world leadership in the last thirty years. This point Lewis misses. To the many hypotheses about campus unrest, Lewis adds a new twist which might be called the theory of red tape. As he says (p. 183), "Who could blame a 20-year-old for not knowing what academic life was all about and how fragile the social bonds were between professor and student, teacher and teacher and student and student in multiversities of 30,000 students and as many rules, routines, functionaries, and miles of red tape?" Faculty "went through the acts of teaching and research but the rituals were empty of meaning and ideas. . . ."

This vast assertion comes near the end of a book that lacks a single live description of a teaching encounter and too frequently relies on heresay evidence, as when he says (p. 186) "one hears reports of lectures delivered from notes yellowed with age." This cliché aside, we have no real sense that Lewis has either observed teaching or has any fresh observations to make about it today as compared with years past.

He also argues that universities have become top-heavy with administrators. But he presents no evidence to us of how much growth has occurred or in what proportion. There are no ratios, for example, of the number of deans or vice presidents to numbers of students today as compared with 100 or 50 years ago. He fails to distinguish patterns of bureaucratic growth by level of institution, which has meant less erosion of faculty authority in some types of institutions than in others. One wonders if he has a longing for a past that never was when he writes, "few individuals spend their hours doggedly working through an intellectual problem, and more research teams spend their afternoons writing progress reports, cultivating strategems to assure the refunding of a project and ordering about research assistants" (p. 188). Certainly some of that goes on and he makes it sound as though all of it is Sisyphean and pointless. It is as though all those faculty who have government grants are engaged in wheel-spinning kinds of research. But he gives us no guidelines nor indicates any distinctions. Would Lewis say, for example, that James Coleman's federally-funded research on equality of educational opportunity was activity at the level of ordering assistants about?

Lewis has the conventional academic's sneer for the administrator. Those who are not scholars "need only to provide space and equipment to enable students (scholars)—young and old—to pursue their activities; it is not necessary for them to continue to introduce new sideshows to an already centrifugal campus merely to justify their existence" (p. 191).

This does not accord at all with my view of administrators, whose moral and intellectual leadership (or the lack of it) vitally affects the institutions we teach in; they are not simply those who pay the light bills. Lewis writes that "the activity of teaching cannot be regulated and all that can be done with reference to it is to make sure that there is a wide selection of courses available to the student, that these are not all offered at the same hour, that there are well ventilated, well supplied classrooms, so that distractions are minimized" (p. 191). Yet the most important curricular experiments in America have been led by administrators—men like Robert Hutchins, Scott Buchanan, Alexander Meiklejohn, Joseph Tussman, and many others. This jaundiced, cynical view of administrators is so pervasive among faculty yet, as in this case, scholars, in condemning administrators, are seldom very scholarly in the kind of evidence they supply.

Special Education: A Sociological Study of California Programs, by CARL MILOFSKY. New York: Praeger Publishers, 1976. 177 pp. $17.50 cloth.

CELESTINO FERNANDEZ
University of Arizona

The title of this book is somewhat of a misnomer, not because it isn't a study of special education programs in California but because it is much more than this. It is an insightful qualitative study of the totality of educational institutions. As the author points out, in order to fully grasp the meaning of special education programs it is essential to understand the educational system in its totality since special education operates within the structure of educational institutions and not in isolation.

The overall theme, then, is on the total educational system with the particular focus on the Educationally Handicapped Minors (EHM) program in California's public schools. ("Educationally handicapped pupils" are defined as students who exhibit learning or behavior disorders due to a neurological handicap or emotional disturbance.) Since there is no means of diagnosing these "disorders" conclusively, EHM classes have become "dumping grounds" for poor and minority students who are too lively and independent and who do not accept the rigid order imposed in our schools.

The author presents both sides of the story justly. We get an insider's view of what it means to be involved on a day-to-day basis with special education programs at various levels—students, teachers, parents, administrators, school psychologists, and state officials. Particularly interesting, often both funny and sad, are the descriptive accounts of situations encountered by some of these individuals. On the other hand we get the outsider's sociological assessment of special education, both in particular settings and in its totality. And this is well done.

In short, this is an excellent book which should be of wide interest to educators, sociologists, and psychologists, in general and to anyone directly or indirectly involved with special education programs, in particular.

Universities in the Western World, edited by PAUL SEABURY. New York: Free Press, 1975. 303 pp. $11.95 cloth.

PHILIP G. ALTBACH
SUNY/Buffalo

This volume, which stems from an international conference held in 1973, takes a critical and generally conservative view of the "university crisis" of the 1960s and 1970s. The volume was sponsored by the International Council on the Future of the University, an international umbrella organization of academics who have opposed many of the reforms of the past decade and who take a traditional view of the role of the university. The essays in this volume are in general well-written, informative, and thoughtful. The conservative bias of the book will not please some readers, but it provides one of the most stimulating collections of essays on the problems of higher education in various countries that is now available. This is true despite the fact that some of the papers are somewhat dated since they were written for a 1973 conference.

The focus of the volume is on the difficulties of universities in Western industrialized nations. While many of the authors have somewhat differing views, they are united by a conviction that the traditional values of academia are worth protecting, and many of the reforms of the past decade are subversive of these values. Traditional scholarship, a research orientation, and the separation of the university from political affairs are in general held as primary values. Recent "threats" include affirmative action, which may demean the concept of appointment to university posts by merit alone, reforms in the curriculum in the name of "relevance" which weaken the traditional curriculum, and similar changes. Student activism is in general seen as an unmitigated evil in that it has "politicized" the University and infused it with oppositional politics.

Some of the strongest criticism is levelled against recent changes in governance patterns, especially in Western Europe. Essays dealing with changes in university governance in Denmark, France, West Germany, and Holland are featured in this volume. In these essays, the trends toward diminishing university autonomy, limiting the power of the senior faculty, and enhancing the "participation" of students and others in the academic community are roundly attacked. These reforms, it is argued, will weaken the traditional academic ethos, will increase bureaucracy, and will inevitably politicize the universities. In some of the essays, these evils are taken as articles of faith rather than persuasively proved. Most of the analysts see that university reform was forced on reluctant universities by a combination of outside politicians eager for peace to be restored to the campus and student radicals and their few allies among faculty intent on radicalizing the universities without much thought to the academic consequences.

This volume includes several thoughtful philosophical essays which deserve serious attention. Edward Shils writes on "the academic ethos under strain" in which he argues that political, fiscal, and internal crises have weakened the resolve of the academic profession in many nations. German Richard Lowenthal and Australian Zelman Cowen consider university autonomy. German sociologist Ralf Dahrendorf and American Alexander Bickel write about the conflict between academic "standards" and the role of the university in providing equality of opportunity.

If one approaches this book sharing the value assumptions of the contributors, the book will be fully satisfying, as it provides a series of essays dealing with some of the key issues facing higher education in a range of national settings. This reviewer wonders, however, whether there might possibly be something in higher education worth reforming and whether all traditional notions about the university are fully relevant. Were all student activists motivated only by mendacity and a desire to bring down the university, or were there other social issues which were involved? Despite the ideological bias of this volume, it remains a valuable collection of literate essays on higher education in the industrialized nations.

Public Higher Education in California, edited by NEIL J. SMELSER and GABRIEL ALMOND. Berkeley: University of California Press, 1974. 318 pp. $12.50 cloth.

WALTER PHILLIPS
University of Toronto

Although ostensibly only edited by Smelser and Almond, half of this volume consists of a monograph-length analysis by Smelser of the problems confronting public, post-secondary education in California during the period, 1950–70. Almond's contribution, on the other hand, seems limited to an introduction which routinely summarizes Smelser's effort and the other, much shorter, papers. These papers, written in response to Smelser's, are by an assortment of individuals who, with the exception of Talcott Parsons, were connected with the California system in one capacity or another during the period in question. While Smelser's own contribution represents a rare attempt to apply the functional paradigm for the analysis of change to a substantive area and a contemporary problem, on first reading the papers that follow seem barely related to his analysis. It is only after much re-reading, considerable reflection, and probably some stretching of meanings as well, that any connections between the two halves of the volume emerge.

There seems, for example, to be a suggestion in papers by Rosemary Park, John Vasconcellos, and Patrick Callan, that the basic problem confronting public, post-secondary education in California has not so much been the reconciling of the conflicting value-orientations of "competitive excellence" and "equality of opportunity," to which Smelser anchors his analysis, but the open-endedness of those value-orientations; that is to say, the persistent failure on the part of those charged with the governance of the California system to answer the questions: excellence in what, and opportunity for whom? To be sure, it is precisely Smelser's argument that given the political nature of the solutions to the problems confronting the California system during the period in question, the terms of the Master Plan of 1960, and the weaknesses of the Coordinating Council for Higher Education created by that legislation, the functions of the various levels of the system so over-lapped that structural differentiation in the form of more specialized institutions with distinctive competences was precluded. As a consequence, he observes, the structure of the system changed very little between 1950 and 1970. Instead, growth took the form of sheer increases in scale, excessive segmentation and duplication of facilities, as well as the proliferation of ad hoc structural additions, in the form of problem-centered institutes, centers, and interdisciplinary programs, bearing little relation to each other.

Nevertheless, one would have expected that the University of California, at least, in view of its vaunted constitutional autonomy, would have proved less vulnerable to the pressures to be "all things to all people," than similar institutions elsewhere. However, as Robert O'Neil points out in one of the more analytical papers in the second half of the book, the legal autonomy of the University of California has meant freedom within the limits of their tenure for the Board of Regents, and therefore weakness and vulnerability for the administration of the affairs of its campuses. This is at least consistent with Smelser's subsequent argument to the effect that the reluctance of the Regents to delegate direct controls to the endpoints of administration, taken with the failure to develop adequate indirect controls at the center, resulted in the growth of powerful centrifugal forces within the University. As a consequence, the more prestigious faculty and their more talented, more experienced, graduate students were propelled toward the peripheries of the institution, thereby creating an instructional vacuum at the nominal centers of its campuses: the Colleges of Arts and Sciences.

Perhaps the most serious shortcoming of Smelser's analysis, however, lies in his refusal to take seriously, even as data, the rhetoric surrounding the events of the 1960s, on the grounds that his is a macroscopic rather than a microscopic analysis of social change. At least some of his readers will be surprised to learn that a macroscopic orientation to data precludes a discussion of the ideological defenses of conflicting organizational aims or interests. For, the truth of the matter is that it is not the level of sociological analysis, but the level of generality on which the functional analysis of change typically proceeds, that precludes such discussions. To be sure, "the commitments of the system" are precisely the subject of Talcott Parson's "Epilogue" to the present volume. One cannot help but feel, however, that Parsons's emphasis on the increasing primacy of "cognitive concerns more or less for their own sake" is more reminiscent of the ideal of Wissenschaft that may have pervaded the Prussian universities between 1850 and 1870, than it is of whatever principle served to legitimate the activities of the "typical high-level American university" between 1950 and 1970.

More to the point is the "idea of the university" that emerges from Kenneth Thimann's paper, "The Social Role of the University and Its Science Departments." As Thimann unwittingly makes clear, it is the land-grant tradition of service to economically (and perhaps politically) interested groups that supplies the key to an understanding of the macroscopic significance of public higher education in California, and in particular the activities of the University of California, during the period in question. It is in this light, rather than in the light of conflicts between the pursuit of excellence and equality of educational opportunity, or a commitment to "cognitive concerns more or less for their own sake," that one appreciates Henry Nash Smith's complaint that in the world of the multiversity those who do not service a powerful constituency in the state or the nation-at-large—namely the humanities—must service those who do. In so doing, as Roy Harvey Pearce suggests in a related paper, humanists are forced into technical (i.e., partial) modes of thinking, thereby undermining their "commitment to wholeness" and to undergraduate teaching. For, as Harvey Brookes argues in still another paper in this volume, from the standpoint of employment opportunities, support for research, and the inordinate length of time required for maturation and recognition, "the humanities look almost wholly to the academic system for reward and recognition." It is only necessary to add that too often during the period in question, the outlines of that system were barely distinguishable from those systems that constituted its environment.

The Young People of Leningrad: School and Work Options and Attitudes, by EVELINA KARLOVNA VASIL'EVA. Translated by ARLO SCHULTZ and ANDREW J. SMITH. White Plains, N.Y.: International Arts and Sciences Press, 1976. 177 pp. $15.00 cloth.

JIRI KOLAJA
Western Virginia University

Vasil'eva has focused on three issues: (1) the relationship between more educated parents with higher jobs and less educated parents with lower jobs and the scholastic achievement of their children, (2) the problem of equality between men and women in schools and occupation, and (3) the working conditions of native Leningradians and migrants to Leningrad.

The author finds that a majority of high school graduates will not be accepted by university level schools when they apply for admission, quite a few of them will reapply after some time, but eventually they will seek admission at a training institution.

What factors were considered as influencing postschooling of graduates? In addition to the universal institutional factors and particular region or industry factors, individual factors such as abilities, interests, and general educational background were considered, as well as the family and its cultural-educational and socio-economic status, and the economic, moral, and psychological atmosphere of the family. A large number of children of less educated parents were found to have poorer grades. However, if one non-working adult interacted with the children, the grades appeared to be more favorable.

The author of this book was concerned with the status of women in school and employment situations. It was reported that women got better grades in educational institutions but that there has been some bias against women in employment.

The problem of occupational mobility is also considered. It is encouraging that Vasil'eva argues that there can be several causes of occupational movement and that the official record has simplified it. Interestingly the book uses only the term "migration" instead of "mobility" that was popularized by another former Leningradian who later became a professor of sociology in the United States—P.A. Sorokin.

In the geographical and occupational mobility investigation, it was found that at the beginning the more educated immigrants usually had to start their work in factories while corresponding Leningradians preferred to work in scientific institutions. Though outsiders later would obtain somewhat higher salaries, they also showed a greater degree of critical attitude. Occupational mobility from a societal viewpoint is detrimental because of the learning time but it also has a positive effect because of a greater satisfaction of migrants.

In concluding the author asks for more data and quantitative parameters as well as for the cooperation not only of educational specialists and psychologists but economists and physicians as well. Let us finally mention that Dobson, in the twenty-three page introduction to this book, shows a good familiarity with Soviet researchers such as Shubkin, Kon, and others.

Critically considered, there appears to be an absence of familiarity with what has been published in other countries on similar problems. To do justice to the author, there is one reference to a Polish-Soviet researcher but otherwise her bibliography shows nothing but Soviet publications.

Further, there is no consideration of informal group influences. Why consider mostly parent-child relationships? After all, chapter two is titled "The Beginning of Independence in Young People's Lives." Since more or less "officially" informal groups do not or should not exist in Soviet organizations, Vasil'eva is probably prohibited from refering to them.

Finally, the general theme is a desirability of converging personal and socio-cultural systems. Note that a criticism addressed, for example, to Parsons and the General Theory of Action convergency could also be applied to this Soviet assumption.

Family and Intimate Lifestyles

Here to Stay: American Families in the Twentieth Century, by MARY JO BANE. New York: Basic Books, 1976. 195 pp. $11.50 cloth.

ROGER W. LIBBY
SUNY/Albany

In this book the author attempts a demographic analysis of family formation and dissolution, living arrangements, and related variables, but neither demography nor selected historical, social, and legal sources are adequate to the apparent goal of determining family trends and consequent policy issues.

The book is divided into two barely connected essays—the first part is largely based on historical and census data, while the second section explores policy issues related to the delicate balance between the privacy of the family and the social responsibilities of the state. Had the second part been developed with more precise and articulate recommendations for policy and law, a fully justified and much needed book would have resulted. Instead, the reader is faced with the often arduous task of wading through a series of legal cases and abstract conclusions. Rather than new ideas and precise recommendations, the book is largely a disorganized, boring, descriptive account of trends already described in several recent books on the family.

Bane's belief is that demographic statistics "give a more accurate picture of what people actually do than reports of what outside observers think they do" (p. xv). It would have been more scholarly and holistic to complement demographic statistics with more sociological and social psychological studies. Self-report data are sparingly cited; the book suffers from this decision.

Implications of trends are usually not well explained. The reader is told to provide explanations for the descriptive observations and trends, but this is hardly a fruitful approach for such a complex subject as the interrelationship between the family, the government, and other social institutions.

A chapter on kinship and friendship networks is several grades above the rest of the book, but even this treatment suffers from a lack of recognition of key research. The coverage of sexual equality and the Equal Rights Amendment is fair, but more thorough analyses are available in other recent books.

Methodological limitations of research are not typically discussed, and *there is no real use of social theory in the entire book!* The intriguing issues of the *forms* the family and marriage will take are neglected, and we are left with an entire book which argues the obvious—that the family is well and alive.

The place of singles, cohabitants, and others not committed to traditional marriage and family life is not explored. In fact, the entire literature on alternative life styles is not acknowledged. This is a major oversight.

This book will be widely quoted by journalists to "prove" that the family is "here to stay." Some social scientists will also cite it as basis for a sign of relief when those who discuss alternatives to traditional marriage and the family (let alone the death of the family) are heard or read.

One does not expect an author to solve social problems, but one hopes for more definite recommendations and ways to implement them. There are fewer than three pages of conclusions. Without tables, footnotes, and a bibliography, the book would be 143 pages. This is hardly a thorough, sensitive, or creative treatise on today's family.

Power in Families, edited by RONALD E. CROMWELL and DAVID H. OLSON. New York: Halsted Press, 1975. 264 pp. $16.95 cloth. $6.95 paper.

MIRRA KOMAROVSKY
Barnard College/Columbia University

This book has achieved one indubitable distinction. It would be foolhardy now to embark upon a study of power in families without having read it. Power, like creativity or aggression, is an evocative word creating an illusion of familiarity and clarity. It is not surprising that researchers who plunged headlong into measurement of power should have encountered perplexing and inconsistent results. This in turn has generated a thrust toward conceptual and theoretical clarification.

The two sections of this book, "Conceptual and Theoretical Issues" and "Methodological and Substantive Research," contain nine chapters by different authors. Introducing each of the two sections is a chapter by the editors attempting to provide an overview.

The dominant stance of the authors in the theoretical section appears to be critical. Acknowledging the contributions of the pioneers (Herbst, Strodtbeck, Blood and Wolfe, among others), Sprey, Turk, Weiting and McLaren, and Broderick consider the current model of studies of family power—"who decides what," to be simplistic. Nor are the critics appeased when students raise the prior question as to which member of the conjugal pair controls the allocation of decision-making in various spheres. Study of victories in *contested* cases represents some, but not sufficient, progress.

These critics propose a variety of new theoretical questions. For example, the relative power of a family member to attain private goals is to be contrasted with the ability to influence critically choices of the family as a group. The very emphasis on "winning and losing" has allegedly led to a neglect of processes, e.g., threat, flattery, compromise, appeasement, and other strategies in the play of power. Exchange and game theories are believed to hold great promise for this processual analysis. Similarly, the preoccupation with the immediate outcome of a contest obscures from view its long-range consequences for the victor and the relationship in question.

The advocacy of a more complex model is repeated in other proposals. Both the types of governance (i.e., unilateral imposition of one's will, rule enforcement, or principled interaction) and the outcomes are said to vary from sphere to sphere in the life of a family. Each family represents, therefore, a complex mix of modes that cannot be depicted by simple categories of husband- or wife-dominance. Again, a new range of problems arises when the study of power makes the group and not the individual its unit of analysis. Several chapters reiterate the need to conceptualize group properties, to discern different rules concerning power operative in families, and to study the effects of group-structured properties of power upon individual members. This theme reflects the structuralist theoretical orientation.

The methodological issues are discussed in the second part of the book in chapters by Cromwell, Klein, and Weiting; Johnson; Corrales; and Raven, Centers, and Rodrigues. The limitations of the prevalent measure of family power, the self-report of the wife, stimulated experimentation with other techniques, e.g., observation, post-experimental recall as to who controlled the outcome, "predicted power" (estimates made by individuals about future outcomes, tested by experimental design). The intriguing result of these attempts is the repeated lack of congruence between various measures.

The editors in their introductory chapter at first appear to advocate the combined use of self-report and observation as "the best of both worlds." Self-report allegedly presents the subjective perception of power, whereas field observation describes the reality as seen by the outsider. However, each of these two measures of power has serious limitations and I find the final assessment of the editors most persuasive: "To date, the richness and the complexity of power dynamics of families have not been adequately dealt with . . ." (p. 150).

In sum, this symposium contains a number of interesting programmatic essays, research reports, and proposed research strategies. As for the editors, they correctly claim that an efficient interdisciplinary paradigm for the study of family power is a distant goal. Offering as they do a very useful survey of the field, they fall somewhat short of codifying the diversity represented in their collection. Which of the various theoretical approaches are complementary and which competing? Which disagreements about methods turn out to stem from different questions underlying the inquiries? What other pseudo-issues are produced by latent premises? The reader would have profited by a more analytical scrutiny of the relationships between the various perspectives.

The Violent Home: A Study of Physical Aggression between Husbands and Wives, by RICHARD J. GELLES. Beverly Hills: Sage Publications, 1974. 230 pp. $11.00 cloth. $6.00 paper.

DIANA E.H. RUSSELL
Mills College

I would not have taken the time to review *The Violent Home* by Richard Gelles were it not for the fact that insensitivity to the significance of the power relationship between the sexes in understanding violent behavior, is so wide spread in and outside of sociology. (Incidentally, this book is the thirteenth publication in "The Sage Library of Social Research" only one of whose volumes includes a female as even a second author.)

Using phrases like "marital violence," "conjugal combat," "intrafamily violence," and the like, Gelles effectively obscures the fact that the violence of husbands is a far more serious problem than the violence of wives in the US and other patriarchal cultures. Neither the strength differential between most men and women, nor the power relationship built into the traditional patriarchal family and the entire society, are ever credited by Gelles as significant factors in the higher prevalence and seriousness of husbands' violence towards their wives. Indeed, though he does concede that "the husband is the more violent of marital partners" (p. 50), at other times he conveys the opposite picture. "Many wives argue," Gelles writes, "that they cannot match their husbands in physical strength, and thus, when they initiate attacks or retaliate, they do so in the extreme. The only individual who actually stabbed a spouse was a wife . . ." (p. 52). No attempt is made to ascertain what percentage of violent acts by wives are in self-defense or retaliation. While Gelles refers to a "protective-reaction violence" where "the wife commences a premptive attack because she fears that her husband is getting ready to hit her" or "*after* the husband has initiated the attack," as a form of "female violence" (p. 79), nowhere does Gelles consider what percentage of the wives' violence is of this type.

According to the most recent figures, only 10% of all violent crimes are perpetrated by females compared to 90% by males (*Uniform Crime Reports,* 1975). Even if it were true that say, double this percentage of women were violent toward their husbands in the home, it would still be necessary to recognize that violence is primarily a male problem. The fact that 63% of homicides are men on men compared with only 4% women on women substantiates this point (*National Commission on the Causes and Prevention of Violence*). It also suggests that where women are violent toward men, it is likely to be in response to men's violence, for the most part. While on the one hand Gelles really obscures this point, it comes through vividly in many of the quotes, and from time to time, in his own statements. For example: "our respondents who did not fight back were still the recipients of repetitive aggression from their husbands. On the other hand, the respondents who *did* fight back were also hit often, so we are left with no real answer as to what posture by the victim reduces the occurrence of beatings'' (p. 82).

On the topic of child abuse—a secondary focus of *The Violent Home*—Gelles's blindness to sexism leads to similar errors. For example, a whole chapter is used to make the point that ''Abused children are likely to become abusive adults'' (p. 171).

But men and women are affected differently: men become abusers of women and children, women become abusers of children but *abused by men*. This difference is never recognized.

At the end of the book Gelles develops a familiar theory: structural stress leads to frustration which leads to violence. If this were true, women would be the more violent sex! No. Male violence is caused by extreme patriarchal notions of appropriate male behavior, plus a social system which condones their abusing their power, particularly in relation to women. Until the dangerous consequences of this culture's idea of masculinity (toughness, superiority, competitiveness, power, conquest, invulnerability) is recognized and changed, male violence toward females, as well as their violence toward other males, will not be halted. But in *The Violent Home* we hear instead about so-called ''victim precipitation''—how ''the role of the victim in intrafamily violence is an important and active one'' through behavior such as nagging. And we learn nothing about how trapped women feel in their violent marriages because they have nowhere to go.

Aside from being sexist, *The Violent Home* is also laboriously written, repetitive, simplistic, and sometimes totally unclear. In addition, it suffers from some fatal methodological flaws. Because of these, this study does not even provide us with valuable data. Half of the small sample of eighty families were selected from police and social agency records because they were believed to be violent. The other forty families, intended as a control group, were their neighbors. However, only one in ten of those approached consented to be interviewed! (p. 50). Yet Gelles naively writes, ''We hoped that interviewing these families would provide data on the incidence of violence in the general population . . .'' (p. 36). In his concluding remarks Gelles states that, ''In no way are the 80 individual family members we talked to representative of any population'' (p. 191). However throughout the book this appears to be forgotten, and Gelles sees fit to estimate the incidence of family violence on the basis of his study, as well as the relationship between family violence and social class, age, religion, number of children, pregnancy, alcoholic consumption, jealousy, etc., etc.

In summary: Gelles's analysis of the tremendously important problem of marital violence—chiefly taking the form of wife abuse—is worse than useless. It blinds us to what is really going on in the patriarchal family, and leads us in the wrong directions in both theory and research.

Family Roles Interaction: An Anthology, 2nd ed., edited by JEROLD HEISS. Chicago: Rand McNally, 1976. 495 pp. $7.95 paper.

IRWIN KANTOR
Middlesex County College

Rather than focusing upon the various approaches to the family (such as the institutional, historical or structural-functional), Heiss has compiled a book of readings relevant to a single theoretical perspective, that of role interaction and role integration. Maintaining that sociological role theory has a dichotomous tradition, exemplified by Meadian social-psychological processual concerns as well as Linton's structural-content analyses, he has revolved the articles around the former tradition. Heiss believes that exploring a single theoretical framework permits the articles to complement each other, thus forming a coherent orientation.

The writing styles presented in the book are varied. For example, Letty Pogrebin's article, ''Down with Sexist Upbringing,'' is largely anecdotal, Frederick Elkin's article is basically a descriptive presentation of Goffman's dramaturgical approach as it relates to the socialization of the self, while the interesting article by Sara Kiesler and Roberta Baral is an attempt to empirically assess the influences of individuals' self-esteem upon their romantic behavior. In general, their findings reveal that human beings desire to select situations which tend to offer them positive self-evaluations and to avoid those situations which threaten their self-esteem. These types of presentations, interspersed throughout the book, prevent the reader from becoming overwhelmed with one particular writing style or research method.

The format of the book is appealing. Prior to each article is an introduction which highlights its central features. Postscripts, added to several articles, help the reader to relate to other works on the same topic. A final editorial postscript summarizes Meadian role theory and discusses how the various studies integrate this theory within the dimensions of the family.

The book could be used by students in a Marriage and the Family course, either as a supplement or as the main text. The articles are well-written, interesting, and relevant.

Medical

The Social Setting of Mental Health, edited by ALFRED DEAN, ALAN M. KRAFT, and BERT PEPPER. New York: Basic Books, 1975. 405 pp. $17.50 cloth.

The Changing Mental Health Scene, edited by RALPH G. HIRSCHOWITZ and BERNARD LEVY. New York: Spectrum Publications, 1976. 382 pp. $25.00 cloth.

MURIEL W. PUMPHREY
University of Missouri, St. Louis

Those who like to think that sociology is a useful as well as a highly theoretic discipline will find plenty to substantiate their convictions in these two volumes. If we sociologists need to be able to see ourselves as others see us, there hardly could be a better device than to analyze what these editors have to say about the contributions sociological thought can make to psychiatric diagnosis and treatment. They provide a kind of mirror image of our body of knowledge and its disseminators. All the editors have been teachers and administrators in departments of psychiatry.

The audience to which Dean, Kraft, and Pepper address themselves is clear: mental health trainees, particularly aspiring psychiatrists. The consumers anticipated by Hirschowitz and Levy are not as specifically identified. Trainees, present practitioners, and social scientists, all of whom ought to keep abreast of innovative experiments and who need to be reminded of the abysmal examples of cultural lag in mental health services, would find these essays stimulating and informative.

Both books are committed to the idea that many emotional disturbances derive from the patient's intimate relationships and in reaction to norms common in the larger society. Both see a carefully trained awareness of these pressures to be an essential part of mental health workers' equipment for helping patients improve and for evaluating the efficiency of the mental health institutional system.

The two collections complement each other. Dean et al. identified sociological concepts they repeatedly had found helpful in teaching an understanding of people as social beings, and proceeded to select key articles and empirical research to illustrate the classic abstractions. Explanations of the meaning and significance in lay (to the social scientist) language in editorial introductions and suggested discussion questions are designed to help sophisticated novices in social science see how the material is applicable to their practice perplexities and working atmosphere. To the sociologist most of the content on culture, status and role, primary groups, deviance, etc. may seem self-evident and elementary. Yet the selections differ from a beginning sociology text by the inclusion of complicated theoretical analyses of the ramifications of classic ideas. Much is not easy reading. The editors have provided tools with which mental health practitioners may examine their own performance and occupational location.

In *The Changing Mental Health Scene,* the editors have used a different approach. They invited innovators and recognized experts to provide graphic descriptions of recent attempts to solve problems in the burgeoning demands for mental health services. Trainees will be nudged to take a hard look at some of the traditional sacred cows of their future profession such as the medical model itself and the uncertainties of the diagnostic process. Hirschowitz and Levy then examine the implications of why some new techniques or innovative delivery arrangements failed or succeeded. For example, among the considerations of how preventive psychiatry might be devised, there is an account of the prior planning and implementation of educational seminars to teach people how to cope with normal changes in the human life-cycle (p. 71). The social science concepts of "transition," "adaptation," and "strategy" pointed to the value of structures that would combat feelings of helplessness during unavoidable shifts to new behavior patterns. Sociological theory concerning group functions helped the experimenters to decide whether groups or dyads would likely be the most effective tools to attain preventive goals.

No scholars in organizing two similar readers, whether moving from concept to practice modality, or practice to concept would have selected exactly the same offerings. After years of attempting to explain the importance of intimate groupings to students in the psychiatric disciplines this reviewer has some doubts that Shells and Janowitz's "Primary Groups in the German Army" (in *The Social Setting of Mental Health,* p. 68) is the illustration of primary group theory that would be the easiest for young psychiatrists to relate to the problems of their diagnostic team, but it is *an* example of an important concept which they should learn to apply. Experts in the field may wonder whether Rakoff and Lefebvre (Hirschowitz, p. 115) provide the best possible explanations of "Conjoint Family Therapy" but the student cannot escape knowing this is an increasingly common therapeutic approach.

The frequent medical criticisms of sociological appraisals of psychiatric endeavors—that they have pointed out flaws but offered no remedies—is somewhat answered by these efforts to make the system respond. Sociologists no doubt will meet the challenge with new theoretic criticisms of new models. Meanwhile, it is difficult to fault any of the contents of these two books on grounds of irrelevancy to mental health or unfair representation of sociological contributions.

The Rise of the Medical Profession, by NOEL PARRY AND JOSÉ PARRY. London: Croom Helm, 1976. Distributed by International Publications. 282 pp. $17.50 cloth.

DOROTHY DOUGLAS
Madison, Wisconsin

The authors examine, through an indepth historical perspective, the way in which the medical profession as an archetypical case has achieved unity and an established place in the middle class through a process of collective social mobility. They place this case study in the context of a theoretical and conceptual scheme which allows them to view the process of collective social mobility as part of a larger process which they term class or even social "structuration."

The Parrys bring a variety of social class theories to bear on the rise of the medical profession. They move among Weber, Marx, Durkheim, Prandy, Parsons, Giddens, and, finally, Freidson (whom they regard as providing the missing link between class theory and professionalism).

The authors make use of copious quotes in their historical-theoretical treatment. Although these are necessary for the flow of the argument, the style in which they are formatted works against a coherent reading of this section. The entire book, in fact, is rather badly put together (little white space, no subheadings, for example) and rather poorly edited with many printing errors.

The main body of the book is a well documented rendition of the development of the medical profession in England since 1790. If the book has a major fault, it lies in its pedantic, single-minded approach to the multifaceted phenomenon it is examining, the rise of the medical profession as illustrative of and therefore partial proof of the theory of collective social mobility as presented by the authors. Taken as a whole, however, it is an excellent, if highly specialized addition to the growing literature on the medical profession as well as a careful treatise in social stratification (its major focus).

Finally, the Parrys treat sexual divisions in society as a structural factor of equal importance with social class and include a chapter on the exclusion of women from the medical profession and the consequent impact of this exclusion.

The Medical Establishment and Social Responsibility, by DUANE F. STROMAN. Port Washington, N.Y.: Kennikat Press, 1976. 193 pp. $12.95 cloth.

THOMAS J. SULLIVAN
Northern Michigan University

Stroman aptly states the principle which underlies his approach toward problems in the health field: "the rights of patients are primary in the organization and financing of care. Medicine exists for man, not man for medicine" (p. 152). There follows an elaborate documentation of the ways in which this principle is frequently violated with castastrophic results. After discussing changes that have occurred both within and outside of medicine, Stroman argues that our health care delivery system has not adapted to these changes. He documents four symptoms of the problems that result: the unmet medical needs of many groups, the poor quality of much medical care, unnecessary surgeries and other medical services, and the rapidly rising costs of medical care. One of the stronger points of Stroman's book is his attempt to relate these problems to particular structural deficiencies in the American health care delivery system: (1) inadequacies in planning and organization of health care services (including limited consumer involvement and an underemphasis on preventive care mechanisms), (2) shortages and maldistribution of health care providers (including the lack of accountability on the part of the medical profession for the planning and allocation of programs), (3) deficiencies in cost control (including minimal consumer involvement, and a reliance on fee-for-service mechanisms), (4) deficiencies in quality control (insufficient professional constraints and consumer involvement). Stroman especially emphasizes the role of the medical profession in creating these problems and deficiencies through their efforts to retain professional autonomy and self-regulation over their work.

Stroman concludes with a discussion of a social ethic which he feels should guide the organization of health care, and he offers some program implications of his analysis. Although Stroman's argument is convincing and well-documented, it has some limitations. For example, there is little discussion of health professionals other than physicians. Many of his proposals are radical departures from current practice; yet he does not discuss how physicians (or other health professionals) can be convinced that such mechanisms are both necessary and desirable and what detrimental consequences of such innovations might result. These and other intricacies of Stroman's proposals about health care organization are slighted in this brief work. However, Stroman has presented an intriguing framework that can serve as a springboard for developing politically and economically feasible solutions to medical problems in the United States.

Methods

Social Effects of Computer Use and Misuse, by J. MACK ADAMS and DOUGLAS H. HADEN. New York: John Wiley & Sons, 1976. 326 pp. $11.50 paper.

The Social Use of Information: Ownership and Access, by ANDREW E. WESSEL. New York: John Wiley & Sons, 1976. 244 pp. $15.95 cloth.

HARVEY E. RICH
California State University, Northridge

The titles of these two books might lead one to conclude that their content is quite similar. In fact, the only similarity is in the subject matter, computers. Adams and Haden have designed their work as an introductory level treatment of the positive and negative effects of the interaction of computers and society. Wessel's book on the other hand, does not appear to have a clearly defined audience. It is addressed, as he puts it, "to those who wish to continue their participation in the making of informed decisions" (p. vii).

To this end, his stated premise is that information systems benefit large institutions and the powerful because only they have the resources necessary to fully utilize them. This, in turn, leads to manipulation of individuals and increased concentration of power in the hands of elites. This theme then should be the basis for a thoughtful treatise on the potential and/or actual abuses of power through computers. However, the level of social commentary in the book does not extend beyond this simple statement. The reasons why social information should be made available on a massive scale to the average person are never examined. Simplistic assumptions about the needs and uses of information by the "common man" abound.

The most useful aspect of the volume for educators and researchers is the author's somewhat detailed treatment of second generation information retrieval systems which are only now beginning to be made available on experimental bases. The need for sophisticated and easily usable information systems should be abundantly clear to all who have experienced the travail of searching for literature through the relatively inefficient sources which presently exist. Unfortunately, even with this benefit, the book suffers major limitations: several of the "technical" chapters tend to be overly detailed and filled with jargon; the cost analyses read more like a National Science Foundation grant proposal than a book geared toward a general audience; and, finally, a whole chapter, is devoted to an updated medieval allegory which seems completely inconsistent with the tone of the remainder of the text.

In *The Social Effects of Computer Use and Misuse,* Adams and Haden set out to acquaint the reader with the numerous ways computers have permeated society. This they accomplish in an appealing manner. The book is easy to read and enjoyable. Approximately one-half the volume is devoted to the computer, its history and usage; the other half discusses the "social, economic and philosophical implications" of the computer revolution. Although the treatment of any single topic is somewhat limited, the text is supplemented by an ample selection of articles which give the overall volume considerable depth as well as breadth for an introductory text. This book would provide excellent material for a "computers and society" course and probably ought to be required in an introductory computer science course because of its treatment of the philosophical and ethical implications of computerization. It certainly would be a welcome addition to various other sociology courses such as social problems or methods of social research.

Professional Mail Surveys, by PAUL L. ERDOS. New York: McGraw Hill, 1970. 289 pp. $25.00 cloth.

DAVID BILLS
University of Wisconsin, Madison

Drawing on his 30 years' experience in market research, Paul Erdos presents information on nearly every aspect of the mailed survey in a twenty-six chapter book. While Erdos's emphasis is always on the practical, workaday problems of mail surveys, the atheoretical nature of the book is more than compensated for by the sheer abundance of useful information. Given the author's goal "to describe the techniques used for professional mail surveys in sufficient detail to enable readers to conduct their own surveys, to evaluate those made by others, or simply to become acquainted with proven procedures used in mail surveys," he has succeeded admirably.

The author covers a wide territory. He gives particular emphasis to the problems of bias, nonresponse, and questionnaire construction, and also presents useful discussions of such topics as mailing lists, cost estimating and scheduling, incentives, mailing procedures, data processing, and editing and coding. The book is packed with practical suggestions. For example,

> Paper. The stock used should be pleasant to look at, substantial to handle, thick enough to be printed on both sides without showing through, light enough to fit within the planned weight of the mailing piece, suitable for writing on with pen or pencil, and hardy enough to take some handling in tabulating. Very light, opaque stock should be used for research conducted entirely by air mail and especially for international surveys, where the difference in weight can make the difference between 25 and 50 postage for mailing.

The book also contains a twelve-page glossary of survey-related terms, an appendix entitled "Percentage and Speed of Response," and an exhaustive, 56-item checklist for evaluating mail surveys. Numerous examples and illustrations are presented throughout the text.

Particularly in the early chapters, Erdos seems overly intent on "selling" the mail questionnaire technique. Further, in addition to the rather low level of scholarship, the reader often wishes for a more extensive list of references. Another consideration is the substantial cost of the book. While the practicing researcher will probably save money in the long run from information contained in the book, many students will likely find the cost prohibitive. Finally, the reader familiar with the survey research literature must also take exception with Erdos's constant emphasis on the necessity of keeping the mail questionnaire as short as possible, a rule of thumb that has not been supported in the literature.

Whatever flaws Erdos's work may have, it is a valuable guide to anyone interested in the mail survey. Erdos offers a wide range of insights into all phases of the survey process, and his book is an important source for anyone engaged in this type of research.

Introduction to Statistics for the Social Sciences, by FREDERICK D. HERZON and MICHAEL HOOPER. New York: Thomas Y. Crowell Company, 1976. 492 pp. No price listed, cloth.

Intermediate Politometrics, by GORDON HILTON. New York: Columbia University Press, 1976. 282 pp. $15.00 cloth.

Nonparametrics: Statistical Methods Based on Ranks, by ERICH L. LEHMANN. San Francisco: Holden-Day, 1975. 457 pp. $22.95 cloth.

Ideas and Data: The Process and Practice of Social Research, by SHELDON OLSON. Homewood, Ill.: Dorsey Press, 1976. 513 pp. $12.95 cloth.

Fundamentals of Behavioral Statistics, 3rd ed., by RICHARD P. RUNYON and AUDREY HABER. Reading, Mass.: Addison-Wesley Publishing Company, 1976. 446 pp. $12.95 cloth.

CHARLES E. STARNES
Oregon State University

The methodological training received by most undergraduate sociology students rarely entails more than a single "methods" and a single "statistics" course. The former are generally very broad and eclectic, the latter very narrow and elementary. The result one may suggest, is a general feel for strategy-of-research options without much hope of implementation, on the first count, and revived arithmetic skills without purpose or perspective, on the other. The methods training rarely allows "getting one's feet on the ground"; the statistical training rarely enables one to "get off the ground."

The book by Olson is the only one of those reviewed here which can be viewed as essentially a "methods" text. Despite the author's introductory concern that "learning the methods of social science is one of those occasions when you don't really learn without doing," it is his own doings rather than the reader's which occupy central place in the text. Olson does, perhaps, bring the student closer to the actual struggles with doing research than many authors of methods texts. But, he does this primarily by (a) a greater than usual emphasis on observational, field research problems, and (b) exceptional illustrations of actual studies and potential data sources. Examples of the latter are reproductions, for discussion, of such as the 1970 U.S. Census Form, 1973 Uniform Crime Reports, the NORC General Social Survey form, and data from the Human Relations Area Files. Fieldwork methods occupy a considerable part of the text and are used to introduce the overall framework (translation of the "folk system" of participants into the "analytic systems" of outsider scientists) which guides his presentation. Olson's own fieldwork serves to illustrate many of the problems he discusses as well as various approaches to meeting them, though he shows a solid acquaintance with the works of others and utilizes them often. The text is weakest on topics or issues of more formal or technical nature.

Experimental design and measurement procedures are, perhaps, most inadequately developed and Olson admits that his review of statistical techniques is "too quick an overview for any more than a tentative grasp of the issues involved." In general, it is my feeling that the text suffers from a failure on Olson's part to decide upon the target audience and, perhaps, a fundamental ambivalence about the value of attention to formal, especially technical, procedures of research. Olson cautions those who oppose "analytic" models that among the reasons for studying them is the dictum that one should know the "enemy." Of course, that rule of thumb should apply as well in the opposite direction. For such self-protective purposes Olson's text should serve adequately whether one lives in the analyst's office or with the "folk." For others it can only be a good beginning.

The books by Runyon and Haber and by Herzon and Hooper are designed for an introductory course in statistics. The former is in its third edition and essentially follows the organization of former editions. There are only modest revisions of most chapters, but these are clearly designed to make the text more generally attractive to students. The probability chapter is extensively rewritten and each chapter now has a final summary, glossary, and numerous exercises. Answers to selected exercises are provided along with tables, glossary of symbols, and a math review in appendices. Useful computational formulae are printed on the inside front and back endpieces. In general, errors and misprints have been rooted out over the three editions, although the review copy has the outlines for chapters fourteen and fifteen interchanged.

Sociologists may be rather disappointed with Runyon and Haber's continued relative neglect of measures of association and total avoidance of multiple regression. Whereas techniques rarely seen in the sociological literature, such as Sandler's A and Mann-Whitney U, are amply covered, there is no mention of such measures as *lambda, gamma,* or *tau*. Further, the exercises and illustrations reinforce the general impression that the text is oriented more toward students of psychology, business, and education rather than those of sociology, political science, or anthropology.

Herzon and Hooper, by contrast, emphasize topics, illustrations, and exercises oriented toward political science and sociology. They also make a special effort to reach the student with weak math training or great fear of math. Presentation of symbols and formulae is kept at a minimum and the reader is drawn into topics cautiously. A review of math is built into the text as a device for accomplishing this. This review, incidently, is one of the best I have seen in an introductory text. The cautious approach and avoidance of unnecessary formalism, however, forces lengthier verbal presentations and may irritate the instructor who wants to "get on with it." It also produces a relatively long text despite the sacrifice of some useful topics. Thus, one-way ANOVA and bivariate regression are presented, but higher order ANOVA is not, and multiple regression gets only very brief and sketchy treatment. Simple nominal and ordinal measures of association (e.g., *lambda* and *gamma,* but not *tau*) are treated, but no hint is given of the log-linear methods which have recently revolutionized the analysis of contingency tables

—an unfortunate lag affecting nearly every introductory or intermediate text I have seen.

Whether either of these texts enables the student to get off the ground is better left to experience. Runyon and Haber's text should appeal more to those with experimental bias; Herzon and Hooper's text is more likely to appeal to those within the survey research tradition. Neither prepares one for coping with the tremendous growth of research reports using structural equations models or related multivariate techniques.

Until recently many of us could lament the difficulty of plunging into these matters because they required the study of rather advanced statistics in econometrics texts. The need for more practical introductory texts is now being met from several corners. Such is the object of Hilton's step-by-step tour from simple regression methods through multiple regression to elementary multi-equation structural models. His *Intermediate Politometrics,* despite its awkward and disciplinary title, could effectively bridge the gap between a good general statistics course and Duncan's *Introduction to Structural Equation Models* or the major econometrics texts.

The expert statistician may feel discomfort from time to time by Hilton's relatively loose use of certain terms or abbreviated treatment of special problems in regression analyses. But the text was not written for the expert. In any case, except for a few innocuous misprints, I have found no serious errors. The book is unusually effective in covering most of the special problems of regression without getting bogged down in notational gymnastics or substantive trivia. The discussion avoids proofs by substituting several simple and persuasive diagrams and worked examples. Even the introduction of matrix notation to facilitate discussion of multiple regression and structural models is done smoothly and effectively. Considerable attention is given to underlying statistical assumptions and the consequences of violating them. Treatment is given topics such as, for example, autocorrelation, generalized weighting to correct heteroscedasticity, multicollinearity, specification bias, lagged variables, restricted coefficients, dummy variables, nonlinearity, identification, and others. While each topic is only briefly covered, on the whole the book will give one sufficient preparation for tackling more technically advanced texts. Part 3, on multi-equation models, provides only a basic introduction to the topic. It is, perhaps, the weakest part of the book and, in any case, must be supplemented by those who wish to understand such models.

Lehmann's *Nonparametrics,* unlike the above, is unlikely to find use in traditional coursework within sociology. This is, perhaps, unfortunate since many data situations in sociology would best be tackled with nonparametric procedures and recently extraordinary progress has been made in their development. Lehmann's text requires greater mathematical sophistication than is ordinarily expected of sociology students, yet the required level is still not great. Those solidly familiar with probability and estimation theory should have no difficulty.

The text should not be seen as either a cookbook or encyclopedia of nonparametrics. If one can handle the mathematics, it is actually a very good presentation of the data analysis problem from a nonparametric standpoint. A central feature is the distinction between population (sampling) models and randomization models, with unusually clear discussion of their relative advantages and limitations. There is, also, a very good treatment of the problem of ties.

The text covers each of the following contexts: rank tests for comparing two treatments, comparing two treatments or attributes in a population model, blocked comparisons for two treatments, paired comparisons in a population model and the one-sample problem, comparison of more than two treatments, randomized complete blocks, and tests of randomness and independence.

The discussion of each context features one procedure and its assumptions, properties, and variants. Each context is developed in terms of models, tests, multiple decision rules, and point and interval estimation. Many texts on nonparametrics fail to go far beyond the presentation of models and tests. Lehmann's is unusual in its exploitation of recent developments in the area of estimation. For professional self-study of nonparametrics, Lehmann's text offers much reward.

Comparative Methods in the Social Sciences, by NEIL J. SMELSER. Englewood Cliffs, N.J.: Prentice-Hall, 1976. 253 pp. $7.50 paper.

HENRY TEUNE
University of Pennsylvania

In this book, comparative methods are conceived broadly, embracing theoretical, substantive, epistemological, and technical issues, reflecting both a long standing dialogue of the author and his current appraisal of the state of comparative research.

Contemporary research, especially of the last twenty years, is linked to the work of de Tocqueville, Durkheim, and Weber. Smelser argues that the methodological issues faced by current comparative researchers have not changed as much as the data, theories, and observational techniques. About two thirds of the book is a critique of these three, largely from a contemporary perspective. The critique of them is sharper and stronger than that of current research.

The fundamental assumption of the book is that there is no such thing as *the* comparative method—in contrast to experimental and statistical methods. What distinguishes comparative research is the *degree* of dissimilarity, making certain problems "complicated and intractable." The logic of scientific analysis requires control; comparative data present control problems, resulting from the magnitude of variance requiring control.

Comparative research perhaps has reached a plateau after the large scale research projects of the 1960s, such as Inkeles's on modernization and Cantril's on human concerns. It is not yet clear what has been learned from these projects. But "comparative" no longer has the attractiveness of something different and challenging.

Smelser's assumptions reflect this. Although comparative research may be more complicated because of the dissimilarities, it is similar to other social science research. Smelser has concluded that his earlier view of *the* comparative method was "erroneous."

Was his earlier view erroneous? Is the reformulation of the discontinuous into the continuous a more sophisticated perspective? Do ecological fallacies become ecological biases, aggregation errors become aggregation bias? Does *the* comparative method become the study of dissimilar units with limited cases for statistical control? I no longer think so.

One distinguishing characteristic of Weber, Durkheim, and de Tocqueville was their effort to link the macro system to micro processes, in Durkheim, for example, societal organization to individual suicide; or the micro to the macro, for example, egalitarian interpersonal relationships to the power of the government. Further, they were sensitive to the history of the system, the acts of the French nobility, and the disposition of the French people to revolutionary destruction.

The comparative research problem is more than the degree of dissimilarity of the units. It is cross-system (two or more social systems), cross-level (the system and groups or individuals within them), and cross-time, (the past as it is structured into the present). The structure of the relationships sought may set aside comparative research from other kinds, not whether the units examined are cities within a country or countries, or independent cultures or ethnic groups within a single society. Comparative research in this sense is distinct from research that stays at the same level, either the macro (such as correlations of GNP and per capita taxes of countries), or the micro (such as correlations among attitudes of individuals within various countries).

One critical ingredient in the development of social theory has been the stimulus of new variances or greater dissimilarities, which call for theories to summarize and explain them. Marx, Weber, and de Tocqueville had the new variances of a new country, industrialization, and non-Western religions. In the early twentieth century, the improvement in the quality of national data fostered a retreat from the comparative. After World War II, a new dimension of variance became available and accessible in new nations and old societies. There were case studies of whole systems, and in the 1960s major comparative research programs. The next infusion of dissimilarity may come from linking historical data to system comparisons. This merger of the historical and comparative is now underway, based on quantitative observations. This combination may move comparative research off its plateau, and, once again, there might be talk of *the* comparative method.

Apart from its insights into some classics, this book brings comparative research back to the mainstream of theoretical developments in social sciences, and, consequently, forces thinking about the basic enterprise of all of its disciplines. It is a worthy contribution to a continuing dialogue.

Organizations

Social Control in Industrial Organisations: Industrial Relations and Industrial Sociology: A Strategic and Occupational Study of British Steelmaking, by PETER BOWEN. Boston: Routledge & Kegan Paul, 1976. 270 pp. $13.50 paper.

Systems of Organization: Management of the Human Resource, by DAVID G. BOWERS.

Ann Arbor: University of Michigan Press, 1976. 166 pp. $6.95 cloth.

Industrial Society: Structures, Roles, and Relations, by EDWARD B. HARVEY. Homewood, Ill.: Dorsey Press, 1975. 417 pp. $13.95 cloth.

Autonomy at Work: A Sociotechnical Analysis of Participative Management, by GERALD I. SUSMAN. New York: Praeger Publishers, 1976. 230 pp. $18.50 cloth.

GEORGE H. WESTACOTT
SUNY/Binghamton

Here is an intellectual feast for industrial and organizational sociologists that includes an overall treatment of the field (Harvey), two weighty theoretical-empirical studies (Bowen and Susman), and a summary of a major theorist's work (Bowers).

To begin with the broadest work, Harvey did his scholarly homework well and has written a highly competent introductory industrial sociology text which, despite its dry title, is consistently interesting. His goal is to make industrialization's multifaceted impact on societies understandable. This he does with an artful blend of theory and vast empirical detail that is informed throughout by historical and worldwide perspectives.

Focusing from the general to the more specific, he outlines sociological inquiry and theories of industrialization before analyzing institutions such as the occupational structure and large-scale work organizations. Then he examines managerial, white-collar, and blue-collar roles before returning to the more general problem of integrating the materials through a discussion of industrial relations and the linkages between occupations, education, and stratification. Finally, the future of industrializing societies (all are industrializing) is glimpsed via considerations of growth, energy use, innovative work arrangements, and leisure.

A persistent theme is industrialization's negative impact on the quality of life as reflected in employee alienation and environmental degradation, but the tone is rational, not frantic. Complemented by lucid chapter summaries and extensive documentation, the book should become a favorite among industrial sociology texts.

Bowen has produced a minutely detailed historical case study of labor-management relations in the British steel industry, with special emphasis on one plant he studied in depth. His overriding concern is to demonstrate an applied role for the industrial sociologist in the analysis and design of industrial relations systems. He outlines the sociological concepts and techniques available for this task, and applies them to problems of work regulation. Social control, his major concept, is understood as joint influence over the regulation of work activity.

His theoretical perspective derives primarily from the sociotechnical school, as reflected in major concerns for both organizational system requirements and the exigencies of work-people. He incorporates an open-system model by demonstrating that key survival problems in steel's history have arisen from technological innovation by competitors in the "task environment." Management and labor's lagging awareness of these problems led to faulty decisions (excess manpower) regarding work regulation, which might have been averted through the services of an in-house sociologist. Bowen's survey of blue and white-collar worker attitudes at the Ironhill plant reveals basic patterns of conflict between unions and management, yet sufficient consensus for joint control of work.

The study is thorough and competent, and will provide empirical fodder for organizational analysts for years. However, he might have more widely generalized the model and findings to other industries and organizational types. In addition, the reader will need keen motivation to cope with the wordy and often abstract style. Thus, the book is for serious sociologists and practitioners of industrial relations.

Susman creates a complex theoretical framework for designing work organizations at the lower levels so they may accomplish both social and technical objectives. He is extremely well grounded in the literature of organizational sociology, being particularly influenced by Emery and Trist's thinking. His framework incorporates elements of field theory, open-systems theory, and the notion of the causal texture of system environments. Motivation is viewed as springing from the individual's need for self-enhancement, which is to be attained through "directed action" (participation) in self-regulating, autonomous work groups.

He criticizes the scientific management/bureaucratic model of organization for using the employee's body (mechanistic behavior) but not his or her mind (purposive behavior), with resulting social and economic costs. He then suggests work group autonomy as a mechanism through which to pursue such desired ends as joint optimization of the technical and social systems, improved quality of work-life, and general post-industrial society values. Work group autonomy is enhanced as groups gain responsibility for reducing variances (uncertainty) in the boundary transactions and conversion (transformation) processes of their units. To support the case for autonomous work groups, evidence is presented from numerous studies, particularly from the author's own design experiments in the coal mining industry.

The book is directed to committed students, researchers, and designers of organizational behavior, but not to neophytes, for it is extremely abstract and demands both familiarity with the discipline and strong motivation. The language will be largely unintelligible to managers, upon whose organizations Susman has designs, so perhaps jobs will be created for Bowen's organizational sociology practitioners. I strongly resented the difficulty of the prose but willingly note that there are conceptual insights which should contribute to the advancement of organizational theory and understanding.

Bower's book might have been titled, "Likert's Systems of Organization," because it is a smooth, concise summary of Rensis Likert's contributions to organizational behavior. It covers the latter's thinking on such topics as: the role of the work group, participative decision-making, motivation, communication, the linking-pin coordinative function, supervision and peer group loyalty, measuring human resources, and finally, implementing System 4 (the participative, and favored, one).

In spite of Bower's articulate achievement, there are several shortcomings which render the book of questionable value. First, Likert's work is left dangling in intellectual space, unconnected to either past or present research and theory on organizations. This flaw reveals itself in the text and more clearly still in the references and bibliography, which are 95% Likert and associates. In addition, perplexingly, the book appears to stop in the 1960s, with hardly a mention of later contributions. Finally, System 4 is claimed to have been proven effective in numerous research studies, but insufficient evidence is presented to convince the reader of this. People interested in Likert's work might better consult his 1967 work, *The Human Organization,* still the best expression of his ideas.

Worth noting in conclusion is the common element of democratic-participative ideology expressed in all of the books.

Modernization and the Japanese Factory, by ROBERT MARSH AND HIROSHI MANNARI, Princeton, N.J.: Princeton University Press, 1976. 437 pp. $27.50 cloth. $11.50 paper.

ROBERT E. COLE
University of Michigan, Ann Arbor

This volume constitutes a major contribution to the social science literature on the social organization of Japanese factories. Yet, it also contains fundamental flaws which invalidate some findings and lead one to question the relevance of others.

Marsh and Mannari have brought together the results of their exhaustive survey of Japanese employees in three firms in three different industries. The 1,695 respondents are drawn from a 525 employee sake firm, an 18,000 employee ship-building firm, and a 13,500 employee electric machinery firm (household appliances). In all three cases they investigate specific plants of the larger units. Some of the findings have appeared before in various journal articles but they benefit from the broader framework in which they are now presented. For the first time, American and Japanese social scientists have applied the techniques of multiple regression systematically to examine the various determinants of institutional arrangements in Japanese industry. To be sure, economists have examined some of these variables in a peripheral fashion, but none has looked at the range of social organizational variables that Marsh and Mannari examine. Briefly put, the book is an attempt to examine the determinants of seventeen dependent variables through an examination of some thirty-five independent variables. The variables to be explained are: knowledge of procedures, job satisfaction, value orientations (pleasure versus work versus family), pay, job classification rank, perceived promotion chances, employee cohesiveness, paternalism, residence (company housing versus private housing), participation in company activities, concern with company, perceived relative advantage of current employer, lifetime commitment, performance, recruitment route, and the consequences of previous inter-firm mobility. We do not have the space to consider the various operationalizations of these measures except to note that many are sophisticated indices while some (such as concern with company) rest on single measures of dubious validity.

To their credit, the authors do not adopt a shotgun approach to the analysis of the determinants of these variables. Rather, they develop a variety of competing hypotheses to explain each dependent variable using stepwise regression to sort through the independent variables. Generally speaking, the choice is conceptualized as between propositions derived from the paternalism-lifetime commitment (PLC) model proposed by James Abegglen and the convergence theory of modernization. Particular attention is paid to the degree of social integration of the employee into the firm and its determinants; it is here that the book probably makes its major substantive contribution.

Although some support is found for the PLC model, particularly on those predictions which are consistent with the modernization model, the bulk of the evidence argues against the PLC model. Many of the best predictors of behavior and attitudes are those variables we commonly expect to be operative in Western organizations (age, education, rank, organizational status, and job satisfaction). Thus, Marsh and Mannari make a strong contribution to the further "demystification" of the social organization of the Japanese firm. They avoid the common error of confusing the distinctive characteristics of Japanese organizations with their most important characteristics (p. 336). They also display in convincing fashion a range of differences among employees in the three firms which contributes further to demolishing the image of the uniformity of social organization practices and attitudes in Japanese firms.

What then are the problems? Above all, the book attempts to fit the Japanese experience into the image of modernization that has until recently dominated American sociological thought. It is typical of that class of modernization theories dominant in the 1960s which assumes a bipolar characterization of the development process, based on ideal-typical categorizations of social organization forms. Such formulations appear sterile and evidence little understanding of the dynamics of non-Western nations. If the study represents an advance in application of measurement techniques to Japan, it is a step backward in conceptualization.

Marsh and Mannari label practices thought to exist in the United States as modern and label their absence in Japan as non-modern, with the process of change always operating toward the idealized Western patterns. The worst or best example is chapter six where the authors define the situation in which pay is determined predominantly by seniority as traditional and the one in which it is determined predominantly by job classification and performance as modern. Marsh and Mannari idealize the American pattern, ignoring the significant role of seniority in wage determination in the United States. Indeed, Rees and Schultz in their book, *Workers and Wages in an Urban Labor Market,* found seniority to be the single most important determinant of individual earnings in their study of the Chicago labor market. More importantly, even a minimal familiarity with human capital theory would suggest the folly of categorizing seniority as a traditional principle. By simplistically dichotomizing a more complicated phenomenon, they thereby lose sight of more subtle relationships.

One can only admire the heroic attempts by the authors to derive testable propositions from what are extremely abstract theories. However, the reader's belief in a tight relationship between the theories and the derived propositions repeatedly is called into question. This is especially true when we read such sentences as, "Although this goes beyond Durkheim, it is at least not inconsistent with what he might have said" (p. 270).

This leads to a more fundamental problem. The PLC model postulated by Marsh and Mannari is their representation of James Abegglen's well-known position. Indeed, the authors seem obsessed with destroying this image of Japanese factories. In effect, the authors select the most extreme version of the model and develop propositions to test it. When they do not find it verified, they claim to have demonstrated the emptiness of the PLC model. To put it differently, they construct overly strict tests which Japanese employees could pass only if they were mindless robots at the disposal of a very unintelligent management. Needless to say, they fail such tests.

Now, it may be that the image of Japanese organizations held by most Western scholars is so naive that it is necessary to repudiate the more extreme caricatures of the Japanese worker. My own impression, however, is that one seldom sees Abegglen cited in the social science literature anymore. For those with an interest in the Japanese experience, there is now a wealth of materials available which contradicts his presentation. To be sure, recent publications by Ronald Dore (*British Factory—Japanese Factory*) and Thomas Rohlen (*For Harmony and Strength*) return to the uniqueness of the Japanese experience but these are far more sophisticated versions of the PLC model. The problem with Marsh and Mannari's presentations is that by focusing on the extreme version of the PLC model, they do not allow themselves the opportunity to examine its persistence in more modified form. Indeed, in one of the few cases in which they constructed a strong form of the model and a weak form, they were unable to reject the weak form (pp. 249–250).

More generally, this is a cross-sectional study (data collected in 1969) with three cases and this engenders the usual host of limitations. Although the authors would like to see their study as a confirmation of the convergence theory of modernization, they have no longitudinal or nationally aggregated data to sustain such a position.

Finally, Marsh and Mannari appear unusually insensitive to the assumptions of the regression technique. Stepwise regression is their chosen instrument, a data search technique which requires cross validation on a different sample for valid controlled inferences. No such procedure is forthcoming. There is a heavy reliance on the interpretation of r^2 with a consequent tendency of the research exercise to turn into the question of "whose variables explain the most variance." Yet, often the direction of the relationship, whether the relationship is statistically significant and whether the theory can predict shifts in the form of relationships, would be better measures. These problems come to the fore when we see that there is relatively little variation of responses to some of the key measures in the PLC model; for example, only about 8% of the sample live in company housing and the responses on the paternalism measures are also highly skewed. To interpret the failure of these independent variables to explain much of the considerable variance in the dependent variables, as a demonstration of the invalid character of the PLC model, is quite misleading. As is common with the heavy-handed use of regression technique, the book may have added more to our ability to predict relationships than to our understanding of them.

Policy

Birth Control and Foreign Policy: The Alternatives to Family Planning, by NICHOLAS J. DEMERATH, III. New York: Harper & Row, 1976. 228 pp. $6.95 paper.

CHARLES F. HOHM
San Diego State University

Professor Demerath attempts to accomplish two major goals: (1) explaining why family planning programs have failed in adequately reducing fertility in underdeveloped countries, and (2) outlining an alternative to family planning. In this reviewer's opinion, the author has succeeded. The manuscript, which according to the author is not aimed at experts but at students and policy makers, should be recommended reading in any college course dealing with human fertility.

Demerath's work is unique in a number of ways. First, while many scholars have criticized family planning programs, none have included a detailed description of the "family planning establishment" as has Demerath. The cooperation, overlap, and interchange between private organizations (such as the Population Council and Ford Foundation) and public organizations (such as the US Agency for International Development) are discussed. Demerath argues that the family planning or contraceptionist approach has been promoted worldwide, albeit unsuccessfully, by the US Eastern Establishment through the Family Planning Establishment.

In his indictment of family planning, Demerath has indeed "bitten the hand that fed him" for he was employed by the Ford Foundation as a program specialist in India from 1965 to 1966. The above leads to the second manner in which the work is unique. Most critics of family planning are outsiders. Demerath however, observed the family planning approach from the inside while in India. As other critics of family planning, Demerath argues that fertility reduction does not occur in a vacuum, that the major institutions (which Demerath calls "primary institutions") must undergo change first. What Demerath contributes to the dialogue is a sociological analysis of *specific* institutions in a *specific* society, namely India. Indeed, one of the author's major points is that the idiosyncratic institutions of a society are very important with regard to that society's fertility and must be understood and dealt with.

The third way in which Demerath's book is unique is in its detailed outlined alternative. Expanding on the Davis-Blake framework, Demerath's "societalist" model features the primary institutions (which are subdivided into the environment, social structure, culture, and polity) affecting reproductive practices (factors such as age of marriage, percent remaining celibate, etc.) which subsequently affect fertility behavior. The societal model incorporates certain aspects of the developmentalist approach (which sees economic and social development as necessary preconditions to fertility reduction) but in addition, identifies those institutions of a specific society that must be changed in order to achieve the desired demographic goals. Demerath is careful to add that changing primary institutions in order to reduce fertility should be part of a larger, more comprehensive strategy of socioeconomic development. Cuba, Tunisia, Singapore, and the People's Republic of China are cited as cases where the societal approach was utilized successfully. A total chapter is devoted to the analysis of what primary institutions were changed in China and how these changes resulted in subsequent fertility reductions.

The last chapter delineates "what the United States can do," i.e., the necessary changes that need to be made in our foreign policy with regard to socioeconomic development and fertility reduction in the developing world.

Doctoring Together: A Study of Professional Social Control, by ELIOT FREIDSON. New York: Elsevier Scientific Publishing Company, 1976. 298 pp. $13.50 cloth.

NANCY R. CHISWICK
Pennsylvania State University

Freidson has hit on an intriguing way to get across some interesting ideas about social policy. He actually takes us into and around and through that most forbidden sanctuary: a group of medical doctors. For those of us who have observed from the outside and often wondered what it is really like on the inside, the intimate glimpses of the inner circle that are interspersed throughout the book make reading *Doctoring Together* a much less ponderous task than if Freidson had presented his thesis using another setting as a model.

The thesis is this: something called "social control" underlies all human organization. It is different in different settings. In a professional setting such as medicine, the social control system is not very clearly understood, and in fact is seemingly misinterpreted on a number of scores. These misperceptions lead to errors in social policy. For example, a program such as Medicare is instituted on the basis of assumptions about the underlying social control system in the medical profession (i.e., that a different administration can make the product different). As Freidson shows, however, the real social controls are not in the administration, but in the providers of service themselves (i.e., the medical doctors), and that this is what policy changers need to attend to in their decision-making. The obvious conclusion Freidson draws from this is that a clear understanding of the underlying system of social control is a necessary precursor to social policy planning, and that policy changes made without thorough investigation of these underlying factors are likely as not to lead to situations in which the product is not affected in the ways the policy changes were meant to effect.

Freidson has a lot of fine things in this book, not the least of which are the appendices, in which he addresses himself more specifically to the methodology of the study. Here included are parts of the grant proposal, the rationale of the study, methods of data collection, even the interview formats: one can only wish that more social researchers were so generous to the social science student.

Sociology and Public Policy: The Case of Presidential Commissions, edited by MIRRA KOMAROVSKY. New York: Elsevier Scientific Publishing Company, 1975. 183 pp. $10.95 cloth.

RICHARD ROSENFELD
Rensselaer Polytechnic Institute

This interesting and disturbing little volume resulted from (then) President Mirra Komarovsky's call for an analysis of the problem of applied sociology in the context of two plenary sessions of the 1973 ASA annual meetings. The state of the art of applied sociology was addressed in those sessions by way of participant-observer accounts of the operation and impact of four recent Presidential Commissions, these followed by three papers whose purpose was to codify the findings of the Commission case studies, as well as derive from them "higher order" generalizations. The case studies were prepared by Otto N. Larsen, James F. Short, Charles F. Westoff, and Lloyd E. Ohlin who, respectively, served on the Commissions on Obscenity and Pornography, the Causes and Prevention of Violence, Population Growth and the American Future, and Law Enforcement and the Administration of Justice. The discussion papers were written by Paul F. Lazarsfeld and Martin Jaeckel, Raymond W. Mack, and Robert K. Merton. All appear in this volume, along with a brief introduction by Komarovsky.

We have then the published report of a Presidential "commission" on Presidential Commissions. Unfortunately, not unlike the final reports of national commissions, this one offers provocative empirical materials, but disappoints in its summary analysis and recommendations.

The case studies are rich in illustrative detail concerning the why's and how's of the establishment of the Commissions, their formal and informal structure, the formulation and subsequent reformulation of their mandates, their internal functioning, procedures for gathering (and, in some cases, suppressing) information, staff recruitment, time and budgetary constraints, internal conflicts, external relations, achievements, failures, and much, much more. It is of some interest to learn, for example, that young lawyers are generally more policy-wise than distinguished sociologists; that it is not easy to recruit academic sociologists for Commission work during the months of June, July, August, and October; that "effects" studies *can* alter opinions (excepting, apparently, Presidential ones) on emotionally charged issues; and that Commission public hearings can be profitably analyzed as a form of political vaudeville, complete with pie throwing. The participant-observer reports read like Hammond's *Sociologists at Work*—but this time at work on comparatively unfamiliar, sometimes hostile, terrain.

To what, precisely, do the separate accounts add up? What do they suggest regarding the contemporary uses, mis-uses, and non-uses of sociological perspectives and knowledge in the formation of public policy? At this point the book falters. The three discussion papers are not systematic codifications of the case-study findings. The Lazarsfeld-Jaeckel discussion comes closest to that objective, but even here "examples" from the case studies are used primarily to clarify a conceptual framework devised by the authors for the empirical study of Commissions. However, if not strict codifications, the discussion papers do contain useful elaborations of themes running through the case studies. Thus Lazarsfeld and Jaeckel illustrate the problem of the divergence between social science findings and Commission summary analyses by contrasting a content analysis of the "official" Kerner Commission explanation of the causes of last decade's ghetto revolts with that of an assessment, which the Commission subsequently suppressed, prepared by a team of social scientists. Valuable, too, is Merton's discussion of Marx's use of data gathered by the British Royal Commissions, which serves as an important reminder that, whatever their failings, governmental commissions do produce enormous quantities of information that might not otherwise be available to students of society—information that inevitably contains nuggets that can be mined by societal critics.

The basic problem with the discussion papers has to do not with their organization of the case study findings, but instead with an unexamined assumption that underlies their recommendations concerning the relation between the sociologist and the policy maker. To put it somewhat baldly, the assumption is that the discipline and the profession are not *useful* enough to the policy maker. This concern is most clearly evidenced in Mack's analysis of the case studies, from which he derives three generalizations, one in the form of a question. He suggests (1) that Commission service is worthwhile for the discipline and the society, and (2) that social science findings and recommendations are usually ignored by the White House. He then asks (3) "if we believe the first generalization," why are we "such reluctant handmaidens to public policy-makers . . ." (p. 147). Perhaps, the reader guesses, because we believe the second generalization. However, Mack attributes the problem to a lack of organizational preparedness to respond to calls for public-policy service and to a generalized "theory-shyness" among sociologists. Similar concerns are voiced by all of the contributors to this volume.

It may be that the legal profession is better able to respond to policy challenges and that, as Lazarsfeld and Jaeckel propose, a greater emphasis on applied research ought to be included in the graduate training of sociologists. Yet surely sociologists are not so much theory shy as they are hesitant to define their theoretical and empirical work in explicitly policy relevant terms. And that may indeed have less to do with a failure of intellectual nerve, as Mack seems to imply, than with its opposite—fundamental unwillingness to allow officially defined "social problems" to predetermine *sociological* problems. The proper connection between the intellectual concerns of sociologists and the informational requirements of policy makers is of course not a new issue, but neither is it one with respect to which a high level of consensus has been achieved within the discipline. Hence what is ultimately disturbing about this book is its implicit premise that broad agreement has been reached concerning this most fundamental question of disciplinary and professional policy and that essentially all that remain to be debated are questions of organizational effectiveness.

Political

When Farmers Voted Red: The Gospel of Socialism in the Oklahoma Countryside, 1910–1924, by GARIN BURBANK. Westport, Conn.: Greenwood Press, 1976. 224 pp. $13.95 cloth.

ELLEN ROSEN
Vassar College

Burbank explores the cultural and ideological basis for the support of agrarian socialism in Oklahoma. He explains it as culturally rooted in the indigenous religious (Protestant, Fundamentalist, and evangelical) traditions of Oklahoma farmers and tenants who, presumably, were the scions of white upcountry southern hill-farmers. Although E.J. Hobsbawm is mentioned only tangentially it is clear that his "primitive rebel" thesis has informed Burbank's discussion.

In seeing Oklahoma socialism as "primitive" Burbank replies to the work of James Green (*Socialism and the Southwestern Class Struggle,* Ph.D. dissertation, Yale, 1972) who sees this movement as "class conscious" and "modern." Yet, while Burbank's carefully mustered evidence convinces me that Hobsbawm's conceptualization "fits" the case in Oklahoma, Burbank's reading of Hobsbawm appears itself to be "primitive"; he misrepresents Hobsbawm's concern.

Hobsbawm argues that some types of peasant insurgencies (millenarian movements) can be culturally and structurally absorbed or transformed by modern social movements. These movements, most likely led by urban intellectuals can help to bring pre-modern populations into the modern world. Of course any specific movement of this type usually embodies both primitive and modern elements. Yet Burbank fails to understand this. He translates Hobsbawm's primitive-modern distinction into one which is uni-dimensional and dichotomous. The question then becomes for him whether Oklahoma socialism was a manifestation of "real" proletarian socialism or only a "primitive" approximation. In Burbank's view of Oklahoma socialism as "primitive," the ideology and commitment of those involved is understood as only a thin veneer which was easily eroded by political repression, individualism, and the post-World War I prosperity.

Unlike Hobsbawm, who uses conceptions of "primitive" and "modern" specifically to refer to the *structure* of the movements themselves, (see Hobsbawm, *Primitive Rebels,* p. 93) Burbank searches for evidence which would clarify the *mentality* of the grass-roots Oklahoma socialists. Scratching the surface of official Party doctrine he finds an individualism and religiosity in the people which are incompatible with a more collectively oriented, scientific, and class-conscious socialism; this latter, more "real" version, he believes, is the one found among more modern, "rational" urban workers and intellectuals.

Finally, Burbank sees the religiosity as having transformed the socialism that the urban intellectuals brought to the rural hinterland. Yet, Burbank's evidence suggests the reverse just as well. The socialism brought to Oklahoma from the outside was successful there because it was able to build upon the religious millenarianism it found. Thus, the culture of religiosity not only transformed the socialism *but was itself transformed by it*.

The evidence that Burbank offers suggests that, of any cultural elements, it was the role of individualism which led to the demise of socialism. This element, rather than their religiosity or their lack of class consciousness, as Burbank shows very clearly, was the most salient problem for the socialist farmers and tenants in the Oklahoma movement. The Party's eventual failure therefore may have owed more to its constituents' familiarity with *modernity* than with the "primitive."

Perhaps the most significant contribution that Burbank makes is to thoroughly document the struggle Oklahoma socialists waged with individualism; not only the individualism of their opponents, but the individualism which they had themselves so deeply internalized. It is Burbank's confrontation with this dilemma which makes his book an important contribution, not only to the study of Oklahoma, but to the larger scholarly concern with the role of socialist ideology in American life.

The Twilight of Capitalism, by MICHAEL HARRINGTON. New York: Simon & Schuster, 1976. 446 pp. $10.95 cloth.

LLOYD DAVIS RAINES
ABT Associates
Cambridge, Massachusetts

Thought provoking yet terribly vexatious would be the terms used by many a befuddled scholar to describe Michael Harrington's new book. For this work could have and perhaps should have been two distinct books: one being a "scholarly rediscovery of Marx" and the other an "analysis of the twilight of welfare capitalism." By trying to achieve the stupendously difficult goal of linking these two important topics together in a way that is coherent and useful to both the intelligent general reader and the specialist, the author has attempted to do too much.

While serious scholars generally agree that the financial crisis, as well as the crisis of confidence, which is presently afflicting almost every capitalist nation of the Western World (though not all, as the author states), is not merely a matter of unpropitious exogenous circumstances—poor harvests, political turmoil, OPEC power and concomitant pricing policies—most of us would object rather strenuously indeed to the author's contention that this extraordinary situation "can be understood only in the light of themes developed by Karl Marx in *Das Kapital* and, above all, in its first chapter."

Many of us would concur with the author's assertion that the welfare state, which has effected profound modifications of the capitalist structure and is even potentially anti-capitalist, still follows the basic logic of privately owned profit maximizing corporations—in the last analysis. There is reason to suppose, however, that the socialization of the economy has bought a significant period of survival time for capitalistic economies. For example, after a traumatic but relatively short adjustment period, massive outflows of currency to buy OPEC oil have led to dramatic increases in OPEC investments in the industrial plant and pecuniary institutions of the advanced countries of Christendom, as well as mammouth new orders for goods and services, rather than to severe international currency instability and economic collapse with concomitant social tensions, as the author seems to infer. While it is true that the welfare state is a *transitional* phenomenon which probably portends the demise of capitalism, as suggested by the author and others, it matters a great deal just how long this transitional period is. There is a world of difference whether this transition era lingers for a mere three decades or for three centuries. Certainly, the inability to place a time parameter on this prediction of capitalism's destruction makes it a less interesting point and impossible to falsify.

From a British perspective, one finds the author's use of the terms "the future Marx" and "the new Marx" most perplexing indeed. Harrington, himself, quite correctly criticizes Althausser for making Marx a Cartesian thinker. Had the author discussed the brilliant work of Maurice Dobb, he would have been compelled to note the "Oxbridge" influence. In a similar manner, Harrington's *new Marx,* "rescued from a murky past" and developed from an "underground European tradition," is very much an *American* Marx. Leaving aside the question of why so few Europeans have any cognizance of this phantasmagoric tradition, one may still express delight that this new American Marx, no matter how he is derived, has so many desirable traits: he is scholarly, non-didactic, observant, idealistic, and most importantly optimistic. Certainly, there is little harm in conveying this vision of Marx; indeed, it may serve as a useful myth (in Sorel's sense), but it is not entirely accurate.

Although we must find much to admire in the author's attack on those who have utilized a deterministic Marxism to obfuscate reality in such manner that the status quo of Eastern European bureaucratic centralism (state capitalism) could be better defended *against* the working class, we think that the "open-endedness" which he purports to find at the very "core" of Marxism is just not there. As Thorstein Veblen sagaciously noted more than fifty years ago, the essence of Marxist political-economy was teleological. There were inexorable forces (inner necessities) mandating an eventual elevation of the consciousness of the proletariat, their organization as a political force desirous of overthrowing an oppressive and alienating capitalist mode of production, and ultimately their success in establishing a new government which would transcend capitalism and embark upon the journey to socialism and then communism. Despite some fragmentary evidence that Marx had his doubts about this process occurring in Asia and the United States, Harrington steadfastly maintains his faith. For him, Marxism, though not a doctrine, has become a morality and a methodology. We should not quarrel with this, however, since it is far better to have a coherent, systematic world-view (paradigm, if you prefer) which suggests salient questions and identifies important quandaries for future research than to adopt a workaday sophistic one stressing elegance and techique for their own sake, while implicitly supporting the status quo. Likewise, it is better to have an unwarranted faith in the working class than a virtually unmitigated contempt for it.

One suspects that Michael Harrington already knows that. For his gentle and intelligent criticism of Erich Fromm illustrates that he was not willing "to go the whole route" in accepting Marx merely as a brilliant Western humanist, noting that "it is dangerous to sentimentalize or overspiritualize Marx—though not as dangerous as turning him into a philosopher of totalitarianism." We concur with Harrington's comment about Fromm. In fact, we should like to apply Harrington's assessment of Fromm's work to *The Twilight of Capitalism*: "I deal, then, with an understandable, fruitful error."

Self-Governing Socialism: A Reader, Volumes 1 & 2, edited by Branko Horvat, Mihailo Marković, and Rudi Supek. White Plains, N.Y.: International Arts and Sciences Press, 1975. Volume 1: 490 pp., $21.50 cloth, $9.95 paper. Volume 2: 327 pp., $18.50 cloth, $8.95 paper.

Self-Management: Economic Liberation of Man: Selected Readings, edited by Jaroslav Vanek. Baltimore: Penguin Books, 1975. 479 pp. $5.95 paper.

George Fischer
Graduate Center/CUNY

Together, these two books go a long way to break down some antinomies we live by.

They serve to blur lines we like to draw—sharp lines that set off socialism from capitalism, economics from politics, Marxism from anarchism, communist countries from the West. And, not least, the left thought of the 1970s from that of the sixties.

Though they do not stress it, both books bring out a continuity with themes that came to the fore in the struggles of the 1960s. For not just these books but a great deal of thought and politics right now go back to a worldwide call of the mid-sixties: direct, participatory democracy. In this way, current themes link up with those of a time that seemed to have left no such seeds.

We can see this all the way from feminism to rank and file insurgency, from Self-Reliance to Appropriate Technology, from Community Development Corporations to Economic Democracy. And we can see it in these books.

Each book consists of selected readings plus long syntheses by its editor(s). High quality and utility mark both the selections and the editors' essays. The same goes for the translations into English by Assistant Editor Helen Kramer; they make *Self-Governing Socialism*, the longer and more historical of the two, much easier to read than most collections that reach us from the continent.

Two volumes make up *Self-Governing Socialism*. The first deals with historical development and then with social and political philosophy. The second volume starts with a section on sociology and politics, followed by one on economics.

The three editors of *Self-governing Socialism* live in Yugoslavia. All are well known Marxists of a humanist, anti-authoritarian type. Branko Horvat, an economist, put together the historical section of the book and a brief one on economics. (The editors refer readers to the other book for more economic material.) Mihailo Marković, former head of Belgrade University's institute of philosophy, gives us a long section in his field. The section on sociology and politics comes from Rudi Supek, heart and soul of the international journal of anti-authoritarian Marxism (*Praxis*) that Yugoslav officials closed of late.

The editor of *Self-Management,* Jaroslav Vanek, teaches at Cornell and writes widely on economic modes of participatory democracy.

In his introduction, Vanek treats self-management as conceivable under both capitalism and socialism. As long as a market economy and localized decisions show some strength, he looks to a wide range of self-management. The modes run from producer and consumer cooperatives to what Vanek calls worker-managed and labor-managed enterprises.

In a worker-managed system, "the income of any capital is basically assigned to the active participants and not to capital ownership which in Yugoslavia is taken to be social [community as against state] ownership." Labor-managed systems, on the other hand, "pay an economic or scarcity-reflecting remuneration for the use of capital to its owners, whoever they may be . . ." (p. 15).

I do not hold to Vanek's faith that self-management can grow in full under benign forms of capitalism as well as socialism. Yet he serves us well by his clear specifications, in this and other books, of just what it might take to shift control to producers under this or that economic arrangement.

The editors of *Self-governing Socialism* share Vanek's view that economic self-management lies close to the heart of any non-authoritarian social structure. This view runs through their readings (from some twenty countries in all three worlds) and their own syntheses. But here the likeness ends.

For Horvat, Marković, and Supek, socialism of a non-authoritarian Marxist kind stands as the one sure base for self-management. More than that, they part ways with Vanek in terms of the line drawn between politics and economics. To the editors of *Self-governing Socialism*, economic self-rule calls for no less of political self-rule. That is why they speak not of management but government. Full self-rule means to them the whole polity and not just the economy. It means nothing less than "the organization of society as a federation of workers' and citizens' councils . . ." (p. ix).

This split in views brings out an issue that runs as deep now as it has in the past. That is the issue of transition, from status quo to self-rule.

If participatory democracy must await the end of capitalism (or Soviet-type statism) and the coming of political self-rule, then how do we bring on the change? How do we get to non-authoritarian rule if not by Small Deeds, bit by bit struggles and shifts within a status quo? Be that status quo capitalist or communist, on the other hand, won't the ensuing reforms from the top down block self-governing socialism?

The Yugoslav editors come back to this issue more than once. The way they do that raised a problem in my mind. In the main they specify only the problems and possibilities inherent in a benign communism like Yugoslavia's. Other modes of transition and self-rule are touched on but not elaborated or specified.

For one, they seem to blur the line between communist countries and the West. They put stress on shared problems and possibilities. At the same time, all of them dwell on Marx as the holy of holies. They do not share the doubts anti-authoritarians in the West now raise on economic growth: above and beyond the need for an ecologically more sane world, must we now slow down growth so as to make room for conventionally less efficient self-rule from the ground up?

By the same token, the line between anarchism and Marxism gets blurred in *Self-governing Socialism*. It does so explicitly in the synthesis by one of the editors (Supek) and in a few selections (notably from Proudhon and Barcelona's CNT in 1936). In the book, too, Proudhon himself equates self-management with anarchism. The editors stop short of questioning that line still more.

The same problem comes to the fore when Horvat, Marković, and Supek deal with the over-all, macro structures of a self-governing socialism. They make clear that such self-rule calls for optimal direct participation all the way to the top, by means of anarchist-type federations. Once more, though, they tend to hark back to the benign communism of their native land.

Finally, neither of these books quite give up one more antinomy. Nor do most of us. I have in mind a sharp line that sets off politics and economics writ large from the personal ties and face to face acts that add up to daily life.

Here we see authoritarianism at work close to home. For daily life keeps up in us the ways of masters and servants. Next to great shifts and hopes, our age still breeds inequality, domination, and manipulation in all we do. It leads us to treat as a given, as part of Nature or Social Order, that we boss and get bossed day in and day out. To set off this side of life from society as a whole makes no sense, of course.

All I have said goes back to the sharp lines we draw and live by. Now, half way between the sixties and 1984, is a good time to put in doubt each of our old antinomies on self-rule. These fine collections will help us.

Social Control of the Welfare State, by MORRIS JANOWITZ. New York: Elsevier Scientific Publishing Company, 1976. 170 pp. $9.95 cloth.

GØSTA ESPING-ANDERSEN
University of Wisconsin, Madison

Liberal social theorists, inspired by Keynes, attached great hopes to the modern welfare state's ability to strengthen the capitalist economy, assure the provision of economic security to the working class, and thereby integrate the poor into society as social as well as political citizens. Today, the welfare state has become the center of conflict, not of social harmony. We have discovered the crisis of the welfare state; its contradictions are being exposed, and its ability to solve those problems it was developed to solve is questioned. The economics of the welfare state crisis have received most attention, and such conservative thinkers as Milton Friedman have with new ammunition argued that a large unproductive public sector is incompatible with political democracy: large welfare state spending absorbs the available surplus for economic growth and produces crises that cause a drift toward authoritarian regimes.

Janowitz addresses himself to the same problem from the perspective of a liberal sociologist (he labels himself a social democrat, but the ideological and theoretical links to the 2nd Internationale are unclear), and the book is therefore a valuable contribution toward a theory of the welfare state crisis. With Friedman, Janowitz shares the fear that the present format of the welfare state may lead to the ascendance of authoritarian politics; not because the state necessarily contradicts democracy, but mainly because the manner in which it has become institutionalized has created new problems of social control and self-regulation. His analysis does not suggest a return to the "night-watchman" state; instead, we should reform the way it performs.

The book should be commended for its attempt to establish, at the macro-sociological level, a theoretical connection between the legitimation problems of the modern welfare state and the issues of fiscal crisis, political instability, social inequality, and social control. Many recent sociologists employ the latter concept to denote imposed social conformity and acquiescence by those who command power. Janowitz wishes to restore it to its classical usage. Social control refers to the ability of a system, or an institution, to regulate itself and maintain stability. The problem with the welfare state in Janowitz's analysis is that it has lost this vital capacity. The book does not deal with the question of power and, in the context of a social control model, that seems problematic. The ways in which the state intervenes in society cannot be divorced from the ways in which power is exercized within the state, and also toward the state. In fact, it may be unrealistic to assume that social control is at all possible under conditions of unequal power.

The author seeks to explain the erosion of legitimacy and social control of the welfare state by setting forth a multi-stage causal argument. First, industrial development allows a sufficient surplus to be taxed for welfare. But, with the expansion of public welfare and service delivery, contradictory demands crystallize as claims for economic equity escalate. Such pressures stimulate budgetary problems and crises, politicize social needs, and since state intervention transforms the system of stratification, stable political coalitions tend to break up. The end product of this causal sequence, then, is the rise of unstable and fragmented political alliances. The political system fails to produce working majorities. Such instability can be viewed as an expression of declining social control.

The causal link between the welfare state and the decline of political stability seems to be the weakest part of the total argument. Janowitz presents data on trends in political participation and party strength for the United States and, as W.D. Burnham has previously demonstrated, there has been system decomposition over the past thirty years. While Janowitz wishes to establish a causal relationship or, minimally, a suggestive correlation, the evidence that is presented does not directly pertain to the hypothesized relationship. Indeed, the link between the welfare state and political instability may prove to be spurious. Instead, political instability may reflect a more deep-seated structural incapacity of anachronistic political institutions in dealing with the fundamental problems of contemporary capitalism.

Janowitz suggests that the welfare state generates claims for economic equity and contradictory demands which strain its capacity. Equity claims and contradictory demands are hardly new to capitalist societies, but the novelty of this analysis is that the stratification system which underlies such demands has become restructured by welfare state activities. It is not the worn out argument that workers are becoming bourgeois; rather, the welfare state adds new dimensions to the system of inequality and thereby cross-cuts and intersects established cleavages. Accordingly, traditional class based politics will give way to new, more volatile, patterns of political expression. Given the mode of participation institutionalized from the past, the system now loses capacity for social control. In the concluding chapter, Janowitz suggests that these problems may be remedied by instituting reforms aimed at securing more effective democratic participation around the welfare state. Here Janowitz is on firm social democratic terrain.

Considering the importance attached to the concept of social control, it is puzzling that it is not systematically analyzed. Instead, it gains the appearance of being pasted onto the argument presented in each chapter. The reader is, to some extent, forced to share Janowitz's assumption that social control is possible in the first place. It is interesting to observe once again, that despite policy differences, conservatives and liberals tend to start from the same underlying assumptions about society.

Friedman and Janowitz raise very important questions that touch upon the most central issues of contemporary capitalism. With such people as Claus Offe and J. O'Connor, a Marxist theory of the welfare state crisis is simultaneously emerging. Such a theory will tend to argue that it is but a symptomatic expression of the general capitalist crisis: the contradiction between the maintenance of social and political legitimation and the necessity of maintaining private capitalist accumulation. The modern welfare state illustrates the basic point that the state embodies the contradictions of the system, and may even intensify them. It does not create them.

Ethics and Profits: The Crisis of Confidence in American Business, by LEONARD SILK and DAVID VOGEL. New York: Simon & Schuster, 1976. 251 pp. $8.95 cloth.

MICHAEL USEEM
Boston University

The political and economic dislocations of the past decade have profoundly altered the political culture of all segments of American society, including the business elite. Corporate executives have become anxious and distressed by the government regulation and public hostility they increasingly encounter. Their political philosophy has come under challenge as well, and the resulting crisis is the subject of this volume by Leonard Silk, an economist and member of the New York *Times* editorial staff, and David Vogel, an academic political scientist.

In 1974–75 the Conference Board, a research organization founded by and serving the needs of large corporations, arranged eight meetings of top business executives for the sole purpose of allowing a candid exchange of views on the changing social and political role of American business. In groups of thirty-five to fifty-five, the executives informally discussed their concerns in three-day meetings, which Silk and Vogel had been invited to observe. *Ethics and Profits* is a summary and synthesis of the themes dominating these discussions. The executives are allowed to speak for themselves; the major motifs of their thought are identified and analyzed, but there is little effort by the authors to assess the validity or origins of the business philosophy they describe. Though the authors have necessarily been selective in the preparation of this volume, there is no reason to believe that *Ethics and Profits* is not an accurate rendering of what was expressed in these off-the-record sessions of peers. Access to these meetings provided Silk and Vogel with a rare research opportunity to observe the kind of business discussion that presumably transpires in executive offices, board rooms, and private clubs. It should be noted however, as the authors fail to make fully clear, that the 360 participants are not a cross-section of the business community; rather, they are nearly all chief executives of the nation's 1,000 largest industrials. Financial, insurance, and other sectors are poorly represented, as are the second echelon of corporate managers and other important functionaries, such as corporate lawyers.

Business legitimacy has suffered a precipitous decline over the past decade. The fraction of the public holding a great deal of confidence in the heads of large corporations has, according to Harris polling, plummeted from 55% to 15% between 1966 and 1975. Yet while the public has lost faith, Silk and Vogel report that the executives are as confident as ever in their own leadership and the private enterprise system. Indeed, the dictum that what is good for business is good for America remains an abiding principle. "We owe all good things in America to the free market," averred one conference participant, and virtually all agreed that the pursuit of corporate profits was synonymous with the achievement of national purpose. The belief that accumulating capital, at whatever temporary social costs, can only serve—and in fact best serves—the public interest is still a genuine article of faith in the business community, and it explains much of their reaction to contemporary conflicts. Were the identification of business and societal interests a cynical, self-serving rationalization, suggestions by business critics that public and private interests do not coincide would be understandable to corporate leaders. But since the classical free enterprise ideology is deeply and genuinely held, attacks on the profit motive are perceived as not only personally insulting but also as threatening the very institution that has made America prosperous and free. As a result, the business leaders have come to regard themselves as the trustees of capitalism and, ultimately, the final guardians of the American way of life.

It is hardly surprising, then, that the business elite has been bitterly antagonized in recent years by institutions that have circumscribed their prerogatives to maximize profits and that have even gone so far as to challenge the legitimacy of the free enterprise system. Business frustrations have been manifested in an intense antipathy toward these institutions, of which the federal government is perceived as the leading villain. Both elected and appointed officials are viewed with hostility which verges on contempt, and the perception of the electorate is hardly more flattering. International communism is no longer seen by the corporate chieftans as capitalism's prime threat; government intervention at home has become the real enemy.

Second only to the state as objects of business loathing are the institutions blamed for thwarting corporate efforts to "communicate" the merits of free enterprise to the public. Foremost among these institutions are the media and higher education. The media are condemned for creating an anti-business mood in the country (Watergate stories were partly viewed as spiteful smears of business), and the college and university system is attacked for mis-directing youth. ''Why do we continue to contribute money to institutions that graduate our foes?'' wondered one executive. Among the concrete counter-attacks suggested at the conferences were programs to provide financial rewards to schools which espouse the ideology of free enterprise and to underwrite seminars for instructing professors in the values of capitalism. Perhaps the most imaginative of the proposals was one suggesting that twenty of the executives band together to acquire a controlling interest in ABC so that ''at least one network will present a balanced viewpoint.'' Ironically, organized labor is identified as one of the few remaining friends of business; George Meany is the ''best ally we have,'' observed one executive in urging that capital and labor unite to ''protect the free enterprise system against everybody else.''

Predictably, the executives take an extremely dim view of reform movements. Conference participants ridiculed the idea of corporate ''social responsibility,'' attributing the concept to a figment of a sociologist's imagination, and virtually all major efforts to protect the environment, alter hiring practices, and democratize the work place were roundly condemned. More surprising, however, was the widespread distrust of the democratic system. While Silk and Vogel assert that few of the executives ''can fairly be regarded as 'fascist,' '' they nonetheless conclude that many of them ''wonder whether democracy and capitalism are compatible.'' Popular pressures are seen as responsible for the government's anti-business policies, and although the executives remain publicly committed to democratic norms, privately they express grave doubts about the viability of the present political arrangements. Enamored with the autocratic efficiency of their own organizations, they have nothing but contempt for the sluggish, irrational administration they see as inherent in a political system subject to the vagaries of public opinion. The evidence presented in *Ethics and Profits* thus suggests that a conventional sociological thesis should be inverted, for it is apparent that ''capitalist class authoritarianism'' has now reached massive proportions.

Though largely descriptive, *Ethics and Profits* does offer an occasional analytic assessment. Perhaps most provocative is the authors' contention that since the American business elite, unlike its European counterparts, has had to struggle against neither an entrenched aristocracy nor a socialist labor movement, little coherence and leadership have emerged in the American business community. Yet the increasingly forceful challenges of various business practices may now be generating such a unity (and the Conference Board meetings can be seen as one small step in that direction). Even academic social science has played a role in sharpening the contradictions now mobilizing the business elite to defend its collective interests. There is widespread concern among the executives, according to Silk and Vogel, about the ''leftward bias of economics professors,'' and one executive even suggested that ''nineteen out of the top twenty graduate departments of economics are hostile to free enterprise'' (Chicago, of course, was the twentieth). Sociological critics of business will be heartened to learn that ''the economists appeared to receive less blame for the miseducation of the young than 'social scientists,' especially sociologists.'' Whatever one's own view, *Ethics and Profits* is required reading for anybody with an interest in the political consciousness of the American business elite.

Race and Ethnic

Race and Ethnic Relations: Sociological Readings, edited by GORDON BOWKER and JOHN CARRIER. New York: Holmes & Meier Publishers, 1976. 400 pp. $18.00 cloth. $7.95 paper.

JOHN W. MARTIN
University of Illinois, Chicago Circle

This collection, edited by two English social scientists, continues what seems to be a trend toward a comparative structural approach to the study of race and ethnic relations and away from the more social psychologically oriented investigations of the attitudes and prejudices of dominant segments of ethnically and racially stratified societies.

''Thirty-five extracts, taken from both sides of the Atlantic, are organized around key issues—sociological perspectives, ethnic stratification, and institutional discrimination.'' Also included is an essay on race-relations theory prepared especially for this volume by Percy Cohen of the London School of Economics.

Cohen's incisive essay raises important questions concerning four alternative explanations of racial antagonism: (1) theories of stratification, (2) ideologies of race, (3) the psychology of racial consciousness, and (4) the importance of *racial* differences as such.

An important theoretical issue in the study of stratification is the relationship between class and race domination. Although some Marxist scholars and activists explain racial oppression entirely in terms of class, Cohen suggests that in many multi-racial class societies there is also something distinctively racial about the structure of social relations that is not reducible to class.

A similar issue—one that has been debated in the United States by Blauner and Glazer—turns on the question of whether or not there are any important differences between race relations and ethnic relations. Cohen's position is that race relations are, indeed, qualitatively different, but the drives they generate need not be more powerful nor more antagonistic than are drives that are based exclusively on cultural differences.

In part one the editors include selections that reflect three sociological perspectives: (1) order (e.g., Park, Myrdal), (2) conflict (e.g., Cox, Blauner), and (3) interaction (e.g., Schutz).

Ethnic stratification, the key issue in part two, includes selections on slavery, caste, race, and pluralism—four major types of ethnic stratification, according to the editors. Some of the familiar contributors to this section are Jordan, Genovese, Warner, Cox, Berreman, Banton, Drake and Clayton, and Glazer, and Moynihan.

The final section is on institutionalized discrimination, "that is, discrimination as part of the economic, political, legal and educational arrangements within a society" (p. 228). Among the contributors are Katznelson on the extension of the colonial tradition in the British response of West Indians, Kuper on apartheid in South Africa, and Liebow on the world of the black, lower-class male.

Teachers of race and ethnic courses, who are seeking a textbook with a comparative, structural approach, would do well to consider this book of readings.

Ethnicity, Denomination, and Inequality, by ANDREW M. GREELEY. Beverly Hills: Sage Publications, 1976. 85 pp. $3.00 paper.

DOROTHY WERTZ
Suffolk University

This monograph documents the rise of ethnic Catholics, now the most financially and educationally mobile group in America. Greeley's surprising statistics show that Irish Catholics have more education and higher family incomes than any other white gentile group; Italian Catholics rank second in income, but are the most upwardly mobile. Although Protestants of English background still rank highest in occupational prestige, proportionately more ethnic Catholics are entering graduate schools. Greeley attributes this astounding success, of which most Catholics are still unaware, to an "overthrust phenomenon" of achievement, and suggests that Eastern European Catholics will be next, perhaps followed by blacks and Spanish-speaking peoples.

The data were gathered from a composite sample of twelve National Opinion Research Center (NORC) surveys (N=17,770) between 1963 and 1974. The author is candid about potential shortcomings in method: Catholics were disproportionately represented in some surveys, although later computations allowed for this; some subgroups are very small (only fifty Episcopalians, for example, in cities over 2,000,000); none of the surveys asked for parental occupation, so parental education became the only measure of intergenerational mobility; there is no scale indicating the occupational achievements of ethnic women. Greeley states that census data or a current population probability sample of 25,000 or 50,000 would be better than his composite sample, but that responses from 18,000 people are far better than no data at all. He has tried to compensate for the skewed geographical distribution of Protestants (southern and rural) and Catholics (urban and northern) by making comparisons within metropolitan areas; he has also omitted blacks and Spanish-speaking peoples in the interests of clearer comparison.

Further research should be done in this hitherto neglected area. Meanwhile, Greeley's monograph should be read by every student of sociology of religion or stratification, especially by Catholics as yet unaware of their own group's success.

A Comprehensive Bibliography for the Study of American Minorities, 3 vols., by WAYNE CHARLES MILLER. New York: New York University Press, 1976. 1,380 pp. $85.00 cloth.

FRANCESCO CORDASCO
Montclair State College

The publication of Wayne Miller's bibliography is an auspicious event for American ethnic studies in a number of ways: it at once affirms the importance of the vast (if undisciplined and uncharted) resources which delineate the American ethnic experience, and the bibliography clearly establishes the legitimacy of ethnic studies in the academic community; if anything, what Professor Miller has done is to put academicians on guard against the neglect of ethnicity and the American minority communities, reaffirming that any study of the American experience which is guilty of such neglect distorts the reality out of which American identity evolves. And there is a patent irony in the fact that a Professor of English (University of Cincinnati) has placed all of his colleagues in the social/behavioral sciences (who should have undertaken the task) in his debt. The quality and high standards evident in the bibliography's conceptualization and design-implementation were augured by Miller's earlier *A Gathering of Ghetto Writers: Irish, Italian, Jewish, Black, Puerto Rican* in which he skillfully presented a sheaf of literary chronicles whose interrelationships he lucidly explained.

No bibliography exists which approaches the range and scope of Miller's volumes: neither Richard Kolm's *Bibliography of Ethnicity and Ethnic Groups,* nor Meyer Weinberg's *The Education of the Minority Child,* which is a specialized unannotated bibliography of 10,000 entries, is truly comparable; and if compendious bibliographies for many of the individual minority groups exist, Miller's achievement is even more remarkable in acknowledging his harnessing all of these multifarious sources, and his articulation of the materials into a single bibliographical resource, at once dimensional, and meaningfully useful.

The bibliography includes 29,300 entries, most of which are annotated. Groups have been arranged in a set of tableaux, i.e., *From Africa and the Middle East* (Blacks, Arabs); *From Europe* (French, German, Spanish/Portuguese, Irish, Italian, Jewish, Greek, Swedish, Norwegian, Danish, Icelandic, Finnish, Scandinavians as a group); *From Eastern Europe and the Balkans* (Slavic, Polish, Czech, Slovak, Yugoslav, Slovenian, Croatian, Serbian, Bulgaro-Macedonian, Ukrainian, Russian, Roumanian, Lithuanian, Latvian, Albanian, Hungarian); *From Asia* (Chinese, Japanese, Filipino, Asian/American); *From the Islands* (Puerto Ricans, Cubans); *Native Americans* (Indians, Mexicans), with a section on multigroup studies. For each group, entries are arranged into categories: bibliographies, guides, collections, periodicals; history (subdivided into periods); sociology; education; economics; politics; religion; biography/autobiography; literary history/criticism; fiction; poetry; drama; folklore; music/dance; and plastic arts. The entries are limited to English language materials. Preceding the entries for each of the groups is a historical-bibliographical essay, essentially an overview, and these essays have been gathered together and constitute the text of volume III which is entitled *A Handbook of American Minorities.* The main work (vols. I, II) is further enhanced by both an author index (209 pp.), and a title index (197 pp.).

Wayne Miller is keenly aware (see Miller's comments on the bibliography in *Melus,* III, Winter 1976, pp. 8–9) of the bibliography's limitations: the entries are almost totally English language materials; for some groups, extant sources are clearly inadequate; and for many other groups the bibliography is, at best, a guide to the work which remains undone; and, of course, the matter of supplements will have to be addressed. Yet, the work stands as a significant achievement, a bibliographical watershed whose influence in American ethnic socio-historiography will continue for years.

Urban Social Segregation, edited by CERI PEACH. New York: Longman, 1976. 443 pp. $20.00 cloth. $13.50 paper.

Variations in Black and White Perceptions of the Social Environment, edited by HARRY C. TRIANDIS. Urbana: University of Illinois Press, 1976. 202 pp. $15.00 cloth.

RICHARD S. STERNE
University of Akron

Triandis's studies attempted to "learn about the generalities of the ways of thinking found in the black ghetto . . ." in order to to teach whites to understand the ways of thinking of blacks, so that the two groups could get along better. Despite the efforts of Triandis and his co-authors to explain their methods for readers without statistical backgrounds, a large portion of the book is given to discussion of involved procedures, and exposition of semantic differential scales, which the average reader is not able to understand. Nor is it easy to determine exactly how the samples were drawn. The terms "hardcore" and "middle-class" white and black groups are used, but whether the samples are generalizable is not made explicit. On the other hand, the very complexity of technical material makes it valuable to individuals working on studies, and especially semantic differential scales.

The stated purpose of promoting understanding of blacks fails on strictly empirical bases. Some of the more effective statements made by the authors employ subjective interpretations, often using qualifiers such as "perhaps," "it would seem," and "may." The discussion of implications is good (e.g., 78f and 118ff), but interpretations are not necessarily drawn directly from the data—nor are they self-confirming.

There is an excellent bibliography; many of the references are to writings of the editor himself (who has worked extensively in the field) but readers must go to Triandis's own articles to get a wider bibliographic base, if they are depending on this book.

An interesting feature of the book is the inclusion of 128 microfiche tables. These contain material not necessarily discussed in the text, but usable for further analysis. Altogether, this volume is more successful as a technical treatise than as a popular explanation of "ecosystem distrust in the black ghetto."

Urban Social Segregation is an interesting collection of articles on social geography. Peach, a geographer, offers a volume for geographers and sociologists. It compares to Theodorson's reader on human ecology, but there is practically no duplication between them, and Peach has a different purpose. As stated in a useful introduction, he intends to study relationships between social distance and geographical space. A division of existing work, "spatial sociology," is suggested: human ecology, social area analysis, factorial ecology, and dissimilarity studies. Peach wishes to relate more to human ecologists and dissimilarists, and a specific argument for the use of the Duncan index of dissimilarities as opposed to the Gini index and others is provided in the introduction.

It is argued that analyses can proceed at three levels: macro and meso and micro, that is, going from the aggregate to the individual level. Peach hopes his volume will help span these levels.

Most of the articles are on "racial" or religious segregation and not so much on socioeconomic, age, or other differentials. A large portion of the material concerns the United States, but there is also the United Kingdom, including Australia and the West Indies. Many articles have appeared in journals inaccessible to American sociologists: Berry, published in England; Boal, from Belfast; Stimson, from Holland; Burnley, from Australia; and Rowland from New Zealand.

In general, the statistical techniques of "factorial ecologists" are not represented in this volume. The book however, is useful in the field that Peach intends to cover. The volume is recommended for library purchase, for sociologists and geographers and for general technical reference in inter-group relations.

Both Triandis and Peach have a normative orientation toward inter-group tensions. Triandis attacks the problem by studying the psychology of the individual and Peach by studying spatial locations. Between these two books, the reviewer feels that Peach's volume deals with the issue more effectively even if less directly.

Introduction to Black Sociology, by ROBERT STAPLES. New York: McGraw-Hill Book Company, 1976. 338 pp. $6.95 paper.

REYES RAMOS
University of California, San Diego

Staples's purpose in this book is to present and discuss something new: a black perspective as an alternative approach for the study of the black community. To illustrate the salient features of a black perspective, the author discusses several substantive areas such as race and racism, black culture and personality, institutions in the black community, black family, black religion, social class in black America, black crime and delinquency, majority groups, and social movements and social change.

The book is a disappointment since there is very little new in it. Staples rejects what he calls racist white sociology, and yet he bases his black perspective on the same theoretical and methodological principles which form the framework of the racist white sociology that Staples rejects. Since the theoretical framework of "white" and "black" sociology is the same, Staples states that the difference between the two must come from the attitude of the researcher. In doing sociology from a black perspective, researchers will be sensitized to seeing the black community in a positive fashion. How this sensitizing process is to happen is not made clear and Staples gives the impression that all we need to have is a positive attitude toward blacks. As he weaves this idea of the positive attitude throughout the book Staples makes a number of generalizations. He uses terms such as "white sociology" and "white sociologists" to define all of American sociology. In doing this he glosses over a great many things, including the qualitative differences between various sociological perspectives and between the proponents of different sociologies.

By locating his work in traditional sociology and by seeing black behavior as normative behavior, Staples provides a black perspective which is nothing more than a cultural determinist model, which in turn provides us with one more stereotype of the black community. The only difference between Staples's work and traditional sociology is that, in Staples case, the stereotype is a positive one. But, the fact still remains that we are told that blacks manage their everyday lives solely in terms of the social scientist's categories and not in terms of what the persons under study take into account and use in coping with their practical circumstances.

It is unfortunate that Staples did not provide us with a theoretical paradigm that has the potential for viewing behavior in ways other than those specified by a normative paradigm. In order to begin defining what he proposes as "black sociology," Staples needs to determine for himself just what he is rejecting and what he is accepting from "traditional" sociology; he might then look toward a new and perhaps more radical paradigm.

Sexual Racism: The Emotional Barrier to an Integrated Society, by CHARLES H. STEMBER. New York: Elsevier Scientific Publishing Company, 1976. 234 pp. $13.50 cloth.

PAUL D. STARR
Auburn University

This book is either profound or gravely mistaken; no scholar seeking to understand the roots of racial hostility or the nature of interracial sex or marriage will be able to avoid some of the hypotheses it contains. Although the title suggests a study of sexism/racism, the book is more precisely about the sexual dimension in race and ethnic relations, particularly those between black and white Americans. Stember's basic contention is that males of both the dominant and minority groups desire the females of the dominant group and that the dynamics surrounding this desire influence the character of intergroup relations in a society. In accordance with this view, the roots of white racism in America lie in the threat that white males feel regarding the possibility of sex between black males and white females. The evidence which the author presents is diverse and impressive but only rarely the result of systematic social research. This use of "soft data" as well as modern fiction to illuminate his points is impressive. Aside from the imaginative work of Gary I. Schulman, social scientists have rarely examined the sexual threat hypothesis among blacks and whites in spite of the significance many have attributed to it in other circles. Sociologists have consistently either minimized the role of sex in social life or employed rather simplistic Freudian models.

Although many readers will find Stember's conclusions insulting, electrifying, or at least controversial, he has done an important service by boldly sticking his neck out and directly confronting an issue of fundamental importance. I hope the strongest reaction will come from hard-nosed researchers who will use their skills to put Stember's hypotheses to the test.

Sex Roles and Behavior

Women Alone: The Disaffiliation of Urban Females, by HOWARD M. BAHR and GERALD R. GARRETT. Lexington, Mass.: Lexington Books, 1976. 206 pp. $17.00 cloth.

HELENA ZNANIECKI LOPATA
Loyola University of Chicago

This volume contains a wealth of information about currently unmarried, poor, older women living in selected areas of New York City. This information has not, however, been digested into a book. The research took place in four areas, selected to meet different criteria and referred to throughout as Tract 56, Tract 76, Tract 159, and Women's Shelter. Tracts 56 and 76 were selected initially because they contain a "low median number of persons in occupied dwelling units, low median income of families and unrelated individuals, and high median age of females" (p. 5). These areas did not produce a sufficiently large sample, so a third tract, characterized by "a large population, a high median age, an overrepresentation of females, and a substantial number of poor people," was added. The tracts vary in the proportion of respondents living in one room units (from 97% to 25%) with cooking facilities (from 41% to 96%) as well as in other socioeconomic and neighborhood features. The Emergency Assistance Women's Shelter is located in lower Manhattan and its temporary residents most resemble the homeless men studied previously by the team involved in the Columbia Bowery Project. The interview schedule administered to all of the 383 women is based, with modifications, on the men's study and includes scales of anomie, misanthropy (faith in people), powerlessness, self-esteem, and self-estrangement. Much additional data were collected on the background and current affiliations of the women. Comparisons across tracts (there must be a better way of identifying people than by the census tract they live in!!!!), and with the Shelter women and the men often provide illuminating glimpses, although the reader feels uncomfortable over the scientific comparability of these groups.

The authors are right in stating that disaffiliated women have not been studied directly in the past. An additional reason to those they listed for their invisibility to our society (and to its sociologists) is still the interest in women mainly as potential or present mothers of small children and wives of occupationally active men. The definition of the population of women from which they drew is also biased in that it contains the assumption that non-married women are automatically disaffiliated because they do not have a husband, although the study actually focused on women who are disaffiliated or "unjoined" in many ways. Even the disclaimer "We would not assert that all single women, widows, or women divorcees are disaffiliated" is followed by a "But. . . ."

What the study needs is another volume, fleshing out the forms of affiliation of all urbanites, as well as a more complete, digested picture of these particular women. Such a volume must pull together the different scales and forms of analyses in a meaningful and integrated way. This work contains only 137 pages of text, followed by four unintegrated appendices. Presentations of distributions on complex scales or factors are set alongside abbreviated and choppy descriptions of people or areas. The method of presentation frustrates a reader who is interested in this type of woman. The disjointment can be exemplified by the fact that the same aspect of one of the charts is described in a similar way twice on two successive pages (pp. 72 and 73). There is no mention of race as a variable except in the more detailed descriptions of the Shelter women. We then find out (in chapter 6) that 44% of the Shelter women, who are younger and the most disaffiliated, are black, but there is no discussion of the significance or implications of this fact. It is also difficult to understand the assignment of these two women, describing their activities the previous day, to the same level of disaffiliation:

> (After morning grocery shopping) I go back to bed just to waste time because there is nothing else to do . . . I go to bed early because I can't read or watch TV and get bored (Age 69). Went to a matinee with a relative; met another friend for dinner . . . went to another friend's home and played cards for the evening (Age 68) (p. 37).

In addition, it is worrisome to find so much reliance for judgments of past social integration placed on childhood memories, elicited by questions such as "How often did your parents attend religious services?" "Were they active in any organizations?"

The saddest commentary on how quantitative sociology can reduce human beings into unrotated or rotated loadings on factors is that the authors had to turn to novelists for pictures of "reactions to disaffiliation among aged women" (Appendix D), in spite of the richness of the data they themselves collected. As yet, is it fair to fault these authors for not being able to reconstruct the women, boxed into census tracts, from the statistical distributions of answers to narrow questions? How many of us have been able to accomplish that with any depth? Maybe it is a good thing that William Proxmire and Jack Anderson are helping to reduce our opportunities for survey research, forcing us to increase our resourcefulness in using other methods for understanding human beings and their interrelations. In the meantime, this book should be read, in spite of its problems. It contains much data on a human condition we as sociologists need to know more about.

What Are Little Girls Made Of? The Roots of Feminine Stereotypes, by ELENA GIANINI BELOTTI. New York: Schocken Books, 1976. 158 pp. $7.95 cloth.

KAREN M. JENNISON
University of Northern Colorado

Given the increased sociological concern with sex-role socialization, this book is of interest in that it attempts to describe the Italian version. The process of learning sex roles, considered similar to that in other Western nations, is examined from before birth when parents exhibit preferences for male offspring to the child's experience of nursery school. Primary and secondary educational institutions are very briefly reviewed.

Of interest is her discussion of how children in nursery school learn sex-appropriate behavior under the unaware eyes of their female teachers as well as to the material on children's games, toys, and literature. Unfortunately, Belotti bases her assertions about socialization differences on unsystematic observation. For instance, her explanation of sex-role stereotyping in children's literature contains numerous examples but no systematic content analysis. Similarly, observations were done in nursery schools but there is no indication of their extent and nature.

Some parts of the book emphasize the differences between Italian and American culture. For example, Italian mothers typically want a daughter to nurse quickly and be weaned early, in marked contrast to her indulgence of a son. Differences between males and females noted by teachers may be more extreme than would be the case in this country, although they are of the same type.

On the whole, the tone of the book is not scholarly; at some points, it is strident in emphasizing all the ways in which females are discriminated against. Thus, other than for developing ideas to be researched, its use to sociologists is probably limited. However, it would be quite valuable in raising the consciousness of those who are or will be teaching young children.

The Proper Sphere: Woman's Place in Canadian Society, edited by RAMSAY COOK and WENDY MITCHINSON. Toronto: Oxford University Press, 1976. 334 pp. $6.75 paper.

SUSAN MANN TROFIMENKOFF
University of Ottawa

Books of documents are hard to read and harder to evaluate. By rights they should be taken in small doses only, savored of an evening or scrutinized in a seminar. Only then can one appreciate their full flavor or test their representativeness. This book, the first of its kind in Canadian history, offers a sampling of women's "views and activities [largely 1870–1920] in a number of realms"—law, education, work, organizations, morality, and the suffrage—all introduced and suffused by varying notions of "the proper sphere" of women. The editors encompass their female spokespersons in male opposition: men define the proper sphere at the beginning and men delineate the limits of women's public behavior at the end. The middle is designed to show the how and why of women moving into the public domain. The pattern is promising, the selections sparkling, the lasting impression—unintended I suspect—somewhat disconcerting.

For what this book documents is not in fact what it claims to do: the tale of women moving out of the home and knocking down the educational and legal barriers to their equal participation in Canadian society. That aspect is of course there and students will be delighted to encounter some of the "firsts" in Canadian women's history. But what emerges from this collection is something hinted at in Kraditor's political study and in Naomi Griffith's reflective essay *Penelope's Web*: the path has not always been upwards in the tale of women's emancipation. Through these documents one can spot a peculiar trend: women were preparing to fly in the 1870s and 1880s and early 1890s. But then something happened. They turned upon themselves, clipped their own wings and began arguing for domesticity as a science. They did not thereby relinquish their claims upon the public domain; they merely argued that their domestic capabilities, their feminine qualities, their moral superiority could and should exercise some cleansing power in that domain. The turning point seems to come sometime in the late 1890s. Thereafter only one voice—that of a man no less—echoed the earlier protest against the artificial barriers placed in the way of women undertaking anything for which they had taste or talent.

And so there are many intriguing questions which the documents suggest. Why the change of heart? How many women did these grave public questions touch? What impact did these pamphleteers and publicists have? How in fact did these outspoken women live? And in what way were their lives reflections of the experiences of other women in Canadian society? A lot of digging therefore remains to be done before we have even an adequate context in which to place these documents.

In short, this book constitutes a rich and provocative collection. Women's studies courses throughout the Western world will want to use it for comparative purposes. If non-Canadian students find nothing very different in the listing and challenging of forty-two objections to woman suffrage, they will certainly be startled by one surely typically Canadian objection to higher education for women: female students would have difficulty clambering over the snowbanks on their way to class!

Dilemmas of Masculinity: A Study of College Youth, by MIRRA KOMAROVSKY. New York: W. W. Norton, 1976. 274 pp. $9.95 cloth.

KRISTIN LUKER
University of California, San Diego

Dilemmas of Masculinity, like its predecessor, *Blue Collar Marriage,* seems destined to be a classic in the field. Addressing herself to the reality that "few would deny that gender roles today reflect massive institutional and cultural disorganization . . .," Komarovsky critically assesses most of the current crop of books on "men's liberation" as being assertions that men "reap dubious rewards for the alleged advantages of masculinity superiority," or are pleas for liberation from the more restrictive aspects of the traditional male role (p. 2). That the path of men toward "liberation" is infinitely more complex than a simple escape from the traditional male role is what this book is about.

As was the case in *Blue Collar Marriage,* this is a small, insightful study which unfolds in unexpected directions the more you think about it. It is not, alas, the definitive work on men faced with the "new woman" or a new and sometimes contradictory social order. The sample consists of sixty-two men who are college seniors at an eastern university. They tend to represent the class distribution of college students, although the sample was stratified in terms of race, religion, and education of father. Still another problem in generalizing these data is that they were gathered in 1969–70, when the women's movement was just beginning and before backlash movements of any significance had appeared on the scene.

However, the methodology that the author uses—a case study approach with repeated intensive, open-ended, semi-structured interviews—is one which lets the men in this study speak for themselves. And therein lies the beauty of it. Komarovsky, as we know from her previous work, is a skilled and often critical interviewer. Thus when men in the present study tell her that they approve of mothers with pre-school children working, she also elicits the doubts, hesitations, and reservations surrounding this opinion which (in her words) "virtually nullify it."

The picture of the "dilemmas of masculinity" which emerges from this study is an intriguing one. Perhaps as a product of the time in which the data were gathered, Komarovsky's respondents are neatly torn between an expressed, verbal, ideological commitment to women's liberation (a commitment they genuinely feel), and the entailing sacrifices of carrying through such a commitment. These men have serious problems integrating their ideals with their reality, but the most interesting part of the study is the extent to which these men are unaware of the gap between the two.

These men are caught in a cultural double bind. They ideologically support equality for women, although it is interesting to note that the few sex role traditionalists in this study scored lower on Well-being and Intellectual Efficiency in the California Psychological Inventory. They want an equal, but an equal who will never threaten them or have divergent or contradictory needs. An equal, in short, who is always willing to subordinate herself. But the double bind occurs because once a woman subordinates herself she is no longer by definition an equal, and (to use a variation of an old line) the man loses respect for her. The most striking example of this double bind in *Dilemmas of Masculinity* are the men who confidently expect that their future wives will be intellectual and professional equals, women who have jobs that are challenging and creative. (Although several men specified that they wouldn't want a wife or a lover to be in the *same* career or profession.) It is also confidently assumed that these same women will cheerfully leave their jobs and careers upon the birth of the first child and stay off the labor market until the youngest child is in school.

The men in this study seem to have no inkling that leaving the labor market for several years can have high professional costs, and that the women most likely to have exciting and creative jobs (an aspect which enhances their stature in male eyes) are also probably the least likely to enthusiastically put such jobs and careers aside, especially in an era of high inflation and high divorce. Someone is in for a rude shock.

Implicit within *Dilemmas of Masculinity* are some clues for the future of relationships between men and women, as well as the future of marriage and the family. To the extent that men in this study have mutually exclusive expectations, women are going to face contradictory pressures in relationships where they are damned if they do and damned if they don't. To the extent that men don't see any conflict between their needs for an equal defined in achievement terms and their needs for a traditional wife and mother, some education about structural realities seems in order. Sociologists and feminists alike need to think about the dilemmas Komarovsky presents in this book, and to clarify and examine the social and structural implications of this set of male dilemmas. Otherwise, these are dilemmas in which there are doomed to be no winners.

Sex Differences: Social and Biological Perspectives, edited by MICHAEL S. TEITELBAUM. Garden City, N.Y.: Anchor Books, 1976. 232 pp. $2.95 paper.

JANET SALTZMAN CHAFETZ
University of Houston

This book consists of an introduction by the editor and five chapters, each representing a review of the research relevant to sex differences (and similarities) in a different field of study. Data from biology, animal ethology, anthropology, sociology, and the history of science are presented. The theme which pervades each chapter is the interactive nature of biological, environmental, and socio-cultural variables for explaining gender-related characteristics among human beings. A secondary theme stresses the tremendous variance within sex, hence the large overlap between sexes, on virtually every behavioral, psychological, and intellectual attribute.

The various contributions are of uniformly high quality. They are written well and avoid highly technical language which only those in the particular discipline would understand. Indeed, if one did not know that each chapter was separately written, one would think that the book was authored by one person, so consistent is the writing style and so integrated are the contents. While I, as a sociologist, can scarcely judge the accuracy of the chapters written by a biologist or animal ethologist, I was struck by the balanced approach taken by all of the authors. They avoid facile generalizations and analogies and go to great lengths to point out inconsistent findings and gaps in our knowledge.

The chapter on biological perspectives presents little material with which the sociologist of sex roles is likely to be unfamiliar. In effect, it covers the same content as Money and Ehrhardt (*Man and Woman, Boy and Girl*), but the chapter is a highly concise statement of the relevant research. The chapter on social influences is likely to be the least useful for sociologists since it represents an equally concise summary of our field of specialty. The remaining chapters should, however, provide considerable insight and data to student and professional alike, in fields about which most sociologists are comparatively ignorant.

I believe this book is very important for all sociologists (and students) interested in the study of gender roles. It presents the newly emerging perspective of bio-sociology, namely, the need to move beyond the old nature *versus* nurture controversy by examining the interaction of nature *and* nurture. The authors appear to be feminist in their orientation, yet the articles are refreshingly free of rhetoric. In presenting so many different approaches in a scholarly yet readable and succinct fashion, it stands virtually alone among available books. My judgment of this book is best expressed by the fact that, after reading only the first three chapters, I had already decided to adopt it as required reading in my course on the sociology of sex roles.

The Social Psychology of Sex, edited by JACQUELINE P. WISEMAN. New York: Harper & Row, 1976. 406 pp. $7.50 paper.

JETSE SPREY
Case Western Reserve University

Human sexuality means many things to many people, including social scientists. The current book market contains a wide choice of monographs and readers on the topic, each, in its own way reflecting the special interests of its authors or editors. The reader under review here is no exception, it approaches the understanding of human sexual conduct within a clearly stated theoretical perspective. This is a plus, since it prevents confusion. Its focus is social psychological, and more specifically is in the symbolic interactionist tradition. This should be noted, because so far a self-conscious attempt to deal with sexual relationships in such a context is lacking.

The editor, Jacqueline Wiseman, justifies the choice of a symbolic interactionist approach by pointing at its dual social psychological and sociological nature, and the structure of her book indeed reflects this double coverage. After a brief introductory chapter, presenting the conceptual scheme, the bulk of the book is structured into six major chapters. Each of these focuses on one specific realm of sexual interaction. For the purpose of this review it seems appropriate to briefly identify each chapter and direct further specific comments toward the general structure and contribution of this reader.

The first chapter deals with the ways in which sexual relationships are originated and negotiated in our contemporary society. This realm of interaction does lend itself quite well to a social-psychological analysis, and the various individual papers in this section bring this out. Sexual exchange and negotiation are phenomena we know very little about and the contributions in this chapter, each in their own way, furnish insight, and a basis for further questioning. Unfortunately, this analytical focus on the mutually bargained for aspects of sexual exchanges does evaporate as a guiding theme throughout the remainder of the book. We are confronted, respectively, with a discussion of the variety of sexual relationships, a rather polemical treatment of the erotic aspects of sexuality, followed by a chapter on the interconnectedness—or lack of it—between the phenomena of sex and love. The final two chapters deal with sexual stratification, and the implications of the so-called "sexual revolution" in our society.

Social science readers are difficult to review, and this one is no exception. As a result of the amorphous nature of its subject-matter the quality of its individual contributions ranges considerably. Several of the papers that make up the chapter on sexual pleasure seem trivial and of questionable validity. The same can be said about some of the more polemical attacks on our hypothetical system of "sexual stratification" in the fifth chapter. On the other hand, a reader of this nature needs papers of this kind if it at all wishes to convey the contradictions, confrontations, and paradoxes that characterize the real socio-cultural context within which contemporary individuals experience their sexual relationships. It is to the credit of the editor that the triviality and one-sidedness that characterizes some of its contributions indeed can be seen as simply representative of our current social scene.

The reader as a whole, therefore, is far from irrelevant. It presents us with a meaningful conceptual approach toward the understanding of current patterns of sexual interaction. Some of its chapters, especially the first one, present original and provocative insights, others are more conventional in their coverage. None are out of place, however, in this well-designed book.

Social Problems

Social Problems, by AMITAI ETZIONI. Englewood Cliffs, N.J.: Prentice-Hall, 1976. 182 pp. $7.50 cloth. $3.50 paper.

Social Problems in American Society, 2nd ed., edited by JAMES M. HENSLIN and LARRY T. REYNOLDS. Boston: Holbrook Press, 1976. 381 pp. $7.95 paper.

Analyzing Social Problems, by JEROME G. MANIS. New York: Praeger Publishers, 1976. 194 pp. $3.95 paper.

Sociology and Social Problems: A Conceptual Approach, edited by JON M. SHEPARD and CYRUS S. STEWART. Englewood Cliffs, N. J.: Prentice-Hall, 1976. 301 pp. $6.95 paper.

Passion, Action, and Politics: A Perspective on Social Problems and Social-Problem Solving, by IRVING TALLMAN. San Francisco: W. H. Freeman & Company, 1976. 299 pp. $11.95 cloth. $5.95 paper.

ARMAND L. MAUSS
Washington State University

Those who have been following the publication of books and articles about social problems will be aware of the sustained emergence in recent years (or re-emergence) of a theoretical perspective that is variously called "subjectivist," "interactionist," or "collective behavior" in nature. Akin to the "labeling perspective" in deviance theory, this emerging perspective holds that social problems have their origins *not* in "objective" social conditions, but rather in a political process through which powerful interest groups and/or segments of the public determine what issues shall be placed on the "national agenda" and duly labeled "social problems." Of course, many theorists recognize a greater or lesser role for public opinion and political activity in the definition and genesis of social problems, but it makes a great deal of difference whether one takes the position (on the one hand) that social problems are "objective" realities which *generate* collective behavior and political action, or (on the other hand) the position that social problems are essentially *generated* by collective behavior and political processes. The former position we might call "objectivist," and the latter "subjectivist." If we visualize these as conceptual poles to a continuum, then the present books would arrange themselves with the Henslin & Reynolds reader at the "objectivist" extreme, the Tallman treatise at the "subjectivist" one, and the others in between, but clearly closer to the former than to the latter.

The real masterpiece of this group of books, in my opinion, is Irving Tallman's, and it is a shame, in a way, that it is not getting a separate review in *CS*, for it is a class apart, both in its scholarship and in its innovativeness. (Those who know of my own book on social problems will recognize that I share Tallman's theoretical perspective almost totally, so this bias of mine should be taken into account here.) The great theoretical accomplishment of this book is that it succeeds in taking due account of "objective" realities, such as social structure, while still essentially spinning a "subjectivist" theory. This is *not* done, however, by the ritual nod in both directions; i.e., by noting that "of course" both objective and subjective realities must be taken into account. Rather, Tallman takes a clear and uncompromising subjectivist position and then goes on to explain thoroughly how social structure and the socialization process *create differential perceptions* about what shall be labeled "social problems." This is quite different from the "objectivist" stance, which holds that social structure (among other realities) *creates the problem conditions per se*. Tallman offers us an innovative synthesis of social structural and social psychological theory in explaining a genesis and etiology of social problems that takes place essentially *independent of* any putatively problematic condition in society. At the same time, however, this is somewhat different from the "collective behavior" approach used by other "subjectivist" theorists like Blumer, Kitsuse and Spector, or myself.

Tallman begins with the "central assumption . . . that social problems are not created by societal conditions but by the perceptions and actions of men and women responding to such conditions" (p. 4). "A social problem, then, is a social condition that has been *politicized*" (p. 18 my emphasis). It would be an oversimplification, but an essentially accurate one, to say that the book then is a study of why and how some societal conditions get politicized. The theory might be conceived in terms of an "etiological chain" (my conception, not Tallman's), in which we begin with social structural realities like the differential distribution of wealth and power, link to these a variety of social psychological conditions like identity-formation, self-esteem, and moral development, and mediate all this through differential socialization in which the family, in particular, has a central function; this differential "mix" of social structural and social psychological variables produces, of course, differential perceptions in different segments of the population about what constitutes a "social problem," and what ought to be done about it. These differential perceptions lead, in turn, to differential levels of "passion" (emotional commitment), of political action, and of problem-solving efforts. The outcome of problem-solving efforts, as often as not, is the genesis of new "social problems." In the process of laying out this developmental model, Tallman is able to explain the parts played by factors so often overlooked in other theories of social problems, such as relative deprivation, distributive justice, differential perceptions and expectations, the disproportionate involvement of the middle- and upper-middle classes in generating social problems, the special proclivity of open, democratic societies for generating social problems, the marshalling and application of political power, and differential problem-solving training in the family setting. While eschewing a "natural history" notion as such, Tallman does see a general rise-and-fall pattern in the careers of most social problems, including stages that can be characterized roughly as "beginning," "growth," and "decline."

In its nine chapters, the book ranges over an enormous body of literature, from Asch to Terkel, and weaves judicious selections and references from all of them into a single, well-reasoned, and strongly supported synthesis. The first two chapters are of an introductory nature, in which Tallman reviews earlier social problems literature and then sets forth the outline of his own theory. The second part of the book (chapters 3, 4, and 5) lays out the important social structural and social psychological factors in the theory; and the third part (chapters 6, 7, and 8) deals mainly with processes (socialization, politics, and problem-solving). The last chapter is an epilogue. The book is obviously too complex and sophisticated for the standard lower-division class in social problems, and it makes no attempt to "survey" the usual substantive problems. It would be a valuable resource in several kinds of graduate courses, and would go well also in advanced and/or able upper-division classes.

My criticisms of this book have to do mainly with certain emphases and lapses that I see in it. While the book attempts to offer us a truly generalizable theory of social problems, its emphasis, amounting indeed to a preoccupation, is upon those problems in which *injustice* or *inequality* of some kind is implicated. On page 197, he even says that "perceived injustices" are a "necessary condition for the development of social problems." Most of his illustrations and references about specific social problems throughout the book show a decided emphasis upon racial injustices, poverty, and the like. While the theory clearly is applicable to such other problems as sexual "deviations," pornography, environment, and even crime and delinquency, these receive little attention in the narrative. Also, while the book is in large part concerned with political processes, it seems in places to overemphasize the importance of *popular* opinion compared to political pressure groups (including those from within government) that may be very effective without any popular support. Governments, and pressure groups closely associated with them, in other words, are quite capable of generating and initiating "social problems" on their own, with seventeenth century witchcraft being only the most extreme example. Of course, Tallman knows that, but it was not as clear to me as it might have been. Another criticism is also a matter of emphasis: in discussing the "decline" of social problems, Tallman deals mostly with their "solution," and how the latter tends to generate new problems and start the "cycle" over again. Insufficient attention, for my taste, was given to the tendency (probably the most common one) which social problems have, *not* for getting "solved," or even ameliorated, but for simply "petering out" and leaving the "objective conditions" unchanged (or worse).

While assuming a posture in this book that is essentially detached, scholarly, and relativistic, Tallman does occasionally lapse into comments that show his own deep feelings about the kinds of "objective conditions" that bother him most, namely poverty and discrimination, and that suggest a certain compromise of an essentially "subjectivist" viewpoint. When he comments, for example, on the "general squalor" and "frustration bordering on futility" of the urban poor, or on how "our society degrades many of its members" (pp. 52, 53, 55, et passim), he seems to me to be lapsing into a partisanship which, however understandable, is not faithful to the main thrust of his theoretical perspective.

The Manis book (which has a foreword by Arthur J. Vidich) is a carefully reasoned theoretical essay on social problems and contains no chapters or sections on any *particular* social problem. It is thus clearly not intended for use as an undergraduate textbook. In his preface, the author tells us that he has written this book out of a concern over our customary ways of looking at social problems, and that he is proposing changes in our ways of identifying, assessing, and resolving social problems. Those proposed changes then become the topics for the main chapters of the book, following two introductory chapters. There are five chapters altogether. In his beginning chapters, the author first reviews the various theoretical perspectives in the literature on social problems, elevating these, curiously, to the status of "paradigms" in Kuhn's terms. Thus we have the social pathology paradigm, the social disorganization paradigm, and so forth, down to the public opinion paradigm. He is critical of all these paradigms, particularly the last, and it is clear that he has little patience for those who think that social problems are "merely" whatever people say they are. In his hasty dismissal of "subjectivist" (or, in his terms, public opinion) paradigms, the author seems actually to be criticizing *popular* opinion, and he seems irritated that we can allow it to get us off the track, as it were, so that our attention is diverted to such "spurious" social problems as long hair. In such a contention, Manis seems to me to be greatly exaggerating the national preoccupation with long hair and to be largely unaware of the important *political* processes implied in the social scientist's usual use of the term "public opinion." In any case, Manis assures us, social problems *are* "objectively" real: they are "those social conditions identified by scientific inquiry and values as detrimental to human well-being" (p. 25). This scientific inquiry is ideally free or neutral of values in the ideological sense, but it is committed to the "knowledge values" of science. These Manis identifies especially as "intrinsic values" (the rules of seeking and accumulating knowledge, such as empiricism); "contextual values" (societal conditions conducive to the quest for knowledge, such as freedom of inquiry); and "social responsibility," including "meliorism." Guided by these values, says Manis, *real* social problems, as opposed to "spurious" ones, can be identified, assessed, and solved or prevented. This is an appealing thesis, of course, especially to social scientists, and he develops it in great detail. It is a truly valiant effort at a viable and useful scientific definition from an "objectivist" theoretical viewpoint, and I regret that there is not space here to do it justice. Nevertheless, the book and its thesis does not quite "come off," in my opinion, because whenever the author moves his level of discourse from the abstract down to the concrete, he betrays value commitments that turn out, after all, to be subjective and ideological, rather than the "scientific" ones that he thinks they are. For example, on pages 88 and 89, he distinguishes "demonstrable" social problems from other kinds on the basis of what is "detrimental to human well-being." Just what this phrase means, beyond simple physical survival, is not too clear, though the author continually refers us to what "factual knowledge" indicates. In all this, he seems totally unaware of competing definitions of "human well-being" that have nothing to do with physical survival or health, nor even anything to do with facts or scientific values per se. In thus insisting on distinguishing "spurious" from "real" social problems, no matter on how firm a "scientific" or "factual" basis, the author is, in my opinion, stressing a distinction without a difference, as far as *consequences* are concerned. (W. I. Thomas still lives!)

Now we turn to the Etzioni book, which resembles Manis's in its uncomplicated faith that both the identification and the amelioration of social problems will yield to a systematic, scientific process of rational research and action. This book too (as part of the Prentice-Hall "Foundations" series) is a treatise for advanced students and professionals, rather than an undergraduate textbook. Though it gets into such specific social problems as alcoholism, urban renewal, health, farmworkers, and civil rights, it does so only by way of *illustrating* basic parts of the book's framework. After an introductory chapter criticizing other perspectives on social problems, the author then sets forth, in the second chapter, his "societal guidance" approach to social problems. The remaining five chapters and postscript dissect and elaborate this approach under the headings "knowledge," "goal-setting," organization," "power," and "consensus."

The distinctive character of *social* problems, for Etzioni, in contrast to other kinds of problems, is that people are expected (collectively) to do something about them. Thus, natural disasters are not social problems, because nothing can be done about them through collective societal action, but both poverty *and* cancer *are* social problems, because both will yield to the right kind of societal response. Etzioni prefers the term "societal guidance" for this response, rather than "social control" or "social management," which have somewhat less satisfactory connotations for his purposes. The need and the motivation for societies to apply "guidance" to the solution of some of their collective problems comes from certain "givens" about human nature, societal reality, and societal dynamics. These "givens" are basically of a Maslovian kind, as far as human nature is concerned, and they include important symbolic, as well as objective, elements as part of the societal reality. Where the third area (societal dynamics) is concerned, Etzioni bases his conceptualization on a cybernetic model of the operation of society, with a capacity to "read" the world, digest the information, and feed it into the decision-making process. His overall image or metaphor of society is an underpowered ocean liner. Every society has what he calls a "core project" (or principal collective goal) that charts the course of the "ocean liner." He advocates that *our* "core project" will have to be changed from the pursuit of material affluence to improvements in self-awareness and interpersonal relations. In any case, the "societal guidance" approach to social problems involves choosing the "right" core project, attending to the "givens" or imperatives in human nature and in society, and doing all that through a process which consists of (1) acquiring knowledge; (2) developing strategies and institutions for effective goal-setting and organization; (3) providing power bases to support needed changes; and (4) developing an authentic consensus. All of this, for Etzioni, adds up to achieving a "responsive" society in which alone "societal guidance" is possible. For me, this all adds up to a verbose and sophisticated way of saying simply that our social problems come in large part from our materialistic inclinations, and that, in order to solve them, we have to bring to bear knowledge, organization, and politics—not a particularly novel perspective, even if it is called a "theory" of "societal guidance."

The Henslin-Reynolds and the Shepard-Stewart books are both readers; both seem aimed at rather unsophisticated (probably lower-division) students, both are composed primarily of selections that have not been widely published elsewhere (indeed, a large number of the Henslin-Reynolds articles seem to have been written originally for this book); and neither has an index. The H-R collection deals primarily with various issues of injustice and inequality, such as poverty, racism, sexism, ageism, the "subservience" of major institutions to corporate wealth, with some articles also on population, energy, and other environmental problems. It has none of the conventional topics usually denoted as "deviant behavior," such as crime, sexual deviations, mental illness, alcoholism, etc. Self-consciously and explicitly abandoning any pretense of scholarly detachment, the editors employ throughout the basic thesis that the "root causes" of social problems are to be found in the "ascendance of corporate capitalism" and in the "subservience of our social institutions" to the same (p. 5). This preoccupation gives the book a "handwringing" quality (nowhere more evident than on its final page), and saddles it with an oversimplified definition of social problems as "conditions of society that have negative effects on large numbers of people" (p. 5) as though such terms as "negative" and "large numbers" have self-evident definitions. This general definition, and its accompanying critique of American social structure, is sustained in the introductions to each major section of the book, and in its fairly lengthy introductory and concluding chapters.

The Shepard-Stewart reader has some general resemblances to the above (H-R) collection, but it is much shorter, not as "heavy," and covers a wider range of problem topics. Like H-R, this reader locates social problems "objectively" in social conditions, but it recognizes the part that governments and powerful interests can play in bringing social problems to the attention of the public. Again there is a rather simplistic definition of a social problem as "an undesirable condition in the social relationships among persons" (p. 1), and the book has a generally structural perspective. Unlike the H-R reader, however, the present one deals with such social problems as sexual, drinking, mental illness, and crime, as well as racism, sexism, the unequal distribution of power and wealth, and so on. The former kinds are seen as attributable to *deviance* vis-à-vis the social structure, while the latter are explained as *conformity* to the social structure. In the extremely brief general introduction and section introductions, a variety of theories about deviance and social injustice are employed in a rather superficial and disjointed way to "explain" the respective social problems. There is no conclusion for the book. Overall, one would have to say that although these two readers might be very useful in undergraduate classes, they make no particular contribution to the literature on social problems (they probably were not intended to), and they are not very different from scores of other readers available for classroom adoption. The earlier three books under consideration here, however, were all serious efforts at scholarly contributions to the social problems literature, and all are important to some degree at least.

The Study of Social Problems: Five Perspectives, 2nd ed., edited by EARL RUBINGTON and MARTIN S. WEINBERG. New York: Oxford University Press, 1977. 253 pp. $5.00 paper.

JAMES D. ORCUTT*
Florida State University

This thorough revision of *The Study of Social Problems* retains the strengths of the popular first edition and overcomes some of its weaknesses. Rubington and Weinberg have clarified their systematic discussion of the five perspectives and have selected a number of new readings which will be more understandable to undergraduates. Only the sections on Social Disorganization and Deviant Behavior contain the same readings as the first edition. Improvements are particularly apparent in the section on Labeling, where new selections by Becker, Erikson, Bustamante, and Nettler offer students a better overview of the central ideas of this perspective. New readings by Platt and Slater on Social Pathology and by Westhues on Value Conflict strengthen these respective sections.

The major gap in this edition, as in the first edition, is the lack of attention to recent critical analyses of social problems from a Marxist or structural conflict perspective. Discussion of this emerging "sixth perspective" is limited to a brief footnote (p. 100). Also, this edition fails to touch on Kitsuse and Spector's efforts to extend the boundaries of the labeling perspective beyond deviance to social problems in general. Nonetheless, instructors who wish to base social problems courses on a solid theoretical foundation will welcome this revision of *The Study of Social Problems.*

* Not the reviewer responsible for the listing in "Delinquent Reviews."

Urban and Rural

The Evolution of American Urban Society, by HOWARD P. CHUDACOFF. Englewood Cliffs, N.J.: Prentice-Hall, 1975. 280 pp. $12.50 cloth. $5.95 paper.

MATTHEW EDEL
Queens College/CUNY

This is an historical overview, useful to supplement topical readings but neither comprehensive nor lively enough to carry a course as sole text. The 1850–1920 period receives most detailed treatment. Chapters treat growth and suburbanization, immigration and mobility, boss politics, and reform. Earlier and later history receive two chapters each. Pictures and charts are well-chosen. The field is well-surveyed, with few errors of detail, but little new material.

Lack of a theoretical focus is a problem. Chudacoff neither picks one analytical paradigm nor explicitly contrasts different theories. Varying causal notions occasionally contradict each other. The concentration of migrants in inner cities is explained once by cultural characteristics and later by analysis of costs and incomes. The role of conflict is also presented inconsistently. Turn-of-century reform is attributed to the attitudes of upper-class reformers, while 1960s reform is presented as reactive to protest, although parallel debates over cause exist in both cases.

This shifting theoretical focus, symptomatic of a crisis in American historiography, is not unique to Chudacoff. For the instructor who can raise theoretical issues in class, or for students interested in chronology, the book will serve well. One could, however, have hoped for more from a book about "evolution."

Latin American Urban Research, Volume V: Urbanization and Inequality: The Political Economy of Urban and Rural Development in Latin America, edited by WAYNE A. CORNELIUS and FELICITY M. TRUEBLOOD. Beverly Hills: Sage Publications, 1975. 316 pp. No price listed, paper.

WILLIAM L. FLINN
Ohio State University

This volume is a refreshing look at the urbanization process. Instead of viewing urbanization in the traditional manner, as a process which distributes the population and skills according to where the resources and demand for labor are located, urbanization in Latin America is seen as a concentration and centralization process which has led to unequal development and exacerbation of social, economic, and spatial inequalities. The city is viewed as having exploitive relationships with the hinterland. The presumed "trickle down" process of economic growth from the city to countryside is seen to be really a "pouring up" or decapitalization of the countryside by the city which is produced both by conscious and unconscious governmental policies and profit-making objectives of multinational corporations. The development programs in Latin American countries are viewed as being little more than "paper" programs and rhetoric which give lip service to reducing spatial and social inequalities, but which actually encourage types of urban-industrial development which only exacerbate, rather than ameliorate, existing inequalities. Moreover, these state policies are seen to be an integral component of the larger process of internal colonialism and uneven development.

The Latin Americans and Latin Americanists who contribute to the volume include five economists, three sociologists, three anthropologists, one political scientist, one geographer, and one urban and regional planner. The volume is thus quite interdisciplinary, which proves to be both a strength and a weakness.

The introductory chapter, "Internal Colonialism," by John Walton forms the theoretical underpinning for the book and deals with the familiar problem of defining and measuring internal colonialism. In the final analysis, Walton sees the concept "as a process that produces certain intra-national forms of patterned socioeconomic inequality directly traceable to the exploitive practices through which national and international institutions are linked in the interests of surplus extraction and capital accumulation" (pp. 34–35). Cornelius is correct in asserting that this reformulation of internal colonialism will not satisfy the critics of the concept. It is difficult to see how Walton's redefinition and measurement would differ significantly from a class analysis conducted by a dependency theorist. One might say that Walton has taken steps to *synthesize* internal colonialism and dependency approaches to Latin American underdevelopment. In any event, Walton's analysis establishes the general tone for the succeeding chapters, although several chapters in parts 3–5 employ more or less conventional econometric or planning perspectives. Most authors, however, see metropolitan systems as the lever of the surplus extraction and transmission processes of internal colonialism. Thus governmental plans for decentralization of urban-industrial growth remain only plans because they are in contradiction with the overall process of internal colonialism.

Part 2 focuses on the micro-level changes which have occurred in rural communities as a consequence of national level policies on urban-industrial development. The two case studies on Peru and Mexico reach similar conclusions—urbanization and state intervention have increased local inequalities. Part 3 is concerned with intra-urban rather than rural-urban or interregional consequences of social inequality. Part 4 examines the determinants of inequalities in national distribution of population, income, and developmental possibilities. The last section analyzes regional development programs and rural-urban inequalities by using case studies from Colombia, Mexico, and Chile.

While in general the volume is well done, it suffers from the usual problem of edited books—unevenness. The review of internal colonialism literature is useful for anyone interested in the debate. The data on the various countries are thorough and presented in detail. Consequently, the book may be best suited for advanced courses on Latin America. I found many of the chapters useful in my graduate course on the sociology of economic change.

Theoretical Perspectives on Urban Politics, edited by WILLIS D. HAWLEY et al. Englewood Cliffs, N.J.: Prentice-Hall, 1976. 229 pp. $13.95 cloth. $3.95 paper.

Essays on the Study of Urban Politics, edited by KEN YOUNG. Hamden, Conn.: Shoe String Press, 1975. 208 pp. $15.00 cloth.

ELLAN ODIORNE DEROW
McMaster University

These two volumes manifest contrasting approaches to the study of urban politics. In editing *Essays on the Study of Urban Politics,* Ken Young "celebrates," among other things, the "maturation of British urban political science" and suggests that the contributions will delineate and review the separate areas of the field in order to clarify and relate them and suggest alternative avenues of exploration. Willis D. Hawley and Michael Lipsky in the introduction to *Theoretical Perspectives on Urban Politics* maintain that the field of urban politics cannot progress or mature in the sense of generating a unifying set of concepts and "discriminating theory." Rather they suggest that urban politics be approached as an "area study" in which important and interesting political phenomena are studied both in and of themselves and in relation to more general contexts and problem issues. Their efforts stem, not from a desire to celebrate, but from feelings that the study of urban politics is adrift and that new orientations grounded in appropriate sorts of theorizing are needed.

Each of these collections contains a variety of papers which should not be missed by either urban or political sociologists or those who wish to see how far the study of urban politics has come since the days of Hunter and Dahl.

There is some substantive overlap between the books in (a) treatments of the importance of the bureaucratic structuring in the provision of policy, services, and opportunities, and (b) concern for metropolitan integration. The Young volume aims to produce conceptual frameworks and theory, while the contributors in the Hawley et al. volume, in spite of the title, are more problem-oriented and are closer to various sorts of American data. Although both collections do bear the imprint of their national origin, the conceptual frameworks developed, for the most part, could be modified for use in either Britain or the United States or other industrialized urban nations, as for example, in Canada. Noteworthy in this regard are Elkin's discussion of organizational networks in urban contexts in Young and the development of decentralization models by Douglas Yates in Hawley et al.

The Young volume opens with a foreward by Edward C. Banfield which might well have been an afterthought or a critique to judge from its lack of integration with the general aims of the editor. Banfield suggests four difficulties standing in the way of urban political science: the inability to specify the object of investigation, the variety of concepts and theories, the lack of "one best way" to go about the study of urban politics as far as methods are concerned, and the non-cumulative nature of knowledge in the area. Next is Young's preface to the volume which contains a statement of his overall approach to the area and the collection.

The first contribution, by Kenneth Newton, examines the traditions of early community power studies in the United States in order to suggest their inapplicability to the British scene. Jeffrey Stanyer constructs a model for reinterpreting the relation of local elections and decision-making with the aim of linking more precisely urban and national political behavior. Janet Lewis discusses the interaction, structure, and attitudes of participants in urban political systems. She focuses on lay-professional relationships in order to elaborate a theoretical model showing how various factors effect policy output. Bleddyn Davis discusses a causal model of factors and their relative importance in the production of policy outputs.

The next three essays relate to one another in a fashion most pleasing to the critical reader. Oliver Williams views urban politics as part of the relationship between spatial and social structures. He provides a framework describing the control of access to resources and facilities in a socio-spatial context. He stresses how contemporary urban structures reflect the ideology of dominant sectors operating within the constraints of production. Providing a contrast to the emphasis on locality is Ken Young's innovative application of an international perspective on political integration conceptualization of the urban metropolis. Stephen L. Elkin's contribution criticizes what he calls the essentialist argument which is illustrated by Williams in this volume and suggests that organizational theory offers a better perspective in that, first, spatially-related goods and services are no different from other goods and services, and, second, exogenous factors are basic to the understanding of urban politics.

The Hawley et al. volume opens with an excellent contribution by Hawley and Lipsky summarizing their views of the field of urban politics. Martin Shefter then offers a model of political machines developed from his careful use of historical data. Karen Orren examines the role played by big business in the city. She sees corporations operating with great discretion and compliance in the US case. Only recently she feels that corporations have had to deal with social groups in the inner city hostile to corporate interests. Paul Peterson and J. David Greenstone use data from urban participation programs to test a pluralist model based on electoral interests and a conflict model based on ideologies. They find that in US urban politics, when racial issues are involved, ideological concerns are more important than considerations of the maintenance electoral hegemony. Willis Hawley discusses the factors important in metropolitan political integration. He sees two basic considerations: indigenous versus imposed integration and change versus no change in lifestyle due to integration. Stanley Greenberg constructs and tests a model of the relationships between dimensions of political alienation and various responses. Michael Lipsky describes the work situation and constraints of city employees dealing with the public. Douglas Yates, in a particularly inciteful contribution, develops five models of urban decentralization based on a detailed analysis of the political economy of various experiments in the US. Ira Katznelson discusses the nature of the crisis of the city from a Marxist perspective. Using the ideas of colonialization and dependency, he presents an analysis of the growth of bureaucratic social control mechanisms in the city.

With such an impressive and varied list of contributions to the two volumes, evaluation is difficult. The only serious omission to my mind is a lack of effort in the delineation of structures and processes relating urban to national or intermediate-level political phenomena. Both volumes suggest that there is a lack of definitive boundaries of the urban or local, yet both fail to indicate the type of boundaries which do exist.

Both collections suffer from a lack of a good summary chapter. This is not even attempted in Hawley et al. Young's final overview leaves much to be desired. No longer does he consider urban politics a mature study but now suggests it is underdeveloped. Additionally, he concludes that considerations of value have unified the concerns of the different contributors. He does not illustrate how or why he came to this conclusion. He goes on to suggest that "three key concepts with the field of urban political analysis" have "significant value content." These are urban imagery, localism, and professionalism. These may well be useful concepts to study; however, it is debatable whether they are key concepts in the area and the relation to notions of value needs to be discussed more fully.

After working through these sets of essays, the sociologist might well question the extent to which it is possible or advisable to separate political phenomena from other urban phenomena. These volumes do advocate such a separation and, to a certain extent, bemoan the difficulty of neatly delineating *specific* urban politics. To what extent, however, does such a position serve to erect or maintain false boundaries between social phenomena and social sciences? It may well be that such boundaries, have in fact helped to create the very dilemmas to which these books address themselves.

A Strategy for Rural Change, by CHARLES P. LOOMIS and J. ALLAN BEEGLE. New York: Halsted Press, 1975. 525 pp. $19.50 cloth.

GENE F. SUMMERS
University of Wisconsin, Madison

Strategy is the large scale planning and directing of operations in anticipation of and adjustment to opposition in the struggle to achieve a pre-determined goal or set of objectives. *A Strategy for Rural Change* is none of this. Indeed rural change does not appear to be a goal for Loomis and Beegle and they do not present a strategy for its accomplishment.

This volume is a revised version of *Rural Sociology: A Strategy for Change*. It is a textbook for an introductory course in rural sociology. If you are not in the market for one, skip the book and this review.

The conceptual framework for the book is Loomis's version of the social system; not to be confused with the work of Parsons. The first chapter provides a brief summary of Loomis's idea which is illustrated in the succeeding chapters as the authors describe major institutional and organizational facets of rural America. The table of contents indicates the usual cafeteria menu: Family, Education, Religion, Government, Health, and Stratification. There are chapters on locality systems and informal systems. On the organizational side, the authors cover agricultural production, farmers organizations, federal agencies, and the library and mass media. There are concluding chapters on behavioral change strategies and the uses of rural sociology.

Undergraduate sociology courses ought to be an experience in discovering society, not sociology; the ideas and methods of the discipline being merely implements to structure and guide the learning experience. If one accepts these assumptions, adoption of the Loomis and Beegle textbook will be problematic.

The book is heavily committed to explaining and illustrating the social system. It is not clear whether the authors desired the student to discover rural society or the Loomis social system. There are times when the viewing instrument distracts from what one is intended to view.

The social phenomena displayed distort the meaning of rural. The items arrayed are primarily from the United States, almost exclusively agricultural, and presented with little attention to historical context. The rural society which students will discover via this book has a dominant motif of self-sufficient family farms and small agricultural towns whose existence is threatened by government programs and corporate invasion.

Students will learn nothing about mining or lumbering families or their towns. They will learn little about rural industries, dormitory towns, or recreational, retirement, or energy-generating communities. They will be spared the conflicts surrounding land use and land use planning, growth vs. no-growth or pollution control. They will not discover the small town residential preferences of great numbers of Americans and the fact that many rural communities are growing after years of decline.

Rural America incorporates much more than farmers, farming, and agri-business. In fact, these are the numerical minorities of social groups, economic activities, and the social realities in rural America in 1975. The guide to its discovery ought to reveal its wealth of social variabilities.

Planning for an Urban World: The Design of Resource-Conserving Cities, by RICHARD L. MEIER. Cambridge, Mass.: MIT Press, 1974. 515 pp. No price listed, cloth.

JOHN D. KASARDA
University of North Carolina, Chapel Hill

Richard Meier, a leading American planner, has written another good book. In this latest effort, he spins concepts and ideas from general systems theory into cybernetic and ecological models which provide an analytical framework for projecting alternative urban futures. This framework treats cities as the organizational nuclei and driving engines of national and international ecosystems with the primary function of converting human capital and natural resource input into societal output.

Meier's main substantive concern is reflected in the book's subtitle. Building on the Malthusian premise that demographic growth and human consumption are rapidly exceeding the expansion of natural resources, he argues for the exigency of designing "resource-conserving" cities. By this, he means planning the future spatial and institutional structure of urban systems, which are conceptualized for heuristic purposes as roughly analogous to machines, such that they generate greater human capital and material output for each unit of resource input they expend. Without introducing these structural changes, Meier contends, we may expect a substantially reduced level of living for the bulk of human societies, and a less than adequate standard of living for an increased portion of the earth's inhabitants.

How does Meier get his message across? His primary instrument is scenario writing, a technique whereby images of the future are projected along evolving chains of interdependent events. Scenarios have become vogue in the planning literature and Meier writes them well. While I question the scientific merit of scenarios (which necessarily involve many dubious ceteris paribus assumptions), I should note that when Meier's first-hand knowledge of urban structures and conditions throughout the world become flavored by his rich imagination, the scenarios he extrapolates provide rather interesting reading.

In step with those of today's ecological alarmists, Meier's scenarios typically culminate in dismal urban futures: energy crises, famine, physical catastrophe, breakdowns in the public order, etc. Unlike many alarmists, however, Meier does not view these outcomes as inexorable, and it is here that he proposes implementing the knowledge and practice of urban planning as a preventive medicine. His underlying assumption is that planners can intervene into urban evolutionary processes with innovative strategies and designs that will prevent ecological disaster and redirect change to much more favorable outcomes.

Meier explicates a variety of planning strategies and urban spatial designs that he believes would serve the dual purpose of easing pressures on natural resources while improving the production and distribution of goods and services to guarantee adequate standards of living for all. In general, his strategies and designs focus on the spatial redistribution of population and commercial and industrial activities in metropolitan systems, new methods of food and consumer goods production (e.g., nuclear-powered agro-industrial complexes), and improved forms of energy capturing and conversion from steady state sources such as the sun. Nonetheless, Meier returns to his Malthusian premise in admitting that even these changes will not elicit a balance between natural resources and human consumption in the long run unless rapid population growth is brought under control. He, thus, argues for family planning programs to be introduced in concert with the strategies and designs he proposes.

Meier is by no means a naive or sociologically simplistic planner. He is well aware of cultural lags and ideological obstacles that must be overcome if redirected change is to occur. Take energy conservation in local transportation as a case in point. Despite widespread knowledge that mass transit is more "energy efficient" and less costly per passenger mile than the automobile, Western society (with few exceptions) continues to abandon public mass transportation in favor of greater reliance on the private automobile. Why? To quote Meier, "The reason seems to be that the real service provided by a bus or electric train misses what is believed to be ideal by a large measure. The auto approaches the ideal of personalized transport much more often ('I go when I am ready, not when the schedule says I can, and I arrive in the style I wish to appear'); therefore people will spend three to ten times as much money on necessary trips and save little, if any, personal time, but gain real satisfaction from remaining in control of their movements" (pp. 251–252). Insights into behavioral patterns, such as the above quote, provide more credibility to Meier's viewpoints than to those of many planners from engineering-type backgrounds who, I find, often fail to consider adequately social resistances to their planning strategies.

My general enthusiasm for this book is tempered by two mild reservations: one substantive and the other technical. Substantively, Meier touches down on so many diverse ecological issues and problems that topical continuity and depth of treatment is frequently sacrificed. Sociologists, in particular, should not look to this book for an intensive treatment of ecological problems and their potential solutions. If they do, they will likely be disappointed. Technically, I feel that the MIT Press did less than adequate service in the book's physical appearance. The tiny print, short lines, and corresponding massive margins give one the impression of a book typeset more for speed reading than for scholarly rumination. These minor shortcomings should not, of course, obscure the basic merits of the book. My hunch is that most human ecologists, environmental sociologists, and others concerned with the important issue of energy and society will find the book provocative. Those with academic interests in the sociology of the future would also be advised to consider what Meier has to say.

Power, Politics and Progress: Social Change in Rural Peru, by WILLIAM FOOTE WHYTE and GIORGIO ALBERTI. New York: Elsevier Scientific Publishing Company, 1976. 307 pp. $15.00 cloth.

WILLIAM L. CANAK
University of Wisconsin, Madison

Whyte and Alberti utilize this book to provide an English speaking audience access to the results of their long term (1965–1973) research on agrarian community development in Peru, and to summarize and integrate the variety of case studies that made up the bulk of this coordinated research program carried out by the Instituto de Estudios Peruanos and Cornell University.

The major objective of the book is to use the various case studies as a basis for generating an historical-structural approach to micro-level analysis. Especially emphasized is the importance of regional, national, and international economic and political relations in the determination of local community structure and agrarian social movements. The historical awareness evidenced in the book, however, encourages one to recall Mill's admonition against "sketching in historical background" as a mode of explanation. The structural linkages of individual communities with larger contexts are depicted as "power" relations at the level of interpersonal relations. Thus it is not surprising that the attempt to generate a theory from these various studies focuses upon a typology in which cooperation and conflict are the most important criteria.

After a brief historical review of economic and political development in Peru, the body of the text summarizes case studies in twelve agrarian communities. The focus is on land tenure and "peasant" social movements oriented to changing land tenure systems in each area. Data were gathered by both anthropological field methods and survey research, although the former clearly dominated the interests of the researchers. The sections on theory and methods are found at the end of the book. A fragmented quality thus pervades these summaries of case studies, resulting no doubt from (1) the divergent observational and reporting skills and interests of the individual researchers; (2) the general lack of integration in the two methodological techniques employed; and (3) the lack of any analytic notion of the modes of structural determination between micro and macro levels.

An enormous amount of rich descriptive material is provided in the book. It should be especially useful to those interested in collective behavior, rural class structure, and the political economy of agrarian development. Sadly, the authors, after concluding that the various "modernization" theories emphasizing psychological dimensions of "peasant" culture were irrelevant, did not seem prepared to conceptualize the class structure, the role of different agricultural production sectors in the development process, the relationship of state policy toward these sectors with the larger interests and structure of the state, the process of capital accumulation within the nation, the relationship of the economy with the world market, etc. These seem reasonable requests since the book itself states as its goal the development of an integrated view of these various structural levels. Moreover, the case studies seem to provide ample data for the depiction of many of these structural relationships. Yet it is not done.

The data on specific agrarian social movements are quite extraordinary in their detailed presentation of the class structure, the interests and capacities of specific class factions, the role of political parties and union organizers, the impact of both reactionary and revolutionary ideologies, and the policies of the state and military. A strongly materialist analysis of the structure and goals of specific social movements is presented throughout the case studies. However, the central focus of the authors is the way in which attitudes become transformed by this experience.

The conclusion provides an attempt to use inductive logic to locate some crucial and common qualities in the twelve areas studied and to discuss the evolution of the research project itself. Yet the originally stated goal of focusing on micro-macro relations in historical perspective here receives short shrift. The concepts of cooperation and conflict, which are the heart of the authors' theory of community development, reveal essentially micro-level relations in an ahistorical model. The interest of the researchers is upon "perceived" conflict and cooperation. Moreover, conflict and cooperation are considered dependent on the existence of projects aimed at improvement in the community. These collective projects are seen as "shaping" attitudes. Yet the nature of this shaping remains vague. Do they set limits on the variation of attitudes? Do they structure the categories? Do they mediate the effects of macro-historical forces? Of interest to all researchers, however, is the admirable section that attempts to directly discuss the evolution of the project itself and how the structure, goals, and conceptualization of the problem became reformulated during the process of the study.

Additional Reviews

"Sesame Street" Revisited, by THOMAS D. COOK, HILARY APPLETON, ROSS F. CONNER, ANN SCHAFFER, GARY TAMKIN, and STEPHEN J. WEBER. New York: Russell Sage Foundation, 1975. 410 pp. $15.00 cloth.

GLADYS ENGEL LANG
SUNY/Stony Brook

This is the *first* publication of the Russell Sage Foundation series "Continuities in

Evaluation Research." Each volume is to report a study commissioned to evaluate the methods, findings, and conclusions of "important" evaluation research. The research under scrutiny here is the Educational Testing Service's assessment of the first years of "Sesame Street," which was awarded "straight A's" by *Time*.

One marvels, given the stormy history of this effort, that there will be a *second* volume in the series. Though Howard Freeman, then the responsible program officer at the Foundation, insists in his foreword that the undertaking "was not intended to create adversary relationships between the original evaluation groups and the investigators" (p. xiii) or "to destroy any social action effort" (p. xi) like that of the Children's Television Workshop. It certainly aroused some strong emotions with both ETS and CTW; anxious about continuing support, they mobilized in self-defense.

The nub of the controversy revolves around the decision of the investigators, Thomas D. Cook et al., to go beyond the assigned mission and look at "Sesame Street" as a "public good." They have re-analyzed the data, to which they were given open access, not only to determine whether the program had some learning impact on viewers, a question addressed by the primary evaluators, but to ask whether "Sesame Street" was reducing the achievement gap between middle-class (economically advantaged) and lower-class (economically disadvantaged) children. Their rationale for this extension of the inquiry is that this reduction was a goal, albeit ambiguously stated, in the original funding proposal.

Not only do Cook and his co-researchers find that the program did *not* reduce this gap but they refer frequently to the possibility that it may have an adverse educational impact by widening it. The evidence for this possibility is mighty slim, yet the authors sometimes treat evidence they themselves refer to as "weak" (for example, p. 310) or "circumstantially indicated by the data" (p. 324) as proved fact. What is first advanced as a "possibility" is then discussed as a creditable threat, as when we are imploringly asked in chapter 10: "Are the gains of knowing more worth the costs of falling further behind?"

So strongly do the secondary evaluators come to believe in their "circumstantial findings" that they make this extraordinary recommendation: CTW should be required to *prove* through audience and impact studies that the program is not widening the achievement gap. If the proof is not forthcoming or "if the data turn out unfavorably" (p. 381–382), funds should be cut off or given only if the program is selectively disseminated to the economically disadvantaged. I take it this could include forbidding its over-the-air broadcast.

The book necessarily includes a rejoinder by Ball and Bogatz, the original evaluators, which is short, succinct, snide, and, for the most part, fair. They deny that "reducing the achievement gap" was a major purpose of the program; any group whose aim was to close the gap, they point out, would certainly not use a universally available educational innovation as the delivery medium. They also make a spirited defense against criticism of their findings as exaggerating program impact, i.e., on whether viewing causes learning.

Here the quarrel between primary and secondary evaluators is more common to social research—less political and more academic. Ball and Bogatz claim that the evaluators, in assessing the impact on learning, failed to understand the data base and research design employed in the original study. When they also say they had some difficulty in understanding what conclusions, if any, the secondary evaluators came to, this reader sympathizes. Still, both groups are most competent researchers, psychologists familiar with the pitfalls of experimental designs. The presentation of methods, analysis, findings, assumptions, and conclusions is detailed. Especially those chapters that focus on the impact of encouragement-to-view and viewing make this book what the Russell Sage Foundation meant it to be—a valuable case study that will serve in training future evaluation researchers.

One hopes that the book—and others in the series—will turn attention to broader questions about evaluation research. Evaluation for what? Why the need to assess the *net impact* of "Sesame Street" in its infancy? Because in this, as in the case of other educational innovations, "scientific" proof of quick payoff was the key to financial survival for the innovators. Given the keen competition for funds, small wonder that research findings, however well-designed the research, are subject to different interpretations which become the stuff around which political battles are waged. "Sesame Street," after nearly a decade, has obviously had an extraordinary impact, but one doubts we shall ever come up with the kind of "scientific proof" that will satisfy those who doubt it.

The New Psychohistory, edited by LLOYD DE MAUSE. New York: Psychohistory Press, 1975. 313 pp. $12.95 cloth. $5.95 paper.

LLOYD S. ETHEREDGE
Massachusetts Institute of Technology

This collection of ten articles selected from the first three years of *The History of Childhood Quarterly: The Journal of Psychohistory* represents an effort to dramatize the appeal, accomplishments, and promise of what the editor enthusiastically maintains is "the first new discipline to be born in the social sciences in this century" (p. 3). It is a stimulating collection, closely tied to data, whose authors have tried to penetrate to the inner emotional dynamics and sensibilities of their subjects. Prepared to be skeptical of a new fad, I found myself learning some new things and grasping some historical issues with an empathy that was missing from my previous education in history. For example, William Langer's "Infanticide: A Historical Survey" was gruesome and Marvick's detailed discussion of the bizarre child-rearing practices used on Louis XIII opened a new door to speculating about the sources of his decisions as king.

This volume, and especially the first essay by deMause, will be of particular interest to sociologists of science. The new psychohistorians and the older traditional historians have been engaged in heated internal fights about legitimacy for several years, living their own psychohistory as a discipline. One of the pioneers and the editor of this collection, deMause, here puts forth a new challenge (psychohistory should split off and become a separate discipline), and calls implicitly on young, idealistic, and humane graduate students to abandon the stuffy and hopelessly old-fashioned Establishment and follow him into the future. He portrays traditional historians as so dehumanized as to make their conversion impossible: "as a result of my personal contacts over the past decade with perhaps a thousand historians . . . I no longer believe that most traditional historians are emotionally equipped, even with training, to use their feelings as psychohistorical research tools, although there is a whole new generation of psychohistorians just now beginning to write who *are* able to do so. . . . [Traditional historians are averse] to psychological insight into themselves or their historical material . . ." (p. 23). (The author does not say *directly* that the fight has involved implicit fantasies, wishes, and fears about who will control new generations of graduate students, but the inference is plain because in the pages immediately preceding the passage just cited deMause has discussed his recent research interest that past international wars have involved their protagonists in birth fantasies and concerns over the fate of children. And as a good psychohistorian would assure us, such juxtapositions are never accidental.)

It is clear that psychohistory is a movement with a mission: deMause writes, "psychohistory is a science in a hurry, racing against man's spiralling ability to destroy himself . . ." (p. 5). There is a strong undercurrent of liberal humane values running through this collection. The faith that psychoanalytic psychology is a therapeutic that can save the world is apparently an important group fantasy in this new field. Such a normative viewpoint underlies a number of the case studies: Kern's exposé of the Victorian family, Ward's study of Kissinger, Dunn's study of the childhood of Vissarion Belinsky, Binion's study of Hitler, Marvick on Louis XIII, and Davis on Theodore Roosevelt can be read as "bad examples," that is as examples of failure to achieve the secular grace of an unconflicted, fully sucessful, fulfilling life when one lacks the access to the intimate awareness and perspective on one's feelings produced by a psychoanalytic sensibility.

Psychohistory as practiced by these authors is essentially restricted to psychoanalytic history. And it is a selective Americanized version of psychoanalytic theory which, for example, avoids the darker hypotheses of an aggressive drive and Freud's belief that social order must be built upon repression—i.e., internalized fear and guilt. More love of children can probably help to create a better world, but I would be more comfortable on scientific grounds if theorists who maintain that compassion and humility come partly from suffering, that rationality and individuation are purchased at costs of bearing loneliness, uncertainty, fears of death, and identity struggles were somewhere in evidence. Romantic humanism may not teach the potentially harder lessons about life, about the trade-offs in culture and society, that a more careful reading of even analytic theorists would at least suggest, ought to be addressed.

I found myself at times impatient with these authors' tendencies to explain everything on the basis of inadequate evidence and single theories. For example, Ward writes of Henry Kissinger's foreign policy as primarily a function of a depressive personality syndrome. But one could also profitably use Kohut's narcissistic personality syndrome or Pye's adaptation of Freud's concept of secondary narcissism or Witkin's field dependence syndrome or Winter's N-power syndrome or Christie and Geis's Machiavellianism syndrome; a careful weighing of the evidence for each would have illuminated different aspects of Kissinger's complex personality as well as clarifying those behaviors potentially dissociated from deeper emotional drives altogether. Such a strategy would probably have saved Ward from wrongly concluding that Kissinger lacked empathy with others (p. 125) since some of these alternative models (e.g., Kohut's) would explain Kissinger's extraordinary gift of sensitivity to other powerful men like himself. Such explicit weighing of evidence would not only engage readers in solving a mystery, but would move psychohistory more toward a style of scientific integrity.

Or to take another example: not all sons are driven by consuming hatred of their fathers—so for Davis to suggest, in the face of Theodore Roosevelt's manifest great love and admiration of his father, that T.R.'s love for killing big game animals was a displacement of such hatred, forces the available evidence, to say the least. It seems more plausible to consider that T.R. was trying to reject the effeminizing influence of his mother and to live up to the high standards a loved and admired father held for him. Killing for sport, like taming big business, can show a desire to achieve mastery and prove oneself a man and does not in an obvious way flow from seething hostility to masculine authority.

One of the worst-kept secrets of psychiatry is that experienced clinicians frequently disagree with one another about diagnosis even when they have first-hand knowledge: theoretical classification and diagnosis become awkward when one deals with unique complexities of a specific case. The "next assignment" of psychohistorians (to use Langer's phrase) is probably to develop multiple psychological models and assess explicitly the power and limitations of each.

Insult and Society: Patterns of Comparative Interaction, by CHARLES P. FLYNN. Port Washington, N.Y.: National University Publications/Kennikat Press, 1977. 131 pp. $9.95 cloth.

ALFRED MCCLUNG LEE
Brooklyn College/CUNY

Insulting behavior or its threat does much to bolster a human's sense of worth, to maintain sexual, age, ethnic, racial, class, and caste differences, and to preserve hierarchies of status within organizations. Perhaps because insults constitute such a demeaning aspect of human behavior, are such a dehumanizing crutch for the ego individually or in a group context, a systematic, over-all, special consideration of them has been lacking.

Using a synthesis of symbolic-interactionist, ethnomethodological, and culture-and-personality theory, Flynn examines insults in a number of societies in relation to the self's thought processes, their social interactional contexts, and their relations with many societies' culture and social organization. To do so, he has drawn and analyzed a wealth of examples from the comprehensive Human Relations Area Files on tribal-village and caste-estate societies and from contemporary literature on modern industrial situations. He divides his treatment so that each chapter compares patterns of insult behavior dealing with a central institution or social process in each of the three major types of sociocultural situations he examines.

Flynn defines an insult as "an act, remark, or gesture which expresses a severely negative opinion of a person or group." And then he immediately adds, "But does its significance end with those who insult and are insulted?" (p. 3). It is to this question that he gives most of his attention. Both the universality of certain insult behavior and its tremendous variety raise intriguing problems of context, and in going from one context to another there can be a reversal of who is insulting and who insulted by a given "act, remark, or gesture." Universal patterns include identifications with dogs and pigs, allegations of incestuous relationships, and spitting. Among wide variations in patterns, Flynn points to the curious discrepancy between what contemporary Americans now take to be modest or immodest and the valuations of our past and other societies.

Perhaps more striking than the patterns of insult are those of response to insult. These vary from counterinsults and suicide to property damage and murder. Many tribal peoples, aware of the possible launching of a chain-reaction of revenge and counterrevenge, have institutionalized ways of "shrugging off" insults. Curiously enough, when violent counter-response is not sanctioned, suicide may be.

The declining importance of the extended family in industrialized societies has in general made reactions to insults less collective. Among tribal-village and caste-estate peoples, an insult to a person from outside becomes a derogation of an entire family. Within such families, males can with inpugnity use insults—gestures of contempt and other reminders of inferiority—to continue their patriarchal domination. On the contrary, the "success" values associated with modern industrial societies not only undermine extended family ties but pave the way for women's liberation. The wife's basic sense of purpose is directed toward what she can make of her husband's potentialities. This "social climbing" takes the form many times of insult behavior—nagging—toward the husband. This "equalizer" then serves as a step toward a more egalitarian type of relationship.

Tribal-village and caste-estate societies exhibit insult behavior that maintains stratification, but it is often behavior that appears to us to be arbitrary and even capricious. A Maori chief might inflict a disastrous reprisal for an offhand or mistaken gesture. The absurdities of dueling among Prussian Junkers and early American whites persisted as a presumed price paid for certifying the alleged innate superiority of upperclass males. Insults still function to keep lowerclass people "in their place" in our allegedly egalitarian society, but in general they now have to be used more subtly and indirectly.

In discussing the relations of insult and deviancy, the emergence of gay activists provides an example of current change. It enables Flynn to illustrate, among other things, the insulting character of tolerance as a gift from "superiors" in contrast with unadorned acceptance.

Flynn illustrates how insults function in legal, religious, and political procedures, in humor and other aspects of socialization with alternations between affection and offense, and in aggression and war. Perhaps his most poignant chapter deals with insults employed in education and especially in modern academia. As he concludes, "Unfortunately, it often happens that the scholar most qualified to review a book in a special area happens to be a prestige-rival of the writer. Because of this, book reviews often turn into insult games between academic titans, who, rather than objectively reviewing each other's work, use the review as a vehicle for deflating one another's status" (p. 115). The insights of this and other chapters make the book perceptive and stimulating reading.

An Introduction to Program Evaluation, by JACK L. FRANKLIN and JEAN H. THRASHER. New York: John Wiley & Sons, 1976. 233 pp. $12.50 cloth.

DAN S. GREEN
Alabama State University

This book will help those who wish to learn about the complexities and considerations involved in the wide world of program evaluation and accountability. Program evaluation, or evaluation research as some seem to prefer, is an important sociological endeavor and there is every indication, as this book implicitly points out, that it will become even more significant. The authors predict that program evaluation is going to become more visible and more frequently demanded by funding agencies; in short, they see increasing demands for program accountability. This text is an accurate and adequate introduction to the field of evaluation for students, novice evaluators, evaluators-to-be, and program administrators.

The central point of the book is that program evaluation, basically a long-term investment, is possible, worthwhile, and necessary. The concept, program evaluation, usually suffering from definitional ills, is explicitly, simply, and elegantly defined as "the determination and assessment of the results (outcomes/impact) of program activities." Here, the authors manifest a bias for the goal attainment model of evaluation. The authors argue, rather effectively, that evaluation is a utilitarian phenomenon rather than an academic one; it is significant that the book is generally written from the viewpoint of the program or program manager rather than from that of the outside, academically-oriented evaluator.

There are few introductory books in this key research area and this may be the only one which emphasizes program exigencies as crucial when considering when and how to perform an evaluation. Conversely, another recurring theme of the authors is that program evaluation has been seriously hindered by program constraints, program organization, and managers with little knowledge about evaluation. One of the major conclusions is that "the major problems in evaluation are not so much methodological difficulties as those of the organizational settings in which evaluation must operate" (p. 201).

The authors are to be complimented for keeping the traditional evaluation jargon to a minimum.

The Comparative Reception of Darwinism, edited by THOMAS F. GLICK. Austin: University of Texas Press, 1974. 505 pp. $15.00 cloth.

NICHOLAS C. MULLINS
Institute for Advanced Study, Princeton, and Indiana University

The *Origin of the Species*, by Charles Darwin, presented a challenge to the scientists of the nineteenth century. The response to this challenge varied by individual, institution, and also by national culture. Anyone working in the social study of science will find interest in these narrative accounts of the reaction to Darwin, in England, France, Germany, the United States, Russia, The Netherlands, Spain, Mexico, and the Islamic World.

Burkhardt's essay on the learned societies in England and Scotland is of particular interest. Burkhardt reports the response among others of the Royal Society, The Geological Society of London, The Linnean Society, the Zoological Society of London. The variety of response to Darwin, its hidden and delayed character, both positive and negative, is most interesting. The impact of the Baconian and Newtonian tradition in English science is seen in the lack of theoretical discourse in regular papers presented to these societies. The major exceptions to this are some Presidential addresses which are more discursive, theoretical, and responsive to Darwin.

The essay on the United States by Pfeifer reports the debate between Aggazi, the most notable biologist in the United States at the time, and Rogers, a supporter of Darwin. Rogers's apparent victory carried great weight in the acceptance of Darwin; however, the slavery question and the earlier impact of a book by Chambers modified it. The American debate was heavily theological, and religious opposition to Darwinian theory still exists (e.g., creationist textbooks in public schools).

As with most good history, the first point that strikes a sociologist who is an inveterate theorizer is the difficulty of generalization along any of the usual lines. For example, both the most rational discussion *and* legal proscription appeared in the United States.

Most essays report that there was some debate over Darwin (or what were believed to be Darwinian theories). That debate occurred in the scientific press, in the popular press, in formal debates, and in critiques and commentaries in private letters, in short in some combinations of the varieties of public and private formus in which ideas might exist. In no culture is Darwin's work taken solely or even primarily as a theory about natural selection and animal species. It always is given a moral, religious, political, economic, or some other broader interpretation.

The varieties of response do not appear to have a simple relation to those factors which have been isolated by sociologists as bearing on the scientific status of a culture. The issues are muddied by the use of the scientific argument about Darwin as a resource in debate about more general societal matters. The use of Darwin by radicals in Russia and Spain are marked examples, but every national story has some element of this.

Several of the analyses implicate changes in economic arrangements (such as the embourgeoisment of the Netherlands), political changes (such as revolution in Spain or the Crimean War in Russia), or changes in the structure of the academic profession (such as the multiple university system in the United States). The variety and difference of the descriptions create a strong suggestion to the sociologist that the wrong unit of analysis is being used. The intellectual community within each country has different relations to the international scientific and intellectual community and to other communities within its national boundaries. The view that there is a response from a culture area is clearly wrong in detail, and the reconstruction for the purposes of generalization probably should not use the national culture as the appropriate unit.

Like most history, the book is almost completely free of tiny sociological discussion of science or indeed of generalization about intellectuals and their society. There are no references to sociologists or their ideas and very few to generalizing historians.

For the sociologist, however, this book provides counter examples, complexities of theorizing, and issues usually ignored. They are not presented in a systematic way, but scattered through the chapters. There is, however, a good index.

The bibliographic essays and other sources cited, while intended for the historian, are a useful resource to the sociologist who wants to follow out a problem. As with all conference books, themes suggested in one essay are not followed out in others, but the obvious effort of the organizers of this conference to promote some unity of papers has resulted in a useful and interesting book.

Stratification, Class, and Conflict, by IRVING KRAUSS. New York: Free Press, 1976. 502 pp. $12.95 cloth.

PAUL BLUMBERG
Queens College/CUNY

This new text in stratification faces tough competition from a number of others that have appeared recently: Daniel W. Rossides's tour de force in *The American Class Structure*: Judah Matras's intensive mobility analysis in *Social Inequality, Stratification, and Mobility*; and Charles H. Anderson's formidable Marxist perspective in *The Political Economy of Social Class*. In scope, if not in substantive achievement, Krauss surpasses them all, for he has written here not one but two books. The first is a standard run-through of the conventional materials in the stratification field. The second is a whirlwind Cook's tour through the social, economic, and intellectual history of Europe and America from the ancient world to the present, with emphasis on matters hierarchical. Such grandiose ambition must be commended, but attempting such historical sweep in so short a space inevitably culminates in superficiality. More appropriate for a stratification text would have been the tried but after all true device of detailed case studies of individual caste, estate, and class systems. What would have been lost in breadth would have been more than gained in depth.

Where Krauss covers the basic stratification material, he touches most bases but does not break any really new ground. His chapter on mobility I find somewhat curious, for in nearly forty pages, he neglects any mention of the actual amount and extent of mobility in America, as measured by contemporary studies. His sources here, as elsewhere, tend often to be aging. In a discussion of social mobility in the 1970s, he relies too heavily on Sorokin, the fiftieth anniversary of whose book on mobility ought to be honored in some other way.

Krauss's discussion of some of the key dimensions of stratification is adequate. In his treatment of occupational structure, he lays the census data out for the reader, but doesn't explore the crucial theoretical issues associated with occupational change in our century, e.g., the post-industrial society debate, the meaning of the white-collar/white-blouse explosion, the future of the old working class and the relevance of the new. Nor is his discussion of the vital subject of the concentration of wealth in America as thorough as one might wish.

Toward the end of the book, the author's facile acceptance of many standard beliefs about the American class system is disturbing. While he acknowledges that income distribution has not changed substantially in the postwar period, his celebration of increasing affluence ignores—as do most writers—the most crucial fact about class in America today: that the postwar era is over and the drive toward the affluent society that characterized that era has been stopped dead in its tracks. Real median income of American families has not increased since 1969, and real take-home pay of production workers has not increased since 1965! While Krauss applauds the educational mobility of the American population and accepts the conventional wisdom that more education leads to better jobs, he ignores the new and serious problem of the growing disjunction between education and jobs, specifically the growing underemployment of the college-educated mass.

What we need now is not the usual chronicle of increasing American living standards, but an analysis of the recent stagnation of American capitalism and the enormous impact that it is having on the American class structure.

Finally, I do not understand why sociologists guarantee instant obsolescence for their texts by writing about the past as if it were the latest model of reality. In a section on *current* class inequities of American society, Krauss devotes three pages to the military draft, writing the whole time in the present tense. Certainly there *were* class inequities in the draft, but this book was published some three years after the draft had been abolished. Does sociology, after all, deserve its reputation of being little more than "slow news"? In the interests of "relevance", or, if that word is no longer fashionable, "timeliness", the author might have made passing mention that the draft is no longer with us, but that the present all-volunteer army has its own class inequities.

The Chinese: A Study of a Hong Kong Community, by CORNELIUS OSGOOD. Tucson: University of Arizona Press, 1975. 1,264 pp. $45.00 cloth.

CHONG-CHOR LAU
The Chinese University of Hong Kong

The author of this three-volume work has come very close to the ideal of reconstructing the developmental history of a culture. After spending some five hundred workdays on a Hong Kong island, he came out not only with a rich amount of data on the cultural patterns of his "tribe," but also with a clear picture of how these patterns were linked to a larger social context. Specifically, this book should be welcome by sociologists for the following reasons.

First of all, Hong Kong society has experienced radical social change in the past quarter century. Various manifestations of this transformation process have fascinated many people and attracted groups of social scientists to study this small colony. One of their findings is of special interest to students of community: that social life in the peripheral villages is as affected by rapid developments as is Hong Kong proper. The once rural and isolated communities are overwhelmed by waves of industrialism and urban lifestyle. The metropolitan culture has become a major source of the village culture. Osgood's study contributes to the understanding of this process by presenting a lively account of what has happened to such a community.

This work, differs from most community studies on Hong Kong. It tries to capture the whole picture of a community system. Like most community systems in Mainland China, the one reported here consists of three hierarchies: the village, the intermediate town, and the metropolitan city. The first two parts of the book are devoted to detailed descriptions of aspects of life in two small villages, while the remaining pages focus on the town and its suburb, with some sketchy data on Hong Kong society as a whole.

Readers who are attracted to the book by its title will find part one satisfying. Here, an intimate history of three farming families is presented. Keen observations of life details yield a concrete picture of "the Chinese" seldom found in other writings on the same subject. Fine ethnography, however, is not the only strong point, conscious efforts have been made to understand this small group of Chinese people systematically and historically.

In part two the research focus shifts to the development of a village culture. Of interest to sociologists here is the account of how a group of less than two dozen people developed a new community with distinctive values in a span of three decades. In this part as well as in part one, the author's invaluable contribution lies in his itemized analysis of cultural persistence and change. It is interesting to find, for example, that the impact of modernization is less important with respect to material objects, such as the food and the homes of the people, than non-material aspects such as education and the clan system.

The first two parts stand for me as the highpoint of the book. The remaining three parts, which comprise the bulk of the text, are, in contrast, somewhat of a letdown. A sharp decline in the intimate quality of description is felt when one moves into part three. Though this can be defended by reference to a shift in focus to the economic activities of the townfolks, one suspects that the reason lies somewhere else. The anthropologist has left the "tribe" and plunged into the many unknowns of a central place of nearly nine thousand people and the object becomes too big to portray with the same intimacy. Restricted by time and methodology, the description of the life of people living in the town and its suburb on the island can only be relatively sketchy, despite the author's skillful combination of first-hand and documentary materials. These limitations notwithstanding, the last parts of the book are justifiable considering the author's objective of examining the cultural links between the villages and the larger society. In short, while the attempt to account for the growth of a culture in a bigger social context must be praised, the main achievement of the work rests on the fine ethnography of a transitional village community.

Max Weber Bibliographie: Eine Dokumentation der Sekundärliteratur, by CONSTANS SEYFARTH and GERT SCHMIDT. Stuttgart: Enke, 1977. 208 pp. No price listed.

Wirtschaft und Gesellschaft, by MAX WEBER. 5th, rev. ed., 2 vols. edited by JOHANNES WINCKELMANN. Tübingen: Mohr (Siebeck), 1976. 940 pp. With a volume of annotations by Winckelmann. 303 pp. No price listed.

GUENTHER ROTH
University of Washington

The authors of sociological classics are more than solemn faces appearing on photographs that commonly portray their subjects with some of the cultural attributes of the decades before the First World War. They may be said to be authors whose "influence" amounts for the most part to a diffuse reception, leading to wide name- or issue-familiarity at the same time that the critical features of their work tend to become blurred, sometimes to the point of indistinctness. In particular, the response to the works of Marx/Engels, Durkheim, and Weber has been so broad and diverse that the notion of a complete bibliography becomes senseless. Instead, some statistical sampling methods might be employed to measure degrees of intensity of reception.

Bibliographies of the secondary literature are, however, useful insofar as they succeed in presenting a manageable selection. This is true of the Weber bibliography assembled by Seyfarth and Schmidt, although it contains more than 2,300 entries—a project that originated many years ago in Johannes Winckelmann's Max Weber Institute at the University of Munich. The bibliography can easily be used by English readers, because the editorial principles of selection and the general apparatus appear in English and German. The entries have been broken down into three sections: (1) Weber's works published and translated since 1920 (for an almost complete bibliography of Weber's writings, see Dirk Käsler, *Kölner Zeitschrift für Soziologie,* 27:4, 1975, 703–30); (2) books and dissertations on Weber, and (3) articles and chapters or sections from books. The editors decided in favor of a chronological presentation, because they believe, with considerable justification, that an arrangement of such a large number of publications by subject matter creates serious classification problems. However, they have appended not only an index of persons and publications in twenty-two languages (including Japanese but omitting English and German) but also a subject index limited to about fifty categories.

The third section permits a rough numerical measurement of the fluctuating attention given to Weber's work and person. If we look at ten-year intervals from 1922, we find the following number of items: 1922: 20; 1932: 14; 1942: 7; 1952: 22; 1962: 42; 1972: 100—this last figure having remained roughly constant each year for the first half of the seventies. This is certainly an indication of a Weber renaissance, which is intertwined with the recent resurgence of Marxism.

The editors did not attempt to include reactions to Weber's work in his own lifetime nor for that matter try to identify the literature that most influenced Weber. This extremely difficult task has now been impressively concluded by Johannes Winckelmann as the satisfying endpoint of his long career as editor of and commentator on Weber's works. His fifth, revised edition of *Wirtschaft und Gesellschaft* contains as a third volume 300 pages of annotations in small print. These identify the large literature used by Weber mostly without citation and provide cross-references to his other works, explanations of hundreds of difficult legal and religious terms, and to a lesser extent references to more recent literature. However, Winckelmann is careful to point out that even this last edition should not be understood as "historico-critical." This will be the long-range task of the critical edition of Weber's works now being prepared by a group of scholars under the sponsorship of the Bavarian Academy of Sciences in Munich.

Editor's Note: Reinhard Bendix's *Max Weber: An Intellectual Portrait* has been re-issued with an introduction covering some of the major publications on Weber since it first appeared in 1960, and the Guenther Roth and Klaus Wittich edition of *Economy and Society* 1968, which has been out of print for several years, will also be re-issued by the University of California Press and made available for the first time as a paperback.

Contemporary Transformations of Religion: The Riddell Memorial Lectures, Forty-fifth Series Delivered at the University of Newcastle upon Tyne on 2, 3, 4 December 1974, by BRYAN WILSON. New York: Oxford University Press, 1976. 116 pp. $6.50 cloth.

THOMAS ROBBINS
Queens College/CUNY

The theory of "secularization," as it is presently manifested in the sociology of religion, has two complementary versions. A neo-Durkheimian analysis emphasizes the degree of structural differentiation in modern society and the consequences in terms of subcultural pluralism, impossibility of societal integration through value concensus, and the "privatized" encapsulation of religion. A neo-Weberian analysis reaches similar conclusions by stressing the bureaucratization of society and the withering of socially transformative prophecy in the "iron cage." Some analyses of today's "secularization" trends combine elements of both approaches (e.g., Peter Berger's *The Sacred Canopy* and Thomas Luckmann's *The Invisible Religion*) while a number of Weberians and Durkheimians reject the notion of secularization and stress the persistence of religious imperatives (e.g., Robert Bellah, Talcott Parsons, Andrew Greeley). The work of Bryan Wilson represents a relatively "pure" and elaborate development of neo-Weberian secularization theory.

Wilson stresses the increasing dominance of bureaucratic forms of social organization and the growing importance of impersonal mechanisms for social control (e.g., parking meters), which are impervious to religious influence. "Our world has been *de*-moralized as we have replaced human involvement in many areas of activity by technical controls . . . . As our society has become less dependent upon moral regulation, and as our relations to each other have become more role-regulated and less personally involved, so the functions of religions have declined, and men feel less need for religion." This theme is developed in the first chapter, which also delineates the ultimately self-defeating responses of the mainline churches to the functional decline of religion.

Chapter two contrasts the role of religious movements in modernizing societies, where religious prophecy may still operate as a powerful agent of social transformation, with the ultimately trivial expressivity of flourishing "new religions" in Europe and North America. Wilson doubts that the nouveau religions and "consciousness" movements currently arising in the West will ultimately be institutionalized, "but are to be as ephemeral as each generation," with the result that "one powerful force for civilization will be lost to man, and there may not be adequate new devices to function in its stead."

The final chapter expands the theme of the ultimate triviality of the present spiritual ferment. The "new cults" actually confirm the process of secularization; they reduce religion to an exotic consumer item and thus "add nothing to any prospective reintegration of society, and contribute nothing towards the culture by which a society might live." Prior periods of spiritual ferment and evangelical revival took place when "society was still largely regulated by personal relationships" and thus could be transformed by the upsurge of new moral ideologies and spiritual orientations. As hopeless expressive protests against ongoing rationalization, the "new cults" are inherently marginal and socially irrelevant, unlike movements such as Chilean Pentecostalism or the Kimbanguist church in Zaire, which "still organize men into stable communities and elicit from them high levels of personal commitment."

Enthusiasts of exotic spiritual diversity such as Harvey Cox or myself may find Wilson's conclusions depressing. The argument is nevertheless provocative and provides a counterpoint to the views of Andrew Greeley and others who straightforwardly interpret the present sectarian upsurge as prima facie evidence for the undiminished potency of religion. "Sociotheologians" who stress the universal need for "meaning" may be partly missing the point. The need for orientation continues but meaning systems may be increasingly *personal* and are thus encapsulated in what Benita Luckmann has called "the small life-worlds of modern man." "Privatized" spiritual disciplines and moral systems have few implications for either directly legitimating or challenging dominant bureaucratic structures. They are irrelevant to both societal integration and societal change.

Wilson's analysis of today's "new cults" is essentially a replay of Max Weber's comments on neo-romanticist movements in Germany in the early twentieth century. The Weberian analysis, which has been replayed many times before, is trenchant, but somewhat familiar and slightly unimaginative. With a little imagination today's yoga, meditation, and sensitivity-encounter groups can be viewed as variations on a single theme reminiscent of Durkheim's "cult of the individual" and "moral individualism" which provides the consensual substratum for organic solidarity in a highly differentiated society (something like this has recently been suggested by Frances Westley in an unpublished paper). Continually comparing today's "cults" to wild asocial patterns such as vandalism or soccer hooliganism, Professor Wilson may understate the degree to which new religious commitments may contribute to both individual social adjustment and societal integration, in part by providing non-vocational sources of personal identity and thus encouraging the impersonal role-orientations which a bureaucratic society requires of its employees. Neither Weber nor Wilson may have the last word on religion in modern society.

Pop Music in School, edited by Graham Vulliamy and Ed Lee. New York: Cambridge University Press, 1976. 207 pp. $11.50 cloth. $4.95 paper.

Peter Hesbacher
University of Pennsylvania

Pop music has, for the most part, *not* been taught in schools. In the capacities of editor and contributor, both Vulliamy (sociology) and Lee (English and music) examine the absence of pop music from traditional music education and explore the prospects for formal instruction in pop as well as serious music. Other contributors are Dave Rogers, Piers Spencer, Malcolm Nichols, and Tony Robins. Not only sociological (using longitudinal and comparative approaches) but also musicological (style analysis and instructional assessment) evaluations are made.

Pop music is shown to have emerged as the dominant music form. School music teaching, however, evolved from a serious music tradition which did not recognize the presence of two different aesthetics, one from Western art music; the other from Afro-American based pop. Education offered music much the way it offered other courses—the teacher-directed approach dominated. Recently, pupil-centered music instruction has been successfully introduced as an approach for learning pop.

Musical illustrations for purposes of teaching and analysis are used throughout the second half of the volume. A demonstration of blues instruction to minimally experienced students of mixed ability employs sequences of convention followed by improvisation, building from different kinds of riffs into full blues composition. Organizational options are described through the operation of an "open" music department and the incorporation of pop music within a more traditional music program. These presentations isolate the central instructional problem—the provision of group and individual performance experience according to taste and talent—and suggest strategies for attacking it.

The authors contend, using notation conventions for pitch, melody, harmony, orchestration, and rhythm for support, that popular music compared to classical music is less often defined by the score. They argue that pop music with Afro-American antecedents grew out of an oral tradition while serious music enjoyed a written tradition within the same educational system that taught its disciples. The development of jazz and blues underlined the separation between oral and written tradition: more complex rhythms, the blues scale, and a variety of harmonic structures offered a new context within which performers *composed* their melodies. Matching instrument sonority and vocal sounds further limited the utility of notation as common language. Musicians seldom crossed over: those from the oral tradition without formal training were frequently bewildered by serious music, while musicians proficient within the written tradition found the essence of pop elusive.

The care with which the authors isolate one kind of pop music—that which is Afro-American based—makes the strongest case for two largely separate aesthetics. Rock, the predominant music form today, is includable, since it often incorporates elements of the Afro-American tradition. This position excludes most low quality pop, but also ignores a wealth of traditional pop music, those ballads and upbeats that comprised the "mainstream" before rock.

The authors believe that pop has been unfairly judged according to serious music standards; they would incorporate it within the formal educational system by implementing "open" programs with pupil-centered techniques. Conventional wisdom asserts that "bad" music drives out "good." This volume counters with two musically acceptable aesthetics. Can a predominantly oral and a predominantly written musical tradition thrive within an educational system that would encompass both? If others within music education consistently blend such sentiment with expertise, the thesis of *Pop Music in School* might be proven right.

Psychodrama: Resolving Emotional Problems through Role-Playing, by LEWIS YABLONSKY. New York: Basic Books, 1976. 293 pp. $10.95 cloth.

KURT W. BACK
Duke University

Role-playing and psychodrama are today well-known techniques. For people who are unfamiliar with them, this book gives a number of striking examples which show that, given the right conditions, people can act out their problems in a very dramatic way. This performance is impressive for the audience and even the transcripts can fascinate the reader. One would expect, however, a treatise on psychodrama to include some assessment of conditions, favorable and unfavorable, justification of different approaches and techniques, successes and dangers, characteristics of different participants. In short, something beyond a wide-eyed excitement that role-playing is possible and impressive.

None of these expectations are fulfilled. The settings of the examples are not clearly identified. Only gradually does it become clear that they come from a variety of conditions, from performances which are open to anybody who buys a ticket to therapeutic sessions to work with convicts and addicts. The effects of the performances are treated in a similar cavalier manner. We find some off-hand comments of better understanding reached by the protagonist and some feedback of group discussion, but all this is mentioned in an off-hand manner, as if not really important to the beauty of the psychodrama itself.

The lack of perspective on psychodrama is aggravated in the later chapters. While the earlier chapters describe typical scenes and incidents in what can be called classical psychodrama, the later part shows the pervasiveness of role playing, first in different psychotherapeutic conditions, then in everyday life. Finally, the discussion spills over the borderline of dramatic performance and psychodrama, analyzes the current cultural conditions from a psychodramatic perspective (with the obligatory obeisances to Auschwitz, My Lai, and Watergate). The discussion reaches some of the most grandiose statements of L.J. Moreno, the founder of psychodrama proper.

The last chapter gives a clue to the apparent diffuseness of the volume. It is a heartfelt eulogy to Moreno, who had been the author's mentor and friend. Moreno was a strong, almost charismatic personality, gifted, contradictory, often infuriating, who could have had a tremendous impact on his disciples. At the shock of his death, a eulogy like this volume may have been called for, directed to the appropriate audience. But reading this book and reviewing it becomes as embarrassing as intruding on somebody's private grief. As a memorial addressed to Moreno's circle, this book could have been a fitting tribute. For a general audience, something different is called for. Moreno was a fascinating person in many ways. His work, with all its limitations as well as contributions, deserves careful scrutiny. The author was too closely involved to keep the requisite distance for such a task. Moreno and his work deserve a thorough biography and analysis, warts and all. In the long run, Moreno's memory could be served better by such disquisition than the passionate admiration of the present book.

PUBLICATIONS RECEIVED

(Listing of a publication does not assure nor preclude its subsequent review.)

ADLAM, DIANA S. *Code in Context.* Routledge & Kegan Paul, 1977. 253 pp. $14.50 cloth.

AIGNER, D. J., and GOLDBERGER, A. S., eds. *Latent Variables in Socio-Economic Models.* North-Holland, 1977. 383 pp. $48.95 cloth.

ALLEN, IRVING LEWIS, ed. *New Towns and the Surburban Dream: Ideology and Utopia in Planning and Development.* Kennikat, 1977. 285 pp. $13.50 cloth. $6.95 paper.

ALMÁSI, MIKLÓS. *Phänomenologie des Scheins: Die Seinsweise der gesellschaftlichen Scheinformen.* Akadémiai Kiadó, 1977. 340 pp. $12.00 cloth.

ARGYRIS, CHRIS. *Increasing Leadership Effectiveness.* Wiley, 1976. 286 pp. NPL, cloth.

ARONSON, ELLIOT, ed. *Readings about the Social Animal,* 2nd ed. W. H. Freeman, 1977. 414 pp. $14.00 cloth. $6.50 paper.

ATTENBOROUGH, DAVID. *The Tribal Eye.* W. W. Norton, 1976. 144 pp. $14.95 cloth.

BADER, BERGER, GANBMANN, and KNESEBECK. *Einfuhrung in die Gesellschaftstheorie: Gesellschaft, Wirtschaft und Staat bei Marx und Weber,* vols. 1 & 2. Campus Verlag, 1976. 517 pp. NPL, paper.

BALBUS, ISAAC D. *The Dialectics of Legal Repression: Black Rebels before the American Criminal Courts.* Transaction, 1977. $4.95 paper.

BANDURA, ALBERT. *Social Learning Theory.* Prentice-Hall, 1977. 247 pp. $9.50 cloth. $5.95 paper.

BARRETTO, LEFTY. *Nobody's Hero: A Puerto Rican Story.* New American Library, 1976. 258 pp. $1.75 paper.

BARTON, ALLEN H., et al. *Decentralizing City Government: An Evaluation of the New York City District Manager Experiment.* Lexington, 1977. 279 pp. $19.00 cloth.

BEACH, FRANK A., ed. *Human Sexuality in Four Perspectives.* Johns Hopkins University Press, 1977. 330 pp. $15.00 cloth.

BECKER, HOWARD S., et al. *Boys in White: Student Culture in Medical School.* Transaction, 1977. 456 pp. $7.95 paper.

BEN-DAVID, JOSEPH. *Centers of Learning: Britain, France, Germany, United States.* McGraw-Hill, 1977. 208 pp. $12.50 cloth.

BHATTACHARYYA, GOURI K., and JOHNSON, RICHARD A. *Statistical Concepts and Methods.* Wiley, 1977. 639 pp. $14.95 cloth.

BINSTOCK, ROBERT H., and SHANAS, ETHEL, eds. *Handbook of Aging and the Social Sciences.* Van Nostrand Reinhold, 1976. 684 pp. $32.50 cloth.

BLOCK, FRED L. *The Origins of International Economic Disorder: A Study of United States International Monetary Policy from World War II to the Present.* University of California Press, 1977. 282 pp. $14.00 cloth.

BOGUSLAW, ROBERT, and VICKERS, GEORGE R. *Prologue to Sociology.* Goodyear, 1977. 303 pp. NPL, paper.

BOLTON, JOHN R. *The Legislative Veto: Unseparating the Powers.* American Enterprise Institute for Public Policy, 1977. 50 pp. $2.25 paper.

BOOT, ADRIAN, and THOMAS, MICHAEL. *Jamaica: Babylon on a Thin Wire.* Schocken, 1977. 95 pp. $6.95 paper.

BOURGUIGNON, ERIKA. *Possession.* Chandler & Sharp, 1976. 78 pp. $2.13 paper.

BRITTAIN, JOHN A. *The Inheritance of Economic Status.* Brookings, 1977. 185 pp. $9.95 cloth. $3.95 paper.

BROOM, LEONARD, and SELZNICK, PHILIP. *Sociology: A Text with Adapted Readings,* 6th ed. Harper & Row, 1977. 619 pp. $13.75 cloth.

BUCHANAN, A. RUSSELL. *Black Americans in World War II.* Clio, 1977. 148 pp. $14.95 cloth.

BURKE, W. WARNER, ed. *Current Issues and Strategies in Organization Development.* Human Sciences, 1977. 448 pp. $24.95 cloth.

BUSSINK, TINE; VAN DER TAK, JEAN; and ZUGA, CONNIE S., eds. *Sourcebook on Population, 1970–1976.* Population Reference Bureau, 1976. 72 pp. $3.95 paper.

BUTLER, ROBERT N., and LEWIS, MYRNA I. *Aging and Mental Health: Positive Psychosocial Approaches.* C. V. Mosby, 1977. 365 pp. $8.50 paper.

CARLTON, ERIC. *Ideology and Social Order.* Routledge & Kegan Paul, 1977. 320 pp. $18.00 cloth.

CARTWRIGHT, ROSALIND DYMOND. *Night Life: Explorations in Dreaming.* Prentice-Hall, 1977. 148 pp. $8.95 cloth. $2.95 paper.

CHAFE, WILLIAM H. *Women and Equality: Changing Patterns in American Culture.* Oxford University Press, 1977. 207 pp. $8.95 cloth.

CHERRY, GORDON E., ed. *Rural Planning Problems.* Barnes & Noble, 1976. 286 pp. $19.50 cloth.

CHILAND, COLETTE. *Long-Term Treatments of Psychotic States.* Human Sciences, 1977. 696 pp. NPL, cloth.

CHIROT, DANIEL. *Social Change in the Twentieth Century.* Harcourt Brace Jovanovich, 1977. 273 pp. $5.95 paper.

COHEN, ABNER. *Two-Dimensional Man: An Essay on the Anthropology of Power and Symbolism in Complex Society.* University of California Press, 1976. 156 pp. $3.25 paper.

COLLETT, PETER, ed. *Social Rules and Social Behaviour.* Rowman & Littlefield, 1977. 185 pp. $14.00 cloth.

COREY, LAWRENCE; EPSTEIN, MICHAEL F.; and SALTMAN, STEVEN E. *Medicine in a Changing Society,* 2nd ed. C. V. Mosby, 1977. 236 pp. $5.25 paper.

COSTELLO, V. F. *Urbanization in the Middle East.* Cambridge University Press, 1977. 121 pp. $11.50 cloth. $3.95 paper.

COTT, NANCY F. *The Bonds of Womanhood: "Woman's Sphere" in New England, 1780–1835.* Yale University Press, 1977. 225 pp. $12.50 cloth.

CREMIN, LAWRENCE A. *Traditions of American Education*. Basic Books, 1977. 172 pp. $8.95 cloth.

CRICK, MALCOLM. *Explorations in Language and Meaning: Towards a Semantic Anthropology*. Halsted, 1976. 212 pp. NPL, cloth.

CUMMINGS, THOMAS G., and SRIVASTVA, SURESH. *Management of Work: A Socio-Technical Systems Approach*. Kent State University Press, 1977. 247 pp. $15.00 cloth.

CURTIS, RICHARD F., and JACKSON, ELTON F. *Inequality in American Communities*. Academic Press, 1977. 354 pp. $19.50 cloth.

DANIEL, WAYNE W. *Introductory Statistics with Applications*. Houghton Mifflin, 1977. 475 pp. $13.95 cloth.

DE LAGUNA, FREDERICA. *Voyage to Greenland: A Personal Initiation into Anthropology*. W. W. Norton, 1977. 285 pp. $9.95 cloth.

DICKSTEIN, MORRIS. *Gates of Eden: American Culture in the Sixties*. Basic Books, 1977. 300 pp. $11.95 cloth.

DONOGHUE, JOHN D. *Pariah Persistence in Changing Japan: A Case Study*. University Press of America, 1977. 117 pp. NPL, paper.

DOUGLAS, JACK D., and JOHNSON, JOHN M. *Official Deviance: Readings in Malfeasance, Misfeasance, and other Forms of Corruption*. J. B. Lippincott, 1977. 426 pp. $5.95 paper.

DOWNIE, N. M., and STARRY, A. R. *Descriptive and Inferential Statistics*. Harper & Row, 1977. 362 pp. $11.50 cloth.

DRINNON, RICHARD, and DRINNON, ANNA MARIA, eds. *Nowhere at Home: Letters from Exile of Emma Goldman and Alexander Berkman*. Schocken Books, 1975. 282 pp. $12.95 cloth. $6.95 paper.

DUMONT, LOUIS. *From Mandeville to Marx: The Genesis and Triumph of Economic Ideology*. University of Chicago Press, 1977. 236 pp. $16.50 cloth.

DUNN, JUDY. *Distress and Comfort*. Harvard University Press, 1977. 127 pp. NPL, cloth.

DUVALL, EVELYN MILLIS. *Marriage and Family Development*, 5th ed. J. B. Lippincott, 1977. 559 pp. $12.95 cloth.

EDWARDS, GRIFFITH, et al., eds. *Alcohol Dependence and Smoking Behaviour*. Lexington, 1976. 268 pp. $17.50 cloth.

EDWARDS, GRIFFITH, et al., eds. *Drugs and Drug Dependence*. Lexington, 1976. 252 pp. $17.50 cloth.

EDWARDS, ROMAINE V. *Crisis Intervention and How It Works*. Charles C Thomas, 1977. 78 pp. $8.00 cloth.

ELMENDORF, MARY. *Nine Mayan Women: A Village Faces Change*. Halsted, 1976. 159 pp. $12.50 cloth. $5.95 paper.

ENGLER, ROBERT. *The Brotherhood of Oil: Energy Policy and the Public Interest*. University of Chicago Press, 1977. 337 pp. $12.50 cloth.

ERICSON, RICHARD V. *Criminal Reactions: The Labelling Perspective*. Lexington, 1975. 170 pp. $14.50 cloth.

ERICSON, RICHARD V. *Young Offenders and Their Social Work*. Lexington, 1975. 225 pp. $18.50 cloth.

FAIRLEY, WILLIAM B., and MOSTELLER, FREDERICK, eds. *Statistics and Public Policy*. Addison-Wesley, 1977. 397 pp. $14.95 cloth.

FASS, PAULA S. *The Damned and the Beautiful: American Youth in the 1920's*. Oxford University Press, 1977. 497 pp. $15.95 cloth.

FISHEL, ANDREW, and POTTKER, JANICE. *National Politics and Sex Discrimination in Education*. Lexington, 1977. 159 pp. $15.00 cloth.

FISHER, ROBIN. *Contact and Conflict: Indian-European Relations in British Columbia, 1774–1890*. University of British Columbia Press, 1977. 250 pp. $18.00 cloth.

FOGELSON, RAYMOND D., and ADAMS, RICHARD N., eds. *The Anthropology of Power: Ethnographic Studies from Asia, Oceania, and the New World*. Academic Press, 1977. 429 pp. $19.50 cloth.

FREEMAN, M. D. A. *The Legal Structure*. Longman, 1974. 243 pp. NPL, paper.

GAGNON, JOHN H. *Human Sexualities*. Scott, Foresman, 1977. 432 pp. $9.95 paper.

GALASSI, MERNA DEE, and GALASSI, JOHN P. *Assert Yourself! How to Be Your Own Person*. Human Sciences, 1977. 237 pp. $7.95 paper.

GALE, Raymond F. *Explorations into Humanness: The Common Strivings of People, A Cross-Cultural Study*. Christopher, 1977. 92 pp. $4.95 paper.

GALLIHER, JOHN F., and McCARTNEY, JAMES L. *Criminology: Power, Crime, and Criminal Law*. Dorsey, 1977. 548 pp. $13.95 cloth.

GARNER, ROBERTA ASH. *Social Change*. Rand McNally, 1977. 430 pp. $6.95 paper.

GARNER, ROBERTA ASH. *Social Movements in America*, 2nd ed. Rand McNally, 1977. 233 pp. $4.95 paper.

GARVEY, CATHERINE. *Play*. Harvard University Press, 1977. 133 pp. NPL, cloth.

GERSHENFELD, WALTER J.; LOEWENBERG, J. JOSEPH; and INGSTER, BERNARD. *Scope of Public-Sector Bargaining*. Lexington, 1977. 211 pp. $16.00 cloth.

GIBBONS, DON C. *Society, Crime, and Criminal Careers: An Introduction to Criminology*, 3rd ed. Prentice-Hall, 1977. 582 pp. $12.95 cloth.

GIELE, JANET ZOLLINGER, and SMOCK, AUDREY CHAPMAN, eds. *Women: Roles and Status in Eight Countries*. Wiley, 1977. 443 pp. $17.50 cloth.

GIL, DAVID G. *The Challenge of Social Equality: Essays on Social Policy, Social Development and Political Practice*. Schenkman, 1976. 225 pp. NPL, cloth.

GINZBER, ELI, ed. *Jobs for Americans*. Prentice-Hall, 1976. 210 pp. $8.95 cloth. $4.50 paper.

GLASGOW UNIVERSITY MEDIA GROUP. *Bad News*, vol. 1. Routledge & Kegan Paul, 1976. 310 pp. $14.00 cloth.

GLAZER, NONA, and WAEHRER, HELEN YOUNGELSON, eds. *Woman in a Man-Made World*, 2nd ed. Rand McNally, 1977. 443 pp. $6.95 paper.

GOLDSTEIN, HAROLD M., and HOROWITZ, MORRIS A. *Entry-Level Health Occupations: Development and Future*. Johns Hopkins University Press, 1977. 100 pp. NPL, cloth.

GOODY, JACK. *Production and Reproduction: A Comparative Study of the Domestic Domain*. Cambridge University Press, 1976. 157 pp. $14.95 cloth. $4.95 paper.

GREENWOOD, PETER W.; CHAIKEN, JAN M.; and PETERSILIA, JOAN. *The Criminal Investigation Process*. Lexington, 1977. 326 pp. $15.00 cloth.

GRONBERG, KIRSTEN A. *Mass Society and the Extension of Welfare, 1960–1970*. University of Chicago Press, 1977. 266 pp. $16.00 cloth.

GROSS, BEATRICE, and GROSS, RONALD, eds. *The Children's Rights Movement: Overcoming the Oppression of Young People*. Anchor Press, 1977. 390 pp. $3.95 paper.

HAAN, NORMA. *Coping and Defending: Processes of Self-Environment Organization*. Academic Press, 1977. 346 pp. $17.50 cloth.

HAMBLIN, ROBERT L., and KUNKEL, JOHN H., eds. *Behavioral Theory in Sociology: Essays in Honor of George C. Homans*. Transaction, 1977. 546 pp. $29.95 cloth.

HAMERMESH, DANIEL S. *Jobless Pay and the Economy*. Johns Hopkins University Press, 1977. 114 pp. $8.50 cloth. $3.25 paper.

HAMILTON, MARSHALL L. *Father's Influence on Children*. Nelson-Hall, 1977. 203 pp. $9.95 cloth. $5.95 paper.

HARRINGTON, MICHAEL. *Fragments of the Century*. Simon & Schuster, 1977. 246 pp. $3.95 paper.

HART, RODERICK P. *The Political Pulpit*. Purdue University Press, 1977. 141 pp. $7.95 cloth. $3.50 paper.

HARTJEN, CLAYTON A. *Possible Trouble: An Analysis of Social Problems* (with teacher's manual). Praeger, 1977. 351 pp. NPL, cloth.

HARWOOD, ALAN, *Rx: Spiritist as Needed: A Study of a Puerto Rican Community Mental Health Resource*. Wiley, 1977. 251 pp. NPL, cloth.

HASSAN, RIAZ. *Families in Flats: A Study of Low Income Families in Public Housing*. Singapore University Press, 1977. 249 pp. NPL, cloth.

HAUSER, ROBERT M., and FEATHERMAN, DAVID L. *The Process of Stratification: Trends and Analyses*. Academic Press, 1977. 372 pp. $19.50 cloth.

HAVEMAN, ROBERT H., ed. *A Decade of Federal Antipoverty Programs: Achievements, Failures, and Lessons*. Academic Press, 1977. 381 pp. $17.00 cloth.

HAWKINS, P. R. *Social Class, the Nominal Group and Verbal Strategies*. Routledge & Kegan Paul, 1977. 242 pp. $20.25 cloth.

HAY, DOUGLAS, et al. *Albion's Fatal Tree: Crime and Society in Eighteenth-Century England*. Pantheon, 1975. 352 pp. $5.95 paper.

HAYES, FREDERICK O'R. *Productivity in Local Government*. Lexington, 1977. 295 pp. $22.00 cloth.

HINKLE, LAWRENCE E., JR., and LORING, WILLIAM C., eds. *The Effect of the Man-Made Environment on Health and Behavior*. US Gov. Printing Office, 1977. 315 pp. $3.25 paper.

HOE, BAN SENG. *Structural Changes of Two Chinese Communities in Alberta, Canada*. Canadian Centre for Folk Culture Studies/ National Museums of Canada, 1976. 385 pp. NPL, paper.

HOERDER, DIRK, ed. *American Labor History: Research, Teaching, and Bibliographic Aids*. Library of the John F. Kennedy—Institut für Nordamerikastudien Freie Universität Berlin, 1976. 181 pp. NPL, paper.

HOROWITZ, DONALD L. *The Jurocracy: Government Lawyers, Agency Programs, and Judicial Decisions*. Lexington, 1977. 145 pp. $14.00 cloth.

HOROWITZ, IRVING LOUIS, ed. *Cuban Communism*, 3rd ed. Transaction, 1977. 576 pp. $8.95 paper.

HOWE, IRVING. *World of Our Fathers*. Simon & Schuster, 1976. 714 pp. $6.95 paper.

HOWE, MICHAEL J. A. *Television and Children*. Linnet, 1977. 157 pp. $7.50 cloth.

JACOBS, JAMES B. *Stateville: The Penitentiary in Mass Society*. University of Chicago Press, 1977. 281 pp. $12.50 cloth.

JACOBSON, GEORGE R. *The Alcoholisms: Detection, Assessment, and Diagnosis*. Human Sciences, 1976. 414 pp. $19.95 cloth.

JENCKS, CHRISTOPHER, and RIESMAN, DAVID. *The Academic Revolution*. University of Chicago Press, 1977. 580 pp. $7.95 paper.

JEWETT, ROBERT, and LAWRENCE, JOHN SHELTON. *The American Monomyth*. Anchor, 1977. 263 pp. $8.95 cloth.

JOSHI, HEATHER, and JOSHI, VIJAY. *Surplus Labour and the City: A Study of Bombay*. Oxford University Press, 1976. 189 pp. $8.25 cloth.

JULIAN, JOSEPH. *Social Problems*, 2nd ed. Prentice-Hall, 1977. 588 pp. $12.95 cloth.
JUNGK, ROBERT. *The Everyman Project: Resources for a Humane Future.* Liveright, 1977. 288 pp. $10.95 cloth.
JUNIPER, DEAN F. *Decision-Making For Schools and Colleges.* Pergamon, 1976. 302 pp. $16.00 cloth. $10.00 paper.
KANDO, THOMAS M. *Social Interaction.* C. V. Mosby, 1977. 349 pp. $9.25 paper.
KANTER, ROSABETH MOSS. *Work and Family in the United States: A Critical Review and Agenda for Research and Policy.* Russell Sage, 1977. 116 pp. NPL, paper.
KAUFMAN, HAROLD F.; SINGH, AVTAR; and DASGUPTA, SATADAL. *Villages upward Bound: Community Structure and Technological Development in Selected Indian Villages.* Editions Indian, dist. by South Asia Books, 1975. 188 pp. $11.00 cloth.
KEPHART, WILLIAM M. *The Family, Society, and the Individual,* 4th ed. Houghton Mifflin, 1977. 546 pp. $12.95 cloth.
KEYES, CHARLES F. *The Golden Peninsula: Culture and Adaptation in Mainland Southeast Asia.* Macmillan, 1977. 370 pp. $6.95 paper.
KRADER, LAWRENCE. *Dialectic of Civil Society.* Van Gorcum, dist. by Humanities, 1976. 279 pp. $22.00 cloth.
KRAUSE, ELLIOTT A. *Power and Illness: The Political Sociology of Health and Medical Care.* Elsevier, 1977. 383 pp. $12.95 cloth.
LABOVITZ, SANFORD. *An Introduction to Sociological Concepts.* Wiley, 1977. 244 pp. $6.95 paper.
LAUDAN, LARRY. *Progress and Its Problems: Toward a Theory of Scientific Growth.* University of California Press, 1977. 257 pp. $10.95 cloth.
LAUER, ROBERT H., and HANDEL, WARREN H. *Social Psychology: The Theory and Application of Symbolic Interactionism.* Houghton Mifflin, 1977. 467 pp. $11.95 cloth.
LAWRENCE, P. A. *Georg Simmel: Sociologist and European.* Barnes & Noble, 1976. 275 pp. $13.50 cloth.
LEE, GARY R. *Family Structure and Interaction: A Comparative Analysis.* J. B. Lippincott, 1977. 343 pp. $9.95 cloth.
LEE, TREVOR R. *Race and Residence: The Concentration and Dispersal of Immigrants in London.* Oxford University Press, 1977. 193 pp. $15.25 cloth.
LEGER, ROBERT G., and STRATTON, JOHN R., eds. *The Sociology of Corrections: A Book of Readings.* Wiley, 1977. 557 pp. $9.95 paper.
LEMASTERS, E. E. *Parents in Modern America,* 3rd ed. Dorsey, 1977. 210 pp. $5.95 paper.
LENERO-OTERO, LUIS, ed. *Beyond the Nuclear Family Model: Cross-Cultural Perspectives.* Sage, 1977. 226 pp. NPL, paper.
LEVIN, BETSY, and HAWLEY, WILLIS D., eds. *The Courts, Social Science, and School Desegregation.* Transaction, 1977. 432 pp. $24.95 cloth.
LEVIN, JACK. *Elementary Statistics in Social Research,* 2nd ed. Harper & Row, 1977. 293 pp. $12.95 cloth.
LEVITAN, SAR A., and TAGGART, ROBERT. *Jobs for the Disabled.* Johns Hopkins University Press, 1977. 129 pp. $9.00 cloth. $3.50 paper.
LIBO, LESTER. *Is There Life after Group?* Anchor Press, 1977. 148 pp. $1.95 paper.
LIPSKY, MICHAEL, and OLSON, DAVID J. *Commission Politics: The Processing of Social Crisis in America.* Transaction, 1977. 476 pp. $14.95 cloth.
LOBE, THOMAS. *United States National Security Policy and Aid to the Thailand Police.* University of Denver/Graduate School of International Studies, 1977. 161 pp. NPL, paper.
LOWRY, RITCHIE P., and RANKIN, ROBERT P. *Sociology: Social Science and Social Concern,* 3rd ed. D. C. Heath, 1977. 716 pp. NPL, cloth.
MACFARLANE, AIDAN. *The Psychology of Childbirth.* Harvard University Press, 1977. 140 pp. $6.95 cloth. $2.95 paper.
MACHT, LEE B.; SCHERL, DONALD J.; and SHARFSTEIN, STEVEN, eds. *Neighborhood Psychiatry.* Lexington, 1977. 221 pp. $17.50 cloth.
MACKENZIE, NORMAN, and MACKENZIE, JEANNE. *The Fabians.* Simon & Schuster, 1977. 446 pp. $12.95 cloth.
MAGARO, PETER A., ed. *The Construction of Madness: Emerging Conceptions and Interventions into the Psychotic Process.* Pergamon, 1976. 221 pp. $13.50 cloth. $7.00 paper.
MANARD, BARBARA BOLLING; WOEHLE, RALPH E.; and HEILMAN, JAMES M. *Better Homes for the Old.* Lexington, 1977. 152 pp. $15.00 cloth.
MANHEIM, HENRY L. *Sociological Research: Philosophy and Methods.* Dorsey, 1977. 391 pp. $12.95 cloth.
McCUE, GEORGE, ed. *Music in American Society, 1776–1976: From Puritan Hymn to Synthesizer.* Transaction, 1977. 201 pp. $14.95 cloth. $3.95 paper.
McPARTLAND, JAMES M., and McDILL, EDWARD L., eds. *Violence in Schools: Perspectives, Programs, and Positions.* Lexington, 1977. 185 pp. $15.00 cloth.
MENOLASCINO, FRANK J. *Challenges in Mental Retardation: Progressive Ideology and Services.* Human Sciences, 1977. 362 pp. $16.95 cloth.
MENZIES, KEN. *Talcott Parsons and the Social Image of Man.* Routledge & Kegan Paul, 1976. 197 pp. $9.50 cloth.
MERON, THEODOR. *The United Nations Secretariat: The Rules and the Practice.* Lexington, 1977. 208 pp. $19.00 cloth.
MOFFITT, DONALD, ed. *The Wall Street Journal Views America Tomorrow.* American Management Associations, 1977. 184 pp. $9.95 cloth.
MOORE, MARK HARRISON. *Buy and Bust: The Effective Regulation of an Illicit Market in Heroin.* Lexington, 1977. 291 pp. $16.00 cloth.
MORALES, ARMANDO, and SHEAFOR, BRADFORD W. *Social Work: A Profession of Many Faces.* Allyn & Bacon, 1977. 286 pp. NPL, cloth.
MOSCOVICI, SERGE. *Social Influence and Social Change.* Academic Press, 1976. 239 pp. $15.25 cloth.
MUELLER, JOHN H.; SCHUESSLER, KARL F.; and COSTNER, HERBERT L. *Statistical Reasoning in Sociology,* 3rd ed. Houghton Mifflin, 1977. 544 pp. $13.95 cloth.
MUIR, WILLIAM KER, JR. *Police: Streetcorner Politicians.* University of Chicago Press, 1977. 306 pp. $15.00 cloth.
MUNNELL, ALICIA H. *The Future of Social Security.* Brookings, 1977. 190 pp. $9.95 cloth. $3.95 paper.
NAROLL, RAOUL; MICHIK, GARY L.; and NAROLL, FRADA. *Worldwide Theory Testing.* Human Relations Area Files, 1976. 131 pp. $5.00 paper.
NELSON, MARIE COLEMAN, ed. *The Narcissistic Condition: A Fact of Our Lives and Times.* Human Sciences, 1977. 300 pp. $18.95 cloth.
NORTH, DOUGLASS, C., and THOMAS, ROBERT PAUL. *The Rise of the Western World: A New Economic History.* Cambridge University Press, 1976. 171 pp. $11.95 cloth. $4.95 paper.
OVERBEEK, JOHANNES, ed. *The Evolution of Population Theory: A Documentary Sourcebook.* Greenwood, 1977. 277 pp. $14.95 cloth.
PAOLUCCI, BEATRICE; HALL, OLIVE AL; and AXINN, NANCY W. *Family Decision Making: An Ecosystem Approach.* Wiley, 1977. 190 pp. NPL, paper.
PATTISON, E. MANSELL. *The Experience of Dying.* Prentice-Hall, 1977. 335 pp. $10.95 cloth. $4.95 paper.
PELLETIER, KENNETH R. *Mind as Healer, Mind as Slayer: A Holistic Approach to Preventing Stress Disorders.* Dell, 1977. 366 pp. $10.00 cloth. $4.95 paper.
PERRUCCI, ROBERT; KNUDSEN, DEAN D.; and HAMBY, RUSSELL R. *Sociology: Basic Structures and Processes,* with instructor's manual and student guide. Wm. C. Brown, 1977. 606 pp. NPL, cloth.
PHAYER, J. MICHAEL. *Sexual Liberation and Religion in Nineteenth Century Europe.* Rowman & Littlefield, 1977. 176 pp. $15.00 cloth.
PITT-RIVERS, JULIAN. *The Fate of Shechem or The Politics of Sex.* Cambridge University Press, 1977. 193 pp. $15.95 cloth.
POPENOE, DAVID. *Sociology,* 3rd ed. Prentice-Hall, 1977. 588 pp. $12.95 cloth.
POPENOE, DAVID. *The Surburban Environment: Sweden and the United States.* University of Chicago Press, 1977. 275 pp. $19.00 cloth.
PRUS, ROBERT C., and SHARPER, C. R. D. *Road Hustler: The Career Contingencies of Professional Card and Dice Hustlers.* Lexington, 1977. 178 pp. $15.00 cloth.
RABINOVITZ, FRANCINE F. *Minorities in Suburbs: The Los Angeles Experience.* Lexington, 1977. 100 pp. $12.50 cloth.
RADZINOWICZ, SIR LEON, and KING, JOAN. *The Growth of Crime: The International Experience.* Basic Books, 1977. 342 pp. $11.95 cloth.
RANNEY, AUSTIN. *Participation in American Presidential Nominations, 1976.* American Enterprise Institue for Public Policy Research, 1977. 37 pp. $2.25 paper.
REES, P. H., and WILSON, A. G. *Spatial Population Analysis.* Edward Arnold, dist. by Academic Press, 1977. 356 pp. $35.50 cloth.
RETTIG, RICHARD P.; TORRES, MANUAL J.; and GARRETT, GERALD R. *Manny: A Criminal-Addict's Story.* Houghton Mifflin, 1977. 264 pp. $5.95 paper.
RICHARDSON, ANN. *Vouchered Skill Training in WIN: Program Guidelines and Selected Empirical Findings.* Bureau of Social Science Research, 1977. 117 pp. NPL, paper.
RICHARDSON, C. J. *Contemporary Social Mobility.* Nichols, 1977. 340 pp. $17.50 cloth.
RICHEY, RUSSELL E., ed. *Denominationalism.* Abingdon, 1977. 288 pp. $15.95 cloth. $6.95 paper.
ROBERTS, CECILIA M. *Doctor and Patient in the Teaching Hospital: A Tale of Two Life-Worlds.* Lexington, 1977. 140 pp. $15.00 cloth.
ROBERTSON, IAN. *Sociology,* with instructor's manual by Donald P. Irish and study guide by Diana K. Harris and William E. Cole. Worth, 1977. 603 pp. $13.95 cloth.
ROBINSON, FRANK S. *Machine Politics: A Study of Albany's O'Connells.* Transaction, 1977. 262 pp. $12.95 cloth.
ROBINSON, JOHN P. *How Americans Use Time: A Social-Psychological Analysis of Everyday Behavior.* Praeger, 1977. 209 pp. NPL, cloth.
ROCK, PAUL E., ed. *Drugs and Politics.* Transaction, 1977. 331 pp. $12.95 cloth. $3.95 paper.

RODMAN, F. ROBERT. *Not Dying*. Random House, 1977. 216 pp. $7.95 cloth.
ROSENBLATT, PAUL C.; WALSH, R. PATRICIA; and JACKSON, DOUGLAS A. *Grief and Mourning in Cross-Cultural Perspective*. HRAF Press, 1976. 231 pp. $9.00 cloth. $4.50 paper.
ROSENFELD, STEPHEN S. *The Time of Their Dying*. W. W. Norton, 1977. 189 pp. $7.95 cloth.
ROSS, JENNIE-KEITH. *Old People, New Lives: Community Creation in a Retirement Residence*. University of Chicago Press, 1977. 227 pp. $13.50 cloth.
RUBIN, BERNARD. *Media, Politics, and Democracy*. Oxford University Press, 1977. 192 pp. $8.00 cloth. $4.00 paper.
RUTTER, MICHAEL, and MADGE, NICOLA. *Cycles of Disadvantage: A Review of Research*. Heinemann, dist. by Humanities, 1977. 413 pp. $13.00 cloth. $5.00 paper.
SAFILIOS-ROTHSCHILD, CONSTANTINA. *Love, Sex, and Sex Roles*. Prentice-Hall, 1977. 150 pp. NPL, cloth.
SAKS, MICHAEL J. *Jury Verdicts: The Role of Group Size and Social Decision Rule*. Lexington, 1977. 136 pp. $15.00 cloth.
SCAGEL, ROBERT F., ed. *Mankind's Future in the Pacific: The Plenary and Special Lectures of the Thirteenth Pacific Science Congress, August 1975*. University of British Columbia Press, 1976. 198 pp. NPL, paper.
SCANZONI, JOHN H. *The Black Family in Modern Society: Patterns of Stability and Security*. University of Chicago Press, 1977. 365 pp. $5.95 paper.
SCHAFFER, RUDOLPH. *Mothering*. Harvard University Press, 1977. 120 pp. NPL, cloth.
SCHMIDT, STEFFEN W., et al., eds. *Friends, Followers, and Factions: A Reader in Political Clientelism*. University of California Press, 1977. 512 pp. $20.00 cloth.
SCHUTTE, JERALD G. *Everything You Always Wanted to Know about Elementary Statistics (but Were Afraid to Ask)*. Prentice-Hall, 1977. 230 pp. $6.95 paper.
SENN, MILTON J. E. *Speaking Out for America's Children*. Yale University Press, 1977. 214 pp. $13.50 cloth. $4.95 paper.
SINGH, ANDREA MENEFEE. *Neighbourhood and Social Networks in Urban India*. Marwah, dist. by South Asia Books, 1976. 230 pp. $11.00 cloth.
SIVACHYOV, N., and YAZKOV, E. *History of the USA since World War I*. Progress, 1976. 501 pp. $5.75 cloth.
SPANN, OWEN, and SPANN, NANCIE. *Your Child? I Thought It Was My Child!* Ward Ritchie, 1977. 176 pp. $8.95 cloth.
STEIN, PETER J.; RICHMAN, JUDITH; and HANNON, NATALIE. *The Family: Functions, Conflicts, and Symbols*. Addison-Wesley, 1977. 452 pp. NPL, paper.
STEPPACHER, ROLF; ZOGG-WALZ, BRIGITTE; and HATZFELDT, HERMANN, eds. *Economics in Institutional Perspective: Memorial Essays in Honor of K. William Kapp*. Lexington, 1977. 218 pp. $14.00 cloth.
STERNBERG, DAVID JOEL. *Radical Sociology: An Introduction to American Behavioral Science*. Exposition, 1977. 338 pp. $15.00 cloth. $7.50 paper.
TAYLOR, ROBERT. *Welcome to the Middle Years: A Doctor's Guide*. Acropolis, 1976. 206 pp. $10.00 cloth.
THOMPSON, E. P. *Whigs and Hunters: The Origin of the Black Act*. Pantheon, 1975. 313 pp. $5.95 paper.
TOURAINE, ALAIN. *The Self-Production of Society*. University of Chicago Press, 1977. 467 pp. $27.50 cloth.
TSUR, JACOB. *Zionism: The Saga of a National Liberation Movement*. Transaction, 1977. 112 pp. $3.95 paper.
TWADDLE, ANDREW C., and HESSLER, RICHARD M. *A Sociology of Health*. C. V. Mosby, 1977. 349 pp. $8.95 paper.
UNGER, STEVEN, ed. *The Destruction of American Indian Families*. Association on American Indian Affairs, 1977. 90 pp. $3.50 paper.
VAN MAANEN, JOHN, ed. *Organizational Careers: Some New Perspectives*. Wiley, 1977. 199 pp. $13.95 cloth.
WALSH, MARILYN E. *The Fence: A New Look at the World of Property Theft*. Greenwood, 1977. 215 pp. $13.95 cloth.
WALSH, MARY ROTH. *"Doctors Wanted: No Women Need Apply": Sexual Barriers in the Medical Profession, 1835–1975*. Yale University Press, 1977. 303 pp. $15.00 cloth.
WALUM, LAUREL RICHARDSON. *The Dynamics of Sex and Gender: A Sociological Perspective*. Rand McNally, 1977. 246 pp. $6.95 paper.
WEIDMANN, MAX. *Das Drogenverhalten von Basler Schulern*. Social Strategies Publishers Cooperative Society, 1977. 124 p. NPL, paper.
WEISS, CAROL H., ed. *Using Social Research in Public Policy Making*. Lexington, 1977. 256 pp. $19.00 cloth.
WESSON, DONALD R., and SMITH, DAVID E. *Barbiturates: Their Use, Misuse, and Abuse*. Human Sciences, 1977. 144 pp. $14.95 cloth. $4.95 paper.
WESTOFF, CHARLES F., and RYDER, NORMAN B. *The Contraceptive Revolution*. Princeton University Press, 1977. 388 pp. $18.50 cloth.
WHINERY, LEO H., et al. *Predictive Sentencing: An Empirical Evaluation*. Lexington, 1976. 209 pp. $17.50 cloth.
WHITE, JAY DIXON, coordinator. *The General Systems Paradigm: Science of Change and Change of Science*. Society for General Systems Research, 1977. 524 pp. $15.00 paper.
WILES, PAUL, ed. *The Sociology of Crime and Delinquency: The New Criminologies*. Barnes & Noble, 1977. 237 pp. $14.00 cloth.
WILKINSON, DORIS Y., and TAYLOR, RONALD L. *The Black Male in America: Perspectives on His Status in Contemporary Society*. Nelson-Hall, 1977. 375 pp. $17.50 cloth. $6.95 paper.
WILLIAMS, JUANITA H. *Psychology of Women: Behavior in a Biosocial Context*. W. W. Norton, 1977. 444 pp. $13.50 cloth. $8.95 paper.
WILSON, AMY AUERBACHER; GREENBLATT, SIDNEY LEONARD; and WILSON, RICHARD WHITTINGHAM. *Deviance and Social Control in Chinese Society*. Praeger, 1977. 227 pp. $5.95 paper.
YOUNG, MICHAEL, and WILLMOTT, PETER. *The Symmetrical Family: A Study of Work and Leisure in the London Region*. Penguin, 1977. 398 pp. $2.95 pp.
ZARIT, STEVEN H., ed. *Readings in Aging and Death: Contemporary Perspectives, 1977–1978 Edition*. Harper & Row, 1977. 305 pp. $6.95 paper.
ZEITLIN, MAURICE, ed. *American Society, Inc.: Studies of the Social Structure and Political Economy of the United States*, 2nd ed. Rand McNally, 1977. 590 pp. $7.95 paper.
ZIMBALIST, SIDNEY E. *Historic Themes and Landmarks in Social Welfare Research*. Harper & Row, 1977. 432 pp. $10.95 cloth.

NOVEMBER 1977 – VOLUME 6, NUMBER 6

ONTEMPORARY SOCIOLOGY

A JOURNAL OF REVIEWS

IN THIS ISSUE

Symposia on
1. *The Dialectic of Ideology and Technology*, by Alvin Gouldner
2. *Social Evolution and Social Categories*, by Paul Hirst

Surveys of recent literature on
1. Social Exchange Theory
2. Mass Communications

Featured essays on
1. Field research
2. *Popular Culture and High Culture*, by Herbert Gans
3. *Astronomy Transformed*, by David Edge and Michael Mulkay
4. *The Form of Sociology*, by Shmuel Eisenstadt

On the back cover. A poem for authors on the publication of a first book

BLICATION OF THE AMERICAN SOCIOLOGICAL ASSOCIATION

contemporary sociology

a journal of reviews

November 1977 • Volume 6, Number 6

Concerning advertising, change of address and subscriptions, address: Executive Office, American Sociological Association, 1722 N Street, N.W., Washington, D.C. 20036.

Concerning manuscripts and book reviews, address: Editor, *Contemporary Sociology: A Journal of Reviews,* C-002, University of California, San Diego, La Jolla, California, 92093.

Contemporary Sociology: A Journal of Reviews is published at 49 Sheridan Avenue, Albany, N.Y. 12210, bi-monthly in January, March, May, July, September, and November.

Annual membership dues in the American Sociological Association, $30.00–$50.00. Student Member, $15; Associate, $20; International Associate, $12; Student Associate, $10.

Subscription rate for members, $10; non-members, $15; institutions and libraries, $20; non-member students, $10. Single issues $4.

New subscriptions and renewals will be entered on a calendar year basis only.

Change of address: Six weeks advance notice to the Executive Office, and old address as well as new, are necessary for change of subscriber's address.

Claims for undelivered copies must be made within the month following the regular month of publication. The publishers will supply missing copies when losses have been sustained in transit and when the reserve stock will permit.

ISSN 0094–3061

Second class postage paid at Washington, D.C. and at additional mailing offices.

Book reviews from *CS* are indexed in *Book Review Index,* published by Gale Research Company.

ASA Multiple Submission Policy: Submission of a manuscript to a professional journal clearly implies commitment to publish in that journal. The competition for journal space requires a great deal of time and effort on the part of editorial readers whose main compensation for this service is the opportunity to read papers prior to publication and the gratification associated with discharge of professional obligation. For these reasons, *the American Sociological Association regards submission of a manuscript to a professional journal while that paper is under review by another journal as unacceptable.*

Cover designed by Kenneth E. Anderson, A.I.A.

TABLE OF CONTENTS

LETTERS 631

SYMPOSIA

Gouldner: *The Dialectic of Ideology and Technology: The Origins, Grammar, and Future of Ideology* ....Anthony Giddens
Benton Johnson
Frederick R. Lynch 635

Hirst: *Social Evolution and Sociological Categories* ....Randall Collins
Guenther Roth 641

SURVEY REVIEWS

Chadwick-Jones: *Social Exchange Theory: Its Structure and Influence in Social Psychology;*
Ekeh: *Social Exchange Theory: The Two Traditions;*
Heath: *Rational Choice and Social Exchange;*
Kuhn: *The Logic of Social Systems;* and
Powers: *Behavior: The Control of Perception* ....Harry C. Bredemeier 646

Alexander: *The Role of Communications in the Middle East Conflict: Ideological and Religious Aspects;*
Carpenter: *Oh, What A Blow That Phantom Gave Me!;*
Hoggart: *On Culture and Communication;*
McQuail: *Sociology of Mass Communications;*
Olson: *Media and Symbols: The Forms of Expression, Communication, and Education;*
Seymour-Ure: *The Political Impact of Mass Media;* and
Wells: *Mass Communications: A World View* ....Gladys Engel Lang 650

FEATURES

Douglas: *Investigative Social Research: Individual and Team Field Research* and
Lofland: *Doing Social Life: The Qualitative Study of Human Interaction in Natural Settings* ....Raymond L. Gold 654

Edge and Mulkay: *Astronomy Transformed: The Emergence of Radio Astronomy in Britain* ....Thomas F. Gieryn 656

Eisenstadt: *The Form of Sociology: Paradigms and Crises* ....Jeffrey C. Alexander 658

Gans: *Popular Culture and High Culture: An Analysis and Evaluation of Taste* ....Bennett M. Berger 661

BOOK REVIEWS

COMMUNICATION/LANGUAGE

Brislin: *Translation: Applications and Research* ....Roger Spielmann 664
Sobel: *The Manipulators: America in the Media Age* ....Lowndes F. Stephens 665
Thorne and Henley: *Language and Sex: Difference and Dominance* ....Katherine Newman 666

COMMUNITY

Abrams and McCulloch: *Communes, Sociology and Society* ....Myron Orleans 667
Duncan, Schuman, and Duncan: *Social Change in a Metropolitan Community* ....Ellan Odiorne Derow 668
Popenoe: *The Suburban Environment: Sweden and the United States* .....Alison E. Woodward 668

CRIME, LAW, AND DEVIANCE

Quinney: *Class, State, and Crime: On the Theory and Practice of Criminal Justice* ....Robert G. Seifert 669

Sells: *The Effectiveness of Drug Abuse Treatment:*
Volume I: *Evaluation of Treatments*
Volume II: *Patient Profiles, Treatments and Outcomes*
Sells and Simpson: *The Effectiveness of Drug Abuse Treatment:*
Volume III: *Further Studies of Drug Users, Treatment Typologies, and Assessment of Outcomes during Treatment in the DARP*
Volume IV: *Evaluation of Treatment Outcomes for 1971–1972 DARP Admission Cohort*
Volume V: *Evaluation of Treatment Outcomes for 1972–1973 DARP Admission Cohort* ....John A. O'Donnell 670

Smart: *Women, Crime and Criminology: A Feminist Critique* ....Mildred Daley Pagelow 672

EDUCATION

Astin: *Academic Gamesmanship: Student-Oriented Change in Higher Education* .... Rosalyn Weinman Schram 673
Baird: *Using Self-Reports to Predict Student Performance* .... Joyce L. Epstein 674
Carnoy and Levin: *The Limits of Educational Reform* .... Gene Grabiner 674
Fitzpatrick: *Women's Inferior Education: An Economic Analysis* .... Judith Caditz 677
Itzkoff: *A New Public Education* .... Ronald M. Pavalko 678
Juniper: *Decision-Making for Schools and Colleges* .... John F. Glass 678
King, Moor, and Mundy: *Post-Compulsory Education II: The Way Ahead* .... Gordon G. Darkenwald 679
Lecht: *Priorities for Planning in Vocational Education: Alternatives for the 1970s;*
Moor: *From School to Work: Effective Counselling and Guidance;* and
Zymelman: *The Economic Evaluation of Vocational Training Programs* .... Robert B. Everhart 679
Levine and Bane: *The "Inequality" Controversy: Schooling and Distributive Justice* ...... Joyce A. Kozuch 680
Peterson: *School Politics Chicago Style* .... David B. Carpenter 681
Pusey: *Dynamics of Bureaucracy: A Case Analysis in Education* .... Edward Gross 682
Rosenbaum: *Making Inequality: The Hidden Curriculum of High School Tracking* .... Martha A. Cook 682
Sewell, Hauser, and Featherman: *Schooling and Achievement in American Society* .... Margaret Mooney Marini 683
Sheps: *Higher Education for Public Health: A Report of the Milbank Memorial Fund Commission* .... Angus E. Reid 684
Stubbs and Delamont: *Explorations in Classroom Observation* .... Candace West 685
van Geel: *Authority to Control the School Program* .... Wilfred B.W. Martin 685
Van Til: *Issues in Secondary Education: The Seventy-Fifth Yearbook of the National Society for the Study of Education, Part II* .... Audrey James Schwartz 686

FAMILY AND INTIMATE LIFESTYLES

Peristiany: *Mediterranean Family Structures* .... Panos D. Bardis 686
Prothro and Diab: *Changing Family Patterns in the Arab East* .... Mohamed El-Assel 687
Sebald: *Momism: The Silent Disease of America* .... David Kent Lee 688
Weeks: *Teenage Marriages: A Demographic Analysis* .... John Kantner 689

MEDICAL

Caplan and Killilea: *Support Systems and Mutual Help: Multidisciplinary Explorations* .... Jonathan A. Freedman 690
Carstairs and Kapur: *The Great Universe of Kota: Stress, Change and Mental Disorder in an Indian Village* .... Robert H. Lauer 691
Levin, Katz, and Holst: *Self-Care: Lay Initiatives in Health* and
Lewis, Fein, and Mechanic: *A Right to Health: The Problem of Access to Primary Medical Care* .... Bebe F. Lavin 692
Marmor: *Psychiatrists and Their Patients: A National Study of Private Office Practice;*
Mulhearn and Momeny: *The Psychiatric Hospital Today: A Quality Profile;* and
Rosenberg and Raynes: *Keeping Patients in Psychiatric Treatment* .... Jan Hankin 693
Mechanic: *The Growth of Bureaucratic Medicine: An Inquiry into the Dynamics of Patient Behavior and the Organization of Medical Care* .... Marshall W. Meyer 694
Szasz: *Schizophrenia: The Sacred Symbol of Psychiatry* .... R.J.M. Lavizzo-Mourey 695

METHODS

Asher: *Causal Modeling* .... Robert B. Smith 696
Boissevain and Mitchell: *Network Analysis: Studies in Human Interaction* .... Benjamin D. Zablocki 697
Clark: *Experimenting with Organizational Life: The Action Research Approach* .... Ruth A. Schwartz 698

POLITICAL

Baechler: *Revolution* .... John Leggett 698
Gold, Christie, and Friedman: *Fists and Flowers: A Social Psychological Interpretation of Student Dissent* .... Peter M. Nardi 700
Horowitz: *Ideology and Utopia in the United States 1956–1976* .... Doris Y. Wilkinson 701
Mamdani: *Politics and Class Formation in Uganda* and
Shivji: *Class Struggles in Tanzania* .... Judith Van Allen 702

North and Thomas: *The Rise of the Western World: A New Economic History* .... Michael S. Kimmel and Walter Goldfrank 703
Schran: *Guerrilla Economy: The Development of the Shensi-Kansu-Ningshia Border Region, 1937–1945* ....Kevin Danaher 704
Veenhoven: *Case Studies on Human Rights and Fundamental Freedoms: A World Survey, Volumes 1 and 2* ....Gail Omvedt 705

RACE AND ETHNIC

Barclay, Kumar and Simms: *Racial Conflict, Discrimination, and Power: Historical and Contemporary Studies* ....Loretta J. Williams 706
Conyers and Wallace: *Black Elected Officials: A Study of Black Americans Holding Governmental Office* ....James H. Laue 707
Gropper: *Gypsies in the City: Culture Patterns and Survival;*
Rehfisch: *Gypsies, Tinkers and Other Travellers;* and
Sutherland: *Gypsies: The Hidden Americans* ....Marcello Truzzi 709

SEX ROLES AND BEHAVIOR

Chafetz et al.: *Who's Queer?* ....Meredith Gould 711
Plummer: *Sexual Stigma: An Interactionist Account* ....William Simon 713
Safilios-Rothschild: *Love, Sex, and Sex Roles* ....Natalie Allon 714
Sokolowska: *Frauenemanzipation und Sozialismus: Das Beispiel der Volksrepublik Polen* ....Julius A. Roth 714
Whitehurst: *Women in America: The Oppressed Majority* ....Elizabeth Briant Lee 716

SOCIAL POLICY

Demerath, Larsen, and Schuessler: *Social Policy and Sociology* ........C.L. Estes 716
Ornstein and Miller: *Policy Issues in Education* ....Rosalie A. Cohen 717
Rein: *Social Science and Public Policy* ....David G. Gil 718

SOCIAL PSYCHOLOGY

Lauer and Handel: *Social Psychology: The Theory and Application of Symbolic Interactionism* ....Peter and Patricia A. Adler 719
Lifton: *The Life of the Self: Toward a New Psychology* ....Roberta Lynn Satow 719
McClelland: *Power: The Inner Experience* ....Lauren Langman 720

THEORY

Baldamus: *The Structure of Sociological Inference* ....Marshall Elliott Shumsky 721
Busino: *Sociologia e Storia: Elementi per un Dibattito* ....Joseph Lopreato 722
Flew: *Sociology, Equality, and Education: Philosophical Essays in Defense of a Variety of Differences* ....Richard A. Hilbert 723
Freidheim: *Sociological Theory in Research Practice* ....Garth Massey 724
Lasky: *Utopia and Revolution: On the Origins of a Metaphor, or Some Illustrations of the Problem of Political Temperament and Intellectual Climate and How Ideas, Ideals, and Ideologies Have Been Historically Related* ....Gwynn Nettler 724
Lawrence: *Georg Simmel: Sociologist and European* ....Lewis A. Coser 726
Ortega y Gasset: *Phenomenology and Art* ....Don Martindale 726
Slater: *Origin and Significance of the Frankfurt School: A Marxist Perspective* ....Barry M. Katz 728
Warshay: *The Current State of Sociological Theory: A Critical Interpretation* ....David R. Simon 729

ADDITIONAL REVIEWS

Barash: *Sociobiology and Behavior* ....John D. Baldwin 731
Cheek and Burch: *The Social Organization of Leisure in Human Society* ....Bill Devall 731
Chickering: *Public Employee Unions: A Study of the Crisis in Public Sector Labor Relations* ....Martin Oppenheimer 732
Cohen and Lee: *Conflict, Conformity and Social Status* ....Cecilia L. Ridgeway 733
Combs and Mansfield: *Drama in Life: The Uses of Communication in Society* ....Peter K. Manning 733
Davis and Flaherty: *Human Diversity: Its Causes and Social Significance* ....Jeffrey Scott Johnson 735
Freedman: *Labor Markets: Segments and Shelters* ....Paul Osterman 736

Gerstl and Jacobs: *Professions for the People: The Politics of Skill* and
Martinez: *The Human Marketplace: An Examination of Private Employment Agencies* .... Gerald Rosenblum 737
Granet: *The Religion of the Chinese People* .... John F. Manfredi 739
Heilman: *Synagogue Life: A Study in Symbolic Interaction* .... Jack Nusan Porter 740
Henshel: *Reacting to Social Problems* .... Malcolm Spector 740
Hobbs: *Issues in the Classification of Children,* Volumes 1 and 2 .... Richard A. Hilbert 741
Hufton: *The Poor of Eighteenth-Century France, 1750–1789* .... Allan Silver 742
Mauss: *Social Problems as Social Movements* .... Bruce D. Johnson 743
Ornauer et al.: *Images of the World in the Year 2000: A Comparative Ten Nation Study* ... . Bettina J. Huber 744
Perlman: *The Myth of Marginality: Urban Poverty and Politics in Rio de Janeiro* .... Alejandro Portes 745
Pickvance: *Urban Sociology: Critical Essays* .... Roy Childs 746
Stewart: *Children in Distress: American and English Perspectives* .... Jane D. McClure 748
Vidich: *The New York Cab Driver and His Fare* .... John Wildeman 749
Vree: *On Synthesizing Marxism and Christianity* .... Nancy DiTomaso 749

DELINQUENT REVIEWS 750

PUBLICATIONS RECEIVED 750

INDEX OF REVIEWS, 1977 755

"Beginning January, 1978 a processing fee of $10 will be required for each paper submitted; such fees to be waived for student members of ASA. This reflects a new policy of the ASA Council and the Committee on Publications affecting all ASA journals. It is a reluctant response to the rapidly accelerating costs of manuscript processing. A check or money order, made payable to the American Sociological Association, should accompany each submission. This fee must be paid in order to initiate the processing of the manuscript."

LETTERS

From the Editor:

In this, the last issue of *CS* under our editorial direction, it is time to offer thanks to those without whose efforts this journal could not have regularly appeared in the mailboxes of readers: to our Associate Editors who, without compensation, did most of the work of fitting books to reviewers; to Jane Geddes, who knew where everything was and kept it all together; to Sondra Buffett and Cathy Ryan, graduate students at UCSD, who did a lot of editing, and listened to and participated in a lot of our policy discussion, and in the process became more sophisticated about sociology than we can reasonably expect graduate students to bear; to the Office of Graduate Studies and Research at UCSD, which provided the funds to support Sondra and Cathy; to Alice Myers, the ASA, and its Publications Committee, which supported everything else; to other UCSD graduate students, like Karen Theobald and Alexandra Todd who helped out from time to time, and to Jean Mayer who got nothing for her work except a wallet in which to keep the money we didn't pay her; to Ken Anderson who designed our cover and our stationary; to my colleagues at UCSD whose expertise and whose contacts we unconscionably exploited for competent reviewers and counsel on problems and policy, but especially to Joseph Gusfield who gave generously of his wisdom and experience and his unfailing wit and good humor; to Henry Quellmalz and Boyd Printing Company, who print *CS* and who were co-operative and helpful with technical information for us novice editors; finally to the entire group which, as a collectivity, made our offices at UCSD a gathering place for visitors and local sociologists, the place where it was at for talk, gossip, crisis-resolution, coffee, wine, and the ritual solidarities which didn't do our proof-reading any good, but which were sure as hell a lot of fun. We wish Norval Glenn the best.

BENNETT M. BERGER

To the Editor:

Please allow us to clear up some important confusions in Inger Sagatun's review (March 1977) of the general theory we state in *Elite Structure and Ideology: A Theory with Applications to Norway.*

First, the theory contends that, within a specified universe of discourse, unified elites will maintain political stability regardless of non-elite configurations. The implication is that this holds for developed societies as well as developing ones. But the main evidence for the contention comes from the history of societies before they attained full development. There are some indications that unified elites in developed societies may not be able to maintain political stability. While we discuss these, we do not reach the conclusion, attributed to us by Sagatun, for developed societies, "the result will be political instability."

Second, one of the new problems in developed societies is the greater similarity of elites *and* non-elites and, as a consequence, the growth of considerable empathy among elites for non-elites. It is not at all the case, as Sagatun has us saying, that increased similarity among elites insulates them from non-elites.

Third, it is not our contention that a welfare state weakens political support for itself by its success in reducing dependency. Evidently, this is Sagatun's own idea, which she assigns to us. In our view, the viability of the welfare state *may* be limited by inflationary tendencies inherent in the work force structure on which it rests and by a growing disjunction between the large nonmanual component of this work force and other population groupings.

Fourth, the Norwegian elite has only been unified since the 1930s at the earliest. It is not true, as Sagatun asserts, that the homogeneity of a society like Norway makes the elite more consensual. Indeed, the major effort of our book is to sketch a paradigm for political sociology which denies that elite structure and behavior can ever be inferred reliably from the characteristics of non-elites.

JOHN HIGLEY
The Australian National University
G. LOWELL FIELD
The University of Connecticut
KNUT GRØHOLT
The Royal Norwegian Ministry of Local Government and Labour

To The Editor:

I was saddened to see Neil Henry's 170 word review of Cohen and Cohen's *Applied Multiple Regression/Correlation Analysis for the Behavioral Sciences* (May 1977, Vol. 6, No. 3). The reason for my sadness is my high regard for the book combined with Henry's thoughtless and glib dismissal of it. Culminating a decade of effort, the book is both comprehensive and clear; it is both technically sound and research relevant; it is both mathematically proper and understandable. Indeed, the Cohens have provided a much needed bridge over the canyon that separates statisticians from substantive researchers. The topics covered in the book include a variety of persistent and difficult issues in social data analysis such as: missing data, change scores, nominal variables, curvilinearity, interactions, and multicolinearity, just to mention a few. For their efforts in this regard, the Cohens deserve our attention and our gratitude.

If the Cohens are as good as I assert, then why would they be summarily dismissed by a competent quantitative sociologist such as Neil Henry? The answer, I believe, has to do with differences of opinion concerning the level of mathematical sophistication to be expected of substantive researchers. To this question, the Cohens (1975:13) assert:

> MRC [Multiple Regression/ Correlation] is itself a product of mathematical statistics, based upon matrix algebra, the calculus, and probability theory—branches of mathematics familiar only to math majors. There is little question that such a background makes possible a level of insight otherwise difficult to achieve. However, since it is only infrequently found in behavioral scientists, it is bootless to proceed on such a basis, however desirable it may be in theory. Nor do we believe it worthwhile, as is done in some statistical textbooks addressed to this audience, to attempt to provide the necessary mathematical background in condensed form in an introductory chapter or two and then proceed as if it were a functioning part of the reader's intellectual equipment. In our experience, that simply does not work—it serves more as a sop to the author's conscience than as an aid to the reader's comprehension.

In discussing the methodological literature, Asher (*Causal Modeling*, 1976:68) states:

> The problem is that little attempt is made to present this work in terms that the layman might comprehend and thereby exploit. This results in a gap between what can be done in data analysis and what is actually being done.

The Cohens have attempted to present competent data analysis in terms that the researcher can comprehend and use. In my judgment, they have succeeded. Neil Henry blithely dismisses the Cohens' work, I believe, because it does not appropriately worship the idol of mathematical elegance. Indeed, statisticians have attempted to create a priesthood of the formula by unnecessarily obfuscating their material. Such an artificial priesthood is supported by flippant disregard of serious attempts to democratize the principles of data analysis. In attempting to democratize these principles, the Cohens have drawn the wrath of the clergy of mathematical statistics. They deserved better than that.

RICHARD A. ZELLER
Bowling Green State University.

To the Editor:

My only response to Zeller is that readers look up what I actually said in those 170 words.

NEIL W. HENRY
Virginia Commonwealth University

To the Editor:

I wished that Scott McNall had read the Segal & Segal selection more carefully when he read Goldman & Segal's *The Social Psychology of Military Service*. If he had I think he would have taken issue with some of their conclusions, particularly the one he cited in his review (May 1977, *6*, 3, p. 325):

This is echoed in the Segals' comparison of Detroiters who served in Vietnam and those who didn't. They found no meaningful attitudinal differences.

Yes, reviewing an edited volume is a chore—particularly if it is multi-disciplinary. Yes, primarily, the reviewer's task is to report what was said and not look for methodological flaws. Yes, the Segal & Segal paper is only one of many and not the central thesis of the book. But, his review has given me an opportunity to point out the flaw I discovered the first time I read it when I attended the IUS meeting two years ago.

True, Segal and Segal (1976) found that veterans and nonveterans differed significantly on only two of twenty-three "trust in government and isolationism-interventionism" attitudes. Unfortunately, the results add little to our knowledge of the adjustment problems of the Vietnam veteran since (a) a very small percentage of the veteran population was sampled (113/29 million), (b) all veterans were analyzed as a group even though strong evidence exists that there are basic differences among veterans of different eras (Peck, C. P., Lorr, M. & Stenger, C. A. Interpersonal and Life Style Characteristics of Veterans in VA Health Care Facilities. Unpublished manuscript available from the VA Central Office, Washington, D.C., 1974), (c) separate analyses were not computed to compare combat and non-combat veterans (Figley, C. R., Ed. *Stress Disorders among Vietnam Veterans: Theory, Research, and Treatment Implications*. New York: Brunner/Mazel, 1977 in press), and (d) only *13* Vietnam veterans were sampled including an unknown number who actually went to Vietnam and saw combat.

The nature of the Segal and Segal paper appeared to border on a diatribe, refuting claims by Lifton (*Home from the War*) and Helmer (*Bringing the War Home: The American Soldier in Vietnam and After)*. New York: Free Press, 1974) that the Vietnam veterans were for example, hostile toward the government and alienated.

Further, Segal and Segal (1976) noted that ". . . in contrast to this view, we find research reporting that middle-aged civilian women are more favorably disposed to violence than Vietnam era enlisted personnel" (Brady, D. & Rappoport, L. Violence and Vietnam: A Comparison between Attitudes of Civilians and Veterans. *Human Relations*, 1974, *26*, 6, 735–752). At a closer reading of the Brady and Rappoport article, however, it is clear that: (1) the differences in mean scores between the female and Vietnam era veteran sample were not significant, (b) the "veterans" were still in the military, awaiting discharge, and (c) the *latter* group was separated by combat involvement. Brady and Rappoport point out that "those who report heavy combat experience have the highest general violence scores" (p. 735), which is consistent with the Figley research which will be published later this year.

I hope more sociologists become interested in veteran studies in general and the Vietnam veteran in particular. A few of us are working in the area, but it sure is lonely.

CHARLES R. FIGLEY
Purdue University

To the Editor:

Although a negative review, or one dwelling more on weaknesses than strengths, is always disheartening to an author, a second hard look frequently reveals some points of agreement as well as disagreement. Such is the case with my own reaction to Barry McPherson's review of my monograph *Sport and Social Organization* in the May 1977 issue of *CS*, and I would like to indicate where I agree and disagree with him.

First, I agree that my treatment of sport sociology literature is incomplete, and would even be willing to concede that it may not be "representative of the current state of the art." In addition, I would be the first to admit I have not provided an intensive analysis of all or most of "the most significant research and writing on central theoretical and methodological issues" in the field—which is what Bobbs-Merrill "Studies in Sociology" selections are supposed to do. In truth, my slim volume of 75 pages was not meant to be an exhaustive treatment of sport sociology literature, and it was not meant to be a major theoretical or methodological treatise of sport sociology. However, even though my book may not realize the stated (lofty) intentions of the Bobbs-Merrill series in which it appears, I still feel it may have some value for students being introduced to the sociology or sociology of sport fields or perhaps even for students of sport sociology seeking some direction for their study. My modest intention was to provide some integration and critical review, from an explicit sociological perspective, of a number of interesting observations and findings from various sources about sport and some basic aspects of social organization. Surely, I missed some major studies, placed too much emphasis on certain studies—even with six pages of bibliographic references, and was selective in focusing on American sport and on a particular set of general themes concerning social organization. I also faced a dilemma common to all who do literature reviews. A number of significant studies—like the Brookings Conference papers about government and the sports business cited by McPherson—were published or became available after most of my writing was done, in 1973. Despite these limitations I still believe one can gain from my work a firm grasp of the kinds of insights and findings sport sociologists possess or want to derive about sport and social organization.

There are two other major criticisms presented in McPherson's review that merit response. First is his contention that my book "consists of a potpourri of unrelated minichapters. . . . " Response to this criticism is important because it allows me to point out the need to look to sociology rather than sport to find the organizational framework within which major topics were discussed, developed, and integrated. I think one can understand the interrelationship of these major topics if one recognizes my effort to relate sport to central aspects of social organization, rather than organize the book around all the basic topics studied by sport sociologists. This seemed to me an appropriate way for a sociologist to approach the study of sport, and it seemed no more arbitrary or random than the approaches used by other sociologists in surveying topics in their particular fields or sociology in general.

The other major criticism requiring response is McPherson's contention that my presentation of concepts was too superficial and of concrete examples was too elementary to allow "any meaningful analysis." I must admit to being a bit puzzled here, since the major concepts I used in discussing or analyzing topics of sport and social organization were ones I defined and illustrated at the beginning of each "minichapter." Furthermore, even though I left the most difficult analytical tasks of explanation and prediction largely to others, I did occasionally attempt some "meaningful" sociological analysis of my own—especially in the concluding chapter about social change in sport. It would have been helpful if McPherson had been clearer about the meaning of "meaningful." He cited other general overviews of sport he apparently considered more meaningful; and I would fully concur that there are numerous other materials—like the review articles by Page and by Snyder and Spreitzer, books like Ball and Loy's *Sport and Social Order*, and a number of readers—that have a great deal of utility for people wanting to learn about sport sociology and basic patterns of sport and society. In fact, I would suggest that the value of my book in serving this end would be greatly enhanced by using it with materials of this sort that expand on or complement its basic coverage of the field. This combination of materials is the most meaningful way I can imagine to study and learn about sport sociology. I am sorry McPherson does not share my (admittedly biased) perception of the potential utility of my monograph. However, I would welcome a fuller elaboration by him of the reasons for its ostensibly limited utility, for like him, I am also interested in expanding people's awareness of sport sociology and in encouraging increasingly better contributions of knowledge to it.

HOWARD L. NIXON II
The University of Vermont

To the Editor:

In response to Professor Nixon, I will illustrate some of the criticisms presented in the review, and elaborate on some others, all of which were not possible within the 300-word limit imposed on the original review.

First, as an aside, it should be noted that Professor Nixon has completed some good theoretical and empirical work on cohesion in sport groups, and chapter 4 clearly reflects this expertise. Chapter 4 is by far the most analytical, comprehensive and insightful theoretical and empirical section in the monograph, although for some reason he neglects to mention his own work. In fact, a monograph on the more limited subject of cohesion in sport groups would have been a worthy contribution to the subfield.

My first major concern was that the material in the monograph was dated. It is unfortunate that a 75-page manuscript had to remain on the shelf for three years before publication, without any opportunity to up-date the material. This time-lag is even more serious and obvious in that studies answering some of the questions posed by Nixon for future work had already begun to appear by 1976 at meetings or in journals. Regardless of where the responsibility for this time-lag lies, it is a fact and a weakness in the monograph.

A second concern was the structure of the monograph into a series of "mini-chapters," all of which, I would agree, do pertain to social organization. However, there was no rationale presented as to why these topics were included and why other aspects of social organization were not included; why they were presented in a particular order; or, why a comparative perspective was not selected (e.g., the Eastern European vs. the North American model of sport and social organization). The author does state, "this focus is a function of the personal biases, interests, or expertise of the author, as well as the availability of relevant literature" (p. 8). This is a serious caveat that should have been given greater attention as the manuscript was being written. To illustrate, one very common framework might have been to move from the micro to the macro level; or, to discuss the interpersonal level, then the group level and finally the social system level. Furthermore, to illustrate my first point, additional relevant literature, published and unpublished, was completed, and "available" in 1973, although it might not have been "available" to the author.

A third criticism in the review dealt with the superficial treatment of concepts. To illustrate, Professor Nixon states "we can define a social class in a loose sense as being a stratum of people sharing approximately the same economic privileges, and hence, life chances, in a society" (p. 33); or, "Commercialization refers to the business-like pursuit of financial gain" (p. 52); or, "Bureaucratic organization refers to large-scale social units with highly specialized divisions of labor, elaborate hierarchies of authority; highly rationalized, formalized goal pursuits; and normative goals" (p. 52). These concepts, once defined, need further explanation and need to be linked with one or more theoretical frameworks, especially for students in an introductory sociology course or for physical education students who may have had little, if any, sociology prior to studying sport from a sociological orientation. Otherwise, unless sociological concepts and theories are fully understood and utilized, a social issues or a social significance of sport perspective will result, rather than a *sociology* of sport perspective.

This leads to the fourth major criticism included in the review, namely that "the review and discussion of research findings tend to be highly selective and descriptive, rather than explanatory, and no alternative explanations are proposed." It is for this reason that there appeared to be little "meaningful analysis." As Professor Nixon stated "this reliance on limited materials implies that caution must be exercised in drawing conclusions, that much of the ensuing discussion will be limited in depth and sociological sophistication" (p. 53). More specifically, the monograph is over-dependent on anecdotal, journalistic examples to illustrate points (e.g. conformity and deviance) which are then accounted for by brief summary statements such as "patterns of rule violations and exploitation of athletes can be explained in terms of the extreme strains, tensions and uncertainties of the big-time coaching role." Here, only one major explanation for deviance in sport is presented, namely, social strains in the system. To illustrate further, in the discussion of conformity in American sport, examples of athletes (e.g. Joe Namath, Derek Sanderson) who were able to assert their individuality and survive were not included. A more "meaningful analysis" might have sought to account for why some survive in the social system and others do not, or at least suggested some possible alternative explanations for the phenomenon being discussed.

Finally, I commend Professor Nixon for his honest and rational reply and would like to reiterate his concern for "encouraging increasingly better contributions" to the sociology of sport. In order for this to occur constructive debate among those "inside" the sub-discipline must be increased, but more importantly, competent scholars must be attracted to the field. In this light, a book reviewer must be concerned with quality control for the sub-discipline, especially for those not actively involved at the present time. For those who are active researchers, or who teach in the field, I assume most will have read the monograph and formed their own opinion prior to my review. Therefore, my review was directed more to those "outside" the sub-discipline who need to be informed as to whether the publication is an accurate reflection of the state of the art, and of the possible utility of the monograph for teaching or research purposes.

In summary, taking into consideration my knowledge of the field, my reading of the monograph, and Professor Nixon's own caveats, I reported that the publication was uneven in depth and breadth and therefore not an accurate reflection of the theoretical and empirical work completed in the sociology of sport. Moreover, the monograph was not as up-to-date as of 1976 as it could have been. While no publication can ever be complete and totally current, this monograph could have come closer to the mark, and hopefully will if it can be revised in the future. Given the impact which sport has on contemporary life-styles, a monograph of this length could serve as the basis for a unit on sport in an introductory sociology course.

B. D. McPherson
University of Waterloo

From the Editor:

We would like to apologize for an error in our May 1977 issue: In Zoltán Tar's review of *The Social Structure of Eastern Europe* (p. 381) the word "poverty" instead of "property" appeared. The sentence should have read: "A 'new class' (Djilas) with rights over property has appeared all over Eastern Europe."

SYMPOSIA

The Dialectic of Ideology and Technology: The Origins, Grammar, and Future of Ideology, by ALVIN W. GOULDNER. New York: Seabury Press, 1976. 304 pp. $14.95 cloth.

ANTHONY GIDDENS
University of Cambridge

In this book, Alvin Gouldner develops and amplifies themes introduced in his previous works *Enter Plato, The Coming Crisis in Western Sociology,* and *For Sociology*. Together with two projected volumes on Marxism and revolutionary intellectuals, these constitute an integrated and highly ambitious project which is nothing less than an attempt to trace the origins and formulate a critique of the leading strands in contemporary Western political culture. Like the earlier books, the present one is very much a personal document as well as an academic study. The author does not conceal his presence in these pages. He is, he says, a "Marxist outlaw," "half sociologist and half Marxist, and rebel against them both"—a High Plains Drifter of modern sociology, unable to ally himself permanently with any camp, yet deadly when he turns his guns against his antagonists. *The Coming Crisis* documented Gouldner's disavowal of the main traditions of orthodox American sociology, but also indicated a critical attitude toward the dominant forms of Marxism. The latter attitude now has become the focus of Gouldner's concern: having attempted the "demystification" of academic sociology, he wants to conjoin this to demystifying Marxism, to explore what he has elsewhere called the "dark side of the dialectic."

The Dialectic of Ideology and Technology is intended to lay the groundwork for such a task. It is in some part an endeavor to rescue ideology from its critics, Marxist and non-Marxist. In both traditions of thought, ideology is treated as "defective discourse," or as "false consciousness." Marx's writings are predicated upon a critique of ideology, and in the works of Comte sociology is decisively separated from religion and from metaphysics. Marxism and positivistic sociology each begin with the object of transcending these residues of the past, except that whereas Comte sought to replace them by knowledge grounded in empirical observation, Marx saw the overcoming of ideology as entailing the practical transformation of society through class struggle. Marx's notion of ideology, Gouldner says, in one sense signalled a major advance over prior social theory insofar as relationship of ideologies to class divisions (and thereby to the conditions of social existence) enabled Marx to identify historically located limitations upon the progress of human reason. But it was also the source of an uncertain legacy regarding the status of Marxism: does Marxism transcend all ideologies, or is it itself an ideology linked to the interests of the working-class movement? In Marx's writings, ideology is not studied as a phenomenon in its own right: Marx was above all concerned with the critique of bourgeois consciousness as an integral element in the transformation of capitalism. Hence Marx did not confront the general problem of the interconnections between social theory and ideology in the modern era. For Gouldner, Marxism is indeed an ideology, but the latter term is not to be understood as necessarily pejorative, nor as referring to idea-systems that are either obsolete or—like bourgeois ideologies—presumed shortly to become so. "Ideology" is rather to be seen as the outcome of the same currents of rationalism and anti-traditionalism which have given rise both to Marxism and to modern sociology.

Ideologies come into being, Gouldner argues, with the formation of a "public sphere" of discourse, freed from the restraints of traditional, hierocratic orders, in which the framework of beliefs tends to be fixed and stereotyped according to established habits. This is true even of conservative ideologies, such as those developed in reaction against the excesses of the French revolution: the defense of tradition involves a distancing from it, a rational comprehension of it that is not possible in a society in which traditionalism still dominates. An "ideology," as Gouldner uses the term, is a secularized idea-system, involving knowledge-claims that its advocates believe can be rationally defended, mobilized in the furtherance of a practical program of social change. There is thus a close relation between the rise of ideologies and the diffusion of the printed word. Printing separates communication from the immediacy of conversational talk, concretizing the public character of discourse; books, journals, and newspapers decontextualize information, helping both to express and to generate ideologies. Ideology is thus in a basic sense a product of bourgeois society. It is a fundamental characteristic of the latter, Gouldner claims, that its dominant class, in contrast to ruling classes in earlier types of society, is not directly involved either in the production of culture or in the administration of the state. The rule of the capitalist class is a "mediated rule": ideology thus comes to assume a particular importance in social solidarity, since the position of the hegemonic class cannot readily be directly sustained by force. Some of the major tensions in the modern order stem from this situation, since although the system of class domination depends more than ever before upon ideology to support its domination, its members do not directly control the cultural apparatus, which consequently may create ideologies counter to those favored by the ruling class. Hence there comes about an increasing reliance upon ideologies of "the end of ideology," or of technocratic legitimation; and "all capitalist economies possess an inherent vulnerability to ideological crisis."

There is a strongly Habermasian strain in this, as at many points in the book. Gouldner frequently acknowledges his indebtedness to Habermas, and while offering various criticisms of Habermas's views, lends his qualified support to Habermas's attempt to ground social critique in the conception of an ideal speech situation. Those who accuse Habermas of lacking a political practice fail to grasp the significance of his commitment to emancipation rather than to equality alone. Gouldner affirms the need for "a critical theory focussed on the production of change in language, in communication, and in media." He only gives a few indications, however, of what form such a "media-critical politics" might take, and one presumes that we shall have to wait for Gouldner's other forthcoming works for a fuller exposition. Certainly some of the basic problems of the "reflexive sociology" introduced in *The Coming Crisis of Western Sociology* appear to remain largely unresolved. In recognizing the public character of discourse and the redemption of truth-claims, Gouldner has definitely moved beyond his earlier portrayal of reflexivity in social theory. Ideology is "one-sided," not merely because it is partisan, but because, like "normal sociology," it does not incorporate self-reflection on its own grounding. But the characterization of critical theory which Gouldner gives at the conclusion of the book, which is "grounded in justified interests" and which makes "a continuous effort to deepen its reflexive understanding of its own commitments," remains only weakly elucidated. I certainly accept the need for a critical theory of some such kind as this, but its formulation demands a head-on confrontation with metatheoretical issues that, in this volume at least, Gouldner skirts.

BENTON JOHNSON
University of Oregon

The Coming Crisis of Western Sociology was the high-water mark of the prophetic style in recent American sociology. It was by far the most widely read and prominently reviewed critique of academic sociology that has appeared during the new upsurge of radical thought in the field. Though repetitious and speculative, its story line was clear and its language eloquent. Above all, its moral perspective was unambiguous. It was an expose of the abominations of academic sociology and of its leading Man of Sin, Talcott Parsons.

The Dialectic of Ideology and Technology is a different sort of book. To be sure, it has the same speculative quality that *The Coming Crisis* had, and it has the same tendency to make assertions not backed up with evidence and careful argumentation. It is also repetitious and occasionally eloquent. But its focus and temper are different and its story line is obscure. Its focus is on ideology, with particular attention to Marxism. Its temper is not prophetic. Gouldner apologizes for his lack of "moral generosity" in *The Coming Crisis*. He has transformed himself from a seer into a seeker. As for the book's story line, Gouldner jumps from topic to topic in a manner reminiscent of free association. He makes pronouncements on more issues than can possibly be summarized or discussed in the short space of a review.

Gouldner considers himself a Marxist of sorts, but few classical Marxists will be satisfied with the book. It contains neither an orthodox perspective on class nor a "proletarian perspective" on the question of political truth. It accuses Marxists of ideological distortion. Its sharpest attacks are directed against the socialist states, with their rhetoric of equality and proletarian rule, and their reality of repression and state control. Talcott Parsons could not have said it better. Gouldner considers himself close to the perspective of critical theory, but many critical theorists will dislike what they read. He argues that Marcuse and Habermas have underestimated the value and viability of free institutions, including the mass media, and have thereby contributed to a politics that destroys freedom. He is more sympathetic to Habermas's recent work on communicative competence, but then many critical theorists regard this work as a scholastic and unpolitical digression. As for all those academic sociologists who were titillated by *The Coming Crisis* (Parsons was never as influential as Gouldner claimed), they may be amused by Gouldner's liberal turn, but his current preoccupations are not theirs, and they may well be bored. All in all, the book is likely to be less influential and less widely read than *The Coming Crisis*.

This is a pity, for it is an important book and it deserves to be taken seriously. A clear theme unites Gouldner's meanderings. It is the problem of rationality, the question of whether and how it is possible to achieve a commonly accepted basis for arriving at valid theoretical and practical judgments. The problem is urgent for Gouldner because Marxism, which now prevails on much of the earth, seems unable to deliver on its promises. Although he confesses to a sense of "being lost in history," and he worries about the emergence of a tragic vision among disillusioned ideologues, he does not wish to give up the hopes for greater freedom and equality that Marxism nourishes.

For Gouldner, ideology is a relatively rational form of public discourse made possible by mass literacy and the mass media. It provides a language that transcends the particularities of conventional experience and discourse, and opens up a more general perspective on society and history. Its superior rationality rests on the fact that it is self-grounded, i.e., its claims to validity are not based on the authority of scriptures or sages, but rather on arguments that can be criticized according to presumably universalistic criteria of truth. Its "grammar" therefore implies the practice of self-reflexivity, namely the critical examination of its own assumptions and their alteration in the face of superior arguments. Yet its rationality is limited by its failure to recognize that it too is generated by particular people in particular circumstances, and that its insights are only partial. All ideologies are silent about precisely those aspects of reality that would prove embarrassing to their pretensions.

What is urgently needed, Gouldner argues, is the greater exercise of the self-reflexivity implicit in the grammar of Marxist ideology. He understands that it is impossible to criticize all assumptions at once, and he realizes that the critical posture undermines that sense of "surety and purity" necessary for the "high and sacred moments of practice." Nevertheless, Marxist theory and practice have not produced the kind of world that many in the West would care to live in. The costs of self-reflexivity are worth paying, for Marxism is in danger of negating its own vision. Marxism needs to speak where it is silent. Among other things, it needs to develop a theory of politics and it needs to think about freedom. In this connection, Gouldner doubts that equality and freedom are perfectly compatible, or that complete equality is achievable or desirable, but he is certain that where freedom is denied equality is also impossible. As for the standard Marxist critique of "bourgeois freedom" as a mask for bourgeois interests, Gouldner suggests that there was genuine insight in classical liberalism's assertion that some particularistic interests are socially useful. In any event, he is sure that the claim to speak single-mindedly for humanity as a whole is a "basic source of false-consciousness among Jacobin-leaning intellectuals." These considerations underlie his cautious neo-liberalism.

Denominational Marxists and other seers of the left will regard Gouldner's book as an exercise in naval-gazing. For them, the critique of ideology has already taken place and the main point now is to gain a political victory and let the future take care of itself. But Gouldner's is not an isolated voice on the left. An increasing number of Marxist intellectuals are worried about the very tendencies in their own tradition that disturb Gouldner. Those who believe that rationality is a scarce and precious resource for the shaping of theory and practice will welcome this timely book about issues that may ultimately affect us all.

FREDERICK R. LYNCH
California State University, Fullerton

The intellectual odyssey undertaken more than a decade ago by Alvin W. Gouldner in constructing an historically informed sociology of social theory continues in his newest book, *The Dialectic of Ideology and Technology*. In this study, as in several before it, Gouldner seeks to penetrate to the very epistemological core of sociology, not only by examining the social bases of social theories but also through comparing and linking it to other modes of cognition. In *The Dialectic of Ideology and Technology*, he employs both approaches, hoping to understand the evolution and nature of sociology by juxtaposing it with the history and grammar of ideology. It is also his aim (in this and future studies) to contribute to a demystification of Marxism.

Gouldner has long been intrigued by the processes whereby various values and ideas come to serve and reflect the interests of different groups. While this sociology-of-knowledge or Marxist outlook was muted by a more dominant, middle-range functionalism in some of his early organizational analyses, this critical focus became much more pronounced in "Anti-Minotaur: The Myth of a Value-Free Sociology." Gouldner revisited the Weberian doctrine and discovered an ideology which has, among its other consequences, served to foster a "false consciousness" of *apparent* objectivity in the social sciences. In fact, he noted, many "value-free" social scientists have tacitly accommodated themselves to the goals of the Welfare State in exchange for its favors.

This sobering appraisal of the social origins of the value-free myth apparently reinforced Gouldner's belief that a new critical examination of the entire history of social theory was in order. "The history of social theory has failed," he pointedly proclaimed in *Enter Plato,* the first of a new series of critical studies of the social bases of social thought. In *Enter Plato,* Gouldner set forth his aims and commitments for the writing of a new history of social theory;

> The task of the historian of social theory is to reveal the different levels on which a theory lives; to show it as a response not only to the technical, intellectual problems, but also to problems in the larger culture; to appraise a theory by comparing it with alternatives shown and known to be historically feasible; to explore the extent to which the triumphs and the flaws of a theory are not only those of the individual theorist but are culture-linked; and, in revealing this for the past, to press home the point for the present (p. 167).

Judging by the preface to *Enter Plato,* Gouldner found its writing to be a deeply moving and "reflexive" experience. Indeed, I suspect that it would be correct to characterize this book as something of a "labor of love" which clearly supplied motivational power and metaphysical desire for his future projects as well as a set of goals and orientations.

"The task here is essentially the same as that undertaken in *Enter Plato,*" Gouldner stated in his second study of the social bases of social theory, *The Coming Crisis of Western Sociology.* Unlike *Enter Plato,* however, *The Crisis* encountered a storm of criticisms. What really seemed to trouble most thoughtful critics was not that Gouldner had shifted his time reference from the past to the present, from Plato to Parsons, rather, they were upset by the implications and the questions raised by Gouldner's bold expansion of his "Anti-Minotaur" theme. Whereas in "Anti-Minoutar" Gouldner had held that a specific professional doctrine fostered a bogus objectivity or false consciousness, Gouldner argued in *The Crisis* that entire social theories masked personal and social interests, values and sentiments. Beneath the explicit theoretical corpus, Gouldner maintained, lies an implicit "infrastructure" of metaphysical background assumptions and sentiments, shaped by the scholar's total social existence. Whether a social theory gains currency depends, in part, upon whether it "resonates" the background assumptions and sentiments of professional audiences.

Maurice Zeitlin was among those who complained that Gouldner "verges on sociological solipism, so that 'ideology' seems to swallow up and absorb all valid knowledge of the objective world. . . . Social theories all but become transformed, in the course of Gouldner's discussion, from imperfect and limited answers to specific questions—from summary explanations which others can understand and test by practical activity—into mere 'mappings' of the social world in competition with other such equally subjective mappings" (*AJS*, 1977:312). Alain Touraine issued this challenge: "We have to choose: either refuse to recognize the existence of sociology as a positive knowledge and denounce it as a ruling class ideology, as the mask of bourgeois society; or recognize its existence and face head-on the problem of relations between science and ideology in sociological knowledge" (*AJS,* 1977:317).

The Dialectic of Ideology and Technology is going to satisfy neither the critics *nor* many of the defenders of *The Crisis.* Marxist and other Leftist readers who warmed to the demystification of Parsonian functionalism in *The Crisis* are not likely to be as gleeful with Gouldner's incisive probing of the contradictions in the neo-Marxist writings of Jürgen Habermas. And critics of *The Crisis,* such as Zeitlin and Touraine, will remain displeased because Gouldner seems to have blurred the boundary between ideology and sociology even more. Indeed, he states that "when the problem of ideology is placed upon the agenda of sociology it has not simply set itself the task of researching another object but of defining its own purposes." Ideology remains "a boundary wall that is manned, watched and recurrently repaired" (p. 10). And Gouldner is quick to remind us that early sociological positivism was a self-defined ideology, designed to promote social cohesion and a new order rather than merely seeking pure knowledge in itself. Marx saw this and said so. Following this Marxian lead, Gouldner is out to demonstrate that sociology has underestimated the rationality of ideology while overestimating its own autonomy from both metaphysics and its own grounding in society.

The social sciences and ideologies both arose during the transition from feudal to bourgeois orders. This transition fostered profound linguistic changes as religious symbolism and traditional forms of legitimating social and personal action were increasingly replaced by a rational mode of discourse. The maturation of the modern grammar of rationality, therefore, was premised in class conflict, urbanization, increases in commerce and travel, and two other highly important factors: (1) The technological revolutions in printing and (2) The rise of the bourgeois "public."

"The culture of discourse that produces ideology was historically grounded in the technology of a specific kind of mass (or public) media, printing, and its specific mode of production: privately-owned, small scale, widely diffused, competitive, and decentralized units" (p. 39). Printing, of course democratizes the culture of writing. It also effectively decontextualizes discourse, forcing greater detail and precision of argument. For "printing separates the talk from the talker, allowing and requiring it to be appraised without the seen-but-unintended supports of the nonlinguistic modalities of communication" (p. 41). But printing also serves to limit rationality by defocusing the social identity of the speaker and the social sources behind his statements. This aspect of printing, in addition to the relatively one-way aspect of printed communication (which does not permit ongoing criticism and feedback by a live audience) inhibits the critical or reflexive function of rationality. "Rationality is here construed as the capacity to make problematic what had hitherto been treated as given, to bring into reflection what before had only been used; to transform resource into topic. . . . This view of rationality situates it in the capacity to think *about* our thinking" (p. 49).

Rational discourse would have been most difficult, however, without the growth of what Gouldner terms the "public" of bourgeois societies, cleared safe spaces in which people could communicate freely. Though rooted in the "private" sector of property and male-dominated family matrices, the public sector became the "marketplace of ideas" in which the ideas, information, and "news" being merchandised by the mass media could be discussed freely and critically in such face-to-face settings as taverns, coffee houses, "public squares," and the like. Censorship, of course, was (and remains) the primary menace to free public discourse and discussion. And, while rational accountability was increasingly employed in the public realm, older, more traditional patterns of thought still held sway in the private sector.

Now, what *is* ideology? Gouldner defines, deepens, and expands the definition of ideology throughout the book. Generally, ideologies are symbol systems, substantially premised upon rationality, which are distinguished by their concern for "what is" and by their world-referencing reports. These reports, in fact, are social theories that are both rationally and empirically supported. Also, on the general level, ideologies can be seen as ontologically-integrative and future-oriented: "Ideologies are project-seeking moralities tacitly seeking to reconstruct a frayed, fragmented whole" or to build an entirely new totality. They "reconstruct the moral grounding of human solidarity" (p. 250).

"More narrowly, ideologies are symbol systems which serve to justify and mobilize projects of social reconstruction" (p. 55). In order to link a variety of personal interests with a public goal, ideologies must serve to blur or conceal more concrete, specific, and personal conceptions of what is "good" ("paradigms") and symbol systems of restricted communicability which are bounded by limited group contexts (the "paleosymbolic"). Ideologies respond to the increased need for meaning and interpretation as the flow of news and information provided by the spreading mass media dramatically increases.

Ideology inevitably entails a politics of change on the personal, linguistic, and social levels. Ideology's descriptions of "what is" immediately suggest "what ought to be" though the latter (in true ideology) is a function of "what *can* be." Ideology insists upon the unity of theory and praxis mediated by rational discourse. Ideology is *critical;* it makes the "given" problematic. Ideology is generic; it stresses the power and potency of ideas and the actions of ordinary people. Ideological thinking surmounts the tragic tradition inherited from classicism and Christianity. Ideology, in short, is "can do" thinking. Its mappings of the world imply imperatives.

But ideology fails by the criteria of its own rationality in one crucial respect: ideology lacks reflexivity. Ideologues cannot make their own interests and social bases problematic—as they do in the cases of others. Of course, this lack of reflexivity is also the major failing of another mode of rational discourse, the social sciences.

In one of the best sections of the book, Gouldner renders intelligible key elements of one form of social thought which *is* seriously attempting to grapple with the problems of rational discourse and reflexivity: the neo-Marxist critical theory of Jürgen Habermas. Yet Goulder sees a central dilemma in the value-groundings of Habermasian theory. "Habermas sought to integrate classical German philosophy's stress on freedom with socialism's stress on equality in a transcending linguistic theory of 'communicative competence.' He sought to establish the character of 'the ideal speech' situation that would permit *all* to participate in a public discourse productive of truth, freedom, justice, and which discourse would constitute the site of a developing rationality" (p. 142). However, the egalitarian, socialist politics of critical theory and of the Left in general tends to favor the growth of a powerful centralized state. And the state can (and has) become an abusive censor of public debate and personal freedoms as well as a leveller of inequalities. Therefore, if the theory "does what it must to foster the equality necessary for communicative competence, it inevitably undermines the freedom it also prizes" (p. 151). Critical theorists and the Left tend to ignore the problem posed by the absence of free publics in the state socialist societies, Gouldner contends. They must focus more upon "media freedom."

The maintenance of a public characterized by freedom of rational discourse in face-to-face contexts is the cornerstone of Goulder's own critical theory and politics of modern societies (especially the capitalist ones). The existence of the public, in his view, is crucial to the future of ideology because "word-of-mouth is the ultimate medium of the masses, if not the newest innovation in media. In the end, there is probably no more powerful mechanism of social change than people's talk" (p. 149).

Both Gouldner and Habermas wish to maximize the possibility for free, rational, reflexive discourse. But, whereas Habermas seems resigned to the waning of the public in capitalist society, Gouldner would rather utilize the contradictions in the capitalist system to maintain the public.

Gouldner provides a portrayal of capitalist society in which the dominance of an hegemonic economic class has become increasingly mediated by two other semi-autonomous classes: state administrators and full-time party politicians. With regard to the middle classes, Gouldner posits a widening split between those who are propertied and those who are highly educated. The Welfare State provides employment for the latter class through the taxes of the former. The propertied middle classes resent this while the more educated classes have tended to become more radicalized. The sources of critical reason in modern capitalist societies are found in the "cultural apparatus." But these creators of culture must obtain their audiences through the property-rooted consciousness industry, the machinery of the corporate mass media. While this might seem to doom radical critique, the consciousness industry is caught in a contradiction as long as there exists a relatively uncensored public. Driven by the imperatives of profit, the consciousness industry must compete with anything that sells in the "marketplace of ideas," the public sector. This includes ideological wares hostile to the existing order. (Thus, the consciousness industry merchandised the critical counterculture of the 1960s.) Gouldner's politics, therefore, exploits this contradiction while amplifying "the common values and hostility toward censorship shared by the consciousness industry and the cultural apparatus" (p. 178). Attention must also be given to institutions mediating the state and language—especially the public schools. More pessimistically, however, Gouldner (following Habermas to some extent) notes that the consciousness industry—especially television—tends to encourage less rational modes of consciousness. The rationality of the public is dulled by the pursuit of leisure and privatized life-styles and by the growing interest in religion, mysticism, and the occult. The university community, which now provides employment for most ideologues, may well become the last, best bastion of the public.

In critically evaluating *The Dialectic,* it must first be said that a tighter and more explicit organizational structure might have made for a better book. In view of the diversity and complexity of materials in *The Dialectic,* a summarizing and concluding chapter would also have been a welcome addition. Granted that Gouldner is one of sociology's most gifted writers and that he is, after all, dealing with two of the most (needlessly?) difficult modes of discourse in the social sciences (sociolinguistics and critical theory); nevertheless, there are passages in the work in which one wonders whether it is the reader or the author who is losing sight of the aims of the book. It might also have helped to ground the overall analysis in *examples* drawn from a *variety* of ideologies. Of course, this might have forced discussion of the non-rational and non-scientific elements of ideology which Gouldner underestimates in his desire to show that other sociologists have tended to over-emphasize these same features. The use of examples might also have led to at least brief discussion of ideology's frequent connection with (or embodiment in) *charismatic personalities*. Indeed, it is most puzzling that the Max Weber Research Professor of Social Theory would not look into this relationship much more closely. Such a focus is undoubtedly planned in the promised forthcoming volume on *Revolutionary Intellectuals*. But some discussion of charisma and its relationship to various ideologies in different cultural and historical settings would have helped to *re*contextualize somewhat all those printed abstractions.

Finally, after all is said and done, how much more have we learned about the nature of sociology as a result of the depth study of ideology? Those who have been attentive to Gouldner's previous calls for a more critical and reflexive sociology will simply find a variation of that important theme. Gouldner's analyses of sociolinguistics and critical theory, however, are refreshing and stimulating. His sociology of the media and his sociology of modern societies (capitalist and socialist) are both compelling and much-needed as is his discussion of the tension between equality and liberty within the infrastructure of neo-Marxist theory. While the liberty-equality issue is hardly new to many historians and political philosophers, the problem needed a forceful restatement in sociology.

Gouldner is in the unenviable position of having this and all future works compared with the enormous accomplishments he achieved in *The Crisis* and *Enter Plato*. *The Dialectic,* I believe measures up fairly well to these works, though it is different—it seems more complex, more abstract, more esoteric. But, then again, it is much the same in both its purpose and its message. Gouldner is still calling our attention to sociological-epistomological questions and problems. He does this better than almost anyone else in the field. Yet his answer seems to be that we must ask more and *better* questions of one another and ourselves, stimulating rational, critical, dialectical discourse. In addition, whereas sociology asks that we obtain knowledge about society by studying others, Gouldner insists that we must also understand ourselves.

Plato would have smiled.

Social Evolution and Sociological Categories, by PAUL Q. HIRST. New York: Holmes & Meier Publishers, 1976. 135 pp. $15.00 cloth.

RANDALL COLLINS
San Diego

British sociology underwent a quantitative expansion with the revolution in higher education of the last two decades, and along with it has come an expansion of intellectual frontiers as well. British theorists have crossed the channel, and the Atlantic, and come back with important critiques (and new developments as well) of Marxism and ethnomethodology. In *Social Evolution and Sociological Categories,* Paul Hirst uses a sophisticated Marxism to mount the strongest critique of Max Weber I have yet seen.

Hirst's book is intense, concentrated, and energetic. In 110 pages of text Hirst closely argues two theses on the general topic of sociological classification and typification schemes. In one section, he shows that Charles Darwin, Herbert Spencer, and Lewis Henry Morgan all had different versions of evolution, and that Marx was not an evolutionist in any sense applicable to these (and that this is so even though Marx and Engels took certain materials from Morgan, and dogmatic Marxists still tend to regard Morgan as part of the canon). In the other, longer section, Hirst analyzes Weber's sociological typologies, pointing up their philosophical biases and theoretical shortcomings. I shall confine myself to the latter section here.

Hirst begins his Weber critique by examining Weber's epistemology, which he describes as "neo-Kantian positivism." It is neo-Kantian in the sense of distinguishing nature, as the realm of mechanical causality, from culture, as the realm of teleological causality; it is positivism in the sense of rejecting subjective and objective idealism, and instead regarding cultures as *historical facts* to be investigated. In this way, Weber is able to recognize that all cultural objects, as products of human wills, are value-related, and yet to distinguish the factual aspect of investigation from the values, precisely because these values are the objects that are to be investigated. Cultural values do not form a unified system; they are frequently in conflict, and the object of sociology is to describe and understand them as human activities in the world.

One result of this stance is that Weber does not look for causal laws or mechanisms. His analytical tools, the ideal types, are heuristic devices, pincers between which one can locate the concrete details of history in all their uniqueness. Thus, Hirst argues, Weber's philosophical grounding upon the primacy of the human will leads to a relativistic and historicist conception of the limits of sociology. From this viewpoint, general theory is impossible; general causal mechanisms do not exist. Hirst contends that this is not only an inferior stance to that of Marxism, which he regards as a basis for a true sociological science, but that it allows free play for a number of biases in Weber's work. In the sphere of action, it leads to "irrationalism and a cult of personal freedom to choose." In the scholarly sphere, it imposes ideal types of the economy and polity which rule out *a priori* both socialism and popular democracy.

In Weber's categories of social action, the emphasis on the teleology of human wills leads to a distinction based on whether relationships between means and ends are calculated (another subjective act) or not; thus the ideal type of *Zweckrationalität* is the vantage point from which all else is surveyed. This leads to a definition of economic action which Hirst regards as unduly restrictive, ruling out everything but a pure marginalist economic model as not only irrational, but even non-economic. Thus all pre-capitalist economies cannot be conceived as economies at all. Further, all subordinated workers are ruled out as economic actors as well; they may do the hard labor of material production, but they do not make calculated economic decisions; this latter is reserved for the capitalist entrepreneur and the rational consumer, who alone are true economic actors.

Thus, Hirst argues, Weber glorifies capitalism and capitalists as the only true subjects of economics; and adopting the arguments of the Austrian marginalist economist Eugen von Böhm-Bawerk (who was, incidentally, Finance Minister in the Austrian government), concludes that socialism is impossible. For all the changes it may make in ideology, the only real economic change made by socialism could be in the distribution of its products. It cannot do away with bureaucratic organization of production, with control by abstract financial calculations, or with the split between calculating economic masters and mindless laborers who carry out their orders.

Similarly, Hirst argues that Weber's categories of legitimate domination prestructure one's view of political phenomena so as to make authoritarian control seem both natural and inevitable. Social relations are defined as inter-subjective relations of freely willing, value-oriented individuals. Hence any stable form of authority must be two-sided. It must involve belief on both sides, that of the ruled as well as the ruler, in the worthiness of obedience. Although Weber recognizes that domination also involves an organizational staff and material means to enforce orders, he places the decisive emphasis for classifying types of domination upon the notion of willing compliance, be it for reasons of belief in charisma, tradition, or enacted law. That people might obey because of coercion or material interests is for Weber not a sufficient condition for a stable, legitimate authority. Weber, and his followers, nevertheless go ahead and use the classification of legitimacy types for virtually all states, thus providing, Hirst charges, an ideology obfuscating the real bases of authoritarian rule.

One consequence of this is that democracy occupies a peculiar place in Weber's sociology. Democracy is a form of *legitimation,* in that it gives a certain form of charismatic sanction to the selection of leaders, but it is not a form of *rule.* The people do not rule themselves, and cannot; as Hirst points out, this ideal cannot even be *thought* in Weber's categories. Any effort at direct democracy is essentially anti-authoritarian, and hence not a form of legitimate domination at all. (Thus Guenther Roth accurately sub-titles the section of *Economy and Society* that deals with urban politics—the section separately published as *The City*—"Non-legitimate Domination."

Instead, what we have under the name of "democracy" is inevitably a system of rule by bureaucratic elites (or sometimes the aristocratic or financial elites that Weber referred to as "local notables") operating through the pressures for specialized administration that Weber's friend Robert Michels called the "Iron Law of Oligarchy." Weber, in his own political writings, showed his willingness to work within such a system. His primary concern was with a competitive electoral mechanism for selecting leaders, but not in order to ensure representation of public interests. Weber merely wished to provide that truly creative human individuals would be found at the top. His ideal politician emerges in the market of mass politics as the entrepreneur does in the economy. In either sphere, the individual will alone is the source of social creativity. In all spheres, Hirst concludes,

Weber places all social value, and all analytical stress as well, on the Nietzschean *Übermensch*.

Hirst's argument is carefully documented from Weber's writings, and I found it impressive, as far as it goes. Unquestionably, Weber's typological formulations are rooted in his epistemology, and Hirst has drawn out the connections in a sophisticated fashion that places his critique many levels above the usual run of anti-Weber polemics. Hirst clearly shows the political and economic limitations of a strict construction of these categories, at the same time that he shows his own intellectual calibre by recognizing that Weber is no polemicist either, but follows out his analytical premises with great consistency.

Yet the question remains of how far Hirst's critique goes. Like most Weber-critics (and many Weberians as well), Hirst concentrates on Weber's methodological essays, and on the definitions that make up part one of *Economy and Society*. Weber's actual analyses of economics and politics, however, are much broader, and suggest lines of development which go far toward overcoming the problems Hirst highlights. I shall mention just a few.

Weber's ideal type model of a pure, calculable economic system does excellent service in analyzing world economic history, and certainly does not prevent him, in the four completed volumes of the comparative world-religions studies, in his *General Economic History,* and in almost 1,000 pages of part two of *Economy and Society,* from analyzing pre-capitalist economies. The rational-calculation ideal type provides the baseline from which other forms of economy can be surveyed. And it does more than that: Weber mounts a strong theoretical and empirical argument that the industrial breakthrough could occur, *for the first time,* only in the form of a capitalist market that approximated the ideal type of calculable movement of resources in the areas of trade, finance, and labor. He was thus able to show the obstacles to the rise of calculable market conditions in each area, and to trace back successively the roles that politics and religion played in preventing or promoting capitalist development throughout the world. This is a massive accomplishment, one that remains obscured behind a simplistic notion of Weber's theory as consisting only in "The Protestant Ethic," and one that is likely to remain obscured by more sophisticated versions of Weber which concentrate only on his methodological essays and his introductory categorizations. I would contend, moreover, that it is as yet our most comprehensive and empirically best founded view of world economic history, one which is larger than, and capable of subsuming, the best of Marxist efforts, including the world-economy view of Wallerstein.

It was in the process of pursuing this question of interpreting economic history that Weber found it necessary to deal with the forms of politics throughout world history. Here, too, Weber's actual work is broader and more realistic than the view Hirst derives from Weber's conceptual introduction. Surely there has been no comparative sociologist who writes of historical states with more realism and detachment than Weber, nor one who has done more to focus our attention on the material conditions of domination, the importance of various material innovations in arms and military supplies, and in the material means of administration of the state (and by extension, of all areas of organization). The tendency to one-sided idealism found in Weber's conceptual writings is nicely balanced in his comparative work, and I would contend that it has been the latter that has been so fruitful for the development of a serious and realistic explanatory theory in sociology. (To mention just one example: Etzioni's empirically-grounded theory of organizational compliance is explicitly Weberian in derivation, and attends to just those variables of coercion and material interests that an idealistic view would appear to overlook.)

In other words, there is no reason why we are stuck with Weber's original epistemology, or with his narrowly historicist view of sociology as illuminating only particulars in their individual complexity. All empirical analysis implies some causal generalizations in the very process of formulating its statements, and those lying implicit in Weber's work are an especially rich source for developing a type of theory that Weber himself did not intend. After all, it has been by being disloyal to some of the claims of one's predecessors that any science has been able to advance.

Hirst has convinced me that there is no value in any canonical loyalty to the specifics of Weber's typologies and philosophical methodology, or even some of his theoretical assertions. Still, I am not going to stop reflecting on Weber's themes and materials just because of these faults, no less than I would stop reflecting on the themes of Durkheim or Marx just because of theirs. Intellectuals are at best salvage-divers from the sunken wrecks of the theories of the past. In any larger sense, Weber carries too much treasure for us to forget him yet. Much of what is empirically and causally powerful in current sociological knowledge has been built upon Weber. And "Weber" is really a gloss for the synthesis and guide to the achievements of nineteenth century scholarship upon which he himself built. That was a great period of scholarship, especially in Germany, and Weber was expert in some of its most important fields: the comparative history of economies, laws, religions, and politics. It is the best of this historical research that Weber has brought down to us, presented with the analytical sophistication that emerged at the turn of the century out of the high-level dialogue that took place in Germany between Marxists and anti-Marxists (and out of which came the leading ideas of Schumpeter, Michels, Oppenheimer, Lukács, and Mannheim as well). Weber is thus, for the present, our connection with wide-lensed historical scholarship in its greatest period of development; and he worked in a situation of fruitful, nondogmatic intellectual discourse across radical lines like that which is reemerging only today.

So there you have it: the best-argued book of sociological theory I have read in some time. It is the best critique of Weber I have yet seen, even though it fails to go far in exploring what can be gained on the positive, and empirically useful, side of Weber. In the latter direction, Hirst might find much in the Weberian vein that would prove useful in his efforts to develop a realistic and scientifically powerful extension of classical Marxism. But whatever comes of this, it is apparent that Hirst's books will be well worth reading for some time to come. How good is British sociological thinking these days? Take a look at Hirst if you want to see how good it can be.

GUENTHER ROTH
University of Washington

Robert Bierstedt found nothing good to say about Hirst's *Durkheim, Bernard and Epistemology* (cf. *CS*, 1976:5:6:828). I have nothing good to report about Hirst's next exercise. In fact, I consider it the most wrong-headed book ever written by a native English writer about Weber, taking its place next to the similar work by the Swedish Marxist-Leninist, Goeran Therborn, *Science, Class and Society* (cf. my review in *CS*, 1975:4:4:371). Here is another Marxist exercise designed to deal a death blow to bourgeois social science by finishing off Weber once and for all. Hirst undertakes to accomplish this in a mere seventy pages, after a thirty-four page discourse on Herbert Spencer and Lewis Henry Morgan, in which he picks a quarrel with another Marxist, Emmanuel Terray. Hirst insists that his political opposition to Weber (and social scientists in general) should be considered separately from his "logical and conceptual critique. . . . whether it is right or wrong is a strictly theoretical matter" (p. 122). Well, let's take him up on it.

Hirst's "general thesis . . . is that classifications of social forms are dependent on and products of specific social theories" (p. 49). In his case, this is an Althusserian credo. In a way the thesis is quite compatible with Weber insofar as his views on capitalism and Western rationalism in general were formulated within a particular tradition of economic and constitutional theory and in a particularly critical period of scholarly dissensus about the nature of concept formation in the social sciences. But Hirst's claim that theories cannot be derived from facts in a positivist manner is meant to be the baseline of his attack on Weber.

Hirst employs a number of Marxist strategies, reinforced by some Althusserian variants. First, there is the epistemological attack. As in his critique of Durkheim (cf. Bierstedt's review) Hirst tries to reduce Weber to absurdity by claiming that his epistemology must vitiate his historical analyses. Being a neo-Kantian positivist, Weber is "relativist and irrationalist" (p. 64), that is, incapable of a rational choice of values. He can't have a truly scientific theory of capitalist or any other society, only a series of arbitrary typifications (ideal types or models). Since Weber's sociology is purely formalist, it cannot provide an "objective" theory of society. This argument allows Hirst to dismiss the fact that Weber tried to reconstruct the path of western rationalism, especially of rational bourgeois capitalism, through a series of specific historically causal explanations on the secular level.

The second strategy (employed in ch. 4) is the old one of concentrating narrowly on Weber's definition of social action and his championship of methodological individualism to the exclusion of his practiced methodology: "Central to Weber's sociology is the teleology of human wills; society is the product of meaningful inter-subjective action" (p. 948). It is well-known that Weber reacted against the fashions of evolutionism, organicism, and other reifications of groups and processes with a fierce insistence that on the empirical level only human beings act, not collectivities. It is also true that Weber denies the empirical relevance of the notion of the social totality and historical teleology—as all empirical social scientists must do. But individuals, whether "great men" or multitudes acting out "collective behavior," play almost no role in Weber's research. Instead we find an overriding concern with the dominant economic, political, legal, and religious structures of Western history and of China and India as main comparisons. All of these structures were full of internal contradictions, and in all of them people suffered the fate of unanticipated consequences. Weber did not differ from Marx in believing that human beings make their own history but under iron constraints.

The third strategy is to claim that Weber's types of legitimate domination deal only with "the problem of legitimacy" in a purely subjective sense (cf. p. 80), as if the bulk of his sociology of domination did not deal with structural sources of conflict between rulers, staffs, and subjects, with the struggle over the control of the means of administration and production, and always also with the economic presuppositions and consequences of a given kind of rulership. Hirst adds an additional twist to this interpretation. After accusing Weber of radical personalism, he himself personalizes Weber's vivisection of bureaucracies as "Weber's bureaucracy" (p. 118). But Weber's statements on the relative efficiency of bureaucratic administration were highly qualified historical judgments, not managerialist pronouncements about organizational efficiency; his comparative longitudinal analysis of bureaucracy was supplemented by his blunt exposure of the Prussian and Russian bureaucracies as entrenched vested interests and outright parasites. After charging that Weber had no general theory of domination, Hirst reverses himself immediately by asserting that Weber believed in Michels' iron law of oligarchy (cf. 111 and 114ff), when Weber demonstrably, if unsuccessfully, spent much effort dissuading Michels from his deterministic view. Hirst also uses a guilt-by-association technique in extravagantly exaggerating the similarities between Nietzsche and Weber, construing a Weberian conception of the *Übermensch,* as if Weber had ever used this term positively and had not viewed Nietzsche's notion of the will to power as typical of the mentality of a German philistine.

So much for Hirst's theoretical critique. His political disagreement with Weber is simple: Weber was no adherent of Rousseau; he was committed to the separation of powers. Hirst happens to believe that political centralization and the abolition of the separation of the legislative and the executive are compatible with, if not favorable to, "democracy"—a clearly Leninist notion (cf. 119ff). Hirst ends up asserting hyperbolically that "the idea that . . . a socialist society might compel bureaucrats and Heidelberg professors to do manual work and to accept workman's wages never enters Weber's head" (p. 119), and this of a man who proudly called himself a "class-conscious bourgeois." Weber was probably quite aware of this possibility, but I tend to agree with Hirst that it was "unthinkable for [Weber] that the result might be an infinitely more 'rational' system of production." It is undeniable that Weber and many of his peers were incompetent at manual work; but it is worthwhile remembering that the mode of academic production, whether privately or state-supported, was more favorable to scholarly productivity in Heidelberg before the First World War than it is today, when American professors are too busy fixing their houses, working their gardens, repairing their cars, and doing without servants, ever to be able to compete effectively with the productive scholarly generations of that period.

SURVEY REVIEWS

Social Exchange Theory: Its Structure and Influence in Social Psychology, by J. K. Chadwick-Jones. N.Y.: Academic Press, 1976. 431 pp. $29.25 cloth.

Social Exchange Theory: The Two Traditions, by Peter P. Ekeh. Cambridge, Mass.: Harvard University Press, 1974. 237 pp. $8.95 cloth.

Rational Choice and Social Exchange, by Anthony Heath. N.Y.: Cambridge University Press, 1976. $16.95 cloth.

The Logic of Social Systems, by Alfred Kuhn. San Francisco: Jossey-Bass, 1974. 534 pp. $15.00 cloth.

Behavior: The Control of Perception, by William T. Powers. Chicago: Aldine Publishing Company, 1973. 296 pp. $8.95 cloth.

Harry C. Bredemeir
Douglass College, Rutgers University

It is too bad the term "exchange theory" was ever invented. As George Homans, who is nearly always (including by most of the authors reviewed here) called an exchange theorist, has recently said, "Since much social behavior may . . . be looked on as exchange, some social scientists have tended to call the type of explanation we put forward 'exchange theory.' We believe this practice should be given up. It implies that exchange theory is somehow a distinct and independent theory, whereas in our view it consists simply of behavioral psychology applied to the interaction of men."

The last eight words in Homans's statement are notoriously controversial, and I shall return to their import below. But they are not the only focus of the controversies that developed once the term "exchange theory" was created. Among the other issues the term—or writings under its umbrella—has raised and caused to be endlessly argued about are such questions as: What is the difference between "social" exchange and "economic" exchange? Is exchange theory "reductionistic"? What is its relation to other "theories" (symbolic interaction theory, cognitive dissonance theory, conflict theory, functionalism, etc.)? Is it too individualistic to be sociological? Does it assume rationality? How can you measure costs and rewards? Can it account for altruistic behavior?

These books are part of the stream of such arguments. Heath's is a well-written, critical, thoughtful, and an urbane guided tour through much of the literature. Chadwick-Jones's is a much more detailed road map (I use the contrasting metaphors deliberately) to scores—perhaps hundreds—of laboratory experiments and other research efforts based more or less explicitly on Homans, Blau, and Thibaut and Kelley. It is also a somewhat pedantic step-by-step summary of those four theorists' books. Ekeh's is a polemic on how Blau and Homans reflect the individualistic tradition of British utilitarianism and neglect the French collectivistic tradition developed by Durkheim and continued by Lévi-Strauss. Neither Powers nor Kuhn styles himself an exchange theorist, but they both cut through a great deal of the confusion that characterizes much of the literature under the exchange rubric. Unfortunately, neither of their reviews of one another's books in this journal in 1975 did justice to either book; and Marion Levy's review of Kuhn's book in the November, 1975 *AJS* told about Levy but not about Kuhn. For those reasons, I include them in this essay.

An essay review cannot hope to cover all the details of all the discussions; but I think some needed clarification is now possible.

The "Behavioristic" Argument

One elementary but always ignored fact merits stating first. It is that B. F. Skinner unquestionably engages in mutually adaptive transactions (I'll avoid "exchange" for a while) with his pigeons. For some reason (not hard to explicate, but we need not bother now), Skinner wants a pigeon to do something like peck a round dot; and the pigeon wants some food. Under certain conditions, each gets what he or she wants. The emphasis is usually put on how Skinner gets the pigeon to peck the dot; but it is equally true—and vital—that one of the conditions under which Skinner gets rewarded by the pigeon in that way is that Skinner does what the pigeon requires him to do—all of it: food at the end of those pecks, a reasonably dry and warm box, no lunging cats, ample water, and on and on. You will find all of the conditions implicit in Skinner's approach made explicit in a place that will probably surprise many readers—namely, in Talcott Parsons's theory of socialization as developed, for example, in *Family, Socialization, and Interaction Process*. (Note that "*interaction* process.") Moreover, of course, Skinner *never* makes the food contingent on the pigeon's singing "Ave Maria."

Why not? Because, deny it as much as he likes, Skinner always operates with at least an implicit model of the internal state of the pigeon. William Powers makes this abundantly clear, as does Alfred Kuhn.

Given the cultural codes that control Skinner and given the genetic codes that control the pigeon, their mutual adaptation follows—if they are to be mutually adapted at all. Let Skinner hypothesize that the pigeon values (will respond in order to obtain) dollar bills or cheese, and you have one frustrated Skinner. If Skinner hangs in there, he'll have to change his hypothesis, and Skinner's learning will take place, as Heath, Kuhn, and Powers (and Parsons) all make clear in different ways, in accordance with much the same principles as the pigeon's.

The operating word is "control." Skinner and the pigeon are both control systems, or negative feedback systems, as are you and I and all the "subjects" and "experimenters" Chadwick-Jones reports on. In Powers's vocabulary, we all have reference signals (values, goals) which prescribe the desired state of our relation to environing others; perceptual signals, which tell us the actual state of those relations; and a repertoire of actions operating to keep discrepancies at zero. Kuhn has a slightly different vocabulary for the same elements: Selector functions, Detector functions, and Effector functions. Each set of terms refers respectively, for example, to the setting of a thermostat; the thermometer registering the actual temperature; and the operation of the furnace to keep discrepancies at zero—a familiar model of a negative feedback control system.

When the nature of the things wanted by a person is established and the question is *how much* of it will get the person to act in a certain way, we have Thibaut and Kelley's concept of the person's "Comparison Level," and Homans's "Q"—the quantity that would satisfy. Chadwick-Jones has an extended discussion of this, and also of Thibaut and Kelley's companion concept, a person's "Comparison Level for Alternatives." Most simply put, this refers to the fact that person A is not likely to continue transacting with person B if A thinks C offers a better deal.

Powers offers a model for the human case of a nine-level hierarchy of reference signals, with a person's "system concept" being at the top—that is, most controlling. By this he means that everyone has some image of some system, the welfare of which his or her actions are designed to further. Powers doesn't quite say so, but I interpret him to be referring to the difference, say, between someone whose governing system concept is his or her own immediate interest (a psychopath), at the one extreme; and toward (not at) the other extreme, someone whose governing system concept is his or her country (Nathan Hale). Kuhn adds the point that people differ in their time perspectives, or as the economists say, their time discount rates.

Both sets of concepts together obviously make ample room for altruism, for the sacrifice of present and subsidiary goals for future and higher order goals, and for "conscience"—phenomena which seem to bother critics of "exchange theory" who take too naive a view of Skinner's actual transactions with his pigeons, and too naive a view of "economic" exchange.

"Social" Versus "Economic" Exchanges

Sociological and social psychological critics of exchange theory are often as bothered by the borrowings from economics as by the borrowings from psychology; and not a few words are invested in efforts to distinguish different kinds of exchange theory in terms of whether they rely chiefly on economics or on "behaviorist" psychology. Peter Ekeh, for example, argues that a major difference between Homans and Blau is that the former relies on operant theory and the latter on economic theory; and that both consequently miss the difference between "social" and "economic" exchanges. Ekeh even quotes James Coleman's lament that, since his initial 1958 paper, "Homans has . . . by degrees led himself away from . . . an [economic] approach into that of operant conditioning" (Ekeh, p. 181).

It is hard to understand what all the fuss is about. Open negative feedback control systems necessarily and by definition have interchanges with one another. They are genetically and/or culturally characterized by reference signals to obtain from environments certain kinds of things at certain rates, and to dispose to environments certain kinds of things at certain rates. If inputs to them rise above their programmed par rates (their reference signals), they will experience the error signal we call surfeit; if inputs fall below the reference signal, they will experience deprivation. If demands for outputs from them rise above their reference signal rates, they will experience strain. Accept outputs from them below their reference signal rates, and they experience slack.

Some people at some times seek to obtain and dispose of, at various rates, such things as money, labor services, cars, and ice cream cones. These are conventionally called "economic" interchanges. Some people at some times seek to obtain and dispose of, at various rates, such things as expressions of affection, symbols of respect and praise, or kisses. These interchanges are sometimes called "social." If you obtain a car by paying someone money for it, some people like to call that an economic transaction, whereas if you obtain it by leaning on your brother-in-law's mercy, some people want to call that social. If you obtain it by filling out a requisition to the transportation department, it is "bureaucratic."

This is sound and fury, signifying something, all right, but not as much as tends to get made of it. Whether they are kisses or cars, different people will have different reference levels for obtaining or offering different kinds and amounts of them; and if you want to affect someone's behavior, you had better proceed exactly as Skinner does (no matter what he says he does)—namely, figure out what the person's reference signal is, how much deprivation (for example) he or she is experiencing; and then try to arrange matters so that you can help the person reduce the deprivation by doing what you want him or her to do—without too great a cost. You might also, of course (as Skinner habitually does), first contrive to create in the person some error signal, and then offer to relieve it at a price, the price being the person's giving you the reward you are seeking. Kuhn's discussion of such pre-transactional impositions of "stress" is excellent, and cuts through a large amount of verbiage about the role of "coercion" and "power" in "exchange theory."

When Skinner tries to get the pigeon to peck the dot, he is in effect testing a series of hypotheses about the pigeon's control systems. What he discovers or demonstrates is that if pigeons are deprived of grain long enough (but not too long), they will value receipts of it enough to peck around at everything until they hit on the peck that reduces their deprivation. He also discovers that pigeons can peck and that their perceptual apparatus can distinguish between round dots and square dots—or whatever. That's the same sort of discovery you make when you test the hypothesis that the car salesman will respond to a hundred dollars, three hundred, etc.

Norms and Indirect Exchange

Another area of confusion in many discussions concerns the notion of "norms" as "causes" of behavior and of "indirect" exchange. Peter Ekeh, for example, strongly criticizes Blau and Homans for focusing on "restricted" exchange, and contrasts this with Lévi-Strauss's concern with "generalized" exchange. (An example of generalized or indirect exchange is the situation in which A gives something to B who does a service for C who rewards in some way D who reinforces A.) Chadwick-Jones comes at the distinction in discussing Blau's emphasis on the importance of norms in social exchange. "Thus, Blau argues that social norms substitute indirect exchange for direct transactions between individuals, and that exchange between the collectivity and its individual members replaces direct transactions as the result of conformity to norms. For instance, in groups of friends each one feels obliged to help others without thought of return, and while there is no direct exchange of favours, the group norm assures that each will receive help when he needs it" (p. 321).

Such language is loaded with confusions. Patently, there is no such thing as a "group norm" which goes around giving assurances; and patently to speak of an exchange between an individual and a collectivity is metaphorical speech. I like metaphors; but it is essential to keep them in their place.

None of this really distinguishes between "social" and "economic" exchange. Nearly all exchanges called economic are indirect, in the sense that I give my labor services and get money in return, some of which I then give to my barber for a different service; and so on. I am willing to accept the money because I think other people will go along with the group norm which makes money legal tender. (*I,* a person, think other *people* will do so; I don't think any norm will do so.) Similarly, the friend who helps a friend expects some expression of gratitude, one dictionary definition of which is the expression of "warm feelings of good will"—a symbolic communication that the favor *will* be reciprocated at an appropriate time. Let some A repeatedly give some B some costly service with no return at all, and after a while such giving will stop.

As Talcott Parsons (who nearly everyone forgets has been from the outset an "exchange theorist") has gone farthest in pointing out, the different symbolic sanctions involved in different kinds of indirect exchanges; but it is always some *individual* who shows his or her right to some good or service from some other *individual,* whether the "showing" consists of flashing money, friendship, insignia of authority, expertise, or weapons.

I cannot think of anything I get from a "collectivity." I get things from grocery clerks, librarians, bank tellers, barbers, friends, college deans, students, and so on. Apparently it cannot be stated too often: "collectivities" do not act; only people act. Collectivities are organized patterns of inter-personal actions; and patterns cannot exchange with people. It is convenient to use such metaphors as, "The United States wages war on Vietnam," but sanity requires that it always be remembered that the metaphor is shorthand for a long series of sentences of the order, "Some person occupying the status of President gives orders to some persons occupying the status of generals to give orders to some persons occupying the status of bomber crews to drop bombs on some persons occupying the status of Vietnamese . . .; and under certain conditions (but not others) all those orders get obeyed by the people involved."

To repeat, giving an order is like offering money or conditioning a pigeon: A wants B to do some X; and B will do it if he or she thinks that's the best way to get what he or she wants. I do not want to minimize the differences among market, bureaucratic, friendship, or influence patterns of relationships; but I do want to stress their similarities. They are all "social" by any reasonable definition of the term; they all involve an A and a B; in all of them, the As and Bs are negative feedback control systems, and they will do whatever they can to keep their error signals at zero—which is another way of saying, get rewards and avoid costs.

Furthermore, not so incidentally, they all involve people "defining situations" all over the place, trying to manage one another's impressions, trying to protect their self-images, and so on. They unambiguously involve, in other words, "symbolic interaction"—necessarily so, since the controls governing the actors are *cultural* controls, and when you say "culture," you necessarily say "symbolic." Symbolic interaction involves people trying to obtain and dispose of various kinds of information, and Homans's basic propositions apply as well to information as they do to bars of soap or dollars. On this whole matter of symbolic interactions and management of definitions, Alfred Kuhn is excellent.

The Measurement and Calculation Problem

Both Ekeh and Chadwick-Jones refer often to the 1965 Morton Deutsch and Robert Krauss criticism of Homans, which Chadwick-Jones says "preempted" most of the later criticisms. Ekeh quotes approvingly the Deutsch and Krauss statement that Homans "implies that there is a common currency or a single dimension to which the value of different experiences ('getting a B+ on an exam,' 'being kissed by one's sweetheart,' 'hearing a Beethoven quartet' . . .) can be coordinated, so that the value of a 'unit' of one such activity received can be compared with the value of another unit" (Ekeh, p. 203).

The plain fact is that people successfully make such comparisons all the time. At some point, a person listening to a Beethoven quartet will stop doing so and kiss his or her sweetheart, and after a while will stop that and start studying for an exam. He or she will have been behaving in each case in accordance with Homans's "rationality proposition," which, as he says, sums up eighty percent of his basic propositions: "In choosing between alternative actions, a person will choose that one for which, as perceived by him at the time, the value, V, of the result, multiplied by the probability, k, of getting the result, is the greater."

Both Kuhn and Powers elaborate this basic notion (without referring to Homans) elegantly; and Kuhn successfully weaves into his account an evolutionary analysis of *why* another twenty percent of Homans's propositions (the frustration-aggression proposition) obtains.

It is true that we do not have an instrument which we could attach to the person and watch it record on moving tape the unit-by-unit decrement of satisfaction being obtained from the quartet, and on the same scale the unit-by-unit growth in the person's hunger for kisses or anxiety about the exam. It may be that in some positivistic dream such an instrument ought to exist; but the real world simply happens to be different. What the exchange theorists are telling us largely is that in the real world, the likelihood that a person will engage in some action (call it X) is great to the degree that he or she thinks the probable benefits will exceed the probable costs, and to the degree that she or he thinks she or he can manage it. They are not telling us it is easy to ascertain the values of the variables controlling a person's action; in fact, much of the content of these books (perhaps especially Chadwick-Jones's) is all about how hard it is. But they are saying that if you want to practice Verstehen, those are the variables, the values of which you need to ascertain.

Power and Bargaining Power

Chadwick-Jones also presents an extended discussion of Homans's, Blau's, and Thibaut and Kelley's analysis of "power." The best discussion, however, is provided by Kuhn, who makes it clear that in most cases Homans and Blau are really talking about *bargaining* power, which is different from "plain" power. (Kuhn does not, however, tie his discussion explicitly to Homans or Blau.)

Chadwick-Jones quotes Blau's proposition that "the greater the difference between the benefits an individual supplies to others and those they can obtain elsewhere, the greater is his power over them likely to be." He then paraphrases Blau's elaboration of this by writing that in the exchange between high status and low status persons, "the benefits afforded by high status members are exchanged for the compliance of low status members" (p. 300).

The term, "compliance," is misleading here (as it is also in Blau); and the notion of "power over" someone is also troublesome. What is always going on in a transaction or exchange, as Kuhn makes clearer than anyone, is that some person, A, has a desire for something, Y, he doesn't have, and will have to give up some X to get it, while the other person, B, has Y but wants X. *Each* is trying to get "compliance" from the other, never mind any difference in "status." (Just like Skinner and the pigeons.)

Now there are two separate questions: (1) What determines the probability that A will get Y and B will get X? (2) What determines the *terms* on which each will get the other's compliance—*how much* Y for *how much* X? The first is a question of power (likelihood of successful adaptation); the second is a question of bargaining power.

Kuhn's clarification can be summarized as follows: A person's power is great to the degree that six things are true: (1) Her/his potential offerings are greatly valued by others. (2) There are lots of such others. (3) There aren't many people like her/him. (4) Those others are willing and able to meet his/her needs. (5) she/he is willing and able to make her/his potential offerings available. (6) Her/his desire for what the others control is great.

A person's bargaining power, however, is a different matter. It is great to the degree that the first four of those things are true, but to the degree that the last two are *not* true. An interesting corollary, if you stop to think about it (as Kuhn does), is that the strongest competitor always has the least bargaining power.

Summary

Among these writers, you will find the most elegant analysis of interpersonal transactions (and attendant norms) in Kuhn's book; (which, incidentally, Kuhn has also "written down" to the introductory text level in *Unified Social Science*); the clearest analysis of people as negative feedback control systems in Powers's book; the most readable short introduction in Heath's book; the most detailed review of the research literature in Chadwick-Jones's book; and the bravest effort to defend Lévi-Strauss against Homans and Blau in Ekeh's book.

The Role of Communications in the Middle East Conflict: Ideological and Religious Aspects, by YONAH ALEXANDER. New York: Praeger Publishers, 1974. 287 pp. $17.50 cloth.

Oh, What a Blow That Phantom Gave Me! by EDMUND CARPENTER. New York: Bantam Books, 1974. 196 pp. $2.25 paper.

On Culture and Communication, by RICHARD HOGGART. New York: Oxford University Press, 1971. 111 pp. $5.95 cloth.

Sociology of Mass Communications, edited by DENIS MCQUAIL. Penguin Books, 1972. 477 pp. $3.95 paper.

Media and Symbols: The Forms of Expression, Communication, and Education, edited by DAVID R. OLSON. Chicago: University of Chicago Press, 1974. 508 pp. $10.00 cloth.

The Political Impact of Mass Media, by COLIN SEYMOUR-URE. Beverly Hills: Sage Publications, 1974. 296 pp. $15.00 cloth.

Mass Communications: A World View, edited by ALAN WELLS. Palo Alto: National Press Books, 1974. 276 pp. $3.95 paper.

GLADYS ENGEL LANG
SUNY/Stony Brook

Edmund Carpenter, a Canadian anthropologist, views the media with distrust in *Oh, What a Blow that Phantom Gave Me!* Media are so powerful, he tells us, that they swallow cultures and even people like his colleague, McLuhan, become their victims. In this little, lively book, with the curious title taken from *Don Quixote*, he addresses both the question of the ways in which people change media and the ways media change people. Still, he regards people as essentially powerless to resist the inevitable changes that follow their encounters with new media.

This is the message he means to convey, using a "hot" medium, to reach the largest possible audience. Writing the book seems—my inference—to be a kind of penance for having contributed, along with all the anthropologists he loathes, to destroying the primitive cultures they set out to study. His particular sin was to have accepted an invitation from governmental officials in New Guinea to advise them on more effective uses for electronic media. However well intentioned these officials were, Carpenter now believes, they were using the media for human control. Example: when villagers ignore their leader, the government tape-records his orders and broadcasts his voice. Hearing the leader's voice coming from a radio held in their own hands, they obey.

But whether or not the introduction of new media is intended to change minds, it does change them, Carpenter tells us. He reports the fear-gripped villagers at Sio when they were first shown Polaroid shots of each other, when they first heard their voices on tape. Yet in a short time they were taking pictures of each other (some wearing their own on their foreheads) and endlessly playing with equipment. Months later they were wearing European clothing, carrying themselves differently, building houses in a new style, some moving away, torn out of tribal existence, detached, lonely, no longer at home anywhere. All this, according to Carpenter, because of the presence of the new media. Vulnerable people, already in process of change, the media tipped the scales.

The power of the media to shape and change society. The power of the people to determine the use of media power: these are old but still sociologically-relevant themes running through this odd assortment of books sent to me for review. *On Culture and Communication* is a delightfully perceptive book by Richard Hoggart whose *Uses of Literacy* is by now a classic. It was put together from a series of BBC Lectures delivered at the time Hoggart, former Director of the Center for Cultural Studies at Birmingham, was serving as Assistant Director-General of UNESCO in Paris. There his daily contacts with representatives of so many cultures seem to have impressed on him not only the obvious diversity of societal arrangements and communication modes but their malleability and potential for change.

As a result, whereas Carpenter, looking at communication in many cultures, concluded that the media make the country, the sum of Hoggart's message is "what countries make of the media depends on what the country is made up of." Society, for him, is always in a state of change and more varied than most people, especially broadcasters, want to believe. And what the media—TV, for example—can accomplish depends on the constant testing of its potentialities by interactions between the possibilities of the medium and the texture of society.

Though Hoggart joins Carpenter in regarding the media as more than inert channels, he rejects completely the notion that broadcasters should be or must be mere "reflectors" ("which in most countries means reflections of someone-in-power's idea of what a culture should look like"—[p. 84]) and says they have the freedom to be active agents of change. Broadcasters ought to be given the greatest possible freedom from interference provided they keep in touch with the variety of their culture, think about the responsibility of the medium and come under the regular scrutiny of the right kind. Those in power do not welcome use of the media to produce change but he is saying where there is a will, there is a way.

Like Hoggart, Denis McQuail, a British sociologist at Southampton and one of the most prolific scholars working in the field of mass communications, also stresses the variety of societal arrangements and the diversity of communication modes that result. So, in organizing his reader, *Sociology of Mass Communications,* he deliberately overloaded it with articles from the non Anglo-Saxon world. He wanted to make available to the student of sociology a sampling of the widely scattered, not easily accessible literature as well as to encourage and contribute to the cross-cultural study of mass communications.

McQuail focuses, also, on the nature of the interdependence between communication systems and the changing society. Reiterating a theme of his earlier book, *Toward a Sociology of Mass Communications* he sees the mass media in their present institutional form taking their predominant character from other features of society—the economic level, the level of technology, the class and status structure, its political forms, the organization of work and leisure. Thus media have to be regarded not as a stable given but as variable and in some degree unstable in respect of product, content and audience behavior.

I have to quibble with McQuail when, critiquing sociological research in mass communications, he deplores the failure to treat media content as an object of cultural analysis, i.e., to seek knowledge about the culture, values and living ideology of a society by examining the content of its media. He attributes this omission to the intellectual history of sociology which, in the past, emphasized the study of culture expressed in behavior and action rather than in symbolic form. Perhaps so and more so in Britain but I think he overlooks the role that technology and institutional arrangements play in the study of communication as well as in the communications studied. The idea of using media content as a social (cultural) indicator preceded "modern" communication research and was an important and popular subject of post-1945 research. The advance of computer technology as well as large-scale and organized support for social science research has just meant that researchers, like those at the Annenberg School where McQuail was visiting around this time, have been able to be more quantitatively sophisticated and to develop study on a larger scale. That "cultural indicator" or "cultivation analysis" study of the media is no longer neglected is testified to by the inclusion of articles by George Gerbner in both the McQuail and Olson selections.

Both McQuail and Welles include readings from many cultures that bring evidence to bear on this continuing theme: if content reflects the living ideology of a society, do the media inevitably reinforce those values or can the media be agents of change as Hoggart optimistically believes? *Sociology of Mass Communications* brings non Anglo-Saxon contributions from Poland (Zygmunt Baumann), Germany (Hans Magnus Enzensberger), Sweden (Karl Rosengren and Sven Windahl), USSR (W. A. Piramidin), France (Olivier Burgelin), Finland (Kaarle Nordenstrang) and Israel (Elihu Katz). From Italy (Francesco Alberoni), comes a particularly suggestive piece on the phenomenon of "stardom," the powerless elite created by the media, as a subject in need of study.

Alan Wells's *Mass Communications: A World View* is a resource for courses in international communications. One central concern is the variation in media systems with special stress on the third world press and media independence. In part two ("Global Village") we confront directly the dictum that the media reflect the country. Back-to-back articles on Russia and China offer the reader a contrast between media systems, both authoritarian but each reflecting the character of the society in which it operates. Both were written before Nixon's tours offered so many, so wide, but refracted, a view of these societies.

Mark W. Hopkins, a journalist, elaborates the inexorable process by which the structure and function of mass media institutions are altered as other social institutions change, even where political leaders and their communication managers do not plan these adaptations. Even in so completely state-controlled a media system as that of the USSR, he points out, there is an unpredictability about the effects of mass media communications—especially those of TV—on public moods and attitudes. The Soviet managers, previously unconcerned with the process through which media change people, had, according to Hopkins, begun by 1960 to be concerned and to modify their communications behavior to understand and exploit that process. (This new awareness was reflected in the large number of media sociologists from Eastern Bloc countries who turned up for the ISA Congress in Varna by 1970). As I write this report (1977) massive plans are underway in the USSR to increase the number of color sets and to extend coverage in time for the 1980 Olympic Games in Moscow. A Soviet official was quoted as saying that the games have always been accompanied by a significant leap in the development of the host country's broadcasting.

The tandem article by Alan P.L. Liu, a political scientist, emphasizes not adaptation but destruction of the mass media in China in response to the Cultural Revolution. Newspapers were transformed into propaganda pamphlets while radio and film content were totally politicized. This destruction he attributes largely to Mao Tse-tung's stress on peasant mobilization and his belief that radio was more effective than print for this purpose. This article, like Hopkins's, is time-bound but more so. The media system that Liu writes about might be more aptly contrasted with the Soviet system in the 1930s. Russia's communication system changed (though not in purpose) as it evolved from a peasant to an industrialized society and so China's communication system has changed (though not in purpose) as its society has evolved. Though the Chinese radio and newspaper agencies may not yet have fully recovered from their near dissolution during the Cultural Revolution, there is more reliance on more conventional media for mass persuasion—and, no doubt, there will be more.

The Wells reader also includes discussions of the media systems in France, the Netherlands, Italy, Sweden, Japan, Africa, the United Arab Republic and Southeast Asia. A resource.

Beyond any doubt, the gem in this assortment of relatively recent books is Colin Seymour-Ure's *The Political Impact of Mass Media*, the fourth in the fine series on Communication and Society edited by Jeremy Tunstall. His is a study of mass media effects and he need not apologize for this. That there might be such a felt need may puzzle readers less acquainted with latest trends in the world of communication research. Responding to the many findings of "no demonstrated direct effects" in survey research—mainly in studies during political campaigns (the Great Debates, etc.) but including inquiry into the consequences for individual behavior of violence, pornography, and specific communication efforts—it has lately become fashionable to decry the search for effects and call for concentration on the *who* or the *what* or the *how* in the communication formulas. Still, whatever the starting point of inquiry, the understanding of impact is what the study of communication is all about.

In part one, Seymour-Ure has done a masterful job in presenting a cogent, straightforward framework for analysis of a broad range of effects, particularly political effects defined as "any change within the political system induced directly or indirectly by the mass media." Many illustrations used in presenting his frame of reference introduce the case studies presented as part two.

These case studies, which evidence the variety of political communication effects, should be informative for political sociologists and students of bureaucratic organization. I found especially interesting the studies of the aftermath of Enoch Powell's 1968 speech on immigration, the British "satire boom" launched on TV by David Frost hosting *That Was The Week That Was* and in print by *Private Eye*, a satirical fortnightly, and an analysis of the role of *The Times* in the appeasement of Hitler.

A case study of Parliament and television further elucidates the nature of mutual influences between changing media and changing institutions. Seymour-Ure writes: "Since democratic values stress communication processes, institutional forms must necessarily change in response to developments in media" (p. 155). Yet, as late as 1974 Britain remained "one of the more conspicuous countries with no form of parliamentary broadcasting at all. . . . The institution simply closed its eyes and ears and pretended the media did not exist." MPs who argued against letting TV in stressed their desires for the survival of the institution as the embodiment of representative and responsible government, failing to recognize that the survival of representative and responsible government required adaptation.

Still, the institutional forms did respond to developments in the media even while not appearing to. If TV could not go to the institution, MPs could go to TV. As government leaders, unable to debate on TV, carried the debate onto TV, made important speeches on televised occasions, and televised political party conferences, parliamentary debate became a familiar staple on current affairs programming. Parallels with developments in American political institutions come readily to mind: excluded from legislative debate, television stages the debate outside the hall and in the corridors. Public affairs programs become the televised equivalent of the *Congressional Record*.

Yonah Alexander's book, *The Role of Communications in the Middle East Conflict* emerged as part of a larger project on the role of mass communications in the advancement of international understanding sponsored by the Columbia Graduate School of Journalism. In it he attributes cultural conflict not to the lack of communications between cultures—a common interpretation—but to the nature of existing communications. He diagnoses the root of continued conflict in the collision between two zealously-held ideologies—Arab Nationalism and Zionism—with self-righteous attitudes firmly reenforced on both sides through a *deliberate* substitution of distorted communication in the form of psychological warfare and propaganda for information and negotiation. Writing just after the May-June 1967 War, this Professor of International Studies looked toward a pacific settlement of further disputes through religion-oriented communications.

The emphasis here is on illustrating the offending propaganda—with illustration after illustration—as transmitted in the press and, especially, over state-controlled radio. I find it disturbing that Alexander who must be thoroughly acquainted with media institutions in Israel and the Arabic countries offers no more than superficial references to the variety of media organizations and media practices in the involved countries. Nor is there a systematic analysis of the process by which the messages he deplores come to be sent: who? when? where? how? how often? Information and analysis along these lines would make it easier for the reader to assess the viability and prospects of his recommendations for avoiding further violent conflict (which, of course, did erupt). These proposals include the establishment of an "ecumenical hotline"—cable with teletype machinery in both alphabets at both ends—for use in emergencies.

Finally, the book edited by David E. Olson, an applied psychologist teaching in Canada, is part one of the 73rd Yearbook of the National Society for the Study of Education—an impressive series emanating from the University of Chicago. The titles of these volumes dating from 1902 index the changing theoretical and practical problems that have concerned those dedicated to promoting investigation and discussion of educational questions. The last yearbook that took the mass media and education as its theme appeared two decades earlier in 1954 when television, the newest mass medium, could no longer be ignored as an educational force. Its potential for both good and evil was the subject of inquiry. This volume, drawing on decades of experience, zeroes in on both the instruction potential and limitations of new technologies of communication, locating limitations both in the failure of educators to exploit the potential and in the deliberate restrictions educators, threatened by the changes new technology sets in motion, have placed on usage.

If the communications revolution necessitates a broadening of the education process, a possibility Olson examines in his preface to *Media and Symbols,* George Gerbner, given the last word in this volume, thinks this kind of institutional response to technological development unlikely. While new media have the same potential for altering the educational process as did the old ones, the question is whether communication revolutions lead to fundamental change or only extend the reach and scope of present structures. The answer resides not in the potential of technology, he writes, but in the response of institutions. And institutions use technology to further their own purposes. In his most quoted dictum: "No society trains its young to live in a different society." Something these books reviewed here tell us in one way or another, although maybe not deliberately.

These are all books that should interest not only media sociologists but sociologists who still believe society exists only in and through communications and that the study of communications, and certainly mass communications, is a central part of their discipline.

Features

Investigative Social Research: Individual and Team Field Research, by JACK D. DOUGLAS. Beverly Hills: Sage Publications, 1976. 229 pp. $11.00 cloth. $6.00 paper.

Doing Social Life: The Qualitative Study of Human Interaction in Natural Settings, by JOHN LOFLAND. New York: John Wiley & Sons, 1976. 328 pp. $14.95 cloth.

RAYMOND L. GOLD
University of Montana, Missoula

As I look over my notes on these two books, I find that I have many more on the one I dislike than on the one I like. Thus, let me make clear at the outset that I think Lofland's book is a solid contribution to the mainstream of qualitative analysis whereas Douglas's technically and morally unacceptable treatment of field observation appears to me to be heading full-speed toward an evolutionary dead end.

In his preface, Douglas says, "the focus is on the *problems* our kind of society poses for field researchers trying to study it, on the evasiveness, secrecy, deceits, frontwork, and basic conflicts and problems of our society, rather than on its openness and truthfulness. This must be kept firmly in mind in reading the book" (p. xii). Elsewhere he makes fuller statements on the book's focus (on pages 55–56, 138–139, and 178, for example) which clearly show that he is inclined to view informants as marks and/or enemies; he feels no obligation to protect confidences or process guilty knowledge with those concerned in order to determine what to do with it; he is unconcerned about keeping the door to investigated social scenes open to further research; he is convinced that in interactions with potential or actual informants the field observer's motto must be "Dupe, lest ye be duped!"; and he gives the strong impression that he believes that he and John Johnson should be considered the gurus of truth-seeking field observation and that he is the very model of a modern sociological hit man.

He starts his assault on the field observation establishment by trying to discredit what he calls the "classical" University of Chicago field researchers and their ilk and, to be sure that he kicks out all such rascals, he tries to give the knee to ethnomethodology as well. Distortions in his portrayals of standard ways of doing social science fieldwork suggest that his research on mainstream field observation leaves a lot to be desired. He asserts, but makes no attempt to demonstrate, that traditional fieldworkers are easily misled by informants, fail to concern themselves with presenting representative findings, and are hung up on making like scientists. Any experienced ethnographer knows that in these assertions Douglas has things bassackwards. What seems to bug him most about enthnomethodology is that it "sees all accounts [of human behavior] as equally valid" (p. 53). This ethnomethodological (and, I might add, ethnographic) position is unacceptable to him because throughout the book he is obviously hell-bent on getting at *The Truth* about what is *Really* important about human behavior, namely, what people prefer to keep to themselves or to their in-groups instead of eagerly sharing with guys like Douglas who are inclined to share it with the rest of the world. His attacks on conventional field observation strike me as serving no other purpose than to help Douglas to present himself as a new broom that is sweeping clean in order to show us the Light about fieldwork and the Way to do it. In this respect, he succeeds only in presenting himself as a pugnacious sectarian whose attempted conversion from logical positivism to "investigative sociology" (better called guilty knowledge sociology) is obviously still only in its early stages because he has never done any longitudinal community research, and I doubt that he has ever even worked with any ethnographer who has, else he would not be so distressingly naive and misinformed about so many aspects of field observation, the little things (like the use and abuse of tape recorders) along with the big (like his utter misunderstanding of what sociology's general societal mandate and informant-specific mandates to do field observation are all about). He seems to believe that we sociologists should unilaterally decide all data-gathering and data-reporting matters by and for ourselves, even if it means employing devious methods to gather information and blowing the whistle on informants in our (publicly available) reports. Evidently, he would have us be faithful only to ourselves and to treat any and all potential and actual informants as outgroupers and therefore fair game for whatever we might wish to do to obtain and publish information. He fears that sociology is largely a study of people's fronts. In the first place, if he had not skipped over an apprenticeship in ethnography, he would know that in ethnographic research there is no way of avoiding acquisition of more guilty knowledge (i.e., knowledge of "backs") than one needs or wants for strictly research purposes. In the second place, there is no reason to believe that a back is any more or less an instance of a really real reality or is otherwise any more or less sociologically relevant than a front. Indeed, I would argue that no account can be faithful to the empirical world of human behavior if it deliberately seeks to put down or take out of consideration ordinary, surface social accounting, which is the primary stuff of human existence. This means that field observers have to be especially sensitive to reality making, testing, changing, etc. in all surfacely interpreted and processed senses because these are the senses in which the primary working and workable consensuses and actualities of life exist. Douglas's concern is with another level or dimension of reality—a sort of insider's reality. His is not the real, working realities of the people he studies. His repeated references to getting at "the truth" are absolutistic hokum. In *T*ruth, he does not *R*eally understand the idea of definition of situation very well at all. The social worlds out there consist of a helluva lot more than the subsurface, the unglossed, the unfronted, the unvarnished, the unembellished, the unlied-about stuff which Douglas fundamentalistically, absolutistically, and therefore ethnocentrically insists is the only real reality worth its sociological salt.

Douglas assumes that informants are not trustworthy and that people who do not cooperate with him in research are "enemies" (keep in mind that an "enemy" is anybody who has sense enough not to be truthful to him when he is inclined to abuse the privilege of receiving such information). He even admits that they have no more reason to trust him than he has to trust them. His definition of the field observation situation amounts to advocating a conflict model of social research as the only way of getting at *T*ruth. In light of the foregoing, one marvels at how he is able to say (apparently with a straight face) that he considers people "dishonest" when they withhold information from a researcher whom they have every reason to distrust.

At this point it should come as no surprise that I strongly advise any would-be reader of Douglas's book who is not a sophisticated social science field observer to pretend that this well-written and occasionally entertaining book is a grand put-on, a curiously inept attempt at satire which was written to serve as a blood-boiling conversation piece for complacent and jaded ethnographers. To find out what field observation is and should be about, the unsophisticated should turn to such standard works as those by Junker and Schatzman; and to learn about investigative news reporting, they should see Woodward and Bernstein. After doing this reading, it should be clear that Douglas's "investigative paradigm" is indeed technically and morally unacceptable to social science—and maybe even to newspeople as well.

Lofland's *Doing Social Life* comes across like the good guy with the white hat after meeting up with Douglas in the act of advocating that the end of digging out *T*ruth justifies just about any and all means. Whereas Douglas feels it unnecessary to explain why he thinks the logical positivists are taking sociology on the road to nowhere, Lofland, who feels the same way about them, shows in his characteristically thorough and well-reasoned way why trying to study society at a distance, making instrument-dependent research a way of life, and so on are keeping the survey research types from achieving "intimate familiarity" with whatever they study. One of the points which Lofland makes in this regard is worth quoting because it is such a refreshing contrast to what one finds throughout the first-mentioned book: "the process of attaining intimate familiarity in some realm of life or social setting is a *humbling* experience" (p. 14). Lofland then goes on to present an impressive, encyclopedic assemblage of classifications, guidelines, and thoughtways which represent the collective experience and seasoned judgment of social scientists who have been obtaining and analyzing field observation data to try to make social scientific sense out of "how people do social things." As a qualitative sociologist, he gently but firmly takes readers by the hand and leads them through the "intimate familiarities," "disciplined abstractions," and other empirically grounded analytic categories he employs to examine highlights of the myriad of intricacies of how people explore, routinize, change, and reflect on trying to fit their behavior together, do things social, and make society. From the very beginning, it is clear that Lofland makes an impressive effort to collate and codify the situation-making and situation-defining that people continually engage in. Yet, at times his approach is so taxonomic, archival, and jargonistic that even those of us who are heavily into this sort of stuff would have found the reading more enjoyable (albeit probably no more profitable) had he made a more determined effort to write in plain English. But every time I started to doze off I was happily revived by Lofland's skilled inventorying of various dimensions of behavior and his indications of gaps and weaknesses in our knowledge of how people do things social.

This book should serve as a very useful reference work for any social scientist who has occasion to lecture about or do qualitative analysis of human behavior. Lofland has done a scholarly job of systematically presenting numerous parts of our humanity. Remaining to be presented is an equally enlightening analytic view of the fullness and wholeness of our humanity.

Astronomy Transformed: The Emergence of Radio Astronomy in Britain, by DAVID O. EDGE AND MICHAEL J. MULKAY. New York: John Wiley & Sons, 1976. 482 pp. $25.00 cloth.

THOMAS F. GIERYN
Columbia University

These days, the scientist who claims that his or her discipline has just survived a scientific revolution is likely to meet a ho-hum response. In all corners of the academy, calls to the barricades are sounded and once-accepted paradigms are toppling, I am told, in everything from etymology to entymology. After all, is it really a *science* if revolutions cannot be announced with routine frequency? In this kind of climate, it seems safe to forecast a revolution in sociological studies of scientific revolutions, and this is just what David Edge and Michael Mulkay might achieve.

In 1930, Karl Jansky of the Bell Telephone Company began investigating sources of static which were interfering with transoceanic radio-telephone circuits. Jansky found that at least some of the radio wavelength "noise" came from the Milky Way. In 1974, the Nobel Prize for Physics was awarded to Martin Ryle and Anthony Hewish for the development of radio astronomy and for research leading up to the discovery of pulsars in 1968. *Astronomy Transformed* is one story of the years between, and Edge and Mulkay with great care narrate the cognitive and technical advancements and the social institutionalization of radio astronomy in Britain.

A two-page Entr'Acte divides the book in half. The first part is an explicit historical narrative of events (informed by sociological ideas and concepts), while the second is an explicitly sociological investigation of scientific change (though more historical narrative creeps in). As it happens, the story does not begin with Jansky (his discovery goes down as an example of prematurity in science), but in the laboratories for radar research of the British Army Operational Research Group during World War II. There, the physicist J. S. Hey made three discoveries which provided postwar radio astronomers with their earliest research agenda: detection of radio emissions from the sun, detection of radar echoes from meteor trails, and observation of discrete sources of radio energy in the direction of the constellation Cygnus. These findings raised a number of questions that were picked up in varying fashion by the two research centers instrumental in shaping radio astronomy in Britain: the Jodrell Bank site of Manchester University and the Cavendish Laboratory at Cambridge.

The authors choose to provide closest examination of the third set of problems, those dealing with discrete radio sources in space. At both Jodrell Bank and Cambridge, investigations proceeded through four loose-fitting phases: (1) exploration and increasing the amount of observational data; (2) implementation of "technical programs," research agendas based primarily on the design and application of new instruments and techniques; (3) attainment of consensus over the legitimacy and meaning of the findings, as comprehensive maps of heavenly radio sources were produced; and (4) emergence of anomalies such as pulsars and quasars which raised new and important theoretical questions about, for example, the origin and morphology of the universe.

This fine-grained analysis of intellectual and technical progress is preceeded by a malapropos chapter on the relative contributions to radio astronomy by scientists from several nationalities. The sweep by Americans of the 1976 Nobel prizes is no indication that scientists in the United States are equally advanced in all sectors of scientific research: American interest and facility in radio astronomy reached its crescendo well after the burst of activity in England. This chapter would sit more comfortably in the second half of the book which, unlike the first half, is organized not by chronological sequence, but in terms of discrete sociological problems. Among the topics discussed are: the nature of discovery, competitive pressure among scientists, effects of funding patterns, and the comparative styles of leadership and of problem-selection at Jodrell Bank and Cambridge.

Edge and Mulkay have gathered an impressive array of empirical materials to document the growth of radio astronomy. Transcripts of twenty personal interviews are supplemented by content analysis of scientific publications, historical and biographical writings, and citation analysis. The detailed technical and intellectual history unfolds at a laborious pace, and will tire those not familiar with recent astrophysics. A primer on radio astronomy would have served the non-specialist well. The deft handling of astrophysical details is in part a measure of the hybrid background of David Edge, now historian of science, but once member of the radio astronomy shop at Cambridge. Some sociologists will pass briskly through the technically rigorous discussions of interferometry or aperture synthesis as they seek the sociological generalizations that lie within. However, abstract theoretical speculation on specialty formation in science is not to the taste of the authors: "We would present our results with a minimal theoretical commitment."

Have they? Their choice of a *pointillist* portrait of the history of radio astronomy results from a theoretical commitment to a certain explanation of scientific change, and not from theoretical agnosticism. Edge and Mulkay criticize studies of specialty formation which fail to balance investigations of *social* structure (such as the formation of scientific networks) with equally detailed descriptions of *cognitive* structures and technical developments. Existing knowledge, techniques, and technical equipment constrain the further accretion of scientific knowledge, in much the same way that institutionalized social norms constrain the procedures through which contributions to scientific knowledge are presented and evaluated.

Time after time, the authors call up details from their rich historical narrative to illuminate developments that would have remained dim if, say, only citation patterns or social network data were available. For example, the postwar migration of physicists into radar meteor astronomy at Jodrell Bank is detected (though not explained) by charting the number of authors of relevant papers over time. To account for the pattern, the authors draw on their familiarity with the cognitive structure of the field, and find that critical problems in related research areas had evaporated: "the really exciting days of cosmic rays were over. . . ."

In the same way, readers who struggle through the tedious descriptions of this technique or that instrument are rewarded by coming to see that the tools of astronomy are so important in shaping the development of the field that a technological determinist could *almost* smile. Differences in the social relations at Jodrell Bank and Cambridge (traced out in network analyses of collaboration and citation patterns) are in part a result of investments in distinct kinds of tools. The lag in American involvement in radio astronomy is in part explained by investments in costly optical instruments such as the 200 inch telescope at Mt. Palomar, first put to use in 1949. And, in that most British idiom, American astronomers "were keen to exploit it to the full."

Plainly, the authors avoid a pitfall common to the case study: lack of comparative points of reference. By pitting Jodrell Bank against Cambridge, and these in turn against developing centers in Australia, Holland and the United States, the reader is able to compare the interaction of social cognitive, and technical factors in a variety of settings.

In the final chapter, the authors relate their case study to the half-dozen or so earlier studies of specialty-formation in science. When compared to like investigations of bacteriology, nascent psychology, phage biology, physical chemistry and x-ray protein crystallography, radio astronomy is peculiar in its symbiotic relationship with the parent discipline of astronomy. Optical astronomers were briefly skeptical of the astronomical utility of radio research, but quickly came to see its complementary contributions. No specialty journal for radio studies of astronomical problems has been established, and about 30% of the articles in the leading British and American astronomical journals report research using radio techniques. To those who view science as a perpetual Thermopylae, and scientists as more interested in recognition than in extending knowledge, Edge and Mulkay reply: "we have found little evidence of an *active* concern among scientists with safeguarding either personal or disciplinary prestige."

All this raises doubts about theories of scientific change put forth by Warren Hagstrom and Thomas Kuhn. Edge and Mulkay find little support for Hagstrom's prediction that new specialties which redefine disciplinary goals will be seen as threats and thus resisted by scientists of the parent field. Also, in contrast to what many hear Kuhn to say, the case of radio astronomy suggests that extensive changes in the social and cognitive structures of a discipline need not be accompanied by a revolutionary crisis. The transformation of astronomy was a bloodless one.

Astronomy Transformed has raised the ante for future sociological studies of specialty formation in science. In its sensitive attention to the details of cognitive structures and in its creative emphasis on the role of technical commitments and instruments in scientific change, the work is a masterpiece of the historical sociology of scientific knowledge.

The Form of Sociology: Paradigms and Crises, by S. N. EISENSTADT with M. CURELARU New York: John Wiley & Sons, 1976. $17.95 cloth.

JEFFREY C. ALEXANDER
University of California, Los Angeles

The condition of sociological theory in the 70s puts one in mind of the epitapth for Louis XV: in relation to the past, it has forgotten nothing and learned nothing new. Nowhere is this malady more evident than in the murky problem of so-called "paradigm conflict." Sociological understanding of theoretical "crisis" has remained mired in notions of incommensurability, total communications breakdown, sui generis revolution, concepts generated by Kuhn more than a decade ago and tenaciously promoted by participants in the crisis ever since. Yet the sociological translation of Kuhn's ideas, once so fresh and original, has become reified into the sterile conventional wisdom. S. N. Eisenstadt's *The Form of Sociology: Paradigms and Crises*, written with the collaboration of M. Curelaru, breaks this impasse. It is an extremely important book, one which will be widely read and which should have a significant impact on sociological theory.

Eisenstadt sets himself an ambitious task. Conducting simultaneously a sociology of knowledge, an analytical history, and a systematic theoretical discussion, he traces the development of sociological theory from its primordial origins to its present predicament. Yet Eisenstadt is more than a match for such a challenge; few sociologists combine theoretical sensitivity with such attention to empirical variation, such comprehension of the symbolic realm with attention to group interests and conflict, such emphasis on the distinctiveness of modernity with encyclopedic historical and comparative knowledge. *The Form of Sociology* succeeds beyond any general treatment yet produced.

Eisenstadt links the origins of sociological inquiry to the themes of protest that accompanied post-Reformation European modernization and secularization, particularly to the tension between the transcendent cultural emphasis on voluntarism and equality and the more constraining and exclusionary reality of the given institutional order. Secular social thought can be viewed, then, as the transformation of such protest themes into more strictly analytical frameworks, viz. the concern of Hobbes, Locke, Rousseau, and Machiavelli with such "theoretical" controversies as the complexity of the division of labor versus the value of unmediated, direct social participation, the ideal of distributive justice versus institutional stratification, the autonomous self versus social constraint. The push to bring such themes of protest to analytic self-consciousness came to a head with industrialization. In this period, there developed most of the specific topical divisions of contemporary sociological study: authority and power, ascriptive traits like race, sex, and age, stratification, family life, secularization, bureaucratization. Such scientific studies, Eisenstadt insists, inevitably interwove normative and descriptive elements, for it was the struggle to achieve normative clarification that produced such specific concerns in the first place. In fact, the very positivist notion of seeking out alternative cases for experimental control can be linked to the normative search for alternative structural forms that accompanied the response to industrialization. Moreover, the questions that constitute today's more general analytic disputes—debates over role autonomy, stability and change, norms versus instrumentalism—are similarly rooted in such an analytic translation of the major themes of ideological and social protest. On the basis of this insight, Eisenstadt can argue that placing the "problem of social order" at the center of sociological theory is , in one particular sense, a revolutionary rather than conservative act, for it can occur only in periods where social transformation produces historical alternatives to any given "order." Finally, and this is only the logical conclusion of his argument, Eisenstadt contends that the tension between normative and analytic components can never be obliterated. Rather, what the history of sociology and its institutionalization trace, in effect, is the "secularization" of this tension, achieved through the development of a self-consciously differentiated mode of discourse called "sociology." The discipline's boundaries with extra-sociological concerns remain as sources of periodic crisis and upheaval, for they are the basis of our analytic emphases in the first place.

These general and specific analytic foci were points of debate throughout the 19th century, in idealist and utilitarian philosophy, in social reform movements, in critical journalism. In order to turn them into specifically sociological questions, however, they had to be further distinguished from their political and ideological boundaries. The crucial additional variable was the growing prestige of the scientific method; with its adoption by social analysts, the period of classical sociology ensued. Weber and Durkheim, more than any other classical thinkers, produced the final step in this analytic transformation, reformulating the original themes of protest into potentially empirical problems, into the vocabulary of "conditions" and "mechanisms." Combining these general disputes and specific problem foci, classical sociology created the familiar analytic starting points around which theoretical conflict continues to revolve: (1) What is society: individuals, organizations, cultures, or ecological environments; (2) What is social regulation: is it systematic or fluid, is it organismic or internally differentiated; further, is this regulation harmonious or conflictual; (3) What is the basis of legitimizing this order: coercion or solidarity? In Eisenstadt's language, these levels and their components can be combined in a "closed system" or an "open system." In the former, each level or component is viewed concretely, hence as separated from every other, and the relationship among levels and components is viewed as fixed in some form of dominance/subordinance pattern. For example, in Lockean utilitarian theory, the individual level dominates other social components; regulation is never systemic, organic, or conflictual; legitimation is purely instrumental. An open system approach, to the contrary, views levels and parts analytically, recognizing their concrete interdependence, and considers the question of dominance versus autonomy in a more flexible way. Most classical sociologists, for example Marx and Durkheim, formulate closed-systems approaches; only Weber, in Eisenstadt's view, consistently explored the possibility of an open system model.

Despite their great strides toward analytic translation, these classical formulations necessarily remained tied to extra-scientific sources of concern. It is not surprising, therefore, that this very period of classic clarification both produced and responded to the first great "crisis" in sociology, a period of intensive and extensive conflict over definitions of disciplinary boundaries, over the methodological choices that would distinguish this discipline from others, over ideological and philosophical concerns.

Eisenstadt's talent for interweaving comparative intellectual history, analytic theory, and organizational analysis emerges strikingly in his discussion of the interwar period. At that time, despite intermittent advances in both the institutionalization of structurally independent sociology departments and of middle-range research, no real advances in broad theoretical paradigms occurred. Only in the post-war period was the organizational reconstruction begun that established the institutional setting for theoretical development beyond the classical period, a development that occurred largely in the US. Here, for the first time, was the empirical potential of the classical analytical translations pursued in systematic research and initial empirical codification begun. The emergence of structural-functional theory was connected to this development as well as to the ongoing process of institutionalization. Eisenstadt argues that Parsonian structural-functionalism, with its great diversity of application, represented the first major theoretical breakthrough since the classical period. Its power, in principle, rested on its sophisticated open system model, which allowed a thoroughly analytic approach to levels and parts and encouraged an agnostic approach to ultimate questions of "the last instance" variety. For these reasons, the theory also offered a synthetic framework for empirical research.

Yet Eisenstadt emphasizes the cautionary "in principle," for he acknowledges the tendency of Parsonian structural-functionalism toward closure in practice. In fact, he utilizes such strains in the model to locate the theoretical controversies of the last 25 years, which he describes as polemics over the Parsonian definition of the relation of levels and parts—over the question, as Gouldner raised it, of autonomy, relative autonomy, or domination of system parts. As Eisenstadt sees it, this challenge to structural functionalism has been conducted in two ways.

In the "abdicative mode," these analytic disagreements have been conflated with the broader controversies generated by sociology's boundaries with other disciplines (particularly philosophy), with non-scientific forms of critical thinking (journalism), and with ideological social movements (the 1960s student rebellions). On the one hand, theoretical discussion and research has become Balkanized, with movement toward closed system approaches undermining the potential for further theoretical development. On the other hand, sociological activity focuses increasingly on the marginalia of extra-sociological problems, implicitly or explicitly denying the possibility of a differentiated mode of discourse and thereby, in Eisenstadt's words, escaping "the challenge of crisis into philosophical meditation, dogmatic-metaphysical assertions . . . , formalistic definitions . . . , or pure technicism." (p. 327). Ironically, this second great crisis of sociology has occurred in response to the second great period of theoretical creativity; in fact, the very act of reinforcing the theoretical distinctiveness of the sociological enterprise placed further pressure on its necessarily delicate boundary relations. Yet this purely intellectual phenomenon can by no means explain the depth and timing of the present crisis, for the intellectual development also coincided with massive ideological movements that revivified the themes of protest upon which the analytic transformations of sociological theory and research are inevitably based. The crisis has deepened in those institutional settings that have, on the one hand, rigidly separated the activities of theory, research, and instruction and, at the same time, failed sufficiently to separate sociological roles from the pressures of other disciplines and ideological centers. For such reasons, Eisenstadt contends, the movement toward fractionalization has been particularly apparent in the sociology departments of Italy, France, and Germany.

The "constructive mode," the alternative response to renewed theoretical controversy and the one that Eisenstadt wishes to pursue here, capitalizes on the critiques of structural-functionalism, regarding them as potentially complementary "openings" in the model itself. As he has done in preceding work, Eisenstadt here utilizes these critiques as opportunities to reconsider, within the broad functionalist framework, the problems of individual creativity and role autonomy, the greater independence of culture vis-à-vis social structure, the omnipresence of conflict and group interest, and the problem of historical variation within an evolutionary framework. In establishing previously unrecognized points of convergence among critics and between critics and structural-functionalists, Eisenstadt's discussion is a highly sensitive one. For example, he conducts a masterful analysis of the treatment of ritual in sociology and anthropology over the last 25 years, indicating how theoretical argument has, in effect, sought to interrelate levels, combine conflictual and cooperative forms of regulation, explore both coercive as well as solidary modes of legitimation. Equally important is Eisenstadt's attention to the patterns of conflict that have evolved within the functionalist school itself, often with respect to these same issues. Finally, Eisenstadt is not only commenting on the work of others; he is also developing an outline, concretized in the book's final chapter, of his own suggestions for analytic reformulation. In the process of taking social interaction from the generic problems of existence, to concrete individual interaction, and finally to the broadest level of systemic organization, he develops a more open conceptual apparatus. While relying generally on Parsons, this conceptualization goes beyond him in its attention to interactionism, exchange, domination, and conflict.

An extremely brief outline to be sure, but perhaps an indication of the strength and breadth of the argument. Despite its profundity, however, significant problems do remain.

(1) Eisenstadt's conceptual tools are not exact enough, not sufficiently specified for the task he has set himself. Comparing "sociologistic" theories (theories emphasizing the organizational level of society), for example, he must turn to ad hoc categories. This problem stems, first, from not systematically incorporating his discussion of types of integration and legitimation with his focus on the different levels of order (individual, social, cultural, ecological). More generally, it stems from employing "open" and "closed" as his major explanatory schema, distinctions which though suggestive are simply not specific enough. Eisenstadt cannot make definite statements about which theoretical properties, at all three theoretical levels, *facilitate* "openness" and "closedness." Most broadly, the

problem relates to Eisenstadt's insufficient attention to recent debate over the "paradigm" concept, a word he uses far too loosely. As this recent discussion in the philosophy and sociology of science indicates, "paradigm" is too clumsy a term; it does not delineate the autonomy of different levels of scientific discourse (models, presuppositions, ideological constructs, concepts, etc.). Its use, therefore, partly undermines Eisenstadt's attempt to establish the precise properties of different theoretical statements at each level of analysis.

(2) For this reason, Eisenstadt's very sensitivity to the numerous cross-cuttings in contemporary debate ends up blurring the precise lines of concrete theoretical conflict. Without sufficiently differentiating levels of scientific paradigms and their properties, Eisenstadt is unable to define which components of a theoretical work are central and which are peripheral: which components force the theory to present a closed system vis-à-vis other theories and which components can be defined as analytic openings to other theories. It is revealing in this regard that Eisenstadt never distinguishes between an "opening" and a residual category, with the result that he will describe theorists as complementary to each other (e.g., as "open" theorists) in one instance, as antagonistic (e.g., as "closed") in another. For example, in one context, he treats Homans's attention to the norm of "distributive justice" as an opening to normative theory; in another, he describes Homans as an exchange theorist of the closed system type, a characterization which would involve treating the distributive justice concept as residual. I think it is this general problem that prevents Eisenstadt from engaging in any intensive analysis of individual theorists, a failure that presents one of the major frustrations of the volume. For example, Parsons, though clearly the pivotal figure in the book, receives no sustained analytic treatment; instead, "purported" (Eisenstadt's word) problems in Parsons's theorizing are utilized as a basis for analyzing contemporary debate.

(3) This problem in turn creates ambiguity in Eisenstadt's evaluation of the contemporary period in general. Has the recent period of criticism been conducted in the kind of open system manner that allows convergence or has it been closed system argument? The fact that Eisenstadt himself impressively essays the possibilities for "constructive," convergent discussion in no way indicates that this has been the actual tendency. Indeed, the particular references he uses as illustrations for his convergence argument often duplicate his references to the crisis dimension of the present period. Once again, I believe this problem can be traced to Eisenstadt's lack of attention to the controversy over paradigms, in which great effort has been devoted to defining the scope and nature of possible theoretical conflict. For example, as Toulmin has pointed out, even in times of rather extreme disagreement, a "disciplinary matrix" is usually maintained; such an agreement over methodological canons of evidence and vague disciplinary divisions virtually guarantees that there will be theoretical accumulation over an extended period. Yet the existence of this disciplinary matrix, with its gradual accumulation, does not mean significant theoretical commonality.

(4) Finally, the precise conditions of "crisis" are occluded in Eisenstadt's analysis. Although he discusses a number of factors and emphasizes the kind of mixed empirical situations that are possible, it is not ultimately clear whether he sees sociology as moving toward differentiated institutionalization that would avoid severe crisis—although not, of course, theoretical conflict—or whether this very progress actually generates greater potential crisis as sociology's boundary relations are drawn more taut. Certainly, many of the conditions cited as typical of crisis periods, such as a vested interest in ensuring followers, are basic to theoretical conflict at any period.

Written by a sociologist who has weathered the recent crisis and has learned from it, *The Form of Sociology* is by far the best discussion extant of the long and short term roots of our contemporary theoretical situation. Although it leaves important questions unanswered, it provides the basis for pursuing them.

Popular Culture and High Culture: An Analysis and Evaluation of Taste, by HERBERT J. GANS. New York: Basic Books, 1974. 179 pp. $10.00 cloth. $3.95 paper.

BENNETT M. BERGER
University of California, San Diego

Medical sociologists don't on the whole seem to be healers manqué, though they often don't like physicians. Sociologists who study suicide are not, as a group, particularly morbid. Most sociologists of law are not frustrated attorneys. Scratch a sociologist of religion, and chances are probably not better than fifty-fifty that you'll find a guru lurking underneath. But almost all the sociologists I know who study art and/or symbolic culture are themselves in one way or another arty or tasteful (As Lily Tomlin might say) or "cultured." People who do sociology of art are themselves often at least part-time artists, or fall in love with artists, or run with an arty crowd, or try to write especially well or elegantly so that their work will not seem ugly by comparison to their subject matter. They often regard their "expressive" data as somehow nobler than the common run of data from demography or political sociology, and they seem to borrow prestige from their subject matter in a way exactly opposite to that in which Robert Merton once attributed sociology's early stigmatization as a discipline to its association with the data of social pathology. It would probably not displease most sociologists of art if artists liked their work better than sociologists did.

Herbert Gans is a major exception to these non-rules. His subject matter, culture, high, low, and in between, gets no *special* respect from him. He does not fawn before artists and media freaks. He practices a plain, serviceable, expository prose style, bereft of literary allusion, complex metaphor, or emotional high points. My guess is that he has no secret easel tucked away in a hidden studio, no plans for a Great American Novel, no dreams of getting to Carnegie Hall (except perhaps for an orchestra seat), no barely suppressed wish to produce (direct, star in) the definitive film of *Don Quixote* (although he does review movies for *Social Policy*). Unlike most sociological esthetes and other intellectuals who regard themselves as Guardians of Culture, Gans has the chutzpah to say outfront that he thinks it more important for people to be provided with good jobs and decent incomes than that they adopt elevated tastes.

Popular Culture and High Culture (reviewed here almost four years after its original publication and almost that long waiting for a promised review in *CS*) is less the expression of a Guardian of Culture than one more part of Gans's continuing efforts at pluralist planning (from a sociologist trained as a planner) and at promoting more equality, topics on which he has already published a lot. The argument of this book is not a complicated one; it is in fact so simple that it comes as a surprise to discover that it has not been seriously and systematically made by sociologists earlier. Like everything else, culture (so the argument goes) is stratified. Just as education, income, and occupation are indicators of whether people belong in the upper or lower reaches of a class system, their particular patterns of selections from the available culture can be used to characterize their lifestyles in similar hierarchical terms, because such patterns are strongly affected by the major stratification variables.

Gans refers to these lifestyles as "taste-cultures," to the groups who share them as "taste-publics," and he describes their moral and esthetic preferences by reference to their typical selections in reading, music, TV, movies, painting, and other arts and entertainments. (Extend the idea only slightly, and it also includes the games we play, the clothes we wear, the decoration of our homes, the food we consume, and the spectacles we attend.) Gans describes the content of five major taste-cultures (from upper to lower), a few minor ones (youth, ethnic, folk survivals), and the social backgrounds of their respective publics. Although it is possible to quibble here and there with Gans's characterizations of each taste-culture, his treatment seems to me on the whole fair and reasonably accurate.

The argument thus far is not greatly different from those made by Van Wyck Brooks, Russell Lynes, and others, about highbrows and lowbrows, except that Gans is more comprehensive, specific, and analytic; but the greatest difference is that Gans's distinctions are not made in an invidious spirit. Unlike Lynes, Dwight McDonald, and other Guardians, Gans does not believe that the taste-cultures of higher-class publics should be regarded as morally or esthetically superior to those of lower-class publics. Given their resources in income and education (and the access to culture which these and other features of social background provide), lower class publics go about selecting material from the available culture like anyone else: in terms which are meaningful for them and which express their own moral and esthetic standards—even if these are not the standards cultural elites might want them to express.

It is this stance—Gans's refusal to regard the moral and esthetic standards which define high culture as inherently superior to the standards of production in the mass culture industries—which has earned him a lot of criticism from "elitists," who regard him as a cultural barbarian. Gans is a relativist and a strict pluralist here: moral and esthetic standards are the expressions of differentiated social groups, and it is blatantly self-serving for elites to affirm their own standards and to express contempt for other standards—one more expression of their cultural domination. Gans treats culture as a social good, like any other to which groups have a right (and a right to selection)—so long as it is not demonstrably harmful. He believes it unrealistic or impossible to expect the bulk of people who are poor or uneducated or ethnically insulated or otherwise provincial (or all of these combined) to dig madrigal or John Cage or conceptual art or the novels of Thomas Pynchon or *The New York Review, Kojak,* Lawrence Welk, *Happy Days, Jaws,* Broadway musicals, Led Zeppelin, *Sports Illustrated, True Romances,* The Super Bowl, Irving Wallace, Harold Robbins, "Mediterranean" furniture, McDonald's hamburgers, and *National Enquirer* are OK, since it seems likely that these do in fact reflect to a reasonable extent the moral and esthetic standards of their publics.

Indeed, although he isn't *against* the elevation of tastes, Gans the planner is not particularly interested in probably unfeasible attempts to promote large-scale social mobility of taste (there aren't sufficient financial or educational resources to create the necessary conditions); he's more interested in proliferating taste-cultures further, so that they can better represent the variety of taste-publics out there. The Gans of *More Equality* speaks clearly when he urges greatly increased programming for the aged and the poor, who are particularly badly served by the mass media. To these ends, Gans makes a variety of proposals aimed at decentralizing the media and reducing the size of the mass audience, so that (perhaps like the structure of the magazine industry) advertisers could select the relatively special audiences they want to reach through differentiated subcultural programming designed to interest not masses but taste-publics.

Gans makes these proposals (with more detail and rebuttal to anticipated criticism than I have space to recount here) diffidently, without much hope for their implemenation, fully aware of the megabucks at stake and the political-bureaucratic problems involved, not at all confident that his ideas are ideas whose time has come, not even very sure that the planning of culture is an entirely good idea. The motive force for this book, then, comes not from Gans's hopes for the adoption of his proposals but from his irritation with the elitist critics (who range from Right to Left) of mass culture, like Dwight McDonald, Ernest van den Haag, Herbert Marcuse, Bernard Rosenberg, and many others.

But unlike these Guardians, whose analytic gifts are often combined with cultural criticism laced with scorn, invective, black humor, Olympian wrath, and other polemical tidbits, Gans controls his irritation rather well. Instead of joining the issues in the polemical style of The New York Intellectuals, he systematically considers the four major themes which characterize their collective critique of mass (or popular) culture, and concludes that they are mostly without merit, either logically or empirically. Gans does this calmly, without invective, and that is a great strength of this book. His socio-logic, which asserts that esthetic standards are the expressive property of social groups, and his moral judgment that all social groups should be valued equally, seem sound to me, and should be persuasive to readers with democratic and pluralist sympathies. He is sensitive enough to see the self-serving character of the arguments by elitists: they are esthetically revulsed by mass culture, see its practitioners as mere hucksters oriented to audiences (the *users* of culture) rather than to artists and intellectuals (the *creators* of culture), fear the seduction of high culture audiences by the popularity of mass culture and the consequent loss of their own privileged status as pundits and arbiters of culture.

Nevertheless, Gans should know that pointing out the self-serving character of an argument does not dispose of its substantive assertions. Despite the studies Gans cites on the effects of popular culture, many of the questions raised by the elitist critics have not been definitively answered by any empirical research I know about. Moreover, although Gans's socio-logic about esthetics *in general* seems sound to me, he does not apply his insights to the analysis and criticism of specific cultural objects, except in a tangential and superficial way (soap opera *does* help people to deal with their problems; homemaking magazines *do* release housewives from their provincialisms), and therefore he does not really engage his elitist critics in the arena where they are strongest: the analysis of works of art.

Gans's strength, then, is in sociological argument rather than in cultural commentary. He functions best in this book as a democratic spokesman for more equality and greater diversity in culture. There are two ironies worth pointing out here. Although Gans cites T.S. Eliot as an elitist several times in this book, he may not realize how close some of his own ideas come to those expressed by Eliot in the 1940s (during the period in which he took tea frequently with Karl Mannheim, and shortly after which Mannheim became a member of the Church of England). In his neglected little book, *Notes toward the Definition of Culture*, Eliot (Aristocrat, Monarchist, Anglican) argued against upward social mobility on grounds that might have pleased Edmund Burke: the culture of a nation is organic and the separate cultures of social classes are necessary constituent parts of it. If the most creative and gifted members of the lower classes leave their places of origin for mobility upward, the culture of the lower classes will decline and the culture of the nation will be impoverished. It is an arresting and *very* conservative argument, but in some respects not at all unlike the argument of Gans, who is not very conservative. I mention this irony in order to re-point out (it's been pointed out before) that cultural pluralism, like cultural elitism, can come both from the Right and the Left, and that cultural policy is unreliable as a guide to political ideology in general.

The second irony is that although most of the elitist critics never entertained much hope for actually shaping public policy toward art and culture, much of their writing shows the esthetic confidence of a Commissar who *knows* what is esthetically good for the people, and a readiness to impose that vision should any of them be called to Office. On the other hand, Gans the planner, much of whose work is explicitly directed at influencing public policy, doesn't seem at all confident when it comes to esthetic judgment—other than his belief that people have a right to the culture they want. Are we, then, left with Yeats's observation that the best lack all conviction while the worst are full of passionate intensity? Not exactly, for Gans doesn't lack *all* conviction, only esthetic conviction, which suggests that it might have been the better part of valor for him to stay out of esthetic combat. But the final irony is that I'm glad he was not so discreet. This is not an exciting book, but it's a good book, and its argument needed to be made. No student of the sociology of art and popular culture can afford to ignore it.

BOOK REVIEWS

Communication/Language

Translation: Applications and Research, edited by RICHARD W. BRISLIN. New York: Halsted Press, 1976. 312 pp. $14.50 cloth.

ROGER SPIELMANN
University of Texas, Arlington

This volume is a collection of some of the most significant articles on translation theory written over the past several years. It fulfills an urgent need for a representative anthology which reflects the development of translation theory and its applications to specific translation/interpretation problems. The purpose of this book is to explain the workings of translation theory to the uninitiated.

This collection is divided into three main sections; (1) the language sciences, (2) the social and behavioral sciences, and (3) applications. The authors come from various backgrounds, including linguistics, psychology, sociology, and education. The effort of translating from one language to another is a complex event deserving the consideration of researchers from a multitude of disciplines. This anthology is largely devoted to the measurement of translation and interpretation quality, and the use of translation as a research tool in cross-cultural studies. "Translation" is the processing of written input, while "interpretation" is the processing of oral input from one language or code to another.

Eugene Nida's paper contains an analysis of the types of interlingual communication involved in translating, and a description of the role of both the primary source and the translator. His paper provides an excellent framework for the analysis and evaluation of translation theory, particularly for those who would develop an empirical understanding of the interacting patterns of translation technique.

The paper by Danica Seleskovitch outlines the skills demanded of a good translator or interpreter. She views interpretation from language to language primarily as a psychological process. This paper describes the interpretation process and the importance of the role played by extralinguistic knowledge over and above purely linguistic information. Seleskovitch distinguishes between the formal memory and the semantic memory in interpreting, a distinction which may prove relevent to students of other cognitive processes as well.

The perspectives and limitations of a didactic framework for teaching translation presented by Wolfram Wilss should be of interest to the sociologist as well as the linguist. This paper focuses on the extent to which translation can be systematically taught and learned. Wilss insists that, due to the intervention of cognitive-code learning theory, translation is re-establishing itself as a useful and legitimate tool of foreign language teaching. He defines the basic task of the science of translation as the amalgamation of theoretical, descriptive, and applied aspects of interlingual transfer.

Ryan Tweney and Harry Hoemann's review of previous research on translation concludes the first section of this volume. Their paper provides an overview of the simultaneous interpretation process and a discussion of the simultaneous generation of spoken and signal messages. The authors make it clear that the research on simultaneous interpretation/translation should help in understanding the cognitive processes that occur during language encoding by monolinguals as well as interpreters.

The second section begins with an investigation of simultaneous interpretation in which David Gerver indicates various positive effects of translating from documents having a great amount of redundancy and contextual detail. Gerver points out that very few psycholinguistic or sociolinguistic studies even mention the complex skills involved in simultaneous interpretation. This paper attempts to provide empirical evidence relevent to simultaneous interpretation by measuring the effects of poor listening conditions on interpreters' performances, segmentation of the source-language message, and an analysis of simultaneous listening and speaking. Gerver provides an excellent preliminary model of the processes involved in simultaneous interpretation.

Harry Triandis adapts the emic/etic analysis developed by the linguist Pike for use in linguistic analysis in describing a specific language to the analysis of translation. He devises different procedural questions for each culture under investigation in his study, based upon the underlying argument that to get a good translation one needs to have culture-specific (emic) analysis.

R. Bruce W. Anderson handles the role of the interpreter in an informative fashion by skillfully using concepts drawn from sociological theory. He notes that, though there has been little interest in the past by sociologists in translation and/or interpretation theory, societal problems related to translation and interpretation have forced a review of the situation. This paper summarizes the basic elements of the interpretation problem and offers insight concerning the role of the interpreter, and some hypotheses about the interpreter's behavior. Anderson discusses the ambiguities and conflicts of the interpreter role; as the person in the middle, but, note, that this is not a powerless position since "the interpreter's control over the interaction pattern that develops, and thereby over the structure of the triadic relationship, is founded in his ability to translate selectively" (p. 218).

Peter Toma begins the third section by pointing out that, in an operational machine translation system, there exists the necessity for linguistic analysis of both the source and the target languages. (Nida comments in his chapter that the machine translation system designed by Toma is the world's only commercially successful operation of its kind). Toma's conclusion is clear; there are no secrets to success in translation outside of hard work and thorough linguistic analyses of both languages.

The primary concern of the translator should be the getting across of information in another language. The clearest example of this is in the translation of literature, and Lila Ray's paper contributes greatly to translation theory in this regard. Her illustrative analysis of the poem, "Déjeuner du Matin" documents how certain information that would be a concern of practical translation is conveyed by the way certain words are used in a cultural context.

Rudolf Kassühlke addresses the linguistic and cultural implications of translation, focusing on the specific problem of Bible translation. The author, as a member of the United Bible Society, faces the task of communicating cross-culturally the documents of the Bible. Kassühlke gives examples of how the meanings of Biblical passages are dependent on the historical setting that provides the background for the passage.

The potential use of translation theory in the future is unlimited as the current trend in social science research continues to concentrate on learning, communication, and information theory. Editor Brislin mentions that the increase in contact among social scientists from varying cultural backgrounds will create a demand for translation theory and methodology. This collection of papers will benefit readers from a variety of disciplines in its presentation of the essentials of translation theory.

The Manipulators: America in the Media Age, by ROBERT SOBEL. Garden City, N.Y.: Anchor Press, 1976. 458 pp. $9.95 cloth.

LOWNDES F. STEPHENS
University of South Carolina

In a recent interview, Robert Sobel, an historian at Hofstra University, argues for deregulation of and first amendment guarantees for the American broadcast industry. In recommending a policy of *caveat emptor* in the market for ideas, Sobel stands beside respected mass communication law scholars such as R.H. Coase and William F. Baxter.

In recommending abolition of government regulation of the broadcast industry, Sobel stands against respected economists such as Roger G. Noll, Merton J. Peck, and John J. McGowan, who advocate redirecting government policy to alleviate the problems of economic concentration, too little program diversity, and too few program options. While Noll, et al. argue for redirecting government policy to foster development of cables (CATV), subscription television (STV) and satellites as ways to help alleviate these problems, Sobel suggests there is no need for government policies because economic concentration and program content, per se, pose no problems.

Sobel says very little about the substance of his book in the interview on National Public Radio, though the purpose of the interview was to explore the implications of his text. In the book Sobel states that five information and entertainment industries constitute the most important power centers in America: newspapers, radio, movies, television, and colleges. Universities in the 20th century are producing "mass" intellectuals who for the most part are users rather than generators of ideas. The information-seeking needs of these intellectuals, born during the college years, are met during adulthood by the mass media which also amuse and entertain this largest of media publics.

The inventors and innovators gave us the technology of mass communications, corporate sponsors were responsible for expediting the diffusion of it, but the performing artists taught us how to utilize it to gain power over the "mass" intellectuals. Sobel defines power as "the ability to make people see the world the way you want them to and then make them act in accordance with your beliefs." Professional journalists have become "performers," and the best columnists, reporters, and commentators are paid big-star salaries. Politicians have become performers, e.g., John Lindsay, and performers have become politicians, e.g., Chet Huntley.

Since the entertainment and the news functions of television and newspapers have become one and the same, we can't expect, nor are we likely to demand, that fact be separated from fiction. Unfortunately, Sobel never completes the scenario, never gets around to proscribing the media, as might Herbert Schiller or Alan Wells.

Neither is *The Manipulators* prescriptive in tone. Sobel's book can best be characterized as an anecdotal history of American mass media which falls short of being an historiography. Rich in particulars, and readable chapter-by-chapter, *The Manipulators* overall provides little sense of understanding because the particulars are not synthesized into an organized narrative text.

Difference and Dominance, edited by BARRIE THORNE AND NANCY HENLEY. Newbury House Publishers, 1975. 311 pp. No price listed, paper.

KATHERINE NEWMAN
University of California, Berkeley

The field of sociolinguistics has spawned many a subdiscipline in recent years, each of which has been concerned with the influence of various sociological variables (race, class, sex, etc.) on linguistic behavior. This subject matter lends itself rather easily, and appropriately, to a dual goal. Within the academy, sociolinguists have had to demonstrate the legitimacy of their interests to mainstream theoretical linguists who have placed a much higher priority on the analysis of formal language structure than on language in use. Thus, the key figures in the sociology of language (Gumperz, Hymes, Fishman, Labov, and others) argued for the importance of understanding the "ethnography of speaking," the social context of linguistic behavior. Other sociolinguists have attempted to identify and comment upon problems of a social and political nature which are reflected in language use. Studies of phonological variation and social class membership, dialectology and ethnic affiliation, and code-switching were partly political commentaries upon language behavior in a stratified society.

This dual purpose is very much in evidence in *Language and Sex*. On the one hand the authors have defended the idea that the study of sex differences in language use is a bona fide topic for academic investigation. On the other hand they have argued that these differences in language use are the basis for evaluative judgments of character, competence, and intelligence—judgments of a "micropolitical" nature which have serious negative repercussions for the job mobility, personal satisfaction, and self-image of the female sex. The scientific and the political are combined in an effort to discover what the nature of the differences between men and women are in the area of language use and how those differences affect the life chances of both groups.

It is precisely this combination of goals which makes the book a difficult one to evaluate. The articles presented in it adequately establish that there are sex-linked differences in non-verbal communication, turn-taking behavior, phonetic variation, intonation patterns, etc. More importantly, the book shows that whatever the "actual" differences between male and female linguistic behavior, the "perceived" differences are great indeed. Women are said to talk incessantly, with a higher pitch, and in more tentative terms than men. From the sociologist's point of view, the evaluation of these characteristics in the minds of social actors is most important. *Language and Sex* devotes a considerable amount of space to showing that such an evaluation takes place—that women are considered to be incompetent chatterboxes (or worse, sexually loose and morally suspect). In short, the authors should receive high points for having substantiated their claims that sex differences in language exist, are perceived, and form the basis for potentially damaging stereotypes which may have little to do with language behavior itself.

Unfortunately, the leap between demonstrating these differences and explaining their wider consequences is a large one—one which the political commitments of the authors makes difficult. Even if one shares the feminist perspective of Thorne, Henley et al; one may find it hard to accept some of their conclusions, e.g., that becoming conscious of the "nonverbal symbolism of power" will help to "reverse the power relationships" perpetrated upon women by those who claim "foreskin privilege." The causes of sexual stratification are complex, as are the results—results which are evident in language use and elsewhere. However, there is a tendency in these articles to confuse the causes with the results and thus to advocate consciousness raising as an antidote to subjugation.

The authors are certainly entitled to their political perspective. However, it is often difficult to see how the wider political conclusions are derived from the data in these essays. Given the inherently politicized nature of the topic, I suppose this problem is unavoidable. However, it should not overshadow the primary goal and the primary achievement of the book, namely the establishment of language and sex as a topic of sociolinguistic inquiry.

Community

Communes, Sociology and Society, by PHILIP ABRAMS and ANDREW McCULLOCH. New York: Cambridge University Press, 1976. 226 pp. $16.95 cloth. $5.95 paper.

MYRON ORLEANS
California State University, Fullerton

Abrams and McCulloch provide a valuable, if flawed, analysis of contemporary secular communalism. Although they offer a comprehensive survey and interpretation of communes in Great Britain, their work is entirely relevant to communal experience in the United States. Effectively employing the classic tradition of sociology, they examine the reflexive construction of self and extended domestic group.

The authors vividly portray the projects, settings, personalities, and dilemmas of a few of the many communes they visited. Unfortunately, they set these descriptive portions apart from their analytical discussions. Thus their interpretations are deprived of potentially rich empirical substance and much of the text becomes too abstract and tedious.

After overcoming their hesitancy in applying a sociological approach to the study of communalism, the authors establish a useful focus on communes as mundane social organizations immersed in "everyday practicalities." They avoid rhapsodic odes to love and ecstasy, and view self-formation, Aristotelian friendship, and a negotiated division of labor as the intentional foundations of communalism. They recognize the fluid, fragile interactive processes constituting the secular commune while rejecting as inappropriate the images of total commitment and submergence of self which have been emphasized in the literature on historical utopias and religious communes.

The aspirations of some communards to create new family styles and to transform conventional definitions of sex roles and childhood are doomed, according to Abrams and McCulloch, because of the tendency of an "antistructure" to emerge. The forging of personal identity within a nonreified domestic context seems to preclude the creation of any system which might foster alternatives. Thus, one cannot expect the communal movement to serve as a model for socio-cultural change or as a revolutionary political force. The authors suggest that through organic solidarity and negotiative interactions communalism can serve the more modest purpose of permitting members to shape the facticities of their domestic existence in such ways as to fulfill their personal and collective projects.

The authors neither systematically interrelate their arguments, nor fully explore the implications of their analysis. But they do make a definite contribution by encouraging us to think of communes as ordinary options of domesticity which serve as temporary sanctuaries for a variety of people. By drawing us away from the usual romantic visions of utopian otherness, Abrams and McCulloch promote a realistic, reasonable, and promising approach to the study of contemporary communalism.

Social Change in a Metropolitan Community, by OTIS DUDLEY DUNCAN, HOWARD SCHUMAN and BEVERLY DUNCAN. New York: Russell Sage Foundation, 1973. 126 pp. $7.95 cloth. $3.95 paper.

ELLAN ODIORNE DEROW
McMaster University

This book, a volume in the social change series by Sage, presents a pulse-reading of Detroit, the survey sociologists' Chicago of the mid-twentieth century. It compares a series of items from various Detroit Area Studies of the early 1950s (the racial attitudes are replicated from surveys conducted in the 1960s) with similar items derived from a 1971 survey. The questions selected for replication in 1971 were chosen, as the authors state, in a fashion somewhat "opportunistic and eclectic" in approach (p. 2). Overall the book achieves the limited analytic import for which it aims. It contains many caveats concerning the comparative meaning of responses from the different surveys.

We need more than pulse-readings. Without theoretical understanding of the nature of social change and some idea of the context of that change, one struggles to make sense of the reporting of unvarnished survey results on a variety of diffuse topics (e.g., marriage, rearing children, communal involvement, values, public affairs, etc.).

Every heartbeat is calibrated in the book. The techniques used in the collection of the data are flawless in themselves, but the arms-length attitude of the authors suggests an alienation from the patient. Frequent admonitions against drawing conclusions and the expressed attitude of "for what its worth" are puzzling.

The book is admittedly an interim report. The authors suggest that further work on these data is forthcoming; this the reader is advised to await.

The Suburban Environment: Sweden and the United States, by DAVID POPENOE. Chicago: University of Chicago Press, 1977. 275 pp. $19.00 cloth.

ALISON E. WOODWARD
University of California, Berkeley

Do widely differing suburban environments affect the social behavior of their residents? David Popenoe's comparison of Levittown, Pennsylvania and a planned Swedish suburb demonstrates that environments at least shape life styles through the options and services they provide.

In a lively way, the book gives a picture of the physical environment from the viewpoint of residents at different stages of the life cycle. Less vividly presented are the ways in which the physical environment actually affects social interaction in the community.

Popenoe rejects crude environmental determinism. Instead he adapts the concept of environmental congruence to examine the degree of fit between residential lifestyles and the environment. Using interviews with twenty-five families in each locale and detailed descriptions of the community, he makes conclusions about what lifestyles and types of residents best fit the two environments.

People in the modal nuclear family fare well in both Vallingby and Levittown. In fact, most people are highly satisfied with their communities. However, other types of people, such as single mothers, teenagers, and the elderly are uncomfortably fitted in Levittown. Vallingby on the other hand, seems to have few non-congruent types.

Divorced women and teenagers are misfits in Levittown while the lonely and ruralists are misfits in Vallingby says Popenoe. The difficulty with this argument is that lonelinesss and dependency are more clearly psychological and economic problems than they are environmental. Thus conclusions about the role of the environment must be tentative, as Popenoe acknowledges. His generalizations about the problems teenagers and working men face in Levittown could have been strengthened with more concrete examples. Suggestions about sources of problems seem highly tentative without this support. By grouping his data into ideal types, Popenoe loses both believability and liveliness, the strengths of good community studies.

Still, his actual portrayal of the two towns is very convincing. The book includes detailed descriptions of the demography, history, and ambience of the two settings. This colorful backdrop seldom appears in sociological studies of the community.

The presentation of the communities gives great attention to the Swedish rationale in planning service-oriented, high density towns. He gives less time to an analysis of the forces that brought Levitt to plan a low density, no-service community. However, Vallingby is no mere "package" suburb. The Swedish satellites were intended to be largely self-contained and to provide social services in a centralized manner. Levitt communities were intended to provide housing alone. Regional decentralization, unity of home and work place, and efficiency of transportation concerned the Swedes. Profit and speed motivated the Levitt organization.

Popenoe includes extensive background information on the Swedish decisions, gathered from interviews with influentials. Parallel material is lacking for Levittown. This failure obscures some important background factors that differentiate the two places.

With his examination of these two older communities Popenoe feels able to draw conclusions about their success and their implications for future planning decisions. He praises the latest US experimentation in planning, while criticizing the latest concrete jungles in Sweden. British new towns are a middle way for future urban development, he suggests.

For the planner, this book is clearly written and without heavy quantification or unnecessary jargon. For the sociologist, the book treads a peculiar middle ground. It provides neither a complete structural comparison of the two communities, nor a vital ethnographic picture of their social interaction. Still it does some of both, and as such makes a first step toward a sociology of the environment.

Crime, Law, and Deviance

Class, State, and Crime: On the Theory and Practice of Criminal Justice, by RICHARD QUINNEY. New York: David McKay Co., 1977. 179 pp. $4.95 paper.

ROGER G. SEIFERT
University of California, Santa Barbara

Class, State, and Crime can be broken down into three essential components: a review and critique of traditional—as well as neo-conservative—conceptions of "criminal justice" (chapter1), a theoretical and empirical inquiry into the "meaning of crime in capitalist society" (chapters 2–4), and a concluding discussion on the necessity for building a socialist alternative, both in theory and in practice (chapter 5). For those of us who are concerned with constructing a coherent Marxist analysis of crime and criminal justice, Quinney's latest effort is at once exciting and disappointing.

On the positive side, Quinney has clearly transcended the limitations that hampered his earlier attempts at developing a Marxist criminology. Relying heavily on James O'Connor's *The Fiscal Crisis of the State*, Quinney now analyzes what the state in general and crime control agencies in particular actually do, as opposed to simply noting the class nature of those in charge. The state, he observes, must endeavor to perform two contradictory functions—to legitimate the capitalist order on the one hand, and to provide the necessary conditions for the continued accumulation of capital on the other. The current "criminal justice movement," which is a reincarnation of the "law and order movement," is best understood in this context. It is "a state-initiated and state-supported effort to rationalize mechanisms of social control," with the larger purpose being "to secure a capitalist order that is in grave crisis," and "likely in its final stage of development" (p. 10).

On the negative side, *Class, State, and Crime* suffers from a slight case of shoddy scholarship. A case in point is the presentation of a graph (p. 135) which shows a significant positive correlation between unemployment rates and admissions to *federal* prisons from 1960 to 1972. This evidence, Quinney submits, "clearly" supports his proposition that the criminal justice system operates to control the "surplus population"; moreover, that "control is especially acute in those periods when the economic crisis is most obvious—during periods of depression and recession" (p. 134). What Quinney fails to deal with are the correlations prior to 1960 which—upon investigation—appear to be quite *insignificant*, especially during the era of the Great Depression. Furthermore, careful analysis of co-variation in unemployment rates and admissions to *state* prisons and *county jails* might well have enhanced the validity of his proposition.

This work fares best when viewed as a programmatic statement of what *still* needs to be done in the development of a Marxist criminology. Despite its shortcomings, its utility as a pedagogical tool cannot be overstated. The ideas Quinney so forcefully presents cannot rationally be disregarded, and no doubt will serve as a focus of debate and a guide for research in years to come.

The Effectiveness of Drug Abuse Treatment.
Volume I: Evaluation of Treatments, edited by S. B. SELLS. Cambridge, Mass.: Ballinger, 1974. 532 pp. $19.50 cloth.
Volume II: Patient Profiles, Treatments and Outcomes, edited by S. B. SELLS. Cambridge, Mass.: Ballinger, 1974. 313 pp. $17.50 cloth.
Volume III: Further Studies of Drug Users, Treatment Typologies, and Assessment of Outcomes during Treatment in the DARP, edited by S. B. SELLS and D. DWAYNE SIMPSON. Cambridge, Mass.: Ballinger, 1976. 463 pp. $22.50 cloth.
Volume IV: Evaluation of Treatment Outcomes for 1971–1972 DARP Admission Cohort, edited by S. B. SELLS and D. DWAYNE SIMPSON. Cambridge, Mass: Ballinger, 1976. 483 pp. $22.50 cloth.
Volume V: Evaluation of Treatment Outcomes for 1972–1973 DARP Admission Cohort, edited by S. B. SELLS and D. DWAYNE SIMPSON. Cambridge, Mass.: Ballinger, 1976. 522 pp. $25.00 cloth.

JOHN A. O'DONNELL
University of Kentucky, Lexington

In the late 1960s the NIMH Division of Narcotics and Drug Abuse—now the National Institute on Drug Abuse—began a program of supporting community treatment agencies for drug users. With admirable foresight, the Division recognized the need for evaluation of its program, and contracted with Saul B. Sells and his research team at Texas Christian University's Institute of Behavioral Research to conduct it.

The Drug Abuse Reporting Program (DARP) was established in 1969, with six NIMH-funded agencies furnishing data. By the end of the first year six more were added, there were agencies in the second year, in the third, and in the fourth. Annual admissions into these agencies grew from 3,000 to almost 17,000, with a total of 44,000. Some were not drug users, but persons seen in prevention programs; other completed the admission process but did not enter treatment. With these deleted, the "research sample" of DARP was 38,433. This number represents first admissions, but the number of different persons would not be much smaller, since few were likely to be known to more than one reporting agency.

Data were obtained from the reporting agencies on two forms. The Admission Report covered demographic data, family background, criminal history, employment history, alcohol and drug use history. Detailed questions were asked about the latter areas for the two months preceding admission.

The Status Evaluation Report was submitted every two months up to the termination of treatment. It contained items on the components of treatment the patient had participated in, on drug and alcohol use, living arrangements, employment, role activities, sources of support, criminal activities, and on patient status at the close of the reporting period.

By comparison with earlier drug studies, DARP produced enormous quantities of data on a very large sample. This is not to say that the data are ideal. For practical purposes, especially to maintain the cooperation of agencies, the forms had to be short; the Admission form had ninety-four items, the Status Evaluation form fifty. Sells' staff visited the agencies regularly for educational and motivational purposes, and there was an elaborate process of editing, and referring errors and inconsistencies to agencies for correction.

The sheer administrative problems of such a research program are obvious. Sells and those NIMH and NIDA staff who served as project officers deserve much credit for handling them well. Less than eight years after the program began, five large volumes of analysis have been published.

Like the first two volumes, the recent three consist of from five to nine separate studies. All studies deal with the same data set, and all fit into the grand research design, but they are independent in the sense that they could be read in any order without loss.

No one is likely to read any volume from cover to cover. The more sensible plan is suggested by the organization of the publications. The first two volumes contain twelve studies in Cohort 1, the 11,000 patients admitted during the first two years of the program, June 1969 to May 1971. Volumes 3 and 4 contain fourteen studies on Cohort 2, the 14,000 admissions from June 1971 to May 1972, and Volume 5 seven studies on Cohort 3, the 14,000 admissions from June 1972 to March 1973. The DARP program continued a year after that, so that all admissions, in all cohorts, could be followed through the first year of treatment, if they remained in treatment that long.

Since the questions asked about each cohort

were the same, or similar, the five volumes contain several sets of three studies, similar but not identical, because experience suggested new or improved approaches, and emphases changed. The reader who is intensely interested in an area, therefore, will want to follow that interest through studies in three of the five volumes, temporarily ignoring other studies in each volume. The reader who is less interested can begin with the appropriate sutdy in one of the later volumes, since it will recapitulate the major findings of the earlier volumes. There is much repetition within and between volumes, but this may be necessary, given that they will not be read to the same extent or in the same sequence by all readers.

There are long—six to ten chapters—"Evaluations of Treatment" for the three cohorts in volumes 1, 4 and 5. Studies on behavioral measures and criteria for assessing outcomes during treatment are found in the same volumes, as are studies on retention in treatment. Death rates in 1971–72 are analyzed in volume 2, death rates in 1972–73 in volume 5. In each case, the analysis in volume 5 contains enough data on the earlier studies for all except those interested in the fullest details.

While the substantive content of earlier studies can be gleaned from the later studies, methodological improvements, and what led to them, will be missed. Methodologists in general, and those interested in evaluation studies, will profit from tracing through the full series of studies the development of thinking about, and of techniques for measuring, criteria for assessing outcomes and typologies of patients and of treatment agencies.

Perhaps half of each volume consists of such studies, more or less replications on one cohort of studies on other cohorts. But there are also many studies which stand alone, or are so much more detailed in one place than another as to constitute quite different entities. Thus volume 2 contains a study of the use of alcohol by patients in treatment; volume 4 has one on the use of alcohol during methadone maintenance only; and volume 5 examines the differential use of illicit drugs by methadone maintenance patients. Criminal behavior is touched on in several volumes, but in detail in volume 4. Volume 3, constructing developmental models of nonmedical drug use, contains an excellent review of the literature; the writers are psychologists, but display a comprehensive knowledge of the sociological literature too.

The complexity of the data, and therefore of the analysis, was great. For example, it originally seemed that patients could be regarded as having entered one of four treatment modalities: Methadone Maintenance, Therapeutic Community, Outpatient Drug Free, and Detoxification. But studies of the agencies showed that there were large differences within modalities—differences in philosophy, goals, strategies, and procedures. The first attempt at taxonomy produced eleven Treatment Types, reduced to nine in the latest revision.

Similarly, an attempt was made to develop a typology of patients, based on cluster analysis of nineteen demographic, drug use, and patient background items. Twelve types were identified for the 1969–71 admissions, but the typology did not prove to be useful, and was abandoned.

Evaluation focused on retention of patients in treatment, death rates and causes of death, and above all on criterion measures of patient behavior, the most important of these relating to opioid use, alcohol use, use of other drugs, criminality and employment.

The general plan of analysis in the central series of studies is threefold. First, treatment effects are estimated by examining gross changes on the criterion measures from pretreatment to the first two months of treatment and to the total time in treatment. The method is tabular analysis of difference scores, separately for the sexes, with single controls on such variables as Treatment Type, ethnic group, and age.

Second, the analysts look for differential effects on the criterion measures attributable to pretreatment criterion levels, treatment factors, and patient classification factors (age, ethnic group, drug use patterns). Covariate analysis is used for this purpose for the second cohort, and this plus profile analysis for the third cohort.

Third, individual patient background variables are examined to see if they account for criterion variance over and beyond the variables of the previous analyses. Methods include partial correlation and computation of semipartial beta weights.

The meticulous statistical procedures, fully described and with data presented in hundreds of tables, greatly increase the reader's confidence in the findings. Unfortunately, the findings become complex, difficult to state in any simple sentence, and even difficult to identify. As one example, the age at which a user becomes involved in a drug subculture is included as one of the twelve background variables in the third analysis above. But evaluation of its effects on criterion measures requires examination of seven panels in each of six tables, spread over twenty-five pages in chapter 6 of the fifth volume, and this is for only one of the three cohorts.

These volumes will be difficult reading for anyone who is not at least moderately competent in statistics and in the techniques of multivariate analysis. The largest natural audience would be the staff of treatment agencies, but many of these lack the background necessary to read the volumes. Even those who have it will sometimes be unable to make the comparisons they would like between their own clientele and the data of these volumes, because some of the variables used are insufficiently described. Age at involvement in the drug subculture, to use that example again, is based on adding the ages at which five events occurred. But the otherwise detailed description of index construction fails to say how one handles it if one or more of the events never occurred.

Sociologists active in the drug field will want, at the least, to be familiar with the contents of these volumes, so as to consult them when relevant to their own work. Those interested in evaluation problems and techniques, in any area, may want the same familiarity. Those engaged in evaluation of drug programs or in follow-up studies will find it essential to review the work Sells and his colleagues have done. Some may be interested in secondary analysis of the DARP data, which are available from the Drug Abuse Epidemiology Data Center (DAEDAC) at T.C.U.

Among the findings, a major one is a substantial reduction in drug use and criminality and an increase in employment during treatment, especially in Methadone Maintenance. When such changes occurred they normally occurred early, in the first two months of treatment. Unfortunately, the baseline from which change was measured was the period of two months immediately prior to entrance into treatment. These are months in which drug use and criminality hit peaks, and employment a nadir, for many users. The comparison used here, therefore, is biased toward a finding of treatment effectiveness. This is not, however, a criticism of Sells; it was from his early reports on the DARP data that we learned the weakness of this basis of comparison.

Another problem that plagued Sells was that patients in different Treatment Types differed not only in background characteristics like age and ethnic group, but also in the extent to which they were at risk on outcome criteria like drug use and employment, so that some variables were inextricably confounded. But this was so during treatment, and analysis should be simpler, and results clearer, on post-treatment variables.

It is therefore encouraging that NIDA has funded and Sells has conducted follow-up studies on large samples from Cohort 1 (1969–1971 admissions) and Cohort 2 (1971–1972 admissions). Field work (by NORC, which did the superb field work on Lee Robins's follow-ups of Vietnam veterans) has already been completed, so we can look forward to future reports from Sells. Our debt, for these volumes, is already great; our anticipation can be even greater.

Women, Crime and Criminology: A Feminist Critique, by CAROL SMART. Boston: Routledge & Kegan Paul, 1976. 196 pp. $10.50 cloth.

MILDRED DALEY PAGELOW
University of California, Riverside

Women, Crime and Criminology: A Feminist Critique is a recent import from England which will be welcomed by many social scientists, particularly teachers of undergraduate students in sociology. This short text will be useful for supplementary reading in courses on deviance, criminology, juvenile delinquency, women, social problems, etc., as well as women's studies courses addressing contemporary social issues. Carol Smart provides a needed and welcome addition to the literature in two important ways. First, as a new arrival to the recent proliferation of feminist literature, her book attends to issues largely concerning working-class women and traditional gender-role (feminine) socialization. The book helps to counterbalance expostulations reflecting middle-class perspectives concerning middle-class values and objectives by focusing on the relationship between increasing powerlessness and decreasing socioeconomic status. Second, a probably more important need is met by providing an extremely scarce resource: a well-organized examination of women's position in crime and criminology. Students and instructors have explored subject matter pertaining to human behavior (and misbehavior) within social systems, while treating one-half of the human population as absent or peripheral to almost all scholarly discussions. The preponderance of literature on homosexuality, for instance addresses male behavior only (sometimes even without reference to such exclusivity), or gives cursory recognition to the existence of lesbians. Criminology and juvenile delinquency literature has similarly scarcely noticed females.

Although it is a scholarly work, *Women,*

Crime and Criminology is written in a style which will make it easy to grasp even by readers who are not specialists in the field. Also, the author is acquainted with American and English theorists and empiricists, and introduces their major works for critique. The American reader may begin by being sharply aware of differences in English and American laws and social structures, but these differences begin to shrink in importance as the similarities become strikingly evident.

Smart weaves her overview chronologically, beginning with "common-sense" and so-called "scientific" explanations generated from theological and paternalistic views of women, progressing through classical, then contemporary studies of female criminality. She maintains that (male) criminology has progressed from early positivistic-deterministic theorems to liberal, New, Radical, and Critical Criminologies, but female criminology lags at least thirty years behind. Among other things, she provides a definition of sexism, discusses the fallacy of bias-free research, decries the tendency of social scientists to concentrate on individuals as pathological rather than on restrictive social structures, and reminds readers of the close relationship between criminological theory and social policy. The author also introduces the interesting concept of "sexualizing crimes," cautions against relying on official statistics for determining the extent or types of crimes committed by females, raises questions about the "creation" of crime by (powerful) definers, and exposes both the working-class bias and the tendency to blame the victim—particularly if the victim is female. To support this viewpoint, she spotlights two sex-specific crimes: prostitution, where females are defined as the perpetrators, and rape, where females are the victims. Beginning with the legal codes, then law enforcement and judicial practices, and finally disposition of cases, it becomes apparent that legal structures operate differentially, depending on the sex of the perpetrator/victim. From Smart's feminist viewpoint, the female systematically becomes the victim, whether she is a prostitute, rape victim, battered wife, or a woman seeking abortion.

Man-made laws, Smart maintains, were created by those with the power to define, in their own interests, not only what is legal, but also what is "natural," moral, and mentally healthy. The author examines "mental illness" as a functional alternative to crime, and concludes that traditional sex-roles create a double bind for women. She notes the consistent tendency for agents of control, in both the legal and medical fields, to apply the "sickness" label to women.

Women, Crime and Criminology is not only a worthy addition to the scarce literature on female criminology (Smart suggests formulation of a feminist criminology), but the book's most valuable contribution probably is that it raises more questions than it attempts to answer. It generates interest and excitement in a largely unexplored field, even for scholars whose attention and expertise have been directed to other substantive areas. The book is recommended especially to those who are searching for stimulating topics for socially useful and policy-oriented research projects.

Education

Academic Gamesmanship: Student-Oriented Change in Higher Education, by ALEXANDER W. ASTIN. New York: Praeger Publishers, 1976. 206 pp. $17.50 cloth.

ROSALYN WEINMAN SCHRAM
Middlesex County College, New Jersey

The author of this book served as the director of an American Council on Education study that had a rather unique purpose. A varied group of 19 colleges and universities were provided with comprehensive data showing the effect that each college was having on its students. The researchers wanted to determine the influence that this student data would have in stimulating changes in policies and programs that would be formulated to improve the educational environment for students. The American Council on Education had already developed a comprehensive core of student data from a national sample of 300 institutions. The enormous amount of data allowed for the analysis of the comparative impact of different types of institutions on their respective students.

The results add to our knowledge of higher educational institutions and their policy making procedures. The likelihood of an institution using student data to effect changes was found to be correlated with less selectivity in recruitment policies, a relatively innovative curricula, and "gate-keeping" policies. The specifics of this particular research design may be less useful than the author's critical discussion of modifications and refinements of it. These modifications would lead to an even more effective strategy for use in future attempts to encourage institutions to utilize student data for planning and decision-making.

Directors of institutional research, administrative personnel, and faculty who have decision-making power concerning student development, would do well to review this publication. Policies such as open admissions and programs such as women's studies and honor's studies could be implemented and revised based on data regarding levels of student satisfaction, attrition, and choice of major. The questionnaires used in this study could be successfully employed by other institutions.

Those interested in adding some new bureaucratic atrocity stories to their repertoire, will thoroughly enjoy Astin's humorous yet insightful chapters, "Academic Games" and "Making Communities Work." The former addresses itself to defensive tactics (such as rationalization and passing the buck) that are employed by people to avoid dealing with the data. The latter describes the various participants (such as the "antidata" person and the "opportunist") who invariably appear on academic committees.

One of Astin's conclusions is difficult to accept. The author asserts that the single most important influence on institutional conservatism is the faculty, with administration and external demands playing lesser roles. Given the complexities of both formal and informal sources of power exercised by faculty, administration, and external structures (i.e., boards of trustees, state departments of education, accreditation agencies, etc.) the relative influence of each of these groups seems undiscernible without further research and study.

Using Self-Reports to Predict Student Performance, by LEONARD L. BAIRD. New York: College Entrance Examination Board, 1976. 90 pp. $5.00 paper.

JOYCE L. EPSTEIN
The Johns Hopkins University

Educational psychologists have rediscovered student surveys and are encouraging their use in nonexperimental settings. Survey questionnaires are called "brief assessments" ("brief" compared to the elaborate inventories or traditional tests we usually associate with psychology). Well, okay. Sociologists, who have long acknowledged the benefits and problems of survey data, may be tempted to scowl disdainfully at this apparent reinvention; but Baird's short monograph is still a useful review of studies and ideas on student self-reports.

He addresses important questions. For example, how do we know respondents don't lie? Actually, there are circumstances under which respondents do lie, and, we need to know more about the environmental conditions, personality characteristics, and question formats that increase distortions and guesses. Yet Baird's review of research is convincing that self-reported biographical data are usually accurate and valid.

Then, how can we best use self-reported truths? Baird's interest is in the prediction of grades, college success, and adult accomplishments. He also makes important points about affirmative action programs, the current limited definitions of "success," and the need for research on the students for whom predictability of success is low. The reviews and comments address current interests of sociologists of education in the better estimation of school effects through the measurement of nonacademic outcomes, the use of subjective educational indicators, the use of student evaluations of environmental characteristics, the identification and analysis of person-environment interaction effects, and the careful and creative design and analysis of nonexperimental data.

Researchers should overlook the weaker sections of the monograph that offer cursory treatments of system designs and statistical methods, but should carefully look over the reviews of research and the cross-discipline communications.

The Limits of Educational Reform, by MARTIN CARNOY and HENRY M. LEVIN. New York: David Mckay Company, 1976. 290 pp. $4.95 paper.

GENE GRABINER
SUNY/Buffalo

With no mention of the struggles for integrated and democratized, free higher education, Martin Carnoy, Henry M. Levin, and other members of the Center for Economic Studies at Stanford University have given us a book which purports to assess the effects and parameters of reform of public education.

A positive virtue of *The Limits of Educational Reform* is the hardnosed approach the authors present to those limits. They do not, as do so many other commentators, romanticize educational reform programs and the place of such programs in terms of real social change. Hence, in the introduction, while discussing the possibility that educational reform might eradicate social problems such as poverty, the authors make it clear that only the destruction of monopoly capitalism can eliminate poverty and reduce economic inequality. Having made this disclaimer, however, they present a structural-functionalist conception of how educational institutions work. At the heart of it is the "correspondence principle" which, rather than being discussed in terms of domination (as in the work of Bowles and Gintis), is composed of accommodative mechanisms. These mechanisms are overlaid with categories familiar to liberal sociologists such as: "industrial democracy," "polity," the scarcity postulate, and a general interest group perspective.

"Correspondence" is a theoretical expression of the authors' view that educational reform in the United States has been the outcome of and a victory for "capitalist industrialization." Introducing their functionalist conceptions (with the work of Henry M. Levin providing the major character to the book), the Stanford Group focuses upon the "correspondence principle," which they claim demonstrates that schools, in a complementary relation with home and work (work being central), produce a differentiated working class in response to differential capitalist requirements at the point of production.

Disregarding material conditions, capitalist relations of production, labor strife, and the internal dynamics of the public school, it is argued that, because of "correspondence," "children of working-class families will be more adept at taking orders" (p. 32). We are told that "little imagination" is needed to see the "correspondence between grades for school performance and wages for work performance" (p. 28). Actually, much imagination is required to argue that working-class youth are more capable of taking orders, particularly when "poor performance," according to capitalist norms of schooling, is "punished with detention, other coercive sanctions, and low grades" (p. 36). Such sanctions might actually be responses to individualistic, inverted, and distorted "misconduct" on the part of working-class children.

The inability of input-output models, such as that used by the Stanford Group, to look *within* the schools places the "correspondence principle" in a dubious position as an analytic tool. "Correspondence" theory does not assert that elements of class struggle and the contradictions of bourgeois society are reproduced in the classroom and the school.

Turning from the failure of educational reforms, Carnoy, Levin, et al. suggest that today only workplace reform can prepare the ground for further educational reform. Yet, the suggested workplace reform, "industrial democracy," does not call for a change in the class structure and only obscures the deeper questions of political and economic democracy which are necessary for the destruction of monopoly capitalism. Therefore, it is merely an ameliorative, liberal reform. This is clear in the authors' shared prescriptive view that "industrial democracy" is needed to curtail wildcat strikes, worker absenteeism, turnover, sabotage, and increased quality-control costs. Hence, inasmuch as "correspondence" is used to look at the workplace, it is employed as a means to recommend strategies for capitalist management so as to achieve greater labor conformation to the demands of capital rather than having production correspond to the human needs of the producers.

In discussing "industrial democracy," Michael A. Carter, of the Center for Economic Studies, presents a sophisticated argument with implications for the development of capitalist strategies of plant stabilization. The workgroup, production team, and "democratic work structure" are offered as models for industrial reform.

Distinguishing between primary routinized and secondary labor segments, Carter notes that the former makes difficult any discipline involving direct supervision and attribution of poor performance to specific individuals. Attempts only result in time and productivity losses, adding to those already occurring. In contrast, the social organization of production among the secondary labor segment involves immediate feedback, direct supervision, and threat of dismissal as disciplinary elements. Exemplary of the secondary segment is the waiter/waitress-busboy "workgroup." The skills generally required for both labor market segments involve short time-learning. However, within the secondary segment, while there is some task specialization, there is also some rotation (e.g., within the foodservice group), one of the hallmarks of "industrial democracy."

As Carter indicates, capitalist labor discipline is less successful among the primary routinized group than the secondary group. Therein lies the real thrust of "industrial democracy." Seeking to extend the management benefits of the secondary segment to the mass factory, the workgroup model would physically and socially fragment assembly-line workers into small isolated production teams. In my opinion, while potentially creating greater social connections at the team level this strategy would sever such connections at the general level of the mass factory. Production teams would then be more amenable to direct supervision and threat of dismissal than assembly-line workers. This has serious implications for unions, particularly since it is offered in a book in which wages are attacked as "consumerism" and the labor movement's victories in obtaining weekends, vacations, and retirement are cynically treated.

Job rotation within the workgroup or production team is an element of "industrial democracy." Supposedly, as suggested in this book, skilled and interesting work is to be learned and rotated within the group, leading to a decline in wildcat strikes, etc. However, on-the-job training is a cost in both constant and variable capital and so contributes to a fall in the rate of profit. Since the capitalist aims for profit maximization, the tendency within "industrial democracy" would be to organize production teams around tasks requiring no more training than presently called for in assembly-line production. I think that it would of course be possible to showcase a few highly skilled teams for public relations purposes, such exceptions, however, would only prove the rule.

Neglected as workers within the educational system, teachers are attacked in this book. They are blamed as part of the reason for either (a) the lack of compensatory education's ever having been tried or, (b) its failure. In the latter case, teachers are said to fulfill powerful and "hierarchical" roles relative to students. Surprisingly, even Martin Carnoy incorrectly states that because they are "outside" the culture of some groups of students, teachers don't understand the "differential reward systems" of different cultures. This use of bureaucratic models of hierarchy and theories of cultural pluralism obscures the class content of both capitalist education and the struggles of public school teachers.

The anti-labor sentiments typical of Michael A. Carter's overview of workplace reform via "industrial democracy" are preserved in Henry M. Levin's discussion of compensatory education and educational workers. Levin, asserting that compensatory education has never been tried, characterizes teachers and their unions as seeking selfish gain behind a "rhetoric of educational improvement" (p. 185). This egoistic self-interest is supposedly manifested in teacher unions' fight for "reductions in class size, increases in remedial specialists [and] extra pay for planning time" (p. 183). Rather than acknowledge that these goals might benefit poor and educationally low-skilled youth, Levin charges that such aims are only to "increase the employment and job benefits of teachers . . . [by] narrowing the scope of normal duties to increase the number of tasks that require extra remuneration" (p. 183).

Levin is correct in that there is not, in all cases, a necessary connection between teachers' economic interests and students' educational interests. And, in fact, there are and have been struggles where they are at variance (e.g., Ocean-Hill Brownsville). At the same time, however, he does not indicate the *contradictory* character of these struggles where, in the majority of cases, teachers' and students' interests are not at variance.

In contrast to the teachers, Levin presents the school board as an embattled conflict regulator; even while it attempts to force teachers to work in ever more crowded classrooms. Additionally, allowing abstracted empiricism to get the best of him and apparently ignorant of Martin Carnoy's criticism of the role of intelligence tests as instruments of ruling-class control in education, Henry M. Levin asserts that teachers are "intellectually less able" (p. 35) as per their low scores on standardized tests of intelligence. The general line of argument in this section, as throughout the book, suggests that the authors have no theory of praxis outside of structural-functionalist theory and that they have a mechanistic and linear view of education, the workplace, and social change.

Given the lack of any systematic and extended discussion of educational reform and the university in this volume, we find only one passage devoted to the academic rebellion of the 1960s and early 1970s. In attempting to trivialize, discredit, and obscure the democratic and progressive character of the student anti-war movement, Henry M. Levin asserts that students turned upon and tried to smash their "father image" universities and not the "munitions plants" out of frustration (p. 24) with an unresponsive government. Such psychological reductionism ignores the fact that at places like Berkeley, the Institute for Defense Analysis, MIT, the Stanford Research Institute, Stanford University, and the University of Wisconsin at Madison there were and are many millions of federal grant monies invested in counter-insurgency research, chemical and biological warfare research. It was already well-known that the university was involved in war research. War complicity in the academy was not hidden behind the analyst's couch.

In a critical mood, the entire collective authorship of *The Limits of Educational Re-*

form (William H. Behn, Martin Carnoy, Michael A. Carter, Joyce C. Crain, and Henry M. Levin) takes on the Report of the Panel on Youth of the President's Science Advisory Committee, *Youth: Transition to Adulthood*. However, their critique is blunted. Rather than criticize the Report for its attacks on the working class, calls to lower the minimum wage and cut back on education as a social right, the Stanford Group merely charges that the workplace is not yet sufficiently reformed and therefore it's simply better to stay in school. While compared to the *Youth* Report their criticism may seem a bit better, it never attains a satisfactory depth.

The Limits of Educational Reform is important as it highlights the limits of certain sociological and economic perspectives in education. The problem is that while criticizing bourgeois rule in education, the authors of *The Limits of Educational Reform* have never mentioned the workers' struggle against that rule. To the degree that only bourgeois norms are acknowledged as a force we have "correspondence" (accommodation), and the researchers themselves can come to doubt the historical possibilities for substantive change. Because of the type of thinking reflected in the structural-functionalist version of "correspondence," not only do Carnoy, Levin, et al. have an erroneous analysis of industrial production under capitalism, they also have a one-sided view of teachers, compensatory education, and education in general. This is reflected in their policy recommendations which imply that they are better managers and can do a better job of securing capitalist interests at school and at work.

Women's Inferior Education: An Economic Analysis, by BLANCHE FITZPATRICK. New York: Praeger Publishers, 1976. 189 pp. $16.50 cloth.

JUDITH CADITZ
Immaculate Heart College, Los Angeles

Is there really sex discrimination in institutions of higher learning? After all, many of us see women in universities and colleges, on both the undergraduate and graduate level. Today, women are visible in law schools, medical schools, and other professional training grounds in the past only open to males. Thus, we wonder: What is the charge leveled by women that there is sexism in educational settings? At the same time, when we have an opening for a position, we wonder why "so few qualified women apply."

Women's Inferior Education addresses issues central to this dilemma. Fitzpatrick argues that women are denied equal opportunity in the educational system after high school. They are restricted to second ranked schools and find themselves in dead end or low paid, low status jobs. She examines educational and vocational institutions in twenty states, with particular detail to the pattern of discriminatory enrollment. She carefully documents her contention that there are economic rewards for perpetuation of sex discrimination. Qualified women are either explicitly or implicitly denied equal admission to top ranked universities; they are denied adequate financial aid available to equally qualified men. Sex stereotyping persists in educational and vocational training programs funded by the federal, state, and local governments and private foundations. As a consequence, women suffer not only from low aspiration levels (perpetuated by counselors, school administrators, and textbooks) but also from discriminatory admissions policies. Leaders in top ranked universities, dependent upon their reputation for obtaining research grants, laboratory and library facilities, etc., are engaging in economically rational decisions; they know that if women represent a sizable proportion of the student body, the reputation of the institution will be lowered, thus threatening financial support. Further, the resources of the university will be wasted if talented women, entering a sexist job market, do not become physicists, lawyers, business executives, bankers, judges, doctors, or senators. Also, if more women enter a particular university, they would lower the rank, prestige, and earnings of decision-making administrators and faculty. Rational decisions are thus based on the knowledge that the relative standing of equal admissions institutions will decline. In addition, she asserts that if women are admitted, they will tend to come from higher income families, since the university resources and reputation will be less affected than by lower class women.

Fitzpatrick suggests some practical methods of promoting equal opportunities for Jane without denying Joe his chance: (1) economic sanctions for unequal admissions, i.e., withholding tax funded grants, contracts, and scholarship funds from institutions and union organizations not using equal admissions policies; (2) election of state and local officials and administrators supporting equal admissions policies; (3) use of texts depicting equalitarian sex roles; (4) opening of enrollment in math courses, shop physics and athletic programs to women. The benefits of equal opportunities will help not only women, but men who will gain from women taking on a greater share of responsibility for family income.

The work would be improved by inclusion of current US Supreme Court cases addressing issues of "reverse discrimination"—*Bakke, Vorchheimer, Flanagan*. Also, for the sociologist, incorporation of theory (for example Weberian analysis of status groups) would increase the implications of the work. The main asset of the book is its careful documentation of the existence of unequal educational opportunities for women; statistical tables offer evidence often lacking in works alleging sex discrimination. The book provides needed information for undergraduate and graduate courses on sex roles, occupations and professions, education, and stratification. It is also helpful as a reference work for administrators and educators concerned with equal educational opportunities for women and for minorities.

A New Public Education, by SEYMOUR W. ITZKOFF. New York: David McKay Company, 1976. 372 pp. $5.95 paper.

RONALD M. PAVALKO
Florida State University

It would be much easier to review Itzkoff's book if I had a clear idea of the audience for which it is intended. The audience could be the general public, educational leaders and administrators, university students in education, or other professors of education.

The central concern of the book is educational reform. Wait; please continue reading. Itzkoff's goals go well beyond the tinkering, manipulation, and reorganizing frequently associated with the term "educational reform." The objectives here are much more ambitious. The "new" public education would require a substantial change in present educational systems. More specifically, "What is needed is a move away from the domination of schooling by the stagnant, politicized, and bureaucratized state systems of education. Education must be given over to those who will be the ultimate beneficiaries of this social service and who are paying for it in the first place" (p. 271). Thus, reform boils down to "the gradual establishment of voluntarism, wherein parents and children can exercise some initiative in deciding which schools best reflect their own values" (p. 11).

Itzkoff's major complaints are excessive bureaucratization, standardization, and centralization. These are not new issues by any means. They have become conventional jargon in the arguments of numerous critics of education in the 1970s. What is different about Itzkoff's argument is that these features of education are seen as historically evolved expressions of the disjuncture between contemporary human needs and both the content and structure of education. In addition, the current malaise in education is seen as rooted in deeper social changes, primarily the demise of community and the (artificial) separation of socialization (which the author calls "informal education") from formal education.

Unlike other recent critics of education, Itzkoff is neither a romantic nor an anarchist. From his perspective, the trick is to return education to the people, the community, parents, and students. How is this to be attained? It is not uncommon for reformers to be long on goals but short on means and Itzkoff is no exception. He stakes most of his hope on the widespread adoption of the voucher system of payment. This, it is argued, would break up the state monopoly on education, bring competition into the picture and provide choices, options, and citizen involvement.

In the process of developing his argument and proposal, Itzkoff presents a detailed and informative commentary on the history of American education, focusing on philosophical assumptions, social values, and social change. Should sociologists of education give this work their attention? Yes, I think so. The discussion of the development of American education is worthwhile in and of itself. Whether or not one agrees with the suggested mechanism of reform, the analysis of how and why education got into its present predicament is fresh, well-grounded in specifics, and useful to anyone concerned with institutional change.

Decision-Making for Schools and Colleges, by DEAN F. JUNIPER. New York: Pergamon Press, 1976. 302 pp. $16.00 cloth. $10.00 paper.

JOHN F. GLASS
Antioch College, West Los Angeles

In this age of variety and increased options in life styles, the need for learning skills that would increase control over one's life and enhance the possibilities for achieving what one values, seems indisputable. Such education is sadly lacking, according to Juniper, and this book seeks to help correct this deficiency by presenting a classroom program for high school and college teachers who wish to teach decision-making principles useful for life and career planning.

The program is divided into four stages, Aim, Information, Evaluation, and Decision, and is further subdivided into sixteen units, each covered in a separate chapter. Units include the use of expectancy tables, checklist analyses, contingency, impulse decisions. The techniques employed in the program include questionnaires, algorithms, personal histories, group discussion, outside activities, role playing, and simulations.

Little advice on how, where, and when to use the program is given beyond saying that it lends itself to team teaching, requires some expertise in group dynamics, and should not be approached by the "faint-hearted, the fretters, or the good opinion seekers" (p. 9). Although each unit was classroom tested, no indication of success is given. In some of the exercises, terms and examples from British life would need to be altered for American students.

This book is useful as a collection of imaginative classroom techniques for teaching logical thinking, problem solving, and decision making. However, Juniper's discussion of values and the valuing process, which underlies decision making, is far too brief and superficial. Instructors considering using this book may find it helpful to supplement it with material on Values Clarification, an approach that allows students to identify, choose, and act on their own values. *Values and Teaching*, by Louis Raths, Merrill Harmin, and Sidney Simon, is a good place to begin.

Post-Compulsory Education II: The Way Ahead, by EDMUND J. KING, CHRISTINE H. MOOR and JENNIFER A. MUNDY. Beverly Hills: Sage Publications, 1975. 200 pp. $12.00 cloth. $6.00 paper.

GORDON G. DARKENWALD
Rutgers University

The theme of this volume is that post-compulsory education for sixteen to twenty year olds in Britain and Western Europe is in a period of crisis and that policies, institutions, and curricula for this age group need to be thoroughly overhauled. The authors base this contention on a five-country survey reported in an earlier volume entitled *Post-Compulsory Education I: A New Analysis in Western Europe*. Regrettably, the present work does not adequately describe the procedures of the survey, so the reader must take it on faith that the interpretations in this report are supported by reliable evidence.

The book is written for policy-makers, teachers, and administrators concerned with the education of young adults. While the volume is organized after a fashion into five chapters, the reviewer was unable to identify precisely what each chapter was intended to communicate. The problem is partly due to the authors' presumption that readers are familiar with British educational terms such as A-levels, GCE-O, CSE, Sixth Form College, and so on.

The principal conclusions and recommendations will seem quite unimaginative to an American reader. The authors come out in favor of expanded options, learner-centered teaching, provision of guidance services, and the development of a delivery system modeled after the American community college. Given the rigidity of upper secondary/lower tertiary education in Britain, the recommendations may be bolder than they appear.

Specialists in comparative education may find the book of value, but despite its enlightened perspective it adds little to our understanding of educational theory or practice.

Priorities for Planning in Vocational Education: Alternatives for the 1970s, by LEONARD A. LECHT. Washington, D.C.: National Planning Association, 1975. 48 pp. $3.00 paper.

From School to Work: Effective Counselling and Guidance, by CHRISTINE H. MOOR. Beverly Hills: Sage Publications, 1976. 192 pp. $13.50 cloth. No price listed, paper.

The Economic Evaluation of Vocational Training Programs, by MANUEL ZYMELMAN. Baltimore: The Johns Hopkins University Press, 1976. 122 pp. $6.00 paper.

ROBERT B. EVERHART
University of California, Santa Barbara

Some ten years ago, John Seeley noted the difference between the "making" and "taking" of social problems. To "take" a problem is to adopt the consensual view of a problem and, accepting it as such, to investigate it within that framework. "Making" of a problem, on the other hand, involves treating the consensual point of view as problematical and re-organizing that view as an object of inquiry itself rather than assuming the accepted problem definition to be legitimate.

All three books under review here, in their own way, are "taking" rather than "making" studies in the field of vocational education. Since the role of schools and training institutions in the preparation of individuals for extant and necessary work roles in industrialized or industrializing societies is not questioned, the authors proceed to discuss how the transition from school to work can be effectuated most efficiently. The current popularity of this perspective as illustrated in these books is important to note, for vocational/career education has received and apparently will continue to receive ever increasing attention and funding, and presently is one of the fads in policy making circles.

Lecht's short monograph amply illustrates the "taking" perspective, as his study notes early that "training in occupational skills is increasingly important as the economy moves to higher levels of technology and specialization" (p. v). Without questioning the *type* of work for which people are being prepared, Lecht proceeds through a standard fare of facts and tables to reveal the general "responsiveness" of vocational educational programs to changing economic conditions. His major policy recommendation is for the government to streamline the funding of vocational education through a revenue sharing approach. Lecht's findings are not surprising, considering the study was sponsored by the National Planning Association, a "non-political" organization committed to "the preservation of private economic initiative" (p. 45). This monograph is of little substantive use to sociologists except as it represents the ideolgies of most business organizations on vocational education.

Zymelman, who is education advisor at the World Bank, seeks to understand the practicality for third world nations of utilizing various models of vocational training. On-the-job training, classroom training, and apprenticeships are among the models discussed. Utilizing econometric models to assess the economic returns of each mode, the author concludes that no one model is conclusively superior. Those interested in cost-benefit models might have some interest in the approach used by Zymelman, but, because consideration of the social dimensions of vocational education is absent, the substance of the monograph seems of little interest to sociologists.

Moor's book has the greatest potential interest, but, unfortunately, this potential is scarcely realized. The book, organized around a social psychological orientation of how occupational choices are made, begins by asking why youth who leave school at the end of the compulsory period have difficulty in obtaining work and what could be done to ease the transition from school to work. The author advertises the study (done in Newcastle, England) as based upon "fieldwork" among fifteen year old boys in five schools in the spring of their last year in school and six months thereafter. In reality, however, the study is based almost solely on structured interviews that reveal little about the cognitive framework and culture of boys in transition to the world of work. Instead, it presents answers to a pre-conceived list of questions reflecting the author's view of what is important to understand about how youth learn about work opportunities and make occupational choices. The author, in the last half of the book, presents a model for providing more complete career information.

Frank Tracy Carlton, in a speech to the NEA in 1910, said that the "industrial organization quietly forces its peculiar impress upon us all." The extent to which that statement is true yet today in schools and training institutions is readily apparent in these books. They do little more than to provide narrow perspectives on how schools and training institutions should reproduce the current work and social structure. The work of Arthur Wirth and Marvin Lazerson/Norton Grubb provides a beginning for those who want to move beyond this ideology.

The "Inequality" Controversy: Schooling and Distributive Justice, edited by DONALD M. LEVINE and MARY JO BANE. New York: Basic Books, 1975. 338 pp. $17.50 cloth. $6.95 paper.

JOYCE A. KOZUCH
Virginia Commonwealth University

According to the editors of this collection, their goal is to dispel confusion about the analysis and purpose of Jencks et al.'s *Inequality: A Reassessment of the Effect of Family and Schooling in America* by addressing two basic questions: (1) what can and should education do? and 2) how does education fit "into the longer-term goals and structures of our society"?

The editors, one of whom co-authored *Inequality*, are to be commended for attempting to provide a broader-based approach to these issues than the study did. This is an interdisciplinary collection which draws on a number of recognized, and sometimes controversial, contributors from various social sciences and philosophy. Thus, there is direct philosophical consideration of the moral issues involved. The volume also recognizes relevant work in economics by including a number of selections from the human capital school of thought. A second strength of the collection, is that the editors are aware that policy formation involves questions of value, as well as questions of adequate information.

However, the potential of a collection of this sort is never fully realized. When the reader looks at the collection as a whole, s/he realizes that it is not so much an attempt to explore a "controversy," as it is an apologia. The various selections all reach conclusions compatible with those found in *Inequality*, although the contributors take their own distinctive, often circuitous, routes. I suspect that even people who concur with the basic position may tire of the one-sidedness of the collection. Other reactions will range from amusement to outright anger, depending on the selection and the reader's stance on the issues. The other problem is that social scientists are not necessarily skilled at addressing questions of value. Unfortunately, the philosophical excerpts exhibit the same deficiency.

The major dilemma is to identify a possible use for the book. The editors' introductory material and two concluding chapters offer little that is thought-provoking. The articles vary in their readability. Some are too technical, others too turgid, for the student and the public sector (and for some academics). There is a lack of coherence within the major sections of the book. While isolated articles may be of use to a social scientist or instructor interested in this particular area, the collection as such would not be. Thus, this reviewer is at a loss to identify any audience for the book.

School Politics Chicago Style, by PAUL E. PETERSON. Chicago: University of Chicago Press, 1976. 304 pp. $15.00 cloth.

DAVID B. CARPENTER
University of Illinois, Chicago Circle

Political scientist Paul E. Peterson of the University of Chicago here presents a carefully researched, lucid account of recent policymaking in the Chicago school system, with primary documentation taken from the 1967–70 period. With research funds from the Danforth Foundation, supplemented by university support, Peterson has had the research assistance of a large number of students in Education and Political Science as well as the counsel and assistance of colleagues in these and related fields. Documentation reflects access to Chicago School and Chicago School Board records and to records of the Chicago Teachers' Union.

Peterson emphasizes three areas of primary disagreement in Chicago school policy formation: racial desegregation, collective bargaining, and political decentralization, as he seeks to explicate and test four alternative models of decision making. With the *pluralist bargaining* model of the political pragmatist he pairs the *ideological bargaining* model of the true believer who is prepared to sacrifice all in the pursuit of a principle. In contrast to the two bargaining models are posed two models which emphasize unity within the decision-making body: the *organizational* model, which treats the school bureaucracy as an interdependent whole with its own interests, values, and operating routines; and the *rational decision-making* model, which borrows from the literature of international relations and its view of national states as rational, value-maximizing, goal-oriented decisionmakers. ". . . I employ bargaining models—both pluralist and ideological—to demonstrate the plurality of forces shaping urban school policy. But I also apply unitary models to the same set of policies to illustrate the extent to which a single set of factors constrain the alternatives considered" (p. xiii).

Peterson utilizes carefully researched records of Chicago School Board votes in documenting coalition patterns over time and issues. He relates the dominant machine-reform split within the Chicago School Board to decision-making, as issues such as school desegregation, collective bargaining, and school decentralization become successively more or less salient. He concludes that consensus and rational decision-making are as relevant to policy outcomes as division, dissensus, and conflict.

Students of urban politics will find Peterson's analysis of the Daley regime illuminating. Students of bureaucratic process will value the case studies of abortive attempts at integration by school administrations in South Shore and South Chicago, and the studies of initially inept efforts at collective bargaining.

But Peterson's particularly significant contribution is in proposing and testing the utility of his two bargaining models and his two unitary models in understanding the decisions and actions of the Chicago School Board and the Chicago Schools as they confront issues associated with declining central city economic resources, changing population, increasing obsolescence, declining student performance, rising minority group aspirations, and rising economic demands from school employees.

Dynamics of Bureaucracy: A Case Analysis in Education, by MICHAEL PUSEY. New York: John Wiley & Sons, 1976. 160 pp. $19.50 cloth.

EDWARD GROSS
University of Queensland, Brisbane, Australia

The author, a former teacher and educational researcher and presently a fellow at the Australian National University, seeks to account for the failure of a Tasmanian government sponsored program change. The program sought a shift in emphasis from fact-memorization to learning of intellectual skills, an attempt to improve the relationships between teachers and students so as to make the former more supportive and concerned with the self-esteem of students, and greater citizen involvement. Two years after implementation, a study of a sample of the high schools reported no sign of substantial change. Pusey relates this result largely to the centralized, bureaucratic character of the school system. That system developed, paradoxially, from the Australian emphasis on egalitarianism. Unlike its American variety, however, Australian egalitarianism is not concerned so much with increasing potential (equality of opportunity) but rather with making sure that no one gets too far ahead or is too different, a concern with "cutting down the tall poppies." That end was achieved, as Australian Professor Sol Encel explains, by a reliance on the authority of the state, hence giving rise to a sort of benevolent bureaucracy. When power is heavily centralized in the hands of Minister and the Director-General of Education in the state, rather than at the local level, Pusey feels any program that seeks to "loosen" relationships at the school level is doomed to failure. Rather the dynamics of relationships at that level have to be dealt with in their own terms. To do this, Pusey takes us on an excursion through elementary organization theory, distinguishing between what he calls the three "dimensions" of formal structure, technology, and social system. He sees the need for direct changes in the last, an end he seeks to achieve through informal committees of teachers, principals, and superintendents, greater "community involvement" (though this was also a goal of the state plan), limited-term contracts for principals and other shifts in career plans, as well as a repeal of a repressive regulation preventing school personnel making public comment on education.

All of Pusey's proposals make sense but we are left with the reality of the failure of one program, which we are to contrast with the promised hope of a new one. And there seems to be a contradiction between the author's attribution of blame to the centralization of power in the Director-General's hand, a fact which is still unchanged, and the promise of the new proposals. In the end, Pusey's analysis remains useful for the explanation it offers of why the government program failed. As to preventing future failures, we shall need not merely analysis but also an applied sociology, one which is concerned with the cultural emphasis on equality and apparently with the power structure itself.

Making Inequality: The Hidden Curriculum of High School Tracking, by JAMES E. ROSENBAUM. New York: John Wiley & Sons, 1976. 238 pp. $13.95 cloth.

MARTHA A. COOK
The Johns Hopkins University

In the preface to *Making Inequality*, Rosenbaum announces his intentions to address the book to both academics and "citizens"—to "preserve the rigor of an academic monograph" while relegating "any social science terminology and complex statistics to footnotes." One can applaud his intentions but not his success; an academician will find his effort extremely disappointing.

Rosenbaum *may be totally correct* in his conjectures regarding tracking in Grayton high school, and his concern with the restriction of opportunity in secondary education is laudable. However, although he *may* be correct, he draws his conclusions from data that do not necessarily support his contentions despite his numerous protestations to the contrary. One cannot say that he is wrong; one *can* say that he has not, in fact, maintained the professional rigor to which he aspired and which he would lead us to believe underlies his conclusions. Unfortunately, therefore, Rosenbaum's book either misleads trusting citizens and academics or disappoints those who read it carefully and examine his documentation.

Space prohibits a listing of *specific* inconsistencies and incorrect statements in the text. However, I will note several general sources of my previously acknowledged disappointment; other readers can discover the specific inadequacies for themselves.

Rosenbaum shows a distressing disregard for reporting and heeding case bases in his analyses. Numerous samples (ranging from 50 to over 400 individuals) are employed in tables and discussions and the reader is either kept guessing from whom the generalizations were derived or driven to detective exercises. Conclusions based upon twelve persons are as confidently advanced as those based upon several hundred. Often unrecorded (and unreported) conversations with students, counsellors, and teachers are used as solid documentation of important points in his arguments. Rosenbaum also displays marked inconsistency in the number of curriculum classifications employed in his analyses: tracks are identified in the student handbook; by some means (unknown to the reader) he identifies five tracks; in some tables he employs all five tracks, sometimes four or two, but not three. One gets the uncomfortable feeling that the data are being manipulated to an unknown degree for unknown purposes. Tables which present regression (rather than cross-tabular) results are confusing in content and format, and the reader is given no direction as to the proper method of interpretation. Additionally, Rosenbaum habitually and somewhat irresponsibly overstates the degree to which (1) his data support his conclusions, (2) the work of other researchers support his conclusions, (3) the work of other researchers is deficient, and (4) his work is exceptional in technique (case study), sample (an homogenous working class school), analytic strategy (multiple data sources and approaches to the analysis), and insight.

In short, Rosenbaum is at his best when unencumbered by data. If the book were advertized as (1) an essay on the insidious nature and consequences of rigid tracking systems, (2) written from a definitely biased perspective, (3) by a concerned, liberal academic, (4) employing impressionistic data collected in a single high school, I would react to it with much more enthusiasm. Academics would benefit from exposure to his thoughts concerning the "tournament model" of selection and perhaps be moved to examine aspects of tracking in public education which have, admittedly, been sorely neglected in most survey investigations of curriculum effects. Laypersons might be shaken somewhat in their complacent belief in the operation of the "contest model" in secondary education and attempt to discover the realities of the world inhabited by the children in their communities, but neither academics nor "citizens" would be lulled into supposing that the author's opinions were soundly backed by empirical evidence.

Schooling and Achievement in American Society, edited by WILLAIM H. SEWELL, ROBERT M. HAUSER, and DAVID L. FEATHERMAN. New York: Academic Press, 1976. 535 pp. $24.00 cloth.

MARGARET MOONEY MARINI
Battelle Human Affairs Research Centers

This book is very much in the tradition of other work by the editors with respect to the high overall quality of the selections, the substantive issues with which it is concerned, and the use of sophisticated quantitative methods. It is an outgrowth of an interdisciplinary seminar on "achievement processes" and, as such, is a collection of papers dealing in one way or another with variables and issues relevant to the study of individual differences in academic and socioeconomic achievement. Schooling is given prominent attention in most selections, although in the first section of the book the emphasis is primarily on the manner in which students pass through and are influenced by an essentially invariant institutional structure, acquiring a certain level of assets or achievement as a result of the schooling process. In the second section, the emphasis is more on differences in the school environment and the effect of these differences on academic and socioeconomic achievement.

Overall, the book is an impressive collection of papers on the forefront of research in educational sociology and social stratification and employs some of the most sophisticated statistical methods now in use in the social sciences. However, the book is also limited in the area of its concern—certainly more than the title would suggest. The authors are concerned with the effects of schooling and other factors on individual differences in achievement, i.e., they seek to examine the effects of variables influencing the relative positions of individuals within the hierarchy of achievement. They do not examine the relationship between schooling and achievement at the societal level, i.e., they do not seek to determine the way in which the distribution of schooling, or the amount of educational inequality, is related to the distribution of achievement (the amount of income inequality). Although the book is an excellent source of information about the micro-social effects of schooling on the achievements of individuals within the United States at a given point in time, it does not examine the macro-social relationship between schooling and achievement as it might be assessed, for example, over time.

A second limitation of the book is that the research, particularly that on socioeconomic achievement, is based almost exclusively on a single segment of the US population—white males. Although the editors are sensitive to the fact that a large number of the analyses in the book are based on regional samples which are not representative of the US population, they appear less concerned about the fact that all of the analyses of socioeconomic achievement, with the exception of the analysis of educational attainment by Hauser et al., ignore minorities and women. Although it could be argued that more limited data are available for groups other than white males and that the failure to incorporate analyses of these groups is due to a lack of papers on them presented at the seminar, one is then led to speculate on why analyses on these subgroups were not presented at a seminar on achievement processes in the United States. Certainly, inequality of achievement among racial groups and between the sexes is one of the major social concerns of our time. Moreover, there are data available for these groups, as evidenced by analyses reported elsewhere.

A third limitation of the research is that it is largely based on cross-sectional with some subsequent follow-up data and not on experimental data. Because of the covariance in the general population between individual resources and the quality of schools attended, even the best statistical efforts (and they are well represented in this volume) to sort out the two sets of covarying influences remain unsatisfactory. In order to unambiguously identify the effects of differences between schools and, more importantly, to assess the potential effect which educational reform based on a change in the relationship between individual resources and the quality of schooling might have, experimental data are needed in which individual resources and the school characteristics of interest are orthogonal.

Higher Education for Public Health: A Report of the Milbank Memorial Fund Commission, by CECIL G. SHEPS, Chairman. N.Y.: Prodist, 1976. 218 pp. $12.00 cloth. $7.95 paper.

ANGUS E. REID
University of Manitoba

Commissioned by the Milbank Memorial Fund in 1972 at the request of the Association of Schools of Public Health, this report contains an assessment of the current state of higher education for Public Health and a series of proposals for rationalizing the training of Public Health personnel. It will no doubt hold great interest for those in the Public Health field especially members of schools of Public Health since it calls for a number of major changes in the curricula of these institutions—away from the training of "front line" Public Health workers and toward the development of Public Health researchers, educators, and managers; all grounded in biostatistics, epidemiology, and management science. This recommendation will likely be the source of considerable debate not only because of its elitist overtones but also because in its investigations the commission itself appears to have fallen well short of the standard of excellence it proposes. Thus, in spite of its call for an objective and scientifically based Public Health training the commission's own work appears neither objective nor scientific. Rather than critically addressing the need for and function of specialized schools of Public Health, the commission simply assumes that such schools are necessary and sets out to legitimize their role. Even worse, the report contains little "hard data" or statistical analyses on which to rest its case (indeed some of its most important assessments are based on "personal communications").

For the sociologist interested in the health sector of American society this report contains little of value as a commentary on the state of the art of training for Public Health. It may prove useful however as a specimen of the contradictions between ideology and practice in the health industry.

Explorations in Classroom Observation, edited by MICHAEL STUBBS and SARA DELAMONT. New York: John Wiley & Sons, 1976. 221 pp. $14.95 cloth.

CANDACE WEST
Florida State University

This is a collection of readings which makes an important contribution to a much neglected field of educational research—ongoing interaction in the classroom. The book's central argument is that most educational research is conducted outside, and without regard for, the actual social situations in which teachers are expected to teach and students are expected to learn. Various selections focus on the in situ, micro interactional processes through which different forms of educational experiences take place, whether conducting language lessons, carrying out laboratory excercises, or developing classroom jokes.

Data collection techniques represented in this volume are diverse, and include participant observation, interviewing, questionnaires, and audio-tape recordings. Most studies employ several of these procedures, but of special interest are those which utilize analyses of verbal interactions. The transcribed excerpts discussed in these chapters allow the reader to see precisely *how* students' and teachers' practical concerns are communicated to one another. The result is a finely balanced tension between empirical investigation and theoretical commentary.

The individual contributions are organized into four parts. Their synthesis is effected to a great extent by the genuinely informative introductions to each chapter. However, the major theoretical integration of chapters is contingent on part one of the book, "Classroom Research: A Critique and a New Approach." There, Delamont and Hamilton furnish an excellent critical overview of the interaction analysis tradition within American classroom research, in particular its reliance on prespecified behavioral categories. Delamont and Hamilton also express a concern for the future of classroom research in Britain—a concern which is sustained throughout the collection. The alternatives to viewing the classroom as a "black box" are provided in parts two and three of the volume, focusing on students' perspectives and student-teacher interaction respectively. A consistent substantive emphasis is placed on the social production of education, e.g., how students "make sense of" teachers; how classroom identities are established, maintained or changed; and how teachers manage routine practical problems (e.g., maintaining attention, sanctioning, or monitering classroom talk). Part four consists of the specific application of the observational techniques and insights of earlier chapters to the analysis of a practical concern, the introduction of a new curriculum.

While each paper individually reflects an explicit interest in socially situated interactions, the institutional context within which classroom processes occur is given less systematic treatment. The ethnographic emphasis of the book could potentially provide for a deeper understanding of the micro-macro relationship. In this regard, the editorial introductions provide prototypical suggestions for integration—e.g., the comparison of a predominantly immigrant and working-class educational setting of one chapter to observations made of a private girls' school in a later chapter. Unfortunately, but perhaps inevitably in an exploratory volume, direct theoretical linkages are left to the reader and to future research.

On the one hand, this book will probably be most helpful to sociologists of education, given its relatively "new" treatment of their "old" substantive issues. On the other, its diversity of theoretical and methodological approaches will make it interesting reading for a wider audience, including qualitative methodologists, social psychologists, and sociolinguists. Since the former was the aim—and the latter the hope—of this collection, the book may be viewed as successful with regard to both its intents and purposes.

Authority to Control the School Program, by TYLL VAN GEEL. Lexington, Mass.: Lexington Books, 1976. 249 pp. $15.50 cloth.

WILFRED B. W. MARTIN
University of New Brunswick, Fredericton

The issue of control over the school program (curriculum) is by no means a new one. Its present significance can be readily appreciated when one realizes that what is taught in the school has important implications for the future of society. As noted in this book, the newer models of control of the school program are exemplified by greater centralization and bureaucratization, greater involvement by the courts, greater influence exerted by the federal government, and a greater part played by teachers' unions in the development and implementation of the school program.

Professor van Geel uses the principles that have counted in the allocation of authority in education (paternalism, the rights of parents, state and national interests, liberty and democracy, principle of affected interests, no delegation of legislative power, community control, equality, efficiency and effectiveness, and keeping education out of politics) to assess the patterns for school governance. The governing structure for controlling educational programs is analyzed in terms of a variety of tasks including establishing minimum standards, determining the content of courses, determining the political and cultural bias of courses, setting up pupil classification systems, and exempting students from courses. The societal implications of control over these and related tasks are not covered here.

This is a well-documented book on the control of educational programs in the United States. Statutes, regulations, and court cases are analyzed in assessing the legal authority of the federal government, the courts, boards of education, teachers, and parents in public and private schools. The author has done an admirable job in detailing the complexities concerning who has the authority to control the school curriculum, and his book will become a useful point of reference in this regard.

Issues in Secondary Education: The Seventy-Fifth Yearbook of the National Society for the Study of Education, Part II, edited by WILLIAM VAN TIL. Chicago: University of Chicago Press, 1976. 350 pp. $12.00 cloth.

AUDREY JAMES SCHWARTZ
University of Southern California

Efforts to expand educational opportunities have brought more homogeneity than diversity to public schooling. Rather than change secondary schools, reforms seem to extend existing practices to larger proportions of American youth. An illustration of this is the massive consolidation of school districts since 1950 in which 100,000 separate districts merged into 20,000 larger ones, each with standardized education. Some contemporary movements also equate sameness with equity. For example, arguments before courts for resource equalization across districts and to legislatures for "mainstreaming" disadvantaged students frequently presume that life chances are best provided by identical educational experiences.

The twelve contributors to this handbook believe that secondary schools should offer more options; although uncritical of past or even present education, these university educators argue that contemporary times demand educational change. Van Til expresses this pervasive theme in his introduction: "has there ever been a time in human history when the surrounding social realities so threatened mankind's very survival?" and "In a time of disillusion and cynicism following the Watergate Horrors, what an awesome task confronts American secondary education . . ." (pp. 16–17). That these concerns are graver than those of other generations is disputable, but the notion that schooling should be different has broad support within, and outside, the Academy.

The authors call for educational goals which teach the individual how to cope with crises. Their preferred tactic for school reform is *pluralism*: pluralistic programs and curricula since school goals should be pluralistic; pluralistic settings for education since alternative environments provide greater linkages with society; and pluralistic teaching strategies since all children do not learn in the same way.

These essays are addressed to lay readers as well to professionals. They are filled with definitions, classifications, and descriptions of current educational practice and provide vast insight into the thinking of today's influential educators.

Family and Intimate Lifestyles

Mediterranean Family Structures, edited by J. G. PERISTIANY. New York: Cambridge University Press, 1976. 414 pp. $32.50 cloth.

PANOS D. BARDIS
Toledo University

The author of Joshua called it "the great sea" (15:12); and Herodotus, the father of ethnography, who flourished in the fifth century B.C., described some of the most fascinating social institutions of the Mediterranean Sea. But the first scholar to write scientifically about the great cultures of this magnificent crucible of human progress was Ibn Khaldun (1332–1406) who, in his *Al-Muquaddimah,* dealt with social phenomena by means of *umran,* the science of civilization.

Since then, myriad authors have studied every aspect of Mediterranean social institutions and given us interesting and valuable accounts of the genesis, development, maturity, decline, and death of these social systems. One of these studies, *Contributions to Mediterranean Sociology,* which appeared in 1968, was edited by J. Peristiany, the editor of the volume under review.

In his new volume, Peristiany, of the Social Research Centre in Cyprus, presents twenty original studies based on field research and organized geographically. These studies are social-anthropological and investigate the family systems in ten Mediterranean countries: Spain, Italy, Yugoslavia, Albania, Greece, Turkey, Israel, Lebanon, Tunisia, and Morocco. Actually additional geographical areas are covered, since many family practices are also found beyond the aforementioned ten nations. For instance, "incestuous" marriage to the daughter of one's father's brother has been observed among Arab-Berbers, as well as in certain Christian communities. The volume, which stresses three main themes—methodological issues, the nature of the family, and the influence of social change on the family institution—is intended for professional persons specializing in Mediterranean cultures and for those interested in social relations in general.

Some of the contributors' findings suggest that the extended family is vanishing; that polygyny is rapidly becoming obsolete; that family privacy is gaining ground at the expense of public elements; and that patriarchy is declining, while woman's social status is rising. More importantly, as one scrutinizes this book, one is reminded of Wilbert Moore's concept of global society. Indeed, many behavior patterns are common to the Mediterranean cultures, rising and emerging everywhere like the cerulean, sapphirine waves of "the great sea" and the golden-maned, brazen-hoofed horses of Poseidon.

Two of the most interesting contributions are those by Tullio Tentori and Carmelo Lisón-Tolosana. The former describes the evolution of the family in Matera, a south Italian town of 40,000 people. Up until a few years ago, the lower classes lived in "caves dug into the rocks of a canyon. . . . Each cave was inhabited by one family, composed of a married couple and all their unmarried children. A cave was usually only a single room" (p. 273). The family donkey stayed in the back of the cave, the chickens under the beds, and the pig wherever it pleased. Lison-Tolosana's study explores the relations among family types, moral codes, and inheritance practices in Galicia, Spain. He thus refers to what he terms "the ecological background of morality" (p. 305).

Edited volumes such as this are usually marred by eight weaknesses: emphasis on breadth at the expense of depth, omission of important subjects, inconsistent theoretical interpretations, methodological chaos, lack of synthesis by the editor, stylistic heterogeneity, careless translations, and arbitrary transliterations. This work, however, is much above average in most respects. Peristiany's own introduction is brilliant. But why does eta become both y and e in the same sentence on p. 358? And why is the diphthong ei transliterated differently in two consecutive lines on p. 401?

Finally, I wish the index included authors, too, and the price were not astronomical!

Changing Family Patterns in the Arab East, by EDWIN TERRY PROTHRO and LUTFY NAJIB DIAB. Beirut: American University of Beirut Press, 1974. 240 pp. $10.00 cloth.

MOHAMED EL-ASSEL
San Diego State University

Many will undoubtedly share the sentiment of one of the authors when he states: "In reading on the subject of the family, I was surprised to find that there has been 'far more systematic field research among the Bantoid people of Africa' than among the peoples of Arabic Islam, one of the world's major cultures" (p. vii). *Changing Family Patterns in the Arab East* is a very much welcomed contribution to a long neglected area of knowledge, namely, the sociological and anthropological aspects of the Arabic Islamic family, particularly in the Arab Levant, which includes the countries of Lebanon, Syria, Jordan.

The book is more than a simple survey of the state of the Arabic Islamic family of the Levant. Rather, it is, as the title justifiably implies, an empirical study of the changes in family life in that part of the world. The authors secured an overall total of 1,944 interviews from four of the largest cities in the area (Aman, Jordan; Beirut and Tripoli, Lebanon; and Damascus, Syria) as well as two villages, one Lebanese and the other Jordanian. Aside from being a demanding undertaking and quite an accomplishment in that part of the world, these interviews provided data about the state of the Arabic Islamic family for at least two generations. By combining and comparing these data with data compiled from a variety of other sources including records of religious courts, census reports, statistical abstracts, as well as finding of other studies, the authors were able to provide meaningful comparisons of various aspects of family life in the area across five decades, viz, before 1930, the 1930s, the 1940s, the 1950s, and the 1960s. A variety of changes were therefore ascertained in an array of family aspects such as courtship, engagement, age at marriage, duration of marriage, divorce, polygyny, residential patterns, religious observance, decision-making, recreation, education, employment, as well as changes in the role and status of women.

The book is detailed and thorough. It is well researched and well documented, and includes an elaborate bibliography, more than 130 entries, which makes it also an excellent reference book. Its findings confirm some previously established notions, but is also dispels many misconceptions. For example, the authors conclude that "the myth of the Arab male divorcing casually and callously on his slightest whim is hardly compatible with what we know of marriage courts" (p. 178). "Indeed, in some courts, the wife is recorded as requesting the divorce in a *majority* of cases" (p. 187). "Polygyny was found to be rare and becoming rarer" (p. 187). Child brides have long disappeared, although grooms' age did not change much over the years. Before 1930 the average age of brides ranged from fourteen to eighteen and the age of the husbands of these women ranged from twenty-one to thirty. In the 1960s, the corresponding ages ranged from seventeen to twenty-two for women and twenty-four to thirty for men (pp. 30–31).

All in all, the book is too rich with data and supporting evidence. So much so, in fact, that it will certainly give a respectable dose of mental indigestion to the reader who is not versed in reading reports which are incessantly cluttered with tables. For example, almost half the text consists of tables—103 tables reported in 99 pages of total text of 210 pages. The reader will undoubtedly find some tables very useful and enlightening; but that many is sheer clutter. Many could be omitted or simply appended. Only authors' obsessions or lack of editorial help, or both, would result in the inclusion of that number of tables as part of the text in a book of this sort. Certainly, this will not make the book appealing to lower-division college students or to the general reader.

Aside from that, the book is valuable indeed for professionals, experts, or serious students of the family, the Middle East, or social change. It is an original, well documented, and solid work.

Momism: The Silent Disease of America, by HANS SEBALD. Chicago: Nelson-Hall Publishers, 1976. 318 pp. $8.95 cloth.

DAVID KENT LEE
California State University, Sacramento

A new disease is abroad in our land, albeit a silent disease, and its name is "Momism." It is a bad disease—Sebald has nothing good to say about it; in fact, one is struck by the many pejorative terms he uses in describing "Momism." It is of recent origin, not going back much beyond two generations, and it appears mainly in the American middle-class, as a result of urban-industrial factors.

"Momism" is the unconscious process in which a neurotic mother rears a neurotic child, usually a son. The mother's neurosis centers on her need to live through the child and her inability to grant him emotional and intellectual independence. The main technique she employs is conditional love. The neurosis that the child manifests in adulthood is characterized by immature emotions, extreme dependence, and a strong need to be guided and approved. It is not apparent to the casual observer, and thus Sebald calls it "the silent disease."

With the continuing development of urbanization and industrialization, modern homemakers spend less time on menial tasks and thus have more freedom and time to spend with their children. Urban-industrial developments have also brought about the small, individually-oriented nuclear family with fewer members available to rear children. These developments set the stage for the emergence of the specialized role of Mother and the associated "Motherhood Myth," which not only glorifies being a mother, but mystifies it as well.

For many mothers, rearing children becomes a project which primarily involves the "manufacture of personality," carried out with the advice of legions of child-rearing experts. "Producing" a child is seen by Sebald as a way in which women can partake of the glories of successful work and thereby experience self-realization. Women's liberation enters into all this by promoting not only equality, but the desire to create and achieve. Other opportunities not being readily available in our sexist society, child production, in which the child is an object, becomes the vehicle whereby many American mothers can satisfy their desires to achieve.

Much of what Sebald has to say in this book is not new, but in fairness to him, it should be pointed out that he makes no claim to that effect, but instead describes the major contribution of his work as an integrating of separate ideas and observations into a coherent picture of "momism." Insofar as this is the major goal of the book, Sebald has done a satisfactory job; however, he also claims that, "the primary purpose of the book . . . is to analyze and diagnose Momism" (p. 239). With respect to these tasks, Sebald's work is less satisfactory. His analysis is adequate, but it might have been improved had he not neglected the excellent structural analyses of Rose Laub Coser and Philip Slater in this area of investigation.

Teenage Marriages: A Demographic Analysis, by JOHN R. WEEKS. Westport, Conn.: Greenwood Press, 1976. 171 pp. $13.75 cloth.

JOHN KANTNER
Johns Hopkins University

This is not so much a study of teenage marriage as it is a study of reproduction among females aged fifteen-nineteen. "The crux of the question of early marriage lies in the birth of children" (p. 4). If there are no children, inside or outside of marriage, the social and personal problems, concern over which motivates this study, would vanish. It would have been more satisfactory and a good deal less confusing to address the main problem—teenage fertility and its consequences—with marital condition treated as a significant part of the context in (or out of) which children are born and nurtured. But that could not have been done with the approach taken here which was to select a marriage cohort, 1966 marriages in California, and match these marriages with births registered in California from 1965 to 1969. The result of this approach and a major limitation of the study, is that fertility that occurs to teenage females who have never been married—and that's the greater part of teenage fertility—does not come into the picture. Ordinarily, I would not criticize a study for not being something other than it purports to be but since the argument is made that fertility is the important thing to study, that teenage marriage per se is less important, then it must be recognized that this way of going about it provides only a pinched view of the subject.

Over one-fifth of the text is devoted to a discussion of the record linkage which by linking marriage to vital events provides the basic data for the study. Two different matching schemes are described, one of which obtains a substantially higher proportion of matches (from 19 to 115 percent better depending on the type of case). One would assume that the analysis would be based on the matching scheme which secured more matches (the author gives several reasons apart from relative performance why one is the better scheme) but this is nowhere indicated. In one of the infrequent tables to provide N's, the totals derived from the inferior matching procedure are shown! If this is not an error (the book is full of them) and the analysis is based on those cases which were obtained as the result of an admittedly poor matching procedure, what do we have? Certainly not a valid sample of the vital events which occurred to 1966 California marriages let alone a valid treatise on teenage marriages. Moreover, out of state marriages are not included in the analysis and for a study of California marriages this is potentially a very large problem (for Easter readers—Washoe County, Nevada lies adjacent to California) because of the selective bias that almost certainly is involved. Fortunately, for the study of teenage marriages in California this appears to be less of a problem than it would be for a study of all marriages since the Reno-Sparks area is less accessible to them for marrying and unmarrying than it is for more affluent adults.

The book is the despair of any reader who worries when data manipulations are not clearly described. For example, the exposition of such a crucial matter as estimating the populations at risk of birth or divorce is quite unsatisfactory and is not helped by tables which are improperly titled and labelled, misnumbered, without indicated sources and, in one instance, even placed in the wrong chapter. Without doubt this is one of the most poorly proofed volumes I have ever examined. On top of this are a number of erroneous and dubious interpretations which do nothing to inspire confidence in the reader. A shame, too, since a lot of hard work went into preparing the data for analysis.

Much of the problem appears to lie in a lack of precision in language and thought. For example, an increase in the percentage of married teenagers who "had borne a first child within twelve months after marriage" (p. 25) is "generally accounted for by the increases over time in the number of brides who have borne an illegitimate child prior to marriage" (p. 26). That of course is the very best time for bearing illegitimate children but beyond that is the logical contradiction in the explanation. Turns out that while his statement is erroneous he was on the trail of the correct explanation when he was unhorsed by his language.

There is also scattered throughout much partial explanation which either fails to fit all the facts or else overlooks ready alternatives. To illustrate a case of the first type, take the explanation of the recent decline in teenage marriages as being due to the inflation of the 60s and 70s and the recession of the 70s (p. 16). This interpretation is followed immediately by a table which shows that while the percentage of married female teenagers did decline in those years, the percentages for males went up. Similarly, the assertion is made that *changes* in the proportion of married teenagers are related positively to *changes* in the rate of economic expansion (p. 17). When plotted, his data which cover the period from 1910 to 1920 are a text book illustration of a spurious relationship with the change from 1940 to 1950 accounting for all there is of a positive relationship. Or the statement that the 1972 liberalization of the California abortion law had an effect only on younger teenagers (15–17) "but had no appreciable effect overall for 18–19 year olds" (p. 30). The fact is, as his data show, that teenage fertility rates declined from 1972 to 1973 in California at each age. For older teenagers this represented a continuation of a downward trend; for younger teenagers (15 and 16) there was more of a kink in the curve but who's to say on the basis of such gross trends which was more affected by the change in the law?

Illustrations of conceptual haziness abound especially in Weeks's treatment of premarital conception and illegitimacy. He seems to forget that he is dealing with only married teenagers when he makes broad statements about premarital pregnancy among teenagers; he takes evidence on the timing of births after marriage as the basis for generalizations about the propensity of premaritally pregnant teenagers to resolve their problem via marriage; he overlooks abortion as a factor in accounting for differences among groups in the timing of postmarital births; he generalizes about the proportions of brides who were pregnant at marriage using data only for those who gave birth, and in similar fashion draws conclusions about the "chances of premarital conception" from those cases which were followed by marriage and the birth of a child; he makes statements about differences in premarital contraceptive effectiveness again from evidence from those who marry and have a child. I could not find a cautionary statement anywhere warning the reader that generalizations along these lines were severely limited by the nature of the data. The discussion proceeds without qualification on a plane of high generality.

There is, however, some interesting and valid material in the book relating to such things as the causes of infant death by age of mother and marital status at conception. Intriguing questions raised by the data are not pursued however. With respect to marital stability to which he devotes a chapter, Weeks presents data which challenge Winch's thesis that the correlation between marital instability and age at marriage is a function of premarital pregnancy since he finds that during the first thirty-six months of marriage at any rate, the arrival of a child is an equally destabilizing influence whether conceived before or after marriage. Age is more important than timing of the birth.

This is an exasperating book. One learns next to nothing about teenage marriages and what leads to them, and one has to pick carefully through the interpretations that are proffered relative to the consequences of early marriage. For some readers the most exasperating part could be the penultimate paragraph (the ultimate is an elongated period to the piece) which with no connection to anything that goes before argues that "future levels of unwanted teenage fertility . . . depend much more heavily upon the birth prevention motivation of women than of men. The equality of the sexes as well as the female-oriented direction of the family planning movement and of welfare services all place the onus of responsibility for preventing a birth much more on the woman involved than on the man" (p. 113). Alas.

Medical

Support Systems and Mutual Help: Multidisciplinary Explorations, edited by GERALD CAPLAN and MARIE KILLILEA. New York: Grune & Stratton, 1976. 325 pp. $19.50 cloth.

JONATHAN A. FREEDMAN
Hutchings Psychiatric Center and *Upstate Medical Center, Syracuse*

As funds get tighter in the human services, as the Carter administration looks for better ways to deliver mental health services, more professional interest is being paid to the natural and planned ways persons can support each other. Such support costs little or no public funds. In the last two years, special issues of journals, several books and articles, and multidisciplinary conferences have rediscovered how important support can be in aiding persons through life crises and that many support networks are flourishing without professional involvement.

Sociologists should take special note of this expansion of interest. Support systems rely upon bonds between persons organized into families, groups, organizations, or communities. Support systems aid people through rites of passage and can encourage persons to accept deviant labels and to work on changing public attitudes toward deviant groups.

This clearly written collection of the recent work of Harvard University's multidisciplinary Laboratory of Community Psychiatry will prove useful to the reader looking for a detailed introduction to support systems and peer self-help groups. For those who are already interested, there are reports of action-research involving work with single parent families, persons newly separated through divorce or widowhood, clergy, the mentally ill, and organizing civilian support systems during a war. Theoretical issues spotlighted include the family as a support system, religious support, going public, etc. Particularly useful is an interpretive conceptual bibliography by Marie Killilea that is the best overview of thinking on ways of viewing most support systems that this writer has discovered.

The Great Universe of Kota: Stress, Change and Mental Disorder in an Indian Village, by G. M. Carstairs and R. L. Kapur. Berkeley: University of California Press, 1976. 176 pp. $12.50 cloth.

Robert H. Lauer
Southern Illinois University, Edwardsville

This straightforward and well-written book reports a study that compared the prevalence and patterns of mental disorder in three communities in South India. The communities provided the researchers with a certain diversity in the context of a similar environment and culture. This, the authors argue, allows a "methodologically sound cross-cultural" study by avoiding such problems as comparable definitions of psychiatric symptoms between cultures with diverse languages. Whether one accepts the argument depends upon how one defines "cross-cultural." In any case, the authors have provided us with a useful comparative study that attempts to deal with certain well-known difficulties in trying to assess the prevalence of mental disorders in a society.

In addition to the difficulty of making definitions comparable across cultures, the authors identify two other problems which they have tried to overcome. One is the inadequacy of both the survey based on clinical assessment and the survey using a standard questionnaire. The clinical approach yields notoriously variable results, depending upon who does the evaluation, while the questionnaire approach (such as the Midtown Manhattan survey) neglects the respondents' definitions of their mental well-being or stress. The Kota study used a "structured interview" method which provided flexibility without impairing reliability. The interview schedule measured the presence or absence of 125 psychiatric symptoms. It was developed particularly for the South Indian area. The second problem attacked by the authors is the nature of psychiatric "need." It is difficult to get consensus among researchers as to when a psychiatric need (that is, the need for help) exists. In the Kota study, a need was defined as present if a respondent had one or more symptoms and had, in addition, either attempted to get help or had expressed an inability to cope or had manifested a diminishing ability to function in his or her social life (as measured by a "social functioning" questionnaire).

Substantively, the study largely supports the findings of previous research. The prevalence of psychiatric symptoms was significantly greater among women than among men; among those forty years of age and older than among those younger; among the lesser educated; among those defined as poor (this was true for males only); and among those living in a joint family than among those in a nuclear family. There were also caste differences. Three castes were included in the sample. The highest caste, the Brahmins, had the lowest prevalence of symptoms. Overall, 37% of the respondents had psychiatric symptoms. Those who had four or more symptoms, who had sought help, and who had expressed an inability to cope were classified as having the highest need for help. Six percent of the respondents fell into the highest-need group. The authors also combined the symptoms into categories and made some additional conclusions—e.g., women have a higher prevalence of somatic symptoms and are more likely than men to have multiple symptoms.

The sub-title of the book is somewhat misleading. Stress is inferred rather than measured, and change is only a minor concern. The authors do show a significantly higher prevalence of symptoms among women (but not men) who were involved in the change from the traditional matrilineal to a patrilineal pattern of residence and inheritance. The transition appeared to subject the women to insecurity and to the stress of coping with an unfamiliar and perhaps unsatisfactory mode of living. There was also a higher prevalence of symptoms among members of a caste whose social status was threatened by the rising fortunes of a previously inferior caste. These findings are congruent with others which indicate that change leading to altered patterns of interaction may increase stress and the prevalence of mental disorders.

One of the more valuable aspects of the book is the close attention given to the research process. In many ways, the book reads like a methodological diary. The authors are candid about their failures as well as their successes. They point out revisions they had to make in the midst of a pilot survey. They discuss the failure of one of their instruments; the questionnaire designed to measure social functioning did not differentiate between those with and those without psychiatric symptoms. They highlight the value of a pilot survey by listing seven things they learned from the survey.

Because of the effort to cope with methodological problems in psychiatric epidemiology and because of the detailed discussion of the research process, this book should be read by all those concerned with the study of mental disorders. We do not learn a great deal more about the patterns and prevalence of those disorders except that findings from Western nations are supported by and similar to findings in South India. Once again we are reminded that no society is immune from the problem of mental disorders. The rural Indians may have as great a need for psychiatric care as the Western urbanites. The authors conclude their work, therefore, by discussing how this need can be addressed in developing nations.

Self-Care: Lay Initiatives in Health, edited by LOWELL S. LEVIN, ALFRED H. KATZ, and ERIK HOLST. New York: Prodist, 1976. 133 pp. $8.95 cloth. $3.95 paper.

A Right to Health: The Problem of Access to Primary Medical Care, by CHARLES E. LEWIS, RASHI FEIN, and DAVID MECHANIC. New York: John Wiley & Sons, 1976. 367 pp. $17.95 cloth.

BEBE F. LAVIN
Kent State University

The authors of both these books address themselves to the problems of how and by what mechanisms the quality, availability, and access to primary medical care can be improved. Unlike the blind describing the elephant, which in this case is primary care, both sets of authors do agree as to the nature of the beast. Both describe it as an unresponsive structure, essentially undeterred by varied efforts made to produce an arrangement more accommodating to the needs of the public who use it. Where these books differ is in their perception of what can now be done. *Self-Care* promotes a new direction while *A Right to Health* suggests a reorganizing of several old ones.

Although both books are valuable reading for anyone concerned with resolving medical delivery problems, *A Right to Health* is more definitive. In particular, the eleven case studies describing major programs attempted as means to improve access to primary care, are excellent reviews, afford a consistent framework for evaluating such efforts, and a sense of what might work in the future.

Self-Care reflects the insights which Levin, Katz, and Holst garnered from discussion with twenty-six other social scientists, health administrators, physicians, and educators from various countries at a symposium held in 1975 at Copenhagen to evaluate the role of lay persons in the primary care process. The authors conclude that by adding lay persons to the process as partners with health expertise, there can be a remedy for some of the problems of health care delivery and, furthermore, that the signs are "green and go" for a self-care movement. They make several cogent arguments for increasing lay initiative in the medical system, arguments bolstered by prior research. For example, they point out that the professional care system has been only moderately efficacious in improving longevity or reducing morbidity. And, more to the point, much of health care is already self care. Primary care physicians, it is suggested, would do better to spend more of their effort in improving the health competency of lay persons, transferring certain skills to the laity. They believe, this would, in the long run, produce such advantages as a reduction in the costs of the present system as well as enhance the doctor-patient relationship by increasing the dignity and independence of the patient.

The development of self-help health groups as well as the popularity of "how to" books are limited evidence that consumers want a more active partnership in health care decisions. There is support for the idea that most lay people can do more to care for themselves when educated to do so, as with chronic illnesses. Perhaps the time is ripe for a self care movement, but what is not addressed is that for most populations health seems to have so little salience compared to other societal values (e.g., Goochman, D. S. *Journal of Health and Social Behavior,* 12, No. 2, June, 1971: 148–154). All three authors, as medical educators, have undoubtedly experienced the frustration of motivating people toward enlightened health care. Persistent cigarette smokers or unvaccinated children attest to the difficulty of changing people's life styles, and doctors may be less willing to try than medical educators.

Although the public may want more input into health decisions, it is doubtful if they are willing to take on what they and physicians have defined as the doctor's work role. One wonders if the latent effect of what these authors suggest would be to give professionals one more reason to blame consumers of health services for defects in the system if they fail to become "educated partners" in the process.

A Right to Health does not raise such problematic issues. It is rather an excellent compendium of what has been done in the past in the United States to resolve inequitable access to primary care and suggests how the past can enlighten future efforts. Access barriers suggested by these authors are those agreed to by most researchers: barriers inherent to the system, such as distribution of services, and those inherent to the consumer, such as sociocultural factors. A welcome addition is a framework useful for evaluating the point at which any program intervenes in the process to affect these barriers.

This book is a worthwhile attempt to chronicle resolutions for a major health system problem. The evaluations are critical, not polemical. The suggestions as to the future are refreshingly not "pie in the sky."

Psychiatrists and Their Patients: A National Study of Private Office Practice, by JUDD MARMOR. Washington, D.C.: American Psychiatric Association, 1975. 181 pp. $7.50 cloth.

The Psychiatric Hospital Today: A Quality Profile, by JOHN MULHEARN and GAYLE MOMENY. Cambridge, Mass.: Ballinger Publishing Company, 1976. 138 pp. $15.00 cloth.

Keeping Patients in Psychiatric Treatment, by CHAIM M. ROSENBERG and ANTHONY E. RAYNES. Cambridge, Mass.: Ballinger Publishing Company, 1976. 167 pp. $16.00 cloth.

JAN HANKIN
The Johns Hopkins University

These three books examine quite different aspects of mental health care, including psychiatrists in private office practice, structural characteristics of psychiatric hospitals, and patients who drop out of psychiatric treatment. Taken together, the books present useful data for persons involved in the delivery of mental health care.

Psychiatrists and Their Patients reports the results of a survey conducted by the Joint Information Service of the American Psychiatric Association. Questionnaires were mailed to a ten percent sample of all psychiatrists who reported spending fifteen or more hours per week in direct patient contact in their private offices. The response rate was 73%, representing 440 psychiatrists. The psychiatrists responded to queries about their practice, as well as data on the last ten consecutive patients seen in their office. Marmor summarizes the data on psychiatrists (including regional location, subspecialty, age, number of patients seen, number and duration of patient visits, and fees charged) as well as patient characteristics (including sociodemographic characteristics, psychiatric diagnosis, and psychiatric insurance coverage). Marmor finds that managerial workers and professionals are overrepresented in the patient population as compared to blue- and white-collar workers. Patients are more likely to be twenty-five to forty-five years old, and depending upon the type of practice, 50–59% female. The majority of patients were seen on a one-to-one basis. Marmor's discussion of the data is followed by commentaries by practitioners, researchers, and politicians.

While the Joint Information Service is to be commended for providing the first data on the content of private psychiatric practice, this study suffers from two serious methodological problems. First, by sampling psychiatrists engaged in fifteen or more hours of private practice, psychoanalysts were oversampled (29% of survey respondents versus 10% of all psychiatrists are analysts). Second, psychiatrists were asked to report on ten consecutive patients. Whether these patients are representative of all private psychiatric patients is very questionable. In addition, the reporting by the psychiatrist of patients' sociodemographic characteristics and psychiatric insurance coverage may be inaccurate. One of the reasons for undertaking the study was to provide information to planners of national health insurance concerning current psychiatric utilization patterns as well as data on psychiatric insurance coverage. However, given the aforementioned methodological problems, data on utilization and insurance must be cautiously interpreted. Thus, while the book provides valuable data on the content of private psychiatric practice, more systematic study of this mode of psychiatric practice is required.

The Psychiatric Hospital Today examines a different component of the mental health care delivery system. The data for this book were obtained from the Accreditation Survey of Psychiatric Hospitals conducted by the Accreditation Council for Psychiatric Facilities of the Joint Committee on Accreditation of Hospitals. Mulhearn and Momeny tell the reader everything you wanted to know about bathing facilities, living quarters, fire prevention equipment, staffing, medical records, and the like, in 366 psychiatric hospitals; the data merely reflecting the requirements for psychiatric hospital accreditation. These requirements relate to structural measures of quality of care, as opposed to measures of process and outcome. While the data on structural characteristics are unexciting, the authors do present some interesting differences between public, private, and Veteran's Administration psychiatric hospitals.

Mulhearn and Momeny are justly skeptical about the high compliance rates on structural characteristics which are reported by the hospitals: "While these high compliance rates no doubt reflect, for the most part, the real world, they reflect also, we suspect, the fact that most of the items are of such a fundamental nature that hospitals of necessity would respond affirmatively, even if it did imply the bending of reality to a greater or lesser extent (p. 80)." An interesting sequel to this book would be a comparison of reported compliance with actual compliance, as ascertained by the accreditation site visit teams.

In *Keeping Patients in Psychiatric Treatment,* the authors analyze a multitude of studies about dropping out of psychotherapy. They examine three correlates of leaving psychiatric care: patient related variables, therapists' characteristics, and treatment variables. In addition, Rosenberg and Raynes briefly discuss help seeking behavior and compliance. The summary chapter presents an interaction model to explain patient dropouts. This model needs additional theoretical development and, in its present form, is simplistic.

The book serves a useful function, as it collects the empirical evidence on the topic of keeping patients in treatment and also organizes the studies in a rational manner. However, the style of presentation is uneven. Study after study is cited, sometimes with little explanation of the research strategy employed. While the authors do discuss methodological problems, these issues are raised intermittently. The studies cited raise numerous questions, including: what are the difficulties in defining a dropout? How does the nature of the psychiatric illness affect dropping out? How does accessibility to psychiatric care influence the decision to stay in treatment? Rosenberg and Raynes, in their summary of previous research, thus point the way for the directions of future research.

These books analyze three separate components of the mental health care delivery system and demonstrate the difficulties and problems inherent in such research. Sociologists would do well to study these authors' techniques in order to develop improved theoretical and methodological approaches for the study of psychiatric sociology.

The Growth of Bureaucratic Medicine: An Inquiry into the Dynamics of Patient Behavior and the Organization of Medical Care, by DAVID MECHANIC. New York: John Wiley & Sons, 1976. 345 pp. $14.95 cloth.

MARSHALL W. MEYER
University of California, Riverside

One cannot read a book by David Mechanic without learning a great deal about medicine, about behavioral research on medical practice, and about ethical dilemmas confronting physicians, social scientists, and policy makers involved in medical care delivery. Consider the following observations by Mechanic:

—Even though most medical care is mundane (p. 19), its value is rarely questioned, except perhaps by social scientists (p. 21).

—"No system of care in the world is willing to provide as much care as people will use" (p. 315).

—Hence some form of rationing of medical services, whether by the market or by bureaucracies, is inevitable.

—Social class, social setting, and certain (typically middle class) attitudes predict the use of preventive medical practices rather well (chapter 10).

—Health maintenance organizations (e.g., prepaid group practices and foundations such as Kaiser Permanente) are more economical than fee-for-service arrangements, but patient satisfaction is lower (chapter 7), and physicians' perceptions of patients' complaints as trivial are much more frequent (chapter 6).

—Mechanic would like to see medical practice "based on a humane, social ethic and involving a greater sense of sharing and sacrifice. Numerous indications suggest that our society, and even our helping institutions are becoming more bureaucratic and less humane'' (p. 77).

There you have the dilemma in a nutshell. Society's infinite appetite for medicine creates demands for greater equality of services, hence the substitution of bureaucratic for market allocation of them. But bureaucratization of medical care breeds dissatisfaction among patients and physicians, and threatens to dehumanize the care of people in distress. Mechanic and his colleagues recognize this problem and, wisely, do not propose utopian solutions. Indeed, their greatest contribution may be in articulation of the complexities of the dilemma rather than in advocacy of a particular course of action. Clearly, they recognize that some inequity in the distribution of medical care is inevitable. Whether the market or public bureaucracies coordinate services, the middle class will almost always use more than its proportionate share.

Aside from the central theme of the book, bureaucratization of medicine, Mechanic touches upon several other issues of current concern. He is worried about the erosion of physicians' authority of which the medical malpractice crisis and human subjects review committees are but symptoms. (The adversary process, Mechanic reminds us, may be much cheaper than automatic compensation of victims of medical error.) He is concerned lest evaluation research focus too rigidly and conservatively on quantifiable outcomes of medicine and suggests that a broader view of evaluation will include the education of physicians in assessing their own performance. He is also skeptical of the impact of academic social science on public policy, noting that until social scientists move into advisory capacities in government, its effect will be mostly to shape public opinion rather than policy options available to decision makers.

I do have some reservations about *The Grown of Bureaucratic Medicine,* indeed important ones. First of all, neither Mechanic nor his colleagues have a consistent definition of bureaucratization. Sometimes size is the culprit; sometimes rules are; sometimes there are vague notions about organizational ponderousness. Second, the conception of organizational theory in the book is extremely narrow, limited basically to the work of Herbert Simon and Chris Argyris. Newer structural, as opposed to social-psychological, theories of organizations are overlooked almost entirely. Third, there is at several points in the book a naivete about the range of possibilities for organizing medical care. At the end of the book, Mechanic suggests a ''loosely organized administrative structure'' for national health insurance (p. 323). This is an open invitation to corruption as recent experience with Medicaid shows. Similarly, Mechanic favors regulation of biomedical experimentation, but regulation that is both simple and responsive to needs of patients as well as the research community. I think this a contradiction in terms. Finally, I find the system of references frustrating and irritating. Large numbers of footnotes are appended to each chapter and they do not give specific page references to the materials cited.

In sum, students of the sociology of medicine and of bureaucracy will find it hard to avoid Mechanic's *The Growth of Bureaucratic Medicine*. It is the work of a man who has mastered his field. The social policy and social research questions raised in this volume will be with us for a long while.

Schizophrenia: The Sacred Symbol of Psychiatry, by THOMAS SZASZ. New York: Basic Books, 1976. 237 pp. $10.00 cloth.

R. J. M. LAVIZZO-MOUREY
Boston College

This book is the outgrowth of an invitation to Szasz to speak before a group of Japanese psychiatrists and neurologists (in Tokyo, 1975). Szasz sat down to prepare a lecture, and had a book length manuscript by the time he finished ''rethinking'' his previous contributions. For persons unfamiliar with Szasz this is an excellent place to begin since the book is inadvertently a primer. It contains the essential Szasz, but substantively, little if anything that is new.

The book rambles but it is never boring. Szasz is a master of metaphor and analogy, and a vitriolic rhetorician who verbally excoriates his predecessors and peers (both establishmentarians and anti-psychiatrists). For example, Kraepelin, Bleuler, and Freud are referred to as ''conquistadors and colonizers of the mind'' (p. 22) because they uncritically accepted the concept of disease as the leitmotif for psychiatry. Laing, Cooper, and Esterson are characterized as closed minded religious zealots who are paternalistic toward, and contemptuous of, their patients (at Kingsley Hall) because they tried to destigmatize the status of being schizophrenic and did not charge for services (p. 65).

Szasz's unrelenting wrath is perhaps more justifiably directed at what he calls "scandals" of psychiatry, e.g., the practice of prefrontal lobotomy as a "cure" for madness, and the so-called psychiatric "treatment" of dissidents in the Soviet Union. Szasz claims that "the greatest scientific scandal of our scientific age . . . is . . . the ceaseless manufacture of disease names in psychiatry, together with a total lack of evidence that any of them—from agoraphobia to schizophrenia—are caused by demonstrable brain lesions on the model of paresis" (p. 190). How was this possible?

Szasz suggests that the medical perspective on schizophrenia has been fashionable because (inter alia) "no other model of comparative scope and power has been offered for it. Nor indeed could such a superior model possibly be offered" (p. 141). To the reviewer this seemed a rather curious statement since Thomas Scheff's work (which temporally parallels Szasz's work) indeed outlines a basically sociological model of the phenomenon of madness (including "schizophrenia") that rivals a strict medical perspective. Why does Szasz choose not to mention Scheff's work? Szasz claims that he is not a believer in social science which he refers to as "fake science" (p. 203), but Szasz's quarrel with the medical perspective is fundamentally consistent with the labeling perspective on mental illness!

If a thesis is discernible at all it would have to be the eclectic synthesis of Szasz's previous work. Stated most generally: madness is not a disease, it is a form of social deviance. This, as adumbrated in his previous work, is certainly not news to sociologists. Specifically, Szasz maintains that mental illness is a myth, and there can be no such thing as a mental *disease*. Szasz's conception of psychiatric evils includes: institutional or bureaucratized psychiatry which is coercive—involuntary hospitalization is tantamount to imprisonment. Involuntary hospitalization and involuntary treatment of individuals accused of being "mentally ill" is to shut away and punish persons who become unbearable nuisances to others (p. 124).

Szasz's vision of psychiatry's mission can be stated as follows: Many of us suffer from ethical dilemmas. These ethical dilemmas, or problems in living are problematic enough for some adults to voluntarily seek out psychiatric help on a fee for service basis. A contract should be entered into between a client and a practitioner (psychiatrist)—a relationship tenable so long as the client consents (p. 49).

But even if one agrees in principle with this program, there are very serious and very real problems that remain. Therapy is not cheap. Szasz's model of what psychiatry should be, completely limits psychiatry to treatment of those few who can afford to pay. The poor cannot pay and Szasz dislikes third party payments which introduce the evils of bureaucracy (etc.) into the relationship. So what can be done for someone who most assuredly has problems in living but cannot afford to seek psychiatric help? What about people who become nuisances (yet break no laws) and do *not* want psychiatric help—regardless of ability to pay? It is laudable to try and protect individuals from being scapegoated by their families and close "friends." But it is much easier for outsiders to say "be more tolerant!" than it probably is for the family to try and live with someone who exhibits much bizarre behavior. How would Szasz's model of private, voluntary (upper middle class) psychiatry answer such questions? These issues are not broached in this book.

In conclusion, this highly readable book would be most useful to persons unfamiliar with sociological criticism of medical dominance in the conceptualization and treatment of madness.

Methods

Causal Modeling, by HERBERT B. ASHER. Beverly Hills: Sage Publications, 1976. 80 pp. $3.00 paper.

ROBERT B. SMITH

ABT Associates, Inc.
Cambridge, Massachusetts

This paper is one in the Sage Publication series: Quantitative Applications in the Social Sciences. This series, designed for readers with a limited background in mathematics and statistics, aims to make quantitative analysis techniques more readily accessible. Given this goal, Asher's monograph is most successful. It is a simple and direct introduction to causal modeling as taught at the summer workshops of the Inter-university Consortium for Political Research. It explicates the Simon-Blalock technique for testing linkages, path analysis, and simple simultaneous equation models.

Asher's primary concern is with confirmatory, rather than exploratory, causal analysis techniques appropriate for measured interval variables. Consequently, his discussion of measurement error and applications to ordinal data is brief. His explication (pp. 44–45) of the meaning of the path coefficient does not remove all the ambiguity of this concept. His justification for treating ordinal variables as interval can be challenged.

Following the political scientist Donald Stokes's "Compound Paths in Political Analysis" (*Mathematical Applications in Political Science* V, pp. 70–92), Asher's exposition differs from those by sociologists in that he explicitly uses the technique of instrumental variables, and begins with nonrecursive models with reciprocal causation. He prefers these because they are more realistic and do not require uncorrelated residuals. His explication of Identification in Nonrecursive Systems (pp. 52–61), and the work as a whole, is an exemplary primer for more advanced texts.

Network Analysis: Studies in Human Interaction, edited by JEREMY BOISSEVAIN and J. CLYDE MITCHELL. The Hague: Mouton & Company, 1973. 271 pp. No price listed, cloth.

BENJAMIN D. ZABLOCKI
Columbia University

The first question that one may reasonably ask about this collection of readings is whether it is out of date. The book, published in 1973, is a collection of papers presented at a symposium organized by the Afrika-Studiecentrum at Leiden in 1969. So much has happened in network methodology since 1969 that it would be easy to presume that no paper from this period could have other than historical interest to the contemporary sociologist.

Although I would certainly not recommend using this book as a basic text in a course in network analysis, it is not true that this book may be safely neglected by researchers currently working with networks. While considerably more powerful analytic tools have been developed in the last five years, the trend of methodological development in the field has not been well-grounded in empirical research and has been increasingly concerned with the analysis of local structure as opposed to total structure. Such emphases are an almost inevitable result of reasonable attempts to bring statistical rigor to a perspective that has evolved from such diverse origins. The American literature, on the whole, is seriously deficient in examples of the problems that occur in adapting network techniques to specific empirical settings.

There are notable exceptions of course. The writings of Edward Laumann are only the most prominent example. But for a sense of the richness of settings to which network analysis might be profitably applied, one could do no better than to consult this collection of readings edited by Boissevain and Mitchell.

It is important to recognize that most of the collected readings stem from the British tradition of social anthropology rather than the American tradition of sociometry. These two traditions came to the investigation of relationships as fundamental units of analysis from diametrically opposed directions. The social-anthropological tradition discovered networks in its flight from the reification of group level properties and in recognition of the fact that individuals derive their identities from multiple group memberships. Sociometry, on the other hand, was developed by researchers rejecting the reification of the individual as the fundamental unit of survey analysis, recognizing that individuals take on different identities as parts of different relationships. The sociometric tradition has, therefore, had little to say about such things as norms, ideologies, and other emergent properties of collective life.

The most valuable papers in the volume from this theoretical perspective are those of Mitchell and Van Velzen. The latter of these, although not grouped with the other theoretical papers in part one, is still one of the best available statements of the relationship between coalition theory and the network perspective.

The empirical papers are grouped in parts two and three of the book. The presentations by Cubitt, Kapferer, Trouwborst, and Boissevain contain material which is somewhat dated. It is, however, still worthwhile to scan these papers in order to get a sense of the diversity of problems to which network analysis has been applied.

The paper by Jongmans, "Politics on the Village Level," seems to me to be the outstanding empirical contribution of the volume. Without having any of the more recent computational techniques at his disposal, Jongmans was able to ransack the contents of his network matrices in a way which makes this paper a classic of its kind. The notion of the network matrix as a rich bank of potential inferences about the population, which is at the heart of Jongmans's approach, is perhaps the most important single contribution which the social-anthropological tradition has to make to American researchers.

In summary I would argue that this book is a valuable but not indispensible reference volume for American sociometricians. It is important for students to be exposed to the social-anthropological tradition of network analysis, and, although there are a number of ways to gain this exposure, reading this book may be the most convenient.

Experimenting with Organizational Life: The Action Research Approach, compiled by ALFRED W. CLARK. New York: Plenum Press, 1976. 259 pp. $25.00 cloth.

RUTH A. SCHWARTZ
New York University

Experimenting with Organizational Life is a collection of sixteen essays written to enhance the social scientists' understanding of the "Action Research Approach." This approach, which had its origins in the Human Relations school of social science, is concerned with expanding the base of social science knowledge, as well as assisting organizations undergo planned change.

Clark has divided the book into two parts, with the first part covering the history of action research, as well as highlighting some of the conflicts faced by researchers in their relationships with their clients and the social science establishment. In addition, some attention is paid to the ways in which the researcher can maximize the potential for collaboration with the client.

The second part provides detailed descriptions of the action research process at work. Through the use of case studies, the articles describe the properties of the distinct client-practitioner systems, highlighting their differences (i.e., environment, goals, needs), as well as their potential for collaboration, with particular emphasis placed on the role played by the mediator in these proceedings.

In particular, emphasis is placed on the means which can be used to reduce the incompatibility between action and research: "by heightening awareness of design properties, types of scientific contribution, and varieties of valid and useful data" (p. 117).

The majority of these articles were either written specifically for this volume or are based on papers read at conferences held during the early 1970s.

Despite the wide variety of theoretical and empirical articles included in this collection, there is a weakness in the methodological distribution, with only the case method being used. This is unlike other excellent readers in the sociology of organizations (cf. Grusky and Miller, Heydebrand) which have included a variety of methods, including comparative analysis, laboratory studies, organizational analysis, participant observation, and secondary analysis.

The case-study method has two shortcomings: (1) it emphasizes the individual in organizations, as opposed to the organizations' relation to its external environment; and (2) it generalizes from the particular, without there being any justification for doing so.

In addition to the lack of methodological diversity, the sections are not sufficiently broken down. I would have preferred to see separate sections dealing with the empirical, theoretical, and historical nature of the field, as well as with the type of organization studied, i.e., industrial or governmental.

These shortcomings, as well as its high price make this book a poor choice as a major text for courses in methodology or the sociology of organizations, but would be useful to have as a desk copy for reference purposes.

Political

Revolution, by JEAN BAECHLER. New York: Barnes & Noble Books, 1976. 208 pp. $15.50 cloth.

JOHN LEGGETT
Livingston College/Rutgers University

In fields as contentious as the sociology of revolution, an analyst must precisely state: (1) the problem under investigation, (2) theory and evidence, (3) counter-theory and counter-evidence, and (4) the connection between concern and relevant current events. Here we would expect a French writer to discuss the relationship between his theory and the Indo-Chinese War, the Post-World War II Madagascar Insurgency, The Battle of Algiers, the larger Algerian Revolution and the Paris events of May, 1968.

The problem addressed by the writer is by no means clear. Is it the "study of all methods of challenging the social system" mentioned on page one, or is it the palace-political-total-distinction advanced by him with several amendments on page ninety-two? The author never chooses one or the other, observing now suicide, later mafia machinations and finally multiple forms of revolution. Perhaps because of this scatter-shot approach, the writer develops a new theory every chapter and predictably concludes with "The way I conceived and wrote this book made it impossible for it to end in a firm conclusion" (p. 205).

The firmest statement on what the book is about can be found in the preface and chapter 4. There his Paretian theory explicitly incorporates some of Marx's assumptions and purportedly attacks some of Marx's weaker points. The writer agrees with Marx that social classes both exist and struggle. But he parts from Marx's alleged assumptions that "struggle necessarily leads to a revolution" and that "revolution is a good thing" (p. 131). Were Marx alive to witness Baechler's simplification, Karl would revise his oft quoted condemnation of simplistic dogmatic Marxism—"Above all, I am not a Marxist"—to read that most certainly he is not a Paretian but a Parisian—perhaps even a Berliner. How could Baechler reduce Marx's theory on revolution to four propositions and expect to get away with it?

For struggle to lead to successful revolution, argues Baechler, the ruling class must be divided. Why this fissure should develop commands our respectful attention for a goodly portion of that fourth chapter. The author indicates the multiple sources of elite disintegration. These causes range from inability of the elite to fulfill promises associated with military success to the frustrations and angers common to both the elite and the masses following a disastrous war.

Certainly, the origins of elite disunity are often neglected by armchair Marxists, as they do spend entirely too much time on the falling rate of profit, rates of exploitation, the organic composition of capital and like considerations to the exclusion of elite failure of nerve.

However much, as is often the case amongst current-day Marxists, the writer also weakens on matters of evidence. He refuses to develop a valid method. He prefers instead to use numerous illustrations and endless typologies to convince the readers of propositions concocted. That just won't do. Brief stories and strings of definitions aren't enough. Tempted to count the hundreds of ideal types set forth by Baechler, this reviewer settled instead for this observation: the writer too frequently skipped the stage of evidence, offered another pantheon of types, cited fascinating illustrations and concluded with what he had earlier assumed to be the case.

Perhaps it was another approach (this time more empirical and systematic and hence more tedious to the author) that most irked Baechler when in the preface he reviewed caustically James Davies's "J Curve Theory" on revolution. Certainly Davies's theory is open to criticism on the necessity of elite willingness to abdicate for a successful revolution. However, the author's citation of Davies's weaknesses does not constitute justification for the introductory section's omission of Marx and the book's later bowdlerization of Marx's writings. Nor was Marx the only alternative theorist mishandled.

What's missing are the observations of Lenin and Trotsky on the question of upper class abdication and associated revolutionary translation of events into the seizure of state power. After all, Lenin did dissect *all* those not yet on his side with the strategic intent to convert, neutralize, or isolate. And much as Malaparte noted in a work favorably cited by Baechler, Trotsky did write at length about a St. Petersburg confrontation between street-marching revolutionaries and wavering military personnel to demonstrate the conditions under which sections of the elite had not only abdicated their power but had gone over to the revolution. Shortly thereafter Trotsky again sensed failure of elite nerve when he led the October seizure of St. Petersburg power by first shutting off everyone's utilities! After he got by with that one, Clausewitz's most apt pupil successfully sought to win the battles of War Communism, especially on matters of transport and military hardware repair, through the enlistment of thousands of former Czarist military officers! Either the author is unaware of *What Is To Be Done, The Russian Revolution,* and *My Life,* or he has deliberately omitted relevant information, in which case there are problems. Further, if he is to oversimplify and/or omit the observations of Edwards, Brinton, Meusel, Marx as well as talented Bolsheviks and Mensheviks, surely the author must counter-attack with more than Konrad Lorenz on inherent aggressiveness.

Despite the book's occasional reference to matters French, such as the alleged irrelevance of matters economic for the origins of the French Revolution, the book suffers from absence of a pertinent French scan of current events. There is little or less than little on the 1912–75 Indo-Chinese war, the Madagascar massacre willfully conducted by the post World War II French elite, and the tortures and murders of Algerian revolutionaries. In each case the anti-imperialists won despite the initial and obvious presence of imperialist cohesion and nerve. In each case the French elite had retained the zest to kill until it had become obvious that the revolutionaries were going to win. Whereupon a growing number of the French elite came to prefer a compromise with the revolutionaries to prolongation of a hopeless war. During the revolutions themselves, it was not the failure of elite nerve that gave rise to revolutionary victories, but the prior military successes which helped to create loss of colonial élan. And these insurgent victories stemmed in part from strategic directions propounded by Benn Bella, Mao, Ho, and Giap. Witness the brilliant combination of theory, practice, and measurement realized at Dien Bien Phu. That was a chess game which yielded results that went well beyond the author's footnoted arrogance:

> Book VI of Clauseuitz's *On War,* entitled 'On Defence,' contains the definitive theory of this type of war. It is impossible, with the best will in the world, to find the slightest trace of new theoretical material in the military writings of Mao Tse-tung or Vo Nguyen Giap (p. 99).

For revolutionary theory derived not only from great nineteenth century writers such as Clausewitz but the lessons of numerous military defeats suffered by the guerilla revolutionaries themselves, as Frantz Fanon observed. Not so strangely, Baechler *ignores* this revolutionary French West Indian on every question, including his dictum on the need for guerilla warriors to murder the colonizer as part of his/her personal, and hence revolutionary, liberation from centuries of colonizer cultivation of self-hate. The Fanon omission no doubt stemmed from Baechler's repeated disdain for revolutionary force. Still, the reader legitimately wonders how and when might colonized murderous violence promote a decline in colonial cohesion?

His personal bias against Fanonesque revolutionary theory notwithstanding, the author's promised next book must not only state precisely the book's concern and pertinent types but carefully specify alternate theory. From there he must move beyond his present rejection of systematic evidence to all-inclusive data collection in order to do battle with theories he rejects.

Fists and Flowers: A Social Psychological Interpretation of Student Dissent, by ALICE ROSS GOLD, RICHARD CHRISTIE, and LUCY NORMAN FRIEDMAN. New York: Academic Press, 1976. 204 pp. $11.50 cloth.

PETER M. NARDI
Pitzer College/The Claremont Colleges

The current mood on college campuses belies the tumultuous events during the late 1960s. The political climate, the educational issues, and the social events of the time dramatically converged and were made manifest through the actions of so-called campus radicals. Much has been written about those days and events, but until *Fists and Flowers* relatively little has been said about the participants who were energetically involved.

What Gold, Christie, and Friedman do is report their findings from several surveys conducted during and around the 1968 Columbia University protests. Armed with a ninety-item questionnaire containing Machiavellian-type scales and newly constructed New Left items, the researchers sought out information to answer the question about who becomes radicalized and under what conditions.

Data collection occurred over a two year period and involved the class of 1972, a one year follow-up survey, subsample interviews two years after entrance, and a variety of samples for comparative purposes which included community colleges, a counterculture group, police, construction workers, high school students, New York City adults, and so forth. Several other pilot studies and surveys were also conducted. In fact, the variety of samples and surveys used is both a major weakness as well as a major strength of the book. The comparative data and the admirable testing of alternative hypotheses lend support to the findings, yet it becomes the most confusing aspect of the research. Often it is not clear what sample is being discussed or which survey is being used (the ninety item version or the shortened sixty item form or the revised sixty item version), or why one particular group is being compared to the Columbia students. There is also quite a bit of post hoc rationalization of the numerous non-significant results.

However, one of the major findings that does seem to emerge from this study that contradicts previous work on radical students is the relatively little contribution of familial background variables. Although there was some relationship between politically active parents and sons' activism (no explanation is given as to why daughters weren't studied in this part), family status did not play a major role in the later stages of the New Left movement. According to the findings, existence in two separate peer subcultures (tastes in music, reading, and other life style variables) and the friendship patterns that emerged were better indicators of radical involvement than the demographic variables (sex, social class, religion, academic major, etc.) traditionally associated with dissident students.

Despite attempts to relate these specific findings to a generalized theory of radicalization and to update the study in a cursory "where-are-they-now" concluding page, this remains simply a correlational survey of 1968 Columbia students. It certainly adds to our store of social psychological correlates of radicalism, but it contributes little new to our knowledge of social psychological theory and socialization. As an historical look at a fairly selective and unique sample of college students at one point in time, *Fists and Flowers* gives a data-oriented person much information. But as a source for better understanding present-day moods and political behaviors, the book is less successful.

Ideology and Utopia in the United States 1956–1976, by IRVING LOUIS HOROWITZ. New York: Oxford University Press, 1977. 464 pp. $17.95 cloth. $5.95 paper.

DORIS Y. WILKINSON
Macalester College

Horowitz is one of those rare perceptive and creative thinkers who makes sociology an enchanting intellectual endeavor. His writings are provocative, readable, and transcend the romantic and irreverent preoccupation with the quantitative ethic. This work, a highly informative compilation of stimulating essays published over a twenty year period, is augmented with pertinent up-to-date sociological commentary. From a dissection of Presidential Politics to a questioning of the End of Politics, this valuable reference encompasses an impelling excursion into class-race, ideological, sociological, and military politics. In contrast to his claims, the period 1956–1976 was one of unique historical importance. For as his essays demonstrate, it was during that epoch that issues of ideological polarization became openly pronounced, class and race perspectives and cleavages permeated the consciousness of America, presidential militarism gained a new momentum, assassination emerged as a mode of ultimate censorship, a phenomenon known as Watergate became an "apocalpytic event in American morality" (p. 46), ethnicity represented a tactical and definitional construct relating "more to sentiment than with science" (p. 59), and the new conservatism reflected "an attempt to anchor, the middle class to something more fundamental than the shifting sands of James's pragmatism" (p. 149).

"The Pluralistic Bases of Modern American Liberalism" (pp. 162–179) is a probing exposé of its rise and demise?! This new brand of liberalism *was* and *is* confronted with contradictions and challenges: "the desperate search for individuation in a mass society which has taken a distinctively nonliberal turn" (p. 174). It was threatened in 1968 by "American Radicalism and the Revolt Against Reason" (pp. 180–193).

Horowitz's dissection of sociological politics is revealing not only for what it asserts with respect to "social-science federal bureaucratic relations" (p. 274), but for its hints about the future governmental utility of the discipline. In contrast to the reasoning and commitment of the new civilian militarists, "the purpose of scientific inquiry is to arrive at accurate forecasts" (p. 313). Although the question is perhaps no longer pertinent, the laity may still be asking whether social science is actually a scientific endeavor.

It is in the final section that the historical and social science affinity and potency of this work are crystallized. In 1968 Horowitz reconceptualized conventional modes of translating deviance in the kaleidoscope of sociological epistemology. He prodded the community of abstract empiricists to consider that the conceptual differentiation between social deviance and political marginality represented an obsolete one. Citing examples of the fusion of deviance with marginality, he appears to obfuscate ideological persuasions of the Right with the "*behaviorism*" of rioters, the cosmological perspectives of freedom movement participants, and the expressive acts of the New Left. Moreover, assassination is much more than a deviant act. Conceptualizing it as deviance results in speaking of it euphemistically and hence inhibits focusing on causes and possible "cures."

The section on "The End of Politics?" (pp. 377–438) uncovers problems and prospects in the federal administrator-social scientist alliance, the middle class suburban basis of the ecology movement, and the maturation of American philosophy after posthypnotic shock of Third World expectations. Like Mills, Horowitz recognizes the linkage between character and social structure: "What takes place in the individual's life has major political ramifications in contemporary society" (p. 396). Overall, this is an enthralling and passionately portrayed chronicle. It provides an empathetic voyage into the thinking of an eminent sociologist. I strongly recommend it for those interested in the drama of political turbulence revolving around ideological convulsions between 1956 and 1976.

Politics and Class Formation in Uganda, by MAHMOOD MAMDANI. New York: Monthly Review Press, 1976. 339 pp. $16.50 cloth.

Class Struggles in Tanzania, by ISSA G. SHIVJI. New York: Monthly Review Press, 1976. 182 pp. $9.50 cloth.

JUDITH VAN ALLEN
University of California, Berkeley

In the last few years many studies have been done that apply dependency theory to Africa. One weakness of dependency theory in its original Latin American form was a tendency to ignore or underplay class formation and class conflict within dependent capitalist societies. These studies by Mamdani and Shivji are framed within dependency theory, but they are primarily concerned with elucidating the class bases of independence movements and post-independence class struggles.

Both authors are strongly interested in convincing their African and non-African readers of the legitimacy of applying Marxist analysis to Africa. Their most convincing argument is their ability to identify significant stratification within Ugandan and Tanzanian society—within rural and urban areas and within African and Asian (Indian) communities—and to make connections between various groups' class positions and their political action.

Mamdani and Shivji try to "unmask" conflicts that are experienced by their participants largely as religious and ethnic antagonisms, and to draw out the economic, or class, base of these conflicts. They see ethnic and religious divisions not as explanations for conflict (as they are often seen in conventional—or bourgeois—social science), but as themselves something to be explained. Thus, the Asian-African conflict that has led, in both countries, to expropriation of Asian property and extensive Asian emigration, and, in Uganda, to Asian expulsion, is explained by the history of economic conflict between Africans and Asians, in which Asian traders and businessmen served to extract surplus from Africans and accumulate it in the interest of the metropolitan bourgeoisie.

Shivji is more explicitly concerned than is Mamdani with practice as well as theory, and this unfortunately sometimes seems to lead him into substituting polemics for evidence. This tendency weakens his argument that the leading revolutionary force in Africa is the working class, not the peasantry. He is highly critical of the "labor aristrocracy" thesis, arguing that what is significant is not workers' income level but their strategic economic position and the potential radicalization produced by their daily contact with better paid non-African workers. But to support *this* thesis one would need a detailed analysis of the class position of the different sorts of "workers" and of their historical roles in nationalist and national liberation struggles. What we get is mainly Shivji's assertion that "There has been no example in Africa where the peasants have played a leading revolutionary role while the workers have sided with the dominating classes."

Mamdani's detailed and careful history of the formation of classes in Uganda from the pre-colonial period through the first years after Amin's coup is a more convincing application of Marxist analysis to Africa than is Shivji's fairly abstract and schematic analysis of post-independence Tanzania. Mamdani's work is solidly based in history, although a particular kind of history. In his words, "we de-emphasize psychology, for we seek to understand the social formation and not the individual personality, to write history and not biography." Both he and Shivji direct their analyses almost wholly to the objective material interests of their subjects. In Marxist terms, they have chosen not to deal with the cultural level. But what is needed to make the categories of class analysis "real" is to make connections between culture and economy, between people's experiential reality and their objective material interests.

It is different to be "petty bourgeois" in the United States than it is in an African society where the "petty bourgeoise" can take state power and act largely in its own class interest; it is different to be a "worker" in an advanced capitalist society and in an African society where there is little industry and the tiny sector of regular wage labor is economically privileged. These differences raise serious questions about the use of European-derived class terminology for Africa, and ignoring them is what gives rise to charges about the "imposition" of "foreign" ideas. When conditions differ, terminology should differ. New terms that capture the uniqueness of African class formations under dependent capitalism are needed, not the old terms loaded with European content and imagery.

Mamdani's and Shivji's major break with the old terms and concepts is in their use of "bureaucratic bourgeoisie" to identify the top stratum of government officials whose economic "base" lies in their control of government posts and policy and in their connections to the metropolitan bourgeoisie. Even this minor deviation from orthodox Marxist categories has met resistance from some Marxist critics. But if class analysis of African societies is to progress, what we need is more deviation.

The question of class is an extremely difficult one in Africa. These books are convincing in showing the relevance of class analysis for understanding African politics, even if the reader does not wholly accept the argument that all racial, ethnic, and religious cleavages can be explained by reference to class. They advance the dialogue about African class analysis, and should be read by anyone concerned with that dialogue.

The Rise of the Western World: A New Economic History, by DOUGLASS C. NORTH and ROBERT PAUL THOMAS. New York: Cambridge University Press, 1976. 171 pp. $11.95 cloth. $4.95 paper.

MICHAEL S. KIMMEL
University of California, Berkeley
and
WALTER GOLDFRANK
University of California, Santa Cruz

Within the past few years there has been a veritable renaissance of social scientists attempting to analyse the transition from feudalism to capitalism in Western Europe. The same sociologists who, a few years ago, were writing about the structure of dependency in Africa or the impact of multinational corporations in Chile are now arguing about the significance of the corn trade in sixteenth century Poland or the tensions between a centralizing state and a nobility oriented to decentralization in seventeenth century France. Actually, this is not as surprising as it first appears; the current search is a search for origins of those structures that have developed into the present capitalist world-economy. Further, there is a growing interest in the mechanisms of a transition between modes of production, as we seek a handle on the transition in which we find ourselves.

Douglass C. North and Robert Paul Thomas's recent book, *The Rise of the Western World: A New Economic History,* is another contribution, this time by two economists, to this growing body of literature. But while Perry Anderson and Immanuel Wallerstein (two of the better known groundbreakers in this field) have promised four volumes (and each a gargantuan effort), employing materials from a variety of sources (Anderson, for example, reads in at least nine languages), North and Thomas propose a theoretical alternative to *any* Marxist-informed model of the rise of the West in 158 pages and using only sources published in English. Despite their brevity and Anglo-centric bias, however, they have constructed an important model of the development of capitalist society.

The theoretical thrust of their model is that the ascendance of certain countries in Western Europe (England and the Netherlands) and the decline and/or stagnation of others (Spain and France) hinges on the institutionalization of property rights (so that individuals will be motivated to invest in enterprises that will promote growth) and the creation of an efficient economic organization to protect those individuals' investments and stabilize the market.

In order to present this theoretical explanation, North and Thomas construct a developmental perspective which periodizes eight centuries of Western European history into two long Malthusian demographic cycles. Each cycle depends on the dynamic elasticity of the population and the ability of a society to respond institutionally to dramatic population growth; that is, "to bring private returns into parity with social returns" (p. 5). The first cycle, from 900 to 1500, entailed a growth in population leading to the development of medieval markets and towns, which in turn led to further population growth. However, as no nation developed the type of economic organization that could effectively protect property rights (e.g., the Spanish *Mesta* retained the right to run their sheep across privately owned manorial lands), the growth of population yielded diminishing returns leading to economic crisis and contraction. Ultimately, the common Malthusian checks of "famine, pestilence and war" (p. 72) return the population to a manageable level.

With population again low, the second cycle (1500–1700) began with demographic growth leading to the redevelopment of markets and a resurgence of cities. However, in this cycle, we observe the divergence of Spain and France on the one hand and England and the Netherlands on the other. To North and Thomas, this divergence marks the fundamental set of events in the development of the West. Spain and France (the "also-rans") declined because, "both absolutist monarchies, caught up in a race for political dominance, failed to create a set of property rights that promoted economic efficiency" (p. 120). They were therefore condemned to suffer the effects of a new round of Malthusian checks, this time, however (although North and Thomas do not note this) in the context of an international arena dominated by the successful nations.

England and the Netherlands escaped forever from these checks and experienced a Malthusian breakthrough since "both the Dutch and the British economies had succeeded in increasing the per capita income of a growing population despite the continued pressure of diminishing returns in agriculture," (p. 117) they therefore achieved "a rising standard of living in the face of a growing population" (p. 118). The Netherlands accomplished this "not by violence but by price competition resulting from more efficiency in both ships and economic organization," (p. 122) while the English, "after an inauspicious start . . . had developed an effective set of property rights embedded in the common law" (p. 156).

Throughout their exposition of these cycles, North and Thomas argue that while the growth of population is the dynamic element to which social institutions must respond, it is the state that must stabilize the market and provide the organizational efficiency necessary to economic development. Here, however, North and Thomas run into very serious difficulty, for their economism leads them to reduce the state to an agglomeration of economic forces. For them, the state is, "primarily an institutional arrangement that sells protection and justice to its constituents. It does so by monopolizing the definition and enforcement of property rights over goods and resources and the granting of rights to the transfer of these assets. In return for this service, the state receives payment in the form of taxes" (p. 97). Thus, the state is reduced to a series of economic exchanges and develops no autonomous interests of its own.

Later, however, they argue that the reason that France was an "also-ran" was the "failure of the French state to develop an efficient set of property rights" (p. 127). Suddenly, then, we see an ad hoc explanation that locates the source of the failure in the state, when, theoretically, the state is but an emanation of the economy.

But what is most striking about *The Rise of the Western World* is not so much this classical economic reduction of the polity to the economy (or the simultaneous reduction of religion and ideology), a reduction that renders an adequate explanation of the transition from feudalism to capitalism impossible. What is so remarkable to sociologists is how much of North and Thomas's "new" and "innovative" economic insights are nothing more than a translation of classical sociological theory into economic jargon. For what are "property rights" but a neutralized Marxist description of the class power of a rising bourgeoisie (and gentry)? What else is "efficient economic organization" but the Weberian notion of rationalized commercial, legal, and administrative structures? And what, after all, is "population growth" but the dynamic density which, for Durkheim, led to social differentiation and urbanization?

North and Thomas have attempted to provide an alternative explanation of the rise of the Western world. However, what they subtitle as "A New Economic History" turns out to be selective and highly schematic "history," "economic" only in that it reduces all superstructural variations (i.e., culture and polity) to economic forces, and "new" perhaps only to those who are unfamiliar with classical sociological theory.

Guerrilla Economy: The Development of the Shensi-Kansu-Ningshia Border Region, 1937–1945, by PETER SCHRAN. Albany: State University of New York Press, 1976. 323 pp. $25.00 cloth.

KEVIN DANAHER
University of California, Santa Cruz

Schran examines the economic problems faced by the Chinese communist movement during the consolidation of the famous Yenan base area. He asserts that "the communists developed a particular strategy and related tactics which were quite effective in meeting the basic needs not only of the communist movement but also of the base-area people" (p. ix). He lends insight to the process by which the communists successfully handled the dual problem of fighting the armies of Japan and the Kuomintang while securing the allegiance of the masses by organizing the overall development of the region.

After laying out the initial conditions of the SKN border region he gives detailed accounts of how the communists formulated economic policy, how they mobilized the population for the development of production, and how they handled the problems of trade, finance, and fiscal responsibility. The content of the book is weighted in a quantitative rather than qualitative direction. Schran gives so much space to tables and the citation of figures (all based on admittedly questionable data) that readers interested in the more qualitative aspects of the Chinese revolution may find a linear reading of this book somewhat tedious. The book should be regarded as a reference work which brings together the extant statistical data in an outline format which makes the information readily accessible.

In a century where the wealth-gap between poor and rich countries has grown remarkably, the experience of the Chinese provides basic guidelines for third world countries desirous of achieving non-dependent development.

Case Studies on Human Rights and Fundamental Freedoms: A World Survey, Volumes 1 & 2, edited by WILLEM A. VEENHOVEN. The Hague: Martinus Nijhoff, 1975. Vol. 1: 582 pp. Vol. 2: 555 pp. No price listed, cloth.

GAIL OMVEDT
University of California, San Diego

"Human rights" has become one of the major political issues of our time, and source material dealing with it is very welcome. "Source material" is what these two massive volumes claim to be, but the contributors' political persuasions are evident.

The purpose of the volumes is to present a scholarly "reply" to third world charges of "racism, imperialism, zionism" etc. in the United Nations, that is, to uncover the Hutu skeletons in African closets, the repressed women in Muslim harems, and the dissidents in Soviet mental hospitals. Thus, the issue of "political prisoners" in countries such as Iran, Korea, Chile are ignored in order to focus on discrimination against "ethnic minorities" throughout the world, and the greatest number of pages, fully a third of the book, are devoted to Eastern European countries and China.

This by itself would not be objectionable, were not the nature of the authorship of the articles so striking. The fact is that the only members of discriminated-against groups who write about their problems are those from centrally planned societies, whereas, *all* the articles about the USSR, China, and Eastern Europe are by refugees. No Blacks, Chicanos, Native Americans, nor Australian Aborigines write about the position of their people. Nor does any woman (with the partial exception of the piece by the assistant editor which deals with Britain but considers the "women's liberation" movement to be "lacking in a sense of humor") write about sex discrimination. Instead—hold your breath—Israelies write about Israel *and* two of the six chapters on Arab countries (a third is written by a Hungarian refugee); a white South African analyzes South Africa *and* white South Africans write on ethnic conflict in Africa and on race relations in Australia. Given the vast amount of often sophisticated material available on most of these countries and issues, this kind of presentation represents a clear political choice.

The result is that in most of the articles the general misleading analyses and frequently superficial coverage override whatever informational base is available, though some of them (for instance those on Wisconsin Indians and on Japan) are detailed and useful. The chapter on India is illustrative of the problems: one is given a running survey of India, touching down on all the bases of untouchables, tribal groups, linguistic divisions, women, etc. but without any solid data. Moreover, in it are unsupported and ultimately erroneous generalizations, turning Brahmans into outcastes (p. 174), referring to the Bangladesh war simply as a result of cultural life style differences (p. 166), and claiming that Marxist parties are unable to operate in the rural areas because of lack of class awareness (p. 173). The credibility of the South African chapter must be weighed against the fact that in it the concept of the "plural society" is given a basis of assumed *innate* tribal-ethnic differences and turned into a justification for apartheid, with the astounding claim that the government has moved boldly forward "in ideologically reaffirming its objectives of eliminating discrimination based on grounds of color" (p. 298). Also, illustrative of the frequent lack of depth in the volumes, women in Muslim countries are discussed, but with a mere description of religious-legal discrimination which neither examines the social forces behind the widely different position of women in Muslim countries throughout the world, and no attempt is made to provide a comparative look at other major cultural traditions, including the Judaeo-Christian. It is a cliche to say of a collection that it is of uneven quality; but it has to be added of this one that the median of that quality is low. The Foundation for the Study of Plural Societies, which published this, puts out an occasionally interesting journal, but this effort does them little credit.

Race and Ethnic

Racial Conflict, Discrimination, and Power: Historical and Contemporary Studies, edited by WILLIAM BARCLAY, KRISHNA KUMAR and RUTH P. SIMMS. New York: AMS Press, 1976. 436 pp. $15.00 cloth. $5.95 paper.

LORETTA J. WILLIAMS
University of Missouri, Columbia

The editors of this collection have attempted to group together in one volume analyses demonstrating the grounding of both cross-cultural racial stratification and international development in the fifteenth century expansion of Europe throughout the non-European world. It is their unifying thesis that the basic pattern of race relations that emerged has been maintained in many of its universals due to the continuation of colonization processes, albeit different in form, down to the present. The editors, utilizing a macro, world system model, view the labor factor as crucial to power and conflict processes.

The editors set up the framework for the collected readings by, in essence, castigating the emphasis on consensual values and norms inherent in the social systems model; they praise the clarity and wisdom of the power conflict model.

The selections include the standard formulations one would expect given this perspective—that is, selections from Oliver Cox, Basil Davidson, Frantz Fanon, John Horton, Donald Noel, E. J. Rose, and others—but they also include articles by less familiar scholars and from journals such as: *America Indigena, Journal of Modern African Studies, Journal of Peace Research, Race, Radical America, Review of Radical Political Economics,* as well as the more familiar sociological journals and books. This feature in itself adds to the character of the book and its utility in familiarizing students with the diversity of pertinent journals.

The arguments are not universally radical or universally cynical. (Inclusion of Edward Shils's argument from *Daedalus*, 1967, is indicative of this point!) While the collection is by no means representative of all sides of the sociological coin, the editors must be congratulated for attempting to compile in one volume diverse perspectives supportive of their strong belief that more attention must be spent in the examination of historically consistent patterns of social, economic, and political stratification. Race relations as an area of emphasis within sociology has too long been considered as the step-child, the crisis explainer or describer. Here we have a compilation of essays demonstrating the importance and continuity of world-wide racial dimensions in the international social system.

Several books are now on the market attempting to broaden the sociological perspective on comparative race relations; most deal with the various Anglo-fragmented societies. One strength of this book is the broader focus; the move from conceptualization and historical development of theory to four case studies representative of a spectrum of adaptations to color stratification processes in England, US, South Africa, and Central America. The section on Central America, which includes pieces by Andre Frank, Pablo Gonzalez-Casanova, Magnus Mörner, Arnold Strickon, and Rudolfo Stavenhagen, is a definite asset. Most readers do not include such an extensive discussion of Indo-American race relations.

Barclay et al., are clearly making a statement that sociological explanations of the emergent world system of the late twentieth century must recognize both the historical continuities from the past and the potential benefit of renewed input from an interdisciplinary focus on race relations.

Dale Johnson, operating from an internal colonization model in "Marginal Classes, Internal Colonies and Social Change," suggests that the strategizing of marginal underclasses is pivotal in the containment or advancement of basic structural changes in any society. The difficulties in mobilizing that segment of society in the development process of a country are carefully delineated. This article and others focus not upon race relations as a factor expediting social change but as an explanation for the slowness of change toward a reasonable level of independence. The arguments chosen to illustrate the case studies, while distinguishing dissimilarities as well as similarities, argue that the "postcolonial society" is not a reality. While there may not be an on-the-spot colonial administrator, the thrust of the argument is that European expansion was so thoroughly accomplished that the "international system of racial domination and subordination can now reproduce itself without the violence of colonial conquest" (p. 369).

The last section of the book is a collection of essays reintegrating the material into a world model. The publication of this book at a time of increased focus upon world systems à la Wallerstein may be a serendipitious occurrence for the editors. Their thesis that the "global distribution of power and privilege along the lines of color'' (p. iii) was secured in the sixteenth century and remains virulent in current international power struggles, although not new, will now be perceived with greater receptivity. Graduate students intrigued by macro level studies might easily plug into the economic and political emphasis in their race relations analyses. A major strength of the collection is the placement of an extensive bibliography at the end of each of seven sections. These, in addition to the various references in the individual articles, provide a resource for fledgling scholars. Those scholars working in the area of international labor relations will also be pleased to have a handy collection of articles which, although published, in the main, during the late 60s and very early 70s, still remain valid.

Some of us might find this book difficult to use as the main text for graduate seminars on race relations. I can see myself best utilizing it as one of several books or as supplementary reserve reading. However, those interested in either race relations or development would do well to examine the vital questions raised by Barclay, Kumar, and Simms.

Black Elected Officials: A Study of Black Americans Holding Governmental Office, by JAMES E. CONYERS and WALTER L. WALLACE. New York: Russell Sage, 1976. 206 pp. $8.95 cloth.

JAMES H. LAUE
University of Missouri, St. Louis

In the few years since the Selma bridge in 1965, we have experienced perhaps the most profound political changes in the United States since the Civil War: widespread Black enfranchisement in the South, a dramatic increase in the number of Black elected officials throughout the nation, the realignment of southern politics with national politics (now one can generally recognize a southern Republican by party label, for example), and the election of the first southern president in more than a century with Blacks carrying the swing vote in key electoral states.

Black Elected Officials offers the first detailed description of one major impact of the new enfranchisement. The authors, note that in 1964, one year before the Selma-induced Voting Rights Law of 1965, only thirty-eight percent of the potential Black voters in the South were registered, and the elections that year yielded only 280 Black Federal, state and local public officials. By 1971, registration had reached fifty-nine percent, and 1,860 Blacks were holding elective government office throughout the country. The authors estimate that the figure reached more than 3,500 by late 1975—an impressive gain, but still only about .6 of 1 percent of all elected officials in the United States.

This book is the result of a 1971 sample survey conceived by Conyers (who also ''supervised the collection, coding, processing and transcription'' of the data), with data analysis and writing by Wallace. A thirty-minute self-administered questionnaire was completed by 805 Black office-holders (forty-three percent of the national total of 1,860, all of whom were mailed the instrument), and by 486 White elected officials (a thirty-nine percent return from a sample of 1,252, roughly matched for type of office and geographical location). In addition, interviews were conducted with thirty-four Black elected officials, including several members of the US House of Representatives.

The study was organized around eight ''principal questions'' (p. 11, emphasis in original):

1. What *political beliefs* do Black elected officials hold?
2. What are their *motivations for seeking office?*
3. What are their *personal background characteristics?*
4. What are the characteristics of the *election districts* they represent?
5. What are their *party affiliations* and *types of elective office?*
6. What *sources of election* help did they draw upon?
7. What *impacts* did they have?
8. What *expectations* do they have?

The authors' answers to these and related questions are presented in four chapters of tables (mainly cross-tab marginals, with occasional tests of significance) and a running commentary on the tables, surrounded by a brief introductory chapter, a chapter of extensive direct quotations from the interviews, and a short concluding chapter. The result is a book that, to me, is generally informative but sluggish, extremely timely but disconnected from realpolitik, and, most seriously, lacking a theoretical framework and a related research design. *Black Elected Officials* is an example of a kind of flat empiricism, without peaks of theoretical interpretation or insightful, risky leaps.

Still, Conyers and Wallace's work is important as the first serious effort to describe and analyze the characteristics of the rapidly increasing group of Black elected officials in the United States. The book is introduced in the context of the question of whether the country is experiencing a "Second Reconstruction," and the inevitable next question about an ensuing period analogous to white supremacist restoration—not an idle concern during the Watergate years in which the data were processed and written up. The gains analyzed in the book are called "slight" in several places, but the authors do note structural, demographic, political, and legal changes that make the power of Black elected officials more likely to endure than was the case 100 years ago.

Three sets of "interrelated" findings are presented, all in large aggregations against personal and social/situational variables: the "ideological attitudes" of Black officials, their perceptions of their constituencies, and their perspectives on the future. In chapter 2 on "Political Beliefs and Motivations for Seeking Office," the authors explore the relationships between three types of ideological positions for both Black and White officials: racial "hereditarianism," direct action vs. conventional action strategies, and Black independence (i.e., separation or self-determination) vs. integration as goals. They find some moderately strong correlations between Black independence positions and sentiments against urban renewal, birth control, and metropolitan government (p. 26). They find a correlation between independence and direct action, and between integrationist ideology and adherence to conventional action. White "socioeconomic conservatives" and Black "racial radicals" find the hereditarian assumption "at least not uncongenial" (p. 34).

But already in this first of the data-reporting chapters two disconcerting and persistent tendencies emerge. One is the manifestation of imprecise editing which results in such sociological bromides as "officials may be motivated toward gratification of self through gaining acceptance from some group that is the source of the gratification" (p. 44). The other is a repetition of lukewarm interpretations of data which appear in such sentences as, "In this relationship, logically speaking, either could be means or either could be end" (p. 45). These kinds of phrases abound, I am convinced, because the authors never developed a commitment to a particular theoretical stance in the data and, accordingly, virtually every possible interpretation of every demonstrated relationship is mentioned as "plausible" or "logical."

In chapter 3 on "Personal Background and Social Setting," the two racial samples are compared on length of residence in the jurisdiction, education, memberships, and age, and found to be virtually identical. Age emerges as a key predictive variable; older Black officials are found to be more integrationist, more socially conservative and less accepting of direct action strategies (p. 60), while younger Black officials more consistently advocate Black independence (p. 62).

It is questionable whether "Sex Differences" merits its own chapter, but the authors deliver empirical verification among their samples for some informal observations held by students of the women's movement for some time: birth control and creation of child care centers (but not women's rights) were more significant issues for female Black officials than for male Black officials, and women's rights were more significant to female White officials than for male White officials (p. 97).

Some of the potentially most valuable findings appear in chapter 5 on "Who Helped Elect Them and Why." Four "Constituencies" are examined: the Black community and the White community (both sources of votes), and political parties and the media (sources of certification and visibility). It is clear from the data that Blacks perceive a broader base of support from their own race as well as Whites in their election efforts than do Whites (p. 104). Black officials see themselves as more secure politically than Whites. Officials of both races feel they appeal more successfully to "grass roots" constituencies of their own race, but to the "leadership" in the other race. Of greatest interest were findings concerning the relationship of Black population concentrations and Black voting and political influence. In urban areas with low percentages of Black population, North and South, advocates of Black independence reported receiving more help from the Black community than did Black integrationists (pp. 134–35).

The sixth chapter on "Perceived Impact and Expected Future" contains eighteen pages of direct quotes from the thirty-four interview schedules, differentiated only in terms of "Impact on the Black Community," "Impact on the White Community," and "Future." The major impact on Black communities is seen to be an escalation of Black confidence that important changes can be achieved through politics within the system (p. 137). Black elected officials report greater confidence in themselves vis-à-vis White communities (p. 143). The "Future" is four pages of direct quotes representing a predictable mixture of optimism and pessimism.

The concluding chapter is symptomatic of concluding sections in the other chapters: it does not conclude. Rather, as with the other chapters, it simply runs out the string of findings, and stops.

A dip into the appendices is rewarding, especially the marginals in appendix D on "Selected Characteristics Not Included in the Analysis," where one learns that educational level of Black and White elected officials in the sample is identical, but that a greater percentage of Blacks is involved in continuing education than Whites. Other striking differences are revealed, especially regarding the sanctity of certain American institutions and practices.

Near the end of my reading, I finally pinpointed my discomfort with the book. It was not due to the "methodological" problems which the authors note at too-great length near the beginning, but rather to the fact that data were collected without a coherent, theoretically grounded design—then counted, correlated, and commented upon without possibility of solid conclusion, interpretation, or recommendation specifically because of the lack of theoretical context. Aggregation without prior design or purpose beyond exhaustive description does not lend itself easily to sociological interpretation.

I look forward to a second edition on this critical topic, perhaps with a shortened and tightened questionnaire flowing from a theoretical commitment, and an analysis plan that disaggregates to at least the level of the individual community so the findings may become connected to the exciting political changes being wrought by Black elected officials and their constituencies in the United States.

Gypsies in the City: Culture Patterns and Survival, by Rena C. Gropper. Princeton, N.J.: Darwin Press, 1975. 235 pp. $9.95 cloth.

Gypsies, Tinkers and Other Travellers, edited by Farnham Rehfisch. New York: Academic Press, 1975. 303 pp. $15.25 cloth.

Gypsies: The Hidden Americans, by Anne Sutherland. New York: Free Press, 1975. 330 pp. $13.95 cloth.

Marcello Truzzi
Eastern Michigan University

It is remarkable that given the attractiveness of the topic of Gypsies for the average person (who has romanticized them as figures of mystery and occultism) and the frequent journalistic reports on them and their way of life, this ethnic minority has largely escaped the close attention of sociologists. This is all the more surprising since Gypsy culture so markedly deviates from so much of the normative order present in American society and thereby presents us with an excellent testing-ground for so many of our supposedly general theories about intergroup behavior. Census figures on Gypsies are few and estimates of their number vary considerably from 5 million to about 1.5 million for the world and from 300,000 down to merely 20,000 for the United States. Despite these figures, textbooks dealing with racial and ethnic minorities almost all completely ignore Gypsies. Yet this ethnic minority has hardly been neglected by others, for the literature on Gypsies is immense (even that on American Gypsies is surprisingly large), and the *Journal of the Gypsy Lore Society* has been published (in three series) since 1888. Unfortunately, most of the literature on Gypsies is highly unreliable and full of contradictions and mythology, much of which was spread by Gypsies to mislead outsiders (*gaje*).

Gypsies have been categorized into Nomadic and Sedentary groups. Nomadic Gypsies are called *Rom*, and most scholars agree that there are four major tribes: Kalderasha, Machwaya, Lowara, and Churara. The tribes are sub-divided into bands called *vitsi* (*tshera* by the Lowara), and each *vitsa* is broken down into *familiyi*. The normally largest social and ceremonial unit is not necessarily a kin group but is a territorially defined *kumpania*. Most, but by no means all, Gypsy groups speak *Romany* (*romanes*), a language akin to modern Hindi.

Gypsies maintain rigid boundaries between themselves and the non-Gypsy host society, and this is strongly reflected throughout their cultural system. This has minimized their assimilation into the cultures around them and has often led to their being viewed as a parish group. Parallels between the social conditions of Gypsies and Jews are well documented, and the Nazis conducted mass exterminations of Gypsies as well as Jews; but little comparative analysis has been done. Study of Gypsies is an especially difficult task for any non-Gypsy and is further compounded by the necessity of learning Romany. However we also have surprisingly little survey data on attitudes towards Gypsies by non-Gypsies, and this is an area where sociologists could make a swift and valuable contribution.

Despite this indifference from their peers, a number of sociologists and anthropologists have now turned their attention to the fascinating and complex culture of the Gypsies, and the three books here reviewed are among the best and latest of such efforts joining the recent field-studies of those like Werner Cohn, Bertha B. Quintana, Lois G. Floyd, Patricia Kirby, William Kornblum, Carol Miller, and others.

Anthropologist Rena C. Gropper's ethnography of New York City Gypsies is certainly the most readable and in some ways the most ambitious of the books under review. *Gypsies in the City* is an updating of, and expansion upon, her 1950 doctoral dissertation *The Fork in the Road: A Study of Acculturation among the American Kalderas Gypsies* (a work frequently cited in the literature on Gypsies under her former name: Cotten). I would recommend Gropper's book, along with Jean-Paul Clebert's *The Gypsies* and Werner Cohen's *The Gypsies*, as an excellent introduction for those wishing to begin investigations into Gypsy culture, particularly for her annotated bibliography which for many may alone be worth the price of the book. Her ethnographic survey of New York Gypsies is broken down into chapters on: Gypsies in the United States and New York; the economics of being a Gypsy (and their *symbiotic* relationship with non-Gypsy society); the socio-political organization of the nomads; the Gypsy system of justice and social control through the *kris*, or Gypsy trial; Gypsy religion and philosophy; Gypsy childhood; marriage; maturity, decline and death; and a discussion of the mechanisms by which Gypsy culture has managed to survive without assimilation into non-Gypsy culture. Gropper follows this excellent ethnography with a final chapter outlining a "choice-taking" conceptual framework (prematurely called a theory) to be used for analyzing social life. She offers this perspective to replace current anthropological theories which she found not "to be adequate for a meaningful organization of the data on the Gypsies I have collected or for an explanation of what I have observed" (p. 194). Since this failure of existing theories is not demonstrated, since her proposed framework shows little connection or systematic influence upon virtues found in her book, and since her model suggests little new for those in social psychology or actor-viewpoint centered sociology, this is the weakest part of Gropper's book. This formal attempt at theorizing aside, however, Gropper offers revealing insights and commentary throughout her study. One of the most interesting parts of the volume is her discussion of the functional advantage in the "miniaturization" in Gypsy social structure whereby each larger Gypsy social unit is a logical outgrowth of similar form to the next smaller unit.

In contrast with Gropper's twenty-five years of participation observation as an "adopted daughter" in the Gypsy community (a role she unfortunately little describes), Anne Sutherland's ethnography results from a mere nine-month involvement as the Principal of the "Romany School" set up for Gypsy children in "Barvale," California, in 1970. Despite this short period of contract (Gropper states that three to five years of field work should be a minimum [p. 199]), during which Sutherland remained an outsider with very little knowledge of the Gypsy language (Romany), she has given us a highly detailed, skillfully analyzed, and in some ways technically superior book to that of Gropper, particularly for the discussion of kinship and relational terminology. Sutherland's research had the advantage of building upon Gropper's pioneer work (with which she takes issue on some points) but presents us with much new and important information. It is especially revealing about the often incredible manipulations of our complicated welfare system by these largely illiterate but clever recipients.

Direct comparison of the Gropper and Sutherland books is further confounded by each having dealt with somewhat different Gypsy groups. Gropper is primarily concerned with Gypsies from the Kalderasha tribe whereas Sutherland's study includes members from the Kalderasha, Machwaya, and Churara groups. The small differences in detail between Sutherland's and Gropper's Gypsies (Sutherland's Gypsies impressed me as often more "orthodox" or traditional and less assimilated than Gropper's) may be the result of tribal rather than geographic differences. Unfortunately, both Sutherland and Gropper fail to consistently distinguish *which* Gypsy groups demonstrate *which* practices. Important differences are noted between the various Gypsy tribes, but the discussions of beliefs and practices too often seem to be generalized to all Gypsies (a methodological error warned against by Sutherland which she does not always observe). Sutherland gives us far more detail about her role as a participant observer than does Gropper, but both supply insufficient information for reliability and validity measures on field work data that are now possible through qualitative analysis. In working with such secretive groups, it is especially important that we know a great deal about the role of the observer so we can assess possible limitations for data obtained. Since both of these field workers are women gathering data in a strongly patriarchal culture, that fact alone is likely to produce much information that may be one-sided. It will be particularly interesting to obtain reports from future researchers some of whom may be male and, hopefully, may even have been born and raised as Gypsies.

The Rehfisch collection presents twelve excellent field studies describing American Rom Gypsies (by Anne Sutherland and by Carol Miller), Gypsies in Southern England (by Judith Okely), Gypsies in North Britain (anonymously authored), Boyash Gypsies around Paris (by William Kornblum), Alsatian Mānus Gypsies (by Aparna Rao), Spanish Urban Gypsy settlements (by Teresa San Román), Czechoslovakian Gypsies (by Willy Guy), Irish Travellers (by Bettina Barnes and by George Gmelch), Scottish Travellers (by A. and F. Rehfisch), and Norwegian Taters (by Fredrik Barth). The essays are concerned with varied problems, but they are uniformly valuable. Sutherland's article is an effective summary of much of her book but contains additional material as well. I found Carol Miller's analysis of American Gypsy views on purity and defilement particularly useful. The individual essays contain many important observations, some of which may surprise the reader (for example, unlike the Gypsies who originate from India and speak Romany, and who are found in England and Wales, the Travellers are probably of Celtic origin, speak Cant, and are found in Ireland and Scotland). Unfortunately, however, this collection of papers is merely that. The editor has provided us with no integrating or organizing materials but has written merely a one and one-half page preface and given us a combined glossary-index. Let us hope that the growing literature on Gypsies will soon include an over-view that will properly classify, if not explain, the variety of social forms found among these fascinating nomads.

Sex Roles and Behavior

Who's Queer?, by Janet Saltzman Chafetz, Paula Beck, Patricia Sampson, Joyce West and Bonnye James. Sarasota, Fla.: Omni Press, 1976. 190 pp. $8.95 paper.

Meredith Gould
New York University

In our society, where individuals and groups of actors gain and recede in importance for study, one would be hard pressed to find an area of investigation more persistently overlooked than lesbian experience and culture. Lesbians are virtually ignored by anthropology, subjected to hopelessly intricate etiological theories by psychology, and maligned by literature. The ethnographic spirit which captured sociology in its early years failed to produce either descriptive accounts or hard data. While those concerned with deviance and social problems, labeling theorists in particular, quite appropriately used the male homosexual experience to illustrate processes of identity, the lesbian remained unremarkable. Since her identity is inimically bound in with that of being a woman, those roles, social worlds, and ways of knowing and expressing social reality as a woman, are highly congruent to lesbian experience. The dearth of either descriptive or explanatory literature about lesbians, essentially up until the women's movement, eloquently expresses lesbianism as only one subset of the heretofore invisibility of women in general.

Consequently, when choosing course texts advancing a sense of the lesbian qua woman, should we opt for the rich, qualitative experience as lived and interpreted by the actors themselves? Or the interpretations of those viewing and documenting that experience? Do we have a choice? During the past decade, several books have formed a core focused around the interaction between lesbianism and womanness. These books are those most consistently chosen for courses dealing with deviance and gender roles, ranging on a continuum from quantitative data and sociological analysis in principle, to the general public type. While we often embrace what ostensibly seems to be good quantitative data in the sometimes verified belief that it will "prove" and "explain" at last, or even advance theory, I would maintain that in this particular area we are limited by our conceptual background from asking those questions which begin to elucidate the lesbian experience. We are bound by previous interpretations of what the etiology of lesbianism should be and are thus hampered from integrating an understanding of lesbianism with a more general theory of identity.

Who's Queer? is one recent addition to the growing literature exemplifying this problem of preconceptualized categories and processes in part illustrated in the questionnaires included at the end of the text (pp. 138–188) where we find familiar questions about childhood friendships, parent identification, body image, etc. which undoubtedly shape the data. Where are the questions, difficult to tabulate, but nevertheless critical, about the experience of being a woman in the world? Since the lesbian sample was matched with a sample of heterosexual women, this book could have been particularly important if we had seen solid evidence of that "conformity greater than deviance" (Simon & Gagnon, *Sexual Conduct*, 1973, pp. 176–217) which prompts us to speculate what, if anything, there is about female socialization which moves some women to become lesbian in theory or practice while others do not. Of critical interest for we who might be tempted to use this book is what part does gender role socialization play in the development of lesbian identity in conjunction with female identity? Are the reciprocal dynamics of identity and community the same for lesbians as they are for homosexual men? Which community is salient? Could those characteristics identified as lesbian be manifestations of feminist ideology and have little or nothing to do with sexual and affectional preference? That these types of points drift through the text and are not seized upon for development is a serious flaw. It is often unclear whether the authors are citing what sound like psychoanalytic theories of lesbianism because they may be substantiated by the data, or in order to refute the arguments to begin with. For example, there is considerable attention paid to the role of parents and parenting, a familiar theme in psychological and psychiatric literature. With characteristic ambivlance toward the validity of their own data, the authors state "The gay and straight samples also differ in their attitudes toward children, childbirth and pregnancy, but not as substantially as might be expected. . . . While the majority of gay women thus seem to be uninterested in raising children, it is nonetheless the case that a substantial minority does desire the experience." Later in the same data analysis they assert "Childbearing is one of, if not the most central aspect of the traditional feminine sex role, it is clear that the majority of gay women reject this task . . . " (p. 24). This passage also reveals a disturbing lack of terminological precision. In the introduction, the authors state they "seek to understand better the ways in which the label 'gay' impacts the social existence of lesbians . . . " (p. 6) however, the terms "gay," "female homosexual," and "lesbian" seem to be used interchangeably—and they may well be. Yet given the connotative assumptions those terms have acquired in the everyday world, it seems self-defeating not to make an explicit attempt at clarification.

As faulty as the data seem they support in some way the findings of earlier studies, mostly undertaken by psychologists using both patient and non-patient samples. The authors even tentatively advance a structural explanation for interpersonal phenomenon, e.g., the discussion of homosexual "marriage" (p. 25), but these potentially exciting observations occur almost parenthetically and are not central to analytical development. In the preface, the senior author on behalf of her co-authors tells us they "approached this project as feminists, deeply aware of the lack of sociologically relevant information about female homosexuality and deeply committed to exploding the common myths surrounding this phenomenon" (p. v.). The body of the book belies this fine intent. In more than one place the reader is cautioned against accepting the data. The last chapter in particular catalogs faults with data collection and sampling procedures quite convincingly, citing high refusal rates, the problems of matching the heterosexual sample to a previously gathered lesbian sample, and the different methodology employed for each group—the lesbians received oral interviews, the heterosexual sample used paper-and-pencil questionnaires (p. 123). The increasing reliance by social control agencies upon sociological research bears too many consequences for the lives of sexual minorities to afford any sort of ambiguous research, no matter how hypothetical or exploratory in nature.

Consequently, although they lack the ballast of hard data, we still must return to the classic accounts of *Lesbian/Woman* (Martin and Lyon, 1972) and *Sappho Was a Right-On Woman* (Abbott and Love, 1973). They provide us with definitions of lesbianism derived from both homophile and feminist perspectives, as well as a passionate history of the lesbian movement from its homophile beginnings to the feminist agony of N.O.W's Lavendar Menance scandal during the mid-1970s. However, of even more importance, these books written by lesbian authors, map out lesbian experience in such a way that the reader is compelled to make a critical analysis of those rigid gender roles expectations which significantly affect the lives of women and men in American society no matter where they fall in the Kinsey scale. I strongly feel these personal expressions of oppression are excellent catalysts for working toward theories of human identity in a world rapidly moving toward androgyny. Ironically, the authors of *Who's Queer*? readily acknowledge their indebtedness to these two books, presumably for their conceptual content. Unfortunately, whatever insight these books offer is not adequately reflected in the *Who's Queer*? data analysis. I would suggest that for now we are better off presenting this material in its overwhelmingly descriptive form since, with perhaps two exceptions, it has not been translated into solid empirical research.

Sexual Stigma: An Interactionist Account, by KENNETH PLUMMER. Boston: Routledge & Kegan Paul, 1975. 258 pp. $18.50 cloth.

WILLIAM SIMON
University of Houston

Sexual Stigma is a thoughtful and scholarly work that should be high on the reading list of all social scientists concerned with deviance, human sexuality, and/or theory. Indeed, it might well be considered as important reading in advanced classes dealing with any of these topics. Going beyond the promises of many who have written on deviance, including the present reviewer, the author extends a concern for stigmatized sexual actors to focus attention upon both the larger social context as well as the larger context of whole lives; the deviant behavior does not occupy its more typical center stage position.

The difficulty as well as the value of this perspective, however, rests with this focus upon the significance of deviant commitments for non-deviant behavior (which must remain for all but precious few the larger part of all lives) and the interfacing of deviant and non-deviant actors. The reader must come away with a more complex sense of the salient aspects that must be considered, but, at the same time, there is a loss of coherence in the ordering of social life; a loss of coherence that is almost proportionate to the increase in complexity. The loss of coherence may partly derive from the abandonment of the equally costly tendency in most previous work to allow the area of deviance to both conceptually organize and explain virtually all of the behavior of the deviant. In part, moreover, this loss of coherence may reflect the contemporary social world which is manifestly less constrained by, or committed to, consistency and/or continuity than is sociological theory in conventional practice.

The author describes his work as being "at least four minature studies." The first "is a study of the symbolic interactionist perspective." Plummer also insists that this is broadened to include insights of the ethnomethodologists. The uses of ethnomethodology or the phenomenological perspective are limited to the most accessible of that tradition; one still finds the conceptual framework far more firmly rooted in Berger and Luckman than Schutz or Garfinkel. The second is "a study in the sociology of sexuality." The third, "a study of the labelling approach to sexual deviation." That is a remarkably ambitious undertaking, particularly for a text that runs (excluding notes and bibliography) barely two hundred pages. Clearly, not all promises are kept, but what remains is still a great deal to digest.

The organization of the fourth study would appear to suggest the movement from a broad theoretical base, progressively narrowing, to a specific category of actors: the male homosexual. The work, thus, would appear ideally to culminate in a fairly finely textured sense of the underlying human experience. Indeed, the author rejects both Freudianism and sociological functionalism precisely because they fail to provide access to the fully dynamic nature of social life, e.g. "seeing socialization as a 'printed circuit' in which men are programmed to behave in the 'right way.' . . ." However, upon arriving at the case in point, the male homosexual, we find a rather abstract figure; the homosexual in discussion turns out to be almost as remote to a textured sense of the human experience as that which might be derived from a statistical table or correlational matrix.

The problem is hardly unique to Plummer; it plagues the entire symbolic interactionist tradition; the theoretical perspective that seemingly forces the textured questions precludes appropriately textured responses. The problems of the variable complexity of observations as well as those of handling multiple observations (or multiple observers) appear as remote to solution as ever. If the fragmentation deriving from quantitative approaches that Plummer would avoid derives from the implicit challenge of accounting for variance, his own approach remains trapped in a measure of central tendency which resists admitting to all but the most primative charting of variance: the linguistic metaphor. It is this reliance on metaphor which produces the abstract quality of discourse as well as a sense of discontinuity in the different sections of the work, e. g., the society looking at the homosexual and later the homosexual looking at society. One is never sure that the homosexual being looked at by society is the same one that is looking back. Moveover, the impulse to ask how much of a change in the perception of one is required to produce or fail to produce a change in the other must either be denied or frustrated. Plummer predictably rejects, at the outset, "structural role theory." However, not even all forms of a dramaturgical role theory are acceptable. The reader is cautioned to avoid producing "classical dramas" (presumably those where the script or form provides the greatest predictability) in favor of improvisational dramas (with a greater emphasis upon the actor's need to size up the situation). Unfortunately the work culminates in highly provocative but still very "classical" vignettes. Both the potential and implicit limits for improvisation remain unclear, as does the way in which the various vignettes articulate with one another.

But we may not be ready to ask even the correlational question, leaving to the structuralist the task of sustaining the illusion that the world is both whole and ultimately explicable. It is perhaps enough that we begin by focusing upon the questions Plummer would have us ask, and, more importantly, understanding why they must be asked. Clearly, they have not been pursued extensively in research on deviance to date. This is the real value of *Sexual Stigma*: the thoughtfulness and thoroughness with which such questions are asked. The book will prove both valuable and embarassing in the teaching of deviance or social problems. In requiring that we understand more about the deviant actor than we were previously expected to know, we also quickly become aware of how limited are the substantive theories "explaining" deviance (or deviants), including some of those favored by Plummer.

A last point. In his discussion of the interactionist perspective, Plummer makes reference to that part of role theory that he refers to as "dramaturgical," attributing it to Erving Goffman. An earlier and more general source, influencing others as well as Goffman, is obviously the wide-ranging works of Kenneth Burke. One possible reason that the author fails to mention the work of Burke is that its uses within and by sociologists has been, at best, unevenly acknowledged, I raise this not as some petty point of scholarly clarification or sociological trivia, but rather to regret the failure as it further obscures a signpost pointing to an intellectual storehouse far richer than current uses by sociologists—acknowledged and unacknowledged—might lead one to expect.

Love, Sex, and Sex Roles, by CONSTANTINA SAFILIOS-ROTHSCHILD. Englewood Cliffs, N. J.: Prentice-Hall, 1977. 150 pp. No price listed, cloth.

NATALIE ALLON
Hofstra University

Safilios-Rothschild pithily presents an insightful and comprehensive descriptive and analytical overview of the independence and interdependence of sexuality, emotions, and sex roles. She clearly discusses the meanings of love and of the notion of "sex object" applied to both women and men. She astutely compares potential and actual feelings of love with the dehumanization and alienation of the stereotypes of femininity and masculinity with which we have been socialized. One central theme is that when women occupy an inferior and disadvantaged sociological position, they become psychologically unequal. Being unequal, men and women cannot understand each other.

Safilios-Rothschild is sensitive to dynamic and transitional processes in the evolution of past, present and future orientations toward love and sexuality. The author describes and deplores how women and men work hard to perform, achieve, compete and succeed with each other, so concerned about power, prestige and social conformity, that they lack mutual trust and openness with each other. With the integration of sexuality into one's total personality, Safilios-Rothschild stresses that there are many viable types of meaningful human relationships.

The author sometimes seems to overgeneralize her ideas to apply to all women and men, but this book will have greatest appeal to white middle and upper middle class audiences, probably in contemporary America, who will see themselves clearly in the analysis.

Frauenemanzipation und Sozialismus: Das Beispiel der Volksrepublik Polen, by MAGDALENA SOKOLOWSKA. Reinbek bei Hamburg, Federal Republic of Germany: Rowohlt Taschenbuch Verlag GmbH, 1973, 172 pp. No price listed, paper.

JULIUS A. ROTH
University of California, Davis

This book is important for people interested in the women's movement and in changing sex roles, not only because it provides an Eastern

European comparison, but because it details some of the ways in which government policy, economic conditions, institutional structures, and concepts of interpersonal relationships affect the degree and manner in which equality of the sexes is or is not attained. The parallels with the development of the women's movement in the United States are as striking and hold as much interest as the contrasts.

Marxist-Leninist ideology proclaimed equality of the sexes and appropriate declarations appear in the constitutions of Poland and other socialist states of Eastern Europe. But ideological statements do not in themselves bring about fundamental change in social practices. The author shows how industrialization and the labor shortage following World War II aided in increasing educational and vocational opportunities for women.

Since World War II and the establishment of a socialist regime in Poland, the encouragement of the training and employment of females has gone through three phases. From 1947 to 1954, a period of reconstruction and the development of heavy industry and consequent labor shortage, training and employment opportunities for women were maximized. Government programs not only provided for increased training and employment of women in technical occupations and in job categories where they had previously been scarce, but also provided child care facilities, job-based food canteens, and other supports aimed at making it more feasible for women to work outside the home. A labor glut began to develop during 1954 and in the period 1955 to 1957, when many new female job seekers could not be placed, the encouragement of female labor was reduced, the family and child-care role of women was emphasized, and opponents of vocational equality for women became more prominent and blamed the disintegration of the family and the rowdyism of youth on working mothers. During this period there was also increasing criticism of women as inefficient workers. From 1958 on (the author takes her description to about 1971) there is another phase in which the economy is stabilized at a fairly prosperous level, there is a political reaction to the opponents of vocational equality for women, and a policy of support for working women is renewed, but not with the single-minded vigor of the first phase. During the third phase there is also an increase in focus on interpersonal dynamics of family life rather than simply promoting women's access to training and employment.

One government approach to encourage female employment outside the household is to provide various ways to lighten housework—public laundry, cleaning and repair services, food canteens, better distribution of groceries, partially prepared foods, and of course, child-care services. There are also special protections provided for pregnant women and women with young children, including long motherhood leaves with no loss of seniority. Such protections run the risk of being turned into discrimination against women.

Government efforts to change sex-related patterns of employment take the form of quotas designed to reduce the proportions of women in female-dominated occupations (e.g., dentistry, nursing) and increase their proportions in male-dominated occupations (e.g., engineering, technical trades). Minimum scores for entry into training programs were manipulated for this purpose. Although these efforts had some effect, discrimination patterns are still evident. Women continue to predominate in the low-income sectors of the economy. Women are still disproportionately low in leading positions. Managers in traditionally male-dominated occupations (especially technical professions where pay scales are highest) resist the employment of women. Family roles have not changed sufficiently in many cases to encourage the pursuit of an independent vocation by the wife and mother. "The consciousness of people changes more slowly than political and economic institutions" (p. 129).

American students of sex-role changes will find some striking paralleles in the Polish situation. For example, it is among married women that the proportion in the work force has been rising most rapidly in recent decades. Working women are often burdened by most of the housework in addition to their outside job. Among "progressive" families—dual career, trend toward sharing household tasks—the birth rate has fallen sharply.

The author is a physician turned sociologist and is well-known in international "social science and medicine" circles. Her book was written in Polish. This review is based on the German translation which should be readily available from its West German publisher. The author (who is fluent in German and English) considers this a faithful translation. She has also stated that she expects a portion of the book to be published in English, but I do not know whether this has occurred.* I have avail-

* Editor's note: Some of this material is now available in English in a chapter by Sokolowska in *Women: Roles and Status in Eight Countries,* edited by Janet Zollinger Giele and Audrey Chapman Smock. (John Wiley & Sons, 1977.)

able a few copies of my own crude unauthorized English translation which I am willing to lend to interested parties for short periods or to supply copies to persons willing to pay for duplication (about 230 typescript pages).

Women in America: The Oppressed Majority, by CAROL A. WHITEHURST. Santa Monica, Ca.: Goodyear Publishing Copany, 1977. 164 pp. $8.95 cloth.

ELIZABETH BRIANT LEE
Short Hills, New Jersey

Within the last decade or so, we have had a vast mushrooming of many organizations and groups, loosely referred to in countless books, magazines, radio, and television programs as "the women's movement." Scarcely a week goes by but here comes still another book extolled as "much-needed" exposition of some aspect of the life of women in our society. While the contribution of women to the culture of their time and place has all too often been overlooked, misinterpreted, or minimized, the current spate of writing about and/or by women is not so much a freshet as a deluge. To keep apace leads one to resort to choice and elimination through reviews, through collections of selected excerpts, and similar cullings.

Along this line, it may be useful to know that Carol A. Whitehurst's *Women in America: the Oppressed Majority* grew out of her teaching of courses in sex roles and, for such, is intended as an introduction and an overview of pertinent sociological literature dealing with the status of American women today. It is much more the former than the latter. Whitehurst deliberately narrowed her field to eliminate treatment of any but white, middle class, somewhat educated women. She pays almost no attention to accounts of earlier attempts toward raising the status of women, and cuts off her beginning perspective at 1963 with the publication of Betty Friedan's *The Feminine Mystique*. Further, we are told that discussion of such large aspects of society as women's relationship to the arts and to religion as well as their sexuality are sidestepped because the literature is so vast, while anything dealing with minority group and working class women is omitted because the literature is so scanty.

In short, Whitehurst provides us here with the usual middle class oriented sociology text, based chiefly on current literature in the field of women's studies or sex roles. She is evenhanded in her treatment of such source material, which can be an admirable stance *if* it is well supplemented by the teacher or by wide reading in depth on the part of the student. As it is, here the superficial stands equally recognized, alongside the well researched and insightful.

The writing itself goes smoothly, perhaps because the book has the general nature of a beginning text, thus it is not loaded down with much in the way of sociologese, a merit.

Perhaps it is unjust to fault one book for the inadequacies found in much of the current literature in sociology. However, objection must be made to the use of a title that suggests treatment of more than one-half of the human race on this continent. Then, beneath it there runs a text that speaks of only part of the lives of some of the middle class, white, better educated women, principally within the past twenty years and within the USA. Students who use this book should be reminded with each chapter how limited a view they are being given, for once the disclaimers are made in the preface, generalities flow about womankind regardless of the narrowness of the base, the lack of historical perspective, and the largeness of the areas uncovered.

Social Policy

Social Policy and Sociology, edited by N. J. DEMERATH, III, OTTO LARSEN, and KARL F. SCHUESSLER. New York: Academic Press, 1975. 365 pp. $17.50 cloth.

C. L. ESTES
University of California, San Francisco

Social Policy and Sociology contains a series of papers and commentaries drawn from a 1972 A.S.A. sponsored conference on the topic. In the first part of the book (Assessment of Policy Research), more than thirty-five "distinguished" sociologists critique or comment on the policy implications of specific exemplars of sociological research which are organized into three areas: (1) Social Inequities and Their Effects, (2) Individual Stress in the Family Cycle, and (3) American Youth and Their Problems. Section one contains papers on poverty, race relations, metropolitan services, and population issues by Peter Rossi, Robert Alford, Howard Schuman, John Kasarda, and Samuel Preston, followed by seven short commentaries. In section two David Mechanic, Joan Aldous, Robert Strauss, Kurt Back, and

Nicholas Babchuck discuss medical care, mental health, sex roles and the family, alcohol, and aging; seven commentaries follow. Section three contains papers on delinquency, drugs, adolescence, and schools by James Short, Albert Reiss, Lois DeFleur, James Davis, and Doris Entwisle, with eight commentaries. The book's second and shorter section is on graduate training and federal funding.

Central themes of the book are the promise and problems of policy research, its appropriateness for the discipline, the prostitution of scholarship in such pursuits (raising issues of academic freedom, moral autonomy, objectivity, and the primacy of theory and truth), issues of graduate training, professional rewards and practice in view of the academic marketplace, and the extent to which policy research calls for the "best" of the discipline's theoretical development, specificity, and methodological rigor.

One closes the book with a sense of the negligible role and impact of sociology on public policy and some understanding of why this is so (and probably will continue)—the continuing classic tensions around whether policy research is a valid objective of the discipline, the lack of sufficient knowledge and theoretical specificity for designing and testing social policy models, methodological short-comings (including inadequate samples and the use of non-manipulable variables which are not subject to change by policy makers), the persistent emphasis on negative findings (what doesn't work rather than what does), and the rejection of findings which are directly translatable into policy because of their radical implications.

Many facets of policy research and its implications are discussed in this volume. One aspect on which a number of authors agreed was that policy research differs from "pure" research in that consequences other than knowledge are significant. The dual focus on the consequences of policy research and the limited applicability of sociological knowledge led to sobering discussions of the risks involved for the discipline in exposing itself to policy endeavours "where the sparceness of our talent may lead to disastrous results" (Winch, p. 344). The justification for a concern with social policy is lodged in the social and moral obligations of the discipline to respond to social problems and in the exposure of the discipline to "the abrasions of reality [which] may be intellectually fruitful" (Demerath, p. 345).

The book provides a valuable review (without resolution, of course) of the broad range of issues which confront sociology's merging of science and policy roles. The papers on the policy-relevance of specific topical research pieces will be of interest to social scientists working in the substantive areas covered (e.g., poverty, delinquency). Less valuable, largely because it is "dated," is the section on graduate training and federal funding. Yet Richard J. Hill's report on a survey of graduate training, Howard Freeman, Edgar Borgatta, and Nathaniel Siegel's remarks on the changing relationship between government support and graduate training, and Nelson Foote's discussion of the role of the sociological perspective capture the continuing national trends and debate on the subject. Kenneth Lutterman provides the only paper from the viewpoint of a government agency, arguing that sociologists contribute little to the amelioration of social conditions because the discipline is concerned with teaching rather than research. Demerath's epilogue contains an informative, accurate overview of the issues.

This book will be of primary interest to social scientists and policy makers concerned with obtaining a relatively non-controversial perspective of main-line sociologists on social policy and sociology.

Policy Issues in Education, edited by ALLAN C. ORNSTEIN and STEVEN I. MILLER. Lexington, Mass.: Lexington Books, 1976. 159 pp. $15.00 cloth.

ROSALIE A. COHEN
Temple University

Books on policy issues in American education are few and much needed. Because schools represent the only compulsory "normal" social setting, modifications in their structure or curricula reflect major themes in social change, and, in future-oriented societies, explicit efforts at social reform. Authors of the eleven essays in this collection present overviews of some contemporary educational issues arising out of major social transformations. Some essays deal with the legitimation of public policy—expressing the editors' biases toward linking research and advocacy. Other papers deal with conflicts arising from enforced structural changes as they affect decision makers and student bodies. Authors present the policy making arena accurately—as political. The papers are sophisticated and the discussion is of the sort engaged in by state or federal commission members or agency administrators. As a result, this book is most useful for their staffs. For university students, however, most missing is an organizing theory, explaining why social structural changes are reflected in contemporary educational policy. The emergence of teacher unions, Affirmative Action conflicts, and accountability themes are discussed without pointing to commonalities among them in a shifting occupational market and in changing legal codes. *Policy Issues* is, thus, an excellent sourcebook on some of these concerns, but recommendations for reform appear more to engage than to enlighten.

Social Science and Public Policy, by MARTIN REIN. New York: Penguin Books, 1976. 272 pp. $2.95 paper.

DAVID G. GIL
Brandeis University

Works of fiction tend to use autobiographic material but scholarly writings are supposedly personal life histories. Rein's book is self-reflective, yet its scholarly quality seems enhanced by this. It is an attempt to search for meaning in his work, and to understand, and convey to others, his personal positions and values, and his approach to policy analysis and social research. Few writers on social policy have shared their philosophical struggles and dilemmas as freely as Rein has in these essays.

Rein's arguments are not original but this does not detract from the book's importance. They reflect his encounter with sociology of knowledge, critical theory, phenomenology, philosophy of science, and radical philosophy. The book thus reveals a stage in the intellectual development of one student of social policy.

Rein's view, that policy analysts specify their values, should apply also to reviewers of books. My work is based on egalitarian, libertarian, and democratic values, and my reactions to his book are influenced by this.

The book's central theme, on which Rein develops numerous variations, is that perceptions and interpretations of facts cannot be disentangled from values, when studying and developing social policies, and when conducting social research and implementing public services. This circumstance leads, in Rein's view, to nearly unresolvable complexities and dilemmas for policy analysts and researchers. Positivist approaches to these issues are judged inadequate by Rein. His tentative solutions include scepticism toward all positions, eclecticism in the use of interpretive paradigms, and a "value-critical" stance which involves analyzing the sources and dynamics of one's own and other actor's values. Rein doubts the feasibility of discovering general laws for social processes and recommends greater reliance on idiographic approaches including case studies, analogues, and "story-telling," the truth and relevance of which can be challenged and tested.

Due, perhaps, to the breadth of issues explored, there are oversights and conceptual problems. Rein overlooks authors who have identified equality as the central value criterion of social policies, and distribution of resources, statuses and rights as central processes. When he describes his own "value-critical" position as non-ideological (p. 79), Rein overlooks that his ideology to be non-ideological is a tacit acceptance of the status-quo.

Rein fails to define the term "value," a central concept of his book. He uses it interchangeably with "goal," "ends," and "purpose." His analysis is largely ahistorical: he fails to trace values to their sources in perceived interests of societies or their subgroups. He also fails to define the meaning of equality and liberty and accepts as a given the myth of an inevitable conflict or trade-off between equality and liberty. Critical analysis would reveal that genuine liberty and genuine equality depend on one another and are unattainable one without the other.

When discussing stratification, Rein considers occupation, income, and education, but neglects a fundamental aspect of stratification systems, namely, the historical process of the acquisition by expropriation of productive wealth (land, natural resources, tools, knowledge, etc.) and subsequent legitimation of this process as "law and order." He also neglects the multiple consequences of this for the division of labor, the organization of production, the distribution of rights (social, economic political, civil, etc.) and for values, consciousness, and social dynamics. When wealth is disregarded, social problems defy solutions.

Judging Rein's development, by comparing this book with his earlier writings, he is likely to confront, before long, the issues he overlooked and seems to have misunderstood in the present book.

Social Psychology

Social Psychology: The Theory and Application of Symbolic Interactionism, by ROBERT H. LAUER and WARREN H. HANDEL. Boston: Houghton Mifflin Company, 1977. 467 pp. $11.95 cloth.

PETER and PATRICIA A. ADLER
University of California, San Diego

This work is a good, representative and recommendable text with a symbolic interaction perspective. It presents a dynamic, processual analysis which differentiates it from the more behavioristic, cognitive, and experimental approaches. Oriented in both writing style and level of presentation toward the beginning student, the book is divided into three segments: part one offers a systematic presentation of symbolic interaction theory; part two examines its substantive application to a number of conceptual areas; and an in-depth depiction of some diverse but exemplary proponents of the perspective is considered in part three.

Well grounded in the general social psychological literature, Lauer and Handel make edifying use of a comparative technique to clarify the position of symbolic interactionism vis à vis other relevant approaches. Sociological and psychological (as well as other disciplinary) influences are delineated, although the authors' orientation is clearly closer to the former. Commendable also is the use of explanatory studies as illustrative examples for general points; the further purpose of acquainting students with considerable germane empirical work is also served.

Of more questionnable value here is the authors' decision to portray symbolic interactionism's ideological jungle as a "consensual body of theory." While we applaud their inclusion of the full range of interactionist notions (Chicago school, Iowa school, Goffman's dramaturgy, labelling theory, and even ethnomethodology), these varied and often conflicting belief systems are incorporated into a single artificial unit whose parts do not always mesh successfully. In addition, the creative idea of utilizing four depth biographical studies (Blumer, Strauss, Shibutani and Goffman) to illustrate the possible clash of various eclectic syntheses within the field fails to achieve full potential for two reasons: (1) Lauer and Handel neglect to draw out the salient theoretical differences, concentrating almost exclusively on presentation of each man, and (2) the proponents chosen do not exemplify anything near the diversity that exists within this paradigm.

Unfortunately, this work is uneven in quality, falling from its original good start to some rather poor chapters on ethnomethodology, labelling theory, and Goffman. Important philosophical roots of the tradition, which could have been employed to reveal the development of thought and add greater understanding, are given scant consideration. Reflections on the shortcomings endemic to the perspective are also inadequate, particularly in the methodological realm. Finally, we note the absence of a glossary or general bibliography at the end of the text which could have been particularly useful to introductory students.

Nevertheless, despite its flaws, this book can be recommended. It is clearly written, understandable, and abounds with interesting material. An excellent instructor's manual, containing a nice summary of each chapter and suggested exam questions, accompanies the text.

The Life of the Self: Toward a New Psychology, by ROBERT JAY LIFTON. New York: Simon & Schuster, 1976. 190 pp. $7.95 cloth.

ROBERT LYNN SATOW
Brooklyn College/CUNY

While Robert Jay Lifton's other books deal with survivors in a literal sense—survivors of Hiroshima or Vietnam—in this book Lifton generalizes his understanding of survivor psychology to a general psychology because he believes that not only holocausts, but rapid social change makes survivors of us all. Lifton argues that death and discontinuity have replaced repressed sexuality and identity conflict as the major sources of our psychological impairments, and the most basic difficulty is the impaired capacity to feel and to order our inner experiences. A new psychology is emerging, according to Lifton, a new paradigm based on the organizing principle of death versus continuity—he calls it "the formative paradigm in death psychology."

While in the Freudian model the most basic concepts are instincts, repression, and defense, the concept of "psychic numbing" is the central concept in the formative paradigm. Psychic numbing is a desensitization, an incapacity to feel or confront certain kinds of experience because of an absence of inner imagery that can connect with the experience. It is the result of an impairment of the human's essential ability to form symbols. Human beings cannot receive information nakedly, there must be an inner re-creation, or symbolization, but when the experience is too overwhelming, there is psychic numbing—or "death in life."

Freud viewed anxiety as related to the threat of unbridled instincts, but for Lifton all anxiety relates to death. But Lifton does not speak of death simply as the end of life. Death imagery encompasses separation and loss, disintegration, and stasis; while life symbolizes attachment, integrity, and movement. The fear of death is seen as similar to what Erikson calls "basic mistrust" and the sense of immortality if viewed as similar to "basic trust." Death is also symbolic of formlessness, while the sense of immortality symbolizes a sense of form and order. Thus, although Lifton ardently rejects Freud's instinct theory and any notion of a death "instinct," he does broaden the meaning of death and the sense of immortality to such an extent as to make one think about a life force (eros) and a death force (thanatos).

The early chapters in which Lifton compares his formative paradigm as well as his formative experiences to those of Freud and Erikson are much less interesting than the later chapters in which he discusses the survivor as creator and his notion that we must confront our living deadness by re-creating modes of symbolic immortality. Some of his most interesting comments are about the "pornography of death"—the presentation in literature and movies of extreme violence and end-of-the-world imagery. Lifton says this is an extreme rendition of our state of desymbolization—it is revelation by excess. While some might argue that excessive violence in books and movies actually encourages psychic numbing, Lifton argues this end-of-the-world imagery must be confronted so that we can unblock our imaginations and overcome our living deadness.

Ironically, Lifton is most fascinating as social and literary critic, as well as psychohistorian, and least interesting when he discusses basic psychological processes and compares himself with Freud and Erikson. In general, this book is a loosely organized group of essays which includes some very insightful ideas about why death has become a major theme in psychology, but it does not add up to a new psychology.

The Inner Experience, by DAVID MCCLELLAND. N.Y.: Halsted Press, 1975. 427 pp. $15.95 cloth.

LAUREN LANGMAN
Loyola University, Chicago

McClelland is a bright, creative psychologist whose work should be known by sociologists. In *The Achieving Society*, he attempted to explain economic growth on the basis of the levels of individual needs for achievement. In his latest book, war, peace, religion, and the growth of organizations and empires are seen as social manifestations of needs for power. This book is more than an empirical study of the psychology of power; it is also a philosophy of life, with a mystical vision of a just world through submission to a higher power. Since the book contains a good deal of autobiographical material, we see how McClelland's vision is rooted in his own Quaker background. The book cannot therefore be evaluated solely on scientific criteria.

The need for power is seen as a need to *feel powerful*, to have an impact; influencing others is only one form of its expression, albeit the one sociologists are most interested in. The manifestations of the need for power differ according to sex, social class, and level of emotional development. Power can be experienced as coming from within or without, and directed toward the self (to feel strong) or others (to influence). This typology corresponds to the Freudian theory of development. In Stage 1 (oral) power comes from others and strengthens the self, in Stage 2 (anal) power comes from the self and leads the feeling of strength through self assertion and control. In Stage 3 (phallic) power comes from within and is used to influence others; in Stage 4 (genital mutuality) power comes from without and is used to influence others. McClelland then goes on to demonstrate that these four stages are universal. In empirical studies, projective measures of power, combined with questionnaire measures of emotional development, revealed interesting patterns of the many ways the need for power is expressed. Individuals can express power through giving, drinking, competitive sports, reading sexy and/or sporty magazines, collecting credit cards, etc.

McClelland illustrates the relation of power to the traditional feminine role—giving, nurturing, and supporting. He calls this the Demeter-Persephone life style, illustrated by the life of his devoted mother-in-law. His analysis of India, based on written texts such as the *Bhagavad Gita* and *Ramayana*, indicates that India is a Stage 1 society, where power, expressed in the feminine modes of giving and supporting, is the dominant psychological theme. In Mexico, McClelland finds combinations of Stages 1 and 2, in which power is manifested by familial loyalty and assertion of the self. He calls this the "Icarus Complex," rising up and falling down. The "macho" pattern is interpreted as a manifestation of self-assertion.

McClelland analyzes the issues of power in a variety of mystical religions, and "the imperial pattern" of industrial managers and complex patriarchal social systems. He hypothesizes that when the society shows the "imperial pattern" a cycle of war or violence results. After war there tends to be a rise of the need for affiliation. When power and affilative motives are balanced religious revivals occur, but this balance is unstable and there is a subsequent drop in the need for affiliation, the basis of war. In his analysis of English and American history, he uses power imagery in literature, ballads, and hymns to support his hypotheses. He sees the current situation as the period of religious revival that precedes war. But war is not inevitable: we can embrace religions that renounce violence like Buddism or change religions that do not embrace pacificism.

This book is not easily evaluated. As an empiricial study its methods are often dubious, the data seem selective, the interpretations forced, the generalizations extreme, and the conclusions speculative. There are many contradictions and biased interpretations of reality. Yet the work is imaginative, provocative, and worth reading. We are reminded that we cannot ignore human motivation as *a* factor which influences society and its institutions, though McClelland's position is far too reductionistic for most sociologists. As a Messianic vision of a just world, and/or a mystical sense of life through union with God and membership in a religion that renounces violence, McClelland's visions go beyond social science.

Theory

The Structure of Sociological Inference, by W. Baldamus. New York: Barnes & Noble, 1976. 238 pp. $17.50 cloth.

Marshall Elliott Shumsky
University of Virginia

In this book the author investigates methods of sociological theorizing. In fact, quite early (introduction), Baldamus asserts that there is only one single theoretical method in sociology: Max Weber's method of constructing ideal types. The justification for this claim comes later (chapter III.1) when Baldamus reveals the latent theoretical structure of the conventionally used "2x2 table." Here his reasoning is quite convincing in two (overlapping) ways. First, the use of graphics poignantly displays concrete examples of a general logic which he has stipulated in advance. Second, his prose is focused and specific to particular activities used by working sociologists rather than diffuse and general, which, unfortunately, is his tendency toward the end of the book (chapter IV.3, appendix).

But, once again, Parsons stands firmly as the head of the dominant class. This time *The Social System* is viewed as functionalism's major theoretical accomplishment while various brands of Marxism provide the only major challenge. The varieties of neo-phenomenologies—while interesting, incisive, and insightful—provide little more than temporary havoc for functionalism. It seems that while these neo-phenomenologies have, in the short run, identified gaps in the functionalistic paradigm, they do not possess, individually or collectively, the stamina for seriously challenging functionalism in the long run.

But the long-term interaction effect between functionalism and Marxism is not without consequence. To a certain degree, mostly in terms of theoretical methods, a good deal of functionalism has been assimilated by Marxist sociologists. Partly, at least from Baldamus's point of view, the anti-functionalist orientation in Marxism has, inadvertently, in long-term effects, eroded the distinctive quality of Marxism. It should be noted that his sample of Marxist sociology is drawn from one major (untranslated) work *Wörterbuch der marxistisch-leninistischen Soziologie*, by Eichhorn, et al. These authors, while aggregately criticizing the contributions of all the prominent figures of Western sociology (e.g., Comte, Spencer, Durkheim, Weber, Simmel, Parsons, Merton, Mills, etc.) have, nevertheless, without exception, partially taken them over in a positive sense. The grain of truth in Western sociology, when suitably corrected or readjusted, is acceptable within a Marxist framework. The contamination of functionalism in Marxist theory is further illustrated by the topics addressed in the Eichhorn collection: Organization Analysis, System Theory, Communication, and Cybernetics. And the ultimate indictment of Marxism by Baldamus is that, in similar fashion to functionalism, Marxist sociology has directed its energy to establishing adequate validation criteria for social knowledge. The consequence of this orientation for Marxism, as well as for functionalism, is that there are no cumulative, concrete, substantive findings.

Another highlight worthy of mention is the convergence Baldamus sees between the explicit theory of theoretical functionalism (e.g., Parsons) and the implicit theory of empirical functionalism (i.e., The Sample Survey). The connective between them is Parsons's theory of socialization which is used axiomatically by both paradigms (explicitly in the former and implicitly in the latter) to the degree that the stability properties of the normative structure of modern industrial society are stressed. Once specific statistical innovations of sample surveys had made possible the manipulation of specific independent variables (e.g., age, sex, race, region, occupation, education), so as to extricate from the flow of data solely the socialization-specific aspects of social behavior, uncontaminated by biological, technological, or economic components, then these variables could be explanatory because they could be viewed as internalized orientations toward social action (i.e., stable properties, relatively independent of external circumstances). For Baldamus, this convergence of two independently-generated systems of knowledge ranks as one of the most extraordinary events in the history of the social sciences.

But without doubt, one of the lasting contributions of this book will be Baldamus's recasting of the Kuhnian notion of paradigm. Relying on the work of Ludwig Fleck (*Entstehung und Entwicklung einer wissenschaftlichen Tatsache. Einführung in die Lehre von Denkstil und Denkkollektiv*), also cited by Kuhn as his inspiration, Baldamus defines paradigm as a collective thought style, from which discovery emerges as the outcome of a prolonged and often intractible "zigzag" process, permeated with countless errors, false starts, and unsuccessful efforts. The paradigm progresses as a disorderly and imperceptible sequence of overstatement errors and their gradual elimination. Only in long-term trends are the structural continuities, present during all these overstatement errors, visible. Scientific progress is more a matter of uncovering these long-term continuities than of the writing of distinctly different paradigms. Baldamus has utilized this approach in delineating the theoretical methods in sociology.

It seems quite evident that this book will be important for those who are involved in working through the "crisis" in modern sociology. Although some of Baldamus's suggestions are somewhat unsatisfying, and stated too often in obscure and terse language, nevertheless his syntheses and insights should have long-term positive consequences for sociology.

Sociologia e Storia: Elementi per un Dibattito, by GIOVANNI BUSINO. Napoli: Guida Editori, 1975. 515 pp. No price listed, paper.

JOSEPH LOPREATO
University of Texas, Austin

Sociology owes Giovanni Busino (a sociologist at the University of Lausanne) a large debt not only for his scholarly work on Pareto's sociology but also for having recently undertaken the monumental task of editing for republication Pareto's sociological works and correspondence.

The present volume brings together some of Busino's own writings. It is divided into four parts. One part, "Switzerland: Between History and Sociology," contains material useful to scholars of ethnic contact and the sociology of education. Another is entitled, "In Search of a Rapprochement between History and Sociology," and contains chapters, among others, on "the history of economic and social facts" and on Guglielmo Ferrero, sociologist and social historian. Ferrero's *The Symbols* (1892) is one of the best contributions to an understanding of the relation between society and culture. And as co-author, with Cesare Lombroso, of *La Donna Delinquente*, he must have been chiefly responsible for the first truly sociological theory of criminality to enter one of Lombroso's volumes.

The remaining two parts are of great importance. One, entitled "Remarks for a Debate," includes essays on "the sociologist's craft," "sociology and history," "history and sociology," and "history of economic science or history of analysis?" The subject, clearly, is the relationship between history and sociology. In Europe, especially in those centers of learning where sociology departments are missing, the debate is still on. A significant point transpires from Busino's treatment: the interdisciplinary contention is the work of minds avidly frozen in narrow perspectives that deny the creative unfolding of knowledge; like a tree, knowledge grows both vertically and horizontally—a narrow mind cannot sit comfortably on a branch. The truth, of course, is that sociology and history are complementary disciplines. Sociology lends history the theoretical apparatus to nomothetically organize the chronology of social facts and the synchronic perspective, epitomized by the system concept, to illuminate the organic interdependence of facts constituting a sort of barrier which the "arrow of time" must pierce. At the same time, history sensitizes sociology to the implanted nature of social facts. I rather suspect that, as the evolutionary paradigm becomes entrenched in sociology, and history develops a less frugal conception of time, the two disciplines will learn to live in each other's company with gusto.

The remaining part, "The Lausanne School," is the most important and contains essays on "the sociology of art of Léon Winiarski," "Ernest Roguin astride jurisprudence and sociology," and several excellent chapters on Pareto. In one of these chapters, "Pareto the eternal malcontent," Busino presents a detailed and acute analysis of Pareto's work on socialist systems. In the process, he creatively underscores the significance of the class struggle and revolution in Pareto's work and in the historical process. Above all, Busino has the almost unique virtue, among Paretean students, of recognizing the pivotal point that power plays in Pareto's sociology.

But the heart of Busino's book is a superb chapter in which he presents and discusses the once famous debate between Pareto and Benedetto Croce, the foremost Italian philosopher of the past two centuries and veritable scourge of Italian social science. Very few sociological events, in my opinion, would be as useful for a historical understanding of sociology, and for a more complete understanding of one of its giants, as a translation and publication of Busino's essay in one of our principal sociological forums. Hopefully, this review will catch the eye of some enterprising editor.

Busino's careful treatment of the debate helps clarify the intriguing fact that Italian sociology practically went into hiding early in this century—victim of a logomachy tyrannically executed by Croce and the other metaphysicians and marionettes who surrounded him. It clearly suggests, too, that much of that sarcasm in Pareto's *Treatise* that has, ironically, angered many readers and driven them away, is in fact an implicit defense of sociology against Croce and the entire metaphysical tradition that denied an intellectual niche to sociology.

Finally, Busino's treatment of the debate shows the incapacity of the metaphysician to grasp the basic principles of scientific thinking and methodology. Where Pareto argued that knowledge cannot develop beyond a certain point without compartmentalizing it for purposes of isolating hidden relationships and then attaining a higher synthesis, Croce was horrified by the idea that reality in its "totality" could be fragmented and packaged into little "bundles." Where Pareto argued that mere reflection and intuition were inadequate to the discovery of scientific laws, Croce incomprehensibly held that social facts were "spiritual" and could only be apprehended through "spiritual intent." (A few years later, Croce crossed swords with Max Weber on this same score and was told, to no avail, that he confused knowledge with *Erleben* and *Einfühlen*, and that *Verstehen* without *Begreifen* could not yield clear and operational concepts.) Where Pareto argued that one could analytically subtract a part of a phenomenon for heuristic purposes, Croce maintained that to do so required an unjustifiable assumption about what can be focused upon and what can be left to one side. Where for Pareto, theory was the result of the manipulation of empirically verifiable observations, for Croce it was "the result of contemplation."

If there is one thing on which one can take issue with Busino it is his underestimation of the fundamentally biosocial-ethological nature of Pareto's analysis—a fact that, however, Busino himself recognizes in the introduction to the volume. This failure leads him to a number of errors. He, for example, approvingly quotes (pp. 62–63) Maurice Halbwachs's criticism of Pareto's "sentiments," or "instincts," as "abstract kernels." Again, on page 299 he finds simplistic and "circular" Pareto's explanation of the historical fatigue of the bourgeoisie. Pareto's explanation, in fact, is complex, direct, and fundamental; it concerns a large series of social events that weakened, in the bourgeoisie, the sentiments of "persistence" and of "the integrity of the individual." But these are almost esthetically pleasing blemishes on a beautiful volume.

Sociology, Equality, and Education: Philosophical Essays in Defense of a Variety of Differences, by ANTONY FLEW. New York: Barnes & Noble, 1976. 143 pp. $13.75 cloth.

RICHARD A. HILBERT
University of California, Santa Barbara

The seven essays in this book are intended as logical-philosophical critiques of current trends in sociology and educational theory. The central thrust of the work is directed against what the author identifies (p. 1) as a "new egalitarianism." This egalitarianism, Flew believes, is rooted in flawed social science theory, especially the sociology of knowledge and social construction perspectives. Such theorizing, argues Flew throughout the book, is illogical and leads to all sorts of Trouble in Academia. To begin with, it denies the existence of an objective, culturally independent reality in terms of which cultures, groups, and individuals can be comparably evaluated. This, says Flew, is due in part to fallacious reasoning: sociologists identify examples of socially constructed reality and conclude that *all* reality is socially constructed (chapter 2). Carried to its logical conclusion, this would deny the very possibility of social science to begin with (chapter 3). But having committed these errors, sociologists foreclose upon research they would not like to see happen, e.g., questions of inherent, objective qualitative differences between individuals or racial groups (chapters 4–5). Educators, furthermore, fall prey to a view that would deemphasize the distinction between competent and incompetent, between teacher and student, leading to politically interested concepts like "student power" and "academic freedom" (chapters 6–8). Flew does little to conceal his intellectual disdain for those embracing such "metaphysical idealism." He suggests they are either scholastically incompetent or secretive regarding their own hidden purposes, i.e., their Leftist leanings. At any rate, such theories, if taken seriously, are to be regarded as educationally subversive.

Sociological Theory in Research Practice, by ELIZABETH A. FREIDHEIM. Cambridge, Mass.: Schenkman Publishing Company, 1976. 325 pp. $7.95 paper.

GARTH MASSEY
University of Wyoming

Why study the classical theorists? The simplest reason is that, despite our sophistication, much can be learned from them. If their facts are dated or discredited, there remains a valuable lesson in their methods. Even at their worst, students are told, they grappled with problems that remain fundamental to the discipline, e.g. empiricism, subjectivism, the nature of groups, sources of conflict, power, and change.

It was bound to be written: classical theory and research in one easy volume. The author presents seventeen "sociologists," from Auguste Comte to Herbert Blalock (this chapter was co-authored by Daryl Chubin), in an attempt to show students the Masters' relevance to research strategies and problems. (Albion Small is included, despite the author's view that his, "principle merit does not lie in his original thought and sophisticated research.") Each chapter contains an introduction, some intellectual background, an image of sociology, the focus of research, a view of science, a section called "Research—The Practice," a conclusion and bibliography. It is simply too much in too little space. The result is a negligible presentation of each person's contribution to sociological research.

The book was written to give undergraduates a theory-research background, to show them the unity of theory and research. Like so many recent text-oriented books on sociological theory, it probably does more harm than good. Through such extreme abbreviation, oversimplified presentations commit a variety of distortions and misrepresentations. More importantly, it leaves the reader with a sense that these Masters' works are ultimately insignificant, so obvious are their ideas and so trivial are many of their approaches and conclusions. When the complexity of a problem or contribution is presented within the abbreviated presentation, it is nearly meaningless to the reader.

The author works in various dichotomies, such as the "natural" versus the "cultural" sciences, claiming that these "persist in modern sociology as a tension between *reliability* and *validity*." The author also contrasts the study of "men's interaction in society" to what is seen as the holistic approach of Spencer, Lundberg, Marx and others, and juxtaposes quantification to interpretive understanding. These are all important concepts for students to confront, but the author's tendency to promote her preferences by cursory analysis leaves the reader asking: "What is the fuss all about?"

This book makes clear that, despite a worthy goal and talented author, the idea of creating textbooks of classical theory should be abandoned.

Utopia and Revolution: On the Origins of a Metaphor, or Some Illustrations of the Problem of Political Temperament and Intellectual Climate and How Ideas, Ideals, and Ideologies Have Been Historically Related, by MELVIN J. LASKY. Chicago: University of Chicago Press, 1976. 726 pp. $35.00 cloth.

GWYNN NETTLER
The University of Alberta

Students of the social scene suffer an occupational hazard. They are vulnerable to a schizophrenia, a splitting of their souls by the tension between knowing the truth and doing good.

On the one hand, it is difficult to live in these modern aggregations that are vaguely called "societies" (but that are seldom nations and rarely communities); it is difficult to live among such hordes of strangers without thinking of a better world.

On the other hand, to propose a better world, as a scientist rather than a seer, is to claim to know something of the workings of the world. Marx and Engels were only seconding the pretensions of the Philosophes when they promised a *scientific* socialism. Given today's secular assumptions, the better world is no longer to be a reward for good behavior provided out of the benevolence of a god. Now it is to be achieved through a doing guaranteed by a knowing.

Melvin Lasky's powerful work is a history of this schizoid tension. *Utopia and Revolution* traces in fine detail the recurring longing for more satisfactory social arrangements, a longing that is repeatedly channeled into a revolutionary ideology by manufacturers of promises.

Lasky's history illuminates the origins of revolutionary ideology in figures of speech used to characterize such dramatic natural events as holocausts, storms, and the whirl of cosmic objects. The reference of these metaphors moves with other ideas, of course, and Lasky notes how the inventors and guarantors of utopian promises have been transformed from prophets and their gods into philosophers, theorists, and social scientists.

Such intellectual transformation represents shifts in the grounds of argument, in the guarantees given to devotees, but these changes in justification do not reflect changes in motive. A Paretian residue remains in the desire to manipulate the world and its denizens toward a promised land that recedes as we reach toward it. Utopia, we remember, is not a place (*ou,* not; *topos,* a place).

Lasky charts a cycle, a cycle that repeats itself on different levels of justification. Utopia once received a sacred justification and a heavenly location. Today utopian thought seeks secular justification and an earthly site. Yet a circle of ideas and actions is discernible and Lasky draws it this way: Promising Utopia and acting to realize it convert hypotheses into ideologies and theorists into dogmatists. Dogma, in turn, provokes doubt. Given the persistence of human curiosity, and given the imposition of a reality upon our dreams, the gap between promise and actuality stimulates heresy. Doubters and dogmatists then do terrible things to each other, and the spiral begins anew.

Lasky's history of ideas does not show utopian theories to be disproved by reasoned argument so much as defeated by realities. The defeat results in disillusion for some and in redoubled efforts for others. However, whether devotees of promise remain faithful or not, each disillusionment is succeeded by a new delusion. Promises are endless.

Lasky's study is a stimulating interpretation of the movement of ideas. It is worth reading for the intellectual exercise alone, but Lasky has learned some lessons which he passes on as prescriptions.

A first lesson is that, unless one is wary, language corrupts thought. If "progress," "revolution," and "utopia" are metaphors, and if such metaphors motivate, a therapy for ugly action is semantic sanitation. Lasky calls for "social reorganization without bewitching metaphor." But this prescription runs against the nature of language which, as Lasky knows and as Malinowski told us, is "a mode of action" as well as "an instrument of reflection." Reasonable persons—disinterested ones, that is—may discipline themselves into separating denotation from connotation and map from metaphor. But most of us, and more particularly the Hopeful among us, cannot abide such clean language.

Lasky's second recommendation would have us reason "humanely" without yearning for perfection. Zeal frustrates rationality. Great expectations promote that hatred which is 'the higher love" and reproduce that circle of injury in which we kill each other, one more time, for the last time. "The better is the enemy of the good," some of the French believe, and moderation has always been sound advice. But, while it may be rational to be prudent, it is more fun to be passionate, and it is doubtful whether ambitious actors can listen to history.

Lasky translates a third lesson into the recommendation that it would be wiser of us to conceive of a better world as something other than a termite society. The visions of better arrangements given us seriously or satirically by Plato and Huxley, Orwell and Skinner have been images of Utopia as a formicary. It would be an ant-heap in which, as a recent president of the American Psychological Association prescribed it, one world is people by one species organized as a Good Society of Good Persons (the capitals are the psychologist's).

But, of course, it is conceivable that Utopia

as harmony may not suit *Homo sapiens*. It may not fit this mammal's character. The recurrently dreamed Good Society would have to operate with creatures and physical laws so different from recognizable beings and known worlds that we can have no basis for comparing the satisfactions of such present and future states. More than this, we have no *knowledge* that allows us to construct such New Persons and Better Worlds.

Saying this, and confirming it by a history of social thought, are one thing; accepting the consequent prescriptions is another matter. Lasky, like Santayana and James before him, recognizes the will-to-believe to be a matter of temperament. A few intellectuals may have a choice, however, between being intelligent and being faith-full. The choice brings us full circle to the risks of schizophrenia assumed in becoming professionally thoughtful. Faith is required as a societal cement and personal integrant. Truth is required if we are to act without vicious consequence. The effort to remain sane engages us in a balancing act in which we teeter between hope and truth, passion and prudence. Lasky has dramatically described this act and has shown how few have kept their balance.

Georg Simmel: Sociologist and European, by PETER LAWRENCE. New York: Barnes & Noble, 1976. 275 pp. $13.50 cloth.

LEWIS A. COSER
SUNY/Stony Brook

This work is a welcome addition to the growing number of contributions by and on Simmel available in English. The first part consists of a lucidly written, unpretentious, and fairly comprehensive introduction to the life and sociological work of Simmel by Peter Lawrence of the University of Southampton. He breaks no new ground, but provides a primer to Simmel that will be useful in directing the attention of students to the continued relevance of his mode of analysis and substantive ideas.

The bulk of the book consists of samples of Simmel's work. Some of these are taken from earlier translations, but most are now translations by D. E. Jenkinson of the University of London. He renders Simmel's thought faithfully and in idiomatic English. Two excerpts come from Simmel's earliest (1890) sociological work, *On Social Differentiation*, which has not previously been available in English. In this work Simmel was still groping toward the mature position attained in his later writings. His sociological thought at that early time was still encrusted with questionable analogies from biology and physics, derived, at least in part, from Spencer and the social Darwinists. These excerpts hence are more important for the history of Simmel's thought than for their intrinsic significance.

In contrast, the excerpts from *The Philosophy of Money* (1900) show Simmel at the height of his analytical powers. The continued absence of a full translation of this major work is deplorable indeed. With the ninety pages or so translated here, together with over forty pages earlier made available by Donald Levine, at least the lineaments of Simmel's complex argument can be discerned by readers who do not have access to the original. Particularly the first part of chapter 4 of the original, here entitled "Individual Freedom," develops an essential strain in Simmel's writings about the liberating impact of money as a medium that helps free the individual from personal bondage. Excerpts from a later chapter record Simmel's contrapuntal observations that once a monetary system dominates the economy and replaces personal and subjective standards by "shared objectivity," it constitutes "a breeding-ground for economic individualism and egoism" (p. 182). This chapter, in addition, develops Simmel's highly suggestive ideas about the parallel development of monetary relations and rational structures of thought.

The final section of the book contains a number of excerpts from other writings of Simmel that are mainly concerned with what he saw as the fatal disjunction between the rapid development of "objective culture" and the inability of "subjective culture" to come to terms with the profusion of offerings and the bombardment of stimuli of modern civilization. These trains of thought are more fully developed in Peter Etzkorn's translation, of which Lawrence does not seem to have been aware.

This book is indispensable for anyone who wishes to gain access to the intricacies of Simmel's thought.

Phenomenology and Art, by JOSE ORTEGA Y GASSET. Translated by Philip W. Silver. New York: W.W. Norton, 1975. 220 pp. $8.95 cloth.

DON MARTINDALE*
University of Minnesota

Unlike most creatures spawned, hatched, or born which come equipped with biologically

* Editor's Note: Not the reviewer responsible for the listing in "Delinquent Reviews."

preprogrammed sensitivities and responses to experience, humans must learn or invent their own. Culture, the accumulating stock of social learning which humans substitute for instincts, is shot through with myths, fantasies, and archaic notions, hence it is constantly subject to alteration in which new forms (including myths and fantasies) are added even as old ones are replaced and corrected. Philosophy and the social sciences seek to account for the moral and aesthetic as well as for the factual aspects of human behavior. In this sense they have a more complicated task than the physical sciences, which need concern themselves only with how things behave.

In the vision of classical philosophy (Plato), the Good, the True, and the Beautiful are one. In modern thought this vision was retained, though Descartes had elevated the investigation of nature to a level of equal importance with the understanding of mind and spirit. Descartes proposed a daring project, to radically doubt everything we think we know until we reach what we experience and know beyond doubt and then to build up the complete system of thought with the certainty of a mathematical demonstration. Descartes assumed, that in the end moral, aesthetic, and factual knowledge would prove to form a single unified system.

The story of recent Western thought following Descartes consists in a series of brave efforts to realize his program, either starting from the side of mind (the Rationalists) or from the side of matter (the Empiricists). Alas, effort after effort repeatedly came to grief: a contradiction turned up, something had to be left out because it did not fit. In time a sense of impending disaster developed. Immanuel Kant eventually turned his powerful intellect to the task of resolving the crisis of Western thought. In a series of critiques he undertook to formulate definitely the sphere of science (pure reason), of morality (practical reason) and, of aesthetics (judgment).

As admiration for Kant's intellectual carpentry paled, scholars developed an acute sense of uneasiness. Kant's solution to the unity of thought was to seal its major subdivisions into airtight compartments, operating on contradictory principles and between which there was, in principle, no interrelation. Science, for example, required necessity; morality required freedom. Kant's formulations were a disaster to the program of the unity of thought.

In various ways the absolute idealists (Hegel), the monocausal materialists (Marx), and, the sociologists (Comte) explored an entirely new approach: they shifted the arena of thought to the collective mind (culture), they treated the basic bearer and agent of culture to be society, they explored the possibility that the true, the good, and the beautiful were phases of a single historical development. The resultant collectivistic philosophies have dominated much contemporary social thought. At first only dyspeptic holdovers from the Eighteenth Century, such as Schopenhauer, complained. But in time the new-found unity of thought began to break up on the rocks of cultural relativism. Toward the end of the Nineteenth Century a major counter reaction took shape under the battle flag "back to Kant."

Unfortunately, the neo-Kantians had to face the very limitations in Kant's theories that had been partly responsible for the rise of collectivism. This was the predicament that faced philosophers and social scientists at the turn of the century.

Confronted with the sterility of neo-Kantianism, a number of thinkers laid the foundations for phenomenology and existentialism. Kierkegaard opposed the individual existence to the Hegelian absolute, accepted the inability of reason to resolve ultimate problems and rested human hopes upon an act of faith. Influenced by the psychological phenomenology of his teacher Franz Brentano, Husserl proposed resumption of the task of Descartes, but with a more rigorous method of analysis to lay bare the intuitional sources of logical and mathematical ideas. Bergson reanalyzed the forms of perception (space and time) to demonstrate that Kantianism overlooked the more fundamental character of time as an internal sense and source of moral creativity.

The essays in the present collection, prove beyond dispute that Ortega was among the earliest and most creative of the founders of the phenomenological and existentialist movements. Ortega had studied with Herman Cohen, one of the most eminent neo-Kantians. Ortega attempted to go beyond the limitations of neo-Kantianism, the problem that haunted so many of his more sensitive contemporaries, by tackling the meaning of human fate by way of the aesthetic judgment (it is noteworthy in this connection what in Kant's treatment the judgment of taste occupied an anomalous position between the pure and practical reason, between morality and science). Ortega's intellectual biography (intended originally as a preface to the German editions of his writings) traces the extent to which in his first book *Meditations on Quixote*, he had laid down a phenomenological program quite outside the influence of Husserl. Ortega had proposed to explore the condition of people in their circumstances at the point where, in the novel, the worlds of fantasy and fact intersect. The essay also traces in detail Ortega's relations to the early phenomenologists and existentialists.

In other essays Ortega analyzes various problems which concerned the early phenomenologists. The essays on aesthetics and the arts derive much from Brentano's phenomenological psychology, and illustrate the operation of Ortega's phenomenological methods. Limpid clarity and dazzling metaphors, as in other of Ortega's writings, make the book a joy to read.

In view of the mounting interest by sociologists in phenomenology and existentialism and the number of works by would-be sociological phenomenologists which commit so many of the mistakes phenomenology originally proposed to correct, *Phenomenology and Art* is must reading.

Origin and Significance of the Frankfurt School: A Marxist Perspective, by PHIL SLATER. Boston: Routledge & Kegan Paul, 1977. 185 pp. $13.75 cloth.

BARRY M. KATZ
University of California, Santa Cruz

Since the publication in 1973 of *The Dialectical Imagination*, Martin Jay's history of the Frankfurt Institute for Social Research has dominated the field of English-language Frankfurt School studies. Jay argued the unsettling thesis that it may well have been the "relative autonomy" of the group of neo-Marxists around Max Horkheimer, and indeed, their practical isolation from day-to-day political conflicts, that contributed to their theoretical achievements in the 1930s and early 1940s. A serious challenge to this interpretation is now available in the recent book by Phil Slater (not to be confused with Philip *The Pursuit of Loneliness* Slater), where exactly the opposite claim is argued, that in fact the most fundamental of the theoretical—not to say political—errors shared by members of the Frankfurt School can be traced to their conscious distance from the political and ideological struggles swirling around them.

Slater directs two important charges against the Critical Theory of the Frankfurt School. First, their own methodological injunctions notwithstanding, it is alleged that they never succeeded in achieving "a critical relation to political praxis"; the second, related, problem with their work appears to be that their studies in ideology, social psychology, and aesthetics were misdirected or inadequate insofar as they failed to support them with a sustained economic analysis. Nobody who has studied the writings of Horkheimer, Adorno, Marcuse, and their colleagues, and takes their work seriously, can afford to ignore these challenges, and it is unfortunate, then, that having raised them, Slater does not carry us as far as he might in developing the two prongs of his argument.

To support his central contention that despite its lasting contributions, the work of the Frankfurt School represents "the break in the historical materialist theory-praxis nexus," Slater offers a sort of roster of what may be interpreted as alternative contemporary political orientations: the KPD; Brandler's opposition; Council Communism; left-wing Social Democracy; Trotsky, and others, suggesting that of the parties of the left, it was principally among the Frankfurt School that " 'praxis' became a theoretical, methodological category rather than a concrete notion of historical class struggle" (p. 63). Little is said about the unhappy fates of these various, more practically-minded groups and movements, however, and almost nothing—surprisingly—about the overwhelming forces against which they were arrayed, namely the National Socialist "Behemoth." Slater makes an important general criticism, but dubiously interprets the Frankfurt School position of the thirties, when it was already patently obvious that the fate of Europe would be decided in war, and not in the polemical pages of emigré newspapers, as a comprehensive orientation toward politics. Max Horkheimer might have been speaking directly to Slater when he wrote, in a 1973 essay from which the author draws liberally, that many intellectuals

> cannot bear the thought that the kind of thinking which is most topical, which has the deepest grasp of the historical situation, and is most pregnant with the future, must at certain times isolate its subject and throw him back on himself.

The other side of Slater's thesis—that the most creative intellectual undertakings of the Frankfurt School have been "superstructural" and are not rooted in an economic analysis—again raises a formidable challenge which was inadequately met by members of the Frankfurt School, and their advocates. But again, there is almost no concrete indication of precisely *how* this shortcoming might be rectified, along what lines an economic analysis might be constructed.

Finally, a word about form and content is apposite. The format of this study resembles certain logic textbooks, where nearly every paragraph is titled and numbered: 71 chapters, sections, and subsections in a text of less than 150 pages! This becomes a problem insofar as so many subdivisions fragment Slater's presentation with the result that a great many provocative and illuminating insights—on Brecht, Lukács, the student movement—are stated, barely developed in three or four paragraphs, and left behind at dizzying speed.

The Current State of Sociological Theory: A Critical Interpretation, by LEON H. WARSHAY. New York: David McKay Company, 1975. 231 pp. $4.95 paper.

DAVID R. SIMON*
University of North Florida

Perhaps the best that can be said about this volume is that it constitutes a modest beginning in assessing the state of contemporary sociological theory. The depth of discussion in the volume does not get much beyond Warshay's own summaries.

(1.) Modern sociology is dominated by small theories and empiricism rather than by large theories or schools. Some explanations are offered for this domination and it is treated with some sympathy (chapter 1).

(2.) Examination of current large theories shows continuing interest in organizational, interactionist, and, perhaps, functionalist theories and increasing interest in ecological, exchange, conflict, and phenomenological theories (chapter 2).

(3.) Other trends are considered including tendencies to open systems theories and to integration of consensus and conflict theories. Also examined are renewed directions toward comparative and interdisciplinary sociology. There is the further conclusion that sociology retains a micro orientation despite some macro attempts (chapter 3).

(4.) The field is polarized philosophically by a (new) humanist-positivist split, this having frustrated the Theory-Method integration hopes of the 1950s. The historic basis for that split is analyzed (chapter 4).

(5.) Other controversies over theory and method are examined. Sociologists are accused of lagging behind other behavioral and natural sciences in that sociologists almost unanimously retain their expectation, or wish, for a single general theory for all of sociology (chapter 5). The disputes over the appropriate structure or form for theories and over the existence of a single method for all sociology and all science are appraised (chapter 6).

(6.) The last part of the book attends to perennial ethical and political issues, recently revived in sociology. Chapter 7 evaluates mutual criticisms between radical and liberal (and conservative) sociologists. Chapter 8 discusses some implications of these issues and disputes. (xvii-xviii)

Given the generality of description, there arises a real question concerning the intended audience of the book. Undergraduates taking their first course in theory should be largely bewildered by this superficial collection of descriptions. To them sociology will not look like a discipline as much as it will history's worst case of multiple personality. While many will admit the discipline has some dandy theoretical disputes, it also possesses some interesting attempts at synthesis which Warshay has chosen to downplay. Marxists, for example, have seriously looked into the works of C. Wright Mills, Weber, symbolic interactionists, ethnomethodologists, exchange and systems theorists, and not without some interesting results.

Perhaps, beginning or advanced graduate students will find this a useful summary, but to me this seems unlikely. While there is a useful bibliography here, Warshay's arguments are made in such haste that one feels the author is tacitly saying to the reader "you know what I mean, of course." All too often it is not apparent what is meant. For example, the criticism is made throughout that elementarism characterizes sociological theory as a whole, as well as many specific theories. Nowhere are we given a definition of elementarism which would allow students to comprehend what would be required for theory to move beyond the elementary (concept) level. Many other terms are sorely in need of explicit definition (e.g., humanism, historicism, formalistic determinism). It is not that these terms are totally

---

Editor's Note: Not the reviewer responsible for the listing in "Delinquent Reviews."

undefined in the book; it is that Warshay's definitions are ambiguous in many instances.

Regarding humanism, the serious differences between certain branches of humanistic sociology have been neglected. To list both Peter Berger and Alvin Gouldner in the same paragraph, and to claim that the tie which binds them is "involvement in several senses of the word—theoretical, methodological, and activist," without specifying which adjective applies to whom is an unfortunate misrepresentation. In fairness, Warshay does state that "humanism has several meanings, not all of which are shared by all new humanists" (p. 86). But this could easily be interpreted to mean that the differences between humanists may be those which differentiate theory from method. In fact, the well known statements of both Berger ("Sociology and Freedom") and Gouldner (*The Coming Crisis of Western Sociology*) serve to indicate profound (conservative-radical) ideological differences, which Warshay, later on, claims are so basic that they could disrupt the sociological status quo!

Professionals might find the work a useful guide to assessing their own biases, but I am skeptical. Warshay says virtually nothing concerning mass society theory, which is to my mind the great intellectual underpinning of both contemporary theories and ideologies. The theory, which Daniel Bell termed the most influential in the world, and Leon Bramson's *The Political Context of Sociology*, handily exposed for its elitism, biased characterizations of the lower classes, and disturbing pessimism and fatalism, still haunts conservative and liberal sociology. Worst of all, Warshay tries to defend these faults in the name of liberal tolerance. To reveal adequately the biases of a discipline, one must not typify what one wishes to expose.

This brings us Warshay's critique of radical sociology, which is viewed as intolerant and potentially destructive of both the sociological and societal status quo. The dubious assumption upon which these barbs are levied concerns a conservative phenomenology: "too strong an emphasis on conflict" invites "negative sanctions upon conflict theorists until or unless a revolutionary situation should emerge" (p. 29). The message seems to be that there are no faults in the status quo; it is those who criticize it which force it to be repressive! In the end, Warshay pleads for a "liberal" sociology; it's the only type which is benevolent enough to tolerate conservative and radical sociology. Tolerance, here, seems to indicate a form of social control where liberals defend radical sociologists' intellectual inquiries into the social order, but quickly withdrawn support when talk "degenerates" into meaningful social change.

Radical sociologists, especially those connected with *The Insurgent Sociologist*, should respond to summaries of criticisms leveled at them by conservative and liberal sociologists. These are contained in Warshay's last two chapters, and are the outstanding features of the volume. This is not because these remarks have validity; it is merely that this is the first time they have all been listed in one place. As in the other chapters of the book, Warshay pretends merely to be engaged in summarizing such criticism. He thus includes *some* radical criticisms of conservative and liberal sociology, but his biases clearly allow him to portray radicals as advocates of violent revolution! This is the most tragic misrepresentation in the entire book, and in making it Warshay clearly indicates the nature and limits of his own "liberal" tolerance. His fear is that "the increasing gulf between . . . radical and . . . liberal sociologists will lead the latter not only to re-emphasize liberal principles more forcefully, but also increasingly to use more conservative ones. . . . The near future may well see liberal sociologists, for defensive reasons at least, increasingly receptive to conservative and right-wing politics and sociology. . . . To the new radical sociologists, such a development would reveal the liberals' true colors to one and all however, it might actually be more a case of a radical self-fulfilling prophecy" (p. 151).

Liberalism has thus come a very long way since Jefferson's advocacy of revolution and equality of property. What we have here is a morally bankrupt defense of the status quo, replete with exercises in blaming the victim and Orwell's doublethink. One wonders, for example, how Warshay would explain Michael Harrington's promising Democratic Socialist Organizing Committee which (1) includes the likes of "liberal" Robert Dahl and "radical" Norman Birnbaum, (2) supports a socialist alternative for American society, and (3) works peacefully within the Democratic Party in order to bring about such a change. What a pity it is that Warshay's energetic and bright mind has resulted in a tragically superficial and biased product! It is as if Gouldner's attack on Parsons was undergoing a sad form of retaliation. The advocacy for reflexive sociology is now endangered by another sort of reflex; knee-jerk liberalism.

Additional Reviews

Sociobiology and Behavior, by DAVID P. BARASH. New York: Elsevier, 1977. 378 pp. $9.95 cloth. $4.95 paper.

JOHN D. BALDWIN
University of California, Santa Barbara

Barash's goal is to provide a clear, informative introduction to sociobiology for the student and social scientist who have not had prior exposure to the topic. The book succeeds admirably: it is a well organized, interesting overview of modern sociobiological theory, nicely documented with animal studies and referenced to the current literature. In addition, the book is graced by attractive illustrations and useful diagrams.

The "Central Theorem of Sociobiology" states: "When any behavior under study reflects some component of genotype, animals should behave so as to maximize their inclusive fitness." That is: animals should behave such that they leave behind the maximum possible number of their own genes. An animal that did not behave this way would be put at a competitive disadvantage by those who did. For example, under many conditions promiscuous males would be expected to leave behind more offspring than monogamous males; hence, under those conditions male promiscuity would be at a selective advantage compared with monogamy. Barash provides numerous examples to support the thesis that reproductive strategies along with inter- and intragroup social relations are explained by the Central Theorem.

Barash openly admits that he is taking an advocacy role, seeking to "push" (p. xi) the evolutionary perspective. Nonsupporting data and critical viewpoints are not included. Barash gives several token apologies for not looking at developmental, cultural, and learned components of behavior; then proceeds to push the evolutionary perspective as far as possible.

Sociobiologists are especially eager to apply their theory to human social behavior, though there is a paucity of relevant empirical data on humans. Barash asks us to be playful and speculate along with him about the causes of human behavior from the evolutionary point of view. However, in the foreword, E. O. Wilson warns us that although the book is "swift and light in style . . . it is entirely serious in content." Throughout the book we get the double message: the sociobiological analysis of human behavior is playful speculation, yet deadly serious. The ultimate cause of behavior—natural selection of the fittest individuals—is based on the evolutionary principle in which "differential reproduction is all that counts" (p. 100). Proximal causal mechanisms for behavior—physiology, development, learning, culture—will presumably have to fall in place to support the ultimate causes (or become extinct). For those who like single factor theories, why not use the *ultimate* explanatory variable.

Barash argues that in spite of the lack of data, we must study the biological bases of human behavior. He criticizes the behavioral view for assuming a "tabula rasa" position (though behaviorists have never held this view [see Skinner, *Contingencies of Reinforcement*]). If not a tabula rasa, then what? Barash makes it look like sociobiology is our only choice. However, admitting the relevance of biology does not automatically mean that sociobiology has *the* interpretation of how our biology affects us.

Perhaps books by enthusiastic advocates are more interesting and spark more debate than books by overly cautious scholars. A lively course or seminar could be constructed around this book, especially if an advocate from the other side (e.g., Marshal Sahlins's *The Use and Abuse of Biology*) were read simultaneously.

The Social Organization of Leisure in Human Society, by NEIL H. CHEEK, JR. and WILLIAM R. BURCH, JR. New York: Harper & Row, 1976. 275 pp. $10.95 cloth.

BILL DEVALL
Humboldt State University

As a substantive area of sociology the sociology of leisure and recreation is important for theoretical sociologists interested in social change, patterns of social organization and attitudes, and for sociologists interested in community planning and utilization of natural resources. A growing list of universities offer undergraduate majors in recreation planning and management. A concise, relevant, and comprehensive textbook for undergraduate courses providing a sociological perspective on leisure and recreation in advanced industrial societies is needed.

When I began reading Cheek and Burch's book on social organization of leisure in human society, I hoped this would be the definitive and timely textbook I have been looking for. But I found the book only partially satisfying and some chapters downright irritating.

Cheek and Burch are leaders in the field of Sociology of Leisure. They have done recreation research, worked for government agencies, and hold academic appointments. Thus, they have excellent qualifications for writing a textbook.

In this book they do not claim to present much original research or original theory but to examine first a set of "empirical regularities common to one industrial society at one particular time" and then discuss the different cultural meanings of time and the "bonding mechanisms" which hold individuals together. They discuss "taste as a cultural mechanism that builds upon a biosocial character of the species" and end the book with a brief review of the rise of recreational institutions in America, the rationalization of recreation, and various theories explaining how play, games, and sport assist in sustaining social unity.

The survey data they present indicates regularities of frequency and timing (daily, weekly, monthly) of recreational activities, but the limited historical perspective for trend analyses of these surveys and the generalized terms used for activities (i.e., "driving for pleasure," "camping," etc.) make it difficult to understand the social meaning of these terms for different aggregates of the population. My own research, for example, leads me to conclude that "camping" has lost any analytical usefulness for the sociologist. The term is used to refer to everything from using huge motorhomes to backpacking with a tent many miles into a wilderness area.

Recreation within group context and recreation as a means of formation of "social bonds" in small groups and larger groups is the primary focus of this book. In chapter six, the authors introduce the concept of *taste*. Using taste as a major theoretical concept, the authors argue that "matters of taste are the social property of small groups, and as such they may provide useful indications of group boundaries," but that "intergroup solidarity requires that such boundaries be permeable."

I have two major criticisms of the book. First, the authors do not get to routinization of enjoyment and the historical development of recreation in capitalist societies until the end of the book. Then they provide a very unsophisticated and brief description of major factors which led to the interest of capitalists in recreation. They virtually ignore the political economy of recreation and the interaction between capitalist, tastemakers (such as professional athletes), and the demand to "consume more" in later capitalist societies. Furthermore, comparison of Japan (never mentioned in the book), America, and socialist countries would be most enlightening for the modes of control of recreation exercised by capital and government.

My second major criticism is the style of writing in the book. Both authors have written many research reports for the National Park Service and other agencies. The bureaucratic style seems to have influenced their writing in this book. It is turgid, dull, and excessively academic.

In sum, while many of us may use this book as a text in the Sociology of Leisure, it is not the book we have been waiting for. When sociologists studying leisure and recreation get off their kick of quantification of "users activities" which satisfies the bureaucrats for whom they work and begin to write critical, historically grounded analyses of recreation such as Dean McCannell's excellent analysis of *The Tourist*, then we may perhaps get a textbook useful for undergraduate courses in the Sociology of Leisure which is lively, timely, and relevant to theoretical issues and practical concerns.

Public Employee Unions: A Study of the Crisis in Public Sector Labor Relations, edited by A. LAWRENCE CHICKERING. San Francisco: Institute for Contemporary Studies, 1976. 248 pp. $14.50 cloth.

MARTIN OPPENHEIMER
Livingston College/Rutgers University

It is startling that in an anthology subtitled "A Study of the Crisis in Public Sector Labor Relations" there is not a single serious discussion of the sources of the fiscal crisis in government. Nor, in a bibliography of some 160 items, is a single work in macro-economics listed—much less James O'Connor's, by now well-known, *The Fiscal Crisis of the State*. It is as if the city's "eroding tax base," its "mounting economic difficulties," its state of "permanent austerity" (to use some favored expressions) simply just happened (partly, one is given to understand in some of these essays, because unions are greedy and some mayors inept), and that this condition is here to stay, for each city to cope with in isolation from, and in ignorance of, the larger political-economic structures of our society and the world. The word "recession" appears in one sentence.

(Incidentally, the title should really have been "Municipal" Public Employee Unions—the book does not deal with state or federal unions, and, as already implied, fails to discuss state or national, much less international, labor relations and their interconnections with crises.)

The main focus of the more technical discussions by such labor relations experts as Theodore Kheel, and Harry Wellington and Ralph Winter (in an essay published originally by the Brookings Institution) is that public sector unions are different from private, in that their funding is different, they provide services rather than commodities for profit and (the view of most of these contributors) they ought not strike. Thus, it would seem to most of these observers, unions create inflationary pressures, at least in part because they have political clout, and therefore need to be held in check (or somehow to achieve more responsible leaders). Professor Nisbet, indeed, believes it's probably already too late, that we are headed for a "new feudalism" in which corporations and unions fight it out due to a "decline in trust" in the State's mechanisms to provide social solidarity. At the same time, oddly, he thinks workers shouldn't trust unions either because "The rise in wages and improvements in working conditions during the last two centuries has had little to do with the activities of unions . . . ," a statement contradicted by virtually every other contributor.

The Kheel, Wellington and Winter, Jack Douglas, Daniel Orr, and David Lewin essays all contribute some historical-descriptive data, the latter two being of particular interest to students of wage levels and strike incidents. Raymond Horton's piece on New York City's financial mess isn't newsworthy—and carefully avoids any attention to the macro-level issues, e.g. the role of the banks. Lipset wanders, and wonders, about Russia, China, Sweden, Israel, etc., and the relationship between "equity" and "equality," by which he seems actually to mean the functional necessity for inequality. The *New York Times's* ace labor columnist A. H. Raskin is against strikes, for compulsory arbitration, and hopes we can all learn to "coexist constructively." The mayors of Seattle and Kansas City gripe about unions, and the heads of the AFL-CIO and the American Federation of State, County, and Municipal Employees tout them (two chapters that could have been dispensed with), and finally editor Chickering reviews the book in a "postscript" which should have come first.

Altogether not very edifying, and if this is the level of analysis being put forward by intelligent spokespersons for the enlightened section of the Establishment we are in for a long crisis and we had better look to other quarters for help.

Conflict, Conformity and Social Status, by BERNARD P. COHEN and HANS LEE. New York: Elsevier, 1975. 203 pp. $13.50 cloth.

CECILIA L. RIDGEWAY
University of Wisconsin, Milwaukee

The fundamental processes by which groups influence their members to conform are still surprisingly poorly understood. The problem, according to Cohen and Lee, has been a failure to link systematic, appropriately conditional theories with rigorous methodology. Cohen's answer in the past has been to conceptualize conformity as a conflict resolution process which can be represented by a Markov chain model (Cohen, Bernard, *Conflict and Conformity,* 1963). In this book, Cohen and Lee construct from Asch-situation data a revised Markov model which, unlike Cohen's earlier one, reasonably reflects the effects on conformity of variables such as a member's status in the group. Since the authors wish as much to advocate a particular research strategy as propose a new model, they describe in detail the specific failures and pragmatic searches for workable alternatives out of which the new model developed.

The work is intelligent and thorough. But the emphasis on making the model work at all costs creates a nagging uncertainty about the ultimate validity of the representation of the conformity process which finally results. The model's usefulness for generating fundamental insights or testing existing hypotheses about conformity is not convincingly shown. But the book remains thought provoking enough to require the attention of any serious student of conformity.

Drama in Life: The Uses of Communication in Society, edited by JAMES E. COMBS and MICHAEL W. MANSFIELD. New York: Hastings House, 1976. 444 pp. $18.50 cloth. $10.50 paper.

PETER K. MANNING

Michigan State University, East Lansing

Playing on and with meanings is one of the several themes within symbolic interactionism;

it is, as it were, an ineluctable characteristic. The terms, "dramaturgic" and "dramatistic" stand in ambiguous relationship to referents, and maintaining that ambiguity, multivalence, and indexicality has as much as anything been the substance of dramatism as a subperspective of symbolic interactionism. Assembling basic statements of this pleiomorphous perspective is something like trying to nail down mercury. To do so, one must obviate the blurred edges, drawing freely from psychiatry (Berne) organizational analysis (Thompson), dramatic criticism (Burke), political science (Edelman, Merelman), and anthropology (Warner), obviate the significant divergences within the perspective, within the perspective over time, and within the ideas of given figures such as Goffman (compare *Presentation of Self* with *Frame Analysis*) and eschew close definitions of key concepts, especially perplexing matters of metaphor: is life a drama, is there only drama in life, or is life like a drama or vice-versa? This is as fine a collection of basic statements as could be managed (one could always argue about a few of the inclusions and exclusions). Within the structural limits outlined above, it is superb. It should be a part of the library of all sociologists interested specifically or generally in symbolic interactionism and its variants. It is carefully and systematically organized into an introductory section "variation in perspectives," and a concluding section, with the intervening sections on "social interaction as drama," "mass communications as drama," "public dramas," "organizational dramaturgy," and "culture and history as drama." It is filled with essays by Berger, Burke, Duncan, Edelman, Goffman, and Gusfield, as well as mini-classics by Merelman, Warner, Messinger et al., Klapp, and Garfinkel. It importantly extends the horizons of conventional symbolic interactionism by including papers on complex organizations and social structure, heretofore rather vaguely indicated as a concern in work done within that perspective. The problem with the collection is substantial, not with the particular pieces. It is essentially flawed.

The problem of symbolic interactionism, reflected in this collection, is that it has become a litany, a responsive reading, a ritualized program to be extolled on cue, performed mechanistically, exhorted and exclaimed. Rituals are not easily eviserated; etiolated or not, they continue to mark the outer boundaries of a sacred concern, and lie at the heart of any perspective. It has been increasingly evident at least to me that ossification of the litany into a Mosaic proceeds apace. The variegated meanings of "dramaturgy" offer a case in point: (a) analysis of events that are highlighted and set apart from everyday life; (b) the conventions defining drama; (c) the use of these dramatic conventions as if they applied to everyday life; (d) the use of the language and perspective of the theater insofar as actors are aware that they are "playing roles," "doing drama," or experiencing "stage fright"; (e) the use of language and metaphor of the theatre to analyze social life; (f) analysis of events perceived by actors to be salient or dramatic; (g) analysis of media fictions and conventions which either produce "dramatic effects," *or* the rules by which such effects produce the experience of drama; (h) historical analyses of dramatic conventions and their roots in contemporary social life in whatever period; (i) an analysis of the doing of drama or of dramatic everyday events. This set offers an unbounded, open semantic field. It is, therefore, rather easy for example to cluster a symbolic interactionist interested in the drama of everyday life (e) such as Orrin Klapp, a later day Goffman (post *Relations in Public*) whose sociology is increasingly structuralist (g, h, i), and a political sociologist interested in the analysis of the symbolization of politics employing a variety of symbols and conventions—theatre, past politics, and religion. This clustering, however, obscures the differences between employing a root metaphor such as "drama" and drawing upon the institution itself as a symbol system with its own conventions, techniques, history, and production modalities.

Further, an unexplicated dramatism which makes obedient bows in the direction of existential thought (as does this book), can obscure the structural bases of social thought and action, while perpetuating the unexamined assumption that all "dramaturgical analysis" is "existential." Is all dramaturgical analysis "humanistic," or rooted in concern for the individual, his/her feelings, moods, and situationally negotiated choices? I would argue it is not, and would further argue that although Goffman is consistently labeled here as a dramaturgical sociologist, that he is not focused upon or concerned with interaction (*Encounters,* 35); is interested in the rules that *organize* and make meaningful experience, not experience itself (*Encounters,* 28, 41; *Frame Analysis,* chapter 1); and is not interested in individuals, but their situations (*Interaction Ritual,* 3). Rather than showing the inherent freedom of individuals, Goffman aims to show the profound limits upon them. Rather than elaborating the joy of creative meaning construction, he trods on the balloon of meaning showing that it, like computer tape, is as thin as any other strip of human doing. The orderly nature of human society is not fragile, not constructed by humans (as the litany goes), but in Goffman's terms, is based upon an ever-so-powerful invisible code. That it may be occasionally perceived as being fragile is an important datum, but its abiding invisibility is far more significant. We have often in employing dramaturgical analysis grasped at straws, failing to see what winds were carrying them.

There is, as these selections show, a kind of nice midwestern (in the tradition of Mead and Cooley) commitment to democracy and to the symbolization of a consensual democratic order in dramaturgical political analysis. As incisive as they are, the articles by Warner, Merelman, and Edelman hold out hope but perhaps fail to grasp that although all drama is a display of consensus, it is also an omission of meanings, a closing off of optional readings, a "mobilization of bias" as Schattschneider calls it. Rituals, being partial in their symbolic capacity, capturing the acceptable and the overtly public side of a dominant political position, do not reveal the extent of "submerged" conflict and thus generate resentment as well as value conflict and integration. (We occasionally are given clues to these alternative meanings when "counter inaugurals" or counter parades are held.) No one has written more brilliantly of the hegemony of "consensual" political rituals and the consensual bias of Durkheimian analysis than Steven Lukes ("Political Ritual and Social Integration," *Sociology* 9, 1975:289–308). Thus Durkheim and Mead, at once, do not fit but split. Efforts of many innovative and creative analysts, Bernstein being supreme among them, to sew together this tattered coat, colorful and Jacobean as it is, have not been completely successful. But Bourdieu, Bernstein, Leach, and Goffman do hold forth a less eclectic version of drama, a vision rooted, not floating, in neo-symbolic meanings unattached to the system of signs constituting the rules of experience.

For this book: plaudits as a superior collection, recommended to all, and as enormously useful. The intellectual task still lies ahead, now that source material has been assembled. This task will seek to reduce the positivistic individualism of American sociology while dramatizing that which is out of sight, the reproductive structures of experience.

Human Diversity: Its Causes and Social Significance, edited by BERNARD D. DAVIS and PATRICIA FLAHERTY. Cambridge, Mass.: Ballinger Publishing Company, 1976. 248 pp. $13.50 cloth.

JEFFREY SCOTT JOHNSON
Institute for Society, Ethics, and the Life Sciences, Hastings-on-Hudson, New York

This book recounts discussions sponsored by the American Academy of Arts and Sciences, in 1973 and 1974, in which evolution, genetics, and psychometrics are reviewed to evaluate the contention that the lack of academic and occupational success of poor Americans, especially black Americans, is largely a consequence of a deficiency in native intelligence. Ernst Mayr, Irven DeVore, Robert Trivers, and E. O. Wilson present human evolution; Bernard Davis, George Brewer, and Luigi Cavalli-Sforza explain genetics; Gerald E. McClearn, Seymour Kety, Steven Matthysse, and John Loehlin treat topics in behavior genetics; Lee Cronbach and Lloyd Humpherys present the logic of intelligence testing; while Arthur Jensen makes the case for a black genetic inferiority in intelligence. Davis has organized, introduced, and summarized the presentations from all these biological areas in support of Jensen's contentions, though the discussants themselves often come short of such support, and Davis's logic is strained beyond holding. David Layzer and Cavalli-Sforza argue that the use of *Heritability* to measure genetic determination of IQ is *invalid,* failing to distinguish direct genetic determination from genetic/environmental interaction and thus confounding genetic inferiority with the consequences of socio-economic deprivation and racial discrimination.

The central arguments of this book do nothing to repair this fatal flaw in Jensen's reasoning, and are rather a misuse of genetics to sidestep a political dilemma. In spite of a short historical section by Mark Adams, and some clear thinking by Christopher Jencks, the book deals only weakly with the socio-political meaning of genetic explanations of inequality, for which I would recommend two current books: Allan Chase, *The Legacy of Malthus: The Social Cost of the New Scientific Racism;* and Jeffrey M. Blum, *Psychometrics and Mental Ability: The Origins and Fallacies of the IQ Controversy*. Davis and Flaherty's book falls short even as an uncritical overview, since it lacks citations for most of the empirical work discussed. For this overview, see Loehlin, Lindzey, and Spuhler, *Race Differences in Intelligence*.

Labor Markets: Segments and Shelters, by MARCIA K. FREEDMAN with the assistance of GRETCHEN MACLACHLAN. Montclair, N.J.: Allanheld, Osmun & Co., 1976. 202 pp. $18.50 cloth.

PAUL OSTERMAN
Boston University

The distribution of money, status, and power in America can be best understood by examining the operation of the labor market. Poverty is a labor market outcome, social struggles such as civil rights and the women's movement focus on the distribution of occupational opportunities and rewards, and recent debates about the equity of income distribution center on the labor market. It is not surprising, then, that the sharpest ideological debates in the economics profession have occurred in the sub-field of labor economics. Nor is it surprising that the best opportunities for cooperation between economists and sociologists are found in this area.

Most economists interpret the labor market much as they do all other markets, in terms of the interaction of supply and demand. Drawing deductively from the core concepts of microeconomic theory, this view holds that the demand for labor is determined by its (marginal) productivity, the supply of labor is determined by the individual's choice between wages and alternative uses of time, and the observed distribution of wages and employment results from bidding in the market. Differences among individual outcomes result largely from individual choices about investment in education and training as well as from differences in ability and taste. Institutions such as unions and internal labor markets are seen as pesky intrusions which interfere with the smooth functioning of the market and are generally accorded little long-run importance. Politics, power, social groups, custom, and class are all virtually ignored.

This interpretation of the labor market has great power and appeal. It draws from a body of theory which is unified, coherent, and successful in many areas. This standard theory was also very influential in shaping employment and training policy during the War on Poverty years. Its central message is that people are poor because they are unproductive and thus cannot command high wages, and the emphasis on training and education which characterized policy flows from this view.

The failure of those policies as well as more general dissatisfaction with the individualistic and anti-institutional biases of standard theory led in the late 1960s to new efforts to develop alternative theories of the labor market. One strand was a Marxian approach which emphasized the role of schools in stratification and which also sought to demonstrate that job structures and production systems result from conscious efforts to stratify and control labor, rather than from the dictates of technology.

A different approach, different in spirit as well as content, sought to model the labor market in institutional terms rather than as an impersonal competitive market. Drawing upon the work of earlier institutionalists such as Commons, Rose, Schlicter, Reynolds, and Dunlop, these economists focused on internal labor markets, social networks, bargaining, and structural differences among firms with respect to hiring patterns, training, promotion, and product markets. The institutionalists drew upon sociological notions of inter-group relations, social custom, and family and neighborhood networks. Fundamental to the institutional view is the belief that the behavior of groups, as opposed to the atomistic economic human, determine labor market behavior and that institutions do more than merely reflect underlying market forces.

The debate among neoclassical, Marxist, and institutional economists has occupied a considerable fraction of recent labor economics research. Interpretations and policy with respect to poverty, racial and sexual discrimination, income distribution, and undocumented workers—to name a few issues—all vary according to which school of thought one believes.

Labor Markets: Segments and Shelters, by Marcia Freedman, assisted by Gretchen Manlachlan, is an effort to describe the labor market from an institutional viewpoint. Freedman, who in earlier work contributed important research to understanding the labor market adjustment of young workers, makes the important point that a driving force behind the labor market is the effort by workers, or group of workers, to erect institutional barriers which shelter them from both competition by other workers and the actions of employers. A variety of mechanisms, including licenses, certification, unions, work rules, seniority systems, and political action resulting in protective legislation, help workers protect their jobs. A useful approach to studying the labor market is to examine the nature of these shelters and how some people get under them while others do not. It is in forcefully making this point that the importance of Freedman's book lies.

Freedman uses Census data to construct an industry-occupational matrix containing mean annual earnings in each cell and then derives "segments" or clusters of cells along a set of independent variables intended to capture degree of sheltering. She uses an analysis of variance routine called Automatic Interaction Detector (AID) to rank the independent variables by the contribution to reducing the variance in earnings. The variables she considers are employment class of the job, percent of employees full time and full year, internal labor market structure, industrial concentration, and establishment size. Having derived job clusters and ranked each of the independent variables by their explanatory power, she writes short interpretive essays on each variable. She then repeats this procedure for variables which measure the characteristics of the people in jobs—sex, age, race, and education.

Unfortunately, the methodology is not as interesting as the fundamental idea of the book. The dependent variable—annual earnings—is a poor choice since it is the product of hourly wage and hours worked. The joining of the two confuses wage effects with employment patterns and labor supply, and this limits the power of the analysis. Furthermore, the AID program is a black box without desirable statistical properties. Its most unfortunate characteristic is that when faced with two or more collinear variables it attributes all of the explanatory power to the (perhaps only slightly) more powerful variable rather than providing unbiased estimates. Finally, the separate analysis of job characteristics and personal characteristics obscures the simultaneity of the process.

Freedman's short essays on each of the variables are, next to the central notion of sheltering, the most valuable element of the book. The essays on establishment size and family income packaging are the most useful. However, the book would have been better had the author paid more attention to just how and when shelters are successfully erected and how they are maintained and/or changed in the face of market forces, individuals left out, and employers who find them inconvenient.

In short, this book advances an idea which contributes to understanding the labor market from an institutional perspective and should be valued for that contribution. However, work remains to give the idea more life and greater depth.

Professions for the People: The Politics of Skill, edited by JOEL E. GERSTL and GLENN JACOBS. New York: Halsted Press, 1976. 230 pp. $9.50 cloth.

The Human Marketplace: An Examination of Private Employment Agencies, by TOMAS MARTINEZ. New Brunswick, N.J.: Transaction Books, 1976. 159 pp. $8.95 cloth.

GERALD ROSENBLUM
McMaster University

The original contributions that form the bulk of the Gerstl and Jacobs volume address the specific occupational areas of law, medicine, the arts, athletics, and teaching. Much attention is devoted to dissident movements within these occupations which call into question the manner in which vital services are distributed and performed in American society. An introduction by the editors and a concluding essay (the one previously published article in the book) by Robert Perrucci serve as critical overviews of the professions, broadly surveys these movements, and appears to have provided a point of departure for many of the contributing authors.

Though the book serves the important purpose of exposing the reader to these phenomena and the innovations that practitioners employ in serving relatively neglected sectors of the population, the material is frequently not marshalled in an effective manner for the apparent challenge to established sociological thinking on the professions. The articles on medicine (Resnick), athletics (Juliani), and teaching (Wenger) are, in varying ways, characterized by clumsy expository styles (e.g., long digressions and excessive pursuit of obvious issues) together with failings in conceptual clarity. By contrast, the discussion of "deviant" legal practice (Kidder) stands out with regard to economy and clarity of writing. Here greater length (rather than the careful trimming that should have been performed elsewhere) would have permitted elaboration of what seemed to this reviewer to be generally sound insights. The article on the arts (Sanders and Lyon) informs the reader of interesting parallels between criticism of the "new artists" and other dissident professional movements, but the nature and boundaries of the groups from which they drew their information was unclear. The arguments surrounding de-licensing of doctors and lawyers during the Jackson era (summarized by Tabachnick) was instructive but the article ends inconclusively with respect to implications for the contemporary concerns of this book.

If any place, a rigorous confrontation with existing work on the professions should have occurred in the editors' introductory remarks. It did not. While vigorously asserting the inadequacy of recent literature, precious little of that work is directly considered. The rejection, for example, of "altruism" as a distinguishing feature of professions, contains not a single citation to the offending writers, let alone a consideration of how the matter is treated by them. One can maintain a critical view of sociological thought on the professions and at the same time be concerned by the assertion (without an effort at substantiation) that it is congenial to "corporatist" ideology (p. 17) which, earlier in their piece, the authors have associated with the rise of fascism (p. 13).

Production problems in the volume were an annoying distraction. The list of references to Perrucci's article was missing. There were an inordinate number of typographical errors, some so obvious as to make one wonder how they were overlooked. There was no index. This book addresses an important subject and issues are raised at several points that merit attention, but the authors neglect to generate the kinds of theoretical tools that would move research on the subject forward.

The often-observed phenomenon of occupational incumbents' manipulation of the prestigious symbols of professionalism in the interest of rewards rather than content, considered at various points in the Gerstl and Jacobs book, is also taken up by Tomás Martinez. Applying the criteria of service orientation and knowledge base to private employment agents, he finds their professional claims to be vacuous. They are essentially salespersons.

This is but one of several topics concerning private employment agencies that Martinez considers. In this brief book he also surveys the history of their emergence, their abuses, government efforts at control and, finally, their present-day operations as depicted by a study of applicant-agent interaction. Martinez thus attempts to close in on his subject from a variety of perspectives, any one of which might have merited more extended consideration. A short book of very broad scope, it was perhaps inevitable that the outcome would be uneven and somewhat fragmented.

This is most evident in the historical overview where the author examines predecessors to the contemporary role of employment agent. Referring to this as an "occupational regression," the ensuing discussion contains such substantial leaps in time and space as to lead one to question its rigor. Within periods, too, the analysis is far from exhaustive. For example, the consideration of turn-of-the-century US practices might have been considerably enriched had the author consulted more than the few sources he cites on labor agents serving immigrant groups. The "padrone system" of immigrant labor agents dealing with later-arriving compatriots was, after all, a rather important influence on labor distribution in the US, partly accounting for the concentration of particular ethnic groups in particular industries. Indeed, the spectacular size *and* diversity of the immigrant labor force goes quite far to explain the flourishing of private labor middlemen during this period. These practices were dealt with at the time in government reports and continue to be an object of scholarly interest today. I believe that Martinez missed an important opportunity to emphasize this linkage (though he does not totally ignore it) between labor force composition and the proliferation of middlemen that the rise of a market economy cannot alone explain.

The author deals with a somewhat surer hand as the work progresses. The abovementioned discussion of what Martinez calls "pseudoprofessionalism" is an instructive case study of such tactics. A useful chapter containing details on the evolving legal status of private employment agencies provides information on court decisions and their rationale, conveying the changing climate of legal opinion. Finally, a chapter based on an interview study of former job applicants (supplemented by the authors' participant observation experience some years ago together with informal interviews during the intervening period) explores in some detail the actual procedures within these agencies. A scale of dependency (associated with the degree of urgency confronting the job hunter) is related in quite an interesting fashion to the client's perception of his/her interaction with the agency and the impact of this experience on such matters as self-esteem and career plans. The relatively small size and unrepresentativeness of Martinez's sample provokes his own comment that "the findings should not be considered conclusive, but suggestive" (p. 114). This reviewer would agree and apply that comment to the book as a whole.

Martinez's contribution is diluted by the broad scope of his study which deprives it of analytical unity and, at times, his material is stretched rather thinly over the terrain considered. Nevertheless, he draws attention to a phenomenon that the structure of the labor market permits to thrive and which would repay further intensive investigation.

The Religion of the Chinese People, by MARCEL GRANET. Translated by Maurice Freedman. New York: Harper & Row, 1976. $17.50 cloth.

JOHN F. MANFREDI
University of Massachusetts

Marcel Granet's *The Religion of the Chinese People* is a masterful exercise of the sociological imagination. First, it is Durkeimian in a phase that is perhaps difficult for American sociologists—the Durkheimianism of *The Elementary Forms of Religious Life* which is, I think, as uncongenial to us as its barely known 1903 successor, *Primitive Classification* (with Marcel Mauss). Parrotting its definition of religion is easy. It is another thing to follow a complex analysis that supposes a familiarity with obscure ethnographic data and epistemologically complex reasoning. Raymond Aron perhaps said it for us when he admitted in *Main Currents in Sociological Thought* that he quoted it frequently because he did not trust himself to describe it sympathetically. *Primitive Classification* is still more recondite and Rodney Needham, while admitting the value of the idea itself, found it a hotbed of non sequiturs and sloppy scholarship. (The chapter on China, incidentally, adumbrates the present work.) Few American sociologists empathize easily with the Durkheim these works exemplify, but they probably have been the most influential outside of sociology. Ethnologists, archeologists, and paleographers have found them highly useful starting points. It is among paleographers' work that Henri Maspero's posthumous essays *Le Toaism et les Religions Chinoises* and the present work can be placed. The editor, Maurice Freedman, calls Granet a sociologist and he was certainly this and more too. He was, however, trained in history and learned Chinese when he was twenty-five. He never left Sinology after that and it constitutes his entire scholarly publication. It ranges from minute paleographic studies to the important synoptic works, *La Civilisation Chinoise*, *La Pensee Chinoise*, and the present work. This is a stunning tour de force that he wrote in six weeks, mainly on a commuter train, without notes, and with such expertise that he never changed anything of importance later!

The first problem illuminated is whether one can speak of a Chinese religion at all. Much expert opinion from James Legge, Herbert Giles, to Derk Bodde emphasized the agnostic character of Confucianism and saw religion as unimportant to Chinese civilization. C. K. Wang properly protests that such views leave "unexplained the Universal presence of religious influence." Granet's work evades such doubts. If you consider theology the systematic articulation of religious beliefs to ethical and epistemological systems to be central to religion, it is, indeed, absent. The Chinese moral community under both feudalism and the empire seemed to be action itself and little more. The search for transcendental truth so dear to Western theology is not there. However, if the core of religion is the sensus numinus, gut night terrors, and supernatural powers, religion was (and probably is) omnipresent in China. Granet not only treats these continuous popular beliefs, but isolates three coherent levels of religious belief. The first was an ancient chthonic peasant faith that arose out of the articulation to the natural order through dances, chants, and festivals, and emphasized the polarities of male and female, damp and dry, light and dark, warm and cold, and ecstasy and restraint. A second religious system arose in the towns centering around feudal chieftains whose Virtue to rule arose out of the rituals of vassalage of the great families who surrounded them. Peasant work organization separated the sexes seasonably, but in the towns there were continuous interactions of man and woman as well as lord and vassal and living and ancestors that were governed by a careful etiquette. The third arose with the evolution of the imperial system by 200 BC under a Confucian literati who codified interactions meticulously and considered the social system its protocols which even assured cosmic regularity. The sovereign Virtue need for this was considered an emergent of correct thinking that could only arise out of correctly observed relationships. Failure, human or cosmic, was blamed upon a corruption of imperial Virtue caused by the failure to observe the system of protocol at some inferior level. (This may seem like heads-I-win-tails-you-lose reasoning, but see Granet, pages 101–102.) However, these upper-class beliefs never attempted to deal with dangerous numinous realms. If you consider these the central Chinese beliefs, Bodde's contention is hard to answer, but Confucianism has often been questioned by the Chinese themselves and ad hoc popular cults, Buddhism, and Taoism have been ubiquitous. In fact, it becomes clear in Granet that Taoism did for peasant practice and belief what Confucianism did for upper class practice and belief—it gave it intellectual coherence. Granet calls it all religion. Moreover, he is always a good Durkheimian. Religion is always ultimately an emergent of society.

Finally, Granet's major feat here is this: The greatest difficulty in describing an exotic religious life is to give to the outsider the understanding of the believer. Granet does this. One may not end believing it, but one can certainly understand it.

Maurice Freedman's editing is superb.

Synagogue Life: A Study in Symbolic Interaction, by SAMUEL C. HEILMAN. Chicago: University of Chicago Press, 1976. 306 pp. $12.95 cloth.

JACK NUSAN PORTER
Boston, Massachusetts

This book is a participant-observer study of an Orthodox *shul* (Yiddish for "school," referring to the synagogue's role as a house of study). Heilman's book *feels* right. His *shul,* located in "Sprawl City," may not be typical of all Orthodox congregations (it has no rabbi for example), but it does tally with what my *shul* was like. Some of what he writes about will not be new or exciting to any Orthodox Jewish sociologist (a rare breed, I might add) but much of it will engender the sense of authenticity one gets from first reading Erving Goffman (a major influence on Heilman), C. Wright Mills, the Lynds, and Robert Merton, among others. If you like ethnography and symbolic interaction, you will like this book.

Heilman was already a member of the *shul* even before he decided to embark on the research. His advantages were that he was an Orthodox Jew and had established a degree of intimacy with the congregants. His disadvantages were that he was an Orthodox Jew and had established a degree of intimacy with the congregants. Heilman has this to say about the dilemma: "I have . . . suggested the epistemological liability of taking too much for granted. This danger . . . was intensified by my being not only Orthodox but also a member. . . . There were personal drawbacks as well. Relationships which I had over time developed on emotional grounds would have to become instrumental; friends would be transformed into informants and I into primarily a collector of social facts" (p. xi).

Heilman admirably surmounted these problems and went on to write a book full of rich detail. Some may quarrel that it is too rich. Others may revel in his description of kinds of *yarmulkes* (skull caps) worn by members; the kinds of hats worn by women; and other memorabilia. I was especially fascinated by Heilman's analysis of what Goffman calls the "sheath," the "shell" in which individual members wrap themselves—their appearance, their clothing (both religious and secular), their grooming, etc. For example, in such a *shul* one can immediately differentiate between married and unmarried males because only married males can wear the *talis* (prayer cloak). I disagree with Heilman, however, that only *married* members can be full-fledged members of an Orthodox *shul* (p. 56). While unmarried men are pitied, I have noticed from my experience that they are still respected by others and even hold high office in the congregation.

Many reviewers of Heilman's book will no doubt seize on one fascinating area—the social usage of gossip among the Orthodox. They seem to be "cursed" with this trait. To gossip, halachically it is called *lashan horah*, ("evil tongue"), turns out to be more complex than I had thought. I loved his chapter on this subject. I highly recommend the book to all sociologists, and especially to graduate students in field-methods courses.

Reacting to Social Problems, by RICHARD L. HENSHEL. Don Mills, Ontario: Longman Canada Limited, 1976. 191 pp. No price listed, paper.

MALCOLM SPECTOR
University of Montréal and *McGill University*

This book, the sixth volume in the Longman Canadian Social Problems series is a solid and serious discussion oriented to undergraduate students. It is clearly organized and generously supplied with references to related literature, both Canadian and American. This will be very useful to advanced and more enthusiastic students and to instructors looking for materials to fill out their lectures. It is well written and, for once, not in the insulting baby talk that many publishers seem to think is all the student can make sense of.

Henshel classifies and describes the different strategies that societies have used in defining and reacting to those conditions and groups they regard as offensive. He groups these into two large categories, preventive and restorative, each of which has several sub-types. After considering the logic and rationale for each strategy, he outlines the objections to each one and finally shows how new modes of intervention have emerged to replace and supplement older remedies. A chapter on evaluation research shows how experimental designs might be used to discipline folk notions about what is good for society, but also describes how political and ethical considerations may compromise such research. The final chapter describes the role of the expert and the rise of technicism in treating social problems. Henshel persuasively argues that while competence is desirable, the current forms in which it is available have many undesirable aspects.

Henshel does not align himself with either side of the recent debate over the objective or subjective definitions of social problems. Rather, he finds a framework within which the substance of both functional and labeling approaches provide examples of how solutions to social problems may fail. Here the general notion of unanticipated consequences (latent functions and dysfunctions) is put to work, not as a general programmatic statement about society, but as a tool for thinking about how a proposed solution may fail to alleviate a problem, exacerbate it, or create a new one. The voluminous literature on the labeling of persons as mentally ill provides both a nice case in point and lets the author show an unnoticed convergence between the two rival formulations in the fields of deviance and social problems.

Issues in the Classification of Children, Volumes 1 & 2, edited by NICHOLAS HOBBS. San Francisco: Jossey-Bass, 1975. 1,040 pp. $35.00 cloth.

RICHARD A. HILBERT
University of California, Santa Barbara

Children, some insightful philosopher remarked, will always be with us. The question "What should we do with them?" seems to be a perplexing one. To a large degree, answers are generated by bureaucracies designed for purposes of handling children. To use the Weberian term, the socialization of the young is becoming increasingly "rationalized." This rationalization process is furthered when problems arise as to what to do with children who fail to respond to established normal treatment, that is to say, "exceptional" children.

Issues in the Classification of Children deals with the problem of identifying, defining, diagnosing, and treating children deemed "exceptional" for a wide variety of reasons: various mental, physical, and cultural deprivations; emotional disturbances; "learning disabilities"; behavior resulting in legal action; and so forth. The ninety-three contributors to these volumes represent a wide cross section of the social sciences, as well as the legal, medical, and public administration professions. Taken as a whole, the authors of the thirty-one papers attempt to summarize, clarify, and improve existing categorical devices and procedures for classifying exceptional children. Overriding concerns include the accuracy of categorical schemas (either proposed or currently in use), the effect of labels on categorized children and their families, the practical utility of classification for various organizations intended to deal with exceptional children (schools, hospitals, social work agencies, correctional institutions, etc.), and specific public policy recommendations. Thus much of the work presented here deals with the traditional concerns of validity and reliability when it comes to the diagnosis of specific pathologies among children. It also deals with issues of administrative policy, especially questions of legal access and confidentiality.

The articles in these volumes are addressed primarily to policy implementers, legislators, bureaucratic decision makers, and others incidentally interested in these issues. They will therefore be particularly helpful to those professionally involved in the administrative handling of children. They will also be of interest to social scientists concerned with the finer methodological points of validity and reliability or the paradoxes associated with classification itself, e.g. the "self fulfilling prophesy" which is often the result of categorization.

The papers derive from the Project on the Classification of Exceptional Children, initiated in 1972 by Office of Child Development director Edward Zigler in response to some concerns of HEW secretary Elliot L. Richardson. They are *not* the final report, but are the works of a number of task force groups organized by members of the project. As such, they do not present a single, characterizable point of view. Nor does the editor attempt to unify them in a systematic way, though his grouping of the papers into six content areas as well as his very helpful abstracts will be of value to the discriminating reader. The papers draw upon a wide range of different literatures and perspectives unique to their authors' respective disciplines, and in the main they tend to address the problems described above. While space does not permit an itemized list of noteworthy articles, several can be touched upon. Prudence M. Rains's et al. "The Labeling Approach to Deviance" is well handled, but seems somehow out of place in a work devoted primarily to the solution of practical problems. William C. Rhodes and Mark Sagor optimistically predict an emergence of understanding and caring in the classification and treatment of deviant individuals. Kathyrn A. Gorham et al., in perhaps the most sensitive and compassionate essay in the two volumes, graphically describe the agony families often experience in their endeavors to obtain required special (or indeed normal) services. Edward A. De Avila and Barbara E. Havassy, using empirical findings, make the interesting argument that Piaget-based assessment techniques lack the built-in cultural biases of traditional standardized intelligence tests. David L. Kirp et al. note that no amount of judicial mandating is sufficient for procedural change without the active participation of those bureaucracies in which the change is to take place. Finally, John W. Filler et al. suggest a method of extending systematic diagnosis and instruction to infancy, enabling specialists to predict and possibly prevent potential learning disabilities otherwise not recognized until the child is well into his/her educational career.

The competence of the contributors to *Issues in the Classification of Children* is not in question. All of the work presented in these volumes is of the highest professional calibre. The reader should be forewarned, however, that the "issues" announced in the title, by and large, revolve around questions of practical utility. Where "humane treatment" is an issue, it is raised as one resolvable (if only *somehow*) through methodological and bureaucratic improvements. Thus Marxists, for example, should know that issues concerning the political and economic contexts of child-managing institutions are not being raised. Neither are issues related to the taken for granted right of the adult world to monitor and evaluate the generation about to replace it. Rather, what is presented is a series of thoughtful, well researched, and for the most part methodologically precise papers which, taken together, summarize current thinking about the categorization of exceptional children by those who categorize them.

The Poor of Eighteenth-Century France, 1750–1789, by OLWEN H. HUFTON. New York: Oxford University Press, 1975. 414 pp. $29.00 cloth.

ALLAN SILVER
Columbia University

This study deals with the one-third of the French population—during the last decades of the *ancien regime*—who lived in families which could not be supported by the labor of one person, and only very tenuously, if at all, by that of two or more persons; or which died in short order after illness, accident, or old age. We are not here dealing with such matters as cultural (or relative) deprivation, discrimination, alienation, or with inequality of result or opportunity in any sense which implies a common standard of reference. Rather, this book is concerned with the unceasing struggle for life itself.

Hufton argues that the poor of mid-eighteenth century France were not a "traditional" class; indeed, they came into being largely through forces in play during the century itself. The population increased from about 19,000,000 in 1720 to roughly 27,000,000 at the end of the century. Pressure on resources was heavy, despite the slow expansion and distribution of resources through the activities of bureaucratic administrators and grain merchants and purchasing agents who dealt in foodstuffs moving across local markets.

Plague and famine, the great Malthusian scythes of earlier centuries, struck particularly hard at the young and the unborn, depressing the reproductive potential of the population. The forms of chronic misery prevailing in the eighteenth century, however, saw the diminution of the great plague and famine cycle, but continuing vulnerability to other diseases which tended to carry off the youngest and oldest, leaving the poor with high reproductive capacity. The demographic potential of the eighteenth century poor was enhanced, too, because chronic misery did not disrupt the process of family formation—indeed, in some ways it encouraged it. Finally, these demographic processes interacted with social structure, as the continuing process of *morcellement*—the subdivision of inherited land among heirs in peasant families—forced younger males and their families into increasingly tenuous access to life-sustaining resources.

Drawing on the wide variety of sources that characterizes contemporary social history—reports by travelers, administrators, local clergy, doctors—Hufton develops a rich picture of the survival strategies of the poor. The structure of biography and of the family, patterns of migration, the logic of the agricultural trade cycle are invoked to situate the character of eighteenth century poverty. Thus, a "pre-career," between the ages of about fourteen to that of marriage—at twenty-seven or twenty-eight—was often employed by men to learn a marketable skill, and by women (usually in domestic service) to save money which, as a dowry, could attract a mate with potentially high earning capacity. Hufton estimates that for between 50% to 90% of the rural poor, the resources thus amassed were insufficient for survival, once family life had begun, and had to be supplemented by rural industry, especially by women.

A complex system of credit and debt was a normal part of the rural poor's way of life; existence was possible only as a debtor, involving a struggle, often a losing one, to retain the ownership of land. The rural poor, however, were forced to sell their crop at harvest, when supply was greatest and prices lowest, to liquidate debts; and to buy at times of scarcity, when prices were highest. Hence, even long-term price rises for their products did not result in higher income.

Orderly systems of migration were also strategies for survival. At periods when their labor was not needed, adults migrated to regions where it was; this did not so much add to income as remove from the household a certain number of mouths to feed at times in the crop cycle when food was in shortest supply. Such migratory patterns expressed not a lack of attachment to land, but a strategy for avoiding debt and penury in order to keep it.

Much of the book is given over to the policies of church and state with respect to the poor. Catholic voluntarism—in which the relief of the poor was a means to religious merit—was gradually giving way to government-sponsored administrative remedies. Neither, however, had much actual impact on the poor and are of less interest to the sociologist than Hufton's richly elaborated analysis of the eighteenth century poor's situation and strategies of adaptation. The book is, appropriately enough, quite a-theoretical, and is all the more rewarding as a source of material. As a picture of a setting for poverty quite different both from the medieval, early modern, or the industrializing nineteenth century, this study of the *ancien regime* contributes some needed historical specificity to the over-generalized sociological perspectives on poverty which rely excessively upon such interpretative writers as Simmel or Polanyi, or on an excessively global notion of "tradition." Hufton's book, widely acclaimed among social historians, repays close attention by sociologists as well.

Social Problems as Social Movements, by ARMAND L. MAUSS. Philadelphia: J. B. Lippincott, 1975. 718 pp. $11.95 cloth.

BRUCE D. JOHNSON
New York State Office of Drug Abuse Services

This book is an ambitious attempt to provide a new theoretical paradigm for the analysis of social problems. The basic thesis, clearly stated in the title, hypothesizes that specific historical social movements generate the publics' perception of some phenomena as a social problem. Further, the continued moral concern and public policy directed at that phenomena is the product of actions by historical individuals, pressure groups, and issue-specific publics. Mauss generally ignores mainline sociological theories of social problems, such as functionalism, strain and control, learning, anomie, interaction, and conflict theories in his analysis of various social problems.

The first two chapters outline his theory and establish the analytic framework employed in the subsequent chapters on specific social problems. Mauss notes that a variety of groups in society have their own, frequently different or opposed, definitions of whether and how a phenomenon is a problem. Consensual reality, what the general public believe to be real, generally emanates from persons or institutions regarded as authorities, although informal beliefs (myths, folklore, etc.) are frequently important. Nevertheless, most social problems are not concerns of the majority of citizens, so the role of important elites and the media at disseminating ideas and "facts" is frequently crucial in influencing public opinion. For any given phenomenon, an issue-specific public, those who are concerned about an issue, provide the basis for the emergence of social movement. From such publics, are drawn the specific individuals ("moral" or "economic" entrepreneurs), organized pressure groups, and affiliated interest groups (church, business, etc.) wishing to influence public policy and the public's perception of the phenomenon.

The natural history of a social movement has five stages: (1) incipiency—uncoordinated efforts of individuals interested in an issue; (2) coalescence—interest and pressure groups begin organized action to influence the government, public opinion, and opposition groups; (3) institutionalization—when the government and other traditional institutions begin to react to the movement, be rejecting, coopting, or adopting the movement's goals and support; (4) fragmentation—occurs if the movement's goals are adopted, coopted, or repressed but the movement remains active; and (5) demise—occurs when the pressure groups give up organized action, are completely coopted, or repressed.

This theoretical model is successfully applied in fourteen subsequent chapters. A great deal of relevant historical information about common social problems topics (crime, delinquency, corrections, radicalism, drugs, alcohol, mental illness, and sexual behavior) is presented in refreshingly new light. This reviewer gained a vastly better insight into the origins and continued activities of relevant pressure and interest groups associated with each of these social problems. The subsequent chapters on women's liberation, abortion, marriage, race environment, and population provide excellent commentaries on contemporary social movements. The chapters on corrections, mental illness, environment, and population seem particularly excellent in exemplifying Mauss's theory and providing superior summaries of crucial socio-historical data generally ignored in other social problems texts.

This book is designed as a major text for a one semester social problems course. Such use may be questioned. The presentation of a relatively simple theory, perhaps too simple, consistently applied to fourteen social problem topics may be appealing. But the relative absence of other theories may make it difficult to teach sociological analysis of theoretical models. Although many historical facts about social movements are fascinating, the student and teacher may feel that the book provides a history course under a sociological cover.

There are other difficulties. The socio-historical evidence in most chapters seems to fit the theory too well. Perhaps the theory is so broad as to be all inclusive or the historical materials were carefully selected to fit the theory. Some relevant and contradictory material is not cited. For example, David Musto's superior history of the Marihuana Tax Act implies that Anslinger, of the Narcotics Bureau, was opposed to the Act; however, Musto's evidence fits Mauss's theory well. The many statistics presented in the consensual reality section of each chapter seems fragmentary and relatively unrelated to the main theme of most chapters.

Nevertheless, Mauss presents a refreshingly new theoretical perspective on that old battered-to-death topic of social problems. He does a masterful job at synthesizing much socio-historical material unknown to the average sociologist, thus providing a gold mine of information for future use. Whether the book, as a required text, will work effectively in a social problems course is less clear.

Images of the World in the Year 2000: A Comparative Ten Nation Study, edited by HELMUT ORNAUER, HÅKAN WIBERG, ANDRZEJ SICIŃSKI, and JOHAN GALTUNG. Atlantic Highlands, N.J.: Humanities Press, 1976. 729 pp. $45.00 cloth.

BETTINA J. HUBER
University of California, Santa Barbara

The authors of this book discuss a remarkable achievement: the successful completion of a comparative study involving two Asian (Japan and India), three East European (Czechoslovakia, Poland, and Yugoslavia), and five West European countries (Finland, Norway, Great Britain, Spain, Netherlands, and a later replication in West Germany). A uniform questionnaire, focusing on diverse aspects of the future and prospects for war/peace, was administered to representative national samples (the Indian sample is an exception), and the uniformly coded data were used by project participants for the cross-national comparisons reported upon. Having such diverse nationalities participate equally in all research phases is most unusual. Under the circumstances, it is inevitable that a compendium of results contain some analytic limitations and considerable repetition.

The authors are aware of the shortcomings of the survey instrument they employ, but often procedures for minimizing these are not undertaken. Probably it was unavoidable that most questions be closed, but the "open" items might have been delimited less stringently (this applies especially to the modification of Cantril's Striving Scale). Most data analysis employs percentage differences, although several contributors use more sophisticated techniques, usually isolating the most intriguing findings reported. With these exceptions, authors tend to focus on single item analysis, and when not, the combination of diverse items sometimes yields variables whose character is ill-defined (i.e., the measure of "social position"). An overwhelming focus on gross distinctions also circumscribes some data discussions. National differences are articulated in dichotomous terms, such as socialist/capitalist or developed/developing, rather than in terms reflecting degrees of difference. Similarly, rather than examining the relationship of individual hopes and expectations, aggregate differences are discussed by comparing national hopes-expectations proportions (there are a few exceptions).

The end-result is that much discussion remains descriptive without examining the data in depth. There is little underlying theory, perhaps because the futures field has little, and explanations are often ad hoc. Several contributors refer to Galtung's theory about systematic distinctions between the center and periphery of society. Delineated to account for divergent perceptions of international relations, this reformulation of the "trickle effect" may not be as applicable to attitudes in general as is assumed.

The study's major finding is that nationality is a potent distinguishing characteristic. Future-related questions, encompassing hopes and expectations for various occurrences, differ in terms of technical-economic development; highly industrialized countries anticipate fewer accomplishments by the year 2000 than do others. Attitudes toward war and peace tend to diverge along the socialist/capitalist axis, though rejection of armed conflict and desire for international harmony are almost universal. Social characteristics such as age, sex, and socio-economic status have only a limited impact on attitudes. Lack of age variation suggests the research probes not only "youth's" anticipations for the year 2000, but also those of national populations. Although not commented upon, it is possible that the over-fifty set differs little from the respondents between fifteen and forty who were studied.

In sum, this book contains a gold mine of data, especially since the appendix lists national marginals. Various chapters tell a great deal about what people anticipate for the future; less about why they think as they do. With more ruthless elimination of repetition, the reported findings might have been dealt with in half the space, no doubt leading to cross-national ego bruising, but insuring a considerable price reduction and wider exposure. As it is, the book may be too expensive for many, even though it contains material relevant to diverse research (e.g., the future, peace research, international relations, public opinion, comparative studies, attitude formation, etc.). It ought to prove a useful source for locating single-nation studies within a broader comparative framework.

The Myth of Marginality: Urban Poverty and Politics in Rio De Janeiro, by JANICE E. PERLMAN. Berkeley: University of California Press, 1976. 341 pp. $14.95 cloth.

ALEJANDRO PORTES
Duke University

Brazilian sociologist, Fernando Henrique Cardoso once remarked that intellectuals in Latin America are important for they are the voice of those who cannot speak for themselves. This book subscribes to that idea, undertaking in unambiguous terms, the defense of the urban poor.

The book evolved out of the author's doctoral dissertation. It is based on interviews with samples of 250 inhabitants and fifty leaders in each of three Rio de Janeiro *favelas*: one in the wealthy South Zone of the city, another in the working-class North Zone, and a third in the peripheral lowlands. More fundamentally, the study is based on the author's experience while living and working for several months in the three squatter settlements. The main study took place in 1968–69, with an informal follow-up in 1973.

Perlman organizes her argument around seven stereotypes which are labelled the "myths of marginality." They range from the imputation of political radicalism to the urban poor to the belief that they are trapped in a crime-ridden, apathetic "culture of poverty." The strategy is to lay out each "myth" and then demolish it on the basis of the survey data.

It is not difficult to predict that she will succeed and this constitutes a major theoretical miscalculation. In essence, she has chosen to use the data in an effort to discredit theories of poverty which an abundant research literature has already proven untenable. The author appears unwilling to confess herself a latecomer to the task and thus engages, repeatedly, in an exercise at dead-horse beating. With a research literature dating back to the 1960s and consistently reporting the same basic findings in a number of cities, those who still adhere to "culture of poverty," "marginality," "radical anger," and similar stereotypes about the urban poor in Latin America are either uninformed or engaged in a transparent defense of their class interests.

A renewed critique of the stereotypes of urban poverty could be justified if it were based on a more compelling empirical analysis. However, a number of methodological problems renders many portions of this analysis weak and unconvincing. To begin with, no evidence of reliability and validity of variables or internal consistency of measures of the same dimension are presented. Though the last line of the appendix states that reliability and validity checks were "highly satisfactory," no data are presented to back this assertion.

The commendable effort to defend the *favelados* against the different marginality myths leads Perlman into several contradictions. For example, the modernity syndrome is criticized as ethnocentric and as providing "an ideological rationale for U.S. domination in Latin America" (p. 114), yet the attempt is made, forty pages later, to prove that *favelados* are really "modern." Two negatives do not make a positive. Furthermore, the author reports that "many items" in Inkeles OM measure of modernity "vary independently" (p. 142) and that, in several instances, their meaning in the Brazilian context is different from that originally intended. If this is the case, the value of such measures as indicators of modernity is much reduced. Three negatives do not make a positive either.

Along the same lines, the almost complete independence among items supposed to measure political radicalism is interpreted as proof of the absence of a "radical syndrome" in the *favela*. A more plausible conclusion is that this pattern is the result of measurement error, an interpretation supported by the failure of these items to correlate with a number of other variables. It appears that radicalism items do not measure what they were intended to measure for a very good reason. There is a contradiction in portraying, on the one hand, the political alertness of the *favelados* and the repressive political milieu of Brazil in the late sixties and expecting, on the other, that they would give naive "open" answers to highly political questions. Authoritarian Brazil is a place where an intelligent person, especially if he or she is politically defenseless, will try to dodge precisely such questions as whether the government is "good or bad" for the country or whether "profound changes going to the root of problems" are needed.

There is a touch of irony in some of the *favelados's* answers to the political items. Asked what are the most important rights that Brazilian citizens have, most responded: "the right to support the government" or "the right to respect the authorities." Conformism? Powerlessness? Or merely a cautious answer to an implausible question under the circumstances.

It should be said, however, that Perlman's book contains many valuable and interesting contributions. They are not found in the review of myths or in the predictable success at demolishing them. They are found rather in those sections based on the author's direct experience while living in the *favelas* and the information on government policy gathered then. Chapter two on the origins and development of the three *favelas* is, for example, an interesting and useful description of these areas.

More important is chapter seven on the program of the Brazilian military government for *favela* removal. This chapter is important because not enough has been written on the specific strategies of "development-oriented" authoritarian regimes for dealing with the problems of urban poverty. Naive social scientists are still liable to take shiny new housing projects in the periphery of Third World cities as evidence of real solutions. Many such settlements, bearing names like "Villa Kennedy," represent veritable concentration camps punishing the most defenseless urban groups for their poverty. Perlman's account in this chapter is a forceful and informed description of the coerced removal of many of Rio's *favelas*. It portrays the tragedy that the program represented for most of its inhabitants; the futility of their resistance against the power of the military; the convenient solution which the removals provided for real estate and construction interests; and the perversity of a program which advertised itself as protecting the very human needs and rights which it was violating.

Mounting resistance and criticism at home and abroad have been instrumental in forcing the Brazilian government to suspend its *favela* eradication program in Rio. Still not enough has been written or is known about the present situation. It is my belief that the perspective opened by studies such as the one in this chapter, dealing with policies of the State toward the urban poor and their implementation, represents a true frontier for future comparative urbanization research.

Urban Sociology: Critical Essays, edited by C. G. Pickvance, New York: St. Martin's Press, 1976. 223 pp. $14.95 cloth.

ROY CHILDS
University of the Pacific

Urban sociology usually reaches for its roots in the writings of Louis Wirth, or in the earlier Chicago school of sociology. In this sense urban sociology seems to differ from many other sociological fields which, one way or another, are more likely to draw on European sociologists. Although Leo Schnore once argued the existence of ties between urban ecology and Durkheim's social morphology, legitimating the former as a valid field of sociological study, few have seriously followed his lead. In this context *Urban Sociology: Critical Essays,* edited by an English sociologist, is of interest. The book is poorly titled, giving no hint as to its content or focus. Who would suspect from the title that the French speaking sociologists included in the book are attempting no less than a Marxist interpretation of urbanization. Karl Marx, the father of urban sociology? Louis Wirth would turn over in his grave!

Nevertheless, the reader will find the book engaging and suggestive of new research directions. But as one might expect of an attempt to develop a coherent theory of urban sociology from any single paradigm, school, or research strategy, a Marxist theory of urban sociology leaves much existing research and many legitimate research concerns completely out of the picture (including, for example, a good deal of the ecological research on occupational and residential segregation, studies of social participation and affiliation, social network analysis, and community organization). Still, the book makes worthwhile though spotty reading for what it does accomplish, which is to provide an *alternative focus* for the field.

The book contains readings by Francois Lamarche (French-Canadian), Jean Lojkine (French), and Manuel Castells and José Olives (both Spanish), and divides naturally into three parts which are sandwiched between critical introductory and concluding essays by Pickvance. Except for the introductory and concluding essays the articles in the book were originally published in French and Pickvance has done the translations.

The first part, containing a critique of existing urban sociology by Manuel Castells, unfortunately contains little that is new. Defining science as the application of historical materialist concepts, and urban sociology as the study of the mechanisms for allocating urban space, Castells reviews the urban literature (with which most readers will already be familiar) and concludes that most of it is not properly urban sociology, and that it is not scientific. This is hardly surprising given the restrictive scope Castells sets out for the field and his particular conception of science. Pickvance rightly comments in his introductory essay that while the perspective adopted by Castells has utility, this should not preclude others from elaborating other theoretical perspectives.

Logically following the Marxist perspective suggested in the first part of the book, readings in the second part attempt to deal with the dynamics of property capital, its relations to other forms of capital, the expropriation of labor value, and the dynamics of political and planning superstructures characteristic of property capitalism. Writings in the third part apply Marxist concepts to the study of urban social movements.

Among the key ideas in part three is the proposition that given adequate organization—i.e., an organizational capacity adequate to mobilize an affected public, or "social base"—the greater the "stakes" in an issue, the greater the likelihood that resolution of the issue will produce "effects" beneficial to the mobilized. The proposition is explored by José Olives through an analysis of sixteen cases of urban protest in a district of Paris. It is concluded that the proposition holds, particularly where strategies used involved direct adversary action (as opposed, say, to more polite forms of indirect, "reformist" activity). Unfortunately the concept of "stakes" does not appear to be clearly defined (does it relate to the immediate costs and benefits to those involved? to implications for the maintenance of capitalist structures? or both?); and the stakes in the cases studied did not always seem high to this writer, although without a clearer definition of the term it is difficult to tell. (A typical issue might involve the provision of facilities in publicly sponsored housing, hotel accommodations for immigrant workers, etc.) Pickvance notes that research in England, which he reviews to some degree in his concluding essay, suggests a number of differing interpretations. He also points out that some of Olives's cases do not appear consistent with the proposition, raising the methodological issue of the appropriate use of case study materials.

The real strengths of the book come out in the second part by Lamarche and Lojkine, which elaborates historical materialist interpretations of "capitalist urbanization" and property development. In one sense the writings in this part seem little more than materialist interpretations of the basic principles of urban economics (rather than urban sociology) by drawing upon appropriately informing passages from *Capital.* But these writings accomplish much more by offering a social class analysis of business and commercial groups at the local level, while at the same time pulling urban sociology much closer to contemporary concerns in urban political economy, and in fact much contemporary thinking in urban planning and policy analysis. Property capitalism, according to these writers, must not be viewed as adding value to production capital; but rather, through the efficient spatial and technological organization of production and service activities, it must be viewed as facilitating the extraction of that value. Economic groups which gain control over space become dominant, institutionally (and also in a traditional ecological sense), and hence are in a position to expropriate the profits of production for their own ends (through such means as the regulation of rents). To maintain their position, these dominants must concentrate on developing around what planners might call the "highest and best [most economically productive] uses" of land, generally to the exclusion of residential interests, and especially the needs of the lowest income groups. Property capitalism thus supplies the organizing focus for contemporary urban land use. Coordinated planning is of obvious value in achieving the most efficient means of extracting value; and hence pressures are created for the cooptation of planning by private, capitalist organizations.

It is unfortunate that the formulation is presented as an established principle, apparently beyond scholarly dispute, rather than as a set of guiding research concerns. Nevertheless, it goes a considerable distance in integrating essentially social institutional concerns within the fabric of ecological generalizations about the spatial organization of cities; and in the process it offers an explanation for this ordering alternative to the market competition (or sub-biotic) processes assumed by the early ecologists. Finally, the analysis contains the rather interesting implication (though it is not pursued) that the class interests of production and property capitalism, or perhaps of production capitalism efficiently and inefficiently situated, might develop in opposition to one another. It is especially the formulation of property capitalism which makes this volume well worth reading by American urban sociologists.

Children in Distress: American and English Perspectives, by PATRICIA R. STEWART. Beverly Hills: Sage Publications, 1976. 285 pp. $12.00 cloth. $7.00 Paper.

JANE D. MCCLURE
University of California, Santa Barbara

Patricia R. Stewart, in *Children in Distress* starts with the following question: What different personality characteristics can be found in those children who perceive themselves (or are perceived by others) as alienated, compared to those children who experience themselves as participants in the society in which they find themselves? The intent of the study is to compare normal and deviating children within their own culture as well as across two cultural settings, the United States and Great Britain.

This study fits in nicely with much recently done work in the area of cross-cultural differences in psychological functions. Stewart's emphasis is primarily on adaptation and maladaptation processes. But this work is unique in that it fills some previous gaps in what has come to be known as the subdiscipline of cross-cultural psychology. First, while most other research in this area has dealt with adults, this study investigates the effects of the cultural shaping of children's maladaptive behavior patterns. Second, correlation is made on both normal personality characteristics as well as psychological deviations in relation to culture. Finally, in the process of developing a new personality measure, consideration has been given to the cultural variable. For these reasons, this book should appeal to persons interested in culture, children, psychopathology, and test response patterns. Essentially this book is a basic research enterprise and as such makes its major contribution to cross-cultural psychology. Applied clinicians might also find useful the new information regarding the effects of cultural variations in the development of psychopathology. Furthermore, anyone interested in the development of a projective yet objectively scored personality test will find this book provocative.

In answer to the question of whether the definition of "normal" is dependent upon the dominant cultural setting, the author finds supporting evidence for other research in psychopathology. While there appear to be some characteristics of mental disorder which are common to the English-speaking matrix under investigation, there also appear to be other mental disorder traits which are specifically related to the sociocultural setting, some of which have specific sex-role interactions. Interestingly, one of the implications of this study is that normal American children are more conventional than are English children, and that the deviating American children are less seriously emotionally and mentally disordered than are their English counterparts. Stewart attributes this situation to the culturally diffuse attitudes of these two countries which eventually result in American children being referred more readily for psychotherapy.

The New York Cab Driver and His Fare, by CHARLES VIDICH. Cambridge, Mass.: Schenkman Publishing Co., 1976, 186 pp. $11.25 cloth. $5.95 paper.

JOHN WILDEMAN
Hofstra University

Without rhetoric and without forcing facts to fit theory, Vidich has produced an outstanding study of the New York City taxi cab industry that amounts to an empirically based argument for socialism. This book is in some ways similar to Eli Chinoy's classic study of another segment of the United States labor force, automobile assembly line workers. When laissez faire capitalism failed to regulate the development of monopoly in the taxi industry in New York, things went badly enough; but they really turned sour when the state stepped in. Vidich chronicles the successive failures of fleet owners and city government to help the taxi industry provide New Yorkers with safe, inexpensive transportation.

On one side of the stage are the profit hungry fleet owners, the taxi cab manufacturers, the corrupt unions frequently allied with organized crime, and inept and election-minded city administrations (especially under Wagner and Lindsay). On the other side are the taxi cab drivers and the public. Guess who has consistently lost out, beginning back in 1897 (the year of the first commercial use of the battery-powered automobile in the United States: the New York City cab). In this case study, capitalism and liberal democracy simply failed to work.

Those interested in the meat of Vidich's historical analysis can skip the anecdotal material of the first two chapters, material which constitutes a fascinating description of the nightmare it is to drive a cab and to use a cab in New York City. One suspects the publisher insisted this material be placed up front. It is the following seven chapters that define the historical relationship in the New York taxi cab industry between the profit motive, public service, and labor under conditions of private ownership. In the final two chapters we have a concise, clear analysis of the gypsy versus medallion cab battle, as a series of violent and often bloody skirmishes in the class struggle.

On Synthesizing Marxism and Christianity, by DALE VREE. New York: John Wiley & Sons, 1976. 206 pp. $14.95 cloth.

NANCY DITOMASO
Northwestern University

This is a terrible book. It is poorly written, the scholarship is sloppy, the logic faulty, and the focus is on strawmen. Vree claims to use the techniques of "analytical-philosophy" to show that Marxism and Christianity are incompatible, and then he proceeds to violate all of the usual canons of logical thinking. His premises are wrong or misstated, and his conclusions do not follow. The only similarity to analytical philosophy is Vree's misunderstanding of the meaning of contradiction in dialectical, especially Marxist, thinking. The focus of Vree's work is what he calls "normative" Marxism (by which he means the Soviet Union) and "normative" Christianity (it is not clear what he means by this term, but his discussion of it is entirely pre-Reformation). It is not true, as he claims, that what he calls "normative" is what most Christians and Marxists affirm, but his definitions set the tone for the rest of the book, which is a series of games with words.

The book, at best, is fifteen years out of date (with a red cross and a red hammer and sickle on a black background on the cover). He persists in discussing the "Marxist-Christian dialogue," but most of the serious work being done currently in which Christians appropriate aspects of Marxism has moved beyond dialogue to what is called "the theology of liberation," especially important in the Latin American continent.

Vree pointedly ignores the work in this area, including Gutierrez, Bonino, Miranda, and Coats, each of whom would provide a better contemporary introduction to the relationship of Marxism and Christianity than Vree. Each of them is also sympathetic to the attempted synthesis, while Vree is not, but one can only develop a systematic critique after taking the work of one's opponents seriously. Vree does not do so.

DELINQUENT REVIEWS

This list is intended as an explanation to authors of why no reviews of their books have yet appeared in *CS*. As of press time we had not received reviews of the following books. Our reminders have been either ignored or met with apologies and promises.

BURCHETT, WILFRED. *China: The Quality of Life*. Penguin Books, 1976.
DAHRENDORF, RALF. *The New Liberty: Survival and Justice in a Changing World*. Stanford University Press, 1975.
DUBEY, S.M. *Social Mobility among the Professions: Study of the Professions in a Transitional Indian City*. Popular Prakashan, 1975.
DUBIN, ROBERT, ed. *Handbook of Work, Organization, and Society*. Rand McNally, 1976.
GOLDTHORPE, JOHN H., and HOPE, KEITH. *The Social Grading of Occupations: A New Approach and Scale*. Clarendon Press, 1974.
GRUBER, CAROL S. *Mars and Minerva: World War I and the Uses of the Higher Learning in America*. Louisiana State University Press, 1975.
HALLER, ARCHIBALD O., and MILLER, IRWIN W. *The Occupational Aspiration Scale: Theory, Structure and Correlates*. Schenkman Publishing Company, 1971.
HILL, M. J., et al. *Men Out of Work: A Study of Unemployment in Three English Towns*. Cambridge University Press, 1973.
HOLLANDER, EDWIN P. *Principles and Methods of Social Psychology*, 3rd ed. Oxford University Press, 1976.
HOLLANDER, EDWIN P., and HUNT, RAYMOND G., eds. *Current Perspectives in Social Psychology: Readings with Commentary*, 4th ed. Oxford University Press, 1976.
JOHNSON, DALE L. *The Sociology of Change and Reaction in Latin America*. Bobbs-Merrill, 1973.
KANTOWICZ, EDWARD R. *Polish-American Politics in Chicago, 1888–1940*. The University of Chicago Press, 1975.
KART, CARY S., and MANARD, BARBARA B. *Aging in America: Readings in Social Gerontology*. Alfred Publishing Company, 1976.
KNUDSEN, HARALD. *Expropriation of Foreign Private Investments in Latin America*. Universitets Forlaget, 1975.
LUKES, STEVEN. *Power: A Radical View*. Humanities Press, 1975.
MANDELL, BETTY REID, ed. *Welfare in America: Controlling the "Dangerous Classes."* Prentice-Hall, 1975.
MERKIN, DONALD H. *Pregnancy as a Disease: The Pill in Society*. Kennikat Press, 1976.
MONTEFIORE, ALAN, ed. *Neutrality and Impartiality: The University and Political Commitment*. Cambridge University Press, 1975.
RAPHAEL, DANA, ed. *Being Female: Reproduction, Power, and Change*. Aldine, 1975.
RUBIN, VERA, ed. *Cannabis and Culture*. Aldine, 1976.
RUSSETT, BRUCE M. and HANSON, ELIZABETH C. *Interest and Ideology: The Foreign Policy Beliefs of American Businessmen*. W. H. Freeman, 1975.
SCANZONI, JOHN H. *Sex Roles, Life Styles, and Childbearing: Changing Patterns in Marriage and the Family*. Free Press, 1975.
SECORD, PAUL F., et al. *Understanding Social Life: An Introduction to Social Psychology*. McGraw-Hill, 1976.
SEIBEL, HANS DIETER. *The Dynamics of Achievement: A Radical Perspective*. Bobbs-Merrill, 1974.
SKLAR, RICHARD L. *Corporate Power in an African State: The Political Impact of Multinational Mining Companies in Zambia*. University of California Press, 1975.
SPENGLER, JOSEPH. *Population Change, Modernization, and Welfare*. Prentice-Hall, 1974.
THEBERGE, JAMES. *Soviet Presence in Latin America*. Crane, Russak & Company, 1974.

PUBLICATIONS RECEIVED

(Listing of a publication below does not assure nor preclude its subsequent review.)

ABEL, ERNEST L., and BUCKLEY, BARBARA E. *The Handwriting on the Wall: Toward a Sociology and Psychology of Graffiti*. Greenwood, 1977. 156 pp. $14.50 cloth.
AHMAD, SAGHIR. *Class and Power in a Punjabi Village*. Monthly Review, 1977. 174 pp. $8.95 cloth.
AHMED, AKBAR S. *Social and Economic Change in the Tribal Areas, 1972–1976*. Oxford University Press, 1977. 81 pp. $5.00 paper.
AL-QAZZAZ, AYAD. *Women in the Middle East and North Africa: An Annotated Bibliography*. Center for Middle Eastern Studies/University of Texas, 1977. 178 pp. $6.50 paper.
AMERICA, RICHARD F. *Developing the Afro-American Economy*. Lexington, 1977. 110 pp. $14.00 cloth.
AMUNDSEN, KIRSTEN. *A New Look at the Silenced Majority: Women and American Democracy*. Prentice-Hall, 1977. 172 pp. $8.95 cloth. $3.95 paper.
ANGLIN, JEREMY M. *Word, Object, and Conceptual Development*. W. W. Norton, 1977. 302 pp. $14.95 cloth.
ARONOFF, MYRON J. *Power and Ritual in the Israel Labor Party: A Study in Political Anthropology*. Van Gorcum, 1977. 184 pp. NPL, paper.
BAIRD, LEONARD L. *The Elite Schools: A Profile of Prestigious Independent Schools*. Lexington, 1977. 163 pp. $15.00 cloth.
BARAKAT, HALIM. *Lebanon in Strife: Student Preludes to the Civil War*. University of Texas Press, 1977. 242 pp. $12.95 cloth.
BARCUS, F. EARLE. *Children's Television: An Analysis of Programming and Advertising*. Praeger, 1977. 218 pp. NPL, cloth.
BARDACH, EUGENE. *The Implementation Game: What Happens After a Bill Becomes a Law*. MIT Press, 1977. 323 pp. $17.95 cloth.
BARTON, WALTER E. and SANBORN, CHARLOTTE J., eds. *An Assessment of the Community Mental Health Movement*. Lexington, 1977. 194 pp. $18.50 cloth.
BAUMHOVER, LORIN A., and JONES, JOAN DECHOW, eds. *Handbook of American Aging Programs*. Greenwood, 1977. 188 pp. $17.50 cloth.
BEBARTA, PRAFULLA C. *Family Type and Fertility in India*. Christopher, 1977. 147 pp. $8.95 cloth.
BEDNAR, MICHAEL J., eds. *Barrier-Free Environments*. Dowden, Hutchinson and Ross, 1977. 278 pp. $22.00 cloth.
BENVENISTE, GUY. *Bureaucracy*. Boyd & Fraser, 1977. 247 pp. $9.95 cloth. $5.95 paper.
BERK, RICHARD A.; BRACKMAN, HAROLD; and LESSER, SELMA. *A Measure of Justice: An Empirical Study of Changes in the California Penal Code, 1955–1971*. Academic Press, 1977. 312 pp. $17.50 cloth.
BERRY, BRIAN J.L., and KASARDA, JOHN D. *Contemporary Urban Ecology*. Macmillan, 1977. 497 pp. NPL, cloth.
BLAU, FRANCINE D. *Equal Pay in the Office*. Lexington, 1977. 143 pp. $15.00 cloth.
BLAU, PETER M. *The Organization of Academic Work*. Wiley, 1973. 310 pp. NPL, cloth.
BLEACKLEY, HORACE. *State Executions Viewed Historically and Sociologically*. With Commentary by John Lofland. Patterson Smith, 1977.
BOCOCK, ROBERT. *Freud and Modern Society: An Outline and Analysis of Freud's Sociology*. Holmes & Meier, 1976. 200 pp. $18.50 cloth.
BOULDING, ELISE. *The Underside of History: A View of Women through Time*. Westview, 1976. 829 pp. $24.75 cloth.
BOURDIEU, PIERRE. *Outline of a Theory of Practice*. (Tr. Richard Nice.) Cambridge University Press, 1977. 248 pp. $18.95 cloth. $5.95 paper.
BOURQUE, GILLES. *L'État capitaliste et la question nationale*. Les Presses de l'Université de Montréal, 1977. 384 pp. $18.50 paper.
BREARLEY, C. PAUL. *Residential Work with the Elderly*. Routledge & Kegan Paul, 1977. 107 pp. $10.25 cloth. $2.75 paper.
BROWN, HELENE. *Yesterday's Child*. New American Library, 1976. 230 pp. $1.75 paper.
BUCKLE, SUZANN R. THOMAS, and BUCKLE, LEONARD G.. *Bargaining for Justice: Case Disposition and Reform in the Criminal Courts*. Praeger, 1977. 181 pp. NPL, cloth.

BULL, HEDLEY. *The Anarchical Society: A Study of Order in World Politics*. Columbia University Press, 1977. 335 pp. $20.00 cloth.
BULLINGTON, BRUCE. *Heroin Use in the Barrio*. Lexington, 1977. 179 pp. $16.00 cloth.
BURCH, WILLIAM R., ed. *Readings in Ecology, Energy, and Human Society: Contemporary Perspectives*, 1977–1978 edition. Harper & Row, 1977. 308 pp. $6.95 paper.
BURSTEIN, JULES QUENTIN. *Conjugal Visits in Prison: Psychological and Social Consequences*. Lexington, 1977. 134 pp. $14.00 cloth.
BUSFIELD, JOAN, and PADDON, MICHAEL. *Thinking about Children: Sociology and Fertility in Post-War England*. Cambridge University Press, 1977. 312 pp. $15.95 cloth.
CAMILLERI, JOSEPH A. *Civilization in Crisis: Human Prospects in a Changing World*. Cambridge University Press, 1976. 303 pp. $17.95 cloth. $5.95 paper.
CARO, FRANCIS G., ed. *Readings in Evaluation Research*, 2nd ed. Russell Sage, 1977. 436 pp. $15.00 cloth.
CASTRO, JOSUÉ DE. *The Geopolitics of Hunger* (updated). Monthly Review, 1977. 524 pp. $18.50 cloth.
CATER, LIBBY A., and SCOTT, ANNE FIROR. *Women and Men: Changing Roles, Relationships, and Perceptions*. Aspen Institute for Humanistic Studies and Praeger, 1976. 270 pp. $17.50 cloth. $3.95 paper.
CHANG, YUNSHIK, and DONALDSON, PETER J., eds. *Population Change in the Pacific Region: Papers Presented in the Symposia on Pacific Populations during the Thirteenth Pacific Science Congress*. Thirteenth Pacific Science Congress, 1975. 206 pp. $4.00 paper.
CIACCI, MARGHERITA, and GUALANDI, VITTORIA, eds. *La costruzione sociale della devianza*. Società editrice il Mulino, 1977. 363 pp. NPL, paper.
COHEN, ROBERT, et al., eds. *Working with Police Agencies*. Human Sciences Press, 1976. 200 pp. $9.95 cloth.
COHEN, SHIRLEY. *Social People: A Brighter Future for Everyone with Physical, Mental, and Emotional Disabilities*. Prentice-Hall, 1977. 177 pp. $8.95 cloth. $3.95 paper.
COLLIER, ANDREW. *R. D. Laing: The Philosophy and Politics of Psychotherapy*. Pantheon, 1977. 214 pp. $10.00 cloth. $3.95 paper.
COLLIER, PETER, and HOROWITZ, DAVID. *The Rockefellers: An American Dynasty*. New American Library, 1976. 774 pp. $2.75 paper.
CONNELL, JOHN,, et al. *Migration from Rural Areas: The Evidence from Village Studies*. Oxford University Press, 1976. 228 pp. $7.00 cloth.
COSER, LEWIS A. *Masters of Sociological Thought: Ideas in Historical and Social Context*, 2nd ed. Harcourt Brace Jovanovich, 1977. 611 pp. $13.95 cloth.
CORSINI, RAYMOND J., ed. *Current Personality Theories*. F. E. Peacock, 1977. 465 pp. $12.95 cloth.
COX, FRED M., et al. *Tactics and Techniques of Community Practice*. F. E. Peacock, 1977. 441 pp. $8.50 paper.
CURRAN, JAMES; GUREVITCH, MICHAEL; and WOOLLACOTT, JANET, eds. *Mass Communication and Society*. Edward Arnold, 1977. 479 pp. NPL, cloth & paper.
CUSACK, DAVID F. *Revolution and Reaction: The Internal and International Dynamics of Conflict and Confrontation in Chile*. University of Denver/Graduate School of International Studies, 1977. 146 pp. NPL, paper.
DALLMAYR, FRED R., and McCARTHY, THOMAS A., eds. *Understanding and Social Inquiry*. University of Notre Dame Press, 1977. 365 pp. $16.95 cloth.
DENTLER, ROBERT A. *Urban Problems: Perspectives and Solutions*. Rand McNally, 1977. 438 pp. $9.95 paper.
DIAMOND, EDWIN. *The Tin Kazoo: Television, Politics, and the News*. MIT Press, 1975. 269 pp. $4.95 paper.
DIAMOND, IRENE. *Sex Roles in the State House*. Yale University Press, 1977. 214 pp. $12.50 cloth.
DONELSON, ELAINE, and GULLAHORN, JEANNE E. *Women: A Psychological Perspective*. Wiley, 1977. 342 pp. $13.96 cloth. $9.95 paper.
DONNISON, JEAN. *Midwives and Medical Men: A History of Inter-Professional Rivalries and Women's Rights*. Schocken, 1977. 250 pp. $14.95 cloth.
DOUGLAS, MARY, ed. *Rules and Meanings: The Anthropology of Everyday Knowledge: Selected Readings*. Penguin, 1977. 319 pp. $2.95 paper.
DUNCAN, STARKEY, JR., and FISKE, DONALD W. *Face-to-Face Interaction: Research, Methods, and Theory*. Lawrence Erlbaum Associates, 1977. 361 pp. NPL, cloth.
DURAND, PIERRE. *Nanacatlan: Société Paysanne et Lutte des Classes au Mexique*. Les Presses de l'Université de Montréal, 1975. 257 pp. $14.25 paper.
EAMES, EDWIN, and GOODE, JUDITH GRANICH. *Anthropology of the City: An Introduction to Urban Anthropology*. Prentice-Hall, 1977. 344 pp. NPL, paper.
ECKELS, JON. *Pursuing the Pursuit: The Black Plight in White America*. Exposition, 1977. 84 pp. $5.50 cloth.
ECKSTEIN, SUSAN. *The Poverty of Revolution: The State and the Urban Poor in Mexico*. Princeton University Press, 1977. 300 pp. $17.50 cloth.
EGGLESTON, JOHN. *The Sociology of the School Curriculum*. Routledge & Kegan Paul, 1977. 171 pp. NPL, cloth.
EISENBERG, MELVIN A. *The Structure of the Corporation: A Legal Analysis*. Little, Brown, 1976. 333 pp. NPL, cloth.
ELIAS, MERRILL F.; ELIAS, PENELOPE KELLY; and ELIAS, JEFFREY W. *Basic Processes in Adult Developmental Psychology*. C. V. Mosby, 1977. 336 pp. NPL, cloth.
ELIAS, NORBERT. *Human Figurations*. Amsterdams Sociologisch Tijdschrift, 1977. 463 pp. NPL, paper.
EPSTEIN, IRWIN, and TRIPODI, TONY. *Research Techniques for Program Planning, Monitoring, and Evaluation*. Columbia University Press, 1977. 178 pp. $12.50 cloth.
ERIKSEN, KARIN. *Human Services Today*. Reston, 1977. 198 pp. $9.95 cloth.
EYSENCK, H. J. *Crime and Personality*. Routledge & Kegan Paul, 1977. 222 pp. $8.95 cloth.
FELIX, JOSEPH L. *Proud Parenthood*. Abingdon, 1977. 158 pp. $6.95 cloth.
FERNANDEZ, RAUL A. *The United States-Mexico Border: A Politico-Economic Profile*. University of Notre Dame Press, 1977. 174 pp. $10.95 cloth.
FIGUEROA, PETER M.E., and PERSAUD, GANGA, EDS. *Sociology of Education: A Caribbean Reader*. Oxford University Press, 1976. 284 pp. $5.50 paper.
FREESE, ARTHUR S. *Help for Your Grief*. Schocken, 1977. 207 pp. $9.95 cloth.
GAGNON, GABRIEL. *Coopératives ou Autogestion: Sénégal, Cuba, Tunisie*. Les Presses de l'Université de Montréal, 1976. 482 pp. $16.50 paper.
GENTRY, W. DOYLE. *Geropsychology: A Model of Training and Clinical Service*. Ballinger, 1977. 137 pp. $15.00 cloth.
GERSHON, MICHAEL, and BILLER, HENRY. *The Other Helpers: Paraprofessionals and Nonprofessionals in Mental Health*. Lexington, 1977. 268 pp. $19.00 cloth.
GIBBONS, DON C., et al. *Criminal Justice: An Introduction*. Prentice-Hall, 1977. 195 pp. $12.95 cloth.
GLASNER, PETER E. *The Sociology of Secularisation: A Critique of a Concept*. Routledge & Kegan Paul, 1977. 137 pp. $11.00 cloth.
GOLDBERG, HERB. *The Hazards of Being Male: Surviving the Myth of Masculine Privilege*. New American Library, 1976. 195 pp. $1.75 paper.
GORDON, SUZANNE. *Lonely in America*. Simon & Schuster, 1976. 318 pp. $3.95 paper.
GOSCIEWSKI, F. WILLIAM. *Effective Child Rearing: The Behaviorally Aware Parent*. Human Sciences Press, 1976. 158 pp. $9.95 cloth.
GOTTESFELD, MARY L., and PHARIS, MARY E. *Profiles in Social Work*. Human Sciences Press, 1977. 238 pp. $14.95 cloth.
GRAHAM, DAVID *He Walks with Me: The Religious Experiences of Country Music Stars*. Simon & Schuster, 1977. 210 pp. $7.95 cloth.
GREENWALD, JERRY. *Is This Really What I Want to Do?* Ward Ritchie, 1977. 207 pp. $8.95 cloth.
GRIFFIN, DONALD R. *The Question of Animal Awareness: Evolutionary Continuity of Mental Experience*. Rockefeller University Press, 1976. 135 pp. $8.95 cloth.
HAAS, J. EUGENE, et al. *Reconstruction Following Disaster*. MIT Press, 1977. 331 pp. $12.95 cloth.
HAGAN, JOHN. *The Disreputable Pleasures*. McGraw-Hill Ryerson, 1977. 254 pp. $5.95 paper.
HALL, RICHARD H. *Organizations: Structure and Process*, 2nd ed. Prentice-Hall, 1977. 356 pp. NPL, cloth.
HANDELMAN, DON. *Work and Play among the Aged: Interaction, Replication and Emergence in a Jerusalem Setting*. Van Gorcum, 1977. 193 pp. NPL, paper.
HANNAN, DAMIAN F., and KATSIAOUNI, LOUISE A. *Traditional Families? From Culturally Prescribed to Negotiated Roles in Farm Families*. Economic and Social Research Institute, 1977. 227 pp. NPL, paper.
HARLOE, MICHAEL, ED. *Captive Cities: Studies in the Political Economy of Cities and Regions*. Wiley, 1977. 218 pp. $17.50 cloth.
HASSAN, RIAZ, ed. *Singapore: Society in Transition*. Oxford University Press, 1976. 371 pp. $23.25 cloth.
HATTON, CORRINE LOING; VALENTE, SHARON McBRIDE; and RINK, ALICE. *Suicide: Assessment and Intervention*. Appleton-Century-Crofts, 1977. 220 pp. $9.75 paper.
HAVILAND, JOHN BEARD. *Gossip, Reputation, and Knowledge in Zinacantan*. University of Chicago Press, 1977. 260 pp. $20.00 cloth.
HEISERMAN, ARTHUR. *The Novel before the Novel: Essays and Discussions about the Beginnings of Prose Fiction in the West*. University of Chicago Press, 1977. 238 pp. $15.00 cloth.
HELMREICH, WILLIAM B., comp. *Afro-Americans and Africa: Black Nationalism at the Crossroads*. Greenwood, 1977. 74 pp. $12.95 cloth.
HELMREICH, WILLIAM B. *The Black Crusaders: A Case Study of a Black Militant Organization*. Harper & Row, 1973. 186 pp. NPL, paper.
HENLEY, NANCY M. *Body Politics: Power, Sex, and Nonverbal Communication*. Prentice-Hall, 1977. 214 pp. $9.95 cloth. $3.95 paper.

HENNIG, MARGARET, and JARDIM, ANNE. *The Managerial Woman*. Anchor Press, 1977. 221 pp. $7.95 cloth.
HILTZ, STARR ROXANNE. *Creating Community Services for Widows: A Pilot Project*. Kennikat, 1977. 166 pp. $9.95 cloth.
HIRSCH, ERNEST A. *Starting Over: The Autobiographical Account of a Psychologist's Experience with Multiple Sclerosis*. Christopher, 1977. 169 pp. $6.95 cloth.
HIRSCHMAN, ALBERT O. *The Passions and the Interests: Political Arguments for Capitalism before Its Triumph*. Princeton University Press, 1977. 153 pp. $10.00 cloth.
HITE, SHERE. *The Hite Report: A Nationwide Study of Female Sexuality*. Macmillan, 1976. 438 pp. $12.50 cloth.
HODGES, ALLEN. *Psychosocial Counseling in General Medical Practice*. Lexington, 1977. 116 pp. $12.50 cloth.
HONG, SUNG-BONG, and WATSON, WALTER B. *The Increasing Utilization of Induced Abortion in Korea*. Korea University Press, 1976. 181 pp. NPL, cloth.
HOOVER, DWIGHT W. *The Red and The Black*. Rand McNally, 1976. 469 pp. NPL, paper.
HOROWITZ, IRVING LOUIS, ed. *Equity, Income, and Policy: Comparative Studies in Three Worlds of Development*. Praeger, 1977. 298 pp. NPL, cloth.
HY, RONN J. *Using the Computer in the Social Sciences: A Nontechnical Approach*. Elsevier, 1977. 155 pp. $10.95 cloth. $5.95 paper.
ISHWARAN, K. *Family, Kinship, and Community: A Study of Dutch Canadians: A Developmental Approach*. McGraw-Hill Ryerson, 1977. 181 pp. $5.95 paper.
JAMES, WILLIAM. *A Pluralistic Universe*. Harvard University Press, 1977. 488 pp. $20.00 cloth.
JANOWITZ, MORRIS. *Military Institutions and Coercion in the Developing Nations*. University of Chicago Press, 1977. 211 pp. $12.50 cloth.
JOFFE, CAROLE E. *Friendly Intruders: Childcare Professionals and Family Life*. University of California Press, 1977. 172 pp. $10.95 cloth.
KANTER, ROSABETH MOSS. *Men and Women of the Corporation*. Basic Books, 1977. 348 pp. $12.00 cloth.
KAPLAN, H. ROY. *American Minorities and Economic Opportunity*. F. E. Peacock, 1977. 387 pp. $10.00 cloth.
KARABEL, JEROME, and HALSEY, A. H., eds. *Power and Ideology in Education*. Oxford University Press, 1977. 670 pp. $15.00 cloth. $9.00 paper.
KASTENBAUM, ROBERT J. *Death, Society, and Human Experience*. C. V. Mosby, 1977. 328 pp. NPL, paper.
KIM, CHOONG SOON. *An Asian Anthropologist in the South: Field Experiences with Blacks, Indians, and Whites*. University of Tennessee Press, 1977. 155 pp. $8.95 cloth.
KRIM, ARTHUR J. *Northwest Cambridge: Survey of Architectural History in Cambridge, Report Five*. Cambridge Historical Commission, 1977. 206 pp. $9.95 paper.
KURTZ, RICHARD A. *Social Aspects of Mental Retardation*. Lexington, 1977. 176 pp. NPL, cloth.
LADNER, JOYCE A. *Mixed Families: Adopting across Racial Boundaries*. Anchor, 1977. 290 pp. $10.00 cloth.
LAITIN, DAVID D. *Politics, Language, and Thought: The Somali Experience*. University of Chicago Press, 1977. 268 pp. $19.00 cloth.
LANGBEIN, JOHN H. *Comparative Criminal Procedure: Germany*. West, 1977. 172 pp. $4.95 paper.
LASSWELL, HAROLD D. *Psychopathology and Politics*. University of Chicago Press, 1977. 339 pp. $5.95 paper.
LEVY, CHARLES S. *Social Work Ethics*. Human Sciences Press, 1976. 266 pp. $14.95 cloth.
LEWIS, OSCAR; LEWIS, RUTH M.; and RIGDON, SUSAN M. *Four Men: Living the Revolution: An Oral History of Contemporary Cuba*. University of Illinois Press, 1977. 538 pp. $15.00 cloth.
LIGHT, DONALD, JR., and SPIEGEL, JOHN. *The Dynamics of University Protest*. Nelson-Hall, 1977. 198 pp. $12.00 cloth.
LIVI-BACCI, MASSIMO. *A History of Italian Fertility during the Last Two Centuries*. Princeton University Press, 1977. 311 pp. $16.50 cloth.
LONDON, HERBERT I. *The Overheated Decade*. New York University Press, 1976. 200 pp. $14.00 cloth. $6.95 paper.
LONDON, HERBERT I. *Social Science Theory, Structure and Application*. New York University Press, 1975. 361 pp. $15.00 cloth.
MacAVOY, PAUL W., ed. *Federal-State Regulation of the Pricing and Marketing of Insurance*. American Enterprise Institute for Public Policy Research, 1977. 105 pp. $3.25 paper.
MacAVOY, PAUL W., ed. *OSHA Safety Regulation: Report of the Presidential Task Force*. American Enterprise Institute for Public Policy Research, 1977. 104 pp. $3.25 paper.
MACINTYRE, SALLY. *Single and Pregnant*. Prodist, 1977. 201 pp. $14.00 cloth.
MACKINNON, KENNETH. *Language, Education and Social Processes in a Gaelic Community*. Routledge & Kegan Paul, 1977. 222 pp. $10.50 paper.
MARKIDES, KYRIACOS C. *The Rise and Fall of the Cyprus Republic*. Yale University Press, 1977. 200 pp. $12.50 cloth.
MARTIN, RODERICK. *The Sociology of Power*. Routledge & Kegan Paul, 1977. 203 pp. $12.95 cloth.
MATRAS, JUDAH. *Introduction to Population: A Sociological Approach*. Prentice-Hall, 1977. 452 pp. $14.95 cloth.
MATTHEWS, FRED H. *Quest for American Sociology: Robert E. Park and the Chicago School*. McGill-Queen's University Press, 1977. 278 pp. NPL, paper.
MAUSS, ARMAND L., and WOLFE, JULIE CAMILLE, eds. *This Land of Promises: The Rise and Fall of Social Problems in America*. J. B. Lippincott, 1977. 452 pp. $5.95 paper.
McCONVILLE, SEAN, ed. *The Use of Imprisonment: Essays in the Changing State of English Penal Policy*. Routledge & Kegan Paul, 1976. 128 pp. $8.25 paper.
McCORD, WILLIAM, and McCORD, ARLINE. *Power and Equity: An Introduction to Social Stratification*. Praeger, 1977. 316 pp. NPL, cloth.
McCOURT, KATHLEEN. *Working-Class Women and Grass-Roots Politics*. Indiana University Press, 1977. 256 pp. $10.00 cloth.
McKELVEY, BLAKE. *American Prisons: A History of Good Intentions*. Patterson Smith, 1977. 408 pp. $16.50. $7.25 paper.
MEYER, MARSHALL W. *Theory of Organizational Structure*. Bobbs-Merrill, 1977. 82 pp. $3.50 paper.
MICHELSON, WILLIAM. *Environmental Choice, Human Behavior, and Residential Satisfaction*. Oxford University Press, 1977. 403 pp. $10.50 cloth. $6.50 paper.
MIERS, SUZANNE, and KOPYTOFF, IGOR, eds. *Slavery in Africa: Historical and Anthropological Perspectives*. University of Wisconsin Press, 1977. 474 pp. $17.50 cloth.
MUKHERJEE, RAMKRISHNA. *Social Indicators*. Macmillan Co. of India, 1975. 146 pp. NPL, cloth.
MULLINS, CAROLYN J. *A Guide to Writing and Publishing in the Social and Behavioral Sciences*. Wiley, 1977. 431 pp. $18.95 cloth. $9.95 paper.
NADER, RALPH, and ABBOTTS, JOHN. *The Menace of Atomic Energy*. W. W. Norton, 1977. 414 pp. $10.95 cloth.
NARAIN, IQBAL, et al. *The Rural Elite in an Indian State: A Case Study of Rajasthan*. South Asia Books, 1976. 256 pp. NPL, cloth.
O'MUIRCHEARTAIGH, COLM A., and PAYNE, CLIVE, eds. *The Analysis of Survey Data, Volume 1: Exploring Data Structures*. Wiley, 1977. 273 pp. $19.95 cloth.
O'MUIRCHEARTAIGH, COLM A., and PAYNE, CLIVE, eds. *The Analysis of Survey Data, Volume 2: Model Fitting*. Wiley, 1977. 255 pp. $23.95 cloth.
OSKAMP, STUART. *Attitudes and Opinions*. Prentice-Hall, 1977. 466 pp. $14.95 cloth.
PALUMBO, DENNIS J. *Statistics in Political and Behavioral Science*, rev. ed. Columbia University Press, 1977. 469 pp. $15.00 cloth.
PARSONS, TALCOTT. *The Evolution of Societies*. Jackson Toby, ed. Prentice-Hall, 1977. 269 pp. $11.95 cloth. $6.95 paper.
PHILLIPS, DEREK L. *Wittgenstein and Scientific Knowledge: A Sociological Perspective*. Macmillan, 1977. 248 pp. NPL, cloth.
PILLAI, S. DEVADAS, ed. *Aspects of Changing India: Studies in Honour of Professor G. S. Ghurye*. Popular Pradashan, 1976. 414 pp. NPL, cloth.
PINE, VANDERLYN R. *Introduction to Social Statistics*. Prentice-Hall, 1977. 415 pp. NPL, cloth.
PREGEL, BORIS; LASSWELL, HAROLD D.; and McHALE, JOHN, eds. *World Priorities*. Transaction, 1977. 281 pp. NPL, paper.
PUNCH, MAURICE. *Progressive Retreat: A Sociological Study of Dartington Hall School 1926–1927 and Some of Its Former Pupils*. Cambridge University Press, 1976. 185 pp. $11.95 cloth.
RADIN, BERYL A. *Implementation, Change, and the Federal Bureaucracy: School Desegregation Policy in H.E.W., 1974–1968*. Teachers College Press. 1977. 239 pp. NPL, paper.
RADINE, LAWRENCE B. *The Taming of the Troops: Social Control in the United States Army*. Greenwood, 1977. 276 pp. $25.00 cloth.
REAL, MICHAEL R. *Mass-Mediated Culture*. Prentice-Hall, 1977. 289 pp. $11.95 cloth. $8.50 paper.
RIST, RAY C., and ANSON, RONALD J., ed. *Education, Social Science, and the Judicial Process*. Teachers College Press, 1977. 130 pp. $5.95 paper.
ROBERTSON, JAMES. *Power, Money, and Sex: Towards a New Social Balance*. Humanities Press, 1976. 149 pp. $10.00 cloth.
ROGERS, JOSEPH W. *Why Are You Not a Criminal?* Prentice-Hall, 1977. 160 pp. $9.95 cloth.
ROSS, MURRAY G. *The University: The Anatomy of Academe*. McGraw-Hill, 1976. 310 pp. NPL, cloth.
RUBEN, BRENT D., ed. *Communication Yearbook I*. Transaction, 1977. 656 pp. $24.95 cloth.
SAMORA, JULIAN and SIMON, PATRICIA VANDEL. *A History of the Mexican-American People*. University of Notre Dame Press, 1977. 238 pp. $9.95 cloth. $5.95 paper.
SANFORD, MARK. *Making It in Graduate School*. Montaigne, 1976. 121 pp. NPL, paper.
SAUL, LEON J. *The Childhood Emotional Pattern: The Key to Personality, Its Disorders and Therapy*. Van Nostrand Reinhold, 1977. 323 pp. $15.95 cloth.
SCHLOSSMAN, STEVEN L. *Love and the American Delinquent: The Theory and Practice of "Progressive" Juvenile Justice, 1825–1920*. University of Chicago Press, 1977. 303 pp. $15.00 cloth.
SCHMIDT, JANET. *Demystifying Parole*. Lexington, 1977. 177 pp. $19.00 cloth.
SENNETT, RICHARD, ed. *The Psychology of Society: An Anthology*. Vintage, 1977. 264 pp. $4.95 paper.

SHANAS, ETHEL, and SUSSMAN, MARVIN B., eds. *Family, Bureaucracy, and the Elderly*. Duke University Press, 1977. 233 pp. $12.75 cloth.
SHAPIRO, R. DIANE. *Foundation for Sociology: A Self-Learning Text*. Rand McNally, 1977. 407 pp. $7.95 paper.
SHAVER, KELLY G. *Principles of Social Psychology*. Winthrop, 1977. 636 pp. $14.95 cloth.
SHEEHAN, SUSAN. *A Welfare Mother*. New American Library, 1977. 144 pp. $1.50 cloth.
SHEPARD, MORRIS A., and BAKER, KEITH. *Year-Round Schools*. Lexington, 1977. 124 pp. $13.00 cloth.
SIMON, RITA JAMES, and ALTSTEIN, HOWARD. *Transracial Adoption*. Wiley, 1977. 197 pp. $14.95 cloth.
SIMPSON, ELIZABETH LÉONIE. *Humanistic Education: An Interpretation*. Ballinger, 1976. 328 pp. $16.00 cloth.
SLATER, PHILIP. *Footholds: Understanding the Shifting Family and Sexual Tensions in Our Culture*. E. P. Dutton, 1977. 227 pp. $4.95 paper.
SLATER, PHILIP. *The Pursuit of Loneliness: American Culture at the Breaking Point*, rev. ed. Beacon, 1976. 206 pp. $8.95 cloth. $3.95 paper.
SMITH, JESSICA; LAIBMAN, DAVID; and BECHTEL, MARILYN, eds. *Building a New Society: The 25th Congress of the Communist Party of the Soviet Union*. N.W.R., 1977. 224 pp. $3.75 paper.
SORRENTINO, ANTHONY. *Organizing against Crime: Redeveloping the Neighborhood*. Human Sciences Press, 1977. 272 pp. $14.95 cloth.
STEIN, EDWARD V., ed. *Fathering: Fact or Fable*. Abingdon, 1977. 190 pp. $6.95 cloth.
STEWART, FRANK HENDERSON. *Fundamentals of Age-Group Systems*. Academic Press, 1977. 381 pp. $26.00 cloth.
SULNICK, ROBERT H. *Civil Litigation and the Police: A Method of Communication*. Charles C Thomas, 1976. 143 pp. $10.75 cloth.
TEGGART, FREDERICK J. *Theory and Processes of History*. University of California Press, 1977. 323 pp. $4.95 paper.
TEPPERMAN, LORNE. *Crime Control: The Urge toward Authority*. McGraw-Hill Ryerson, 1977. 256 pp. $7.95 paper.
TIMMS, NOEL, and TIMMS, RITA. *Perspectives in Social Work*. Routledge & Kegan Paul, 1977. 233 pp. $10.50 cloth. $5.25 paper.
TINKER, HUGH. *The Banyan Tree: Overseas Emigrants from India, Pakistan, and Bangladesh*. Oxford University Press, 1977. 204 pp. $11.00 cloth.
TROLL, LILLIAN E.; ISRAEL, JOAN; and ISRAEL, KENNETH, eds. *Looking Ahead: A Woman's Guide to the Problems and Joys of Growing Older*. Prentice-Hall, 1977. 216 pp. NPL, cloth.
TUNSTALL, JEREMY. *The Media Are American*. Columbia University Press, 1977. 352 pp. $14.95 cloth.
TURNER, JONATHAN H. *Social Problems in America*. Harper & Row, 1977. 555 pp. $12.95 cloth.
VALENZUELA, ARTURO, *Political Brokers in Chile: Local Government in a Centralized Polity*. Duke University Press, 1977. 272 pp. $13.75 cloth.
VAN DYKE, JON M. *Jury Selection Procedures: Our Uncertain Commitment to Representative Panels*. Ballinger, 1977. 426 pp. $15.00 cloth.
VENTURI, ROBERT; BROWN, DENISE SCOTT; and IZENOUR, STEVEN. *Learning from Las Vegas: The Forgotten Symbolism of Architectural Form*, rev. ed. MIT Press, 1977. 192 pp. $9.95 paper.
WALLIS, ROY. *The Road to Total Freedom: A Sociological Analysis of Scientology*. Columbia University Press, 1977. 282 pp. $12.00 cloth.
WARNER, DAVID C., ed. *Toward New Human Rights: The Social Policies of the Kennedy and Johnson Administration*. Lyndon B. Johnson School of Public Affairs/University of Texas, 1977. 448 pp. NPL, paper.
WARREN, RACHELLE B., and WARREN, DONALD I. *The Neighborhood Organizer's Handbook*. University of Notre Dame Press, 1977. 237 pp. $9.95 cloth. $4.95 paper.
WARREN, ROLAND L. *Social Change and Human Purpose: Toward Understanding and Action*. Rand McNally, 1977. 348 pp. $9.95 cloth.
WATT, KENNETH E.F., et al. *The Unsteady State: Environmental Problems, Growth, and Culture*. University Press of Hawaii, 1977. 287 pp. $12.95 cloth.
WECHSLER, HAROLD S. *The Qualified Student: A History of Selective College Admission in America*. Wiley, 1977. 341 pp. NPL, cloth.
WEEKS, SHELDON G. *The Social Background of Tertiary Students in Papua New Guinea: A Survey of Students in Fifteen Institutions*. Educational Research Unit, 1977. 106 pp. NPL, paper.
WEINBERG, MEYER. *A Chance to Learn: The History of Race and Education in the United States*. Cambridge University Press, 1977. 471 pp. $27.50 cloth. $6.95 paper.
WEISBERG, HERBERT F., and BOWEN, BRUCE D. *An Introduction to Survey Research and Data Analysis*. W. H. Freeman, 1977. 243 pp. NPL, paper.
WEITZ, SHIRLEY. *Sex Roles: Biological, Psychological, and Social Foundations*. Oxford University Press, 1977. 283 pp. $10.00 cloth. $5.00 paper.
WERKING, RICHARD HUME. *The Master Architects: Building the United States Foreign Service, 1890–1913*. University Press of Kentucky, 1977. 330 pp. $18.75 cloth.
WICKMAN, PETER, ed. *Readings in Social Problems: Contemporary Perspectives*, 1977–1978 ed. Harper & Row, 1977. 279 pp. $6.95 paper.
WILCOX, SANDRA GALDIERE, and SUTTON, MARILYN. *Understanding Death and Dying: An Interdisciplinary Approach*. Alfred, 1977. 474 pp. $8.95 paper.
WILDHORN, SORREL; LAVIN, MARVIN; and PASCAL, ANTHONY. *Indicators of Justice: Measuring the Performance of Prosecution, Defense, and Court Agencies Involved in Felony Proceedings*. Lexington, 1977. 321 pp. $16.00 cloth.
WINTER, J. ALAN. *Continuities in the Sociology of Religion: Creed, Congregation, and Community*. Harper & Row, 1977. 308 pp. $11.95 cloth.
WISEMAN, JACQUELINE P. *People as Partners*, 2nd ed. Canfield, 1977. 495 pp. NPL, paper.
WONNACOTT, THOMAS H., and WONNACOTT, RONALD J. *Introductory Statistics for Business and Economics*, 2nd ed. Wiley, 1977. 753 pp. $15.95 cloth.
YOUNG, DENNIS R., and FINCH, STEPHEN J. *Foster Care and Nonprofit Agencies*. Lexington, 1977. 265 pp. $18.00 cloth.

U.S. POSTAL SERVICE

STATEMENT OF OWNERSHIP, MANAGEMENT AND CIRCULATION

(Required by 39 U.S.C. 3685)

1. TITLE OF PUBLICATION	A. PUBLICATION NO.	2. DATE OF FILING
Contemporary Sociology	9 9 6 8 8 0	9/30/77

3. FREQUENCY OF ISSUE	A. NO. OF ISSUES PUBLISHED ANNUALLY	B. ANNUAL SUBSCRIPTION PRICE
Bi-Monthly	6	$15.00

4. LOCATION OF KNOWN OFFICE OF PUBLICATION *(Street, City, County, State and ZIP Code) (Not printers)*

1722 N. St. NW Washington DC 20036

5. LOCATION OF THE HEADQUARTERS OR GENERAL BUSINESS OFFICES OF THE PUBLISHERS *(Not printers)*

1722 N. St. NW Washington DC 20036

6. NAMES AND COMPLETE ADDRESSES OF PUBLISHER, EDITOR, AND MANAGING EDITOR

PUBLISHER *(Name and Address)*

American Sociological Ass'n 1722 N St. NW Washington DC 20036

EDITOR *(Name and Address)*

Prof. Bennett Berger Univ. Calif. San Diego, La Jolla CA 92093

MANAGING EDITOR *(Name and Address)*

7. OWNER *(If owned by a corporation, its name and address must be stated and also immediately thereunder the names and addresses of stockholders owning or holding 1 percent or more of total amount of stock. If not owned by a corporation, the names and addresses of the individual owners must be given. If owned by a partnership or other unincorporated firm, its name and address, as well as that of each individual must be given.)*

NAME	ADDRESS
American Sociological Ass'n	1722 N. St. NW Washington DC, 20036

8. KNOWN BONDHOLDERS, MORTGAGEES, AND OTHER SECURITY HOLDERS OWNING OR HOLDING 1 PERCENT OR MORE OF TOTAL AMOUNT OF BONDS, MORTGAGES OR OTHER SECURITIES *(If there are none, so state)*

NAME	ADDRESS
None	

9. FOR COMPLETION BY NONPROFIT ORGANIZATIONS AUTHORIZED TO MAIL AT SPECIAL RATES *(Section 132.122, PSM)*
The purpose, function, and nonprofit status of this organization and the exempt status for Federal income tax purposes *(Check one)*

[X] HAVE NOT CHANGED DURING PRECEDING 12 MONTHS
[ ] HAVE CHANGED DURING PRECEDING 12 MONTHS
(If changed, publisher must submit explanation of change with this statement.)

10. EXTENT AND NATURE OF CIRCULATION	AVERAGE NO. COPIES EACH ISSUE DURING PRECEDING 12 MONTHS	ACTUAL NO. COPIES OF SINGLF ISSUE PUBLISHED NEAREST TO FILING DATE
A. TOTAL NO. COPIES PRINTED *(Net Press Run)*	9300	9250
B. PAID CIRCULATION 1. SALES THROUGH DEALERS AND CARRIERS, STREET VENDORS AND COUNTER SALES	None	None
2. MAIL SUBSCRIPTIONS	7405	7973
C. TOTAL PAID CIRCULATION *(Sum of 10B1 and 10B2)*	7405	7973
D. FREE DISTRIBUTION BY MAIL, CARRIER OR OTHER MEANS SAMPLES, COMPLIMENTARY, AND OTHER FREE COPIES	None	None
E. TOTAL DISTRIBUTION *(Sum of C and D)*	7405	7973
F. COPIES NOT DISTRIBUTED 1. OFFICE USE, LEFT OVER, UNACCOUNTED, SPOILED AFTER PRINTING	1895	1277
2. RETURNS FROM NEWS AGENTS	None	None
G. TOTAL *(Sum of E, F1 and 2—should equal net press run shown in A)*	9300	9250

11. I certify that the statements made by me above are correct and complete.

SIGNATURE AND TITLE OF EDITOR, PUBLISHER, BUSINESS MANAGER, OR OWNER
Alice F. Myers
Alice F. Myers
Administrative Officer

12. FOR COMPLETION BY PUBLISHERS MAILING AT THE REGULAR RATES *(Section 132.121, Postal Service Manual)*

39 U. S. C. 3626 provides in pertinent part: "No person who would have been entitled to mail matter under former section 4359 of this title shall mail such matter at the rates provided under this subsection unless he files annually with the Postal Service a written request for permission to mail matter at such rates."

In accordance with the provisions of this statute, I hereby request permission to mail the publication named in Item 1 at the phased postage rates presently authorized by 39 U. S. C. 3626.

SIGNATURE AND TITLE OF EDITOR, PUBLISHER, BUSINESS MANAGER, OR OWNER
Alice F. Myers
Alice F. Myers
Administrative Officer

PS Form Mar. 1977 3526 *(Page 1)*

INDEX OF REVIEWS, 1977

(Code—Year:Volume:Number:Page)

A

ABADAN-UNAT, NERMIN. *Turkish Workers in Europe, 1960–1975: A Socio-Economic Reappraisal.* Jonathan Matthew Schwartz. 1977:6:5:559.

ABRAMS, PHILIP, AND MCCULLOCH, ANDREW. *Communes, Sociology and Society.* Myron Orleans. 1977:6:6:667.

ADAMS, HOWARD. *Prison of Grass: Canada from the Native Point of View.* Joe T. Darden. 1977:6:1:69.

ADAMS, J. MACK, AND HADEN, DOUGLAS H. *Social Effects of Computer Use and Misuse.* Harvey E. Rich. 1977:6:5:576.

ADLER, RICHARD, AND CATER, DOUGLASS, eds. *Television as a Cultural Force.* Paul Dimaggio. 1977:6:5:545.

ADORNO, THEODOR W. *Introduction to the Sociology of Music.* Judith Adler. 1977:6:3:301.

AHLSTRÖM-LAAKSO, SALME. *Drinking Habits among Alcoholics.* Odis E. Bigus. 1977:6:1:30.

ALBERONI, FRANCESCO. *Italia in transformazione.* Edith Kurzweil. 1977:6:2:206.

ALEX, NICHOLAS. *New York Cops Talk Back: A Study of a Beleaguered Minority.* Michael Williams. 1977:6:3:375.

ALEXANDER, YONAH. *The Role of Communications in the Middle East Conflict: Ideological and Religious Aspects.* Gladys Engel Lang. 1977:6:6:650.

ALFORD, ROBERT R. *Health Care Politics: Ideological and Interest Group Barriers to Reform.* Scotty Embree and Rosemary C. R. Taylor. 1977:6:5:529.

ALTHAUSER, ROBERT P., AND SPIVAK, SYDNEY S. *The Unequal Elites.* Ray C. Rist. 1977:6:1:69.

ALTHEIDE, DAVID L. *Creating Reality: How TV News Distorts Events.* M. G. Dunn. 1977:6:5:546.

ALTHUSSER, LOUIS. *Politics and History: Montesquieu, Rousseau, Hegel and Marx.* Arthur W. Frank, III. 1977:6:2:252.

ANDERSON, CHARLES H. *The Sociology of Survival: Social Problems of Growth.* Allan Schnaiberg. 1977:6:2:235.

ANDERSON, RALPH E., AND CARTER, IRL E. *Human Behavior in the Social Environment: A Social Systems Approach.* Gregory Williams. 1977:6:1:112.

ANDREASEN, ALAN R. *The Disadvantaged Consumer.* Susan Maizel Chambré. 1977:6:2:263.

ANGRIST, SHIRLEY S., AND ALMQUIST, ELIZABETH M. *Careers and Contingencies: How College Women Juggle with Gender.* Bettina J. Huber. 1977:6:4:452.

ARAFAT, IBTIHAJ, AND YORBURG, BETTY. *The New Women: Attitudes, Behavior, and Self-Image.* Nona Glazer. 1977:6:1:89.

ARENS, W., AND MONTAGUE, SUSAN P., eds. *The American Dimension: Cultural Myths and Social Realities.* Lester R. Kurtz. 1977:6:5:552.

ARIETI, SILVANO. *Creativity: The Magic Synthesis.* William A. Sadler, Jr. and Sallie Green. 1977:6:2:156.

ARNOLD, FRED, et al. *The Value of Children: A Cross-National Study. Volume 1: Introduction and Comparative Analysis.* Moni Nag 1977: 6:3:339.

ARNOLD, FRED, AND FAWCETT, JAMES T. *The Value of Children: A Cross-National Study. Volume 3: Hawaii.* Moni Nag. 1977:6:3:339.

ARONSON, ELLIOT. *The Social Animal,* 2nd ed. Morris J. Daniels. 1977:6:2:241.

ASHER, HERBERT B. *Causal Modeling.* Robert B. Smith. 1977:6:6:696.

ASHKAM, JANET. *Fertility and Deprivation: A Study of Differential Fertility amongst Working-Class Families in Aberdeen.* Hyman Rodman. 1977:6:1:44.

ASTIN, ALEXANDER W. *Academic Gamesmanship: Student-Oriented Change in Higher Education.* Rosalyn Weinman Schram. 1977:6:6:673.

ATCHLEY, ROBERT C. *The Sociology of Retirement.* Sarah Matthews. 1977:6:1:109.

AUSTIN, LEWIS. *Japan: The Paradox of Progress.* Brian S. Vargus. 1977:6:4:439.

B

BAECHLER, JEAN. *Revolution.* John Leggett. 1977:6:6:698.

BAHR, HOWARD M., AND GARRETT, GERALD R. *Women Alone: The Disaffiliation of Urban Females.* Helena Znaniecki Lopata. 1977:6:5:597.

BAILEY, F. G., ed. *Debate and Compromise: The Politics of Innovation.* Michael Lewis. 1977:6:3:313.

BAIRD, LEONARD L. *Using Self-Reports to Predict Student Performance.* Joyce L. Epstein. 1977:6:6:674.

BALDAMUS, W. *The Structure of Sociological Inference.* Marshall Elliott Shumsky. 1977:6:6:721.

BALDWIN, ELAINE. *Differentiation and Cooperation in an Israeli Veteran Moshav.* Selma Koss Brandow. 1977:6:2:172.

BALL, DONALD W. *Microecology: Social Situations and Intimate Space.* Arthur H. Patterson. 1977:6:2:186.

BALL, DONALD W., AND LOY, JOHN W. *Sport and Social Order: Contributions to the Sociology of Sport.* Gregory P. Stone. 1977:6:1:110.

BANE, MARY JO. *Here to Stay: American Families in the Twentieth Century.* Roger W. Libby. 1977:6:5:570.

BARASH, DAVID P. *Sociobiology and Behavior.* John D. Baldwin. 1977:6:6:731.

BARCLAY, WILLIAM; KUMAR, KRISHNA; AND SIMMS, RUTH P. eds. *Racial Conflict, Discrimination, and Power: Historical and Contemporary Studies*. Loretta J. Williams. 1977:6:6:706.

BARKER-BENFIELD, G. J. *The Horrors of the Half-Known Life: Male Attitudes toward Women and Sexuality in Nineteenth-Century America*. Michael Gordon. 1977:6:1:89.

BARNLUND, DEAN C. *Public and Private Self in Japan and the United States*. Minako K. Maykovich. 1977:6:3:378.

BARON, SALO W. *A Social and Religious History of the Jews*, 2nd ed. *Volume XVI: Late Middle Ages and Era of European Expansion*. Francesco Cordasco. 1977:6:4:463.

BARON, SALO W. *The Russian Jews under Tsars and Soviets*, 2nd ed. Francesco Cordasco. 1977:6:4:463.

BARTOLLAS, CLEMENS; MILLER, STUART J.; AND DINITZ, SIMON. *Juvenile Victimization: The Institutional Paradox*. Roy L. Austin. 1977:6:4:430.

BARTOS, OTOMAR J. *Process and Outcome of Negotiations*. Bernard P. Cohen. 1977:6:1:94.

BASCOM, WILLIAM R. *African Dilemma Tales*. Steven S. Jones. 1977:6:4:436.

BATES, FREDERICK L., AND HARVEY, CLYDE. *The Structure of Social Systems*. Richard A. Peterson. 1977:6:2:253.

BAUER, ARNOLD J. *Chilean Rural Society from the Spanish Conquest to 1930*. Peter Singelmann. 1977:6:4:425.

BAYLEY, DAVID H. *Forces of Order: Police Behavior in Japan and the United States*. Jerome H. Skolnick. 1977:6:3:375.

BEAVER, STEVEN E. *Demographic Transition Theory Reinterpreted: An Application to Recent Natality Trends in Latin America*. Shirley Foster Hartley. 1977:6:5:556.

BECKER, SELWYN W., AND NEUHAUSER, DUNCAN. *The Efficient Organization*. Gerald R. Salancik. 1977:6:1:59.

BECKFORD, JAMES A. *Religious Organization: A Trend Report and Bibliography*. Wade F. Hook. 1977:6:1:81.

BELL, DANIEL. *The Cultural Contradictions of Capitalism*. Jonathan Rieder and Norbert Wiley. 1977:6:4:411, 416.

BELL, GWENN, ed. *Strategies for Human Settlements: Habitat and Environment*. Howard M. Hammerman. 1977:6:4:445.

BELLAH, ROBERT N. *The Broken Covenant: American Civil Religion in Time of Trial*. Benton Johnson. 1977:6:1:82.

BELOTTI, ELENA GIANINI. *What Are Little Girls Made Of? The Roots of Feminine Stereotypes*. Karen M. Jennison. 1977:6:5:598.

BENN, S. I., AND MORTIMORE, G. W., eds. *Rationality and the Social Sciences: Contributions to the Philosophy and Methodology of the Social Sciences*. J. David Lewis. 1977:6:2:254.

BENNETT, CARL A., AND LUMSDAINE, ARTHUR A., eds. *Evaluation and Experiment: Some Critical Issues in Assessing Social Programs*. Lynne G. Zucker. 1977:6:3:316.

BERELSON, BERNARD. *The Great Debate on Population Policy: An Instructive Entertainment*. Nancy E. Williamson. 1977:6:1:35.

BERES, LOUIS RENÉ, AND TARG, HARRY R., eds. *Planning Alternative World Futures: Values, Methods, and Models*. Elise Boulding. 1977:6:1:62.

BERG, ALAN; SCRIMSHAW, NEVIN S.; AND CALL, DAVID L., eds. *Nutrition, National Development, and Planning: Proceedings of an International Conference Held at Cambridge, Mass., Oct. 19–21, 1971*. Roy Wehrle. 1977:6:3:315.

BERNARD, JESSIE. *The Sociology of Community*. Philip Olson. 1977:6:2:173.

BERNSTEIN, ILENE N., ed. *Validity Issues in Evaluation Research*. Lynne G. Zucker. 1977:6:3:316.

BERSHADY, HAROLD J. *Ideology and Social Knowledge*. Barclay D. Johnson. 1977:6:1:97.

BÉTEILLE, ANDRÉ. *Six Essays in Comparative Sociology*. Joseph R. Gusfield. 1977:6:3:357.

BEYNON, H., AND BLACKBURN, R.M. *Perceptions of Work: Variations within a Factory*. James W. Rinehart. 1977:6:1:53.

BIANCO, CARLA. *The Two Rosetos*. Paul J. Campisi. 1977:6:1:70.

BIRNBAUM, PIERRE, AND CHAZEL, F., eds. *Theórie Sociologique*. Phillip Bosserman. 1977:6:1:99.

BLACK, CYRIL E., ed. *Comparative Modernization: A Reader*. Randall G. Stokes. 1977:6:4:432.

BLACKEY, ROBERT, AND PAYNTON, CLIFFORD. *Revolution and the Revolutionary Ideal*. Ronald Y. L. Cheng. 1977:6:3:329.

BLACKWELL, JAMES E., AND JANOWITZ, MORRIS, eds. *Black Sociologists: Historical and Contemporary Perspectives*. Albert J. McQueen. 1977:6:1:71.

BLALOCK, H. M., et al., eds. *Quantitative Sociology: International Perspectives on Mathematical and Statistical Modeling*. Nancy Brandon Tuma. 1977:6:3:317.

BLAXALL, MARTHA, AND REAGAN, BARBARA, eds. *Women and the Workplace: The Implications of Occupational Segregation*. Virginia Olesen. 1977:6:3:376.

BLOCH, MAURICE, ed. *Political Language and Oratory in Traditional Society*. Lloyd Etheredge. 1977:6:3:330.

BLOCK, N. J., AND DWORKIN, GERALD, eds. *The IQ Controversy: Critical Readings*. Barbara G. Cashion. 1977:6:2:242.

BLUME, STUART S. *Toward a Political Sociology of Science*. Lowell L. Hargens. 1977:6:1:64.

BLUMENTHAL, MONICA D., et al. *More About Justifying Violence: Methodological Studies of Attitudes and Behavior*. Daniel B. McGillis. 1977:6:2:194.

BOGDAN, ROBERT. *Being Different: The Autobiography of Jane Fry*. Imogene L. Simmons. 1977:6:1:90.

BOGDAN, ROBERT, AND TAYLOR, STEVEN J. *Introduction of Qualitative Research Methods: A Phenomenological Approach to the Social Sciences*. Kathy Calkins Charmaz. 1977:6:1:114.

BOISSEVAIN, JEREMY, AND MITCHELL, J. CLYDE, eds. *Network Analysis: Studies in Human Interaction*. Benjamin D. Zablocki. 1977:6:6:697.

BOTTOMORE, TOM. *Marxist Sociology*. Michael Burawoy. 1977:6:1:9.

BOWEN, PETER. *Social Control in Industrial Organisations: Industrial Relations and Industrial Sociology: A Strategic and Occupational Study of British Steelmaking*. George H. Westacott. 1977:6:5:580.

BOWERS, DAVID G. *Systems of Organization: Management of the Human Resource*. George H. Westacott. 1977:6:5:580.

BOWKER, GORDON, AND CARRIER, JOHN, eds. *Race and Ethnic Relations: Sociological Readings*. John W. Martin. 1977:6:5:593.

BOWLES, SAMUEL, AND GINTIS, HERBERT. *Schooling in Capitalist America: Educational Reform and the Contradictions of Economic Life*. Michael Useem. 1977:6:1:19.

BOYD, WILLIAM L. *Community Status and Conflict in Suburban School Politics*. Regina H. Kenen. 1977:6:5:564.

BOZEMAN, ADDA B. *Conflict in Africa: Concepts and Realities*. David D. Laitin. 1977:6:3:359.

BRAGG, MELVYN. *Speak for England*. Joan Gilbert. 1977:6:4:500.

BRAIN, ROBERT. *Friends and Lovers*. Craig Calhoun. 1977:6:4:447.

BRALY, MALCOLM. *False Starts: A Memoir of San Quentin and Other Prisons*. Peggy Ann Thoits. 1977:6:2:175.

BRAROE, NIELS WINTHER. *Indian and White: Self-Image and Interaction in a Canadian Plains Community*. Philip A. May. 1977:6:3:342.

BREWER, MARILYNN B., AND CAMPBELL, DONALD T. *Ethnocentrism and Intergroup Attitudes: East African Evidence*. Stanley J. Morse. 1977:6:4:465.

BRISLIN, RICHARD W., ed. *Translation: Applications and Research*. Roger Spielmann.1977:6:6:664.

BRODSKY, ANNETTE M., ed. *The Female Offender*. Harriet Engel Gross. 1977:6:1:31.

BROWN, ARCHIE, AND KASER, MICHAEL, eds. *The Soviet Union since the Fall of Khruschev*. Alexander Matejko. 1977:6:2:207.

BROWN, GARY D., AND BROWN, DUANE. *A Survey of the Social Sciences*. Sharon McPherron. 1977:6:2:263.

BRUGGER, WILLIAM. *Democracy and Organisation in Chinese Industrial Enterprise, 1948–1953*, Gary G. Hamilton. 1977:6:1:53.

BULATAO, RODOLFO A. *The Value of Children: A Cross-National Study. Volume 2: Philippines*. Moni Nag. 1977:6:3:339.

BULMER, MARTIN, ed. *Working-Class Images of Society*. Patricia Voydanoff. 1977:6:1:54.

BUNCE, RICHARD. *Television in the Corporate Interest*. Robert G. Dunn. 1977:6:1:113.

BURBANK, GARIN. *When Farmers Voted Red: The Gospel of Socialism in the Oklahoma Countryside, 1910–1924*. Ellen Rosen. 1977:6:5:587.

BURBY, RAYMOND J., III, AND WEISS, SHIRLEY F. *New Communities U.S.A.* Sally S. Rogers. 1977:6:2:259.

BUSINO, GIOVANNI. *Sociologia e Storia: Elementi per un Dibattito*. Joseph Lopreato. 1977:6:6:722.

C

CAHALAN, DON, AND ROOM, ROBIN. *Problem Drinking among American Men*. Howard M. Bahr. 1977:6:3:305.

CALHOUN, DONALD W. *Persons-in-Groups: A Humanistic Social Psychology*. Morris J. Daniels. 1977:6:2:241.

CALVERT, BARBARA. *The Role of the Pupil*. Rosalie Cohen. 1977:6:2:181.

CAMP, JOHN. *Magic, Myth and Medicine*. Miriam Sonn. 1977:6:1:49.

CAMPBELL, ANGUS; CONVERSE, PHILIP E.; AND RODGERS, WILLARD L. *The Quality of American Life: Perceptions, Evaluations, and Satisfactions*. Richard M. Cohn. 1977:6:4:489.

CAMPBELL, CARLOS C. *New Towns: Another Way to Live*. Sally S. Rogers. 1977:6:2:259.

CAMPBELL, COLIN. *Toward a Sociology of Irreligion*. Rolf Schulze. 1977:6:1:84.

CANTRELLE, PIERRE, et al., eds. *Population in African Development*, Vols. 1 & 2. Karol J. Krótki. 1977:6:5:558.

CAPLAN, GERALD, AND KILLILEA, MARIE, eds. *Support Systems and Mutual Help: Multidisciplinary Explorations*. Jonathan A. Freedman. 1977:6:6:690.

CAPLOVITZ, DAVID. *Consumers in Trouble: A Study of Debtors in Default*. Julius A. Roth. 1977:6:1:115.

CARLSMITH, J. MERRILL; ELLSWORTH, PHOEBE C.; AND ARONSON, ELLIOT. *Methods of Research in Social Psychology*. Royce Singleton, Jr. 1977:6:3:319.

CARNOY, MARTIN, AND LEVIN, HENRY M. *The Limits of Educational Reform*. Gene Grabiner. 1977:6:6:674.

CARPENTER, EDMUND. *Oh, What a Blow That Phantom Gave Me!* Gladys Engel Lang. 1977:6:6:650.

CARROLL, BERENICE A., ed. *Liberating Women's History: Theoretical and Critical Essays*. Marilyn J. Boxer. 1977:6:2:230.

CARSTAIRS, G. M., AND KAPUR, R. L. *The Great Universe of Kota: Stress, Change and Mental*

Disorder in an Indian Village. Robert H. Lauer. 1977:6:6:691.

CARTER, ANTHONY T. *Elite Politics in Rural India: Political Stratification and Political Alliances in Western Maharashtra*. Richard P. Taub. 1977:6:2:208.

CARTER, ROBERT M., AND KLEIN, MALCOLM W., eds. *Back on the Street: The Diversion of Juvenile Offenders*. Roy L. Austin. 1977:6:4:430.

CHADWICK-JONES, J. K. *Social Exchange Theory: Its Structure and Influence in Social Psychology*. Harry C. Bredemeier. 1977:6:6:646.

CHAFETZ, JANET SALTZMAN, et al. *Who's Queer?* Meredith Gould. 1977:6:6:711.

CHATTERJEE, PRANAB. *Local Leadership in Black Communities: Organizational and Electoral Developments in Cleveland, in the Nineteen Sixties*. Leslie G. Carr. 1977:6:1:73.

CHEATWOOD, DERRAL, AND LINQUIST, THEROLD, eds. *The Human Image: Sociology and Photography*. Philip H. Ennis. 1977:6:3:302.

CHEEK, NEIL H., JR., AND BURCH, WILLIAM R. *The Social Organization of Leisure in Human Society*. Bill Devall. 1977:6:6:731.

CHEKKI, DANESH A. *Modernization and Kin Network*. A. A. Khatri. 1977:6:1:46.

CHICKERING, A. LAWRENCE, ed. *Public Employee Unions: A Study of the Crisis in Public Sector Labor Relations*. Martin Oppenheimer. 1977:6:6:732.

CHOMSKY, NOAM. *Reflections on Language*. William L. Raiser. 1977:6:2:188.

CHUDACOFF, HOWARD P. *The Evolution of American Urban Society*. Matthew Edel. 1977:6:5:606.

CLARK, ALFRED W., compiler. *Experimenting with Organizational Life: The Action Research Approach*. Ruth A. Schwartz. 1977:6:6:698.

CLARK, BURTON R. *The Problems of American Education*. Daniel L. Kegan. 1977:6:4:434.

CLARK, NORMAN H. *Deliver Us from Evil: An Interpretation of American Prohibition*. Marston M. McCluggage. 1977:6:5:549.

CLARK, S.D. *Canadian Society in Historical Perspective*. Jean Leonard Elliott. 1977:6:2:174.

CLAUDE, RICHARD P., ed. *Comparative Human Rights*. Harry M. Johnson. 1977:6:3:307.

CLAYRE, ALASDAIR. *Work and Play: Ideas and Experience of Work and Leisure*. Andrea Fontana. 1977:6:2:197.

CLIGNET, REMI. *Liberty and Equality in the Educational Process: A Comparative Sociology of Education*. Ronald P. Dore. 1977:6:2:181.

COHEN, BERNARD, AND LEE, HANS. *Conflict, Conformity and Social Status*. Cecilia L. Ridgeway. 1977:6:6:733.

COHEN, JACOB, AND COHEN, PATRICIA. *Applied Multiple Regression/Correlation Analysis for the Behavioral Sciences*. Neil W. Henry. 1977:6:3:320.

COLE, LEONARD A. *Blacks in Power: A Comparative Study of Black and White Elected Officials*. Leslie G. Carr. 1977:6:1:73.

COLLETTI, LUCIO. *Marxism and Hegel*. Arthur W. Frank, III. 1977:6:2:252.

COMBS, JAMES E., AND MANSFIELD, MICHAEL W., eds. *Drama in Life: The Uses of Communication in Society*. Peter K. Manning. 1977:6:6:733.

COMMONER, BARRY. *The Poverty of Power*. Noman Miller. 1977:6:2:187.

CONSTANTINE, LARRY L., AND CONSTANTINE, JOAN M. *Group Marriage: A Study of Contemporary Multilateral Marriage*. Stephen K. Sanderson. 1977:6:1:44.

CONYERS, JAMES E., AND WALLACE, WALTER L. *Black Elected Officials: A Study of Black Americans Holding Governmental Office*. James H. Laue. 1977:6:6:707.

CONZEN, KATHLEEN NEILS. *Immigrant Milwaukee, 1836–1860: Accommodation and Community in a Frontier City*. Eric H. Monkkonen. 1977:6:4:501.

COOK, RAMSAY, AND MITCHINSON, WENDY, eds. *The Proper Sphere: Woman's Place in Canadian Society*. Susan Mann Trofimenkoff. 1977:6:5:599.

COOK, THOMAS D., et al. *"Sesame Street" Revisited*. Gladys Engel Lane. 1977:6:5:612.

COOPER, CHESTER L., ed. *Growth in America*. Albert J. Mayer. 1977:6:4:445.

CORDASCO, FRANCESCO, ed. *Studies in Italian American Social History*. William P. Nye. 1977:6:1:74.

CORNELIUS, WAYNE A. *Politics and the Migrant Poor in Mexico City*. Bruce Harris. 1977:6:3:360.

CORNELIUS, WAYNE A., AND TRUEBLOOD, FELICITY M., eds. *Latin American Urban Research, Volume V: Urbanization and Inequality: The Political Economy of Urban and Rural Development in Latin America*. William L. Flinn. 1977:6:5:607.

COSER, LEWIS A., ed. *The Idea of Social Structure: Papers in Honor of Robert K. Merton*. David Caplovitz, Randall Collins, and Maurice R. Stein. 1977:6:2:142, 150, 154.

COUCH, CARL J., AND HINTZ, ROBERT A., JR. *Constructing Social Life: Readings in Behavioral Sociology from the Iowa School*. Santo J. Tarantino. 1977:6:2:243.

COX, OLIVER C. *Race Relations: Elements and Social Dynamics*. Don O. Watkins. 1977:6:4:466.

CRAIB, IAN. *Existentialism and Sociology: A Study of Jean-Paul Satre*. Dean MacCannell. 1977:6:4:493.

CRIDEN, YOSEF, AND GELB, SAADIA. *The Kibbutz Experience: Dialogue in Kfar Blum*. Selma Koss Brandow. 1977:6:2:172.

CROMWELL, RONALD E., AND OLSON, DAVID H., eds. *Power in Families*. Mirra Komarovsky. 1977:6:5:571.

CROSS, GEORGE LYNN. *Blacks in White Colleges: Oklahoma's Landmark Cases*. Sethard Fisher. 1977:6:2:216.

CROZIER, MICHEL, et al. *Oú va l'administration française*. Ezra N. Suleiman. 19776:3:331.

CSIKSZENTMIHALYI, MIHALY. *Beyond Boredom and Anxiety: The Experience of Play in Work and Games*. Murray S. Davis. 1977:6:2:197.

D

DANIELS, LES. *Living in Fear: A History of Horror in the Mass Media*. Nathan Weinberg. 1977:6:1:116.

DASHEFSKY, ARNOLD, ed. *Ethnic Identity in Society*. Douglas S. Snyder. 1977:6:2:217.

DAVID, DEBORAH S., AND BRANNON, ROBERT, eds. *The Forty-Nine Percent Majority: The Male Sex Role*. Jane H. Scheff and Thomas J. Scheff. 1977:6:3:379.

DAVIN, DELIA. *Woman-Work: Women and the Party in Revolutionary China*. May N. Diaz. 1977:6:3:377.

DAVIS, BERNARD D., AND FLAHERTY, PATRICIA. *Human Diversity: Its Causes and Social Significance*. Jeffrey Scott Johnson. 1977:6:6:735.

DAVIS, LOUIS E., AND CHERNS, ALBERT B., eds. *The Quality of Working Life. Volume 2: Cases and Commentary*. Craig C. Lundberg. 1977:6:1:55.

DAVIDSON, W. PHILLIPPS; BOYLAN, JAMES; AND YU, FREDERICK, T. C. *Mass Media: Systems and Effects*. Herbert I. Schiller. 1977:6:5:548.

DEAN, ALFRED; KRAFT, ALAN M.; AND PEPPER, BERT, eds. *The Social Setting of Mental Health*. Muriel W. Pumphrey. 1977:6:5:574.

DEITCHMAN, SEYMOUR J. *The Best-Laid Schemes: A Tale of Social Research and Bureaucracy*. David R. Segal. 1977:6:4:502.

deKADT, EMANUEL, AND WILLIAMS, GAVIN, eds. *Sociology and Development*. J. Bernard Murphy. 1977:6:4:441.

deMAUSE, LLOYD, ed. *The New Psychohistory*. Lloyd S. Etheredge. 1977:6:5:614.

DEMERATH, N. J., III; LARSEN, OTTO, AND SCHUESSLER, KARL F. *Social Policy and Sociology*. C. L. Estes. 1977:6:6:716.

DEMERATH, NICHOLAS J., III. *Birth Control and Foreign Policy: The Alternatives to Family Planning*. Charles F. Hohm. 1977:6:5:584.

deNEUFVILLE, JUDITH INNES. *Social Indicators and Public Policy: Interactive Processes of Design and Application*. Brian Vargus. 1977:6:3:320.

DENTON, DAVID E., ed. *Existentialism and Phenomenology in Education: Collected Essays*. John M. Johnson. 1977:6:1:22.

DESPRES, LEO A., ed. *Ethnicity and Resource Competition in Plural Societies*. Aubrey W. Bonnett. 1977:6:1:75.

DINNERSTEIN, DOROTHY. *The Mermaid and the Minotaur: Sexual Arrangements and Human Malaise*. Miriam M. Johnson. 1977:6:4:476.

DOSMAN, EDGAR J. *The National Interest: The Politics of Northern Development 1968–75*. Stephen O. Murray. 1977:6:2:218.

DOUGLAS, JACK D. *Investigative Social Research: Individual and Team Field Research*. Raymond L. Gold. 1977:6:6:654.

DOUGLAS, MARY. *Implicit Meanings: Essays in Anthropology*. Bennetta Jules-Rosette. 1977:6:5:554.

DROZ, REMY, AND RAHMY, MARYVONNE. *Understanding Piaget*. Kathryn P. Meadow. 1977:6:1:100.

DUBERMAN, LUCILE. *Social Inequality: Class and Caste in America*. Joan Huber. 1977:6:2:250.

DUNBAR, TONY, AND KRAVITZ, LINDA. *Hard Traveling: Migrant Farm Workers in America*. David Harvey. 1977:6:4:453.

DUNCAN, OTIS DUDLEY; SCHUMAN, HOWARD; AND DUNCAN, BEVERLY. *Social Change in a Metropolitan Community*. Ellan Odiorne Derow. 1977:6:6:668.

DUNKERLEY, DAVID. *The Foreman: Aspects of Task and Structure*. Richard K. Brown. 1977:6:4:454.

DURKHEIM, EMILE. *Textes*. Volume 1: *Eléments d'une Théorie Sociale*. Volume 2: *Religion, Morale, Anomie*. Volume 3: *Fonctions Sociales et Institutions*. Edward A. Tiryakian. 1977:6:1:17.

DWORKIN, ANTHONY GARY, AND DWORKIN, ROSALINE J., eds. *The Minority Report: An Introduction to Racial, Ethnic, and Gender Relations*. Joseph S. Roucek. 1977:6:3:343.

E

ECKSTEIN, HARRY, AND GURR, TED ROBERT. *Patterns of Authority: A Structural Basis for Political Inquiry*. Anthony Orum. 1977:6:4:455.

EDELSTEIN, J. DAVID, AND WARNER, MALCOLM. *Comparative Union Democracy: Organisation and Opposition in British and American Unions*. Edna E. Raphael. 1977:6:1:60.

EDGE, DAVID O., AND MULKAY, MICHAEL J. *Astronomy Transformed: The Emergence of Radio Astronomy in Britain*. Thomas F. Gieryn. 1977:6:6:656.

EDWARDS, ANNE R., AND WILSON, PAUL R., eds. *Social Deviance in Australia*. Frances H. Lovejoy. 1977:6:1:30.

EISENSTADT, S. N. *The Form of Sociology: Paradigms and Crises*. Jeffrey C. Alexander. 1977:6:6:658.

EKEH, PETER P. *Social Exchange Theory: The Two Traditions*. Harry C. Bredemeier. 1977:6:6:646.

ELAZAR, DANIEL J. *Community and Polity: The Organizational Dynamics of American Jewry*. Irving Louis Horowitz. 1977:6:3:287.

ELKANA, YEHUDA. *The Discovery of the Conservation of Energy*. Robert Cameron Mitchell. 1977:6:3:379.

EMERY, F. E., AND TRIST, E. L. *Towards a Social Ecology: Contextual Appreciations of the Future in the Present*. Richard O. Mason. 1977:6:4:494.

ENGELMANN, F. C., AND SCHWARTZ, M. A. *Canadian Political Parties: Origin, Character, Impact*. Paul Lamy. 1977:6:4:457.

ERDOS, PAUL L. *Professional Mail Surveys*. David Bills. 1977:6:5:577.

ERICSON, EDWARD E. *Radicals in the University*. Henry Pachter. 1977:6:4:457.

ETZIONI, AMITAI. *A Comparative Analysis of Complex Organizations: On Power, Involvement, and Their Correlates,* revised and enlarged. Paul M. Hirsch. 1977:6:4:503.

ETZIONI, AMITAI. *Social Problems.* Armand L. Mauss. 1977:6:5:602.

F

FABER, BERNARD LEWIS., ed. *The Social Structure of Eastern Europe: Transition and Process in Czechoslovakia, Hungary, Poland, Romania, and Yugoslavia.* Zoltán Tar. 1977:6:3:381.

FAINSTEIN, NORMAN I., AND FAINSTEIN, SUSAN S. *Urban Political Movements: The Search for Power by Minority Groups in American Cities.* George W. Dowdall. 1977:6:1:104.

FAIRFIELD, ROY P., ed. *Humanizing the Workplace.* Craig C. Lundberg. 1977:6:1:55.

FARMANFARMAIAN, KHODADAD, ed. *The Social Sciences and Problems of Development.* J. Bernard Murphy. 1977:6:4:441.

FEINBERG, WALTER, AND ROSEMONT, HENRY, JR., eds. *Work, Technology, and Education: Dissenting Essays in the Intellectual Foundations of American Education.* Zelda F. Gamson. 1977:6:1:23.

FELDSTEIN, STANLEY, AND COSTELLO, LAWRENCE, eds. *The Ordeal of Assimilation: A Documentary History of the White Working Class.* Harry Cohen. 1977:6:1:76.

FICHTER, JOSEPH H. *The Catholic Cult and the Paraclete.* Marion Dearman. 1977:6:2:226.

FIDEL, KENNETH, ed. *Militarism in Developing Countries.* Stephen P. Cohen. 1977:6:3:324.

FILSTEAD, WILLIAM J.; ROSSI, JEAN J.; AND KELLER, MARK, eds. *Alcohol and Alcohol Problems: New Thinking and New Directions.* Marston M. McCluggage. 1977:6:5:549.

FISHBEIN, MARTIN, AND AJZEN, ICEK. *Belief, Attitude, Intention and Behavior: An Introduction to Theory and Research.* Richard J. Hill. 1977:6:2:244.

FITZPATRICK, BLANCHE. *Women's Inferior Education: An Economic Analysis.* Judith Caditz. 1977:6:6:677.

FLETCHER, COLIN. *Beneath the Surface: An Account of Three Styles of Sociological Research.* Kathy Calkins Charmaz. 1977:6:1:114.

FLEW, ANTONY. *Sociology, Equality, and Education: Philosophical Essays in Defense of a Variety of Differences.* Richard A. Hilbert. 1977:6:6:723.

FLINK, JAMES J. *The Car Culture.* George H. Lewis. 1977:6:3:345.

FLYNN, CHARLES P. *Insult and Society: Patterns of Comparative Interaction.* Alfred McClung Lee. 1977:6:5:615.

FORCESE, DENNIS. *The Canadian Class Structure.* Jean Leonard Elliott. 1977:6:2:174.

FORD, AMASA B. *Urban Health in America.* Jennie J. Kronenfeld. 1977:6:2:261.

FORD, ANN SUTER. *The Physician's Assistant: A National and Local Analysis.* Michael Yedidia. 1977:6:1:49.

FORM, WILLIAM H. *Blue Collar Stratification: Autoworkers in Four Countries.* William H. Friedland. 1977:6:2:159.

FORMAN, PAUL; HEILBRON, JOHN; AND WEART, SPENCER. "Physics circa 1900: Personnel, Funding, and Productivity of the Academic Establishment." David A. Woodrow. 1977:6:3:382.

FORMAN, SHEPARD. *The Brazilian Peasantry.* Peter Singelmann. 1977:6:4:425.

FOSTER, JOHN. *Class Struggle and the Industrial Revolution: Early Industrial Capitalism in Three English Towns.* Mary Ann Clawson. 1977:6:3:289.

FRANCIS, EMERICH K. *Interethnic Relations: An Essay in Sociological Theory.* Richard T. Schaefer. 1977:6:4:466.

FRANKLIN, JACK L., AND THRASHER, JEAN H. *An Introduction to Program Evaluation.* Dan S. Green. 1977:6:5:616.

FRANKLIN, JOHN HOPE. *Racial Equality in America.* William P. Nye. 1977:6:4:467.

FRAZIER, CHARLES E. *Theoretical Approaches to Deviance: An Evaluation.* Lee Ellis. 1977:6:3:307.

FRAZIER, E. FRANKLIN, AND LINCOLN, C. ERIC. *The Negro Church in America* and *The Black Church since Frazier.* Russell R. Dynes. 1977:6:1:84.

FREDERICKS MARCEL A., AND MUNDY, PAUL. *The Making of a Physician: A Ten-Year Longitudinal Study of Social Class, Academic Achievement, and Changing Professional Attitudes of a Medical School Class.* Robert H. Coombs. 1977:6:2:191.

FREDERICKSON, GEORGE, AND O'LEARY, LINDA SCHLUSTER. *Measuring Power, Public Opinion and Policy: A Case Study of Syracuse, New York.* Martin J. Murray. 1977:6:2:209.

FREEDMAN, MARCIA K. *Labor Markets: Segments and Shelters.* Paul Osterman. 1977:6:6:736.

FREIDHEIM, ELIZABETH A. *Sociological Theory in Research Practice.* Garth Massey. 1977:6:6:724.

FREIDSON, ELIOT. *Doctoring Together: A Study of Professional Social Control.* Nancy R. Chiswick. 1977:6:5:585.

FRENCH, DAVID, AND FRENCH, ELENA. *Working Communally: Patterns and Possibilities.* Paul Goldman. 1977:6:2:199.

FRIEDLANDER, PETER. *The Emergence of a UAW Local, 1936–1939: A Study in Class and Culture.* James P. Mulherin. 1977:6:2:203.

FRIEDMAN, LAWRENCE M. *The Legal System: A Social Science Perspective.* Allan Horowitz. 1977:6:3:308.

FRIEDMANN, F. G. *Youth and Society.* Judith D. Handel. 1977:6:1:116.

FRY, PETER. *Spirits of Protest: Spirit-Mediums and the Articulation of Consensus amongst the Zezuru of Southern Rhodesia.* Bennetta Jules-Rosette. 1977:6:4:471.

FUMOLEAU, RENÉ. *As Long As This Land Shall Last.* Stephen O. Murray. 1977:6:2:218.

G

GAEV, DOROTHY MEYER. *The Psychology of Loneliness.* Robert A. Stebbins. 1977:6:4:490.

GANS, HERBERT J. *Popular Culture and High Culture: An Analysis and Evaluation of Taste.* Bennett M. Berger. 1977:6:6:661.

GASSON, RUTH M.; HALLER, ARCHIBALD O.; AND SEWELL, WILLIAM H. *Attitudes and Facilitation in the Attainment of Status.* James R. Lincoln. 1977:6:2:245.

GEER, BLANCHE, ed. *Learning to Work.* Jeylan T. Mortimer. 1977:6:1:57.

GELLES, RICHARD J. *The Violent Home: A Study of Physical Aggression between Husbands and Wives.* Diana E. H. Russell. 1977:6:5:572.

GERSTL, JOEL E., AND JACOBS, GLENN, eds. *Professions for the People: The Politics of Skill.* Gerald Rosenblum. 1977:6:6:737.

GIDDENS, ANTHONY. *New Rules of Sociological Method: A Positive Critique of Interpretative Sociologies.* Aaron V. Cicourel and Thomas F. Gieryn. 1977:6:5:533, 535.

GLAZER, NATHAN. *Affirmative Discrimination: Ethnic Identity and Public Policy.* Andrew Billingsley, Jack D. Douglas, and Joan W. Moore. 1977:6:5:537, 539, 542.

GLASSIE, HENRY. *All Silver and No Brass: An Irish Christmas Mumming.* Roger Abrahams. 1977:6:4:437.

GLICK, THOMAS F., ed. *The Comparative Reception of Darwinism.* Nicholas C. Mullins. 1977:6:5:617.

GLOCK, CHARLES Y., et al. *Adolescent Prejudice.* Jane R. Mercer. 1977:6:2:219.

GLOCK, CHARLES Y., AND BELLAH, ROBERT N., eds. *The New Religious Consciousness.* Roy Wallis. 1977:6:4:472.

GOLD, ALICE ROSS; CHRISTIE, RICHARD; AND FRIEDMAN, LUCY NORMAN. *Fists and Flowers: A Social Psychological Interpretation of Student Dissent.* Peter M. Nardi. 1977:6:6:700.

GOLDBERG, STEVEN. *The Inevitability of Patriarchy.* Rayna Rapp Reiter. 1977:6:1:91.

GOLDE, GÜNTER. *Catholics and Protestants: Agricultural Modernization in Two German Villages.* Eleanor Meyer Rogg. 1977:6:4:441.

GOLDEN, M. PATRICIA, ed. *The Research Experience.* Norman K. Denzin. 1977:6:3:321.

GOLDHAMER, HERBERT. *The Soviet Soldier: Soviet Military Management at the Troop Level.* David R. Segal. 1977:6:1:117.

GOLDMAN, NANCY L., AND SEGAL, DAVID R., eds. *The Social Psychology of Military Service.* Scott G. McNall. 1977:6:3:325.

GOLDTHORPE, J. E.. *The Sociology of the Third World: Disparity and Involvement.* Randall G. Stokes. 1977:6:4:432.

GORECKI, JAN, ed. *Sociology and Jurisprudence of Leon Petrazycki.* J. G. Hund. 1977:6:2:176.

GORHAM, WILLIAM, AND GLAZER, NATHAN, eds. *The Urban Predicament.* Joseph M. Conforti. 1977:6:3:372.

GOULDNER, ALVIN W. *The Dialectic of Ideology and Technology: The Origins, Grammar, and Future of Ideology.* Anthony Giddens, Benton Johnson, and Frederick R. Lynch. 1977:6:6:635, 636, 637.

GRABER, DORIS A. *Verbal Behavior and Politics.* M. Glenn Newkirk. 1977:6:3:332.

GRACE, JOHN. *Domestic Slavery in West Africa: With Particular Reference to the Sierra Leone Protectorate, 1896–1927.* Edward Reynolds. 1977:6:2:221.

GRANET, MARCEL. *The Religion of the Chinese People.* Translated by Maurice Freedman. John F. Manfredi. 1977:6:6:739.

GRAS, ALAIN. *Sociologie de l'education: Textes fondamentaux.* Remi Clignet. 1977:6:1:24.

GREELEY, ANDREW M. *Ethnicity, Denomination, and Inequality.* Dorothy Wertz. 1977:6:5:594.

GREENBERG, LOUIS. *The Jews in Russia: The Struggle for Emancipation.* Francesco Cordasco. 1977:6:4:463.

GREENBLAT, CATHY S.; STEIN, PETER J.; AND WASHBURNE, NORMAN F. *The Marriage Game: Understanding Marital Decision Making.* Charles T. Hill. 1977:6:1:45.

GRIFFIN, KEITH. *The Political Economy of Agrarian Change: An Essay on the Green Revolution.* William L. Flinn. 1977:6:3:313.

GROOMBRIDGE, BRIAN. *Television and the People: A Programme for Democratic Participation.* Robert G. Dunn. 1977:6:1:113.

GROPPER, RENA C. *Gypsies in the City: Culture Patterns and Survival.* Marcello Truzzi. 1977:6:6:709.

GROSS, NEAL, AND TRASK, ANNE E. *The Sex Factor and the Management of Schools.* Patricia Yancey Martin. 1977:6:2:231.

GUBRIUM, JABER F. *Living and Dying at Murray Manor.* Juanita Wood. 1977:6:2:192.

GUILLEMIN, JEANNE. *Urban Renegades: The Cultural Strategy of American Indians.* Joe T. Darden. 1977:6:1:69.

GURIN, PATRICIA, AND EPPS, EDGAR. *Black Consciousness, Identity, and Achievement: A Study of Students in Historically Black Colleges.* A. E. Paris. 1977:6:1:25.

GURR, TED ROBERT; GRABOSKY, PETER N.; AND HULA, RICHARD C. *The Politics of Crime and Conflict: A Comparative History of Four Cities.* Michael Polen. 1977:6:5:550.

GURR, TED ROBERT. *Rogues, Rebels, and Reformers: A Political History of Urban Crime and Conflict.* Michael Polen. 1977:6:5:550.

H

HABERMAS, JÜRGEN. *Legitimation Crisis.* Translated by Thomas McCarthy. Jonathan Rieder and Norbert Wiley. 1977:6:4:411, 416.

HAHN, HARLAN, ed. *People and Politics in Urban Society, Volume 6: Urban Affairs Annual Reviews.* John B. Williamson. 1977:6:2:261.

HANSON, F. ALLAN. *Meaning in Culture.* Robert A. Paul. 1977:6:5:555.

HARDOY, JORGE E., ed. *Urbanization in Latin America: Approaches and Issues.* J. John Palen. 1977:6:1:105.

HARRIES-JENKINS, GWYN, AND VAN DOORN, JACQUES. *The Military and the Problem of Legitimacy.* Richard Machalek. 1977:6:3:326.

HARRINGTON, MICHAEL. *The Twilight of Capitalism.* Lloyd Davis Raines. 1977:6:5:587.

HARTLEY, SHIRLEY FOSTER. *Illegitimacy.* Jennie J. Kronenfeld. 1977:6:2:264.

HARTZLER, H. RICHARD. *Justice, Legal Systems, and Social Structure.* A. J. Bergesen. 1977:6:3:310.

HARVEY, EDWARD B. *Industrial Society: Structures, Roles, and Relations.* George H. Westacott. 1977:6:5:580.

HAVIGHURST, ROBERT J., AND DREYER, PHILIP H., eds. *Youth: The Seventy-fourth Yearbook of the National Society for the Study of Education, Part I.* Judith D. Handel. 1977:6:1:116.

HAWKINS, GORDON. *The Prison: Policy and Practice.* Robert Sommer. 1977:6:2:177.

HAWLEY, AMOS H., AND ROCK, VINCENT P., eds. *Metropolitan America in Contemporary Perspective.* Mary Donahue Stearns. 1977:6:2:262.

HAWLEY, WILLIS D., et al., eds. *Theoretical Perspectives on Urban Politics.* Ellan Odiorne Derow. 1977:6:5:608.

HEATH, ANTHONY. *Rational Choice and Social Exchange.* Harry C. Bredemeier. 1977:6:6:646.

HEILMAN, SAMUEL C. *Synagogue Life: A Study in Symbolic Interaction.* Jack Nusan Porter. 1977:6:6:740.

HEISE, DAVID R. *Causal Analysis.* Doris R. Entwisle. 1977:6:2:194.

HEISS, JEROLD. *The Case of the Black Family: A Sociological Inquiry.* Elizabeth Higginbotham. 1977:6:2:265.

HEISS, JEROLD, ed. *Family Roles and Interaction: An Anthology,* 2nd ed. Irwin Kantor. 1977:6:5:573.

HENRIQUES, FERNANDO. *Children of Conflict: A Study of Interracial Sex and Marriage.* Robert Staples. 1977:6:1:76.

HENSHEL, RICHARD L. *Reacting to Social Problems.* Malcolm Spector. 1977:6:6:740.

HENSLIN, JAMES M., AND REYNOLDS, LARRY T., eds. *Social Problems in American Society,* 2nd ed. Armand L. Mauss. 1977:6:5:602.

HERZON, FREDERICK D., AND HOOPER, MICHAEL. *Introduction to Statistics for the Social Sciences.* Charles E. Starnes. 1977:6:5:577.

HESS, IRENE; RIEDEL, DONALD C.; AND FITZPATRICK, THOMAS B. *Probability Sampling of Hospitals and Patients,* 2nd ed. Coralie Farlee. 1977:6:2:195.

HESS, THOMAS B., AND BAKER, ELIZABETH C., eds. *Art and Sexual Politics: Why Have There Been No Great Women Artists?* Robert D. Leighninger, Jr. 1977:6:3:303.

HEWITT, JOHN P. *Self and Society: A Symbolic Interactionist Social Psychology.* Sylvia Clavan. 1977:6:2:247.

HIGLEY, JOHN; FIELD, G. LOWELL; AND GRØHOLT, KNUT. *Elite Structure and Ideology: A Theory with Applications to Norway.* Inger J. Sagatun. 1977:6:2:210.

HILBERMAN, ELAINE. *The Rape Victim.* Lynda Lytle Holmstrom. 1977:6:2:178.

HILTON, GORDON. *Intermediate Politometrics.* Charles E. Starnes. 1977:6:5:577.

HINDESS, BARRY, AND HIRST, PAUL Q. *Pre-Capitalist Modes of Production.* J. Craig Jenkins. 1977:6:2:254.

HIRSCHMAN, CHARLES. *Ethnic and Social Stratification in Peninsular Malaysia.* John A. Lent. 1977:6:3:361.

HIRSCHOWITZ, RALPH G., AND LEVY, BERNARD, eds. *The Changing Mental Health Scene.* Muriel W. Pumphrey. 1977:6:5:574.

HIRST, PAUL Q. *Social Evolution and Sociological Categories.* Randall Collins and Guenther Roth. 1977:6:6:641, 644.

HOBBS, NICHOLAS, ed. *Issues in the Classification of Children,* Volumes 1 & 2. Richard A. Hilbert. 1977:6:6:741.

HOBSBAWM, E. J. *The Age of Capital, 1848–1875.* S. D. Berkowitz. 1977:6:4:428.

HOGE, DEAN R. *Commitment on Campus: Changes in Religion and Values over Five Decades.* Zelda F. Gamson. 1977:6:4:474.

HOGGART, RICHARD. *On Culture and Communication.* Gladys Engel Lang. 1977:6:6:650.

HONDRICH, KARL OTTO. *Demokratisierung una Leistungsgesellschaft.* Gianfranco Poggi. 1977:6:3:350.

HONDRICH, KARL OTTO. *Menschliche Bedürfnisse und soziale Steuerung.* Gianfranco Poggi. 1977:6:3:350.

HONDRICH, KARL OTTO. *Theorie der Herrschaft.* Gianfranco Poggi. 1977:6:3:350.

HONIKMAN, BASIL, ed. *Responding to Social Change.* Galen Cranz. 1977:6:2:235.

HORN, PAMELA. *The Rise and Fall of the Victorian Servant.* Jane E. Prather. 1977:6:1:58.

HORVAT, BRANKO; MARKOVIĆ, MIHAILO; AND SUPEK, RUDI, eds. *Self-Governing Socialism: A Reader,* vols. 1 & 2. George Fischer. 1977:6:5:589.

HOROWITZ, IRVING LOUIS. *Ideology and Utopia in the United States 1956–1976.* Doris Y. Wilkinson. 1977:6:6:701.

HOSTETLER, JOHN A. *Hutterite Society.* Allan W. Eister. 1977:6:1:85.

HOWITT, DENNIS, AND CUMBERBATCH, GUY. *Mass Media, Violence and Society*. Nathan Weinberg. 1977:6:1:116.

HUFTON, OLWEN H. *The Poor of Eighteenth-Century France, 1770–1789*. Allan Silver. 1977:6:6:742.

HUNDLEY, NORRIS, JR. ed. *The Asian Americans: The Historical Experience*. Rawlein G. Soberano. 1977:6:3:345.

HUNT, LEON GIBSON, AND CHAMBERS, CARL D. *The Heroin Epidemics: A Study of Heroin Use in the United States, 1965–1975*. Paul Attewell. 1977:6:1:31.

HYMAN, HERBERT H.; WRIGHT, CHARLES R.; AND REED, JOHN SHELTON. *The Enduring Effects of Education*. Jerry L. Fletcher. 1977:6:2:182.

HYMES, DELL. *Foundations in Sociolinguistics: An Ethnographic Approach*. Beryl L. Bellman. 1977:6:2:189.

I

IGLITZIN, LYNNE B., AND ROSS, RUTH, eds. *Women in the World: A Comparative Study*. Janet Zollinger Giele. 1977:6:4:478.

INKELES, ALEX, AND HOLSINGER, DONALD B., eds. *Education and Individual Modernity in Developing Countries*. Scott Chrisopher Wren. 1977:6:3:314.

ISAAC, RAEL JEAN. *Israel Divided: Ideological Politics in the Jewish State*. Rita J. Simon. 1977:6:3:346.

ISAACSON, DEAN L., AND MADSEN, RICHARD W. *Markov Chains Theory and Applications*. Robert McGinnis. 1977:6:3:322.

ITZKOFF, SEYMOUR W. *A New Public Education*. Ronald M. Pavalko. 1977:6:6:678.

J

JANOWITZ, MORRIS. *Social Control of the Welfare State*. Gøsta Esping-Andersen. 1977:6:5:590.

JEFFERY, PATRICIA. *Migrants and Refugees: Muslim and Christian Pakistani Families in Bristol*. Sharlene J. Hesse. 1977:6:5:560.

JONES, GAVIN. *Population Growth and Educational Planning in Developing Nations*. Pranab Chatterjee. 1977:6:1:36.

JONES, KATHLEEN. *Opening the Door: A Study of New Policies for the Mentally Handicapped*. Morton O. Wagenfeld. 1977:6:2:192.

JONES R. KENNETH, AND JONES, PATRICIA A. *Sociology in Medicine*. Thomas J. Sullivan. 1977:6:3:383.

JORDAN, Z. A., ed. *Karl Marx: Economy, Class and Social Revolution*. Michael Burawoy. 1977:6:1:9.

JULES-ROSETTE, BENNETTA. *African Apostles: Ritual and Conversion in the Church of John Maranke*. Daniel J. Crowley. 1977:6:4:475.

JUNIPER, DEAN F. *Decision-Making for Schools and Colleges*. John F. Glass. 1977:6:6:678.

K

KAHL, JOSEPH A. *Modernization, Exploitation and Dependency in Latin America*. Ira Studin. 1977:6:4:442.

KANE, ROBERT L., ed. *The Challenges of Community Medicine*. Laurie Engelberg. 1977:6:1:50.

KAPLAN, LAWRENCE J., AND KESSLER, DENNIS, eds. *An Economic Analysis of Crime: Selected Readings*. Herman Schwendinger. 1977:6:5:551.

KARAN, PRADYUMNA P. *The Changing Face of Tibet: The Impact of Chinese Communist Ideology on the Landscape*. Mario D. Zamora. 1977:6:4:444.

KARP, HERBERT H., AND KELLY, K. DENNIS. *Toward an Ecological Analysis of Intermetropolitan Migration*. Gregory Williams. 1977:6:1:37.

KASINSKY, RENÉE GOLDSMITH. *Refugees from Militarism: Draft-Age Americans in Canada*. John C. Leggett. 1977:6:2:211.

KATZ, DANIEL, et al. *Bureaucratic Encounters: A Pilot Study in the Evaluation of Government Services*. Theodore L. Reed. 1977:6:1:64.

KATZ, FRED E. *Structuralism in Sociology: An Approach to Knowledge*. Ino Rossi. 1977:6:2:255.

KATZ, MICHAEL B. *The People of Hamilton, Canada West*. Jean Leonard Elliott. 1977:6:2:174.

KATZELL, RAYMOND A., AND YANKELOVICH, DANIEL. *Work, Productivity, and Job Satisfaction: An Evaluation of Policy-Related Research*. Craig C. Lundberg. 1977:6:1:55.

KAUFMAN, GIANNI. *Il Sistema Globale: Immagini e Modelli*. Edith Kurzweil. 1977:6:2:206.

KAUFMAN, HERBERT. *Are Government Organizations Immortal?* Marshall W. Meyer. 1977:6:3:382.

KAYAL, PHILIP M., AND KAYAL, JOSEPH M. *The Syrian-Lebanese in America: A Study in Religion and Assimiliation*. William P. Nye. 1977:6:1:74.

KESSLER, EVELYN S. *Women: An Anthropological View*. Judith Caditz. 1977:6:1:92.

KING, EDMUND J.; MOOR, CHRISTINE H.; AND MUNDY, JENNIFER A. *Post-Compulsory Education II: The Way Ahead*. Gordon G. Darkenwald. 1977:6:6:679.

KITANO, HARRY H. L. *Japanese Americans: The Evolution of a Subculture*, 2nd ed. Darrel Montero. 1977:6:4:467.

KLEIN, LISL. *New Forms of Work Organization*. Paul Goldman. 1977:6:2:199.

KLEIN, MALCOLM W., ed. *The Juvenile Justice System*. Roy L. Austin. 1977:6:4:430.

KOMAROVSKY, MIRRA. *Dilemmas of Masculinity: A Study of College Youth*. Kristin Luker. 1977:6:5:600.

KOMAROVSKY, MIRRA, ed. *Sociology and Public Policy: The Case of Presidential Commissions*. Richard Rosenfeld. 1977:6:5:585.

KRADER, LAWRENCE. *The Asiatic Mode of Production: Sources, Development and Critique in the Writings of Karl Marx*. Gail Omvedt. 1977:6:4:495.

KRAUSS, IRVING. *Stratification, Class, and Conflict.* Paul Blumberg. 1977:6:5:618.

KREILKAMP, THOMAS. *The Corrosion of the Self: Society's Effects on People.* Sylvia Clavan. 1977:6:2:247.

KRICKUS, RICHARD. *Pursuing the American Dream: White Ethnics and the New Populism.* Paul D. Starr. 1977:6:1:77.

KUHN, ALFRED. *The Logic of Social Systems.* Harry C. Bredemeier. 1977:6:6:646.

KUPER, LEO, ed. *Race, Science and Society.* Hugh H. Smythe. 1977:6:1:77.

L

LADD, EVERETT CARLL, JR. *Transformations of the American Party System: Political Coalitions from the New Deal to the 1970s.* Steven E. Deutsch. 1977:6:2:213.

LAMB, CURT. *Political Power in Poor Neighborhoods.* George W. Dowdall. 1977:6:1:104.

LANDERS, DANIEL M., ed. *Social Problems in Athletics: Essays in the Sociology of Sport.* Carolyn R. Dexter. 1977:6:2:249.

LASKY, MELVIN J. *Utopia and Revolution: On the Origins of a Metaphor, or Some Illustrations of the Problem of Political Temperament and Intellectual Climate and How Ideas, Ideals, and Ideologies Have Been Historically Related.* Gwynn Nettler. 1977:6:6:724.

LAUER, ROBERT H., AND HANDEL, WARREN H. *Social Psychology: The Theory and Application of Symbolic Interactionism.* Peter and Patricia A. Adler. 1977:6:6:719.

LAVE, CHARLES A., AND MARCH, JAMES G. *An Introduction to Models in the Social Sciences.* David D. McFarland. 1977:6:2:196.

LAWRENCE, PETER. *Georg Simmel: Sociologist and European.* Lewis A. Coser. 1977:6:6:726.

LAZARSFELD, PAUL F., AND REITZ, JEFFREY G. *An Introduction to Applied Sociology.* Michael Hennessy. 1977:6:1:118.

LEACH, EDMUND. *Culture and Communication: The Logic by Which Symbols Are Connected.* Robert D. Leighninger, Jr. 1977:6:4:496.

LEBRA, JOYCE; PAULSON, JOY; AND POWERS, ELIZABETH, eds. *Women in Changing Japan.* Cornelia Butler Flora. 1977:6:2:232.

LECHT, LEONARD A. *Priorities for Planning in Vocational Education: Alternatives for the 1970s.* Robert B. Everhart. 1977:6:6:679.

LEE, ALFRED MCCLUNG. *Toward Humanist Sociology.* David O. Arnold. 1977:6:2:266.

LEHMANN, ERICH L. *Nonparametrics: Statistical Methods Based on Ranks.* Charles E. Starnes. 1977:6:5:577.

LEIBENSTEIN, HARVEY. *Beyond Economic Man: A New Framework for Microeconomics.* Duncan MacRae, Jr. and Samuel H. Preston. 1977:6:3:298, 300.

LENZER, GERTRUD, ed. *Auguste Comte and Positivism: The Essential Writings.* Donald N. Levine. 1977:6:3:352.

LEVESON, IRVING, AND WEISS, JEFFREY. *Analysis of Urban Health Problems.* Jennie J. Kronenfeld. 1977:6:2:261.

LEVIN, LOWELL S.; KATZ, ALFRED H.; AND HOLST, ERIK, eds. *Self-Care: Lay Initiatives in Health.* Bebe F. Lavin. 1977:6:6:692.

LEVINE, DONALD M., AND BANE, MARY JO, eds. *The "Inequality" Controversy: Schooling and Distributive Justice.* Joyce A. Kozuch. 1977:6:6:680.

LEVITAN, SAR A., AND JOHNSTON, BENJAMIN H. *The Job Corps: A Social Experiment that Works.* William S. Bennett. 1977:6:1:119.

LEWIS, CHARLES E.; FEIN, RASHI; AND MECHANIC, DAVID. *A Right to Health: The Problem of Access to Primary Medical Care.* Bebe F. Lavin. 1977:6:6:692.

LEWIS, LIONEL S. *Scaling the Ivory Tower: Merit and Its Limits in Academic Careers.* Gerald Grant. 1977:6:5:564.

LEWIS, MICHAEL, ed. *Origins of Intelligence: Infancy and Early Childhood.* Barbara G. Cashion. 1977:6:2:242.

LEWIS, ROBERT A.; ROWLAND, RICHARD H.; AND CLEM, RALPH S. *Nationality and Population Change in Russia and the USSR: An Evaluation of Census Data, 1897–1970.* D. Peter Mazur. 1977:6:5:561.

LEWY, GUENTER, *Religion and Revolution.* Roger O'Toole. 1977:6:1:86.

LIEBERT, ROLAND J. *Disintegration and Political Action: The Changing Functions of City Governments in America.* Warner Bloomberg, Jr. 1977:6:3:373.

LIEBMAN, SEYMOUR B. *Exploring the Latin American Mind.* Edgar G. Nesman. 1977:6:4:438.

LIFTON, ROBERT JAY. *The Life of the Self: Toward A New Psychology.* Roberta Lynn Satow. 1977:6:6:719.

LIN, NAN. *Foundations of Social Research.* Roger Spielmann. 1977:6:4:449.

LINDBERG, LEON N., et al., eds. *Stress and Contradiction in Modern Capitalism: Public Policy and the Theory of the State.* Michael Useem. 1977:6:3:333.

LIU, ALAN P. L. *Political Culture and Group Conflict in Communist China.* Martin K. Whyte. 1977:6:3:361.

LIU, BEN-CHIEH. *Quality of Life Indicators in U.S. Metropolitan Areas: A Statistical Analysis.* Kirsten A. Grønbjerg. 1977:6:1:107.

LOEHLIN, JOHN C.; LINDZEY, GARDNER; AND SPUHLER, J. W. *Race Differences in Intelligence.* Edward E. Harris. 1977:6:1:78.

LOFLAND, JOHN. *Doing Social Life: The Qualitative Study of Human Interaction in Natural Settings.* Raymond L. Gold. 1977:6:6:654.

LOJKINE, JEAN. *La politique urbaine dans la region lyonnaise, 1945–1972.* Edith Kurzweil. 1977:6:3:374.

LOOMIS, CHARLES P., AND BEEGLE, J. ALLAN. *A Strategy for Rural Change*. Gene F. Summers. 1977:6:5:609.

LORSCH, JAY W., AND MORSE, JOHN J. *Organizations and Their Members: A Contingency Approach*. Johannes M. Pennings. 1977:6:1:61.

LUKER, KRISTIN, *Taking Chances: Abortion and the Decision Not to Contracept*. Ruth B. Dixon. 1977:6:1:51.

LYMAN, STANFORD M., AND SCOTT, MARVIN B. *The Drama of Social Reality*. James M. Henslin. 1977:6:1:95.

M

MACCANNELL, DEAN. *The Tourist: A New Theory of the Leisure Class*. Suzanne Wedow. 1977:6:2:200.

MACCOBY, ELEANOR EMMONS, AND JACKLIN, CAROL NAGY. *The Psychology of Sex Differences*. Elizabeth M. Almquist. 1977:6:2:233.

MALTHUS, THOMAS R. Edited by Philip Appleman. *An Essay on the Principle of Population: Text Sources and Background Criticism*. Etienne van de Walle. 1977:6:3:340.

MAMDANI, MAHMOOD. *Politics and Class Formation in Uganda*. Judith Van Allen. 1977:6:6:702.

MANDEL, ERNEST. *Late Capitalism*. E.K. Hunt. 1977:6:3:335.

MANIS, JEROME G. *Analyzing Social Problems*. Armand L. Mauss. 1977:6:5:602.

MANN, MICHAEL. *Workers on the Move: The Sociology of Relocation*. James W. Rinehart. 1977:6:1:53.

MANTELL, DAVID MARK. *True Americanism: Green Berets and War Resisters*. Charles P. Flynn. 1977:6:1:65.

MARCH, JAMES G., AND OLSEN, JOHAN P. *Ambiguity and Choice in Organizations*. Charles Perrow. 1977:6:3:294.

MARCUS, STEVEN. *Engles, Manchester, and the Working Class*. Evan Stark. 1977:6:1:100.

MARMOR, JUDD. *Psychiatrists and Their Patients: A National Study of Private Office Practice*. Jan Hankin. 1977:6:6:693.

MARRIS, PETER. *Loss and Change*. Fred Davis. 1977:6:2:160.

MARSH, ROBERT, AND MANNARI, HIROSHI. *Modernization and the Japanese Factory*. Robert E. Cole. 1977:6:5:582.

MARTIN, TONY. *Race First: The Ideological and Organizational Struggles of Marcus Garvey and the Universal Negro Improvement Association*. Douglas S. Snyder. 1977:6:4:468.

MARTINEZ, TOMÁS. *The Human Marketplace: An Examination of Private Employment Agencies*. Gerald Rosenblum. 1977:6:6:737.

MATEJKO, ALEXANDER. *Social Change and Stratification in Eastern Europe: An Interpretive Analysis of Poland and Her Neighbors*. Szymon Chodak. 1977:6:4:486.

MATTER, JOSEH ALLEN. *Love, Altruism, and World Crisis: The Challenge of Pitirim Sorokin*. Don Martindale. 1977:6:3:353.

MAUSS, ARMAND L. *Social Problems as Social Movements*. Bruce D. Johnson. 1977:6:6:743.

MAYS, J. B. ed. *The Social Treatment of Young Offenders*. Roy L. Austin. 1977:6:4:430.

MCCAFFREY, LAWRENCE J. *The Irish Diaspora in America*. John Murray Cuddihy. 1977:6:3:344.

MCCAGG, WILLIAM O., JR. *Jewish Nobles and Geniuses in Modern Hungary*. Robert Blumstock. 1977:6:1:78.

MCCLELLAND, DAVID. *Power: The Inner Experience*. Lauren Langman. 1977:6:6:720.

MCCONVILLE, SEAN, ed. *The Use of Imprisonment: Essays in the Changing State of English Penal Policy*. Robert Sommer. 1977:6:1:32.

MCCUBBIN, HAMILTON I.; DAHL, BARBARA B.; AND HUNTER, EDNA J., eds. *Families in the Military System*. Athena Theodore. 1977:6:3:327.

MCCULLUM, HUGH, AND MCCULLUM, KARMEL. *This Land Is Not for Sale*. Stephen O. Murray. 1977:6:2:218.

MCDONALD, LYNN. *The Sociology of Law and Order*. John Hagan. 1977:6:2:161.

MCINTOSH, MARY. *The Organisation of Crime*. John L. McMullan. 1977:6:3:310.

MCKENZIE, ROBERT H., ed. *The Rising South. Volume 2: Southern Universities and the South*. Alvin L. Bertrand. 1977:6:3:389.

MCQUAIL, DENIS, ed. *Sociology of Mass Communications*. Gladys Engel Lang. 1977:6:6:650.

MECHANIC, DAVID. *The Growth of Bureaucratic Medicine: An Inquiry into the Dynamics of Patient Behavior and the Organization of Medical Care*. Marshall W. Meyer. 1977:6:6:694.

MEDNICK, MARTHA TAMARA SHUCH; TANGRI, SANDRA SCHWARTZ; AND HOFFMAN, LOIS WLADIS. *Women and Achievement: Social and Motivational Analyses*. Sandra Harley Carey. 1977:6:1:93.

MEHAN, HUGH, AND WOOD, HOUSTON. *The Reality of Ethnomethodology*. Bruce M. Hackett. 1977:6:1:101.

MEIER, RICHARD L. *Planning for an Urban World: The Design of Resource-Conserving Cities*. John D. Kasarda. 1977:6:5:610.

MERNISSI, FATIMA. *Beyond the Veil: Male-Female Dynamics in a Modern Muslim Society*. Janet Abu-Lughod. 1977:6:3:364.

MESAROVIC, MIHAJLO, AND PESTEL, EDUARD. *Mankind at the Turning Point: The Second Report to the Club of Rome*. J. Allen Whitt. 1977:6:1:38.

MICHEL, ANDREE. *Sociologie de la famille et du mariage*. Saskia Sassen-Koob. 1977:6:1:47.

MICHELMAN, CHERRY. *The Black Sash of South Africa*. Linda Stoneall. 1977:6:4:469.

MICHELSON, WILLIAM, ed. *Behavioral Research Methods in Environmental Design*. William R. Burch, Jr. 1977:6:4:450.

MILETI, DENNIS; DRABEK, THOMAS E.; AND HAAS, J. EUGENE. *Human Systems in Extreme Environments: A Sociological Perspective*. Verta A. Taylor. 1977:6:1:119.

MILLER, ARTHUR SELWYN. *The Modern Corporate State: Private Governments and the American Constitution*. Stephen J. McNamee. 1977:6:3:337.

MILLER, JEAN BAKER. *Toward a New Psychology of Women*. Nancy Chodorow. 1977:6:4:479.

MILLER, WAYNE CHARLES. *A Comprehensive Bibliography for the Study of American Minorities*. Francesco Cordasco. 1977:6:5:594.

MILLER, WILBUR R. *Cops and Bobbies: Police Authority in New York and London, 1830–1870*. Eric H. Monkkonen. 1977:6:5:552.

MILLMAN, MARCIA, AND KANTER, ROSABETH MOSS, eds. *Another Voice: Feminist Perspectives on Social Life and Social Science*. Myra Marx Ferree. 1977:6:2:256.

MILOFSKY, CARL. *Special Education: A Sociological Study of California Programs*. Celestino Fernández. 1977:6:5:567.

MONKKONEN, ERIC H. *The Dangerous Class: Crime and Poverty in Columbus, Ohio, 1860–1885*. David Lewis Smith. 1977:6:1:33.

MONTAGU, ASHLEY. *The Nature of Human Aggression*. Richard McClintock. 1977:6:3:384.

MOOR, CHRISTINE H. *From School to Work: Effective Counseling and Guidance*. Robert B. Everhart. 1977:6:6:679.

MOORE, JOAN W. *Mexican Americans*, 2nd ed. Audrey W. Forrest. 1977:6:4:470.

MORIOKA, KIYOMI. *Religion in Changing Japanese Society*. David W. Plath. 1977:6:2:227.

MORRIS, PAULINE, AND FARIDA, BEVERLY. *On License: A Study of Parole*. F. William Howton. 1977:6:2:178.

MOSCOVICI, SERGE. *Society against Nature: The Emergence of Human Societies*. Richard McClintock. 1977:6:3:384.

MOSKOS, CHARLES C., JR. *Peace Soldiers: The Sociology of a United Nations Military Force*. Phillip Butler. 1977:6:2:214.

MULHEARN, JOHN, AND MOMENY, GAYLE. *The Psychiatric Hospital Today: A Quality Profile*. Jan Hankin. 1977:6:6:693.

MURTON, THOMAS O. *The Dilemma of Prison Reform*. W. David Watts. 1977:6:1:34.

MYERS, LONNY, AND LEGGITT, HUNTER. *Adultery and Other Private Matters*. Louis Rowitz. 1977:6:4:448.

N

NACHMIAS, DAVID, AND NACHMIAS, CHAVA. *Research Methods in Social Sciences*. S. Padmini Ravindhran. 1977:6:3:323.

NEAVE, GUY R. *How They Fared: The Impact of the Comprehensive School upon the University*. John C. Weidman. 1977:6:1:26.

NEE, VICTOR, AND PECK, JAMES, eds. *China's Uninterrupted Revolution: From 1840 to the Present*. Ben Stavis. 1977:6:2:236.

NEEDHAM, RODNEY. *Belief, Language, and Experience*. Beryl L. Bellman. 1977:6:3:385.

NELSEN, HART M., AND NELSEN, ANNE KUSENER. *Black Church in the Sixties*. David O. Moberg. 1977:6:2:221.

NELSON, DANIEL. *Managers and Workers: Origins of the New Factory System in the United States, 1880–1920*. Marshall W. Meyer. 1977:6:2:204.

NELSON, WILLIAM E. *Americanization of the Common Law: The Impact of Legal Change on Massachusetts Society, 1760–1830*. Allan Horwitz. 1977:6:3:308.

NETTLER, GWYNN. *Social Concerns*. T. P. Schwartz. 1977:6:2:237.

NEWMAN, DOROTHY K., AND DAY, DAWN. *The American Energy Consumer*. Robert Cameron Mitchell. 1977:6:3:379.

NICKELL, PAULENA; RICE, ANN SMITH; AND TUCKER, SUZANNE P. *Management in Family Living*, 5th ed. Rela Geffen Monson. 1977:6:4:449.

NIEMI, RICHARD G. *How Family Members Perceive Each Other: Political and Social Attitudes in Two Generations*. Suzanne K. Steinmetz. 1977:6:3:387.

NISBET, ROBERT. *Sociology as an Art Form*. Frederick R. Lynch. 1977:6:3:354.

NIXON, HOWARD L., II. *Sport and Social Organization*. Barry D. McPherson. 1977:6:3:388.

NOBLE, DONALD R., AND THOMAS JACOB L., eds. *The Rising South. Volume 1: Changes and Issues*. Alvin L. Bertrand. 1977:6:3:389.

NORLÉN, URBAN. *Simulation Model Building, A Statistical Approach to Modelling in the Social Sciences with the Simulation Method*. Theodore L. Reed. 1977:6:3:323.

NORTH, DOUGLASS C., AND THOMAS, ROBERT PAUL. *The Rise of the Western World: A New Economic History*. Michael S. Kimmel and Walter Goldfrank. 1977:6:6:703.

NYE, ROBERT A. *The Origins of Crowd Psychology: Gustave LeBon and the Crisis of Mass Democracy in the Third Republic*. Maurice Jackson. 1977:6:2:268.

O

OAKLEY, ANN. *The Sociology of Housework*. Jane E. Prather. 1977:6:1:58.

O'BRIEN, DAVID J. *Neighborhood Organization and Interest-Group Processes*. George W. Dowdall. 1977:6:1:104.

O'CONNOR, JAMES. *The Fiscal Crisis of the State*. Jonathan Rieder and Norbert Wiley. 1977:6:4:411, 416.

OLDENBURG, PHILIP. *Big City Government in India: Councilor, Administrator and Citizen in Delhi*. Mark Spevak. 1977:6:3:366.

OLSON, DAVID R., ed. *Media and Symbols: The Forms of Expression, Communication, and Education*. Gladys Engel Lang. 1977:6:6:650.

OLSON, MANCUR, AND LANDSBERG, HANS H., eds. *The No-Growth Society*. J. Allen Whitt. 1977:6:1:38.

OLSON, SHELDON. *Ideas and Data: The Process and Practice of Social Research*. Charles E. Starnes. 1977:6:5:577.

OPPONG, CHRISTINE. *Marriage among a Matrilineal Elite: A Family Study of Ghanaian Senior Civil Servants*. John Mogey. 1977:6:1:47.

ORLAND, LEONARD. *Prisons: Houses of Darkness*. W. David Watts. 1977:6:1:34.

ORNAUER, HELMUT, et al. eds. *Images of the World in the Year 2000: A Comparative Ten Nation Study*. Bettina J. Huber. 1977:6:6:744.

ORNSTEIN, ALLAN C., AND MILLER, STEVEN I. eds. *Policy Issues in Education*. Rosalie A. Cohen. 1977:6:6:717.

ORNSTEIN, MICHAEL D. *Entry into the American Labor Force*. Jeylan T. Mortimer. 1977:6:1:57.

ORTEGA Y GASSET, JOSE. *Phenomenology and Art*. Translated by Maurice Freedman. Don Martindale. 1977:6:6:726.

OSGOOD, CORNELIUS. *The Chinese: A Study of a Hong Kong Community*. Chong-chor Lau. 1977:6:5:618.

O'TOOLE, JAMES. *Work and the Quality of Life: Resource Papers for "Work in America."* Craig C. Lundberg. 1977:6:1:55.

OVERBEEK. J. *History of Population Theories*. G. Edward Ebanks. 1977:6:3:341.

OVERBEEK, JOHANNES. *The Population Challenge: A Handbook for Nonspecialists*. Paul R. Williams. 1977:6:5:562.

OXAAL, IVAR; BARNETT, TONY; AND BOOTH, DAVID, eds. *Beyond the Sociology of Development: Economy and Society in Latin America and Africa*. Patricia Madoo Lengermann. 1977:6:1:65.

P

PAK, HYOBOM B. *China and the West: Myths and Realities in History*. Francis L. K. Hsu. 1977:6:3:362.

PARKER, STANLEY. *The Sociology of Leisure*. Worth C. Summers. 1977:6:4:506.

PARRY, NOEL, AND PARRY, JOSÉ. *The Rise of the Medical Profession*. Dorothy Douglas. 1977:6:5:575.

PEACH, CERI, ed. *Urban Social Segregation*. Richard S. Sterne. 1977:6:5:595.

PÉREZ, LOUIS A. *Army Politics in Cuba, 1898–1958*. George A. Kourvetaris. 1977:6:3:328.

PERISTIANY, J. G. ed. *Mediterranean Family Structures*. Panos D. Bardis. 1977:6:6:686.

PERLMAN, JANICE E. *The Myth of Marginality: Urban Poverty and Politics in Rio de Janeiro*. Alejandro Portes. 1977:6:6:745.

PESCATELLO, ANN M. *Power and Pawn: The Female in Iberian Families, Societies, and Cultures*. Marta Tienda. 1977:6:3:363.

PESSEN, EDWARD, ed. *Three Centuries of Social Mobility in America*. S. M. Miller. 1977:6:1:40.

PETERSON, PAUL E. *School Politics Chicago Style*. David B. Carpenter. 1977:6:6:682.

PETTIT, PHILIP. *The Concept of Structuralism: A Critical Analysis*. Ino Rossi. 1977:6:4:497.

PIAGET, JEAN, AND INHELDER, BÄRBEL. *The Origin of the Idea of Chance in Children*. Kathryn P. Meadow. 1977:6:1:100.

PICKERING, W. S. F., ed. *Durkheim on Religion: A Selection of Readings with Bibliographies and Introductory Remarks*. Tendzin N. Takla. 1977:6:2:163.

PICKVANCE, C. G. ed. *Urban Sociology: Critical Essays*. Roy Childs. 1977:6:6:746.

PINKNEY, ALPHONSO. *Red, Black, and Green: Black Nationalism in the United States*. Paul T. Murray. 1977:6:3:347.

PIPES, RICHARD. *Russia under the Old Regime*. Alexander Matejko. 1977:6:2:207.

PIPES, RICHARD, ed. *Soviet Strategy in Europe*. Paul Hollander. 1977:6:4:459.

PLATT, JENNIFER. *Realities of Social Research*. Bob Hinings. 1977:6:4:451.

PLUMMER, KENNETH. *Sexual Stigma: An Interactionist Account*. William Simon. 1977:6:6:713.

POMPER, GERALD M. *Voter's Choice: Varieties of American Electoral Behavior*. Carl A. Sheingold. 1977:6:3:337.

POPENOE, DAVID. *The Suburban Environment: Sweden and the United States*. Alison E. Woodward. 1977:6:6:668.

POWERS, WILLIAM T. *Behavior: The Control of Perception*. Harry C. Bredemeier. 1977:6:6:646.

PRESSER, HARRIET B. *Sterilization and Fertility Decline in Puerto Rico*. John J. Macisco, Jr. 1977:6:3:342.

PROTHRO, EDWIN TERRY, AND DIAB, LUTFY NAJIB, eds. *Changing Family Patterns in the Arab East*. Mohamed El-Assal. 1977:6:6:687.

PULLUM, THOMAS W. *Measuring Occupational Inheritance*. Paul H. Tress. 1977:6:1:42.

PUSEY, MICHAEL. *Dynamics of Bureaucracy: A Case Analysis in Education*. Edward Gross. 1977:6:6:682.

Q

QUINNEY, RICHARD. *Class, State, and Crime: On the Theory and Practice of Criminal Justice*. Roger G. Seifert. 1977:6:6:669.

R

RAFFAELE, JOSEPH. *System and Unsystem: An Ethnic View of Organization and Society*. A. Barrett Fields. 1977:6:2:222.

RAUSH, HAROLD L., et al. *Communication, Conflict and Marriage.* Suzanne K. Steinmetz. 1977: 6:3:387.

RAVEN, BERTRAM H., AND RUBIN, JEFFREY Z. *Social Psychology: People in Groups.* Morris J. Daniels. 1977:6:2:241.

REHFISCH, FARNHAM, ed. *Gypsies, Tinkers and Other Travellers.* Marcello Truzzi. 1977:6:6:709.

REIN, MARTIN. *Social Science and Public Policy.* David G. Gil. 1977:6:6:718.

REISMAN, DAVID A. *Adam Smith's Sociological Economics.* Louis Schneider. 1977:6:4:497.

REMMLING, GUNTER W. *The Sociology of Karl Mannheim.* H. C. Greisman. 1977:6:4:499.

RICH, ADRIENNE. *Of Woman Born.* Nona Glazer. 1977:6:4:480.

RILEY, MATILDA WHITE, AND NELSON, EDWARD E., eds. *Sociological Observation: A Strategy for New Social Knowledge.* Norman K. Denzin. 1977:6:3:321.

ROBERTS, JOAN I., ed. *Beyond Intellectual Sexism: A New Woman, A New Reality.* Athena Theodore. 1977:6:4:482.

ROBERTSON, LEON S., AND HEAGERTY, MARGARET C. *Medical Sociology: A General Systems Approach.* Judith Blackfield Cohen. 1977:6:2:193.

ROBINSON, DAVID. *From Drinking to Alcoholism: A Sociological Commentary.* Walter Davis. 1977:6:4:507.

ROBISCHON, THOMAS G.; RABOW, JEROME; AND SCHMIDT, JANET, eds. *Cracks in the Classroom Wall.* Daniel L. Kegan. 1977:6:4:434.

ROBY, PAMELA, ed. *Child Care—Who Cares? Foreign and Domestic Infant and Early Childhood Development Policies,* student edition. Marijean Suelzle. 1977:6:2:268.

RODGERS, FREDERICK A. *The Black High School and Its Community.* James P. Pitts. 1977:6:2:183.

RODNITZKY, JEROME L. *Minstrels of the Dawn: The Folk-Protest Singer as a Cultural Hero.* R. Serge Denisoff. 1977:6:2:269.

ROEBUCK, JULIAN B., and FRESE, WOLFGANG. *The Rendezvous: A Case Study of an After-Hours Club.* Edward F. Vacha 1977:6:1:35.

ROGERS, EVERETT M., AND AGARWALA-ROGERS, REKHA. *Communication in Organizations.* Rita Braito. 1977:6:4:500.

ROGERS, FRANCIS M. *Americans of Portuguese Descent: A Lesson in Differentiation.* William P. Nye. 1977:6:1:74.

ROGERS, SINCLAIR, ed. *Children and Language: Readings in Early Language and Socialization.* Robert Williams. 1977:6:1:120.

ROHRLICH-LEAVITT, RUBY, ed. *Women Cross-Culturally: Change and Challenge.* Judith Caditz. 1977:6:1:92.

ROSE, JERRY D. *Peoples: The Ethnic Dimension in Human Relations.* Douglas S. Snyder. 1977:6:2:217.

ROSE, PETER I.; ROTHMAN, STANLEY; AND WILSON, WILLIAM J., eds. *Through Different Eyes: Black and White Perspectives on American Race Relations.* John W. Martin. 1977:6:1:79.

ROSEN, GERALD PAUL. *Political Ideology and the Chicano Movement: A Study of the Political Ideology of Activists in the Chicano Movement.* Lionel A. Maldonado. 1977:6:3:348.

ROSENBAUM, H. JON, AND SEDERBERG, PETER C., eds. *Vigilante Politics.* Harold A. Nelson. 1977:6:3:338.

ROSENBAUM, JAMES E. *Making Inequality: The Hidden Curriculum of High School Tracking.* Martha A. Cook. 1977:6:6:682.

ROSENBERG, CHAIM M., AND RAYNES, ANTHONY E. *Keeping Patients in Psychiatric Treatment.* Jan Hankin. 1977:6:6;693.

ROSENBERG, CHARLES E., ed. *The Family in History.* Bernard Farber. 1977:6:2:167.

ROSETT, ARTHUR, AND CRESSEY, DONALD R. *Justice by Consent; Plea Bargains in the American Courthouse.* Jerald W. Cloyd. 1977:6:3:311.

ROSOW, JEROME M. *The Worker and the Job: Coping with Change.* Craig Lundberg. 1977:6:1:55.

ROSS, MARC HOWARD. *Grass Roots in an African City: Political Behavior in Nairobi.* Robert Cameron Mitchell. 1977:6:2:237.

ROSSI, JEAN J., AND FILSTEAD, WILLIAM J., eds. *The Therapeutic Community: A Sourcebook of Readings.* Judith Blackfield Cohen. 1977:6:2:193.

ROSSI, PETER H.; BERK, RICHARD A.; AND EIDSON, BETTYE K. *The Roots of Urban Discontent: Public Policy, Municipal Institutions, and the Ghetto.* Albert J. Reiss, Jr. 1977:6:1:108.

ROTHMAN, JACK. *Planning and Organizing for Social Change: Action Principles from Social Science Research.* Carole Joffee and Joan Mandle. 1977:6:2:238.

ROTSTEIN, ABRAHAM, ed. *Beyond Industrial Growth.* Irene Taviss Thomson. 1977:6:4:487.

ROZMAN, GILBERT. *Urban Networks in Ch'ing China and Tokugawa Japan.* Theda Skocpol. 1977:6:1:120.

ROZMAN, GILBERT. *Urban Networks in Russia, 1750–1800, and Premodern Periodization.* Theda Skocpol. 1977:6:1:120.

RUBINGTON, EARL, AND WEINBERG, MARTIN S., eds. *The Study of Social Problems: Five Perspectives,* 2nd, ed. James D. Orcutt. 1977:6:5:606.

RUDOFF, ALVIN. *Work Furlough and the County Jail.* W. David Watts. 1977:6:1:34.

RUESCHEMEYER, DIETRICH. *Lawyers and Their Society: A Comparative Study of the Legal Profession in Germany and in the United States.* Albert J. Bergesen. 1977:6:1:59.

RUNYON, RICHARD P., AND HABER, AUDREY. *Fundamentals of Behavioral Statistics,* 3rd. ed. Charles E. Starnes. 1977:6:5:577.

RUSHING, WILLIAM A. *Community, Physicians, and Inequality: Sociological Study of the Maldistribution of Physicians.* Victor W. Marshall. 1977:6:1:52.

RUSSELL, DIANA E. H., AND VAN DE VEN, NICOLE, eds. *Crimes against Women: Proceedings of the International Tribunal.* Teresa D. Marciano. 1977:6:4:483.

RYNKIEWICH, MICHAEL A., AND SPRADLEY, JAMES P. *Ethics and Anthropology: Dilemmas in Field Work.* Elvi Whittaker. 1977:6:4:508.

S

SACKS, MICHAEL PAUL. *Women's Work in Soviet Russia: Continuity in the Midst of Change.* Marilyn Power Goldberg. 1977:6:3:378.

SAFILIOS-ROTHSCHILD, ÇONSTANTINA. *Love, Sex, and Sex Roles.* Natalie Allon. 1977:6:6:714.

SALBER, EVA J. *Caring and Curing: Community Participation in Health Services.* Laurie Engelberg. 1977:6:1:50.

SAMPSON, EDWARD E. *Social Psychology and Contemporary Society,* 2nd ed. Mary Ann Groves. 1977:6:2:248.

SAMUDA, RONALD J. *Psychological Testing of American Minorities: Issues and Consequences.* Carl C. Jorgensen. 1977:6:2:223.

SANCHES, MARY, AND BLOUNT, BEN G., eds. *Sociocultural Dimensions of Language Use.* Beryl L. Bellman. 1977:6:2:189.

SANDERS, IRWIN T., AND MORAWSKA, EWA T. *Polish American Community Life: A Survey of Research.* Eugene E. Obidinski. 1977:6:3:390.

SANDERS, WILLIAM B. *Juvenile Delinquency.* Roy L. Austin. 1977:6:4:430.

SCHELSKY, HELMUT. *Die Arbeit tun die anderen: Klassenkampf und Priesterherrschaft der Intellektuellen.* Gerd Schroeter. 1977:6:4:438.

SCHIFFRIN, HAROLD Z., ed. *Military and State in Modern Asia.* Stephen P. Cohen. 1977:6:3:324.

SCHOENBERG, BERNARD, et al., eds. *Bereavement: Its Psychosocial Aspects.* Jeannette R. Folta. 1977:6:2:193.

SCHRAN, PETER. *Guerrilla Economy: The Development of the Shensi-Kansu-Ningshia Border Region, 1937–1945.* Kevin Danaher. 1977:6:6:704.

SCHULBERG, HERBERT C., AND BAKER, FRANK. *The Mental Hospital and Human Services.* Judith Blackfield Cohen. 1977:6:2:193.

SCHULZ, DAVID A. *The Changing Family: Its Function and Future,* 2nd ed. Rela Geffen Monson. 1977:6:4:449.

SCHULZINGER, ROBERT D. *The Making of the Diplomatic Mind: The Training, Outlook, and Style of United States Foreign Service Officers, 1908–1931.* Donald P. Warwick. 1977:6:2:202.

SCHUR, EDWIN. *The Awareness Trap: Self-Absorption Instead of Social Change.* Louis Rowitz. 1977:6:2:239.

SCHWARTZ, BARRY. *Queuing and Waiting: Studies in the Social Organization of Access and Delay.* David Glanz. 1977:6:2:165.

SCOTT, JOAN WALLACH. *The Glassworkers of Carmaux: French Craftsmen and Political Action in a Nineteenth-Century City.* Gregg Carr. 1977:6:2:214.

SCOTT, JOHN PAUL. *Aggression,* 2nd ed. Karl Schonborn. 1977:6:1:123.

SEABURY, PAUL, ed. *Universities in the Western World.* Philip G. Altbach. 1977:6:5:567.

SEBALD, HANS. *Momism: The Silent Disease of America.* David Kent Lee. 1977:6:6:688.

SEIDENBERG, BERNARD, AND SNADOWSKY, ALVIN, eds. *Social Psychology: An Introduction.* Mary Ann Groves. 1977:6:2:248.

SELG, HERBERT, ed. *The Making of Human Aggression: A Psychological Approach.* Karl Schonborn. 1977:6:1:123.

SELLS, S. B., ed. *The Effectiveness of Drug Abuse Treatment, Volume I: Evaluation of Treatments.* John A. O'Donnell. 1977:6:6:670.

SELLS, S. B., ed. *The Effectiveness of Drug Abuse Treatment, Volume II: Patient Profiles, Treatments and Outcomes.* John O'Donnell. 1977:6:6:670.

SELLS, S. B., AND SIMPSON, D. DWAYNE, eds. *The Effectiveness of Drug Abuse Treatment, Volume III: Further Studies of Drug Users, Treatment Typologies, and Assessment of Outcomes During Treatment in the DARP.* John A. O'Donnell. 1977:6:6:670.

SELLS, S. B., AND SIMPSON, D. DWAYNE, eds. *The Effectiveness of Drug Abuse Treatment, Volume IV: Evaluation of Treatment Outcomes for 1971–1972 DARP Admission Cohort.* John A. O'Donnell. 1977:6:6:670.

SELLS, S. B., AND SIMPSON, D. DWAYNE, eds. *The Effectiveness of Drug Abuse Treatment, Volume V: Evaluation of Treatment Outcomes for 1972–1973 DARP Admission Cohort.* John O'Donnell. 1977:6:6:670.

SEVERY, LAWRENCE J.; BRIGHAM, JOHN C.; AND SCHLENKER, BARRY R. *A Contemporary Introduction to Social Psychology.* Mary Ann Groves. 1977:6:2:248.

SEWELL, WILLIAM H.; HAUSER, ROBERT M.; AND FEATHERMAN, DAVID L. *Schooling and Achievement in American Society.* Margaret Mooney Marini. 1977:6:6:683.

SEYFARTH, CONSTANS, AND SCHMIDT, GERT. *Max Weber Bibliographie: Eine Dokumentation der Sekundärliteratur.* Guenther Roth. 1977:6:5:619.

SEYMOUR-URE, COLIN. *The Political Impact of Mass Media.* Gladys Engel Lang. 1977:6:6:650.

SHAPIRO, THEDA. *Painters and Politics: The European Avant-Garde and Society, 1900–1925.* Barbara Rosenblum. 1977:6:4:509.

SHARMA, BALDEV RAJ. *The Indian Industrial Worker: Issues in Perspective.* Rudi Volti. 1977:6:3:368.

SHARMA, K. L. *The Changing Rural Stratification System: A Comparative Study of Six Villages in Rajasthan, India.* Santosh Kumar Nandy. 1977:6:2:250.

SHARP, RACHEL, AND GREEN, ANTHONY. *Education and Social Control: A Study in Progressive Primary Education.* Rosalie Cohen. 1977:6:1:27.

SHEEHY, GAIL. *Passages: Predictable Crises of Adult Life.* Michael S. Kimmel. 1977:6:4:490.

SHEPARD, JON M., AND STEWART, CYRUS S., eds. *Sociology and Social Problems: A Conceptual Approach.* Armand L. Mauss. 1977:6:5:602.

SHEPS, CECIL G. *Higher Education for Public Health: A Report of the Milbank Memorial Fund Commission.* Angus E. Reid. 1977:6:6:684.

SHERIF, CAROLYN WOOD. *Orientation in Social Psychology.* Sylvia Clavan. 1977:6:2:247.

SHILS, EDWARD A. *Center and Periphery: Essays in Macrosociology. Selected Papers of Edward Shils, Vol. 2.* Ellen R. Robert. 1977:6:2:257.

SHIMAHARA, NOBUO KENNETH, AND SCRUPSKI, ADAM. *Social Forces and Schooling: An Anthropological and Sociological Perspective.* Daniel L. Kegan. 1977:6:4:434.

SHIVJI, ISSA G. *Class Struggles in Tanzania.* Judith Van Allen. 1977:6:6:702.

SHNEIDMAN, EDWIN S., ed. *Suicidology: Contemporary Developments.* James F. Short, Jr. 1977:6:4:511.

SHOHAM, S. GIORA. *Social Deviance.* Nanette J. Davis. 1977:6:3:312.

SHORTER, EDWARD. *The Making of the Modern Family.* Bernard Farber and Michael Gordon. 1977:6:2:167, 169.

SILK, LEONARD, AND VOGEL, DAVID. *Ethics and Profits: The Crisis of Confidence in American Business.* Michael Useem. 1977:6:5:592.

SINGH, VIJAI P. *Caste, Class and Democracy: Changes in a Stratification System.* Baidya Nath Varma. 1977:6:4:488.

SKIDMORE, WILLIAM. *Theoretical Thinking in Sociology.* Deena Weinstein. 1977:6:1:103.

SKIDMORE, WILLIAM L. *Sociology's Models of Man: The Relationships of Models of Man to Sociological Explanation in Three Sociological Theories.* Deena Weinstein. 1977:6:1:103.

SKULTANS, VIEDA. *Madness and Morals: Ideas on Insanity in the Nineteenth Century.* Miriam Sonn. 1977:6:2:180.

SLATER, PHIL. *Origin and Significance of the Frankfurt School: A Marxist Perspective.* Barry M. Katz. 1977:6:6:728.

SMART, CAROL. *Women, Crime and Criminology: A Feminist Critique.* Mildred Daley Pagelow. 1977:6:6:672.

SMELSER, NEIL J. *Comparative Methods in the Social Sciences.* Henry Teune. 1977:6:5:579.

SMELSER, NEIL J., ed. *Karl Marx on Society and Social Change.* Michael Burawoy. 1977:6:1:9.

SMELSER, NEIL J., AND ALMOND, GABRIEL, eds. *Public Higher Education in California.* Walter Phillips. 1977:6:5:568.

SMITH, DONALD EUGENE, ed. *Religion and Political Modernization.* Thomas C. Bruneau. 1977:6:2:228.

SMITH, T. LYNN. *The Race between Population and Food Supply in Latin America.* William E. Bertrand. 1977:6:3:369.

SMITH, WHITNEY. *Flags Through the Ages and across the World.* Sasha R. Weitman. 1977:6:1:96.

SMOCK, DAVID R., AND AUDREY C. SMOCK. *The Politics of Pluralism.* Paul D. Starr. 1977:6:3:368.

SOBEL, ROBERT. *The Manipulators: America in the Media Age.* Lowndes F. Stephens. 1977:6:6:665.

SOKOLOWSKA, MAGDALENA. *Frauenemanzipation und Sozialismus: Das Beispiel der Volksrepublik Polen.* Julius A. Roth. 1977:6:6:714.

SOMERVILLE, JOHN. *The Peace Revolution: Ethos and Social Process.* Duane K. Friesen. 1977:6:1:66.

Sotsiologicheskie Issledovaniya. Jiri Kolaja. 1977:6:2:266.

SPENGLER, JOSEPH J. *Population and America's Future.* Paul R. Williams. 1977:6:1:43.

SPILLANE, WILLIAM H., AND RYSER, PAUL E. *Male Fertility Survey: Fertility Knowledge, Attitudes, and Practices of Married Men.* Teresa D. Marciano. 1977:6:1:48.

STAATS, ARTHUR W. *Social Behaviorism.* Morris J. Daniels. 1977:6:2:241.

STAPLES, ROBERT. *Introduction to Black Sociology.* Reyes Ramos. 1977:6:5:596.

STEBBINS, ROBERT A. *Teachers and Meaning: Definitions of Classroom Situations.* Thomas J. Cottle. 1977:6:1:28.

STEIN, BRUNO. *Work and Welfare in Britain and the USA.* Marie Withers Osmond. 1977:6:2:202.

STEIN, MORRIS I. *Stimulating Creativity, Volume 2: Group Procedures.* William A. Sadler, Jr. and Sallie Green. 1977:6:2:156.

STEINBERG, STEPHEN. *The Academic Melting Pot: Catholics and Jews in American Higher Education.* John Murray Cuddihy. 1977:6:2:184.

STEINER, STAN. *The Vanishing White Man.* Joe T. Darden. 1977:6:4:446.

STEMBER, CHARLES H. *Sexual Racism: The Emotional Barrier to an Integrated Society.* Paul D. Starr. 1977:6:5:597.

STEPHENS, JOYCE. *Loners, Losers, and Lovers: Elderly Tenants in a Slum Hotel.* Andrea Fontana. 1977:6:3:391.

STEWART, PATRICIA R. *Children in Distress: American and English Perspectives.* Jane D. McClure. 1977:6:6:746.

STEWART, PHYLLIS, AND CANTOR, MURIEL, eds. *Varieties of Work Experience: The Social Control of Occupational Groups and Roles.* Craig Lundberg. 1977:6:1:55.

STODDARD, ELLWYN R. *Mexican Americans.* Jaime Sena-Rivera. 1977:6:1:80.

STRATTON, BRIAN. *Who Guards the Guards?* 2nd. ed. Robert Sommer. 1977:6:1:32.

STROMAN, DUANE F. *The Medical Establishment and Social Responsibility.* Thomas J. Sullivan. 1977:6:5:575.

STRUENING, ELMER L., AND GUTTENTAG, MARCIA, eds. *Handbook of Evaluation Research,* Vols. 1 and 2. Howard E. Freeman. 1977:6:1:122.

STUB, HOLGER R., ed. *The Sociology of Education: A Sourcebook,* 3rd. ed. Josephine A. Amato. 1977:6:2:185.

STUBB, HOLGER R. *Status Communities in Modern Society: Alternatives to Class Analysis.* James Murtha. 1977:6:3:356.

STUBBS, MICHAEL, AND DELAMONT, SARA, eds. *Explorations in Classroom Observation.* Candace West. 1977:6:6:685.

SUSMAN, GERALD I. *Autonomy at Work: A Sociotechnical Analysis of Participative Management.* George H. Westacott. 1977:6:5:580.

SUTHERLAND, ANNE. *Gypsies: The Hidden Americans.* Marcello Truzzi. 1977:6:6:709.

SWINGEWOOD, ALAN. *Marx and Modern Social Theory.* Michael Burawoy. 1977:6:1:9.

SZAMUELY, TIBOR. *The Russian Tradition.* Edited by Robert Conquest. Alexander Matejko. 1977:6:2:207.

SZASZ, THOMAS. *Heresies.* Robert S. Broadhead. 1977:6:3:391.

SZASZ, THOMAS. *Schizophrenia: The Sacred Symbol of Psychiatry.* R. J. M. Lavizzo-Mourey. 1977:6:6:695.

T

TAFT, JOHN. *Mayday at Yale: A Case Study in Student Radicalism.* Richard G. Braungart. 1977:6:4:461.

TALLMAN, IRVING. *Passion, Action, and Politics: A Perspective on Social Problems and Social-Problem Solving.* Armand L. Mauss. 1977:6:5:602.

TAYLOR, IRVING A., AND GETZELS, J. W., eds. Perspectives in Creativity. William A. Sadler, Jr. and Sallie Green. 1977:6:2:156.

TEDESCHI, JAMES T., AND LINDSKOLD, SVENN. *Social Psychology: Interdependence, Interaction, and Influence.* Mary Ann Groves. 1977:6:2:248.

TEITELBAUM, MICHAEL S., ed. *Sex Differences: Social and Biological Perspectives.* Janet Saltzman Chafetz. 1977:6:5:601.

TEPPERMAN, LORNE. *Social Mobility in Canada.* Jean Leonard Elliott. 1977:6:2:174.

THOM, RENE. *Structural Stability and Morphogenesis: An Outline of a General Theory of Models.* Timothy W. Collins and Hector J. Sussman. 1977:6:5:543, 544.

THOMPSON, RICHARD. *Retreat from Apartheid: New Zealand's Sporting Contacts with South Africa.* Remi Clignet. 1977:6:2:250.

THOMPSON, VICTOR A. *Bureaucracy and the Modern World.* Robert N. Stern. 1977:6:3:391.

THORESEN, TIMOTHY H. H., ed. *Toward a Science of Man: Essays in the History of Anthropology.* Lola Romanucci-Ross. 1977:6:1:103.

THORNE, BARRIE, AND HENLEY, NANCY, eds. *Language and Sex: Difference and Dominance.* Katherine Newman. 1977:6:6:666.

TILLION, GERMAINE. *Ravensbrück: An Eyewitness Account of a Women's Concentration Camp.* Translated by Gerald Sotterwhite. Nancy R. Chiswick. 1977:6:3:339.

TOMASI, SILVANO M. *Piety and Power: The Role of the Italian Parishes in the New York Metropolitan Area, 1880–1930.* Oscar Handlin. 1977:6:1:88.

TRIANDIS, HARRY C., ed. *Variations in Black and White Perceptions of the Social Environment.* Richard S. Sterne. 1977:6:5:595.

TRUZZI, MARCELLO, AND SPRINGER, PHILIP B., eds. *Solving Social Problems: Essays in Relevant Sociology.* Henry M. Barlow. 1977:6:2:240.

TULLOCH, G. JANET. *A Home Is Not a Home: Life Within a Nursing Home.* Thomas J. Cottle. 1977:6:4:512.

TURNER, BARRY A. *Industrialism.* Randall G. Stokes. 1977:6:4:432.

TYBOUT, RICHARD A., ed. *Environmental Quality and Society.* Arthur H. Patterson. 1977:6:2:186.

U

UNGER, ROBERTO MANGABEIRA. *Law in Modern Society: Toward a Criticism of Social Theory.* Allan Horwitz. 1977:6:3:308.

V

VAN DEN BERGHE, PIERRE L., ed. *Race and Ethnicity in Africa.* Sharon Stichter. 1977:6:4:470.

VAN GEEL, TYLL. *Authority to Control the School Program.* Wilfred B. W. Martin. 1977:6:6:685.

VAN TIL, WILLIAM, ed. *Issues in Secondary Education: The Seventy-Fifth Yearbook of the National Society for the Study of Education, Part II.* Audrey James Schwartz. 1977:6:6:686.

VANEK, JAROSLAV, ed. *Self-Management: Economic Liberation of Man: Selected Readings.* George Fischer. 1977:6:5:589.

VASIL'EVA, EVELINA KARLOVNA. Translated by Arlo Schultz and Andrew J. Smith. *The Young People of Leningrad: School and Work Options and Attitudes.* Jiri Kolaja. 1977:6:5:569.

VAYDA, ANDREW P. *War in Ecological Perspective.* Richard Machalek. 1977:6:3:326.

VEENHOVEN, WILLIAM A. ed. *Case Studies on Human Rights and Fundamental Freedoms: A World Survey,* Volumes 1 & 2. Gail Omvedt. 1977:6:6:705.

VIDICH, CHARLES. *The New York Cab Driver and His Fare.* John Wildeman. 1977:6:6:749.

VIEL, BENJAMIN. *The Demographic Explosion: The Latin American Experience.* Barry Edmonston. 1977:6:5:563.

VOGEL, EZRA F., ed. *Modern Japanese Organization and Decision-Making.* Batia Sharon. 1977:6:2:205.

VOIGT, DAVID Q. *America through Baseball.* Carolyn R. Dexter. 1977:6:2:249.

VREE, DALE. *On Synthesizing Marxism and Christianity*. Nancy DiTomaso. 1977:6:6:749.

VULLIAMY, GRAHAM, AND LEE, ED., eds. *Pop Music in School*. Peter Hesbacher. 1977:6:5:621.

W

WAGENHEIM, KAL. *A Survey of Puerto Ricans on the U.S. Mainland in the 1970s*. David Jess León. 1977:6:2:224.

WAKIL, S. PARVEZ, ed. *Marriage, Family and Society: Canadian Perspectives*. Marylee Stephenson. 1977:6:2:270.

WALLER, IRVIN. *Men Released from Prison*. F. William Howton. 1977:6:2:178.

WALLIS, ROY, ed. *Sectarianism: Analyses of Religious and Non-Religious Sects*. Harry H. Hiller. 1977:6:2:229.

WARSHAY, LEON H. *The Current State of Sociological Theory: A Critical Interpretation*. David R. Simon. 1977:6:6:729.

WAX, MURRAY L., AND BUCHANAN, ROBERT W., eds. *Solving "The Indian Problem": The White Man's Burdensome Business*. Joe T. Darden. 1977:6:1:69.

WEBER, MAX. *Wirtschaft und Gesellschaft*, 5th, rev. ed., 2 vols. Edited by Johannes Winckelmann. Guenther Roth. 1977:6:5:619.

WEBER, WILLIAM H., III. *Socioeconomic Methods in Educational Analysis*. David E. Drew. 1977:6:1:124.

WEEKS, JOHN R. *Teenage Marriages: A Demographic Analysis*. John Kantner. 1977:6:6:689.

WEIL, MILDRED, AND HARTLEY, DUNCAN. *The Sociology of the Arts*. Richard W. Christopherson. 1977:6:1:125.

WEINBERG, MARTIN S., ed. *Sex Research: Studies from the Kinsey Institute*. Marjorie K. Little. 1977:6:2:234.

WEINSTEIN, JAY A. *Demographic Transition and Social Change*. Shirley Foster Hartley. 1977:6:5:556.

WEIZENBAUM, JOSEPH. *Computer Power and Human Reason: From Judgement to Calculation*. John F. Crowther. 1977:6:1:125.

WELLS, ALAN, ed. *American Society: Problems and Dilemmas*. Henry M. Barlow. 1977:6:2:240.

WELLS, ALAN, ed. *Mass Communications: A World View*. Gladys Engel Lang. 1977:6:6:650.

WERTMULLER, LINA, Director. ROMANO CORDARELLI, Producer. *Swept Away*. Chandra Mukerji. 1977:6:4:483.

WESSEL, ANDREW E. *The Social Use of Information: Ownership and Access*. Harvey E. Rich. 1977:6:5:576.

WESTBY, DAVID L. *The Clouded Vision: The Student Movement in the United States in the 1960s*. Peter K. Manning. 1977:6:3:348.

WESTERGAARD, JOHN, AND RESLER, HENRIETTA. *Class in a Capitalist Society: A Study of Contemporary Britain*. Rochelle Feldman. 1977:6:2:251.

WEXLEY, KENNETH N., AND YUKL, GARY A., eds. *Organizational Behavior and Industrial Psychology: Readings with Commentary*. Bert R. Brown. 1977:6:1:62.

WHEELER, MICHAEL. *Lies, Damn Lies, and Statistics: The Manipulation of Public Opinion in America*. David V. McQueen. 1977:6:2:215.

WHITEHURST, CAROL A. *Women in America: The Oppressed Majority*. Elizabeth Briant Lee. 1977:6:6:716.

WHYTE, WILLIAM FOOTE. *Organizing for Agricultural Development: Human Aspects in the Utilization of Science and Technology*. E. A. Wilkening. 1977:6:1:109.

WHYTE, WILLIAM FOOTE, AND ALBERTI, GIORGIO. *Power, Politics and Progress: Social Change in Rural Peru*. William L. Canak. 1977:6:5:611.

WIEBE, PAUL D. *Social Life in an Indian Slum*. Jay Weinstein. 1977:6:3:370.

WILLIAMS, J. E. HALL. *Changing Prisons*. Robert Sommer. 1977:6:1:32.

WILLIAMS, RAYMOND. *Television: Technology and Cultural Form*. Robert G. Dunn. 1977:6:1:113.

WILLIE, CHARLES V. *Oreo: A Perspective on Race and Marginal Men and Women*. James H. Laue. 1977:6:2:225.

WILSHER, PETER, AND RIGHTER, ROSEMARY. *The Exploding Cities*. J. John Palen. 1977:6:1:105.

WILSON, BRYAN. *Contemporary Transformations of Religion: The Riddell Memorial Lectures, Forty-fifth Series Delivered at the University of Newcastle upon Tyne on 2,3,4 December 1974*. Thomas Robbins. 1977:6:5:620.

WILSON, BRYAN R., ed. *Education, Equality, and Society*. Daniel L. Kegan. 1977:6:4:434.

WILSON, PAUL R. *Immigrants and Politics*. Mark Tannenbaum. 1977:6:1:67.

WINTERSMITH, ROBERT F. *Police and the Black Community*. Gwynne Peirson. 1977:6:1:80.

WISEMAN, JACQUELINE P., ed. *The Social Psychology of Sex*. Jetse Sprey. 1977:6:5:601.

WOLCOTT, HARRY F. *The African Beer Gardens of Bulawayo: Integrated Drinking in a Segregated Society*. Craig MacAndrew. 1977:6:2:180.

WOLFE, ALAN. *The Seamy Side of Democracy: Repression in America*. Albert Szymanski. 1977:6:1:68.

WOLFF, JANET. *Hermeneutic Philosophy and the Sociology of Art: An Approach to Some of the Epistemological Problems of the Sociology of Knowledge and the Sociology of Art and Literature*. Batia Sharon. 1977:6:3:304.

WOLFF, KURT H. *Trying Sociology*. Robert Jackall. 1977:6:2:258.

WOLTERS, RAYMOND. *The New Negro on Campus: Black College Rebellions of the 1920's*. Ronald W. Saufley. 1977:6:1:29.

WOOD, JAMES L. *The Sources of American Student Activism*. Richard G. Braungart. 1977:6:4:461.

Y

YABLONSKY, LEWIS. *Psychodrama: Resolving Emotional Problems through Role-Playing*. Kurt W. Back. 1977:6:5:622.

YAUKEY, DAVID. *Marriage Reduction and Fertility*. Ruth B. Dixon. 1977:6:5:563.

YOUNG, KEN, ed. *Essays on the Study of Urban Politics*. Ellan Odiorne Derow. 1977:6:5:608.

Z

ZIMMERMAN, DON H.; WIEDER, D. LAWRENCE; AND ZIMMERMAN, SIU, eds. *Understanding Social Problems*. Malcolm Spector. 1977:6:3:392.

ZYMELMAN, MANUEL. *The Economic Evaluation of Vocational Training Programs*. Robert B. Everhart. 1977:6:6:679.

NEW FOR 77

THIS LAND OF PROMISES

The Rise and Fall of Social Problems in America

Edited by **Armand L. Mauss,** *Washington State University; and* **Julie Camille Wolfe,** *University of Montana*

A stimulating collection of twenty-five articles structured around a central theoretical perspective: that social movements are closely related to, and in some sense reinforce, social problems. The articles range over problems of inequality, crime and sex, alcohol and drugs, political protest and the environment. The author-editors have prepared an extensive general introduction outlining their theoretical stance, introductions for each section and an epilogue.

452 pages/1977/paperbound, $5.95

Second Edition

CORRECTIONAL INSTITUTIONS

Edited by **Robert M. Carter, Daniel Glaser,** *University of Southern California; and* **Leslie T. Wilkins,** *State University of New York, Albany*

This well balanced introduction to corrections comprises thirty-eight articles — of which twenty-seven are new to this edition —that cover the history and current status of prisons and prison systems, with particular emphasis on the problems of the inmate. While retaining the structure of the first edition, this new edition stresses new approaches to correction, including community programs and innovative programs within prisons.

571 pages/1977/paperbound, $7.95

Lippincott

Author! Author!

Shout Halleluja
When my book's in press.
It may not be
The first book written
But it is my first.
Sing Halleluja
To draw my soul out
Playing like that marching band
In Sheboygan
And the heat of Midwest summer
To celebrate bratwurst
With the international baton-twirling
Champion
Flat chested but unafraid
To strut little white boots
In public.
Say Halleluja
As though your mouth were filled
With sausage, sauerkraut and mustard
And your eyes were slow
To look at one more single, supple body
Getting bloated by the beer
And you're sinking into lawns and trees
To find neglected dew
To cool in
Looking at the traffic which will
Slow the ride home.
And even then
Think Halleluja
When you've broken through
The bottleneck before
The two-lane highway out of town
Because your brakes are good
And now that traffic's moving
The battery won't die
If the air-conditioning's on.
Perhaps no Halleluja
Should go to that sunset
Since no one really noticed
And all knew the sun returns
Like a manuscript from publishers
With comments, red marks,
Questions, answers, crowds of voi
Saying nothing
Resembling
Halleluja.

—Chandra